Navigating the Rapids

Books by Adolf A. Berle

The Modern Corporation and Private Property
(with Gardiner C. Means)

Liquid Claims and National Wealth
(with Victoria J. Pederson)

The Natural Selection of Political Forces

New Directions in the New World

The 20th Century Capitalist Revolution

Tides of Crisis

Power Without Property: A New Development in
American Political Economy

Latin America: Diplomacy and Reality

The American Economic Republic

The Three Faces of Power

Power

Leaning Against the Dawn

Adolf A. Berle in his office in the State Department, Washington, D.C., 1942

Navigating the Rapids
1918 ~ 1971

From the Papers of Adolf A. Berle

Edited by
BEATRICE BISHOP BERLE
and
TRAVIS BEAL JACOBS
Introduction by
MAX ASCOLI

New York
HARCOURT BRACE JOVANOVICH, INC.

To the children
and grandchildren of
Adolf and Beatrice Berle
and to their children in turn

May faith in the tradition
of personal responsibility
give them the strength to
sustain the knowledge that
ideas become real slowly

"In longer vision, men will carry on the work of discovering intellectual tools and philosophic principles, in the hope of enlarging the capacity of generations yet unborn to confront conditions and dangers no dawn has yet revealed."
—Adolf A. Berle, *Leaning Against the Dawn*

Contents

I. 1917–1932   1

"Inexperienced as we were, I think we did foresee, accurately, that a treaty based on hatred and irritation, and an endeavor to perpetuate the advantage of war in favor of the Allies under the cover of a so-called peace, would produce nothing but long drawn out misery."

". . . when you are sitting in a little office watching the elevated trains go by . . . and do not have enough clients to occupy your time and have to work your head, thinking may determine what happens to you later."

"The translation of perhaps two-thirds of the industrial wealth of the country from individual ownership to ownership by the large, publicly financed corporations vitally changes the lives of property owners, the lives of workers, and the methods of property tenure. The divorce of ownership from control consequent on that process almost necessarily involves a new form of economic organization of society."

II. 1932–1936   29

"So far the brain trust rides high; but I have a vague feeling that the rapids are near and require some careful shooting."

"I am by no means clear that the intelligentsia who had a hand in the campaign will retain any position now that the campaign is over. If they do, I shall choose merely that of being an intellectual jobber and contractor from time to time when jobs come forward."

"It will be said in years to come that an administration came into office at the precise moment when a crisis almost unparalleled in modern history had reached its peak. . . . It will be pointed out that whenever such a crisis has occurred elsewhere in the world, its swift sequel has been a revolution. . . . In the United States, however, life goes on with no such violent aftermath."

"A La Guardia intellectual in New York is a political asset both to you [Roosevelt] and to him; another 'Brain Truster' in Washington is a liability."

CONTENTS

III. 1936–1939

". . . plainly what is needed here is not an Assistant Secretary of State, but a Chancellor; and the experiment of Moley shows pretty well that no subordinate official can play that part."

"The prospect of spending any considerable amount of time in the poisonous atmosphere of Washington is appalling. However, the danger of war is growing so great that there can be no declining. I only hope that something can be done."

IV. 1939–1940

"Yesterday a rather shattering day; as during the day the nerve ganglia of Europe began to decay, I have a horrible feeling of seeing the breaking of a civilization dying even before its actual death."

"The last couple of days have produced almost exactly the sensation you might have waiting for a jury to bring in a verdict on the life or death of about ten million people."

". . . the Western world is besieged on the two Americas; and the rest of my life, or at least most of it, will be spent trying to defend various parts of this world from the economic, military and propaganda attempts to establish domination over it."

V. 1940–1945

"What I think [the Lend-Lease bill] means is a steady drift into a deep gray stage in which the precise difference between war and peace is impossible to discern."

"Navigating the rapids in the next few months is going to be difficult, if not impossible, and it will require pretty careful steering to remain both honest and American, and at the same time see that all of the interestss which have marched together are kept together, going in the same direction and for an ultimate victorious, and I hope somewhat idealistic, end."

"Many of us represent a rather vigorous moderate development which has nothing in common either with the chauvinism of the Right or the sheer tyranny of the Left. Were we doomed to be ground out of existence as the Liberals and Social Democrats have been?"

"Somewhere a voice must be found for the voiceless: the little people who fought in our fight, and are being condemned to death by our common victory. I am rapidly getting to the point where I have had all of this I can take. But until the Germans are beaten, we have to follow the rule either to be quiet or to be helpful."

VI. 1944

"No greater tragedy could befall the world than to repeat in the air the grim and bloody history which tormented the world some centuries ago when the denial of equal opportunity for intercourse made the sea a battleground instead of a highway."

CONTENTS

"Again the problem of how to connect the intellectual with dynamic forces."

"The life of any Ambassador is incomplete without a scrimmage with the international oil people, and my turn has come."

"There is always an element of tragedy in the end of an administration. This one had in general dealt well with its people. It had been, in general, humane. As dictatorships go, it was about as good as one is likely to find. But the weaknesses of dictatorship in the long run outweigh its strengths; for it still is true that power corrupts and absolute power corrupts absolutely; and the strength of Getúlio [Vargas] was being eaten away in a thousand ways which perhaps he never knew."

"I walked a little around Rio yesterday and today. This is a sweet city, fragrant and tender, a kind of graceful iridescent jewel; worthy of more love than these politicians give it."

"The election returns are in, which merely confirm what anybody could see coming. The New Deal dissolved with Roosevelt, and the country is voting for another shot at the laissez-faire economy."

"Apparently you must choose between a popular revolution already battered by Russian imperialists, on one side; and well-dressed black reaction on the other; and I do not see that the little people will get a break either way."

"And how—oh, how—to explain that opposition to Russian expansion is opposition to expansion and not to Russia. . . . We opposed German expansionism and now Russian and I hope we shall be patriotic enough to oppose expansionism in the United States."

"It is hard to learn that ideas become real slowly."

"In politics you only get what you ask for; the problem is to ask the right thing."

". . . the Caribbean Sea has been to me what a mistress has been to other men and when she calls it is generally because she feels she is entitled to more attention than she has been getting. Her claims have been extravagant in the last few months. There is always a degree of delight in meeting her."

"I should rather spend the last few years meeting and, if need be, fighting with reality than in anyone's palace by the sea."

"A President who is willing to use some of his political capital can put measures forward and get them through. A President who is content to sit and let nature take its course will get nothing through."

"Foundations sit on a very padded cushion."

"I said that Latin America wanted Castro stopped and wanted the luxury of criticizing us."

CONTENTS

Preface

Adolf A. Berle began to keep a "diary file" in 1937. The last entry was made in January 1971, one month before his death. In it he noted his resolve, made with his publisher, William Jovanovich, to prepare and publish a book based on his diary.

For the diary file, entries and memoranda were dictated at daily, weekly or monthly intervals, with carefully appended dates, though the text was not always corrected by the diarist when it came from the typist. There are periods with no entries for several months, because of lack of time or the feeling that there was nothing worth noting. Lapses during World War II were deliberate:

Nov. 2, 1942: This is the first entry in this Diary for a long time, partly due to the fact that I have been up to my neck in plans for North Africa and I wished to have nothing in writing about it. If any advance information were derived from anywhere on that score, I did not wish it to be from any scrap of writing in my possession.

No diary file has been found for the years 1918–1936. This means that the record for the early days of the Brains Trust and the first La Guardia administration in New York City has been put together from documents, personal letters, a handwritten diary covering the years 1923 and 1924, excerpts from the diary of his wife, Beatrice Bishop Berle, and oral history interviews given in 1969 and not revised by the author.

The present volume is not a biography. It is not a history of the times in which Adolf Berle lived and worked. It is intended for the general reader, so that he may follow Berle's own account of his adventures, whether academic, political, economic, international, or familial. His comment on many a current scene, often written from the center of action, is characteristically impersonal and always in the service of what he saw and defined as the paramount public interest. His diary is innocent of gossip, but what he has to say of men and events and the exercise of power is often profound and prophetic.

In order to meet the requirements of a manageable single volume, the diary file has been reduced to approximately one-fifth of its original length. A few extracts from published works, unpublished speeches, and correspondence have been included to insure clarity and improve continuity. Representative materials from Adolf Berle's long career make up the text. Editing has been confined to deciding what material to use, dividing the text into parts, adding identifications, writing transitional material, and excising to maintain pace and interest. The editors have not introduced substantive corrections into the text. Names have been supplied and their spelling corrected where it was possible to do so. Some persons are identified at first appearance in the text and again if their position changed. Figures who appear once sometimes are not identified. Excisions are noted by the conventional ellipses. Material not used, often of compelling historical interest, is of the following kinds:

> speeches and drafts of speeches for public figures;
> detailed accounts of diplomatic and political negotiations;
> technical memoranda considered to be of marginal interest to the general reader;
> reports of events or conversations peripheral to the author's central activities;
> some references to persons still alive;
> incidents that would require lengthy explanatory footnotes;
> repetitions or redundancies (there are few in the original).

The editors have worked together harmoniously. They trust that their selections will epitomize, not distort, the ideas and spirit of Adolf Berle. They acknowledge a special debt to the staff of the Franklin D. Roosevelt Library at Hyde Park, New York, for its help in locating material not in the Berle papers themselves, and to William R. Mizelle for his indefatigable zeal and expertise in determining the correctness of Latin-American spellings and other detail.

The Berle papers will be available in due course to students of modern American history.

BEATRICE BISHOP BERLE
TRAVIS BEAL JACOBS

September 30, 1972

Introduction

by Max Ascoli

Precocity first made him known when he was a boy at Harvard, and from then on he kept doing uncommon things at his own brisk pace until death stopped him well beyond retirement age. He skipped both adolescence and senility. During more than fifty years he developed into a many-sided personality: he was the tireless critic of the power of wealth when management is disassociated from ownership; his name became a synonym for democratic inter-Americanism; he acquired eminence as a scholar, a teacher, and a practitioner of the law, but consistently he thought of his professions as accidental escapes from his real calling, which was public service.

The public servant in him was never spoiled by too many rewards from his master, but apparently he did not care much. He was an odd character, anyway, that wiry, relentless little man, driving hard at one difficult task after another, and frequently several at the same time. In the opinion of many he was arrogantly self-centered, and this was true in the sense that within the range of extremely broad interests he invariably followed the dictates of his well-trained conscience. As a good Calvinist, he must have thought that if others failed to realize this, too bad for them.

Fortunately, when his life was in mid-course, he decided to keep in a diary enough of the private and of the public self to appear less as a disparate collection of institutions and more like the man he was. The idea was pursued by him to the end, though its ultimate realization would not have been possible without the active participation of the surviving part of himself—his wife. This had been their way of living since the day they were married, on December 17, 1927.

When he was still a child, things happened to him that mark the outline of his destiny. He had direct encounters with poverty in Chicago, where his father was a Congregational minister. He remembered going to school on early winter mornings and seeing frozen bodies in the streets. They might have been dead or dying, but there seemed to be nobody who cared. From Chicago, the Berles went to minister to a congregation in

xv

Brighton, a suburb of Boston that included people of various economic and social backgrounds. The family lived at the end of the streetcar line, and served hot coffee to the motormen late at night. Much before learning about poverty from statistics and treatises, young Berle knew what it does to the individual it has ensnared. He never forgot it, and for him a person's destitution, caused by circumstances beyond his control, entitles him to help in attaining a decent level of subsistence.

Before her marriage, his mother had done missionary work among the Sioux Indians. The American Indians appeared at a formative stage of Berle's own growth, not long after he indignantly came home from the Versailles Conference. He had already made his first acquaintance with American gunboat diplomacy and native lawlessness in the Caribbean republics. The state of affairs in those offshore islands remained one of the objects of his thinking and action as long as he lived. He could not shake off the anguish of peace-making after having personally suffered the shock of the Versailles Conference.

True, he had not been in favor of American intervention in the war, just as when the Second World War became increasingly close he did all he could to keep our country neutral. He hated war, and on this he never changed. His mind could never be reconciled with the notion of bloody fighting for ideas. But when he first saw that ideological barriers were being created in an international conference to bring peace into the world, when he saw that there were victors and vanquished largely because of the American intervention that had been brought about to bar both, then Berle could not help crying "foul." The League of Nations, particularly close to the heart of President Wilson and conceived by him as the means to establish justice, appeared to many Europeans and Americans, including Berle, as a Holy Alliance against Germany and Russia. Two great nations were put beyond the pale as criminals. When this happens, nations so treated can easily fall under truly criminal leaders. This apprehension was quite widespread among the protesters at the Versailles Conference.

Berle had been made a Russian expert by the whims of military bureaucracy, but it did not take him long to realize what was involved in relations, or lack of relations, with Lenin's Russia. He sided with William Bullitt in wishing for the establishment of some serious contact (now we would call it co-existence) with the Soviet Union. He frequently met with French Socialist leaders, and with Englishmen who thought as he did. But there was nothing one could do. The leaders of the Allied powers who had defeated Germany in spite of the Russian revolution could not consider the Soviet regime as legitimate. Younger people who had a more realistic view of the way relations with Communist Russia should be directed, the Keyneses, the Berles, had better go home and work out their different destinies.

Berle wrote a couple of bitter articles but never became a dogmatic believer that the resumption of diplomatic and trade relations with Russia was a necessary condition for American well-being. Neither did he ever become what he called a paranoid anti-Communist. Even toward the end of the Second World War, he had no liking for the "Soviet haters," and as long as Communism was the internal regime of the Soviet Union, he had no qualms about accepting the notion that it had shown its interest in the welfare of the masses. Only when it became abundantly clear that the Soviet government could not be restrained by any international commitment from interfering in the internal affairs of other countries did Berle become acutely aware of its potential danger.

He left the Army in August, 1919, returned home, and resumed the practice of law, which he had started with the firm of Louis Brandeis in Boston. In New York, working with Rounds, Hatch, Dillingham & Debevoise, and for more than forty years in partnership with his brother, Rudolf, at Berle & Berle, he could not expend all his energies for the exclusive benefit of his clients. His search for the causes of juridical trends and for the laws of economics made his mind burrow into ground, lying at the boundaries between economics and jurisprudence, that had had little exploration. Economics had taken unprecedented forms and substance in the United States. Jurisprudence provided for the safe expansion and the self-preservation of economics. Was there a limit anywhere? Could economic power, constantly growing and in the hands of fewer and fewer men, be left free to move as far as it could, shielded by the protection of lawmakers and judges? The son of the Congregational minister was convinced that a check had to be found.

It was not right, in the eyes of the young scholar, to have the wealth of the nation unevenly distributed to the point of assuring no protection, aside from casual philanthropy, to millions of workers tossed around by ever-recurrent depressions. True, Berle was making no discovery. Marx had drawn from what he thought was ever-increasing, unredeemable poverty a dramatic conception of history. He was sure things were bound to roll their irreversible way, the origin of each crisis of misery inherent in the preceding one down to the inevitable terminal upheaval. Berle could not see the built-in catharsis; he could not make himself into the prophet of any fancied necessity. He wanted to find the basic trends of economics and their alternatives, if any. This implied the stamina to remain exposed to experience, and to examine facts at a closer range than from papers collected at the British Museum.

Whenever it was asked of him, he made himself available to disentangle human conflicts of interest from the clutches of the law, for he knew there was no better way to increase his knowledge of both. Easily, he volunteered his services on behalf of people who could not hire defenders. This was the case in 1923, for instance, when the American Indian Defense Association asked his firm to provide legal assistance for the Pueblos in New Mexico and Arizona. They were in danger of being deprived of their lands by an act of Congress. Berle went, attended the Indians' discussions and ceremonies, and found there was no reason why the Pueblo Indians had to be scattered around a land that was once their possession. They were doing no harm to white Americans, unless having different ways of living constituted a threat, which it did not. Their ignorance of our laws of property was no reason why they should not receive the benefits of those laws.

Berle was sent to Santo Domingo by the War Department in 1918, before being ordered to the Versailles Conference. On his way, he stopped in Puerto Rico, and for a long time remembered the misery of that American colony, which later became a sort of adopted country for him. In 1921, he published a number of articles on Santo Domingo, Puerto Rico, and Haiti, in various ways critical of American misrule, and particularly of the heavy-booted Marines. In Santo Domingo, he did not like how "a friendly government [has] been so thoroughly destroyed and a friendly country so completely submerged."

Haiti was particularly bad. "The worst of Haiti is not the effect on the Haitians—it is the effect on Americans. We lose something of our honor, and we blunt our national sensibilities in permitting it. The numbing of moral sense which is the inevitable effect of militarist occupation is a danger which no thoughtful American dares overlook."

The judicious respect for the Pueblo Indians, the denunciation of colonialism in the raw, seemed to be a far cry from his study of the new dimension and complexity economic power was reaching at home. Moreover, he was also a practicing lawyer. Berle's mind had a singular gift for finding links and precedents among facts in different areas, thus extending his realm of knowledge and of action. Intellectual principles were dear to him, but even dearer was the ethical urge that brought him to the heart of the facts observed.

In New York, he was a diligent observer of city politics and of how the poor lived. For three years, his residence was the Henry Street Settlement, and whatever time he could make free he liked to spend with young people who could not know yet whether they would be able to make a decent place for themselves in the world. The borders of the underworld lay near, and the temptations were many. But those whom Berle took care of found in him an understanding brother. He knew how to speak their language. One of them, who had kept in touch with the Berles, wrote to Mrs. Berle after Adolf's death: "How gratifying it would be to search my memory and set down the many things, which affected my life to the good, were ascribable to the Berle influence. How I wish I could write a small tract which treated only with my friend's great heart and his lifetime of giving to the ghetto kids, me, and hundreds like me."

Yet, the reputation for superciliousness and arrogance was his steady companion. When he was expressing himself on subjects where he was politically or morally involved, his voice was never high-pitched, but the words were invariably trenchant, and sometimes hurtful. But when he was talking to children or simple people, his tone was low and intimate—as it must be if a sense of equality is to be established.

In 1924, he became a teacher at the Harvard Business School. In 1927, he was appointed Professor of Law at Columbia University. Teaching was one of the inevitable outlets of his personality, though by no means the only one. In this trade he was one of the best; his ideas on corporations and on the role of law could grow and, at the same time, be tested anew in the minds of his students. He was an enthusiastic and disciplined teacher when he himself was young, and he remained the same to the end, after he had become Emeritus.

Some of his students later became his political opponents, yet even antagonism could never be bitter on the part of those who once worked under Professor Berle. It was a two-way proposition. Occcasionally, about some Columbia Law School graduate who had acquired an unsavory reputation, he would say, with a faint smile: "Yes, but he was a very good student of mine." A number of his friends started their relations with him in the classroom. Berle knew well that the end of a course marks the beginning of new associations, different from case to case, where the ideas and the skills that one acquired as a student could sometimes demand the assistance of the former teacher. Berle was always ready.

Berle's disciples, even before he started teaching, were among lawyers and economists in every university. His articles on preferred stock, on convertible bonds, his *Studies in the Law of Corporate Finance* and *Corporate Powers as Powers in Trust,* to mention only a few of his technical writings on financial matters, are all steps leading to the book he wrote in collaboration with Gardiner Means, *The Modern Corporation and Private Property,* first published in 1932.

It is difficult to describe what this book has done to the study of law and of economics in this country and all over the world. It became a classic almost as soon as it appeared. Since then, it has been rewritten or plagiarized down to our day, and there is no reason to assume that the series has been brought to an end. In fact, it cannot and should not. That school of thinking cannot be damaged by sloppy or overbrilliant variation. What is still talked about as if it were one name, Berle-Means, has acquired a sort of canonical quality, and, as with reproductions of traditional images of saints, real or marginal economists or sociologists feel obliged to give us their own versions.

Yet it is not a particularly revolutionary book. It is based on a set of facts that had long cried out to be acknowledged, objectively and unrhetorically. Essentially, it is the critical list of the traits to be found in impersonal, corporate property since its predominance was established over individual and family property. In our time, the atomization of wealth has given a new, fantastic impetus to the production and distribution of goods. It is organized in new institutions, the giant corporations, led by managers who have symbolic responsibilities toward the stockholders, and none toward the workers and the community at large. Ownership is too diffuse to be actually effective, and government too distant. In this anarchic situation, the economic and political orders have managed to exist as if each had its own realm and a common domain: us.

Since *The Modern Corporation* was published, notable changes have occurred in this state of things, and one of the major causes for these changes has been the publication of the book itself. Of all the rewriters of *The Modern Corporation,* the most thorough and assiduous was Adolf Berle himself.

He did it in a number of successive books, and in a large section of *Power,* the last one he wrote. His most utopian conclusions are to be found in his preface to the last edition of *The Modern Corporation and Private Property,* written thirty-five years after its original publication.

Fortune, alertness in recognizing the proper time for action, were on the side of Adolf Berle. He could not possibly sulk in Hamletlike contemplation of the wide range of potentials. In fact, 1932, the year when his reputation as a scholar was firmly established, gave him the chance to become a shaper of public policies, and to acquire a more intimate knowledge of national affairs. The Depression had been torturing Americans for over two years. There was going to be a change in the national administration; the prospective Democratic candidate who seemed to have the best chance to win the nomination, in spite of the scorn on the part of a large number of intellectuals, was Franklin D. Roosevelt. He needed ideas on facts—a commodity with which Berle was oversupplied. When Berle joined the Brains Trust at the suggestion of Raymond Moley, he started pouring out concrete proposals for legislation on railroads, employment, banking, and other subjects. It was an active atonement for having spent so much energy in research and meditation. Now the time had come when he could contribute to the building of mechanisms designed to provide greater stability to the national economy and put some brakes on the whims of management.

President Hoover had long insisted on what the classical economists used to call "individualism." Actually, this meant the lucky few who were supposed to provide the evidence of what might happen to others. But this lottery system did not make much sense to Berle; neither did it to Roosevelt. During the campaign, Berle worked prodigiously to provide position papers, speeches, articles, which only occasionally bore his name. Why should he have cared? Anyway, much of what came out of Democratic headquarters was quickly recognized by anybody who had a sense of his style as pure or slightly watered-down Berlese. The dilemma of the modern corporate system was to be found over and over again. Which of the two should prevail: the economic or the political government? The harrowing thought for Berle was that neither of the two seemed fit to accept its share of responsibility toward the other, and toward the whole. But the immediate need was greater power for the federal government.

With Roosevelt's victory, the federal or political government (Berle used the old European term, the state) acquired a much better chance to assert itself and to assume an active role in assistance to the underprivileged. As for Berle, he was used occasionally by the administration, and given an appointment of some importance: General Counsel of the Reconstruction Finance Corporation. There he had a chance to do useful work, particularly on account of the reciprocal liking that quickly developed between two radically different kinds of men: the salty Texas banker, Jesse Jones, a man with a green thumb for business, and Professor Adolf Berle, of Columbia University, the tireless critic of wealth. They had in common their dedication to the good of the country.

In the same year, 1932, Berle got to know Fiorello La Guardia, who had been impressed by the book on the modern corporation. The Boston-born Berle had to be more than just a resident of New York City. At the Henry Street Settlement, he had learned what poor people get from the clubhouse as a reward for their loyalty to the boss. Moreover, as a lawyer he had occasion to observe the complacency of too many of the well-to-do toward the misgovernment of the city.

For all his ebullience, the indomitable Little Flower was, like Berle, a long-range reformer. A Congressman for twelve, nonconsecutive, years, he was one of the most dedicated friends of labor on Capitol Hill; yet he knew that one day the country would have to face the arrogance of big labor, just as it had faced for decades the greed of big business. Berle, too, knew how to be patient and uncompromising in the conflict between political and economic power. There are conflicts that can only find their solution in the course of generations and not in a spasm of revolution.

Berle and La Guardia took to each other nearly from the first time they met. La Guardia, who had been defeated for re-election to Congress in the Democratic sweep in 1932, wanted to set the example of an honest, effective municipal government in New York City. The example still has significance even after its memory has turned into a myth: New York had a thoroughly honest, competent administration. The first time he was elected, in 1933, no one of his friends was as skillful and resourceful as Adolf Berle. The nominal Republican La Guardia, whom the New York GOP politicians could not abide, gave to the Brains Truster of FDR the chief administrative job, City Chamberlain, which meant, in the intention of both men, the financial house cleaning of the city. Toward the end of La Guardia's first term, in 1937, his re-election was considered impossible even by some of his most devoted supporters—but not by Berle.

With the influence he had gained in Washington, reinforced by the record as public servant he had established in New York City, Berle was extremely active in trying to bring harmony and co-operation between the two leaders he had served. Already by 1937 the administration had offered him tempting jobs, including the ambassadorship to Cuba and the counselorship at the State Department. La Guardia would have liked to have him as president of the City Council, or as a candidate for governor.

Berle could find some attraction in a foreign policy appointment if the American diplomacy he believed in had a chance to be pursued. His was a policy of hemispheric neutrality, with no intercourse with any belligerent beyond either ocean. It was not for Fortress America, but for Fortress U.S.A., dedicated to protecting the freedom of the other American nations. What, above all, was needed, as he put it, was the high quality of the man at the top—a quality of character, something incorrupt and austere. In 1938–39, he was looking around for such men—or such a man.

His confidence in FDR had started to waver. In his eyes, Franklin Roosevelt was looking and acting more and more like a lame-duck President: he had entered the second half of his second term. Even so, when he was asked to become Assistant Secretary of State, in February 1938, Berle could not refuse the chance, at long last, to work more closely with Roosevelt. True, the New Deal, for all its social reforms, had failed to bring about the hoped-for changes in the economic structure of the country. The number of unemployed was still staggering. To many, the Depression was not a bitter memory of the too-recent past but a dismal, recurrent prospect for the indefinite future.

Assistant Secretary Berle was kept busy at State, but he had little influence on the conduct of foreign affairs. Whenever possible, he made his opinions known to the Secretary of State, Cordell Hull, or to Sumner Welles, the Under Secretary. Like the others there, he had to keep a death watch on Europe, and guard against overreactions on our part. The President had created enough of a stir in the country when, in October 1937, in Chicago, he urged an international quarantine of aggressors as the only means of preserving peace. A year later, Berle was one of those in charge of keeping our country and its southern neighbors quarantined from aggression. In fact, he had accepted the job at State on the assumption that it was going to be a short stint. Even his friend La Guardia said of Berle's nomination, "It will be a great loss to the City of New York . . . but I hope that very soon the peace of the world will be so secure that within a short time he will be able to come back to us."

Berle, after scarcely five months in office, thought that he had had enough of it and offered his resignation. His foreign policy viewpoint seemed to be shared by the men in command at State, while the internal situation, the one the New Deal had been pledged to repair, was getting uglier. It was turning into the primary concern of the old Brains Truster. The general state of things was reflected in the leader, who, on March 4, 1933, had taken possession of the tools of power like a man born to be sovereign. With the end of the second term approaching, he looked worn out to Berle, and not to Berle alone.

Or was it that Roosevelt could not accept the idea of retirement when so many heavy clouds hung over the nation? He did not accept the old New Dealer's resignation, but asked instead for a postponement of a few weeks. Berle resigned formally on August 16, 1938, and thought that this time it was for good. For once, the scholar and the teacher tried to assert the right to resume his own work. The President reluctantly agreed, then let Berle know that the international situation was still rather tense but Berle could resign when it had cleared up. Berle was trapped: public duty comes first.

Public duty also imposed some action on his part on the issue that was acquiring greater momentum every day: who was going to replace Roosevelt? Or at least who was going to receive the Democratic nomination? For Berle, there was only one solution, or perhaps two, that could be combined according to the democratic game: Hull or La Guardia, or maybe Hull for President and La Guardia for Vice President. A moderate, leaning toward liberalism on a few issues, and a tough progressive: that was what the country needed after Roosevelt. Berle would have liked the ticket even better if it had been the other way around, and probably the team of Cordell Hull first, Fiorello La Guardia second was the maximum concession Berle could make to political realism.

A number of other people were in favor of such a peculiar team, including the two protagonists. La Guardia was particularly outspoken: he thought that his time had come. For two terms as mayor of New York, he had followed the line of the Democratic national administration, thereby saving the city from the Tammany Democrats. Berle, who could be called, if anything, a La Guardia man in Washington, thought that the Little Flower had abundantly reached national stature. The former Republican could save the Democratic party after its national leader had returned to Hyde Park.

The leader-to-be-retired was, in a talk with Berle, uncharacteristically blunt in turning down the notion of a La Guardia Presidency or Vice Presidency. He listed all the reasons that would have been advanced against the New York Mayor. On the whole, it was the same list of prejudices that was supposed to have caused the defeat of Al Smith in 1928, except that La Guardia, while thought to be Catholic, was a Protestant, and his mother half Jewish. These still-invincible liabilities in late 1939 proved to be enough for Berle, and that was enough for La Guardia, too.

Then war came to Europe, that *drôle de guerre* after the quick massacre of Poland, then a nightmarishly cruel one—and Franklin D. Roosevelt, as if he had never thought of it, found himself renominated.

At the end of the First World War, Adolf A. Berle, Jr., an intelligence officer at the War College, chanced to be put at the Russian expert's desk, and quickly learned to behave accordingly. When the Second World War became a hideous reality that had to be kept away from this country, Berle did not refuse to stay on a job he had been holding for a few months—long enough to be sure he did not like it. His devotion to Roosevelt was such that he could not say no to him when the threat of war, still remote, had to be dealt with. There was a deep optimistic streak in this Calvinist: maybe he could contribute to keeping the danger away. Perhaps he would have a chance to do some good while entombed in the third-rank position of assistant secretary in a somber, dark-leathered suite at the State Department. With his marginal authority and national prestige, he could quietly work at establishing smoother relations between his reciprocally uncongenial superiors, Cordell Hull and Sumner Welles. Berle respected them both, was close to the President, and his minor position on the team was a modest price to pay if it might bring some harmony into the State Department's leadership.

Among our diplomats at that time, none could be compared to Sumner Welles. The cool clarity of his mind, the awareness of the demands events could make on our country, allowed him to see things in perspective while history was being disfigured by the demonic evil of Adolf Hitler. A friend of the President, he could perhaps better than anyone else make him aware of the chasm between our military unpreparedness and the naïve confidence in us felt by frightened people abroad. Cordell Hull, the respected old judge from Tennessee, was dedicated to two causes: neutrality and free trade. He knew that both his causes, far from being self-sustaining, were at the mercy of adventurers who grab total control of powerful states. Such was the case in some of the countries lying on the other side of the two oceans.

Berle had realized early the irrationality both of war and of peace-making. He firmly believed that the people's well-being can best be attained and peace established if a process of economic unification is pursued on a continental basis. The American hemisphere was the one to set the example. Within a continental common market, individual nations would still have a role to play. But while nationalism in itself tends to become obsolete, and universalism of the League of Nations type is still remote, unified continents can provide the basic pillars on which a peaceful world can be built.

Berle's continentalism was thought out as a pattern that could be adopted, with due variations, by other continents or subcontinents. True, the Western hemisphere was hardly suited to set the pattern, because of the staggering differences in economic and cultural resources. Yet Berle's faith never faltered. He was for keeping this nation out of war, and with this nation the whole hemisphere. For this loyal citizen of the United States, the Americas were his country. A united hemisphere was, for him, the firebreak that could prevent the ravages of war from engulfing the lands of the hemisphere and perhaps some of those of Asia. He was for our quick rearmament, and for assistance to a few neutral countries.

At the State Department he could work for the hemisphere as he had done before his appointment as assistant secretary, but just because of his versatility he had a staggering number of other jobs thrust upon him. The men in charge of the department had to assess every turn of events and anticipate what the next one might be. In 1939–40, they were brusquely brought to engage in contingency thinking. Becoming quickly adept in the theory of games, the American leaders learned to delineate a series of conceivable options that, according to the circumstances, could be followed should the Nazi-Soviet side win and partition Europe and the Middle East between them. Then as now, the State Department was not the sole headquarters where possible alternate decisions were defined and then submitted to the President for ultimate choice. The President kept the military departments busy with analogous assignments in futurology, and if, in his judgment, there were not enough agencies in the same area, he was glad to create new ones.

Berle and his State Department colleagues had been trying to envisage a number of alternative scenarios at the time of the phony war, that eight-month spell of no-peace, no-war from the crushing of Poland to the invasion of the Low Countries. A disarmament conference or a reduction of armaments was authoritatively suggested, with the pious hope that a war-preventive peace conference would follow, under the auspices of the least armed among the great powers. Confidence in the magic of sitting around a negotiating table—even when the sitters are irreconcilable enemies—is an undying American superstition. The memory of the Prinkipo Conference, devised at Versailles to find a compromise between Bolsheviks and White Russians and that never took place, was not so old as to be forgotten by some of the men who had advocated it, Berle included. Sumner Welles, on February 17, started a round of visits to the capitals of the belligerent powers to meet the antagonistic leaders and search for some area of mutual interest where their aims could be reconciled. On March 28, he reported to Roosevelt on the irrepressible aggressiveness of Hitler.

Berle had to write a contingency plan examining the choices available to the United States should the Nazi-Soviet allies aim at extending their conquest from Europe to the Western hemisphere. Should we defend ourselves by crossing to the other side of the Atlantic, or wait on our shores for the inevitable enemy attack? There could be only tentative answers to tentative questions, and Berle's recommendation was to develop our military strength and fortify our shores. Or if the defeat of England brings the war to Canada, could we remain at peace with Nazi Germany after it had reached our northern boundaries? One of the possible answers, according to Berle, might be yes, *if* the Germans stopped their intrigues in this hemisphere. Incidentally, since the idea of inter-American hemispheric unity was conceived, Canada had constantly refused to be a part of it.

The President, from the glimpses of him in Berle's diary, appears as the nation's vital nerve throughout the war. There are little sketches of him, and what Berle reports on the President shows the mettle of both. In May 1939, for instance, Roosevelt told Berle that a German and Italian victory could not be excluded. Their combined navies were equal to ours, and once they had disposed of the French and British fleets, the shores of the Americas were in danger. That would have taken care of Berle's hemispheric unity, and the tale was tailored to convey the notion that the hemisphere could not be protected by a hemispheric navy. Another revealing episode is Roosevelt's answer to Hull, who, on September 21, 1939, in preparing a message on the repeal of the neutrality arms embargo had suggested it might be expedient to include a commitment that we would never, under any circumstances and whatever happened, go to war. The President looked at him, quite simply, and there was dead silence for some seconds. Then he said: "Can you guarantee that? Can I guarantee it?"

In April 1940, when the German army occupied Denmark, the Danish Minister to Washington, Henrik de Kaufmann, went to see Berle in a state of great anguish. There was no more Denmark, he said, and a country that has ceased to exist cannot have representatives abroad. Berle answered him nobly, saying that there was still a Denmark as long as it held the loyalty of a few brave citizens abroad. He even found the way to help the Danish Minister maintain the essence of his function and to live a modest, austere life.

Greenland, an icy hunk of Danish territory in the Western hemisphere, was populated at that time by about 20,000 people, mostly of mixed Eskimo-Danish descent. A year later, after American landing fields had been established there, a *de facto* government was recognized, endowed with the true Danish sovereignty that the Germans had reduced to a mockery. The German-appointed government in Copenhagen did not like the whole scheme, but the American position was stated by the President in the strongest terms: since Greenland is in the Western hemisphere, no change of sovereignty from Denmark to another European power can be tolerated.

A test had already come in September 1940: a supposedly Norwegian but actually German ship was moving toward Greenland for alleged scientific exploration and with plenty of arms aboard. Who should take care of it? An American destroyer when we were not at war with Germany? Or should a British warship do the job in Western hemispheric waters? The question was brought to the President, whose answer was quick: Leave it to the British (or to the Canadians, which was about the same), and tell them not to get ideas, for Greenland was part of the Western hemisphere.

The Greenland episode constitutes one of Berle's most notable achievements at the State Department. His hemispheric theories, backed by the President, prevailed. The Roosevelt that Berle shows us in brief sketches is firm, genial—somehow of another world, although capable of communicating with all sorts of men. In the first years of his administration, Berle used to start his letters to him "Dear Caesar," a jocular habit that had to be suddenly abandoned when the Supreme Court controversy was raging and one "Dear Caesar" letter nearly leaked out. For Berle, there was a Caesarian quality in Franklin Roosevelt that gave finality to his major decisions. Yet Berle was the opposite of a courtier, of which there was no lack around the President. His Caesar had a list of things likely to happen during his term of office that might demand risky action when inaction could be an even greater risk.

Berle was for neutrality to the limit as long as this hemisphere was left untouched by transatlantic or transpacific powers. He had no liking for Germany, and an innate, old-fashioned distrust of perfidious Albion. It is not inconceivable that during the war he gave to his dislikes a somewhat excessive expression. Who was not excessive in the expression of his emotions in those days? In their antagonism toward the Free French movement and Charles de Gaulle personally, the President, Berle, and most of official Washington went to the extreme. It took time for many authoritative people to get rid of the notion: there was no France.

The President never assumed that the war would spare us. It could be delayed but not avoided. The neutralist Berle, a member of his administration, made his opinions heard inside its councils, but after the President had reached a decision out of line with his own thinking, was ready for new assignments. He was one of the most active among high administration officials in drafting, or contributing to the drafting, of the Presidential messages and legislative measures repealing, one layer after another, the main items of the Neutrality Act. In the memoranda about postwar Europe, he was for the punishment of Nazi officialdom, but the demand for the unconditional surrender of the Axis powers could not but disturb the veteran of Versailles.

Berle had no qualms about the destroyer deal with England, by which fifty overage ships were bartered for land bases in the Western hemisphere, but he had serious doubts about Lend-Lease and the principles and freedoms proclaimed by Roosevelt and Churchill in the Atlantic Charter on August 14, 1941. Roosevelt had already listed the Four Freedoms seven months earlier, in his message to Congress on January 6, 1941. Berle had been a believer in more freedoms than four, but for him "freedom from want" was the key one, on which all others depend. In all government pronouncements there is an element of destiny when formulated by the leader one trusts. Yet, a free man must question in his own conscience the pronouncements of destiny, particularly when they are in the making.

In 1939, he notes that American opinion, to judge by the utterances of journalists and commentators, was overconcerned with Europe but did not seem to care much for what was happening in Asia. Later, when the extreme militarists got control of Japan and to the war in China added the conquest of French Indo-China, a number of highly placed people in the administration started pressing hard for a showdown with Japan. After Indo-China, what next? The Philippines, and Malaysia, and the Dutch East Indies? Cordell Hull started negotiations with the Japanese special envoy, Admiral Kichisaburo Nomura, in search of a settlement, both economic and territorial. The Japanese-American negotiations had to be kept going at the highest possible level, including the President, for our leaders knew that the Japanese navy had orders to go so far as to attack U.S. territory. Chance brought Berle, too, onto the team of American negotiators, when a projected loan to the Thai government had run into snags, for Berle had a well-established reputation as a repairman of certified ingenuity.

One day, he happened to find the President in a humorous mood. FDR regaled him with a probably enriched account of an act he had put on for Nomura. War between the two countries, he said, must be avoided at all costs, for nobody knows what implacable fury can sweep the American people when they are outraged. He gave the Japanese envoy a few examples—the Spanish-American War, first of all—as if he himself, the President, were terrified at the prospect of what might lie ahead should Japan inflict some hurt on America. For all its corniness, it was as good a way as any to let the Japanese know how risky it was to challenge the United States.

Ten months later, the attack on Pearl Harbor occurred. Our intelligence services had foreseen the Japanese blow for the 8th—a mix-up in military intelligence that probably happens frequently in those tumultuous hours when warfare replaces diplomacy as a medium of communication between nations. A proper comment came from Berle in a letter to Hull a week later. He congratulated his old chief for having protracted the negotiations with the Japanese envoy until a time when Germany, having launched its attack on Russia, was no longer in condition to help Japan. In fact, while our country declared war on Japan on December 8, Hitler's Germany and Mussolini's Italy waited until December 11 before declaring war on us. Roosevelt, too, waited, for the two European Axis powers to join Japan in infamy. That day, December 11, should be remembered as the one when neutralism came to an end in our country—for that season.

Berle had been right when he felt that his position at the State Department was unsuited to bring out the best in him. It was not to his measure and did not offer enough scope for his different and sometimes contradictory talents. A good writer himself, at the Department he had to practice to an even greater degree than during the battles for the New Deal the art of ghost-writing and ghost-thinking. Moreover, he had a rather dangerous habit: whenever asked to do something difficult and that others could not have done as well, his quick answer was likely to be "Why not? I will try."

At the Department, he was given an exorbitant number of assignments, but mostly of the thinking variety. Thinking, well-articulated thinking, came disturbingly easy to him—disturbing for his Puritanical conscience, which could justify his facility in the formulation of ideas only when put at the service of a grand purpose, like the ultimate unity of the Americas or the coming into being of institutions designed to provide individuals with a greater and greater measure of equality.

Before Pearl Harbor and to a feverish degree afterward, new supranational structures were designed by the highest officials of the State Department and other concerned branches of the government, in close cooperation with representatives of Allied governments—first of all, those of the United Kingdom. That was the case with the Bretton Woods Conference on monetary problems, which led to the creation of the International Monetary Fund and the International Bank for Reconstruction and Development. Shortly afterward came the Dumbarton Oaks Conference, where the vague principles of inter-Allied organization for peace and security, relief and rehabilitation were brought together in a broad framework designed to be far more resilient than the then-dying League of Nations.

Among the highest American officials appointed to draw, together with British and other Allied counterparts, the features of the postwar world, the name of Adolf Berle is never to be found. As he put it himself at the end of his service at the State Department, he had been made to play second fiddle. Yet most of the debates on the new supranational order were on the terrain where economics is the subject matter of law-making. He had been working on that terrain from the end of the First World War to the beginning of the Second. Why was he left out? One of the answers may be that he was not a careerist and had little taste and no skill for bureaucratic in-fighting. When the expression "premature anti-Fascist" was already common in bureaucratic language, Berle was perhaps handicapped by his premature search for continental units that could check and spur the development of continental economies.

At the Department's committee or subcommittee level, his mind was kept fully employed. His beloved hemisphere, however, was rather forgotten by the world planners. When the United Nations Declaration was announced on January 1, 1942, it was considered by its twenty-six original signers to be a network of functional agencies already in existence or to be created, not as a potential sovereign, world-wide entity. Berle was never among the believers in One World, to be brought into being by the instant abolition of all sovereignties. Rather, he thought that, at the initial stage, the new world should be a U.S.-U.N. venture, never U.S.-U.K., and was not displeased that among the twenty-six nations, nine were Caribbean republics. To a good legal mind, there is happiness in setting down the norms in anticipation of the facts to which they should be applied.

In his contingency planning, Berle could not avoid the inclination neatly to legislate the future on the assumption that existing trends, with not much change in their rate of development, may prove enduring. He was singularly skillful at this game, except that no human can play it to perfection because man's view of things to come is inevitably distorted by his prejudices or passions. One of Berle's pet abominations was British mercantilism, but in his view of the postwar world he failed to realize that two world war victories had spent the power of Great Britain. He recognized the imperialistic drive of the Soviet Union, particularly in the Middle East, but thought that in eastern Europe the Russians could guarantee a zone of peace more or less as we had in the Caribbean. In the postwar world, we should use abroad just enough of our power to give our diplomacy room to maneuver.

On one occasion, Berle had an opportunity to show himself as a prophetic lawmaker. In December 1944, the era of air travel was dawning in the civilized world, and everyone who had thought about it could not help seeing the ascending curve of a predictable future. Berle had long studied the subject and was prepared. Appointed chairman of the United States delegation, he was elected president of the International Air Conference that opened in Chicago on November 1, 1944. Fifty-seven nations were represented. The Soviet Union withdrew its delegation as the conference opened, declaring in preparatory meetings that it would not allow foreign planes to violate Soviet skies or land on its territory, and that the closest airport from which travelers could board Soviet planes was, significantly enough, Cairo.

Among the members of the American delegation was Fiorello La Guardia. He and Berle knew each other so thoroughly that an uncanny similarity of instinct and reaction had developed between these two immensely different men. They knew at the moment the conference was assembled how formidable was the strange alliance of prejudices and lobbies that stood in the way of what could be called a common law of international aviation. There could not be a world-wide agency to impose its will across the borders of nations, and nationalism in many a country— Russia was an example—found a new chance to assert itself by holding tight to its skies. The principle was: my sky is not made for any other country's traffic or trade. The achievement of the conference was described by Berle in a speech he made commemorating the twentieth anniversary of the International Civil Aviation Organization by contrasting it "with the two centuries of delay, six or seven wars, and endless savage struggles required to establish freedom of navigation on the seas. We entered the Chicago conference amid fears of the sixteenth century. We closed it with the freedoms of the twentieth."

One of the strongest obstacles Berle had had to overcome was the shortsightedness shown by the heads of the two major Western airlines, Pan Am and BOAC, in judging the future of transatlantic aviation. Technological inventiveness was supposed to have stopped with the DC-4 or its equivalent; air travel was going to remain a marginal form of transportation between continents. Other nations considered the skies over their lands like the cover of a box in which narrow openings could be made, on a case-by-case basis, for loading, unloading, and refueling. At the end, the International Civil Aviation Organization was created. It was an international clearinghouse, where such issues as the landing or discharging, the loading or unloading of passengers and cargo among nations willing to co-operate could equitably be settled. The process of settlement is constantly going on, for new issues keep arising because of technological advances, fluctuations in traffic, competition, and the like. But the center around which the whirling changes occur is the one laid down in 1944, in Chicago.

The same technical language is spoken between pilots and control towers all over the world. The same air tunnels are followed in the skies of the earth. There cannot be lawlessness in the skies, although piracy has managed to stage a comeback. Neither can there be a supranational law-enforcement agency. The flexibility and the creativity of the common law have been brought to operate above the boundaries of nations. For this historic feat, the major credit goes to Adolf Berle.

Six days before the conference closed, Assistant Secretary Berle received a telegram, signed FDR, asking him to take over the embassy at Rio de Janeiro. What had happened was only too clear. The ailing Cordell Hull's resignation had caused a change in leadership at the State Department. Berle was supposed to keep his rank of Assistant Secretary but with such trifling assignments that there could be no doubt about the meaning of the whole thing: Berle had been resigned. He complied, and sent a formal letter of resignation.

Embittered as he was by his humiliation, he could not ultimately refuse the appointment to Rio without exposing himself to criticism from his enemies (he had collected quite a few in Washington) for letting the President down in wartime. His long-time friend Stephen Early, Press Secretary at the White House, somehow patched up the whole thing. The news releases about Berle's resignation and his appointment to the most important embassy in Latin America were nicely doctored. The President, who was at Warm Springs in the days of Berle's crude liquidation, had a good talk with him on December 21. The Roosevelt charm was turned on, together with expressions of gratitude for the eminent services Berle had rendered at the Department. The President genially went on to say that the ambassadorship to Brazil had "a return ticket" attached. After V-J Day, if not before, there would be important economic assignments for him in Washington.

Berle, of course, accepted, and arrived in Rio on January 24, 1945. A noncareer diplomat, he was still struggling to get the hang of his job in a messy embassy when, on April 12, the news came that Franklin Roosevelt had died. Few men had known the President for such a long period of time, served him in so many capacities and, no matter what use was made of their devotion, been so loyal to him. His Caesar capriciously rewarded the services rendered him. Yet, the pages of the diary written at Roosevelt's death carry no trace of criticism or resentment. They are like a prayer to the spirit of his fallen chief, who, in death, had regained his wholeness. If he had seemed at times lighthearted or playful, it was because his gallantry did not allow him to let other people know how heavy were the burdens he had to carry. He had made deals with questionable characters at home, and with unwholesome foreign rulers, because he knew how to keep himself beyond good and evil when this was demanded by the interest of the nation. The last time Berle saw him, he had felt that the end was near.

He went to Brazil, and did a superb job in the short time he was there, learning to know the country and its immense potential, establishing enduring relationships with some of the best Brazilian minds. Two American ambassadors were in Rio for the price of one, for his Latin-educated wife took to the imperial republic of Brazil with passionate enthusiasm. A medical doctor, she exhibited in her work there a rare virtuosity in the practice and theory of modern medicine that is still considered a model of excellence. Visiting and exploring the country with a care for people well beyond the limits of diplomatic protocol, the Berles exerted an influence on the intellectual and political life of the country that lasted long after their return home.

Berle used his return ticket on February 21, 1946. In the thirteen months of his stay, things of major importance happened in Brazilian politics, all characterized by that unique blend of radical change and bloodless revolution—Brazilian style. Popular discontent had forced President Getúlio Vargas, who had ruled with absolute power for fifteen years, to call general elections. The feeling was strong that elections with Vargas still in power were unlikely to be honest, or to take place at all. Ambassador Berle, as a representative of the major democratic power in the hemisphere, had felt it was incumbent on him to intervene with a public address to express his confidence in the representative process and in the Brazilian electorate. He went so far as to show Vargas his speech before delivering it at a journalists' club. In spite of Vargas's words of approval, Berle had qualms up to the last minute, for, with that candor he exhibits frequently in his diary, he was "natively a timid soul."

The pro-Vargas papers protested fiercely at this intervention on the part of a representative of a great power. Anyway, Vargas was forced to resign on October 29, before the election took place. It did Berle good to see Brazilian men and women going joyously to the polls on December 2. General Eurico Dutra, leader of the Social Democratic party, was elected. After General Dutra, Vargas was re-elected, but, four years later, rebellion in the armed forces led him to commit suicide. Then came Kubitschek, the maker of Brasília, and then Quadros, who resigned after one year, but had time enough to receive Berle and be extraordinarily rude to him, thereby proving how Berle's devotion to Brazil could never be forgiven by the native demagogues. Neither is it forgotten by the best minds Brazil has, irrespective of the regime in power.

INTRODUCTION

With the good-by to Rio, the longest phase of Berle's work for the government came to an end. The economic assignments that Roosevelt had mentioned to him were not forthcoming under Truman, and, as for many of those whose energies had been used by Franklin Roosevelt, it took time to become reconciled to the fact that the great magician was no longer in the Oval Room. In more than one way, Berle was fortunate: he had a world of his own waiting for him. He went back to teaching and the practice of law; he resumed his unending work on the corporate system. He had never liked living in Washington, and the cocktail party–dinner circuits of the capital were obnoxious to him. In no place on earth was he as happy as in his house on Nineteenth Street, in New York, unless it was his farm, in Great Barrington, where the cultivation of the soil with his own hands gave him, season after season, the happy rewards of the loving gardener.

The end of eight years of full-time work for the government at high, even if sometimes unsatisfactory, levels leaves a man disoriented, at least for a while. Berle mentioned it poignantly several times, and frequently his diary comments on current events, learned from public sources, sound like sharp editorial notes of a paper without circulation. The criticism is particularly insistent when addressed to a former colleague of his at the State Department, Dean Acheson. Both had worked there for four years as assistant secretaries, tied to each other by reciprocal dislike. At the end, Berle found himself out of the Department, and Acheson, after a series of up and down and out, became Secretary, from January 1949 to January 1953.

The assignment of both men to practically the same area of responsibility proved to be one of those sources of friction so characteristic of the Roosevelt style of administration. In common, they had first-rate legal minds, both of them sharpened under the influence of Louis Brandeis. Incidentally, both were sons of ministers, of different denominations and different ranks, but prone to the traditional Protestant reliance on personal judgment. Berle's mind was dominated by a few essential principles, half gained through scientific research and half prophecy, like hemispheric unity and the need to overhaul the nation's corporate structure by carrying into economics the equalitarian principles of political democracy. Acheson's mind could expatiate over the vastest areas of the law, domestic and international, unencumbered by prophetic callings. He was also served well, sometimes even too well, by an acerbic tongue that could hurt somebody he did not like to the point of exacting from him at least redoubled antagonism.

Berle pursued with single-minded tenacity a number of callings throughout his life; he was a source of inspiration for radical social and institutional reforms, a stubborn believer in regionalism and continentalism as the pillars of a world peace, but the ideological reticence of the Calvinist never allowed him to give full systematic expression to his beliefs. Acheson was a master craftsman in handling the foreign policy of our country according to the exigencies of the present and of that rim beyond the present where, with all its promises and threats, the future may lie.

Berle's and Acheson's incompatibility generated the occasions for their conflicts. It is a pity that these two men who rendered eminent services to their country remained attached by their reciprocal dislike to the end of their lives. But it would be a far greater pity if their interoffice conflicts were to linger on as footnotes to the history they made.

Berle could be as devoted a friend as, when provoked, he could repay enmity with enmity. His friendship with Fiorello La Guardia is perhaps the best evidence of the reciprocal loyalty that can bind together two entirely different men, one relying on the other so thoroughly and for such a long period of time that the very differences between them become the cement of their amity. The Little Flower was a man of the people in the most thorough sense of the term, with more than a touch of that flamboyance, showmanship, and uncompromising integrity that, from time to time, brings onto the stage of history popular heroes. Berle, an intellectual's intellectual, needed to test his ideas by trying them out on La Guardia. Who gained the most from the interchange nobody could say; what is certain is that it did honor to both.

Toward the end of La Guardia's life, when many thought he was an odd relic, Berle had him appointed as one of the American delegates to the international air conference. Ambassador La Guardia was sent to represent the United States at the inauguration of President Dutra of Brazil. When Berle resettled in New York, professional and academic work could scarcely be enough for him. He needed what he had when he left: active participation in politics, in partnership with a full-fledged politician. La Guardia was still there, but his day had passed, and death was close. When it came, on September 20, 1947, it was a cruel blow for Berle. One of his tenets, admirably expressed in a letter to James Perkins, was the Calvinistic obligation to keep a balance between the search for ideas and the performance of deeds.

There was a maverick party in New York State that offered Berle a chance to play a political role independent of the Democratic party and not too removed from it. The Liberal party, after a series of internal strifes, had freed itself from Communist influence by breaking away from the Communist-dominated American Labor party. It elected Adolf Berle as its chairman in 1947. The newly installed Chairman thought the whole thing slightly foolish. A year and a half later, he found the right words for his outfit: it is a pressure group on the Democratic party. And that it remained until, in July 1955, in agreement with the professional Liberal party leaders, he resigned the chairmanship. The pressure group had managed to keep a measure of independence from the Democratic party, and to avoid having its support taken for granted. Berle had in David Dubinsky something like an equivalent to La Guardia—although there never could be another La Guardia for him.

On a minor scale, the experience with the Liberal party is pure Berle: eager to assume a public responsibility, he has misgivings when formally burdened with it, sticks it out until the foreseen consummation comes, and then rumination begins, sometimes quiet, sometimes protracted, never without pain. This was the pattern of his long years at the State Department, from the time Roosevelt dragged him there to the bitter end which vindicates his foresight. The Liberal party provided him with a few distasteful situations when his leadership proved little more than nominal. He saw what was ahead of him when, after bickering with himself and John F. Kennedy's entourage, he assumed the chairmanship of the Task Force on Latin America, a job that gave him more aggravation than recognition. But throughout these different episodes, no matter what discomfort they imposed on him, Berle would not have wanted to be exempted from the tests. He never reached the high policy-making position he aspired to, yet he never lost public prestige or self-confidence.

In one area particularly, the quest for service was incurable: Latin America, the region in the world that concerned him the most. He was a dejected man when he left the State Department in July 1961, after six months in office. In accepting that job he had failed to listen to his own judgment, which had told him not to accept a government position with greater responsibility than power. But if Lyndon Johnson had asked him to return to Washington and work on Latin America, he would have gone. The persistency and the continuity of his efforts on behalf of the unity of the hemisphere never slackened. When he could no longer pursue it inside U.S. diplomacy, he kept it going as his own private diplomacy, in alliance with a few Latin-American friends. Whenever one of these friends was the target of right- or left-wing attack, his answer was: he's a New Dealer.

Berle's concern with the countries south of the Rio Grande started early in life, and in the long series of inter-American conferences held during the Roosevelt administration Berle's influence was dominant—beginning with the ones in Buenos Aires in 1936 and Lima in 1938, where he won the admiration of Alfred Landon. Then, he was not yet in the government, as he was totally out of it at the Rio Conference in 1947, when his major aim was finally achieved: each American republic guaranteed the integrity of the others against attacks from non-American powers. The enforcement of the Monroe Doctrine had become the responsibility of each American nation, and of them all. Berle felt that the basic law of American unity had, at long last, been laid down. In December 1961, at the end of a diary entry on the Cuban fiasco, he wrote: "I should be wiser than I will be if in the coming year I stick to academic economics and political science. There is, however, a difficulty. All the best academic work in the world counts for nothing if the essential integrity of the American system is not preserved."

In February 1962, Adolf and Beatrice Berle went on a tour of Central America. "Only in a long lifetime," he wrote later, "I have learned that when the Caribbean calls, it is wise to go." The eleven countries of the Caribbean Sea were among the lands most in need of a New Deal. Here and there, a few sturdy New Dealers were facing the internal and external attacks of gangland characters. Eminent among Berle's associates was José (Pepe) Figueres, of Costa Rica, junta president, then twice elected president of his country, and uninterruptedly a force for democracy over a score of years. Another precious friend was Luis Muñoz Marín, who did not need defense against foreign aggression (at least not until Castro showed himself a Communist), because of the special association of his island with the United States. The list could be much longer. It includes good guys and bad guys, with Berle constantly trying to prevent warfare between them.

The Berle private diplomacy was principled, and politically somewhat left of center. It could not play its game openly. Yet it contributed to some remarkable changes for the better, like the return from exile of Rómulo Betancourt and his election to the presidency of Venezuela, where he served his full term, from 1959 to 1964, and laid the foundations for democracy in a country that had been under dictatorship for most of half a century. It was a major achievement of the diplomacy that had its unofficial headquarters at 142 East Nineteenth Street.

One could conclude from this that Adolf Berle was obsessed with Latin America. And this would be true for anyone but Adolf Berle—a man who cultivated some other obsessions at the same time, and managed to keep his mind alert to new ones. He kept on teaching and writing more books to pursue further the theme that had first brought acclaim to *The Modern Corporation;* every four years, in the months preceding a Presidential election, he was feverishly at work for the Democratic candidate, showing the unmistakable characteristic of the pure-blood politician: my candidate is sure to win. Other passionate men find themselves in trouble for putting all their eggs in one basket, but there never were baskets enough for all of Berle's eggs.

In a single diary entry in March 1957, he lists four big foundations that had asked for his talents: The Fund for the Republic, the Rockefeller Brothers Fund, the Rockefeller Foundation, the Committee on Human Ecology. He said yes to all, and very close to his heart was the Twentieth Century Fund. It is an old trait with him: as an individual, he feared loneliness and, although he worked hard with so many persons, seldom escaped it. He had several lines of interest, each pursued with extraordinary vigor. Their sum total could have entitled him to a position of singular distinction among humanists. And, indeed, one of his best and least-read books, *The Natural Selection of Political Forces,* shows the humanistic side of him. But his eagerness to be as close as possible to action made him shun the humanist's calm, detached view of things. Rather, he was a restrained radical.

A good-neighbor policy does not necessarily mean that the Americas have to act as if they were one country—a conviction that Berle lived long enough to see shattered by the encroachment of Communist imperialism into the hemisphere. Even more radical was his conception of economic versus political power. On a number of occasions, from the papers written for the first election of Franklin Roosevelt on, the line of conflict is stretched out and its ultimate conclusion drawn—or nearly drawn. The political power of the state is bound to take over the impersonal power of so-called private wealth. Several times in his writings, he mentioned that, when the banks were closed as the Roosevelt administration took office, the idea occurred to many a New Dealer to continue government control of the banks. In general, one can say that nationalization of large areas of the economy was, according to Berle, bound to come. But he found little use in being an advocate of the inevitable.

As a New Dealer, he preferred combined planning by government, business, and labor on the assumption that progress would result for the community as a whole. But he was never quite persuaded that this could happen in an ever-normal way, or that built-in stabilizers could be engineered strong and flexible enough to withstand the pressure of the most destabilizing circumstances. Economists, even of the hard-nosed variety with limited respect for classical theories, could be satisfied with low percentages of unemployment, or with moderately bumpy trends.

Berle's concern for the individual made him indifferent to averages. He opened a way to look at economic factors as they affect the human person, and are influenced by the people's reactions. His equalitarianism made of him a radical of the American variety, called populism. Sometimes, American populism goes so far as to border on chaos—Berle's word for ultimate horror. His mind was too sophisticated not to see the danger inherent in populism, and even in his own brand of it. The major restraint on his radicalism came from the fact that he had always been a Jeffersonian, and a Jeffersonian society, with the citizen free to do or not to do what he pleases, could scarcely be the outcome of a Hamiltonian superstate.

He never finished his running study of corporate and political power, of the way they grew, each in itself and with respect to the other. Perhaps he did not want to finish. He wanted to create and maintain the alertness to both while providing, to the end of his life, tentative but probably never definite alternatives. His disciples were countless and unrestrained. Berle maintained a tolerant attitude even when, among the many transcriptions of his theories, some gained acclaim that pretended to make of economics the undismal, frivolous science. But all this is trivial. The copies and caricatures of Berle's theories can only serve to put in the proper light the real Berle: in his unique way, and in his many ways, one of the major forces for good in our time.

I

1917~1932

In his diary on November 19, 1960, Adolf A. Berle, Jr., then sixty-five, wrote a short memorial of his father. His mood was one of reminiscence—a rare mood for him—not untouched with pride. It provides an appropriate place to begin this book made from his papers.

My father was 95 years old [when he died]. He was born just at the close of the Civil War—just before the assassination of Lincoln. His father, a '48 immigrant, settled in St. Louis, went into the Union Army, was naturalized an American citizen in 1866 and had an honorable discharge. He died two years later. He was a Catholic and I suppose my father was baptized a Catholic. He had done some of the decoration in the old cathedral in St. Louis but my father soon came into the Protestant Church with which German Catholics had close relations—many of the '48 Catholics were Protestants anyway. My father's family was divided. Their little castle at Berleburg was a petty principality. In the War of the Reformation, the family divided and in that area the Protestants won so it is Lutheran now. The Catholic parts of the family went south—this is probably why my grandfather was a subject of the Grand Duke of Baden when he was naturalized. It is interesting to note that in my father's lifetime Germany came into existence (1871) and its empire fell (1918) and the Nazi empire came (1933) and went (1945). He himself went to Oberlin and took his Divinity degree [1887], there meeting my mother. They were married by President Fairchild of Oberlin in the Oberlin Chapel. She was the daughter of Professor G. Frederick Wright who combined natural geology with theology at Oberlin.

But before, he had gone to Harvard, taking his A.B. in 1891 and [had had] himself ordained as a Congregationalist clergyman. His years in Boston (1891–1903) and his subsequent years in Salem and Shawmut, Massachusetts (1904–1910) were, I think, the most fertile for they brought him in contact with men as diverse as Winthrop Murray Crane [owner of a paper mill in Dalton, Mass.; U.S. Senator] and Louis D. Brandeis and with a number of figures in New York like Lillian Wald of the Henry St. Settlement. So he became a part of the liberal movement which brought into existence the first program of social legislation in Massachusetts and

3

the first attempt at educational reform. He spent much of his time in New York after he left Shawmut Church in Boston.

The evolution is fascinating. The son of an immigrant, he really made a break-through when he was graduated from Harvard; Harvard remained to him a kind of spiritual homeland. It is not accident that at 95, six months before his death, he insisted on attending the Harvard Commencement though it nearly killed him. A certain passionate energy brought him into quite unnecessary conflict with all sorts and kinds of people; but it also brought him into contact with a great many people who renewed his strength as one draws strength from a blood transfusion. It also brought him in a strange way into a ruling class—the class of militant intellectuals who drove through the plutocracy regnant from 1890 to 1914 and opened the way for the beginning of a civilized social system in the United States. I have two photographs—one given by Louis Brandeis in memory of the many struggles in the public service; and another by Fiorello La Guardia (for whom he campaigned in 1933) inscribed: "To the Noblest Roman of them all." At 95, it was time to go. Beatrice and I had been there two weeks earlier. We thought the sands were running out.

. . . In one sense all the ends have been tied up; for he had seen his great grandchildren and had enjoyed them. He had seen Peter and Peter's bride on their honeymoon. He was passionately hoping that Peter would come back safely from the service; the prince of the house was the most important to him. He had refused to have anything changed at Kinderhof in Boscawen; it was almost a perfect museum of a late Victorian intellectual, with the most fascinating private library I know. His theory was that if ever you sat down in a comfortable chair, you would find an interesting book within reach.

So passes an era. The reformers of today do not think of free men but of the aggregates they would like; the result is not the same.

Adolf Augustus Berle and Mary Augusta Wright Berle had four children: Lina Wright, Adolf Augustus, Jr. (born on January 29, 1895), Miriam Blossom, and Rudolf Protas. Adolf Berle, Jr., graduated from Harvard in 1913 and received a master's degree the following year. In 1916 he finished Harvard Law School and began practicing with Brandeis, Dunbar & Nutter in Boston. When the United States entered the war in 1917, he enlisted in the army.

The Oral History Project at Columbia University began an interview with Berle in 1969. The interview stopped at 1932, however, and Berle never reviewed the typescript. Selections from the interview follow and are indicated by quotation marks.

"It is fair to say I knew I would have been drafted if I had not enlisted. I was unhappy. I didn't like the idea of being in the Army. Young men rarely do. And I didn't like the idea of getting killed, which is natural. Most of all I did not like this war. The idea that you would revolt and say 'Hell no, we won't go,' was foreign to the whole manner of thinking of that time. But this did not prevent many young men from feeling towards that war very much the way some people feel about the Vietnamese war today. There's a slight difference. Today many people are prepared to go against their own country. That kind of thinking was practically unknown in 1917. Then, the few who acted in this way were considered traitors.

"I wasn't a conscientious objector. I couldn't say that I never believed in any war at any time. On the other hand, I did feel that this was a European war primarily, that it was not a war that we had caused or had much interest in, and I found it difficult to believe that a Europe dominated by the Hohenzollerns would be very much different from a Europe dominated by the French, which seemed to me the main item in the picture. This feeling for me really only changed when Mr. Wilson began to lay out a policy which appealed to my own sense of idealism. If that would be the result then maybe it was worthwhile.

"This kind of thinking had made me very unpopular in my undergraduate career. Harvard declared war in 1914, right off the bat. They had no interest in any other point of view. I had a German name, inherited from my grandfather, so I was besought either to change my name or to join in anti-German manifestoes which I didn't believe in. The actual persecution, if you want to call it that, of anyone supposed to be pro-German then was as great or greater than the Joe McCarthy persecution of Communists. This was a rather bitter period.

"I enlisted in the Signal Corps. The Signal Corps was then a *corps d'elite* and sounded to me like rather fun. I stayed a private for a couple of weeks. When I was asked whether I wanted to go to Plattsburg and train for an officer, I accepted. In November 1917, I was commissioned as second lieutenant of infantry and was sent to the Army War College in Washington. . . .

"The equivalent of the War Production Board of that period was seeking to increase the production of sugar. Accordingly, in February 1918, Mr. Ralph Rounds, a New York attorney whose firm represented the South Puerto Rico Sugar Company in Puerto Rico with a subsidiary, Central Romana, in the Dominican Republic, requested the War Department to place me on 'inactive duty' for the purpose of going to Santo Domingo in connection with land titles and the movement of the sugar crop in the island.

"In March 1918, I landed in Santo Domingo City and went to work on clearing the land titles for the South Puerto Rico Sugar Company and any other company that would produce more sugar and export it to the United States. I may note that the program succeeded, although I don't think the sugar production came in until after it was far too late to be of great use in the war effort. I was learning then that economic planning and military planning are not necessarily coterminous. I was working with a first-rate Dominican lawyer, Francisco Peinado. Eventually we worked out a theory of land titles and a land court which would clear title to land and permit immediate sugar production. (This law was adopted by the military government and is still in operation.)

"The Dominican Republic at that time was occupied by the United States and the military governor was H. S. Knapp, an American admiral.

5

This was a dictatorship, full, complete, absolute, and total, no doubt about it.

"I soon became involved in Dominican politics. Peinado, like most Dominicans, didn't like the American occupation. He said, 'We can't fight the United States. But we must negotiate out of this somehow.' So he was heading a kind of group asking for the liquidation of the American occupation.

"I was working in the province of Seibo, on the extreme eastern end of the island. There was a small contingent of Marines there. The Marines were organizing a supplementary Guardia Nacional composed of Dominicans. My impression is that only the least capable Marine officers were left in the Dominican Republic, out in the districts, where they virtually had absolute power. . . . In Seibo, on one occasion, the Marine captain had been ambushed from behind a tree and killed. The second in command, who was a Guardia Nacional Officer—a Dominican—at once shot ten hostages against a blank wall. [Berle reported this to headquarters in Santo Domingo.] Admiral Knapp was a very honest man. An investigation was carried out—a court-martial was held—two or three men wound up in military psychiatric hospitals. . . .

"The situation for me, that phase of it, came to an end because in the summer of 1918 I went back to Washington.

"I reported in to the Adjutant General's office and was directed to the War College for an Intelligence assignment. I went into a large room. A lot of officers were working at desks and there was no place to sit down. As I was standing next to a desk, an orderly came in and called for Lieutenant Cushing. The man immediately next to me stood up. The orderly said, 'You're in luck, you've got orders for Siberia.'

("We were sending General [William S.] Graves to Siberia at that time, in the hope of controlling the Japanese. It was then that I reached a convinced dislike of sending American troops to Asia—not perhaps on the moral grounds that our youths urge today, but on the cold grounds that you can never control events there.)

"Anyhow, Lieutenant Cushing got up, and parted from the story of my life. His chair and desk were left vacant, so I sat down. Presently an orderly came in from the Colonel's office calling for the expert on Russian economics.

"I said, 'If you mean Cushing, he's gone to Siberia.'

"He said, 'Oh, has he? What do I do with this?'

"I said, 'What is it? Give it here.'

"It was a request from the Colonel to know the present rate of exchange on Finnish marks, Finland then being, of course, part of Russia. I fished a copy of the New York *Times* out of the wastebasket, looked it up on the financial page, wrote it out on a piece of paper, and sent it along back.

"Similar requests kept coming through all day; about the end of the day came the Colonel himself, inquiring for the expert on Russian economics. His name was [H. C.] Mason. I knew him later, delightful fellow.

"When he realized that Lieutenant Cushing had gone to Siberia and that I had been covering his desk, he asked, 'Who are you?' So I stood up and gave him my name. He looked at me, looked at the desk, and said, 'You're the expert on Russian economics. Give me your full name, number, and so forth, and I'll put it through.'

"So this is how I became an expert on Russian economics—pure chance! This meant trying to follow the economic side of the Russian involvement. This was positive intelligence, so called, not strategic. I was a bit stumped because I had never been in Russia. I wrote to my grandfather, who was then alive, and got all of the wisdom and notes I could out of him on Siberian geography and general sociology. Since this was precisely the area in which the play-off came at the close of the war, some of it was very useful. The rest of it I naturally studied as best I could. Anyhow, nobody challenged it.

"I was in Washington when the war ended. I never did get to Europe during the war.

"November 11, 1918 was the Armistice, and immediately thereafter the organization of the Paris Peace Conference. Six generals, not on the State Department list, had many experts on their staffs whom they thought would be useful for the conference. I don't think they were ever invited, but they went anyhow. They picked their staffs, and I was asked whether I would accompany them as one of the Russian experts. We all got our orders and were duly loaded off, first to England and then by boat to France."

The following passages are diary entries.

December 7th, 1918   Saturday
     Arrived last night in Paris, after a wild day.
     We came down from London to Southampton on Thursday, and took a transport to Le Havre—it was a converted cattle boat without accommodations except wooden coffin-like shelves—and we slept in our overcoats. It was cold work. We were treated with rather marked discourtesy by the British.
     At Le Havre, the only efficient Q.M. sergeant I ever met headed us for Paris, which we reached at midnight.
     We looked up the Railway Transport Office, and found the following —'6 officers coming. If assigned to Peace Conference put them in the Hotel Crillon; if to Supreme War Council, Versailles, nothing to be had!'
     Our orders read to Supreme War Council; and as we obviously couldn't tell the R.T.O. Corporal that this was camouflage to enable some Intelligence men to get into the Conference, our only course was to drive to the Crillon and try our luck. Which we did. Captain Pier emerged, he having gone ahead, and fixed things somehow. A palatial palace with Marie-Antoinette furnishings!
     This morning after any amount of red tape we reported. I looked up Mr. Storey, chief of the Political Intelligence (Moorfield Storey's son); shook hands with his aide, my old classmate Vanderbilt Webb, and was examined by an absolute stranger named [Royal] Tyler as to linguistics

and my desire to go to Russia (I do desire it. I desire more to stay here.)

This afternoon to Versailles, reported to General [Tasker H.] Bliss' [American Military Representative at the Supreme War Council] aide, Colonel U. S. Grant, and was duly assigned to the Peace Conference. Unlike the rest of the group I played it in the open, and said we had been sent to Bliss as a temporary assignment pending the arrival of the Secretary of War, or in any case, General [Marlborough] Churchill [Assistant Chief of Staff]. We were kindly heard; it appeared Bliss hadn't been taken into the scheme, and as a matter of fact there is a plain indication that we have mixed quite unwittingly in some one of [Chief of Staff] General [Peyton C.] March's intrigues.

The evening we spent at 'Thais'—Ten bars of Massenet's music, and the Conference, the Generals, the war, Paris, and the shifting pictures of the past week were left far behind . . . music is the Great Release. . . .

December 8, 1918   Sunday
"A leisurely morning—coffee in bed (a new experience to me—not altogether pleasant) and a late déjeuner. Got organized a bit in the morning: [Captain Stuart] Montgomery in charge of the Russian work, with [Walter] Pettit and myself as assistants. Looked over the recent digests here—apparently in Washington we have been rather closer to things than this group.

The Crillon is a curious sight. It has been taken over by the U.S. gov't for the Peace Delegation. It shelters a motley crew: Col. [Edward M.] House [adviser to Wilson] is there, also Admiral [W. S.] Benson [Chief of Naval Operations], and Gen. Bliss is to arrive soon; and besides these, there are hosts of minor retainers, gold-plated secretaries swaggering in splendid and unused uniforms, chargés drawn in from our legations, State Department officials and the like. Many are intriguing for themselves, but most are endeavoring to find themselves in a rather inchoate mass. The organization is in process of formation, and is slowly taking shape. [Joseph C.] Grew, as secretary of the Delegation, is really the most powerful man here. The surroundings are luxurious. . . . As a matter of fact life is very pleasant, tempered only by a wonder (on the part of the poorer members like myself) whether we are to be presented shortly with an enormous bill.

It is obvious that the United States stands as a strange isolated Parsifal among nations, with Wilson as the great idealist. The socialists make of him a messiah; their posters say—'A President Wilson—La France prêtera la plume avec laquelle sera souscrit une paix durable et juste'—or some such effect. . . .

December 12th, 1918   Thursday
. . . We are evicted from the Crillon, to make room for part of the President's party. Spent yesterday looking over the Latin Quarter the Luxemburg, etc. etc. and finally located a room in an old palace on the Rue de Varennes. In my search I came on [General John J.] Pershing's residence: a splendid place, in really ducal style; there is something sinis-

ter in the great American general's living on that bank of the Seine, and having nothing to do with the Peace Mission and diplomats on this side; and it is open talk that there is a great feud brewing between Pershing and March, whereby the latter has eliminated the Generalissimo from any part in the Peace. Perhaps it is as well. Why should generals make peace? On the other hand, why should diplomats? Oxenstierna's [17th-century Swedish statesman] little dictum [probably *"Bellum se ipse aleat"* (Let war feed itself)] is more and more pungent.

Walter Lippmann [editor, author] is to be our rédacteur; Col. Mason, to be our immediate chief. This means the old days back again.

The State Department is making as much of a bungle of this business as is conveniently possible.

December 14, 1918   Saturday

Wilson's triumphal entry. Place de la Concorde was solidly packed with thousands upon thousands—we could look down from our window in the Hotel Crillon opposite the Obélisque. A lane was cut from the Pont Alexandre III, and edged with blue soldiers in double line—there were mobs everywhere, even on the quai. I came to work about 9, and there had been crowds for hours. At half-past ten the guns saluted, and a little time later the Republican guards galloped down the lane, and then came a couple of automobiles; and then open carriages, Wilson, Poincaré, Mrs. Wilson, Bliss, Pichon, Castelnau, Jusserand, Pershing, etc.—amid cheers. Then the blue lines folded inward and the lane was lost in a seething mass. I thought there was not much enthusiasm. . . .

The boulevards have been crowded ever since with holiday crowds. Tonight it was as much as one could do to keep from losing hat or handkerchief.

. . . Noted also, that after the Wilson parade a lot of British soldiers paraded with a large banner "British—vos alliés 1914–1918!" It had a rather sinister look.

The fact is that both France and Britain have their own fish to fry. They don't want an effective League of Nations; Freedom of the seas; general reconcilations; and a square deal. France especially is for seizing everything in sight. Rhine Valley and all. The saner people want neutralization of the Left Bank (except, of course, Alsace Lorraine).

After leaving the Crillon, Berle ran into Robert Lord, one of his Harvard professors and the specialist on Russia and Poland. Lord invited him to become his aide and to help set up his office, above Maxim's restaurant, across from the Crillon.

"The same night, we got a communication from the Hoover Relief Organization to the Peace Conference, in this case to Robert Lord, chief of the East European divisions. It said, 'We have 10,000 tons shiploaded with food, where shall we send it? Candidates appear to be Odessa or Riga. In both places starvation is reported. Kindly advise where to send it.'

"Lord asked me to settle the question. It was assumed that eight or

9

ten thousand people would die wherever you didn't send it, so, this was life or death, theoretically, for eight or ten thousand people, and how do you decide questions like that?

"I sat up all night, partly studying and partly thinking. I finally sent it to Riga. This may not have been the right thing to do. My decision was based on the fact that the Latvian population had a somewhat higher degree of education, was somewhat more organized, more likely to make good use of it than the population in Odessa, caught in the full tide of the Russian Revolution. Thereafter the office got organized. Robert Lord was presently joined by a young man who had drifted in, of all things, in striped pants and a cutaway coat. His name was Samuel Morison—great historian—and when we saw him in striped pants we thought, 'Oh my God.'

"He had a forbidding mien. The next thing he said was that he wanted to borrow some money. There was nothing unusual about that. Pay at that time was interrupted. He was just out of the army as a private. He said he'd give us a note for it, and this made it still worse. Nobody gave notes for debts of that kind. So we took up a collection. I contributed and lent him I think about $30 or $40. He sat down and wrote out a note. I am sorry I didn't keep that note. It was funny. It was in Russian characters, 'I owe you so many rubles, payable as when the Czar is restored,' something like that, something foolish.

"This looked better. Actually under this stern New England profile he was one of the kindest, one of the most humorous, in some ways one of the tenderest men I've ever known.

"It developed that the Peace Conference had decided simply to put Russia into the Deep Freeze. But there were a lot of questions, notably Poland, where we did have business. After a while, Robert Lord was sent off as high commissioner to Poland."

Commenting on this situation, Berle wrote his father on February 17, 1919:

You will be inclined to laugh: but the fact is that Pettit and myself are the Russian experts here—Dr. Lord being away in Poland. *There is no one in the Government Service, except ourselves, who has followed the situation closely.* It is all wrong of course; no youngster of twenty-four ought to be making policy. But the simple fact is that there is no one else to make it. When I get free of this business I can tell you the tale.

The last couple of days have been as exciting as can well be; for the League project is out (you have it in America by this time), and to tell the honest truth, not much of anyone is satisfied. As will appear, it has thrown a bomb into my own little dugout. I had a little to do with putting some of the sections of the draft into their final form, though it was more mechanical revision and translation work.

But my own sensations are the same as those of Marcel Cachin, the Socialist editor here: he wrote in *L'Humanité* that he could not conceal his disillusionment. The same afternoon he ran into Sam Morison, our new office mate, at one of [journalist] Lewis Gannett's teas; and the discussion waxed warm, concluding with Cachin's remark that the Socialists in France, to whom Wilson had been a Messiah until six weeks ago, felt that he had failed them in a crisis, and though they would not oppose him, they would search elsewhere for the great idealistic leadership which they sought.

. . . What struck me however was this. The League is so far at least only a closer cementing of the Entente. Under the current proposals there must be two great outlaw nations—Germany, which is not to be let in for a considerable period, and then only by two-thirds vote, and Russia, in like position. The result is to put an irresistible pressure, military, economic, moral, on these countries to ally, unite, smash the buffer states of Poland and Bohemia, and with the greatest resources of manpower, raw material, and technical, organizing ability in the world, defy the whole League. They would have the power to do this. To me it seemed childishly simple to come at this conclusion; and there is every reason to believe the idea has occurred to both Russians and Germans. Such an entente could start the whole game of competitive armaments on a bigger scale than ever; it is economically independent, and the League could do nothing effective save to start another war. The remedy would be a rapprochement with the one or the other. . . . It is manifestly a political impossibility at the present time to get any sympathy for a rapprochement with the Germans. Personally I should think a German rapprochement would be desirable to a Russian one, but it can't be done. . . .

"In the meantime, [British Prime Minister] Lloyd George had decided to send a mission to Russia to see if terms could be made with Lenin. William C. Bullitt [attaché to the American Commission and responsible for Current Intelligence Summaries] was picked for that mission. He had his instructions from Lloyd George's private secretary, Philip Carr (Lord Lothian), who later became ambassador to Washington. The Bullitt mission was duly organized. He took with him Lincoln Steffens and Walter Pettit. Bullitt was the only one who really got into Russia. The other two men stayed in Finland.

"Bullitt did negotiate a treaty with Lenin. Since he was reporting to our office, we knew the details of it. Before he returned, the French Intelligence got the text, and on Clemenceau's orders started a campaign against it. They called Bullitt an adventurer, with no real standing. Lloyd George said he knew nothing about it. We of course had a copy of the instructions Bullitt had from Lloyd George's private secretary. Wilson denied knowledge of it. I've never known even today whether Wilson knew about it or whether Lloyd George and Colonel House put this one over behind his back."

To his father, May 6, 1919

The thrill over Wilson's Fiume statement lasted about two days; then there came the Shantung-Kiauptschan business and the miserable compromise even on Fiume; and I have come to the conclusion that no statement of ideals by anybody will ever get any reaction from me again. If I can trust myself, I shall be happy; if I trust anyone else, I shall be a fool. Once in a lifetime a Wilson may capitalize your ideals; but the next man has a different proposition. In practice of course it does not make much difference because the forces unloosed are far too elemental to be tamed by any treaty; and perhaps as to the other matter, the lesson is well learned early.

Yesterday Bullitt called me in and asked that an offensive and defensive alliance be made; wanted to start a new drive on the Russian situation, and asked me to come in on it; and I will though Bullitt is in disgrace in a sense, and though it is taking one's life in one's hands. The proposition was attractive; I went out to lunch and pondered it, considering the matter over a mug of beer; and came to the conclusion that it would be better to tie to a man who was at least trying to get something done than to a bunch who consider that 'watchful waiting' is slowly letting the matter straighten itself out—as though a straightening which already counted ten million deaths by starvation and the wreck, devastation and anarchy of the greatest country in Europe was a solution. . . .

To his sister Lina Berle, May 8, 1919

The peace terms are out, and I suppose somebody is satisfied with them; in any event we are not, and the unforgivable sin is the sanctifying to Japan of the Shantung concessions. It is a plain case wherein the principles on which we theoretically fought have been betrayed; and there is no excuse for it on any explanation. The French are measurably pleased with the ensemble, but I must confess that to me it seems as great a crime as Brest-Litovsk—Jeremiads aside, however. The Jeunesse Radicale [an informal group of young officials who protested the treaty] are contemplating action, though we don't as yet know what it will come to.

Bullitt resigned on May 17. The daily report to the peace mission dated May 22, 1919, quoted an article from the London *Daily Herald*.

"SENSATION AT CONFERENCE—NINE AMERICAN PEACE DELEGATES RESIGN FROM MISSION TO PARIS—DISGUSTED WITH TREATY. It says that practically the whole of the membership of the American Commission at Paris are disgusted and disappointed with the Peace Treaty. You will not find a half dozen of them who approve it. They are convinced that so far from being a basis of lasting peace, the Treaty will be the direct and certain cause of further wars. And they are beginning to say so distinctly. Already resignations are beginning. Bullitt, Young and Isaiah Bowman have resigned. *Six other highly placed members of the delegation staff* have tendered their resignations. They find they have assisted in the making of a peace based, not on the ideals for which America fought, but upon the greeds and ambitions of European Imperialists. The general feeling of the delegation is that they have been duped. They resent keenly the manner in which the peace has been framed; the secrecy, the autocratic methods of the Big Four; the refusal to listen to criticism; the contemptuous flouting of the will of the people."

A few days previously the Jeunesse Radicale, including Lincoln Steffens, Samuel Morison, Joseph V. Fuller, Christian Herter, George Noble, and Berle dined together at the Crillon. Recalling the episode in 1940, Berle wrote to Bullitt, then U.S. Ambassador to Paris:

. . . I told Upton Sinclair about your chucking the red roses to the people who had resigned from the peace conference and the yellow jonquils to the people who hadn't. . . . As I have your signature on the menu card for that dinner, I can prove your presence by documentary evidence, though the incident abides merely in a rather vivid recollection of the evening.

Bullitt and other civilian members of the Jeunesse Radicale could resign; Berle, in the army, could only ask to be relieved of his duties, which he did.

AMERICAN COMMISSION
TO NEGOTIATE PEACE

May 15th, 1919.

From: A. A. Berle, Jr.

To: Mr. Grew (for the Commissioners).

After reading the summary of the terms of the proposed German treaty, and examining its text, I feel bound in honor to place on record my protest against American acquiescence in it.

The American war was declared, supported, and fought to a victorious conclusion on and for certain fundamental principles, stated by the President, to the attainment of which the United States pledged itself. The treaty as prepared seems in large measure to have abandoned both letter and spirit of these pledges. The abandonment seems to include not merely the compromises necessary to achieve a humanly workable scheme, but in many cases, a surrender of the principles involved. In certain striking instances (notably the Japanese clauses), the treaty threatens also to create a situation thoroughly dangerous to the interests of the United States.

Bearing in mind the difficulty of securing persons acquainted in detail with the subject matter of my present duties, and having no desire to hinder the work here in any way, I leave to the Commissioners the question of my continued connection with the Commission. My single desire is to serve faithfully the United States, and to assist in realizing, so far as possible, the ideals expressed by the President prior to the proposal of the treaty. But, (if by no other considerations), the honorable fulfilment of my oath as a United States Officer would constrain me to a statement that conclusion of the proposed treaty will not, in my judgement, serve either the idealistic or material interests of America, or, indeed, of humanity.

Grew, replying on May 20, stated that the Commissioners desired "further time" to consider his request. In mid-June, however, Wilson's assistance to Admiral Alexander Kolchak's anti-Bolshevik drive prompted Berle to insist upon a reconsideration. Writing to the American Commissioners Plenipotentiary on June 17,

13

he said: "I find myself in the peculiar difficulty of wholeheartedly disagreeing with the proposed line of action, and completely unable to secure its alteration, yet . . . under military orders to further it. . . ." Unable to get Berle to change his mind, Grew wrote on June 25: "I beg to advise you that the Commissioners, on June 23d, approved your request to be released from the Commission."

Berle received orders to sail for home on June 30; this action was followed by a certificate of honorable discharge, on July 9, and a promotion to first lieutenant, dated August 28, 1919.

Reflecting on Versailles thirteen years later, Berle replied to an inquiry from John Bassett Moore, an eminent authority on international law:

July 27, 1932

The Versailles incident has not, I think, been very much in print. I was not a member of the legal staff, but was a member of the expert staff, doing Russian and Baltic affairs.

Some ten or twelve of the staff resigned at the same time. They were: Joseph V. Fuller, Samuel Eliot Morison, William C. Bullitt, George Noble, and two or three other men whose names I do not now recall. We did not get up a joint memorandum; and the reasons were all different though they revolved around a central conception. This was that when you make war you try to win; but when you make peace, you try to reach a real peaceful solution, permitting nations to live together happily. I recall writing when the treaty was in draft that it did not forward any interest of the United States nor did it advance the interests of the World in general; that the Shantung clauses violated our whole policy with regard to China and that the European clauses violated every principle on which we had gone to war.

In the flush of great bitterness, I wrote an article in *The Nation*, "The Betrayal at Paris", [August 1919] and stated, though I think with more feeling than wisdom, what I then felt.

At the time of our resignation, the Paris newspapers attempted to make a good deal of it, but the French censor cut out the story; and two or three papers appeared next day with front pages almost wholly blank.

Mr. [Robert] Lansing [Secretary of State 1915–1920] in his autobiography mentions the fact that various individuals, when the draft treaty appeared, indicated their dissatisfaction with it. I believe also that it was at this time that [British economist] John Maynard Keynes and one or two other men resigned from the British delegation for about the same reasons.

At twenty-four (accident had put me in an interesting position when I was still extremely young) one has not the maturity to deal with these situations very effectively. And yet, thirteen years after the event, I am not disposed to apologize. Inexperienced as we were, I think we did foresee, accurately, that a treaty based on hatred and irritation, and an endeavor to perpetuate the advantage of war in favor of the Allies under the cover of a so-called peace, would produce nothing but long drawn out misery. I am glad to find that you agree; there were few enough then to lend even moral support in what seemed like—and of course was—a futile gesture. . . .

After Versailles, Berle entered the law firm of Rounds, Hatch, Dillingham and Debevoise in New York as an associate.

"In 1923 I had a case which was fascinating to me. The secretary of the American Indian Defense Association, who later became Commissioner of Indian Affairs, John Collier, came to the firm looking for advice in connection with the defense of the titles of the Pueblos of New Mexico and Arizona. At that time, in the Harding administration, the Secretary of Interior was taking some of their lands, and there was a bill introduced in Congress by Senator [Holm D.] Bursum [R., N.M.] which might have stripped them of their lands, and they were looking for legal advice. Nobody in the firm had much interest in it. In the Dominican Republic I had become quite familiar with old Spanish colonial law. Under this law the Pueblos are themselves entities. Collier asked if I would act as attorney for the Pueblos.

"So I took a vacation. I went out and lived with the Pueblos for a while to try to get the drift of the case and how the situation worked and likewise the facts as nearly as you could, via the tribal saga, because it really is that, as to what had actually happened, so that I could come back and either try a case in the courts or, as we finally did get it worked out, get an act through Congress. Quite a bit of brouhaha had been stirred up about the violation of Indian rights, and you'll recall that the fate of the officers of the Harding Cabinet was not too good—Albert B. Fall and others."

Berle and a friend, Charles Fabens, went by train to New Mexico. The following entries are from his handwritten diary.

August 5—Santa Fé and Domingo
    To Sunmount Sanitarium to see Mrs. Mary Austin [author of *Earth Horizon*], who is ill; Mrs. Mabel Lujan (née Mabel Dodge!) and Antonio Lujan joined us. A.L. is chief of the Pueblo of Taos; where Mabel picked him up and married him I don't know. He speaks fair English; good Spanish; was, in fact, the majestic burnous-clad Indian [we met] yesterday.
    We conferred two hours or so, agreeing to call a conference for Monday, and a general meeting of all the chiefs of all the Pueblos on the 25th. . . .

August 6th—Santa Fé
    Wandered about the old Palace of the Spanish governor in Santa Fé Plaza, browsing among the historical library there: came on Twitchell's 'New Mexican Archives' and much valuable data on pueblo history etc. —To the Federal Court where were Charles and Francis Wilson [former government counsel for the group of Indians] and we consulted about divers matters; F.W. firmly convinced that the Pueblo Indians must be protected against their own generosity to Mexican squatters; but that these last must not be unduly harmed where they have built on land in good faith; went over the record of Twitchell's test case to prove that statute of limitations does not run in favor of squatters against Indian pueblos (*U.S.* vs. *Candelaria*)—and a worse test case I never did see. . . .

August 11, Taos

. . . forth-with out, with A. Lujan, Antonio Romero, the cleverest of the Taos Indians, and Mary Austin, Collier, and Mrs. Lujan, to Glorieta, the sacred grove of the Taos Pueblo, to dine by an open fire. An eerie grove; with occasional Indians riding by on horseback, their white burnouses over blue smocks looking more Bedouin than ever: three passed at dusk, chanting as they went. We fed well, and to Taos Pueblo, to the Governor's house.

[August 15]

It seems that a man is Governor for a single year only; then he becomes a Principal; so that there is always a young Governor to act on the advice of older ex-governors or principals. Usually he has been lieutenant-governor before his term of office. In some cases there is an historian—who by oral tradition—singularly exact—keeps the history of their land matters alive. Some Pueblos have also a reigning hereditary Cacique, of less actual than symbolic importance.

Aug. 11

When we came in the Council was assembled: silent Indians, arriving like white-coated ghosts; throwing back their burnouses as they entered the little room. It was a low-raftered, whitewashed room in a 'dobe house —not in the tiered pueblo itself—with a Crucifixion and a calendar, and the two canes—Spanish and American—symbols of the Governor's office —hanging on the wall. . . .

The Governor sitting silently on his bed; the interpreter talking at intervals; the information proceeding largely from a deaf old man "Viejito"—who remembered back to the old grant, which they produced. It was signed by Abraham Lincoln.

An oil lamp over the fireplace. A low bed for Collier, Charles, and me to sit on. The Indians, sitting against the wall. I started in Spanish—but legal Spanish proved too complex so that Tony Romero finally interpreted from English—the Indians murmuring "m-m" at the end of each sentence. We explained our hopes and fears; our proposed legislation; asked their advice. They agreed in general, wished to talk; announced that they would come to the grand council on the 25th and we came away, —all gravely shaking hands—greeting us in Spanish—standing, white-clad in the darkness as we got into the automobile A. Lujan drove us away.

To Mrs. Lujan's; and Charles and I put in an evening hour outlining the legislation. We have scrapped our first and second drafts.

Learning is bad business. It upsets one's ideas fearfully.

A good day—

August 12—Picuris Pueblo—Taos

A long ride over the hills to Picuris Pueblo where I sketched the lands from the top of their circular *Kiva* or temple. This Pueblo once had three valleys: Picuris, Penasco, Llano. Now they have 100 acres of arable land in Picuris: there are 85 left out of 3000 in 1700.

This is the worst case I have seen so far. The encroachments are fairly recent. The men said they had, as boys, herded cattle on the bottom lands now totally taken up by Mexican squatters.

But it is no joke to evict the Mexicans. They are humble people; working hard; their little houses are well cared for: it goes against my grain to throw out a family whose land is tilled and whose house is surrounded by hollyhocks and larkspur. No help for it, though. We must get them some compensation. . . .

August 16

. . . to Nambe where we found the Governor a Mexican half-breed, cutting alfalfas and requisitioned a room from him in his summer house —a 'dobe dwelling in the fields; sent him to the Pueblo to call a council while we picknicked on corned beef and coffee; and to the Pueblo to discuss.

Next to Picuris this is the most unlucky of all; because the Indians have intermarried and their organization is corroded; also they have traitors who have sold their land. We had three chairs; the council squatted against the wall. An oil lamp on a discarded stove gave a dubious light. The old chief—whose treason had caused some of the Nambe grant to be sold—was the man to whom we had to appeal for information. He spoke in Indian, which was interpreted into Spanish—it seems there are two claims—one of the Romeros to whom he had sold against protest of the tribe. This sale had been assisted by an exaggerated claim by Romero: and was confirmed in court after litigation. The other was regarding land lent to one Armijo who had assisted the Indians in ancient times against Navajo raids. They there lent him land for three years. Whereon Armijo forged a Spanish "merced" and claimed title. To get him from under their walls they exchanged a piece of land down the Nambe river, near the border—where there is now a little church and a cluster of houses. Strange business, this raising of Spanish ghosts long dead, to untangle present injustice.

A dramatic interlude. The head-man of the heirs of the last of the Pojuaque Pueblo—eight miles away, but now deserted—asked what could be done for his people. And it appearing that some nine of them had taken refuge at Nambe; still have organization, and still claim their land, and have defended it at times, I told them to keep up their Governor and their Council; to go, once a year to the deserted Pueblo; to hold their meeting there; formally to take and hold possession of their cities and their lands; and to send a representative to the All Pueblo Council at Santo Domingo Pueblo on the 25th. . . .

August 25—Domingo Pueblo—The Grand Council

Early up and to Domingo with Charles, J. Collier, Mrs. Atwood. The council assembled and after a secret meeting invited us in. The whole New Mexican Association on Indian Affairs on hand. Likewise Crandall, Indian agent, who sympathizes with us: Mrs. Austin; etc. Debate in Spanish. I opened; much discussion on the townsite matter—the Indians finally agreeing to cede the townsites; and squarely against the Lenroot

Bill [to settle land claims, land grants, and reservations in New Mexico].

Raid by the New Mexican Association, they having undertaken to break up the meeting. M. McKittrich leading the raid. Witter Bynner and W. Henderson [members of New Mexican Association] following. After which J. Collier spoke. The Indians asked to have the resolution read; and unanimously adopted our program. Amusing side-play when, after the New Mexican Association raid a Laguna delegate, Presbyterian preacher, lectured us all on the values of Christian-unity and brotherhood! Quite right, say I. The White men can learn a lot from these dignified, courteous Indians.

. . . So the campaign ends for a time.

There have been annoyances and sorrows. But there have been compensations and the thing was worth doing. The moonlit nights of Taos; the stately courtesy of the Pueblo Indians; the glorious quality of their character—their home-loving and their enthusiasm—are things I shall long remember. The "Vaya: Taos!" as our car came back to Taos plain and the Taos delegates cheered the sight of their home and their sacred mountain, was a real delight.

It is a real job, this building walls around a creditable race whose only fault is that their spiritual, idealist civilization fares ill in competition with our more grasping ideas of life. The stakes are worth playing for. —There is no villain in the play. The Indian enemy is no single man or group. It is the whole drive of the white materialistic political and economic organism—

"What we succeeded in doing was to draft a bill in which, first, the existence of the Pueblos was recognized. They were recognized as bodies corporate having rights. Second, their rights under Spanish law were recognized. Third, a commission was to be appointed to survey out and go over the lands which the Pueblo Indians claimed and which were in dispute, and fourth a procedure was determined with standards to determine the rights which the Pueblo Indians had, as against the possessions of outsiders. The problem was not free from doubt. If the Pueblo Indians had rights, as they did, there were in a number of cases occupancies going back a couple of centuries of Mexicans who had either descended from the Spanish armies that had been there many many decades ago or others that had been there and the families had continued to occupy the land. So it wasn't quite as clean cut as one might expect.

"The commission was appointed. Likewise right was given to the Pueblos to bring action in a federal court to determine and have decreed to them the titles to the lands to which they were entitled. The general outline of those rights, more or less delimited by the Spanish law, was likewise recognized, so they had a forum in which the claim could be presented, a basis by which the claim could be recognized, and a prohibition of further interruption of their rights until the final delimitation of land could be worked out. There were additional provisions which I think assisted the Indians, at least the Indians thought they did, and certainly the result has been fairly good. Those Pueblos are there today, many of them flourishing. They have their lands and they raise their cattle and they have their water rights, and if there were any mining rights—I haven't heard of any—they would have those also. It also meant that if they did choose to allow outsiders, that is to say non-Indians, in their territory, they could collect rent for them, and have the land tenure such that the Pueblos could take it back.

"I haven't maintained connection with it, so I don't know what the situation is today. . . .

"After the Indian adventure, I returned to practicing law in New York and in January 1924 I formed a partnership with a man I had met in the Dominican Republic and with whom I had worked there, Guy Lippitt. The firm was named Lippitt and Berle, and we hired, chiefly on our nerve, a small office at 67 Wall Street, and started in for ourselves. This was the time when you hoped your retainers and payments would cover the rent and leave you a little over to live on, and when at the end of the first year we checked out with about $4,600 apiece as net profits, we considered we'd done very well.

". . . The important thing about that situation to me, strangely, came in a different direction.

"First, I had been asked to be lecturer in finance at the then nascent Harvard Business School. This meant that I gave three classes in finance once a week, Mondays, usually, in Cambridge. This was in 1925. This brought in a little revenue, which I needed. It also made some contacts, some of which I still have.

"While working as an instructor in corporation finance, I began to study the corporation as an institution. Specifically I began to write articles. One of them ["Non-cumulative Preferred Stock" 23 *Columbia Law Review* 358, 1923] I'd written before I got out of Rounds, Hatch, Dillingham and Debevoise, but I began to write a few others, and one or two of them were published in the *Harvard Law Review* ["Non-voting Stock and 'Bankers Control' " 39 *Harvard Law Review* 673, 1926], most of them in the *Columbia Law Review* ["Participating Preferred Stock" 26 *Columbia Law Review* 303, 1926; "Problems of Non-Par Stock" 23 *Columbia Law Review,* 1925]. This was unpaid work. You don't get paid for writing articles for law reviews.

"The attempt I was then making was to assert the doctrine that corporate managements were virtually trustees for their stockholders, and that they could not therefore deal in the freewheeling manner in which directors and managers had dealt with the stock and other interests of their companies up to that time. It was the beginning of the fiduciary theory of corporations which now is generally accepted.

"I mention that because that set of articles led to the next stage in my career. The whole handling of corporation law, both academically and in the courts, shocked me at the time. Finally I made a very youthful move. I asked for an appointment with the Dean of the Columbia Law School. He was Harlan Stone, who later, as you know, became Attorney General and then a justice of the Supreme Court and finally Chief Justice of the United States. . . .

"I told him I thought the course in corporation law given at Columbia was no good. He grinned and replied courteously that it was given by his partner, who had not changed the course for thirty years. He asked what I thought ought to be done. I replied I thought corporation law could not be taught without paying a good deal of attention to the realities and to the law of corporation finance. I did not see how you can simply go on repeating the rules that applied to the little corporation of twenty, thirty, forty years ago, and pay no attention to what goes on in the stock market, the bond market, the flotation of securities markets, and the whole financial processes with which corporations are not only intimately associated, but of which they're the principal cause. 'I think the material ought to be amalgamated. We ought now to bring finance right in as part of corporation law.'

"Stone said, 'I'd like to think about that a little. These things don't happen quite as rapidly as you seem to think they do, but I'm wondering. Would you consider perhaps giving a seminar, say one day a week or something of this kind. Will you try to teach corporation finance tandem with corporation law? And let the subject develop a bit.'

"I said, 'I think that will be interesting.'

"I ought to add that something else had happened about the same time. Some of the articles I had written for the Harvard and the Columbia law reviews had come to the notice of a Harvard professor of economics named William Zebine Ripley. Ripley had been discussing this academically in his classrooms at Harvard. He used some of my material in a book which he published called *Main Street and Wall Street*. This was a smashing success from the point of view of circulation. He discussed these doctrines of corporation finance and the fiduciary capacity or obligation of directors in connection with the public utility holding companies which were then building to massive proportions; in the course of it we met. . . .

"About the same time there was being formed the Social Science Research Council, in effect to spend money on research in various economic and social subjects, financed by the Laura Spelman Rockefeller Foundation. William Zebine Ripley was on the organizing committee of that; [Boston merchant Edward A.] Filene was on the board, and my meeting with him at this time resulted later in my association with the Twentieth Century Fund.

". . . I presented a project toward the study of corporations, and very much to my surprise got a grant from the Social Science Research Council. It was not, as you would think today, a very elaborate one. I think it may have amounted all together to about $7,000. I've forgotten the exact figures. But the Social Science Council stipulated that the research should be carried on in connection with some recognized university. I hadn't any recognized university; I was alone in my glory at 67 Wall Street. So I went looking for a university.

"My first visit was to the Dean of the Yale Law School. His name was Robert Hutchins. He had no interest in this at all. Then I went to Harlan Stone again and suggested that I would like to give a course at Columbia and do the research at the same time.

"I joined the faculty of the Columbia Law School in 1927 and left the Harvard Business School at the end of that year.

"The research gradually took form. I needed an associate as statistical and economic research assistant. I found an old bunkmate of mine from Plattsburg days. His name was Gardiner C. Means. He had done his undergraduate work at Harvard in economics and was enrolled at the graduate school at Harvard as a candidate for a Ph.D. in economics. I asked Gardiner if he would join me, which he did. We shared a little office in Kent Hall at Columbia and eventually on the grant we got a stenographer assistant.

"As a result of this research the book *The Modern Corporation and Private Property* emerged. It was completed in 1931 and published in 1932. Gardiner Means contributed so much through his statistical studies that I considered his name should appear on the title page. We were finally able to persuade the authorities at Harvard to accept the work on this volume for his thesis requirement and as a result he obtained his Ph.D.

"In the course of preparing this book, the financial situation of the country was changing rapidly. While analyzing the methods of financing current on Wall Street during the period 1927–1930, I became very critical of them. The public seemed to be totally unprotected. The ideas expressed by William Zebine Ripley in *Main Street and Wall Street* were proving to be only to correct. The freewheeling corporation that could do anything it pleased with no consideration for either production or the public seemed intolerable to me. Many of these ideas and the possible legal remedies are expressed in *The Modern Corporation and Private Property*. Actually, though we didn't know it at the time, we were laying down the principles on which the securities-and-exchange legislation in force today is based. I subsequently was active in drafting some of the legislation."

Diary, June 27, 1947

When *The Modern Corporation and Private Property* was brought out it was first published by the Corporation Clearing House. Mr. Darr (now of the West Publishing Company, publishers of my law case books) handled the matters connected with its publication in 1932. The Corporation Clearing House was a law book publishing company, the stock of which was owned by the Corporation Trust Company.

Shortly thereafter a representative of the Corporation Clearing House called on me to say that they thought they could not handle the book properly and wished to transfer the contract to some other publishing company and arrangements were finally made to transfer the contract to Macmillan, which then took over the book.

Darr tells me that the story behind it was this:

One of the large corporation clients of the Corporation Trust Company (Darr believes the General Motors Corporation) read a review of the book and then called on the Corporation Trust Company explaining that in the view of that corporation no such book ought to be published.

The Corporation Trust Company agreed that they would require CCH to drop it at once. This the CCH did.

That was in 1932. It would be interesting to know whether a corporation of that size and standing would do the same thing in 1947.

"An arrangement finally was worked out by which we peddled the plates of the book to Macmillan and Co. Just prior to that, the book had been discovered by the *Nation,* then a liberal paper, edited by Oswald Garrison Villard. I think Stuart Chase was assigned to review it, which he did handsomely. The *New Republic* did somewhat the same thing. It began to attract some attention, and in Columbia it was very well considered.

"I may add that the crash of 1929 had somewhat changed the views of a good many people on the immutable brilliance of the preceding system of corporation finance. A great many people were prepared to accept criticism of the system that perhaps they might not have been prepared to accept earlier. In financial circles and circles of great wealth, the book was very unpopular.

"In tribute to Columbia University I wish to state that during this and the ensuing period of the New Deal, the university never even indicated that it might be inconvenient for it in relation to possible donors on whose gifts Columbia then, as now, depends. Nicholas Murray Butler was president. He rallied me a couple of times on it and said 'Stay with it.' The Columbia Law School faculty, far from disapproving, approved it. They seemed to think that the law was sound. I had a little luck in that the courts cited the book two or three times in connection with decisions, which indicated perhaps that it was entitled to be taken seriously. The book is still used as a text, and a revised edition was published in 1968.

"The story really has significance in the fact that when you are sitting in a little office watching the elevated trains go by—they did go by then—and do not have enough clients to occupy your time and have to work your head, thinking may determine what happens to you later. I could not have guessed that at the time, nor did I realize that the training in teaching the subject plus a lot of thinking and writing really was important."

Charles A. Beard, reviewing the first edition of *The Modern Corporation and Private Property* in the New York *Herald Tribune* on February 19, 1933, wrote: "In the time to come this volume may be proclaimed as the most important work bearing on American statecraft between the publication of the immortal 'Federalist' by Hamilton, Madison, and Jay and the opening of the year 1933. . . . if there is any intelligence among Americans supposed to be intelligent, 'The Modern Corporation and Private Property' will mark a sharp turning point in fundamental, deep-thrusting thinking about the American State and American civilization. Nothing less should be said in introducing to the public this masterly achievement of research and contemplation."

In 1968, Harcourt Brace Jovanovich published a revised edition. Robert Lekachman commented in the New York *Times Book Review* on September 15, 1968: "The 36 years since the original publication have certainly not diminished the social significance of the large corporation, any more than time has weakened the power of Berle's and Means's analysis of its operations."

In the preface to the revised edition, entitled "Property, Production, and Revolution," Berle noted:

More than thirty years ago, in the preface of this book, I wrote: The translation of perhaps two-thirds of the industrial wealth of the country from individual ownership to ownership by the large, publicly financed corporations vitally changes the lives of property owners, the lives of workers, and the methods of property tenure. The divorce of ownership from control consequent on that process almost necessarily involves a new form of economic organization of society. . . .

The effect of this change upon the property system of the United States has been dramatic. Individually owned wealth has enormously increased. It is today reckoned at more than 1,800 billion dollars. Of more importance is the distribution of that figure. Relatively little of it is "productive" property—land or things employed by its owners in production or commerce—though figures are hazy at the edges. The largest item of individually owned wealth, exclusive of productive assets, is described as "owner-occupied homes" (approximately 520 billion dollars). These, of course, are primarily for consumption, though a fraction of them are probably farmsteads. The next largest item—consumer durables—accounts for 210 billion dollars more; these are chiefly automobiles and home equipment, again chiefly used for personal convenience and not for capital or productive purposes.

. . . "Individually owned" enterprise is thus steadily disappearing. Increasingly, the American owns his home, his car, and his household appliances; these are for his consumption. Simultaneously, he increasingly owns stocks, life insurance, and rights in pension funds, social security funds and similar arrangements. And he has a job, paying him a wage, salary or commission. . . .

. . . In crude summation, most "owners" own stock, insurance savings and pension claims and the like, and do not manage; most managers (corporate administrators) do not own. The corporate collective holds legal title to the tangible productive wealth of the country—for the benefit of others.

The word "revolutionary" has been justifiably applied to less fundamental change. The United States is no longer anticipating a development. It is digesting a fact. . . .

We must note an enormous expansion of the scope of the term "property" in this connection. Not only is it divorced from the decision-making power of its supposedly beneficial holders (stockholders and their various removes), but it has come to encompass a set of conceptions superimposed upon the central reality of domination over tangible things. Businessmen describe an enterprise, great or small, as "the property." They do not mean merely the physical plant. They include access to all the facilities necessary to produce, transport, distribute and sell. They mean an entire organization of personnel without which the physical plant would be junk; they mean a hierarchy of executives, technical experts, sales managers and men; as well as the dealer organization and the labor-relations habits. . . .

A counterforce registers the impact of this extension. Literally enormous quantities of technical information have been accumulated by government and thrust into fields of non-statist enterprise. Resources of nuclear energy and nuclear physics are the most dramatic—but by no means the only or even perhaps the most significant—of these intrusions. Nearly two-thirds of all technical research is now financed by the federal government. Through a great number of modern industries—one thinks at once of electronics, of aviation, and of space-satellite communication—this government-financed technique enters the process of corporate explosion. By no stretch of imagination can it be described as property primarily created by private enterprise. Like it or not, these assets are social and statist in origin. Complete turnover of these assets to "private" (that is, non-statist) ownership seems wholly unlikely. Illustration of the impact—and of a compromise—is found in the Communications Satellite Act authorizing creation of ComSat, a corporation owned one-half by the federal government and one-half by private investors. . . .

"Property" when used in connection with and as adjunct to legal (that is, corporate) ownership is thus changing its import—not because the old rules relating to ownership of a plant have changed, but because of the addition of an enormous proportion of new content differing both in kind and in origin from the old. . . .

A mature corporation typically does not call for investor-supplied capital. It charges a price for its products from which it can pay taxation, costs, depreciation allowances, and can realize a profit over and above all these expenses. Of this profit item, approximately half goes as income taxes to the federal government, and 60 per cent of the remaining half is distributed to its shareholders. It accumulates for capital purposes the undistributed 40 per cent and its depreciation charges. This is a phenomenon not of "investment," but of market power. Since corporations legally have perpetual life, this process can continue indefinitely. The result has been that more than 60 per cent of capital entering a particular industry is "internally generated" or, more accurately, "price-generated" because it is collected from the customers. Another 20 per cent of the capital the corporation uses is borrowed from banks chiefly in anticipation of this accumulative process. The corporations in aggregate do indeed tap individual "sayings," but for only a little less than 20 per cent of their capital, and mainly through the issuance of bonds to intermediate savings-collecting institutions (life insurance companies, trust funds, pension trusts and savings banks). . . .

Not surprisingly, therefore, we discover a body of law building up to protect and deal with this remarkable phenomenon. To that fact itself perhaps is due a continuing tendency: subjection of property devoted to *production*—that is, chiefly in managerial hands—to legal rules requiring a use of it, more or less corresponding to the evolving expectations of American civilization. . . .

Increased size and domination of the American corporation has automatically split the package of rights and privileges comprising the old conception of property. Specifically, it splits the personality of the individual beneficial owner away from the enterprise manager. The "things" themselves—including the intangible elements noted earlier in this essay—"belong" to the corporation which holds legal title to them. The ultimate beneficial interest embodied in a share of stock represents an expectation that a portion of the profits remaining after taxes will be declared as dividends, and that in the relatively unlikely event of liquidation each share will get its allocable part of the assets. . . .

Yet this is only the "top level" of passive property-holding. A very large number of shares are not held by individuals, but by intermediate fiduciary institutions which in turn distribute the benefits of shareholding to participating individuals. One of the two largest groups of such intermediary institutions is that of the pension trust funds maintained by corporations or groups of corporations for the benefit of employees; these collect savings in regular installments from employers to be held in trust for their employees and subsequently paid to them as old-age or other similar benefits. The second is the relatively smaller group of institutions known as mutual funds; these buy a portfolio of assorted stocks and sell participations in the portfolio to individuals desiring to hold an interest in diversified groups of stock instead of directly holding shares in one or more companies. Through the pension trust funds not fewer than twenty million (probably a great many more) employees already have an indirect beneficial claim both to the dividends proceeding from shares and to their market value in the pension portfolio—even though their interest is non-liquid, and is received only on retirement, death or (occasionally) other contingency. Perhaps two million holders of shares in mutual funds are likewise indirect beneficiaries, although they receive current return, and can promptly convert their shares into cash.

. . . Comparatively speaking, all these institutions combined probably own a relatively small fraction of all stocks outstanding—perhaps between 5 and 10 per cent. Yet the rapidity of their growth—especially striking in the case of pension trusts—indicates that this form of stockholding is likely to become dominant in future years.

The significance of the intermediate institutions is twofold. First, they vastly increase the number of citizens who, to some degree, rely on the stockholding form of wealth. Second, they remove the individual still further from connection with or impact on the management and administration of the productive corporations themselves. . . .

. . . The purchaser of stock does not contribute savings to an enterprise, thus enabling it to increase its plant or operations. He does not take the "risk" of a new or increased economic operation; he merely estimates the chance of the corporation's shares increasing in value. The contribution his purchase makes to anyone other than himself is the maintenance of liquidity for other shareholders who may wish to convert their holdings into cash. Clearly he cannot and does not intend to contribute managerial or entrepreneurial effort or service.

This raises a problem of social ethics that is bound to push its way into the legal scene in the next generation. Why have stockholders? What contribution do they make, entitling them to heirship of half the profits of the industrial system, receivable partly in the form of dividends, and partly in the form of increased market values resulting from undistributed corporate gains? Stockholders toil not, neither do they spin, to earn that reward. They are beneficiaries by position only. Justification for their inheritance must be sought outside classic economic reasoning.

It can be founded only upon social grounds. There is—and in American social economy, there always has been—a value attached to individual life, individual development, individual solution of personal problems, individual choice of consumption and activity. Wealth unquestionably does add to an individual's capacity and range in pursuit of happiness and self-development. There is certainly advantage to the community when men take care of themselves. But that justification turns on the distribution as well as the existence of wealth. Its force exists only in direct ratio to the number of individuals who hold such wealth. Justification for the stockholder's existence thus depends on increasing distribution within the American population. Ideally, the stockholder's position will be impregnable only when every American family has its fragment of that position and of the wealth by which the opportunity to develop individuality becomes fully actualized.

Privilege to have income and a fragment of wealth without a corresponding duty to work for it cannot be justified except on the ground that the community is better off—and not unless most members of the community share it. A guaranteed annual wage for all, a governmentally assured minimum income, a stockholder's share in the United States distributed to every American family—these are all different ways of giving Americans capacity to settle their own lives rather than having their lives settled for them by blind economic forces, by compulsions of poverty or by regulations of a social-work bureaucracy.

Wide distribution of stockholdings is one way of working toward this.

Such distribution is indeed proceeding—rather dramatically in terms of statistics, all too slowly in terms of social ethics. The generation since 1932 has multiplied the number of direct stockholders tenfold. If indirect stockholdings through intermediate institutions are included, a vast indirect sector has grown up as well. Yet distribution of wealth generally is still in its infancy. One per cent of the American population owns perhaps 25 per cent of all personally owned wealth* and undoubtedly more than that percentage of common stocks. Plainly we have a long way to go. . . .

One would expect therefore that the law would increasingly encourage an ever wider distribution of stocks—whether through tax policy or some other device. It would encourage pension trust or social security trust entry into stockholder position. The time may well come when the government social security funds are invested, not wholly in government bonds as at present, but in a broadening list of American stocks. As social security and pension trusts increasingly cover the entire working popula-

* *The Share of Top Wealth-holders in National Wealth 1922–56,* Robert J. Lampman (Princeton, N.J.: National Bureau of Economic Research, 1962), p. 208.

tion of the United States, the stockholder position, though having lost its ancient justification, could become a vehicle for rationalized wealth distribution corresponding to and serving the American ideal of a just civilization. The institution of passive property has an advantage which, so far as we know, is new to history in that distribution and redistribution of wealth-holding can take place without interruption of the productive process. Ancient Hebrew law required redistribution of land every half-century through the institution of the "Jubilee Year," but ran into operational difficulties, as might have been expected. The great revolutionary movements of 1848 and, in our time, in Russia, China and Cuba involved extreme productive losses, none of which has yet been recouped (though after half a century the Soviet Union may finally be at the point of doing so). The corporate system, accompanied by reasonably enlightened tax policies and aided by continuously growing productivity, can achieve whatever redistribution the American people want. . . .

Though its outline is still obscure, the central mass of the twentieth-century American economic revolution has become discernible. Its driving forces are five: (1) immense increase in productivity; (2) massive collectivization of property devoted to production, with accompanying decline of individual decision-making and control; (3) massive dissociation of wealth from active management; (4) growing pressure for greater distribution of such passive wealth; (5) assertion of the individual's right to live and consume as the individual chooses.

Of this revolution, the corporation has proved a vital (albeit neutral) instrument and vehicle. It has become, and now is, the dominant form of organization and production. It has progressively created, and continues to create, a passive form of wealth. It is, in great measure, emancipated from dependence on individual savings and "capital" markets. Nevertheless, like the slave of Aladdin's lamp, it must increasingly follow the mandate of the American state, embodied in social attitudes and in case, statute and constitutional law. This mandate changes and evolves as a consensus is developed on values and their priorities in American life.

We are well underway toward recognition that property used in production must conform to conceptions of civilization worked out through democratic processes of American constitutional government. Few American enterprises, and no large corporations, can take the view that their plants, tools and organizations are their own, and that they can do what they please with their own. There is increasing recognition of the fact that collective operations, and those predominantly conducted by large corporations, are like operations carried on by the state itself. Corporations are essentially political constructs. Their perpetual life, their capacity to accumulate tens of billions of assets, and to draw profit from their production and their sales, has made them part of the service of supply of the United States. Informally they are an adjunct of the state itself. The "active"—that is, productive—property of an organization increasingly is prevented from invading personality and freedom, from discriminating in employment and service against categories of men, in recklessly using their market control.

Passive property—notably, stock—increasingly loses its "capital" function. It becomes primarily a method for distributing liquid wealth and a channel for distributing income whose accumulation for capital purposes is not required. The corporation may, and indeed is expected to, retain earnings for the maintenance and enlargement of its capital plant and operations. The stockholder's right to spend the income from or use the liquid value of his shares as he pleases is guarded as a defense of his right to order his own life.

Far beyond this summary, the real revolution of our time is yet faintly perceived. If the current estimate that by 1980 our total productivity will double (approximately 1.2 trillion of 1960 dollars) and personally received income will reach approximately one trillion dollars proves true, the entire emphasis of American civilization will appreciably change. Philosophical preoccupation will become more important than economic. What is this personal life, this individuality, this search for personal development and fulfillment intended to achieve? Mere wallowing in consumption would leave great numbers of people unsatisfied; their demand will be for participation. This means, in substance, a growing demand that significant jobs be available for everyone, at a time when automation may diminish the number of all commercially created jobs as we presently know them. It may well mean that the state would be expected to create jobs wherever a social need is recognized, irrespective of the classic requirement for a commercial base. Is it possible, as Walt Rostow maintains, that the population will merely become bored? Perhaps; but if so, it will be because esthetics, the arts, the endeavor to understand, use and enjoy the thrilling prospects opened by science, and the endless search for meaning, will have tragically lagged far behind economic advance. Not impossibly, the teacher, the artist, the poet and the philosopher will set the pace for the next era.

II

1932~1936

From Berle's review of *The Brains Trust* by R. G. Tugwell for the *Annals* of the American Academy of Political and Social Science, 1968

For his pre-nomination and pre-election campaign of 1932, Franklin D. Roosevelt mobilized a handful of intellectuals to work up policies and measures he could propose to the country as answers to the deepening financial, economic and social crisis of the time. Raymond Moley did the recruiting; a preponderant share of the original intellectual work eventually fell on Tugwell and myself. With advice of Louis Howe, James Farley, Basil D. O'Connor, Samuel Rosenman and other party chiefs, Roosevelt mauled our proposals into politically viable and appealing shape. The intellectuals, then an unusual phenomenon in campaigns, were unflatteringly christened the "Brains Trust" by James M. Kieran of the New York *Times*—a jibe parried by Roosevelt, who quipped that he had no "Brains Trust" but trusted in brains. Upon his election, the "New Deal," with the political backing Roosevelt provided, translated the academic solutions thus molded into legislation and government action into a determinative piece of American history.

From "The Reshaping of the American Economy," *The Centennial Review*, Spring 1965

My own first memorandum to him [Roosevelt] (May of 1932) was predicated on the theory that the millions of individuals and families in distress were probably the key to the situation; if we could make these families reasonably secure in current income, in such savings as they still had, in their jobs, and give them some confidence in the economic future, they would cease to be frightened hoarders of cash, would resume consumption and thereby reactivate manufacture and production:

"Both as a matter of sound economics and decent humanity, an economic policy of the government ought to be adopted towards the restoration of individual safety," and suggested a series of concrete measures. All connoted the entry of the federal government into fields it had, theretofore, considered outside its function. Roosevelt had without anyone's help determined on federal entry; the problem was whether to start at the bottom or the top. Serious consideration, so far as I know, was never given toward Socialization—that is, government take-over—of production in general. . . .

THE NATURE OF THE DIFFICULTY

This memorandum of May 1932 was written by Berle and Louis Faulkner, of the Security Research Department, Bank of New York and Trust Company. The comments in brackets are marginal notes made later by Berle, probably when he used the memorandum as the text for a seminar on the New Deal. On the first page is the comment: "Discussed at Albany with Gov. Roosevelt, Raymond Moley, Jim Angell, Rex Tugwell, Sam Rosenman late May, 1932. Generally adopted. AAB."

INTRODUCTORY

The Nature of the Difficulty

It appears to us that the economic depression has heretofore been analyzed with a wrong emphasis. Substantially all of the thought has proceeded along the line that the mechanics were wrong, notably in two particulars: (a) that money and credit had contracted; and (b) that industrial capacity was not being used to the full.

From this we derive difficulties on the one hand with the banking system and the structure of corporate securities. On the other hand, we have unemployment, lack of purchasing power and the like. The very terms suggest that the system has been looked at from the point of view of a credit and money circulation system, or a manufacturing system, or a selling system.

Fundamentally, the entire system can only rest on the individual. Proper functioning of the system rests on the twin factors that an overwhelming majority of the individuals in the country have money or credit and are willing to spend or lend money or credit. The first factor is present. The second—willingness to spend or lend—is not.

Credit and money can be either *sterile* or *live*. A hoarded dollar is sterile and it contributes nothing (for the time being) to the system. The same is true of potential credit, of which borrowers are afraid to avail themselves or which lenders are afraid to extend. The two are interrelated. Under our system, the amount of credit is dependent on the amount of currency; but a large amount of currency will not necessarily create a large amount of credit. In normal times, the amount of deposited currency multiplied by ten will be equal to the amount of potential credit. Currency withdrawn from banks, however, ceases to be a basis of credit; a potential credit of ten dollars is wiped out for every currency dollar withdrawn from the banking system. A currency dollar taken out of the banking system and hoarded, contributes nothing to credit and little to purchasing power. The only force which can stimulate it into action is the feeling of the individual who has it, that he can safely deposit it in a bank or buy something with it. At that point, and dependent on his will, it becomes live.

Sterility extends to credit. Deposit of a dollar in the banking system does not make it live, nor liven the potential ten dollars of credit which may be based on it, unless someone is willing to borrow and a bank is willing to lend. Individuals must feel that they can afford to borrow, do something useful with the money, and ultimately repay it; banks must feel that they may lend with reasonable degree of safety.

Industry, manufacture and employment: (the three are all linked together), present a similar situation. That there is the desire for a large enough proportion of the output of our present plant capacity to keep the system running more or less normally seems unquestionable. But desire has to be effective to translate itself into economic demand. The difficulty seems to be far more lack of willingness to use these goods and services rather than lack of ability to command them.

Why the stoppage? The causes seem to be two:

(1) Individuals have not confidence in the future permitting them to believe that they can safely entrust such money or resources as they have to the banking system by way of deposits, by way of loans or credits, or investment in securities. There is fear that the deposit will not be available in case of future need; that loans will not be repaid; that securities either will not pay interest or will so fall in value that the investment cannot be repaid. In either of these cases the individual's resources become useless to him. His natural idea, therefore, is to keep them in such position that they will always be available. The logical result of this is hoarding.

(2) On the side of employment, no individual feels that his job or present salary is secure. With a guaranteed job, even at a low wage, individuals can safely spend money. With a job, however good, which may go by the board within a few weeks or months, the only possible individual course is to spend as little as possible, that is to say, use as little purchasing power as possible, to borrow no money, to save everything possible and to await contingencies.

This is the problem of millions of individuals and families to whom little, if any, attention has been paid. They appear to be the key to the situation. In our view, the sound approach to the situation is to begin by looking at him and the millions like him, and to tackle the job of making him more secure, (a) as to his savings and (b) as to the continuity of the activity producing his livelihood, and crucially, to bring home to him his own part in the picture. Were this done, even on a reduced scale, he would cease to endeavor to reduce his savings into cash; cease to deny himself goods and services which he really wants; he would begin to purchase the things he needs and lend his money in the form of bank deposits, securities or mortgages, as the case might be. In that reversal of opinion the entire trend might be started in an upward direction.

Both as a matter of sound economics and decent humanity, an economic policy of the government ought to be adopted towards the restoration of individual safety. The following suggestions are all constructed with a view to this end:

I SECURITY OF SAVINGS

Generally

One major difficulty with the present situation is that substantially every individual in the system has a prevailing feeling of insecurity as to those resources which he has put away for use in bad times, old age, or sickness. With a safe reserve against contingencies he can afford to make his money live instead of sterile. But if he believes that these resources have been or are about to be wiped out, his natural instinct is to cut down the satisfaction of every desire, however legitimate, until he can be sure that his reserve is intact.

This interacts with another situation, namely, the ability of industry to pay its debts currently. It would matter relatively little that industry cannot pay its debts if the effect were not receiverships, suspension of activities and employment for a more or less long period of time, and waste and chaos pending readjustment. During this process savings invested in such industries temporarily, (perhaps permanently) lose any value to the individual. It is of no interest to the individual that a bond which he bought at 90 and which during receivership is worth 10, will in five or six years from now be worth 85. During the five or six years, it is of little use to him. For his purposes he must assume that he has lost his savings and curtail his activities.

This is true even though most individuals hardly realize that they own securities. They have savings bank books or policies in an insurance company, or deposits in a commercial bank. If a sufficient number of bonds—that is to say, debts of the industrial system, as it now stands—go into this process of adjustment by receivership, the savings bank closes, the life insurance company suspends payment, the commercial bank fails.

So strong is the feeling on this subject that the mere apprehension that such a process of readjustment may take place is sufficient to incite the individual to sterilize his savings at once by withdrawing them hastily from the commercial bank, or from the savings bank, or borrowing on his insurance. This means that the banks and the insurance companies are asked to provide him with cash; to do this, they must sell securities; these are thrown upon a market which has, under our system, no reserve whatever to meet that contingency; the good go with the bad; apprehension spreads until the entire industrial debt is reckoned at far below any true value, based upon probability of repayment of principal, or payment of interest.

A new force here comes into play. Were all debts perpetual, such a system would not of itself affect the great industrial plants of the country, except the extremely weak ones. But even the strongest may have debts falling due from time to time. These are commonly refunded by new borrowings. When there is a general desire of individuals to convert all their holdings into cash, no new borrowings can be made. Then the soundest of industrial loans cannot be met; the strongest plants may find themselves required to go through receivership, disorganization and chaos. Fear that this will happen is the present cause of general fear about security of savings. [Legislation: F.D.I.C.]

Specific Credit Groups

There are eight great groups of bonds outstanding on which individuals, commercial banks, savings banks and life insurance institutions depend. They comprise the savings of the country. These groups are:

1. Railroad Bonds
2. Public Utility Bonds
3. Farm Mortgages
4. City Mortgages
5. Industrial Bonds
6. Municipal Bonds
7. State Bonds, and
8. United States Government Bonds. [Done. Expansion of power of Reconstruction Finance Corp.]

We are leaving out foreign bonds. In normal times they deserve a place in the system, but they are already so deflated that they have virtually vanished from the structure. A small list of foreign bonds, (Swiss, Dutch, Canadian, English) is high in price, reflecting a flight from the dollar. Most of the rest have fallen to so small a fraction of the savings originally invested in them that they have substantially passed out of the savings portfolio of the country. Little is to be feared from further losses in this direction, though the investing public will not (and should not) easily forgive the banking methods which led to the losses already taken.

Of the eight groups mentioned, one group—*railroad bonds,*—is in a dangerous though by no means hopeless state. A second group, *farm mortgages,* is in extremely bad shape. A third group, *mortgages on city property,* as nearly as we can estimate, divides equally. Half is hazardous —the remainder reasonably sound. A fourth group, *municipal bonds,* is in dubious though not hopeless condition. The fifth group, *industrial bonds,* though dangerous in individual instances has, on the whole, been reduced to so small a figure that it does not form a real problem. The sixth group, *public utility bonds,* is, by and large, safe. The seventh and eighth groups are State and government bonds, which are in very good shape indeed.

Danger of financial catastrophe may be appraised from this index. Any one of these groups going to pieces would threaten the system. Two groups going under at once would wreck it. At the moment two groups hang in the balance; a third has danger signals out.

1. *Railroad Bonds*—There are outstanding long term railroad debts amounting to $11,046,000,000. Interest charges on this debt come to $511,-000,000 a year. Accurately, however, the railroads have additional charges to be met in the form of lease rentals and the like; $683,000,000 annually in fixed charges (including interest) has to be met.

Seventy per cent of this entire debt (approximately $7,500,000,000) is held in savings banks, insurance companies and similar institutions. General default would on a conservative estimate affect perhaps twenty million individuals—every holder of a savings bank book or life insurance policy, as well as all colleges and endowed institutions.

The danger in which this group of bonds now stands may be estimated roughly as follows:

In 1931, which was not a particularly good year for railroads, the net corporate income of substantially all railroads was twenty-six millions of dollars, or slightly *more* than their interest charges, and actually *less* than their fixed charges. This year, thus far, the net operating income of railroads has been running at approximately 40% less than the year before. Estimated operating income in 1932 available for interest charges comes to $300,000,000. In other words, the railroads will not earn their interest charges by upwards of $200,000,000; nor will they earn their fixed charges, amounting to $178,000,000 in addition. Barring an upturn, the railroads will be $380,000,000 short of meeting their fixed charges this year.

Maturities for the year 1932 are $181,000,000; and for 1933, $295,-000,000. Normally these would be met by refinancing. This year they cannot be so met. In addition, the railroads owe a volume of short term bank loans. In sum, within the next two years it will be necessary to provide for short term loans and maturities approximating $600,000,000. Together with the deficit in fixed charges for the present year ($380,000,000) and possibly for the next year (another $380,000,000) there is in all a net deficit through the end of next year of well over $1,250,000,000. Any plan of action splits into two divisions. First, the present emergency must be swung. Second, constructive measures must eliminate the causes of the difficulty.

Emergency Measures

The Reconstruction Finance Corporation, together with the Railroad Credit Corporation, have at hand, and apparently will have, control over a sufficient volume of funds to handle the present drafts both for interest and for maturities.

(*Note:* It is assumed that the bill expanding the Reconstruction Finance Corporation's borrowing power in this regard will pass. If not, the Reconstruction Finance Corporation together with the Railroad Credit Corporation has almost enough to handle the situation for the next twelve months.)

A good many railroads have cash reserves sufficient to meet interest charges and maturities for a time. These also can be drawn on to meet the emergency.

The Reconstruction Finance Corporation must be vigorously supported in its relief measures. But it should be plainly recognized that this, in substance, means that the government virtually purchases an interest in the railroad system of the country. The government consequently has a right to demand that the railroads put their house in order.

The second line, *Constructive Measures,* toward relieving the situation relates to this ordering of the railroad house.

(a) *Economic handling of the railroads.* At present, 10% of the railroad mileage carries 50% of the freight of the country; another 60% carries 48% of the freight of the country, and 30% carries only 2% of the freight of the country. The passenger statistics show approximately the same story. Put differently, approximately 12% of the railroads produce 60% of the operating revenues. Approximately 48% of the railroad mileage about pays its fixed charges and breaks even. The balance is a continuing loss to the whole system.

There are only two answers to this situation, and of these only one is really practicable. Either the strong have to contribute to the weak by recapture of earnings; or there must be a process of merger, creating a unified successful system. The recapture clause, (a compromise in our present law) is in practice not possible. It is now an invitation to a law suit every time a railroad has a profitable business. The real answer is consolidation. Previous administrations have flirted with the idea of consolidation; steps have been taken in that direction with little or no practical effect. But if the government is to finance the railroad it can demand consolidation, apportioning earnings over the entire railroad system; and it can demand abandonment of those lines which do not justify their economic existence.

Failure to do this can only mean that one after another the uneconomic lines will fail. Failure of each such line adds to the impossibility of putting even the strong lines on a sound credit basis.

(b) *Guarantee of reduced interest charges.* We believe that the Reconstruction Finance Corporation should follow vigorously the policy which it has laid down in the Frisco situation, by demanding that the holders of bonds, especially junior bonds, shall be prepared where necessary to expect and accept a lesser amount of interest on their bonds, at least during the period of stress. This can be done by exacting as a condition for financing a proper scaling down of interest. [Not done, but RFC did make long-term money cheaper.] In return for the bondholder, assent to such scaling down should be given by a definite commitment from the Reconstruction Finance Corporation that the reduced rate of interest thus arrived at will be maintained for a period of time. The net result of this on the individual may be briefly explained. Railroad bonds paying 5% but in danger of default will sell at perhaps 15. If the same bond be guaranteed a rate of 3%, it will sell for 50. The individual can afford to sacrifice a little of his present income in favor of safety. He will be better off, and so will the railroad and the Financial system.

With this must go a second policy—that the Reconstruction Finance Corporation either obtain extension of the due dates of bonds nearing maturity; or else commit itself to meeting the maturities as they occur.

(c) *Wage Reduction and Job Assurance.* Railway workers both can and should be required to contribute to this situation. Their jobs are unsafe if the railroads go into receivership. We believe there should be a general reduction of wages either through a flat cut of 10% or by elimination of specific wage practices ("Featherbed reduction"). With this should go an assurance that the railroad will be kept afloat, and, in substance, that the men will not be laid off. [Never done. Everybody objected. Pub. Works Administration instead (1934).]

As to both the wage situation and the bond situation, the Reconstruction Finance Corporation ought to be given a certain degree of flexibility, since situations vary. Both can be met without the chaos and waste of strikes or receiverships. The government is in a position, we believe, both as a matter of economics and as a matter of law, to compel the situation.

(d) *Taxing of Truck Competition*. Certain uneconomic competition ought to be eliminated or scaled down. Railways are in competition not only from each other but from trucks and buses. Many of these last are able to exist because they do not have to pay for their rights of way. Some apparently are not aware of the fact that, by failure to provide for depreciation, they are really losing money. This can properly be handled by scientifically worked out taxes. Such taxes might be on (1) gasoline; or (2) excises on interstate tonnage carried by trucks (for instance, a tax on truck freight waybills or the like). Trucks have a legitimate place, supplementing existing railway lines and replacing uneconomic railway lines. They cannot substitute for the railroads. According to an estimate of Professor William Z. Ripley, if an attempt were made to replace railroads by trucks, one ten-ton truck would pass, every twenty seconds, over every mile of improved road in the country.

(e) *Reduction of Local Taxation*. There should be reduction of local (state, county, municipal) taxation. This is taken up later.

2. *Farm Mortgages*

The second extremely bad situation is the farm mortgage group. On this there are about $9,480,000,000 [sic] extant, and they carry an interest of slightly over $560,000,000 annually.

There are no trustworthy figures to indicate the ability of farms to carry their fixed interest charges, but it is fairly plain that the load cannot be carried and has in fact not been carried. The farm mortgage situation presents to the individual a particularly poignant picture. Foreclosure of a farm mortgage means wreck of a home, and as many of the farm mortgages are held by banks and similar institutions, peculiarly in the West, these banks first "freeze" and then fail.

The situation is complicated by the fact that in addition to the farm mortgage interest, farms, like all real estate, bear an extremely heavy share in taxation. The real first mortgage on a farm is the annual tax bill; the first mortgage interest is really a second lien. In many foreclosures, the technical difficulty is not that the farmer did not pay his interest (he did not) but that he could not even pay his taxes.

It is not material here to go into the cause of farm mortgages. Their amount has been attributed in part to the land booms of the War. This is only partly true. They in part represent the unpaid bill for mechanising the farm—a process which proved expensive and ultimately useless. Farmers who kept out of debt and relied on their work were safe. The farmer who went into debt for machinery, relying on it to make money, now is being wiped out. The fallacy lay in the assumption that mechanization could work on the small farm. In fact, it is applicable only on the large farm.

1932

Measures

A vigorous attack on this problem has never been attempted. Certain lines, however, do offer possibilities:

(a) *Federalizing the Marginal Farms*—A definite program of federalization of those farms which are abandoned ought to be carried on. This can be done at a minimum of expense by purchasing farms for taxes where the taxes are in default, and where the mortgagee, as frequently happens, is not prepared to take over the farm. This would permit the government to reacquire large areas of land for use in replenishing the heavily depleted forest reserves; and would tend to diminish farm overproduction since these farms would be taken out of agriculture and put into other use. Individual hardship on the farmer could be mitigated by permitting him to remain on his farm for a time, letting him work out a nominal rental by assisting in the reforestation work. Mere announcement of the policy might have some effect, and by systematically carrying it forward, it would tend slowly to raise the price of commodities produced by the remaining farmers. This in turn would permit the reabsorption of farmers now unable to stand the burden.

(b) *Reduction of Local Taxation*—A second and coordinated line of attack must be accomplished by radically reducing local taxation in these communities.

The individuals here by banding together can assist their own situation materially; they should be given every encouragement to do so. A large part of taxation now goes for road maintenance. At present the farmer has virtually provided a free right of way and free maintenance for the truck transportation system as well as handling local burdens. A part of this burden should be taken off his hands; at least he should not be required to contribute to the maintenance of a branch of the transportation system. The federal truck taxes, proposed above, could be apportioned to lift a part of the load.

(c) *Clearing Obstacles to Foreign Trade*—It must be frankly recognized that the farmer is at least in part the victim of an international situation. He would be one of the principal beneficiaries of any arrangement lowering tariffs and cleaning up international debts. This promises once more the absorption of a part of the surplus of farm products abroad. [Eventually Hull Reciprocal Trade Agreement. Lowered gold value.]

(d) *Reduction of Interest Charges*—The interest burden can be and should be lightened. The banks and individuals which hold farm mortgages are better off with a reasonably safe 4% than a risky 6%. The machinery of farm loans at present permits a certain amount of rediscounting of farm mortgages. This should be accompanied by a policy by which such discount privileges are permitted where banks voluntarily reduce the interest rate. Reduction of farm mortgage interest generally from 6% to 4% would save, approximately, $198,000,000 annually, to American farmers.

Vigorously pursued, we believe that the combination of these measures would materially relieve the farm system and greatly strengthen the credit position of the farm mortgage. [Was done. (a) H.O.L.C. (b) Farm Credit Administration. (c) Farm Bankruptcy Act.]

Urban Mortgages

Figures are not presently available as to the total amount of urban mortgages. They are too widely scattered; held by too many individuals, and aggregates are difficult to ascertain. Some indication of their size may be given by the so-called "real estate bonds", secured by mortgages on property. Of these there are now $12,000,000 outstanding (American Institute of Banking estimate) and of these ten billions are in default. These, however, do not cover the field of those conservative first mortgages held by savings banks and life insurance companies in large amounts. An estimate of $35,000,000,000 of such mortgages is perhaps fair.

This item, many times larger than any other, would present a catastrophic picture were it not for one fact. Much of this figure is due to real estate speculation within the last few years. Urban mortgages in many cases are still held by speculators; foreclosure means merely that a past speculative profit is wiped out. To the individual who is foreclosed it frequently means the failure of an unlucky speculation. This is especially true of mortgages on business property. A great proportion of this paper does not enter into the general credit situation; it does not harbor the dangers inherent in deflation of securities largely held by savings banks and institutions. Mortgages representing such situations, even if wiped out, would occasion relatively little damage to the system.

But there remains a tremendous volume of conservative first mortgages, held by institutions and by individual investors and weighing upon home owners. This group enters vitally into the credit system.

Measures

(a) *Reduction of Taxation*—The first line of attack must necessarily be reduction of local taxes. In many of the larger centers the real estate tax is almost equal to the interest on the first mortgage; the mortgage burden is virtually doubled by the burden of taxation. In part, this must be attributed to municipal waste and to systems of local taxation. Part of this waste is inevitable, perhaps; most of it can be eliminated. Among the methods of such elimination are reduction of municipal salaries, which may be the more drastic because in many cases municipalities employ more men than are necessary to do the work. Municipal taxation can be redistributed through a search for new ways of revenues and the more equitable distribution of taxes, so that the individual who buys a home or the individual whose savings are invested by him or for him, by a first mortgage through a bank or insurance company, is not penalized.

Reduction of local taxation would assist the economic situation in many ways. Construction might revive once more and building might become profitable. The cycle in construction is peculiarly sensitive to the reduction of fixed charges. Rents could be lowered, thereby releasing individual spending power.

Revival of construction deserves a word. It is commonly said that the country is over-built. This is true; but especially in municipalities, a large part of the existing construction consists of tenements which could and should be reconstructed. The line of building from now on, for a time, at least, should be replacement of specially undesirable properties with economic and desirable ones. While large and expensive apartments and houses are overbuilt and lie vacant, the poor home owner or renter has had little benefit from the "boom" construction. The tenement dweller is still a tenement dweller.

Reduction of taxation improves municipal credit; which in turn makes it possible for municipalities to refund present liens at lower rates of interest, still further saving taxes. [Not implemented.]

Municipal Bonds

The amount of municipal bonds outstanding is not easy to estimate, partly because of the different classes of indebtedness which are included loosely under this heading. A fair estimate would be not less than seventeen billions, and, including certain other local government units, the amount might be extended to twenty billions. It is loosely said that most of these loans are precarious; the fact being that a large proportion of this amount is in very good shape. Nevertheless, an amount (difficult to estimate) comprising the borrowings of certain areas and large cities is at or near default.

The cause of the default lies in reckless municipal borrowing accompanied by municipal waste; and the default is precipitated by unduly high taxation bearing on real estate in bad times, leading to taxpayers' strikes, litigation affecting the validity of taxation and lowered municipal revenue. Municipal bonds are largely held by savings banks and insurance companies; they enter into the structure to a very large degree. One large segment is held by individuals who desire tax exempt securities, on whom loss would not bear heavily. But so great a proportion of this is in the system that the danger must be squarely met. The steadily increasing rate of interest demanded by municipal bond buyers indicates the approach of the danger point. This interest burden is being added to increased cost of government, which has risen from 3 billion in 1913 to 13 billion in 1930. [Never done.]

Measures

This is a problem of local government, and local taxation. There is no apt legal method by which interest charges can be scaled down; municipal difficulty means, in the long run, payment of such high rates of interest on new loans as to constitute ultimately a greater burden than before.

The remedy must be rigid municipal economy, which in turn means rigid municipal efficiency. The individuals in urban centers are rapidly approaching the point where they must choose between efficient and economic local government, or municipal difficulties, wholesale mortgage foreclosures and everything that goes with it. There is no other answer to this problem. At this point, the individuals must speak for themselves. One method of bringing this home is to encourage a system by which every rent bill states upon it the amount of the rent which is directly attributable to taxes, so that no individual remains in ignorance of the precise amount of the load he is bearing.

The Remaining Groups

Public Utility Bonds are earning their fixed charges twice over. Certain excrescences on the public utility system, notably the pyramided holding companies representing speculative attempts to get profits and issue of securities capitalizing these anticipated profits have come to grief. Others may follow; but a fair proportion of these losses has already taken place. The normal financial machinery—receiverships and the like—can be used to take care of these situations without endangering anything fundamental. That the individuals who have been induced to participate in such enterprises have a very real complaint against a financial system which permitted the foisting of virtually worthless securities on them is undeniably true; elsewhere, measures for prevention of this are suggested. But the situation does not represent a great danger.

Industrial bonds, as noted above, are small in amount. As a group, the industrial companies are in good shape; in the aggregate, they are perhaps better off than any other single group. The individual situations may be handled, as they appear, either by the normal machinery, or in peculiar cases, possibly by the Reconstruction Finance Corporation. It seems desirable to us that the Reconstruction Finance Corporation should have the power to deal with individual industrial situations where the result of receivership would be to throw men out of work or to create an undue quantity of human misery.

Practically all *state bonds* and *United States government bonds* are in good shape.

Summary

A survey of the situation in the matter of savings-credits indicates that of the eight great groups, two are in bad shape and two are doubtful. One of the doubtful groups does not enter into the system to a point at which it threatens a catastrophe. The three danger spots all seem to be manageable; in them a vigorous policy, though difficult, will afford reasonable assurance to individuals that their savings are reasonably safe. Realization that these problems are being effectively handled will make the individual once more willing to pick up his normal economic life; realization that he has responsibility and power, (particularly in local matters) will conduce to a sound attitude on his part.

II   SECURITY OF WORK

The Problem in General

In our view, the other incentive needed to make the individual once more an economic factor and to translate money held by him or in the banking system from sterile to live dollars and credits is security of work and livelihood.

The heart of the difficulty here lies in the combination of two forces. Men are afraid that their jobs will cease to exist. Consequently, they cease to buy. Consequently, there ceases to be a demand for products they buy and the manufacturers of these products cease to be able to employ labor. The vicious circle spirals in a widening radius. Yet the great majority of American workmen are still at work. They have their normal desires; they can purchase, and they would, were they convinced that their jobs were safe. The difficulty is uncertainty. Men can adjust to the known; they cannot adjust to the unknown, or to a perpetual state of fear.

Were it possible by fiat to guarantee everyone his present job at his present pay for five years, and to guarantee that his savings were safe, the situation would change at once. [Not done.]

Heretofore, depressions have been broken up by an economic miracle or windfall; a gold rush, the opening up of new territory, a war creating demand for goods, or some similar factor. This cannot be counted on at present; such a windfall is not now on the horizon. It is not necessary, for the only result of the windfall is to create an impression on the part of the population that it is secure; this lends support to other groups and thus turns the tide of the cycle. The reality of the security is almost immaterial; the psychological effect of the security is the real force at work.

The problem now is to create this effect by united endeavor; instead of waiting for some economic windfall. The present policy both of the government and the financial communities appears to be to wait for such a windfall to turn up; a policy which is dangerous and speculative in the extreme. No private financial affairs could be run on that basis.

Specific Measures

We suggest, first, that a moderate amount of guarantee of security be provided (in addition to the guarantee of security through strengthening the savings situation) by arranging that loans be furnished to enterprises which employ men, on condition that these enterprises guarantee that their men will appear at work for a period of time, say one year. [No. Now appears in the "guaranteed annual wage"!]

Such loans cannot be made by any central Federal agency, because they are in all cases local in character. A banking system with courage might provide those loans now, on its own initiative. It is urged. [Not done.] Bankers insist that they cannot do this because depositors may demand repayment of deposits which the commercial banks cannot meet, unless they are in a liquid position.

Hence, there is a great stagnant pool in the system, centralized in the commercial banks which have adopted this policy. In following that policy they sterilize most of the money on deposit, and with it the credit which could be based on this money. A bank which has 80% of its reserves in cash or liquid assets is merely a bank which is declining (possibly for good reasons, viewed from its individual point of view) to permit its resources to perform their normal function in the community.

The history of the creation of this stagnant pool need only be touched upon. In 1929, a tremendous amount of credit was tied up in the stock market. After the crash, the banks in substance assumed a large part of these credits; credits which entered into security prices but had little effect on industry. From June, 1930, to the present, credit has been steadily contracting. Such of it as remained was put into government bonds. There, in substance, it remains. The banks felt that they needed immediate liquidity—that is to say, that they had to be prepared to meet the demands of the hoarder and of frightened depositors. This, far more than withdrawal of gold, has constituted the real contraction in the system.

It becomes necessary to release this sterilized credit, and to put it back to work at its normal function of assisting goods to pass from people who make or sell them to people who want them; and to assist people who want goods to satisfy their normal and legitimate desires.

The Reconstruction Finance Corporation, or a similar corporation, should be empowered by the government to rediscount and guarantee repayment of new loans made to concerns which will in turn guarantee employment to individuals for a stated period of time. [Done by RFC.] This policy should be carried out, first, in those industries where it is obvious that the community has a real need of the project. Such rediscounting and guarantee should only apply to two-signature paper, and for this purpose provision should be made for handling trade acceptances. Primarily, the objective should be to finance purchase of materials where the effect is to put men to work and keep them there. The immediate effect of this policy would be to thaw certain quantities of frozen credit; the secondary, but rapid, effect would be to create demand for commodities by the very men thus put to work. Carried out with sufficient vigor, and above all, with sufficient care, the commencement of a turn in the tide could be made.

Demand for commodities occasioned by an appreciable, even though small, amount of individual security, at once tends to stabilize prices, and the price level thereafter begins to take care of itself. This in turn brings back confidence to the dealers in commodities; once more normal stocks are carried; commercial life adjusts itself.

A guarantee of loans of this kind running as high as one billion dollars would be small in comparison with the result. Most such loans would be self-liquidating; even as small a volume of security as this would, in our view, give the start which the system needs.

This is materially different from the sterile credit which the Federal Reserve Bank is pumping into the system by purchasing government bonds and giving credit to the banks. That policy, good as far as it goes, does not do the one thing necessary—it cannot stimulate the use of credit along lines which will tend to give any group of individuals a feeling that their livelihood is safer.

An appropriate system of guarantee stimulating the use of credit, where individuals would benefit from it, is the heart of any constructive solution, and the key to the ultimate return of prosperity.

III · THE LONG VIEW

Generally

In our judgment, certain long range measures are essential.

The so-called "cycle," with periods of depression occurring in every decade, has reached a stage threatening the safety of the American economic system. This is due to the fact that economic life has been, and still is, concentrating to a degree unparalleled in economic history. When most people are on farms, and business is small, a depression merely means a bad time. When most people are concentrated in cities, and most industry is concentrated in a few hundred very large units, depression means dislocation of the entire mechanism; millions of people literally without food and shelter; savings temporarily or permanently wiped out; wholesale misery and disturbance. There is a slow parallel between increasing intensity of depressions in the cycles, and increasing economic concentration. Unless there is some reversal of trend, or some residual control, some depression will ultimately cause a wholesale dislocation amounting to a revolution in fact, if not in name.

Such a dislocation could take place next winter; and might do so were any two of the credit groups, reviewed above, to fall to pieces at any one time. There is perhaps one chance in five that this will take place. For the first time the United States has come within hailing distance of revolution along continental European lines.

Concentration has proceeded to a point at which 65% of American industry is owned and operated by about six hundred corporations; the balance being spread among millions of little family or individual businesses. Nearly 50% of American industry is owned and operated by two hundred large corporations. This means that some six thousand men, as directors of these corporations, virtually control American industry; eliminating the inactive directors, the number of men is reduced to not more than two thousand. These control perhaps 30% of the total national wealth; such wealth being the concentrated industrial wealth which dominates the life of eastern United States.

Concentration appears to be proceeding more rapidly during depression than during prosperity.

The handful of dominant individuals do not agree on a policy; assume little responsibilities to the community, to their customers or to their labor; have no cohesion; fight among themselves for supremacy within their industry. Industries fight against each other.

Through the investment banking system, the public is asked to assume tremendous blocks of credit instruments (stocks, bonds); in fact, this is the principal outlet provided for savings. Fifty-five per cent (55%) of all savings must go, directly or indirectly, into corporate securities, other investments not being available. This means, in substance, that such savings of necessity go into the stock and bond markets.

The true antithesis just now is not, as commonly stated, between the American system and the Russian system. At the present rate of trend, the American and the Russian systems will look very much alike within a comparatively short period—say twenty years. There is no great difference between having all industry run by a committee of Commissars and by a small group of Directors.

Scientific Policies

With this in mind, we think certain policies ought to be adopted. They fall into three groups: (a) Financial reform; (b) Controlled industry; (c) Foreign affairs.

(a) Financial Reform

1. *Publicity of corporate accounts and stock transactions.* [Beginnings of Securities & Exchange legislation.]

Wherever industry is concentrated to the point where properties are primarily represented by securities listed on the stock exchanges or bond markets, a federal law should provide for publicity of corporate accounts and their rendition at frequent intervals, presumably quarterly. With this should go publicity of transactions in the securities of such corporations by their officers and directors whether these transactions are carried on openly or through dummies.

The Stock Exchange in reality is the paying and receiving teller's window of a great savings bank; and it is the measure of value of savings held by individuals and by institutions the country over. To allow these appraisals to vary from day to day and to allow the actual values in exchange to be manipulated, especially by the individuals in charge of the industries in question, violates the underlying function of these markets in the present system.

This seems immediately practicable; and sentiment, even in the financial community, generally favors it.

2. *Federal Control of Security Issues.*

The investment banking community has not concentrated upon a unified policy; and has maintained an attitude of irresponsibility. Investment bankers necessarily hold the position that they are merchants of securities, selling to the public what the public wishes at the moment. Once distributed, their responsibility is over except as they intervene in reorganizations, in which the record is little, if any, better than in selling. The result has been to put the economic system of the country at the hazard of tremendous issues of securities many of which are unsound; some of which are sound but issued at inflated values; and some of which are sound but uneconomically distributed. The tyranny of the syndicate list virtually permits dictation to distributors and small banks throughout the country. When the public (as contrasted with institutions like savings banks and commercial banks) has purchased and holds large amounts of any given security, the banker considers the job well done, irrespective of the fact that the issue may subsequently decline in value. No more cynical statement has ever been made in finance than Mr. Mitchell's testimony before the Senate Committee on Finance upon Senate Resolution 19 in connection with foreign bonds. The losses on foreign bonds by individuals who saved money and invested in good faith, amount to nearly $2,000,000,000. Mr. Mitchell was asked whether the situation was sound. He answered that

"By far the greater part of the foreign issues outstanding in this country are distributed among individuals or institutions other than banks and life insurance companies"

(hearing on Sen. Res. 19—Part I, page 70), estimating the number of foreign security holders at more than a million and a half; and subsequently pointing out that The National City Bank and The National City Company hold only a nominal amount ($350,000) of these bonds (page 73) and concluding that the banking situation was perfectly sound so far as foreign bonds were concerned because the banks held so few of them (page 80). So long as the loss was merely taken by individuals no harm was done.

A similar attitude could be developed in other fields.

It therefore seems necessary that there should be constituted a Capital Issues Board which could perform the functions of a federal Blue Sky Commission, exacting full information about securities sold [SEC]. Such a commission could be gradually developed to the point where it would exercise a real control over undue expansion of groups of credit instruments, where issue of these reached a point threatening the safety of the financial structure. [No, never done.]

3. *Chain Banking.*

The commercial banks are in a somewhat similar position. They are large enough so that individuals have little liberty of action. They are not centralized enough so that there is a unified policy or any single group which can cope effectively with a situation like the present.

When difficulties arise each bank seeks safety for itself at the expense of the system by declining to loan money, contracting credits, calling loans, and forcing liquidation. The money thus realized is invested in short term government securities, and does not enter into industry on any effective scale.

As a result, bank deposits have been falling during the past year at the rate of approximately $100,000,000 per week—each dollar of which represents a called loan and a liquidation of securities or commodities to meet the loan. For a short time after the Federal Reserve Bank commenced buying government bonds in large quantities, this policy ceased; but it seems to have commenced again within the last few weeks.

This must be contrasted with the centralized banking systems of Australia, Canada and England which have avoided violent liquidation even under worse conditions; and have almost entirely avoided bank failures. In America the result has been drastic curtailment of credit; paralysis of business; violent liquidation in the securities and commodities markets; and failure of many thousands of banks.

The answer would appear to be the adoption of the English system of chain banking permitting centralization and giving to each unit in the system the advantage of the liquidity of the entire system. [Turned down flat!] In substance, this makes possible the carrying on of banking even in time of stress without requiring every unit in the chain to reduce its assets to cash. Liquid assets may be mobilized between various units at will.

The foregoing three recommendations all have to do with finance and the handling of long term and short term credits. In these problems, concentration to a point where government control becomes feasible seems absolutely necessary. Credits, both long and short term, are of necessity national in character. We have at present the vice of centralization, in that a few large investment banking houses and a few large commercial banks really dominate their respective systems by one or another device. We have not the advantages, arising from a single policy, and from an ability to mobilize liquid assets where necessary.

The next group of problems has to do with concentration of industry.

(b) *Control of Concentrated Industry* [Never done]

4. *Amendment of the Anti-Trust Laws.*

The Anti-Trust laws were designed, fundamentally, to discourage undue concentration, and to protect small business. This they have not done in many industries. It is the view of some members of this group that the appropriate method of handling this is to amend the Anti-Trust laws so as to permit consolidations and even monopolies at will; but to provide that when, in any industry carrying on interstate commerce, there occurred a concentration of more than 50%, that in two corporations or less (corporations being defined to include not merely technical corporate units but groups of corporate units under the same control), the concentrated units shall be subject to federal regulation.

This would leave each business man freedom of action. He could run a small business if he so desired. If, however, he and his associates desired to consolidate into large units they could do so; but in that case the units would come under government regulation. The underlying theory is that where an industry is concentrated to a point permitting domination of 50% or more by two units or less, these units have actually become objects of legitimate national concern.

Regulation should include power to require uniform prices; to control security issues; and to control further consolidation.

5. *Old Age, Sickness, and Unemployment Insurance.* [This happened.]

Although apparently differentiated from problems of concentration, insurance against old age, unemployment and sickness really becomes necessary as a result of concentration. The theory that such insurance is unnecessary and unwise is based on the premise that individual action at liberty is the best safeguard of the individual. Where businesses are largely small and competitive, this may be true. In concentrated industry, the individual has no real liberty of action; he is at the mercy of a uniform system with which he cannot possibly cope.

Further, the surpluses largely built up by the large units in concentrated industries and apparently retained by such units, represent funds which as a matter of economics should be available to take care of the men employed in those industries in bad times. Industry does not recognize this obligation at present, though the more enlightened leaders are coming to do so, notably Mr. Owen Young and Mr. Gerard Swope. Past surpluses are not available now because they have been locked up in plant investments. It is imperative that this situation be not permitted to occur in the next swing of the cycle.

The answer appears to be government unemployment, old age and sickness insurance; set up as a charge on the earnings of industry, and arranged with sufficient flexibility so that where a corporation provides its own insurance in these regards, within standards laid down by the government, such insurance could be recognized as satisfying the obligation of the company.

To this policy was largely due the stability of German industry from 1880 to the fall of the Empire.

(c) Foreign Problems

There remain a group of problems connected with foreign trade which have an important economic bearing.

6. *Negotiations with Russia* [Done. A failure].

The largest actual market available at the moment is Russia. Faced with a shortage of the wheat crop, it could absorb the American surplus of farm products. It is suffering likewise from acute shortage of practically all products which the United States manufactures. Under our present legal relation with Russia there is a considerable barrier to any real resumption of trade relations. In addition, Russia has not at the moment either credit with which to buy or export surpluses with which to pay. Despite this fact, foreign countries faced with depression, notably Italy and Germany, have worked out trade relations with Russia which are approximately satisfactory through the use of long term, revolving credits; and even despite the barrier of non-recognition, a substantial number of American companies have availed themselves of the Russian market by the same process.

Those corporations which have had most to do with Russia—The General Electric, The Standard Oil Company of New Jersey, the International Harvester Company, are apparently prepared to encourage negotiations looking towards the recognition of Russia, the settlement of the Russian-American claims, and the resumption of commercial relations with Russia. The Russian foreign propaganda in favor of communism seems largely to have died in the Russian preoccupation over success of the five year plan.

Opening of the Russian markets would to some degree afford possibility of working out payment for our exports through the operation of triangular trade not now available. This problem should be carefully studied; and in any such study, purely doctrinaire ideas, as, that communism automatically outlaws a nation, should be discarded.

7. *European Debts and Tariffs.*

A barrier to trade with Europe is our prohibitive tariff; which has occasioned retaliatory tariffs by European nations; and the whole problem is complicated by the debt and reparations question. The three problems—tariffs, debts, and reparations—are inextricably tied together.

This problem can hardly be handled briefly. One conclusion is that:

(a) A settlement by cancellation of debts against cancellation of reparations should be arrived at simultaneously with a negotiation of agreements regarding tariffs, to permit the freest possible exchange of goods between all of the western European countries and the United States. [Done finally.]

(b) In making tariff agreements, a scientific study should be made to ascertain what industries require tariffs and what industries do not. Many industries have no need of tariffs; in other cases, industries which have no legitimate basis exist because of tariffs. In the former instance, tariffs may be reduced or cut out. In the latter case, tariffs may be reduced gradually permitting a readjustment of the plants and facilities to other purposes. In still other cases, tariffs are needed in order to maintain the American standard of living. [Done—Reciprocal Trade Agreements Act.]

It would seem that the true justification for a tariff exists where all competitive factors are equal except the standard of living of laborers of equal efficiency. We should be in a position to compete in any respect, except in standards of living; where competition means matching a lower standard of living of equal efficiency, American labor ought not to be asked to meet the competition.

This solution violates some of the classical concepts of international economists; but it represents what seems to us a practicable present solution.

Problems of foreign exchange are not here dealt with. Mr. Angell is better qualified to cope with these problems than we are. In all of the foregoing, political feasibility has not been considered.

The following is an excerpt from a diary that Berle's wife, Beatrice B. Berle, kept intermittently (henceforth: BBB Diary). Berle added the numbered notes at the end of the entry in the margin of the diary.

October 6, 1932

Here beginneth the history of the Brain Trust! *—so called by the newspaper men. If the Brain Trust continues, this should be one of the materials of history, a primary source for the students of the history of this period.

Knowing how quickly one forgets and alters facts in retrospect, I will endeavor to keep this as a diary setting down A[dolf]'s comments on the day's work and my own observations if I am in a position to make any.

A. is in N.Y. today and I by the fireside [in Great Barrington] on a very wet evening. Today then, I can only put down a few things in retrospect.

Last [spring], A. was in a state of great ferment over the affairs of the world feeling there were only three ways out, (1) inflation and consequent wiping out of all bond holders, (2) continued disorganization of business ending in universal bankruptcy and revolution perhaps, (3) a controlled scaling down of debts which could only be done after careful study and with government assistance.

He felt that the leaders of finance in this country were yellow and short sighted, that nothing could be achieved through them. I told him at the time he should find a customer for his ideas. Shortly after this, he got together with some of the jr. economists of some N.Y. banks and they drew up a memorandum. This got around the town and came to the notice of Raymond Moley, advisor to Roosevelt. A. was accordingly invited to Albany and this was the origin of the Brain Trust. The first debate,[1] I believe was on inflation, Roosevelt at that time being in favor of it.[2] A. convinced him that it was only a last resort. Bernard Baruch then stepped in[3] and wanted F.D.R. to pronounce himself against inflation under any circumstances. A. did not want this and apparently pacified Baruch.

From that time on, A. has been in great and constant demand at Albany and Hyde Park. Moley is the constant companion but A. seems to be the inspirer![4] The other members included Rex Tugwell (whom I have never met), Charles Taussig [author; Board Chairman and President, American Molasses Company] and Gen. [Hugh S.] Johnson, Baruch's representative. Tugwell is the agriculture economist and seems to be going by the board; Taussig contributed some ideas about the tariff but is less active now. The triumvirate of Moley, Johnson and A. remains. A. certainly had a frabjous time! I should add Bobbie Straus, son of the Macy Straus, who contributes much of the cash and liquor and is by way of getting a p.g. course out of this!

[1] Present: Rexford Tugwell, Raymond Moley, Prof. James Angell, Max Lowenthal [New York lawyer] (later ejected).
[2] Or rather, flirting with the idea. This was prior to his nomination.
[3] This occurred the day after R's return from Chicago where he had been nominated.
[4] A masterpiece of overstatement!

* note: the term was not one of endearment. [Berle]

Memorandum to Roosevelt, July 20, 1932

Re: Economic Program of Bernard M. Baruch

The program proposed by B. M. B. was discussed by Moley, Tugwell and myself. Most of the practical proposals seem like sound common sense; we have not discussed the tax program.

When he gets under principle, B. M. B. poses the essential issue between the two wings of the party. Like most eastern business men, B. M. B. wants to permit free play to business, which in practice means freedom to six or eight hundred large corporations and banks to fight out among themselves the ultimate mastery of the situation. He believes individuals must suffer for and rectify their own mistakes. Unfortunately, the result reached is that the "forgotten men" suffer for the mistakes of the industrial leaders, who come off relatively unhurt.

The obvious line is to agree on definite measures without committing on questions of philosophy or principle.

His proposal to get in Charles E. Mitchell [Chairman of the Board, National City Bank] seems dangerous. My contact with some of the higher officers and methods of the bank in question, coupled with the fact that the Norbeck Committee is continuing its investigation [of Wall Street], would seem to indicate the wisdom of giving that institution a wide berth, both generally, and on the specific ground that the Norbeck Committee may, early in the fall, explode information which would make an alliance there very unhappy.

Memorandum to Roosevelt, August 1, 1932

I lunched with Mr. [W. Averell] Harriman today, following your suggestion. He will hand me a copy of a memorandum by Mr. Carl Gray [Union Pacific President], covering some of the matters we have discussed.

Summarizing, Mr. Harriman's views are:

(1) In favor of a program of voluntary reorganization of the weaker railroads through the medium of the Reconstruction Finance Corporation; in place of a guarantee of interest on the reorganization bonds he would prefer a straight loan of a given amount, sufficient to "see the properties through". This is a modification in detail only and not in principle.

(2) He is all in favor of taxing trucks, and would add to that waterway transportation.

(3) He would like to see abandonment of the legislative policy of competition, so that consolidations need not provide that all territories be served by at least two competing lines. Thereafter he would like to have consolidation, but only by agreement of the railroads, accompanied by free permission to abandon uneconomic lines (less in mileage than is generally supposed, he thinks) by permitting drastic cuts in operating expenses through elimination of unnecessary service.

(4) He feels that railroad labor costs must come down but he thinks it would be very dangerous to introduce this into politics.

I gather that he would favor:

1)—A general policy of voluntary reorganizations through the Reconstruction Finance Corporation.

2)—The taxation or regulation of trucks.

3)—A general pronouncement in favor of consolidation along monopoly lines instead of competitive lines.

He does not appreciate that this last necessarily entails a declaration of policy sufficient to make the consolidation serve the public interest.

I gathered that he believed these declarations would materially improve the railroad bond market.

Memorandum, August 1, 1932

There are various views as to what Mr. Harriman really represents. He is heir to a great name and a large fortune; is regarded by the public as merely a figurehead to reconcile warring factions in the Union Pacific; is supposed by railroad men to have done a good job in cutting expenses on the Illinois Central; is generally opposed to government ownership. Like all railroad men he has a firm sense of vested right of a railroad management—a right which is not easy to justify, since the railroad managements do not own the railroads and therefore must stand on their record as expert managers for any title to go on operating systems which they control only by the accident of their being in power. I should estimate that the major portion of the program we envisage could be announced without seriously antagonizing Mr. Harriman himself. We have not yet met up with a hard-boiled variety of railroad men like Mr. [W.W.] Atterbury [Pennsylvania Railroad President] or Mr. [Leonor F.] Loree [Delaware & Hudson President].

Memorandum to Roosevelt, August 2, 1932

In the securities markets the rise in securities values is leading to a good deal of loose talk about recovery.

Actually, the buying comes from European speculative sources. The British and Scotch investment trusts, rumored to be buying, are in fact buying for investment New York real estate at foreclosure.

Practically all business indices show a worse position than before, with third quarter earnings probably at a still lower ebb. Publicity given to public improvement is widely circulated apparently by concerted action of the banks.

On anything now visible this looks like a false start in the stock market.

Improvement in the bond market is more nearly justified; even though, taking into account the present rise, levels are far below any long term estimate of real values.

The foregoing is merely for your information, in the event that the stock market increase figures in any discussion you may have. Views in the New York district are notoriously colored by casual stock market movements.

Memorandum, August 5, 1932

Last night there met at the Governor's Raymond Moley, Samuel Rosenman, Rexford Tugwell, General Johnson (of Baruch's outfit), Max Lowenthal and myself.

Lowenthal came in because [Harvard Law Professor] Felix Frankfurter wanted to bring him in on the proceedings; this over Moley's objection, with which all of us concurred.

The draft speech prepared by Johnson was approved in principal and the governor and Rosenman are attending to the re-drafting.

Lowenthal, after raising a number of objections, wanted to delete anything about inflation of the currency. He put this on strategic grounds, but my impression was that his real motive was something else. Either he was anxious for inflation (reflecting the views of the Amalgamated Clothing Workers' Union, or some other similar group), or he had been in touch with some of the Jewish financiers, possibly Eugene Meyer, [Governor] of the Federal Reserve Board. But he may merely have been endeavoring to make an impression. We were under the disadvantage of having to debate the question with him present.

It presently appeared that Johnson and Baruch had debated the question of inflation considerably with [Treasury Secretary] Ogden Mills, Eugene Meyer, and the Treasury crowd generally; that they had urged that nothing be said about inflation as they wanted to carry through the government program, make the stock markets rise, etc.; and tried to impose on Baruch a patriotic duty not to upset this apple cart. When Baruch declined, pointing out that the result might easily lead to disaster since the inflation once started could not be stopped, Mills apparently arranged to have Owen Young [Chairman of the Board, General Electric] and the National City Bank put pressure on Baruch along the same line.

Johnson feared that a similar epidemic of pressure would be brought to bear on the governor and therefore was not anxious to have Lowenthal or anyone else disclose the outlines of the currency speech; but we none of us quite trusted Lowenthal, who is the typical "liberal on the make", with some sincerity, some good ideas, considerable ability, and no loyalty—except to F. F. and the particular little group that revolves around him.

It was agreed that there would be a number of set speeches, probably eight in all, and several minor ones. The speeches agreed on were:

(1) Stock market publicity, etc. (probably within two weeks);
(2) A railroad speech;
(3) Tariff speech;
(4) Agriculture speech;
(5) Speech on government economy and the budget;
(6) International debts and foreign affairs;
(7) (Possibly, though probably not), General reconstruction measures;
(8) The currency.

There have also to be a number of short speeches, including:

(a) Foreign bonds
(b) Emergency relief
(c) Local taxation; etc.—

These probably will be developed from time to time during the campaign. I think the governor's idea is to make in his set speeches his formal pronouncements; but in his short speeches to elucidate simply and quietly some of the major features touched on in his longer addresses.

The tariff speech is being prepared by Moley and [Kemper] Simpson.

The stock market speech and the railroad speech fall with me.

The currency speech will probably be done by Johnson, with the help of Tugwell and Angell.

The agriculture speech will be done by the governor himself and Tugwell.

Naturally all speeches, with attendant material, are to be handed to the governor, who will chew them over and renew them as seems best.

The Stock Market Publicity Speech.

The governor feels that the government can not at the present time undertake to tell people in what they shall or shall not invest.

He does feel, however, that the government can

(a) Make sure that only men of character undertake the flotation of securities, and
(b) That all material facts in regard to those securities are known; and
(c) That there shall be continuously public accounts; and
(d) That manipulative moves by the corporate insiders ought to be disclosed.

He is undecided as yet on the proposition that banking affiliates in the securities flotation business ought to be divorced from commercial banking. He agrees this is economically sound but wonders whether the time is yet ripe. He seemed generally favorable to the idea; and my own impression is that on further looking into it he will discover not only that it is sound, but that practically every responsible banker wants to do it. He pointed out, rightly, that the federal government could not divorce affiliates from commercial banking except in the national banking field, which of course is a real difficulty.

I have not had time to give thought to this, but it seems to me in the light of the morning after that a good deal could be done by making it a rule of the Federal Reserve Bank that member banks could not engage in the flotation business.

O'Connor, who was also present, took a wholly cynical attitude about the whole stock market idea, believing in general that nothing that could be legislated could not be evaded; that the public were suckers anyway and likely to continue so, no matter what anyone did or tried to do for them. With this, of course, I wholly disagree.

Memorandum to Roosevelt, August 10, 1932

The Policy Regarding Inflation of Currency

Mr. Lowenthal's remarks at Albany, coupled with Professor Felix Frankfurter's letter to me of August 8th, sufficiently indicate that the so-called "liberal" group propose to argue the inflationist policy without openly saying so. Perhaps this is unjust; they may merely desire to keep this as an open line.

Summarizing the situation pro and con, it lines up as follows:

(1) As a matter of ideal economics a "managed currency" might be a good thing. But we have not got as yet the political machinery for that purpose in sight. Witness the bonus agitation; and the several drives on the currency when there is not a treasury surplus.

(2) A certain amount of inflation now exists, and a certain additional amount is inevitable. There has been an increase in treasury and federal reserve circulation of not quite three billions of dollars paper. The deficit indicates that an additional amount of three billions has to be

raised, either by the present inflationary method, or by issuing government obligations purchased for investment. . . .

(3) It would seem that we are in for three billions of inflation already out, and very possibly an additional three billions. Once out these cannot be helped,—a long, slow job of retiring them is necessary.

(4) Conceding that the inflation so far may have been necessary, the problem is whether as a matter of government policy it should go any farther. As to this,

(a) Approximately half the population of the United States (at any rate, a minimum of one-third of the population) are at present creditors in the sense of having savings in one form or another. This is on the assumption that the immediate family of the owner of savings are likewise interested in savings.

(b) To some extent this is offset by the fact that from five to eight million individuals (to whom may be added their families) are also holders of equity stocks and therefore might benefit from inflation, assuming (which is not certain) that stocks would ultimately benefit from inflation.

(c) The entire farm section, south and west, would benefit from inflation. This affects roughly forty per cent of the population. They would suffer, however, in so far as they had savings, as many of them do.

(d) We agree with Professor Gregory that the effect of inflation will not necessarily stimulate business in any way, unless at the same time the attitude towards the currency is changed; and in any case such inflation would be cruelly unjust to those individuals who have already been wiped out through the operation of a non-inflationary, deflation process (foreclosures, receiverships, etc.).

(e) The ultimate effect of inflation would be to lower the wages of labor and the white collar class in the east. We are not able to agree with the labor groups who want inflation at the moment.

(f) Had the labor groups and the individuals interested in savings, and reckoning the various grade groups of obligations outstanding which are likely to be able to maintain themselves as against those not so likely, the statistical balance appears to be against inflation.

(5) The persons benefitting first from the inflation would be speculators in commodities and on the New York Stock Exchange; later, and to a lesser extent, farmers and middle-men; finally, debtors generally; but the results of the inflation would probably pyramid heavily into the hands of the speculative fraternity.

(a) The evils of inflation would probably be a steadily mounting cost of living without accompanying rise in wages, ultimately reacting heavily against the whole urban population of the United States, except the fortunate few who own either stocks, real estate, or commodities, in large quantities.

(b) While it may be conceded that the balance is close, we have not got to inflation yet.

(6) The conclusion is that—

(a) It is not the time to support inflation.

(b) Leaving aside the propriety of inflation, there is no excuse whatever for leaving the country in ignorance of what is being done. A policy of inflation might be undertaken consciously, as in 1870 or in Bryan's time; to undertake it secretly seems little short of folly.

(c) The objective ought to be to stop the inflation which will necessarily exist by March fourth next—that is, hold the situation at the level which will then have been reached. Since the momentum of inflation mounts in geometric progression, if the process is to be stopped, the campaign has to be begun now.

(7) Conceivably the situation may be so bad by March fourth next that inflation is the only way out. But that bridge can be crossed when we get to it.

Memorandum to Roosevelt, August 15, 1932

Casting over the whole campaign, one matter I think should be considered.

We hope you may win; and the chances are rather better than even. Possibility of defeat has, however, to be reckoned on. In that event, you still have your political career to think of.

Should the campaign go off merely on a series of scattering issues, defeat would probably end your career, as it did the careers of [James M.] Cox, [John W.] Davis, and even Al Smith. Should you, however, quite definitely become the protagonist of an outstanding policy, your significance in American public life would continue—as did that of [William Jennings] Bryan and Theodore Roosevelt. The illustrations of course do not suggest any agreement with the policies of these men.

Obviously the line is, therefore, to make some statement analogous to Woodrow Wilson's "new freedom" speech.

The issue I think has been tendered by the President in his constant recurrence to the idea of "individualism". What he means is that government shall keep clear of the entire economic system, confining itself to emergency relief, keeping the peace, and the like. His reference to exploitation by certain financial interests is obviously a minor sop.

Whatever the economic system does permit, it is not individualism.

When nearly seventy per cent of American industry is concentrated in the hands of six hundred corporations; when not more than four or five thousand directors dominate this same block; when more than half of the population of the industrial east live or starve, depending on what this group does; when their lives, while they are working, are dominated by conditions made by this group; when more than half the savings of the country are dominated by this same group; and when flow of capital within the economic system is largely directed by not more than twenty great banks and banking houses—the individual man or woman has, in cold statistics, less than no chance at all. The President's stricture on "regimentation", accompanied by a willingness to let the centralized industrial scheme dominating things occasionally run loose, is merely ironic; there is regimentation in work, in savings, and even in unemployment and starvation.

Were the few thousand men running things a coordinated group, you would at least have a government of sorts. Actually, they are in the state of the political feudal barons in France before a centralized French government unified them; and the result was more individualism, (for men and women), not less.

What Mr. Hoover means by individualism is letting economic units do about what they please.

I can see the opposite view, which is a far truer individualism, and might be a policy by which the government acted as regulating and unifying agency, so that within the framework of this industrial system, individual men and women could survive, have homes, educate their children, and so forth.

The President's program of "moral leadership" envisages a president as a kind of elective autocrat; certainly there is no law or permanent policy in it.

Concretely, the situation would seem to suggest:

(1) A program of legislation under which the government could deal with concentration in industry as and when found; this means among other things—

(a) A revision of the Anti-Trust Act.

(b) A revision of the transportation system in the direction of coordination.

(c) The gradual placing of savings invested in the industrial system under regulation which ultimately might be not wholly unlike the regulation accorded to banks.

(d) A centralized and stable banking system instead of many thousand individual banks struggling with each other to accentuate peaks and depressions alike.

(2) Some kind of governmental machinery along the line of an economic cabinet, though probably not so called, collecting information, and giving an almost continuous economic audit of the situation. The Department of Commerce might perhaps be used for this purpose.

(3) Coordination of the various relief measures such as old age pensions, sickness and unemployment insurance, and the like.

In a word, it is necessary to do for this system what Bismarck did for the German system in 1880, as a result of conditions not unlike these.

Otherwise only one of two results can occur. Either the handful of people who run the economic system now will get together making an economic government which far outweighs in importance the federal government; or in their struggles they will tear the system to pieces. Neither alternative is sound national policy.

I feel that appropriately phrased, some such pronouncement would probably make at once your place in history; and a political significance vastly beyond the significance of this campaign. All of my friends west of Chicago and south of Baltimore are calling insistently for some such pronouncement; and these are rather the substantial citizens than academicians or doctrinaires. To the answer that the government is inefficient they merely suggest that the efficiency of an uncoordinated economic system as it runs now has ruined half the country and threatens to starve a substantial portion of it.

On August 16, Roosevelt wrote to Berle gratefully acknowledging his memorandums of August 1 and 2. "You are," he said, "a wonderful help. See you soon."

August 17, 1932

My dear Governor Roosevelt:

Following up your suggestion at Albany the other night, I tackled the question whether the receivership laws and reorganization procedure could be transformed into something summary and swift, avoiding the general mess of delay, expense, and division of the assets among every member of the bar, in Peter Dooley's phrase.

I am satisfied that the thing can be done. The technical discussion, if you wish, can be left until later. . . .

A campaign is no time to explain technicalities of reorganization procedure; but unless you see some reason to the contrary, I will include for your consideration, a paragraph in the memorandum of material for the railroad speech covering this point.

We have checked and re-worked your outline of the Columbus speech to include a skeleton constructive program.

I am attaching a brief memorandum of Tugwell's "Economic Council".

Memorandum to Roosevelt, August 17, 1932

The "Economic Council"

The liberal wing of the party, particularly the intellectuals, are very firm in favor of an economic council.

In theory, of course, they are right. Practically, all responsible students agree that the present industrial situation can result only in one of two ways. Either the government steps in through some form of economic administration; or the business machinery, by consolidation, merger, or the like, evolves an irresponsible economic government of its own.

Practically, however, the development of such a council is a Herculean job. No mechanism covering the ground has existed, except in war time.

I think the line has to be the slow development of a group which will collect, coordinate and continuously interpret economic information, rendering opinions to the president of the congress at intervals. As these judgments show themselves wise, the group could gather authority and public confidence.

I think the group could be constituted by providing joint action with existing government officials, without setting up another bureau. . . .

August 17, 1932

My dear Governor Roosevelt:

I take this opportunity to congratulate you on the way you have handled the [Mayor James J.] Walker hearing [concerning New York City
corruption]. It excites the admiration even of your enemies. To manhan-
dle a situation of this sort into a proceeding which is both dignified,
pointed, and fruitful, is an achievement of the first order. It is doubly so
since you have not the buttress of a codified procedure which supports
judges on the bench.

I am of course among your partisans; but I should say the same thing
if I were in the opposite camp.

With kind regards.

"My dear Berle," Roosevelt replied on August 22, ". . . I am glad you feel as
you do about my handling of the hearing. It was not an easy task. . . ."

One of Berle's contributions to Roosevelt's speech in Columbus, Ohio, on August
20, 1932 was the *Alice in Wonderland* parody. This is from Berle's original draft.

Alice was now fairly in the Wonderland of the New Economics. The
White Knight had wondrous schemes of unlimited sales in foreign markets, though we had to lend the money to our customers to pay the shot. A
Red Queen in Washington merely remarked "Off with his head!" to anyone who suggested that you cannot, indefinitely, defy the laws of arithmetic; and through it all old Father William balanced the sinuous eel of a
pool-ridden stock market on the end of his nose; while the Mad Hatter
wanted everyone to "have some more tea"—though there wasn't any tea.
Not until long after—August, 1932, to be accurate, did the fantasy fade to
the sobered description of a puzzled Executive acknowledging that there
had been a "soil poisoned by speculation." . . .

"How if I cannot pay my bills?" says Alice. "The moratorium would
come in usefully here." "Never," says the fearless leader. "It is contrary to
our national policy to help individuals out of their difficulties. You have,
however, your intrepid souls."

Replying to a letter from Professor E. C. Branson, of the University of North
Carolina, Berle wrote on September 7, 1932:

It is hardly fair to Mr. Roosevelt to say that he has fallen under the
sweep of my thinking. He was good enough to ask me to act as one of a
trio of economic advisers; so that I have seen a good deal of him in the
past few weeks; and he knows, better than we do, that there has to be a
thorough re-examination of a lot of assumptions on which we have built
the rickety fabric of today. Particularly, I like his feeling that the economic machinery is made for the man and not the man for the economic
machine. And I do not greatly care whether the conservative East considers this radical or not. They can take it as light or take it as lightning,

since it is pretty clear that the industrial system as we know it will not stand much more of the kind of thing we have seen in the last three years.

The denouement in the Walker case ought to satisfy everyone except the Tammany men. Governor Roosevelt has declined to permit publication of what happened on the famous night when Walker resigned. Actually, the entire Tammany group came to Albany and asked whether the Governor would give them some hope. He answered that matters would have to take their course. They spent two hours explaining why they would arrange that he lost New York State, possibly New Jersey, possibly also Massachusetts and may be Illinois. The implication was that if he wanted to lose the presidency the way to do it was to go right through with the investigation. At the end of the two hours he repeated that matters would simply take their course. Somebody apparently then went out to telephone and twenty minutes later Walker resigned. No one had the slightest illusion, I think, as to what the Governor meant.

Since so much has been said about the Governor's lack of courage, I have felt it unjust to himself not to let the story be known, for I know very few comparable acts of political courage. Apparently, however, the policy was not to give this out to the newspapers; and the only recognition was [Judge Samuel] Seabury's remark (which the facts entirely justify) that the action was in the best tradition of a Cleveland or a Tilden.

The rest of the campaign will tell its own story; and you have to remember always that the Governor is working with a party split from end to end. So far he has kept his lines clear and from the point of view of an independent intellectual he has used the political technique to get about the maximum obtainable out of the situation. Many, including myself, would like to see much more done, but politics is a matter of reality, and I think the Governor is doing his honest best,—and a very significant best.

BBB Diary

October 6, 1932

The speeches on the Western trip were all, except the little extempore blurbs of political soft soap, engineered or written by A. and Moley.

The farm speech which I do not understand was put together by Tugwell and A. after consultation with all the experts.

The RR speech was approved by Baruch and [Donald] Richberg the counsel for the brotherhoods but written by A. and delivered almost verbatim. Baruch said it would make the market go up and it did. He was much pleased and paid his debt with a retainer for some insurance cos.[1]

The power speech was written by some of the power authorities.[2]

A. thinks however that the high point of this campaign and in fact of his political ventures past, present, and future was the new individualism [Commonwealth] speech written by us at this table. A. dictated a first draft which I thought very sloppy so I chewed the pencil, and did a powerful lot of pruning and rewriting. By that time he had clarified his thinking and wrote off the end in fine shape thus at last getting off "the princes of property." A. has the draft in our joint handwriting. The editing for delivery spoiled some of our better expressions but I did not mind their cutting out some of my historical prelude. What is Louis XIV to San Franciscans, what indeed? The social justice was discussed by the B.T. and written by Moley, I believe. The style is not as good as ours.

1 This might have been corrupting the expert—but I think not!
2 Leland Olds [Executive Secretary, New York Power Authority], with some help from me.

Telegram to Roosevelt, September 19, 1932

Attention Professor Raymond Moley

Memorandum individualism matter airmailed today . . . Fundamental issue today adaption old principles to new and probably permanent change in economic conditions which can only be done by enlightened government. . . . This means planning and persuading all hands to make plan effective curbing lawless competitor where required but always in interest of workers consumers and owners of savings stop Text less academic than above outline which indicates line of argument only regards

Berle's draft of a speech Roosevelt delivered, with only a few minor changes, at the Commonwealth Club in San Francisco, September 23, 1932

There come times in the life of every nation when a redefinition of fundamental political aims is imperative. During the past generation, our material progress has been so rapid and has wrought so many changes in our daily existence that we have been hypnotized watching the wheels turning faster and faster, little heeding the fact that we ourselves might be ground under them. It is only since the disaster of 1929–1932 that we have begun to realize how far behind our social institutions are in meeting the demands of the machine age and in providing the "right to life liberty and the pursuit of happiness" for our people under modern conditions. This adjustment of social institutions to meet the needs of our times is essentially the task of government. This task can only be accomplished if the leaders will cease for a moment to be politicians working on politically expedient stop-gap devices and will endeavor to take the long view of the statesman who thinks clearly and tries to state the fundamental issue. This, I propose to do in my speech today.

As I see it, the fundamental issue of government has always been whether individual men and women live to serve some system of government or economics, or whether the system of government and economics exists to serve individual men and women. That question has run through history for generations; honest men have differed, and still differ both in theory and in practice, as to the answer. Let me trace briefly the age-old conflict between these two schools of thought.

We tend to forget in the maturity of government how hard won the privilege of government is. The growth of the national governments of

Europe as we know them today was the struggle for the development of a centralized force strong enough to impose peace upon warring barons and thus insure protection from feudal raids to the farmers, the tradesmen and the little people. The strong central government then was a haven of refuge, not a threat to the individual. The disturber of the peace in the fifteenth century was the grand seigneur against whom Richelieu fought. Power thus became centralized in the crown. Louis XIV in France was then able to say, with truth, "I am the State"—and people approved him. But great concentration of power in a few hands, then as now, in the course of time is susceptible of abuse. Kings and king's ministers, like industrial leaders of today, were not always highly responsible men, with an enlightened view of the good of their people at heart. The old creators of national governments were, perforce, ruthless men; they acted from motives of ambition; they were often cruel in their methods; but they did drive steadily toward something Society very much needed and very much wanted: a strong central state, able to keep the peace, to stamp out internecine wars, to put the unruly nobleman in his place; to permit the bulk of individuals to live safely. The ruthless man has his place in a developing country; and Society is willing to reward him for his services in its development. But when the development is complete, and the ambitious ruthlessness has served its turn, it tends to overstep its mark. In Europe there was a growing awareness that government was being run for the private benefit of a few who profited unduly at the expense of all. Almost inevitably Society sought a balancing and limiting force. Gradually, through town councils, trade guilds and national Parliaments there grew the conception not of destruction of the strong national government, but of its limitation by constitution and popular participation; and with this came an insistence that it assume responsibility to its subjects.

The American colonies were born of this struggle. The American Revolution was a turning point in it. The enlightened thought of the World had begun to recognize that the purpose of absolute monarchy had been served and that its danger outweighed its usefulness.

The struggle was by no means over. It continued on this side of the Atlantic during and after the revolution. Men as brilliant, as honest and as able as Hamilton believed fundamentally that the safety of the Republic lay in the strength of its government, that the destiny of individuals was to serve that government and that, fundamentally, this meant a strong group of central institutions guided by a small group of able and public spirited citizens. Hamilton was asked what part the people might play in this scheme of things. His famous answer was, "The people, Sir, are a great beast".

But Mr. Jefferson, in the summer of 1776, after drafting the Declaration of Independence turned his mind to the same problem and took a different view. He did not deceive himself with outward forms. Government to him was a means to an end, not an end in itself; it might be either a refuge and a help or a threat and a danger, depending on the circumstances. We find him carefully analyzing the Society for which he was to organize a government. "We have no paupers. The old and crippled among us who possess nothing and have no families to take care of, but being too few to merit notice as a separate section of society or to effect a general estimate. The great mass of our population is of laborers, our rich who cannot live without labor, either manual or professional, being few and of moderate wealth. Most of the laboring class possess property, cultivate their own lands, have families and from the demand for their labor, are enabled to exact from the rich and the competent such prices as enable them to feed abundantly, clothe above mere decency, to labor moderately and raise their families."

These people, he considered, had two sets of rights, those of "personal competency" and those involved in acquiring and possessing property. By "personal competency" he meant the right of free thinking, freedom of forming and expressing opinions, and freedom of personal living each man according to his own lights. To insure the first set of rights, a government must so order its functions as not to interfere with the individual. But even Jefferson realized that the exercise of the property rights might so interfere with the rights of the individual that the government, without whose assistance the property rights could not exist, must intervene, not to destroy individualism but to protect it.

You are familiar with the great political duel which followed; and how Hamilton, and his friends, building towards a centralized power were at length defeated in the great election of 1800, by Mr. Jefferson's party. Out of that duel came the two parties, Republican and Democratic, as we know them today. It is a matter of irrelevant interest that that election with its declaration for individual rights came exactly thirteen years after the end of the Revolutionary War; just as the present election comes exactly thirteen years after the end of the World War.

So began, in American political life, the new day, the day of the individual against the system, the day in which individualism was made the great watchword of American life. The happiest of economic conditions made that day long and splendid. On the Western frontier, land was substantially free. No one, who did not shirk the task of earning a living, was entirely without opportunity to do so. Depressions could, and did, come and go; but they could not alter the fundamental fact that most of the people lived partly by selling their labor and partly by extracting their livelihood from the soil, so that starvation and dislocation were practically impossible. At the very worst, there was always the possibility of climbing into a covered wagon and moving West where the untilled prairies afforded a haven for men to whom the East did not provide a place. So great were our natural resources that we could offer this relief not only to our own people, but to the distressed of all the world; we could invite immigration from Europe, and welcome it with open arms. Traditionally, at the end of a depression a new section of land was opened in the West; and even our misfortune served our manifest destiny.

It was in the middle of the 19th century that a new force was released and a new dream created. The force was what is called the industrial revolution, the advance of steam and machinery and the rise of the forerunners of the modern industrial plant. The dream was the dream of an economic machine, able to raise the standard of living for everyone; to bring luxury within the reach of the humblest; to annihilate distance by steam power and later by electricity, and to release everyone from the drudgery of the heaviest manual toil. It was to be expected that this would necessarily affect government. Heretofore, government had merely been called upon to produce conditions within which people could live happily, labor peacefully, and rest secure. Now it was called upon to aid in the consummation of this new dream. There was, however, a shadow over the dream. To be made real, it required use of the talents of men of tremendous will, and tremendous ambition, since by no other force could the problems of financing and engineering the new developments be brought to a conclusion. So manifest were the advantages of the machine age, however, that the United States fearlessly, cheerfully, and, I think, rightly, accepted the bitter with the sweet. It was thought that no price was too high to pay for the advantages which we could draw from a finished industrial system. The history of the last half century is accordingly in large measure a history of a group of financial Titans, whose methods were not scrutinized with too much care, and who were honored in proportion as they produced the results, irrespective of the means they used. The financiers who pushed the railroads to the Pacific were always ruthless, often wasteful, and frequently corrupt; but they did build railroads, and we have them today. It has been estimated that the American investor paid for the American railway system more than three times over in the process; but despite this fact the net advantage was to the United States. As long as we had free land; as long as population was growing by leaps and bounds; as long as our industrial plants were insufficient to supply our own needs, society could afford to give the ambitious man free play and reward him with hundreds of millions provided only that he produced the economic plant so much desired.

During this period of expansion, there was equal opportunity for all and the business of government was not to interfere but to assist in the development of industry. This was done at the request of business men themselves. The tariff was originally imposed for the purpose of "fostering our infant industry", a phrase I think the older among you will remember as a political issue not so long ago. The railroads were subsidized sometimes by grants of money, oftener by grants of land; some of the most valuable oil lands in the United States were granted to assist the financing of the railroad which pushed through the Southwest. A nascent merchant marine was assisted by grants of money, or by mail subsidies, so that our steam shipping might ply the seven seas. When some of my friends say with all honesty that they do not want the government in business, I always wonder whether they know what they are saying. For it has been traditional particulary in Republican administrations for business urgently to ask the government to put at private disposal all kinds of government assistance. The same man who tells you that he does not want to see the government in business—and he means it, and has plenty of good reason for saying so—is the first to go to Washington and ask for a government tariff on his product. When things get just bad enough—as they did two years ago—he will go with equal speed to the United States government and ask for a loan; and the Reconstruction Finance Corporation is the outcome of it. No, we wanted the government in business; and in large measure we were right in wanting this. What we did not clearly recognize is that we cannot have it both ways. Either the government was expected to exercise some influence over the situation or else it had no business to assist private enterprise.

In retrospect we can now see that the turn of the tide came with the turn of the century. We were reaching our last frontier. There was no more land and our industrial combinations had become great uncontrolled and irresponsible units of power within the state. Clear-sighted men saw with fear the danger that opportunity would no longer be equal; that the growing corporation, like the feudal baron of old, might threaten the economic freedom of individuals to earn a living. In that hour, our anti-trust laws were born. The cry was raised against the great corporations. Theodore Roosevelt fought a presidential campaign on the issue of "trust busting" and talked freely about malefactors of great wealth. If the government had a policy it was rather to turn the clock back, to destroy the large combinations and to return to the time when every man owned his individual small business.

This was impossible; Theodore Roosevelt, abandoning the idea of "trust busting", was forced to work out a difference between "good" trusts and "bad" trusts. The Supreme Court set forth the famous "rule of reason" by which it seems to have meant that a concentration of industrial power was permissible if the method by which it got its power, and the use it made of that power, was reasonable.

Woodrow Wilson, elected in 1912, saw the situation more clearly than any other man. Where Jefferson had feared the encroachment of political power on the lives of individuals, Wilson knew that the new power was economic. He saw, in the highly centralized economic system, the despot of the twentieth century, on whom great masses of individuals relied for their safety and their livelihood, and whose irresponsibility and greed (if it were not controlled) would reduce them to starvation and penury. The concentration of economic power had not proceeded as far in 1912 as it has today; but it had grown far enough for Mr. Wilson to realize fully its implications. It is surprising, now, to read his speeches. What is called "radical" today (and I have reason to know whereof I speak) is mild compared to the campaign of Mr. Wilson. "No man can deny", he said, "that the lines of endeavor have more and more narrowed and stiffened; no man who knows anything about the development of industry in this country can have failed to observe that the larger kinds of credit are more and more difficult to obtain unless you obtain them upon terms of uniting your efforts with those who already control the industry of the country, and nobody can fail to observe that every man who tries to set himself up in competition with any process of manufacture which has taken place under the control of large combinations of capital will presently find himself either squeezed out or obliged to sell and allow himself to be absorbed." Had there been no World War—had Mr. Wilson been able to devote eight years to domestic instead of to international affairs—we might have had a wholly different situation. However, the then distant roar of European cannon, growing ever louder, forced him to abandon the study of this issue. The problem he saw so clearly is left with us as a legacy; and no one of us on either side of the political controversy can deny that it is a matter of grave concern to the government.

A glance at the situation today only too clearly indicates that equality of opportunity as we have known it no longer exists. Our industrial plant is built; the problem just now is whether it is not over-built. Our last frontier has long since been reached, and there is practically no more free land. More than half of our people do not live on the farms or on lands; and cannot derive a living by cultivating their own property. There is no safety valve in the form of a Western prairie to which those thrown out of work by the Eastern economic machines can go for a new start. We are not able to invite the immigration from Europe to share our endless plenty. Our system of tariffs has at last reacted against us to the point of closing our Canadian frontier on the North, our European markets on the East, many of our Latin American markets to the South, and a goodly proportion of our Pacific markets on the West.

Just as freedom to farm has ceased, so also the opportunity in business has narrowed. It still is true that men can start small enterprises, trusting to native shrewdness and ability to keep abreast of competitors; but area after area has been preempted altogether by the great corporations, and even in the fields which still have no great concerns, the small man starts under a handicap. The unfeeling statistics of the past three decades show that the independent business man is running a losing race. Perhaps he is forced to the wall; perhaps he cannot command credit; perhaps he is "squeezed out", in Mr. Wilson's words, by highly organized corporate competitors, as your corner grocery man can tell you. Recently a careful study was made of the concentration of business in the United States. It showed that our economic life was dominated by some six hundred-odd corporations who controlled two thirds of American industry. Ten million small business men divided the other third. More striking still, it appeared that if the process of concentration goes on at the same rate, at the end of another century we shall have all American industry controlled by a dozen corporations, and run by perhaps a hundred men. But plainly, we are steering a steady course toward economic oligarchy, if we are not there already.

Clearly, all this calls for a re-appraisal of values. A mere builder of more industrial plants, a creator of more railroad systems, an organizer of more corporations, is as likely to be a danger as a help. The day of the great promoter or the financial Titan, to whom we granted anything if only he would build, or develop, is over. Our task now is not discovery or exploitation of natural resources, or necessarily producing more goods. It is the soberer, less dramatic business of administering resources and plants already in hand; of adjusting production to consumption; of distributing wealth and products equitably; of adapting existing economic organizations to the service of the people. The day of the manager has come.

Just as in older times the central government was first a haven of refuge, and then a threat, so now in a closer economic system the central and ambitious economic unit is no longer a servant of national desire, but a danger. I would draw the parallel one step farther. We did not think because national government had become a threat in the 18th century that therefore we should abandon the principle of national government. Nor today should we abandon the principle of strong economic units such as the great corporations, merely because their power is susceptible of easy abuse. In other times we dealt with the problem of an unduly ambitious central government by modifying it gradually into a constitutional democratic government. So today we can develop our economic units.

As I see it, the task of government in economics and business is to assist the development of an economic declaration of rights, an economic constitutional order, which must be the foundation of the coming order if it is to endure.

Happily, the times indicate that such a course not only is the proper policy of a government, but is the only line of safety for the economic organisms we have built up. We know, now, that these economic units cannot exist unless prosperity is uniform—or, to put it differently—unless purchasing power is well distributed throughout every group in the community. That is why even the most selfish of Eastern corporations for its own interest would be glad to see unemployment cease; to bring the farmer back to his accustomed level of prosperity and to assure a permanent safety to both groups. That is why many enlightened industries themselves endeavor to limit the freedom of action of each man and business group within the industry in the common interest of all; why business men everywhere are asking a form of organization which will bring the scheme of things into balance, even though it may in some measure qualify the freedom of action of individual units within the business.

The exposition need not further be elaborated. It is brief and incomplete, but you will be able to expand it in terms of your own business or occupation without difficulty. I think every one who has actually entered the economic struggle—which means everyone who was not born to safe wealth—knows in his own experience and his own life that we have now to rewrite the unchangeable concepts of American government in terms of today.

Government in the United States is, you remember, a social contract by which the rulers for the time being are accorded power, and the people consent to that power, but only on clearly understood terms. I hold this as true today as it was in 1776; but I hold that the application of this principle has widened. The contract is not with formal, office-holding government alone. It embraces the informal economic and business government as well. Enlarging an old phrase, I hold that private economic power is also a public trust; and that continued enjoyment of that power by any individual or group must depend upon the fulfilment of that trust. The men who have reached the summit of American business life know this best; happily, they are foremost among those who urge the binding quality of this greater social contract.

The terms of that contract are as old as the Republic, and as new as the economic order.

Every man has a right to life; and this means that he has also a right to make a living. He may by sloth or crime decline to exercise that right; but it may not be denied him. We have no problem of famine or dearth; our industrial mechanism can produce enough and to spare. Our government, formal and informal, political and economic, owes to every one an avenue to possess himself of a portion of that plenty sufficient for his needs, through his own work.

Every man has a right to his own property; which means a right to be assured, to the fullest extent attainable, in the safety of his savings. By no other means can men carry the burdens of those parts of life which, in the nature of things, afford no chance of labor: childhood, sickness, old age. In all thought of property, this right is paramount; all other property rights must yield to it. If, in accord with this principle, we must restrict the operations of the speculator, the manipulator, even the financier, I believe we must accept the restriction as needful, not to hamper individualism but to protect it.

These two requirements must be satisfied, in the main, by the individuals who claim and hold control of the great industrial and financial combinations which dominate so large a part of our industrial life. They have undertaken to be, not business men, but princes—princes of property. I am not prepared to say that the system which produces them is wrong. I am very clear that they must fearlessly and competently assume the responsibility which goes with the power. So many enlightened business men know this that the statement would be little more than a platitude, were it not for an added implication. This implication is, briefly, that the responsible heads of finance and industry instead of acting each for himself, must work together to achieve the common end. They must, where necessary, sacrifice this or that petty private advantage; and in reciprocal self-denial must seek a general advantage. It is here that formal government—political government, if you choose, comes in. Whenever in the pursuit of this objective the lone wolf, the unethical competitor, the reckless promoter, the Ishmael whose hand is against every man's, declines to join in achieving an end recognizably for the public welfare, and threatens to drag the industry back to a state of anarchy, the government may properly be asked to apply restraint. Likewise, should the group ever use its collective power contrary to the public welfare, the government must be swift to enter and protect the public interest.

Men of high ideals are not wanting who insist that the formal government should itself enter and itself perform this function of economic regulation. Perhaps they are right; but it is a last resort, to be tried only when private initiative, inspired by high responsibility, with such assistance and balance as government can give, has finally failed. As yet there has been no failure, because there has been no attempt; and I decline to assume that the best business brains of the nation are unable to meet the situation.

The final term of the high contract was for liberty and the pursuit of happiness. We have learnt a great deal of both in the past century. We know that individual liberty and individual happiness mean nothing unless both are ordered in the sense that one man's meat is not another man's poison. We know that the old "rights of personal competency"— the right to read, to think, to speak, to choose and live a mode of life, must be respected at all hazards. We know that liberty to do anything which deprives others of those elemental rights is outside the protection of any compact; and that government in this regard is the maintenance of a balance, within which every individual may have a place if he will take it; in which every individual may find safety if he wishes it; in which every individual may attain such power as his ability permits, consistent with his assuming the accompanying responsibility.

All this is a long, slow task. Nothing is more striking than the naivete of the men who insist whenever an objective is presented, on the prompt production of a patent scheme guaranteed to produce a result. Human endeavor is not so simple as that. Government includes the art of formulating a policy, and using the political technique to attain so much of that policy as will receive general support; persuading, leading, sacrificing, compromising, even, in the hope of leading again. But in the matters of which I have spoken, we are learning rapidly, in a severe school. The lessons so learnt must not be forgotten, even in the mental lethargy of a speculative upturn. We must build toward the time when a major depression cannot occur again; and if this means sacrificing the easy profits of inflationist booms, then let them go; and good riddance.

Faith in America, faith in our tradition of personal responsibility, faith in our institutions, faith in ourselves demands that we recognize the new terms of the old social contract. We shall fulfil them, as we fulfilled the obligation of the apparent Utopia which Jefferson imagined for us in 1776, and which Washington, Jefferson, Madison and Jackson brought to realization. We must do so, lest a rising tide of misery engendered by our common failure, engulf us all. But failure is not an American habit; and in the strength of great hope we must all shoulder our common load.

To Raymond Moley, on Roosevelt's special train, September 30, 1932

. . . The bonus. It is becoming increasingly clear that it is extremely poor strategy to delay statement on the bonus indefinitely. The newspapers state that the Governor will make a full length speech on the subject. I don't think it calls for that; he could issue a thousand words of a copyright statement which would do just as well. My idea as to the line would be this:

The bonus cannot be paid. But there is no reason why everybody should raise their hands in holy horror. For years special interests have felt perfectly free to go to Congress and ask for special favors. Every industry has got up a lobby and tried a tariff graft. Some industries have got up a lobby and asked for direct subsidies. It has got to stop; and now is the time. The policy of granting special favors has already nearly bankrupted the economic system; and it simply cannot go farther.

We cannot impugn the motives of five million men. Many of them are in want; and many more are anxious to see something done to relieve their fellows. The right of veterans to get relief is the right of human beings, not the right of a privileged class. As a good navy man, the Governor could take the position, so far as he is concerned, that men, capital, labor are all alike subject to service in war for 'the common defence of everyone.

Some such statement would clear the air very much. . . .

Johnson and I are working up the defensive speeches. [Vice-Presidential candidate John Nance] Garner will tackle part of the defense, I hope [Senator] Carter Glass [D., Va.] the rest. So far the brain trust rides high; but I have a vague feeling that the rapids are near and require some careful shooting.

To Sumner Welles, October 3, 1932

. . . I am flattered that you should ask my views because your own experience has been wider perhaps than any except that of a very few men living.

A purely practical question is whether anything ought to be said about Latin American matters in the campaign as it has developed to date. Something will have to be said sooner or later; the problem is whether a campaign which has thus far gone off exclusively on domestic issues should be widened in scope.

Confidentially, there are those who believe that the Governor should follow the course of a Chinese Buddha and "contemplate his navel" for a while.

This, however, does not let him out from making the pronouncement on foreign affairs at some time between now and March 4th in any event; and he has to have his South American data ready. . . .

BBB Diary

October 6, 1932

Now F.D.R. wants some more speeches but I think it's time he shut up. He'll be all talked out before he gets elected.

The best joke though, is writing speeches for Garner. Johnson wrote the freshman year as he thought A. couldn't drop to that level. But A. wrote the sophomore year, I didn't think he had it in him! It was quite colloquial. I took out all the words of three or four syllables I could find.

There is still one month of the campaign. It looks as if a lot of people would vote against Mr. Hoover and elect Mr. Roosevelt. It is also becoming increasingly evident that the Democrats have many strange bedfellows in their party, that F.D.R. cannot always be all things to all men and to steer a path through all this morass will require extraordinary nicety of judgment.

October 12

A. has read this over and seems to think credit is due some of the other members of the B.T. but after all I'm not their wife. . . .

On Monday the B.T. met again to consider the strategy of the next Roosevelt trip.

Hoover's Des Moines speech has created great surprise and annoyance among the bankers. Lippmann calls it a campaign of panic and apparently it was so taken abroad the $ going down. Hence A. has written a speech today entitled "In Defense of American Finance" showing we had plenty of gold to meet foreign payments and the danger lay in the American flight from the $ caused by lack of confidence in the Administration and an unbalanced budget. My reaction was—"If this is true, why did Hoover make such a noise?" That I believe was the impression intended to be created upon the public. There is also a lot of soft soap about cutting gov't costs, and telling the world the $ is OK—

Charles [Taussig] it seems wants to write another "new individualism." That says A. can only be done once in 20 years—O these prima donnas.

October 16

I met A. in Albany Friday night at what he rightly calls the world's ugliest house. The walls are imitation vermilion leather with gilt edges and brown mahogany wood work. The Roosevelts had left for Hyde Park and Moley was sitting at the desk writing a bologna speech about "F.D.R., The Man" to be delivered by himself in Cleveland.

F.D.R. it seems was impressed by [Senator William] Borah [R., Ida.] and does not consider the gold standard as the basis of all sound economic life. He is flirting with the idea of a managed currency. (Was any one ever able to manage it?)

Garner made his freshmen speech yesterday and it wasn't so bad. We dined at the Fields [Berkshire friends] and Miss Field during the evening asked naively and seriously "Where did Garner go to college?" A. paints a man who has been shell shocked by the amount of noise made by Mills and others; one who can slap Texans on the back effectively but does not understand the demeanor expected in national politics.

A. speaks of F.D.R. as a man whose judgments of people and ideas are primarily instinctive and not rational, who learns not from books but from people. He has his eye on the ball; on things that he thinks he can get done, he is not the champion of lost causes.

A. is wondering where all this will come to as far as he is concerned. Politically he cannot get a big Washington job and he could not afford to take another.

Today A. is off again to Hyde Park.

Memorandum, October 17, 1932

On Friday, October 14th, with Raymond Moley, I met the Governor. The debate was on the bonus question. A statement had been planned for

Wednesday previously; postponed to Saturday. A great many veterans' organizations had been writing the Governor congratulating him on his brilliant stand for veterans' rights.

It was finally determined to issue the bonus statement in connection with the speech on the budget to be given at Pittsburgh.

As we left it, there was a flat opposition, with a possibility that something might be done for veterans in need.

Memorandum, October 17, 1932

On Sunday, October 16th, there was a meeting with the Governor; Raymond Moley, Rexford Tugwell, General Hugh Johnson from Baruch's office; Mr. [Swager] Shirley, formerly chairman of the House Committee on Appropriations; later Mr. William H. Woodin of the American Car and Foundry Company and the Federal Reserve Bank; and Forbes Morgan [Secretary, Democratic Finance Committee]. Samuel Rosenman came in and later Basil O'Connor. In the middle of it Mayor [Joseph V.] McKee [acting mayor, upon Walker's resignation] called up. The difficulty appeared to be that the city was not able to meet its November pay rolls unless the city budget was cut by a hundred millions, which [Tammany boss John F.] Curry had refused to do. The Governor stated that he was ready to call a special session of the legislature and have the city taken over by receivers if it defaulted on November 1.

He then talked it over with Curry on the telephone.

I notice that on October 17th it was announced that Tammany would probably back the budget cut.

The debate was on the budget speech; likewise on a speech answering Hoover at Des Moines. We decided to eliminate the gold standard part, because the financial districts already made that argument; also because the Governor said, "I do not want to be committed to the gold standard. I haven't the faintest idea whether we will be on the gold standard on March 4th or not; nobody can foresee where we shall be." I gathered that the Governor would rather stay on the gold standard than not. But he is not undertaking to say now what the policy will be. In this connection note that Felix Frankfurter and his friends have been arguing for a managed currency along the line of Maynard Keynes.

BBB Diary

October 20

A. is getting somewhat fed up.

The real excitement of last Sunday seems to have been when McKee called F.D.R. and told of the refusal to cut down expenses in N.Y.C. by Tammany. F.D.R. then said he would call a special session of the state legislature to take over N.Y.C. bonds and declare N.Y.C. in bankruptcy. Apparently when he finally gets his back up he does stick to what he says.

October 23

A. considers that an intellectual adventure has been had: that he has been the master mind directing a political campaign or rather the ideas enunciated by a candidate for President.

He apparently went to a small dinner given by Richard Crane [friend of Roosevelt] this week taking in some of the leading lights of the Democratic Headquarters. At this party A. was the grand Mogul and everyone wanted to know what F.D.R. would say next and what A. advised him to do about this that and the other thing. A. was mysterious and non-committal!

A. is worried again about wars and rumors of wars in the Danzig corridor. Thinks there may have to be a special European mission.

And still they go on making speeches. "In Defense of American Finance" is apparently not to be given but F.D.R. gave one dealing [with] various forms of securities and credits which was AAB Jr straight. . . .

But I am thoroughly fed up on speeches and think it's time they quit. Hoover is making a very good stand and I wonder whether he might not be reelected.

To Roosevelt, October 24, 1932

Mr. Baruch has offered me a retainer in connection with the Coolidge Committee of Insurance Companies etc. on railroad policy. It does not take effect until after election.

I write you this only because a group like the "brain trust" becomes worthless if tainted with outside influence. Mr. Baruch has asked nothing indicating that the retainer connotes any influence; there is no apparent reason why I should not take it. If you have other views, please say so; otherwise do not bother to answer. Your time now is far too valuable.

With congratulations on the result of the campaign to date. . . .

Roosevelt responded on October 28, saying he could see "no reason in the world" why Berle should not accept Baruch's offer. "More power," he said, "to your arm!"

Confidential memorandum, November 3, 1932

The Brain Trust has had heavy going.

It started the week with Senator Key Pittman (Nevada) who will be chairman of the Committee on Interstate Commerce in the coming Senate. With him was Senator Jim Byrnes, of South Carolina.

By Monday night both Senators were somewhat the worse for wear and good liquor and senatorial speeches rather than ideas flowed.

By Tuesday night the senior senator from Nevada was half-seas-over, while the senator from [South Carolina] was beginning to recover. As Moley was away, the group developed into Judge Rosenman, General Hugh Johnson, Senator Byrnes and myself.

The following night Senator Pittman from Nevada was completely out of action, and the Senator from South Carolina was needed primarily as nurse. In an endeavor to get together the material for the last three speeches of the campaign, his contribution was primarily keeping Key Pittman from going out and assaulting the taxicab starter in front of the Roosevelt.

Last night (November 2) also General Johnson disappeared, apparently having suffered the same fate as Key Pittman. Byrnes and Rosenman still in the running.

We estimate that by Saturday night there will be nothing left of the Brain Trust but the secretary.

Memorandum, November 7, 1932

I spent Saturday with Governor Roosevelt. Raymond Moley became ill on Friday afternoon and was in bed; General Johnson is still out of action, for the same reason which keeps Key Pittman at the Roosevelt.

On Saturday afternoon, the decks having been cleared, the Governor fell to talking about the prospective Cabinet. I observed that [William Randolph] Hearst had already given him one.

He said that of the elder statesmen the only one with an adventurous mind was Owen Young; that Owen Young had discussed the gold standard with him shortly before the convention when he (Young) had confirmed to the Governor that he was not opposing the Governor's nomination in any way. The Governor had asked what would be the effect of going off the gold standard; Owen Young had said no one could tell but that he did not imagine there would be any catastrophic effects.

He thought [Newton D.] Baker was extremely honest and extremely capable, but timid about adventuring too far in economic matters; and added a phrase indicating the same thing of John W. Davis [1924 Democratic presidential candidate]. Remarking that the average New York person would pick out a Cabinet composed of ten New Yorkers, he said that it was impossible for him to make any suggestions about a Cabinet now because events might so happen between now and March 4th that a quite different type of man might be needed, depending on circumstances.

I said I hoped his majority would not be too large; if it was something amazing—say twenty-five million (It would be ten million, said the Governor)—the country would want economic action far more quickly than any political engineering could arrange it and, not getting it, there might be a very serious situation. His response was that the kind of program he had in mind necessarily would take a certain amount of time; that if the majority were very large there would be instant pressure on Hoover to fire [Henry L.] Stimson, appoint him (Roosevelt) Secretary of State; have [Vice-President Charles] Curtis resign to the President and then have the President submit his own resignation, whereupon Roosevelt would become President. He indicated that he thought there might even be some possibility of this happening, though he did not consider it probable.

We discussed briefly foreign affairs; I brought up the question of [Professor James T.] Shotwell's memorandum;* he said that Europe had taken no interest in the election until a few days ago, when suddenly they have become furiously interested and that he had had three trans-Atlantic calls this morning. Further, that [journalist] Anne O'Hare McCormick (who is intimate at the Roosevelts') had interviewed Hoover and in the course of it had asked whether Hoover was going to say anything about foreign affairs. Hoover answered that he would not unless Roosevelt forced him to. Mrs. McCormick asked whether she could tell this to Roosevelt and President Hoover said that he hoped she would. It is, I believe, the only message even indirect which has passed between the two men from the beginning, at least since Hoover refused to confer on the St. Lawrence waterway.

Of course the fact is that the [French Premier Edouard] Herriot government, threatened with defeat when the Chamber of Deputies convened, has risked its life on a dramatic foreign move, namely, its proposal for a European general staff which it is thought will be pleasing to the American point of view as expressed by Stimson. A harsh word about this program from Roosevelt, amounting to a repudiation of the Stimson negotiations, would probably precipitate the fall of the French cabinet, since Herriot would be accused of making futile gestures and of having been tricked into a weak policy by failing accurately to appraise the political situation here.

* Berle memorandum to Roosevelt, November 4, 1932 re "Disarmament Conferences—Foreign Debt Settlement," discussing Shotwell's role. Shotwell actively supported the League of Nations.

To John Hanna, Professor of Law, Columbia University, November 9, 1932

Thank you for your letter. You persist in giving me more credit than I am entitled to.

As for going to Washington, (a) there has been no suggestion of that; and (b) no job which could by any possibility be offered me as things now stand would be one which I could afford to take; (c) all of us can be a good deal more useful hoeing our own row than monkeying with obscure under-secretaryships or commissionerships.

The thing that counts here is the steady intellectual drive which at long last must condition every political change. This is a conscious sacrifice of today for tomorrow. The politicians and the business men have their hour; and the men who can think straight and be vocal in their thinking have as much of the future as their mental ability entitles them to. I have work enough now, legislative and scholastic, to last for the next five years; and more comes in by the minute. Offhand, I don't see that a government job could add very much. I do hope to have a relationship which will permit my going to the White House occasionally to delve in when various discussions are forward; and that, in all conscience, is responsibility enough.

Memorandum to R. Moley, November 10, 1932

Since the result of election will call for action immediately on inauguration, we have to consider a program which can if necessary be presented at a special session of Congress. I think the economic situation may change very much for the worse before that time, so that many of the following suggestions may have to be shifted as we go along.

Proposals as to the program of legislation will have at least to consider the following possibilities:

Fundamental Legislation

1. The farm relief act—domestic allotment plan or some other plan designed to increase purchasing power of the farmer.

(This is essential. It is also the largest single factor in dispersion of national income with corresponding increase in purchasing power and presumably increase in the industrial market. Vital, therefore, if only as unemployment relief.)

2. (Possibly.) Industrial stabilization—limited permission to industries to get together under suitable supervision on stabilization plans, *provided* they afford reasonable probability of greater employment, protection to the consumer, and are kept in control.

(I am making a collection of these stabilization plans. The work has been foreshadowed by Senate Resolution 273 introduced by Senator David I. Walsh [D., Mass.]. Necessarily this involves at least a limited set of exceptions to the Anti-trust Act. Incidentally, this might strengthen the security markets and correspondingly the banking situation, which will be in bad shape beginning about February 1, 1933.)

3. A relief act, which might be coupled also with an unemployment insurance program.

(We shall be lucky if we get through the winter without having this question badly messed up by the Congressional session. No one yet realizes the extent of the trouble we shall be in by mid-winter.)

4. The currency question.

(This is less a matter of legislation now than determining what the economic policy will be; and that will have to depend on conditions on March 4 next; so that all we can do is study the question theoretically.)

5. Funding or otherwise taking care of the floating debt.

(By the end of the fiscal year (June 30, 1933) this will amount probably to about eight billion dollars. Classical finance would dictate the funding of the long term bonds. It is now merely absorbing all the bank credit—that is, banks call their loans to individuals and buy short term government securities. This situation may blow up any time: the banks may not absorb the treasury offerings; present certificates will drop in value; we should have an epidemic of bank failures at once. Baruch is following this situation.)

6. Taxation—whether by sales tax or otherwise, the budget has to be balanced.

(This question is complicated by the adoption of various excises by the individual states. Some kind of a conference would be desirable, and that very rapidly, before all available sources of revenue are preempted.)

7. Material for tariff negotiations.

Curative Legislation.

1. Federal regulation of security issues and publicity of accounts, covering public utility holding companies, etc.; but to be considered also with reference to companies of large size and national scope bidding in the capital market.

(These were touched on in the Columbus speech and at certain other places in the pre-election program.)

2. A federal incorporation act,—which is tied up with the foregoing. (Our hand is forced on this because the Committee on Interstate Commerce, working with the Interstate Commerce Commission, which is now investigating holding companies, proposes to recommend a federal incorporation act; [W.M.W.] Splawn of that commission has asked me if I would join in drafting one, commencing about January.)

3. Possibly, a branch banking act. This is Carter Glass's proposal. (Scientifically, there is no answer to it, and the American Bankers' Association, after opposing it for years, recently rescinded its resolution opposing it. It needs a great deal of thought. The real difficulty is with the standards of American bankers.)

4. A thorough-going coordination of the various credit emitting agencies such as

> The Home Loan banks
> The Federal Farm Loan banks
> The Federal Joint Stock Land banks
> (Possibly) the Reconstruction Finance Corporation.

(These are in a mess, largely because the detail has not been well enough worked out.)

5. The revision of the federal receivership laws. (This is largely to provide for the probable railway reorganizations which will have to take place; along the lines suggested in the Salt Lake City speech.)

6. Some revision of the Interstate Commerce Act providing for regulation of motor trucks and additional unification of railway facilities to eliminate unnecessary competition.

(A good deal of the spade work here has been done for us by the Interstate Commerce Commission.)

- - - - - - - -

On my own responsibility I have been collecting material in those fields in which I happen to have special facilities, notably:

(A) Industrial stabilization plans;

(B) Federal regulation of security issues, publicity of accounts, etc.;

(C) Federal incorporation (in which I shall be involved, as it seems, any how);

(D) Revision of the federal receivership acts;

(E) Revision of the Interstate Commerce Law—(as counsel for the Coolidge Committee on Railroads, I shall have access to their material; I think there will be no objection to using it.)

I have also been collecting some material on branch banking; and some material on the currency matter; though this is by way of supplementing the collections which must be in existence elsewhere.

It must be remembered that by March 4 next we may have anything on our hands from a recovery to a revolution. The chance is about even either way.

My impression is that the country wants and would gladly support a rather daring program.

After your discussion at Warm Springs, we can arrange about splitting up the work.

When Moley submitted to Berle, before publication, a chapter of his *The First New Deal* in 1966, which included large excerpts from Berle's November 10 memorandum, Berle replied, on February 2, 1966:

You do not mention—and perhaps should—the feeling of most of us, myself especially, that a larger share of the national income ought to be steered toward the lower income levels including farmers. This we did, consciously, through lowering interest rates, credit arrangements and so forth. This was not socialist: it was common sense. They needed the money; business needed the customers; everybody needed employment. We thought private organization would do it, but were prepared to do this through public sectors expenditures if need be—the result, in any event, would be mixed. . . .

I was half-way between a philosophy of "getting the old boat going again," on the one hand, and the socialist and near-socialist conceptions proposed by some of our friends. Essentially the Frankfurter group proposed to depend on ultra free markets and return to a small-scale production. Like you, I thought [Charles R.] Van Hise's *Concentration and Control* was more logical.

I think you should mention one other fact. At that time academic economists did not soil their hands with practical questions. Application of their science is almost entirely a post-New Deal phenomenon.

Memorandum to Moley, November 15, 1932

Re: International Debts

Some study of this situation, and some familiarity with the creation of certain of these debts, suggests the following:

Two questions involved:

(A) Collecting the value by the debtor government

(B) Transfer of that value to the United States through purchase and exchange.

As to these,—(1) Ability to collect: On present government expenditures, I believe collections could be made,

Easily, by France;

With reasonable possibility by Great Britain, Italy, and Greece;

Possibly with extreme difficulty by Jugoslavia and Germany.

The foregoing assumes no change in expenditures and armaments or the like. Diminution of armaments would of course permit collection of the values by all the governments.

(2) Transfer of the funds through purchase of American exchange, Could be done easily in the case of France (whose gold reserve is sufficient);

Could be done, but with extreme difficulty by the British (this might involve a drop of between 10% and 20% in the current value of the pound sterling);

It is practically impossible in the cases of Germany, Jugoslavia and Greece.

I am not clear about Italy; I believe payment could be made without breaking the lira but it is not easy to know.

The debt notes likewise involve two problems:

(1) An immediate arrangement;

(2) Agreement to negotiations.

Anything looking towards an arrangement would be extremely popular in the financial markets and the business communities; and would probably be unpopular elsewhere.

In fundamental economics, any payments from abroad diminish the chance of disposing of an export surplus of farm products. But the debt payments are relatively unimportant in comparison with interest on the private debts (foreign bonds, etc.) and payments on short term bank paper of which eight hundred millions (about) are in New York. The significance of the debt payments is therefore appreciable but not determinative; the psychological factor outweighs the financial or economic. . . .

I am convinced that negotiations will finally have to be entered about these debts, whether we like it or not, but I think that this ought to be postponed if possible until time of recovery, when exchange conditions are more normal. It might not be a bad idea to indicate that the proposed transfer arrangements would be maintained until a general business recovery permitted considering the question of negotiations with more real understanding of the possibilities of the situation.

Special note as to the French:

They are not entitled to much consideration. The drive on the American gold reserve last summer suggests that the Quai D'Orsay would not have been wholly sorry to see the United States go off the gold standard, permitting payment of the American debt in depreciated dollars instead of in gold. The French are strong on the "heads I win, tails you lose" policy in these matters. This is not true of the British; nor of the Germans; nor the Italians, who are in real difficulties.

The Hungarian situation is peculiar; but their financial situation is largely determined in Paris. If possible, it would be wise to evolve a result which would give the Herriot government something that looked like a small success; otherwise the government may fall and we should not have a happy time dealing with the extreme right, which would promptly succeed.

To John Hanna, November 16, 1932

. . . The Berle-for-Attorney General movement seems to have exactly one member—yourself—and even I should not join you in that.

Fortunately, the question is not an issue. I am one of the rare people who happens to have in life the thing that he most wants—the position of an intellectual free lance, with a moderate living, the gracious gift of friendship, and no lack either of color or work. Short of some peculiar set of circumstances imposing a real obligation, I should be merely foolish to trade this for the mazes of official life in Washington. The one time I had that opportunity—in the Wilson administration—it turned out a grand emotional fiasco. I was absurd enough to have views as to the desirability of what the government was doing (this was the Treaty of Versailles) and my resignation hardly reflected the mental agony both before and after it.

I am by no means clear that the intelligentsia who had a hand in the campaign will retain any position now that the campaign is over. If they do, I shall choose merely that of being an intellectual jobber and contractor from time to time when jobs come forward.

As to the rest of the Cabinet, I have not even a guess, let alone information. The only bit of real information is that the Governor I think quite consciously wants to be surrounded by what he calls "adventurous minds" and he will find them where he can.

I still think that a mixture of practical research and university work is about the most effective contribution that can be made.

To Moley, November 28, 1932

I have a couple of matters on my mind—and two men.

Of the two men, if names come up for jobs, I should be glad if you would have in mind,

(1) Fiorello La Guardia. You know all about him. He is going to be important in the short session. I am having him to dinner tomorrow. His career is not over by a long shot and I think he ought to be annexed.

(2) David Lilienthal. He is a member of the Public Service Commission of the State of Wisconsin, appointed by Phil La Follette after a short but brilliant spell of practice at the Chicago Bar. His administration in the Wisconsin Commission has been outstanding. Milo Maltbie [Chairman, New York Public Service Commission] will stand sponsor for him; the two men work hand in glove. He is in no need of a job, because the Democratic party in Wisconsin put as a plank in the state platform a statement that Lilienthal would be continued. We owe him something, because he played a part in swinging the La Follette group to the Governor; but we need him on account of sheer ability. Personally he is very attractive and has many friends, among them Donald Richberg.

So much for the men.

As to the matters, much as I hate to do it, when the Governor gets back I think I shall need half an hour with him.

(1) The railroad receivership bill. This is being drawn for the Coolidge Committee, along the line of the Governor's suggestion in Hyde Park that we try to follow the English procedure. The English Act can be adapted so that it will work here. Before we get the Coolidge Committee

thoroughly sold on it, I would like to have the Governor's blessing. It carries out one of the promises in the railroad speech.

(2) Industrial stabilization, along the lines that we were talking about in your office just before you left for Washington. I have been fussing with this and it now looks as though we could work out something pretty closely along some of the lines Brandeis worked out in his opinion in the Oklahoma Ice case. I have talked with a good many groups of business men and I am inclined to think it would make a ten strike in that quarter—not that this is important, but that it tends towards giving a balance to the whole program. Specifically, if we hand the farmers something, as we are proposing to do, it would help a great deal if we could likewise hand the business men something. I think also it would make possible more employment, release some of the frozen credit at the banks and give us something like a stable industrial structure, for a while, at least. I will get this pretty well forward by the time the Governor comes back.

(3) The Governor asked for some figures relative to the possibility of a 25% cut in all debts—this is an alternative if the creation of an artificial price structure does not work out—or possibly as an aid to it, if no better way can be found. We shall have these figures ready when he gets back; I presume he does not want to be bothered with them now.

You are all over the rotogravure sections by now and, what is worse, about to be written up in "House and Garden". Well, there is no way out of fame when it comes your way.

Memorandum to Roosevelt, December 2, 1932

Congressman Fiorello La Guardia came to see me on Monday. He has a bloc said to be twenty-six in number, mainly western Progressives, which he claims to control in the next House.

I gave him the guy-ropes of the Farm Relief program; likewise some of the legislation we talked about in the campaign, which he expressed himself as very anxious to support. Unless you see some reason to the contrary, it would be well to have him put in touch with [Congressman] Marvin Jones [D., Tex.], so that they work together.

This is the group that wrecked the sales tax last year; and in a close case could control the House; La Guardia insists that with the Democratic contingent they will be able to pass a Farm Relief bill even over a veto.

Berle helped La Guardia draft two major bills that session. The first, bringing the Federal Bankruptcy Act of 1898 up to date, included a section that gave the Interstate Commerce Commission jurisdiction over railroad reorganization. The second, a farm credit bankruptcy bill, was not acted upon before Congress adjourned; the New Deal later passed a similar proposal during the Hundred Days.

Memorandum to Roosevelt, December 16, 1932

Railroad Relief—R.F.C. Act

Mr. Woodin and I were in Washington on December 14th and 15th discussing an amendment permitting the Reconstruction Finance Corporation to lend to railroads on open note against certificates of the Interstate Commerce Commission. The present Act requires such loans to be "adequately secured". The R.F.C. interprets this as requiring collateral—many railroads haven't any.

Key Pittman thought it might be done.

Glass was cool, believing that the government ought not to help out bondholders and that we were in for deflation anyhow.

Garner thought it could not be done because the whole Reconstruction Finance Corporation would be raided by everyone with a flood of unsound legislation. He also thought the Reconstruction Finance Corporation could make open note loans now to railroads if it wished (it has done so to Banks), insisting that the phrase "adequately secured" did not necessarily mean secured by collateral. He suggested that the Reconstruction Finance Corporation Board be approached.

All agreed that nothing could be done unless a farm credit relief measure accompanied it.

Congressman [Sam] Rayburn [D., Tex.] (a very dependable man) agreed to urge this on Jesse Jones [an RFC director]. Mr. Woodin agreed to have the railroad people talk it over with Hoover and the Republican members of the Board.

This is about all that can be done now.

To Roosevelt, January 11, [1933]

Dear Governor—

Raymond will tell you of Felix Frankfurter's telephone call last night regarding the Railway Reorganization (Bankruptcy) Act.

Typically, F.F. comes in at the last minute with many ideas, some very good, none of which could be got into legislative shape in less than a year or got by this Congress; and would like to do nothing unless he can have everything he wants; but will take no responsibility for getting anything done. And he talks of opposing what has been done, using the usual bunch. Which explains why, in his long and interesting career his opposition has been brilliant, but his ideas have never been brought to fruition —except over his protest.

Col. Lawrence, in his "Revolt in the Desert" observed that the men who were best at raising a revolution were usually the world's worst at translating it into a government.

Yours truly, in a mean state of mind, with considerable admiration of F.F.'s public career and an intense personal desire to see him shot.

BBB Diary

March 5, 1933

Home after the inauguration and never have I been so glad to get home.

It was a continuous standing in line going from one place to another and no place worth going to. And as for it being a good show, there was no show. We have lost all color and all sense of pomp and ceremony—

probably there never was any in this country. There was no thrill in the crowd, only idle curiosity.

We heard Roosevelt's speech pushing through the Capitol grounds as the other half of the population was pushing away—bored. It was a great speech and with all the banks closed a few hours before—most timely and dramatic though the crowd showed no indication it thought so.

It may be too that the people as well as I have lost the capacity for that fine frenzy of enthusiasm for any cause. A. is the one person who has not lost it and whose romantic sense is getting plenty of nourishment. But being a god is not all beer and skittles—it's d——d hard work.

I have not spent an evening with him for a week and the only quiet time we have had was yesterday morning. Pulling out from the gov't now may be declining a place in history, said he—Shall I be Alexander Hamilton? A few hours later he went to the U.S. Treasury and has been there ever since. Who knows when he will come home.

Being in public life does mean that your time is not your own and that your personal life is to a large extent drafted. Neither he nor I wish to make that sacrifice, but what must be must be and emergencies I suppose do not last forever.

"There is no room for brain trusts or kitchen cabinets in the American scheme of government," Berle declared shortly after Roosevelt's inauguration in March 1933. "It was intended as a government of direct responsibility. The people elect and the President appoints those charged with the formulation of policy. Necessarily the actions of these officials must be open to public scrutiny and criticism. They should act and live as if in a goldfish bowl." (From a manuscript drafted by Ben Stern in 1939, with corrections by Berle.)

A participant at the famous Treasury Conference during the banking holiday, Berle also served on committees working out legislation for the special session of Congress called by the President. Preferring only a part-time position in the administration, although one with an official status, Berle declined an appointment as a Federal Trade Commissioner. In April he agreed to become a special assistant to the director of the Reconstruction Finance Corporation, to advise Jesse Jones on railroad and banking legislation. Throughout the Hundred Days he commuted regularly from New York to Washington.

Memorandum, April 24, 1933

On Wednesday afternoon the White House tried to find me to go to the Economic Conference which was to be held on that afternoon. The Conference was finally held on that day. Present among others, were [Budget Director] Lew Douglas, James Warburg [financial adviser to Roosevelt], Charles Taussig, [Assistant Secretary of State] Raymond Moley and Secretary [of the Treasury] Woodin. The President greeted everybody by asking whether they had heard about the United States going off the gold standard. Hardly anyone supported this, except Taussig and Raymond Moley. I had previously given my view to Moley in favor of it. Lew Douglas said this was the end of Western civilization.

The theoretical reason was international negotiation.

From my point of view the real reason is as follows:

Some of the banks which were reopened after the holiday are beginning to get into trouble. The difficulty is at Tulsa, Oklahoma, at Birmingham, Alabama, and at Nashville, Tennessee.

The R.F.C. will of course stand by these banks. But if the movement were to grow it could not handle the load.

The burden of liquidation of the banks remaining closed after the holidays and of the rising unemployment and of the falling price level obviously indicated more rather than less trouble.

Estimating the time element as well as I can, it would seem to be as follows:

After the trouble started, and taking the Dawes Bank mess in July 1932 as the beginning, the movement reached a head in February, 1933, a period of seven months.

Allowing for the automatic acceleration usual in these matters, we should expect about one-third the time—that is to say, trouble developing in June at the latest.

Nor can we count on the credit machinery being sufficiently intact to handle the matter by credit inflation (bank credit, government bonds, etc.).

We made a mistake in not guaranteeing bank deposits after the bank holiday. That would have been in effect the same thing we are doing now, but, I think, a sounder basis. That being out, and it being obvious that a mere appeal to people not to withdraw their deposits would not work a second time, a currency solution is the only one.

Possibilities. The rising price level may save things without more. If it does not, the country may go on a currency basis, which means providing currency equivalent to bank deposits. Banks in that case become merely safekeeping agencies, possibly charging a small fee for the job.

Manifestly, three billions of paper will not do this; but cutting of gold content and use of the Federal Reserve note issuing process, however, may fill up the slack.

The problem in my mind is whether the currency bill will get through quickly enough to avoid the banking difficulty.

Problem: Can the commercial banks, as we know them, now exist with the country going on a currency basis?

I have no reason to believe that the Administration has this slant of things in mind as yet.

Memorandum, May 23, 1933

Senate Investigation of Morgan—Glass.

I noticed from the newspapers that Glass was objecting to the investigation of the [House of] Morgan income tax returns by [Ferdinand] Pecora and the [Senate] Committee, on the ground that the Internal Revenue people had done all that.

I happen to know that Pecora has evidence indicating that the Morgan returns were not audited by the Treasury Department which was in the habit of accepting as correct anything that came from Morgan's office. Pecora intends to prove this. Glass objected to the evidence on the ground that the Internal Revenue Department had already audited these returns. I have a great admiration for Glass and dislike to see him put in a false position; for he will be in a position of having attempted to prevent the Committee from investigating, and he will subsequently find that the Treasury had not investigated either. I believe that he does not know this.

In an effort to save Glass I telephoned Baruch, asking Baruch whether he might not suggest to Glass (who is his close friend) that this would be a good line to drop.

Soon after Roosevelt sent to Congress a bill for the regulation of securities by the Federal Trade Commission, Berle sent to Rayburn, who had introduced the measure in the House, a number of specific suggestions for revising the draft. Concerning the memorandum, dated April 3, 1933, Berle noted the same day:

Briefly, our idea is that the bill ought not to lay down specific requirements as to the information which must be filed with the Commission. In place thereof it ought to declare as the purpose of Congress that there must be filed with the Commission, and open to the public, information sufficient to permit a buyer of securities adequately to estimate the risk that he takes, and sufficient to prevent any fraud. The Commission should be given power to prescribe what information must be required, except that such information must be embodied in a formal registration statement executed as provided in the act.

On April 6, 1933, Berle wrote "My dear Frankfurter: . . . It is pretty plain that a good deal more work has to be done on this act. I am terribly afraid to make the mistake the English made after the South Sea bubble, instead of doing the real job which Mr. Gladstone, in his report of 1844, envisaged. . . ." Frankfurter, on April 12, thanked Berle for his letter and helpful suggestions.

To Woodin, April 12, 1933

. . . The new draft has been made up by Felix Frankfurter, apparently without consulting any of the banking or accounting people here. Conceding that all of the banking community are villains (they are not) it still would be useful to have their experience unless, of course, they are to be legislated out of existence which seems not on the program. We hope that some day we will be selling securities again.

Could you suggest that before any draft is shot, Rayburn or someone be asked to call in a few people for practical comment? Felix is a brilliant man with excellent ideas, but some experience sometimes helps in these matters.

You are doing a magnificent job; the unanimity of approval is, I think, unexampled in American life. . . .

To Rayburn, April 27, 1933

. . . In all the talk about the Securities Bill up here two ideas have been produced which might be useful. They are concisely:

(1) A suggestion that the Federal Income Tax Return of corporations be made available to the public.

(2) A requirement that profit sharing arrangements and officers' compensation shall be disclosed.

The President has had in his mind for some time a proposal that corporations selling securities to the public be required to make their accounts public under some kind of supervision which might cover both questions. On the other hand, these might find a place in the proposed bill.

I realize perfectly that ideas, when a bill as far advanced as the present one, even when sound, may be entirely impracticable because the scope of the bill has been thoroughly defined. These are accordingly offered merely for what they may be worth. . . .

Rayburn replied on May 3 that the subcommittee rejected the possibility of the first proposition and that there should be general corporate legislation to cover the second one.

Berle discussed the significance of the Federal Securities Act (signed by Roosevelt on May 27, 1933) and what he considered were the necessary additional steps in the New York *Times* on June 4 ("New Protection for Buyers of Securities"). Later, in the *Yale Review* ("High Finance: Master or Servant," Autumn 1933), he examined at length the inadequacies of the bill. He argued that, although it had eliminated fraudulent finance, there had to be control over the power of investment bankers.

On June 10, 1933, a few days before Congress adjourned, ending the Hundred Days, Berle spoke at the twenty-fifth anniversary of the Harvard Business School. He said in part:

It will be said in years to come that an administration came into office at the precise moment when a crisis almost unparalleled in modern history had reached its peak. . . . It will be pointed out that whenever such a crisis has occurred elsewhere in the world, its swift sequel has been a revolution. . . . In the United States, however, life goes on with no such violent aftermath. American faith in American institutions is surely justified on this record.

To Roosevelt, August 9, 1933. (Draft. Not sent.)

My dear Caesar:

It seems to be necessary to clean up the New York City finances, if possible. This involves winning an election. Hence the activities of which you have heard. I am grateful for your courtesy to Beatrice and have noted carefully what you said.

Merely for your interest, there is some method in this scattered shot. In the long-term finance of the country, the largest situation was the railroad bonds ($11,000,000,000); the next largest single situation, the New York Savings Banks ($5,000,000,000); the next largest, the Guaranty Mortgage situation (nearly $4,000,000,000); the next, the City of New York. I list them where they can be dealt with approximately as a unit. . . .

I haven't asked for instructions from you but have tried to work it out through the responsible officials in each case.

This is really Treasury work and some time I hope you can change the law and have a flying Assistant Secretary of the Treasury to handle this kind of question. But if there is going to be real recovery, these situations have to be swung as they come along. I hope you have a splendid vacation.

On August 21, 1933, Ambassador Sumner Welles, in Havana, asked the State Department to send a financial commission to Cuba as soon as possible to assist in discussions with the Cuban government. Ten days later, the State Department requested that Berle proceed to Havana "in order to make certain studies in connection with Cuban economic and financial matters." Before leaving, Berle resigned as special assistant to the director of the R.F.C.

"A few days after their arrival," a subsequent State Department memorandum noted, "the Government of President Céspedes was overthrown by a new regime, which was not recognized by the Government of the United States. Under these circumstances the Commission returned to the United States after rendering a preliminary report" (September 5, 1933). On September 19 Welles informed Secretary of State Cordell Hull that the report "has been drawn up under Berle's direction, in accordance with my own views," and that "he has been exceedingly helpful."

Years later Berle, commenting on a book, recalled his experience in Havana during Gerardo Machado's revolution: "The book has one error. [R. H. Philipps] tells the story of Sumner Welles sitting between the officers in the Army in the Hotel Nacional in 1933. She speaks of him as talking quietly with his Counsellor of Embassy, Ed Reed. This is wrong. Sumner Welles was talking to me about Emily Dickinson of whose poetry he was fond and of Berkshire flower gardens of which I am fonder" (Diary, July 15, 1959).

Before leaving for Cuba Berle had worked energetically in La Guardia's campaign for the Fusion, or anti-Tammany, nomination for mayor of New York. He had met Congressman La Guardia late in 1932 and had collaborated with him during the lame-duck session of Congress that winter. As Arthur Mann has stressed, in *La Guardia Comes to Power: 1933* (1965), Berle looked to La Guardia "as one of the few leaders in American public life who know *what* had to be done and *how* to get things done." Berle introduced him to Judge Samuel Seabury and prominent civic leader C. C. Burlingham, and their group engineered his nomination for the Fusion ticket.

Telegram to Roosevelt, September 24, 1933

Joe McKee is telephoning you tonight to confirm your part in following arrangement: Joe has been promised by Ed. Flynn [Bronx Democratic leader, Roosevelt supporter] that if he will run for mayor of New York you will furnish Flynn enough patronage to buy Tammany leaders sufficient to assure election. . . . All of us feel strongly you ought to stop this unauthorized use of your name and prestige in a situation which can result in nothing but harm to you with probable effect of exchanging a premier moral position for reputation of second grade politician. [Roy] Howard [Scripps-Howard newspaper publisher] puts it even more strongly. Better adhere to your principle of keeping clear of local fights and especially steer clear of being in position of rehabilitating Tammany. Regards.

To Roosevelt, October 21, 1933

Dear Caesar:

It seems now that La Guardia is likely to win the New York City election by a respectable plurality, perhaps even a landslide.

The night before last Ogden Mills came out for him, uninvited. We had excluded Mills et al. from everything up to then, but we don't own the air. Since there was a large sign in Times Square "A Vote for McKee is a Vote for Roosevelt" Mills' only object was to attack you by attacking McKee. Of course, Mills hates La Guardia and everyone connected with him, including your humble servant; a feeling heartily reciprocated.

I feel that another statement of neutrality might be in order. It will keep the Mills crowd out. It will head off the cry that a La Guardia victory is a reverse for you.

This is a revolutionary year; left sweeps the board. La Guardia, as the left progressive, is simply taking (virtually) the vote you got last fall. The slogan "A Vote for McKee is a Vote for Roosevelt" freely advertised here lets the Millses rage and the Wadsworths imagine a vain thing. I hope it can be stopped. . . .

Don't deliver us into the hands of your (and our) worst enemies.

In 1965 Berle recalled: "I felt that if what the President wanted to achieve was to prove successful, there should be not merely a New Deal in Washington but a score or more similar programs over the nation. I could see La Guardia carrying out such a program, but never so earnest a Tammanyite as McKee." La Guardia "could be and was a gut-fighter in New York politics. The difference was that he knew the difference between gut-fighting and the society he hoped to create. . . . Roosevelt considered he had a half-commitment to support McKee. . . . I like to think that I neutralized his influence. It was difficult to maintain that McKee was a Roosevelt candidate when I was overtly campaigning for La Guardia. I only asked Roosevelt's neutrality—which he gave. . . . Roosevelt said nothing—and stayed out." After being elected, La Guardia named Berle City Chamberlain, a post Berle held throughout the Mayor's first term. (Ben Stern's manuscript, 1939; Berle letter to Arthur Mann March 31, 1965 and April 23, 1965.)

Also during the fall of 1933, Berle was appointed by Roosevelt to two committees, one to study the subject of federal incorporation and the other, known as the Roper Committee, to evaluate the 1933 Securities Act and to propose stock exchange legislation. Before starting work on the stock market project, Berle discussed "The Social Economics of the New Deal," in the New York *Times Magazine*, October 29, 1933.

. . . The New Deal may be said to be merely a recognition of the fact that human beings cannot indefinitely be sacrificed by millions to the operation of economic forces accentuated by this factor of organization.

Further, the mere process of organization which could create the economic mechanism can be invoked to prevent the shocking toll on life and health and happiness which readjustment under modern conditions demands.

Whatever the outcome, President Roosevelt will live in history as a great President if only for this one fact. He not only appreciated the situation, but had the courage to grapple with the cardinal economic problem of modern life. And he did so not in the spirit of hatred manifested by the red revolutionary or the black Fascist abroad, but in the typical American spirit of great generosity and great recognition that individual life and individual homes are the precious possessions; all else is merely machinery for the attainment of a full life. . . .

It remained for the hard-boiled student to work out the simple equation that unless the national income was pretty widely diffused there were not enough customers to keep the plants going. . . .

This is why the experiment of the Roosevelt administration not only is historic, but why it must succeed. This is why the only intelligent attitude to take is one of cooperation. This is why, though all of us will undoubtedly have moments of discouragement at the slowness of it, we build more strongly than we might were we either to attempt a wholesale revolution, or to plunge back into the chaos which was failing dismally only a few months ago. . . .

In a world in which revolutions just now are coming easily, the New Deal chose the more difficult course of moderation and rebuilding. This, in a word, is the social economics—the political economics, in the old phrase—of the New Deal.

Memorandum, November 27, 1933

I lunched today with Mr. Lewis Strauss, a partner of Kuhn Loeb & Co., in the private dining room of that house. No one was present. Mr. Strauss asked me whether I felt free to advise two corporations,— "friends" of his, in respect to loans which they wish to secure from the Reconstruction Finance Corporation. He explained that he did not wish me to arrange for or advocate these loans before the Reconstruction Finance Corporation, but merely to advise whether on the type of project and the local set-up, loans could be granted to them.

I explained that my relations with the Reconstruction Finance Corporation were too close to permit my taking such retainer; further that I considered the information they desired to be in the nature of public information which should be available to anyone without payment of any fee; and that on application to Reconstruction Finance Corporation I had no doubt that his friends would be promptly given the information they desired.

To Roosevelt, December 9, 1933

Dear Caesar:

Yesterday Lewis Strauss . . . came into the office. He said there had been a tacit understanding among the security houses that no issues would be floated for the time being, pending revision of the Securities Act, and possibly a stabilization of money.

I said the financial district would simply commit suicide along those lines. Issues were maturing, and I thought no government would permit a general collapse. If necessary, they would work out some ways themselves to meet the maturity. Strauss said he and the younger men agreed, and he was accordingly working on a method of financing some of the major real estate maturities, which he thought might meet the situation. I told him I thought this was a pious act and that I hoped they would also think along the lines of breaking the jam generally.

If this view prevails, the opposition is weakening. If it does not, I see no escape from giving the Reconstruction Finance Corporation the right to go into the investment banking business.

Thank you for your courtesy to Major La Guardia. It eases things here enormously. . . .

Roosevelt answered on December 15, 1933, saying "That talk you had with L. S. confirms my guess. You are right. Hope to see you soon."

To Jesse Jones, December 28, 1933

Re: Reconstruction Finance Corporation Legislation

I have spent a little time going over the long term financial situation, which bears on the legislation the Reconstruction Finance Corporation will want in the next Congress.

It is plain that investment bankers are not going to float long term bonds for a while, and this is not wholly due to the Securities Act, because they are not floating even bonds exempt from the provisions of that Act. . . .

This money ought to come from true investment money, and not from the banks. A commercial bank has no business to loan money for capital purposes; its liquidity vanishes pretty rapidly if it does so, and it ought to do so only when the securities on which it loans will presently find their way into the true investment market. Handling this kind of credit is the job of the investment bankers; and they are out of action partly because they dislike the Securities Act, partly because they would like to re-establish the political position they have lost, and partly because they are shell-shocked and afraid. On the other hand, a good many investors are quite anxious to buy, if they can be sure that the security is honestly issued and that the enterprise has been impartially gone over.

Finally, the agencies of the United States government, such as the Home Owners' Loan Corporation, and the credit agencies of the Department of Agriculture, are having trouble handling their own bonds, since there is no machinery provided.

I suggest that we take the bull by the horns and ask Congress to authorize the setting up of a Division in the Reconstruction Finance Corporation which can buy, sell and underwrite bonds of federal agencies, municipal bonds, railroad bonds, and, to a limited extent, industrial bonds; and make agreements with banks to do so (to permit bank credit to be loaned against a "take out") on the showing that application has been made for such accommodation through ordinary investment channels and the accommodation is not obtainable on reasonable terms.

I raised this question with the President the other day, and he seems to think that some such method of handling things will be necessary. The Department of Agriculture (Jerome Frank) [General Counsel] seems to have the same idea, and I rather imagine [John H.] Fahay, of the Home Owners' Loan Corporation, will welcome the matter. Specifically, I think Frank will take it up with you in a few days.

I can see no political opposition to this, except from the investment banking community, and they are hardly in a position to object very forcibly. . . .

To Roosevelt, January 9, 1934

Dear Caesar:

[Governor Herbert H.] Lehman's controversy with La Guardia is unfortunate; particularly because La Guardia had asked for a conference and was met with a political blast. I hope to navigate things into a conference and clean things up. Lehman gets support from Republicans who want to take a poke at you; it is of no use to him nor to you and merely muddies the water.

It gives, however, the liberal Republicans the first chance they have had to offer anything to New York City, namely, cooperation with the Fusion Administration . . . for the first time in years a Republican stands a chance to be Governor of New York. . . .

What I want to do is to navigate New York City into a friendly cooperative basis with both the State and National Administrations, and if there is any line to take here, I should be glad of a steer.

The President wrote back to Berle, from Washington, on January 13, 1934: "You are right about navigating New York City. I will talk with you about it when next you come down."

During the fall of 1933, Berle had sent to Assistant Secretary of Commerce John Dickinson, chairman of the Roper Committee, several memoranda concerning the proposed stock exchange legislation, and in mid-January he completed a "Draft of Proposed Report to Secretary [of Commerce Daniel C.] Roper on Stock Exchange Regulation." When the final report was prepared, Berle concurred, but with a number of specific exceptions. James Landis, Federal Trade Commissioner and a member of the committee, wrote to him on February 25, 1934: "Just a word of appreciation of your wisdom in your separate report. As an outsider, if I had been and were such, I should have little difficulty in subscribing to your qualifications. Here as well as elsewhere I find your thought something to respect and admire. . . ." During the spring, Congress passed the Securities Exchange Act, which Roosevelt signed on June 6.

Telegram to Roosevelt, March 1, 1934

[Robert] Moses [Chairman, Triborough Bridge and Tunnel Authority] matter probably will become a national incident within a few days since Triborough funds are still held up stop I think this is one of the things you cannot do unless there are reasons other than personal giving ground for public defense stop Moses will certainly resign not merely from Triborough but from city administration stating his position of which our opposition friends are prepared to make the most stop I hardly know Moses but suggest there might be more real devils to fight stop Remember the execution of the Duc d'Enghien broke Napoleon

Roosevelt replied, on March 2, 1934:

Dear Adolf:

I love your suggestion that Bob Moses' real name is the duc d'Enghien. Also, though I do not mind your calling me Caesar, I hate your suggestion about Napoleon!

As a matter of fact the case of your friend, the duc, is in no sense a personal one. There are, however, a good many cases in other cities and counties and states where it has been necessary to lay down and follow the definite principle that where an independent Authority is set up to carry through a public work, the members of this Authority must be divorced from any other government agency.

I have no objection to your friend, the duc, continuing for a short time as a member of the Bridge Authority, but if an exception is made in his case we cannot well maintain a very necessary and very advisable rule in other parts of the United States. I think you will see the point.

To Roosevelt, March 3, 1934

My dear Caesar:

A few days ago General Atterbury, of the Pennsylvania Railroad, asked me to see him.

He said he and the Morgans had about come to the conclusion that none of the eastern railroads could survive long, though it would be possible for the Pennsylvania to live and make money for a few years. But the struggle for traffic would ultimately break them all.

. . . they contemplated a single operating combination for the entire northeastern district. . . . After asking whether I would act as attorney for the Pennsylvania, and learning that I would not, he asked my views.

I told him that, on the figures, after a few years they would all be bankrupt. A big regional unification probably was the only sound way of handling it, financially, other than government ownership. But a combination as strong as that infringed on the power paramount; the government could hardly allow so strong a combination, unless it were in virtual control.

Atterbury said he realized this, but they were reaching a point which required that something be done, even at that price. He asked whether the definite plan, when worked out, should be presented to [Joseph] Eastman [Interstate Commerce Commission member who wanted to coordinate railroads into regional systems]. I thought it had best be presented to you direct, and referred to Eastman. This gets beyond railroading, and becomes a matter of sovereign economic power.

This is an issue that is going to have to be faced, anyway, before the end of your present administration, and perhaps might as well be faced now.

I gathered that a plan would be worked out within the next six weeks. But if there is anything in it, it should be your plan, not theirs.

I wired you about Moses. I don't know him; he is often impulsive, incautious, and difficult to get on with. But the incident would release a great tide of ill feeling here. All of Moses' friends, including Al Smith, have caucused on it. There may, of course, be a publicly defensible objection to Moses, which we don't know.

Roosevelt wrote on March 10, 1934: "Yours of March third about the eastern roads is most interesting. When the matter crystallizes a little further I should be delighted to talk with General Atterbury or anyone else. Let me know."

To Roosevelt, March 15, 1934

Dear Caesar:

The Duc D'Enghien matter is up again. If you could have [Secretary of the Interior and Public Works Administration head Harold L.] Ickes make a general ruling stating that memberships on federal authorities or fund disbursing bodies must be divorced from political jobs, we can work it out. This, of course, hits other people besides the Duc. We can defend publicly a ruling of general application. We should be glad to do so especially if it could be part of a general move to make wholly non-political the economic agencies of the Federal Government. Following the lines of your ruling about national committeemen practicing law, the move would be not only defensible but very popular. An apparently personal ruling on the Duc, F.H. [La Guardia] could not defend without wrecking his administration and alienate both for him and you progressives everywhere. People here fear the implications of a political organization which has stock in your bank, a mortgage on your house, control of your relief funds and so on. The political job business is working against us rather than for us now; when there are one hundred applicants for five jobs, we make more enemies than friends.

Politics here are chaotic. There is no Democratic Party. There is a Republican progressive movement in the making in the City which has more in common with the New Deal and the independent Democrats than does any "regular" Democratic outfit. . . .

Atterbury and the Morgans are exploring railroad unification; [Thomas W.] Lamont [of J. P. Morgan & Co.] favors it; they are trying to persuade [President Frederick] Williamson of the [New York] Central. Lamont thinks that if it is done here all other sections will rapidly follow suit, adding that he agrees with Atterbury in believing that public control is inevitable. I will keep you advised as the conferences progress.

P.S. Caesar, of course, is historically accurate. A supreme power, elective, subject to Senate and people. I apologize for bothering you with Napoleon. His ghost came in handy along with the Duc.

To Roosevelt, April 23, 1934

Dear Caesar:

Mr. Justice Brandeis has been revolving matters in his head and I think requires some attention. At all events, he stated his view to Jerome Frank the other evening, asking to see me and Rexford Tugwell. His idea was that we were steadily creating organisms of big business which were growing in power, wiping out the middle class, eliminating small business and putting themselves in a place in which they rather than the government were controlling the nation's destinies. He added that he had gone along with the legislation up to now; but that unless he could see some reversal of the big business trend, he was disposed to hold the government control legislation unconstitutional from now on. I think also he regretted not having had a chance to talk to you about it. He, of course, wants drastic taxation of big business units, accompanied by leaving small business, via the N.R.A., strictly alone.

His view, if ever stated, would command wide popular support. But as long as people want Ford cars they are likely to have Ford factories and finance to match.

To Roosevelt, April 23, 1934

My dear Caesar:

It is said here that [Postmaster General James A.] Farley is to dominate the reorganization of Tammany, and that he is opposed to the La Guardia administration.

Since no great change is taking place in Tammany, perhaps it would be wise for the national administration to steer clear. . . . The La Guardia administration and the New Deal are popularly identified; but you are in the happy position of not being responsible for us if we make mistakes. We have kept the La Guardia administration from being forced into the Republican camp thus far; it should not happen now. Yet I see no other result if it were flanked by a regular Democratic organization supported by the national government, with a Tammany label.

We are beginning conferences with the bankers tomorrow morning to try to buy out of the Bankers' Agreement. The City of New York now has credit; and we might conceivably finance without reference to the New York group. One pleasant effect for me is that I can presently abolish the office of City Chamberlain with a clear conscience!

Roosevelt answered on April 30, 1934: "It is good to get your two notes. As to the tiger, you have doubtless seen Farley's statement. Hands off means hands off. As to our friend of the highest court, I expect to have a good long talk with him within the next few days. The difficulty is that so many people expect me to travel at a rate of one hundred miles an hour when the old bus cannot possibly make more than fifty miles an hour, even when it is hitting on all eight cylinders."

To Roosevelt, May 18, 1934

Dear Caesar:

Hugh Johnson asked me to go to Washington to do plain and fancy thinking for the N.R.A. But I think not. Thinking can be done here. A La Guardia intellectual in New York is a political asset both to you and to him; another "Brain Truster" in Washington is a liability. Since the New York finances are coming round nicely, even the taint of impracticality is being removed.

To Roosevelt, May 18, 1934

Dear Caesar:

. . . I have to thank you for keeping the administration out of the Tammany business here; it helps us and I think is sound for you. As to getting fifty miles out of the old bus, it is so much better than the rest of us that I marvel. But, most precious Caesar, there are by actual count eighty-five administratorlets reporting directly to you. No man can do that and live. Make captains of tens and deal only with eight, before Ossa falls off Pelion.

Roosevelt's answer of May 24, 1934 read: "I think you are right about letting the N.R.A. do its plain and fancy thinking for the time being. Pretty soon, however, and very shortly after the Congress goes home, lots of things are going to happen.

"Your old Uncle Franklin thinks that you ought to stick by the pretty good ship you are now voyaging on—at least until you abolish your own job!

"When that times comes, and perhaps sooner, there is a cabin with hot and cold running water ready for you in Washington. We will decide on its location a little later!"

July 16, 1934 [Not sent—hold as memo]

Dear Caesar:

This is merely to put on record the New York City finance situation to date. It will be solved within the next few days.

Having economized and balanced our budget, the time is ripe to fund our floating debt. . . .

Jesse Jones is a better poker player than I am so we turned over the trading to him and I understand that an agreement will be possible the day after tomorrow. So we shall get our floating debt funded and another cycle in the financial history of a tangled city will have ended, and with it the particular job I set out to do a year ago. This is merely so that you know the state of affairs in the queen city of the empire.

God give you pleasant adventures.

Confidential report to Hugh Johnson, of the National Recovery Administration, July 1934

Pursuant to your request, I am making this report on the general outlines of policy of the [NRA]. . . .

I need hardly say that this report is not designed for publication. In the course of collecting information, two or three people got wind of the fact that such a report was in preparation—namely, Secretary Hull and I believe also the President. Unless you object, I see no reason why copies of the report should not be in their hands, likewise on a confidential basis. But I took the position that the report was made for you, and that you would probably wish to show it to [Donald Richberg, chief counsel]. . . .

Memorandum Report on the Underwriting Policy of the National Recovery Administration

I. Introductory—The National Recovery Act to Date.

A. The Purposes of the National Recovery Act

The National Recovery Administration cannot be thought of except in terms of the conditions which called it into existence. These are:

(1) Something over fourteen millions of unemployed workmen, who were inevitably converging on the federal treasury for relief;

(2) A constriction in the area of possible purchasing power by reason of the unemployment, and also by reason of the fact that industrial payrolls had dropped by almost two-thirds since 1929; and

(3) The fact that liquidation, the need for cash, and the constricted market all combined to intensify competition to a point which meant wholesale wreckage in the industrial system. With this went a steady lowering of wages, indicating that the brunt would be borne not merely by industrial enterprise, but by labor also, which in turn continued the vicious cycle of more reduction, less purchasing power, greater constriction of market, and so forth.

These conditions which were present when the National Recovery Act was born are, in less degree, but compellingly, in existence now, save that they have somewhat changed their form. Unemployment still exists, though the figure may be ten million instead of fourteen million odd. A fair proportion of this group has already found its way into the relief system—federal, state and municipal; and the problem of financing this relief is rapidly reaching an acute point. In a sense, the relief problem of the United States is a measure of the territory which the National Recovery Administration and the Agricultural Adjustment Administration combined have been unable to cover, together with the help of private agencies, of families and friends. It can be said that this condition has been mitigated enormously since the inception of the National Recovery Administration; it cannot be said that it has been removed as a major problem in respect of which the bulk of our thinking must necessarily be done.

The constriction of the area of purchasing power likewise remains, though factory payrolls have increased, and though the number of unemployed has decreased. This, however, can only be considered in terms of price levels, since an increase in purchasing power can only be accomplished by a *relative* increase of industrial payrolls and number of employed, over and above the prevailing price level. There is great dispute as to whether this actually has occurred, one group holding that there has been a very considerable relative increase; another, that price levels on the whole have been increased by the National Recovery Act rather faster than have factory payrolls and employed individuals. From my point of view, there is no necessity of resolving the factual dispute. My opinion would be that there has been some relative increase; but it plainly has not been an increase adequate to maintain the industrial system which we had in 1927, 1928 and 1929 on any permanent basis. In this view, which I hold, the National Recovery Act has very materially contributed to the situation. It has not, however, proved a solution; and it is entirely possible that after a few months we shall be once more in the dilemma of having to supply either a speculative fillip through some inflationary measure, or face a general breakdown. There is, however, an alternative possibility, which is almost as unattractive as either horn of this dilemma. This is to excise a whole group of the American people—namely, about eight million of the ten million unemployed, if not more, from the entire economic system, leaving them as permanent recipients of a dole or some other form of subsistence relief, adding to this number the accession of young people who come into employable age now—leaving this group permanently outside the system. The distribution of purchasing power would then have to be limited to the remaining group, eliminating perhaps a large, but not disastrously large, group of industrial concerns, and running the economy of the country for a period of time on this narrow base. Something like this is what happened in England as a result of her unemployment crisis after the war.

The third condition—the violence of competitive practice which, in substance, forced concerns to cut-throat and even absurd tactics, has, in my judgment, largely been corrected—at all events, the pressure is not in the direction of less competition, but more.

In addition, at the time when the National Recovery Act was born it was likewise conceived that with it, as a concomitant of it and as a useful tool in it, certain great social objectives could be obtained. These were: standards of hours of work, standards of wages, and elimination of a certain kind of labor, especially child labor. It was thought that the communities would accept certain standards of operation in these regards, and that if an enterprise could not maintain these standards, the community would rather see that enterprise go under than have a sweat shop, a child labor factory, or the like, which might furnish goods at a lower price to the consumer but in that very process might force all of the industry down to its own standard, and ultimately force the burden of our economic difficulties back upon the laborers and their families.

At the time of the inception of the National Recovery Act, it was the opinion of a group of economists who convened at my house that the National Recovery Act would contribute something towards the mitigation of the general depression; that it would result in the absolute gain of a great deal of employment; that it would be extremely useful in terms of social legislation; but that it would not furnish a complete solution to the problem. This prediction has been, on the whole, verified by the facts; and it answers the criticism both of those who hoped that the National Recovery Act would achieve the impossible, and of those who insist that the National Recovery Act would be better out of the picture. While the National Recovery Act may not have solved the depression, its material contribution of some four million men more at work is so enormous that it cannot be ignored. The problem to be considered is whether the price we have paid to secure this contribution is too great.

The Theory of Operation of the National Recovery Act.

The National Recovery Administration took the view, and in my judgment soundly, that the policy was that outlined by President Roosevelt in his Commonwealth speech during the campaign. This meant, in substance, that the problem was to be put up to industry, and that industry would be implemented, under suitable regulation, with adequate tools to bring about a result.

The principal end which industry was expected to achieve was the net increase of men in employment, and the net increase in industrial payrolls. This, it was thought, would release purchasing power as well as alleviate distress, and tend to start the cycle spiralling upward instead of downward.

The tool with which industry was to be implemented was a freedom in certain aspects from the restrictions of the Anti-Trust Law, particularly in terms of agreements on methods of competition, and possibly, where necessary, agreements on price.

The problem of enforcement from the government angle would be an impossible one without substantial counter-check to employing groups; and this counter-check was conceived to be organized labor.

By using these tools, it was expected that

(1) Hours of labor would be shortened without pay cut, and additional men taken on to fill up the gap.

(2) Unsocial employment (sweat shop, employment at unconscionably low wages, child labor, night work for women, etc.) would be eliminated entirely, thereby accomplishing certain of the social objectives conceived at the time of the birth of the National Recovery Act.

Results

This would increase purchasing power; which would in turn increase consumption; which would in turn increase employment; and so forth.

In my judgment, the theory is sound. Three difficulties, however, necessarily arose.

The first had to do with using organized labor as a counter-foil. Unfortunately, organized labor is a pure abstraction in a great many industries. There is not "organized labor". There are "organizations of labor", in many cases, and in many other cases there are not even those. Further, organized labor as such in the United States has never undertaken to assume responsibility for a major national policy. It conceives itself as a bargaining group, which means in substance that it aims to secure for itself such advantages as it can in a bargain and naturally to put itself in the strongest possible position in making such bargain. There is no criticism of this course, except that it necessarily relegates labor to the position, not of a champion of the popular rights, but to exactly the same position held by an employing group. Labor is a more appealing group because the results of its bargain are more widely distributed, and a distributed purchasing power is always more significant to the community than a concentrated purchasing power, which leads to investment rather than to consumption. But in any given industry or group of industries, the result of an agreement between labor and employing groups may very well be exactly the same as the result of an agreement among employing groups, namely, to raise the price. This tends to destroy the desired increase of wage payrolls in relation to purchasing power—and while it may advantage the particular group, it means that there is no necessary contribution to the general situation. The theory of the Recovery Administration offered to American labor a chance to pull itself together and achieve a unified policy. This, so far as I am able to discover, American labor groups failed to do, preferring to remain as individual bargaining units. While these individual bargaining units may be useful in individual situations as a counter-foil, it necessarily might be impossible as a general governmental counter-foil, save in individual instances.

The result on this line has been to strengthen certain labor units and certain industrial groups and to make them available. It has not been to bring into existence any labor movement in the country conceived in general enough terms to be used as a general counter-foil. I do not believe this is primarily the fault of any conception of the National Recovery Act, unless indeed that we over-estimated the potential statesmanship of American labor. The experiment had to be tried.

The second problem, which is just at the moment a great deal in the public eye, arose in connection with the price policy. Since the objective was continuously to increase the relative factor of industrial payrolls as against purchasing power, a price fixing arrangement, whether direct price fixing or through the medium of open price associations, carried with it the possibility of an immediate run-up in prices. To the extent that such a run-up merely corrected the crazily low prices of 1931 and 1932, this might be discounted; for while wage payrolls were intended to increase more rapidly than prices, it was plain that an unduly low price level would make impossible any such increase. A rise of price beyond a certain point, however, simply eliminated the advantage of the proceeding. A further difficulty in the price field was, of course, that in fixing a price or arriving at a price through open price machinery or otherwise, the problem at once arose, a price based on whose costs? A price based on the cost of the most efficient producer would put the less efficient producers out of business. Contrary to the assumptions of a good many of the so-called "Brandeis group", the fact was that in the spectacular instances the low price could be made by the largest producer, though this was not always the case. In such situation, the low price meant putting the small producer out of business (hence the cry discrimination against small business); and a price made to cover a relatively inefficient producer meant offering stupendous profits to the efficient producer if he could hold his market or increase it, which he naturally attempted to do. In this case, the cry at once was raised that the government was fostering monopoly and taking care of the rich concern, and so forth. In general it may be said that the burden probably did bear more heavily on small industry than on large; my observation of it in the three or four areas around New York and New England, where I had occasion to take first-hand evidence, indicates that the small producer was being hit two ways at once. He frequently was not as efficient a producer; and he was, or thought he was, heavily penalized by the social legislation features, which exacted a minimum wage, short hours, decent conditions of work, and the like. This was particularly true in the so-called service trades, where probably the social legislation had a maximum of effect (indeed, where it was needed most), and it may have been accentuated by carrying some of the regulations to an extreme degree. As will be seen a little later, the so-called competitive practice provisions of the codes had an irritating rather than an actual effect, in that they cut off a good many of the little producers from their normal methods of marketing. Adjustment to this was always possible, but where smaller business failed to see the possibilities of the situation, the effects were often, at least temporarily, unfortunate.

The competitive practices tool with which the National Recovery Act implemented employing groups, in the form of trade associations, has probably occasioned more general comment than any other single provision, other than price fixing. This revolved around a number of foci, many of which are only indirectly related to the main issue.

The first focus is the personnel of the Code Authorities. There is a widespread suspicion that these Code Authorities were largely composed of the major elements of the trade (they well might be, insofar as the principal directive was toward employers of labor, since such units employ and can employ more labor frequently than all of the smaller units put together). This suspicion I believe to be fairly justified by the facts. There was also a suspicion that a great deal of the information which Code Authorities collected was used by the larger and stronger elements as a method of eliminating their competitors. I am unable to verify this suspicion, though I am unable to escape the feeling that in a good many cases it was more or less justified. The smaller man found himself very largely in the hands of his enemies. The Codes with which I am most familiar, when set against the experience of the men in them largely did indicate the collection of three or four large interests of like mind into a group which proceeded to secure and impose policies making it as difficult as possible for anyone else. I am inclined to think this was rather unconscious than conscious. The great lords of the rayon industry, for example, and peculiarly of the sugar refining industry, regard the entire market as their vested right, and anyone else in the field as merely an interloper to be put out of business at all costs. In other cases, the individual administering the Code Authority was not one who commanded the confidence of all the industry; and in any case it was always easy for a small business for whom the going was hard to blame its difficulties on the National Recovery Act, and particularly on the Code Authority.

Memorandum, August 3, 1934

In Washington yesterday Charles Taussig, Sumner Welles [Assistant Secretary of State, 1933–1937], Rexford Tugwell [Under-Secretary of Agriculture, 1934–1936] and I reviewed the state of the nation.

An intimate visitor was Bobby Straus.

Bobby Straus reported that the N.R.A. was practically over; about one-half of the men were resigning, largely because of the affair between Johnson and "Robby" (Miss Robinson) which has now reached an acute stage. Richberg resigned on that account. . . .

A somewhat similar situation on rather the same lines seems to be going on in the Interior.

Rex has just returned from the West. It seems that the drought has reached staggering proportions. About 2,000,000 cattle has to be killed or will die. The corn crop will be about 1,600,000,000 bushels or slightly larger against the normal of 3,000,000,000. There is no carryover in corn. The effect would be a glut of the markets with meat for a short time, followed by a steady rise in the prices of food and milk. The wheat crop is likewise in a serious condition. There is a glut of carryovers but the orders cannot come in which means that the farm implements and other similar machinery will be in very bad shape by next fall or thereabouts. Of course, it is possible that it will begin to rain and fall continuously for sometime, but this requires a miracle. I pointed out that from my own calculations the strain on the local organizations arising from relief would probably become impossible by about next March. We have had a survey made of the operations of the various governmental organizations. The R.F.C. is functioning well; likewise the H.L.O.W. [Home Owners Loan Corporation?] Rex believes the A.A.A. is, but the rest of us would only give it a fifty percent. rate. Public Works is almost at a full stop; the N.R.A., of course, is rather rapidly disintegrating. We have no doubt about the Treasury; I hear it is doing pretty well. The surplus relief corporation is functioning, on the whole, smoothly.

The intrigues are growing; many of them turn on the activities of George Peek who is head of the Export and Import Bank and who has been trying to get the approval of the State Department probably and particularly of Cordell Hull. . . .

In other words, we have an Administration in very bad shape indeed; at least partially corrupt and headed into a crisis less dramatic than a bank holiday but probably as violent, though the banks quite likely may not be affected; but it ought to take place sometime next spring.

It was agreed that as soon as the President gets back I was to see him and ask him to call a conference of Sumner Welles, Rexford Tugwell, Charles Taussig, myself, and possibly one or two others and simply attack the situation on all phases. There is no point in declining to face the issue.

I pointed out that the New York situation has been alienated following an alliance between Farley and Tammany Hall and that probably Seabury would be nominated on the Republican ticket and would win the nomination. It was thought that Farley's political activities were not sanctioned but arose from his desire to be Governor of New York and then President of the United States.

Roosevelt wrote to Berle, August 7, 1934, from Devils Lake, North Dakota: "It was good to get your letter when I reached the coast. Congratulations on the refunding.

"What does one do in cases like that of Portland, Oregon? The city is solvent and this year is running $700,000 receipts in excess of expenditures. They needed some short time money—six months, one year and two years and the best rate they could get from the banks was five per cent. They ought, of course, to get it at somewhere between two and three per cent.

"I wonder what the answer is.

"When I get to Hyde Park about the twenty-fifth of this month, you run up some day and see me."

Welles in a letter to Berle, August 11, 1934, wrote: "One of the things that I am most thoroughly dissatisfied with is the failure of this Department to obtain satisfactory publicity for its principal policies. I refer specifically to the trade agreement policy.

". . . I would like to have your feeling in the matter and any suggestions you may have to offer. . . .

"If, by any chance, you are planning to come to Washington next week, I suggest you try to make it before Wednesday since Mr. Hull is probably leaving for a two weeks' vacation on that day and he told me this morning he was anxious to have a talk with you and myself."

Berle wrote, soon after, an article, "America Embarks on a New Trade Policy" for the New York *Times* of August 26, 1934.

To Roosevelt, August 14, 1934

Dear Caesar:

Thank you for your letter from Devil's Lake. When you get to Hyde Park, I will telephone Mac [Marvin McIntyre, appointments secretary] for a date.

The City of Portland ought to have lower interest rates for short term money. Could not Jesse Jones dicker with the banks? If necessary, he could arrange with banks in New York or Chicago to rediscount for the Portland banks. Credit is an asset of the community, and not of the banks, anyhow.

May I ask your personal advice? [President] Richard Whitney has asked me to serve on this unpaid Board of the New York Stock Exchange representing the public. I think the idea a good one, and worth a shot: these quasi-public bodies ought to have public representation. At least we could try it on until we discovered whether all they wanted was a whitewash committee, in which case I could pull out. The information would be worth having. But I don't want to seem to be crossing from the public side to some supposedly private group.

Roosevelt answered on August 15, 1934: "I think it is absolutely all right to go on that Stock Exchange Board. As a matter of fact, as you and I know, the fundamental trouble with this whole Stock Exchange crowd is their complete lack of elementary education. I do not mean lack of college diplomas, etc., but just inability to understand the country or the public or their obligation to their fellow men. Perhaps you can help them to acquire a kindergarten knowledge of those subjects. More power to you!"

To Roosevelt, September 12, 1934

Dear Caesar:

Cordell Hull asked me to see him tomorrow, which I will do.

It is increasingly probable that the Treasury financing on Friday will fail; and in any case we have to stand by for violent repercussions in the next ninety days. Hull knows this: likewise Raymond Moley [now editor of *Today*]. Both have asked me to join in forming (or reforming) the old "brains trust", except that R.M. would eliminate Charles Taussig and Rex Tugwell. Plainly the thing could be done if at all, only (a) by your direction, and (b) reporting through a cabinet member. In practice, this means Hull, who in any case feels he must take some position in the coming fiscal difficulties,—as, of course, he must.

I have worked out, and am sending you tomorrow a sketch-plan for discounting certain Federal and local bonds without interest, along the line of our talk last week. Something like it has now become a necessity: within a few weeks, indeed, it will hardly be a matter of choice. At that time I hope Hull can see his way clear to going along; for he has the confidence of the country to a very large degree.

The selling of government bonds today seems to have come mainly from the country banks. New York banks are panicky, but feel they cannot let go. This is all reminiscent of Cleveland's time! . . .

To Roosevelt, September 13, 1934

Dear Caesar:

I promised you that I would try to work out some kind of a plan in connection with the matter of handling the relief needs of the country.

After going over the figures, one is compelled to the conclusion that the demands in terms of human need cannot be within the frame of the budget as it now stands. The financial markets know this: which accounts for the steady decline in government bonds and the very real possibility that we may be in for trouble on the federal refinancing on Friday. The problem is fundamental and cannot be met, I think, by any mere financial device.

Two plans, used either separately or together, might be considered.

(1) Creation of credit without interest, and its direction solely towards immediate activity.

A commercial bank "makes" money when it makes a loan, simply by setting up a credit on its books. It can obtain currency by rediscounting that loan at the Federal Reserve. We have no cognate machinery for capital activity. But I see no reason why we could not create such a cognate machinery.

The English banking system does this to a limited extent now.

A set of, say, Reconstruction Banks, with membership in the Federal Reserve, could be created. The capital would be limited. They would be authorized to loan money to the federal government or the local governments, for relief needs only, such loans to be without interest; and as security they should take non-interest bearing bonds of these governmental units.

The machinery would work somewhat as follows:

New York City would apply for a loan at the Reconstruction Bank and deposit its non-interest bearing bonds amortized as rapidly as seemed possible. The Reconstruction Bank would set up a credit to New York. New York City would pay its workmen and contractors with checks on this bank. The contractors would deposit their checks with the Guaranty Trust Company, which would through the Clearing House demand payment from Reconstruction Bank. Reconstruction Bank, having no assets save its capital in the New York City bonds, would rediscount at the Federal Reserve, likewise without interest. It would then pay the Guaranty Trust Company with a check on the Federal Reserve Bank. To the limited extent that currency was needed, it could of course obtain Federal Reserve notes. The effect would be vastly to increase the excess reserves of the commercial banks at the Federal Reserve. This could lead to credit inflation; but the Federal Reserve could check this if it started to run away, by selling government bonds in the open market, which operates to reduce reserves; or by suspending rediscounts.

Logically, the commercial banks ought to do this; but they act only for an interest charge, and as they do not do this you probably would have to create a mechanism of your own.

(2) Relief taxes could be levied in kind, mobilized through, let us say, the Code Authorities of the N.R.A., and redistributed to the various localities for distribution for relief. It is always easier to pay taxes in kind rather than in cash, just as a manufacturer will always prefer to pay his advertising bill in a trade credit rather than in cash. It cuts out the tremendous item of expense involved in selling, financing a sale, collecting the credit and reducing it to a cash profit. The only expense is the direct labor cost.

In practice this would mean that [Federal Emergency Relief Administrator Harry] Hopkins would get in from the various localities their estimates of what they needed in terms of goods. Presumably each state would get in similar estimates from its localities. Hopkins could then work out a relief budget in terms of goods; and this could be passed on into the budget in terms of a tax payable, at the option of the payor, in cash or in kind. The rugged individualist might choose to pay in cash. The rest would probably take the cheapest way out. The job of mobilization, industry by industry, and clearing the various shipments, could then be worked out. This would likewise involve railroads paying taxes in kind, in terms of free transportation, but I see no difficulty about doing this also. Appropriate safeguards to prevent goods so mobilized from entering into competition with goods produced for commerce would have to be evolved; again presumably by taxation in the form of a very heavy sales tax wherever such goods are resold outside the relief requirements.

Since this kind of plan could be used to mobilize raw materials as well as consumption goods, you could have work projects going forward on a very large scale.

Of course I like the second plan better than the first. Finance is a fixed frame, and the real elasticity in the situation is that we have an indefinite amount of productivity. Consequently it is theoretically sound to tackle the line of expansion where the expansion is really needed. Fundamentally our job is to increase the national income by increasing productivity. Any financial mechanism such as playing with credit or fiat money, or what not, has this, and this only, as its objective; and the real objections to them are that they are apt not to be effective; this is particularly true of fiat money. I have tried to work out United States baby bonds circulating as money; but on any real analysis those would be simply treated as fiat money for all purposes, and would have all of the fiat money effects. This means that on the original issue you would get some activity in terms of public works. But they would not go back into the banks. They would immediately be used to buy goods, and after their original issue they would have the same effect on prices that the German marks had. A credit device of the kind suggested would minimize this danger. Since, however, the real idea of such notes is to command the materials and consumption goods needed to take care of the relief lines, it would almost seem sounder to tax, and thereby secure those goods directly, thereby directly increasing the national income.

This is not orthodox finance, but I cannot see that any orthodox system will work out. The English solution of heavy taxation and a small dole means ultimately a debased people, though not a debased currency; and it works now only by socializing capital through inheritance taxes to a degree which our people do not even comprehend. The English solution transposed into the United States would seem infinitely more radical than the entire New Deal. Ultimately, the job comes down to some kind of social reorganization which permits the use of unused productivity against human need; and perhaps the quicker you get at the job the happier we shall all be. There will be a tax in any case, and any use of either currency or credit means a violent fight. Perhaps the fight had better be fought directly on the issue of using idle surplus productivity to meet human need than in terms of complicated and meaningless discussion of currency.

I wrote you last night about the various moves on the board to reconstruct the Brain Trust. The morning's layout of the treasury financing changes the picture a little. The October 15th maturities apparently will be met, largely owing to pressure by the New York Banks. The long term obligations are not being exchanged so well. Briefly, this means that every maturity is a matter for discussion with the banks: the country is thus heading into the position in which New York City was a year ago. That, I think, accounts for some of the worry.

I think a clear-cut financial policy ought to be decided on; laid out; then definitely announced and quite rigidly adhered to. Private business can always adjust to the known; but the knowledge of an impossible budget problem ahead leads to all kinds of wild rumors.

To Roosevelt, October 2, 1934

Dear Caesar:

Last week Cordell Hull asked me to see him, with Sumner Welles and Charles Taussig, about various national problems. As I think I wrote you, Ray [Moley] had suggested a similar group a few days previously.

The situation reminded me of Harold Nicolson's description of Lord Curzon and Lloyd George in 1919. One thing is plain: the historic hatchet between Ray and Hull simply has got to be buried somehow.

We paid the first installment on the mixing of the national machine with Tammany Hall today. Lehman, of course, has to come out for [Frank J.] Taylor as against [Professor Joseph D.] McGoldrick [candidate for comptroller] in New York. This of course means that La Guardia cannot be for Lehman. Nathan Straus [journalist, business executive, civic leader], Langdon Post [Chairman, City Housing Authority] and I are meeting tomorrow night to try to mobilize an independent Democracy. But between Bob Moses [Republican candidate for governor] and the reactionaries on one ticket, and Lehman, flanked by Al Smith and by Tammany on the other, there is not much of any place to go in New York State just now.

To Roosevelt, October 23, 1934

Dear Caesar:

We made a political failure in the attempt to work La Guardia and Lehman into the same boat. Farley's intervention in favor of McKee could have been forgotten and he did stop tying up with Tammany last summer.

But one struggles in vain against some things. . . .

New York finances work towards a climax. The bankers have virtually stated that as a condition of any relief credits, they want a sales tax. They would raise the subway fare (in the name of a transit tax) but there are legal objections. The real question is whether relief taxes will fall on the poor or on the well-to-do. After election we shall have a show-down. The sales tax is the equivalent of a 3% income tax on everybody in New York—70% of whom are operating on a wage of $20 a week; and I cannot see it. I am unwilling to borrow further for relief. We have rehabilitated New York credit which means we have saved the bond-holders. But I dare not borrow any more. One-third of our budget now goes for debt service; so we cannot afford the luxury if we have to pay interest.

Bankers here reacted favorably (!) to my suggestion that the Government create capital credits calling this a useful bit of machinery. A year ago they would have talked of "inflation". Ideas do filter.

To Roosevelt, November 3, 1934

Dear Caesar:

We rounded up on railroads in the R.F.C., the Coordinator's office, and some railroad men. It gets increasingly difficult for the R.F.C. to hold the line: the I.C.C. does not like loans to roads headed for bankruptcy. At present speed, eighty per cent of the mileage will be in receivership next year unless the R.F.C. and I.C.C. loan blind. . . .

The sweeping solution seems the only one possible. . . . It looks like a general take-over; a holding corporation on top; systems covering various areas; preferably headed by a business man—someone like Jesse Straus [President of Macy's, Ambassador to France]. I think the Pennsylvania, the Central, and perhaps the Morgans would support it; opposition from Santa Fe, Union Pacific, western roads.

Security holders don't consent to drastic reorganization, preferring receiverships, hoping something will turn up. But unlike 1893, nothing will turn up. This time there isn't a period of expansion ahead to take up the slack. Jesse Jones has the detailed red ink.

The New York City election goes well enough; Lehman will carry the town; Moses has eliminated himself; we shall elect McGoldrick by a moderate majority. [Lehman defeated Moses; McGoldrick lost.] I wish the Governor had taken more of your advice and less of Al Smith's. He could have kept out of this New York thing altogether. He and we would have been better off.

To Roosevelt, November 8, 1934

Dear Caesar:

. . . Congratulations on your vote of confidence. It is a brilliant result. Oddly enough, we seem to be the only opposition in New York, though you will agree that is the choice of Lehman and the National Committee and not ourselves; we did our best to avoid it. Fix it so that we are not opposition, when you can!

I hope to see you soon.

To Dean Young B. Smith, Columbia Law School, November 7, 1934

You asked for an account of what I have been at from July, 1933 to July, 1934.

The research in connection with problems of liquidity has been finished. The volume entitled "Liquid Claims and National Wealth", written in collaboration with Miss Victoria J. Pederson, will appear published by Macmillan Company on November 13th. It is the first study in the English language of the economics of liquidity with an indication of a parallel in legal machinery.

The research in connection with the study of Blue Sky Acts and the Administrative Law of Securities Regulations is going forward. Due to the fact that this study must now include a study of the new Federal Acts regulating the issue of securities and regulating the stock exchange, this study cannot appear until next Spring. The economic data have been completed; the data as to the State Securities Commissions have been collected; and the data covering the early operations of the Federal Securities Commission are in hand. This research is financed by the Commonwealth Foundation.

Certain public activities may be of interest. During the summer of 1933 I was Special Assistant to the Directors of Reconstruction Finance Corporation, in charge of the Railway policy. With the organization of the office of the Federal Coordinator of Railways I resigned this office, remaining, however, Special Counsel to the Reconstruction Finance Corporation in New York, likewise in connection with Railways. During September, I was Financial Adviser to the American Embassy in Cuba, in connection with the finances of the Republic of Cuba in the period following the fall of the Machado government. From the first of January on, I have been Chamberlain of the City of New York, primarily engaged in the problems affecting the finances of the City of New York, and the rehabilitation of the credit of the City; and in transit problems; and in rehabilitating the trust funds held by the City of New York. I was a member of the Inter-Departmental Committee in Washington, reporting to the President and to the appropriate Congressional Committees upon the proposed legislation for the regulation of the New York Stock Exchange, which now appears as the National Securities and Exchange Act; reporting likewise on the proposed amendments to the Federal Blue Sky Law; likewise on the Committee of the Department of Justice, studying the problem of Federal Incorporation. During the summer of 1934, I was elected by the Board of Governors of the New York Stock Exchange to act as a member of the Advisory Committee to the Board of Governors of the New York Stock Exchange, and I now hold that position on the New York Stock Exchange.

If it is of interest, during the summer of 1933, I likewise was called in to endeavor to work out a plan providing liquidity for the system of mutual savings banks in New York City, working with the savings banks, the Federal Reserve Board and the Reconstruction Finance Corporation. I drafted and secured the adoption of a plan setting up the reserve bank of savings banks, together with a companion institution for the purpose of affording liquidity to mortgages held by savings banks. This plan was set up and is still in effect. I have been acting as Adviser to the City in its negotiations with Transit Companies during most of the past year.

I think these are the main points. There are a good many other smaller ones, which are perhaps of less interest, but this will give the general trend.

If you don't object, I hope you will point out that I did not on this account miss my classes in the Columbia Law School. Unlike the other New Dealers around here, I have taken some pleasure in the fact that instead of abandoning my academic work, I kept it up both on the research and the instruction side.

On February 21, 1935 Berle received a letter from John H. Fahey, Chairman of the Executive Committee of the Twentieth Century Fund, inviting him to become a member of its board of trustees. Fahey said: "I myself believe that the Fund is doing work that is disproportionate in its service to the public to its annual income. In these days when, of necessity, there must be a great concentration of control over our economic life from Washington, it is more important than ever that there be entirely nonpartisan and independent agencies studying

economic problems and formulating constructive policies for meeting them. . . .
I hope you will agree with me that membership on the Board of Trustees of the
Fund offers an opportunity for public service which you cannot but accept."
Berle accepted on February 25.

Dear Mr. Fahey:

It gives me great pleasure to accept your kind invitation to become
a member of the Board of Trustees of the Twentieth Century Fund, Inc.
There is no Fund for whose work I have greater respect: though I have
not studied the pamphlet report you sent me, I am familiar with enough
of it without going farther to make up my own mind.

You are perfectly right in saying that if there is going to be government control, there must be continuous non-partisan economic work
keeping pace.

Please let me take this opportunity to say that I think you have done
a magnificent job with the Home Owners' Loan Corporation Act, and to
wish you all good fortune. Unless all signs fail, there is going to be more
difficulty, and I am glad to know that you are likely to be on deck.

To H. G. Wells, August 27, 1935

. . . The lines are slowly drawing here for a political-intellectual
conflict exceeding in bitterness that which revolved around Mr. Wilson's
head after Versailles. Your little book [*The Shape of Things to Come*] accurately foreshadowed the line. For myself, I am, of course, on the progressive side; but I can get up no heart for bitterness. The Diabolonian
quality of Pareto is having its effect here; the question is to find a philosophy to replace the doctrine that power is justified for its own sake, and
belongs to him who can take it.

To Roosevelt, June 30, 1936

Dear Caesar:

I am writing swiftly and bluntly lest time be lost. A situation has
developed in the State Department with which you are probably acquainted; but I am writing to make sure.

[William] Phillips' appointment to Rome [as ambassador] leaves
the Under-Secretaryship open. Both Sumner Welles and Cordell Hull
consider that Sumner is entitled to it on all counts; and they are right. It
is possible Sumner would not care to remain if passed over. Were Hull
otherwise constituted he would probably say so to you; but as you know,
Hull does not make representations, especially just now.

Hull considers he was personally repudiated and insulted at the
Philadelphia convention. I was there; and I thought he was. He is in no
mood to make requests of the White House just now. Fortunately, the
newspapers have not yet got hold of it. Perhaps to make sure they did not,
Hull left Philadelphia Thursday and has not yet come back to Washington; arranging not to be back till after you leave.

I think it would be wholly unjust not to appoint Welles as Under-

Secretary. He has been substantially doing that work for the last three years; pulls his political weight not only in Maryland but also in the confidence which La Guardia and the majority of the Eastern Liberals have in him. This may make considerable difference both in Maryland and New York; and in the Congressional support we get in foreign affairs in the next Congress. Sumner happens to be the kind of man who asks no favors; but I wish (since Hull will not be available) that you would make an opportunity to talk things over with Sumner.

I am sailing for France July 3, returning August 3. It looks to me like the beginning of a real French revolution. The result may leave Britain and America as the last of the Democratic powers.

My congratulations on the Philadelphia speech! If and when I can be of help, let me know. . . .

I am writing swiftly from the R.F.C., so as not to lose any time.

In 1936, La Guardia, Berle, and other leading progressives supported Senator Robert La Follette's progressive campaign for Roosevelt's re-election and organized the Progressive National Committee at a meeting in Chicago. Unable to attend the conference, Berle received a detailed report from his father and replied:

September 16, 1936.

Dear Father:

. . . Your size-up is much the same as mine. I have stipulated for one statement and one only—to wit, that while we supported the progressive legislation of Mr. Roosevelt, we were unalterably opposed to the continuance of the spoils system. When I saw that that statement came out, I was afraid that something was wrong.

It really comes down to two men in the long run—[Wisconsin Governor] Phil La Follette, for whom I have tremendous respect, and Fiorello. These two men between them, with Sidney Hillman of the Labor crowd, have got to carry the ball. I am sorry to have stuck you with it. I certainly never thought it would have come out that way, or I wouldn't have done it. In fact, the mere accident of the engagement before the Transit Commission alone prevented my being there.

However, there is a long and steady four years' trend ahead of us, which I think now will probably result in conservative reaction. Perhaps it is as well; so far as I am concerned, I have no particular ambition for a political career and I don't see that there is any lack of opportunity for public service, no matter who is in power. In many ventures, the happiest outfit I have found yet is the government of the City of New York under Fiorello, and if I can end that incident honorably and with a good reputation I am quite happy.

I am only sorry you are disappointed. I thought it might be an interesting and pleasant addition to your long string of political experiences. You had better stay by the City of New York with Fiorello and, while results may not be spectacular, we can get a good deal done for the general enhancement of living conditions in a quiet, unostentatious sort of way.

Eventually the empire is going to need men who are honest and experienced. When that time comes, we may be able to note a few. . . .

From Berle's review of *Rexford Tugwell and the New Deal* by Bernard Sternsher, for the *New Republic,* March 7, 1964

. . . In a broad sense, the New Deal was an institutional revolution. It shifted the major centers of economic power from private to public institutions. President Roosevelt and his intellectual as well as political cohorts quite consciously chose not to make it a socialist revolution. Thereby the intellectuals around FDR incurred the lasting enmity of a small but vocal extreme left wing, who hoped—as some still hope—to work up a sort of class war in a country which neither needs nor provides adequate material for that grim adventure. Tugwell (as also this reviewer) at the climax of his career nevertheless was assaulted as a "socialist" by right-wing forces of finance, business and their political representatives who were losing power. Simultaneously the left considered we had missed (or funked) a golden opportunity to force a class revolution, European-style.

Both charges had elements of truth. We certainly followed Franklin Roosevelt in his determination to take economic power from the financial rulers in New York and their satellites, and to place it for the time being in Washington. We certainly refused to take advantage of the economic collapse to set up state socialism (let alone Communism) or to intrigue within the government to prepare such a development. We did undertake through democratically adopted measures to redistribute the national income, steering more of it toward the least-favored among the population. We hoped for a better distribution of wealth. We did intend that the federal government should take over the ultimate controls of currency and credit (as it did), and the power, where necessary, to allocate capital resources as well. We did hope for the location of residual power over the economic system in the hands of the democratically-elected Congress and the United States government, while maintaining non-statist enterprise as the major method of production.

Most of this was achieved, and in doing so Franklin Roosevelt quite consciously made the decisions. Thereby he (and we)—literally—violated dogma right and left. All of us believed in democracy, not in dictatorship of "the proletariat" (or indeed of anyone else), whereas neither the extreme left nor the extreme right really accepts democracy at all. For once in history, the pragmatic, socially-minded reformists won, succeeding in doing what Mirabeau and the moderates attempted but failed to bring about in France between 1789 and 1793.

The left-wing charge may be dismissed summarily. No mandate whatever to convert the United States to socialism was sought in, or could be extracted from, the campaign of 1932. That charge boils down to anger that the "Brain Trust" (and especially Tugwell and myself) did not intrigue, still less plot, against the State to do so. Factually, as Sternsher points out, there were tiny Communist groups (notably the "Ware" group and Lee Pressman) who entered the administration at low levels and who probably wanted just that. Neither President Roosevelt, the public, the Brain Trust nor any of us wanted any part of it. So far as I know, no one even dared to suggest it to anyone in authority. The left-wing extremists joined with the extreme right in attacking Tugwell when he became the chief target of Roosevelt's enemies because they recognized him as an obstacle.

The right-wing Republican opponents for their part, notably the reactionary Liberty League, thought they could defeat Roosevelt in 1936 by creating the impression his administration was an overt socialist and a covert Communist plot to transform the federal government into some sort of personal dictatorship. This was pure political moonshine. Yet, exaggeration aside, the Republican attack had a minimum of intellectual validity. The New Deal did intend to make so-called "private enterprise" and the property involved in it ultimately responsive to the decisions of a democratically-elected political state. That was accomplished, and is the system today. It also intended to maintain non-statist enterprise as a chief method of production—which also is the situation now.

The New Deal and its intellectuals also considered that private property, especially when aggregated in vast corporate organizations, had not, and intended that it should not have, constitutionally (let alone, divinely) guaranteed privilege of economic decision making, beyond the control of democratic political decision and without responsibility for social result. This set up a constitutional battle in the courts as well as political battles in Congress and at the polls. Roosevelt emerged triumphant in both, though in the courts it took the "court-packing plan" and unlimited and magnificent statesmanship by Chief Justice Harlan Stone to establish—subject to the Bill of Rights—the capacity of the Congress to modify 19th-Century conceptions of private "property." In 1964, the results are obvious. Under the old system, substantial evolutionary changes in the economic system would have required change of the Constitution, if not actual revolution. Today these can be obtained by the ordinary political process of winning elections and passing laws.

A major though subsidiary struggle found Rexford Tugwell and me on the same side of a hotly contested issue. His formation was economic (stemming partly from Veblen) and pragmatic, stemming from his critical observation of American and Soviet agriculture. Mine was juridical, with an economic background. Both of us considered that a government should not be continuously at war with its productive machinery. In the American case, most of the industrial production was (and still is) carried on by large corporations. Their success on the productive side was indisputable then as it is today. We therefore tried to work out bases and methods of cooperation. The American corporation is unrivalled as a productive instrument, and can be a good servant; we needed all the production we could get for the things we hoped to do. Equally, these institutions could be and had been extremely bad masters.

Socialist groups, and most non-socialist liberals, despite complete difference in their proposed remedies, objected (they still do) to sympathetic cooperation between government and "business." Both asserted that institutions devoted to private profit must necessarily be opposed to the interests of the community. The non-socialist liberals contended during the New Deal that the only means of curbing the power of corporations was to break them up—"atomize them"—in the interest of democracy. This theory involved a throw-back to the economics of the 19th Century. Essentially it was nostalgia for Adam Smith's "free market" composed of many small competing interests, irrespective of the waste, the human cruelty and the instability that those markets historically entailed.

This school of thought in 1934 had wider polticial support than we did. Enmity to "the interests" and anti-trust action were certainly in classic American tradition. When the Temporary National Economic Commission held its hearings, this conception dominated its proceedings, though that Commission reached no clear-cut conclusions and had little practical result. Today (nearly thirty years later) the situation has stabilized itself more nearly along the lines of our thinking. "Atomization" as a cure for "bigness" is no longer seriously accepted, though bigness may, and frequently does, require restraint and is tolerable precisely because its results are subject to control as need arises. As Tugwell foresaw and as both of us then urged, political-economic progress in the United States moves forward more through national, social and economic planning than through reliance on atomization and "free markets" which destroy themselves unless the political state continuously intervenes to maintain them. . . .

Was Tugwell impatient? Should he have withheld his resignation, staying by, playing through the next administration, hoping to accomplish more? I doubt it. The atomizers (Sternsher calls them "trust busters") leading to the "Second New Deal" were by then in the ascendant. Roosevelt's administration rested on a shotgun political coalition which included many forces antagonistic both to Tugwell's social ideals and to his methods—indeed, not too friendly to Roosevelt himself. Tugwell believed—I think wrongly—that Roosevelt was steadily leaning toward the conservatives in his coalition. In any case, Tugwell yearned for quiet.

The parting of the two men in 1936 was, I think, inevitable. A statesman, or if you choose, a politician, necessarily practices the art of the possible during his term of office. When compelled to leave aside great and sound visions with which he agrees, and with them their chief advocates, the politician is neither deserting a friend nor betraying a principle. He is merely practicing his profession, as he is bound to do. When the Brain Trust was originally organized, President Roosevelt said to me (and he meant it for the whole group), "You study the problems, work out the best answers you can, and bring them to me. Don't mix in politics —it is unpleasant, sometimes a dirty business. Leave that to me."

Steadily, it seems to me, Roosevelt chose as much of the ideas and measures we presented to him as he believed he could translate into reality. I have little patience with those liberals who thought he "let them down" because he did not go all-out for all their measures. He, not they, best knew what could be achieved. Certainly he, far better than they, could estimate the greatest common divisor of effective opinion in the Congress and in the United States. No one understood better than he the difference between "education"—preparing possibilities for tomorrow—and political action—designed to achieve tangible results today. In the grim business of separating today's possibility from dreams later to be achieved, friendship (it was real between President Roosevelt and his Brain Trust) never can and never should control the statesman. Roosevelt knew and appreciated Tugwell's quality. He also knew that Tugwell's ideas were not generally held, let alone likely to attract votes either at the ballot box or in Congress.

In hindsight, one may reason that Roosevelt should have known he would win the 1936 campaign anyway. But there was no such certainty at that time. Also, another element entered—an element ignored by Sternsher. This was the clear possibility that the Democratic Party might break up into factions. Roosevelt once spoke to me about that; he even correctly named the men who might engineer the split. I thought his fears groundless; yet later (as Roosevelt suspected) [Secretary of Agriculture Henry] Wallace himself attempted to form a separate party and a powerful group of Southern Democrats also seceded. Finally, it is fair to say that Tugwell's bent toward collectivism went beyond Roosevelt's own philosophy, and certainly far beyond the philosophy of at least nine-tenths of the United States. The country was not ready to accept economic planning and direct action in the measure Tugwell then wanted, though it clearly is on the verge of adopting such planning today. . . .

A final note—and it is no derogation of Tugwell who knows the score as well as most. Was he—were any of us—other than President Roosevelt himself—as important as biographies seem to make out? I wonder. All of us, however, can rest in cheerful assurance that at long last historians will implacably elevate the important to their real stature, and cut the notorious but unimportant down to size. Irrespective of that verdict, we can comfort ourselves with consciousness that high privilege and great good fortune allowed us to be among the many co-workers in a time of vast change.

In the year 1964, the forces generated by the New Deal have about accomplished their potential. Yet in the light of results, and comparing the situation today with that in 1933, it is impossible to deny that a great advance in American welfare was scored. Equally it is impossible to deny that the American economic system now permits, and social morality demands, a new huge advance of comparable proportion. I agree with Sternsher in believing this requires a far greater measure of forward social planning, a capacity to use new resources of technology to a degree thus far undreamed, and larger visions of the content of life than those dominating the hopes of the Roosevelt Age. This is as it should be. The new generation should begin where we left off.

III

1936-1939

III

1936 ~ 1939

President Roosevelt proposed in early 1936 an Inter-American Conference "to determine how the maintenance of peace among the American Republics may best be safeguarded." It met in Buenos Aires. The American delegation included Berle, who also later served as a delegate to the Inter-American Conferences at Lima (1938), Havana (1940), and Chapultepec, Mexico (1945).

On November 7, 1936, Berle, with Secretary of State Hull, Assistant Secretary Welles, and a number of other delegates from the U.S. and other American republics, set sail from New York on the *American Legion*.

BBB Diary

November 10, 1936

In spite of Hull's statement that there would be no work for a few days, school started on Monday and is regularly held at 4 PM every afternoon; the more advanced students like Adolf also go in the AM and have a lot of homework. The first piece of homework seems to be the President's speech in B.A. The rival ghoster is George Milton, editor of the Chattanooga *Times,* a personal friend of the Secretary's.

Buenos Aires, December 2.

The President arrived two days ago. It was a radiant sunny day with soft warm breezes—the blue acacia trees are still in full bloom and flowers are everywhere. The day was declared a legal holiday; the children scampered across the parks and climbed the large trees. . . .

Adolf spent an hour with the President—the Secretary, the Ambassador, and Sumner present. The speech was gone over, the President overhauling it to the satisfaction of A. and S.W. S.W. trés émotionné as this is the culmination and fruition of many years of work. The President was also advised by Hull to use the "steam shovel" in flattering [Argentine Foreign Minister Carlos] Saavedra Lamas!

The following night at 9:30 was the banquet offered by the President of the Argentine [Agustin P. Justo] to the President of the U.S. It was the most brilliant affair of that kind I had ever attended. Of course it poured as hard as it did in Rio. Soldiers presenting arms with their swords and dressed in blue and red uniforms were stationed on the stairs; all the diplomats wore gala uniforms with plenty of decorations; the tables were laden with flowers. My neighbor, Ibarra García, undersecretary of foreign affairs, had been ordered to stop the band from playing the national anthems but claimed that the order had not come in time. When the Star-Spangled Banner was played, Roosevelt blushed and remained seated; by the time the Argentine anthem started; James Roosevelt and some one else had arrived to help him up.

President Justo toasted Roosevelt seated and Roosevelt rose to his feet to answer which was received with great applause. We are all used to his infirmity and take it for granted—to impose oneself thus on a new people and on a new country takes great courage and he did it very well. (Roosevelt's reply had been concocted by A. and Sumner at 5 minutes notice while getting into their morning coat for the conference in the afternoon.)

That afternoon, at 6, the opening session of the Conference was held. It was a terrible squash for the mere onlookers—6 people at a time in a tiny elevator with the stairs closed off for some reason. The electric fans were going in the top galleries and we were sweating in the first gallery. My first reaction was that there was no need to come and see the performance of the play one had seen in rehearsal. But I got a thrill after a while hearing Adolf's phrases recited before the world. The President had "remanié" Adolf and Sumner's text with success. He had added in the necessity for the belief in God. Adolf's phrase "B.A. the capital of peace" got the headlines. Justo did not say much except for the point that a peace program here must be tied to the League of Nations.

. . . It was still raining when the President left the following day. A. spent some time with him. He said he could make a place in his cabinet for La Guardia and that he wanted A. in Washington. A. wrote an airmail letter to inform F.H. A. and I both agree there is not much point in going to Washington as a subordinate at this stage.

. . . During the ensuing two weeks, the work consisted in trying to tame Saavedra Lamas. He started off by forbidding the Secretariat to publish the American proposal. He also tried to align the Central American countries on his side. A violent set to was had with [Minister of Foreign Affairs José Carlos de Macedo] Soares of Brazil at which point they all called each other "pigs, sinvergüenzas, mentirosos" etc. It develops, as Adolf had surmised a week ago, that S.L. committed himself to England last summer that he would not involve himself in any agreement binding his country to neutrality in the next war.

December 14

Since writing these lines, the consultation treaty has been accepted by S.L. as his own and now rejected again as if he had never heard of it. The rejection has been taking place all day with the help of Uruguay, Bolivia, and Chile. S.L. started by saying to the U.S. the treaty was improperly drafted and to the rest of the world the work was all done and they could go home. . . .

After additional negotiations, the American republics unanimously adopted the declaration: "That every act susceptible of disturbing the peace of America affects each and every one of them and justifies the initiation of the procedure of consultation." Moreover, in an Additional Protocol the signatories declared "inadmissable the intervention of any one of them, directly or indirectly, and for whatever reason, in the internal or external affairs of any other of the parties." The United States ratified the Buenos Aires agreements without reservation.

To Roosevelt, February 4, 1937

My dear Caesar:

In Buenos Aires you asked me whether Mayor La Guardia intended to run again for Mayor of New York; otherwise he might be brought into the government. He expects to run, feeling that if he takes a job with your government and declines to run, he will be accused of making a deal by which in return for a safe berth in Washington he clears the decks for a combination between Tammany and Farley. I think he is right. As things stand now, he has a better than even chance of being elected. Anyhow we would rather be defeated trying to do something we believe in than throwing up the sponge.

I hope you can keep clear of this. As in 1933, there is nothing in this for you; the alleged Democratic machine includes the very people who tried to cut you and did cut Lehman. In return they are apparently asking you to give them the City. . . .

Berle's diary file apparently began with this entry. Unless otherwise noted, all the following selections are from this source.

February 16, 1937

Yesterday at the Stock List Committee meeting the Household Finance Corporation proposed for listing a series of preferred stock. It was created by amendment of the charter adopting the "blank stock" provisions of the Delaware Law which permitted the directors to give to any series of preferred stock any rights they pleased. This was the provision I protested against in April, 1929 when that law was drawn, and again in the *Columbia Law Review* of May, 1929.

I asked the Stock List Committee whether they cared to list a preferred stock as unprotected as this, pointing out that the directors could create new issue redeemable at, say, $1,000 and carrying a dividend of, say, 100% a year.

The Committee declined to list the stock unless some limitations should be worked out. They further proposed that a general ruling be issued making it plain that use of the "blank stock" provisions without limitation would not be permitted by the Exchange.

It took eight years to get this far, but we are making some progress. . . . Apparently the Delaware Courts have come to the conclusion that they also had about enough of this.

February 20, 1937

I talked yesterday to Sumner Welles at the State Department.

[Jefferson] Caffery is being withdrawn from Cuba. Hull was good enough to suggest my taking the Embassy; Welles stated that he would be glad to work it out, but he thought that I possibly would not want it; which I cordially confirmed. We think at the moment it is best to send someone there who will handle merely routine matters until the situation shifts somewhat. —Note, that the influx of German and Italian Fascists to Havana is causing some worry. . . .

David Lilienthal [Director, Tennessee Valley Authority] came in for breakfast this morning. It is his hope that the T.V.A. will presently reach a position where it can buy out the entire Commonwealth and Southern facilities. We talked over methods, a possible approach; and he asked whether I would be free to do the negotiating for the T.V.A. in that case. I said I should be very glad to do so. . . .

February 26, 1937

The President's proposal to reorganize the Supreme Court has aroused the customary storm of debate. In residue, the controversy boils down to three positions:

1. The groups who want no reorganization, no change in the constitution and maintenance of the status quo. This is the conservative position.

2. The liberal groups who want a change in the constitution as now construed by the Supreme Court and who accordingly insist that they wish a constitutional amendment.

3. The groups who are in favor of the change. This is probably the middle group and it appears to be plainly a majority of the country.

After giving the matter a good deal of thought, my conclusion is that the President's proposal ought to be passed; that the more rapidly it is passed, the better we shall be. By the same tokens, what ought to be stressed, however, is that the appointments both to the Supreme Court and to the lower federal courts must be kept of the highest quality and removed altogether from the political dickering which has debased judicial appointments in this administration as in previous administrations. In that case, we shall have nothing whatever to fear.

I believe the first position, maintenance of the status quo, is both impossible and dangerous. Lawyers, of course, have a high degree of respect for the Supreme Court tradition. To the man in the street, however, the Supreme Court has become a kind of Mumbo Jumbo which produces strange results. It says that the federal government cannot regulate child labor. It also says that the state cannot regulate child labor. It says that the federal government cannot tell the elevator boy that his employer must give him one day off in seven. It remains doubtful whether the state can tell him the same thing. It says that the liberty which was intended to protect individuals from invasion by some curious process will protect strange monopolies such as public utilities . . . and so on. Plainly, the Supreme Court has as it does once in so often in our history put itself athwart a current of public opinion. A solution has to be reached; else after an appropriate period of fermentation some kind of an explosion takes place which probably will wreck the court. Plainly the impasse has to be broken. The standpat position cannot be maintained indefinitely with safety to anyone and particularly to the Court.

The second, or liberal position reached, is a position in reverse. Few liberals really want an amendment to the constitution. What they want is the constitution which they always thought they had; most of them have maintained throughout that a reasonable interpretation of the constitution without amendment would have given them everything they desired and at the same time would have preserved the constitution as the firm buttress of civil liberties and individual rights which the liberals peculiarly have defended against all attack. The "amendment" they have wanted is not in the direction of a change in the constitutional system. It is an attempt to restore the constitutional system which they and most of the United States originally thought they had.

Generally speaking all they want is an interpretation of the regulatory powers of Congress over commerce and state created forces such as corporations which shall be commensurate with the development in those fields. Everybody knows that interstate commerce today differs from interstate commerce as it was in 1787. It is plain that state rights in these fields can be broken up, because a state which wishes to create one set of conditions may be blasted out of its policy by some other state which is prepared to adopt lower standards, compete, take away industry from the state of higher standards, and the like. The South has taken the heart out of the New England manufacturers already. The constitution could have been interpreted to prevent this without difficulty; a constitutional amendment ought not to be necessary to bring constitutional law in line with national economics.

This is why liberals find it difficult to agree on a form of constitutional amendment. An amendment broad enough and strong enough to bind the court might easily be so broad that you could drive a Hitler program through the breach thus created. Better to break the impasse by a constitutional amendment than not to break it at all; but the process seems unnecessary.

The third position seems logical. What most liberals really want is a systematic modern interpretation of the constitution in line with actual modern economics. The court has done that from time to time and could carry it further. Most of the younger men of the bar whose lives are not mortgaged to the service of particular interests have been trained for twenty years to set constitutional decisions alongside of economic data; the standard premise of constitutional law today is that the constitution did not freeze the economics of any historical period. On the contrary, it was designed to permit the court and the government to move along with the conditions.

This leaves as the real problem—and it is fundamentally—the question as to the kind and quality of men who would be appointed to the Supreme Court. I think much of the thrust of the President's proposal comes from the fact that the judicial appointments which have been made have been principally political. It is too often obvious that federal judges were not appointed by the President, but by the local political leaders;

and nobody wants any more of that in the district courts and the circuit courts, let alone in the Supreme Court of the United States.

But this is a chance which is always taken with every appointive power. The constitution does let the number of judges be increased and does give the appointment to the President, and it leaves to the Senate to decline to confirm that appointment—which the Senate has freely done in a good many cases. Particularly when public opinion is brought to bear widely as it has been now there is far less danger of depreciating the quality of the court than at any other time.

Finally, the President is safeguarded by the oldest and strongest tradition we have. Once appointed a judge acts and behaves like a judge irrespective of how he got there. Most Supreme Court judges have been appointed because the appointing President inherently liked their views. Practically all of them once on the bench judge fairly and honorably according to their convictions, irrespective of any feeling of obligation to the appointing power. Much of the criticism of the President's proposal is a lack of faith in that tradition and I do not share that lack of faith.

I rather imagine that the passage of the President's proposal will not let us out of a thoroughgoing constitutional debate. But I see nothing to be afraid of in that. In fact, nothing is better for the country than to have occasional discussions of its constitutional system. Ideas are clarified; the courts learn the merits of public opinion; the public learns the position of the courts; the government obtains a clear mandate; everyone is benefitted.

In coming to this conclusion, I do not undertake to defend some of the arguments which were made for the court's proposal. Particularly I am grieved by what must be regarded by some of the Justices of the Supreme Court as repudiation of their long careers of public service some of which in many cases have been splendid in the extreme. It is one of the tragedies of the situation that a man like Brandeis who approaches the sphere of a national hero should find himself in the line of fire. As to this we can only develop a certain kind of philosophy and remember that in a good many judicial systems—that of New York is one of them—judges are compelled to retire at seventy; and that some of the men on the Supreme Court today found merit in that idea before they ascended the nation's highest court.

March 1, 1937

The conference at Harvard [on February 27] was in many ways amazing. There were gathered not only the Harvard, Yale and Princeton students coming from a natural conservative group, but a set of guests representing both the government and business. Practically every round-table emerged with a project for some control using the federal government as a unit, with the exception of the table on the functions of the states in which a majority were members of the Massachusetts State Legislature—where it hardly counts.

Combining this with the breakfast with [R. A.] Gordon [Harvard economics professor] I got a picture of the entire property structure of the country changing. It is, if you choose, a change from control based on position with politics as a railroad of traffic to a control based on position in organizations of all sorts: the corporate manager representing industrial property; the head of a cooperative representing the aggregate buying power; the head of a radio station representing the power to get to people; and so forth and so on. These are not strictly economic interests; they are of kinds without the economic interests at the moment predominating.

This suggests an orientation of the country towards something which we find in the history books where the lords spiritual and temporal (representing two fields) made the merchant and craft guilds and other similar organizations—except that this organization power takes in a vastly larger field. Apparently the amalgamation of this force acts so strongly that if enough of them can be brought into conjunction almost anything can happen. I note the fact without undertaking to explain its implications.

March 4, 1937

Yesterday Colonel McIntyre telephoned from the White House. He said that he had a pencil note from the President suggesting that he point out to me that two or three people on the White House staff read my letters to the White House. After a little fencing it developed that the real thing was my superscription "Dear Caesar". In view of the attack made on the President as a would-be dictator through the Supreme Court bill, it is good for a long and large run for many columnists in the country. . . .

Of course, he is quite right; but there is something more interesting in it. When we started this practice, I pointed out to the President that "Caesar" is technically the title of an elective position. I even have a letter from him on the subject saying that Caesar was all right but Napoleon would be all wrong.

The last letters I wrote were just before the Supreme Court proposal and not after.

March 9, 1937

At lunch yesterday Seabury said that he was anxious that the Mayor should not come out in favor of the President's court reorganization bill. He said that we shall have trouble enough to get a Republican nomination, and they would use that as an excuse to deny the nomination to the Mayor. He had better keep out until after the nomination. . . .

April 13, 1937

Yesterday the Mayor called for me. He had a talk on Monday with the President. They talked politics; it appearing at the moment that the Democratic and Democratic organization people here have nobody in mind as a candidate against him, though they have talked to the President repeatedly. . . .

I see in all this an intrigue to get the President into the picture against the Mayor; and incidentally, if possible, to split up the alliance between the Mayor and myself. Since the President has already offered to make La Guardia a member of his cabinet and make me Ambassador to Cuba, and the Mayor has insisted that I will have to be in his government when I get through being City Chamberlain, I should want more definite proof than I have that the President would lend himself to this. But it is perfectly true that the President's party problems would be very much assisted if both La Guardia and I got out of the way in New York. Of course, we cannot do it. . . .

April 15, 1937

Rex [Tugwell] quoted Harry Hopkins as saying that the President's plan was to be neutral in this election; and among other things to invite La Guardia to the White House for dinner with some pomp and ceremony—the theory being, I suppose, that this will unofficially indicate to the faithful that La Guardia is quite all right in the White House.

In any case it is plain that there is as yet no mobilized opposition and so far at least the President has not permitted himself to become the rallying point.

April 26, 1937

I talked yesterday to Cordell Hull, likewise to Sumner Welles. I understand Sumner will be appointed Under-Secretary of State. . . .

They want me to be Assistant Secretary of State in Washington, commencing any time after the La Guardia campaign. My present feeling is that I would give a good deal to get out of it, unless the European situation at that time indicates that some prospect of a real peace move is going forward. . . .

April 29, 1937

I have been trying to figure out a way of not being caught by one of the two governments. Hull and Welles will try to make me go to Washington as Assistant Secretary; La Guardia and Seabury will try to make me run for President of the Council. In an endeavor to escape both, I have got La Guardia to agree to put in his protest to Washington on the theory that he needs me here; if I can arrange to fix it so that Washington keeps me out of the New York situation, it may be possible to keep clear of both entanglements. . . .

May 24, 1937

The evidence seems to be accumulating that Robert Moses [City Park Commissioner] decided to betray the Mayor if he could. I think he is endeavoring to combine the Al Smith wing of the Tammany crowd with the Republicans and thereby go into the field probably with himself at the head. I have difficulty in believing this, but merely note what seems to be happening:

He waited until the Mayor left for vacation to force a personal fight on the Mayor in connection with the Park budget, even going so far as to close the parks. The Mayor reopened them and the Tammany Board of Estimate in the Mayor's absence primarily took advantage of the situation by calling a special meeting and voting the budget that Moses asked. . . .

The resolution was blocked by Newbold Morris [Assistant Corporation Counsel, member Board of Aldermen] who insisted that a $700,000 appropriation ought to be referred to committee. The meeting was put off until June first when the Mayor gets back. . . .

This is serious business. We expected Tammany against us anyway, but I do not know that we are adequately prepared to take care of treachery in our own ranks.

May 26, 1937

Yesterday in Washington I went with Commissioner [William Fellowes] Morgan of the Department of Markets to look for some Federal money to finance the creation of the Bronx Terminal Market into a primary market. As usual, after the idealists in the Department of Agriculture had arrived nowhere, Jesse Jones provided the answer. Morgan left us and we talked over some matters. Jesse offered me the job of general counsel of the Reconstruction Finance Corporation which I declined because I cannot leave La Guardia until after the election.

Jesse stated that he understood Justice [George] Sutherland was retiring after this term which dropped two of the conservative judges. He had been called in for lunch at the White House to help in passing the court bill. He did so and came to the conclusion that as it stood it could not be passed. When he talked he had concluded that the President could get two judges, but since the upholding of the Social Security Act he doubted even that. The Congressmen were saying that with the Court in its present frame of mind there was no further need; and I am inclined to think that they are right. All that they wanted was some intelligent decisions and not a batch of new judges.

Further, the President is in difficulties. The Senate insists that he should appoint [Majority Leader] Joe Robinson [D., Ark.]. Joe is, of course, as conservative as they make them, and with only two judges to appoint he could have one liberal and one conservative—a perfect stymie. Jesse was at the White House on Monday and the President indicated pretty thoroughly that he was sick of the business and was inclined to drop it.

This is perhaps on the whole a good outcome from every point of view except that of the President's. The effort was well worthwhile since it did convince the Supreme Court that they had to get their thinking within hailing distance of what the country was thinking.

The talk in Washington is that Henry Wallace is to be the rising star for the next President. Talk like this comes easy at this stage.

June 18, 1937

Last week the President called in Charles Taussig. Charles advised him that the country was getting into a state of considerable confusion as to the program and suggested that the President give two or three radio speeches to clarify. The President asked whether Charles, Rex Tugwell and I would draft one of the speeches for the end of next week. He then went into a press conference and announced that he was going to make some speeches. He stated that he wanted to bring up the condition of the lower one-third or 40,000,000 people of the United States. Apparently he said something about taxation which at least led the newspapers to believe that this was primarily a tax program, though I do not understand that that was his idea. . . . Plainly nobody can write any speech for the President about his specific plan without knowing what it is; and the President does not yet know. Actually there is no program; the President has some general ideas as to objective and method. The fact is in connection with the editorial in the New York *Sun* last night which referred to an article of mine in the *Yale Review* ["Redistributing the National Income," 26 *Yale Review* 1937] and pointed out that my ideas are at loggerheads with those of the President as the forthcoming speech will presumably demonstrate. . . .

June 25, 1937

Bernard M. Baruch got hold of me yesterday. He had been approached by various of the people who are working for La Guardia's re-election; he said that he would deal only through me, and would give me some money for the campaign fund. He said further that he plans to support the Mayor unless Alfred E. Smith or Jeremiah Mahoney were nominated in which case he would have to give his support because of his personal friendship for both of those men. But he added that if Smith took such nomination, he ought to have his head examined.

It seems that the Tammany group have been trying to get Alfred E. Smith to run. . . .

August 3, 1937

On Thursday, July 22nd, the question as to whether Mayor La Guardia would be renominated by the Republicans remained unsettled. The Mayor asked me to get into touch with Kenneth Simpson [Manhattan Republican leader], likewise with the Labor people, and arrange a meeting. We were to discuss the constitutional convention and incidentally the City slate. . . .

. . . Meanwhile the Mayor was canvassing possible candidates for Comptroller. He was anxious that I should run and I declined, and we then started looking for other candidates. . . .

[Simpson and the Labor group met at Berle's home for five hours on Saturday.] . . . Kenneth insisted that the Republican Party was against La Guardia; that he thought he could deliver it; that he hated La Guardia's eyes; but that he would go along in order to beat Tammany. What possible objection could La Guardia have to Morris [for City Council president] and McGoldrick [for comptroller]? I pointed out that the Labor Party had to be consulted and that they had more votes than the Republican Party.

. . . the Mayor had made it pretty plain that what he would really like to do was to run as an independent. He likewise feared, as I did, that the Republicans intended to nominate Morris and McGoldrick and not him; meanwhile having secured the Fusion and Labor nominations for these two men and making it possible for them to elect one or two Republican members of the Board of Estimate and leaving the Mayor up on a pole. Accordingly, after the meeting I took Morris and McGoldrick to the Players Club and we sat up to two in the morning. I tried to persuade them to issue a statement that they would run on the Republican ticket if the Mayor also ran, otherwise they would not. Morris agreed that he was willing to do this. McGoldrick said in substance that that was what he intended to do, but he would not say so. It wound up with neither man agreeing to stick by the Mayor in that regard. I left nature take its course accordingly and went to bed. . . .

Yesterday after talking with my father, it seemed something ought to be done about this. Plainly with two-thirds of the Republican organization going in another direction, the Mayor will have a bad time of it in the primaries. In all probability he will wish to withdraw after being designated. I got hold of Judge Seabury, of [Benjamin] Davis [Jr.], of the Progressive City Committee, of Ben Howe of the Fusion Party, and of Alex Rose of the Labor Party, and got substantial agreement on the proposition that they would endorse no candidate who stayed on the Republican ticket if the Mayor were off it.

Paul Kern [member of Civil Service Commission], the Mayor and I went off to the stadium concert which was interrupted (Heifetz playing beautifully) by a very heavy rain storm. . . .

August 5, 1937

On Tuesday, August 3rd, information came in that the American Labor Party was about to make a pronouncement. . . . Accordingly and on La Guardia's advice I asked Rose to have the Labor Party nominate the Mayor at its meeting on Wednesday and hold up all other nominations to a date after the Republican Primary. Rose agreed with me as to the possibility and he issued a story through The New York *Times* analyzing the problem in this general sense. . . .

. . . Meanwhile the Labor Party at their meeting issued a smashing statement for La Guardia which is really conceived as being the charter background of the Progressive Party in New York City and New York State. They have done an excellent job and whoever did the drafting of it deserves all congratulations. It is a first class bit of political work. . . .

Hull and Sumner Welles say that [Judge R. Walton] Moore [State Department Counselor] has an eightieth birthday in the next few months on which date he will retire from the State Department. He then proposes to have me appointed Counselor of the State Department. I am frank to confess I should hardly go across the road to get that appointment. My feeling, however, is that fate opens the way and one cannot indefinitely struggle against fate.

August 11, 1937

The President is out with a statement this morning that he will remain neutral [in the mayoralty election]. I should hope so.

August 12, 1937

By appointment Tuesday night I met the Mayor at his house. We went down and picked up [Thomas E.] Dewey. . . . The object was to persuade Dewey to run for District Attorney of New York County. Dewey's vanity, always disagreeable, was working overtime. He had somehow fallen into cahoots with Ferdinand Pecora. He made a condition that the President and Governor Lehman should ask him to run; that Seabury should guarantee him $300,000 campaign fund (he later reduced this to $150,000); and that he should have separate headquarters, etc. My own thought was that it was better to drop him overboard. Apparently he also wanted to be told that he was essential to the Mayor's victory. I declined to do this. In the first place it is not true; in the second, it would merely mean trouble later. No head of any government should admit that an outsider was essential to his government even if it were true which it is not. The Mayor and Dewey left for the Stadium Concert about nine-thirty; I looked at the river for awhile and then came home to bed.

Breakfast with Fiorello on Wednesday morning. We decided to give Dewey the absent treatment and let him come in or stay out as he felt. I think he will stay out. Word came in that the decision had been made by Al Smith to put Moses into the Republican primary if the Mayor should decline. He thought he could do this by substituting Moses under the technicality of law which permits on the day appointed to fill vacancies to substitute a different name from that for whom the petition was signed, if the candidate petitioned for declines to run. . . . Moses as an honorable man ought not to have even flirted with the proposition. By the same token, however, a couple of people must be folding up very fast. I am more afraid of the Moses treachery than anything else here. Moses has been advising the Mayor to run in the Republican primary; he would therefore have a fairly clear record if the Mayor declined and Moses picked it up himself.

Last night we met on Roy Howard's yacht; Seabury, [City Corporation Counsel Paul] Windels, Tom Thatcher [lawyer, chairman of Charter Revision Commission], Roy Howard, Lee Wood [a New York *World-Telegram* editor] and myself. We persuaded the Mayor to go into the Republican primary. This also was Burlingham's advice given by wire. The Mayor wanted to make the run independently and Farley is of the same view. But I am inclined to believe that he should announce that he is running independently anyway and is willing to put in for the Republican primary. If they want to nominate him, all right; if not, all right. He owes it to a great many Republican friends on strictly personal grounds. Also, there is the Moses business in the offing. It closed up by trying to appoint a campaign manager. They chose me. I said I would clear things from now to some time next week when I would get the responsible heads of the Fusion and Labor Parties together and get a real manager. Who in the devil could you get to campaign for the Republican Party? I insist that the campaign manager must be a democrat or an independent. We have taken enough from the Republican party; they have not the votes in any event. . . .

August 17, 1937

On Thursday, August 12th, we went to work again on Dewey. Dewey had stipulated among other things for three days "public clamour" that he should run. He stipulated that editorials were not enough. He wanted press stories, etc. The young Republicans—Bill Thurston and George Brokaw Compton—came into action; so did Seabury and Thatcher. Thatcher talked most of Thursday afternoon with Dewey who when Dewey asked for $300,000 campaign fund and stated that he would use it to pay workers who had large families and would vote for him, called it off and said he wanted nothing further to do with the matter and went home . . . all of us agreed that the thing to do was to let Dewey stew in his own juice. I went off to address the Kings County Convention of the American Labor Party—an interesting meeting with a running endorsement of [Hugo] Black's appointment to the Supreme Court; and considerable ovation for La Guardia whom I represented. There is a lot of vitality in the Labor crowd.

Friday to the Mayor's for breakfast. It seemed obvious to us that Dewey would give in and the Republicans were beginning to capitalize. Specifically there were repeated intimations that everything would be all right if the Mayor would campaign actively in the Republican primaries and if he would declare that he would have nothing to do with any third party movement. Of course, this would end his connection with the Labor Party; and these Republicans seem to want the Labor Party votes while denying their right to exist. The thing was foolish and I said so.

During the day considerable skirmishing. Dewey put in one additional demand. He wanted a free hand in the Police Department. This transmitted to me through Seabury I turned down flat. I told Seabury that I would campaign against any Mayor who turned over his Police Department to anyone else no matter who he was. Dewey was still pressing this demand at four o'clock when a telephone call came to me from the Mayor. He asked if I were going up to the country for the week-end. I said I would stand by. He said to stay out until Tuesday morning—he was going to do the same. Everything that ought to be done could be done Tuesday; to stay around was simply to invite foolish demands. He thereupon left his house where he had been and cleared away theoretically leaving no trace. Actually he went to the summer City Hall and worked on the budget. . . . [Took] the six o'clock train to Great Barrington and shut off all the telephone wires. Based on the commotion here this morning, I gather the wires must have been pretty hot. . . .

Just before leaving for the train, I learned that Dewey had decided to give in, although he had not announced it. I telephoned this to the Mayor and we then cleared out. On Saturday Dewey announced his candidacy. . . .

We have put together a picture. People who object to La Guardia cannot object to Dewey. Dewey will have to campaign for the Mayor in the Republican Primaries because Dewey as District Attorney would be helpless with a Tammany Mayor. . . .

La Guardia has his own plan to which I have given and will give no commitment. He wants the Labor Party to make an independent nomination for Governor next year. His proposal is that I take that nomination. 1938 is a long way off.

Sumner Welles writes me and asks me to give him an account of the New York situation so that he can keep the President informed. I am arranging to do this.

. . . As a prosecutor Dewey is one of the world's best. He obviously has taken his own build-up seriously and actually thinks of himself as having the entire weight of the United States on his hands. He wants to run for Governor next year on a combined Republican and Labor party ticket which I think is impossible. Government is of two sorts: defensive, the war on crime and the like; offensive, the kind of thing that forces out the proper function of government so that it serves the people better. Dewey can do the first extremely well; I have yet to see that he has even the faintest conception of the second. The Labor Party would not follow him for that in any event. So that I suppose the man is really proceeding on a miscomprehension—the theory that support which is mobilized for him as district attorney would also be available for him when he tries to become Governor. Of course, he may develop and the situation may change; things are certain to look quite different next year.

For the moment the picture is complete; barring a Republican primary angle. As to that, I do not know that it really matters whether the Mayor wins or loses. If [Senator Royal S.] Copeland [an anti-New Dealer] wins, the Democrats are divided; if Copeland loses, there is La Guardia against the world and he does pretty well in that role.

This morning Jimmy Walker was appointed by the Transit Commission to a job primarily to safeguard his pension rights. . . .

August 19, 1937
The Mayor and I checked up on the Board of Estimate's proposals as far as we could. The City will be pretty thoroughly bankrupt in another two years if somebody does not call a halt. Apparently anything goes in an election year and it looks to me as though the City would have to print money if this business goes on.

The Mayor is upset at Seabury's attack on the appointment of Walker to the Transit Commission. He points out it is easy to make Walker a martyr getting nowhere.

This morning the President comes out with the first of a series of speeches which have been written for him by [Thomas G.] Corcoran and [Benjamin V.] Cohen in the R.F.C. building. I cannot say that I think this one is a good job. It answers nothing when the reactionaries call the President a dictator and he responds graciously by calling them Lord Macaulays.

August 20, 1937
Last night John Barriger, head of the Railroad division of the Reconstruction Finance Corporation, came in. . . . At the rate things are going, in another two years Allegheny will be hopelessly bankrupt; Ches-

apeake and Ohio shares will be worth half what they are now; Erie and Nickel Plate will be in receivership; possibly also Pere Marquette.

Present indications are likewise that outside the Van Sweringen interests [which controlled the above railroads] the Baltimore and Ohio and possibly the Southern will go next year; and it is a very open question whether the Illinois Central can swing through. Our program for government ownership of railroads probably could be accomplished pretty cheaply about the year 1940.

This, however, suggests the probable date of the beginning of the next depression. The effect of a series of cumulative railroad receiverships will begin once more to cripple the steel industry say by the middle or end of 1939. We can expect trouble in that case just about 1940—that is just before the next Presidential election. [Note added later: Actually—it started almost immediately!] This, of course, might be distorted by a war.

August 27, 1937

. . . Farley has definitely decided to support Mahoney. It seems that we are once more fighting the Federal Government tooth and nail. This in my judgment is a mistake of Roosevelt. If he would bet on his policies instead of his politicians, he would be obviously better off—especially in view of the kind of political fight he is going into in the next year. He ought to have learned by now that his politicians have no use for his ideas except for patronage. . . .

On Wednesday evening to chat over finances with the Mayor. He is in a very low frame of mind. The Tammany majority in the Board of Estimate has passed every kind of a graft bill commencing from lowering the fare on the Staten Island Ferry to granting pay increases to anybody and everybody who asked for them, with the result that our budget is already at least $20,000,000 higher than last year and will be $40,000,000 higher. . . . If he vetoes the bills, as he ought to, he gains the ill-will of a large number of special groups. The bills are passed over his veto and he piles up a political opposition without getting anywhere. If he signs them, he has a financial jam of the first order on his hands. Of course what is wanted is that he vetoes the bills and for vetoing the bills he should be defeated in the election, after which the bills will quietly die. At the moment I do not see any answer. . . .

August 31, 1937

Fiorello and I took stock of the campaign and decided there would not be any. We will not have headquarters, we will not have marches, we will not have bands and make speeches except those in regular course of events. The Labor Party has its headquarters and so has the Fusion Party and the Republican Party, if it is still there, and I suppose Maurice Davidson [of the Progressive City Committee]. There is no reason why we should do anything except run the City. I made a mental note, however, that we would try to coordinate the election machinery and let it go at that. This will disappoint many politicians, but it will save a large amount of money. This is just as well because we have not got it. Afterwards to the fight to see Louis win by a decision. I thought he deserved it because he boxed well, though the crowd was obviously with Farr because he is a big bruising slugger type. All of the political swells were there, but I confined my attention to shaking hands with Governor Lehman, Arthur Sulzberger [New York *Times* publisher] and Roy Howard. . . .

To Roosevelt, September 1, 1937

The New York situation is clarifying pretty rapidly now. For what they are worth, you might be interested in our estimate as to what will happen.

The Labor Party will cast considerably over 400,000 votes—the optimists claim 600,000, though that is asking a good deal. These will be mainly withdrawals from the regular Democratic machine. . . .

In a straight out fight with Mahoney, La Guardia will win, probably by upwards of 250,000, though he may do a good deal better. I have staked this campaign on the theory that the public followed your policies though it was cool to your politicians; so far the judgment seems to have been justified.

Fundamentally, the Republicans opposing the Mayor are right. They see him as an outstanding outpost of a progressive movement tying up with the New Deal, the La Follettes and the whole northwest and middlewest Progressives; if they can kill him off, it will weaken the movement. They seem, however, to develop no underlying strength, in spite of huge expenditures of money. . . .

It looks now as though the great experiment had come off; and that we may have demonstrated that you can run a big political situation without patronage or the spoils system provided the administration is first-rate and the ideas are progressive and intelligent. I think this will be the first time since Andrew Jackson that the experiment has been successful in any large unit.

You are widely quoted on both sides; we are taking the position that nobody can speak for you except yourself; and that you meant what you said in declaring yourself neutral. I hope, accordingly, that Farley does not go as far this time as he did in 1933, when we actually found ourselves fighting the federal machine tooth and nail—a profitless conflict of advantage to nobody.

I have a private and personal stake in this election. As soon as Fiorello is re-elected I can resign the office of Chamberlain (it is abolished, and, by accident, by a member of the same family that created it in 1671), putting in a decent City Treasurer. I only hope the Tammany majority, which is passing anything to buy votes, will leave a couple of cents in it for the new man to begin on. Whatever they leave, it will be more than I inherited.

September 2, 1937

. . . It is noted, however, that there is some difficulty in the Stock Exchange. The volume has fallen to a point where very little trading goes on; on anything other than the stock of the very largest and best known companies, liquidation of any large amount of securities takes a very long time. This might or might not mean anything; but the banks are beginning to talk of running up the interest on security loans on the theory that the securities are not liquid. Perhaps it really does not matter, provided the public realizes that when it buys stock it cannot sell it at the drop of the hat.

September 14, 1937

Tuesday, September 7th, was a bad day in the Stock Exchange. After the close of the market, both President [Charles] Gay and Frank Altschul [investment banker] rang up. It seemed to me as though everyone was having a bad attack of nerves. . . .

On Thursday, September 9th, I went over to Hyde Park to see the President. It was kept very quiet because, as the President said [in a letter], a visit might have political implications. As a result, the house was as empty (but for the state guard) as any summer house when the family has gone off to the beach for the afternoon. I found the President in bed with a cold.

We talked over a variety of things. He was interested in the New York City situation; said that he estimated La Guardia's chances of winning at about 5 to 4, (I think they are better than that) and wanted to know whether he had been handling it better; whereupon I said he had. He asked what would happen in the Republican Primary; I told him that I thought we had an edge. We then talked state politics generally. The President said that their candidate for Governor next year was Robert Jackson [U.S. Assistant Attorney General], but that he would be a hard man to nominate. He said that there was nobody in New York City who could make the grade. . . . He is convinced that the people are with him on the court plan, and asked what I thought of Hugh Black. He was constrained to appointing a Senator because otherwise Congress would have debated the appointment for thirty days at least during which time nothing could have happened. Since the nomination, and although a good many Southern newspapers disapproved of it, their own people have brought pressure on them to get behind and support a Southern Supreme Court justice.

It was obvious that Sumner Welles and Hull had been talking to him about the State Department. I asked him whether I was to take their talk of the counselorship seriously and the President said "yes". There was much to be done down there and the Department itself needed new blood. . . . He then asked about his western trip. He said that he thought he should preach again. I encouraged this idea as much as I could. I asked him whether he was going to campaign for the court plan. He said that he hated to preach, but that there was not much else that could be done. Both he and Hull propose to keep us out of war. He thought the newspapers did not give a true account of it because they missed the important points; especially, they did not give adequate importance to the fact that the Japanese were getting ready to seize the Island of Hainin which lies half way on the road to Singapore and which accordingly would threaten both French Indo-China and also the British trade route. We had a general rake-over of the Administration in respect of which he told of the removal of [William E.] Humphrey from the Federal Trade Commission. He had enough on Humphrey to remove him because he had taken bribes from two rayon companies and a tinning process concern; but on getting into office he had sent for him and asked him to resign so that there might be harmony in the Administration. Humphrey asked time to consider; two weeks later the President called him up. Humphrey said that he had talked it over with Mrs. Humphrey and was agreeable and thought it would help if the President would write him a letter saying on the whole that he thought it better if Humphrey would simply resign because of fundamental disagreement. Of course, this letter was equal to a certificate of good conduct. Humphrey then declined to resign. Roosevelt removed him; Humphrey brought suit to recover his place and won it, using the letter in evidence. It happened that Humphrey died so that the place was vacant anyway. For the President it was a case of the old kind heart, and he described himself both as an ass and a sucker in the whole proceedings. He asked me that if anything happens in the New York situation, to telephone him; and to see him as soon after November when the unpleasantness was over as I could. He intimated that he had given Farley pretty strict orders to stay out of this. . . .

Last night to dinner with Charles Taussig, who has been working pretty continuously with Cordell Hull. Charles is of the opinion that in order to keep out of war we have to make up our minds to the completest kind of non-intercourse—possibly keeping the trade routes open to the western hemisphere, but not otherwise. This means virtually war controls and spending as much money in subsidizing the American farmers as we should spend in a war itself; and he has been anxious to have Hull begin the long and difficult work of organizing the necessary trade controls and particularly the necessary propaganda so that the country could be kept out. . . .

The Stock Exchange men are still scared to death. Both Gay and Altschul are convinced that there will be a real down-turn in business and that the stock market antics are merely an indication of that fact. What they really want is to have the whole national policy reversed. There is not a chance of that and I think they have a bad attack of nerves. . . .

September 15, 1937

To dinner last night with the Mayor. The plan is to have the American Labor Party make its nomination for Governor next June in advance of the nomination of the Democratic Party. The Democratic Party will then either have to nominate the American Labor Party candidate or resign itself to losing the State. La Guardia wants me to take this nomination; I think it belongs to him. It is not a serious question yet.

September 17, 1937

. . . to Washington on the midnight train to spend Thursday with Charles Taussig. We had lunch with Frank McNinch, the new Chairman of the Federal Communications Commission, and started in on the long job of working out a radio policy. . . . Since Frank has been working exclusively in power, he protests somewhat bitterly that he hardly knows the difference between a wave band and a receiving set. Nevertheless we covered a good deal of territory. Charles especially was making the point that the short wave and ultra short wave licenses ought to be kept for the public; that no vested interests should be built up in them because the time was not very far off when there would be sufficient wave lengths commercially available so that everyone in the United States could have his wave band just as he has his telephone number. There was considerable debate as to whether the F.C.C. had any duty to protect invested capital—that is whether radio stations were entitled to the kind of protection which we have successfully accorded railroads, power plants and lines and telephones.

. . . In the evening Hull came down to Charles' room and we spent the evening going over possible American policy.

The Secretary laid out the problem. He had pointed out, he said, that the Japanese were developing a forced policy in the East. Their occupation of Manchukuo had resulted in the virtual exclusion of all nationalists except Japanese. The same process was automatically followed in north China. The apparent plan was to dominate all of China and ultimately all of Asia as far east as Lake Baikal. This was parallel to the Italian policy in the Mediterranean. The United States had been storm-cellar pacifists with the net result that Japan and Italy, which he called "desperado nations" were encouraged to go on indefinitely. He pointed out that the British after endeavoring to rely on an unarmed appeal to orgnization, had at length been forced to adopt an armament policy costing some $10,000,000,000, with the full support of labor and other groups.

Charles said that it seemed to him that the alternative was between isolation and war; and that isolation was a policy almost as expensive as war. . . .

I inquired whether the isolation was to include South America.

The Secretary said that in that case the Argentine and other South American countries would want to be taken care of too. The Argentine lived on meat, on wheat and other similar products. Chile lived on nitrates. Deprived of their market for these products, they would ask us to take care of their burdens too. This was on the assumption that we could persuade them to forego their war markets which was problematic. This assumed also that we were prepared to dispense with the enrichment of our civilization by free contact with the world, limiting ourselves to this hemisphere.

Charles asked whether the economic pressure, if it could be completely created, would be sufficient to end a war like the present Asiatic war. I said I thought not. The Secretary concurred. We have on this hemisphere only 20% of the world trade. . . .

The Secretary said that there came a point at which failure to be willing to fight led literally to more fighting. The impression he wanted to convey was that America could not be absolutely counted out as a military force under all circumstances.

I asked if the Japanese could not be convinced of this without our actually making a demonstration. The Secretary appeared to think not.

I suggested that in this case some understanding with the British was inevitable. If there were to be a naval demonstration in the Pacific, it would have to be based on an American fleet concentrated at Hawaii with the British fleet off Singapore. . . .

The party broke up without attempting to reach any conclusion—indeed we were only exploring the grounds of all possibilities. Charles likened the suggestion under discussion to a game of stud poker in which we showed that the card still turned down was an ace.

In the little after conversation I pointed out to Charles that we had not more than scratched the surface. For instance, a policy of hemispheric isolation ought to be arranged as a second line of defense. If, for instance, there was a naval demonstration, there ought to be a simultaneous Latin American consultation under the Buenos Aires agreements. Conceivably if we wanted to set up a policy of non-intercourse, we could likewise permit "normal exports" from South America, isolating the balance. We might even, for instance, steer some of these exports in the direction of countries such as Germany and Italy to relieve economic pressure, thereby providing them with peace credits. In that case, the economic influences would work for us as well as against us.

. . . Fundamentally, to push the matter to a war point would be futile; the real use of naval power would be to create what might be called a civilized island in the world composed of this hemisphere, possibly Great Britain and a considerable part of western Europe.

September 22, 1937

The Mayor called me [September 21] and asked if I would meet him for a quiet talk. The only place we could meet was on the grandstand while the Mayor was reviewing the Legion Parade. However, such a place is as private as any other. On one occasion in 1934 we had such a conference while we were marching at the head of the Memorial Day Parade and we never had as quiet or more satisfactory place to talk.

At the end of a small war I reached the grandstand and found the Mayor sitting with Governor Lehman who was very cordial. We detached presently. . . . La Guardia had said that he did not wish to be a delegate [to the state convention], but knew two or three people acceptable to him. Specifically, he named me, Newbold Morris and Nathan Perlman [Judge, Court of Special Sessions of New York City]. He asked us to get in touch both with the Labor Party and with Kenneth Simpson; and to fight out any joint slate in the Labor Party to the last degree. If necessary, he was willing to break with the Labor Party on that issue.

. . . [Simpson] stated that he was proposing to try to have the State Executive Committee accept certain men as delegates at large—La Guardia, myself, Morris, Windels, Nathan Perlman, Judge Frederick Crane and three or four upstate people. I told him that La Guardia was obvious; that the Labor Party would accept Morris and Perlman and I thought Windels. As to the others, I simply did not know. . . .

. . . The difficulty with the Republicans is that they cannot understand that a man might be considered from their point of view progressive and still be no representative of the labor group. I note incidentally that Kenneth had disregarded La Guardia's suggestion that I represent him; natural enough from Kenneth's point of view. But it is once more the amusing situation that these people will buck if ever my own name is suggested and still rely on me implicitly to supply the necessary votes to put their candidates over. Since I have no desire to be a delegate to a Constitutional Convention or any other convention, this can be taken philosophically and with a good deal of humor. . . .

It is interesting to note that the White House is apparently up to its neck in endeavoring to handle the State situation. I happen to approve of what the White House is doing, but indulge a vague wonder if the skipper has not enough on his hands now without trying to run this situation here.

September 23, 1937

I note by the morning papers that Kenneth Simpson and the steering party proposed both La Guardia's name and mine to the full committee and after a vote that must have been a daisy they turned us both down. This would seem to prove merely that they knew La Guardia was not a Republican—which is obvious; that I am not either—which I would think was obvious. In point of fact the Republican nomination would have been rather embarrassing. It is an amusing incident.

But I can understand the professional politician in these matters. It happens that La Guardia is already provided for and, of course, I have no interest one way or the other. But a man whose life depended on a string of nominations would almost have to do anything necessary to get his chance. The nomination could have been had for either of us if we had cared to assist the Republicans in gerrymandering the state against the Democrats which, of course, neither of us would care to be a party to.

September 24, 1937

Yesterday after a day spent mainly with the Mayor on the Constitutional Convention and other similar matters to the meeting of the State Executive Committee of the Labor Party. Everybody's nerves were on edge. [Sidney] Hillman had talked secretly to Farley. Farley had said that if the Labor Party would endorse six or seven members of Farley's slate, Farley would allow the Labor Party to name three delegates at large, but stipulated that they could not include La Guardia or myself. We went over Farley's slate and it is pretty bad. . . .

All that the Labor Party has learned out of this is that they are not very well liked by both the old parties. The Republicans hate them on principles; the Democratic machine hates them because they threaten supremacy. The only person who likes them in the Democratic Party is the President; and as Lincoln once said "he has very little influence in the White House and almost none with the Party".

It is probably healthy for the Labor people to learn that their inherent strength has to rest with the people and not with political alliance. . . .

October 1, 1937

. . . To Carnegie Hall where the Labor Party was having its opening meeting. The place was jammed; everyone made speeches; and it warmed my heart to see Seabury come in unannounced. It had been rumored that the Labor people were against him because he supported [Alfred M.] Landon, yet the entire house roared for Seabury. . . . Seabury got as great a personal ovation as I suppose a private citizen can ever get. It did the old man good.

October 7, 1937

Yesterday chiefly working on the budget with the Mayor: the Board of Estimate is trying to evade the laws of arithmetic, that is, trying to cut the budget revenue and not cut the budget expenses. They want to make the Mayor take the responsibility of cutting expenses after they have cut the revenue. So far he is standing by. . . .

October 13, 1937

In Washington on October 11th, mainly to go over matters with Sumner Welles. The President's speech had been largely drawn for him by Norman Davis [financier, diplomat] with the approval of Secretary Hull; but the President had added the two or three paragraphs which caused the comment; specifically he used the phrase "quarantine" with relation to the militarist nations, apparently without recalling that the phrase was almost a literal translation of the French phrase "cordon sanitaire" which was applied to the isolation of Russia.

Sumner had had a week's vacation in Lausanne but was working the rest of the time. He came back to find some difference in policy between him and Secretary Hull. Hull was feeling increasingly agitated over the so-called "desperado" or bandit nations; and was firmly convinced that there was a working agreement between Germany, Japan and Italy. His idea therefore was that we should convoke the nine power signatories and Russia, and should slowly deliver a preachment against the Japanese policy in China. To Sumner this seemed futile and dangerous. He was convinced that the Germans did not go along with the Japanese policy; they had received that "fat head" [Chinese financier H. H.] Kung extremely well and had promised him the undying support of Germany. I pointed out that from a military point of view any German understanding with Japan would be violated by the Chinese affair. Instead of keeping Russia occupied by getting involved in China, the Japanese had got themselves occupied, leaving Russia relatively free to do what she pleased in the west.

Sumner's plan accordingly was to hold the Nine Power conference not inviting Russia until later; to accompany this with very definite information to the Japs that we would consider her economic and national difficulties; to try to have her there, bringing the Russians in later and endeavor accordingly to work out things by agreement. Apparently he was successful in this because the President included a couple of paragraphs looking towards this end in his speech last night.

He likewise is developing a larger idea, namely, that after the Nine

Power Conference is under way, the President should invite the various foreign diplomats in Washington to the White House; should indicate to them his intention of sending a circular communication to all of the various countries setting out that international life had become increasingly difficult because the norms of international conduct were upset; that he should then announce his intention of choosing a similar group of countries who might be called into conference on the methods and norms of international intercourse in the hope of working out a formula which might be submitted to the rest of the country for acceptance. Of course, this is nothing more than the kind of thing which the League of Nations did except that it is not mortgaged to maintaining the status quo.

If we get out of this business without a war it will be principally due to Sumner. He is the only one who apparently keeps his head working aside from his emotions. . . .

The Reconstruction Finance Corporation is going out of the money lending business; but Jesse wishes to keep it going as an alternative to the New York banking crowd so that it can act whenever it is necessary. They are worried in Washington about the continuous slump in the Stock Market and the apparent downturn of the business index. The President is wondering whether it is not concerted action on the part of the New York financial district to discredit the Administration which both Jesse and I think impossible.

October 15, 1937
    Charles Taussig and I agreed that the economic situation begins to look like a major recession and ought to be tackled on very broad lines. Charles thought that a change in the corporate surplus tax would be sufficient. I doubt that. Either the situation is a great deal less important than that or a great deal more. . . .

October 19, 1937
    Yesterday the 1929 panic was really repeated with more to come today. The Stock Market people are most bewildered and frightened. The Stock Listing Committee was anything but a happy place.
    Charles Taussig came in after work. His theory is that we ought to get the President to renounce something; that would open things up. It is possible that the President has lost a good deal of his magic in this particular regard. For, it is now plain that business is dropping as well as the market—in other words, we are in for a rather bad winter.
    Norman Davis is off for the Brussels conference or the Nine Power Treaty. . . . He is rather pro-English and there is always the danger that he may play the part in this business that Walter Hines Page [Ambassador to the Court of St. James's] played in 1914–1917. I find myself wishing that Sumner Welles had gone himself.

October 20, 1937
    The Stock Market broke loose yesterday as was expected. Gay called me, likewise Altschul. I would have telegraphed the President but as Joe Kennedy [Chairman of U.S. Maritime Commission; former Chairman of

Securities and Exchange Commission] was there I did not see that I could add much to the discussion. This looks to me like 1903—a rich man's panic. Surprisingly enough, everybody is watching the Stock Market—the real danger is the freezing of the bond market which now is practically illiquid. A hard winter will come not from financial fright in the Stock Market, but from a brief interruption of the steady flow of bonds which hits the heavy industry. I wish the R.F.C. were staying in business. The President put it out of business yesterday morning at just about the time when we need it most.

The insane jealousy which [Treasury Secretary Henry] Morgenthau has for Jesse Jones is at least partly responsible—and not creditable. . . .

October 21, 1937

Yesterday the Stock Market cleared itself up a little. The Exchange made arrangements with the banks so that the worst of the brokerage loans were not called, and by consequence the wreckage will not be serious. The bond market continued frozen. The Administration ditched the Federal Reserve people and likewise the S.E.C. and called in Joe Kennedy instead. When asked why the head of the Maritime Commission should be taking care of the Stock Market, Gay, the President of the Exchange, grimly replied that it was because the government was all it was. . . .

The Dewey crowd is getting extremely fresh. Their general line seems to be that if Dewey gives the Mayor assistance, he might perhaps be elected, which is sheer rot. Dewey, of course, is running on a campaign against crime which raises no issue whatever. Of course, he is planning to be Governor next year. . . .

October 25, 1937

. . . On Sunday found a telegram from the counsel of the Stock Exchange asking me to come to a little meeting at the Knickerbocker Club. I got there at nine finding Roland Redmond, Bill Jackson, Bob Lovett, Howland Davis and one of the floor men. They had information on the size of the short sales in the last break. Apparently, there was no increase in the short position throughout. . . . All of this does not prove anything and the figures are too incomplete to make sense. But they believe that the Administration which has come in for a good deal of pounding, is looking for a goat. Joe Kennedy has been acting for the Administration. They understand his plan is to get the Exchange to concede that it has been incompetently managed. . . .

The *Times* estimates La Guardia's majority at 400,000. It was the opinion of the meeting last night that this was a gross under-estimate. I gave that figure to La Guardia myself. But it looks now as though it was more likely to be double that figure. In that case, La Guardia becomes almost as important publicly as Roosevelt, and we are on the long road again of manipulating national sentiment. Curiously, there is a great deal more faith in La Guardia's integrity than in that of Roosevelt. However, another ten days will tell.

October 26, 1937

Chiefly campaigning. The stock market opened badly with a small group of bear raiders driving into it. The Board of Governors circulated the story that they were about to run in the shorts; and the covering was immediate. I think we are over the worst of this. It now develops that the man who divulged the strategy of Joe Kennedy and the Administration's politician is none other than Jimmy Roosevelt. That boy will get his father and himself into trouble yet.

Last night to dinner with the young Republicans. I had to save their position with the Republican organization in the summer time. All the candidates they were able to get on the ticket they got because I intervened with the Mayor and the Labor Party. When the president asked me to say something, I spent ten minutes in giving them unmitigated hell and making them swallow it. This is not done in campaigning. Logically, of course, the thing to do is to aim only at the goodwill of the group; it would have been still more logical not to be there. . . .

October 28, 1937

. . . Welles sent me the draft call for the World Congress; but this was too great an adventure for snap judgment so I put it by. The Chamberlain's Office needed attention as we are gradually completing the transfer of trust funds into Savings Banks. Some political work and then to Columbia; but the Stock Exchange people were bothered about the proposed intrigue of Kennedy and the whole position of short selling. I agreed to meet them after class. At six to meet Charles Gay, Roland Redmond and Dean Worcester at the Knickerbocker Club. Gay was tired out. He means well and takes things hard. They are going to have the Twentieth Century Fund investigate short selling and other S.E.C. regulations, if I can get the Fund to take it on, which I agreed to try to do. To the house to dinner and then campaigning in the Bronx. . . . And then to sit an hour or two in the library and try to think out the implications of Welles' international plan. This required a good deal of reaching into deep memory and silence; to get the same call which Wilson once made and avoid the mistakes he made. I put the conclusions in my letter to Welles; and my redraft of his plan. There ought to be a little more appeal to the tremendous yearning for some sort of peace and security; the emphasis ought to be shifted away from rules of warfare (nobody believes they amount to anything anyhow). Most of all it seemed possible to introduce a new conception in international affairs. We have had international law. Why not international equity as well? —Equity being defined in the old Latin sense of the appeal to justice which can be used to revise legal obligations and be relieved from them if they fail to meet the facts. But I was too tired to work so turned in; and to bed. In the morning I drafted out a revision of the five points changing them to four points, and broadening the phrase "access to raw materials" to include "other necessary elements of economic life" or words to that effect; the intent being to include the possibility of discussing access to markets. Likewise, inclusion of a new point covering pacific revision of international arrangements—a delicate method of opening up the possible defects in the Versailles Treaty.

To the office then to revise very carefully the balance of the statement, keeping Welles' exactitude and perfect form, but setting the basis for a slightly more extended interpretation. I telephoned Sumner and he seemed to agree with the line and the document went forward. Meanwhile arranging with the Twentieth Century Fund to take up the Stock Exchange bid which the Fund agreed to do. I presume it went through the Board of Governors yesterday (I could not go) and we shall be at it in a couple of days.

. . . Home then for a quiet evening with Peyton Rous [Rockefeller Institute] and Gerry Lake [textile executive] discussing the impact of ideas which are still outside the range of immediate experience.

Baruch offered to contribute to clear up any deficit which La Guardia might have in his campaign. . . .

October 29, 1937

To Columbia and to see Nicholas Murray Butler for a few moments; the old man is in fine form but not happy about politics. To Madison Square Garden where the Labor Party turned out for the final campaign demonstration for La Guardia. They obviously think they are beginning a national policy. Everybody had a good time except me. I noticed, or thought I noticed, that the greatest enthusiasm was for one, Michael Quill, who is a typical Irish labor politician and who dominates the Transport Workers Union. He has done a good job with the Transport Workers Union, but politically he is going to go off the deep end. I gathered that he was more interested in using the party as a pressure instrument than in trying to get a political result; and you never can tell when some of these men will sell out. At all events, that particular man bears watching.

Previously, I had dropped in for a moment at the Mahoney big demonstration at the Hippodrome. The place was not one-third full and dead as a door nail. This show is over; and some time between eight o'clock on November 2nd and nine o'clock on November 3rd La Guardia will find himself in national politics. This is first rate. I shall find myself in private life which is also first rate. The certain thing is that both of the old parties would be glad to sink this group as deep as they could.

At lunch with Seabury who said that the Republicans had given orders that he (Seabury) should not be allowed to speak or acquire any prominence in the campaign. Since Seabury is no radical; this can only mean that the gang is afraid of any man whose personal appeal challenges them. I imagine the same orders were given so far as I am concerned, but since I am a Rooseveltian, that is legitimate. It therefore did my heart good to have the spontaneous applause for Seabury from the floor of Madison Square Garden. What the people want just now are some men they can trust and the attempt of both the Democratic and the Republican parties in the state to stand between their public and men who are trusted cannot be successful very long.

The Japanese have refused to go to the Nine Power Conference which looks bad for Sumner's plan; but we may be able to do something about it later on. . . .

November 1, 1937

. . . To the Harvard Club to meet Evans Clark [Executive Director, Twentieth Century Fund]. We arranged the investigation of short selling by the Twentieth Century Fund for the Stock Exchange. I noticed that this was announced later and is hailed as a political master-stroke by the Exchange. . . . It is obviously necessary that the Exchange and the S.E.C. stop fighting each other for political points.

To the farm with a pleasant Saturday off mainly occupied with Halloween pumpkins. . . .

A letter from Sumner which indicates that on last Friday the President was to consider Sumner's proposed draft call for an international conference. I hope he thinks well of it. And yet the forces running in Europe are almost past the stage of conference. I wish I could make sense out of the English policy. They are pursuing the phantom on an understanding with Germany and Italy; a sound idea but neither the Germans nor the Italians are interested in doing more than playing for time while they actually take the territory. It reminds me of [J. L.] Motley's account of the negotiations between the Dutch and the Spanish while Parma was steadily mopping up one-half of Holland.

November 4, 1937

Pretty useless activity preceded and occurred on Election Day. The Mahoney forces staged a Nazi parade inviting us to cancel the permit. They figured that we would have to go back on our principles or else allow the parade and lose a lot of votes. We elected to stand by our principles and risk it. They then hired radio time and got the professional Jews to make trouble. I think we lost between 60,000 and 80,000 votes on that alone. However, it worked.

I spent the day staying by the Labor Party headquarters; and at night handled their party. At ten o'clock reporting in to the Mayor, I found him on the wire with the President; the President apparently wasting no time on congratulations. This is apparently because he feels that way about it. It is also because he proposes to annex this if he can—and he is right. If I had my way, he would have annexed this four years ago; but Jim Farley blocked him.

Then to Seabury's house where there were C. C. Burlingham, Paul Windels and one or two others. The two old men who were more nearly the architects of this than anyone else made a fascinating study. Both were very happy. For it was nearly the end of Tammany Hall and Seabury had at last destroyed what Aaron Burr had built.

To City Hall in the morning where Fiorello was putting on the "business as usual" act, though without much success as it seemed to me. There is some danger that he will start a boom for me for Governor which I think unrealistic.

I do not like the way the Nine Power Conference in Brussels is going.

One of my fears is that it will demonstrate that any conference is a war conference and not a peace conference.

November 8, 1937

On Thursday night Fiorello asked to have dinner with my father and with me; and there offered to pay all debts like a gentleman. Specifically, he asked me to consider my own career and to take whatever plunder the City of New York might offer to advance it. He explained that he thought that no man with an Italian name could be elected President; that in any case when his term was over he would be too old (he will be fifty-eight); that the youngsters who are widely acclaimed, like Morris and Dewey, do not really amount to much and would not have emerged except that they tagged onto his coattails; and that we might as well go ahead and play for the governorship. He inspired the article in the *News* nominating me for Governor.

We are to discuss again today, but there is nothing that we can do. Obviously it is not often that a man in public life offers to recognize his obligations as Fiorello did so I was deeply grateful. But it cannot be done.

Meanwhile, I was sick and tired and unhappy and on Beatrice's advice went swiftly off to the country to untangle my head. There were a number of things that annoyed me; Newbold Morris, for instance, and some of the other men who at least owe me a courteous word in view of the fact that they owe their entrance into public life and their election to me because the Labor Party who supplied the necessary votes to elect them were dead against them and accepted them only on my say so. However, that is usual in public life; and it is probably typical of the nice people in politics that they do not observe the courtesies which the crude politicians do.

Two days of walking untangled a good many things and today we are going to put the City government together and I am going to make a graceful exit.

The foreign news is bad. Poor old Davis is just barely keeping himself out of trouble in Brussels. The Dominican border has blown up and there will be a mess in the Caribbean unless it is handled with care. With Brussels in trouble I do not see that it is wise for the President to push Sumner's plan of an international conference and the best I can do is to tell him so when I get to Washington.

To Roosevelt, November 9, 1937

. . . The campaign being over, I hope to see you some time. The real difficulty begins now. The Democratic machine,* thanks to Tammany and Lehman, has to be completely remade if there is to be a Democratic party at all.

* Berle's note at bottom of letter: "It first tried to stop being Democratic—and ended by ceasing to be a machine."

November 10, 1937

On Monday night I had dinner with the Mayor as agreed. He still has the Governorship idea for me. I told him it was all right to try, but my own opinion was that it would end by his having to take a combined Labor and Republican or Democratic nomination for the Governorship. My private intention is to keep the Labor Party together; to make it as influential as possible; and, when it becomes apparent that the Party cannot nominate a Governor of its own, then to put the whole force behind the most progressive candidate we can find. Logically, this should be La Guardia. Conceivably, it might be Seabury. I think the Republicans now might accept Seabury. I am pretty sure they would accept La Guardia if he declared for them. I doubt if the Democrats would accept me or anyone else. The machine here wants nothing but jobs and graft; no one we could support could make the promises necessary to get a Democratic nomination unless Roosevelt steps into the matter which I asked him to do yesterday. . . .

The Transit Commission has suddenly got busy on a plan of unification. Since at the moment they represent nothing and nobody, the movement is one to try to save their job. They are proposing to buy the lines outright with city bonds for a lower price. This is quite all right as far as it goes, except that the City cannot afford to use the bonds; and all of the city credit would be shot on a single transaction leaving us nothing to build schools with when we got through.

November 17, 1937

Various jobs including trying to work out a plan by which New York can take advantage of the Wagner Housing Act. Lang Post came in to see me; and we got to work on a scheme to use the relief moneys. We now spend $32,000,000 a year relief money to pay for rent. Why not use part of this to pay instead interest and Sinking Fund on municipal housing; in return for which the Housing Authorities supply quarters for relief families. At least we would then get some tangible result, namely, good housing for our relief money. The idea appealed to Lang and I think we can go forward. . . .

The course of foreign affairs runs badly. . . . It looks to me as though Norman Davis was making the same mistake as was made by Colonel House and Page in 1916 and 1917, that is, he plays too close to the English. There is a lot of talk around that the democracies of the world must now stay together and fight. I do not yet see that we lock in destiny with either Great Britain or France. Our experiment the last time was certainly no success.

November 23, 1937

Variety of places yesterday chiefly with La Guardia inducting Henry Curran as Deputy Mayor. He will do well. It was a little funny. About one o'clock Curran asked weakly "when do they eat around here"? On being told that you generally do not eat around there at lunchtime, he seemed disturbed; but on my advice knocked off, and went out and had a square meal. Of course, the only penalty for walking out on the job of government is that somebody else does the governing. . . .

Reviewing the business situation a little. The actual drop in business activity has been sharper and more precipitant than any on record. This probably means among other things that it will not continue very long; but it is going to be a bitter winter; and there is trouble in the offing. . . . The President is ill, tired and obviously confused.

November 29, 1937

Pretty nearly a solid week of trying to put a government together which I can claim to be a distinct success; La Guardia usually emerging with the answers before I found them. . . .

On Saturday, Seabury, the Mayor and I lunched together to go over the state of the nation. Seabury asked the Mayor where he was going to be sworn in; the Mayor promptly answered "in your library" which was the right answer and warmed the cockles of the old man's heart. . . .

. . . The Mayor suggested that I take the purely courteous title of financial adviser to the Mayor which is quite all right with me.

But this morning (Monday, Nov. 29th) Sumner Welles writes "The way is now cleared in the manner, I hope, is agreeable to you for you to come to Washington" which must mean that Ambassador [William E.] Dodd has resigned from the Berlin Embassy; Hugh Wilson will go; and there will be an Assistant Secretaryship of State vacant.

I wish I had more enthusiasm for the idea. Only I think the Roosevelt Administration is making heavy weather and is going to make worse; for everything devolves into a mess of trouble . . . the last couple of years of the Roosevelt regime will be very bitter bread to eat. The foreign affairs of the United States, however, have to go on and somebody has to do the work and I would rather do it myself than leave it to some second-rate intriguer picked from the political basket who will get us in a British alliance and a European Asiatic war.

December 2, 1937

By arrangement, I went yesterday to Washington to find out about this job that Sumner wished me to take.

Leaving the train, I went to the Carleton where Charles Taussig and I had breakfast. I told Charles that . . . I surmised that [Sumner] wanted to ask me to replace Hugh Wilson as Assistant Secretary of State. Thereupon Charles laid down the law. He insisted that that was the last thing in the world that ought to be done. He gave a brief and terribly searching analysis of the present situation in the Administration. The President was trying to placate big business; but lest he lose the Progressives, he is making Progressive appointments; hence Jerome Frank, whom we had been persuading to take the job in the S.E.C. The President was now in the grip of ineluctable political forces he could not control; and since he had not developed any great austerity, there was a very real question whether the near brilliance of politics could bring anything out. By consequence, any member of the Administration would have almost no effect.

I left there and went over to see Sumner Welles. We reviewed the situation a little in New York: I pointed out that even the Labor Party people here with the balance of power were distrustful of where the President's political maneuvers might lead them. They trusted him personally, but not the machinery.

Sumner spoke with extreme frankness as usual. The position, as I thought, was Hugh Wilson's; Dodd will leave Berlin and Hugh Wilson will replace him on January 1st. This leaves a job open. . . . I have no joy of the adventure as Assistant Secretary of State.

Sumner said that his plan was not limited to any Assistant Secretary of State. The President now had virtually no advisers who amounted to anything with the possible exception of Henry Morgenthau and, of course, himself on foreign affairs. At a recent cabinet meeting where Sumner had been acting for Hull, the President had had a dramatic and violent time. Everyone in the cabinet had been telling him how bad things were getting; the President asked whether anyone had any specific suggestion to make; and not one turned up, except Morgenthau's; he, of course, was pressing taxation. The President, it seems, got angry and told them what he thought about them which was not much. Everyone was trying to be a Crown Prince and the results were bad. Sumner's plan was to put a Brain Truster in immediate contact with the President and thereby try to take over the situation, restoring something like order in the government.

I said that I would consider this and get hold of the President as soon as he got back. Obviously, no such plan as that could be consummated unless the President had at least some idea that he wanted this. I did not gather that he had any such desire when I saw him last at Hyde Park. If it were merely a question of being an Assistant Secretary of State, there are plenty of routine men in the Department who could do that better than I. If it were a question of a general Brain Truster, the President could say so. But I pointed out that what the country needed was not merely ideas, but character: they want something they can trust as they trusted Andrew Jackson; something incorrupt and austere. For the President's reliance on his political machinery had at length failed him; and unless he was prepared to be, not a political organizer, but an intellectual leader in his own light, the next three years would be merely fighting a political rear guard action, with nothing to be accomplished and so far as personalities were concerned, everything to be lost. Sumner said that he knew all that and that we had better go ahead and clear it up with the President.

I suppose that next week I shall have to go down and see the President. It will be a stormy and difficult interview. For, plainly what is needed here is not an Assistant Secretary of State, but a Chancellor; and the experiment of Moley shows pretty well that no subordinate official can play that part.

In the foreign field, Sumner believes that we still can have a general international conference. . . . Sumner noted that the British who have been pressing us for cooperation, military, naval, economic and otherwise, had not felt it necessary to inform us of what they proposed to do. . . . I pointed out that this was reminiscent of 1916. The same pressure had existed, but no one had felt it necessary to tell us of the secret treaties.

Actually, according to Sumner, the Germans are being reasonable. . . . The President had agreed in principle to Sumner's draft call for an international conference to take the place of the Congress of Berlin; and Sumner's plan now was to try to put that as a seal on the political solution if any worked out in Paris, London and Berlin. This, of course, leaves the Italians out of it.

December 6, 1937

Thursday to Cambridge; and breakfast with President [James B.] Conant of Harvard. He is an interesting, quiet and sincere man. . . . We talked chiefly foreign affairs; likewise a little of the conflict between the idea of administrative law developed at Harvard and the idea of self executed law as we try to think of it at Columbia. Then to a conference in the Senior Common Room of Winthrop House where there were some forty odd boys and various Professors; and a full day. Most of us were trying to block off the rise of the war spirit here. . . .

To dinner with Anna Brock and very glad to see her. At seventy-five she is still as active and keen as she was when she taught [me in] the third grade. . . .

December 7, 1937

Various jobs at the Chamberlain's Office . . . and the clearing away for the new Treasurer . . . I turned in my resignation; which was duly noted, but seems to make no difference to anybody. It will have to, however. . . .

December 10, 1937

. . . the Stock Exchange decided to appoint a committee to study and work out the reorganization of the Exchange. I agreed to go on that committee at the request of Mr. Gay. This will make some of my beloved friends in Washington angry; that is their lookout. The Stock Exchange has quite as much right to the service of liberals as anyone else.

I took the mid-night to Washington. Arriving in Washington I telephoned to find that Beatrice had already gone to the hospital, though nothing was expected until late in the evening. . . .

As not infrequently happens, [the President] took the bit in his teeth and started to give a clear-cut résumé of the politics of the nation and his own plans. He was anxious that Fiorello should not get a swell head. He said that he would, so far as all personal reasons were concerned, support Fiorello 100% as a first-rate liberal President who was easily the ablest of the lot. As a practical matter, however, although he had been brought up in the west and was a Mason and a Protestant, the country was not ready to elect an Italian whose mother was partly Jewish as President of the United States, and his language and accent were those of New York. This would not go over so well in the farm belt. I told him that I thought those things were loosening up even along these lines. . . . He stated frankly that he did not know what conditions would look like in 1940, but the bets were that he would be able to dominate the Convention; in other words, to force a liberal on the Democratic Party.

I was thinking about Beatrice and the baby; and likewise that the liberals might disagree with Mr. Roosevelt on what was a liberal.

He continued that if a liberal President were elected with a split Congress that poor devil would have the worst time anyone ever had since the Civil War. . . .

We went to work on New York State. He stated that . . . [for] the Governorship, there was the possibility of Robert Jackson, myself, Jim Farley. . . .

I observed that he could write me off; I had no ambition and was not on the make. He said that that had nothing to do with it; being on the make would get no one anywhere anyhow; but we had to take matters as they were. I said that I had some leadership in the Labor Party and proposed to keep it as trustee for the situation. . . .

He said another possibility was to bring La Guardia to Washington and put him in the cabinet; I held my peace knowing that La Guardia would not go. Actually I doubt if La Guardia would go to Albany either; so it will finally come down to [Senator Robert F.] Wagner and Jackson or Wagner and myself assuming (it is a violent assumption) that the President can control the situation here. I am not clear that he can.

We got to work on the Mexican business. He was at odds with the State Department because they wanted to collect American claims more vigorously than he did. . . .

We got to the proposed job in the State Department. I pointed out to the President that what the State Department wanted was not a third Assistant Secretary of State; they want to plant a Brain Truster in the White House. In other words, after spending a year to get Raymond Moley out, they want to put another Raymond Moley back. The President riled a little and said that it was not the State Department who got Raymond out. He is right about that; it was the President himself. But he thought the State Department needed a Brain Truster. Hull was magnificent in principle but timid; Sumner was fundamentally a "career man". I then said that I was more useful in New York; the situation would probably run loose here. He said that he thought not and there we left it. I was still thinking about Beatrice; and wanted to get swiftly away. So I cleared out of there . . . and left for New York. . . .

At ten o'clock Wednesday night (December 8th) my son Peter Adolf Augustus was born. Beatrice was wonderful as always.

December 13, 1937
A full day Friday trying to lend a hand on winding up the Chamberlain's Office. . . .

Chiefly with Beatrice during Saturday and Sunday; but on Sunday night I went to work to settle the State Department matter in good earnest. Charles Taussig and I talked until one o'clock in the morning, at the close of which I cleared my own mind in the matter and decided it could not happen. Today and tomorrow I must get to work on clearing the decks.

Charles had spent four days in Washington. Rex Tugwell had been with him; Rex and the President had lunched together, joined by Charles. The economic situation is getting worse by the minute; and the President has no particular ideas as to what to do nor has any of his group.

Later Rex and Charles sat down with John Lewis [President of the United Mine Workers] and his counsel Lee Pressman. They have not any ideas either. If the way out is by housing, then the President is right in wanting a lower wage for the building trade accompanied by a guaranty of employment (which is entirely sound). Lewis said that the only guaranty which would be acceptable would be that of the Federal Government. This was as far as they got. Charles proposed a conference to work out policy between Lewis and an industrialist, presumably Owen Young, and a couple of bankers. He took this up with me. Of course, programs do not come out of those conferences unless someone makes a program first. I proposed that we have a conference presumably at my house of Lewis, Young, T. W. Lamont, [Edward R.] Stettinius [Chairman of Finance Committee and Director, U.S. Steel] (to represent steel) and himself and myself. . . . The program would have to be an agreement to spend money on relief preferably by guaranteeing wages in certain industries beginning with housing, and an increase in relief appropriations.

This means balancing the budget is impossible.

It means also inflation unless wealth is created almost to the extent of the relief expenditures.

It probably also means taking over the railroads and doing some repair and reequipment work.

Of course, this implies taking over both housing and construction; and railroads; which is another way of saying that we have opened a wide gate in what is called private property. But I do not see that it can be helped.

Plainly, if this kind of thing has to go on, Hugh Wilson's office in the State Department is the world's worst place to try it. You would be limited by a small job which carries with it no political protection because it is unimportant. I will try to get to work on it during the day.

December 14, 1937

The committee to reorganize the Stock Exchange meets to organize today. Somebody is threatening to make me Chairman which I could do without. It is ghastly irony that at the time you really need to organize the social system the nearest you can get is to reorganize the Stock Exchange.

To have drinks with La Guardia and go over the state of the nation. Alex Rose saw him and I gather the result was very unhappy. The Labor Party thinks that it can do what no other Party has done, that is, dictate appointments. Nevertheless, I recognize Rose's difficulty. To be elected seems to involve ingratitude; to inspire hopes in a lot of people that they will get jobs when it is perfectly apparent that nothing can be done.

Last night to dinner with Charles and Rex. The night before Rex had had dinner with the President. Rex was trying to educate the President in general economics. The President was interested in steering the income stream into productive investment. He really wanted the N.R.A. back. He also wanted to have some group of individuals write him a letter saying that it was necessary to take care of the people on relief even though the budget was unbalanced, to get him out of a difficult situation. . . . I explained that I thought there was no point in this unless the program which created wealth would accompany it; and that I was afraid that what would happen would be the easy thing, namely, spending money without the necessary concomitants. Rex thought that we ought not to bargain with the President. I tried to point out that a democracy differs with any other kind of government in that you can bargain with the President. In fact, that is the way it originated. I cannot say that we got very far. What began with a program could easily dissolve into a mess of third-rate politics. . . .

December 16, 1937

A bad day on a great many counts. The Stock Exchange reorganization committee met and determined to be called the Organization Study Committee so as to be known by the initials O.S.C. They elected as Chairman [Carle] Conway who is head of the Continental Can Company. They think they are going to study officials of the Exchange. I think they are going to be forced into the middle of a really fancy discussion of what the Exchange is all about. As is the case with all business men, they are interested in machinery and afraid of fundamentals.

. . . to see T.W. Lamont. I told him briefly of the expedient which Charles Taussig had suggested and got his program. Briefly what he wants done is to allow for relief and an unbalanced budget but in addition (1) repeal the surplus profits tax; (2) modify the capital gains tax; (3) make peace with the utilities; (4) undo some of the deflation measures; and (5) make some peace with business. This is all right as far as it goes aside from the utility matter which I am not clear about; but it may carry a great many matters in its train. Making peace with business all too frequently involves whitewashing a lot of things that ought not to be allowed anyway. . . .

Yesterday I went to the Chamberlain's Office and cleaned up; then to the Sinking Fund where (since it is my last appearance there) I took [daughters] Alice and Beatrice. They sat with the Commission and a very pretty sight they made; the Mayor duly noted their presence in the record. Immediately afterwards I had [Almerindo] Portfolio sworn in [as treasurer], but the Mayor doesn't want me to announce my resignation. This is partly because he is sentimental about keeping his Chamberlain right there and partly because he hates to have a public record of my getting out. Then to the office to start Portfolio off and say farewell to the shop. . . .

Getting out of an office is a curious sensation. The office is not worth anything and I am glad to be clear of the nuisance; nevertheless there is a certain curious disappointment about leaving.

To Sumner Welles, December 20, 1937

Charles Taussig and I went to Washington last night to talk to the Secretary. My plan was to try to find you if I could . . . we did not get through talking until eleven so I gave up the idea and came home to New York where there is threat of a combined taxi strike and teamsters strike which I have to go to work on this morning.

Since I saw you things have been moving pretty rapidly on all fronts. There is no program in Washington and the President has not got any. He is waiting for the logic of circumstance to appear which in practice means either that the situation becomes acute or that a group emerges whose strength creates logic. Accordingly, Charles Taussig, Rexford Tugwell and I are having John Lewis, T.W. Lamont and Owen Young meet on Wednesday to see what we can do. This is getting back to the 1932 days.

But, as I told the Secretary, if this kind of thing is going forward, I cannot be Assistant Secretary of State or, for that matter, anything else. The men who ought to be doing that work for the government are the cabinet ministers. Failing that, it can be done from outside. But it cannot be done by anyone in a subordinate position in any department for reasons which you understand only too well. Hull promptly agreed, pointing out that it would mean merely exchanging a relatively safe position for a completely vulnerable one. He was very kind about it and very understanding.

I had best end the letter here since there is no point in putting on paper a lament that the world is not ordered better. The next stage of this is going to be brain-trusting on a large scale at the close of which the President will emerge with a program amply supported by the right, the middle and the left; and the President will get great credit for bearance, patience, wisdom in making up a program and leadership when it will do most good.

Meantime, I propose to be in Washington as often as I can and to see you as often as I can.

December 23, 1937
. . . The committee to organize the Stock Exchange convened and got started. I do not think they intend to do very much except to put in a different type of administration leaving the economic questions unsolved. At work arranging for a conference on national policy [Advisory Council]. . . .

December 23, 1937
Minute of a conference between Mr. John L. Lewis, Mr. Thomas W. Lamont, Mr. Owen Young, Mr. Charles Taussig, Mr. Rexford G. Tugwell,

Mr. Lee Pressman, Mr. Philip Murray [Vice-President of the Committee for Industrial Organization] and A.A.B., Jr.

This Conference met at the Century Club. . . .

The aim of the conversation was to discover whether the group could reach an agreement as to points of national policy which would tend toward alleviating the distress caused by the present depression in business and which might bring about recovery.

1. It was agreed, without reservation by anyone, that the present disunity in industrial, financial, and political circles and in labor could not continue. The existence of constant recriminations, of failure to agree on policy and the inability to constitute any concerted national effort, was obviously bad for business, for domestic tranquillity; for the prestige of government and for the steady employment of labor. One object of national policy should be to bring about a harmonious agreement, so far as possible.

2. It was generally agreed that relief appropriations must be sufficient to take care of the increasing number of unemployed. If this meant a continued unbalance of the budget, the interest in balancing the budget must be subordinated to the major human need. . . .

3. It was generally agreed that the policy of the Federal Reserve Board in restricting credit, especially through the raising of required bank reserves and the sterilization of gold, ought now to be reversed. . . .

There was general agreement that the present gold price of the dollar would have to remain fixed until such time as, through a stabilization agreement with Great Britain, at least, taken after an international agreement on other matters which should include, if possible, the lowering of trade barriers, parity could be restored. Such a conference was probably impossible at the moment, but policy ought to steer toward that end.

It was suggested that the lowering of bank reserves would probably be the most effective immediate move which might be made, with desterilization of gold as a following move.

4. It was agreed that the problem of the heavy industries was in considerable degree bound up with the fact that the capital markets were substantially closed. . . . The group was not in agreement as to the importance of the Undistributed Surplus Tax . . . there was no disagreement that its repeal was indicated.

It was agreed that the Capital Gains Tax in its present form should be modified. The specific suggestion was that the Capital Gains Tax be approached from the point of view of producing the greatest amount of revenue, rather than from the point of view of taxing capital gains as such; and that the lowering of the rate to a flat amount which would permit a large number of transfers, would add to the revenue, tend to open up the capital markets, and increase liquidity. Mr. Lewis agreed in general, with the same reservation as in connection with the surplus profits tax.

It was agreed, however, that in repealing the surplus tax and modifying the Capital Gains tax, care must be taken to point out that the object was not to shift the burden of taxation to groups less able to bear it. Specifically, this must not be thought to be merely a wedge to permit introduction of sales or consumption taxes. Mr. Young suggested that in lieu of the Undistributed Surplus Tax a flat rise in the corporate income tax might be considered; pointing out that in his company they distributed all their surplus and that the tax would fall more heavily on General Electric in that form. Nevertheless, he considered the change desirable from the general viewpoint.

5. It was agreed that utilities and their expansion could be of some use in stimulating heavy industry. To this end, some understanding must be reached permitting the utility industry to finance and to go forward; the belief being that the utility companies were ready to do this and in a position to do it, provided certain fears were removed.

To accomplish this, Mr. Young suggested and the group agreed, that government competition with utilities ought to be discarded, and in place of that, a policy should be definitely adopted that duplication of facilities was undesirable. Accordingly, where government felt it desirable to enter the utilities business, a method should be found of taking over the private utilities. As a possible illustration, the T.V.A. might enter negotiations to purchase the properties of the Commonwealth and Southern Lighting within its area. The result aimed at would be some areas in which utilities were government owned; some in which they were privately owned; but that a destructive competition ought not to be a part of the policy. . . .

[Marginal note:] Mr. Berle notes as a comment that abandonment of competition might be possible now that a more reasonable attitude had appeared among the utilities; and that he believed the policy to date had been necessary to induce that attitude.

6. It was agreed that a vigorous and very large housing program should be entered upon; the feeling being that this could be effective only if done through one or more national corporations, possibly acting under the existing powers of the R.F.C., which could directly construct houses. . . . A program which might run to, say, two or three billion dollars, was indicated.

The problem of wages in the construction industry came up. Mr. Lewis said he did not consider them important but noted that lowered wages would become possible only if a guarantee of, say, 225 or 250 days' employment could be given to the men. In substance, this could only be done by or through the agency of a national construction unit: individual contractors were not in a position to do so. Prices of materials likewise should become less as volume of use was assured. . . .

7. It was agreed that the long expressed policy in favor of railroad consolidations ought to be pushed to a point where consolidation actually took place. . . .

8. The drift of the country towards war was noted; and it was agreed that all possible measures should be taken to steer public opinion and public policy away from that danger.

9. It was suggested that an essential to general harmony was the maintenance of the National Labor Relations Act, and the passage of a wages and hours bill. . . .

10. Monopoly: It was the view of the group that the proposed wide program of anti-trust prosecutions offered very little hope of anything. Mr. Lewis and Mr. Lamont, among others, agreed that the result of the anti-trust laws had been negligible . . . and that the uncertainty caused by such prosecutions added very little to the process of recovery. . . .

Charles Taussig, Tugwell and I have agreed that we will chat the matter over with the President, with a view to seeing whether the study ought to be continued.

December 24, 1937

Yesterday we went on with the conference except for Phil Murray who was not there. The aide-memoire which I dictated yesterday covers the conclusions and I suppose we now have to go to the White House. It is extremely interesting that John Lewis is the man who now wants peace in the country. If he means that, it will help considerably.

The tough spot, of course, is the utility question. I think the formula of public ownership or private ownership, but no indeterminate field of competition, is the right one; but it ought to be made plain that this is possible now only because Lilienthal and the rest of the boys put up a splendid fight. Today the utilities might be reasonable. In the early days of the discussion they were too arrogant for words. It is interesting to find Owen Young with this view. . . .

December 27, 1937

Christmas Eve at home; Alexis Carrel [Rockefeller Institute] and his wife came in for Christmas Eve with the rest of the family. The family again united at Christmas dinner. . . .

This morning [Robert] Jackson is out with a speech blaming the present depression on monopolies and promising trust prosecutions. This is Jackson's bid to be Governor of New York and I think he has ambitions for the White House. Somehow I do not think it will do. Undoubtedly prices were pushed too far and too fast; but I have a theory that the public is a little fed up with this line of attack—certainly a mess unless some very real and tangible results are promised.

A letter from Sumner indicates that they do not want to close the State Department issue without a fight. We will deal with that later in the week.

December 29, 1937

Monday to Atlantic City where was the meeting of the American Economic Association and other similar groups including the American Accounting Association. There I spoke just after [Robert E. Healy] of the Securities and Exchange Commission. His chief accountants were there. I made the point that the S.E.C. could get to be very arbitrary in accounting unless they were careful about allowing open arguments. Quite a debate because Healy announced they plan to issue rules codifying accounting. . . .

In New York yesterday working on various matters and to find that Rex Tugwell had gone to Washington, talked to the President and the

President had thereupon invited the group consisting of Lewis, Lamont, etc., to meet him at the White House on January 5th. I am to arrange to have them all there. This is rushing it a bit and I so told Lamont though we may be able to get somewhere. Charles is optimistic and I am not. The morning newspaper does not indicate to me the remotest possibility of getting a policy of the kind suggested. Bob Jackson is going on a career of trust-busting with the full support of the Administration and while I have no objection to trust-busting, it accomplishes exactly nothing. . . .

Dewey has announced his appointments which look to me, on the whole, about as political as they could well be.

December 30, 1937

To meet Charles and Rex . . . We had especially for discussion Robert Jackson's anti-trust speech. If on top of this we are to take Lewis and Lamont to the White House, I am afraid we may be luring them into a political trap—to which I do not care to be a party. Actually, analyzed I can see nothing but rather second rate demagogy. It is merely amusing that about half of it is taken from *The Modern Corporation and Private Property.* . . .

It appears that the President had told Rex that he wanted the interview [with the Advisory Council], but he wound up saying that he thought we could scare these people into doing something, which I doubt. His real point, of course, was that Jackson wanted to shave off at the top and bring up at the bottom, but how in the world anti-trust cases will do that I am not altogether clear. Also, I suppose I am merely politically inept in this kind of business. I know too much about the two hundred corporations to make a personal devil out of them. I know too much about sixty families to think that they will amount to very much. And I do not see that anything is accomplished by calling the particular group "Bourbons". Generally speaking it was a bad evening.

December 31, 1937

Yesterday morning the Mayor called up and sent his car down. I found him in the Empire State Building where he was struggling with the Planning Commission. He finally threw the Chairmanship at me to hold until the right man is found to head it permanently. But the real reason was different. He wants someone to stay alongside. I do not blame him: governing the City of New York is a lonely business at best. I arranged to have Phil Thurston on hand to be Secretary for technical legal work and to get the group together to look for a chief of staff today. And that will be that. Later somebody turned up with the fact that the job has a $15,000 salary. I had not even known about it. . . .

January 10, 1938

Tuesday evening, January 4th, back to the City and, generally speaking, a mess of trouble. We solved the City Planning difficulty (it is a full job) by having me sworn in not as Chairman, but as a mere member with the designation to act as Chairman, but this is not public. The Commission has no quarters and nothing to work with. Nevertheless, on Wednesday morning we had a meeting and organized, making Phil Thurston Secretary (he had been working over the week-end in preparing a tentative set-up and getting the routine started along.)

. . . To Washington on Friday to talk to Sumner Welles. I have outstanding a tentative commitment to go to the State Department. I meant to get out of it, but all I did was to get myself farther in. They think the time is ripe for another Raymond Moley and they do not like the domestic situation. This is beginning to handicap them in their foreign affairs work. I should think it might. Sumner Welles is obviously having an unhappy and bad time. It still sounds romantic to me; and I said that I would come along provided the situation indicated that it was possible to get something done; which I think will not be. . . .

Saturday at various jobs and then to lunch with La Guardia at the Century Club and for an afternoon's ramble, inspecting the City with him. . . .

Jackson announced his candidacy [for governor]. I never saw less enthusiasm in my life. They seem very sure of the Labor Party endorsement. This must be because they have talked to Hillman for the Party people know nothing about it. Yet the fact is that if the election were held today Jackson could not be elected.

A quiet day Sunday, but I have been evolving in my mind the making of some kind of a political manifesto. We cannot run any national affairs in an atmosphere of congealed hatred.

January 11, 1938

To the Planning Commission to get things set up. At least we had desks and stenographers. . . .

To the office and then to the Committee to Reorganize the Stock Exchange. We are getting to the point where a draft report has to be made. I want it broad; some of the Committee don't want to go that far. . . .

January 17, 1938

On Thursday we tried again to find John Lewis; Lewis saying that he would go with us to see the President with Owen Young and T.W. Lamont. . . . Lamont said that he did not want to go without Lewis and I agreed. So we put it up to Charles Taussig to find Lewis and Charles came through as usual and did. At seven o'clock I learned that Lewis had been found and would come. A leak from the White House gave the whole story to the newspapers: this is definitely a White House leak because it included a summary of Rex's discussion with the President on, I think, Monday.

On Friday we met at the Mayflower in Owen Young's room; discussed matters, and Young proposed that the President form a small committee to try to make definite recommendations. We went to the White House in some style; and suggested it to the President. Lewis stated that the structure of prices, wage levels, etc., had to be maintained. The President spent a good deal of time insisting that the various business associations misrepresented his appeals. He agreed, I think, with some enthusiasm to Young's proposal. We left amid a battery of photographers: Lewis, by nomination of Lamont, acting as spokesman. We then went back to Young's room where we roughed out the drift of a possible committee. Back to New York with Lamont.

On Saturday a bad day. The Planning Commission has no staff, no money and still a tremendous amount of public work to do. We shall get at that this morning. To the Stock Exchange to draft a report for the reorganization of the Stock Exchange. I have the outline of the report, but they want to stick to machinery and I want to talk about fundamentals which probably means that we will have two reports—one about reorganization and another by me on economics.

A quiet Sunday; I ought to have worked, but the machine was overloaded and I could not think very well. Alexis Carrel came in to lunch; he is still interested in his lay order which I think is essential. We have to have men who will work on these matters without ambition. . . .

January 18, 1938

To the Planning Commission and various places; to a brief lunch with Charles Taussig who had some news from Washington. It seems that the extreme left faction in the C.I.O. want to block any agreement between Lewis, Lamont and the White House. . . .

January 19, 1938

Lamont is anxious to get forward with the memorandum for presentation to the President and I am trying to do so. To Columbia and then home. . . .

Yesterday the *Tribune* had Lippmann calling us a group of "economic symbols"; today the *Times* with Arthur Krock called the Lamont Lewis Committee "Mr. Berle's economic zoo", which will do for one day.

January 20, 1938

Yesterday to the first public meeting of the Planning Commission; then to the Annual Meeting of the Savings Banks Trust Company. . . .

This morning's papers record that the President came out for the Advisory Council yesterday in talking to the Roper Committee. So it seems we are there.

January 21, 1938

Yesterday to work via the City Treasurer's Office . . . To the Planning Commission . . . then to the Stock Exchange to work on the report. It is getting down now to a question of words. . . . To City Hall to find the Mayor; he was back from Washington where he had a good time before the Senate; had had lunch with the President; and was not impressed with Washington at all. He said that if I went there I would be very unhappy and that the latch-string was out in New York. I suggested that I go with a return ticket plainly marked at the beginning. I do not think that he knows all that is involved, but I think that his conclusions are probably sound. But I do not see any way out of trying.

I am pretty clear now that the impetus behind the Washington drive is a double one. Hull and Welles are alone and unhappy and want help very badly indeed. Mr. Roosevelt wishes to have the decks clear for his campaign for Jackson [whom he later appointed Solicitor General]; and several people have learned that it is not altogether safe to leave me loose. They did that once in the City situation and have not got over it yet.

Politically, of course, this is not my fault. I suggested that the Administration back La Guardia in the first instance. If they had, they would have been better off now.

January 25, 1938

To the Planning Commission and then to lunch with my brother and Charles Taussig. Sumner telephoned that the wires were pretty well cleared for the matter he and I worked on—mainly, the proposed conference of powers. He likewise wants to put my name through for the State Department so that we can get the preliminary work forward. The work itself would be interesting; Washington itself is the last place in the world any sensible person would like to be in. It is a good deal of a sewer just now.

. . . We are getting forward with the Lamont-Lewis-Young arrangement for an Advisory Committee. The President seems to think well of it.

. . . Everything is all right except that I am sick at heart about this Washington business, but can see no way out of it.

January 31, 1938

We finished up the Stock Exchange report on Wednesday afternoon and left it to the two youngsters in the Commission to check. Bill [William McChesney] Martin took on the job and he did it well. . . . To Washington on the midnight.

On Thursday breakfast with Charles Taussig. There has been no end of a split in Washington over our maneuvers with Lewis and Lamont. Corcoran and Cohen think their position is threatened and have started a row. Charles blocked it off and made tentative peace. But there is no peace with other peoples' egos as I know very well. To the State Department where there were assembled Welles, Norman Davis and a group of the Department's experts and we went over the call to the International Conference which Welles had framed and I had worked on late last Fall. While we were working on it the President's message on naval affairs came over for revision by the Secretary. In the afternoon we went to work on it with Secretary Hull. It was pretty well finished when I left. I interrupted for a few minutes at twelve o'clock to hand the Stock Exchange report to [William O.] Douglas at the S.E.C.

On Friday to see Lamont. Both he and Young are unhappy at the turn of affairs in Washington. They planned a real attempt to reach an understanding with the Government and apparently it had been used to make third rate politics. Young is pretty well off the boat; so is Lamont, though he still would like to help if he could see a way. We will have another attempt on Monday to see what we can do. . . .

Word from Washington indicates that the President's naval message which came out on Saturday is well received and he plans to carry it forward with a general conference in about ten days. Then there will be some real fireworks.

To dinner with the Gordon Bells [old New York friends] and after to hear some music at Mrs. [Reginald] de Koven's. A party reminiscent (as all her parties are) of the great days of the Gilded Age. There are not many left like it.

To Roosevelt, January 28, 1938

In connection with my proposed appointment as Assistant Secretary of State, Secretary Hull suggested that you were waiting some definite word from me. . . . I tried to give you that word when the recent conference at the White House broke up, but, of course, that was a bad time to do it. I should, of course, be glad to accept the appointment if you wish it.

As you know, I have never sought either appointments or nominations in New York, Washington, or anywhere else; but if I can help there, I am, of course, very glad.

I should like to feel free to ask for my release when the step you have in mind as an active search for peace has been finally brought to a conclusion. It would be something of a relief to feel that an understanding could be made that those of us who are working for you could be freed from sniping by other people who are likewise working for you. Taking office means assuming the risk of what our political enemies do to us; but I wish we could work out some way of being safe from our colleagues.

February 1, 1938

Yesterday a meeting of the Planning Commission and various odd jobs. The Stock Exchange adopted the Conway report and appointed a committee of three to draw the amendments. It would seem as though we were off to a fair start.

A quiet evening at home and to see father. Nothing new from the Washington front. I am pretty well resigned to whichever way it comes out.

February 7, 1938

Thursday, February 3rd, in Washington principally to talk to Sumner Welles . . . The Washington situation is confusion worse confounded; literally there is no program. The suggestion that I go as Assistant Secretary of State seems to have stirred up [people], particularly Ben Cohen and Tommy Corcoran. It does not greatly matter.

Hull finally opposed the theory of a general negotiation. His idea was to make a trade treaty and a loose understanding with England and after some months offer substantial assistance to Germany on the condition that they would be good and behave themselves. Sumner objected that this did not take account of the political realities which were quite as pressing as the economic realities. I understand the President backs Sumner's plan. I agree with Sumner in this, though it is not a clear case: there are dangers either way, but I think less by following Sumner's plan than by taking the Secretary's view which is, in substance, not unlike the view that Colonel House took in 1915. There might be implied out of the latter policy some kind of an alliance which might lead to our participation in a new war. I am desperately afraid of this and I know, of course, that Hull does not have that idea.

With Mayor La Guardia on Friday mainly about City finances. . . .

Saturday to the Planning Commission. But before going down T.W. Lamont telephoned me. What he said was disturbing to a degree and very confidential. The automobile people and others talked to the President. They had a pleasant time, but got nowhere in any real discussion of fundamentals. They were accordingly planning to take it up with the labor people themselves; were to agree on a policy with the labor groups; and then take their desires directly to Congress. I could say nothing except that this was a free country and there was absolutely no reason why they should not do so. [The Advisory Council ceased to function at this time.]

But this, of course, is exactly what the Administration ought never to have permitted. The White House and its executive departments ought to have been the focus. They could be so long as all groups were acquiescent and looked to the President for leadership. Once convinced that they cannot find it there, they will, of course, try to develop their own as and when they can; which in practice means the creation of a new political bloc, assuming, of course, that they can get together as I think they can. . . .

It seems to me as though something like a big wind ought to strike pretty soon clearing out a lot of this second-rate barking and talking in terms of real business.

February 9, 1938

To the Planning Commission and various jobs; later opening the work in the Seminar at Columbia. . . .

February 10, 1938

The President sent my nomination as Assistant Secretary of State to the Senate yesterday. I am sorry because I had hoped that he had about decided not to do it. The prospect of spending any considerable amount of time in the poisonous atmosphere of Washington is appalling. However, the danger of war is growing so great that there can be no declining. I only hope that something can be done. The passive assumption that we have to go to war is growing rapidly and dangerously. I do not think we do; nor do I think it absolutely necessary to have a general European war. There must be some way by which the human mind can drill a hole in the situation. . . .

From the New York *Times,* February 10, 1938

Commenting on his nomination as an Assistant Secretary of State, A. A. Berle, Jr., head of the City Planning Commission, yesterday said:

"My understanding is that the particular job which the department has in mind for me may not last more than a few months. I am accordingly retaining my professorship at the Columbia Law School."

Mayor La Guardia said:

"Naturally it doesn't come to us as a surprise. I know of no one who is better equipped, who has more information about foreign affairs, than Professor Berle. It will be a great loss to the City of New York, of course, but I hope that very soon the peace of the world will be so secure that within a short time he will be able to come back to us."

February 11, 1938

Various jobs . . . The correspondents' stories about Hull not wanting me in the State Department appear to be true. . . .

February 14, 1938

Two days off in the country and well spent too. I gather from the general drift of affairs that there is going to be a hard road to hoe in Washington including a good deal of opposition in various parts. Well, there is nothing to be done about it except to lace in and try.

It is going to be difficult to clear the decks here.

February 16, 1938

Meanwhile the European situation is working overtime. The German ultimatum to Austria has been accepted and I suppose to all intents and purposes Austria has fallen into the German camp. . . .

February 18, 1938

. . . Then to the Planning Commission and we arranged to get under way the big zoning problem for the East Side—the first and probably the last big project the Commission will work out under my chairmanship. . . .

The Nazi coup in Austria is complete and obviously will be followed up by a drive through Hungary and Rumania. The great question is what will happen to the Czechs. But direct contact between the German and Russian front is now established. From here out anything can happen.

The reconstitution of the Austrian Empire unit under Germany is probably necessary and probably not alarming. But what Hitler will do with it nobody knows. Dorothy Thompson [columnist] seems to think democracy committed suicide this morning in the *Tribune;* but this is slightly emotional. Anyway we are in for fireworks.

February 21, 1938

. . . The Austrian Anschluss is supposed to mean here that the German Empire is on the march; which is another way of saying that the

Great Congress which Sumner had persuaded the President to call is now too late, and that we are in for a period like that of Frederick the Great.

I am not so clear. . . .

February 23, 1938

. . . Tuesday was a holiday; but I did get a long over-due article written for the *Virginia Law Review* ["The Lost Art of Economics"]. To see Judge Seabury and the Mayor about transit. . . .

The morning newspapers carry the story of the British negotiations with Italy; Dorothy Thompson is running a war party all by herself. From now on we shall have the romantic liberals wanting war; and the hard-boiled conservatives looking for peace. At least so it would seem from the papers here.

February 24, 1938

To work yesterday chiefly at the Planning Commission and we started three big blanket zones—Fourth Avenue, East Side and Fieldston. This job is beginning to get interesting. . . .

As far as I can see my appointment as Assistant Secretary of State is peacefully sitting in the Senate which pleases me. If they keep on this way the winter will be over and about the only effect will be that I had my picture in the magazines. Perhaps by that time Mr. Neville Chamberlain, Mussolini and Hitler will have settled all outstanding questions and we can have a nice quiet time.

March 1, 1938

Not very much. I am still waiting for the Senate to confirm my appointment which I suppose will happen whenever Key Pittman gets back. . . . Last night with Dean Smith, [Huger] Jervey [Director, Institute of International Affairs], [Professor of Law Richard R. B.] Powell and [Professor of Economics Elliott E.] Cheatham trying to plan out a scheme for a legal center at Columbia to enlarge the work of the Columbia Law School.

March 3, 1938

Yesterday a meeting of the Planning Commission and we started some more zones. Then to lunch with Bernard Baruch to discuss various things. . . . Then as a result of a telephone call, to Albany to attend a hearing on a bill to abolish the Transit Commission. I summed up at the end. Then back with Seabury . . . to New York in time to turn in about 1:00 A.M. A full day.

March 4, 1938

. . . The Senate Committee voted out my nomination so I suppose the next thing happens in order. . . .

March 9, 1938

Yesterday at the White House I reported in and discussed various matters with the President.

He was in favor of making the Massachusetts speech for Labor's Non-Partisan League and suggested a possible outline. Labor had been told in Massachusetts in 1912–16–32 and 36 that the factories would shut down if a Democratic Administration were elected and especially if anyone were so heterodox as to attempt tariff reform. Nevertheless, this had not happened. Further, that the necessary development of the country would automatically lead to developing manufactures elsewhere, notably in the far west, the south and southwest, which, of course, would tend to draw from New England. Their export trade thus became increasingly important; also, more attention ought to be given to diversifying manufactures in New England, especially to take care of their local requirements.

I told the President that I was studying the question of capital credit. There was no reason why capital markets should ever be closed. He outlined his own ideas and asked me to discuss the matter with [Marriner] Eccles [Chairman of Board of Governors, Federal Reserve System]. He had been considering a plan for having regional capital credit banks, which could make capital loans. The Government might subscribe the initial capital, the banks might sell their own debentures, possibly through the post offices or otherwise; (he had not thought this out), local industry would be able to borrow through this system only in the office of the region in which it was located, each bank in each district would be obliged to purchase some of the debentures from the banks in the other districts, so that the holder of a debenture in any one bank would hold a credit document backed by the diversified capital instruments of the whole country; apparently the Treasury was interested; I gathered the Federal Reserve was frightened at this proposal. I agreed to go to work on it and see what could be done.

We discussed the Mexican negotiations. His primary interest there is that, while we have no quarrel with any government which elects to set up an internal dictatorship, we must take a different point of view if a dictatorship is set up backed by foreign money, propaganda or support, such as shipment bonds. Obviously, the difficulty, of course, is in determining at what point foreign influence really begins. . . .

March 10, 1938

After going over things as well as I can, and having talked now with the Federal Reserve Board, Treasury people, some of the S.E.C. people, heads of several of the large labor unions, it seems to me that the tangible and realizable program is roughly this:

(1) Creation of capital credit mechanism so as to reopen the capital markets.

(2) The passage of a railway consolidation bill. . . .

(3) The stimulation of rapid use of the Federal housing credit. This seems to be happening anyway so that all that will need to be done would be publicity.

(4) The closing up of the T.V.A. Commonwealth and Southern controversy by appointing a couple of negotiators to trade for the southern properties.

(5) The problem of taxation seems to be taking care of itself in Congress automatically.

This program appears to be possible* because:

(a) The President, Douglas and Eccles appear to be in agreement on creating capital credit mechanism. The fancied opposition on Eccles' part was obviously not present.

(b) There seems to be a general unanimity about railroad consolidation. The danger is that we may find ourselves in a controversy as to who will administer the act. This the White House can settle when it desires.

(c) The President has indicated a basis of a settlement of the utility controversy regarding Commonwealth and Southern, but the symbol of the special negotiators would have to be appointed so that the matter was not indefinitely held up by the Morgan controversy.

We should likewise be deriving continued and increasing benefit from the trade treaties, but these will tend to operate slowly. . . .

* It wasn't. AAB—Apr 25

On March 11, 1938 Berle prepared a memorandum on the proposed railroad consolidation act. Two weeks later, in the Non-Partisan League speech in Massachusetts, which he had discussed with Roosevelt on March 9, he noted:

The situation with respect to our railroads is not good. We need some additional legislation to make the railroads fit conditions in transportation which have come about through the development of the highway and the airways; legislation that will give some governmental agency authority to compel railroads to do that which they seem unable to do voluntarily.

. . . We must have railroads maintained and operated at the highest state of efficiency. We demand the best possible service of them and should not require that this service be furnished at a loss. Just how the problem is to be solved has not been determined, but solved it must be.

March 15, 1938

I talked to the President today about the proposed answer to the Canadian note [of January 27 about power negotiations].

The President thought:

(1) There was no reason why this should not go forward and that the existence of the T.V.A. controversy did not make delay desirable;

(2) He hoped that if negotiations were taken up, we could work towards an international authority analogous to the Port Authority of the City of New York created by a liberal agreement between this Government and the Canadian Government;

(3) That instead of trying to duplicate on both sides of the river power facilities developed on either side of the river ("toss a coin to decide"), to enter an arrangement by which both parties could draw power from the resultant generation;

(4) If the Canadians suggested that they did not need the power, our reply should be that we would be prepared to build the dam entirely at

our expense, taking all the power because we need it; but leave the Canadians an option of thirty days notice to notify us that they needed a percentage of the power . . . in other words, we construct and draw all the power, they to have the option to take any part of the agreed percentage of the power at any time, contingent to their paying that percentage of the cost.

(5) Instead of drawing the power from the Niagara and from the rapids down below, build a flat canal to take the water to a bluff where a fall of 480 feet could be had, thereby getting a great deal more power from the water used;

(6) Construct a reservoir somewhere near Buffalo which could impound sufficient water so that at stated times in the day a full flood could be had for Niagara for scenic purposes.

All this he thought could be worked out once it got into negotiation. His idea was that it might take time. . . .

March 15, 1938

We talked briefly about the proposed flow of capital credit. I pointed out that Eccles had described himself as being in favor of it; Jesse Jones likewise, and Douglas, of course. I have not talked to Morgenthau. The only real issue appeared to be who would run it. Eccles thought it came properly under the province of the Federal Reserve. The President inquired who would own the corporation, to which the answer is that the United States Government should put up the equity. He asked where the ultimate money was coming from, and I pointed out that *prima facie* it would come from the sale of debentures, which today would mean from the commercial banks who would buy them. The office would be under the chief control of the Federal Reserve System.

The President had no doubt as to the result. The Federal Reserve was essentially a control institution. The Credit Corporation would be a lending institution and, therefore, belongs to Jesse Jones. The object, if possible, would be to get these two men to agree among themselves before the project was put up to him.

March 19, 1938

The week has not produced much in Washington since we are practically confined to watching the course of European events without being able to effect their course.

I finally got sufficiently excited to put my feelings on the record in the form of a memorandum to the Secretary and to Sumner pointing out that we were not opposed to the annexation of Austria as such, but we were opposed to the oppressive quality of the Hitler government and we might steer towards trading or recognition of the situation for some concessions along that line. But Hitler is practically impossible to negotiate with in these matters. I was, however, concerned lest the manner of our recognition be such that it will simply strengthen the military party in Germany.

Sumner had been called up by the President. The President wanted to issue some kind of statement at once; I gather a rather condemnatory statement. On Sumner's advice he withheld it for the time being.

The State Department is divided. About half of it is following a Wilsonian moral line which in my judgment would lead eventually to our entry into a war on the British side. The other half, headed by Sumner and myself, is still endeavoring to steer matters into an ultimate conference.

As nearly as I can make out the nice people have declared war already. . . .

For the rest this job at the moment is a ringside seat at a slow movie watching Europe get ready. to tear itself to pieces. The Polish ultimatum expires this morning; there are some grounds for believing that the desire is to permit Poland to take most of Lithuania and the Germans to take Danzig and Memel. The price which the Italians have asked for Austria is already apparent; it is complete domination of Spain. There is obviously more coming since the military movements in Austria would seem to indicate action towards the East.

March 23, 1938

The Secretary called a meeting at three o'clock today to consider the Mexican expropriation of oil properties. They have a right, of course, to expropriate but as they cannot pay, and their promise to pay is a mere formality, this does not solve the situation. We were considering holding up the purchase of Mexican silver, but this might have the effect of lowering the world price; of making unemployment in Mexico and embarrassing Mexican finances. Yet failure to do so would be an indication that we were simply weak.

I note that there is a possibility that we might hold a consultation under the Buenos Aires Resolutions.

March 26, 1938

I went to work last week to try to establish contact with the Left Wing. Rex Tugwell was kind enough to invite Robert Jackson to dinner. Charles, Bob, Rex, Jerome Frank [Securities and Exchange Commissioner] and I hashed over the situation. It was a long night; but they are all thinking mechanically, that is, of various things that can be done. Whereas, in fact, the real difficulties are moral and psychological. The following night I was having a lonely dinner in the restaurant when Cohen came over. He had been dining at the next table. I pointed out that this campaign was the last campaign which the New Deal would have anything to say about and we had better be getting our philosophical legacy to the country in good order. We agreed to get to work on this next week.

Yesterday to lunch with Sumner. I told him quite frankly that what was needed was not a brain truster, but a priest or a psychiatrist, meaning thereby that what we had to do was to change the habit of mind of Washington which is a singularly unreal place.

The State Department work is anything but heavy, but when it does come through, it is important. For instance, we are working on Mexican oil. The Secretary is for taking a much stiffer stand than Sumner; and only the events of the next few days will show what really ought to be done. The danger is that the social movement to eliminate the foreign interests is becoming at the same time a frank anti-American movement which is not so good. There is such a thing as being simply soft about it.

. . . tomorrow to the Labor Non-Partisan League in Boston.

April 1, 1938

I

Last night Mr. Wayne Taylor, Assistant Secretary of the Treasury, Mr. Ronald Ransom, Acting Chairman of the Federal Reserve Board, and I met at Mr. Taylor's house to consider the existing financial situation.

Among other factors, we had in mind (1) the present levels of production; (2) the relative absence of new capital financing; (3) the dropping of the stock market; (4) the fact that the Government bond market had recently required some support from the Federal Reserve; (5) the existing number of the unemployed and the need for relief.

It was generally agreed that the difficulties were as much moral as economic. Nevertheless, there seemed enough chance that the trend would continue to make it urgent that a program be evolved.

II

It was suggested, as an immediate program, that the following might be scheduled for prompt initiation. It was assumed that the Glass Bill, extending the loaning powers of the R.F.C., would be passed within a few days. In such case, it was thought that the immediate situation would be stabilized if—

(a) The public works program was reopened;
(b) A railway equipment corporation were formed to order, finance and provide railway equipment to railroads needing it;
(c) The making of capital loans for business, with special attention to planned employment and construction;
(d) The extension of loans for housing construction, with special emphasis on middle class housing;
(e) The reserve requirements, raised last May, might now be reduced. . . .
(f) Adequate W.P.A. and relief appropriations would have to be asked. This requires legislation; but it appears essential.

III

In view of the actual situation, the tactics are important. They might include:

(a) An appropriate speech, presumably on the occasion of the passing of the Glass Act, outlining the program;
(b) Some forty-eight hours later, the announcement of some dramatic public works job;

(c) Shortly after that, a campaign to form production committees to stimulate private construction financed, if necessary, under the Glass Bill. In that connection organized labor ought to be asked to assist, and ought to be made aware that labor groups are also responsible for creating production, as well as for making demands. In other words, make local labor leaders actually share in the process of putting the job through;

(d) A day or two after that announcement, announce, if possible, some big piece of private construction or of railway equipment contracts, or both;

(e) If possible push the negotiations between T.V.A. and Commonwealth and Southern. . . .

IV

Three points ought to be recognized:

(a) Practically no business group in the country has escaped investigation or other attack in the last five years. Irrespective of their deserts, the result has been shattered morale. We have not, in the absence of a large Government ownership program, any class or group to whom we may turn for economic leadership. It is, therefore, necessary to make that group pull itself together.

(b) There are some remote indications (notably in steel) of an upturn. If, therefore, we can weather the next sixty or ninety days, normal processes very well may "take us out." The next few weeks, however, may determine whether these processes can be set in motion.

(c) It was noted as possible that the railroad bill might be so handled as to provide at least the hope that railroads would do better.

Since the next Presidential message scheduled has to do with monopoly and, (possibly), bank holding companies, it might be well to have that message so handled as to lead into a program of this kind.

April 4, 1938

As agreed, Governor Eccles called me yesterday afternoon.

He was generally in line with the suggestion made by Messrs. Ransom and Taylor; but he was more interested in having a group working on the drawing up of a positive program than in anything else. He understood Secretary Wallace would go along. Eccles accepted the Glass Bill reluctantly, but thought that the principal task was to make the banking system work. . . .

. . . It was relatively obvious to me that with such a difference of opinion regarding persons, nothing will happen here. It seems to me that Jesse, whose Glass Bill has actually gone through, is in a position to act, while the rest of these people are still talking about it.

The President will have to consider whether he wants to leave the whole program in the hands of Jesse or whether he will try to do something else.

April 9, 1938

. . . I got into touch with the President as soon as he got back from Warm Springs. I previously arranged to have Jackson and these men explain to the President that the situation was serious and that it was well to shift the policy towards something productive. I think this did not please Corcoran. . . .

Sunday night there was obviously the battle of the century culminating with the Senate and House leaders telling the President that there was trouble on all sides.

On Tuesday morning I spent an hour with the President and we went over the situation. He laid out in considerable detail what he wanted to do, which followed closely the line of agreement we had worked out—relief expenses were to be taken care of, housing acts enlarged and public works provided for. I wrote to La Guardia and asked him to stand by to offer to put some of the public works money to work. La Guardia actually did this by formulating his program and going to Washington yesterday (Friday).

Tuesday afternoon, Wednesday and most of Thursday Sumner Welles, Cordell Hull, Norman Davis and I went to work drafting the President's message [to Congress on April 14]. This had to involve not only the so-called pump-priming campaign, but also a general address to the country insisting that the time had come to have a unified sentiment instead of fighting. It was difficult because what some of the older men wanted was a real retreat; what I wanted was an agreement to hold the line accompanied by a dramatic insistence on some kind of moral unity. This is necessary from the country's point of view and equally from the President's. He has to be in a position to dramatize his own leadership and I doubt if he could be induced to retreat.

. . . In the course of this, a little dinner with the Latvian Minister [Alfred Bilmanis] which turned out to be a minor celebration of the de facto recognition of Latvia which I recommended at Paris nineteen years ago. This was an interlude. My sister Lina did the honors on our side.

Meanwhile Cordell Hull had got sufficiently steamed up to go over to the President and state his own views for the first time in six years as Prime Minister. He followed the line we worked out and wound up by handing him a copy of the message we drafted. This was followed up on Friday by Sumner Welles and the President agreed to go over it over the week-end.

All of this was conditioned on the idea that the reorganization bill (which is of no importance, but had become a sort of test as to whether the President was still in control) would pass the House probably by a small majority.

I came to New York on the four o'clock train; had my class at Columbia and met Geoffrey Parsons [of the New York *Herald Tribune*] late last night. This was by accident, but I had intended to do so because when the message came out my plan was to have it acclaimed as a real move towards unity. E. J. Marshall [Toledo, Ohio, lawyer] had been in

Washington Friday morning and had agreed to have the Northern Ohio newspapers [support the President]. However, at eleven o'clock last night it appeared that the reorganization bill had lost by a small majority and there the matter stands.

Winning, the President would probably have moved to unify; losing, I am afraid he simply will throw himself into a campaign of bitterness. This will tear the country to pieces without accomplishing anything. We will have both bad economics and bad politics with every kind of Corcoran and Huey Long, etc., coming into action.

April 11, 1938

As agreed, I went to New York Friday evening and arranged to meet Geoffrey Parsons. . . .

I pointed out to Parsons that his newspaper had to contemplate the possibility of the economic distress continuing; that in such case a purely disorganized political situation would be both dangerous and difficult; that I thought that there would be a movement toward general unity and that I hoped, in that event, his paper would do what it could towards helping it along.

Parsons said he regretted that we had not met earlier in the evening, since he had already written his editorial on the defeat of the Reorganization Bill and it was in type. He agreed, however, to try to handle the matter from then out, with a view to playing the differences down. Apparently, he succeeded in doing this on Sunday.

On Saturday I had Mayor La Guardia to dinner. He had been thinking the situation over himself; he agreed that in any event, to the extent that he became the nucleus of any movement, he would move to strengthen rather than weaken the national government. Both he and I had in mind moves both from the extremists of the right and the extremists of the left; and the probable emergence of people like [Father Charles] Coughlin, etc.

He was very firm in his belief that the foreign situation made it imperative that the country should put up a united front and, so far as he was concerned, he would work to that end; he had indicated his views to the President on Friday and . . . (today) at 6:15 over a national network. He agreed that he would likewise do what he could with the Progressives in Congress and we would settle the method of doing that at breakfast on Tuesday morning. Meanwhile, he had announced Rex Tugwell as Planning Commissioner for the City of New York.

In the event that the move which the Secretary advised is made by the White House, there will be, therefore, some considerable support in the New York area. If the Northern Ohio people come through, La Guardia gives at least a tentative outline. . . .

April 26, 1938

Last night Governor La Follette called me up from Madison. He invited me to come to the Progressive Conference to form a third party to be held at Madison on Thursday of this week. He had previously been in touch, by telephone, with Mayor La Guardia, (who is, I presume, at Wichita Falls, Texas). La Guardia had agreed to come and had apparently agreed to send him a telegram, which more or less commits La Guardia to the third party movement. La Guardia had asked Phil to get me out there, if possible.

Phil said that he would understand it perfectly if I did not come because it might lose me my job. I told him that that was the least part of my worries; though I did want to consider the effect on the work. I said I would mull it over and let him know.

I thought this over for five minutes and then called President Roosevelt and asked him what he wanted done. He said that his judgment was that I ought to go; the third party conference was called by Phil; Bob La Follette was not as enthusiastic about it; it was all right if the movement did not get too far away from shore so that the forces could not be joined. He said he thought that the men involved were sincere, but their methods of political attack, while they worked well in their own territory, were hardly adapted to the eastern situation; that, in consequence, it would not be a bad idea to have someone there who would generally keep the lines parallel. . . .

I told the President that I did not wish to turn up at a third party meeting which might prove hostile to him without his entire knowledge and approval because I could not be sure that these people were not ready to go much farther than I personally thought wise. The President said he understood all that perfectly. . . .

April 30, 1938

I arrived in Madison on Thursday noon, April 28th, and went directly to Governor La Follette's house. He outlined to me the general plan. The National Progressive Association (a party) was incorporated in Wisconsin, the signers of the certificate being the Governor and his wife, Elizabeth Brandeis, David Niles of Boston, and a few of the Wisconsin associates. La Guardia was invited to sign; I had his proxy to do so, but felt it unwise.

There was very great interest, but a very distinct feeling that the result of this ought not to divide the liberal forces especially under the leadership of President Roosevelt; and that the third party would become logical if and when the Democratic Party repudiated the Roosevelt leadership. . . .

I think Phil is deceiving himself a little. . . .

I did gather, however, that the Governor was hopeful of getting substantial support in Minnesota, North Dakota, Iowa and possibly Nebraska. In talking to Phil he did not disguise on the whole that he was hostile to Roosevelt. I pointed out that Roosevelt had to govern the country for the next two years and that I saw no reason for turning over the government to a reactionary group for two years in the hope that the 1940 combination might work out. After the meeting I went and had some beer at La Follette's house and then to take the night train to Chicago. Since I had a date to telephone the President at noon, I could not take any of the planes out of Chicago and hung around both lonely and bored until the time came to leave.

The President obviously had the situation pretty well in hand. He was particularly interested in the report that La Follette wanted to do W.P.A. work by private contract and probably was veering towards segregating and earmarking the P.W.A. and W.P.A. funds. . . .

The understanding is that La Guardia will take a sympathetic and parallel line, but will not go off the deep end on the La Follette situation, which I think is exactly right. The American Labor Party feels the same way.

What La Follette is monkeying with is interesting. The Republican papers are making a tremendous play. It is all to the good so far as they are concerned to play up a third party which in any case will be very weak, and will divide the Democratic Party. . . .

The obvious thing to do here is to have the Administration use the third party as a potential threat to the Democrats who desert a reasonably progressive policy. Since a good many of the President's own men have been going off the reservation very freely, I believe this use might be made of it in some places.

I do not here comment on the La Follette program, which strikes me as interesting, but so little worked out as not to be really subject to analysis. The only clear-cut program is for government ownership of the banking system which I think is sound and will have to come.

For me individually, the situation is a little difficult. I was there representing La Guardia. I am a member of the Roosevelt Administration and likewise a friend of Phil La Follette. The best I can do is to be friendly—which was evidenced by my going out there; and non-committal —which was evidenced by my not signing on the dotted line and wearing the button.

My major preoccupation is that I do not know intellectually where Phil is getting himself. His program actually is so close to that of the Italian fascist that it is simply surprising. But, of course, the Wisconsinites know fascism only as a name and they simply did not see it. Neither did Phil. On the other hand, Phil is a young man who means what he says.

I have a distinct feeling that what is going on is a slow movement for a general realignment. The man who is best equipped to meet the problems is obviously La Guardia. Phil is naive; I doubt if he knows how to handle the labor problem.

May 3, 1938

The appeal Phil made ought not to be underestimated. Curiously, it "took" in the New York financial district, and among the white collar classes. I had Louis Faulkner go out to gather opinions; several younger men have telephoned my New York office about it with enthusiasm. The emphasis Phil laid on production, on permitting recognition of superior ability in contrast to the equalitarian talk of the labor unions, on recognition of individual initiative, were popular. I do not think these people understand the implications of the program outlined by La Follette (I doubt if Phil does); and I cannot imagine Wall Street going along with a program to nationalize the banks. The labor policy has not yet been disclosed. Times are hard, however, and the support it gets from disturbed Conservatives, big and little, seems due in part to political intrigue; but far more to a tropism toward another *catharsis* like that which the country wanted in 1932. Especially there was comment that Phil condemned nobody, but talked of sweeping constructive change.

May 26, 1938

At the moment Washington is divided into a medley of personalities, namely, thinking politically, but with a very strong sub-current of memory about the economic situation. There is a very strong view to which I am inclined that some very thorough-going overhauling of the economic system will be necessary. This is particularly true since the number of unemployed namely concentrated in the southeast section must now approximate (including dependents) some thirty-odd million people. The President has begun to age and is a little bitter; he is inclined to ascribe the difficulty to the efforts of a few bankers and businessmen, not realizing, I think, that practically the entire business class concurs in their view. In a sense he is right. The same thing is happening to him that happened to the Ramsay MacDonald government in England; but the class is too large to individualize.

There are three lines of attack on this situation which are discernible:

The first revolves around the remnant of the Frankfurter group which is extremely powerful because it satisfies the President's desire for some personal villains. This group which includes Corcoran, Cohen, Ickes and a few others propose recreating the anti-trust laws in some fashion so as to create a thoroughly competitive machinery. They are bewildered and angry because organized labor does not spring to the support of this policy not realizing that organized labor prefers the large scale quasi-monopoly groups to the small business.

The second group is quite frankly thinking in terms of some wholesale change. I was invited to head that group yesterday by a number of economists who have been working for the State Department, the Tariff Commission and the Federal Reserve. I promptly declined since such a group if it meant anything would cease to be economic and would become an active political bunch very rapidly; and now is not the time. The measures ought to be worked out and exploded if at all in the 1940 campaign.

The third group believes in making peace with business and letting matters run. Eccles of the Federal Reserve shares this view and I see a good deal in it myself. Cordell Hull, Norman Davis and some of the older men in Congress take this tack. They also are blocked by the insistence of most businessmen that, in substance, every social objective of the New Deal be called off. The wiser men know better, but they are promptly taken into camp by the politicians.

Out of all this it is extremely difficult to make a government; and it is only by great effort that we keep the smouldering of war-fear under cover. Eventually it must come to a political issue within the Democratic Party itself; I presume under cover of the primaries this summer and fall.

In foreign affairs we are actively in the Mexican situation, but we prefer not to have a revolution and to trade out the confiscation of the oil properties. Again the oil companies prefer a revolution, not understanding that they may uncork a civil war of some magnitude. I drafted a possible method for the Mexicans which was merely an endeavor to elaborate a suggestion President [Lázaro] Cárdenas made; we are going to work on Friday with the Mexican Ambassador, who now has authority to deal. But it does not follow that the oil companies will deal.

The European situation coasted the fringes of a war last Sunday. When the Czechs finally mobilized, the British indicated some support of the French; the French said that they would probably fight; the whole having been done because the British were convinced that the Germans had mobilized their troops for a dash into Czechoslovakia. This seems to have been a mistake; and our information indicates no movement of German troops, though there may have been plenty of danger. The problem now is to get the Czechs demobilized, which they, not unnaturally, do not feel like doing while the Germans are talking of dismembering their country. The British make foolish moves, urging the Czechs "to be reasonable," which as far as I can see is simply ridiculous. Someone said that when you want to make the lion lie down with the lamb, there is not much point in beating the lamb.

I rather think this matter will preoccupy most of us for some weeks. Our own influence will be no greater than our ability to handle the economic situation here. The British keep making moves, all of them designed merely to bring the United States into an understanding with them, which actually would probably result in our entering the probable war on the British side; but there is no Colonel House in this Administration to make understandings of that kind behind the back of the State Department and the President. We may have to go to war, but if we do, it will be our own decision and not someone else's.

May 27, 1938

I landed in New York at eight o'clock yesterday morning; had breakfast at my house and cleared up a lot of dictation. I then went to my office. . . .

I invited Sir William Wiseman [of Kuhn, Loeb & Co.] to lunch with me at the Midday Club to discuss Mexican oil. . . .

I went to the meeting of the International Industrial Conference Board and made a speech . . . back to 19th Street and taught my last seminar class, finishing up my Columbia work.

I met Frank Altschul at his apartment. There had been a Republican gathering, all of whom had left (which was why we made the appointment so late). Landon and Hoover had been there and had gone. Altschul was firmly convinced that business was simply disintegrating, that the effect of the falling wheat market and the general financial situation here might lead to a collapse. However, he is always a little of an alarmist and over romantic.*

I caught the train with three minutes to spare at one o'clock, AM.

* Note added later by Berle: "It did not prove so, in the play-off."

June 16, 1938

I worked continuously with Jesse Jones to try to arrange an agreed railroad program up to the time that it became obvious that nothing could be done. We thought we had agreed with Senator [Burton] Wheeler [D., Mont.] on legislation on Monday morning, which would permit R.F.C. aid to the railroads, some improvement to reorganization and the railway employees retirement bill. Senator Wheeler wanted assurance from the White House that he would not be attacked for it. I went to the White House on Tuesday, June 14th, talked to Steve Early [Roosevelt's press secretary], who sent a message in to the President and got back a statement that the President wanted this course followed; he would support it more or less in the press conference that afternoon. Actually he did so.

Senator Wheeler apparently attempted to do this and thought he had the Senate lined up, but when he took matters up with the House leaders, they bucked; the labor people still insisting that there should be a provision denying any aid to a railroad which tried to cut wages. Jesse endeavored to compose the differences, but was unable to do so. Accordingly, the legislation lagged. The President did not wish to recede from his commitment not to hold the Congress in session. . . .

Tuesday night it was apparent that any legislative program would fail. I thereupon got hold of John Barriger and outlined a plan by which the R.F.C. might buy the B. and O. Railroad, exchanging R.F.C. securities for B. and O. bonds at slightly over the market value. John went to work on figures and produced a specimen shot this morning. I saw the President at eleven o'clock. He expressed himself as anxious to have this plan, or something like it, go through and asked that I go to work with Jesse Jones; put a plan in the works and have it ready for him to take up seriously on his return to Washington next week. I pointed out that we would have a string of bankruptcies, culminating in the bankruptcy of the New York Central next January, and that we would be in a bad way. The President agreed and said he hoped we could work out this plan as a demonstration of what could be done so that we would have our work pretty well forward when Congress convenes in January. This, he thought, would stabilize things. He said that he really wanted the railroads handed over to some administrator with instructions to see that they got entirely clear from the I.C.C. . . .

I expect to tackle this with Jesse Jones just as soon as possible.

On May 31, 1938, the State Department transmitted to Canada the draft for "a comprehensive treaty which provides for the planned use of the Great Lakes–St. Lawrence Basin. Such use would make possible development of navigation, and of cheap power." At the New York State Constitutional Convention in June, the New York Power Authority proposed that power and power sites always be vested in the people of the State of New York, an amendment bearing upon the U.S.–Canadian negotiations. Berle appeared in favor of the amendment, representing a large federal interest and La Guardia's position, and as a citizen of the state.

June 30, 1938

I arrived yesterday in New York; met Leland Olds and Frank Walsh [of the New York Power Authority] at the Empire State; worked a little with them on the presentation of the case before the Committee in Albany. At Albany we made the presentation before the Committee on Utilities of the New York State Constitutional Convention.

My impression was that the Niagara-Hudson has the Convention thoroughly sewed up; that is, it has all of the Republican members and probably a decent minority of the old line Democrats. Accordingly, I think it would be necessary for the United States to consider seriously putting in a T.V.A. experiment in New York.

Back to New York and to meet La Guardia; we went to the night session of the National Education Association and afterward had a chance to consider matters.

Politically, we think it desirable to drop out of things in New York State for the time being. One thing, there is nothing that can be done; and, in the second place, there is not a clear enough line as yet.

I raised the question as to foreign policy. We have a blunt situation, in which liberal elements prevailing in domestic policy are likewise insisting on anti-fascist policy, which really extends from the Russian Foreign Office line. This is designed eventually to lead us into inevitable war. La Guardia agreed with me that the prevailing desire in the United States was for peace and that no liberal policy could be expected to survive an ensuing war. Politically, this makes matters difficult since we would have all of the Washington liberals on our necks. . . .

. . . the speech I made before the Constitutional Convention . . . goes pretty far towards committing the Government to tackling a TVA experiment in New York.

July 9, 1938

On Wednesday I had a short chat with the President. His idea of the New York State situation was that it should be kept in complete confusion until he got back. . . .

I offered my resignation. He suggested we hold this and go over the matter as soon as he got back in August; and said some nice things about my work on the recovery business, but was not happy about the State Department. There were, he thought, too many careerists and too little free thinking. I pointed out that a junior Assistant Secretary of State could hardly remedy that situation since he could only mess into things.

We got the groundwork laid for some speeches on the St. Lawrence Treaty in August. It appears that he decided to have Sam Rosenman [New York Supreme Court Justice] instead of Tommy Corcoran prepare the speeches on the western trip; and proposed to change the line from an aggressive attempt to eliminate all his congressional opponents to a rather quiet insistence on principles—which I think is all to the good. . . .

So far as Washington is concerned, the scene is filled with politics, but I cannot see that it makes a great deal of sense. The President wants to liberalize the Party. Corcoran and his friends tried to construe this as making a private club limited to the rather narrow academic progressivism, not too far dissociated from the class war. . . . Further, they have just learned that they have no men. Both Hopkins [Works Progress Administrator] and Jackson are out of the question. This leaves only Ickes. . . . I took occasion to say to the President that this simply could not go on, but I am not inclined to think that the President will—or can—do very much to control howling Harold.

Actually, this is slowly lining up as a duel between Garner leading the conservative forces, Ickes leading the progressive forces and Cordell Hull as a moderate in the middle. I propose to hold my forces because there might be a chance for Fiorello; if not, then for a Hull–La Guardia ticket which at least is a possible result. But it is too early to tell, and a great deal can happen. Since the Corcoran contingent are substantially eliminating themselves in two major states—New York and Ohio—and have lost the progressives like La Follette in Wisconsin and got into trouble in Iowa, I do not see that they can do very much, though they have not yet discovered the fact. But politically, they are not right.

July 16, 1938

It seemed advisable to follow, to some extent, Corcoran's activities in political developments of the next few weeks.

Corcoran is assumed to be speaking for the White House by certain departments. . . .

As far as I can discover, the President knows of this—tacitly and cynically allows it to go on. His theory is that conflict between various elements will produce a logic of events suggesting its own solution and, until that logic emerges, either because the departments decline to cooperate or because public relations make it impossible or because the "boys" lose in their political fight, he will simply await developments.

It is interesting to note that, outside various fields, the "boys" have very little influence. They cannot, for instance, impair the standing of people outside their group at the White House or influence any other department. Their support in the press is not great. . . .

Politically, this group can be dismissed as not important. It has not the confidence of the country, commands no men who are available for election. . . . It is really gambling now on its assumed representation of the President to develop popular support and for its actual mechanics it is relying on the purchase of a few corrupt who need help; and occasionally assistance by perfectly honest progressives or progressive democrats, who are out of things, are trying to get in and, therefore, find chances to stand for nomination and possible election. In both these cases, apparently a perfectly cynical, if not corrupt, use is being made. It is also being made directly in the President's interest where there is a clear-cut situation, such as the Kentucky [primary] election. My impression, accordingly, is that political deals will be made in connection with P.W.A. grants and certainly with W.P.A. officials—and probably with respect to certain S.E.C. transactions provided these can be made quietly and there is no danger of getting into print.

A certain amount of "big business" will be done. This will take the form of flirtations with certain interests, such as United States Steel and others acting through the medium of the Department of Justice and the monopoly investigation. My impression is that Thurman Arnold [Assistant Attorney General] is only on the edges of the political design as yet; and that Jackson is, or in general would like to be, straight, but is slowly entangling himself in a mesh of things. Douglas still thinks he is straight, but by now is so far gone that he is unable to distinguish. Hopkins is doing his best with an essentially impossible situation. The three principals in the group who are worth salvaging, if that is possible, are, respectively, Hopkins, Jackson and Douglas. It would probably be possible to salvage the first two, but I am in doubt about Douglas. In all cases the difficulty is that the men are very clear they are serving the Lord on the progressive line and have completely lost their balance.

One immediate difficulty lies in the fact that this group has become definitely hostile to Secretary Hull. I think the real difficulty is not a divergence of point of view, but the fact that Secretary Hull is becoming increasingly popular as the symbol of what the Democratic Party ought to be like, whereas their own first choice was Jackson and then Ickes.

I am not well informed as to how far the rest of the Administration has played the situation. My impression is that Wallace rather carefully keeps out of it and insists on using his own judgment. . . .

At the moment, the issue appears to be between three groups; the people who are essentially trying to govern, Secretary Hull, Wallace and Morgenthau; and within that frame generally trying to support the President. An old line political group who are working the usual political machinery of the Democratic Party as it has been worked for years.

This younger group, who have no roots in the country, are trying to manufacture them through their control of administrative processes; who are trying to carry out the President's policies if they agree with them and, as far as I can see, are perfectly prepared to carry on under cover when they happen to disagree with them.

To Roosevelt, August 16, 1938

I am enclosing my resignation, in accordance with my conversation. I made the date at your pleasure in September, but I hope to get away for a holiday about September 1st.

There was not sufficient time to go over the whole situation with you so that I merely note the following:

In academic work, I have pioneered certain economic fields. Development of them to a point where they may be useful in social evolution seems to me of major importance. I diverted from this some six years ago because of the crisis; and worked at various public jobs as situations arose. They included the campaign of 1933, the finances of the City of New York in 1934 and 1935, with the attendant reorganization of the City Government. 1936 brought a succession of foreign problems, culminating in the Buenos Aires Conference. This Winter, as you know, the thing that brought me here was the necessity of mobilizing some sort of agreement on a recovery plan—that is, that you would get unanimous advice at least on major outlines. We are getting our recovery.

There is a difference between this kind of work and the sort of thing Jackson is doing. He is working on the progressive thesis of the 90's, which was old in the time of McKinley. The hole in the program is a way of supporting the fifty million more people in a country today who live from the proceeds of a large scale industrial system.

The paramount necessity now is to do some thinking at least one lap ahead of the obvious financial and industrial crisis, which is plainly indicated within the next few years. In feeling this, my views agree with those of Marriner Eccles and Wayne Taylor. If Government can only use ideas which are already pretty well developed and discussed, there is no reason now for staying around except to do State Department administrative work, which twenty other men can do better than I, or the purely sentimental reason of staying by Sumner and the Secretary. Both of them seem to be doing pretty well now that the economic decks are clearing. Also things politically were looking bad last winter. Now they are looking very good; and, in any event, you need your supporters in the states and not in Washington.

My plan is to clear out on or about the first of September. I need hardly say that I will defend you against all your enemies, foreign and domestic.

Roosevelt wrote to Berle from Hyde Park on August 23, accepting his resignation as Assistant Secretary of State "with very real regret." Berle was to leave the department September 15, 1938.

August 29, 1938
     The cables over the weekend indicate that Germany is apparently prepared to invade Czechoslovakia in any event. . . .

September 1, 1938
     Yesterday Ambassador Kennedy was frequently in consultation with high officials of the British Cabinet and the British newspapers were playing up. They are, of course, doing the "solidarity in time of war" act. Meanwhile, Kennedy sent here the draft of a speech to be made tomorrow (September 2nd) in Scotland. One paragraph stated that war was unthinkable and asked the British public whether any dispute was worth the life of a son or a brother. He asked immediate approval.

     [Assistant Secretary of State George] Messersmith and I went out to find the Secretary on the lawn at Woodley. Pierrepont Moffat [Chief,

European Division] was there. We all agreed (a) that we were entirely in sympathy with Kennedy's point of view, but (b) that the paragraph ought to be taken out, first, because it constituted an appeal to Englishmen over the head of the English Government and, second, because they served notice on Germany that, so far as the United States was concerned, Germany could go as far as she liked.

Since Kennedy is apparently beginning to go Walter Hines Page on us and run foreign affairs all by himself, I suggested that the cable be sent to the President and that thereafter the Secretary should discuss it with the President before sending his instruction; and that the instruction should indicate that the President agreed. This plan was adopted and I then telephoned the White House, making the necessary appointments. . . .

Personal memorandum to the President, September 1, 1938

It seems that the dénouement of the German situation will be a move by Hitler, followed by the virtual absorption of some, if not all, of Czechoslovakia. This will be successful and the rest of Europe will back down. But feeling will be intense; subsequent moves will bring recurrent crises. American emotion will steadily rise.

I venture to set down an opposite point of view. All thinking just now is emotional, based on our horror at the methods of Hitler and his group. We, therefore, identify Germany with him. Humanly this is sound. Historically there is a different side. During the Versailles Conference one branch of the American Delegation felt it was a mistake to break up the Austro-Hungarian Empire; and, indeed, the result reached was more dictated by French military considerations than by trained political men. . . . Liberal policy and thought favored . . . reconstitution right down to 1933, preferably in the form of a customs union or other cooperative or federal arrangement. The idea foundered always on the rock of the French support of the Little Entente.

The brief point is that our emotion is obscuring the fact that were the actor anyone other than Hitler, with his cruelty and anti-Semitic feeling, we should regard this as merely reconstituting the old system, undoing the obviously unsound work of Versailles and generally following the line of historical logic.

American emotion ought to be reserved to combat the atrocities rather than by entering a general war to try to maintain a situation which was untenable from the time it was created by the treaties of Versailles and Saint Germain.

I take occasion to send you this memorandum because it is both difficult and even dangerous, in the existing state of emotion among a good many of your group, to set out any view other than that fascism must be vanquished. God knows there is so much to support this view that I hardly blame the people who will let loose personal attacks on anyone who lays out a colder analysis. The Russian Foreign Office, however, is taking all the advantage of that view it can; and the generous emotions of

American liberals are as likely to be abused now as they were in 1914. We have yet to encounter the full weight of British propaganda, should they decide to enter. We have not yet developed a Walter Hines Page or a Colonel House, who will secretly start us on the road to war behind your back and that of the State Department; but there are probably three or four candidates for these roles in the offing.

It seems to me, therefore, that we should be developing a north-south axis, and not be swung off base by either diplomacy or emotion. In this connection, requests from [Foreign Secretary Lord] Halifax to Kennedy asking continual consultation and the similar moves of the French Foreign Office could easily and insensibly make us substantially "an associate power" before we knew it.

Summarized, I doubt if what is happening will precipitate a general war; but if it does, I doubt that Europe will disappear; or that even a successful great Germany will be forever the hideous picture it is today; and I reject the thesis that our intervention would have any results other than those achieved last time.

September 2, 1938

We seem to be making some progress in cobbling the machinery. The Secretary took up with the President the matter of Kennedy's speech in Scotland; likewise the fact that Kennedy had been giving out interviews by long distance telephone to certain American papers. It was gently intimated to Kennedy that it would be well to stick by the regular channels. I am particularly happy because it means that the White House and the Department are working in close formation, as they should. . . .

September 14, 1938

Yesterday afternoon about 4:30 [Ambassador] Bullitt telephoned the Secretary from Paris. The Secretary, Moffat and I listened in.

The Czech Government had rejected the [Sudeten leader Konrad] Henlein ultimatum. Bullitt said the British and French were considering a direct three power conference with the Germans in Berlin tomorrow to see if the matter could be settled directly. Of course, other powers would have to come in. The Secretary agreed to turn it over in his mind whether we could join it. We went out to play croquet and considered the idea, but it seemed plain that we could add little to such a conference. The Secretary invited me to dinner alone at his apartment. He got the President on the telephone about nine o'clock and reported the events of the day. The Secretary also asked the President if he would hold up my resignation until we saw where this came out, which the President promptly agreed to do.

At my suggestion, the Secretary asked the President to issue an order to the various agencies to maintain close liaison with the State Department.

I went home and went to bed, but at midnight Jerome Frank of the Securities and Exchange Commission telephoned. They wanted to establish liaison and to know the situation. I agreed to act for them, as I had already agreed to act for the Federal Reserve. Liquidation largely from London and Amsterdam in the last hour of the stock market was heavy. I urged them to keep their shirts on and not consider closing the exchange though tomorrow (today) showed signs of being a very heavy day. . . .

On September 15, 1938, Roosevelt wrote to Berle: "In view of the European crisis I am withdrawing my previous acceptance of your resignation, to take effect today. I am glad that you can continue as Assistant Secretary of State until such time as the situation becomes less serious."

September 19, 1938

A pretty continuous conference has been going on in the Department here, which might almost be called the "death watch" of Europe. . . .
. . . the Secretary, Messersmith, Moffat, [Political Adviser James] Dunn, [Economic Adviser Herbert] Feis and myself. The added cables made it perfectly plain that Hitler had given an ultimatum, demanding Sudeten territory, that he had likewise virtually demanded that the French and British agree to it and, if possible, that the Czechs agree to it. It was likewise plain that both the French and British Governments would agree, though [French Prime Minister Edouard] Daladier stood out.

Meanwhile the Mexican situation is in a mess. . . . The Mexican Embassy is, to all intents and purposes, not functioning. [Ambassador Josephus] Daniels is afraid that material showing the harshness of Mexican policy will make the Department take a strong stand—so he does not permit his subordinates to send it. As a result, we have to get information on important matters, such as the International Labor Conference, and the International Conference against War and the activities of John L. Lewis, etc. from outside sources, frequently irresponsible and untrustworthy. It ought to be noted that John Lewis seems to have been handling himself extraordinarily well there, according to this information, which I personally believe in that regard.
. . . [The Secretary] agreed that he would tackle the job of Mexican relations at the White House, but might want me to follow up. I told him that this meant some trouble with the "Left Wingers" of the Administration, but there was no hope for it—Mexico was already trading oil for German planes, which would mean undoubtedly German instructors, as well, and we had better get to work towards a solution. . . .

In the event that the Czechs fight, even alone (I think they will), Moffat and I have been reviewing in our minds the possibility of a Presidential call to a general European peace conference. Plainly nothing can be done until the sell-out is complete—but it is just about now. In the event that the Czechs do not accept it and there is a threat of general involvement, I am not convinced that the President might not consider some such move. If he moves before the Czechs have acted one way or the other, it will be assumed to be merely added diplomatic pressure on the Czechs.

September 22, 1938

The Secretary, [Moffat, Dunn] and I met yesterday to check up on the European situation. We all agreed that there was nothing for us to do except to steer clear and keep quiet; there was much danger that various powers involved would try to make us the scape goat for their own weakness; the question as to whether there would or would not be fighting was debated a little. I thought the Czechs would fight and was somewhat surprised to find that Pierrepont Moffat agreed.

This morning we met again; likewise to check up. The Secretary felt strongly that the sacrifice of British and French prestige was so great as to virtually make Germany supreme in Europe, especially that the spectacle of [Neville] Chamberlain going back to deliver the goods was still worse. Norman Davis, who was also present, seemed to agree with this. We all still agreed that it was best to say nothing and steer clear. I raised the point that it seemed now that our line was north and south, that this called for swift action to counter weight the inevitable and immediate growth of movements along the line of the German and Italian idea and probably of intrigue with them; we had as a start Mexico and Cuba. I asked that the Secretary take a little time to consider, with the Latin American Division, all of the various problems raised, with a view to seeing what we could do about it. Norman Davis expressed the view that the good neighbor policy would have to be re-stated. Apparently "good will" is not enough and it had to be implemented to some extent so that, in the name of good will, we did not merely surrender everything we had.

September 26, 1938

Friday, September 21st, in New York, in making arrangements to clear the decks at Columbia. I met Harry Norweb [U.S. Minister to the Dominican Republic] in the afternoon. . . . We talked generally of strengthening our lines in Latin America since it is probable that the immediate result of Hitler's move will be to strengthen the Nazi propaganda there. We ought to be ready to defend.

Saturday in Washington. Sumner Welles is back and I am very glad; although the Corcoran boys are laying down a barrage against him, chiefly to cover their failure to defeat [Senator Millard] Tydings [in the Maryland primary]. . . .

The death watch met again on Sunday [September 23]. The question came up as to whether we could say anything; the President is playing with the idea. A general discussion by the Secretary, Sumner, Norman Davis, Moffat, [Political Adviser Stanley] Hornbeck, Dunn and myself, resulted in my volunteering with Moffat to write the draft. I was anxious that the statement should prove not merely an appeal but a definite suggestion that we would use our good offices in a draft leading to the revision of the Versailles Treaty.

In the afternoon we drafted, taking the draft to the Secretary at the croquet ground. At six o'clock he took it to the President, but thought the idea of revision was too dangerous. We met again in the evening; and about midnight evolved the final draft which appears in the papers this morning. Sumner and the Secretary took it to the President, who okayed it, though the Secretary advised against our tender of good offices as being too dangerous and it was struck out. The result, accordingly, is merely a repetition of the Kellogg-Briand Pact, good as far as it goes, although I am afraid not too effective in this situation. . . .

September 27, 1938
    September 26. The President was enthusiastic about the good reception of the message to Chamberlain, Hitler, et al., which Pierrepont Moffat and I drafted on Sunday.
    September 27 (1:00 p.m.) . . . [Last] evening Hitler's answer to the President came in. Messersmith telephoned the substance of it to the President. In the Secretary's office this morning, the Secretary, Judge Moore, Sumner, Messersmith, Dunn, Moffat, [Legal Adviser Green H.] Hackworth and I met in conference. It was decided (1) to send a telegram instructing all our representatives to request their governments to telegraph Berlin suggesting the continuance of negotiations; (2) to draft a personal appeal from the President to Mussolini; (3) to work out, if possible, an answer to Hitler. Sumner and I were asked to draft this, and he and I took the position that we had to act pretty boldly. We then drafted a proposed message to Hitler, calling a conference at The Hague and stressing the fact that all major questions had been agreed upon, yet war was threatened because precise methods had not been agreed to. Sumner and I drafted independently and then met. His draft was infinitely better; so we substituted the last paragraph of my draft for his last paragraph. The Secretary and Sumner then left for the White House, where they are now. We all of us think there is only one chance in a thousand. . . .

September 27, 1938, 4:00 p.m.
    Immediately after lunch I met the Secretary and Mr. Welles, who were just returning from the White House, the main issue being the sending of a call for a new conference. The Secretary had been depressed over the possible danger arising from quite so bold a step; and had instead instructed Sumner to telephone Bullitt in Paris and Kennedy in London, asking them to sound out Daladier and Chamberlain on the possibility of calling such a conference. In that case a message might be drafted to be sent tonight along the lines of the preliminary memorandum dictated by the Secretary by adding a suggestion that a conference might be called at a neutral European capital. Promise of American participation was omitted, though it was open to the governments involved to attend. The theory of this document was that it was a telegram addressed solely to Hitler in answer to his telegram to the President; and it was to conclude with an emotional rather than a factual appeal.
    Sumner and I thereupon evolved a draft . . . which Sumner and the Secretary were to take up with the President at 4:00 o'clock this afternoon.

September 28, 1938, 10 a.m.

Last night (September 27th) after working out the draft the Secretary and Sumner went over to the White House. The President accepted the draft with a few suggestions. There was a two-hour session on the subject. The report was sent over that the Germans might march last night, in which case the President came up, all standing, and said in that case he would go on the air to tell the facts to the American people. He was much impressed by Chamberlain's speech.

The Secretary went home to bed, and Sumner and I finished revising. The draft was done at 9:00 o'clock, signed by the President at 9:30; sent off at once and given to the newspapers this morning. I note with interest that they miss the main point, which was the proposal that existing negotiations be implemented by a general conference.

The telephone reports from both Bullitt and Kennedy were favorable.

The general view here is that there is practically no hope of averting war. Nevertheless, there is an element of irrationality about it, namely:

(1) The bulk of the question is settled—unless, of course, the real desire is for the domination of continental Europe.

(2) Instead of marching at once, Hitler is waiting until Saturday. This does not make sense. If the issue were closed, why four days for other people to mobilize?

(3) In every case where we move up to the point, Hitler shrinks from the final issue. It looks to me, accordingly, as though there might yet be a dramatic turn to events; but this is wishful thinking.

Adolf Hitler has invited Britain, France and Italy to meet him in a four power conference on the Czech crisis at Munich tomorrow morning Prime Minister Neville Chamberlain informed Commons.

Press Flash

The "break"! Thank God.

10:30 a.m.
Sept. 28

September 30, 1938

Neither Wednesday nor Thursday were particularly active; the matter stands in the hands of the conferring powers at Munich. The cables showing the whole dramatic story of the night of Tuesday, the 27th, make a most amazing story. . . .

The knowledge of the calling of the Munich conference was greeted abroad much as was the armistice of 1918.

Yesterday we merely followed the reports of the conference, which reached an agreement. At 8:00 o'clock last night the Czechoslovakians handed us a note agreeing to observe the general terms and adding that if difficulties should arise, the Czechoslovak Government suggests that the entire dispute be settled by an international conference or be submitted to President Roosevelt.

It is difficult to appraise any one part in the transaction. I note that Stephen Early is indicating publicly that all drafting was done by President Roosevelt, who virtually assumed control of the State Department. Of course, the actual documents show the precise contrary; though the President certainly wanted action. My own idea—that of translating the Nietzschean Uebermensch into a pacific animal—was not without a certain charm. After all, if the superman existed by breaking the bonds of convention, why might he not break the bonds of the convention of war as an instrument for realizing national destiny? Since it is plain that Hitler is merely playing Nietzschean, we might try to take the philosophical discussion one stage further. . . .

To Hull, September 30, 1938

CONFIDENTIAL

. . . There is, plainly, the danger that the Czechoslovak settlement will lead to the same impasse which existed after the Austrian annexation of Bosnia and Herzegovina. There, mobilizations and sudden diplomacy resulted in the granting of the territory to Austria; but every party to the discussion proceeded to arm for the ultimate struggle which came only a few years later. Matters move more swiftly now, and instead of having the five or six years we may have only two or three, or even less.

Plainly, we are not in any position to take an attitude regarding the internal government of the German Reich.

The only line we can take, therefore, is to see if an arrangement cannot be worked out looking toward disarmament. A German government which was not heavily armed would be less of a threat to the outside world. Internally, the Germans will eventually have to settle whether they like the Nazi regime for themselves. Our concern is the possibility which is threatening the peace of the world. . . .

Accordingly, it seems to me that we might consider whether, after the lapse of a brief period of time, the President might not send a new circular message pointing out that a substantial victory for peace had been won; that this could be made permanent only through general settlement implemented by disarmament; that, according to Hitler, substantially all outstanding questions had been solved; that, in consequence, the time was ripe to discuss not an armed truce but a lasting peace and real demobilization.

In such case we might offer to become host to a conference looking toward disarmament, with the understanding that a simultaneous conference to settle existing outstanding questions, if any there were, might be held at the same time and place, to which we would act merely as host. The position should be plain that we do not enter into European political solutions, but do enter into disarmament solutions.

This, plainly, could only be done after sounding out the interested parties. I should be inclined to think that such a conference would be confined to ourselves, Great Britain, France, Germany, Italy, and Poland. In view of the elimination of the Russians, special provisions would have to be conceded to Poland.

At least, I think an idea along this line is worthy of serious consideration.

To Roosevelt, October 6, 1938

You were kind enough to accept my resignation to take effect September 15 last. When it became obvious that a disturbed condition required the presence of a full staff, I of course was only too glad to stand by until matters cleared up, in accordance with your letter to me of September 15.

Happily, the crisis is over, at least for the time being; and there seems to be no reason for not asking for my release. It has been, as always, a privilege to work with the Administration during the exciting and crucial days of the past month.

November 1, 1938

Yesterday I spent half an hour with the President.

He was worried about the Lehman campaign; estimates that he may win by not more than 150,000; is afraid Wagner may lose. He asked whether I could get La Guardia to give some help. I told him I would gladly try to do so; but I hoped that he could protect La Guardia as a party matter. Anyway we will see what we can do.

I took up the problem of the St. Lawrence power negotiations. It seemed to me that we needed a strong representation in Canada. The President thought it would be best to appoint a special commissioner who could come and go to Canada—which is Leland Olds' idea; and he will do this when it is appropriate. It ought to be someone who can drop in and see [Prime Minister William Lyon] Mackenzie King, as the President put it, "every Monday morning".

The question of Spain came up. The President is thinking in large lines. If the Vatican would propose it, he would be prepared to name a three-man commission to govern Spain for a period of months, then gradually to associate Spaniards and so ultimately to bring back a Spanish government. He jokingly suggested that he might appoint someone like me. I stipulated for a battleship to bring home our corpses after the inevitable assassination. Actually, my impression is that something like this was done by Metternich a little over a century ago. . . .

We arranged that my resignation should be put through on return from Lima.

November 7, 1938

Following my conference with the President, I took up in New York with Monsignor York (who has been active in supporting Franco) the possibility as to whether the Catholic Church would ask the President to try to compose the Spanish civil war. To my surprise Father York at once said, "Yes; otherwise Spain becomes like the Sahara desert". He thought it could be done either through the apostolic delegate or through direct representations at Rome. He agreed to talk it over with Bishop [Thomas] Molloy [of Brooklyn]. . . .

Memorandum for the President, November 19, 1938

[Regarding the Spanish armistice:] in view of our changed relations with Germany it will be necessary to associate some South American countries with us; and if possible, make it a unanimous act of the Lima conference. A formula has been prepared which Sumner will probably take up with you. It seems to me that some move is essential. I think that Loyalist Spain would accept; there is a possibility that Franco might, but that if he did not, the knowledge that he had declined would liberate political forces which might force peace within a few months. Further, if he did refuse it would clear the way for changing our position in the matter of the Spanish embargo.

What must be done here is to make sure, if possible, that the Vatican goes along. This would have to be handled while we are en route to Lima.

I feel no possible harm would come from making a strong move; great good might result; and the move works along with your policies whether successful or unsuccessful in immediate effect. The career people feel there is at least an even chance of its being successful.

January 10, 1939

As it turned out we got nowhere. The plan was to have the President ask for an armistice in Spain. Mr. Welles proposed that we have many American nations associate themselves with us in the project.

Secretary Hull at Lima took up a Cuban project in somewhat the same sense; but he was unable to secure agreement. By consequence, the matter died before it was born. . . .

On November 25, Cordell Hull, Berle, and the rest of the American delegation had left for the Inter-American Conference at Lima, Peru. During the twelve-day sea voyage the delegation met regularly. Berle was instrumental in formulating the principle of non-intervention that Hull proclaimed in his opening speech: "Each and all of us desire passionately to live at peace with every nation of the world. But there must not be a shadow of doubt anywhere as to the determination of the American nations not to permit the invasion of this Hemisphere by the armed forces of any power or any possible combination of powers." After the conference, Berle had prepared an official memorandum on the negotiations, dated January 2, 1939, and entered in his diary "the personal and individual sidelights . . . of limited interest." The following are excerpts from these two documents.

We arrived in Lima on the morning of the 7th [of December]. The Secretary made arrangements to visit the head of each delegation, including [Foreign Minister José María Cantilo], who while in Lima was taking active control of the Argentine Delegation. During those visits he undertook to acquaint them with the general point of view of the United States and likewise gave them copies of the American project covering solidarity and also the proposed resolution on economic affairs.

Almost at once intimations were conveyed to me through Dr. [Francisco] Castillo Nájera [Mexican Ambassador to Washington], and through Dr. [Carlos] Salazar of Guatemala, that a group was in process of formation composed of the Caribbean Republics and as many of the northern tier governments as cared to join, co-ordinating their efforts towards a solidarity pact. Of this group Dr. Castillo Nájera was the obvious leader for the time, though later the more aggressive leadership was taken by Columbia through its Minister for Foreign Affairs, Dr. [Luis] López de Mesa. . . .

But before the declaration was approved, lengthy and difficult negotiations were necessary to convince the Argentines, who did not wish to spell out the manner in which the principle of consultation was to be carried out. . . .

The Caribbean bloc, represented by the Mexicans, according to Dr. Sierra [of Mexico], left the Argentines to the United States; and met to develop their own ideas. . . . These, in consultation with the various delegations representing not less than 12 countries, produced a draft.

Before this draft was completed, however, the third Argentine draft of December 20 had come to us in strict confidence from the Chileans. . . .

The blunt fact was that on the night of December 22 every Delegation had agreed except the Argentine, and the Argentine Delegation was without authority to do so but was awaiting instructions from its own Foreign Office; and its own Foreign Office knew that Cantilo was committed to the particular text proposed. . . . [On December 23] the Argentine Delegation received its instructions during the day and signed late that night. Dr. Mello Franco [Chief of the Brazilian Delegation] insisted that he had to secure new instructions though [Brazilian Foreign Minister Oswaldo] Aranha insisted that [Affonso Arinos] Mello Franco had full authority, which I think in fact he did have. On the following day Brazil signed the Declaration which was then in shape for unanimous introduction.

Secretary Hull wished to handle negotiations personally and without assistance so far as possible. I surmise this was because in previous negotiations Sumner Welles had taken so much of the laboring oar that the Secretary felt that he himself was not in control of the situation. Accordingly, for the first 3 days, when the Secretary was endeavoring to persuade the various Delegations to adopt the American point of view, he went alone, usually with George Butler [of the State Department] as interpreter. Since his habit is to talk in terms of generalities rather than to sit down and work on drafts, this produced a general feeling of agreement, but it did not lead to a clean-cut result. Three or four days after the Conference was underway, Dr. Carlos Concha, Minister of Foreign Affairs of Peru, came to me and said that the time had come when the Secretary had to make up his mind as to the text of a draft, and asked if I could help, which, of course, I agreed to do.

We then put together the American draft and circulated it during a plenary session. When the Argentines proposed the counter-draft through

Cantilo, we revised that; and practically all of the experts present agreed that that draft was acceptable. As appears from the memoranda it was subsequently adopted.

During a good deal of the negotiations Secretary Hull lent as heavily on Dr. Concha (who speaks English) as he would have on one of his own Delegation; and Concha so far as I could see never once took the slightest advantage of that position, but worked as closely with the Secretary as if he had been Secretary Hull's junior.

In an article, "After Lima," 28 *Yale Review* 1939, Berle wrote:

In this statement, the continent has begun to attain stature as an international factor. With the essential principles of its own being now in form, it has stated its will to exist without falling under the domination of a non-American system, whether imposed by force or created by ideology; and it has erected for that purpose a machinery of consultation to be carried on through the medium of personal conversations between its foreign ministers, convening at the call of any one of them, sufficient cause existing; and a specific reason for such a consultation is a threat from without.

January 10, 1939
    The Secretary was very kind about the work I had done in Lima on the way back, recognizing as he did to all intents and purposes that the work of the Delegation had to be done by himself, myself and Harry Norweb since the rest of the Delegation were either appointed for political purposes or were composed of international law experts ([Professor Charles G.] Fenwick and Hackworth). These last two did a manful job on the international law points—a limited field which they handled excellently but they were of only limited help on the political and economic work.
    Governor Landon proved a delightful travelling companion and a charming addition. He knew enough to know that he knew nothing of the language of the country or the subject matter, and therefore conceived that his job was to back up the Secretary wherever possible and be as pleasant to everyone as he could. As a result, he was an immense favorite in Lima despite the fact that he knew no Spanish; and successfully conveyed the impression that political differences at home do not mean a divided house when we deal with foreign affairs. This was just what he was there for; he did it admirably. I hope we will meet again soon. . . .

January 10, 1939
    The memorandum of April 1st, 1938 set out the outline of the detail agreement reached between the Federal Reserve Bank, the Treasury and myself as to the recovery program which we would recommend to the President who was at that time at Warm Springs. I have reason to believe that it follows the line which Corcoran and Hopkins are tackling, but it was reached independently. . . . The draft message to Congress, drafted

in the State Department on April 10th, formed the basis with very considerable changes of his subsequent message and radio address.

It was the subject of a battle royal between Hull and Davis on the one hand, and Corcoran, Jackson and Hopkins on the other who wished to declare more severely for a warfare against business. I stood in the middle and as usual had some debates with both sides.

I advised the President that I thought that we could see an upturn in general and a very violent upturn by September or October which it seems worked out.

Memorandum to the President, January 12, 1939

Re: St. Lawrence Waterway.

Things seem to have taken a turn for the better in the St. Lawrence Waterway negotiations . . . intimations have reached us that the Canadian Government is working on an answer to our note proposing a draft treaty and that probably they will suggest that conversations begin at once. I am having prepared the necessary material for those conversations. . . . This, of course, is on the assumption that the unofficial intimations which have reached us turn out to be true. But things seem to be loosening up for the first time.

January 16, 1939

The immediate layout as to the Presidential situation is now getting to be fairly clear.

I spent most of Saturday with La Guardia. The President had talked to him very frankly. He had stated first that he was not interested in a third term; that he had about come to the conclusion that the Convention would nominate a middle-of-the-road man; that he was prepared to accept Hull provided the Convention would nominate a progressive for second place. He named as men who would fill that requirement Hopkins [now Secretary of Commerce], Jackson, La Guardia or [Attorney General Frank] Murphy. La Guardia thought that there was no possibility of his name getting through the Convention. I told him that I thought it was just as possible for him to get through as for any of the other men named. The President encouraged the progressives to say and keep on saying that they would run a third party if the result of the Convention left them no place to go.

It looks like a long shot to me, but the President's strategy is, I think, the only possible course to take under the circumstances.

On Thursday, January 12th, I talked to Sumner Welles. He had been to the inauguration of Governor [Herbert] O'Conor in Maryland, and there he met Jim Farley, who fell on his neck. Farley said that he was fighting the Garner candidacy tooth and nail; that he was gathering in all the delegations he could; and that his own judgment was that these ought to be cast for Secretary Hull. Sumner had the distinct impression that Farley rather hopes for second place for himself.

I talked the matter over with some frankness with Secretary Hull just before we left the boat [returning from Lima]. He has made no move in any direction, but realizes that the time has come when he has to take a position. I pointed out to him that his own desires in the matter probably were not conclusive; no one is big enough to decline a nomination for President.

This gives the general outline of the situation. As things look now it seems to me that Hull is likely to become the major candidate for President with the second place in doubt. Mrs. Hull is not anxious to have him President; she believes that if he turns in a perfect eight years as Secretary of State, that is enough; and that a Presidential term would probably almost kill him. Nevertheless I imagine the course of events will override any desire of this kind, though they are obviously sensible.

January 27, 1939
By now, I have got started on a whole set of more or less intellectual adventures: the French book [L'Homme et la Propriété] is to come out in the next few weeks; the book on the new democratic economy [A Banking System for Capital and Economic Credit, 1939] is beginning to be in type; thanks to Nathan Lobel [former law student] the second edition of the Case Book in Corporation Finance is beginning to come around; and there is always that infernal study of the S.E.C. which I agreed to do some time ago and which now has to be finished up [never finished]. I think we will be able to get them done during these four months and after that it looks now as though Washington and the international situation would swamp us.

January 31, 1939
Chiefly plowing along on the intellectual work. I got hold of Peter Nehemkis. He has been appointed to investigate investment banking in this monopoly business, which, of course, is making no progress whatever. . . .

Hitler's speech is wholly unimportant from the point of view of giving any information on the international side. For one thing, none of the information could be believed even if it were in. What strikes me, however, is his exposition of national economics; his statement that currency depends on production; that the emphasis on production is primary. This is so obviously sound that I merely wonder why it is difficult for other people to accept it. The tragedy is to get as simple and economic an idea as that into practice; all of the rest, crazy Nazi ideology, has to be indulged. Of course, all this is the work of [Dr. Hjalmar] Schacht, who must have done a good job at teaching what economics is all about and how to handle a currency and credit system. I could mention among other things the assumption that the gold theory is as dead as a doornail as far as these people are concerned; I myself think it is as dead as a doornail anyhow.

The fact is slowly emerging that the Russian and the German points of view are moving closer together and are finding common enemies. Bluntly, they are both fighting what they conceive to be a capitalist civilization; and they will both wind up together. In this connection I note Max Lerner's wholly unconvincing differentiation of the Nazi's from the Communist's point of view. Obviously the trick has to be a handling of national economy so as to permit individuals to find their own way of life, without mortgaging those individuals to the mechanics of finance or corporations.

Memorandum for Mr. Nehemkis, SEC, February 3, 1939

Re TNEC: Investigation of Investment Banking.

Investment banking is designed to apply capital to the production of capital goods through sale of securities. It has been assumed that the capital drawn upon was "savings". The system today has to be investigated from the point of view of a financial mechanism which has failed—that is, which does not today apply capital to the construction of capital goods in sufficient volume. The object of the investigation ought to be to lay the foundation for the creation of a system which will accomplish the objective.

My feeling is that the new system will have to draw not only on "savings" in offering an attractive interest rate but also on created bank credit through the operation of existing or specially constructed banking units.

All other phases of the investigation must, I think, be wholly subsidiary to this major objective. . . .

My thought is to sketch out in relatively bold lines the major fact that investment banking today can handle only certain strata of capital application; that capital application is no longer limited to "investment of savings" but includes bank credit; that we have no ordinary way of doing this last, except at the old high interest rates; and thus navigate into existence the general possibility of a capital credit banking system. I believe that the Federal Reserve Bank will chiefly assist in this.

In this connection, it is to be noted that in the forthcoming Federal budget provision is being made for the financing of the capital construction of the government, not as a part of the Federal budget, but by taking their own bonds which are then guaranteed by the government and sold in the open market. This is one step towards the segregation of the capital construction functions of the government from the normal budget. It is also one step towards separating capital construction generally from either the "savings" flow or from the old Federal fiscal system.

February 17, 1939

It is pretty plain that we are moving towards more than a usually bitter political situation.

Yesterday at lunch Portfolio, who is City Treasurer in La Guardia's administration, made it plain that he thought La Guardia had a good chance for the Republican nomination. . . . Meanwhile, of course, Corcoran and the White House left wingers are paying great courtesy to La Guardia. La Guardia himself thinks that the Republicans cannot win without him, which may well be true as of today.

This puts me in considerable dilemma. I do not believe that the White House left wingers can get any of their own people by a Democratic Convention, let alone an outsider like La Guardia. They may be able to force a choice between one or another Democrat, but unless all signs fail they would be in no position to dictate anything. La Guardia's chances for one of the top places therefore exists if at all on the Republican side.

Meanwhile it is fairly plain that the movement to make Cordell Hull President is likely to succeed partly because of his own strength and partly because Farley, who is gathering in delegates for himself, will eventually have to throw in his support to someone else and presumably Hull.

It is no great service to the President to point out to La Guardia that his personal interests lie on the other side of the lot and that the left wingers can use La Guardia, and can do nothing for him.

It is certainly no service to La Guardia to encourage him to play along with the Corcoran bunch knowing that he gets left out in the end. . . .

February 20, 1939

Yesterday I worked in Washington primarily because I was uneasy.

I had breakfast with Peter Nehemkis, who is in charge of the investment banking end of the monopoly study. He and I went over his outlines of procedure which follow fairly closely our own attempt to get the thing lined up in New York. The insurance investigation is coming to an end after a lot of pure foolishness; it got nowhere, proved nothing and apparently irritated everyone. Peter's statement of the gossip is that Douglas will go on the Supreme Court and that he may be succeeded by Jerome Frank. Peter was afraid of this and hoped that the gossip that it would be offered to me would turn out to be true. I told him that I did not want it and that my own impression was that the S.E.C. had become so corroded with politics and possibly a little graft that the successor to Douglas would have a bad time cleaning up. . . .

The Secretary was ill with a cold and I saw him for an hour in bed. We went over all the cables including those of the recent Peruvian revolution and then got to work on the European matter. He felt that the President's statement indicating a possibility of a European crisis in the near future which was based on Bullitt's cable about the Italian and French mobilization was somewhat overdrawn, but agreed with me that it was obviously intended for European consumption. But he felt that the situation was serious. . . .

February 22, 1939

In the evening to preside at the meeting of the Youth Congress in honor of Mrs. Roosevelt. I had a chance to chat both with her and Mrs. James Roosevelt and was somewhat surprised to have Mrs. Roosevelt ask whether in the few minutes before she went on the air with the prepared speech she should tell the truth, the truth being in this case that she thought we had still to solve the fundamental problem; that the problem was economic and not political; that it did not matter much which party was in power, we would still have the major question; that the New Deal had bought time to think, but that the thinking had not been done. I was really excited about this because I have been thinking so myself from the very beginning . . . we presently got to work, but it was odd that as to economic prognosis the agreement was complete. "What it comes to is this", she said, "we have possibly a year or two, or until the next war, whichever comes first, and if we do not get something started by then, we are in for trouble." . . .

March 7, 1939

In Washington yesterday. The city is in a typical second Administration state. Everybody's nerves are on edge and the coherence of the crowd seems to be rapidly disintegrating. The President is apparently encouraging business, having been forced into that position by Garner, and the Cabinet is all for it. If they had stayed by when Cordell Hull and I proposed this last year, the Administration would not be in a position of retreating as it is now.

The Italian demands on France are expected to be pushed this week. The British are angling for a position as mediator similar to that which they held at Munich. The European division, notably Moffat and that group, believes that the heavy barrage will be laid down next week; Sumner thinks perhaps earlier. This will pile up to a climax between the end of the month and early in April. The European division thinks it will be touch and go whether war breaks out; I think the odds are greater in favor of peace than they do. . . .

. . . Meanwhile the Secretary, who has not recovered from his cold, is going South to Florida for ten days during which time the European situation should come to a boil. Sumner is carrying on, but I gather the strain is pretty bad. I will have to go down there next week. However, if the dust dies down by the first of June there may be some chance of steering clear during the summer. . . .

The closing years of a second Administration never were very inspiring.

March 10, 1939

The morning newspapers begin to tackle European affairs with something like prescience for the first time in a month.

The Germans' threat to Holland which happened last January has reached the newspapers via the Paris route just about seven weeks late. Chamberlain's plan to steer toward a disarmament conference (it was also Sumner Welles' plan in 1937) likewise reaches the newspapers. . . .

I think the question that the United States will have to determine is whether it could play any part in a peace conference, for the Central powers simply must attain a status which permits them to live. They can live quite handsomely on a peace basis; they would starve on the existing war basis; but they will use the present position to make all kinds of adjustment we shall not like.

At Wesleyan College the night before last there were something over a thousand people there mainly interested in [Professor of Law Edwin] Borchard's vigorous plea for isolation. I did not agree with some of the innuendos or with his speech, but I was glad he made the speech. A little hard-boiled realism ought to be inserted in the discussions every once in a while. . . .

On the Washington front the throat-cutting . . . is amusing. . . .

The left wingers are, of course, not loyal to anyone except themselves; their ethics are not of the best. It will be interesting to see to whom the President finally turns. My private opinion is that he will try to bring the two groups in line and we shall have an inconclusive result.

March 16, 1939

In Washington yesterday. Various problems of the State Department, where the current view is that the German drive to the east continues substantially unchecked; that the Germans will not materially assist the Italians in their drive against the French. During the day, the news of Hitler's annexation of Bohemia and Moravia came in, giving rise to considerable of a state of mind. . . .

To see the President, and we talked for an hour or more, covering an entire range of matters.

He believes that the Germans will go eastward; that they will not make any agreement with Stalin. . . .

As to the state of the Union, he contemplates calling in a few publishers and employers and asking them, in connection with the so-called "appeasement of business", exactly what concrete (not general) suggestions they have to make, as on: taxation, economy, changes in the S.E.C. Act, etc. He plans, I think, to put them in a hole; they will either have to come through with definite and detailed provisions, or have recourse to vague generalities, and in either case he will have them more or less at his mercy.

I urged him to make a speech which would clear the decks here. He said he had been thinking of that. . . . I tried to indicate that I thought he could not only cover the past, but lay out the issues for the future, and I thought that this could be done in a way which did not further divide the United States, at the same time standing his ground on all points. It was obvious that Corcoran and Cohen had been trying to undermine [Under-Secretary of the Treasury John] Hanes. The President complained bitterly of Morgenthau and Hanes on the tax matters, which they had been discussing that day. . . .

I raised the question of the banking and currency system in connection with the budget. At this point, the President fairly exploded. He said he had worked and worked, but the Treasury made no progress in any matter. He pointed out that the T.V.A. was now a revenue-producer; it could issue its own bonds and put a hundred and fifty millions or so back into the United States Treasury; it could finance its own operations, to a large degree; there were other similar assets of that kind. Their expenses ought to show up in the banking system, and not in the budget: he had been unable to get anybody to move. I asked where was the block on the line. He answered, "In the Treasury", and said he would be everlastingly grateful if I could persuade the Treasury to do something about it. I told him that we had Taylor about convinced, but then he resigned. He asked me to try to tackle it with Hanes.

Now of course the real difficulty is Henry Morgenthau, and everybody knows it; but the President does not want to change that.

Back at the State Department, where a conference had been called by Sumner Welles. (He is Acting Secretary this week.) There were present: George Messersmith, Norman Davis, Pierrepont Moffat, Jimmy Dunn, and myself, together with Sumner Welles. After some sparring, the question was laid on the table as to whether we should not break relations with Germany. Sumner was obviously much disturbed and broken up by the events of the afternoon. . . . Behind all this was the fact that Hitler had given his word, as a part of Munich, not to violate the integrity of the Czech Republic, and now, only a few months later, the whole thing had gone by the board. How, therefore, could anybody deal with a country on that basis?

Messersmith and Davis at once advocated the immediate breach of relations. They thought that the moral principle violated here was so strong that there was little left on which national intercourse could be hung; that if we did not withdraw our Embassy, we probably would be forced out, ungraciously. . . .

Moffat and Dunn, the two careerists, thought otherwise. They said that some representation was better than none; that we could protect the Americans and, to a less extent, the refugees, a little, whereas after a breach we should not be able to protect at all; that the act was not very significant in and of itself; that, logically, we ought to do the same thing with Japan, and so forth.

I tried to analyze. Breaking relations of itself means little; there would follow increasingly strained relations, Nazi excesses, demand for reprisals here, and we should drift slowly into a state of war without shooting. Further, we might excite hopes in France and Great Britain that in case of ultimates we would go to war—a process which Welles, Messersmith and Davis agreed would be futile. If we disappointed those hopes, we should have stimulated a course of action which we were not prepared to see through.

Welles raised the question of our relations in South America; we agreed that if we did nothing German prestige probably would rise.

It was understood that we would reconvene and discuss it over the week-end, at which time Hull would be back, and held everything for the time being. The direct point in all this is that while on the surface there is apparently a good deal of apathy, the State Department, at least, is rapidly getting to the boiling point. I gather the President feels somewhat the same way about it; at all events, Bullitt had been telephoning him during the day. While I was at the White House, the President told me Bullitt had just telephoned: [Georges] Bonnet [French Foreign Minister] had shown him a recently delivered German *aide-mémoire,* saying that France had no need to worry in the matter: no breach of the Munich understanding had been made, because the Czechs had requested the Germans to take over—that is, had voluntarily abandoned their sovereignty. Of course all this is pure tripe: they did it with a gun at their head.

March 17, 1939

At work on various things, but generally turning over in my mind the proposed question of breaking relations with Germany. This is a straight question of whether you can appeal to a moral principle in governing the world, or whether we have to be guided by straight Machiavellian policy. Tomorrow and over the week-end we shall be settling the matter in Washington. The principle seems to be this:

1. Whatever we do, we shall have to go alone. Neither France nor Great Britain can be trusted; they are frightened and unfrank. This is particularly true of the British Government.

2. Any move we make will be the first move in a constant irritating policy which will lead to a modified state of war.

3. In the event that the European situation does explode we are then in the war in any event.

4. There is no use merely irritating. Unless we are prepared to knock out the principle, I do not see that we gain much.

Instead of breaking relations, we could consider at least recognizing the existence of a state of war in Central Europe and imposing the Neutrality Act provisions, which means in practice cutting off all trade with Germany.

On the other side is the fact that slowly but steadily the American people are getting increasingly unhappy. Since we are really attempting to defend the United States against going into the militaristic situation which has dominated Europe during the past century, it may be that we may ultimately develop a policy of standing ready to fight any overmastering imperialist power on the other side of the Atlantic. It is interesting to note that as the discussion goes on our real interests become clearer. We are interested in the Atlantic side and not the Pacific: this is because the Atlantic is no longer wide enough to be a defense against attack; the Pacific still is.

No one here has any illusions that the German Napoleonic machine will not extend itself almost indefinitely; and I suppose this is the year. It looks to me like a hot summer ahead.

March 22, 1939

To Washington on the midnight, arriving Saturday morning. The dust had somewhat died down since it had been pretty well decided not to break relations with Germany (this was right), but instead to decline to recognize the Czecho-Slovak seizure. Sumner had issued his statement after consultation with the President. Secretary Hull is away in Florida; he did not like the statement too well, preferring a more socialized statement which would steer less towards a direct break with Germany and more towards an attempt to be a world arbiter. The fact is that the belligerent party in Washington is making headway; indeed, every bit of German news makes it difficult to do anything else.

Dispatches from Prague give a vague outline of the Czech story. . . .

At work over the week-end on possible legislation giving to the President power to prevent mobilization by Germany or any other country of assets within the United States. As to this there is a war going on between the Treasury and the State Department. The Treasury apparently wants to set up an act which would virtually socialize most of the United States. . . . Sumner and I tried to hammer the legislation into something like successful form. After I got finished with this on Sunday I went over to see Jesse Jones; we talked politics, administration and otherwise, for a couple of hours.

On Monday working on various European phases. The Treasury sent over the list of proposed acts suggested (again from the [General Counsel Herman] Oliphant group) at the time of Munich—a pretty immoral list of perversions of Presidential power, again nominally aimed at Germany, but really designed to shift the whole social structure of the United States. To lunch with Sumner Welles and Oscar Chapman, Assistant Secretary of the Interior, mainly discussing plans to make Cordell Hull President. He looks now like the only Presidential possibility. The division in the Democratic Party is growing so strong that it is practically impossible to reconcile unless, of course, Hull can finally do it.

The European situation meanwhile goes from bad to worse. If I were guessing today I would say that there will be war within four months. . . .

As the situation stands at this minute, Germany is on the march principally to the East; all of the surrounding governments, with the possible exception of Hungary, are consulting to see what if anything they can do. The Russians are devious, as usual, and probably are playing all ends against the middle, intending not to do anything themselves. It is going to come down eventually to a French-English combination with whatever help they can get from the smaller countries; Russia and to a less extent Italy are still an open question.

My leave from the State Department has to all intents and purposes been cancelled so I shall be spending three days a week here and four days in Washington, and I do not like the prospect, but there is nothing to be done about it.

IV

1939~1940

March 23, 1939

The foreign news is all bad and getting worse, for it is perfectly obvious that the Rumanian situation is ready to break. It is true that the Rumanians might put up a fight, but they have practically nothing to fight with; the Germans would probably not do the fighting themselves, but would force the Hungarians to do it for them. There is nothing with which to stop the German drive with the possible exception of a comparatively successful stand in the line of the Transylvanian mountains. It is twenty years ago this month that Rumania with the assistance of the French seized Transylvania and a part of the Banat from Hungary, which was then disarmed. Now the tide rolls back.

The morning newspapers yesterday suggested me for the Chairmanship of the S.E.C. in place of W. O. Douglas, who has been nominated for the Supreme Court. I took occasion through The New York *Times* to let it be known that I was not a candidate for the job, and it appeared this morning. There will be plenty of work to do in the State Department. The reason I did this was a triple one. First, there is no point just now in running into a bitter fight with the Corcoran crowd who want that job for themselves. Second, it is not good for me to be appearing to be a candidate for a job which I do not want. Finally, there is going to be heavy firing in the foreign field; if we can get that job done, all is well; if we cannot, the thing to do is to come home, and stay home. . . .

March 31, 1939

. . . To Washington . . . Monday and spent an unpleasant week. In the first place, there is some strain between Hull and Welles. The real difficulty is that Welles goes frequently to the White House and is considered a thoroughly capable man. Hull tends to be silent, cautious and quiet. He was away during the seizure of Czecho-Slovakia and of course during that period Welles occupied all the headlines. A good many of his friends resented this and I think Welles made a tactical error in not bringing the Secretary's name into the situation. At all events an article came out in the newspapers probably from Hull's quarters indicating that he had dictated the messages over the telephone from Florida which, of course, is not true since the statements were entirely written by Sumner save that the President inserted the word "temporary" before the words "extinguishment of Czecho-Slovakia". At all events, Hull is feeling unhappy and Welles likewise. It was inevitable that it should be so. At Lima, for instance, it was prefectly plain that Hull was rather glad not to have Welles there. There is such a thing as having a too capable Assistant from the point of view of the Chief. Yet actually the men complement each other completely; and it is essential that they work together in complete confidence. Meanwhile, Welles is doing his best to see to it that Hull gets the nomination for the Presidency. When we came to grips with the question, I asked Welles (who was furious with the press statement issued on behalf of Hull) whether he wanted to change his line. Welles immediately said "of course not", so I suppose things will blow over, but it is going to be a difficult piece of buffer work.

For the rest, the usual second Administration disintegration is setting in. The Corcoran-Cohen boys are trying to get themselves permanent jobs since it is already plain that none of them will be even remotely around when the show is over. . . .

. . . While this was going on [General Francisco] Franco took Madrid and the "white terror" now begins, for Franco proposes to shoot or imprison pretty much all the members of the old loyalist government—something like a million in all. We tried to arrange the escape of some of them and I have been working on it for the last couple of days. . . .

The general European situation is slowly going from bad to worse; Sumner thinks there will be war this summer. I am not quite so clear. . . .

April 2, 1939
Mémoire: Foreign Policy of the United States
Events of the past few weeks make it evident that this government may soon have to determine its policy vis-a-vis a climax in foreign affairs, offering at least an even chance of a world war.

We may either:

(1) Await that climax on the side-lines, taking the view that it is, fundamentally, no concern of ours, or the equivalent view that, however great our concern, we can do nothing effective about it;

(2) Await that climax, nominally on the side-lines, but actually giving strong intimations of sympathy to one side or the other—actually, to the British and French, since it is unthinkable that we could find any ground to sympathize with the German or Italian governments as now constituted;

(3) Attempt to anticipate or avoid the climax by endeavoring to pledge the support of the United States in advance to one side or the other: actually, to the Anglo-French combination, augmented by Poland and other parties to the British anti-aggression agreement;

(4) Attempt to prevent the climax by endeavoring to call a peace conference of some kind; or

(5) Attempt to reach an understanding with Russia as to a common attitude in the event of war or threatened war.

I

Were our policy to be the first—noted, that is, a policy of true "neutrality," we should, virtually, be standing squarely on our hemispheric arrangements outlined in the Monroe Doctrine and in the Declaration of Lima. We should, without doubt, have to speed up a great deal of strictly defensive work, since both European contesting groups would seek to establish footholds in this hemisphere, partly for political reasons and largely to assure supplies of materials, food and munitions. Any such foothold, no matter by whom established, would be unfriendly to us: just as the British influence in the Argentine has persistently been directed against the United States, going even to the length of an attempt to break up the Buenos Aires Conference in 1936. In the event of war, we should also have to be prepared to assist the entire continent economically to a degree not yet realized in the United States.

II

The second policy, namely that of neutrality with plain indication of sympathy for the Anglo-French group, is that actually being pursued. Since the American form of government permits no commitment in advance for direct military aid, not even a certainty that munitions will be made available to either side, this sympathy can be manifested only as suggesting an attitude of the Executive branch, with the added possibility that public sentiment in the country might follow the line, and that, after a period of time, the Congress might adopt it also, through a series of discriminatory measures, culminating, possibly, in a declaration of War. This was the history of our entry into the World War, commencing in 1915. Certain measures may be taken by the President under powers delegated for other purposes, though this really involves a perversion of the purposes of the acts delegating these powers. This was the import of the suggestions made by the late Mr. Oliphant and certain of his associates at the time of the Munich crisis: suggestions which the Secretary of the Treasury did not adopt. Inevitably the line of "biased neutrality" is urged by our Ambassadors to Britain and France, just as it was urged on Wilson by Page, and later by House. In the event of a prolonged war, this policy can, in my judgement, end only in one of two ways. Either the country utimately accepts the policy, pushes it to a logical conclusion, and we enter the war; or it repudiates the "bias," seeks actual neutrality, and repudiates the executive. The former is far more probable. Neither is a happy result.

III

The third policy—that is a frank pledge to support one side in the controversy, is possible only if the country is consulted through the medium of some declaration of policy, debate thereon, and Congressional action. This is not usual, since the political issues thus raised afford a golden opportunity for opposition politicians. We are, in consequence, constantly open to the charge made against Sir Edward Grey and his government in 1914, viz: that a clear statement of policy was not made, though, if it had been, the war might not have commenced. This objection is less forceful today than in 1914: for the Imperial German Government was at least a rational group capable of weighing possibilities when presented clearly; whereas the present German government makes many decisions apparently on a basis of emotion and superstition, only thinly coated with a veneer of reasoning. In this respect it resembles the latter part of the Napoleonic phase: its mistakes eventually destroy it, but the inevitability of destruction is no deterrent. The real effect of such a policy would be found in the bracing it would give to the British and French governments: an effect which must be discounted considerably because both those governments appear certain that we will, ultimately, support them in any case.

There is a distinct and major difficulty applicable later to this, and to the previous policies. We do not know, with any accuracy, the real designs of British policy, save in a few particulars. I am wholly unable to accept the Russian Thesis (also held by the Left Wing group in America) that the British Government consciously desires to enthrone a fascist regime in Europe to prevent a general revolution. Yet it is certain that she toyed with the idea of letting the Germans meet the Russians in an East Front war, steering clear herself, just as it seems highly probable that the Russians at the time of Munich, were not wholly averse to seeing an Anglo-French German war, Russia remaining out of it and prepared to bring everything possible into her own orbit at the end. Any real cooperation or understanding between two foreign offices as cynically protective of their own nationalist interests as these two appears to me out of the question, though they might work on parallel lines for brief periods in specific matters. No one acquainted with the Russian government will expect it to decline any opportunity to assist or foment revolution in the internal politics of any country with which it is in alliance, just as no informed person would expect the British government not to take advantage of every chance to strengthen her own commercial and naval position at the expense of any ally. In accepting President Wilson's Fourteen Points, the British Foreign Office did not find it necessary to inform us that she had already made inconsistent commitments through secret treaties which she expected to keep. So, today, we do not know, and probably will not be told, what arrangements she has made or will make in detaching Italy from the Axis by concessions in Spain or Africa, or in detaching Japan by concessions in China, Eastern Siberia, or the islands.

A commitment to prevent Germany from dominating Europe, must contemplate an ultimate rearrangement of Europe, and probably Pacific affairs; for after the war of defence there must be a peace. It follows, that before we determine how far we become involved in the defence of Europe, we ought to know what, if any, ideas have been formulated as to the reconstituted Europe. Not much would be gained, for instance, if central Europe were saved from efficient Nazi tyranny and cruelty (as contrasted with the existing inefficient tyrannies now governing that territory) and were turned over to an equally cruel Russian tyranny; or if much of the

Mediterranean basin were turned over to the now obviously waning Italian dictatorship. . . . In short, if the present German government is destroyed (the necessary first objective of any war of defence against her under these conditions) can we assure ourselves that the ensuing and necessarily weaker government will not again be forced into the same position as were [Foreign Minister Gustav Stresemann, 1923–1929] and his associates? Or that the victorious associated European governments will not, promptly, as in 1919, again create a situation of short-sighted advantage to themselves, leaving our own country less happy, less prosperous, and with the prospect of facing, a few years later, the same or a similar, situation?

It is obvious that no such assurances will be, or can be, forthcoming.

IV

Is there the possibility of calling an effective peace conference—i.e., the prospect of calling a conference capable of taking effective action in advance of the war, instead of after it?

Probably Chamberlain hoped to do so at the time of Munich; possibly Mussolini had a somewhat similar idea. In any event, that conference failed, save as a legalization machinery for Hitler's demands. The assurances he gave, in any case, were promptly broken by the seizure of Czecho-Slovakia in March, 1939. So that any similar conference starts with the assumption (a) that it would merely be a forum for exaggerated German and Italian demands; (b) that no agreements made on the German side would be made in good faith. Against this must be set the fact, however, that were war really at hand, the overwhelming public sentiment in all countries, including Germany, would favor its success on almost any terms. . . .

Yet it must be admitted that the moment for calling any such conference might never arise; and that any such attempt taken at the wrong moment would presumably do more harm than good, as evidencing an interest to yield to further threats of force; that initially it would become possible because of the temporary balance of power, and would then have to bridge the supremely difficult gulf between a situation resting on force, and one finding its base on the general satisfaction of popular desires and needs. Finally, it is an open question whether any government or group of governments has moral standing in today's world sufficient to have the degree of popular confidence which alone could make valid any call to such a conference in the first place, or any decision taken in the second. For the result of such a conference, if successful, would have to approximate a revolution in the present political processes of most of Europe; and particularly in the processes used by the Fascist and Communist powers for their various types of endeavor to interfere with the evolutions of other countries.

We must conclude, then, that the fourth alternative is not to be ruled out, but to recognize its extreme difficulty.

V

The policy of a Russian-American understanding is urged occasionally, chiefly by American liberals. We have no reason to suppose the Russian government has ever interested itself in the matter.

To contribute anything to the peace of the world, such an understanding would have to include an agreement to act jointly, through military and naval action, were war to break out. Since the Russian government cannot act (if she is in condition to act at all, which appears not to be the case) save in the Far East and on her own Western Frontier, this means, in practice, an agreement to make a defensive alliance, in which case we should contribute the overwhelming majority of support. We should range against us, not only the so-called "upper classes," but that huge majority of people in the Western world who see little practical difference between living under a Russian or a Nazi tyranny. Nor could any conceivable Russian government be expected to treat such an understanding as anything other than an opportunity to forward their own type of political penetration.

I conclude that any attempt of the kind suggested is as far out of the question as would be an American-German alliance. There is no such community either of understanding or interest as would make the idea feasible or desirable.

This leaves, as practical possibility either (1) strict neutrality (isolationism) or (2) neutrality weighted in the direction of France and Britain, with probable development toward ultimate association in a war; or (3) possibly, the attempt to reach a stage of conference.

April 5, 1939

The news Monday and Tuesday indicated increased activity in Germany and likewise in Italy. Yet it is not clear that the Italian mobilization on the Brenner and the apparent intent to seize Albania are not directed as much against Germany as in implementation of the axis.

The evening brought confirmation of Italian moves accompanied by a suggestion from Bullitt from Paris that we impose stop orders on all Italian funds. This would be equivalent to lining up in a European war. I telephoned Secretary Hull and asked to see him last evening, and did so; he had anticipated my own feeling in the matter, and had telephoned the President at Warm Springs. It is certainly inadvisable to take any such step now. Even the British and French have not gone so far. . . .

In this connection my own ideas on the subject were set out in a memorandum of April 2. I took up the possibility of a last-minute attempt at a conference with the Secretary last night. He thinks we should continuously explore the possibilities. The timing of any such call would have to be perfect if it were to work at all.

The two speeches for Secretary Hull and for the President for Pan American Day have been duly drafted. The choice seems to be between saying the conventional courteous words, or making a strong declaration. In the existing situation it seems a strong declaration is indicated; but in any event the President is thinking of that because his only instruction was that there should be included the idea of a continental defense. I have drafted in that sense, but have tried to slant the draft towards the possibility of a last-minute move should we be able to see a chance. . . .

April 7, 1939

During the night the Italians decided to land [in Albania] and did so this morning. At my suggestion a meeting was held with Moffat, Dunn, and Hackworth, at which Norman Davis sat in. The Albanian Minister will come in at 3:00 o'clock this afternoon. The problem was whether to treat this in the same manner as the Czechoslovak incident.

The Secretary took the view that irrespective of the technical position the move was one more blow at the peace of the world; and that, in consequence, something would have to be said about it. We could hold over for the day but tomorrow would be another story.

. . . My impression is that the Italian movement indicates that probably the Italians have finally decided to throw in their lot with the Germans for the summer's campaign. Up to now I had hoped that they were seriously considering changing sides.

Yesterday to lunch at the Federal Reserve Bank with Eccles, Ransom, Jerome Frank, [Beardsley] Ruml, and [Elliott] Thurston. We discussed the possibility of drafting a more or less permanent plan of economic reorganization which would have to include revision of banking, revision of taxation, direct use of the productive capacities of government and semi-government instrumentality. Frank and I agreed to draft. The theory was that the safest economic policy to follow would be to have the President set up a complete economic program, propose it to the Congress and stand on it as a political platform if the Congress felt unable to go along. This means a couple of weeks' hard work of drafting. . . .

April 13, 1939

At least sixty out of the last seventy-two hours I have put in at the State Department. The European crisis has been moving in all directions. Substantially, men are massed on every frontier in Europe, and the British and French fleets are in the Ionian Sea. The chance of getting off without a general war is not great.

In this contingency, all of our minds naturally turn to any possibility of moves to prevent it. . . . My memorandum of April 2nd forecast one of them. The President's mind had been working the same way. He had drafted a proposed communication to Hitler and Mussolini which he turned over to Secretary Hull at 5:00 on the day he came back from Warm Springs, that is, on Monday the 10th. Hull, Davis, Moffat and I went into executive session and at 9:00 I left them and redrafted. I drafted two documents: a polite diplomatic communication to Hitler and Mussolini, and a manifesto to the Italian and German people calculated to indicate that they were fools to be lead to the slaughter; and then left it. In the morning I redrafted a sort of combination of the two which I submitted. This was further redrafted by Hull, Davis and Moffat and the Secretary took it up with the President on the afternoon of the 11th. The

President thought it still a little weak and redrafted again that night. I was working on it myself and telephoned the President Tuesday evening. He explained the situation as he saw it very cordially. . . . He was worried about the proposal of the English to send their fleet to Singapore. He pointed out that if they lost the Far East they could take it back; but without the Mediterranean they had nothing. We talked over our own fleet and decided to send the Pacific fleet back to San Diego. In the morning Hull, Davis, Moffat and I went to work again on the President's redraft. I did not like it too well, but it was pretty plain that somebody else had better do the drafting, so I pulled out and came up here to teach my class at Columbia. This will hold until Saturday or I miss my guess.

Meantime I have been preparing a statement of neutrality which is really a general statement on foreign policy. That, however, will hold until next week.

I still cannot help feeling that the British have not been entirely frank with us. There is still something left out of the picture. Nevertheless, they are actually trying to close the circle as rapidly as they can and I hope by tonight the news will indicate that they have done so. . . .

April 14, 1939

Yesterday at work on revising the setup of the Savings Banks Trust Company, and then to lunch with George MacDonald and Byrnes Mac-Donald. They really wanted to ask the attitude of the State Department in the event that the oil companies with which George MacDonald is connected should finance a revolution in Mexico to be headed by [Plutarco Elías] Calles [the exiled former President]. The inducements they gave were that the new government would be conservative; would return American expropriated properties; and would recognize American rights and would open Mexico widely to American capital.

I listened sympathetically and then did my best to dissuade them. I said that I thought any party or revolution so financed would immediately excite the anger of Mexico and, for that matter, all the rest of South America. We had given a pledge not to intervene in Mexican affairs and we meant it. They asked if we could not be unofficial about it. I said that I could not distinguish; in the State Department we try to be frank in our relations—either we did the thing or we did not. This was not a thing we could do. They asked whether, if such a government succeeded to be master of Mexico, we would recognize it. I said that our policy was to recognize any government which actually was a government; but that I feared that government would have to develop a great deal more spontaneous support in Mexico than ever could be developed by the kind of thing they envisaged. . . .

April 15, 1939

I left for New York at midnight on Wednesday.

During Thursday and Friday the redrafting of the message to Mussolini and Hitler continued. My redraft was superseded by the President's redraft of that; a further conference was finally held between the President and Sumner, at which the final draft was evolved.

It is immensely improved. . . .

. . . the general outline, however, of a general conference regarding economics and disarmament accompanied by simultaneous conferences in regard to political matters was preserved. This idea was the same as that proposed by Sumner a year ago last November.

There was some question as to the timing, the Secretary believing that perhaps it might wait another day or two, the President feeling that time was of the essence. It was released, accordingly, at 10:30 this morning.

I thereupon put into effect the arrangements previously made to have it broadcast widely so that it would be received by as much of the German and Italian public as could possibly be reached.

This message, as timed, comes immediately after the President's Pan American Day speech (which came out yesterday substantially in the same text as drafted by me). The authorship of the President's address to Mussolini and Hitler is distinctly and definitely his own. No one added anything to it other than the necessary technical development of the ideas which he himself had definitely worked out.

April 19, 1939

It develops that the plan of giving wide radio publicity to the President's message has had some effect in Italy and in Germany. At all events the news which reaches us via Paris is that the rising tide of public opinion, first, compelled publication of the message in Germany, and second, led to the adoption of the policy of a delayed answer to be made on April 28 by Hitler, instead of an immediate and contemptuous rejection.

[Michael] McDermott [Current Information Chief] arranged to have the Latin American replies radioed to Germany and Italy likewise, thereby spiking the propaganda that South America revolted against the American move.

Cornelius Bull [General Counsel, American Veterans Association] yesterday conceived the idea of having the American veterans organizations issue a statement for European consumption. Having in mind the attempt in the German press to make it appear that the President is alone in his move and that the country is not behind him, I helped him draft; this morning he tells me it appears that all of the veterans organizations will join. In that case we may have a statement from the American veterans of the war addressed to their fellow veterans throughout Europe. I am arranging for prompt broadcasts.

The peace societies likewise have the idea of holding a large meeting. I suggested this for early next week. This also ought to indicate a united America and at the same time emphasize that what is desired is peace and not war, if this can be attained.

Whether all this does any good I cannot say. At lunch today Hugh Wilson indicated that he felt the German Government would not relinquish its theory of lebensraum; that is, that there is no way by which we could get a definitive proposal which would represent a definitive solution. I am afraid that he is right.

Some work with Nehemkis on the proposed investigation of investment banking; to see Brandeis yesterday with him. Mr. Brandeis is seeking an organization of business which develops men; and is now really reminiscing of his early days in New England.

April 20, 1939

The previous memoranda give a rough outline of the picture during the past few days. They do not, however, show the obviously growing tension in the State Department. The only attitude one can take is to endeavor to make sure that the two men [Welles and Hull], neither of whom wishes to indulge in personal considerations at all, continue a smooth working program. Since the crisis is forward, and getting worse, there must be no possible shadow which will impair the effectiveness of the Department.

It is already obvious that the Germans are building up a case to present against the President's note on April 28th. They have asked their representatives in practically all of the European countries to inquire in the foreign offices in those countries whether the country was consulted in advance of the President's note; and whether the country considered itself menaced by Germany. Presumably the speech on the 28th will be a summary of all of the answers. Naturally every country will answer no to both questions since the plain implication is that if they answer yes, the Germans will come down on them like a ton of bricks. The President, I think, plans to see that these inquiries have been thoroughly publicized first. We ourselves are asking these countries to allow the President to make public their attitude toward the peace proposal, which they will do, and to do so just before Hitler's speech, which will knock the ground from under Hitler. On this kind of debating the President can give Hitler cards and spades and beat him.

The only encouraging thing about the picture is that the Germans feel that they have to defeat it.

Actually the telegrams for the last two days show large troop movements in all directions on a rapidly ascending scale. The movements spell only one thing to me—a military move on a tremendous scale. I would think, therefore, that the next phase is war unless several miracles happen, of which there is very little pleasant indication. If it were not for the German inquiries mentioned above, I should have a very real fear that Hitler's speech on the 28th might take the form of a general declaration of war. After that, the consequences are simply incalculable.

Joe Kennedy was scheduled to make a speech in England on the 21st (urging Englishmen not to support a war); I got the President to approve a cablegram stopping him. It was a more than usually foolish speech. On the other hand, the President wants to work out a method of stopping all payments to Germany and Italy presumably as an act of apprisal; but, of course, it will be taken as an act of war in spite of the fact that the Germans did exactly the same thing.

We are getting the neutrality legislation into something that may make sense. Briefly, the plan worked out is: no arms carried on American ships; no American ships in combat areas; all possible restrictions on Americans travelling in combat areas. These, with the continued restrictions on credit to belligerents, about cover the field.

April 21, 1939

The German inquiries noted yesterday have already become public, apparently through Paris.

Mussolini's answer is not nearly as bad as the American headlines make out. If he means what he says, of course, there will be no war. But one cannot help wondering why if that is his intent, he has many hundred thousand men mobilized. A purely pacific intent does not go along with so many armies in the field.

April 24, 1939

After working here late I called the President. I had on my mind the matter of the possible reply to Hitler; the conduct of the investment banking investigation by the SEC; and a suggestion in the event that the chairmanship of the SEC remained tied up. The President was rather anxious to discuss things in general. . . .

As to the headship of the SEC, I made the suggestion that in case the President was stymied, he might consider putting in Martin, the present head of the New York Stock Exchange. Martin has consistently followed the President's policy. . . . It would be an amusing idea to put Martin in as Chairman of the SEC. The Stock Exchange could hardly quarrel with this; the business appeasers would be satisfied or at least stopped; the Old Guard having eliminated Bill from the Stock Exchange would meet him coming back as Chairman of the SEC; and I gather that the New Dealers on the whole think well of Bill. The President roared with laughter; he thought that the idea would be, so far as the Old Guard was concerned, almost sadistic. He added that he was trying to put in Jerome Frank but that he needed one vote at the SEC which he did not have. . . .

He took occasion to be very courteous about the Pan American Day speech, of which he thought extremely well.

April 25, 1939

We shall be heading up for a regular party on federal credit about May 15th and after that anything can happen. This, of course, is provided we navigate the next few days without a war. If war does not come now, we shall have another crisis probably in the middle of August; that one should be about the last. I do not think the nerves of Europe will stand another one; there will have to be either a liquidation in some fashion or a war. I am more hopeful about liquidation than I was.

May 8, 1939

Yesterday in an afternoon session we completed the proposed statement of the Secretary regarding the "Neutrality Act". . . .

May 10, 1939

On Monday, Mayor La Guardia came to town in connection with WPA appropriations and we got together for a half hour. He had been seeing the President, who is feeling unhappy as the political game becomes increasingly troubled.

I told him quite bluntly that my own theory for a winning Democratic ticket was Hull for President and himself as Vice President; also that I could see no other ticket which stood a reasonable chance of success. He does not plan to run for a third term as Mayor in any event. . . .

May 16, 1939

The Neutrality Act moves along. Secretary Hull is now taking up matters personally with Sol Bloom [Chairman, House Foreign Affairs Committee; D., N.Y.] and I think in time will quietly get the kind of Neutrality Act he wants. This is better, it seems to me, than the general debate on foreign policy, though I think Sumner Welles would prefer a more dashing attack. . . .

In the afternoon, working at various things of no particular importance, and then to see Nehemkis and the Monopoly Investigation Committee, who are struggling with the problem of capital flow, capital formation and investment banking. The expert witness will be Alvin Hansen, of Harvard, and I think he ought to be extremely good.

Memorandum for the President, May 10, 1939

The hearings of the Temporary National Economic Committee on investment banking open on May 16. I have been giving the boys some help. While the chairmanship of the SEC is undecided, they seemed to want some.

The plan is to ask the committee by interim report to recommend immediately certain legislation, namely:

1. A Public Works Finance Corporation . . .

2. A bill making credit available to small industry . . .

3. If possible, a bill for regional credit banks along the lines we frequently discussed.

There is a fair chance we could get two or perhaps three of these through at this session.

I hoped you might give this part of the investigation a send-off, by meeting Peter Nehemkis, possibly on Monday; and perhaps issuing a letter or press statement somewhat along the lines attached. . . .

May 19, 1939

. . . Jerome Frank has been duly elected Chairman of the S.E.C.; he is going to have a tough row to hoe, because that outfit is in terrible shape.

May 20, 1939

It now develops that the Labor Department proposes not to extend [Soviet Military Intelligence defector General Walter] Krivitzky's non-immigrant visa, and to deport him. This looks to me suspiciously like Communist manoeuvring through the Labor Department to get Krivitzky out of the country. I do not like the idea. If Krivitzky were a Communist who had deserted the Nazi cause and anyone tried to do the same thing, there would be a howl to high heaven. The point is not that he is attacking Communism, but that anyone should have an influence sufficient to permit the immigration law to be used in one way for one kind of people and in another for another. Actually, both the Communist and the Fascist groups alike are doing their best to make trouble for us.

May 22, 1939

Sunday afternoon, at Judge Moore's garden party, I ran into Mrs. [Ruth] Shipley [Chief, Passport Division]. She wanted some help with the Krivitzky case. Briefly, she has the outlines of evidence indicating fraudulent passports for Earl Browder [General Secretary, American Communist party], Browder's sister, and possibly one other person; she knows, also, that they have a counterfeit seal of the United States; that fifty of the passports issued to the Spanish volunteers were taken by the political commissars and sent to Moscow; and she thinks Krivitzky probably knows how to find them. Accordingly, she wants somebody alongside. I telephoned Isaac Don Levine [journalist], who had been in Washington on Thursday, and we may perhaps be able to find out something. . . .

Without wasting too much sympathy on Krivitzky, who is a former chief of spy service who is turning state's evidence now that he has been thrown out, we still have a major political problem. Passports are extended in due course. They have been extended for [Harry] Bridges, who is an ex-Communist, but he is head of the labor union in the State of Washington. They are apparently being denied Krivitzky because he is doing damage to the Communist Party. This looks to me like trouble, and the problem is to get the facts.

May 23, 1939

Then to the T.N.E.C., where I testified for a mortal hour and a half. Old Senator Borah came and he was very kind. The Memorandum was submitted and I suppose there will be the devil to pay in the newspapers tomorrow morning.

The following article appeared in *Common Sense* for November 1939 with this note by Berle:

This article is a summary of a memorandum presented by the writer to the Temporary National Economic Committee. Its object was to stimulate re-examination of our banking and credit system, with a view to determining whether it could not more effectively connect sound money with sound plans and dreams to get needed work done, to get existing productive capacity into action, and to take the product toward known need. The social demands now made by great groups on the Government must be met and particularly since resources are obviously available to meet them. They can be met either by government spending or by change in the banking mechanisms.

A BANKING SYSTEM FOR CAPITAL CREDIT

Since the United States has at its command all necessary productivity, all necessary technical skill, all necessary energy and labor, and substantially all necessary raw materials, any failure of the economic system must be directly due to malorganization.

In a democratic economy, the processes of finance are in large measure relied upon to make it possible for individuals to organize their energy, the materials obtainable, and other necessary elements to produce and distribute whatever the country may, in reason, desire. I suppose the test of a financial system is whether it approximately accomplishes that purpose. The present system apparently does not, and a major difficulty appears to be in the system of handling capital credit.

Classic finance recognizes the sharp difference between short-term credit and money—the sort of function a commercial bank normally performs, and long-term financing—the kind of thing done by the investment banking houses through bond and stock issues.

The short-term credit field has been evolving continuously and rapidly. During the last century the private commercial banks moved steadily forward. As they did so repeated occasional stoppages of currency and credit forced a steady evolution of their theories and their machinery. The result was the organization of the great European central banks and reserve bank systems developed in the latter half of the nineteenth century, and, in the United States, the creation of the Federal Reserve System in 1914.

Briefly, what happened was the creation of machinery so that the supply of money and short-term credit should keep pace and proportion with the need for it, and yet be kept in rough working relation to the floating supply of current goods and services moving towards consumption or final use. In result, the supply of bank credit and bank deposits (in effect, the power of commercial banks to create and circulate money) is rightly considered as much a part of our monetary system as is currency itself.

By contrast, the long-term credit field has had no comparable development since its appearance at and after the time of the Napoleonic wars. A striking fact is that long-term credit—that is, the type of money which normally goes towards construction, public improvements, and permanent acquisitions to plant through investment—moves in much the same way that it did when the House of Rothschild started selling bonds more than a century ago. We have no really modern system of long-term finance.

Meanwhile, certain academic students have developed major discoveries. Outstanding among them is the fact that long-term capital is by no means a thing apart from money and credit.

The studies of Professor Harold Moulton plainly indicated that the whole theory of long-term credit necessarily had to be revised. His major contribution was the discovery that a large part of what had been assumed to be "savings"—that is, money destined for long-term investment —was not different from any other kind of created bank credit. His conclusion, stated concisely, was that a considerable part of what we had called "savings" consisted merely in an excess of money or bank deposits created through the normal operation of the banks and made available for investment.

I do not think that the revolutionary quality of this discovery has been adequately appreciated. If true, it meant that our ideas on the whole subject of capital and capital credit had to change. For, if capital could be created by creating bank credit, we were released from the irregularities of the flow of so-called "savings." Banking mechanisms could be called on to accomplish at least part, and perhaps more than part, of what had been done by a much less dependable process, and with far less regularity. Capital development can go on though there are no savings; or though owners of those savings decline to invest them and wish to hoard. Moulton's study pointed to a definite reorganization of the banking structure. It at least suggested the possibility that long-term investment might be assisted or carried on through properly controlled banking operations.

Likewise, during the past decade, the work of John Maynard Keynes had indicated the importance of capital financing in a national economy. The point of interest here lies in his demonstration that capital financing directly increases the national income by more than its amount. The "Keynes Multiplier" can roughly be taken as a multiplier of two and one-half to one, meaning that national income is increased by about two and a half times the amount spent on heavy capital construction.

The theory of the "Keynes Multiplier" has been both attacked and defended. My own conclusion is that Keynes' demonstration stands up as a matter of theory. There is evidence, based on the work of Schacht, who put the theory into practice in Germany, that it stands up in practice as well.

It is against that theoretical background that we have to work in undertaking to reappraise our theories of capital credit.

Finally, we have the undisputed fact in the United States that the private capital markets have been in large measure closed since the year 1931. Private markets are not funneling capital funds into capital construction at more than one-third to one-half the rate they were doing in the 1920–1930 decade. This means that private activity in heavy industry is not being continuously generated in sufficient volume to keep those industries busy, or to keep the country continuously on an even economic keel.

The slack has been taken up by government financing. It is entirely beside the point to object to this so long as the situation remains unchanged. Irrespective of political complexion, any government faced with a substantial closure of the capital markets would be forced to take measures to keep the heavy industries and the capital goods markets sufficiently active to provide employment. If the only available method was use of government credit, that method would necessarily be used. To attack government spending as such in this situation is simply to ignore realities.

The danger lies in the fact that if wealth is to be created by creation of government debt, the scope of government enterprise will have to be largely increased. Government will have to enter into the direct financing of activities now supposed to be private; and a continuance of that direct financing must be inevitably that the government ultimately will control and own those activities. Over a period of years, the government would gradually come to own most of the productive plants of the United States. This is certainly so fundamental a change in the course of American life that the decision to make it should be the considered choice of the country, and not the result of a policy of drift. The government's ability to create wealth efficiently is denied by a good many people. It seems to me a good many of these blanket attacks are unjustified; but in any case, it is true that there are vast areas in which the government probably cannot act effectively; and, in a democratic organization of economy, the obvious end should be to permit and require private initiative to do as much of the work as it can, consistent with maintaining the national economy on a reasonably even flow. It is the definite function of the financial system to make this possible at all times.

The conclusion seems inevitable. Either we are on the eve of a change in our financial system; or we are on the eve of a change in our social system.

Plainly, a revised financial system should not be conceived to settle the question of whether the United States becomes a Socialist country, which, of course, I am not advocating. That will be determined partly by economic forces and partly by the thinking and the desires of the country itself. In consequence, the system of finance has to be so adapted that it can serve equally well private enterprise, public enterprise, or a combination of both, and any intermediate forms which may appear. The plan must be flexible enough to permit any development—always provided that the development actually does create added tangible wealth. If private enterprise will do it, and maintain an even and expanding national economy, good; if it is unable to do so, the scheme must be drawn widely enough to tap other methods of organization of wealth.

There has been a major change in the relation of public and private activities. As development of a country progresses, I think it will be found on careful analysis that there is an increased need for wealth of the non-profit type. I think that the need for such wealth increases at a rate faster than the development of the country.

Under the traditional businessman's view, this is not usually considered "wealth." The argument is plainly untenable. In New York there are two bridges: the Brooklyn Bridge, which is free, and the George Washington Bridge, which is a toll bridge. The Brooklyn Bridge makes possible the free flow of traffic from one part of New York to another, and therefore adds to the wealth of the entire city, though it does not charge by the unit, and is supported out of the tax roll. The George Washington Bridge is owned by the Port Authority and pays its way by a standard charge collected from each passing car. It is absurd to say that the Brooklyn Bridge is not "wealth," and that the George Washington Bridge is "wealth," merely because of this difference. It is equally absurd to say that a public hospital is not "wealth" because it serves the area gratis, or nearly so; while a private hospital, which is able to pay its expenses through charges made against its patients, is "wealth." In this sense, wealth is anything which satisfies a recognized need. The advance in technical, demographic and cultural development of the country has apparently brought to the fore recognized social needs with greater rapidity than heretofore. These social needs become a logical field for public capital financing.

The machinery we now have is passive. A businessman with a sufficiently strong imagination and will, and sufficient ability to convince the public that there is possibility of profit, can attract towards his enterprise the capital necessary to construct his plant and set up his organization. He cannot, of course, do this in a field where the need is social rather than commercial, and the initiative rests upon the government—federal, state or local. In this last field, there is a whole mine of initiative which could be tapped, were the financial resources readily available, which they are not.

In any new capital credit setup, accordingly, there ought to be not merely a passive mechanism which can be made available; but an active group recognizing the responsibility for filling certain needs of the community, and for finding the means and the men who can fill those needs, and for putting at their resources the capital necessary to do so.

Even a brief review of the major elements tends to indicate the line of solution. In essence it suggests creation of a capital credit banking system which can do for the country what the revised commercial banking system has done in the short-term credit and strict currency field.

It would appear that such a banking system must meet certain major requirements:

(1) It must make available at all times an adequate supply of cash for "investment" purposes, for the purpose of construction of net tangible additions to the wealth of the country. Such cash may be savings withdrawn from the ordinary currency and short-term credit supply; or may be bank credit created for the purpose; or may be a combination of both.

(2) The interest rates must be flexible—that is, adjustable to the need which the country at any given time may have to stimulate capital construction.

(3) As a corollary to that, it is probably necessary that the interest rate should be selective. There may be every reason for asking four or even five per cent return from a commercial enterprise; but there should be the possibility of charging, say, one-eighth of one per cent for a non-commercial enterprise, such as a hospital.

(4) The amortization rate of any loan must be such that the loan will be paid within the life of the asset created by it.

(5) Because a capital credit banking system of this sort must serve

public as well as private ends, it cannot be exclusively in private control. Conceivably, it may be wholly under public control; conceivably, it may have units both private and public.

It must be rigidly non-political. We have been in the frying pan of having the flow of investment credit used in large measure to build up private positions of power; and the resulting dangers are obvious. This is not a reason for jumping into the fire of a public institution under political control whereby a politician uses the mechanism to build up his power instead.

Finally, the capital credit banking system must justify its existence as much by enlarging the basis for capital operations, as by supplying the capital operations which are now conventional. Probably the most constructive contribution it will make will be opening up a new layer of enterprise, which is not now comprehended within the private profit field. For this reason, I have ventured to emphasize the quasi-public and public elements involved. A single illustration may suffice.

According to the hospital survey of New York (United Hospital Fund of New York, 1938), New York City alone will need, over the next twenty years, in capital construction for hospitals (land, buildings and equipment) an investment of $428,000,000. This is not to create a millennium, but to keep the health plant of New York City approximately at par.

Humanitarianism aside, this represents a possible construction market of nearly half a billion dollars in a single activity, and in a single city. It is simply absurd to say that there is no outlet for capital constructive ability with this sort of need in existence. It is possible over a period of, say, thirty or forty years—within the life of the hospitals—for New York City to borrow and repay a half billion dollars. It is probably not possible for it to borrow and repay a billion dollars—the amount of capital construction doubled by the interest rate—without sacrificing a huge amount of other, needed, construction. Eliminate the interest rate, and you have uncovered a new market. It is true that instead of being organized by a private enterpriser, this new market is organized and put into action by public or semi-public bodies; but the economic effect of this construction is quite as great as though a private enterpriser had decided to build a half-billion-dollar railroad.

It is sometimes said that any idea of capital credit banking is "radical." This, though not argument, is worth a word of examination. Actually, it will be found that most business men engaged in actual production—that is, business men who are not in banking—are pretty clear themselves that there must be some radical overhauling of the banking system. Faced with the constriction of economic activity as it flows through the bottleneck of finance-capitalism as at present organized, they seek avenues of escape.

The "radicalism" of the suggestion fundamentally lies only in a single field. Control over economic expansion today lies chiefly in certain groups mainly allied with the investment banking operation. Development of capital credit banking undoubtedly does shift that control. New centers are set up; centers which should be more responsible to the public, and carried on by groups which, by their nature, assume greater responsibility for maintaining a continuous economic flow.

No mere change of the capital banking system will supply the ultimate and basic need for men and organisms whose actual business is organizing production for the creation of useful wealth. The drive which sets men to work is quite as much moral as financial. Plenty of energy certainly exists in the United States. Work like that of La Guardia in New York, of Nathan Straus in the housing field, of Lilienthal and Morgan in the electric power field, efforts of hosts of men in less spectacular areas is quite as significant, today, as the work of a Harriman, a Huntington or a Carnegie of yesterday.

May 26, 1939

Yesterday at work, partly on the proposed Neutrality statement, which the Secretary is not too anxious to deliver, feeling that it may do more harm than good; partly on the proposed statement about Zionists. Quite a bit of mail as a result of the testimony before the T.N.E.C. In the afternoon I went over to the White House with Wallace Murray [Chief, Near Eastern Affairs Division] and for three-quarters of an hour we discussed the state of affairs with the President. The President did not like the proposed State Department release about Palestine, saying concisely that the mandate was not going to be modified substantially for five years; but he doubted the present situation would last five years and that we might cross the Palestine bridge when we came to it, instead of now. The Zionist pressure politically he did not think amounted to anything; and if the pressure group was on Congress, let it stay there. He suggested a brief, one-page statement, which I drafted later. He was quite aware of the rising Arab feeling, but he thought that that could be handled by spending a little money in some appropriate way for use by way of purchasing farms or driving wells, or anything of the kind, so that any Arab who really felt himself pushed out of the city could go somewhere else. . . .

Murray left, and we talked over a more general range. The President told me that he had arranged the tax matters with the Treasury and the Congress leaders. . . . The Treasury had gone along. He seemed happy about my shot at the T.N.E.C.; said we ought to get those bills in order during the summer and be prepared to shoot them likewise. . . .

Regarding neutrality, he said he had taken a strong line with the Congressmen to whom he had talked. He had pointed out that in the event of war, there was at least an even chance that the Germans and Italians might win. In that case, their first act would be either to seize the British navy or to put it out of action. They would then go ahead and establish trade relations with the South American countries and Mexico, put instructors in their armies, and the like. They would probably not touch the British or French or Dutch islands in this hemisphere. But at the end of a very short time we should find ourselves surrounded by hostile states in this hemisphere. Further, the Japanese, who "always like to play with the big boys," would probably go into a hard and fast alliance.

The combined German and Italian navies are about equal to ours; the Japanese is eighty per cent of ours; and the temptation to them would always be to try another quick war with us, if we got rough about their South American penetration.

This he described as possibility only; but a possibility no far-sighted statesman could afford to permit. His job was to make sure that that kind of possibility could not happen. Accordingly, he had urged the repeal of Section I of the present Neutrality Act (embargo of arms) as the greatest single step the Congress could take towards the preservation of peace.

He had already talked over the line which the Secretary is taking and wholly approved of it. . . .

May 27, 1939

Yesterday a full day. We cleared the Zionist statement in the morning, and started that along. We put the Neutrality statement in final form and shipped it along to the White House, where I thought it would be well received. This morning, in fact, it came back: the President thought it excellent, and so we can clear on that. I presume it will go to the public today. . . .

Lunch yesterday with Sumner. He had been seeing something of the President; but meeting Tommy Corcoran and refusing to speak to him. He said he had come to the conclusion that if his relations were so tenuous that they required that he fawn on Corcoran, as Morgenthau does, they had better go by the board; which, of course, has been my own feeling for years. He is anxious that we should work up an intellectual program for what is left of the New Deal, either for adoption or for the purpose of the 1940 campaign. . . .

Corcoran sent along Jay Franklin [commentator, author] to Sumner, to find out whether Sumner would join in the "draft Roosevelt for a third term" movement. Sumner courteously declined, but he took it up with the President. The President got emotional about it. He said he had nothing to do with third term talk; he did not consider it; did not want it; and was violently and vividly opposed to it. This is, of course, obvious, since a third term movement would discredit everything he has done, which would be interpreted as merely serving his ambition. The Corcoran crowd naturally want a third term, because with anyone else in the White House they would not be allowed within fifty miles of Washington.

June 1, 1939

Yesterday at work chiefly on the neutrality legislation; in the late afternoon, Representative Bloom brought down a number of the members of his Committee, including [Pete] Jarman [D., Ala.], [John] Kee [D., W.Va.], Luther Johnson [D., Tex.], etc. They seemed to feel sure that they could get a majority in Committee for a bill embodying the Secretary's proposals. Bloom had introduced, on May 29th, a bill embodying the general ideas; we worked a little on cleaning up the language. I feel that we are coming along. The job seems to be saturating the whole situation with the necessary arguments.

This morning Sumner told me that the President had asked [Speaker William] Bankhead [D., Ala.] and Rayburn to take a poll on the matter and I suppose we shall know within a day or so about how the House will line up. My own guess is that the bill will get through both houses without too much difficulty. This will be at least one job behind us. . . .

The Russians have now thrown down the proposed Franco-English alliance, though negotiations continue. My private hunch is that the Russians will not sign any alliance but will keep the British and French dangling, meanwhile dickering a little with the Germans behind the curtain somewhere. This is a case where a cynical Russian office meets an equally cynical British office. The danger is that in one of their comings apart the Germans may decide the time has come to move. Private advices from Poland suggest that the probable time of moving will be late July—which looks like another mid-summer crisis. Until that time, things will probably be very slow on the surface. . . .

An event of minor international importance occurred yesterday. Secretary Hull and Hornbeck were engaged in a hand-to-hand croquet match: Cassius Clay [Assistant General Counsel, R.F.C.; Berle's brother-in-law] and [his wife] Mimi had come over, bringing with them their Scotty puppy. The puppy bolted for the croquet ground, caught one of the Secretary's best long shots on the fly, and completely wrecked that game before anyone could recover. This amused the children hugely, but not the Secretary, who takes his croquet seriously.

June 6, 1939

We are engaged now in assembling material for the big debate on the Neutrality Act. This will have two phases, one in the House and another in the Senate and unless all signs fail, it will be a job of some proportions. I do not feel certain, yet, as to the outcome, though I think we shall work out of it fairly well. The House Committee seems to be voting on straight party lines. Curiously, it is the New Dealers in the House who are making most of the trouble.

Politically, things are moving towards something of a climax. The Garner people announced their drive. This has been countered by a gang revolving around Ickes and Corcoran, who are putting a third term movement into the field in some proportions. It is said they have tacit White House support, though I doubt this. My sweet and cynical Caesar has just the kind of sense of humor to realize that this would keep a great deal of the Administration in line through sheer fear lest they catch the wrong horse, and let it run, without saying very much one way or the other. Also, knowing the way he works, I am pretty clear that this is a case where Ickes and Corcoran are trying to go out on the end of the limb, believing that the President will take care of them—or rather, not saw them off. Yet it has its extreme dangers. For the Corcoran-Ickes crowd have no particular roots or respect in the country; they really want to keep themselves in power; they have no program; they represent virtually a war party, which the country does not support. To the extent there is such a thing as a confession of faith, it is found in Ickes' article in *Look*, which is, in the main, a venomous attack on pretty much all his associates in the Administration. This plays directly into the hands of the Garner faction, who will probably try to control the nomination for Garner and then vote Republican anyhow. It is a bad set-up and I do not know what, if anything, can be done about it.

To La Guardia, June 6, 1939

The political situation here is beginning to move into a singularly entangled phase. A "Draft Roosevelt for the Third Term" movement is being stimulated primarily by Ickes and by Corcoran, and will, I presume, emerge as some sort of organization, nominally to perpetuate New Deal ideas but really for strictly political purposes. . . .

. . . My fear is that from now on the whole debate will go on the merits of a third term and everything we have tried to do will be forgotten in that singularly sterile issue.

On this layout, all that I can think of doing is to try to keep a position which makes it possible to talk to both sides, in the hope that the extremists on both sides will play themselves off the stage and eventually the solid middle ground, which is progressive, though not extremist, will make itself felt. If it were desired merely to have a minority progressive movement as the final result, that is one thing; but if the desire is to govern the United States, the problem of a politician has to be to get a good working majority of the Party moving in its direction.

The pity of it is that the move towards progressive organization would have been logical and tremendously effective if it had been tackled in 1933 or 1934. But as we found out to our cost, nobody was prepared to do it at that time. I also think that these people are being pretty unjust to Garner; but fairness is not their forte. My private opinion is that it would be well for you to steer clear of any entanglements just now, and make and retain as many friends as you can. Eventually, your own voice will probably decide what ticket can be considered as both progressive and realist; and I think you can build up a little to the point where, some time next year, you make the speech that settles the issue. . . .

June 12, 1939

Over Saturday, Sunday and Monday, we cooked up a pretty full libretto for the debate on the Neutrality Act. This morning I talked to Sam Rayburn, the House leader, about it. Rayburn is by no means clear that the bill will go through, though it will be reported out probably tomorrow. He is anxious to know whether Secretary Hull would not like to have a careful poll of the House taken; and then decide whether he wishes to put the measure to a vote. If it is going to be beaten, the Secretary might not wish to have the vote taken at all.

I personally think the bill will go through the House, in any event. Also, before the poll is taken, someone, preferably Speaker Bankhead, ought to make it clear that this is an Administration measure. A good many people will vote "Yes" if they know it is an Administration measure.

Welles insists that the President has no desire for a third term and that the third term racket is mainly beaten up from outside. I hope so. I should hate to admit that the last eight years have left the collection of policies in which the country is now embarked resting solely on the shoulders of a single man. . . .

June 17, 1939

On Monday I went to see Sam Rayburn to arrange about getting into the hands of various Congressmen "memoranda" (really speeches) which they can use in supporting the change in the Neutrality Act. Rayburn is not so sure about its getting through the House, but I think he had been giving his attention to other matters. We talked easily of old Brain Trust days; then I expressed my regret that the Corcoran crowd had succeeded in antagonizing so much of the Democratic party. With this he cordially agreed, pointing out that practically all of the legislation had got through because Garner had put it through for them; and that now Garner was being held up to every kind of insult and obloquy. He spoke of Hull in the highest terms. I told him I would try to keep a little in touch with him, to see if we could not reduce this quarrel to manageable proportions and eventually get it settled up. . . .

Wednesday, again on Capitol Hill, this time to see Senator [Alexander] Wiley [R., Wisc.], who wanted some stuff on neutrality. He had likewise inserted in the *Congressional Record* a particularly unpleasant article from the Milwaukee *Journal* on my alleged revolutionary tendencies. This came out at the end of a pleasant lunch; when I told him the Milwaukee *Journal* had very courteously corrected it, he agreed to insert the correction in the *Congressional Record,* too, which I believe he has since done. He is a Wisconsin Senator from up-country; used to be the chief lawyer and banker in a small town; tries to be fair and I think is very decent. Naturally, he has a political question on his hands, for Wisconsin is heavily German. . . .

Morgenthau turned up on Thursday and served notice on the Secretary that he hoped I would discuss any further financial ideas with him. This I should be very glad to do. . . .

To play croquet with the Secretary, and he won the game.

The Latvian Minister, Dr. [Alfred] Bilmanis, came in to see me to discuss the structure of Latvia. He is a solid, square-set farmer, very honest and very straight, very anxious that his country should be let alone and not guaranteed by anyone in this Anglo-French-Russian negotiation for an anti-aggression pact. He points out that they have several acres of non-aggression guarantees already and don't seem to gain anything, and he considers that the new one will add very little to the discussion. I said nothing about this, but my private opinion is that he is dead right.

Chatting with [Constantine] Oumansky, the Russian Ambassador, the other day, I am pretty clearly of the opinion that the Russians do not mean to sign anything.

Jobs for the next few days: completing the settling of neutrality; straightening out the new railroad legislation; picking up the Far Eastern situation because Hornbeck has gone away.

June 21, 1939

Saturday morning (June 17th) on various jobs and then to work on the proposed Japanese note with the Secretary, Max Hamilton [Chief, Far Eastern Affairs Division], Dunn and Welles.* The British were pressing heavily for an indication that we were going to do something about it, presumably associate ourselves with them, or more likely get out a little in front. (This is pure irony. When Stimson, in 1931, tried to get the British to join in protesting against the Japanese seizure of Manchuria, they left him flat. Now they are begging for help. Saying "I told you so", however, does no good in this business.) We got the note pretty well forward and knocked off at 3:30.

To work at it again Sunday morning (June 18th). The Secretary had thought things over during the night and decided that he did not wish to be rushed; therefore that the note could wait over while he watched development. Instead, he evolved the policy of putting out a brief press statement indicating interest, which would prevent our German and Italian friends from putting it about that the United States had parted company with Great Britain.

On Monday, June 19th, I recobbled the note, but I think not a very good job; at 12:15 to join the squad in welcoming General [Pedro Aurélio de Goes] Monteiro [of Brazil]. The War Department was out in force. . . . To Annapolis, where General Goes Monteiro disembarked, along with General [George C.] Marshall. (Marshall is the new Chief of Staff; [Malin] Craig retires next week). . . .

[Marshall] said . . . that the army, including Goes Monteiro, was a little offish and that our real task should be to try to convert General Goes Monteiro . . . we discussed American preparations. He said the important thing in preparation these days was materiel; that we had now got the money and at the end of 18 months or two years we should be in a position to be the decisive factor in almost any conflict. As to the Far East, he agreed with Craig that we could do nothing, that we must not get pushed into the front line trench by the British; that the whole system of concessions was doomed, anyway; that we should probably have to meet the Far Eastern situation later. He apparently had been entertained almost to death in Brazil, where they scarcely left him a moment to dress or sleep.

. . . then to Sumner Welles' house in Oxon Hill, where there was an informal buffet dinner for the Little Cabinet, with the President as guest of honor; the President in fine form; but I was dog-tired and could not add much. Somebody touched lightly on the third term. He animadverted to Theodore Roosevelt's statement about the cup of coffee (T.R. said two cups of coffee were enough for breakfast, and in 1912 he said that he had meant he did not want another cup of coffee then, but had not committed himself that he never would want another); wound up by saying that next year this time we should be discussing the formation of a "liberal democracy". This means, to me, that he will not run a third time but will be on a majestic fight for a liberal Democratic party. His plan in Wisconsin was to get a joint Progressive and Democratic nomination for Bob La Follette and put Phil La Follette "on probation" for two years. "He is young yet," said the President. . . .

A very considerable amount of mail from all over the country about reorganization of the banking structure; the White House is beginning to get interested; and while I doubt if we get much in the way of legislation, I think we shall get a study committee and an issue for next year.

Meanwhile, to unsnarl the railroad legislation. . . .

* The long note, which was never formally submitted to Tokyo, mentioned Japan's provocative activities at Tientsin and asserted America's concern about Japan's "new order" in China.

June 23, 1939

Various jobs, chiefly in connection with neutrality, and the Far Eastern situation. As to neutrality, Ben Stern [Secretary to Senator Frederick Van Nuys (D. Ind.)] has been keeping me informed. There are a great many letters coming in to Congressmen, chiefly from Father Coughlin's crowd, and from the Irish districts, especially Brooklyn, where I rather gather my old friend, Monsignor York, and Father Coughlin are getting themselves deeper into politics than they really know. Apparently a small-sized Fascist center has been developed up there, getting its contact through the Franco government sources. . . .

This morning Isaac Don Levine came in to see me at my request. I suggested that he get into touch with Mrs. Shipley in New York and make an arrangement to have Krivitzky talk to her. She has the pictures and assumed names of a good many people using our passports who probably were Russian agents and whom Krivitzky would know. Levine has likewise tracked down the Soviet government's attempt to counterfeit American money in 1929–1932. . . . Krivitzky knew about it because he thought it was foolish; would be discovered; and protested against it, I gather on grounds of expediency rather than morals. According to him, there are two Communist "underground" centers operating here, one having to do with labor circles and fed from the Left Wing group of the C.I.O. (John Lewis is not involved but I am afraid some of his associates are. I wonder about Lee Pressman?) The other has to do with political and military intelligence. . . .

There is some possibility that an attempt may be made to either kidnap or kill Krivitzky; at all events, Levine thinks so. . . .

June 26, 1939

The cables this morning are disturbing. My guess is that in Germany they are beginning to beat the tom-toms for a final work-up to a war psychology. Hitler has had his generals and advisers at Berchtesgaden, and I vaguely suspect that we are heading into the coda that leads to the final crash chord.

To President Nicholas Murray Butler, Columbia University, June 24, 1939

As I think Dean Smith has told you, I have written to him for a leave of absence. . . . Secretary Hull has asked that I stay here until the situation shall become less serious. . . . I endeavored to see whether it would not be possible to commute, teaching my courses as usual; but when times are full of stress, the result of that usually is that full justice is not done to either job.

In justice to Dean Smith, I asked him whether he would prefer to have a resignation, a step which I do not wish to take but which might be forced if the demands of the country unduly upset the work of the Law School, which must be his first concern. The leave of absence suggested itself to him as a more useful step; and I accordingly make this application.

Butler authorized the leave of absence.

June 27, 1939

Monday, June 26th, chiefly at work on the Japanese note; we finally decided to finish it up and went to work on that basis. Accordingly, I redictated half of it in the afternoon; Sumner Welles and Max Hamilton and I polished it toward the end of the day and we got it, we thought, in fair shape. During the afternoon, Sumner and the Secretary had been conferring about the Far Eastern situation; they were pretty well convinced that a move in Europe was imminent; that the best thing to be done was to try to keep the Japanese out of it; and reached a tentative decision to push the fleet into Pearl Harbor. . . .

June 28, 1939

At work yesterday on the Far Eastern situation, which is shifting with great rapidity; likewise, a somewhat disturbing situation in Europe. There is at least some ground for the belief that both the French and the British are preparing to "appease" the Germans, this time on the theory that they were unable to get the necessary assurances from the United States. Of course they cannot get any such assurances, and are not going to.

My own emotions are pretty mixed about this. Readjustments in Central Europe are apparently necessary. On the other hand, they will inevitably be the basis for a still greater imperialist movement. If the result is to create an intolerably strong German-Italian empire, I should guess that it would be only a question of time—two or three years, perhaps—before they undertook to crush England, with whom they must inevitably come into conflict on both commercial and imperial lines. We have no necessary interest in defending the British Empire, aside from the fact that we prefer the British as against the German method of running an empire. But we do have a very real and solid interest in having the British, and not the Germans, dominant in the Atlantic. The minute that starts, we shall be meeting imperialist schemes in South and Central America, not on a paper basis, as we do now, but backed up by an extremely strong naval and military force. This can only mean that the next phase of the United States will be militarist and no mistake about it; or, still worse, that we shall be forced into empire to preserve ourselves, much as the British were. . . .

June 29, 1939

This morning, more work on the Far Eastern note, which we think ought to be sent off promptly.

During the morning, Isaac Don Levine telephoned to say that a notice for the deportation of Krivitzky, apparently dated as of May 2, eight weeks ago, has just been served. The Communists seem to have got to him at last. I could only say that there was no reason now why he should not say anything he wished to to the newspapers; at all events, I could not advise him to be silent. It is a case for a lawyer.

[Diary, February 10, 1941: General Krivitzky was murdered in Washington today. This is an OGPU job. It means that the murder squad which operated so handily in Paris and in Berlin is now operating in New York and Washington. This is not a good idea.]

June 30, 1939

Still on the Far Eastern matters, and on Western Europe, which looks as though the pot were beginning to boil over. Jimmy Dunn, the Political Adviser, says he does not see a war in this—merely a Danzig coup—but I, personally, am not so certain.

The debate on the Neutrality Act went on yesterday; and last night an amendment was adopted putting in the arms embargo. It is one of these things that makes you tired. The night session had lasted until 11:30; a hundred Democratic members had gone home; half of those there had not discovered what it was all about; and the whole thing has to be untangled again this morning—if it can be.

The horrible thing about all this is that about all the Germans need to know to consider that their hour has arrived is (a) that the Anglo-Russian alliance has failed; (b) that supplies cannot be had from here. I think they are pretty clear about (a) already; and the Congress of the United States is doing its level best to demonstrate (b). How many people do we have to kill on this kind of foolishness?

July 27, 1939

Three weeks holiday in the hills, until Monday, chiefly making hay, with a little time out on the long trail in Vermont, mostly with [daughter] Alice.

The immediate question up is that of Japanese relations. During my holiday, decision has been reached to abrogate the trade treaty with Japan, which incidentally prevents any embargo on shipments to Japan. There is a six months waiting period. This is due partly to fear lest we be suspected of the same weakness which the British are forced into by their Mediterranean position; partly because of the fact that the Tokyo government, despite its fair words, is wholly unable to control the armies in China; partly because of the growing sentiment in the United States for embargo on shipments to Japan. It is a curious fact that the United States, which bolts like a frightened rabbit even from remote contact with Europe, will enthusiastically take a step which might very well be a material day's march on the road to a Far Eastern war. Nevertheless, it is a good time to do it; the Japanese are in difficulties in China; are being pressed by the Russians on the Manchurian border and in connection with Sakhalin Island, and have just antagonized the British. I therefore believe that while they would be surprised, especially on the streets in Tokyo, where the people know nothing of the acts of the Japanese army in China, there may be a tendency to be wise.

Theoretically, there has been dead calm in Europe. I do not believe so, but then, I doubt if we are as fully informed as we ought to be on the troop movements on the Continent, and particularly in Italy and the Balkans. . . .

The Krivitzky matter is still delayed; however, he gave us some real help, and certain of the group who have been forging passports may eventually fall foul of the proper proceedings. At least the justice is even-handed here; since I yesterday signed a letter designed likewise to permit investigation of Fritz Kuhn and the [German-American] Bund. I see absolutely no reason for being soft about foreign political organizations who come here and violate our laws.

Raymond Moley's memoirs [*After Seven Years*] have been coming out in the *Saturday Evening Post;* this last one refers to the bank holiday period. In general, I think Moley has tried to give a fair account of what happened; though of course it suffers from the fact that no one knew everything, and that the tempo was so high that the chancest of remarks made little sense to the recipient. For instance, he quotes me as saying that "Only Ogden Mills made sense"—which is true, as far as it went, but which related to a meeting of bankers at which everyone was demoralized except Mills, who still had a cool head; and he likewise quotes me correctly as saying: "There is too much of the Col. House business"—which is likewise true, but which related to my insistence that the Brain Trust was at an end; and that the only way any of us could properly function, if at all (which was doubtful), was through the Cabinet offices to which we were assigned. I was glad to see that he wrote kindly of Will Woodin. . . .

August 4, 1939

. . . Later in the afternoon [July 27], to see Paul McNutt [Federal Security Administrator], now a great figure in politics, whom I had not seen since the Harvard Law School days. He readily accepted the draft of the speech [supporting Hull's foreign policy] which Joe Green [Chief, Division of Controls] and I had prepared for him. . . . It was delivered on Saturday, and had a rousingly favorable reception in the press, with the single exception of Hugh Johnson, who, having praised Mr. Hull and his policies the previous day, proceeded to vituperate Paul McNutt. I gather the difficulties are personal.

Felix Frankfurter is in town and has promptly got in contact with McNutt. This is amusing. When McNutt's appointment was bruited about, all of the Frankfurter boys seemed to indicate that this was Fascism, pure and simple. Nevertheless, I notice they lost no time in endeavoring to make favorable contact with a rising power. McNutt is no fool; and he naturally will get their friendship, if he can. What he intends to do is his own secret, thus far. . . .

In the evening [July 28] a long and very pleasant dinner with my friend E. A. Goldenweiser, the Economic Adviser to the Federal Reserve Board. We speculated on Moley's history of the bank holiday and particularly Moley's statement that Will Woodin had thought up the problem of printing asset currency and otherwise making credit available, while playing his guitar. Actually, the plan had been worked out by Goldenweiser himself, in conjunction with several other people, subsequently recommended to Woodin, and presumably he told it to Moley. It is merely an illustration of the fact that a fraction of the facts may be honestly told; be true from the angle of the teller, and still give a completely false indication as to what happened.

The important part of the evening, however, was devoted to our own syntheses of what would probably happen. I pointed out the social demands and that democratic process would require that they be met. I did not see how this could be done, without a radical change in our whole currency theory. If this meant really creating currency and putting it in the hands of need, on some basis or other, we should be obliged to do that, at least until our productive plant was working at or near capacity. Somewhat to my surprise, Goldenweiser agreed, realizing fully that this was a complete departure from the classic tradition; and we fell to considering what kind of controls would be essential. . . .

Meantime, and behind all of the work of the week, there was the slow and steady grind in connection with the growing tension in Japan. Apparently American public opinion will fight shy of repealing an arms embargo in Europe—though the danger of attack on us from that side is nil. But it will merrily rush into a movement in favor of a complete embargo on shipments to Japan, in spite of the fact that we are in a somewhat exposed position there, and that Japanese attack on our position in China or in the Philippines would mean serious business. Apparently, to American public opinion, getting into trouble is quite all right if the trouble is in the Western Pacific; but very, very bad if in Europe. Yet the immediate dangers are far greater in the Western Pacific.

On Sunday, my old friend James Harvey Rogers, of Yale, was in town, getting ready to sail for Brazil; I fitted him out with letters. [Berle's marginal note: "He was killed in a plane accident on arrival at Rio. A good friend; a good man; a good teacher; a good man."] I tackled with him the same problem as to monetary theory that we had up with Goldenweiser. In a sense, we are now verging on a situation where social demands, which are essentially ethical, are colliding head-on with what has been regarded as "sound finance." Most European revolutions of recent years have grown out of just that problem. Rogers likewise was prepared to ditch the classic theory and see what could be done on expansion of the currency credit system. I think we are slowly beginning to discover a body of opinion which may make possible a solution of the problem by credit means and thereby avoiding a head-on social collision.

Thus armed, I went to lunch with Senator [Sheridan] Downey [D., Cal.] on Monday (July 31st); but Downey can only see one thing [the Townsend Plan]: an old age pension (minimum figure, $7,200,000,000 a year!) raised by taxing everybody else to pay it; or in other words, taking purchasing power from John and giving it to James. Just how the production of the country will be increased by this process, I do not see, and he did not explain, save on the apparent theory that this would soak up all the savings of the country and put them to work. Well, perhaps; at all events, the theory of over-savings which is rife in Washington this week has to be re-examined. . . .

That evening August 1, we suffered our first smashing defeat in the House: the defeat of the so-called "Spending-Lending" bill (which really is a very conservative way of getting capital into action). Two of the Representatives, [Democrats Jerry] Voorhis of California, and [Robert] Allen of Pennsylvania, of whom the latter voted against the consideration of the bill, came with Peter Nehemkis to consider the state of the nation. It was agreed that there had to be some kind of a choate and careful economic program to go to work with, and I agreed to tackle it with the President and see whether we could induce him to go to the country with a careful and highly definite statement which summarized the past economics of the New Deal and indicated what had to be its future. I then put in for a date with the President. It was a long session.

There are, meanwhile, alarums and excursions on the Mexican front. The negotiations between the oil companies and the government have pretty well broken down, now that the Mexican government has really insisted that it continue in possession of the oil fields, no matter what happens. This is a direct collision with the policy of the oil companies, who have a blast prepared. . . . It looks, therefore, as though the oil issue might enter American politics, and incidentally, Mexican politics, where I gather the American interests are prepared to support General [Juan Andreu] Almazán. Meanwhile, it is also said that General Cárdenas proposes to succeed himself, taking appropriate measures to that end. . . .

Thursday, August 3, a really violent day . . . to see the President at 11:45. Freely acknowledging the defeat in Congress, he pointed out that this had happened in 1934, 1936 and 1938; nevertheless, the popular result invariably had supported him. In this he is perfectly right. . . . My speech to the Affiliated Young Democrats last night is in reality a memorandum of the line the President suggested; it is, in fact, as close a memorandum of what the President said as I could make. After some talk, he agreed that he ought to make a set of speeches on the occasion of his Western trip . . . and asked me to get together the material and the outlining for four speeches. . . .

[To New York.] At La Guardia's house to dinner, I outlined my own hope of getting Mr. Roosevelt to accept Hull as candidate for President, provided the Convention would accept Fiorello as candidate for Vice-President—a long shot, but by no means impossible. To this he agreed, though of course it is necessary to re-consider the situation from time to time. We likewise agreed to a caucus to determine whether we would continue to register in the American Labor Party, or do something else. Nobody knows what Party means which, at the present time. . . .

Then to the Piccadilly Hotel to talk to the Affiliated Young Democrats, which I did, saying, among other things (with La Guardia's permission), that unless the Democratic Party were progressive enough to take in a La Guardia, it could not possibly win the 1940 election. The rest of the speech was as per the President's outline.

Midnight, home; and dog-tired after a full day.

Yesterday, I discussed for a brief moment with the President the possibility of a European explosion. He is of opinion there probably will be one; and suggested as a possible date September 10th, though as he humorously said, "I get this by being psychic; if other statesmen are allowed that luxury, I don't see why I shouldn't."

August 7, 1939

A quiet few days, with nothing apparent save the steady piling up of military pressures in Europe.

The Congress exploded and finally adjourned Saturday night. In passing, it defeated several of the Administration's pet measures; the great question is whether these defeats represent an actual ground-swell in the country against the President, or whether they are merely local politics. I personally believe that they are in large measure local, though there is no doubt a certain amount of reaction. In practically every case, one can trace the defeats to intrigues, frequently close to the Administration. Thus the bill to permit guaranteed loans (frequently known as the "spending-lending" bill) was designed to open up credit through the banks. It was really defeated by Harold Ickes, the Secretary of the Interior, who wanted a straight public works administration program, which he hoped to administer. It is pretty clear that he intrigued against it from the beginning. . . .

The same propaganda, of course, made possible the defeat of the Housing Bill, though I am not too clear whether Ickes was part of that, or not. . . .

It is likewise plain that some of the agriculture people were not of too great help on the Neutrality Act. This I think probably reflects a real division of sentiment in the country. . . . Expectations are that during the summer both economic and international forces will tend to indicate that the President's program is essentially sound.

Yesterday was Beatrice's birthday, which we celebrated by taking a canoe on the Potomac. A pleasant day, and a lovely river, though I like the cool northern water better. Off to Denver to make a speech, or possibly two. . . .

August 16, 1939

A bad cable came in from Bullitt last night, expressing the deep fear of the French Foreign Office that war might blow at almost any time. . . .

Before he left, the President talked over with Sumner Welles the possibility of sending a message of some kind, preferably through the King of Italy; the President wishes to be sure that he has left no stone unturned to prevent a war. We occupied ourselves with drafting a possible message in that sense, though of course it may never see the light of day. It could only be based on the President's telegrams of April fourteenth to Hitler and Mussolini. Plainly, the line taken before Munich—insistence on a negotiated settlement—would merely constitute additional pressure to give up something in view of the threat of force. Even so, I wish we were better informed than we are; and Phillips's reports from Rome are meagre; and as far as I can make out, the London Embassy has simply signed off for the summer. We have, on the other hand, been getting fairly good reporting from Berlin, which is interesting, in view of the difficulty proposed; likewise from Paris, where Bullitt is a first-rate antenna for French opinion. My impression is that the next two or three weeks are going to get pretty thick.

A meeting of the Personnel Board this afternoon; there is a certain satisfaction in digging into straight administrative work.

I am still bothered about the efforts of the Tommy boys to weed out of the Democratic Party everybody who has not at once jumped on the third term bandwagon. Specifically, they are trying to do this to Sam Rayburn, who has fought valiantly for us throughout. I am writing Rayburn, telling him I take no stock in any of this monkey business and that these people ought to be looking for friends, instead of enemies. I myself propose to remain on as good terms with all of the groups as I possibly can. If the next election is going to be won, it will be by getting a great many people to agree, and not by getting them to fly off on various tangents, which has wrecked the Democratic Party several times before.

To Rayburn, August 16, 1939

I am prompted to write because of comments reported from this end of Pennsylvania Avenue on the subject of your announced support of the candidacy of Vice President Garner. It is said that the very limited group which the columnists delight to call "the New Dealers" regard this as disloyalty to the Administration, and to the idea of a liberal Democratic Party.

I take this opportunity to say that I do not share any such ideas; that I hope the reports are exaggerated or untrue; and that to the extent they are true, I have no use for them. I do not forget that during this whole period you have put through all the progressive measures whose passage the Administration has actually secured. I do not forget that whenever your advice was asked on drafting them the advice has been uniformly good and that if any mistake has been made it has arisen from too little consultation. My impression is that the liberals in the Administration owe you a great deal more than you owe any one of them, with the single exception of the President himself.

Let me further say that as I understand the rules of the game, until the President speaks, any member of the Democratic Party or the Administration is at liberty to take any position he likes about the nomination of 1940. This is the necessary and logical effect of the traditional two term limitation. I myself do not feel it necessary to take any stand on the subject at this time; but I do not see that anybody has any right to quarrel with people like yourself, who do. I have absolutely no reason to believe that the President feels otherwise about it; nor that the men who are at present behind the third term movement have the slightest right to speak for him. Indeed, no one can speak for him in that regard, except himself.

My own desire is to have a liberal Democratic Party, because I am convinced that people who really wish a conservative or reactionary administration will vote Republican anyhow, and that a sane, liberal point of view is a logical and necessary contribution of the Democratic Party to American public life. . . . If to be liberal the Democratic Party has to exclude men like yourself, I cannot see any sense in it. Still less can I see any sense in not recognizing that legislation, among other things, is a highly technical job; and that a good deal of our difficulties have been due to bad workmanship, in respect of which criticism was justified, and to administrative difficulties, which are always a problem; and that criticism on this score does not imply a desire for reaction, or anything of the sort.

You will pardon this unduly long letter. I merely meant to convey the general idea that the supposed criticism of you which gossip records here strikes me as unwarranted and unjustified, to say nothing of being uncommonly inept politics.

August 17, 1939

Yesterday morning, at Sumner Welles' call, he, Messersmith, [Assistant Secretary] Henry Grady, Pierrepont Moffat, and I met to consider the general situation, which looked bad. I suggested that we ought not to let the coordination of neutrality matters run as was done before Munich, when we hastily got together groups to bring into existence the necessary regulations, etc. for the organizing of American neutrality under the Acts; and that we have some people get started on the general job of doing it. It appears that before he left for his vacation the President left Sumner very wide authority indeed to do what was necessary to prepare for neutrality in case of trouble.

Accordingly, we had a meeting today, consisting of Mr. Welles; Louis Johnson, Acting Secretary of War; Charlie Edison, Acting Secretary of the Navy; Johnny Hanes, Acting Secretary of the Treasury; General Marshall; Admiral [Harold] Stark [Chief of Naval Operations]; Thurman Arnold, who is, I think, now the Acting Attorney-General; Messersmith, Moffat, Feis and myself. Danny Bell was also there, from the Treasury. This was a typical crisis meeting. From a long experience in this Administration, crises always happen when everybody is on vacation; and the seconds in command show up. Perhaps this is why, on the whole, practically every really effective measure has been taken in time of crisis. The second-string men have less ego in their cosmos and get the work done.

We reviewed the various Acts, especially the Neutrality Act, the Emergency Banking Act, and such of the old war legislation as is still in force.

The technical job of taking care of travel control, repatriation of American refugees, arms licenses, etc. falls on the State Department and would normally stay there. The Treasury Department is the normal depository of the powers under the Banking Act.

There is already in existence a War Resources Board which takes care of the Acts for shipment of goods, etc. and in whose jurisdiction falls the task of price control. Something tells me that this Board is going to have the solid enmity of the so-called "New Dealers"; it includes men like [Edward] Stettinius, of U.S. Steel; [Walter] Gifford, of A.T.&T., and so on. That becomes really in large measure the economic administration of the country.

At least partially on my insistence, a committee was set up covering the credit end, under the general jurisdiction of the Treasury but including a representative from State, Treasury, Federal Reserve, Justice and possibly Commerce and Agriculture. This has to determine how far the credits between United States and belligerent countries are to be stopped —that is, the difference between war credits and legitimate commercial credits, unless it is decided to limit these later. I likewise stuck up for having this Committee at least see that there is an adequate line of credit supplied, so that South America is not wiped out in this business. My private belief is that we will have to go a good deal further.

In addition to that, it was decided to have a general or over-all committee which, as nearly as I could make out, consisted of those present. As long as the Cabinet stays on vacation, this is a way of having Cabinet meetings without too much trouble in discussing policy.

Sumner is arranging to make this last committee official by sending a radio to the President; Johnny Hanes is arranging to set up the credit committee, by similar radio.

My object in suggesting this is to try to avoid the wholly unseemly and generally outrageous scramble for power which took place just before Munich. . . .

At least we have a representative committee occupying the territory; and instead of having irresponsible raids from outside sources, they have to be passed through something approximating a responsible and representative group.

. . . Quite bluntly, I see an intra-Administration struggle for power between two groups, one of which, at least, will keep within hailing distance of the normal governmental machinery. The other, a group of men who, however idealistic they are, are actually as ruthless in their desire to get hold of and use power for personal ends as any group of spoilsmen or Tammany politicians. Steering a course between the big business group which is on the War Department horizon and this group of highly inexperienced New York radicals, so that the effect works out a sane, progressive, but efficient, moderate representation of the country, is going to be a political task of some importance; no less so, because it probably never will be known or talked about. Naturally, if war does not ensue (which is almost too much to hope for, on the basis of the day's news), we shall not have any of these problems.

August 18, 1939

NOTES FOR THE PRESIDENT'S FOUR SPEECHES.

It seems to me that these speeches should be in the nature of an intellectual argument [for the New Deal], so handled that they are complete as speeches, but that to them could be appended the statistical and other material which really makes them, in effect, a brief for his economic policy.* As it lies in my mind, these could be taken up as follows:

1. Land & production is the economic base; the claims on that production which a modern government has to satisfy or offer to use as satisfying. This would include conservation, agriculture, utilization of natural resources, including water power; based on the argument that the plant must be maintained and improved; and that the needs of the country must be met from its production.

2. The method of establishing claims. Since this is a democracy and not a dictatorship, the country cannot by fiat decree production and decree that everybody gets a stated share. It can, however, establish minima (the Wages and Hours Act) to protect against undue fluctuations (hence the Agricultural relief); permit the orderly assertion of claims (hence the National Labor Relations Board and the general recognition of organized labor); work relief, and the like.

3. Finance and currency. This distinguishes between purely policing activities (the S.E.C.) and productive methods of finance, commencing with the R.F.C., the R.E.A., the Commodities Credit Corporation, and the like. Attention must be paid here to the phenomenon of concentration of economic and financial power to a point where individual enterprise is stifled on the one hand, and national enterprise is interpreted entirely in terms of a small group which by the rules of the game—its own rules—is bound to think only of the profits of a small number of people, rather than the actual welfare of a very large number of people. This justifies a very real change in the rules. The measures taken; possibilities of the situation. The discussion of "spending-lending"—and of "public spending". This has to be fundamental and very carefully done.

4. Governmental implications. This ought to be a straight political speech and ought to lay out the situation as, in essence, a conflict between people who are content to let things run on the chance that something would show up, when every evidence is to the contrary, and people who insist that there has to be a continuous advance in the art. Emphasis ought to be on government policies which will call out and use non-government initiative in these matters to keep them as flexible as possible. The various pressure groups can be ranged on one side and the other; and something can then be worked out on the line of a liberal Democratic Party.

* Marginal note by Berle: "Never worked out. The war came on."

August 18, 1939

Last evening with Peter Nehemkis, going over the proposed plans for finishing up the T.N.E.C. investigation of investment banking. Since the hearings are scheduled in November, I do not really think their conclusions will amount to very much, at least so far as immediate politics are concerned. Since the Committee shows no signs of writing a real report (despite the fact that Leon Henderson [Executive Secretary] at lunch indicated that he was working on something of the kind), I think we have to assume that as a legislative force, they are out of action.

Today is entirely dead here. It is perfectly plain that the European crisis is fairly rushing on; that the plan is to invade and seize all of Poland, and to do so before effective allied assistance can be brought to bear. . . .

. . . After lunch, Henry [Wallace] talked to me a little about the third term situation. He shared with me the feeling that the politics of the Corcoran crowd were as completely disastrous as anything could possibly be and wondered whether the President really sponsored this business.

. . . I told him what I thought, my ideas cordially agreeing with his own. For it is plain that by the time this business gets through we will have nothing left but a handful of half-baked liberals which might make a good subscription list to the *New Republic* but certainly would not carry an election.

Privately, I have my own idea as to what is happening. Knowing the President fairly well, I know that anyone who acts in his name is permitted to go right ahead. He never disavows anybody. As matters go along, he will eventually take a stand. We will therefore simply watch events.

In this case I think it is a mistake. What is going on here is not merely a balloon ascension: it is the continuous and active process of convincing a very great number of men who would like to belong to the liberal party that they would rather see the Democratic Party beaten than see it wind up in the control of a group of men who, whatever may be said for their liberalism, have in the view of their opponents no character and cannot be trusted. For, on any evaluation it must be agreed that all this particular crowd has done is to substitute for the old monetary corruption a new and no less dangerous political corruption; with the result that there is hardly a New Deal agency in Washington which cannot be "reached" by influence, or which has not in greater or less degree been perverted to political ends. This is the quickest way of smashing any liberal movement, particularly when the process of a movement must involve transfer of a considerable amount of power toward governmental hands.

August 21, 1939

A full day, chiefly occupied in getting things ship-shape in the event that war should break out. In the morning, getting at the various collective orders, regulations, etc. We have drawn some; the Navy has drawn some; and the Treasury. . . .

The question has come up of warning American residents to leave Poland; likewise, evacuating the dependents of our foreign service officers there. We decided to do this, and it was accordingly done.

Further arrangements with the Treasury in respect of the inspection and control of ships leaving port.

The major fight is ahead. It will be to try to prevent some of our friends from using the emergency powers in the event of war to try to take over price and other control of the entire United States, at a single bound. The regulations which Oliphant drew before Munich came perilously close to being a small-sized Fascist revolution. They were held up by Morgenthau, according to Feis, on Feis's advice. We shall undoubtedly have to have this fight out again.

August 22, 1939

The announcement of the German-Russian understanding to conclude a non-aggression pact was flashed in about the middle of yesterday afternoon. The fact is not surprising, since it has been perfectly obvious that the Russians were double-dealing right along; but the timing is unpleasant, for it can only be regarded as an indication by the Russians that the Germans can have a free hand so far as they are concerned. This is as cynical a piece of international business as has happened in a long time. . . .

On its face, and taking at face value the German announcement, there is a bloc running from the Pacific clear to the Rhine. The Baltic states are turned over to Russia, to all intents and purposes; Poland becomes an island in a huge sea. So, also, do Rumania and Hungary. Adding in Italy and Spain, and it would seem that the combined Soviet-Nazi allies now have all Europe, with the single exception of France, England, Holland, Belgium, and the Scandinavian neutrals. The other exceptions in the Near East come down to Turkey and Greece, with the Arabian East, as usual, debatable. This is a picture not unlike the picture of Europe after Napoleon had made his famous Russian treaty at Tilsit.

Analysis on the other side, however, shows a different picture. The axis was built up on the basis of the anti-Comintern pact—that is, was anti-Russian. The adherence of Spain was gathered in on that basis and Franco's government specifically fought its way to power against a Russian-Communist menace. The treaty just made can hardly fail to shake that alliance to its very base. One would expect, therefore, as time wears on to see the Italians shake loose and gravitate into the West European orbit; to see Spain do likewise.

And in the Far East, where Russia is rightly regarded by Japan as her worst enemy, the only effect can be to jar Japan entirely loose from the whole axis situation. Sumner Welles thinks that the immediate effect will be that the British will sell out the Chinese completely to the Japanese in return for an Anglo-Japanese understanding. This would be their idea of capitalizing on a shock which must be felt in Tokyo. One cannot yet tell. Certainly the Tokyo government has something to worry about.

Information has been widely circulated from Germany that the troops are ordered across the border on the 24th or the 25th. . . .

If there is any humor to be extracted from the grim situation, it will be to see the Marxoid group around here, who have been insisting that if we play along with Russia and Communism all will be well, trying to explain themselves out of the situation. This merely completes the bankruptcy of the so-called "liberal" thought of America.

. . . The Secretary of State will be back tomorrow. I personally could wish he had come in today. In this kind of a contingency, the American public trusts Secretary Hull: and nobody else will do. . . .

August 24, 1939

Early on August 22nd, Moffat, Welles and I met in Welles' office. We had before us the draft of the proposed communication to the King of Italy, somewhat rephrased by the President and radioed by him to Mr. Welles. In general, it follows the lines blocked out. . . .

Accordingly, on Wednesday morning or thereabouts Sumner cabled the message to Phillips, instructing him to ask for an audience with the King of Italy. Phillips did so, securing an audience for two o'clock on the 23rd with the King (who is at Turin) and I suppose has delivered it by now. No one else knew it was being sent. We all of us agreed that this is weak; but there is not much else that can be done.

Last Wednesday, the news came, first, that Great Britain had sent a letter to Hitler indicating that she would fight if Poland were attacked; Hitler bluntly answered warning England to get out of the way; the British Ambassador had tried to clarify the situation with [Vyacheslav] Molotov, the Russian Secretary of State, and had been insulted for his pains; Molotov declining to indicate in any way the extent of the non-aggression pact. (Note—it is now clear that he had the text all the time: it is not a non-aggression pact, but in substance an alliance.) Bonnet told Bullitt that he saw no hope of peace, and the French mobilization began; Kennedy, in London, seemed to think that everybody was "punch drunk" and could not think any more, and the British began to get their war machine in order. Kennedy's distinct advice to Secretary Hull was to go slow—"This is one bull whose tail we ought to go slow in seizing"—or words to that general effect. News came of the signing of the actual pact between Russia and Germany and the text came over the press wires last night; the situation, generally speaking, is as bad as it can possibly be.

It seems to me that the British and French now have to fight, whether they like it or not. After all, France is very slightly larger than Poland; if Poland disappears and Russia and Germany are working together, France's own independence is literally at stake. It is therefore a question of fighting now while the Poles are still in the field, or fighting next year alone, with Great Britain. The Germans in various places are talking about starving England, through an air blockade.

I have been tying up as many knots as I can. The Inter-Departmental Committee which Sumner formed at my suggestion has occupied the territory for war measures; my own Liaison Committee occupies some more; the Credit Committee in Treasury is occupying a great deal. . . .

There were only two humorous touches in the day: the *Daily Work-*

er's attempt to explain the situation in mountains of words which explain nothing; and an agonized telephone call from John Hanes at the end of the day. He had a cable from Morgenthau, who is marooned in Norway— (*Why* do Cabinet ministers want to get off the earth, just when they ought to be on deck?)—and he could get no news, and wanted some. So I dictated a résumé of the international situation as it looked to me and shipped it in the direction of Scandinavia, where it will probably die in some German censor's office.

Joe Kennedy telephoned Sumner from London anent the message to the King of Italy. He said it was lousy and a complete flop in London. He said the only proper procedure should have been a strong message to Poland urging her to make the necessary concessions to Germany. He must have been sold a bill of goods, presumably by Sir Horace Wilson [Chamberlain's confidential adviser]. In view of the fact that we have pretty clear information that the Russo-German pact included a secret arrangement to divide spheres of influence, Germany getting western Poland and Russia getting eastern Poland, Russia also getting Estonia and Bessarabia, I am not quite clear how you would word a strong message to Poland. It would have to begin: "In view of the fact that your suicide is required, kindly oblige by" etc.

However, the President, arriving from his vacation, decided that he still ought to make a further attempt. Accordingly, he wished to have a message sent to Hitler and to the President of Poland [Ignacy Moscicki] requesting them to exhaust all possible avenues and especially those of direct negotiation, arbitration, or conciliation. This to be ready for immediate transmission. Sumner tackled the one to Hitler, and I drafted the one to Poland. But I had very little stomach for it, because the one chance is so to handle it that it does not appear to be pressure on Poland to cave in; everybody knows that the real difficulty lies on the other side of the border. My end of the correspondence, therefore, is about as colorless as I could conveniently make it. Sumner, having more latitude in talking to Hitler, did considerably better with his.

My private opinion is that these messages will have about the same effect as a valentine sent to somebody's mother-in-law out of season; and they have all that quality of naiveté which is the prerogative alone of the United States. Nevertheless, they ought to be sent. The one certain thing in this business is that no one will be blamed for making any attempt, however desperate, at preserving peace. . . .

Thus far, I have not even had time to think, let alone write, about the death of a very dear friend of mine, Sidney Howard. I remember him as a friend, in college; as the charming companion of canoe trips along the New Jersey canals; as an intelligent, moon-struck poet, desperately in love with Clare Eames in her greatest days; tragic when his marriage finally broke up, not because they did not love each other but because both loved each other too violently and too much; and his desperate attempts, now that he is one of the most successful of the playwrights in the

Hollywood markets, to keep his old friends and his old contacts with the *New Republic* and the little people. *Sic transit.*

August 26, 1939

Yesterday a rather shattering day; as during the day the nerve ganglia of Europe began to decay, I have a horrible feeling of seeing the breaking of a civilization dying even before its actual death. As the Polish wire went down and Moscicki had to communicate with us by telephone to Moscow or any other place; as the stoppages began to pile up in Berlin; as the direct line sailings left various points without even mail communication, you saw how delicate a fabric this thing we call modern civilization really is. I worked at the Department most of the day; the Inter-Departmental Committee put through the documents in the afternoon and they directed me to report to the President in the morning. And so home, late, to meet Lina, who came to town—and very glad I was to see her. Then back to the Department to read the late cables. These contained a very rough outline of Hitler's proposed "plan" which he gave [British Ambassador] Neville Henderson to take to London; but I couldn't make much out of it. In theory, it reduced Hitler's minimum demands to those he made last Spring, namely, for Danzig and a corridor across the Corridor; but when you added up the rest of it, it amounted much more to a partition of Poland, without saying so.

Meanwhile, Moscicki of Poland had answered President Roosevelt's letter to him; and as agreed, a cable was promptly got off to Herr Hitler advising him that Moscicki had accepted our suggestion. This, as the President put it this morning, "put the bee on Germany"—which nobody had done in 1914. Home and to bed for a night's sleep; and this morning things started fast. We got the file in order and I went over to the President. . . . [He] suggested that now is the time to shoot the gun towards getting our neutrality laws changed. He indicated a couple of speeches which he thought either Louis [Johnson] or I might make. Louis is making one this afternoon and one Monday. So he asked me to draft for him in this connection, which I did, sandwiching in the drafts between a variety of other work.

The President was less than slightly interested in the draft proclamations and executive orders. He assumed they had been gone over and wasn't bothered about explanation. He did, however, make one point, namely, that in the event that there were hostilities and we proposed to him a proclamation of neutrality under the Neutrality Act (which includs embargo of arms) he thought he would refer that proclamation to the Attorney General to see if it was all right. He anticipated that the Attorney General would find a flaw in it and return it to the State Department for redrafting. In that case, the State Department would redraft, which would take a day or so and it would then go through the Attorney General's office. He thought that it would take at least five days after hostilities before the neutrality proclamation could go into effect. Meanwhile, he assumed the British and French would be shipping out of the country their manufactured and partly manufactured stuff.

I told him that I had overlooked the matter of a flaw in the Neutrality Act proclamation but that I would see that one was there. I added that I thought that in that case the proclamation ought to go to the Inter-Departmental Committee again, which would take at least an additional twenty-four hours.*

The President grinned and went on to the next. He had asked at the Cabinet meeting that we discover all of his powers in advance of a general emergency and asked Justice to get to work on it, with the cooperation of Treasury and State. (I had previously heard this from Justice and had directed Hackworth to attend the meeting.) He was interested in a number of matters, such as whether he could call out the Naval Militia, as, for instance, he can call out the National Guard, without a national emergency.

He then launched into what was really on his mind. He wants to find the historical precedents tending to show that the object of the Monroe Doctrine is actually to keep war off the American Hemisphere; that, for instance, in 1798 when England and France were at war, both they and Spain commissioned privateers which preyed on our commerce to the West Indies. We acted first through the War Department (there being no Navy Department) and fitted out six frigates to go out and force the privateers out of our waters. Later [President John] Adams created the Navy Department and bought eighteen frigates. In all, we fought 104 separate naval actions and cleared up the privateers. . . .

Basing on this and on his speech declaring that he would defend Canada, he had in mind undertaking to prevent any hostile action against any European colony in the New World, running all the way from Canada to Guiana. (How about the Faulkland Islands?) He would patrol that line. He would say to all of the belligerents that they did not propose to have the European war invade this Hemisphere; therefore their vessels of war, etc. ought to be kept on the farther side of the Atlantic. Since the boundary of the New World is no longer the three mile limit, obviously, it has to be somewhere in the middle of the Atlantic, lest airships, etc. upset the American peace. He would propose that each side agree to keep outside that line. The British and French would undoubtedly agree to it; the Germans and Italians would not; he would then direct the Navy to make sure that no vessel came on this side of the Atlantic.

This, I thought, was logical and necessary under existing situations. It does really change the status of the New World; a kind of *pax Americana*. I agreed to tackle the historical precedents; but I wished also to think about the possibility of drawing in the Latin American states by way of consultation. Their attitude might be a complicating factor; but I am by no means clear that they would not welcome it. . . .

* Marginal note by Berle: "This we did not do. Better to play straight."

August 28, 1939

The last couple of days have produced almost exactly the sensation you might have waiting for a jury to bring in a verdict on the life or death of about ten million people.

The Department was in practically continuous session. . . .

As of this morning, accordingly, the summary appears to be this: the Germans have stated a set of claims and theses which in fact amount to the destruction of Poland. They have appealed to France and Great Britain not to stand by their guaranty of Poland. France has insisted she would stay by her obligations. The British are answering now; we do not know their answer; it represents a compromise between two groups. In doing so, the British and French have not consulted. The danger is that they may muddle their answer, leading the Germans to believe they are afraid.

Hitler backed up his demands by a letter to Daladier which is a masterpiece of propaganda—the difference being, of course, that the assurances he gives that all will be well after he disposes of Poland are precisely the assurances he gave before Czechoslovakia. It seems to me that the crisis of nerves comes today and tomorrow.

Meanwhile, all the frontiers are being closed, etc., etc. . . .

The next forty-eight hours will tell the story. Curiously, I have a hunch in the back of my head that Hitler is going to recede.* His people have been jarred by the Russian alliance far more than anyone suspects. They likewise have had the firm promise, through all this propaganda, that they were being led not to war but to a greater peace. If both of these promises are belied, it is almost impossible that the internal shock in Germany should not be very great. Hitler's own moves seem to indicate that whatever his ultimate intent, he desperately wants to escape a general war. . . .

* Marginal note by Berle: "No such luck!"

August 30, 1939

Yesterday a quiet morning, chiefly waiting for matters to develop; nothing could be done while Hitler was making up and sending his message to Chamberlain. . . . Sumner briefly outlined the steps he had in mind should war break out; first, a Latin-American consultation (which we had frequently discussed); second, an idea he had for the formation of a congress of neutrals directly on the outbreak of war, who should assert their right to intervene in the resultant peace so as to check the rapacity or emotion of the victor, whoever it might be. I took occasion to say that it seemed to me that we needed not only machinery but content: that what was really needed was the outlining of a new order. I suggested possibly an order analogous to the cooperative peace which we were trying to bring into reality on the Western Hemisphere. We talked a little of various similar dreams, particularly the "Great Design" of Henry IV of France. . . .

To the croquet ground with the Secretary, Norman Davis and Pierrepont Moffat. While we were there, Gray telephoned saying that the Treasury were worried about the fact that we were holding the ships of potential belligerents, particularly the *Bremen*. He wanted the matter brought up as a question of policy. A brief huddle on the croquet ground developed the general feeling that we ought not to hold these ships any longer than reasonable inspection required. . . .

We finished the game; five minutes after the Secretary had left, Cecil Gray, his secretary, telephoned to say that the German Chargé d'Affaires [Hans Thomsen] had requested to see Mr. Moffat about the holding of the steamship *Bremen*. Moffat had suggested he see me. I asked them to make the date for immediately after dinner at Woodley [Henry L. Stimson's home, which the Berles rented until Stimson returned to Washington as Secretary of War in 1940], and thither Thomsen came. He merely made inquiry; I pointed out that we were inspecting the ships to make sure that they would not become commerce raiders at sea in the event of war; we tilted a little about the press; and had a friendly conversation over the coffee cups. I think ghosts may have been walking at Woodley; for in that same room twenty-five years ago, or thereabouts, Colonel House and Cecil Spring-Rice, the British Ambassador, started the long conversations which eventually led us into the war, with Billy Phillips presiding as host. *Non nobis.*

I had telephoned the President, the Secretary and Sumner before talking to Thomsen; and at the President's request I telephoned him afterward. He inquired genially whether I had insulted Thomsen or Thomsen insulted me, but I told him we had had a very friendly time. This was an inquiry, and not a protest. I told him that Thomsen was particularly interested in the President's statement that they would have to make sure that the vessels were not armed at sea, possibly by arms coming from outside the vessel; and I added that this, though a new idea to me, seemed to have some real possibilities. The President said it gave him an idea, too; there were islands in the Atlantic, both Spanish and Portuguese, where a ship might run under the lee of the island and take on a navy crew and a full kit of supplies. He thought it unlikely that they would arm from a mother ship on the high sea. He suggested it might not be a half bad idea if the British or somebody had a destroyer to watch these ships in case they sailed. We traded a couple of shots over the telephone and turned in for the night.

I gather the boats are going to clear at four o'clock this afternoon anyway, and change the issue. But last night Senator [Styles] Bridges [R., N.H.] started an attack on the President, saying that by holding the ships he was getting into war even before it started, and a few other things.

The midnight report of Hitler's reply to Chamberlain seems to indicate that he has gone some distance in keeping matters open for discussion. The President said he thought it indicated that they were scared. I personally do not see it. It seems to me that it has merely reframed the old proposition of having a Pole come to Berlin and be told just how Poland is to be cut up. The text of the note may bring a different impression. We shall know, soon. At least it gives us 24 or 48 hours' breathing spell. . . .

September 1, 1939

Wednesday evening I dropped by the R.F.C. to see Jesse Jones, who had a speech to make; and went over the draft. Jesse is ill now, and no longer young; and whether he can stand the hammering which of necessity must follow in the next few months is a very fair question. I told him that to have him ill was very much like being told that the Rock of Gibraltar had a stomach ache.

During the evening of the 31st, word was received that Hitler had called the Reichstag for the following morning; likewise that the British Cabinet was meeting. The situation was thus at stalemate: the British-German negotiations had failed; the Poles had declined to receive a communication, though the communication was already published.

Home and to dinner; Roger Baldwin [American Civil Liberties Union leader] came in and he, Beatrice and I had a large and friendly evening debating the fate of the world all the way from beavers to the effect of the German-Russian alliance on the soft-headed American liberals. As I went to bed, Hermann [house servant; World War I veteran] came in to observe that by radio there were reports of fighting in Upper Silesia. I thought of them as merely border patrol matters but was uneasy and went to bed and slept badly. At 3:40 a.m. in the morning, Cecil Gray telephoned from the State Department, asking that I come down to the office at once.

It seems that at 2:50 a.m. [Anthony J. Drexel] Biddle, our Ambassador at Warsaw, had telephoned the President to say that Poland had already been attacked and that bombs were being dropped on Warsaw. At 3:10 a.m. Bullitt telephoned the President with the same information. . . . The President thereupon called the Secretary and Sumner Welles; likewise the Chiefs of the Army and the Navy, and got all the machinery started. At 4:00 o'clock or thereabouts, we met in the Secretary's office; the Secretary, Sumner, Messersmith and myself; and gradually, as they got waked up, the Bureau Chiefs came in. Hitler was talking to the Reichstag. The immediate task was to verify whether there really was a war or whether there wasn't; but from Hitler's speech, and the proclamation which he issued, and the reports, it was pretty clear that there were acts of hostility, if not a war.

We at once sent the telegram to our missions requesting that the principal powers concerned agree not to bomb unfortified towns. This must have gone fast; because the Secretary put in a call for Joe Kennedy, in London, within a few minutes and Joe had already got it. Joe said, surprisingly enough, that the British had no official information of anything happening at all; that they were principally preoccupied in publishing the British-German correspondence as a White Paper; that they were stirring around considerably, but this was because of radio reports; and that not a single British mission had checked in. It takes the British every time! Bullitt was later reached by telephone and he confirmed the news; still excited. The Secretary wanted to know whether this was merely a border clash or whether it was serious business and Bill was very sure (from Paris) that it was a full dress war on all fronts. I think he is wrong. I think it will be, later in the day, at the rate things are going; but is not, yet.

Thereafter, Sumner and I foregathered. Sumner had been drafting the telegrams calling for a Pan-American consultation to be held at Panama; he wants it jointly called by the governments of the United States,

Argentina, Brazil, Peru, Mexico and Panama. This was the consultation which we had thought out many years ago; worked out at the Buenos Aires Conference; and further implemented at Lima. . . .

. . . In the course of the day, Lord Lothian, the new British Ambassador, came in with [Victor] Mallet [British Embassy Counselor] merely to say How do you do. I recalled that we had met twenty years ago at the time of the Versailles Treaty. We chatted a little on the structure of the Continent; I tried to make the point that the Continent believed much more in moral forces and structure than perhaps we Anglo-Saxons. He said, "You mean the French are more logical." I tried to conceal my fury at having this ancient and half-baked English canard pulled out and sparred with him a little about the word. But it was foolish to let the word get under my skin, because Lothian after all was merely making a round of official visits and, poor fellow, he must have been having a rough time. Nevertheless I could not help remembering [London *Times* correspondent] Hugh McClure Smith's remark that people thought well of Lord Lothian's intelligence because he thought well of it and for no other reason on God's earth. I hope this proves unjust; for he has a difficult job on his hands.*

* Marginal note by Berle: "It did prove unjust—wholly; Lothian was the best representative G.B. had!"

September 4, 1939

September 2nd was a day chiefly of waiting while the French and British sparred a little. They made a last effort to get the Germans to talk to them; the results were a couple of ultimata indicating that if the Germans did not evacuate Polish territory on or before an hour set on Sunday, September 3rd, war would automatically result. This, of course, was a forlorn hope. During this period I have some reason to believe that Hitler was furiously trying to establish contact with the appeasement group in the British Cabinet, and the defeatist group in France; but the tide was set. The last-minute intrigues we shall probably know after the war is over, but they really do not matter. Fundamentally, Hitler's purpose was perfectly plain: he proposed to mop up Poland and then "give peace", which is another way of saying dictate peace, to the other two. During Saturday the news came of the Russian military mission arriving in Berlin, along with some hysterical French forecasts that the Russians would at once come into the war on the side of the Germans. In this case Bullitt, who is very much excited, thought the defeatist party in the French Government would decide there ought to be no war. The military mission arrived and was received with all enthusiasm by the Germans; but the Russians did not arrange to come in during the day. The ultimata were to expire very early Sunday morning.

Saturday night I had, to me, a singularly unpleasant job. Isaac Don Levine in his contact with the Krivitzky matter had opened up another idea of the Russian espionage. He brought a Mr. X [Whittaker Chambers] around to my house on Saturday evening, after a rather unhappy croquet game had been played between Secretary Hull and some of the rest of us at Woodley. Through a long evening, I slowly manipulated Mr. X to a point where he told some of the ramifications hereabout; and it becomes necessary to take a few simple measures.* I expect more of this kind of thing, later.† A good deal of the Russian espionage was carried on by Jews; we know now that they are exchanging information with Berlin; and the Jewish units are furious to find that they are, in substance, working for the Gestapo.

To bed at 1:00 a.m.; in the early morning the ultimata expired. I slept peaceably through it. Bullitt telephoned the President that the war was on; then he dug out Secretary Hull and Sumner Welles, who turned up at 7:30 a.m. Welles at once sent out the telegrams calling the Latin American consultation. Either he or I will have to go down to do that job; I said, bluntly, I thought he probably couldn't be spared; he said, with equal bluntness, that he had not been getting any sleep and that he proposed to go himself, primarily to get the three or four days' rest on the boat each way. I am in favor of this.

A very gloomy meeting in the Secretary's office on Sunday morning; it was really the last meeting of the death watch over Europe. There was really not very much to be done, save to watch the game play itself out.

On Saturday, September 2nd, we redrafted for the President; but he, I am glad to say, had stated that he was going to draft, himself, on Saturday afternoon. Of this I am extremely glad. When the President really can take time to draft, he can do a better job than anyone can do for him; when he uses other people's drafts, it is commonly because of lack of time. At all events, between an Inter-Departmental meeting on whether we would let American shipping go into war zones (we didn't get anywhere) and some other little matters of that kind, I got out a draft which went over to the White House at 1:30 p.m. September 2nd. Likewise, we got together the historical precedents for the proposal that belligerent ships be barred from the seas adjacent to the American shores, and sent that along. I presume this will be brought up at the Panama Conference. By consequence, on Sunday morning there was not much to do except consider the state of a world slowly smashing itself into fragments, which we did for a couple of hours with Secretary Hull, Mr. Welles, and the whole bunch of us on deck.

Word came from the President that he would send his proposed speech over to the Department in the afternoon for any revision Secretary Hull cared to make. Of this I was extremely glad, remembering how Wilson had done his speeches without telling Lansing anything about it, so that the White House and the State Department were virtually cut off. Accordingly, in the afternoon we came down to the Department, but the President telephoned that he wished we would come to see him, instead. Whereupon, the Secretary, Sumner, Louis Johnson and I met the President about 4:15 in the Lincoln study. The President, in his shirt-sleeves, went over his draft, which was a tremendous improvement over anything I had done; we took out a couple of phrases which, the President readily agreed, indicated bias against the German method (how could any sane person draw any other conclusion?).

Beatrice had been working in the hospital all day long; we met at Woodley and went to swim in [Hungarian Minister John Pelenyi's] pool; . . .

This morning (September 4) to put the final touches on the Declaration of Neutrality. Yesterday, the President indicated that he proposed to issue the General Neutrality Proclamation tomorrow morning; the proclamation under the Neutrality Act of 1937 with the arms embargo, tomorrow afternoon. He does not plan to call Congress for some days; and the main question is whether to declare a national emergency, which gives him a tremendous amount of additional power, or not. . . .

* See entries for Aug. 18, 1948 and March 18, 1952. The Smith Act of July 1940 required registration of aliens.
† Marginal note by Berle: "L. thinks."

September 6, 1939

Late in the afternoon of September 4th, I found the Secretary still worrying about the formula for the description of the British Empire. The law was in favor of the formula we had adopted. But the Secretary was worried about Canadian opinion; and a variety of other things. He finally agreed that the formula might as well be placed as agreed to, and with that we knocked off for the night. The next morning (September 5th) we had the documents fairly in shape. At 11:45, the Secretary, Sumner Welles and I went to the White House, where we found the President and Robert Jackson, Solicitor General. The problem was to get the General Neutrality Proclamation (which is not the proclamation under the Neutrality Act embargoing export of arms) signed and started along. We adverted to the formula about the British Empire. The President raised the question, himself. Jackson said, quite accurately, that no set of lawyers could determine what to do. The law was that when England was at war Canada was at war. Sir Wilfred Laurier [Liberal leader] had said so, twenty-five years ago; and the Attorney General of Canada had ruled so, very recently. Canadian neutrality was equivalent to secession. Technically, the real question before the Canadian Parliament (which meets September 7th) is not whether they will go to war, but the degree of their participation in it.

We pointed out that if we did not include Canada, the British foreign office might accuse us of trying to break up the British Empire. On the other hand, if we included Canada, the Canadians might be angry, on the theory that we had invaded her independence. The President said concisely that if he had to choose between going along with London and going along with Ottawa, he would rather go along with Ottawa; it was nearer; and suggested that we ring up Mackenzie King and find out. From his bedroom, we thereupon put in a telephone call to Mackenzie King; got through in a few moments, and reported that Mackenzie King said to the Secretary, by telephone, that he hoped the Secretary would leave Canada out until the Parliament met on the 7th. The President then took over the telephone and conversed with him for a few moments, saying that of course he would stay by Canada in any event—and that was

that. Since the Union of South Africa is in approximately the same position, we thereupon drafted to read "The United Kingdom, India, Australia and New Zealand"—these last two being the two dominions which
have declared a state of war. The effect of this is to recognize that the
British Empire is no longer one. . . .

To the State Department, where the Secretary affixed the great seal to
the Proclamation, in a battery of Klieg lights. . . .

At 4:30 we went back to the White House; the President had just
finished his press conference, where was a huge throng; he then signed the
second proclamation, under the Neutrality Act, which puts into effect the
arms embargo on exports. Everybody was feeling a bit glum. . . .

Meanwhile, plans had been made to patrol the Atlantic waters some
five hundred miles out to sea, thereby putting into effect the substance of
the suggestion which was made clear back in Jefferson's time. I presume
this will be brought up at the proposed consultation between the American republics; that it is now planned to hold it at Panama on the 21st,
with Sumner Welles heading our delegation; this is a good idea, for a
variety of reasons, but the most powerful reason is that Sumner needs the
sleep.

To the State Department again, to get a raft of regulations, etc.
which the Secretary of State should have signed; but he had cleared out of
the White House and left the Department. We had agreed that we could
take a chance and have them signed in the morning; but my conscience
bothered me and I went down and got him to sign them at his apartment
in the Carlton. . . .

September 8, 1939
    September 7th: a full day . . .
    The Canadians have not yet made up their minds whether they are
at war or not. Lord Tweedsmuir, the Governor General, made a speech
from the throne to the Canadian Parliament on the 7th, indicating that
they were; but Mackenzie King issued a statement saying that it was up to
Parliament. So we are still hanging fire. The President wanted to get out
a proclamation under our neutrality laws indicating that both the Union
of South Africa and Canada were recognized as belligerents. This proved
to be all right for the Union of South Africa, which, when the question
came up, threw out General [J.B.M.] Hertzog's government, declaring a
state of war, and put in General [Jan Christiaan] Smuts as Premier. They
also notified us that they were at war; which settles that. Not so the Canadians. I telephoned the President last night at ten o'clock about it and we
agreed to get up two sets of papers, one for South Africa and another for
the Canadians, and to hold the Canadian papers until their Parliament
had settled it. Apparently we have not only broken up the British Empire, but split the Canadian government in twain.

    Meantime, the President has been at work on an emergency procla-
mation. He wants this because it gives him power to transfer budget
items, and to bring the army and navy to full peacetime strength. At the
same time he does not want to create the impression that we are getting

ready to go to war. In this I believe he is entirely sincere. He wishes to increase the navy strength because we shall presently be patrolling the mid-Atlantic at least as far south as the Virgin Islands, if not farther; and it means more ships. The Secretary disapproves of the idea, feeling that it will frighten the country into believing we are headed for war. The German secret reports seem to indicate that they think we will be in the war in three months; how they know this, I cannot make out, but they do know their war plans, which may include sinking American ships. . . .

September 11, 1939

Sunday was punctuated by the announcement that the Canadians had declared war. We had the Canadian proclamations in the safe; took them out, dated them and proclaimed neutrality with Canada. The British Empire is now reunited. . . .

September 13, 1939

A protocol dinner Monday evening for the Geophysicists, who are here in congress assembled. It was merely a State Department chore, punctuated by a strange and somewhat frightening incident. In the reception line a white-bearded Pole came up and I recognized him. He was Arctowski, the technical assistant who, with Professor Lord and some cub assistants, had drawn the line of the Polish Corridor and indeed the line through Silesia, as well. He had then lived honored in his own country; comes here as delegate from the Cracow University; and while here has again lost his country, as the work which he and Lord did has furnished the material for a new World War.

Tuesday, at various jobs, including the endless and perpetual question of what to do with American ships which wish to ply the seas in spite of wars. To assert our full rights as neutrals means running into the same jam which brought us into war in 1917. To tie them all up means wiping out our world-wide commerce. The middle line, to warn our ships out of danger zones, is the only possible one, if we can agree on a formula. The Secretary asked Hackworth to prepare one; he prepared a very good one. . . .

. . . A little more work on the formula regarding ships; but I feel that time presses, for any night may bring the news that an American ship has been torpedoed and all the world will ask why we let that ship go there at all. . . .

And finally, a ghost walked on two legs into my office. He was Sir William Wiseman, who came to announce that he had been selected as aid to Lord Lothian, to interpret American opinion to Great Britain and English opinion to the United States, and particularly he was interested in how the British had organized their war purchasing, in view of the existing political situation. He said he hoped that I, as an old friend, could give him some steers. Well, I thought, under cover of some courteous remarks, this approaches the fantastic. For Lothian, in an earlier incarnation, was Sir Philip Kerr, Lloyd George's secretary. As young men, he and Wiseman were the brain trusters; Wiseman arranged many of the meetings between Colonel House, Lloyd George's private emissaries and the British Ambassador (then [Cecil] Spring-Rice) and of all things, they took place at a house which Billy Phillips then had, called Woodley, and which I have now. The history of our past English "interpretations" was a history of half truths, broken faith, intrigue behind the back of the State Department, and even the President, and everything that goes with it. To Wiseman, of course, all this is merely a patriotic duty now and I suppose I look like the easiest mark.

If personal ghosts are bad enough, international ghosts are worse. I have been dreaming; though I cannot make the European Division go along with me. (The careerist is taught to stick to facts, which is all right as far as it goes, but is a limitation.) The basis of fact behind the dream are four events. The Russian Soviet authorized its government to break relations with any government which hampered trade relations with the Soviets. The following day announcement was made that the British were hampering such relations. Meantime, several classes of Russians were called to the colors and conscripted for service, destination unknown; actually, the Polish border. Today an unconfirmed report from Moscow (but probably correct) says that Russian ships en route to Great Britain have been ordered to turn around and come back to a Russian or friendly port.

If I am right, this means that the Russians are about to enter, on the German side. They will seize Estonia and Latvia, in substance, if not in name. They will occupy Poland about up to the old Brest Litovsk line; and presumably put pressure, soon after, on Rumania to surrender Bessarabia. I cannot believe that at the same time they will omit to force Turkey into their ambit, which they are almost able to do.

If this nightmare proves real (and it seems only too damnably logical) the state of the world will change overnight. Italy is then forced into the Allied side; but you will have two men able to rule from Manchuria to the Rhine, much as Genghis Khan once ruled; and nothing to stop the combined Russian-German force at any point, with the possible exception of the Himalayan Mountains north of India. Put differently, the Western world as we know it ends at the Rhine River; and for the time being, Europe is gone.

Well, I thought this poses a pretty question. Should we enter the war to relieve the now besieged countries of England and France, which are no longer empires but small nations fighting for a precarious life? Or do we at once commence to treble our fleet, fortify our coast cities, and build an impregnable Atlantic line? For the next phase of this is simply this: the Western world is besieged on the two Americas; and the rest of my life, or at least most of it, will be spent trying to defend various parts of this world from the economic, military and propaganda attempts to establish domination over it. Ultimately, of course, the new empire will break up, as Genghis Khan's did; but so many things will break with it that it may be said, without hyperbole, that an era in history is literally passing before our eyes.

September 14, 1939

Some work with the Secretary regarding a statement reserving our rights in case American ships are stopped at sea; but the real issue will not come until later, when some are actually stopped. Getting together the materials for the campaign to change the Neutrality Act.

Some study and work on the probable redraft of the map of Europe as the Russian troops get on the march. . . .

The only real hope I see of stopping this infernal business is a settled attempt to stir up a row between the Russian and the German troops when they finally meet somewhere in Poland; and if the French and the British could see more than six inches ahead, they would be at that job now. Even the propaganda justifying this partition of Poland is already being made. Moscow is talking about Poland's lack of inner unity, due to her conglomerate race structure. Ukrainian risings against Polish oppression have already started; the kind that come in packages with propaganda and directions attached, ready to use, from Berlin or Moscow. Hungary has been asked whether she wants a chunk of the plunder, which she wisely disclaimed, since the Germans aimed to infiltrate her. Instead, they are demanding that their troops be allowed to pass through her territory near Kass. Nobody seems to bother about the Rumanians. In good time, but slowly, the Russians propose to take Bessarabia.

Cable advices indicate that Russia has already forced Turkey to send her foreign minister to confer with the Soviet authorities. At the moment it looks to me as though the game was wide open. Singularly enough, neither the American press nor the American people, nor, as far as I can see, the Anglo-French combination, has done any thinking about it.

Last night, a quiet dinner party. . . . It was intended to be a pleasant evening. But [Finnish Minister Hjalmar] Procopé came in twenty minutes late, white as a sheet. He had had a cable from Helsinki saying that the Russian troops would be on the march in a few hours. His advices I think were a little bit previous; I should think it would still be a couple of days; but Procopé, who was foreign minister of Finland, knew exactly what it meant. He plucked me by the sleeve and told me this; and I told him I had been considering that situation, and devoted the rest of the evening to trying to buck him up a little. There was no trace of the diplomat left; merely a well-informed Finn seeing the end of one of the most valiant attempts in history to remake a nation. For undoubtedly with the Russians on the march Finland, Estonia and Latvia are gone; Lithuania I suppose will be left as a puppet state, nominally for buffer purposes. . . .

September 18, 1939

Sumner left for Panama on the night of the 14th; I am taking over his desk. . . .

By Saturday morning it had become increasingly clear that Russia was planning to move; Procopé's news had only been a few hours ahead of time. . . .

Sunday morning papers announced that the Russian troops had

crossed the Polish border. Bill Bullitt had got it from the Polish Ambassador in Paris; and he called up the President at 5:30 a.m. to tell him so. . . . The Department meeting in the morning was pretty glum; and I left at 11:30 to go canoeing on the river with Beatrice and the children. There has to be some interval in this ceaseless contemplation of Europe becoming Asiatic, if one is to preserve any sense of balance. . . .

September 19, 1939

About half past ten on Monday, September 18th the President sent for me to come over to listen to something interesting. What had happened was that the priceless adventurer, W. R. Davis, who has been selling oil for the Mexican Government, had finally got an appointment with the President. He had got it through John L. Lewis. . . . The President wished me there as witness; likewise, to do any follow-up which might be necessary. . . .

. . . Then back to the office [after dinner], where we worked on the President's message. The President indicated he was going to draft today, so that there was no chance of cross checking again with the Secretary. We turned in at midnight, or thereabouts, sticking one copy under the President's door at the White House and another under the Secretary's door at the Carlton, which was the best I could do. I realize that the Secretary is entitled to the last O.K. before anything goes to the White House, but sometimes you have to be guided by circumstances and I thought that the Secretary would be covered, because he could put his oar in next morning, if he did not like it. . . .

. . . To the Department and a mountain of papers; then to a conference with the Secretary, Pierrepont Moffat, Joe Green, Hackworth, and pretty much everybody else, on the President's message. It sounded a bit hollow to me, because I had a suspicion that the President had already drafted it. It wound up impossibly, with eight or nine new drafts which were shot at me with instructions to get out a new draft and send it over to the President. I tackled this late in the afternoon, but on instructions from the Secretary called up the President to say we wouldn't be ready until the morning. The President blithely replied that he had eight out of the projected eleven pages already drafted; for which I was naturally glad; and he invited me to come over this evening at 9:15 to work out a draft with him. This appears to settle this phase of the night's work. . . .

. . . I am trying to get a permanent visa for the United States for old Professor Arctowski, and am standing sponsor for him before the Carnegie Foundation, in the hope that he can get something to do now that his native country of Poland has blown up. [On March 14, 1940, Berle wrote: "We straightened out, at last, Professor Arctowski's citizenship, and thereby, I think, paid our debt to a very dear and delightful old man."]

The President telephoned, about noon. He had received an interesting cablegram which had been sent to W. R. Davis. It implemented the intrigue which Davis had sketched out; since it was a request from [Field Marshal Hermann] Goering's secretary, obviously in answer to something Davis had sent him, that Davis influence the President not to revise the Neutrality Act, but support a German peace offer, in return for which the

German Government would accord to the United States an absolutely free hand in the Far East. Leaving aside the essential immorality of this kind of thing, there is a delicious naiveté about it which would be amusing if it were not for the staggering realization that the life, peace and happiness of millions of men are apparently in the hands of people who are behaving like half-ignorant children. . . .

The President was in excellent form; he was interested in this business.

. . . He was thoroughly angry at the Moley book and wondered whether we could not begin checking up. He said he had not read it, but what little he had read seemed to be manufactured out of whole cloth. Certainly this was true of the London Conference account. He proposed to get Herbert Bayard Swope [journalist, publicist] to "spill the beans", and he thought [Arthur] Ballantine [Under Secretary of the Treasury 1932–1933] would be honest enough to admit that he, Ballantine, did not write the famous message which the President wrote following the bank holiday. The President incidentally told me how he wrote that message himself. He said he told Grace Tully [his secretary] to sit behind him; he sat and looked at the wall, trying to imagine a painter on a scaffold at work on the ceiling, a fellow repairing an automobile on one side of the room, and a clerk working a cash register, or some similar person, in the other corner of the room, all of them saying: "All our money is in the Poughkeepsie bank, and what is this all about?" He then dictated just as it came to him, and Grace Tully took it down. He said as nearly as he could recall the draft, for once in a way, came out almost perfectly; he did not change more than twelve words.

September 21, 1939

The Secretary and I went to the White House at 8:30 on the 20th, where we found the President and our old friend, Judge Samuel Rosenman. . . . The President made a few changes on the master copy [of the draft for the message] which Grace Tully is keeping, and corrected my English at various points. He approved, likewise, the rearrangement of the legislative program, which Hackworth and I had followed closely but had rearranged more nearly in the order of the six points presented by Secretary Hull to the Congress last Spring. The Secretary pointed out the political expediency of making a commitment that we would never, under no circumstances and whatever happened, go to war. The President looked at him, quite simply, and there was dead silence for some seconds. Then he said: "Can you guarantee that? Can I guarantee it?"

Nobody said anything and the question came to me. I said that I did not see how anyone could guarantee the future in the next eight months. . . . All we can do is to say that until the Atlantic line is seriously threatened or crossed, we will not go to war; and the statement, accordingly, was left as the President then dictated and as it appears in the final Message.

The Message was to be presented in person at two o'clock on the 21st. . . .

September 22, 1939
We talked a little as [the President] was turning in—very sleepy—for the night. He was mulling over the subject which was most in his mind: what kind of a threat to the United States was this war going to be? He said he had been dreaming over the map of Poland which I sent him and putting in some more of his own. It would be logical to suppose that Stalin and Hitler would not get over-extended but he said in view of the kind of people they were he expected that they would keep on going while the going was good. He thought in the Middle East the agreement probably was that Germany should take a sphere of influence in everything southwest of the Tigris; Russia everything northeast. How far they would go into Persia or towards India was an open question. Likewise, the Japanese solution was entirely obscure.

He then said that undeniably the next thing would be a drive at the west. The real objective would be to get into the Atlantic. . . .

It was a hard night's work for him and he was tired. . . .

September 29, 1939
The President indicated [at the evening conference at the White House] that this was going to be a dirty fight. He thought, indeed, that we ought to be able to fight the battle on the same ground as our enemies. We had, unfortunately, no demagogue like Coughlin to go ahead and call names in the same sense that Coughlin, Borah, [Senator Gerald] Nye [R., N.D.] and the rest of them were doing to us. We tried to think up a few but I must say that this Administration is shyer of silver-tongued orators than one would think. On the whole, Ickes seems to be the best bet; and the demagogue style is right down his alley. I volunteered to see what I could do around; and Frank Altschul, who is in town, agreed to talk to some Republicans. He is trying to get Boston and Vermont to do the job.

The 21st seemed relatively easy, because the message—for whatever it was—was now off the ways; and instead of going up to the capitol to hear it, I stayed by my desk. A day with a good deal of routine in it, including checking Sumner Welles' speech at Panama. . . .

At six o'clock in the evening I went over to pick up Alf Landon and took him out to Woodley for an evening drink. Landon had been with the President at the famous bi-partisan conference [on September 20]. He had come away, he said, almost in tears. Instead of telling him anything about the international situation, the President had only talked Congressional strategy. As a result, knowing nothing about it, he had been pretty cool to the whole proceeding.

I poured him an extra glass of whiskey and undertook to compress a concise view of the international situation into four minutes' talk. I painted the picture of the line to the Pacific combination almost completely dominant; the danger that we ourselves would be besieged; the fact that to all intents and purposes we were supplying this combination via Russia and not supplying the French and the British; that our national interest called for not having another imperialist power in the Atlantic; and that the hemispheric line would certainly be crossed some time. Alf wanted to know why the President had not told us the same thing. I answered that I was talking to him, in my own house, and that he would be discreet. But the last time the President had tried to talk frankly about foreign affairs when he had the Senate Foreign Affairs Committee at the White House, two-thirds of it had leaped to the newspapers in half an hour, and the President been quoted as saying that America's frontier was on the Rhine. Obviously, this could not be done again. "Then," said Alf, "why did he not send [Frank] Knox [1936 Republican vice-presidential candidate] and myself to the Secretary or to you, first?" I told him that I had thought of that; but the President had set up the party and I had decided—erroneously, it seemed—to mind my own business, for a change. . . .

September 30, 1939

Pressure of work has made record almost impossible. The President's message produced a considerable convulsion of feeling in the country. Propaganda began to pour in on the Congress, chiefly in the form of letters and telegrams. We intercepted here telegrams from Berlin to a number of places in the United States asking their friends to send such letters. I arranged to have this cablegram "leaked" in various directions, including Walter Winchell's column, and others, spreading the news rather widely. A considerable number of these telegrams then stopped. Likewise, Steve Early, through T. W. Lamont, arranged to get Alfred E. Smith to make a campaign speech in favor of revision of the Neutrality Act. I finished up the negotiations with Lamont, and Al Smith goes forward. Lamont likewise was working to get President Conant, of Harvard, to make a similar speech.

This is all very well as far as it goes, but it has a terribly suspicious 1914 ring about it. It was the Morgans, the Harvard New Englanders and the like who really influenced our entry into war in 1917; and now, in an endeavor to get our Neutrality Act in shape, we suddenly find ourselves relying on the same group. I am not too happy about this. Our policy is not to get into this, but to stay out; to have a true neutrality.

The international situation has meanwhile moved along, so that we are now able at least to forecast its results. The full extent of the Russian-German arrangement seems to be plain; and more of it is coming along. Besides getting a sphere of influence (in this case not a platonic one, but a real one) covering Estonia and Latvia and Poland lying behind the Brest-Litovsk line and Bessarabia, they also get a sphere of influence in all of the old kingdom of Rumania, namely, a great crescent moon whose southwestern tip adjoins Yugoslavia. The Transylvanian part, bounded by the Carpathian mountains, goes as a German sphere of influence. Already the Russians are somewhat active in Yugoslavia.

It thus appears that the Russians really have taken a great semi-circle from the southern border of Poland clear to the Adriatic Sea. They now surround the German conquests in Danubia. They have cut the Germans off from the Black Sea; and they are neutralizing the Black Sea with the help of Turkey. The Balkan peninsula now falls to Russia; and the Germans are really effectively besieged behind the Baltic—which is thus Russia—the new Russian acquisitions on her western frontier and the Balkan peninsula. . . .

A number of incidental pieces of work; . . . an attempt to back up Welles at Panama. This last broke into a staggering job yesterday (September 29).

The President proposed the inclusion of belligerent operations in zones of war around the American continent. The unfortunate use of the phrase "closed sea" bothered the Secretary, because it is in violation of international law; and he, in agreeing to the proposition, decided to stay silent and let the President work it out with Sumner. Sumner declared for the zone at Panama, in accordance with instructions. Yesterday morning (September 29th), however, the latent disagreements broke; and the result was that Captain Earle, Captain [R. E.] Schuirmann and Captain Moore, of the Navy, arrived in the office, along with several members of the Latin American Division. They stated that in their view a patrol of these waters was impossible. I tackled it with the Secretary, who expounded his disagreement; said that he was loath to send any cables on the subject to Sumner and suggested that I go to the White House and clear matters up. I thereupon made an appointment with the President for four o'clock, and there found him, sleepy on a summer afternoon, and obviously a little tired. He had been having a heavy week. I showed him the proposed cable and indicated the Navy's disagreement and our fears regarding the matter. It then developed that there had not been very much consultation with Navy about it and he sent for Admiral Stark. A swift exchange took place, which wound up with the President authorizing the commissioning of eighty ships, chiefly destroyers, which start for the line, blocking out the general outlines of the patrol, and agreeing that the patrol should be principally for purposes of information and report, with consultation in the event of focal areas.

This left open a knotty point: the eighty ships blockaded in Mexican, Brazilian and Dutch harbors behind the line. We left the Dutch out of the discussion, by common consent, and addressed ourselves to the ships blockaded in Latin American harbors. It is the Latin American idea with which Sumner fell in, that these, now guaranteed from capture, should be allowed to ply in the coastwise trade. Our people do not like this; nor did the Secretary; not the President; nor I. Further, the British had served notice that they would capture such ships, anyway. We considered, accordingly, the proposed transfer of these to neutral flags. The British had served notice that they would not recognize any such transfer but would capture the ships. I obtained authority to try to dicker it out with the British government. . . .

This morning, more trouble in camp. (Saturday, September 30th). The Bolivians at Panama asked an emergency loan of two million dollars from Sumner. News of this had got out in the American papers and this morning's *Tribune* attacks us editorially for considering a loan to a country which has made no payment on existing debts and expropriated American property. I think, myself, that it was rather cool, and I am not clear that Sumner apprehended the whole situation. At all events, Jesse Jones, [Warren] Pierson [Export-Import Bank President], and everyone here opposed making the loan, to which Sumner had half committed us; and Secretary Hull can see absolutely no sense in it; also, he was furious at the editorial attack. The Latin American Division drew a cablegram virtually closing the door to the loan and applied to me for help, as they do when they get into a jam. We tackled it with the Secretary, who thought the cable ought to be sent but wanted me to take it up with the President. The President is on the Potomac cruising in the harbor today, so that it would not seem practical. I accordingly telephoned Welles and told him the state of affairs here, and discovered that it probably would satisfy the situation if we agreed to take the matter up promptly after Panama, in case the Bolivians would send a representative, presumably the Bolivian Foreign Minister. We are altering the cable in that sense and sending it forward. . . .

October 2, 1939

On Sunday to the Department, where were the Secretary, Breck Long [in charge of a special division to handle emergency wartime matters], Messersmith, Moffat, and divers others. We had before us the not too veiled warning by the German government that they were about to open up unrestricted submarine warfare. In consequence we decided forthwith to warn American nationals that they must not travel on belligerent ships—though they have the right to do so, under the law, for the next sixty days. We also decided to consider whether we would warn American ships out of European belligerent harbors. I also brought up for consideration the President's desire to get the blockaded ships in the Caribbean to move somehow; and was met by the insistence of Breck Long, among others, that the thing couldn't be done. Unless I miss my guess, the President proposes to do it anyhow, and I happen to believe that he is right about it. . . .

The neutrality debate opened today; Al Smith duly sounded off on Sunday night and it seemed to be a good speech; and I think things are coming our way. . . .

October 3, 1939

Yesterday . . . in the evening we set up a meeting on the troublesome question of American ships going into European waters. All of us believe that after the peace offer there will follow an unrestricted warfare which will mean that ships in that area are quite generally sunk. There are some one hundred ships either there or loading for that area and they all carry contraband, and as the Secretary wryly observed, you would hardly expect a submarine commander to visit a ship, find contraband on board, and then go away again. I personally think it will go farther; any ship afloat becomes a potential blockade runner, from the German point of view.

Accordingly, this morning we had in [Emory S.] Land and [Max] Truitt, from the Maritime Commission, Captains Moore and Schuirmann, from the Navy, Messersmith, Hackworth and myself. The Commission on the whole thinks its job is to run ships through hell and high water, which is good naval tradition, but the American public won't stand for it. We finally compromised by getting out a warning statement generally indicating that we thought American ships ought to steer clear of this.

Assuming the warning has validity, the problem was then presented as to whether we ought to allow American ships to be transferred to neutral flags—for instance, Panama. The Maritime Commission has to approve such transfers. The State Department was rather careful not to take much of any point of view on this. . . . We would not want American crews on board. I suppose if somebody wants to go into the blockade-running business under the Panamanian or Costa Rican flag, there is no great reason why they shouldn't—though it is a hypocritical business. I think what the Maritime Commission will do is to permit transfers of these boats right and left; but require bonds and agreements that the ownership shall remain American, and that the American owner will re-transfer them on demand to the American flag. In practice this means that the American owners will profiteer in war shipping, but under foreign flags.

In the afternoon at various tasks and at the end Count de Saint-Quentin, the French Ambassador, came in to point out that if German ships were transferred to Latin American flags the French navy planned to capture them, if it could. Note: it couldn't. The English navy would do the capturing; but I let it go. . . .

October 6, 1939
Wednesday . . . Sumner had finished up his Panama Conference in excellent shape; and the Declaration of Panama as adopted embodies the President's idea of a zone of water around the American continent from which war is to be excluded. . . .

The difficulty with this is that Secretary Hull never really liked the idea. He thought in the first place that it was getting outside the framework of international law. In the second place, he thought that some belligerent would commit a belligerent act inside the zone and we would find ourselves committed to go and sink a few ships, with imminent danger of getting into war. He said he had tried to put a little caution into the situation but that both Sumner and the President had overridden him on that point. Accordingly, by Wednesday, and still more by Thursday, the bricks were beginning to come in from several directions. Somebody in the British press has said that it was a violation of international law; and somebody else had said that it was the equivalent of an act of war if we tried to stop anybody from being belligerent; and generally things were getting into a bad way. The Secretary thought of tackling the President but the resolution was passed and out, and public, and obviously nobody could go back on that. . . .

I was still stewing in my head; and likewise working the next morning (October 5th), when Charles Taussig came in and we went out for an early lunch. I mentioned my difficulties and Charles hauled out of his capacious memory the fact that we had declared a special interest and participated in an off-shore patrol of the Guinea coast to stop the slave trade. Coming back from lunch, I discovered that the Secretary had decided to tackle it on all fronts, in the Cabinet meeting; and has required that I furnish him with all the material that I had (I hadn't any, except in my head); and as he had already gone over to the Cabinet meeting, would I send it after him. I dictated a short memorandum on the revitalizing of international law; attached it to the memorandum on historical precedents which we had had earlier, and I put in Charles's invaluable illustration about the off-shore patrol on the slave trade, this last with the silent prayer to the historical gods that his lunch table memory was accurate. Apparently it solved the situation, for the Secretary had a standpoint from which he could at least see daylight ahead, and we went on to attempt to cobble up a memorandum which would serve as a solid legal basis on which this could develop. This I have just dictated. It was the old task of trying to accommodate the Secretary's ideas to those of the President and Sumner; and at the same time give reality to the action taken. . . .

To lunch with John Hanes [October 6]. Hanes thinks he can prevent a war boom in the United States. His plan is eminently sensible; it is, to get to the head of the principal corporation in each of the main industries and induce that corporation to agree not to raise prices but to make its money on increased volume. If any large unit does this, no other can raise its prices, since the competition would make that impossible. In that way, he hopes to increase volume, but at existing price levels. He does not want an excess profits tax; he thinks that is locking the door after the horse is gone; the idea is not to have excess war profits. He is dead right about all of this; it is a good trick if it can be done. I am not clear that it can be done. But it is infinitely saner than the price control statutes which the Tommy boys are working on.

To work again here, but the dramatic moment in the afternoon was when the Finnish Minister, Hjalmar Procopé, came in. His government had been invited to send its Foreign Minister to Moscow—of course to capitulate, just as the Estonians, Latvians and Lithuanians have been compelled to do. This may mean the end of Finland; for plainly the arrangements the three other republics have had to make mean the eventual end of those countries. I thought Hjalmar was in very bad shape; nervous, sleepless. In strict confidence, he said that when he had been received by the President he had asked the privilege if he got into very difficult straits, of going to the President direct. The time for this had not yet come. But he did not know how soon it might. He thought that we still had some moral influence with the Soviet government; that possibly a telephone call from the President to [Ambassador to Moscow Laurence] Steinhardt indicating special interest in the fate of Finland, with whom we were particular friends, might alleviate things. I made a note of this;

because I think there is a real value in the idea. The Russians tap Stein-hardt's wire. They would therefore pick up any conversation the President had. So would the Germans, because the wire runs through Germany. The President might thus in fact talk directly to two foreign offices, without in form doing anything other than talk directly to Steinhardt. I propose taking this up with him on Monday; but I should suggest that he send cable notification in advance, to make the telephone appointment—to make perfectly sure that the right people listen in.

Hitler made his speech in the Reichstag this morning. It purports to be a peace offer. It is, I think, the worst job of that kind I have ever seen done. Surprisingly enough, men who are as intelligent as Halifax are actually prepared to consider it to some extent. But I do not think peace can be made on that basis. . . .

October 10, 1939

October 8th (Sunday) to the Department, in the morning. The usual meeting was had; one situation developed. The Secretary is still unhappy about the special zone declared around the American continent. So much so, indeed, that he is thinking of going on record in formal protest to the President. After which, as he put it, "They can tell me to do what they like." I told him I hoped that he would not feel it necessary to do that until we had worked out a careful statement and that I thought that the points of view could be reconciled.

We then discussed the possibility of the President's acting to mediate in the European war. . . .

But the consensus of the meeting was that while peace ought to be made, now was not the time. At least until the British and French have said something, we cannot. Further, we cannot undertake to advise them. Still less can we undertake to back up Germany. For the moment, therefore, we must watch and we must wait, but the time might come and it might come very soon. . . .

Lunch with Jesse Jones [yesterday]. It seems the Finns have asked him for a loan with which to purchase arms. He is playing it along but wants to have some clear line of policy worked out, first. He knows that the Congress does not like foreign loans for armament; nevertheless, that they do like the Finns. It is typical in American foreign affairs: people want two opposite things at the same time.

Actually, the Finns seem prepared to put up a fight. . . .

October 13, 1939

The evening of the 11th gave me a pretty bad hour. About six o'clock practically every press association in the country descended on our Press Section, wanting to know about a report which had come from Stockholm to the effect that we had participated in a joint move with the Scandinavians; the move being a representation to Russia asking her to let Finland alone. The Chief of the Press Section, McDermott, knew nothing about it and he naturally called me. So did several other newspapermen.

All I knew was that Procopé, the Finnish Minister, had asked the

Secretary to consider such a move, and the Secretary had declined; and that he had indicated that he wished to see the President, because he told me so. He had seen the President; and presumably had asked him to make representations. I knew also that the Scandinavian Ministers had seen the President and it was at least natural to assume that they had joined in the request. But this was the end of my knowledge. The Secretary had subsequently seen the President and it was therefore natural to assume that they had talked it over; but their conclusion, if any, had not been divulged. It later appeared that the President had told the conclusion to Judge Moore; but in the State Department knowledge is power and if you have any you do not give it away. The President had drafted a message which Steinhardt, in Moscow, was to give to Stalin; and the message had actually gone out. This was what we found out, later.

Well, and we were confronted with a pretty clear statement by the Norwegian Foreign Minister which the press men wished us either to confirm or deny. If we denied it flat, we spoiled the effect of the President's move—if any. If we said nothing, it was equivalent to confirming. Mac and I held a council of war. Knowing the President well, I guessed that he would not remain quiet in this matter; I had to urge the Secretary to consider favorably such a move, myself, and I thought the President's mind would run the same way. Therefore I thought he probably had done so. We had to act on this guess, since I could not get through to the President by telephone. He was closeted with Frank Knox, a Republican who is supporting the President's foreign program.

We solved it by a simple denial that any diplomatic action had been taken "as yet" and the newspapers got the idea. By the grace of God it washed out properly the next morning; except that today Arthur Krock is making unpleasant remarks in his column because the State Department and the White House were less frank. Arthur seems to have found out the fact, namely, that some of the information was held out from the responsible people who had to handle the front line.

On the 12th . . . W. R. Davis came in. . . . Davis had used his interview with the President as a springboard; had undertaken to report (in fact, he hopelessly misrepresented) the President's position to General Goering, conveying the impression that the President wholly agreed with the Nazi thesis; and seems to have made, on the whole, as much trouble as one man can. . . .

October 16, 1939

[In New York] there was a car waiting for me, thoughtfully sent by La Guardia; and to Fiorello's apartment for breakfast with him and Marie and the two children. After that we sat in Fiorello's little study chewing over the state of the state of the universe. We decided to go on registering in the American Labor Party, primarily because it is important that Fiorello stay where he is. To register Republican is impossible; they haven't any use for him; to register Democratic is too obvious. Anyhow, if someone bids for him it will be because he is himself and because of his strength with labor; not because of his Party regularity.

We hashed over the whole situation; he thinks that the result of this politically will be a Party squabble, old style. None of us knows how it will come out. Fiorello said that if he had his choice he would like a congressional contract to manage Washington for about ten years. It could be made the most splendid city in the country. He was happy about the opening of the North Beach airport, the preliminary contract for which he and I negotiated several years ago; and now it is a great reality. This will be worth the price, without any doubt. . . .

October 16: . . . I read to the President that part of Davis' letter to him in which he purported to give the President's views, and as I expected, the President squarely hit the roof. . . . I propose presently to advise Davis that we can consider no suggestions unless they come officially, through a government.

. . . Leland Olds [member, Federal Power Commission] had just brought up the problem of possibly getting forward with the St. Lawrence waterway pact as a part of our necessary power defense plans. On his memorandum, the President had written: "Adolfo: Seems to be the time to throw in the clutch. F.D.R."—which seems to be orders to go ahead. Leland Olds came over this afternoon; we agreed to get in the Canadian Minister [Loring Christie] and start going. . . .

October 18, 1939

The President telephoned today. . . . He said he had forgotten to say that he had learned that Christie was prepared to discuss Canadian power matters. He suggested we have Leland Olds in on the discussion and I told him that Leland was coming over to join this interview.

He suggested that we take up with Christie the possibility of making Niagara Falls a free port. Perhaps the Canadians could do the same thing on their side of the Niagara River. The two ports could be operated by parallel commissions, working together. They could then develop the power. He likewise reverted to an idea which he had canvassed before: digging a ditch on our side of the Niagara, so that we could get a 400 foot drop at the lower edge and develop 750,000 HP, as against 180,000 HP now. Leland Olds's plan calls for selling power to them at Niagara and for our buying power at Massena; this would work out eventually a fifty-fifty swap. We may be getting into motion on this. . . .

At four o'clock Christie and Leland Olds duly turned up and Christie announced the glad news. Since we had made a date with him, ourselves, at four o'clock, in the hope of persuading him to take up the St. Lawrence question, this put an entirely different slant on the interview; and instead, we went to work to discuss how the matter ought to be carried forward. It is moving, and I am very much bucked up.

October 31, 1939

Very great pressure has made it almost impossible to keep up to date; this journal therefore reconstructs more salient happenings from the office diary of the various memoranda, and my recollection. . . .

Saturday and Sunday, October 21st and 22nd—two days off. We went to the Blue Ridge; stopped at Skyland and spent two gorgeous fall days walking in the hills. Beatrice and I had the Danish Minister, [Henrik de] Kauffmann, with us. No serious business done; but Kauffmann did tell us of the difficulty Denmark had in maintaining itself, with trade restrictions slowly strangling her from both sides. I must get to work on finding some way of taking care of these small neutral countries. The policy must be to make the United States the rallying point for all solid neutral sentiment. The war will not last forever; some time there will have to be peace; and we might have something to say.

. . . At noon [October 23], Fiorello La Guardia came in; he was seeing the President, in the hope that the President would reverse the War Department and authorize the construction of the Battery-Brooklyn Bridge. I went out to lunch with him afterward, where we met Jesse Jones; and Jesse proposes to build a tunnel, if he can. The whole problem really is the rate of interest; and I rather hope, still, that we can get this done.

To Henry Kinsey, President, The Williamsburgh Savings Bank, Brooklyn, October 30, 1939

. . . Even in the toils of foreign affairs, I try to stay as close to New York City as possible. I want either the tunnel or the bridge—whichever can be had—and as soon as I can get it. . . .

By the way, this incident explains some of the ideas I have about finance which make me unpopular with some of your friends. Everybody knows that the tunnel (or the bridge, as you choose) is absolutely necessary for Brooklyn. . . . Your bank cannot take 2% bonds because savings banks need a higher rate of interest. For this reason, I want a division of the banking system which can take care of needs like these at low rates of interest—which means, of course, on a non-profit or a limited profit basis; and I do not think that they compete with the kind of thing you do, at all. In the City Planning Commission there are projects of equal utility, adding up to roughly half a billion dollars, that ought to be tackled now. This is why, it seems to me, we need some addition to our banking system, so that we can get this work done; and I don't see that it threatens private enterprise, either. The object ought to be to arrange to do the work which private enterprise cannot do. In practice, we can get the tunnel built if we can argue the Federal Government or the R.F.C., or somebody, into providing the money at the lowest rate of interest—which is actually what we are at, at the moment. . . .

November 1939

Thursday, November 2nd, my brother looked in, and I was very glad to see him; then a little swift work with the White House setting up the work. It was anticipated that the Neutrality Act will be passed some time during the day; the Senate having passed it, it merely remains for the House to act. I told General [Edwin] Watson [Roosevelt's military aide] I thought that the proclamations and so forth were in fairly good shape; and called a meeting of the Liaison Committee to discuss the handling of ships and the desirable limits of a combat area—a danger zone within which we do not want American ships. Towards the end of the day we heard the House vote; and it was a larger majority than we had expected. . . . I took occasion first to go down to the croquet ground and congratulate Mr. Hull on what is really a determinative victory, for the vote on the Neutrality Act really amounts to a vote of confidence in the Neutrality policy of the Secretary and the President, giving them a clear field ahead. . . .

Friday, November 3, getting the proclamations in pretty fair shape. . . . Then to lunch with Welles. . . . Some time there must be a statement of war aims and the time has come when we really have to get at it. We talked over various phases of it and agreed that in due time we would get the President for an afternoon and go over the thing as well as we can. . . .

Saturday, November 4th, a full dress day. The President was arranging to sign the Neutrality Act at 12:00 n. and the proclamations and so forth immediately after. So we got everything set, with maps and so forth . . . and thence to the White House. At 12:00 o'clock, in the presence of any God's quantity of Congressmen and so forth, to say nothing of Jack Garner and others, the President signed the Neutrality Act, with Mr. Hull looking over his shoulder; and we pushed in a couple of proclamations and these were signed, too; and then the course of the combat area was mapped. But it still was not settled whether we would run a corridor into the north of Spain or not, and the President told me to produce a naval officer with chart at 2:30.

I got the proclamation finally drawn about 2:25; but the naval officer with the chart proved a problem. The main officers were absent on unavoidable business (which I suspect had something to do with the Navy football game) and it finally got down to Captain Schuirmann, the liaison man. We took a collection of charts to the White House and therewith went to it. The line being finally drawn (we had drawn the proclamation in duplicate, so he could take his choice), the President signed it as of three o'clock and thereupon closed his desk and announced that he was going to Hyde Park to spend two days in serious sleeping. He told me to be quick and call him up when anything happened and that he would be on deck at any hour of the day or night. But there was a faint note of weariness; partly due to the end of a big fight and partly due to the fact that having won his victory he was still wondering exactly how much it was worth.

Back to the State Department to give the proclamation to the press, likewise a statement we had written up trying to give the plain English of it. I was just getting ready to go home when all of the other Departments interested in Neutrality began to call up to ask clearance for various regulations. It seems that the State Department's word was law in the matter —for no reason, so far as I could see, other than that we seemed to be astride of the situation—and for at least an hour I knew what it feels like to govern the United States. The feeling is anything but pleasant. . . .

Monday (November 6th) chiefly working on regulations which permit ships which have started their voyages to continue; and citizens in danger areas to stay there without being liable to be fined, imprisoned or boiled in oil; and some very messy questions during the day, of which the most unpleasant was the desire of American ship owners to turn their ships over promptly to neutral flags (Panama, and the like) so as to defeat the provisions of the Neutrality Act. Well, I thought, I don't like it, but that seems to be exactly the result which Congress wants to get. . . . The Secretary . . . wanted nothing to do with it, so he simply said that no point of foreign policy is involved and that if American ships left the American flag they shouldn't come back to him looking for help. This, I suppose, saved our soul; and accomplishes exactly nothing. But I have a horrible feeling that it is just the way the American people feels about this. They don't want American ships to go abroad because they might get into trouble. Nevertheless, they do want the commerce and the trade there. So a dirty subterfuge like getting behind the flag of a defenseless neutral will probably fit them. Something tells me we are going to have a bad press on it tomorrow, and I must say I think we ought to. But I gather the Maritime Commission has cleared with the President and we have no distinct power or definite duties in the matter. Perhaps a quick and violent reaction may cure the situation; and I think it is not well to take all of the American shipping off the sea, even though it has to be transferred to another flag. That starts something else and perhaps the ultimate economic effects are more important than anybody's conscience. In this case, as far as I can see, the American public does not quite have the courage of its own cowardice. It is really a scheme by which you have your cake and eat it too—have the commerce out from under the American flag, but have the commerce with your left hand. It is not inspiring.

November 13, 1939

The next day, November 11th, was commonly a holiday but not so far as I was concerned. I cruised into the Secretary's office and there we found the whole problem of the transfer of ships to the Panamanian flag fairly boiling. I had had a brain storm and drafted out a statement which I thought settled the matter. The Act permits the transfer of these ships, but the spirit of the Act would indicate the bona fide sale to independent interests. I looked in at the White House with the suggestion that this ought to be introduced in the matter; and sent word over that I was working on it. We were still talking with the Secretary when the word came that the President . . . wanted to see me, and over I went. It was a short session. He indicated that he hoped the United States Lines would withdraw their application, and get to work on a bona fide sale.

We talked very briefly of other things. He said that the threatened German invasion of Belgium and Holland was very much on his mind; he would like to say something, but did not see how he could move in the matter. I told him I feared he could not. Any statement he made would be taken as additional provocation; the Russians were alleging against Finland that they were relying on assurances of outside powers. In the Finnish case, of course, there is more in it, for we now know that the British actually did call in the Russians and tell them that trade negotiations pending between England and Russia would be broken off if Finland were invaded.

Home and to plant bulbs; and Huger Jervey was there; and very glad I was to see him. We talked of Columbia for next year. Not much can be done, I am afraid; I hope to be back; but this tide of events may make a good deal of difference. . . .

November 15, 1939

Tuesday, November 14th; at various jobs, chiefly in connection with the Neutrality Act, and an endless number of rulings. The Secretary left for a vacation last night, and very glad to go. We are still endeavoring to untangle the question of the proposed turning over of ships to the Panama steamship line. . . .

From Sumner it develops that the President has indicated that in the next campaign he will support Mr. Hull. He has apparently given up the idea that anyone else can possibly be elected. Of course he may change his mind, but as usual in political matters, after trying other things he recognizes realities and this seems to be the reality in this case. But there will be some heart-breaks before we are through.

I have been endeavoring to review the situation with the possibility of making some peace for a change. The French war aims are now tolerably plain, though not stated. They propose the reconstitution of Austria, and of Czechoslovakia, and of Poland. They propose to have a monarchy, with Otto of Hapsburg as Emperor of Austria and of Czechoslovakia; and possibly even Poland. I gather that Hungary is to be left out of this, on the general theory that it rests in an Italian sphere of influence.

The British are not so definite, and what they want on the continent they have not said.

I have it in my head that we are approaching the old Wilsonian dilemma. An idealist conception of cooperative peace can be talked about; but it would at once be used as a cover for strictly nationalistic designs. Obviously the Austrian Empire, or something like it, has to be re-invented; obviously a set of regional arrangements have to be made so that the countries are not strangled by their economics and their politics; obviously, all these have to work together. But how? One vague idea floating through my head has been the possibility of three or four great regions based on economics; with national units within the regions; the regions to be recognized by monarchies, or what you will. Thus there might be an Anglo-French-Spanish region; a Danubian region; a German-Dutch-Scandinavian and Baltic region, or the like; an Italian-Balkan-Turkish region. These are extraneous. The real question is the moral, philosophical content within any of these areas. At all events, the mere fact that things are beginning to take concrete shape offers the mechanical possibility of doing something, provided the moral possibility is also there.

November 17, 1939

November 16: A ghastly meeting in the afternoon to try to determine what the Neutrality Act means.

Today (Friday, November 17th), the first meeting of the sub-committees of the Inter-American Advisory Committee. I represent the United States on the sub-committee dealing with financial and monetary affairs; which, as far as I can see, is licensed to do some very free-hand invention in economics, with next to no preliminary notice. The principal preparation for this consisted of a chat with Jesse Jones, riding down to work. I elaborated my theory that we ought to do something in the way of an inter-American financial institution; building presumably on the Export-Import Bank as a base. He thinks well of the idea, and that is a good deal gained. At the sub-committee the question came up almost first out of the box, and we shall be at it continuously from now on. . . .

The European situation is still on a dead center. Such information as we have now indicates that the Germans really did order and prepare a march into Holland on the night of November 11th, or the morning of November 12th. It was this that caused the fright. The German explanation, which is already floating in here by the grapevine route, is that the whole scare was worked up by the British, who propose to put their troops into Holland and wish a decent excuse. This may be true, for all I know; but I also think that the Germans really did plan an invasion but that the saner group in the German high command thought better of the idea and that we have an almost complete absence of plan now prevailing.

If the situation could be held on dead center for two or three months, I believe it might be possible to make peace, for the psychological forces in Germany are running heavily against the present regime. But a gambler who has made a throw and lost is far less predictable than one who has been winning. . . .

The following thesis was presented to the Inter-American Advisory Economic Committee, November 20, 1939.

The group of problems suggested herewith arise out of consideration of certain basic factors.

There is an unbalance in the trade between the countries of the Inter-American group. This is likely to continue for some time.

Were the entire hemisphere under a single government or under a single monetary system, this would not be serious. There is a similar unbalance, for example, in the trade between the various regions of the United States. Yet because all of the trade is reflected in the single banking system of the United States and because currency is always available through the central banking system, there is no reason to balance the accounts at any given time or indeed over a period of many years. A Californian who sells goods in New York has available dollars in New York, and as the banking system readily translates those into dollars in San Francisco at will, a Californian has no interest in forcing their immediate conversion into California currency.

Further, when he does desire currency in California the California bank is quite able to provide him with currency against an asset, namely, the debt of New York, although the debt remains in New York.

If therefore in imagination the twenty-one separate currency systems of the American Republics were replaced by an imaginary single currency system which was implemented by an adequate central banking reserve system, the problems would cease to be acute. Instead of having problems of exchange between the twenty-one countries, there would be merely the problem of an adequate and controlled supply of currency to carry on the operations of the entire hemisphere.

Although this theoretical possibility of a single monetary system is probably not now attainable, we should nevertheless consider the possibility of securing at least some of the advantages of such a system. The prosperity of the United States was due in large measure to the evolution of such a system, though until 1914 this country had within itself many of the problems which now are found in the Inter-American groups because it had no adequate central banking reserve system.

Assuming this central thesis, certain practical problems would approach solution. For instance, a merchant in New York could sell goods in the Argentine or in Chile; he could be paid in whole or in part in dollars through the central pool or institution. This could be done, for example, by having the central institution buy the paper representing the debt of the Argentine or Chilean purchaser. The institution could collect that debt in Argentine or Chilean pesos and hold a balance of such pesos for further use without the requirement that those pesos be used at once to purchase dollars and thereby unfavorably affect the Chilean or Argentine exchange. . . .

It is not unlikely that the central question is not one of values—for the continent is extremely rich—but of liquidity. The developed riches of the Inter-American group of countries are great enough to act as the foundation for a much enlarged credit and currency basis, but the credit and currency basis must serve not the long-term economic needs of enterprises so much as the individual and personal needs of individuals who desire that their funds shall be safe and that they should be available when needed. In addition to this a limited amount of creation of currency through the creation of deposits against long-term values can be used to stimulate development in regions needing or desiring it provided that this process is carefully controlled so that the amount of credit and currency thus created does not upset price levels.

Once these questions are met, it then is possible to determine how the currency levels of the continent should be matched with the currency and credit policies of Europe for the maximum protection of the interests of the continental countries.

November 28, 1939

Monday, November 27th: Arrived in town after a quiet Thanksgiving, Friday, Saturday and Sunday at Westover, [Va.], where everything is quiet, and one would think that we were back in the days before the Civil War.

The desk was mountain high with papers, chiefly relating to the Finnish crisis; the increasing stress of the German free mine war against British shipping; and a whole variety of cognate questions. At ten o'clock, however, the Inter-American Advisory Committee met and we went further with discussions as to the possibility of creating an Inter-American Advisory institution. We have run into a point at which it is impossible to go forward until we find out whether this government will go along; which means, in practice, getting the Treasury to come into the discussion. The idea is now sufficiently concrete so that they at least have something to shoot at. . . .

Tuesday, November 28th (this morning), Sumner told me that Morgenthau had seen something in the newspaper about the Inter-American Advisory Committee and following his usual practice (he is always fearful of his authority) had spent half an hour raising the devil over the telephone. . . .

To see Henry Morgenthau, with Welles. Morgenthau was in one of his worst moods. He seemed to think that the fact that Sumner had been appointed on the Inter-American Committee was a deadly insult to him, Morgenthau. Wished to be offish about the work of the Committee; and if Sumner had not had his temper well in hand, came perilously close to insulting him directly. However, we got matters (I think) straightened out and he agreed to have the Treasury experts assist. I don't know what the matter with this man is; Sumner thinks he is a psychopathic case. . . .

November 29, 1939

[U.S. Consul General to Berlin] Raymond Geist's conversation yesterday gave something to think about. He knows Goering well; has seen the Nazi machine grow from its infancy; has seen the effect of the Russian alliance; believes that the German-Russian machine will not be starved out; that one cannot make peace with it; and therefore that the only ultimate solution is a military victory by the British and French, which will not be forthcoming for a long time; that it is a distinct possibility that the British and French may be worn out; that in that case we shall have to enter the war. Were the Russian-German combination to become dominant, we should have to become a militarized nation; and he is under no illusion whatever as to the extent of the German-Russian dreams. They contemplate air bases and outposts pretty much all over the world. . . .

The Secretary, Moffat, Sumner and I redacted an offer of the good offices of the United States to solve the Russian-Finnish difficulty. I doubt if it will do any good. I think the Russians intend to mop up Finland as soon as the lakes freeze and they can march easily: as cynical a job as was done in Poland; and that all we are doing is making the record. . . .

December 1, 1939

[New York, November 30] To the Twentieth Century Fund for the meeting of Trustees; but the newspapers showed that the Soviet government had bombed Helsinki and probably the most brutal bit of warfare yet perpetrated has already begun. I telephoned to the State Department to get the proclamations of belligerency started, in case they should be needed.

A long Board of Trustees meeting, chiefly concerned with my insistence that we get a committee to work out methods of organizing large housing developments—by large I mean really large, on a stupendous scale—available against the time when a new depression begins to threaten us with wholesale unemployment. . . .

To see La Guardia. I told him that Nathan Straus [U.S. Housing Authority Administrator] had transmitted a message from Farley to me, saying that Farley would be prepared to assure La Guardia a place in the next Cabinet—contingent, I presume, on La Guardia's support of the ticket, whichever it is to be. Apparently the President is prepared to accept Hull; in which case, Farley would presumably be Vice-President. I asked La Guardia whether he was willing to do this. La Guardia thought he had better quit. While he could not see himself on the national ticket as yet, he might want, as he put it, the fun of running on a third ticket; and as he said, there might be an unexpressed side to this, namely, that we turn over the City of New York to Tammany. I told him that this was by no means implied. Possibly we could safeguard the City with it. . . .

[Washington, December 1] The day's news is pretty grim. It seems that the Germans and the Russians consulted; the Germans wishing to rip into the lower Danube situation in order to get more supplies from Roumania. The Russians asked them to delay until they had completely solved the Baltic question. This they thought could be done at once. The result was the invasion of Finland; the theory being that at the end of a very short time the Germans and the Russians together would be in a position to rip up Rumania, which of course means bringing pretty much all the Balkan states into the war.

For the time being, no serious consideration is being given to breaking off relations with Russia, though there is very great popular support for it.

December 5, 1939

Monday, December 4, things moving very fast indeed. The whole Finnish imbroglio is up. Sumner is heavily for breaking relations with Soviet Russia; the Secretary, more cautious, is not; and I think the President agrees with him.

. . . A telephone call from the White House interrupted [lunch] and I went over to the White House. . . . The President was finishing his Monday lunch with Morgenthau and the object was to talk a little on the subject of an Inter-American bank. I went over, guardedly, the ground that Morgenthau and Welles and I had gone over. Morgenthau insisted that because Sumner "felt very deeply" the responsibility for running things, he, Morgenthau, did not feel it right to claim his prerogative of taking over the representation. Which is as complete a misstatement of the fact as anything I can imagine; but as Morgenthau is sincere, it merely shows that men look at things differently. The President went the whole way. He was for having an Inter-American bank, and a new kind of Inter-American currency, preferably to be called "Unitam", and generally shooting the works. Morgenthau was [dead] against the whole thing, and said nothing, and I did not feel like getting myself slaughtered in the process.

The President told a couple of stories and wound up by saying that he would tell a stranger one. He proposed to make peace next Spring on the basis of having everybody produce everything they could; take what they needed; put the rest into a pool; and let the countries which needed the balance draw it as needed, through the cartels. . . . Well, it is as good a way as any other; the conventional methods seem to be landing us precisely nowhere. . . .

[December 5] . . . The move to break relations with Russia has not got anywhere thus far; and I must confess I think that is right. Procopé was arguing for it last night; but these emotional moral gestures do not get very far in the long run. Nor are we going to proclaim a state of war between Finland and Russia. I think it is planned to work out a loan for the Finns. . . .

The change in public opinion here has been remarkable. The Russian invasion of Finland seems to have stopped everyone in their tracks. Particularly since it is known that the Swedes are arming in simple self-defense, it looks entirely possible that this country had had the emotional shock it got when the Germans invaded Belgium. The pacifists of last month are urging all kinds of measures against Russia. Plainly, the neutrality of this country is not as solid as it was a week ago.

This is not surprising. The whole Russian handling of the Finnish invasion is almost the last word in brutality. They have set up a puppet Russian government, described as "burning eyed fanatics" (they were, of course, Finnish Communists exiled in 1918) and propose to deal with that as the government of Finland, which is merely another way of saying that they propose to submerge the whole place. Our Riga despatch of some months ago suggested that, and suggested also that they proposed to take over a part of northern Norway and northern Sweden, so as to control not only the Gulf of Bothnia but also the ice-free port of Narvik. Unless I miss my guess, these pull in all Scandinavia before we are through.

There is the scheduled move in Rumania in a month or two. It is increasingly plain that this brings in all the Balkans. I should estimate that by next June we will see as thorough-going a scramble as ever appeared in any medieval history book.

December 6, 1939

We are making some progress on the Inter-American bank. At all events, the Treasury experts, working with the Federal Reserve, are endeavoring to get to a conclusion. A meeting has been called for tomorrow (Thursday) with the end, aim and object of getting some of the questions answered; but in the process both they and we will have to take positions. By consequence, it involves the closest sort of playing in with the Treasury. I am in a difficult position, because logically the representative on this Committee ought to be the Treasury; and the Treasury feels that way; and nobody can be unhappier than a man from one Department who must take positions which are worthless unless another Department—and a suspicious one at that—backs him up.

Most of the day taken up with a whole variety of neutrality cases which are now coming thick and fast. . . . I have been trying to evolve the doctrine of neutral rights not conceived as protecting a generality of trade, but as protecting the right of the neutral to live—a somewhat different variation on the basis of the theory that the neutral right to live transcends the belligerent right to make things unhappy for his enemy. But unless we send the fleet to enforce this I do not see that we get very far. . . .

December 11, 1939

Monday, December 11th, to the Department; a meeting of the Inter-American Sub-Committee this morning. We are now wrestling squarely with the problem of whether capital can be made safe in Latin America, which means meeting Mexican exploitation, etc., head on. The Committee asked me to propose for Wednesday a declaration on the rights of capital. I observed that the rights of capital had to be so handled that they did not come into conflict with the social development of a country. The problem presents very great difficulties in the existing state of affairs. What would be mild here raises, of course, burning political issues in these countries, which makes everyone gun-shy. . . .

December 13, 1939

In the course of a day, a routine telegram came in from Sweden. They would like to buy some destroyers and a couple of our cruisers: useless, of course, against Germany or England, but perfectly useful against Russia. A routine telegram had gone out, saying "No"—this being our general policy. I flagged it and took it out; for I think that we ought to consider as a matter of policy selling some munitions to Sweden. Unless I misconceive the Russian design, the Swedes are going to need this bitterly. It is by no means impossible that the Russians and Germans may decide to divide Scandinavia between them in the not distant future, thereby ending the independent existence of the most civilized part of Europe; and if American public opinion works in regard to Sweden as it has in regard to Finland, we shall rapidly assume a quite different emotional complexion in this part of the world.

At the end of the day, Secretary Hull, who was just back from the White House, asked me if I would draft for the President a letter which the President wants to write to the Pope. It is in the nature of a Christmas message, designed to lay something of a moral foundation for an ultimate peace. This gives some pause for thought. Somehow, to work with munitions and sale of warships on the one hand, and neutrality policy on the other, and still have enough independent head left to work on peace messages, requires a detached intellectual process which becomes almost impossible at times. Particularly when one has to throw in heavy intellectual work on an inter-American bank.

However, the general guide-line is clear enough. Obviously, the difficulties in the world today are moral, even more than they are mechanical. If some unity of moral action could be had, no matter how elementary, we could then get at the strictly technical work of reorganizing economics sufficiently at least so that everyone could live. The inter-American work is apposite, because we have, within limits, arrived at a moral agreement which permits both justice and generosity; they follow national interest, but national interest, seen in the largest possible lines, is life in a peaceful world. Having got that far, it is legitimate that we should, so far as possible, endeavor to prevent other people from trying to break that up; which is the real reason why we cannot be morally disinterested in, let us say, the Russian invasion of Finland, or attempt to smash up Sweden. So put together, it is possible to make a consistent intellectual picture; a moral synthesis; a cooperative peace; the mechanical and technical work which implements that cooperation; the defense of that cooperation where we find it; the continued attempt to spread the idea of the moral synthesis as a method of liberation for much of the world. . . .

December 15, 1939

Yesterday, December 14th, a full day's work, chiefly running around. . . .

Then into a two hour conference, here, substituting for Sumner Welles, in an endeavor to get the big companies which control the plants, processes, patents and chemical knowledge needed to manufacture high-test aviation gasoline from selling this information to Japan. A stiff tussle; but they finally agreed. After which we held a brief powwow to see whether we would not withhold that information from Russia also, and it was agreed that we should do so. On the whole, the oil men were cooperative, once they absorbed the idea that this probably was needed in the national defense. . . .

To the diplomatic reception in the evening—my first, and a brilliant party, because the diplomats came in uniform with swords, and so forth. After that, a reception at Mrs. Truxtun Beale's, which of course is Stephen Decatur's old house; and I surmise that the house looked very much as it did in the early Washington receptions, for uniforms do not change through the centuries. Beatrice was very beautiful. I met Alice Longworth [daughter of Theodore Roosevelt] and had a pleasant time: the technique of dealing with her is to go for her first, and keep it up. But her hair is growing gray now: *tout passe*.

December 15th—this morning—an Inter-American Sub-Committee meeting, discussing the proposed Inter-American bank. But I was ticklish about it because we did not yet know what the Treasury was going to do; and there is no use in my saying or agreeing to anything unless the Treasury decides that it wishes to go forward. When, later in the day, Harry White [Morgenthau's assistant] (he must have done a magnificent piece of missionary work) telephoned and said a letter from Secretary Morgenthau, saying that a preliminary examination of the proposal [satisfied him, was being sent], I felt as though we had really scored a great advance. Thanks to the President, to Mr. White, and to Mr. Morgenthau, we may get somewhere. I still hope to convert the Federal Reserve; and I have observed in this town that if you ever get the Treasury and the Federal Reserve to agree with any third party on anything, it is pretty likely to be done. Especially, when the President wants it. So we may make some progress. . . .

In the course of lunch with Mrs. Shipley and [Edward] Tamm of the FBI I ran into something which I am going to do something about if it smashes me. As a matter of common decency to illegitimate children, we have been granting illegitimate children of American mothers, born abroad, [passports] as Americans (the law says, I think, "American parents"); and there are many and many people in the United States, some who know of their illegitimacy and some who do not—many of them adopted—who have been traveling on this arrangement. Very recently, some bright, misguided and absolutely idiotic boy in the Department of Justice has sent over a ruling that these must be regarded as aliens from now on, because, forsooth, being illegitimate, they had no legitimate parents, or something of the sort. Accordingly, we are supposed not to issue them passports; and these children are supposed to be deported as aliens illegally in the country, and the Department of Labor is actually blazing along on this singularly inhuman angle.

Cruelty is bad enough when it is purposeful; but the casual cruelty of this sort of thing drives me wild. It means the breaking of many thousands of lives, just at a time when deportation is equivalent to a sentence to variegated forms of hell. I believe something can be done about it, and ought to be done about it, and I am going to do something about it if I have to blow up the Department of Justice.

December 18, 1939

Then to work on the problem which we started last week, namely, to get the owners of plants and processes which manufacture high-test gas not to sell these to the Japanese—and for good measure I added the Russians, with which Secretary Hull cordially agreed. We got out the telegrams. . . .

December 19, 1939

A full day, beginning with the Inter-American Committee and the beginning of the construction of the form of Inter-American bank. We sent the proposed note of the President to the Pope along to the White House, after clearing it with various people.

To lunch with Wallace Murray, of the Near Eastern Division; and because Welles is now stoked above the gunwales with work, the Near Eastern Division will report to me from now on, as on the whole the nearest shoulder to weep on. It is just as well, because the Near East is going to be fairly in flames by next Spring—unless we have some tremendous luck—and for that reason I am glad to be looking into it.

December 26, 1939

December 21. A full day, beginning with the Inter-American Committee; still working on the bank. Then to the Department and a considerable number of jobs, chiefly in respect of neutrality and ships. Meanwhile, La Guardia came down to see the President. After that he came over here and we went out to lunch at the Mayflower. The President and La Guardia talked politics; actually, this is one more of the long moves to try to unify all of the progressive elements in the Democratic Party. I still think it may be possible to have a whole La Guardia ticket; though it is said that Jim Farley wants to be on that ticket, himself. . . .

Then a long meeting of the Personnel Board.

Friday, December 22. Again a full morning. The question of how far we can help the Finns is up; likewise, whether we ought to. . . .

. . . This was interrupted by a call to the White House. Accordingly, I went over and met Mr. Hull there and the President called us in. He had taken my proposed draft Christmas message to the Pope and had redrafted it, inserting some pages of his own and putting in the idea that he would now appoint a representative to the Vatican.

Back to the Department to try to get the documents in order. Three are planned: a message to the Pope, which of course has the important factor of appointing Myron Taylor to the Vatican; a like letter to Rabbi Cyrus Adler [President, Jewish Theological Seminary of America]; and one to Dr. [George A.] Buttrick [President, Federal Council of the Churches of Christ in America].

But of course the major significance is in the move to establish an open line of communication through the Vatican.

The real reason is something more than diplomatic. The President is convinced that there is something more than merely mechanics wrong with Europe. Somehow or other we have to tap the underlying philosophical necessities of the situation; and while the Vatican may not be the best of all possible ways of doing this, it is one of the few ways open. . . .

Back to the White House at 5:30, where we went over the letters; got them signed. The President then telephoned Archbishop [Francis] Spellman of New York to ask about transmission; Spellman agreed to come right down to Washington. . . .

Home and to decorate the Christmas tree. . . .

December 23. The next morning to the White House. I met Archbishop Spellman in the President's bedroom; they had been talking for some time and we went over the general picture. . . .

Thereupon Archbishop Spellman and I went to the house of the Apostolic Delegate, Archbishop [A. C.] Cicognani; and presented the letter for transmission to the Pope. Archbishop Spellman was in a state of tearful exaltation; Cicognani very much impressed, but as a good Papal diplomat, keeping his form. I found myself in the surprising situation of assisting in drafting a telegram from the Apostolic Delegate to the Holy See, in Italian, and I wished my Italian (which is nearly non-existent) was better. There was a brief cut and thrust; for the Apostolic Delegate would like to enlarge the quality of representation to a full diplomatic mission, whereas the President is endeavoring to keep it on a slightly tentative line. . . .

December 25. Christmas day; off. A pleasant day from beginning to end; at lunch Loring Christie, the Canadian Minister; and Procopé, the Finnish Minister, came to dinner merely to play with the children. Except for the fact that Christie said that the Canadian [proposal for the St. Lawrence Treaty] would be delivered the day after Christmas and Procopé is, of course, preoccupied about help for Finland, we knocked off shop; and principally played games with the children. . . .

December 27, 1939

Steve Early tells me that of many, many telegrams about the Papal message there have been very few dissenting. Out of the first three hundred, all but four were whole-heartedly in approval. The European reaction, so far, is thoroughly good.

Thursday, December 28th. Once more at a meeting to organize a peace group. This time it was held in Sumner's office; and then the question came on to be heard as to who should be the permanent, full-time members. The group exhibited a surprising reticence on this point, everybody knowing that membership in this group might very well mean membership in the ultimate peace conference. It was solved by having Sumner take the temporary chairmanship and look around for an executive officer. . . .

After that, the Finnish Minister came in to present, unofficially, a memorandum showing that Finland really ought to have a loan of sixty million dollars, cold cash. I tried to explain that helping Finland presented other problems beside merely the Finnish case. The United States cannot, of course, help everybody in the world, without getting into very serious trouble. And so the real problem is where to draw the line.

Then Hornbeck and [Loy] Henderson [Assistant Chief, European Affairs Division]. In putting on a moral embargo on the sale of the secret processes for making airplane gasoline we have requested some of the companies not to supply these secrets to Russia. This involved asking them not to continue fulfillment of their contracts. Henderson had an attack of conscience and did not like our asking people to break contracts. I pointed out that we have to be a little realistic here. We asked the Russians not to bomb open Finnish towns (they had agreed not to). Nevertheless, they did. If we thereupon supply them with means to keep this process up ad lib, it hardly would do as an excuse to say that we were very jealous that our manufacturers who were selling the tools should have complied with all their contracts. The moral law of contract is a high one; but there are higher, and preventing the indiscriminate killing of women and children seems to me to be the more imperative. . . .

December 29, 1939

. . . To lunch with Sumner Welles to discuss how to organize this committee on peace terms, of which I seem to have the two doubtful assignments of political organizer and, likewise, of economic organizer. Either one of these is a contract and a half. Sumner is for something narrowly approaching the League of Nations, believing that the old one was all right if it had been properly used. I was arguing for something like a symbol. Europe has worked on the symbol, or at least the hope, of a universal empire for so long that it needs something more than merely debate. The debating has constantly needed to be brought to a point by some kind of loyalty. Philosophical; then practical. . . .

A little discussion in the Secretary's office. The Finnish government has asked us to make a new peace move, but it is not clear whether we are to try to mediate the Russo-Finnish war, or hold a general peace conference. I think the Finns are thinking along the latter line.

My private opinion is that the President's mind is working towards trying to summon a general peace conference before the beginning of the spring drives. My own mind is leaning in that direction. I agree that this will not be ideal. But I do not see that it will be any more ideal, no matter who comes out top dog in the spring and summer fighting. In other words, I do not see that the situation is any worse for making a just peace now than it will be later. I have had no experience at attempting to make a just peace when somebody was victorious. But this requires some thinking. . . .

January 4, 1940

Back to work on Wednesday, January 3, after a few days' playing hookey in the Berkshires with Beatrice and the children, chiefly sleeping and rolling around in the snow. There was work in plenty. For I took advantage of the time to do a little thinking about the organization of peace, and likewise about the possible economic problems. One difficulty with work in the Department is that you never get five connected minutes together now, and thereby lose the time needed to meditate on problems. All solutions cannot be instinctive.

It seemed to me that the present war in Europe was largely a civil war to determine how Europe should be organized. On one side there is still a dream of universal empire—a capital of Europe, a superior race, satellite states, and so forth. On the other hand, there is a kind of dream of federalism, which as yet has no clear outline. It is equally plain that our public opinion will not let us participate in any European set-up; and I happen to believe our public opinion is right. I think, instead, that what is possible is the relationship of a Pan American group to a European group—or a series of European groups—and we may be able to string something on that line. I also think that the European habit of seeking a center (a Pope, a Holy Roman Empire, or the like) has to be given scope.

. . . we met to discuss the matter in the afternoon. Sumner's mind moved smoothly and cleanly in the direction of immediate machinery, namely, a conference of neutrals to be called here to discuss the maintenance of neutral rights, and incidentally to suggest, if possible, some plan by way of declaration which might be used as a nucleus for peace efforts. I went farther and tackled the possibility of a long-range organization. . . . But we got only fairly started before we tackled the main question, which is the political organization of peace. . . .

January 4. The Canadians are proposing to negotiate on the St. Lawrence waterway; which means that we shall all have to leave for Ottawa on Saturday night. I hope it is a short session.

January 11, 1940

January 4. Dinner at home, with the Apostolic Delegate, Bishop Molloy, of Brooklyn, Jim Farley, and two or three others. I took occasion to try to explain to Bishop Molloy that the Brooklyn Diocese could not go on messing up with the Coughlin crowd; that our policy toward the Catholic Church was obviously good, as had been demonstrated by the Vatican proposal; but that Coughlin, who had committed himself to "Franco's way", made it very difficult to carry that move forward. I think Molloy got the point. . . .

January 6. At 4:30, got on board the train for Ottawa with Leland Olds and John Hickerson [Assistant Chief, European Affairs Division]. To Ottawa . . . the Chargé, [Jack] Simmonds, and Secretary [David McK.] Key met us; to lunch then with Simmonds and two or three others. Norman Robertson, the Assistant Secretary of External Affairs, was there. We took occasion to throw it into him rather hard in connection with one of the Canadian tricks, namely, to insist that Americans resident in Canada turn over their American bank balances and securities to the Canadian government. Robertson is one of these soft, quiet men, who, when they try extreme measures, go very hard. In this case, he has overdone it. I think we shall come out all right. This pretty well killed the afternoon; then to an early evening dinner with Dr. [O. D.] Skelton, the Under-Secretary (really the Chief) of the Department of External Affairs. Mackenzie King has the portfolio, and the result is that the Under-Secretary does all the work. Skelton is a fine, literate, Scotchman; was Professor of History at Queens; now finds himself running Canadian foreign affairs at a crucial period in their history; is working himself to death. But a singularly attractive, honest and high-grade man. The company included most of the people we were to deal with, including the principal obstacle, MacLachlan. We had had an advance tip that he was opposed, so we went for him. For all his Scotch penury, he did construct a railroad to Hudson Bay which rejoices in having a total traffic season of something like six weeks, and has never made enough traffic even to pay for the spikes in the line. The men were interesting, and chiefly Scotch; the Scotch seem to have abandoned Scotland and undertaken the pleasant job of running the rest of the Empire. . . .

Monday, January 8th. To work at ten o'clock, and a steady, all day session, which did not break up until 7:30. . . . However, we did hammer the St. Lawrence waterway project down to three main issues: the time when the waterway was to be completed, the amount of money that we were to pay, and the question of the diversion of water by Chicago. Someone jocularly referred to the three issues as "time, space, and hell". We shall have no difficulty on time; and I think we can work it out on Chicago, because the Canadians are prepared to give us 5,000 cubic feet of water per second for the Chicago drainage canal. The trouble with this is that the water would make more than 100,000 horse power if it were run through the St. Lawrence River; and will make only about one-third that if it is run through the Chicago drainage canal and used for power at Joliet. The principal reason for doing it is that there are five

Mississippi Valley votes that we need in the Senate. Leland figured out that we were losing a net economic value (present price) of around a million dollars a year, forever and ever, amen, which he thought was a high price to pay for five votes. Hickerson genially suggested that we try to figure it out on the cash basis and see what the Chicago Senators would settle for on the plan of a life annuity to them. It is one of these hateful situations where principle collides with a piece of political expediency: which do you do?

It was pretty obvious that the Canadians are unwilling to take a single dam project; likewise, that they want us to pay for the whole thing, except, of course, what they get from the Ontario Hydro. It happened that [Thomas H.] Hogg, of the Ontario Hydro, was in town; so, after getting the guide wires, we left Leland Olds to dicker with Hogg. They are old friends and it could be worked out. However, the Canadian estimates boosted the values for land, which have to be taken from two million to twelve million, which looks fishy. This is some of MacLachlan's work. What I think will happen is that we knock down their estimate somewhat; raise the price a little which Ontario Hydro is prepared to pay; likewise with the New York Power Authority; and so strike a balance. By the end of the day's work we were all very tired; and had the new Canadian figures.

To a brief dinner with Key, and then to the hotel to tackle the estimates. We knocked off at 1:30. . . .

Tuesday, January 9th. Up betimes, and to breakfast with Hogg. He looked at the Canadian figures, likewise ours, and damned MacLachlan with a series of Scotch expletives which (not knowing the precise habits of the Scotch clans) I was unable to evaluate. The general drift of it was that there was considerable money to be saved here and by the time we got through it was obvious that we were, at a maximum, only fourteen millions apart, and probably could cover that in. So we worked through the morning and then adjourned, to meet in Washington on January 22; and I went over to the formal luncheon given by Jack Simmonds for me, while Leland ducked out to have a quiet, off-the-record lunch with Hogg. After lunch I learned that Leland had done a good job. He pushed up the price Ontario Hydro was willing to contribute by five millions; and will try to sell the same idea to the New York Power Authority; which is ten of our fourteen millions difference. If Hogg can argue MacLachlan out of several millions of his estimates, I think we are there. . . .

. . . To Washington on the night train.

January 11. Some work getting the Canadian–St. Lawrence treaty a little bit better into line; and some work with the Treasury experts on the Inter-American bank; and some with the Personnel Board, including, *inter alia,* my own proposal to reorganize the Foreign Service School. Then to dinner at the [Robert Woods] Blisses', where everybody was discussing the symbolism of medieval art: a fascinating subject, but I was too much tangled with the various tasks of war and peace to be able to make a smooth and easy transition. This is a mistake. I should be able to drop things and glide into another world, without a visible break.

The really important work of the day I imagine was the sub-committee on organization of peace. We are about decided that the next thing to be done is to call a meeting of neutrals, in theory to discuss methods of maintaining their rights during the war period. But the real and inevitable discussion would be whether mediation could not be proposed, together with possible peace terms, and with an insistence that the neutrals sit at the peace table with equal right. This is an evolution of an idea which Sumner put forward several years ago. The real problem is how to give the machinery which will thus be created actual content. . . .

January 12, 1940
. . . The Treasury has finished its draft project of the Inter-American bank. In doing so, they naturally followed their own ideas and left the Federal Reserve out in the cold, so that I went to lunch with Marriner Eccles, Goldenweiser and [Robert H.] Gardiner, and we spent two solid hours pounding out the whole situation. I pointed out that the Inter-American bank was probably a sighting shot at a method of opening trade after there was peace, at which time we should be facing a pretty serious situation. Specifically, there would be no international medium, such as gold; trade would be at a dead standstill, and there would be no normal exchange; Europe would be facing the staggering task of turning its war organization into peace-time economics; we should have to furnish the working capital to get the flow started; and this was, accordingly, a laboratory study in how to get going. I thought that Marriner was impressed. The final point—whether the Inter-American bank should be strictly a government matter or a matter between the Reserve banks—we left open for the time being. Fundamentally, it is less important than many people here seem to think. . . .

January 15, 1940
The high point of the day was a brief talk with the President. He has been working with Joe Davies [Special Assistant to Hull] on a scheme. Believing it possible that the Germans will invade Holland, the question then comes up as to what is to be done with the Dutch islands in the Caribbean. He is evolving a plan by which the United States will lease them from Holland for a dollar, with the right to fortify them, but agreeing to maintain the existing officials in charge, or to appoint Dutchmen, should it be necessary to replace them. Included in this would be the right to fortify the harbor of Curaçao. The President plans an air landing field at St. Eustatia. It is typical of my long-headed Caesar that while he was supposedly engaged in naval maneuvers last year, he used the cruiser to run around these islands, with a view to considering exactly this point. By consequence, he had his plan all worked out. I hope it may not be necessary. I said that it might be necessary by the end of next week. "By the end of this week", said he.

We talked a little of possible peace terms; I reverted to his idea that producing countries might go on producing; pushing their excess production into an international cartel for distribution where needed. He said he thought it was worth working on. "I do not know that we any of us have minds big enough to comprehend this kind of situation", he said, "but we have to work at it, just the same." I observed that the highly classical methods of going at it seemed to be getting us nowhere. We are rather hoping that the Inter-American bank may serve as a laboratory study for some of the things that can be done later on in terms of peace work. . . .

January 19, 1940

Tuesday, January 16. A stiff day, with oral examinations for the Foreign Service; some first-rate men, some pathetic cases, and one in particular, a boy who had passed a brilliant examination; worked his way through college; was living on $75 a month and finishing his graduate work at N.Y.U.; he had all the qualifications except the main one, namely, a physical personality which would carry him through. We had to flunk him, and later I made him come up to see me. I thought it was possible to do something about him in New York, which I am trying to do. . . .

January 19. The traffic is unduly heavy just now; I have Sumner Welles's work while he is away; my own; the Inter-American Committee; the Canadian Seaway negotiations, with the attendant row about power; and most of the regular divisions reporting to me. The Secretary and Henry Grady are up to their necks in the trade agreement fight. By consequence, these are full days, and I shall be glad when things quiet down a little.

January 22, 1940

January 19 . . . The fleet orders seem to have gone out for a visit of the fleet to the West Indies, with particular reference to the Dutch West Indies; indicating that the President not only has a plan, but is prepared to have the people there to put it into effect. I do not know yet whether the Dutch have agreed to it; Joe Davies has this in hand. . . .

At noon, Lord Lothian came in. He came at my request and I handed him a copy of our Aide-Mémoire protesting against their holding up of our ships at Gibraltar. They do this in order to make it hard for our ships, and at the same time they make it easy for the Italian ships, so that the Italians can feel they have discriminatory treatment. Lothian was incautious and he adverted to the fact that the Italians capitalized on their nuisance value. I told him this was what we all of us feared; and perhaps the best way to have our rights respected was to be somewhat of a nuisance ourselves. . . .

January 21 . . . the question about the Finnish loan. The Congress does not like this loan and is going to take its orders from the Secretary of State, who therefore has to determine some very difficult questions. The Finns want a great deal more money than they are getting; we are less anxious about the money than we are about getting tangled up in a situation the precise end of which no one can foresee. In this respect, the Secretary of the Treasury is putting up a terrific fight for a large loan; and he feels he is entitled to more help from the State Department than he is getting; but the State Department is less sentimental.

January 22. At ten o'clock, to the office, to meet the Canadian delegation; and we spent all morning on the negotiations, and most of the afternoon. . . .

At noon, the formal lunch for the Canadians; and in the afternoon, more of it. . . .

January 23, 1940

The day broke with a bang. The Secretary is ill with a head cold and possible flu, and not talking to anyone. Meanwhile, everyone who could give the instructions has cleared out. I telephoned, at Mrs. Hull's suggestion, to Mr. Welles not to come back. The real reason for this is, of course, that Mrs. Hull does not want it thought that the Department can't run while Welles is away.

To the office, to get a few things in shape; and at ten-fifteen to see Henry Morgenthau [and others] in his office and they said they had completed a draft of the Inter-American bank scheme which they were generally prepared to stand by. I stated that I would call a meeting of the Inter-American Advisory Sub-Committee for tomorrow afternoon (the 24th) and meanwhile invited them to thresh out their differences with the Federal Reserve System, if they could—which they are agreeing to do. But I have to vote on a bank scheme which Secretary Hull hardly knows about, which Welles cannot review. I tried to get hold of Secretary Hull, but he is not seeing anyone, and left it to me to clear with the President, which I propose to do.

Meanwhile, the Canadians are in town, and they are continuing to negotiate on the St. Lawrence treaty. We are not getting a good press, and I am unhappy. It seems, somehow, as though all the constructive things run into political obstacles. The destructive ones, however, go through merrily. . . .

January 24, 1940

A bad day, and things getting worse. Secretary Hull is ill in bed with a cold; Welles is away, Grady away, and the volume of work is almost intolerable. The intolerable quality lies not in the quantity, but in the fact that we have the ultimate responsibility, without any ultimate authority: always a bad situation. Mrs. Hull is, properly, very anxious that the Secretary's illness should not be put in the newspapers, because it would be exaggerated.

There were two hours of oral examinations for the Foreign Service; some very good men coming up. Then to the White House. We cleared a little of the policy on the Inter-American bank; the President developed an idea he had to file a sort of public brief for the neutrality patrol, which, in his view, has kept war away from our shores by making it difficult for raiders and warships to move unobserved and to refuel, etc. In this I think he is right; but the difficulty is proving it, since we have only our own navy reports to go on. The President is in excellent form.

A lunch at the neighboring hash house with Leland Olds and Hickerson, and the Canadians were there, too; and then to a meeting of the Canadian and American conferees. We settled up the last outstanding points—they were principally engineering—and anyhow, Leland did most of the work. . . .

January 26, 1940

About seven o'clock last evening, Harold Hinton [New York *Times* Washington reporter] called up. Lester Markel, Sunday editor of the *Times,* had received an article for publication which he described as "a pretty tough piece". Its theme was that the British, under cover of contraband control, were really building up and consolidating a commercial and economic position aimed against us quite as much as against the Germans, and that they were waging their warfare as mercilessly against us as against their enemies. Markel had wired him, asking him to call me and see what advice I could give about printing the piece.

I said that I certainly did not propose to be in a position of advising the *Times* not to publish anything it thought worth publishing. Specifically, I did not care to be in the position of telling the *Times* not to publish an anti-British piece. But, I said, the accusations made were very grave. Unless they were backed up by a pretty solid set of facts, I saw no particular reason for spreading accusations of that kind around. We had been pretty stiff with the British, and the British had had a bad press; and we had reason to believe they were worried about it; and I could see no reason in merely piling on a bad press for the fun of it. If, however, there were some real facts which the American public ought to know, then by all means go ahead.

Hinton said that he had gathered that Markel thought the facts were not as solid as they ought to be to back the accusation and that he would be governed accordingly. I told him that I wanted it perfectly plain that the *Times* would have to use its own judgment in the matter and that I could merely give him my personal impressions as to what I would do if I were in the place of a Sunday editor—without indicating a Department view. Hinton said he understood this perfectly.

January 30, 1940

Friday, January 26. The Hungarian Minister came in today and asked whether the United States would take the lead in proposing to negotiate peace between Russia and Finland. This was done obviously as a result of some kind of an unofficial German maneuver. I think we should be prepared to do it if we thought we could get anywhere. The Germans are interested, I suppose, in getting more supplies from Russia and Sweden; or perhaps they are interested in clearing the decks for a spring Balkan campaign. In spite of this we are prepared to go forward. My reason for doing so is that I think if peace starts anywhere it may spread very rapidly. . . .

. . . The Secretary is still out.

Saturday, January 27. To work on the Hungarian démarche. The President, by telephone, agreed to go forward with this. The reports indicate considerably rising stress in Russia, which may help. Accordingly, we cabled to Steinhardt in Moscow and asked him to start in. . . .

In the afternoon, when the Department had gone home, I tackled the job of drawing an agenda for the proposed neutral conference. It is a staggering thing. It seems to me that if we dealt, not in abstractions, but in tangible problems, it would be more nearly possible to get towards an ultimate scheme of life. Mr. Wilson tried it from the top down. We might try it from the bottom up. So I tried to think of all the difficulties Europe would have to meet as soon as the war ended; and to consider how we could get at them.

[Ernest] Cuneo [former Berle student and former La Guardia law secretary] came in from Baltimore, with a lot of news; he gathers, through Walter Winchell, pretty much all the gossip of the town; but a good deal of it is not altogether accurate. One bit is that the President has been talking about La Guardia as Vice-President along with Cordell Hull. If this should by any chance work out, it would be the fruit of an idea manufactured some two or three years ago; one of the longest political shots on record. I think I can fairly claim to have been the first to think of it. But it was a long way between thinking about it and getting there. Mr. Hull's stock is rising so steadily that it seems to me practically inescapable. But the Vice-Presidency is still open. Garner, I am told, now knows that he is not going to be nominated or elected. Fortunately, he is a very good friend of Fiorello's.

Sunday, January 28. A quiet day; to church with the children, some skiing and fresh air in the afternoon. In the evening the servants were gone and Max Ascoli [Professor, New School for Social Research] came in for a pick-up dinner with Beatrice and me. We talked the evening through about the possibility of making peace. His analysis of the situation is the same as mine: this is a war superimposed on an as yet undefined revolution: Europe in search of a positive, instead of a negative, principle. But when it comes to the actual job of making peace, we differ. I asked one question: Would the end of hostilities liberate positive forces, or sanctify the existing negative forces? To this I did not get a very clear answer. Ascoli was anxious to have the war go on until the Nazis' and Fascists' principle were smashed; but he agreed that the British and French were as likely to make terms with the Italian Fascists as to try to smash them; in a word, that their victory did not promise any particular liberation. Curiously, he was there fighting the forces which exiled him from Italy; the worst kind of fighting, because he is unable actually to get at them.

At the close of the discussion I had about concluded in my own mind that the thing to do is to try to make peace this spring, if possible. There will be, perhaps, a certain apparent renunciation of the smashing of Fascism; but I ended the conversation by being very clear that the negative force theory will not be smashed by the present force of arms, but by the liberation of quieter and more continuous forces; and that these are more likely to be liberated by peace than by a continuation of an economic war to the breaking point. . . .

Monday, Jan. 29. I am glad to note that Eccles and the Treasury did reach an understanding at a conference on Saturday morning. This clears the decks on the Inter-American Bank, always provided we do not run into some other snags. . . .

Dinner at the Canadian Legation: a pleasant evening. I hear that the draft of the St. Lawrence treaty we sent up is in pretty good shape. We may be ready to report in a day or two.

January 31, 1940

. . . Then on the afternoon train to New Haven, where [Professor] Arnold Wolfers met me and I made a speech at the Yale Political Union. Somehow it angered me a little to find these youngsters being ever so afraid of taking themselves seriously. Elsewhere, men of their age are either fighting, or running governments, or otherwise taking a hand in things. I tried to talk about the underlying data of peace; but I do not think it went very well.

February 12, 1940

Sunday, February 4. A quiet Sunday at home; but in the afternoon Miriam telephoned that she had just received word by telephone from Aunt Helen [Berle's mother's sister] that Mother had had a stroke of some kind and was ill in Oberlin and might not live. I communicated with Lina, who communicated with Rudolf; and took the night train to Cleveland.

February 5. At Oberlin. Mother had had a cerebral hemorrhage yesterday, shortly after lunch, and had lost consciousness within half an hour. There was nothing to do but wait. Rudolf and Lina were in Oberlin; but all we could do was to keep watch, and wait. . . .

February 6. Still waiting. Father, who was in Florida, where he had been arranging for an apartment for Mother and himself, was on the way north; but the planes were grounded. We thought Mother was recovering a little in the morning; but by evening it was plain that not much could be done. Certainly I would rather not have any recovery than to have her linger for a few months with a paralyzed body and a clouded mind. —Rudolf was, as always, a tower of strength; as also Lina.

Wednesday, February 7th. Father and Mimi arrived in the morning. Father was frightfully broken up and had a bad time on his way north. He was ill in Jacksonville; and apparently a good Samaritan stranger by the name of Metzger, who runs Crane & Company there, took care of him and put him on the plane to Washington, where Cassius met him.

I think my Mother was probably waiting for Father to get there, though this is difficult to support on any rational grounds. The conscious mind, of course, had stopped functioning; no one knows how much of the unconscious mind may still exist and work. Certainly as soon as he came the end began to come very rapidly, and at seven o'clock she died, almost imperceptibly.

The long vigil of some days, through nights and days, and in the bitter gray fog of the Lake Shore, made for a curious clarity of emotional thought, which there is no point here in setting down. Curiously, there is a crystalline demonstration of the way matters bring themselves to full cycle and when the cycle is completed, end themselves. Even dying, Mother accomplished the last thing she really wished to do.

February 8. Following the family custom and Mother's wish, we did not have any great funeral; merely a prayer and the Twenty-Third Psalm. An old friend of Father's and Mother's, Dr. Van der Pyl, who had been often at our house in the Boston and Salem days, was there in Oberlin.

Home on the evening train. I took Father with us.

On February 8, 1940, Roosevelt wrote to Berle: "I have learned with great sorrow of the loss which has come to you with such crushing force in the death of your dear mother. Mrs. Roosevelt joins me in an assurance of heartfelt sympathy to you, to your father, and to all who mourn with you. Our hearts go out to you."

To Roosevelt, February 12, 1940

Let me thank you, on behalf of my Father and the rest of us, for your kindly letter of February 8th on the occasion of Mother's death.

My Mother was one of the last of the pioneer Christians, whose faith in life was great in its quiet and simplicity. I think that, unconsciously, she knew her work was done; completed her cycle by going back to the town where she had been reared and married and where she had deep roots in the land her family had settled; and then went swiftly home. There was so much of the building of America in that life: the pioneering of the Western Reserve prairie in her father's life, the opening of South Dakota in her own; the intense insistence on a spiritual synthesis and the refusal to accept any hatred, which has kept this country clear of the decay which seems to have characterized this century elsewhere.

February 12, 1940

Friday, February 9. Washington. Sumner told me of the President's plan to send him to Europe—a variation on a procedure we have thought of before, since the explorations I had assumed would be carried on here. I do not know exactly when the change was made, though I suppose it may have been made during the last four days. . . .

Saturday, February 10. More work on this neutral conference. . . .

Fenwick is back from Rio; he says it is positively amazing how the Neutrality Committee has become the symbol of Latin American solidarity. The Good Neighbor policy really seems to be working.

To lunch with Jerome Frank. I tried to put him up to date on some of the longer shot thoughts I was having about what reconstruction of peace must look like. There is a difficulty here. My speech at New Haven seems to have frightened some people and I suppose perhaps it was incautious. My difficulty is that if we are talking about economic reconstruction after the war, either we mean it, or we do not. If we do, the problem, in size and intensity, is staggering; no half measures will do; we shall have to go the whole way, and there is no point in the world in not letting the United States know about it. Accordingly, I was attempting, in a guarded sort of way, to prepare a little for the kind of thing which will have to happen. I notice that it is linked in the editorials here with Welles's trip.

Sunday, February 11. . . . The Berlin cables indicate that something is being said about my New Haven speech, in Berlin; also that a good deal is being said about Welles's mission. This time the German papers are not using it for propaganda, but are reporting it straight. This argues a certain degree of hope.

In the afternoon, walking with the children.

February 17, 1940

February 16. To say farewell to Sumner, who is off on what looks to me like one of the most difficult and unhappy trips a man ever started on. The Chicago *Tribune* is sending along a man to write him up as unpleasantly as possible and make political capital against the Administration. . . .

Home, and in the evening Jesse Jones came in. . . . Fundamentally, I gathered, he thought Mr. Hull would be President. I am not too clear about it; I think the President may decide that a third term is essential. . . .

Today the Inter-American Bank was approved by the plenary session of the Inter-American Economic Advisory Committee. I think I can claim to have got this thing going, though most of the work was done by the Treasury, and I think the principal credit ought to go to Harry White. . . .

Saturday, February 24—Sunday, February 25, 1940

To Des Moines, via Chicago, to cover one of Welles's speaking dates before the National Farm Institute. . . . [Saturday] was a good evening and I enjoyed the outfit. Iowa was the pleasantest thing I have seen in a long time: the prairie, the farmsteads, the whole activity devoted to giving people the materials of life, instead of the materials of death, which seems to be the principal occupation of the industrialized sections of the world. On balance, I am prepared to think that the industrial revolution was one of the greatest mistakes the human mind ever committed.

February 26, 1940

The rest was a mess of continuous economic work on neutrality, and a little serious thinking as to what we can do to cushion the shock when the Allied credit gives out. The deadly probability is that someone will want us to finance the war at that time. In another year we shall be facing ultimates, here. . . .

February 29, 1940

Jim Rowe, from the White House staff, came over to say that the President had decided that in putting the Inter-American Bank through Congress, Jesse Jones ought to take the lead. This is all right, provided Morgenthau and everyone else will (a) let him take the lead, and (b) stand by him when he does. . . .

March 3, 1940

The estimate of things is briefly this:

The Welles mission has developed with us as a country seeking peace, but has proved a theatre for statements in public by the German government as to their real desires. These statements are nothing less than a demand for the domination both of the seas and of the continent of Europe, since they include a free hand in the East, the turning over of the Mediterranean strategic points—Gibraltar, Suez, etc.—either to Germany or to Italy; the relinquishment of the naval base at Singapore; the "freedom of the seas". This is called a "Monroe Doctrine" for Germany, clearing her of danger from foreign interference.

It appears to me that, irrespective of what the statesmen may have said privately, this amounts to a statement which cannot be got out of.

Further, it develops that we are definitely in the hostile range. This has not appeared from anything the Germans have said or done. On the contrary, they are treating us with kid gloves and avoiding every possibility for controversy. But it does appear in the Russian propaganda. They are now flooding Russia with propaganda indicating that the Finnish war was due to three plutocracies, namely, the United States, Great Britain and France. This is launching us definitely as a hostile, or quasi-hostile, power. . . .

The French are now pressing the British to recognize that Russia is an enemy and treat her as such. . . .

Now the Italian relations with Great Britain at the moment are bad. The Italian population wants peace; but the Italian government is sitting to see in which direction her profit lies and to pick a winner. Her greatest profit lies in going with the Germans and despoiling the British Empire; but she is held in check by two fears: first, that the Germans may not win, and second, that if they do win they will limit her participation. . . . Her diplomatic position is still central; the British wooing has not proved successful; and she lies squarely athwart the line to the Middle and Far East.

The German army is probably stronger by a good many divisions than the combined armies against her. The Russians probably will be able to engulf Finland, in the long run, though the cost would be very great. . . . The ghost I saw last spring, of a German-Russian combination substantially dominant from the Maginot Line to the Pacific, is becoming more of a reality than I like to think about. . . .

We are thus drawing visibly nearer to the point noted in my memorandum of last April: namely, whether we will ultimately defend against an essentially hostile Europe in Europe, or on the Atlantic line. Such little naval advice as I can pick up indicates still the Atlantic line, though at a terrific cost of our emotions; and the time is not yet, for it still remains to be seen whether the British blockade will eventually be broken.

On this not very happy layout I should think our policy ought to be more decisive than it now is.

(1) We should not get into this war.

(2) We should and must increase our fleet, and to some extent, our army, and bring them to immediate mobile strength, instead of planning a program due to be complete about 1943.

(3) We ought to be giving economic assistance right and left, to Finland, Sweden and China, which if nothing else occurs will mean a steady attrition of the Russo-German position. If we do get to ultimates, they will be that much weaker.

Our real defense lies in the fact that the cost of a Russo-German success, though it may leave them to dominate the field, will leave them so weakened that they need not be feared; in which case our great test will be economic: can we maintain enough economic life for this Hemisphere so that one after another country in South America will not be forced by trade relations to fall into the Berlin orbit? The Secretary puts it concisely: he says that that success will mean that nobody can trade except by permission of Tokyo or Berlin; and that the South American countries in that case will have to be either supported by us, or drawn into definite political and economic arrangements with the two capitals. . . .

Mr. Hull put it that we were, in a sense, sailing right into a continuously thickening fog so far as we were concerned; and this is, I think, a fair statement of the situation. The uncomfortable fact about it is that the bulk of the United States dislikes to face unpleasant realities; therefore assumes that everything is all right; that if we go our way rejoicing we shall have no major difficulties and will not hear anything different. I proposed telling the truth to the public and that is a question to be considered. But it is difficult, politically dangerous, and probably to anyone in my position at present, impossible. . . .

March 8, 1940

March 5. A string of minor matters which have to be cleared with the White House. Here, however, there is embarrassment. The press stories about Welles having a more intimate contact in the White House than the Secretary have not been helpful; and if one goes to the White House much there will be additional stories of that kind. So I am trying to push as many of these things through the Secretary as I can. Aside from protecting him from publicity, this is scant kindness because it means he has to go through and digest a lot of material about unimportant matters, and this is time-consuming, when his whole energies are naturally in the really important things. . . .

March 7. At work on a long spell of minor things, of one sort and another, but at 6:25 a very unpleasant cable came in from Stockholm. It was [Minister Frederick A.] Sterling, to say that he had learned that the Finns had finally decided to throw up the sponge, tired as they were of Allied promises which did not come true and Swedish pressure on them to make peace at any price, and no real help in sight. The government had already decided to send envoys to Moscow, and they had already gone. Naturally, the Russians are going to make a Carthaginian peace, if they can. [Eljas] Erkko [Finland's Chargé d'Affaires in Stockholm] had asked Steinhardt whether possibly the President could do anything. With a heavy heart, I telephoned Secretary Hull, who had just received a cable, and asked him whether we could not do something. He turned it over in his mind, suggested that we cable Steinhardt to go and see Molotov and tell him that our public opinion would be impressed by a moderate and generous peace; and then telephoned the White House. I drafted, and added the one piece of solid pressure we have: namely, that our people had been pressing for measures affecting economic relations (translate: embargo on Russia) and that these movements would be less active if there were a generous peace. The Secretary telephoned back, having talked to the President; we re-phrased the cable three or four times, and I then rang up the President, who was at dinner. Catching him between the State dinner and the meeting afterward, he approved the telegram and we shot it off. But I am afraid that it is too late. I told the President that to ask generosity from the Russians was much like talking Christianity with a cobra. Perhaps the morning will show a better story. But I think not.

Home, dead tired and unhappy.

Somehow, when this has finished with us I do not give any of us a clean bill of health. We ought to have been more clean-cut in our help. The Allies ought to have made up their minds earlier. The Swedes probably ought not to have yielded to German pressure; but in view of the action of stronger powers, I do not see that it lies in our mouths to complain. The Finns have done all, and more than all, that could be expected of them; and if they choose to make terms now, one cannot even remotely blame them. For the alternative is ultimate conquest and sheer extermination—unless, of course, the Allies do something, which to date they have not done. Their proposed help of 30,000 men and supplies means very little as contrasted with Russian waves of 400,000 at a time surging in and in, and keeping on almost indefinitely. . . .

Saturday, March 9th. To work with the Secretary; and some further work on Finland and Scandinavia. We have been careful to keep Steinhardt informed, and likewise a little withdrawn; he has made his representations asking the Russians to be moderate (not much chance). The rest is trying to estimate how the cards fall. The Allied pressure is rising. It now develops that they have offered to send a full expedition to Finland and on condition that the Finns stay through to the end (I presume an agreement that they will not make a separate peace). They are at last prepared, if necessary, to risk a war with Russia. Actually, however, I think Chamberlain has some idea that a peace will be beneficial, because it will relieve pressure on Russia and thereby make possible a Russian break-away from Germany. This looks to me like a long shot and too clever to get by. . . .

March 11: [At the White House] I asked the President whether I should write speeches for Jim Farley, pointing out that the game was getting so close now that it was embarrassing. The President said that one could not know yet what could be done—I apologized for raising the problem thus obliquely, and indicated that I certainly did not want an answer. He at once disclaimed that; but I gathered from what he said that he is not yearning to let anyone get too close to him just now. This poses a pretty problem, for obviously we have got to keep everyone together if the next election is not to be a complete defeat.

March 18, 1940

Following is a summary of the last few days. It is necessarily incomplete. The pace has been so rapid and the speed in affairs so great that it becomes almost impossible to follow the outlines. Added to this is the fundamental fact that we know very little.

Welles is reporting in cipher to the President; and the Secretary does not have the cipher: he learns what the President tells him. I can only deduce that I am very glad to be in that position. If anything "leaks", I prefer that it does not come down my direction. Also, I gravely doubt whether Welles can have very much causative effect on the situation. . . .

March 14 . . . Welles has almost completed the circuit; will shortly be back in Rome. [He returned March 28.]

The Finnish peace has been made; and the staggering repercussions of it are setting off forces all over Europe. Russia, having ended her war, once more has freedom of action: cannot statesmen ever see that a country which is engaged even in a tiny war has lost all liberty of action? It is obvious that the Russians are re-enforcing their Far Eastern front, having as yet made no arrangements with Japan. The Russians are likewise becoming active in the Balkans, and the Rumanians took due note of what happened to the Finns. They therefore are not planning to stiffen their resistance very much. In this connection, I recall that the Rumanian Minister [Radu Irimescu], spending an evening with me last December, said that Finland's fighting made the Balkans safe. And now, she is no longer safe. The blunt fact is that the Allied governments wanted Finland to fight, but could not help, and their talk of sending an expedition was illusory, because they were not ready, either diplomatically or militarily. . . .

March 15: Another powwow with [F.] Ashton-Gwatkin and [Charles] Rist [special British and French emissaries] and most of the British and French embassies, and our own experts. They wanted to know all about moral embargoes—not that it is any of their particular business—but we are telling them. Their next move will be to complain that we ought to have more embargoes. Query—Why? They cannot quite get it through their heads that the embargoes are for our purposes, and not for theirs. However, our interests may be parallel in certain respects; and there is, of course, the fundamental and underlying national interest that a German-Russian combination with megalomaniac means of world domination shall not break into the Atlantic and start corroding this Hemisphere. We will listen to what they have to say.

The high point in the day was reached when Ashton-Gwatkin served notice that the British propose to intercept our clipper planes, which now, of course, avoid the British censorship by not calling at Bermuda. After a brief moment of silence, I observed that the first time a British air squadron shot at an American plane there would be the deuce to pay. Rist said it was a question of technique. I said that the Germans had said that when they wanted to exercise their right of visit and search by a submarine through the technique of torpedoing without warning. A few months later, we found ourselves at war with Germany. I hoped that new techniques, therefore, would not be relied on too much: better negotiate, instead. This is typical of Ashton-Gwatkin: I should say the least attractive type of British Foreign Office servant. He was trying to talk fair words with one hand and carry a club in the other: treating us as though we were a small European nation—say, Czechoslovakia. The quicker they drop him overboard and take Lord Lothian's advice, the better off we shall be. . . .

Home; and bad dreams of this whole air warfare business. For, if this kind of thing goes on, air warfare will make neutrality nearly impossible. And who can say what power will be master of the air? For air supremacy has vibrated from France to Russia, to Italy, to Germany. It turns on the country which is prepared to organize its industrial life and its production for warlike ends. . . .

March 18: I am glad that the President made the speech [Christian Foreign Service Convocation, March 16] against the peace-at-any-price idea. [The Finnish business, Berle had written Roosevelt, has pretty well proved that peace is not available at that price.] If it has no other effect, it will indicate that Welles is not behind the peace-at-any-price move. The next couple of weeks ought to be interesting: they may even be crucial; and God knows what the result may be. All I can say is that if the Allied governments are not more careful about their military activities than they are about their diplomacy, everyone is in for a bad time.

March 22, 1940

March 19. Michael Straight, son of an old friend, brought in Molly Yard [American Student Union leader], who wants a student conference to interest students in going into politics. I am afraid I was not too encouraging. Perhaps I am getting old, but I do not believe in the youth movement. Youth, cut adrift and operating by itself, produces very unpleasant results, because it is invariably capitalized by an older head. Hitler built his party on the "youth movement". The youngsters ought to get into politics, but they ought to get into politics along with the people who are of a similar way of thinking, some a little older, some much older, etc., so that the experience of the elder generations filters down automatically into the younger ones. Segregated, a youth movement becomes merely a pressure group on a large scale, too easily translated into force. A family, for instance, has children; but it does not have a "youth movement" in it. . . .

March 20. In the evening, Charles Rist, Lauchlin Currie [Administrative Assistant to the President] and [Alaska Governor] Ernest Gruening came to dinner. Rist is one of the most delightful men in the world. . . .

. . . It seems to me that currency ought to be regarded not as an end in itself, but merely as a tool: you put it where you want it, just as you put a steam shovel where you want that, in any form you want it. A light steam shovel for short-term credit; a heavy steam shovel for long-term credit; and your reserve mechanism to keep your currency in order. I suppose this is over-simplifying. . . .

March 21. Lunch with J. Edgar Hoover and Mr. Tamm, anent the affairs of the F.B.I. For an hour and a half we discussed a variety of matters, largely connected with the seamy side of the New Deal. . . . There were a number of matters which J. Edgar Hoover has had to handle and handle quietly at the direct request of a number of people, and his own organization has done far less actual wire tapping than the Treasury, the S.E.C. and several of these agencies. The newer the agency, the less it is anxious to respect the ancient and usual rights. I must say that the feeling one gets is a strong devotion to the anti-third term movement—not particularly on account of the President, but because in eight years little pyramids of power get built up and abused. My present feeling would be that logically we ought to permit a President to have as many terms as he likes, but on condition that he make a clean sweep of his government and get in a new set of men at least once in every two terms—which, of course, is impossible.

A little work on Near Eastern matters, as to which I am trying to study geography and trends. For it is perfectly plain that Turkey is the only reason why the German-Russian combination does not own everything in Asia and part of Africa as well as in Europe east of the River Rhine. . . .

Home, and to church for the evening.

But after, until late at night, stirring matters around in my mind. For the week thus far has been sinister to a degree.

The British-French alliance stands on one side of the West Wall. On the other is Germany—and Russia—with nothing between them and the Pacific. The Scandinavians endeavored to form a defensive alliance: Finland, Norway and Sweden; the Russians indicated that they would object, which is equivalent to declaring that Scandinavia is preempted for future Russian development. The Norwegians, frightened, retired from the defensive alliance, and the Swedes and the Finns are still wondering whether they dare work it out. Or are they already, like the Czechs, enslaved? . . .

To the south is Italy, still an undetermined question. . . .

The reports appear to be that so far as military matters are concerned the Allies cannot advance; the Germans possibly can. I think the British air raid on Sylt was a failure and I think the German air raid on Scapa Flow may well have been a partial success. Things will hold as they are for a time; but eventually there must be a titanic meeting of forces and no one can say how they will come out. If they come out in favor of the German-Russian combination, with megalomaniac dreams dominating the line, we have nothing to do save wait in the Atlantic, becoming as strong as we can to defend.

But the defense must be something more than force. It has to be ideas. If it was possible to get a foothold in ideals of something like love as against something like hatred, in Italy, we might be able to do the same thing in other parts of the world as well—if we are quick enough and clever enough, and sincere enough and straight enough to find a way through.

March 27, 1940
March 22. Morris Ernst [lawyer, author] telephoned from New York. . . . He is very angry with the press attack on J. Edgar Hoover. As he points out, J. Edgar Hoover has run a secret police with a minimum of collision with civil liberties, and that is about all you can expect of any chief of secret police.

A little time reviewing the espionage and counter-espionage work. It is sufficiently plain that in the Communist reaches at least, we are dealing with a large, thoroughly capable and thoroughly well-organized espionage system, reinforced by the ability to create certain centers of disorder through the hold on certain kinds of labor and other organizations. In addition, there is a certain amount of political support arrived at through manipulating the soft-headed liberals. The under-cover skeleton of this, which involves money and men on a large scale, requires a lot more attention than we actually can give it.

Saturday, March 23rd. A little further consideration of the espionage matters. Mr. [Raymond] Murphy [European Division] came in to say that the RCA had been subpoenaed by both the Dies Committee and the Department of Justice and that part of the haul was a complete set of cable instructions from the Russian government to various of the Communists (Browder, the *Daily Worker*) telling them exactly what to print regarding the Finnish war. . . .

March 24th, Easter Sunday. To the early morning service; but it was no good. This was not the fault of the church. It was the fact that in the prayer for the general state of things the admonition was given to pray for a just and moral peace; and since that started in this office, with a message from the President to a not too impressive missionary meeting which happened to time perfectly with events in Europe, it brought my mind back to this endless and tangled operation of affairs on the international front.

To the State Department and to chat over matters with the Secretary. He has been considering the state of affairs, in his ruminative way, and has not been feeling happy. Briefly, he sees, as we all do, the possibility that either by military or diplomatic shift we may find ourselves besieged by this Fascist combination; and in that case force would be the only immediate remedy.

I had been worrying about this, too. By consequence, through the courtesy of Ernest Cuneo, I got Walter Winchell to insert in his Sunday broadcast a stiff editorial on preparedness for the defense of the Hemisphere. We listened in on Sunday night; and an hour later Cuneo telephoned to say that the radio station had been jammed with favorable telegrams and wires. This was interesting: the Secretary had pointed out that it was politically dangerous to tackle this line and he doubted if anyone would have the courage to do it. But the columnist did try it, and the response was overwhelmingly favorable. It seems to me as though our politicians are far more timid than they need to be; maybe Walter Winchell will give them enough of a demonstration so that they can be stimulated to take a strong line. . . .

March 25. Then swiftly home to change and back to the state dinner at the White House for [Rafael] Calderón Guardia [President-elect of Costa Rica].

The President was in good form, but tired, and this cold [weather] is not doing him any good. He animadverted to the fact that the missionary speech seems to have worked out well. "The timing was perfect," he said. "It seems to have made a magnificent splash." There is probably more to that than I know. The British Ambassador turned up to thank Secretary Hull for having the speech made; and I suspect that it probably arrived at a critical juncture in Anglo-French politics. . . .

March 26. . . . I turned in a memorandum [March 23] to the Secretary about the need for national defense in the event that there is an Allied defeat. He called me in to say that he agreed with it entirely, but the thing was too hot to handle; if the memorandum were to "leak", it could be too easily distorted as a concession that the Allies would be defeated. . . . His suggestion was that I talk it over with the President, which I have agreed to do. . . .

> (Circulated. The Secretary noted it but asked that all copies be withdrawn—and that I go at this orally. I did. A.A.B.)

March 23, 1940

A study of the various reports from Europe, augmented by the estimates of certain officers here, would seem to indicate the necessity of the prompt reconsideration of our own position in the national defense. Through the courtesy of the Navy Department, we have had before us an informal estimate of the possible outcome of affairs in west Europe from Admiral Stark. Through the operation of the Liaison Committee we have had informal expressions of opinion of various of the Army officers. We have, likewise, the reports of our own representatives, which are particularly useful in respect of the Baltic region, the Near East, and of the Balkan areas.

A conclusion, which is very nearly inescapable, is that there can be no certainty as to the outcome of the war in west Europe. The possibility of a defeat of the Franco-British alliance must now be squarely reckoned with. There is a balance of chance against such a defeat; but it is so small that in handling our own policy we cannot rely on that fact. . . .

. . . Since Russia and Germany in the event of victory will undoubtedly be joined by Italy, we should then have three Powers in urgent need of raw materials without financial ability to acquire them in the ordinary course, and desiring to acquire them in the Western Hemisphere.

Nor have we any doubt as to the methods which would be used. . . .

It must therefore be assumed that an immediate result of the German victory permitting access to the Atlantic will be an attack politically, economically and, possibly, naval, on the hemispheric block which has been built up here within the line of the Monroe Doctrine. We have no doubt of this; while the process has not gone far, it is sufficiently plain that in a number of South American countries skeleton organizations have already been built up by Germany, which will be available for use whenever opportunity affords.

We know further the immediate course of events following any such victory. Under the terms of the declarations of Lima and the more specific pledges of the declaration of Panama all the 21 Republics are pledged to resist penetration of that kind. The immediate question would be asked of us whether we were prepared to defend the entire situation. This question would require an immediate answer. Any hesitation or delay in answering it would at once lead a wavering South American country to make the best terms it could with the apparently victorious power in the belief that otherwise it would be abandoned as the smaller European neutrals were abandoned in the hour of their danger.

We cannot forecast the time when such a problem might be put before us. . . .

But if we wait until the time actually arises without being fully prepared for eventualities, we shall be entirely unable to answer effectively the appeal for assistance which will at once be sent in our direction. We should be, in a word, in no better relation to South America than Great Britain has proved to be in respect of Finland or of Czechoslovakia. . . .

Recommendations

I accordingly recommend:

1. That the Inter-Departmental Committee on Neutrality be called together and the situation be disclosed;

2. If the Committee agrees in substance with the foregoing estimate, that it present an immediate recommendation to the President asking him to call a conference on preparedness, which will cover military, naval and air defense, and shall also cover the provision of adequate supplies of munitions and war materials, designed to bring the American defense establishment to a high strength within the period of not to exceed six months;

3. That such defensive measures be conceived as dealing with the entire Western Hemisphere;

4. That it be made clear that the force so developed is designed not for service in Europe but for the defense of an Atlantic line roughly corresponding to the line marked out by the declaration of Panama.

5. That if this policy be determined upon, an appropriate message be sent to the Congress outlining it, and

6. That simultaneously appropriate consultations with the governments of the South American Republics be had, primarily for the purpose of explaining the motives and intent of the policy, and for securing such coordination as may seem desirable with the defense measures of the other American Republics.

March 29, 1940

Some miscellaneous jobs, and to lunch with Jesse Jones, chiefly working on the Inter-American Bank, the policy with regard to the loan to

Colombia (they want ten million; will get five million, but only for their necessities in purchases of goods outside Colombia. Jesse thinks, and so do I, that if it is a question of money to spend in Colombia, it is their business to handle their own currency system. Foreign loans should be primarily to give foreign countries a chance to have a free exchange, which they can use outside the country. This is good doctrine: I wish the United States would accept it).

April 3, 1940

To the Pan American Union, where we put in a heavy morning discussing revision of the statutes of the Inter-American Bank; then to lunch with Sumner Welles.

From his European trip he came back with two or three definite ideas. The first is that we ought at once to try to improve our relations with Italy, which are as bad as they could possibly be. He thought this could be done through some economic assistance, including some method by which they could get coal from us. Mussolini, he said, could lead the country into war on the German side, even though there might be trouble six weeks or two months later. The Italian position at the moment was determinative. . . .

April 4, 1940

[Ambassador] Spruille Braden came in from Colombia, where he has done a first-rate job, especially in clearing up the air lines matter. Pan Am had been helping to run a German line in Colombia and had been using it to train German pilots—presumably to bomb the Panama Canal when the time comes. Braden has done a first-class job in clearing them out. . . .

April 5, 1940

At the end of the day the news came that the Senate has passed Secretary Hull's extension of the trade treaty program. We all congratulated the old man on what is, after all, one of the most brilliant and hard-fought victories of his long career. Probably in that vote the Presidency has been really determined; though that we cannot yet tell.

April 9, 1940

April 6. Then the really bad time. The Norwegian Minister [Wilhelm Munthe de Morgenstierne] came in, very much worried; he thinks there will be trouble. He told me that the Russian Ambassador, Oumansky, had been to see him recently, for the first time in months. His purpose was to explain that Russia considered the Finnish adventure liquidated; had no more demands on Finland; that any talk that she wanted part of Norway was anti-Soviet propaganda, etc. This, of course, is a direct lie; their plan did call for taking part of northern Norway. But the sinister question arose: Why should the Russian Ambassador suddenly come up for air to give assurance of this kind? It looked to me as though he were making a record. Further, telegrams from Copenhagen indicated that

Hitler had ordered an advance into Scandinavia; he had done this over the objection of the army people and was preparing to move. We know of troop concentrations at Stettin and naval movements along the coast of Denmark and the southern coast of Sweden, apparently headed in the direction of Norway. This looks like a bad business. . . .

April 7. I was still uneasy, having the Scandinavian situation in mind. But the day passed quietly, without any particular sign of activity so far as we were concerned. . . .

Monday, April 8. A chat with Welles, principally about inter-American bank matters; then to a mortal long meeting at the Pan American Union, raking over the draft convention, charter and by-laws of the proposed Inter-American Bank. . . .

Then to bed, but somehow wakeful. I had barely turned out my reading lamp when the watch officer telephoned.

Tuesday, April 9. The watch officer said that they had just read a telegram from Daisy Harriman [Minister to Norway] in Oslo. It said that the Germans had attempted to land in Norway; the Norwegians had fired, and Norway was now at war with Germany. The British had asked us to take over their interests. I pulled on some clothes and went down to the Department. On the way, I met the *Times* correspondent, [Frank] Kluckhohn. Their office had received a wire announcing that the Germans had landed in Denmark and several places and likewise crossed the border by land; that Copenhagen had already been occupied. Apparently, immediately after this got out, all wires were cut.

At the Department there was little to do, except authorize Daisy Harriman to take over the British and French interests; and to give like authorization to [Ray] Atherton [Minister to Denmark]. We telephoned the news to Welles, who was in bed; to the Secretary, who was in Atlantic City, and who will come back; to [William D.] Hassett, one of the President's secretaries, at Hyde Park, but with instructions to him not to wake the President. (What could the President do at this stage of the game?) Then to the question of ships. We found that the Maritime Commission had got tuckered out and stopped having a watch officer. So I raked Max Truitt out of bed, but he was too sleepy to be articulate. I did extract an idea, namely, that we might get old man [Emmet J.] McCormack, whose line has all our ships in that area, if we could raise him in New York. At two o'clock we pulled him out of bed; and he said he would stop the ships that were going there, or at least see that they did not get into trouble unduly. Fortunately, there are only two or three. A little work on the press announcements for the Department, and by that time the entire staff was on deck in the State Department; then home to bed, for a brief sleep.

I put in about four hours' sleep and then came down to the Department. . . .

. . . A slough of work getting ready for neutrality proclamations; then to the Pan American Union for a final meeting of the sub-committee. We at length approved integrally the charter, by-laws and convention affecting the Inter-American Bank. This brings us one step nearer to a project which was started when the Pan American Union founded itself exactly fifty years ago (specifically, April 14, 1890). Pretty fast work, and not done yet. . . .

Then back to the Department, where we went right into the problem of drawing a new combat area. For, as things now stand, the situation is this:

Norway has told us and Great Britain that she is at war, but it is pretty informal. Nevertheless, I think time will tell that she really is. The Danes have said nothing. Instead, there is confirmation that some kind of an agreement has been reached between Denmark and Germany—an agreement reached at the point of a pistol. From now on, the Danish government can no longer be regarded as a free agent. The Germans have landed at several points on the Norwegian coast, and indications are that the British are going to go after them. One wonders, by the way, where the British navy was all this time, while the Germans were merrily traveling all over the Norwegian coast. . . . Anyhow, the whole of the Norwegian coast is, or may become, a battleground, so that we have to keep our ships out of there.

We held, accordingly, a meeting of representatives of State, Commerce, Maritime Commission and later called in the Navy and Justice. . . .

Between meetings, a really tragic meeting with Henrik Kauffmann, the Danish Minister, whom I have come to like and respect very much. He wanted personal advice as to his own status. He said they did not need Henrik Kauffmann to represent any puppet government run by Germans; and he had to recognize that the Danish government was no longer a free agent. He wondered what to do. I told him that I hardly dared give personal advice, as I realized the tremendous danger to him and to his family and to everyone else. But I said I thought that there was such a thing as Denmark and would continue to be, even though its government was temporarily submerged; that I thought he might say so and continue to represent it, even if it was, for the time being, nothing more than an idea in the breasts of a few courageous Danes. But I told him that the risks involved in this were very great; that no one could really decide for him. I said that I thought a country which lay down could not easily get up again, but if even as few as two or three courageous men declined to lie down, the country might rise up with them in the future, however distant. Henrik clasped my hand and left, in tears.

We have blocked all the Danish and Norwegian balances, knowing perfectly well that the Germans will attempt by force to seize them at once, by the simple process of requiring the Danes and Norwegians who have signatures on checking accounts at our Federal Reserve and New York banks to turn them over to the appropriate German agency. I do not think that we would care to recognize these signatures, at least for the time being. If we hold them on the line, we can determine what to do later, and I think that as to that we may be able to handle the situation so that the money is used for Denmark and Norway, respectively, and not for someone else.

A little liaison work with the Federal Reserve, Maritime Commission, etc. We will have the combat area proclamation prepared for the President; Welles and the Secretary are meeting him at the train. I am going to dine with the Apostolic Delegate and talk about the re-creation of a world based on spiritual values. It sounds a trifle inane, in view of the actual situation, but I am pretty firmly convinced that reality lies more nearly in that direction than in all this shouting Nineveh of forced moves.

April 19, 1940
Wednesday, April 10. A raft of detail, all arising out of the Norwegian and Danish invasions. . . .

. . . we wound up in the President's office. He signed the order [blocking the Danish and Norwegian bank balances], and that was that. He told me that the Danish Minister had just been there and . . . had asked what would happen if the Danish government, now under complete control of the German military, recalled him and sent someone else in his place. Which of the two would the American government recognize? The President told him that we should undoubtedly take the factor of duress into consideration—plain indication that we would not recognize any appointee of the now captive government of Denmark, until such time as that government became a free agent again.

April 11 . . . At 6:30 I got on the train for Houston, Texas; and glad of the sleep.

Friday, April 12. On the train, and doing nothing but watch the country-side.

Saturday, April 13. Arrived in Texas. This was a meeting of the young Democratic Club, chiefly a Garner movement, and very heavily under the influence of Jesse Jones, who had really arranged it. Before I was there more than five minutes, [Mayor] Maury Maverick came in from San Antonio. He is running an opposition, or third term movement. I tried to explain to all hands that it seemed to me that the Garner candidacy was finished . . . and that the delegation would have to do what the President wanted them to do; that my private opinion was that Cordell Hull was as likely to be the candidate as anyone else. . . .

Then to make a speech, which was really a kind of requiem for the Texas conservatives. . . .

April 15. [To New Orleans] By the night train to Atlanta, where, somewhat to my consternation, I was met by a brass band. The show was spoiled, because the train got there five minutes early. So we had to go back and do the brass band over again; then to lunch with several southern bishops . . . and a variety of others . . . and Chief Justice [Charles] Reid, of the Georgia Supreme Court. They insisted, among other things, that the opposition to Myron Taylor's appointment to the Vatican came exclusively from two men . . . and that it excited no sympathy. . . .

The Bishops have been setting up a Catholic conference of the South designed to take the lead in social movements in the South. They have a good program, and may get something done. Naturally, it is on the cautious side; all Catholic action is; but they at least have the right idea. I was glad to find that they are solidly against the Coughlin movement.

Wednesday, April 17. On the train home, and glad to get there.

The high point of the trip came on Monday, somewhere between Houston and New Orleans. In the club car the porter turned on the radio. It was the Pan American Day speech, and not many changes in it. I was glad the President felt that he could make that speech.

Excerpts from Berle's draft of Pan American Day speech

. . . We have no need to seek a new international order. We have achieved an American order. . . .

The cooperative peace in the Western Hemisphere was not created by wishing; and it will require more than words to maintain it. In this cooperative group, whoever touches any one of us touches all of us. We have only asked that the world go with us in the path of peace. But we shall be able to keep that way open only if we are prepared to meet force if challenge is ever made.

. . . We know that old dreams of universal empire are abroad in the world again. . . . We must reckon at least on the possibility that brute force may some day be used even against the Western Hemisphere.

The American family of nations has considered even that possibility. At Buenos Aires we agreed that we would consult, should our peace be threatened. At Lima we agreed to stand together to defend and maintain the absolute integrity of every American nation from any attack, direct or indirect, from beyond the seas. At Panama we worked out ways and means for keeping war away from this Hemisphere. Should there be need, we can be swift to repel attack. I believe we shall not have to meet that test; but should it be necessary, I am convinced that we should be wholly successful. The inner strength of a group of free people is irresistible when they are prepared to act.

April 20, 1940

Yesterday, April 19th, a long and difficult and somewhat disturbed day, what with a variety of miscellaneous affairs. It is obvious that the Baltic situation is rapidly developing, though we cannot tell when things will change. High point in the day came towards the end of the afternoon, when we were called in to deal with the problem of Greenland. The Danish Minister has been setting up committees to take care of Danish affairs here; and regarding Greenland. As to this, we have already warned off the British, the French and the Canadians, on the ground that Greenland is within the Monroe Doctrine area. Although Iceland is within the Western Hemisphere, it is so obviously a part of the European system that we can leave that out. As a result, the Europeans are keeping their hands off Greenland for the time being. But the question is how to act here.

I took the position in the conference that the government in Greenland, although it is rudimentary to a degree, is still a remnant of the sovereign government of Denmark. Any authority the Danish Minister can get from the Greenland councils and the Greenland governors is therefore a full authority to act, and he can act on it if we recognize it.

Consequently, I advocated that we recognize any authority he might thus obtain.

Lunch with Welles, and we hashed over a variety of things. Welles is perfectly certain that the President will not run; that Mr. Hull will be the nominee, and that the President will therefore have complete control of the Convention; and that machinery is unnecessary. I think this is quite likely to be so, but I am not altogether clear. . . .

April 20. A small job with regard to English shipping; and then to work with the Danish Minister. He is now in communication with Greenland and will get authority to act for Greenland; and the next thing that will happen is the Greenlanders will present a request for our protection and assistance. I think it is by no means improbable that we shall do something about it. Henry Morgenthau has agreed to fit out a ship and have it ready to go up there. This is just as well, because during the morning the Royal Canadian Mounted Police had sent word, through the F.B.I., to know if we objected to their sending a force to Greenland to find out what was going on. I think the Royal Mounted should mind its own damned business, and let the governments settle high policy. We politely indicated that, both then and to the Canadian Minister.

Meanwhile, Kauffmann is working along as well as he can, re-creating, with what limited authority he has, some representation for the still independent Danish shipping and business interests here. He will have some real authority from Greenland, however, based on the theory worked out last night. . . .

April 23, 1940

Meanwhile, the Danish shipping committee had come in. They told a tale that makes you angry. As soon as Denmark was invaded, the British announced that they would treat all Danish ships as enemies. These ships, accordingly, went into neutral ports and stayed there. A Danish shipping committee went to work to negotiate—with Ashley Sparks in New York, representing the British government. Sparks coolly asked them to turn over their ships to the British and they would be condemned as prizes. The British government would consider paying for them, as of grace, some kind of a figure. I assume the cargoes, most of which are American-owned, would likewise be taken. After that, the British would consider whether, under the British flag, they might not let some of the Danes work on the ships.

This is a bit of low-grade English piracy. Sparks is head of a competing British company. It is not up to the Nazi piracy, at its best, but it is one of these things that makes you very leery about getting too deeply in with any British interest. The fact that by surrender of the ships, which Sparks asked for, some fifty or seventy-five millions of American cargoes would likewise be confiscated seems not to have been worth mentioning by anybody. I think we shall have to talk to Lothian about it. Incidentally, the politics of it is about as bad as it can be. The British would probably convince the Danes in Denmark that they will fare about as badly under either master. . . .

April 26, 1940

April 24. We figured out a way of doing something about the Danish ships, at least so far as American interests are concerned. I can see no sense at all in having American cargoes go under a British prize court, and so arranged that no Danish ship shall be allowed to clear until our interests are somehow protected. . . .

April 25. An hour in Sumner Welles's office; we discussed, chiefly, the possibility of setting up some kind of coordinated method for working out the national defense. This involved certain prior decisions of policy which, it seems to me, are not being made. Defense is one thing if you are going to defend the Philippines and, let us say, the Dutch East Indies. If you are going to begin at Hawaii, that is something else. It is one thing if you think you wish to defend in Europe; a second thing if you envisage it as a defense of the Atlantic line (which grows in my mind). To the south of us there are like problems. . . .

The end of the day, a little work on trying to find out the exact state of affairs in Greenland. I have been pushing the idea, which originated with Secretary Hull, of sending a consul up there; and I think Norman Davis is considering sending a Red Cross crew, as well. . . .

April 30, 1940

April 27. Thence by plane to New York City, to the La Guardia airport; the first time I had seen it since the early days when it was a mud field which we were thinking of buying. Now it is one of the most magnificent ports in the world, looking like a picture in an H. G. Wells novel. La Guardia was there to meet me. We had lunch at the air port and talked over various and strange things. Particularly, whether he could be Vice-President on a ticket with Hull. Of course this may not work out; for the President may decide to run, himself, or he may try—without success, I think—to make Jackson President in his place. In that case, Jackson will be beaten; no one trusts the younger New Dealers as yet, and there is no particular reason why they should. . . .

It was La Guardia's view that if any movement for Vice-Presidency for him began, the proper place to begin it would be in the South or in the Southwest. . . .

We discussed a little the future of New York City. I told him that I thought his was the last big job that could be done; within the limitations of existing rules of finance, he had taken it about as far as was possible. The next Mayor would be confined merely to managing what La Guardia had set up for him; and La Guardia observed that this was not only true, but that the increasing pressure of the time would mean constant drives on the revenue of New York City. Real estate can no longer supply the demands and New York City could not supply the State and take care of itself, too, particularly in view of the present policies of the federal government. In consequence, the next Mayor of New York would either be nothing to speak of, or he would be the interpreter of a changed financial policy of the government, which was not as yet in sight.

. . . and then went to call on old C. C. Burlingham, now eighty-five years old, but extremely vigorous. C. C. confided that he had tried to get Harvard to give La Guardia an honorary LL.D.; but the Corporation had looked him over and decided that it would not do. This is natural: so far as the Harvard Corporation is concerned, the fact that a man has merely been of service to his country and his kind is no reason for commendation. It has to be done in a particular mode, and with the appreciation of the best thought of people.

I tried to give the general outlines of the foreign policy, so that he could have those in his mind in the event that they came up. We then fell to talking about labor. "It is time that something very solid was said about this", said La Guardia. "We have met the arrogance of organized money. We still have to meet the arrogance of organized labor. They have sabotaged every real attempt to take care of the workmen. We are ready for annual wages and steady employment; but the leaders will have nothing of it; preferring fantastic scales of hourly and daily wages, without work, instead. The racketeering is beyond belief."

. . . We picked out a few speeches to be made in the South and in the Midwest and the West; and that was about all that it came to, save for the pleasure of seeing a man who has done a magnificent job and is entitled to the next step forward, which lesser men are prepared to take away from him if they can—and perhaps they can.

By the night train home.

April 28. . . . I met Lord Lothian. He told me that they had received word from a secret source in the Vatican that the Fascist Grand Council had met, and had agreed to enter the war on the German side. There had been a row about it, but Mussolini had carried the day. Lothian was very blue. . . .

April 29 . . . then some solid work rigging up the general outlines of our provisional consulate to Greenland. The Coast Guard has a cutter which will go as soon as it can. We had selected a boy for the job; but he had been too long in London and gone soft; and when he got to the stage of wondering whether his wine would keep and a seven room knock-down house could be shipped up there, we called that one off and looked over some other candidates. We found a boy who had been at Yunnun-Fu and had gone over the Burma Road alone, and he looks like a better Greenland bet than our other chap. By the end of the day we had things fairly well lined up. The Consulate, of course, will be a gesture suggesting that other people ought to keep out. [On May 8 Berle had lunch with Hugh Cumming (European Division) and the two men being sent to Greenland, James Penfield and George West.]

May 1, 1940

Mussolini received Phillips and gave him the completest assurance that he does not intend to enter the war. He treated the gesture as a very friendly one; Welles thinks this ends the Mediterranean crisis. I question whether it was our influence that did it, but am glad to have the assurance—if assurance it is. Privately, I have only limited faith in assurances;

they may be true at the time, but there is nothing that keeps them good for very long. . . .

Thursday, May 2. There are indications that the St. Lawrence Seaway treaty has struck a snag, but I am not sure whether it is not here, as well as in Canada. The President, I think, believes he has not the votes to put it through; therefore will not force it. Nevertheless, I am trying to keep the flag flying for the next man who wishes to have a whack at it. . . .

Dinner at Mrs. [Florence] Keep's house, principally to see [her sister] Mrs. Murray Crane. This is the first house I dined at in Washington when I was here as a 2nd Lieutenant; and I first saw Washington at breakfast with Mrs. Crane in the year of Grace 1912, when Murray Crane was a reigning figure in the Republican Party.

Friday, May 3. The Norwegian matter grows more complex. It is now plain that the British not only did abandon the Norwegians to their fate, but commenced their retreat and actually took to their ships before they even notified the Norwegian commanders. The result, of course, was to leave the Norwegian units to certain massacre, unless they were able to work out an armistice—which they appear to be doing.

This has two sets of repercussions.

The first is political. No neutral will rely on British promises of aid again. For the British record is pretty nearly perfect. They deserted and betrayed Czechoslovakia—this, no doubt, as they say, because they could not do anything else and to buy time to rearm. But Czechoslovakia ceased to exist.

They agreed to support, and actually went to war over, Poland; but they could give and did give Poland no effective help.

They intervened to assist Norway and did actually do so, but so ineffectively that the help did more damage than good, and the manner of their leaving was such as to create bitterness in every Norwegian heart. The British take the attitude that the neutrals have been hostile to them, in not putting up more resistance, which is the reason they yearn to call the Danes enemies and are endeavoring to do so legally in order to seize the Danish fleet. But on this record their protestations are not likely to be very convincing. Again it is the British desire to act under the cloak of morality always that gets them into trouble. If they said they were merely going to do the best they could and hoped it would be enough, it would be a much easier position for them.

Since the principal defense against an invading empire like Germany is the maintenance of national units inside the empire which will endeavor to make headway and reconstitute themselves, it seems to me that the British policy of grousing about neutrals which they are unable to help is a singularly ineffective one. Whatever they think, I should assume that they would try to foster those national movements for all in sight. . . .

May 4. The Norwegian Minister came in. He has something real on his mind. He fears that the result of the British defeat may be the submergence of the present Norwegian government. He wants to use the power of attorney authorizing him to take over the funds of the Norwegian government, the Norge Bank and a variety of other Norwegian government institutions. He wishes to use this to get the assets into his own account before a new Norwegian government comes in which revokes his power, under German pressure, or before his own government goes under. I thereupon got hold of [Assistant General Counsel Bernard] Bernstein, of the Treasury, and we tried to work out a method of going to work at it. Welles, who is Acting Secretary in Secretary Hull's absence in Atlantic City, is quite agreeable, and I think we shall get something worked out in the not distant future. It means some examination of the legal matters.

During the day a cablegram came in from Mrs. Harriman, through Stockholm, indicating that the power of attorney to the Norwegian Minister had been authenticated by her and had been placed in our pouch headed for the United States. I suppose, therefore, there is a document, and we can act on that. . . .

May 5. For the Germans now claim that in the Namsos fighting they were able to sink a capital ship by air bombardment. If this is true, and it appears that the air can definitely overcome the sea defenses, Britain is in a bad way indeed. She can move her fleet, of course; but this leaves England open to air bombardment at any time, and it is by no means impossible that we are looking down the gun barrels of the end of the effective British defense.

. . . Lothian dropped in to see Welles, chiefly to get information but hazarded a guess that the Chamberlain government might well go under on Tuesday, but there was no one who could act as Premier. . . . Welles said that on the first of the two evenings he saw Churchill he was quite drunk. I asked whether he saw, in his peregrinations, any indication of clear-cut leadership. Welles answered that he saw none. . . .

May 8. As the day closed, a cable came in from Berlin indicating that [Counselor of the Embassy Alexander] Kirk had picked up news that orders were out for the German army to march some time soon; and that they undoubtedly were going forward to Holland and Belgium. This looked bad. I went home, accordingly, to have dinner, but kept in touch. About ten o'clock, or a little later, the watch officer called me. Cables had come in from the Queen of Holland for the President. She referred to a message he had once sent her saying that if she were in difficulties and needed asylum, he would send a cruiser to take her to the United States. She indicated that she had decided to stay by her job, but wondered whether the President would honor the request if it were sent by the Princess Royal. . . . I rang up the White House and talked to the President. He had got the cable and had asked Welles to answer it. Welles was on his way downtown. Since I thought this indicated that German troops might be on the march, I came down to the Department to find Welles, who had gone to bed with a couple of sleeping powders, been routed out, taken some black coffee and showed up very tired, and quite unhappy. Obviously, we cannot send a cruiser through the war zone now, without getting into trouble. I suggested sending a cruiser to Iceland and letting the Princess and her small daughters go there. Sumner had a much better idea: let her take a plane to Lisbon and the cruiser meet her there. We happen to have a cruiser which frequently calls at Lisbon, so we sent the message and waited a while to see whether, as midnight passed and dawn came in Holland, there would be news of any activity. There was none, and we put in for home. We made a pretext of calling by the Metropolitan Club and he there invited me in for a drink, and for one of the few times in his life let down his guard completely. He was furious with desire to sleep and totally unable to do so; and we drank four Scotches in a row, in quick succession. There were a number of things that came out in the course of an hour's talk, between one and two in the morning. It is understood that Roosevelt, unless the situation changes, will wait until the last minute and then issue a statement in favor of Mr. Hull. In event of the election of Hull, Norman Davis will be Secretary of State. Welles thinks there will be nothing for him; London, which he will undoubtedly be offered, would be boring to a degree—besides, he thinks he could not afford it. Bullitt and Kennedy are no longer on speaking terms; Kennedy is full of admiration for Welles; Bullitt hates him. I discount a little of this for the acuteness of great fatigue; but the general outlines are plain enough. . . .

We swapped yarns on old times in Santo Domingo, and wondered where we all would be in another year. Sumner thinks I ought to take Eccles' place at Federal Reserve; but I pointed out that that was practically not much of a post, now. In any event, it doesn't matter; if we can help to pull the country through, ambitions of any individual amount to very little.

We knocked off at half past two and turned in. . . .

Thurs., May 9 . . . A humorous twist at the end of the day. Although we had announced Penfield and West's sailing for Greenland, nobody had noticed it until today, when the newspaper boys picked up the rumor that the Coast Guard cutter on which they are going was loading rifles and other weapons and ready to land a force and run up an American flag and annex the Arctic, and so forth, there. Accordingly, one of the papers wanted to put a special war correspondent on board—I presume to give a careful account of what the porpoises said on the way up. I argued them out of it. . . .

There followed a dinner given by Basil Harris, who is the shipping adviser to the Treasury and owns the United States Line. It was more like the ball Becky Sharp gave in Brussels the night before Waterloo, according to "Vanity Fair", than any dinner I have ever been at. For the company was large and brilliant, and sparkling. But in the middle of it, someone called for Pierrepont Moffat. It was the Secretary; our Minister at The Hague had just telephoned him that the German planes were flying over Holland. The Luxembourg government had already fled to France. The word slowly circulated. The Belgian Ambassador, who has a son and a son-in-law at the front, merely lifted an eyebrow and continued, suavely, to flirt a little with the ladies. Slowly, the State Department men who were there slid softly out: Moffat, Dunn, myself, and later, Breck Long; and went over to the State Department. The Secretary was already there.

The big push was on, in good earnest. The Norwegian tactics were being used; fifth columns to attack the Dutch and Belgian air fields; parachute troops being dropped to seize them; obviously, air reinforcements to follow. It must have been a wild and storm-swept evening. Apparently the Dutch and the Belgians both were fairly well warned; and the Blitzkrieg tactics scarcely worked. There is some reason to believe that the Germans were also landing troops by sea.

We could merely watch the progress of affairs and let it go at that. At one o'clock there was not much to be done, and just at this time Welles arrived—again pulled out of bed, where he had again gone with a couple of sleeping powders. But he had himself well in hand. All we could do was watch things for a little; but The Hague wire was hardly working, though one telephone call came through; and we could not even raise Paris. It was a sort of murk of general destruction, with reports coming in on the radio and occasional cables indicating the long-promised Blitzkrieg, which lived up to the anticipated horror.

There was only one relieving note. After strenuous efforts, we finally got a trans-Atlantic wire through to our Embassy in London, and waked up Joe Kennedy. The Secretary asked him what the news was. Joe hadn't heard of any news; was as innocent as a babe unborn of the whole night's work. The Secretary remarked, when he put down the telephone, "His mind is as blank as an uninked paper."

I stayed until half past two and then decided that there was no point in spending all one's strength on sight-seeing; and thereupon went home. . . .

Friday, May 10th. A pretty mixed-up day, without any clear record of accomplishment. The proclamations of neutrality relating to Belgium, Holland and Luxembourg, were in order, prepared by Mr. [Charles W.] Yost [Division of Controls]. But the Secretary rightly thought that we needn't be in a hurry to put them out.

The orders freezing the Dutch and Belgian balances here are likewise out. The little arrangement we worked out as regards Denmark now proves useful—if it is not pushed too far. The Dutch Minister [A. Loudon], looking very badly, came in at ten o'clock; he had thirty-five dollars in his pocket, and all of the rest of his money blocked. We arranged with the Treasury to give him clearance for what he needed. . . .

A variety of work on other things, including something that, if we get it fairly forward, may be the beginning of a reorganization of our international intelligence service. . . .

May 16, 1940

May 11 . . . To see Secretary Hull. But he is down-hearted with the general bad news of the day. For it is perfectly plain that there is nothing on the Belgian frontier, nor on the Dutch frontier, that can hold anything.

The news indicates a violent attack all along. . . .

The President's speech opening the Pan American Scientific Congress last night was magnificent. . . . I called him up after listening to him on the radio, to tell him how good it was. He was still a little exhilarated from the push of a big effort. For he had said exactly what he wanted to say, and in his own words, and said it extremely well.

I told him . . . [that] Lord Lothian . . . not being able to get hold of anyone, finally caught up with me, and came to see me at Woodley at 11:00 o'clock Friday night. It seems the British had decided to occupy the Dutch West Indies, and he had merely come to deliver a note saying that they did plan to do so, solely for the purpose of preventing sabotage. Just before he came in, the newspapers had announced that the French had landed on the island of Aruba. . . .

The President said he was not happy about the landing, but obviously there was not much that could be done now. He suggested insisting that the troops be landed under the Dutch flag, at the command of the Dutch authorities, and solely for the purpose of assisting the Dutch in keeping order. That was all we could do about it then. He likewise told me to tell Lord Lothian that he had taken note of the British occupation of Iceland and that he had no particular objection to that; but if they tried the same trick as to Greenland, he would be very angry. I told him that the Canadians had been in to see us; that the British were pressing them to occupy Greenland; that the Canadians had countered by proposing that we and Canada together arrange with the Greenlanders to defend the cryolite mine at Ivigtut—presumably by selling to the Greenland government a gun or two and arranging to get a gun crew. The President thought this was a fine idea and said he could rake up a couple of ex-Navy men any time who could handle the guns.

All this I duly reported to Lord Lothian when he came in; and took the note announcing the projected arrival of the British troops, for transmission to the State Department the next morning. . . .

The Secretary was not feeling happy about it. He pointed out that anything that was done in the Dutch West Indies the Japanese would take as an excuse to do the same in the Dutch East Indies. By consequence, he got to work at once with the British and French, and also the Japanese, getting declarations all around that nobody would change the *status quo*. This is all right as far as it goes, but I do not easily see that this is going to stop anyone for very long. . . .

May 14 . . . To dinner and to the Toscanini concert. Toscanini handled his orchestra magnificently, but the last number, the Ravel Waltz, was more nearly like a dance of death than anything else.

On the way home, the Secretary's lights were lighted and I went in. He and the President had been working, and the President had asked him and Pierrepont to draft a message to Mussolini asking him to keep out of war; and they did so. Meanwhile, the President drafted, himself, and he did it, as usual, better than anyone else. He telephoned, and we in the Secretary's room got the general drift of it. One sentence deserves to be famous. He said, as nearly as I can remember, "I am a realist. As a realist, I know that if this war becomes general, it will be impossible for chiefs of state to keep it in control, and no one is wise enough to foresee the ultimate results." The general idea was that here were a set of forces denying everything from reason to God, and that the people who unleashed these forces not only could not control them, but would eventually go down in the general ruin. It was shipped along to Phillips to deliver.

Meanwhile the bass obbligato of the heavy guns was growing. Bullitt in Paris was almost hysterical; thinks the French lines are broken. The Germans not only are driving westward in Belgium, but attacked at Sedan. According to Bullitt, the French government understood that there was now nothing at all between Sedan and Paris. The German tanks had come through the Maginot Line without difficulty; and bombing was miscellaneous all over France. Somehow or other, I cannot make out whether this is a mass of hysteria in Paris, or whether things are really extremely bad. Sumner is inclined to think that they are really bad.

At all events, at the end of the night's work it was perfectly plain that Holland was already gone, and most of Belgium. . . .

Altogether, a highly dramatic and highly unpleasant day. When we finally took account of stock, about 2:00 a.m., there was not much left of any of us. . . .

May 15 . . . Sumner tells me that our communication to Mussolini was received in entire friendliness.

The Belgian Ambassador [Count Robert van der Straten-Ponthoz] came in. He is begging for planes. Can we give him some, sell him some, send him some? The British likewise. Last night apparently Churchill called in Kennedy and begged him to send them some old destroyers, or anything else of the kind. He spoke rather wildly of fighting to the last ditch and moving the fleet to Canada, and keeping it up, even then. These are invitations for us to move into the war now; though if their fright is justified, nothing we could do could get there in time, even if we wished to do that. Instead, it seems plain that our job is to collect the strongest and solidest defense force we can, and not to fritter away small detachments to the other side of the Atlantic. The outcome of the battle which will decide the fate of Europe obviously will be decided before anything can get across the Atlantic.

So I told the Belgians that we would consider the matter. [Paul] Van Zeeland [former Prime Minister of Belgium] is taking it up with the White House. I reported the conversation to the Secretary, who had already got wind of it; and had advised the President to go slow—which I have no doubt he will do. . . .

At the end of a long day of routine, to go and receive at our garden party for the Eighth Pan American Scientific Congress—the party which the White House ought to have given, but didn't. Beatrice had worked very hard on it, between shifts at Gallinger Hospital; and I really think it was up to the South American best—which is a very good best, indeed.

Following a conversation with Maury Maverick in April, Berle wrote him on May 16, 1940:

(Personal)

I really think the question of whether Mr. Roosevelt will run or not is being settled somewhere on the banks of the Meuse River.

You know my private theory. It is that he did not want to run, does not want to run, and will not want to run, unless circumstances are so grave that he considers it essential for the country's safety. This is why I am not particularly interested in a "draft Roosevelt" movement. He knows his own mind; the "draft" will come from the situation, in which case both his nomination and his practically unanimous election will be a foregone conclusion. If the circumstances do not do this, he will not run, and probably ought not to.

My private opinion is that the circumstances are drafting him. I need hardly say that in that case I personally should be very happy.

I should have been very unhappy if pressure succeeded in making him run, against his own better judgment, resulting, perhaps, in his election by a not too large majority, in the face of a suspicious Congress and a suspicious country. That, I think, would result in nothing but tragedy. As stated, circumstances are working the other way. While the circumstances are very unhappy for the world in general, they are very likely to give us another four years for the President.

Memorandum to the President, May 16, 1940

Subject: St. Lawrence Seaway Treaty.

It seems to me that we shall be needing more electric power pretty soon. Do you think it well to push the St. Lawrence Seaway and Power Treaty on this basis? I think it is at least possible that we could get it through as part of a long range defense program; we could get power fairly soon.

Roosevelt answered: "Not now—it would delay adjournment a month."

May 25, 1940

May 17 . . . Good dominie, Dr. [Donald Grey] Barnhouse, came in with his son. He has a thirteen-year-old boy who has been admitted to Harvard; but is studying at Westminster College. He wants to keep him in England, and obviously made up his mind to do so. . . . The interesting fact to me was that Barnhouse simply could not absorb that there was any real danger in the situation. Neither, so far as I can see, has the American public. I suppose it comes hard to realize that the foundations of the order of things as you know it may have ceased to exist. . . .

A little work at getting ships out to the Orient to get the rubber and manganese and tin which we have there coming this way. We have now to reckon on the possibility that if the British cave in the Japanese will move likewise and we shall be a besieged hemisphere.

Meanwhile, the stock market has been cracking off. Jerome Frank called up to know what I thought about closing the stock exchange. I told him Saturday was a short day and if they wanted to do anything let the exchange close to match up orders, but I didn't think this was as stunning as it sounded. Later in the evening, I learned that the President had thought the matter over and decided they ought not to close the exchange.

Saturday, May 18th. As it turned out, the President was right; the exchange took care of itself. It lost more ground, of course. I think the New York community ought to pull itself together. Either the entire social structure goes by the board, or a good many companies are going to make money. So, at least, it has always been.

The military news is worse than ever. . . .

May 18. B. M. Baruch was in town and I went over to find him. We sat in Lafayette Square for an hour, while he dreamed of old times, principally with regard to organizing the national defense. He had been talking to the President. He wanted the President virtually to re-create the War Industries Board as it had been before.

But the trouble with all this business both here and in Europe is that it is not the young men coming forward, but the old war horses, heroes some of them are, but still fighting a war of twenty years ago. In France they have called out the old [Marshal Henri Philippe] Pétain—octogenarian, magnificent, and of the last century. London's best is Winston Churchill, now at last Prime Minister of England and behaving as well as he can, but no longer the young Churchill. . . .

Sunday, May 19th. To the Department. The Secretary and Sumner Welles were already there. They still felt that the country was not coming forward with any unified support of the President. They wanted a group of Italians to send news to Mussolini that the country really was awake and that eventually we should have to be reckoned with. I telephoned La Guardia and he sent a message to the King. It will get to Mussolini, anyway. They also wanted a group of people—non-partisan leaders—to come out with some statements about supporting the President. But nobody was left to bell the cat, and the more they thought about it the less they liked it. . . .

May 21. The question is up as to whether we should move our fleet to the Atlantic. Hornbeck has one set of ideas: thinks the fleet is stabilizing the Far Eastern situation, therefore no need to move it to the Atlantic. . . . As of today, Hornbeck is probably right, but as of tomorrow and on the assumption that the British are defeated, it might be needed. If needed, it might be needed in a hurry. . . .

Meanwhile, in the Secretary's office, the Secretary expressed an interest in having the right to embargo outgoing materials which might be necessary to complete our defense program. I was excited about this because I had been shown correspondence by which several hundred radio compasses for airplanes were being shipped to Japan—this at the time when we are trying to build fifty thousand planes and will need just this sort of thing for ourselves. Apparently not much could be done about it—though I did it, anyway. So I dug around and got hold of some of the army men who are pushing the military authorization bill through: and Col. Brennan and Col. Dinsmore and some of our people got together in my office and drafted a rider to the bill giving the President that power. After we had drafted, I telephoned the President, who approved the draft. They are going to put it through the Senate Committee tomorrow.

A little work with Max Truitt and Tom Woodward [Vice-Chairman, Maritime Commission] about ships in the rubber trade. This is one of the things that makes you sick. The real reason why rubber is not moving eastward from the East Indies—we may need the rubber very badly if the Japanese cork the bottle there—is that our American ships, which are subsidized to the gullet, would rather carry jute at a fifty cent rate than rubber at a thirty-six cent rate. I speculated a little on a system that does this to people. If you asked these people whether they would sacrifice the country for fourteen cents a ton they probably would say no and mean it—but in practice it works out that way.

Meanwhile, the news gets worse and worse. Bombing of the north of France has begun in dead earnest, obviously presaging a drive, not on Paris but to the Channel, with the intent thereafter of attacking England. The radio people naturally are making a horrible holiday out of it all. . . .

The German advance units seem actually to have reached the Channel at Abbeville and to be moving towards the Somme. This traps nearly a million men in Belgium and north France, cutting them off from the French main army. I presume the two will try to rejoin. . . .

Wednesday, May 22nd . . . train to Boston. I went out to see Anna Brock and had dinner with her; then to give the Ware Lecture in Boston. We had had to sit up most of Tuesday evening getting this infernal thing written out; and I must say that to try to write sermons at a time when what you really need is guns seemed right poor sport.

But there was a certain impressiveness in standing up in a gown and hood in the old Boston [Unitarian] church. Had matters been easier, I should have enjoyed it thoroughly. I never did talk from the pulpit before.

The lecture, in part, as printed in the *Christian Register, Unitarian,* July 1, 1940, and also in *New Directions in the New World:*

Samuel the Prophet had grown old. During his lifetime, the people he governed had done that which was right in their own eyes, and had endeavored to maintain both their strength and their freedom by the voluntary acceptance of moral obligation. The intensity of their faith and their willingness to sacrifice for their freedom was growing weak. Even Samuel's sons were becoming corrupt. The individualist life, free from moral restraints, had produced disunion.

Against this nation, which was thus conducting perhaps the earliest recorded experiment in dynamic democracy, there were arrayed powerful enemies, whose force was derived from a strong, centralized government, resting at bottom on a system of control so rigid as to approach slavery. To such enemies, swift military action was both natural and easy; the organization by which armies could be put in the field and swift invasions conducted was always at hand. In the old age of Samuel, Israel was afraid. . . .

But at once this requires translation into effective action. Too often it is said that because of the faults in our social system, our economic system, or our political affairs, nothing can be done; and never was a more vicious idea allowed to grow up. Even a street beggar can spend a little of his strength in making some tiny corner of pavement a little cleaner and a little pleasanter. A quixotic act: but an act which automatically reunites him with civilization. A powerful figure in financial, political or industrial life, after a like meditation, would find in the great range of known experience and interests huge things which had to be done, some part of which he could attack. The act of contribution, is the act of assuming a place in the scheme of things. There is, indeed, no other way by which an individual can become a part of society.

And now let us return to our earlier story of Samuel the Prophet. At the close of this earliest recorded political contest between individualism held together by faith and duty and love, and dictatorship held together by king and force and fear, the old prophet Samuel stood up to give a final account of his stewardship. The king stood before his people, and the prophet was nearing his earthly end. Already the people were realizing that they had lost something which might be difficult to reclaim. They had set up power, and trusted to that, and were finding it a fearful thing. *"Fear not,"* said the old man. *"Turn not aside from following the Lord but serve the Lord with all your heart."* To the old statesman there was but one foundation which was real; and that lay not in the pride and strength of any ruler, nor in the successes of any individual, but in the faith which alone made possible the individual lives, the social achievements, the national life, the universal hope, in which his nation could find continuing life.

May 25, 1940

May 24. Meantime, the President is pulling together the defense program. He seems to be centering very largely on Harry Hopkins, which I think is a mistake, because I do not believe that Harry has that kind of mind. But because Harry can now talk to businessmen there probably are certain contacts gained by it. But I must say I can't see any very clean-cut and unified approach pulling out of this. I should be happier if there were a defense council, a straight line organization and institutions to work fast and without any nonsense about it. . . .

May 25. Lunch with Leland Olds. Hogg, of Ontario Hydro, is coming down here. We decided to recommend to the President that he have the St. Lawrence Treaty signed and put on ice for presentation at the next session. Meanwhile, we would make a gentlemen's agreement covering the St. Lawrence power, so that Hogg could get more power now. What this really amounts to is that we might support the Ontario Hydro as against the private utilities which would put it out of business. . . .

May 29, 1940

May 26. . . . The military news is getting worse by the minute. The country has just begun to wake up to the shuddering possibility that the Germans may win this war, including a seizure of the British fleet—and that then we shall have German interference all up and down the coast of South America, to say nothing of some incidental trouble here.

May 27 . . . Feis came in. We are working on getting rubber and other things out. I tentatively proposed the idea that we now undertake to work up an agreement by which, should Germany undertake trade negotiations with any South American country, we get all the countries to agree that we would trade together. This would help materially.

At the Cabinet meeting Friday, the President suggested that Jesse Jones would handle the legislation on the Inter-American bank. . . .

To lunch with David Lilienthal and Gordon Clapp, Manager of the TVA. They want to be sure that in mobilizing the TVA for defense, the TVA is not virtually mobilized out of existence. For instance, the phosphate plant, which supplies the phosphate fertilizer for most of the Agricultural Department program, is to be shifted over to making ammonium nitrate. For a million and a half it could be equipped so it would produce both. To abandon the phosphate program would mean the wrecking, in a couple of years, of a great deal of what has been done, especially in the Valley. . . .

Tuesday, May 28th. The watch officer telephoned me at half past six to give the news of the surrender of the King of the Belgians. On the situation, it was clear that something was going to happen, though none of us had quite expected this.

In the pocket in Flanders are the bulk of the British trained troops. They may get them out, but only with terrible loss; and there are many hundred thousand (perhaps millions) of refugees jammed into a small corner. It looks as though there were food and munitions for not more than a couple of days.

The question is whether the Germans will strike straight for England or whether they will try to smash up the French army in their rear. Since there is no more offensive, my guess is that the French are digging in to prepare for this last. Military men think that the Germans will try to eliminate the French army. I don't. I think that they have started going and propose to keep right on going, and will risk the French army provided they can get to England, which is their real objective. . . .

Then came in [Moffat, just appointed Minister to Canada], the Belgian Ambassador and M. [Georges] Theunis [Belgian Ambassador-at-Large]. In the morning, Theunis had declined to believe it [the surrender], and then had thought he would stay by the King—for Theunis had served the old King well. The Ambassador was white and unhappy. Theunis lost control of himself, breaking into tears and insisting that the French would blame everything on the Belgians and yet insisting that it was not the Belgian line that had broken but the French line at Sedan; then pulled himself together and said that they had to think about the future, instead of the past, and he had decided that the King was no longer a king and that the Belgian Government in Paris would have to carry on. . . .

May 29. Likewise, a little work on Greenland; they are sending the *Campbell* north tomorrow, with a skeleton or symbolic defense force on board. This is designed primarily to keep the British quiet. Obviously, one coast gun and a few machine guns cannot defend Greenland. Either the British fleet holds; or, if they break, our fleet has to take over. So far as we know, there is only one heavy German ship now capable of taking sea. A submarine might, however, show up. . . .

To Roosevelt, May 31, 1940

Whenever I get the time, I will punch Bullitt's head for using me as a code word for Adolf Hitler.

Roosevelt answered, June 1, 1940: "I rather agree with you about Bullitt's use of your first name, but why not punch your namesake's head instead of Bullitt's?"

June 4, 1940

May 29. Last night, after talking at the Cooperative Forum, I stopped by with David Lilienthal, who is in town, to meet Leland Olds and Tommy Hogg, head of the Ontario Hydro. Since Lilienthal's T.V.A. is really an American version of the Ontario Hydro, it is proper and fitting that the two men should meet. Hogg needs more water, in order to take care of the rapidly rising Canadian demands for power in their defense program, and he needs it from the St. Lawrence. This afternoon Leland Olds and I tackled matters a little, and I hope we shall be able to work out some scheme which meets the situation. . . .

Friday, May 31st. The military news is worse than ever. The best part of it seems to be that the Allied armies are making something of a stand. Meanwhile, the German claque of triumph grows, and of course is having repercussions all up and down South America. Sumner seems unhappy about it, fearing that there might be a breakaway and that the hemisphere would be split up. In that case there is not much question but that we should be in for a chaotic period in South America.

To a meeting of the Joint Committee on Intelligence Services in the office of J. Edgar Hoover. My old commanding officer, General [Ralph H.] Van Deman, was there. We had a pleasant time, coordinating, though I don't see what the State Department has got to do with it. . . .

I was very anxious that there should be not merely the usual espionage, arrest, etc. mechanism, but also a little staff which should work out positive measures. Foreign agents are not frightening unless they can energize masses of our own people. The grievances they use to set up trouble ought to be taken care of ahead of time, if possible, whether by a little labor research, or by W.P.A. work, or whatever may be needed.

Hastily, thence to New York City, there to make a speech before the International Ladies Garment Workers Union. This was a straight plea to labor to cooperate in a national defense program and it seemed to go well.

Then to take the evening train home. Eleanor Belmont [Mrs. August Belmont] was on the train, which made the trip pleasant. She is all for war and helping the Allies and going in the whole way.

There was no point in saying anything about it, but of course the fact is that we have had many requests in the past few days which were really war requests. Thus, the Allies want to buy the planes which we had in the United States Army. Also, they want to buy back the French 75's which we bought from them after the war. Also, they would like us to block all German exchange.

Meanwhile, there is a steady wave of hysteria now developing. For the country has at last got the idea that the war may end in a smashing German victory—so smashing that the British may surrender their fleet. For the first time in over a century, the country is beginning to get a little frightened. . . .

Sunday, June 2. Morning in the State Department, discussing various things. It looks as though the Act we got up giving the power to the President to embargo export of any materials useful in national defense will get through. I think we shall have no trouble.

But the résumé of things this morning was not too pleasant. We have been having continual negotiations with Mussolini, principally in the hope that we can keep him out of the war. . . .

June 3. Then to a knock-down and drag-out fight, first with the British and then with the Canadians. It now develops that the Canadian boat going to Greenland has not merely the naval officer referred to but also a bunch of Royal Mounted Police (they get their man), a few soldiers, several mining engineers, and God knows what. Likewise, the Danish ship which happened to be in England at the time of the invasion is now coming out with three British naval officers on board and perhaps some other people as well. This is all right if these people are going to inspect and go back; but if it is a landing party, we don't like it. I told both [F. R.] Hoyer-Miller [First Secretary], the Britisher, and [Merchant] Mahoney [Commercial Counselor] and Escott Reid [Second Secretary], the Canadians, that Cecil Rhodes had been dead a long time and even if alive, Greenland was hardly a place for his talents. I asked for an immediate answer. This was just as well, because late in the evening Hugh Cumming (a first-rate boy) telephoned to say that a message had come in from Penfield, in Greenland. The Governor there, [A.] Svane, seeing all this battery arriving in Ivigtut, had conceived the idea (not wholly without foundation) that these people were going to occupy Greenland; and he planned to ask the United States to send a landing force and take possession at once. This is plain grand imperialism, on a miniature scale. If there is any more monkey business, we are going to have a destroyer sent up there and stop it. I hope the Canadians and English accept my not too diplomatic invitation to have a drink on the Governor of Greenland and go home. . . .

Then to J. Edgar Hoover's office for a long meeting on coordinated intelligence. We agreed that we would set up a staff that I have been urging, plans to be drawn here. This may transfer some of this paranoid work into positive and useful channels. We likewise decided that the time had come when we would have to consider setting up a secret intelligence service—which I suppose every great foreign office in the world has, but we have never touched. . . .

June 11, 1940

June 4. Lunch with Jesse Jones; we arranged to get the Inter-American Bank a little bit forward, and discussed some of the problems in connection with hemispheric defense. We are likewise looking up an Italian meeting in Baltimore, which Mayor La Guardia will address. It looks now as though the Italians will be in the war by then and we shall need to keep the Italian element here in something like order; and La Guardia is the only one who can do it. . . .

June 8. Then in came Kirk, Chargé at Berlin, who had been ordered home, really to give him a little rest, after a staggering term of duty, first in Moscow and then in Germany. Kirk was eloquent on the subject of the tremendous force of the German *Mystik*. He said it engendered a defeatism all around; that it was marching steadily on; that it had to be stopped, just as Mohammedanism had had to be stopped; that there was only one real way of doing it, and that was for us to send an immediate declaration of war. This he thought would sufficiently stagger the Germans into reality so that they would quiesce. I am perfectly clear that it would not do so, but I was very much interested in his point of view, particularly in his insistence that there would be an ultimate conflict. He was going down the Potomac with the President this afternoon but was going to listen, and not talk. I told him to talk; that the President wanted to hear what he had to say. . . .

June 10 . . . A little work with ships, and some work on Fifth Column activities in South America. Then Harry Hopkins telephoned and suggested that I have dinner with him. He is staying at the White House, and thither I went. We had a priceless evening, discussing every kind of thing that one could think of; dining in his bedroom. The President was in Charlottesville making a speech. . . . There had been great debate over his severe condemnation of Italy's entrance into the war; an entrance which had staggered everyone when it was finally announced at noon, though of course we and all the rest of the world knew it was coming. Sumner Welles apparently had been at the White House in the afternoon, trying to argue the President out of putting in the phrase that Italy's declaration of war was a dagger thrust into the heart of a friend.

Harry felt that the war now definitely threatened the United States. So, he thought, did the President. The problem therefore was to get some help to people now and build up new defenses. As he said, none of us will be here a few months from now unless we actually get things done.

The President [returned], and I went down to find him. Joe Green was already there; the President was in the office. He signed the neutrality proclamations covering Italy. The President was full of the élan of his Charlottesville speech; he had said, for once, what really was on his mind, and what everybody knew; and he could speak frankly, and had done so.

I observed that as the situation now stood, it seemed to me that there were only two men left in the world, himself and Hitler, with any number of lesser Gauleiters in between. That, said the President, is a terrible responsibility.

We chaffed a little, and then turned in for the night.

Tuesday, June 11th. A little work with Harry Hopkins. Then to a two hour meeting in J. Edgar Hoover's office about the distribution of intelligence work. We got a nice line of organization, but what I really want to see is the reports coming in and something actually done. The difficulty of a liaison position (I have nothing but that) is that you can express ideas without responsibility, and get nothing done about them as a result. Fortunately, the three men who have responsibility seem to know their business, in the narrow and technical sense of intelligence.

June 12, 1940

A bad day, with a multiplicity of great and all too unimportant detail.

June 13, 1940

A little work on economic policy, and then home. But not for long, for at quarter of ten the Secretary telephoned and I came downtown.

The news was a cable from London indicating that [Premier Paul] Reynaud had about come to the conclusion that unless the United States could give him definite and immediate and tangible help, in a large way, France could not carry on the struggle. Apparently the Germans were already at the gates of Paris. Churchill had been at a meeting of the French Cabinet in Tours and therefore was urging us to go the limit. An earlier message during the day had been sent, promising that we would send supplies, along the lines of the President's Charlottesville speech. Secretary Hull wanted to be very guarded about this; but at a conference between him and Welles and the President, the President wished to go much farther; Welles had supported him; the Secretary had been silenced, but by no means convinced. That message had apparently been interpreted by Churchill, and possibly by Reynaud, as holding out hope that we would virtually commit ourselves to declare war—which of course nobody here could do.

Time was of the essense, it seems, for the French army was about played out and Reynaud was by no means clear that it could carry on very long.

We cooked up a brief message asking Churchill to explain that we could not go beyond the assistance we were actually giving by way of sale of supplies, and so forth.

I gathered that one of the points at issue was whether, in the event the French should cave in, the French fleet could not be separated from the French and be joined with the British. This had had something to do with the message of the afternoon, the text of which of course I have not seen yet. We called up Kennedy and in a three-way telephone conversation between the Secretary, Kennedy and the President, asked him to have Churchill once more try to make the appropriate arrangements covering the French fleet. Naturally, we do not want to have that fleet against us through surrender to the Germans, in the event that the French turn hostile.

The Secretary was not happy about Welles having over-ruled him in the White House on the message. He likes to mull things over, whereas Welles likes to act fast. But I think in this particular case there is a difference of principle. Welles and the President are emotionally much more engaged than the Secretary. . . .

He is a realist. He was afraid, of course, that the President's impassioned pleas, and the emotion of the situation, might lead to the sending of some message which the French would interpret as a commitment to immediate intervention; which would lead them, accordingly, to continue to fight, in the hope of help which would never arrive; and thereby place on this government the responsibility for killing hundreds of thousands of men who otherwise might live. It was a sound and sane point of view; and it prevailed.

June 24, 1940

The most important things to do:

(1) Get Jesse Jones to go forward with the South American trade plan. This is best done by having the Division of American Republics get together the cables from South America as to what they need.

(2) Get a draft completed of the law for control of associations engaged in subversive activities.

(3) At least get started the idea that we should use the surplus gold for the purpose of paying for the Pan American cartels. This ought to be done directly, through Morgenthau; he would resent any other approach. Practically everyone is in favor of it.

(4) Work out some kind of plan with [Assistant Secretary of War] Louis Johnson for speeding up air defense. We shall probably get plenty of plans; but I am not clear that they will be the right kind, or that there will be any unified command.

(5) See if we can get Lowell Mellett [Executive Office of the President] his money to work out the organization of foreign language groups. He wants $200,000; perhaps $100,000 will do. . . .

June 28, 1940

Two weeks—which has almost been a lifetime in international politics. During this time, the rush of matters was so swift there was not even time to dictate. By consequence, this has to be reconstructed from my notes and appointment books. I think it probably is less important than one might expect, for the reason that Welles has been largely endeavoring to hold matters in his own hand, giving as little information as he could. The intellectual history of two weeks is therefore extremely important, but I am not sure that I know it. . . .

Monday, June 17th. We were at it, with a vengeance. We are beginning to get under way in connection with the South American plan—which in its essence is simple enough. We shall have to buy surpluses, along the lines of the Surplus Commodities Corporation, so as to give the countries cut off from their markets something to go along with. Later, we shall have to work out a method by which we jointly meet the impact of the German economics, instead of being wide open to it. . . .

Then Secretary Wallace telephoned and wanted to bring over Milo Perkins [President, Federal Surplus Commodities Corporation] to work on the South American plan, which is now christened, unfortunately, the cartel plan. We arranged to take care of a number of Congressmen who had various things on their minds; late in the afternoon, Wallace and Milo Perkins turned up. Perkins is proposing a double action currency: a blocked currency, good only in the Hemisphere, and "reciprocal dollars" good outside. The theory is that we can use currency for use, rather than as we use it now, and the underlying idea is right, but it involves some very sweeping decisions. And yet the fact of the matter is that any American integration—for that matter, the European integration—is as much a currency matter as anything else. It is not beyond the bounds of possibility that the war of 1940 will be found to have been a revolution for the purpose of changing the currency-credit system of the world.

To Baltimore, with Beatrice, where was Mayor La Guardia; and we had a meeting designed to reassure the Italian community there. The immediate reaction—that all Italians were Fifth Columnists—of course is wholly unjust and has made a great deal of trouble.

Tuesday, June 18th. A raft of work. The British want us to block export of oil. Of course we cannot do that. Nevertheless, I am being a little bit careful about export of oil in various places in the Atlantic—not to serve the British blockade so much as to assure that hostile German craft do not pocket it around and later use it against us. It is plain that the French phase is over, and the only question now is how soon the Germans can clean up and get to the business in hand, which they construe as attacking England. . . .

June 19. Sumner is still working like a beaver, and the question of the day is "Who gets the French fleet?" . . .

June 24. Then a meeting about Iceland. The Canadians are landing there, and this raises squarely the problem whether we ought to try to extend our influence into Iceland, or regard Greenland as our boundary. The Naval men contributed the bulk of the information on the subject, namely, that while Iceland could be an air base against us, the air route is open over Greenland only in July and August. The thing to do, therefore, was to hold Iceland and let Greenland go. I hope the Navy is right.

Tuesday, June 25th. Louis Johnson came in in the morning and we knocked off for a considerable space of time to go over things. Louis and the President had a scene, which must have been painful. The President had told him that he recognized his commitment to make Louis Secretary of War, but the political situation had not worked out that way. Louis said it was almost worse than being told he was no good and to get out of the way. He thereupon offered his resignation, assuming that [Henry L.] Stimson [just appointed Secretary of War] would want his own assistants. The President declined the resignation, saying that they could not educate a new Assistant and Louis had to go on and do the work, and all would be well.

I told Louis that I was a clairvoyant and that anybody who delivered the goods in the next few months would be well taken care of. Stimson, whatever his great merits and his political symbolism, was, after all, a man of seventy-three, and younger men had to do the job: and that, quite aside from duty to the country, my impression was that people were beginning to notice a sharp distinction between political symbols and the actual combatants. . . .

The news about the French fleet is a little better. Some of it has got to England; some of it is under the guns of the British; some of it is at Alexandria; some in African ports. But what the African colonies will do, we do not yet know.

June 26 . . . Then a rather shattering experience. A Norman Alley, of Hearst Newsreels, came in with a complete story of the German plans. He said they already had a Fifth Column capable of taking over the United States. They plan to conquer England by July 10th; give us three days to deliver a lot of materials, etc.; immediately after that to attack. He obviously believed it. His story of the way the Fifth Column was already in control of New York was so graphic that it frightened me completely. Only after I got the FBI, which had heard the story in detail, to check, did I begin to pull myself together. . . .

July 1, 1940

Saturday, June 29:—A full day, but I couldn't see that we got anything done.

Lunch with [Emilio] Collado [Assistant Chief, Division of American Republics] and Dr. [Antonio] Espinosa de los Monteros of Mexico, who is back to stay by the Inter-American Advisory Committee. We talked over things which must come: of the necessary building up of inter-American economics; of the change in our currency system which is now essential; of the fact that, properly handled, surpluses can be used so effectively in the Hemisphere that we really need not worry about the German desire to monopolize trade; and so on. All this is perfectly possible, if men have minds flexible enough to do it.

The key to the situation really is in our own Treasury; and I am not clear how flexible Treasury is.

The consensus of opinion here seems to be that [Wendell] Willkie will make an extremely strong [Republican Presidential] candidate, if indeed he is not successful. I do not think anyone knows how the election will come out—or, indeed, who will be nominated. The New Dealers are pressing the President to run, or if he does not, to name either Jackson or Douglas, in which case Willkie will win, hands down.

I find myself curiously apathetic on the subject. If Willkie is elected, it will at least end this helter-skelter existence and permit getting some solid intellectual and economic work done. . . .

June 30. All that has been the matter with me was that talk with Norman Alley. . . . He had a complete and paranoid picture of Fifth Columnists; and has succeeded even in frightening me with it.

Paranoia can be catching. Nevertheless, in the quiet of last evening I did some meditation. It comes to the following, and this in spite of the extreme danger which is now everywhere:

(1) By all tests and standards that we know, a personality like Hitler's and a movement like that which he has instituted, smashes up in time. . . .

(2) In a sense, this is very much like the temptation on the Mount; the devil offered Christ all the kingdoms of the world if he would fall down and worship him. The translation "Thou shalt not tempt the Lord thy God" is probably better translated "Thou shalt not despise the Lord thy God". What it comes to is that you cannot indefinitely eliminate the spiritual quality of things, without breaking up the human organism.

(3) A good deal of this fantasy of strength represents not the triumph of the German ideal, but the essential weakness of Europe, which achieved neither the strength of the old-time royalist feudalism nor the strength of the popularly rooted, soil-nourished individuality. . . .

(4) Always the rise of this kind of thing in Western Europe has called into counter-balance something in the East; and vague stirrings of that counter-balance are already apparent in Russia, Turkey, and the like. This does not mean that we shall necessarily be let out of the final struggle; but it means that we shall hit the struggle after the wave has reached its crest, rather than while it is still full on.

This combination, the spiritual with the rational, may be wishful; but at least it comforts me.

So far as policy is concerned, it seems to me that there is only one sane, practicable policy: a line in the Atlantic and a line in the Pacific, and notice to all hands that we are prepared to open economic relations, provided politics on this side of the water are barred. On this basis, I think we can do something. . . .

. . . I am a little philosophical in the event that Willkie should be elected. Perhaps what is really needed is to uncover a new layer of energy; the Roosevelt administration has uncovered one, which will leave its trace and its seal, and a new set of faces, with a new set of enthusiasms might not be a bad idea.

July 8, 1940

Tuesday, July 2. Mr. Atherton came in this morning, the new Chief of EU [European Affairs]. We have been working a little on the possibilities of Norwegian relief. This raises some real questions. A Norwegian committee wants to barter goods for food through a Norwegian committee here, headed by Captain [Torkild] Rieber, head of the Texas Oil Company, who is supposed to have strong Nazi connections. I think that we ought to go as far as we can towards feeding the Norwegians, and I do not have the slightest idea that we ought to join in any blockading of Europe. To my mind, if Europe quiets down, it will be due to Europeans, and to live ones, and not dead ones; and I do not see any point in the starvation technique as getting anyone anywhere. The British blockade will probably do some of that; but when that is out of the way, so far as I am concerned, I would supply food to anyone who is really hungry—including Germans. To my mind, the philosophy of loving your enemies has a very solid common sense to it—partly because I do not believe that the human race is entirely changed. I am inclined to believe that there is a great deal more sentiment for this than one suspects. What we ought to oppose originally is any export of European politics in payment for the food.

Some heavy work in connection with the so-called South American cartel plan (and I am sorry for whoever christened it "cartel"). What it is slowly boiling down to is a policy of lending money to permit South Americans to swing their surplus question until the situation clears up; accompanied by enough organization so that when they do finally trade with Europe, they can trade on even terms. . . .

Sunday, July 7th. At the Department meeting this morning . . . a general review of our foreign situation. The essence of it (Hornbeck dissenting) summed up:

(1) We will not get into a row with Japan. We have to recognize that we cannot now afford a Far Eastern war.

(2) On balance, we do have to recognize that the continent of Europe is now in German hands and likely to stay so for some time; any other idea is simply wishful thinking.

(3) On balance, we believe that probably the forces in Europe will balance each other out; but one cannot count on this; hence every emphasis on armament.

(4) Some extremely tricky questions will arise in Latin America; we shall have to do our best to swing those, at least for the time being. . . .

Monday, July 8th. Work with the Secretary in the morning. It now looks as though I will have to go to Havana. Sumner Welles is staying at home, leaving the Secretary to go, with what help I can give him. I am not quite clear why this is. Sumner has some powerful reason for wanting to stay here, but I haven't yet figured it out. Pragmatically, I should think that he would be more useful in Havana than anyone else. He thinks the conference will be fairly easy, due to the good relations between us, and the people who are coming north; but I can see a certain amount of trouble ahead. For one thing, there will be a Cuban election just about then, and Cuban elections, being unusual, are apt to be unpleasant. The last time [1933] I stopped at the Nacional, if I recall correctly, we were first besieged and later bombarded.

A long lunch with Jesse Jones. We have decided to set up this South American surplus emergency program by increasing the lending power of the Export-Import Bank and removing its restrictions, and getting away on that basis. I think this probably is as good a way of handling it as can be found. . . .

August 2, 1940

The Havana Conference gave no time for anything other than the most semi-occasional memoranda. This record, therefore, merely sums up.

The Delegation was in bad shape. Sumner had set up the conference pretty much without consultation; finally determined that the Secretary ought to go; the Secretary did not particularly wish to, and then laced in to prepare. . . . I went along as Senior Adviser, along with Hackworth, as Legal Adviser. . . .

Arrived in Havana, we found that very formidable propaganda had been made against us by the Germans. Some eight or ten German agents were in town, sent up for the purpose of "observing" and I suppose doing a little influencing on the side. I know, for instance, Leiswitz, the German Gestapo man, was in touch with several delegations, more particularly the Argentine.

The economic resolution, which merely referred a set of questions to the Inter-American Advisory Committee in Washington, got away to a good start, helped naturally, by President Roosevelt's message, which according to schedule, came through on Monday, July 22nd. Since this recommended an increase in the lending power of the Export-Import Bank, it evidenced that we meant business. . . . By Wednesday night, though the Economic Commission was in fairly good shape, there was likely to be disagreement about the wording of the resolution, and a little defense work in beating off some troublesome amendments. The fact of the matter was that the resolution we introduced really blocked out about four months' hard work for the Inter-American Advisory Committee, breaking ground (it was only that) for the economic organization of the Hemisphere.

On Wednesday, July 24th, intimations began to reach me that things were running badly in the political section (Organization of Peace), of which Secretary Hull had been appointed Chairman. This was partly a technical difficulty. In order to give everyone a committee post, the twenty-one Ministers or representatives were split into three committees; the Committee on the Organization of Peace, which had jurisdiction over the vital problem of the European colonies, included the United States and Brazil, and several smaller countries, but excluded Colombia, Venezuela and Argentina, all of whom had had vital interests. Further, our projects had not reached the Argentine in time for them to be discussed with Leopoldo Melo, the Argentine delegate. . . .

I took a walk around the Malecón and did some thinking. It had been my entire plan to keep out of this, leaving the Secretary to do the thing himself. I was convinced he would succeed; but I was also convinced that he wished to do the business himself, and without help. There had been entirely too much talk that the real work had been done by somebody else—Sumner Welles, particularly. Nevertheless, the matter could not be let run. The next morning, I ran into Felipe Espil [of Argentina], and touched off a minor explosion on his part. Accordingly, a few hours later I telephoned and said I wanted to see him. He was not anxious, suggesting I see Melo, but I wanted to begin with him. I told him that as I understood the Argentine position they had two interests only in mind. They wanted to be a member of the Pan American group which became responsible for the colonies; and this was right. They also did not wish to be put into a position where they assumed responsibility for the defense of the Caribbean, which they could not at present undertake; they therefore wished to cast the matter into such form that they were not automatically involved without their desire. . . . Felipe seemed to think that was true. I then . . . asked whether we could not steer the project into a sub-committee on which they were, so that their suggestions could be worked into the draft. Felipe seemed to think this was a good idea.

I thereupon went to the Secretary. He called (I think he had already called) a meeting of his committee for that night, and he authorized me to invite the Argentines, the Venezuelans and the Colombians. He likewise kindly adopted my suggestion that a sub-committee be constituted; but pointed out that there already was a sub-committee which had on it the Cubans and the Panamanians and they could not very well be displaced. At the end of the meeting, accordingly, he asked for authority to add the Argentines to the sub-committee, which was granted. López de Mesa and [Venezuelan Ambassador to Washington Diógenes] Escalante suddenly became unhappy, and immediately I went around to them and invited them to sit with the committee, pointing out that because there were two members on the committee (Cuba and Panama) which could not be displaced, and we did not wish to create a huge sub-committee, the simplest thing to do was to invite the interested parties to join us. This they did. The sub-committee convened at eight o'clock, in the Secretary's office, the following morning—(this was Friday, July 26th)—for six solid hours. At the close of it, we evolved the document which, with a· few amendments later made in full committee, is the Convention; and blocked out the general principles of the Act of Havana, which was built on the consolidated base of a Declaration the Cubans had suggested, and a resolution we had suggested.

The Cuban declaration gave us trouble, not because it amounted to anything, but because it had been dictated by President [Fulgencio] Batista, and showed it. No living being could read the first sentence twice without getting dizzy, and the angel Gabriel could not understand it. But it presently developed that the real desire was not to get any language set down, but to enshrine Havana in history. I cursed the day when we had had the idea of christening the Lima agreement "the Declaration of Lima". . . . It was plainly a case for putting the principles underlying the draft Convention in as the declaratory part of the then nascent "Act of Havana", and this we did. Our resolution . . . was really designed to create a committee to do the work of administering the European colonies until such time as the Convention came into force. . . .

The significance of this [convention] is little short of amazing. For the Act of Havana directly recognized the right of any American nation to take steps to protect the peace and security of itself or of the continent in respect of any of these colonies—which in practice means a blanket authority to the United States to seize any of the islands if there is threatened change of sovereignty, or if there is some kind of indirect control amounting to the same thing, or if they become a menace to the continental peace.

During this time the Germans had been sounding off. Not having any notion of the economic proposals actually being made, Folk [Walter Funk, Minister of Economics?] made a speech in Germany which was widely reported, saying that they would only trade with free and independent South American nations. Since no South American nation considers its independence threatened by anything we did, this sounded like so much junk—which of course it was. So nobody paid any attention to it. . . .

At all events, by Monday there was general agreement, and the German subsidized paper in Havana (*Discusión*—nobody reads it) came out with a banner headline saying that the Havana accords were quite satisfactory to Berlin. One could hardly expect them, after all, to say that they had made a dead set at the beginning to break up the Havana Conference and had failed, flat. . . .

We left Havana on the SS *Oriente* on July 30th . . . in a blaze of glory, and encompassed by a crowd of drunken tourists on the boat.

So to Miami and a hot morning at the Roney Plaza beach; and then the train home. I was glad to see that somebody (I imagine Sumner) had routed out about fifty Congressmen to meet the Secretary at the station. The newspapers seem to have given us a good press. . . .

August 2, 1940

Thursday, August 1:—Arrived at Washington on the 11:00 o'clock train. To the State Department, then to see Jesse Jones, who is piloting our $500 million Export-Import Bank bill through Congress.

He told me the story of the Chicago Convention [which nominated Roosevelt for a third term], and it is not nice; he gave as his own opinion that if the election were today, Willkie would win; felt that the President had not been frank in stating what he intended to do, and that things had left a bad impression everywhere.

August 27, 1940

Arrived in Washington yesterday morning—after three weeks partly at Great Barrington and partly in the woods. It was good to get in the north country again, and out of the range of newspapers. . . .

Then a really tough conference on Greenland—it develops that a project is forward sponsored by the British and Canadians to investigate the possibilities of a landing field in Greenland so that airplanes may leave from Labrador; stop at Greenland; hop thence to Iceland, and so to Europe. The difficulty with this is that if planes can go East that way they can likewise come West; and I'm not enthusiastic about developing an air route which might be used by an enemy to make trouble for us. Also, we have pretty sincerely tried to keep Greenland out of this. And of course the moment it becomes an air ferry station, we should have to contemplate the possibility that the Germans might try to interrupt the place. This brings in the Monroe Doctrine with a vengeance and I regard it as possibly crucial. It is a step eastward which means a step into the furnace which is raging there. The War Department seems to think that it is not interested, leaving the matter to high policy. Yet, the establishment of such a station means pretty plainly an extension of our naval and military responsibilities.

As usual, the solution is practical. Between now and the freeze-up it is impossible to establish such a base; if somebody wants to shelve the possibilities we can review the situation on the basis of information. My own feeling is that if anybody has a base in Greenland I prefer that we do. . . .

August 28, 1940

An endless amount of work—we started machinery to ask the various American companies with interests in South America to eliminate those of their employees and managers who were known to be engaged in anti-American propaganda. Many of them have been using German agents—it is quite all right if the German agent stays out of politics and quite all wrong if he engages in anti-American propaganda. This propaganda has become increasingly anti-American following closely along the line of the alleged secret order of Hitler to his propaganda services in Europe indicating that eventually the war would be prosecuted against the United States. Geist will have charge. . . .

I have been reviewing a little situation in the event of a possible British defeat. My private opinion now is that they would be able to hold, but no one can be sure, and estimates are really worthless.

The thinking is strictly realistic.

The United States is in no mood to try to reconquer Europe, and it probably would have great difficulty in doing so if it tried.

A British collapse would mean that Canada is still at war. Our own arrangements would thus force us either to talk with the Germans at that time or immediately to declare war ourselves. The fundamental consideration would be whether the Germans expected to continue their invasion in this Hemisphere, or whether they would stop at the Atlantic line.

There is reason to believe that they think of a war in this hemisphere. Yet, on cooler consideration they might think otherwise. . . .

. . . I am convinced that the situation in Europe is not static but evolving, and that, at long last, it will be to the interest of everyone not to have a shattered and weakened Europe which we now do have, but a reconstituted and strong Europe—which can only be achieved by recreating the nations which are at present prostrate. . . .

I do not see that the Russians will permit the Germans to dominate the Middle East. Put in a nutshell, the Russians are expanding westward and southward without a war rather faster than the Germans are expanding in Western Europe with a war. . . .

September 5, 1940

Saturday, August 31. . . . Then to the Secretary's office. They are getting ready the announcement of the deal between the British, Canadians, and ourselves by which we acquire seven naval bases in return for fifty destroyers and for a natural confluence of events such as the defense of Canada. It is likewise an assurance by the British that they plan not to sink or surrender the British fleet.

The Secretary told something of what had happened. . . . Some of the British cabinet were for bargaining—getting the best possible price they could for the bases. Finally someone had a touch of statesmanship and said that the real result of this lay not in any technical swap, but in the demonstration of solidarity, the ability of democratic nations to act, and the inevitable repercussions which would follow. This view carried the day.

We worked a little on the statement being the President's letter of transmittal of the Hull-Lothian Agreement to the Congress. . . .

Of course, if this can be done in the Atlantic it can be done in the Pacific also; but before we cross that bridge, it would be well to see whether the country approves the policy we have taken. They will be foolish if they do not. In a single gulp we have acquired the raw material for the first true continental defense we have had since the sailing ship days. I am particularly happy that a base in Guiana is included for I am certain that that will stiffen the morale of some of our South American friends who fear that they may be left out in the cold. . . .

Then to work in connection with the material which we hope will push the Export-Import Bank bill (five hundred million dollars) through the United States Senate. . . .

September 10, 1940

September 4. Then a small question raising some large prospectives. This was the request of the French Government to the Treasury requesting that French-American balances be unblocked sufficiently to permit the Vichy Government to pay their legations and embassies outside of Europe. I came to the conclusion that the funds ought to be allowed at least now if not in the future, and the reason is this:

The movement in France in favor of [Charles] De Gaulle [Free French leader in London] is growing by leaps and bounds. Further, the Germans have been pressing the Vichy Government so hard that there is imminent danger of the worm turning. In that case presumably the Germans would occupy the unoccupied portion of France. . . . Remembering that one determined man, [General Edgard de] Larminat, came from Syria to French Equatorial Africa and single-handed took that whole belt of colonies into camp and turned them over to De Gaulle, and that Morocco, Algiers, and other French colonies are very much in the wash, it is by no means impossible that the immediate result of that would be to throw all Africa back into the scales against Germany. This is a case where strong moral action can bring enormous results. I think the same thing is true in French Indo-China, and I'm certain that it has already proven to be the case in the French mandates over South Pacific islands. . . .

September 5. Greenland is once more supplying a little Arctic excitement. A supposedly Norwegian (certainly German) ship, the *Furenak,* apparently is headed for east Greenland with a set of scientists on board supplied with guns and ammunition. Scientists have strange ways these days! The instructions were to set up some weather stations and presumably to assist aviation and likewise to prepare a landing field on a suitable glacier. Since we hear the German aviators have been practicing on Norwegian glaciers, this sounds like business. This presents a square question, whether we are going to let it go (obviously we cannot) or acquiesce in the British breaking it up (in which case where is the neutrality agreement?), or undertake the work ourselves—which means in substance that an American destroyer would have to be prepared to engage the alleged sailing ship *Furenak*. There is only one way to handle this, and that is to talk to the President. . . .

[Memorandum, September 7: I got the President on the telephone this morning. . . .

Regarding the *Furenak*, the President said at once that the logical thing to do was to make no objection if the British or Canadians took steps to seize the boat. . . .

He suggested, however, that we should address a communication to the British and Canadians, indicating that we consider Greenland as a part of the Western Hemisphere, and therefore that we could not acquiesce in any operations which constituted a permanent occupation or change in the status of the territory. . . .]

Friday, September 6. Our military staff people came in this morning. They are more optimistic about the British fighting than they have been for some time. I think that the Germans have not, and will not be able to put the R.A.F. out of the air; that the losses of the R.A.F. are less than their stream of replacements; that they have an army now large enough and well enough trained to spare some for Near Eastern and African operations; that, generally speaking, the danger is not so great. Things look better. . . .

The big air attack on England began last night and this morning; it promises to be the attacking force which, I am told, our army people have been expecting, as have also the British. The strategy seems to be to send great waves of planes over one after another on the theory that eventually they will tire out or smash up the British air force. . . .

September 9 . . . We had to work out questions with regard to Martinique. I thought that the plan which we evolved was a good one. There are a lot of planes there which could be of use to us or at least somebody; the Island is blockaded by the British. The population in general stands with De Gaulle; the Governor apparently is on the fence. It seems to me this is a chance for the Greenland technique and having our consul there establish direct relations with the Governor on the theory that Vichy is, as Pétain somewhat naively admitted to one of our people, acting under compulsion; then we could purchase the planes. In return for that we shall have to make arrangements to feed the Island. . . .

This was a dinner for the Canadian-American Defense Commission, whose senior member is La Guardia; a fascinating vignette. When La Guardia and I first joined forces many years ago, the dinners were not so splendid, and it was a matter of shirt sleeves and spaghetti. Today it is champagne and diplomats. In the course of the evening the Canadian Minister, Christie, took up with me whether it was not time to revive the St. Lawrence power project—at least so as to get power for the Ottawa Hydro. Since we also need power, I think it ought to be possible.

Tuesday, September 10. Gerald Cruise of the New York Power Authority and his chief engineer were camped on my doorstep this morning. They got Governor Lehman to write a letter to the President suggesting that we start work on the international rapids power development right away. The scheme looks interesting though it has the disadvantage of taking the Great Lakes project in small bites—whereas I like the idea of a big bite.

Then three or four questions of relief, etc.; I then got hold of Leland and we went to bat on the question of Canadian power. I think this will get forward pretty soon. It seems that the President has already asked Leland Olds to go over to the White House on the matter with some one from the State Department, if desirable. . . .

. . . Somehow or other it is difficult for anyone here to realize that if a Germanized Europe attacked the United States it would be in two vast pincer claws, one of them stretching from Norway, to Iceland, to Greenland, to Newfoundland; the other from Africa, to Dakar, to Brazil. Really, this little cut and thrust around Dakar is the logical complement of the new fighting on the coast of Greenland—though they seem far distant from each other. We have the Greenland situation tolerably well in hand (but I think ultimately we will have to include it in a chastity belt patrol). But the naval base in Guiana and some of our measures taken on the Brazilian shoulder gives at least a start there. Dakar has a position in the matter not unlike Iceland—which the British control. But the Vichy Government controls Dakar, and that is a different kettle of fish. . . .

Dinner with Secretary Hull for the Canadian Legation; I sat next to General Marshall, for whom I have unbounded admiration. He has been working like a beaver and I think is really making progress. He thinks that by April, or May at the latest, he will have things in such shape that there cannot be any monkey business here. As a matter of fact, though he does not say so, he probably is more nearly ready now than he cares to admit. He said in quiet confidence that one difficulty had been that the President knows the Navy like a book, but he knows very little about the Army. Yet, every Navy man always thinks he could run the Army, and by consequence he had had trouble in getting either money or men as early as he really wanted. I gathered that he thought that things were better off now. He has not been a swivel-chair general; has a habit of cruising in his airplane and dropping in on garrisons, and one thing or another; has likewise solved the formula that "the staff is always right." He says that taken collectively they can always prove they are right, but if you shoot a couple of them out to get after results, then you find out differently. . . .

September 11, 1940

Jesse Jones telephoned; he's got his [$500,000,000] Export-Import Bank bill through (we shall thus have for the first time ammunition to deal with South America). It is a good job. . . .

September 16, 1940

The Canadian Minister called this morning, at my request. In our previous interview he had asked, and I had agreed to have drawn up, a memorandum covering the plan to get boring and survey work started for the St. Lawrence power development.

I handed him such a memorandum, prepared by Mr. Leland Olds and by Mr. Hickerson. . . .

Mr. Christie said that he had received a telegram from Ottawa, based on some newspaper reports that the President had decided to go ahead with the St. Lawrence power features, eliminating the seaway. This had caused some concern. From reading the memorandum, however, he gathered that this was not the case.

I said that it certainly was not the case. The growing needs of defense, the possible shipping situation now and later, and conceivable changes in the Atlantic all heightened in our minds the need of inland navigation and possibly inland ship-building, as well. The President had expressed himself as not wishing to take the St. Lawrence–Great Lakes matters "in bites", but as a whole, which of course included navigation. All that we were trying to do here was to get matters started so as to make construction necessary for the most immediate requirements, namely, power, but with full intention of going forward with the whole project as rapidly as circumstances permitted.

September 21, 1940

Tuesday, September 17th. Win Crane [Berle assistant] brought his father in to see me briefly this morning; remembering that I was first in Washington as guest of his grandfather in 1909, and my father had been intimate with [Senator] Crane as far back as Theodore Roosevelt's administration, we can really claim to have covered quite a span of Washington history between the two families. . . .

September 18. The great week which was supposed to be that of the German invasion of Britain is now going on, but the invasion is not taking place. Instead, each side is pounding the other to a kind of a bloody pulp. It looks now as though there would be nothing but a long, bitter stalemate; and meanwhile the Germans and Italians are getting active in the Mediterranean. I still do not see the Spanish move which Sumner feared; but I do see the movements looking toward the possible occupation of unoccupied France. . . .

September 26, 1940

Saturday, September 21st. There is a nice little row blowing up over our commercial air policy.

The Pan American Airways have been trying to establish an airtight monopoly—of course with government money. In our desire to extend air facilities for defense purposes up and down South America, the Army is going into a contract with Pan Am the effect of which may very well be to rivet their position in South America so that no one else can get a handhold there. [Thomas] Burke, of our [International] Communications Division, wept on my shoulder, and as a result, Major [Clayton] Bissell came over from the Army and was kind enough to give me the whole picture. But there is a dilemma. We need the air facilities, and need them now. Obviously it is easier to use the Pan Am landing fields which do exist, as a place to begin, rather than to establish new ones. It looks as though we were in a fix. My preoccupation lies in the fact that I do not trust Pan Am any farther than I can see it. They certainly tried to protect German interests in their Colombian company up to the gullet, and are trying to see that the German fliers whom they trained there (. . . for use in bombing the Panama Canal) are taken care of and repatriated to Germany. They certainly have endeavored to stamp out every kind of competition in Central America. . . .

General [Sherman] Miles came in to see me. He has been thinking over some suggestions of several weeks ago, realizing that there is more to this job of internal defense than merely intelligence and police work. He feels that J. Edgar Hoover, who is a good policeman, does not wholly take in the entire situation, and in any event the Intelligence Committee has no directive which enables it to do other things, such as extablishing contact with foreign language associations and with the many groups in the country who yearn to do things and might do the wrong thing, and for making use of the information which the Department of Justice will presently have on hand due to registration of aliens. I think he is right, and as soon as possible will try to get hold of Francis Biddle [U.S. Solicitor General] and two or three others and see what we can rig up. It seems to me that there is a legitimate line between propaganda and control (totalitarian style) and the reasonable handling of groups in this country, aliens and others, who might be made really dynamic democratic forces. . . .

Monday, September 23rd. We are getting the Canadian–St. Lawrence matter a little forward, but as usual the Canadians get tied up in knots between the Dominion government and the government of the provinces—in this case Quebec. . . .

September 24. To the Capitol to appear before the Senate Committee on Foreign Relations urging the ratification of the Convention at Havana, and to explain why the Act of Havana did not need to be submitted for ratification. There was a little friendly ragging from the Republican Senators, but they wound up by saying that it was a diplomatic triumph and the vote was unanimous.

To lunch with Fred Davenport [former Congressman; R., N.Y.], who thinks La Guardia ought to make a great speech showing that the present political campaign is the climax of the thirty years war against corporate and financial control started by Theodore Roosevelt. I think he is true, but I am not clear that we really need to do this to win; and I am not clear whether the issue ought to be drawn between the government and business in the sense that they would draw it. It seems to me our job is less to bang business over the head now than it is to bring it into a solid cooperative frame of mind—at the same time being sure that they do not steal the Treasury. . . .

September 30, 1940

Wednesday, September 25th. A raft of routine work; and a good deal of the day wasted at the Capitol, where the Appropriations Committee of the Senate is sitting on a deficiency appropriation bill, concealed beneath which is the item providing for the Export Line's subsidy making possible a competing line across the Atlantic, to Portugal. Pan Am has been moving high heaven to block the item. It is a surprising thing that the court of the last resort should be a minor and wholly unheralded item in a deficiency bill on which hangs the question of whether our air policy shall be tied to a monopoly, or whether we shall have several companies sailing the air. So quickly do vested interests "crystallize"—and it is not property rights that crystallizes them, either. It is government privilege. The Export Lines are being very good just now. I suppose if they get an intrenched position they will fight us just as fast as the next person. The policy here has been threshed out by us, by the C.A.A., by the Post Office, by the President of the United States, and everybody else—but this does not cover the situation.

A fascinating lunch with General Miles. This was given for General [George V.] Strong [Assistant Chief of Staff], and Colonel [Carl Spaatz?], just back from England.

Strong is convinced (a) that England cannot now be successfully invaded; (b) that the new devices which she is working up will, in the not too distant future, prove an answer to air bombing. . . . I thought, as I heard him talk, that it is the old question of defense eventually balancing offense. . . . The effect of the British defense may very well be to buy just time enough for this balance. In that case, the German adventure is over—though it is not apparent at the moment. For the entire German plan consists of a smashing offense which reaches its objective and digs in before any defense can organize. . . .

Friday, September 27th. The alliance [Tripartite Pact] between Germany, Japan and Italy was duly announced this morning. In general, it follows the lines we had been expecting; but is more obscure than we had thought in the Russian clause. Simultaneously, we are led to believe that there was not adequate consultation with Russia. The Secretary called a meeting to discuss the matter, during which time we hashed over a variety of phases of the agreement. I must say that it was a singularly unhappy meeting. Hornbeck has been all for a stiff policy in the Far East, and has always discounted the strength of the Japanese threat there. Equally, he thinks that the world situation will deteriorate radically if Japan is not checked, and is apparently not worried by the dangers inherent in our getting tied up in operations in the East while there still may be a threat in the Atlantic. (We cannot bet the national safety on English resistance, stiff as it is.) The Secretary took the general line that there was nothing new in the situation; he had assumed that the three powers were acting on parallel lines right along, and that this merely recognized a state of affairs which had existed—though it did not make certain that if there were war on either side of the world there would be war on the other side, at the same time. . . .

A brief talk with old Professor [William H.] Hobbs [former Director, University of Michigan Geological Laboratory], whose explorations in Greenland had been the basis of a good deal of our own work. On his plans, Lacey, of the Coast Guard, explored the west coast of Greenland [where Leif Ericson had his reindeer farm] and probably has located the best spot necessary for an air base, should we need one there—as it seems not improbable we shall. Hobbs was a friend of my grandfather's. . . .

Key Pittman 'phoned today to say that the Convention of Havana was ratified by unanimous vote in the Senate. There had been some debate and they ragged him a little; but all went well, and the game is over. I thanked him.

Saturday, September 28th. In New York, chiefly to make a speech at the State Convention of the American Labor Party. It was a very unimportant speech, but I was glad to be there among old friends, and to get out of the rarefied atmosphere of the State Department and down into the mud, where politics are really made. The fight with the Communists has been won; only ten per cent of the Leftists were there; and they were obviously somewhat confused. Their orders were to have demonstrations against Roosevelt and against conscription, and so forth, though they behaved themselves while I was talking. It so happened that we had intercepted the Comintern orders (which undoubtedly resulted from the Japanese-German-Italian treaty) to the Russian propaganda and other organizations. These were to say nothing unpleasant about the United States and generally play up the friendship angle. Of course they had not yet reached the New York Communist crowd—probably will not for a week or so; and I thought that I probably knew more about what their outfit will do next than they did. . . .

. . . if I could see any way of getting food actually into the hands of starving West Europe, I would do so at once. This does not go along with the thinking around here, which believes in a hard-boiled policy. My reason for feeling a little bit differently is that I think we ought to maintain the bridgeheads of our own influence; that starvation as a policy does not work; that there is no reason for letting us get tarred with the responsibility of blockade, and that, at this stage of things, food blockades are not going to have much effect on the war, anyway. The calculations entering into this, however, have to be checked with great care. For one thing, I am convinced that there will be less starvation in Europe than most people suppose and that what there is will come directly either from German requisitions or from the disorganization of transport, even more than from actual lack of supply. It is, for instance, a little stupid to be sending relief to France at the same time that the Germans are insisting that the Vichy government must force on Frenchmen a ration thirty per cent below the German rations, and are saying that there is no food to feed the French prisoners of war.

The greatest objection to feeding Europe, as it seems to me, is that in these occupied regions the distribution will probably be made by local committees composed of local Nazis—for instance, the Quisling crowd in Norway, than whom there is no more nauseous group of sold-out traitors in the world.

Sunday, September 29th. To the State Department. . . .

The Far East [Division] reported that if anything more were done in the way of aid to China or withholding of supplies to Japan, or the like, the scales would probably be decided and the Japanese would declare war. Hornbeck disagreed with this to some extent; and I am rather inclined to do so, myself, since a declaration of war would then be nothing. . . . It was obvious to everyone that the Germans hope to embroil us in the Far East as rapidly as they can, thereby assuring to themselves—as they think —a clearer prospect in the Atlantic. Despite this, Hornbeck is for sailing into the Japanese. . . . Norman Davis, who was there, agreed in the main with Hornbeck and was pretty bellicose so far as Japan was concerned. I tried to insert a different idea into it. I said that it seems to me that even if we considered the two powers as united, the problem had become a military one. Where, in the event the gun went off, could we put our strength to most advantage? Agreeing that either Germany or Japan could and would declare war on us, based on the aid we were giving to either China or Britain, we should then have to consider whether the greatest military advantage could be obtained on the plains of Europe or by knocking out the Japanese fleet. Hornbeck seemed to think you could do both at once—which may be true, though I have yet to see any army officer who would agree to that proposition.

Actually I think nothing will happen for a time. My own view is that neither the Japanese nor the Germans wish to see us at war; that they will not declare war on us for a considerable time. . . . We are at least clear of the illusion that the balance of power, or the shifts or turns of diplomacy, would either safeguard our people or produce our ultimate safety. We have now learned that if we are going to get our farm work done it is we, and not our neighbors, our friends or relatives, who are going to do it.

But it was unhappy to be thus talking, with ghastly proximity, about war. Twice in a lifetime is too often. . . .

September 30. Some routine stuff; and a visit from the American Export Air Lines in force, to announce that they have just bought up the low-priced freight air lines in Central America. These were owned by a Britisher named Yerex, who also came in, and were under the name of "Taca". The C.A.B. has to bless the arrangement.

This air business is getting to be almost as much of a war as the European war. . . . [Pan American Airways President Juan] Trippe's plan is monopoly or nothing; and he is quite able to play on either side of the belligerent line, or both sides at once. I wish I were happier about some of this business than I am.

October 10, 1940
October 9 . . . Jim Farley came in, now out of his great political role; he wanted to pass the time of day with the Secretary and came in here, as usual. He tells me that all is well, except that he still feels unhappy because the President did not tell him he was going to run for a third term until the Hyde Park conference, which Jim had to ask for. He did not talk bitterly; said he thought the President would carry New York by around 500,000; all is well. . . .

Jim Bonbright [Chairman, New York Power Authority], Olds and Cruise came in. Not having an answer from the Canadians, we had decided that we were going to put through a survey board to take St. Lawrence borings, anyway. But now it looks as though the Canadians were going to answer. I think the fact that we told them that we were going to move anyhow rather jerked things up a little. The fact is that while the Canadians were delaying, the power companies in Quebec were making a huge propaganda, including bringing influence to bear on any of the Canadian government people they could—and they can bring quite a lot of such influence to bear on quite a lot of people. I have not a high regard for the strict incorruptibility of the Canadian government. They have some good Tammany customs there, too.

October 10. The Canadian Minister and Escott Reid, along with Olds and Hickerson, showed up this morning. The Canadians have agreed to the St. Lawrence commission to start borings; and now the question is whether we can get the letters out through the White House. . . .

I was looking over a memorandum I made on June 24th of a lot of things that ought to be done. Jesse Jones did get forward with the South American trade plan; he has 500 millions to work with, and that is something.

We never did get a draft law to control associations engaged in subversive activities. Neither did we get anything done on the idea of using surplus gold to pay for the idea of Pan American cartels.

We got started on speeding up air defense with Louis Johnson; but that died when Louis Johnson went. The Defense Commission is, however, picking up and working hard.

We are still working on organization and foreign language groups and nobody is going to do anything about it. . . .

This strikes me as a pretty poor score for six months. On the other hand, a lot of things have happened. We did get through with Havana; the South American campaign did prevent German revolutions from being exploded during the summer; we have got something done on refugees; we are working on coffee and corn agreements; and if you add up a huge combination of trifles, I suppose something may be said to be going forward.

October 11, 1940

October 10 . . . The President was working on his October 12th speech on foreign affairs, which Sam Rosenman was cobbling up. Sam called me to come over to the White House. It was the old Brain Trust back again, except that the scene was the Cabinet Room, instead of the Hotel Roosevelt; Sam, in his shirt sleeves, Harry Hopkins, Grace Tully, doing the typewriting. Sam had pounded out a very decent draft, developed partly out of some suggestions I had previously made, and between us we mauled and battered and manhandled some difficult material into something like shape. The bulk of the speech was the President's, for he had taken Sam's draft and done things to it himself; and the result was the President's, somewhat hammered. The object was, first, to indicate that we were keeping a stiff upper lip in the Japanese crisis; second, to try to unify the various race groups in the United States; and third, to use the whole thing as a springboard for an eloquent plea for unified action in the hemisphere.

I think we shall have to complete this by a later speech that calls the roll on what has actually been done in terms of defense. This knocked out a day which was already pretty thoroughly scheduled. . . .

Our St. Lawrence waterway matter struck a snag. It is an odd kind of a snag. We had asked the Canadians for an agreement; they had done nothing about it; we had decided to go ahead anyway, and courteously told them of that fact.

Whereupon they agreed.

This meant retranslating unilateral orders; and a raft of papers had to be redone, resubmitted to the Attorney General, the Budget Director, and so forth. We did not get through. I wanted the President to sign them before he left on his speaking trip tonight; but it couldn't be done. . . .

October 11. The matter of handling the English seems to me to require some thought. In the World War we came so into the English camp that we became virtually an adjunct to the British war machine. They kept that position after the war was over, and the result of that was that we got not one single thing that we really desired in the ensuing peace.

This time it seems to me that the thing should be the other way around. We have the ultimate strength. We also have the ultimate consistency of principle; we are the inevitable economic center of the regime which will emerge—unless, of course, we all go under. This is troublesome. There are so many men around here—Felix Frankfurter [appointed Associate Justice of the Supreme Court in 1939] is notable among them—who take the British whole without developing a strictly American point of view, that it becomes difficult. It is horrible to see one phase of the Nazi propaganda justifying itself a little. The Jewish group, wherever you find it, is not only pro-English, but will sacrifice American interests to English interests—often without knowing it. I think the process is unconscious, partly born of their bitter fear, and partly because the British actually have worked out more satisfactory relations with the Jews than any other country in the world. Then there is always the Anglophile group; and the British propaganda is working overtime. There is, of course, a smashing foundation to go on, for the admiration for the British spirit in the defense of London is really immense. London is taking a horrible pounding.

And yet, when all is said and we finally come to grips, the salvation of the world will be the building of a system more nearly like that which we have on this hemisphere than like anything which the British are likely to produce, with their experience, their habits and their all too justifiable hatreds.

At all events, it suggests that we should remember Pershing's famous refusal to fritter his army away in small detachments.

The discussions about naval bases in the Far East have been proceeding with alacrity on the British side and not much on ours. The Secretary asked Lord Lothian quite casually what kind of forces they had at Singapore and thereabouts, and was somewhat flabbergasted when Lothian came back with a note suggesting immediate conversations as to the joint use of these naval bases, which might be carried on either here or in London; Hull quite properly declined to receive the note, saying that there was no foundation for it in anything that anybody had said.

Of course we can use the Singapore base if we want it. Conversations about these naval bases, however, in practice would merely mean our undertaking a unilateral obligation to defend the British empire. There may be some good reasons for doing that, but I am in favor of going a little slow. Not that it needs any voice of mine, because the Secretary is quite as aware of the situation as anybody else.

October 17, 1940

October 14 . . . The Turkish Ambassador [Mehmet Munir Ertegun] came in, at my request. I asked for definite suggestions he might have by which we could improve Russian relations. I don't really know that he has any. He sadly said he thought the time had gone by when much would do, except an outright pledge of support, perhaps by measures short of war, in the event of an attack. He thought that the German drive would begin to blow up the Balkans, possibly within a week's time. Yet, devout Mohammedan that he is, he expressed faith in ultimate victory: the kind of thing going on in Europe simply could not succeed.

There is a great gulf fixed between the devoutness of this wise old Mohammedan Imam and the devoutness of my Mother's New England Puritanism; but somehow the two merged in a fantastic moment of realization that a great faith in a kindly God produces characters that are much alike. Even the voice and the face, for half a second, seemed the same. . . .

Our Canadian notes regarding the St. Lawrence work are now duly agreed to and I suppose will be signed when anybody gets round to it. This has given rise to a fear on behalf of some people that we are going to abandon the seaway, which of course is not true, though I think the President does not want to make an issue of it before election. But because of that the Seaway friends are coming in to ask about it. . . .

October 15 . . . They have asked Louis Johnson to answer [Charles A.] Lindbergh's speech of last night—Lindbergh's brilliant, but I think specious, argument that preserving American independence means chucking all foreign influence out of here, and not antagonizing the strong military nations of Europe and Asia. Of course this is Berlin stuff, pure and simple. . . . Louis had told Steve Early that he would make the speech if I would write it. Whereupon, having cleared the decks a little, we went to work to write it.

Johnson asserted:

Colonel Lindbergh stepped out of his recognized field of aviation . . . and thought we were unprepared for action. . . . In plain English, he now argues that we should appease these powers [the Axis]. . . . We can do, in two years, more than Germany did in seven. . . . When, therefore, Colonel Lindbergh argues that we ought to sacrifice the principles on which the United States was built, and that we ought to have played up to the Axis powers because of their strength, although they were obviously hostile to the United States, when he tells us that we are a weakened nation in the center of an antagonistic world, and therefore ought to be frightened out of our British friendship, Colonel Lindbergh displays alike his ignorance of the United States, of its state of preparedness, and most of all, of its iron will.

October 18, 1940

Louis Johnson came in today, all happy about the reception of his speech.

October 21, 1940

I have been considering a few situations.

Cordell Hull is making it increasingly plain to everybody that he expects to get out when the Administration changes. This means that there will be a new Secretary of State. Bullitt proposes to try to get it if he can; and of course Welles expects it. The problem of Under-Secretary will then be of some importance. Obviously, if I do not have it my own usefulness will be over, just as Welles's usefulness will be over if he is not appointed to the Cabinet. The only other place I could be of much use would be Treasury; and no living being can work in Treasury and live. Morgenthau has destroyed, thus far, every one who has worked with him, with the single exception of Dan Bell, who is merely a quiet Civil Service Clerk. Wayne Taylor today has been appointed Under-Secretary of Commerce, after having been to all intents and purposes Under-Secretary of the Treasury, without the title. The only other financial positions are in the Federal Reserve Board—which has practically been reduced to a nullity by Morgenthau's operations; or in the R.F.C., which again is completely dominated by Jesse Jones. I am proceeding, accordingly, on the theory that my own work here will end some time next spring. Welles himself has no desire for assistance.

My private feeling is that everyone ought to descend on Cordell Hull and make him remain in his present job.

The politicians are in the usual state of dither, believing that matters are going against them. They had exactly the same sensation during the Landon campaign when up to the night before election many people supposed that Landon would win. I think that we shall win, not by as large a majority; but I should not be surprised if Willkie failed to carry more than eight or ten states. The press is allowing the wish to be father to the thought and is practically dead against the President. It is creating an impression which I think the facts do not really warrant.

I am happily out of the great bulk of pre-election intrigue, but there is slathers of it.

October 29, 1940

Tuesday, October 22nd. A fairly stiff day.

The Finnish Minister came in, with his Counselor. He wants support to get some food, chiefly fat, and some clothing and such, through the British blockade. I think the British ought to let it through, and have gone on record in a lengthy memorandum. . . .

Then the Norwegian Minister and the Director General of the Norwegian Relief. They also want food and oil and other things to go through the British blockade. I sympathize, and wish something could be done; but it looks very difficult to me. The Norwegian coast is a part of the battle line. Obviously, therefore, nothing that can be easily requisitioned can be allowed through. But I do think we can help them somewhat in the matter of housing. They can buy pre-fabricated housing in Sweden if they have American dollars to do it with; and I think we can arrange to supply those. I am also going to try to put up a fight to get a shipload of warm clothing into Norway, but that is far more doubtful. . . .

October 23 . . . the French situation is rapidly getting to be a nightmare. Pétain is in his dotage. [Vice Premier Pierre] Laval is taking care of himself, selling out his country and everyone in it. For all I know, he may be sincere in believing this is the only way out; but there is no question that he is, almost systematically, wrecking France. [General Maxime] Weygand has left for Africa and is being well received at Dakar. Whether he will go along with Laval in any proposed treaty we do not yet know. The French Foreign Office has implored us to get a message from the President to Pétain; and the President is doing this in the form of a personal message sent through the Ambassador here, [Gaston] Henri-Haye. The King of England is sending a message, likewise. But Henri-Haye is probably a crook: up to his neck in Laval's affairs, probably working hand in hand with the Germans, and there are ugly reports that he is beginning to organize a "Gestapo" here to spy on the Frenchmen who do not go along with Vichy. As a result of which, their families in France, if any, will be arrested or otherwise made miserable. I hope to find a way of hitting this before very long. Fortunately, we have pretty accurate information. . . .

October 25 . . . Harry Hopkins 'phoned. Accordingly, I went to the White House, there having a sandwich and coffee. We got to work on drafting speeches—this time a speech on defense in foreign affairs. It took, one way or another, most of the night.

The crew working on the President's speeches this year are: Harry Hopkins, Sam Rosenman, and Robert Sherwood, a good playwright. The influences chiefly playing on the situation, however, are Frankfurter and Justice Douglas. This means a highly intelligent crew. . . . How you can put any of the saving grace of solidity of character into this bunch is a question that I have been totally unable to solve. I am afraid we shall get one of these clever, progressive administrations in which the end always justifies the means, as a result of which nobody has any confidence in the outcome. But that is a secondary matter.

October 26. More work on the President's speech; and in the afternoon to the White House.

The President was working on his speech and the crew sat down together as in old times; Hopkins, Rosenman and myself. The President was in good form. He took a few minutes off and did an imitation of John L. Lewis coming to call on him. John Lewis had got the idea that he was being followed by the F.B.I.—which happens not to be true. I accused the President of doing us a dirty trick when he sent Katherine Lewis to Lima with the delegation; he said he wanted to send somebody who would be entirely safe from the blandishments of the State Department. He scored that time: Katherine Lewis, in that sense, would be safe in hell.

He made one somewhat revealing observation. He said that until John Lewis had made his speech, he had had less than no enthusiasm for this campaign at all, and did not greatly care how it came out; but after Lewis had uncorked this singularly dirty line of demagogy, he wanted to be re-elected if only to put Lewis out of public life.

There was the usual bunch of campaign stuff flowing into the White House. . . . All very sloppy, unpleasant and I suppose unimportant. The dregs of a dirty campaign are not nice to look at.

Home, very late indeed.

Sunday, October 27th. In bed with a cold, but about four o'clock Harry Hopkins telephoned to say the draft of the Foreign Affairs speech was done; they wanted to get hold of the Secretary; could they send it out to me? I sent little Alice through the fence to see if the Secretary was playing croquet at Woodley; he was; so we had the speech sent out and I took it over to the croquet court, where were the Secretary and Mrs. Hull, Norman Davis and [Assistant Counselor Carlton] Savage. We went over the general outlines of it and in the main it stood up. That was that.

Then down to the White House, where we cleaned up on the revision; likewise, we cleaned up on a little statement the President is to make when the first drawing under the new draft law takes place; then home and to bed.

October 29. There has been a row in the Intelligence Committee. General Miles, the MID man, who is probably less well forward with his work than FBI or ONI, wants a general overlying picture of the situation made up for his staff work. He is right from his point of view: The Army might have to do the whole job. But the rest of the bunch have no interest particularly in his problems, and the Navy, as always, is a little defensive. It worked out an unhappy meeting for General Miles, with this undersigned endeavoring to keep peace in the family and getting precisely nowhere.

A considerable amount of miscellaneous stuff.

On Monday morning, the Italians duly invaded Greece, as per schedule. It did not go off too well, because the Greeks rather thumped their advance guard; but they have undoubtedly reserve power enough to get through in time. The British promptly seized the island of Crete. . . . At all events, we are off on a Near East adventure which is the complement of the British adventure, and the rest of the pattern is fairly plain. . . .

November 12, 1940

October 31 . . . Harry Hopkins telephoned in, wanting to know whether the Secretary was going to make a good speech in favor of the President—which he is. Mr. Hull did not want, originally, to get mixed up in third term politics. But by the time Lindbergh and [William R.] Castle and the rest of the crowd turned up as vigorous Willkie supporters, he began to get more interested in the campaign. His speech tomorrow night will be in fact a good political endorsement of the President. . . .

Monday, November 4th. The day before election, and everyone more interested in the election than in real work. . . .

Tuesday, November 5. We voted for the President. I registered Democratic this year, instead of Labor Party, because on going over the list practically everyone I was voting for was a Democrat, except Fritz Coudert, and he is a Republican. It happens that in my district the Communists were able to nominate the local candidates.

. . . I was glad to see that New York had done about what we had estimated it would do—a majority of around 300,000 [for the President].

In the course of the day I went to see La Guardia, sitting in a deserted City Hall. . . . La Guardia said that if the election came out right, he expected to serve out the term as Mayor and then go and live quietly on his pension. If not, he was going to settle in some small town and at once start building the Party for 1944. The Administration owes him a good deal in this campaign. I hope they know it and recognize it—but you never can tell.

At all events, at three o'clock in the morning we got, very weary, on a train headed for Washington.

The third term is now a determined fact; another old landmark has gone down; and I must confess that, lying in a singularly uncomfortable bunk, I wondered what the end of this would be.

I think that the third term will be such as to discourage anyone else from wanting another one, for a good long while. Yet the international symbol which Mr. Roosevelt has become is now preserved; and this perhaps beyond anything else is a real justification. . . .

V

1940 ~ 1945

November 7, 1940

I went to see Mr. Hull today to tell him that I thought he ought not to resign from the Cabinet. In New York half the people thought they were voting for Roosevelt and Hull, anyway.

Hull said that he did not want to run out; but that he had been constantly affronted and made unhappy by having Morgenthau or somebody else spring a fast diversion in foreign policy over his head, and finding that the President stood by some favorite. If he could get assurance that this kind of thing would not go on, he would stay. But I am by no means clear what the outcome will be.

We started work on organizing the Intelligence Division for the Department. Intelligence is beginning to be interesting in the Department now, so everybody wants to be in on it. The surprising thing is that what they say rarely, if ever, reveals any great knowledge of what it is all about. . . .

November 8, 1940

The Italians seem to be getting handsomely trounced by the Greeks. All our reports have indicated that things were going badly for the Italians, and the reports this morning come pretty close to confirming it. The difficulty with this is that I fear the Greeks are getting nothing out of it. The Germans will wait until the Italians have been finished off and then quietly appropriate Greece for themselves. . . .

November 9, 1940

I got hold of Welles and told him I thought we ought to be sending someone to North Africa. Welles agreed, but thought that the way to do it was not to start in negotiating at once but to send a really able man to go over the situation and start negotiating on the ground. The Greenland technique might conceivably be applied to Algeria, Morocco and perhaps even Dakar. . . .

November 27, 1940

November 26 . . . My old friend, [Kaarel] Pusta, who first organized the Estonian Committee and made this into the free government of

Estonia and remained in the service of the Estonian State until it was destroyed a few weeks ago, came in to see me. He had been in Paris and succeeded in escaping. I did not tell him that I had facilitated his escape —else he probably would have been in prison or dead by now. The old man is beginning at the bottom again, trying to reorganize the nucleus which once built a free Estonia. I tried to give him such encouragement as I could. He talks of a committee of former European statesmen to study a possible reorganization of Europe. It takes a brave man to say this.

Luncheon with James K. Penfield, who is off for Greenland on Thursday. He is in for long, dark nights; and the dream may be interrupted if the German landing party which is secretly bulwarked on the east coast of Greenland is followed by another and more extensive expedition. But I doubt if this will happen; flying in Greenland is not so very healthy at this time of the year. Still, we can take no chances. . . .

Wednesday, November 27, 1940. Jesse Jones called up and asked me to ride downtown with him—which I did. Secretary Hull had proposed to him a loan of one hundred million dollars to China. Jesse wanted to make a pro-Chinese gesture but does not want to shoot all of his ammunition in one salvo; also, he points out that the five hundred millions for the Export-Import Bank were primarily designed for South America. In any event, he wants a letter from the Secretary covering the matter. I told him that I thought that the gesture was indicated, though it might well be done by lending out the money in small amounts. . . .

To the Secretary's office and we opened discussions as to the possibility of a meeting with the Treasury on general exchange control. . . . Something can be done with the idea, but it is dangerous in the extreme. The trouble with this idea is that it is only half an idea—not really thought through. . . .

Memorandum to Secretary Hull, November 26, 1940

. . . (1) The Treasury memorandum is not clear as to the type of "exchange control".

Presumably, it contemplates extension of the kind of control now exercised—which in practice means not only that funds are blocked, but that approval from the Treasury must be had for each expenditure from the blocked funds. . . .

(2) This places in the Treasury a virtually absolute power over a very large area of foreign relations, and at the same time a life and death power over a very great number of Americans and American businesses. Most large businesses have some international angles, involving a certain amount of transactions with countries other than the United States. A blocking of the balances arising out of transactions with all foreign countries means that the operations of a very large segment of business fall directly under Treasury control. . . .

Our conclusion is that while a measure of further exchange control may be useful and desirable, the shotgun extension of the present control seems dangerous, both as building up an internal dictatorship in the

United States, and as creating an unclear situation here. It is suggested, accordingly, that the Treasury be asked to make a more concrete statement of the order it would like to get out, and of the method it proposes for handling the infinite number of transactions which we do not desire to impede. For instance, the immediate tying up of all transactions with Latin America would undoubtedly create a very great amount of difficulty in those countries, since Latin American balances are frequently carried in New York. The Treasury's ideas as to how these accounts might best be handled to forward our inter-American relationships might or might not be the same as ours; and there is no indication here of a machinery which we might use to carry them out.

In any event, the step is one of such far-reaching importance both in terms of the internal effect on the United States, and the external effect on foreign relations generally, that it ought to be thoroughly canvassed. . . .

December 3, 1940

November 28. Leland Olds came in. We hammered out the policy on the St. Lawrence Seaway and Power project. We tried to get hold of the President—but he is tied up, ill, and a little unhappy. . . .

Home to a little dinner for the Argentine head of the Central Bank, [Raúl] Prebisch, a brilliant man of under 40; Felipe Espil, the Argentine Ambassador; Dick Casey, the Australian Minister; Ronald Ransom; and myself. This was exclusively a party to leave reality behind. I opened by saying that every political consideration was driving us all closer together; every economic consideration was driving us apart. All I could see was a change in the entire financial method—change of which no one was yet completely aware. Thereupon the discussion took off into flights; we planned and replanned a new world of human affairs; a shift in banking and everything else. At the close, Prebisch said that he now saw what the Inter-American Bank was aiming at; and Casey said he was going to attach an economist to the Australian Legation to try to follow the new thinking, and generally speaking it ended on a high note. It was great fun. But I think more important than that, it brought us face to face with the main problem. Ronald Ransom, theoretically a conservative on the Federal Reserve Board, was [as] usual extremely comprehending. We agreed that it was time for somebody to look into the matter.

Friday, November 29 . . . To a meeting of the Twentieth Century Fund where were among others, John Faye, Francis Biddle, Robert Lynd, Bruce Bliven, and some others.

I proposed that we lay aside some of the Fund money and finance a couple of people merely to dream out the kind of problem we shall have to meet when the war is over; the half-revolutionary driving forces of demobilization will drive us somewhere; and we might as well at least lay out a few possible hypotheses. To my surprise everyone, including the conservatives on the Board, agreed.

So we are blazing away and will endeavor to find a few men. But finding men to do this is not easy; it takes great technical equipment, great knowledge of affairs, and an unlimited willingness to dream; an unlimited determination not to be bound by certain of the current economic shibboleths. . . .

Thence to La Guardia Airport, there to meet Fiorello incoming from Washington; and he, Marie La Guardia, and I held our annual caucus to determine what should be done with the State and City of New York.

The first question was what was to happen to him. The President, aside from expressing a general desire to him to have him here, has expressed no detailed proposition. The rumor about the Defense Council is merely rumor. Accordingly he is writing this off as a total loss.

Marie does not want him to run for a third term in New York, and neither does he.

I said that he belonged in the national scene; if he wanted the third term that was that, if not then it was either a cabinet position here or the governorship of New York. . . .

November 30 . . . I also asked [the President] for a snap judgment on how to work out the St. Lawrence waterway business. He agreed that we might as well go ahead after the inauguration; and that it would be better to proceed by concurrent legislation rather than by treaty. . . .

Tuesday, December 3, 1940. The President on his way South signed a message to the St. Lawrence Seaway Council, indicating that he was ready to press for the St. Lawrence Power and Seaway development. Leland Olds drafted the message, and a good job it was. . . .

Thursday, December 5, 1940. In Detroit, the first time I had been there. Had breakfast there with my sister, Leland Olds, Malia, and a variety of people interested in the Great Lakes–St. Lawrence Seaway. At the luncheon I read the President's message. Leland Olds made an excellent speech. The Detroit newspaper people seemed to be in favor of the project—and then after a little walk around the Detroit waterfront I took the train home.

Leland is a man who grows on acquaintance. His father was President of Amherst. He started out in the theological school planning to be a Congregationalist minister. A couple of years of that stopped him completely; whenever he struck a real problem apparently the churches wouldn't let him touch it. Fundamentally his idea is that the social reconstruction of the world is very much involved with its spiritual reconstruction—which I think is plainly true.

December 28, 1940

December 27, 1940. Sam Rosenman telephoned me. He is drafting the President's speech for the evening of December 29th [fireside chat on Lend-Lease]. He wanted some suggestions about labor. . . .

Two minutes later Harry Hopkins telephoned. He says that the speech has to go along with the message to Congress. . . . I went over to the Treasury to witness the signing of the Argentine-American Stabilization Agreement (which fulfilled some promises I had made at the Havana Conference, so I was glad to see it go through) and then came back to see Harry Hopkins in his bedroom at the White House. He asked whether I would make the first draft of the President's message to Congress, which I agreed to do. . . .

January 21, 1941

At the Inauguration luncheon I met Tommy Corcoran, at the White House. I congratulated him on the birth of his daughter. He said he wanted to come in and see me. I told him I should be glad to see him whenever he wished, and he came over. . . .

He wished to clear up and have out some differences. He felt unhappy because I had theoretically thrown him down when he wanted La Guardia to speak for the Progressive Committee in the campaign of 1936, calling him "a stooge of Jim Farley." . . . I told him that I had no quarrel and that what he said did not make any sense to me . . . that the question had come up as to whether La Guardia should speak for Mr. Roosevelt and I had advised the Mayor that since he owed nothing to the Roosevelt Administration he need not speak under Roosevelt auspices unless he chose to, and that probably his support of the President (he did support the President in 1936) would probably be more effective if he made it under his own steam than if he made it as a part of the Democratic machine. . . .

He then got to the real point of his conversation. He was going to practice law in New York . . . he understood that I was interested in the governorship or the mayoralty.

I told him that I had no particular interest in this kind of thing anyway, though one never could be quite sure how things would go. Accordingly, I was not dogmatic about anybody's future, least of all my own. . . .

The conversation was filled with mutual good-will.

February 1, 1941

With Leland Olds and Pierrepont Moffat to see the President. The President has a cold, and is tired. He obviously has a lot on his mind. Pierrepont brought him a personal message from Mackenzie King: Mackenzie King is willing to go along with the St. Lawrence Waterway if the President wants him to. Power is all right; but he thinks that he will be criticized if he forces the Waterway. The President told Pierrepont to go ahead and ask him to go forward, but on an arrangement by which the Waterway can be delayed, if this seems necessary. . . .

February 5, 1941

There is a terrible row about Greek planes. The President promised them thirty good planes. All our planes were committed, and we tried to get the British to let go of some. They started to, and finally decided not to. The Treasury is handling the matter, and finally, at [Secretary of the Navy] Frank Knox's suggestion, called in the Greek Minister [Cimon P. Diamantopoulos] and told him to take thirty obsolete Navy planes, or brush on about his business. The Minister was angry and unhappy about it (thinks we are welching—I think we are), but he nevertheless started in to look over the Navy planes. The Minister meanwhile wanted to see the President; and the President sent word over to me to field the ball. This would seem kindlier than it actually is: the fact of the matter being that the President was in a jam and isn't going to talk to anybody until something shows up. I don't blame him a bit, but it reminds me of William Allen White, who got a nasty letter one day while I was there and asked me what you did with a letter like that. I told him I didn't know. He then said he would show me, and yelled for his son, Bill. When Bill arrived he shoved the letter over to him and said, "Bill, answer this letter. I'm going off for the day." Only in this case, I am in Bill's shoes. . . .

February 6, 1941

A really bad situation is turning up in Greenland. The Canadians and the British are pressing for air bases in Greenland. Professor Hobbs, of Michigan, has told them that they can get a good one down near Cape Fairwell. The Canadians have a battalion lined up and are prepared to take it. We have stalled this off so far, and will send American experts to look the place over. But the sites are actually there; and either the Canadians or the British or we will be moving pretty soon.

I called a conference with the Army and Navy and Coast Guard people this afternoon. They indicated that they thought we ought to go ahead, preferably in cooperation with Greenland, and get at it, since they figure that we would be forced to do so, anyhow, and that air fields were essential for our defense. Sumner Welles agrees. . . .

But, we now have an advance base, close to the water zone, which we are bound to defend. The lines are coming terribly close. Yet we must have the air bases. A German air base in Greenland would make it perfectly possible to bomb New York.

Hell has broken loose in the Near East. The President promised the Greek Minister thirty planes. . . . While the Greeks were still considering this, the Secretary of the Navy announced that they had declined them as a gift. . . . The difficulty with this, of course, is far greater than thirty planes. The Middle East is holding up largely because of faith in us, and hope that we will ultimately navigate their liberation. To have the President's word discredited will run around the Balkans like the germ of a bad disease; and we may lose at one fell swoop the Greeks, the Turks and the Bulgarians. . . .

February 13, 1941

A stiff conference on Greenland. We told the Canadians that they couldn't grab an air base there; instead, we would try to work out with the Greenland authorities that they should build an air field and have it open to the other American nations for purposes of hemispheric defense. This seemed to satisfy the Canadians, and we will tackle it next with . . . the Greenlanders. This of course is the first true "strategic point" (European style)—a case where we are forced into a move primarily lest a military enemy should grab it first and make trouble for us. I am glad that there is not very much territory in the Arctic, and so few people there that it does not complicate the course of world affairs as it does in West Europe. But it is, I think, a distinct new step in the American position. For the first time, the Monroe Doctrine has to be implemented militarily on a frontier.

The Greek Minister came in and I tried to pacify him about the planes. Morgenthau is trying to grab some good planes off the Navy, and the Navy is kicking like a mule. The President has got to settle it. Equally, the Greek has to have his planes. . . .

February 14, 1941

To the Secretary's office. . . .

We likewise got to work on Greenland. We shall be negotiating for a Greenland-constructed and Greenland-owned air base available to the hemisphere. I anticipate some resistance on the part of the Greenlanders, though plainly something is going to have to happen. . . . [On February 28, Berle wrote: "We got started today on sending a survey party in the general direction of Greenland to locate some air fields. Jesse Jones says he will give us some money if we need it."]

A long talk with Tom Burke and [Artemus] Gates, Counsel for the Civil Aeronautics Board. It relates to the American Export Lines' desire to take over TACA, an air line in Guatemala and other Central American countries; and it probably would be the foundation for an air service from New Orleans to Panama. Pan Am is fighting, tooth and nail—as dirty a piece of business as I have seen—and the problem is whether to blow Pan Am out of the water at the forthcoming hearing, or to play it more mildly.

The Swiss Minister [Charles Bruggmann] wants to see the President to protest against freezing, fearing lest Switzerland blow up. The President doesn't want to see him, and has shipped him back to me. I don't blame the President, but it is a hot ball to field. . . .

The European situation is thick, and getting infinitely thicker by the minute. The German invasion of Bulgaria is already pretty well forward. Their "tourists", to the number of some six or seven thousand, are already in Bulgaria and are clustering around the airports. . . .

. . . The Germans are sending "observers" in considerable numbers to the west African ports—Casablanca, and now Dakar. They are really establishing their wings on the Atlantic line—their extreme right resting in Norway; and their extreme left designed to rest ultimately on Dakar. I have been desperately feeling in my mind for some way to stop the process, but the only real way to do that would be to work out a method of landing troops directly at Dakar and Casablanca—which is obviously impossible at the moment. The solution is, of course, to energize, in some fashion, the French North African Government and the French forces; but we do not know altogether whether this will be possible. . . .

The Greek plane controversy came up in Cabinet yesterday, whereupon the President decided to order the Navy to hand over some good planes to the Greeks. The Greek Minister was advised this morning. He is all happy again, and that is one mess out of the way.

This is more important than it sounds. The one antithesis to Hitler is the myth of President Roosevelt; and if that myth were destroyed, as by a flagrant breach of his promise in a case like this, we should lose a moral strength which would be worth many divisions when the ultimate showdown comes.

For come it must, though I surmise it will be political rather than military. . . .

February 16, 1941

A flying trip to New York to see Mayor La Guardia. La Guardia had been talking to Carlo Sforza, former Minister of Foreign Affairs in Italy. . . . Sforza would like to set up the equivalent of a "De Gaulle" government for Italy. La Guardia was interested in following it up. I am tackling it with the Department.

We also talked politics. I told Fiorello that the President would undoubtedly give him the offer of the next main-line Cabinet job that falls open; but he will not create a Cabinet vacancy (at all events, he never has) and the timing may not be right to take care of the New York City election. In consequence, I thought that La Guardia had to consider running for a third term. He said that he had promised his wife that he wouldn't, which Marie immediately and heavily confirmed. He further said that the Democratic aspirants were tearing each other to pieces and that a good thing to do was to keep everything below hatches for quite a while—which is good judgment, but of course means that he will have to take the third term himself, just as the President had to.

Dr. [George] Baehr, his doctor, came in while we were there. He had made Fiorello have some X-ray pictures taken. Fiorello had no sympathy with the proceedings, and stuck a Yale key underneath his shoulder blade, so that the X-ray pictures came out showing a Yale key somewhere in his anatomy, which he insisted he had swallowed by accident in an absent-minded fit of irritation. But on the play-off, Baehr won. He got an extra appropriation of $100,000 for some anti-influenza work he is interested in.

February 17, 1941

We are still having the battle over "fund freezing" with the Treasury. I am maneuvering [Dean] Acheson, the new Assistant Secretary, into the front line on this. Acheson is a pet of Frankfurter's and I think the Frankfurter crowd can deal with the Treasury crowd better than I can.

Fund freezing of course talks like exchange control, but actually consists in making it impossible for the frozen person to pay a laundry bill without a license from the Treasury. It can therefore be complete confiscation. As the proposed order is drawn, alien funds are "frozen"; and alien control is judged by the widest possible test. In one case, a coporation six per cent of whose stock was owned by Luxemburg interests was frozen. On this basis, practically every large interest in the United States could be frozen. The Treasury boys, [Harry Dexter] White [Director of Monetary Research], [Edward H.] Foley [General Counsel] and Bernstein, were explaining how kind they would be and how easily the administration would work out, and so forth. I could not help thinking that if Fascism ever comes to the United States its protagonists will talk in exactly that fashion. Of course it is a war measure, and if we are at war we do things like that: individual justice does not count for much. Short of war, it is a pretty devastating instrument. . . .

February 18, 1941

To the White House with Leland Olds. The President was in excellent form. We were talking about locating the St. Lawrence project between the Federal Government and the State of New York. Since the Canadians have not signed the treaty yet, we have not got the project; so it was like two tramps bargaining to buy and sell a railroad. Properly, this ought to be a new TVA project; but the history runs in favor of a State project, and so the State Government will probably have a major voice in it. The President's main concern was that the State should actually take and run the transmission lines, and not resell to the power companies.

The President told us a variety of things. One of them was the genesis of the Canton-Ederbury Island matter. Americans had discovered the island; then the British had. Americans had taken away guano; so had the British. Nobody had been interested in the islands, but the British mapmakers had the habit of coloring everything red and claiming it as British if no one else had tied it down, and they did this with these islands. At the President's direction, Americans went and occupied the island. . . . Sir Ronald Lindsey [British Ambassador during 1930's], whom the President had known since he was a small boy, came in and the President told him that Americans were there and occupying. "But I say, you can't do that," says Sir Ronald. "But I have," says the President. "But you can't," says Lindsey. "But I am telling you I have," says the President. The President left it to the State Department, which, as he said, wrote notes back and forth, and nothing happened. Finally, he sent a personal message to Neville Chamberlain. He suggested that they agree that the islands be occupied jointly. . . . Any cargoes of beer arriving there were to be divided equally between the two groups. The question of sovereignty, the President suggested, might adequately be decided in the year 1987. He said to Neville Chamberlain that the solid advantage in this clause was that both of them would be dead by that time.

He likewise put on a sketch of his conference with Admiral [Kichisaburo] Nomura [Japanese Ambassador]. Considering that we are supposed to be on the brink of war with Japan, this qualified as a fair-to-middling important conference. He said that he had decided that the best way to do was to be really emotional about it. He would say the speech that he made to Admiral Nomura, interspersing it with sobs. He pointed out how President McKinley had done his best to avoid war with Spain, but then one of these horrid things they call an episode occurred. Nobody knew whether the *Maine* was sunk by the Spaniards or not, but President McKinley and John Hay were unable to resist the insistence of the American people for war. (Sob). When the Japanese sank the *Panay*, a wave had gone over the country. He and Mr. Hull (who was sitting opposite him during this interview) had with great difficulty restrained another wave of indignation, but thank God had succeeded. (Sob). He hoped Admiral Nomura would make it plain to his Government that while everybody here was doing their best to keep things quiet, it trembled on the brink of the indignation of the American people, and should the dikes ever break (three sobs), civilization would be ended.

I doubt if the interview was exactly as stated; at all events, the President's account corresponds only roughly with the memorandum of the conversation written out by Secretary Hull, which I have also seen; but it is splendid to find the President in a mood to joke about these things. . . .

February 20, 1941

A raft of detail, and nothing very important. It seems that the newspapers assume I am going to be La Guardia's candidate for Mayor of New York. . . .

To New York, where I told the Affiliated Young Democrats that it was not time to talk candidacies for Mayor as yet. We have a good one and want to hold on to him.

February 21, 1941

A long conference with Leland Olds and Jim Bonbright. The row is still on as to whether the State of New York or the Federal Government will have the ultimate voice in the St. Lawrence Power Project. If they keep on fighting about it, there won't be any project, and that will settle the matter. . . .

February 24, 1941

A conference in the office about getting the new American planes to Britain. The Treasury was worried about some of our rulings as to pilots, law, etc. On careful examination, I believe that the difficulties are not as great as most people suppose; at all events, I think they can be arranged. Certainly they ought to be. If we are sending planes at all, the object is to have them there, and not somewhere else.

Lunch with Gerhard Colm. He and Gardiner Means have been working on the budget and tax system. They figure that we can do quite a bit by expanding the currency; but that the time will come when we have to guard against inflation. He and Gardiner are suggesting two possible ways: (a) A plan for forced savings by small people, which in practice means a tax something like a payroll tax taken out of their salaries but invested in government bonds and saved up for them. These savings could be made available in case of sickness or need; and after the war, when spending power is needed, the sums could be released. From $1500 to $10,000, the plan is to have part savings and part straight tax. Over $10,000, it is a straight, progressive tax. (b) Or, a tax on the amount of value added—which in practice means a tax on the gross selling price, less cost of materials, etc. Both are designed to diminish consumption and to haul in currency to some extent. The particular trick they have in mind is to have the legislation applicable, not at once, but on the decision of the President, or a defense finance board whose business it will be to study for signs of inflation, and throw in the lever when prices begin to get out of line. It is an ingenious idea, and one well worth considering. I am glad that they are working on it. . . .

February 25, 1941

A conference with the Navy and our aviation people on an attempt to work out an aviation policy. The immediate question is whether we let Congress kill American Export Lines and thereby guarantee Pan Am a pretty permanent monopoly. The Navy had done some valiant work and got the Army to agree not to do it. In other words, to recommend that the American Export Lines get its subsidy to go to Portugal. It is a good job, and we will report to the Postmaster General accordingly. . . .

March 5, 1941

Thursday, February 27th. Juan Trippe came in today and made an impassioned plea for the principle of monopoly—even if government-owned—meaning thereby that he does not want American Export permitted to do business at all. I don't see it. . . .

Monday, March 3rd. Sumner Welles is away, and I have his desk as well as my own, which makes a bad time. There was a raft of fundamentally unimportant detail, though any particular thing in it was tolerably important. For instance, the Federal Reserve wants to get its bill through permitting drafts on frozen funds by accredited representatives of certain countries. We need it, since otherwise the Latvian and Estonian Legations are sunk. . . .

Meanwhile, the boys were fighting the battle of fund freezing. For over the week-end the Secretary of the Treasury decided to do an incautious thing—namely, "rush" Secretary Hull. So they got up all the orders and they were going to have them signed at nine o'clock next morning, this on account of Bulgaria, which is now duly invaded, and whose funds have to be frozen. But we caucused on it, and Secretary Hull declined to be rushed. So I suppose they will be freezing Bulgaria, and the battle will go on. . . .

Tuesday, March 4th. Juan Trippe was in, pleading the case of the Pan American Airways, a few days ago. Accordingly, John Slater showed up to plead the cause of the American Airways. There is not much that can be done about it. . . .

Wednesday, March 5th. We went to work on Near East relations with Wallace Murray; we are trying to get our North African economic agreements forward, and I think will succeed.

Then a big meeting working on Greenland air fields with Hugh Cumming and Jack Hickerson; likewise, the Army, the Navy and the Coast Guard. An impressive meeting. Followed immediately after by a visit from the Danish Minister, and we got the groundwork laid for the diplomatic agreement which must follow. . . .

The superstition about the Dardanelles so far seems to be holding good. A day or so ago the Russians, having sat silently during the occupation, issued a statement to the Bulgarian Government rebuking it for assenting to the German occupation and indicating their disapproval and their belief that the Bulgarian Government has therefore let the war into the Balkans. If they had said this publicly a few weeks ago, things would have been different—but that is not the Russian way. . . . Meanwhile, we have pretty clear information that the Germans propose to attack Russia this summer. . . .

If my guess as to what happens is right, I think I know now how this thing is coming out. The Germans will tackle Russia, and probably will smash her. They will be smashed, themselves, in the process. I think the two dictatorships are going down in one hideous mass of slime and blood and anarchy.

March 7, 1941

A little work with [N.R.] Danielian [Director, St. Lawrence Survey] in setting up the St. Lawrence fight. It is going to be a daisy.

March 8, 1941

After lunch, the White House called up and I went down to see the President. He indicated he was going to have a new head for Military Intelligence, and was casting about in his mind for the proper man. . . .

March 9, 1941

To the office and then to Secretary Hull's apartment, where we cleared a raft of stuff. He has been having a hard time, chiefly because they have put him on the Lease-Lend Bill, and until Saturday he has been seeing every Senator in sight. The Senate vote really ends the fight; and I suppose that the Bill will go through the middle of next week. Thereby we have settled another issue of foreign policy and really moved into another phase of things, a semi-belligerent phase. Curiously enough, I am not sure that it means war, necessarily. I think the Germans simply do not want war with us. What I think it means is a steady drift into a deep gray stage in which the precise difference between war and peace is impossible to discern.

March 11, 1941

A rough day. I went up to the Senate Committee on Appropriations to testify for the item giving the Export Air Lines a subsidy to go to Portugal. Pan American Airways has been lobbying against this like anything. They say we ought to have a single, monopolistic air line. They may be right, but it ought not to happen by a side wind. I asked that the Committee vote the appropriation and keep the question open till it could be decently examined. . . .

March 12, 1941

It is pretty plain now that we shall be able to sign the St. Lawrence Treaty some time next week.

The Swedish Minister came in. The Treasury are freezing some Swedish assets. The Swedes have made advanced payments on a lot of goods they were buying from various countries. They did this by depositing dollars in American banks to cover letters of credit. The countries were then invaded and we froze the funds. The deliveries were never made to the Swedes, and the Swedes are entitled to their money back. The Treasury won't let them have it. They don't say why.

The real difficulty, it seems to me, is that there are two strands of theory going in the Administration. One of them is the Treasury theory, which is also Felix Frankfurter's, and revolves around the idea that the British are the salt of the earth but everything on the continent is hostile by hypothesis. Therefore, whatever you do to the Swiss, the Swedes, the Yugoslavs, and so forth, is immaterial.

The other idea is ours, namely, that the continent of Europe will be conquered by the continentals, and that wherever there are nations which are standing up for themselves as best they can, we ought to nourish them in every way we can. To my mind we ought to go as far as we can towards keeping Finland, Sweden, Switzerland, Yugoslavia, Portugal, North Africa, and so on, afloat. We ought to do this on common sense grounds, if on no other: it will cost the Germans time, money, men and organization to seize them. Most of all, we ought to do it because our whole theory of life contemplates that these people shall some day be free, independent and I hope cooperative.

In the afternoon, a terrible long row with the Russian Ambassador [Oumansky]. He came in to raise the dickens about our stopping the Soviet propaganda. I gave him legalistics, but told him quite bluntly that in a big defense effort nobody would tolerate propaganda directed against that effort. We know, of course, that all of this agitation against defense, against the Lend-Lease Bill, and so forth, was inspired by the Communists —probably by agreement with the Germans.

I pushed at the President a memorandum authorizing the exchange of notes between the United States and Canada indicating that the President wants the St. Lawrence Treaty. Mackenzie King needs this to stiffen his nerve.

March 13, 1941

A slow day. The outlines of the new War Cabinet are pretty plain now; it will be Hull, Morgenthau, Knox and Stimson. In practice, this will mean Welles, Morgenthau, [James V.] Forrestal [Under Secretary of the Navy] and [Robert] Patterson [Under Secretary of War]. Harry Hopkins will be the general coordinator and head of the whole shooting-match. Philip Young [Special Assistant to Morgenthau] is going with Hopkins. . . .

March 14, 1941

The Battle of the Balkans is on in full swing. At the moment the question is whether Yugoslavia signs up with the Axis or sticks out and goes it alone. . . .

The Treasury wants to freeze Yugoslav balances here. They took it up with Dean Acheson, who it appears is this week the Treasury point of contact. We talked it over; took it up with the Secretary of State, and he telephoned the President. The President, on a swift snap judgment, decided no. We can get the bulk of the effect by simply not buying the Yugoslav gold which they wish to sell to the Treasury, after which they wish to take the money out of the country. It is going to be close going, by all standards.

A lot of work, chiefly aviation. I started negotiations with [Paul] Guerin, Weygand's representative here for economic assistance to North Africa. I tried to make it plain to him that it depended at least in part on the different situation which prevailed in North Africa as against the Vichy government. I told him I thought that this would be an added strength to the government of unoccupied France. Of course the plain fact is that if Vichy forces a war with England (they are talking of convoying French ships through the blockade) North Africa will have to decide whether it is going with France or staying out of this and going it alone.

This morning the Treasury sent over a draft agreement they are making with the English for transfer of material under the Lease-Lend Bill. They wanted the Secretary of State to approve it in five minutes and send it back—not a good way to do business, because the Treasury must have been working on it for a week. It is, briefly, an agreement that we transfer stuff to the British; and that they transfer to us at some future time pretty much anything the President wants to take, as a *quid pro quo*. It is a meaningless agreement, because you can't collect on it. The problem that I am wondering about is whether we ought not to have a clause in there providing that the munitions leased or lent shall not be used against someone friendly to us. Bluntly, I trust the British as warriors, but not as statesmen. . . .

March 15, 1941

Mr. Gates, of the Civil Aeronautics Board, came over. He is getting ready to investigate Pan American Airways; but wants to know whether he will be politically crucified. Bearing in mind that Pan Am had succeeded in forcing the Department of Justice to withdraw its anti-trust suit, I think he is up against some pretty stiff firing. On the other hand, there is a good deal of question about Pan Am and I think that he is reasonably safe. . . .

March 16, 1941

Sunday . . . Off.—This is unusual, and worth noting. However, I was asked to go down to the White House with Leland Olds. Whither we went, about half past twelve, finding the President in bed. He was in excellent form and trying to get his affairs into shape so that he could go away for a week's rest on the boat. We got clearance for our plans to support the St. Lawrence Waterway agreement in the Congress: it will be a stiff fight. . . .

He reminisced a little about the St. Lawrence Waterway; pointed out that he, as a youngster in the New York Senate, had had a good deal to do with blocking the aluminum company's attempt to take all the water in the river. The man who had got the grant, and who opposed the repealer legislation, was Leighton McCarthy, now Canadian Minister to Washington, but who subsequently has been an old friend of the President. The President jollied McCarthy about it when he came in to present his credentials as Minister. . . .

March 17, 1941

Increasingly, there is tension in the Administration between the people who take the English view, i.e., that there are only two civilized peoples in the world—English and Americans (I am not sure that they let us in, except when they are talking to us), and that the entire Continent of Europe ought to be written off as a total loss. The Treasury takes this view, and Felix Frankfurter urges it on all occasions. When the fact is that we need every nucleus of continental help we can get. The Hungarians are a case in point. If, for instance, the Germans get involved in a huge southeastern adventure and it were possible to energize the Serbians and the Hungarians at the same time, that adventure would break up like a shot. The President knows this; his individual correspondence with Prince Paul in an endeavor to get the Yugoslavs to stand fast is an evidence of it. But just when he has done something brilliant like this, the extreme Anglophiles come along and sock the European nucleus squarely in the face with something like a freezing order, or a studied insult of some kind. We try to see what we can do—but it is tough going.

Olds left for Ottawa last night and is there now; and with him Jack Hickerson. They have been telephoning about the arrangements for press releases, etc.

I asked Dan Tracy [Second Assistant Secretary of Labor] to see whether he could give us some help with the Labor people on the St. Lawrence, and he says he will do so. . . .

March 18, 1941

At Ottawa. The temperature is ten below zero.

Pierrepont Moffat and the boys have got the St. Lawrence treaty pretty well in hand, and there is not much for me to do.

In the afternoon, a talk with Hugh Keenleyside [First Secretary, Department of External Affairs]. They have proposed a study of economic pooling between the United States and Canada. Their plan is to have a joint study committee—three men on their side, three men on ours, and a couple of liaison men. In part this is to integrate our defense production with theirs: so that we manufacture the things we can do best; they the things they do best, instead of trying to duplicate each other's production, buying, etc.

But the rest of it goes much farther. Keenleyside realizes that this is now one continent and one economy; that we shall have to be integrated as to finance, trade routes, and pretty much everything else; and in this I so thoroughly agree with him that it is refreshing. We talked long and happily about it—though much lies in the realm of dreams. This at least is a new order which can exist without hatred and can be created without bloodshed, and ought to lead to production without slavery.

Dinner at the Legation. Pierrepont Moffat does it up to the nines. I met [Ian A.] MacKenzie, of the National Research Council; General [L. R.] LaFlèche, the best of the French-Canadian officers, and a bunch of other people. The feeling against the British in official circles is very great. For instance, they want the Canadians to build fuselages for airplanes. They don't want them to manufacture engines; and they don't want them to buy American engines. They want them to agree that they will only import British engines, put them in the planes and then ship the planes back to England. . . . Finally, the British imperial officers treat them as though they were Malayans, and issue orders all over the lot (principally paid for with American money), and the Canadians are pretty sore. This, however, is strictly official. The people have been told that it is all out for Britain, and they go the limit.

Well, I suppose this is normal. The British are doing the fighting, and therefore have the center of the stage. It is the British statesmanship that is at fault, as it has been right along.

March 19, 1941

We signed the St. Lawrence Agreement at 2:30 this afternoon. Being the first international agreement I have signed, I found myself too excited to hold the pen properly and therefore blamed it on the Canadian pen— which was merely discourteous. Thereafter, we all went over to the Canadian House of Commons to see Mackenzie King inform the House that the agreement had been signed, and lay on the table the notes exchanged between the Canadian Government and the United States—the last being a personal message from the President to Mackenzie King designed, I regret to say, to buttress Mackenzie King's political position. The fact is that the President is more popular in Canada than King is—and King knew it—and so he arranged to have the President request him personally to execute the agreement. A plain but intelligent girl sat next to me in the visitors' gallery. Presently I was introduced. It was Princess Juliana, of Holland.

Then over to the hotel, where we continued discussions begun in the morning. These were between Leland Olds, and [Clarence D.] Howe, the Minister of Munitions [and Supply], and Diblis, who is batting for Tommy Hogg, the head of Ontario Hydro. It was quite a discussion. The Aluminum Company is borrowing power from Canada to make aluminum at Massena. They want more power. Ontario Hydro has more applications for power than it can satisfy now. They are thinking of cutting down domestic consumption—but this is dangerous, because in Ontario they use electric heat, and many of the houses are built without chimneys. They can't possibly give Aluminum Company any more power. The Aluminum Company ought to have got started on building some new power in the Saguenay, but they didn't. Instead, they want all the power they can get out of the St. Lawrence—or out of Ontario—even though the Canadian Government was prepared to finance their development at Saguenay.

We generally agreed: (a) that we would try to pound some sense into Aluminum Company (a slim chance); (b) that we would try to take all the available sources of power supply on our side of the line and pool resources with the Canadians, and thus try to get things going. Plainly, you cannot ask the Ontario towns to go cold and dark while we run a wide open shop on the other side of the river, with movie lights and everything else. We were pretty well at it when the time came to take the train home. . . .

March 21, 1941

. . . Wallace Murray, with some tragic business of news about the Greek planes. It seems that the British have proposed to substitute British planes for the 30 Grummans we are giving them. The Greek Government was skeptical about getting the planes, and are hanging on to what they have got. Then somebody representing Harry Hopkins telephoned the Greek Minister that they were going to take the Grummans away from them anyhow. And here is another piece of desperate mishandling of one of the principal points of resistance in Europe. I think that Britain, with our help, is going to win this war; but it will only be because of the personal and direct intervention of the Lord Almighty if this kind of thing goes on. . . .

A raft of paper work—not well done.

March 22, 1941

To Congressman [Francis D.] Culkin's [R., N.Y.] office, where were three or four of the brethren interested in the St. Lawrence, and we set up the campaign. Back to the office to do a raft of work. There is a radio speech tonight which will open up the St. Lawrence discussion. . . .

April 15, 1941

I have not made any entries in this diary since March 22nd.

The time has not been wholly unoccupied.

The Lend-Lease Bill went through, and the Treasury proposed a formal agreement by which the British repay us for the articles. I have been endeavoring to try to rephrase this into something like a more sensible agreement, really slanting not towards repayment but towards economic cooperation after the war. . . . This work has gone on intermittently.

Likewise, by direction of the President, we worked out the agreement permitting us to establish landing fields in Greenland. . . . The Danish Minister considered that he would probably be recalled if he executed this agreement; on the other hand, he believed that this was probably the only way to safeguard the position of Greenland; and accordingly, he went ahead. The notes of recall duly came in; and we promptly declined to recognize them. This raises some interesting questions in international law; but I think the outlines are plain. Denmark no longer can exercise sovereignty over her unoccupied territories, namely, Greenland. Greenland is thus a *de facto* government, which carries the Danish sovereignty with it. De Kauffmann is the representative of unoccupied Denmark—

namely, Greenland; and Copenhagen, being occupied by the Germans, has no power to force his recall. In a sense, Greenland is a *de facto* government which we recognize, and Kauffmann is the Minister.

But I am worried about the situation. I should have been glad to delay the agreement.

The past month has seen the situation shift entirely. Yugoslavia was forced to sign a limited treaty joining the Axis, and really making possible a German military operation against Greece. . . .

The military situation is as bad as it can be; but matters are complicated by a diplomatic shift. The Russians have signed a "Neutrality Agreement" with the Japanese, whereby both parties agree to stay neutral if the other goes to war. The Russian side is plain enough: they expect to be attacked by the Germans this summer (which I am pretty clear they will be), and this protects their rear. But to the Japanese it may well prove an encouragement to blast away southward and head for Singapore. . . .

We are beginning today to organize the St. Lawrence project; which is another big one; and I am likewise arranging to send up the Inter-American Bank for ratification. It is about time.

April 17, 1941

The other day Loy Henderson came down to see me. It seemed that old Dr. Pusta, who had represented Estonia at the Versailles Conference, was here in Washington, so broke that he had not paid his rent, nor had they had enough to eat. I got Henderson to get hold of the head of a Society of the Friends of the Baltic Republics and asked him to buy from Pusta an article on the status of the Baltic republics for two hundred and fifty dollars, which I thus secretly supplied. This will enable them to eat. Thereafter, we got a law passed making it possible for the recognized Legation of a recognized government to draw, within limits, on blocked government funds here, and I suppose the Legation can take care of Dr. Pusta.

I believe the Lithuanians are in the same situation—the exiled President of Lithuania is here.

The foregoing was not politics, but ordinary humanity. These men deserve well of their country and the world, and it simply is not right that they should starve to death here.

I saw Senator [Walter F.] George [D., Ga.; Chairman, Foreign Relations Committee] on April 16th, and asked him to bring out the project of the Inter-American Bank. There is no reason now why it should not go forward. I have been waiting for somebody else to do it, with the usual results; and have finally gone to work at it, myself. I think Senator George will appoint a sub-committee of the Senate Committee on Foreign Affairs, and we can get started.

April 24, 1941

I went to the White House with Leland Olds and we talked with the President for half an hour. The President is tired. I hope he gets away very soon.

We talked about St. Lawrence legislation. I told him I did not think that New York state authorities and the Federal authorities could get together and I thought we would do better to bring in an authorization bill with court action with any statement protecting the New York position we thought fit.

The President agreed that we ought to do this and sketched out to Leland Olds the kind of a statement which might be made when the legislation comes up. He added that Mackenzie King had hoped we could get our legislation forward in about two weeks.

I asked about the possible appointments to the committee to work out economic cooperation with Canada. The President first said that he thought the thing might be done directly between the Canadian Purchasing representative and our own. I said that Canada had something much broader in mind, at least judging from their note. They were talking of a committee of three. I thought it required somebody from OPM [Office of Production Management], somebody from Finance and perhaps someone else. . . .

May 26, 1941

It has been a long time between entries. The run of news has been consistently bad. However, there is not much point in making any entries, because I do not think that I have been in on any major decisions and if anything important has been done, it has been chiefly thinking.

The military situation is not good. . . .

The British seem fairly safe from invasion. . . .

It is clear that the Germans have a preponderant force in North Africa, which, however, for some reason they are not able to maneuver very rapidly. . . .

The Germans are undoubtedly getting ready to angle for the shoulder of Africa down to Dakar. It is going to take time. They will not go west until they have gone east. . . .

The Atlantic line is thus beginning to establish itself.

The President is working on what is inevitably one of the crucial speeches in the matter to be given May 27th. [In this first major policy speech in five months, Roosevelt reviewed Nazi war aims and proclaimed a state of "unlimited national emergency."] He sent a copy over to the State Department Saturday, to be looked at. We looked at it. It was calculated to scare the daylights out of everyone (there is some reason for that) but it did not do much else. Secretary Hull commissioned me to go over and try to get a chance to work in on a redraft. I thereupon went over to see Harry Hopkins, and got the President to postpone considering the draft. I then came back to the Department and worked literally all night trying to rearrange the draft, and put in for a couple of hours' sleep just as the rosy dawn was breaking on Sunday morning. . . .

Then Sumner and I went to the White House and there met the President, along with Sam Rosenman and Robert Sherwood, who had been working on the earlier draft. . . .

We worked out a redraft of the speech and had lunch with the President: a quiet little lunch, and as happy as could be under the circumstances. . . .

We finished up about half-past six; home for a snack and then back to go over the new draft with the President in the evening. He redictated a good deal of it; but the result, when it finally came out, was a really good job. It is more explanatory than dispository. In other words, it leaves several main issues to be settled later. The principal problem which is still unsettled is whether the President proclaims a general emergency and goes into the whole business of really heavy preparation. It is obvious now that the German tactic is to keep us clear of this by every means they can. . . .

May 29, 1941

The draft of the President's speech was somewhat changed during Sunday and Monday, principally I think because of various culls made by some of the cabinet ministers. . . . The real highlight was the proclamation of national emergency. This was what I had urged on Hopkins Saturday night. We accordingly included it in the Sunday draft. Hopkins had wanted to take it up with Treasury but it was still hanging in the balance. Secretary Hull weighed the matter and finally determined in favor of it after some consultation with all of us, and it was duly included.

Everybody's nerve was considerably bucked up by the sinking of the *Bismarck*. . . .

But the combined Crete fighting and *Bismarck* incident do change the situation somewhat. So far as I can now see, the Crete fighting proves that Britain cannot be invaded despite the success (at the date of this writing) of the German seizure of Crete. The British do not have any air force based on Crete and their Egyptian forces were too far away. The land based air force could prevent the British Navy from giving any real help; and of course they could land men from the air in very considerable quantities. But I question whether the same thing could be done in England. If it could be done at all, the cost must be staggering; the risk far too great (I should imagine) for a German Army to take on.

Meanwhile, the fact that the *Bismarck* was sunk (substantially) by air power, seems to make it plain that if there is anything like an adequate air force, a naval invasion of the Western Hemisphere is out of the question. Even if the Germans conquered Europe, and if they outbuilt us navally and with merchant marine, it would still be a question whether these ships could live long enough to reach the United States. If there is anything certain, it is that we must have an adequate air force, and lots of it. . . .

The President's speech itself was a brilliant affair. . . .

Yesterday, work with varying degrees of importance (actually little that was very important). And then to Justice Stone's to dinner where were Sir Arthur Salter [Churchill's representative for shipping problems], Francis Biddle, Archie MacLeish [Librarian of Congress], and some others. The only important thing we agreed upon was that we would have to stiffen the morale of the foreign born in the United States and to talk to the submerged populations in Europe. I agreed to go to work on it. Accordingly, today I had lunch with [Harold B.] Hoskins whom I brought down from the Cannon Mills to work on this kind of problem; and finally got hold of Wayne Coy, the new chief of the Office of Emergency Management, to take the baby into his family and raise it. I suppose they will take Hoskins for temporary chief. I am proposing to sell it to La Guardia later, if he wants it. But I think he will be up to his neck in straight defense work for some time. This is the beginning of an entirely new phase for us; and is being done quietly and without benefit of clergy or anyone else. . . .

June 4, 1941

To the Senate Committee, to get it to approve an exchange of notes providing for further diversion of Niagara water. This is because we are already short of power and need a lot of it for the ferro-alloy industries in the Niagara Valley. We shall need more before the summer is over. I couldn't stay through, but left to go to see the President at eleven. . . .

He signed the message recommending the St. Lawrence Seaway. He had discussed the matter with the leaders—Rayburn and [Congressman John W.] McCormack [D., Mass.; Majority Leader], George and [Senator Alben] Barkley [D., Ky.; Majority Leader]. I gathered that they were not too enthusiastic, but the President did give them some help. He thought that if things got really bad we might arrange that the Canadians suggest that they are going to build their half of it anyway and charge us tolls. This would put some squeeze on the Senate. It is a good idea, if it works. We made some jokes and talked over some men; I thought he was standing by beautifully, in view of the fact that all the military news we get is bad, and getting worse.

In the late afternoon cables came in which made it perfectly evident that the French Government had caved in completely; and that they agreed to collaborate pretty thoroughly with the Germans; this includes granting the Germans naval bases at Casablanca and Dakar. I think they have one of these bases actually working now. At all events, there have been submarine sinkings off the Cape Verde Islands. . . .

June 5, 1941

Various work, chiefly on the St. Lawrence, and on some Canadian matters; and we got the note to Canada arranging for a joint study committee initialed and out of the way. . . .

June 19, 1941

We are all rejoicing in the appointment of Harlan Stone [as Chief Justice of the Supreme Court]. I think Bob Jackson wanted it; but he would be the first to recognize that Stone, by every title of intelligence, of legal ability, and of quality as a human being, is entitled to it. Once in a while the right thing happens around here. . . .

On Tuesday, June 17th, the hearings on the St. Lawrence Waterway opened. It is the usual line-up: railroads, railway labor and the utilities on the one side, and about everybody else on the other; but concentrated special interests can very often beat a majority, and they are going to try. Stimson led for the Administration, and after that I spent five mortal hours on the griddle. I think we are making some progress.

Meanwhile, things are going all ways in Europe. The German-Russian show-down is nearing its climax. The armies are mobilized; there are five divisions in Finland (at least) and huge concentrations in Norway, these partly for Russian use and probably for use in an all-over attempt to seize Iceland and Britain a little later. After that, we can count on the probability of trouble, ourselves. The time is getting short. The Germans, I think, believe they will take Russia without fighting; but I am not altogether clear about it. Their real object now is to destroy Stalin and his regime; I cannot but believe that the Russian government knows that; and they therefore have to either fight or die. Death in this case is literal: if the Germans ever get control of the situation they will massacre the regime. . . .

During the last week of June, Berle participated in a conference on Canadian-American affairs at Queen's University, Kingston, Ontario, and received an honorary degree. There are no diary entries concerning Germany's invasion of Russia on June 22.

On June 26 Roosevelt wrote Berle a memorandum saying, "I have not the slightest objection towards your trying your hand at an outline of the post-war picture. But for Heaven's sake don't even let the columnists hear of it. . . . Don't forget that the elimination of costly armaments is still the keystone—for the security of all the little nations and for economic solvency. Don't forget what I discovered—that over ninety percent of all national deficits from 1921 to 1939 were caused by payments for past, present and future wars."

Memorandum to the President, July 8, 1941

It is now evident that preliminary commitments for the post-war settlement of Europe are being made, chiefly in London. Perhaps you are being kept informed of these. I am not clear that the State Department is being kept informed of all of them by the parties. Some have been told to us by the British; others we hear about.

I propose sending you from time to time information as to the post-war commitments as we hear of them. You will recall that at Versailles President Wilson was seriously handicapped by commitments made to which he was not a party and of which he was not always informed.

I have suggested to Sumner that we enter a general caveat, indicating that we could not be bound by any commitments to which we had not definitely assented. . . .

July 11, 1941

. . . I have been working a little on the British peace commitments —if they really are peace commitments. Some of them we know are. One of them, the alleged turning over of Trieste to Yugoslavia, has already been denied. Yesterday, having got hold of Welles and of Harry Hopkins,

I sent a memorandum to the President. I understand that the President wrote a message to Churchill last night in the general sense that the United States could not be bound by any commitments to which they were not a party. . . .

I have asked the Federal Bureau of Investigation to continue their surveillance over Communist activities here. A party line which could change from one of hostility to one of collaboration overnight could change back with equal speed. Anyhow, freedom from subversive activities (in plain English, from plotting, sabotage, political strikes, and in some cases, murder) ought not to rest on the grace of a foreign government. It ought to rest on our own strength.

July 17, 1941

La Guardia is in town; he is staying with me. We have been working somewhat on the New York City election. I had [Harold] Moskovit [leader of the Affiliated Young Democrats] ask Ed Flynn whether he would not simply call off the election and renominate the ticket, as is. Flynn answered yesterday by renominating a full ticket, with [William] O'Dwyer at the head of it; thereby putting himself in flat opposition to the present administration. . . .

The beginning of a first-class battle is going on over the economic frame of post-war Anglo-American relations. Maynard Keynes is here representing the British Government; he is discussing with Dean Acheson the lease-lend compensation. He intimates that all lease-lend stuff is really a gift (I think it is) and also that after the war the only possible economic structure will be one of closed economies—which implies a British economy closed against us. If this is worked out, the only economic effect of the war will be that we have moved a closed-economy center from Berlin to London. In the previous war we moved a militarist center from Berlin to Paris—and not much else was accomplished.

Hopkins is going to London, but I don't know what for. I am hoping that the President told him to take a little time off and assure himself, and incidentally the rest of us, that there are no secret peace commitments made, or being made. . . .

July 23, 1941

The City campaign is on. La Guardia announced that he was running for a third term on Monday. The Republicans have already agreed to accept him, though the Old Guard grumbled. . . .

Last night in a rather moving scene at the Norwegian Legation Sumner Welles opened up on peace commitments; proposed some kind of an association of nations, dedicated first to abolition of offensive armaments under international supervision and control, and second, recognition of the natural rights of all peoples to equal economic enjoyment. I was sorry about the "association of nations" idea, because it is going to draw a picture to everyone in the old League; and I rather wish that he had let the machinery evolve out of the objectives. . . .

A lot of work on the St. Lawrence; legislative work is always time-consuming. I think we shall come out all right, but it will be close going. . . .

To Harry Hopkins, July 30, 1941

The attached memorandum to Welles explains itself. I put it frankly as a precaution lest someone starts the yarn we are "sabotaging" Russian assistance—which God knows we are not.

Having had my fingers burned in Russian affairs several times in my life, permit me to make a point. The Russian dénouement is unpredictable. There might be a Peace of Brest-Litovsk. Or there might be a military coup in Germany with a General appearing as dictator and an immediate Russo-German alliance. . . . The Russian Ambassador here regularly interchanged espionage reports with the Germans up to June 21, 1941; the same personnel is still in the country. The British, glad of the Russian assistance, are at the moment taking no precautions. They did not take any precautions in 1917; as a result nearly lost the war in the spring drive of 1918.

So for God's sake, tell the sentimentalists to watch themselves.

I am in favor of giving all the things we can to Russia for her immediate defense. Whether she comes entirely inside the breastworks will have to turn on future events. Money, guns, planes, machinery she ought to have. But she ought not to have anything she can sell or turn over to someone else should there be a violent change in party line.

I mean this quite seriously. We nearly got killed by it in 1918. The British were betrayed into an almost hopeless position by it in August of 1939. Unless you can foresee the events of the next year on the Eastern Front, you cannot say with certainty that there may not be another change in the situation. . . .

July 31, 1941

Matters move too fast for comfort. On Monday Welles decided that we should get to work on trying to organize the possible handling of a peace conference. There will be a departmental committee with himself as chairman, myself as second in command, Feis, [Leo] Pasvolsky [special assistant to Hull], Acheson, Hackworth, and [Harry] Hawkins [Chief, Commercial Treaties and Agreements]. . . .

The job is a staggering one. It means drawing outlines in two dimensions; the economic and social common denominator of nations; the territories as well. But I have a feeling that circumstances will do this for us.

Likewise, we had a conference on the Russian demand that we turn over our military secrets to her, and give her engineers access to the plants making our secret military weapons. The extreme Anglophile view is that we should turn over everything to the Russians at once. They seem to think that the Russians now love them and will be in all respects a part of their train. . . . I am in no way sanguine. . . . In point of fact, the engineers they have wished to let in the plants are the same ones who were doing espionage for Russia and Germany until six weeks ago. I consequently voted "no" and was glad to see that the Army, Navy and FBI did likewise. We are much better off if we treat the Russian situation for what it is, namely, a temporary confluence of interest.

Then on Tuesday, a worse question. The Russians opened relations with the Poles; the Poles endeavored to insist upon a recognition of their pre-war frontiers; the Russians did not want to do this. The British put pressure on the Poles to accept. Three members of the Polish Cabinet offered their resignations after they found the treaty left the matter open. The Poles wished to put a statement in the newspapers saying that they interpreted this as recognition of pre-war frontiers. The British put pressure on them not to do that and the Poles applied to us for help. They thought, in a word, that they were being squeezed to buy support from Russia. I don't like the situation and suggested that we draft a telegram indicating that we stood flat on our position recognizing no territorial aggressions and insisting that any changes in territorial lines must be reserved for the final settlement. Note that Halifax [Ambassador Lothian's successor] recently requested us to join with them in recognizing the Russian conquest of the three Baltic provinces; Halifax did not think highly of these three peoples.

And so it goes, with an endless amount of departmental detail. . . .

We are working along on St. Lawrence [in Congress] and trying to support Leland Olds in his desperate attempt to keep Ickes from seizing power which he knows nothing about; and I hope to loosen up the Inter-American Bank and a few other things of that kind. But the main preoccupation is how to put together post-war reconstruction for the United States and post-war peace terms. The thing staggers one's intellectual processes. Distinct signs of strain are beginning—not so much in Washington but around the Foreign Service. I don't know that much can be done about it. . . .

August 2, 1941

At work yesterday on peace terms. At the request of some of the men in the European Division we had a meeting here on Eastern Europe. . . .

We got as far as agreeing on three points: (1) We must in honor stick up for the independence of Finland, the Baltic Republics, Poland and Czechoslovakia and Yugoslavia. Boundary questions can be left fluid for the time being, and worked out in a general settlement. (2) We will continue to recognize Finland. (3) We will make a very small beginning at taking care of these situations by asking the Russians if they will receive a Red Cross mission to try to take care of the needs of some of the populations deported from their countries, notably, Poles and Letts.

We will go on debating. . . .

A day's work on St. Lawrence and a whole raft of minor and unpleasant little questions. . . .

I telephoned the President today. This was to inquire whether or not he wanted the St. Lawrence Project tossed into the Rivers and Harbors Bill as Representative [John] Rankin [D., Miss.] and others have been recommending. He asked what we thought. I told him my best guess was in favor of it though one could not of course be sure. We will draft a letter in that sense. . . .

September 23, 1941

We had a pleasant dinner party on Friday night with [Eleazar] López Contreras, [Ambassador Diógenes] Escalante, the Aide, Jurado, the Apostolic Delegate [A. G. Cicognani], Archie MacLeish, and the Britisher, Noel Hall [Minister to Washington], who it seemed ought to be educated in the ways of South American affairs.

All of us were immensely struck with López Contreras. It took a great man and a statesman to bring Venezuela out from under the Gómez regime. He said a number of small things which indicated the way his mind ran: he had carefully educated the country to dissociate the presidency from the military authority by gradually doffing his uniform and appearing in civilian clothes; and then gradually encouraging his staff officers to do likewise.

A quiet day Sunday, marked principally by a heavy tennis game with Nelson Rockefeller [Coordinator of Inter-American Affairs]. I proposed to Nelson that since he now has South American propaganda we tie to that the F.B.I. intelligence service and thereby get a real machine rigged up. Rockefeller agreed, and I think we shall be able to get something done.

On Monday the Secretary delicately opened the question of repealing the Neutrality Act. Judging from the reaction, everybody approves the idea: the Neutrality Act has long since outlived its usefulness. The Secretary described it as a "last year's bird's nest"; the idea that we ship goods to England to defend ourselves and at the same time say we ought not to ship goods, for fear we shall get into war if they are sunk, is only one of many absurdities. . . .

October 10, 1941

This has been an anxious spell. The German armies seem to have broken the Russian front though not as yet the organization of the Russian armies. . . .

The British are pressing the Finns to make peace. Since the Russians have promised to exterminate the Finns if they win, I do not see that there is much in this for Finland. I am trying to think out a way by which we can offer some effective guarantee to Finland, in which case something essential might be done. The trouble with this is that the British guarantee is worthless; they have their hands full now and are certainly not going to open up a new front in Finland. A Russian guarantee is worth exactly what the Russian word is worth—which has not proved much so far. And I do not see that our people are prepared to push armies into Europe for Finland if, indeed, they are willing to move even in their own best interests.

I have been in negotiations with the British, chiefly Sir Ronald Campbell [Minister to Washington], to try to protect Iceland. . . . To my mind, the Icelanders had a legitimate complaint. The British took all their food, declined to give them supplies, asked them to get supplies from us, and if, by any chance, we paid them dollars, tried to insist that the Icelanders should turn over the dollars to the British. The President made some promises to the Icelanders when we agreed to move our troops in; and I have been trying to see that those promises are kept. . . .

October 24, 1941

A long meeting with the Economic Board this morning. There is a good deal of desire for organization there, but underneath it there is a lot of intrigue—largely because a good many of the new men coming in were brought in by Acheson, probably at Frankfurter's suggestion. Frankfurter apparently is getting a little out of scale. At all events, one of his confidants reported to J. Edgar Hoover that Frankfurter was endeavoring to have Secretary Hull removed by a series of whispering campaigns about his health, over-work, etc. Further, that his candidate to succeed Hull was Acheson, and that Frankfurter remarked that when he had accomplished this he would then be in substantial control of every Department of the Government. . . .

Regarding the Frankfurter matter, I think it has come remotely to the ears of Chief Justice Stone; and I think Stone is unhappy and wants to do something about it. If he wants the Supreme Court to be safe, he had better—unless J. Edgar Hoover's information is all wrong, as I fear it is not. . . .

November 3, 1941

During this week likewise the La Guardia campaign was on; and reached very bitter depths. . . .

I made a couple of speeches. . . . I think La Guardia will win by a pretty large majority, despite the current estimates in the situation. At all events, we shall know day after tomorrow.

November 18, 1941

Some of my own babies are working out; next spring or early summer we shall have an air route from Canada to southern Greenland, to northwest Greenland, to northeast Greenland, to Iceland, and so to Scotland. We ought likewise to have expanded facilities between here, New Zealand and Australia. So I think things will move along on that side, also.

On Sunday night, a quiet private dinner with Justice Stone. We talked of many things; I voiced my fear that Frankfurter's operations on so many fronts were beginning to imperil the Supreme Court's position; Stone indicated, with equal caution, that he felt the same way about it. It is not very often that one discusses things of that kind with the Chief Justice of the Supreme Court, and it was, of course, under the seal. This was because of the most recent report, namely, that Frankfurter proposed to direct the State Department through Acheson, making him Secretary when Cordell Hull should finally get through.

The State Department is going to have to do some strictly defensive work. About everyone in town suddenly yearns to run the economic foreign policy of the United States. . . .

Privately, I think Mr. Hull will run it; and I propose to have a word or two to say about it, if I survive that long—which no one can tell.

The fight on the Neutrality Act last week has left some scars. [Abandoning major parts of prewar legislation, this act permitted the administration to arm American merchant ships and to send them into combat zones.] I had something to do with getting the New York delegation to supply at least a fair number of votes; but the result of that is that I have political obligations towards a bunch of Tammany Irish Congressmen who were working both against their district leaders and against (I regret to say) their parish priests. The result of this, plus the election of La Guardia, is that the entire Democratic state situation in New York is in a hopeless muddle—a matter of no great importance were it not for the fact that the governorship election next year will be taken as a plain national signal. . . .

Today we are having a little cocktail party for the Icelandic delegation, which is going home and I believe fairly happy. At all events, we have liberated it from the bonadge of the British exchange agreement; we have provided for markets and free dollar exchange; and we are making at least a token trade agreement for future reference.

I am trying quite definitely now to swing my own mind into the business of the post-defense economic and other settlements. This is because I am perfectly clear, now, how the war will come out—though I cannot tell how long that will be. The first job is to try to get the St. Lawrence through; likewise the Inter-American Bank; and meanwhile to try to create some financial sentiment for the only financial arrangements which will make possible something like open trade.

November 27, 1941

Three days at the farm, over Thanksgiving, with Henrik De Kauffmann as a guest. Then some bad days in the office.

The Germans have forced the Danes to sign the Anti-Comintern Pact; and what is worse, to accede to a secret clause requiring the Danes to conscript and mobilize their people between eighteen and thirty (I wonder if this does not include girls, as well as boys) and to send two hundred thousand men to fight in Russia "when imperative". The Germans mobilized troops and threaten to take over the government. From now on, it is a mere puppet government, and we have to act accordingly.

Henrik is sending out calls to the other Danish diplomats in the Western Hemisphere asking them to join him. We have agreed to endeavor to protect them by causing the governments to which they are accredited to go on recognizing them as Ministers, should they decide to do so. Only the end will indicate whether we are successful. . . .

I have not seen the Secretary for a week. He has been deep in the conversations with [Saburo] Kurusu [special Japanese Ambassador]. These seem to have broken down now; and while I think the Japanese will probably have another stagger at it, my own feeling is that we are getting close to ultimates. Sumner thinks there will be war very soon. I am not sure about this as yet; but I think now we must fight if the Japanese move in almost any direction. . . .

It looks now as though the Inter-American Bank would go into the mill. We might have the outline of a currency system very soon. . . .

The difficulty of working now is that it is hard to keep all the details in one's head, even with as relatively small a sector as I have. There is a steady stream of minor cases of injustice, little problems, and so forth, all of which get into the records, I suppose, but probably will be buried in merciful oblivion.

December 1, 1941

I have got into the Far Eastern business by a curious side door. Knowing nothing about the Far East, up to now I have been left pretty well out of that phase of discussion.

However, on Thursday (November 27th), Sumner called me in and said that it is desirable to make a ten million dollar loan to Thailand in order to stiffen their morale, so that they might resist the Japanese. He asked me to talk to Hamilton and Hornbeck. This I did; whereupon, somewhat surprisingly, both men agreed that there was no point in doing this at all unless the United States were prepared to fight Japan if Thailand were attacked. Otherwise, they pointed out, the Thailanders would resist; would be promptly overwhelmed; the Japanese would have the whole country; nothing would be gained. We should be merely aiding the Thailanders to assist a policy which we ourselves were not prepared to support in any effective way. Since Hornbeck has been urging a militant stand and Hamilton rather the reverse, I was glad to find the men in agreement.

Their arguments were unanswerable, so I promptly took the matter up with the Secretary. I barged into a meeting, finding him with Hamilton, Hornbeck and [Joseph] Ballantine [former Assistant Chief, Far Eastern Affairs; Consul General at Ottawa]. They were discussing the Far East. The Secretary looked up and said, grimly: "Come in. You might learn something." They were apparently rehashing a situation which had been hashed over endless times. Briefly, Hornbeck was urging determination to act by force of arms. The Secretary was pointing out that the army felt it would not be ready for another three weeks and that the navy wanted another three months. Hornbeck pointed out that the navy had asked for six months last February and that the Secretary, through his negotiations, had got them that six months. Now they wanted three more. Hornbeck's idea was that the President ought to stop asking the navy, and tell it. The Secretary, rather wearily, passed it aside and at this point raised another question. The Thai loan was put aside for further reference.

It seemed that Kurusu, on behalf of the Japanese, had proposed a ninety-day truce. During this time we were to supply a certain amount of oil—I should gather around six hundred thousand tons of low-grade crude. We were likewise to permit Japanese troops to remain in Indo-China—including contingents over and above the limited force which was agreed on some months ago between Japan and Vichy. We were likewise asked to relax certain other trade restrictions—I presume, to unfreeze funds. Japan would promise not to move. All hands considered the promise worthless.

It seems that on Saturday night the Secretary called Kurusu and Nomura to his apartment and patiently went over their memorandum. He turned down substantially all of their various points. A ninety-day truce during which nobody moved might be possible; but to permit them to improve their position meanwhile was obviously out of order, and the Secretary turned it down.

Meanwhile, [Hideki] Tojo, the Japanese Prime Minister, had issued a cut-throat statement saying that the time had come to end American and British exploitation in the Far East forever—or words to that effect.

Meanwhile, a new angle had appeared. On Saturday morning the Secretary had indicated that the President might be coming back; that they would be taking up the text of a draft message; that the President might want to present this to the Congress. He asked Hornbeck to join in drafting the message. Hornbeck had said bluntly that he couldn't draft a message unless he knew what was going into it: was it peace, war, or what? This, of course, merely raised the old discussion again—with the Secretary trying to induce the President to take a stiff stand at the same time that the navy was saying that there ought to be more time. I thereupon offered to be of some help in the matter, and the net result of that was that Hornbeck turned over the drafting to me and the Secretary, somewhat wearily, said "yes", and that was that.

On Sunday (I had not known, of course, of the Saturday night conference), Hornbeck came to my house. We were just finishing lunch with Chief Justice Stone and Adolf Miller [Federal Reserve Board 1914–1936], who were saying that if we did not act pretty soon in the Far Eastern matter the United States would lose respect for itself. Hornbeck brought up some notes he had made for the draft, including also some material from Secretary Stimson and Secretary Knox. He likewise had some notes which the Secretary had given him which took a rather different line— namely, the line emphasizing that fundamentally there should be harmony of interest between the United States and Japan. Hornbeck said he was sick and unhappy and disgusted, and so forth, and that he had got to the point where he couldn't see his way clear to going much farther. I tackled the stuff and read it.

On Sunday evening with Beatrice I tried to review the whole situation—in the light of pretty complete ignorance, I am afraid. As occasionally happens, I finally reduced it to a matter of mathematical formulae. Beatrice and I asked why the navy wanted to delay: obviously, because of the possible danger in the Atlantic. To a less extent the same is true in the army. As to the policy of a stiff stand in Japan, we didn't have much doubt, providing, of course, the risk was not too great elsewhere. Thereupon I tried to estimate the various factors of risk. . . . We finally isolated the risk to the United States in the Atlantic as presently dependent on three factors, of which factors: First, the military situation of the Germans in South Russia, particularly in Rostov; that we called "X". The second was the military situation of the Germans and Italians in Libya; that we called "Y". The third was the military threat to West Africa, chiefly Dakar; that we called "Z". Z is less important in the situation at this time, as things look.

Then X plus Y plus Z is the Atlantic danger. If X, meaning the Rostov fighting, comes out all right, and Y likewise comes out right, the Atlantic danger is zero and the President and the Secretary can be as stiff as they feel like. There is a third factor (West Africa, Dakar, Casablanca, etc.) but these are likely to be subsidiary—I cannot imagine the Germans getting really heavily involved in West Africa unless the Libyan situation is in hand.

The attached memorandum gives the solution.

Promptly this morning I went in to see the Secretary. He was alone and unhappy. He said that everybody was trying to run foreign policy: Stimson, who felt bitterly about the Far East; Knox; and pretty much everyone else. "They all come at me with knives and hatchets," he said. "Acheson, yesterday morning, went at me and I had to ask him directly whether he knew what the naval force could do in the Far East."

I told him what I thought, and I thought it interested him, namely, that we ought to hold the line for a week or ten days until we knew the answers to the south Russian fighting and the Libyan fighting. After that we could plot a course—overruling the navy, if all was well, or making some other disposition if it were not; meanwhile we ought to be asking the navy what kind of a demonstration they could make which would keep the Japanese from going too far.

I then departed, and Kurusu and Nomura came in.

After they got through . . . the Secretary said that he had, as he put it, "talked to them with a good deal of bark"; and had given them the devil for what Japan was doing, particularly in view of Tojo's statement and their moves in Indo-China. He had dissociated Nomura and Kurusu from the militarist party in Japan, putting the blame on the militarist leaders there. He had told them that he had done his level best to hold things in line here so as to give them a chance to get something done with their own public opinion, but he could not hold things very much longer.

The Japanese had told him that they had as yet no instructions from Tokyo covering the last memorandum he had sent them—which I presume is our answer to their proposal for a *modus vivendi*. He telephoned Halifax and gave Halifax the general drift of things, and then departed for the White House to report to the President. Unhappily, the strain of a terrific ten days is telling on him and I am afraid he will be in bed with the grippe for a day or so.

December 7, 1941

Sunday night. The war has broken out and there is every reason to believe that during the night Italy and Germany will declare war. My impression is that this is the first time in the history of the United States that any nation has declared war on us. Up to now, we have always done the declaring.

I had substantially nothing to do with Far Eastern matters until the other day; and the mathematics of the situation indicates the way I then felt about it. In the next few days it was interesting to follow the equation. The X factor, namely, southern Russia, came out favorably. The Y factor, being the Libyan campaign, came out badly. The British met certain naval reverses which they have not announced, notably the sinking of the *Barham,* and probably some other losses as well. The Japanese meanwhile were, I am told, full of professions of peace, but their troops continued to move. Especially, there were a couple of naval convoys with troops on board, whose destination was not specified. Sumner had the idea that they probably intended an attack on Thailand; Hornbeck believed that they would get an agreement with Thailand and that the Japanese motion would tend to be rather slow. We were, as it proved, wrong in both instances as to the actual intent of some of the movements. . . .

I am not clear whether Saturday will go down in history as the day when [daughters] Alice and Beatrice went to see *The Student Prince,* or the day when, in practice, the war really started. At all events, we were working on the proposed message which the Secretary was getting up for the President to send to the Congress. It anticipated that the Japanese would break off conversations. The state of the record was that on November 26th we had handed to the Japanese a rather general plan for peace in the Pacific; that thereafter we had inquired of the Japanese what in the devil they were doing moving their troops around in Indo-China; and that the delay in that reply had made it pretty clear that the démarche of November 26th would not be successful. At half past one, or thereabouts, we left the Secretary's office; we then thought that we could get in some intensive work on Monday. I went to join the children at the Hay Adams House, where Freddy Lyon [Assistant Chief, International Conferences] (acting in my name, place and stead) was feeding them eight dollars' worth of lunch; after which we went to the matinee of *The Student Prince.* At quarter of five we came back to the State Department. . . .

I took the children home and had a snack, returning to the Department about seven. Around seven-thirty, the Army Intelligence reported that they had intercepted the text of the reply which Japan was to make. It was not only a flat turn-down, but a coarse and gratuitous and insulting message as well. Bad as this was, the accompanying message, likewise intercepted, was worse. The Japanese envoys were to keep this message locked up in their safe and present it only on the receipt of a signal; and during this time the final dispositions were to be completed. In other words, they were to hold up delivering the answer until certain military dispositions were completed.

We worked up a text of a message; and I turned in to bed about one a.m., feeling very uneasy. The waltzes of *The Student Prince* seemed like a dirge of something that may have existed once, but certainly had very little relation to anything one knew today.

Sunday morning, and to the Department. The Secretary was closeted with Stimson and Knox. We fussed a little more with the message and took a few simple precautions; and when the three Cabinet Ministers adjourned, we went into the Secretary's office. We were discussing the lines of the presentation of affairs to Congress when the Japanese Ambassador requested an immediate appointment with the Secretary. He asked for it at one o'clock—which happens to be eight am. Honolulu time. The Secretary fixed the time for 1:45. Sumner Welles and I stayed with the Secretary until 1:45, and then left, just as the Japanese were coming in. We had lunch at the Mayflower and came back about quarter of three. The Japanese had already gone. The news had come in that the Japanese fleet and air force had attacked Pearl Harbor, Manila (this appears to be wrong—it was probably Cavite). A little later it seemed that one of the Japanese expeditions was headed for a British base in northern Burma. . . . At Pearl Harbor it seems that there has been a great deal of damage. The attempt was made to bomb the army air field and I gather they got two hangars and perhaps 350 men (this is not yet confirmed), and did a very considerable amount of damage to the shipping. The *Oklahoma* seems to have been hit and put out of action. We have as yet no knowledge of the Philippines.

It was a bad day all around; and if there is anyone I would not like to be, it is Chief of Naval Intelligence.

The Secretary has been telling the Navy now for thirty days that some kind of a violent explosion of this kind might happen and that they should be on the alert on all fronts. Nevertheless, the Japanese seem to have been able to arrange for an attack by approximately fifty bombers on Pearl Harbor; and attacks of greater or less degree of strength elsewhere. . . .

The afternoon was spent partly with the Secretary and partly with Welles. Naturally, any message reporting on negotiations did not amount to much, so we recast a statement, in terms of what did happen. Meanwhile, we were taking some measures. Fletcher Warren [Berle's executive assistant] promptly showed up, went over to the Department of Justice. The Attorney General [Biddle] was out of town, and the Solicitor General [Charles Fahy] could not be got at for a couple of hours; but the F.B.I. and Immigration were on the job and anxious to get some instructions. We have been giving them a hand all afternoon. We have endeavored to cover communications, air travel, telephones, and to a less extent railway travel, etc. The thing to do seems to be to paralyze everything during tonight, and reconsider the situation in the morning. We likewise cabled all South American countries, shutting down on Japanese transfers of gold and funds. We formally notified practically everyone in the Western Hemisphere—I say practically, because the political people seem to think that Henrik De Kauffmann does not sufficiently represent a Western Hemisphere power—namely, Greenland—to require notification. I don't know that it matters. . . .

December 8, 1941

A rather nightmarish evening, yesterday. We worked with Sumner on drafting a speech—but I must say that the task of a logothete is not very satisfactory when the guns are actually moving.

The Cabinet met last night; while they met, Sumner and I sat together and redrafted. Afterward, Sumner went over to the White House: I stayed here, working on a variety of things, until he returned.

The problems were swift and large, and settled, as usual, off the bat: the immobilization of Japanese and other enemy aliens; the handling of communications, etc. . . .

At noon the President delivered his message to the Congress, which promptly declared the existence of a state of war between the United States and the Japanese Empire.

The political sentiment is swinging behind the President at once. It is just as well: all hands have their work cut out for them. Everyone thinks this is going to be a short picnic. It is not going to be anything of the kind. It is going to be a long, dirty, painful, bloody business. . . .

December 10, 1941

The night of December 7th remains the outstanding experience and it took a couple of days really to round up on what was done. Being Sunday afternoon, almost everyone was off duty; the FBI was the principal agency on deck; they seemed to want guidance from State and were content to act under my orders. Biddle was out of town.

When the dust had cleared away, we had immobilized Japanese generally, had cut communications, had started procedure to pick up the known foreign agents, and so forth. All these measures filtered into their proper channel the next morning. . . .

I have had plenty of chances to learn the exact military situation but since I could not do anything about it, have turned them all down. Since I presume my house is under pretty full espionage (though I do not know this) it seems best to me to fix it so that there is absolutely nothing there worth getting.

And now a raft of problems, one after another. There is the problem of the French fleet; I think that the French are about to turn it over—or part of it—to the Germans. . . .

The heartening thing in all this is the swift and virtually unanimous support from all the republics of this hemisphere. If ever a policy paid dividends, the Good Neighbor policy has. So far, they are sticking to us with scarcely a break and you will have a united hemisphere. . . .

The President's speech last night was first-rate. There was a complete absence of drama; no heroics, nothing but a very sober statement of a very long and hard time ahead. So I think it will prove to be.

December 13, 1941

The Thai Minister [Mom Rajawongse Seni Pramoj] is heartbroken by the betrayal of his country by the Prime Minister; he is running an insurrection all by himself. He came in to ask for some advice on that point and got it. He is a good boy. He told an amusing incident. He said he had gone to see the Secretary and had expressed his unhappiness. The Secretary had listened and said to him, "Pull yourself together, young man. We are going to lick the Hell out of them." Later I saw the memorandum of conversation which the Secretary had dictated. His memorandum is accurate but runs somewhat as follows: "The Thai Minister expressed his unhappiness at his country's course. I made encouraging remarks." . . .

We have received authentic indication that Admiral Nomura and possibly Kurusu are planning to commit harakiri. The information comes from Nomura's secretary. I do not blame them; it must be an unhappy fate to go down in history as having been the cover men for one of the greatest acts of international treachery in modern times. The Secretary adheres to the theory that Nomura did not know; we are not sure about Kurusu. Anyhow, they ought not to commit suicide here since it would probably he played up in Japan as murder and we want to get Grew [U.S. Ambassador to Japan] out safe and sound. After they get back to Japan, they can do what they please.

The President has decided that we will ignore all declarations of war except those of Japan, Germany and Italy.

The air power–sea power debate is, in my humble judgment, almost ended. The air power is the dominant service; sea power becomes auxiliary. Of course, you need both; air power cannot be without sea power, whereas sea power cannot operate without air. Carried to its logical conclusion, that would mean that the continental units may be divided; that military exigency will require that the Americas are separate from the world island. Our isolationists may thus get what they want in the long pull; the "world islanders" of the German school may get what they want —neither wanting to get it that way. But that is a long way ahead. . . .

To Hull, December 15, 1941

I should like to put on the record my sincere conviction that your handling of the negotiations with Japan, from the time they were initiated up to December 7th, 1941, has proved of inestimable benefit to the United States. As time goes on and more is known, I am convinced that it will be increasingly apparent that the country owes you individually a very great debt of gratitude.

From the outset in the Japanese problem certain groups asserted that the Japanese were bluffing and had little strength with which to back up their threats. They continuously urged that an issue be forced with Japan, claiming that this could be done with relative safety. You did not share that view; and the individuals, private and official, who thus underestimated the potentialities of the Japanese situation have already been proved wrong in their major premise. That premise was, that the risk involved in forcing an issue with Japan was minor, and that the results would be prompt and decisive.

The fact was that with the opening of the German war on France and Britain, the United States stood in grave danger of having to defend the hemisphere, virtually without allies, in the Atlantic. . . . Unless the Japanese resources were negligible—as you rightly estimated they were not—it would have been wholly rash to force a situation which would at once cripple our aid to Britain in the Atlantic, and at the same time expose us to grave attack in the Pacific.

Further, your own knowledge of the exact relationship between Japan and Germany made it clear that, prior to June, 1941, largely owing to the Russo-German alliance of 1939, the Japanese probably would not force an issue by themselves, and probably could not be forced to create an issue by the Germans.

Under these circumstances, war in the Pacific depended almost entirely on the attitude of the United States. In my considered judgment it was a wise and statesmanlike decision to decline to force matters to that point during the entire year 1940 and through the summer of 1941. . . .

Only in the late Fall of 1941 did it become apparent, first, that the British reinforcements in the Near Eastern front were sufficient to afford reasonable safeguard for Suez and the Near Eastern life-line; second, that the German striking power had been materially decreased and probably could not be repaired for some time; and third, that the American aid to Britain had already progressed to a point at which the situation in the Atlantic was more nearly secure. Even then there were, and still are, factors of greater risk in the entire situation than many of the self-appointed diplomatic and military strategists apparently know anything about.

It is never possible to prove a historical "might have been." But, had an issue been pressed and had the Japanese declared war (as we are pretty clear they would have done) in the early Spring of 1941, it is entirely probable that the Germans, instead of attacking Russia, would have concentrated their entire striking force in the Atlantic, at a time when both we and the British were under maximum strain in the Far East, when the Near East defenses were still incomplete, and when the German striking power was at its level maximum. The negotiations which delayed the Japanese attack, due entirely to your wise and foresighted handling of the situation, resulted, I think, in the separation of the German military effort from the Japanese military effort. They resulted in the Japanese war being held off until the German strength was sufficiently impaired so that it could not be of that degree of assistance to the Japanese which otherwise it would have been. In combination, these factors may well prove to be the deciding difference between the victory of which we are, in my judgment, assured, though it may be long coming; and a very grave situation with which we would otherwise have been faced.

I want to place this on the record now. Since I have had no part in Far Eastern affairs or in the Japanese negotiations, I am perhaps free from any charge of endeavoring to defend any personal act or position of my own.

December 18, 1941

There have been a number of bad days. On Sunday we handled the question of cobbling up documents which might provide for an inter-allied war council and, if possible, inter-allied high commands. The situation differs from that of the first World War. Then there was only one front so far as the Allies were concerned, namely, the West Front. They fought two years and lost untold thousands of men before they got an Allied War Council, and kept the losses up again until they got a high command in April of 1918. I did what I could to try to get some of these things forward now, realizing, however, that there would have to be allied commands in various theatres.

The decisions will be staggering, especially in the Far East. For as the Secretary bluntly states it, the job is to build up enough navy to go and root the Japanese fleet out in its own waters; and enough army, if necessary, to conquer Europe—unless developments let us out of doing that, as it is just possible they may. These are huge tasks. Meanwhile, we shall have to find the points at which the situation will be held, and the points which have to be let go until such time as the full striking force is ready.

It has been quite an interesting assignment. We have been working on it intermittently during the week and all day today. . . . The plan is to have (1) a joint declaration, which I suppose is the equivalent of the Axis anti-Commintern pact; and (2) a memorandum of arrangement setting up a war council. I hope this will slant towards a unified command. . . .

I thought the war would stop the intrigue in Washington—but it hasn't, and as far as I can see everybody is grabbing as well as they can.

In the little field in which I have something to do—and wish I didn't —namely, censorship, the thing is going worse than ever. But I suppose these things will get untangled before we get through.

We are all of us heartened by the fact that the South American nations are, in the main, staying by. Even the doubting Thomases in the United States are beginning to see what the Good Neighbor policy was all about. . . .

There is to be an investigation of the responsiblity for the surprise at Pearl Harbor. Since the Secretary as far back as November 27th had been telling the War Cabinet that hostilities might start at any time, when the Japanese replied to his last proposal, his record is clear. . . .

December 19, 1941

More work today with Secretary Hull on the business of a war council; the great question was whether we should bind ourselves not to cease hostilities to all of the many countries or as between four nations, namely, ourselves, China, Britain and Russia. It was finally decided at the last minute that the latter course was safer, lest we find ourselves prolonging the war because a couple of Central European powers insist on keeping up a war that everybody else has decided to stop. I doubt that it makes much difference, though I can see the theoretical possibility. . . .

There are some frightful questions involved in the Eastern Baltic and Central European areas; and I for one do not feel like throwing anyone to the wolves. Either we have a moral position or we haven't, and I prefer myself to stick to the moral position, believing that its strength in the long run is greater than its weakness.

December 26, 1941

Amid a cloud of rumors principally emanating from London, Winston Churchill and a staff of about 80 people did arrive here on Monday. Simultaneous conferences were being held meanwhile in Moscow and in Chungking looking towards the unification of the allied commands. The Department of State's suggestions were duly transmitted to the President and I thought he was interested in them on Saturday night; but not having been anywhere near the conferences myself, I cannot do more than guess how it will come out. There are some cruel decisions to make—or rather, they probably have been made by now.

The underlying fact is that the United States was not set up for an offensive, but instead was diverting such defensive weapons as it had to British use; therefore, we can expect a run of bad news from the Far East; and we are in for the long, slow job of building up the huge matériel needed for an ultimate offensive in the Far East. I should think we should have to do it island by island and the prospect is a long one, though there can be no doubt as to the outcome.

One result of this has been to set me working on the possibility of increasing supplies in the Indian Empire, on the theory that the Japanese striking power cannot get very far into India no matter what happens— even if Singapore were to fall.

Meanwhile, the supplies and work of the British and ourselves in the Middle East seem to be bearing fruit; Rommel's army is pretty well cut to pieces in Libya. However, on the 23rd and 24th we received increasing reports that the Germans were planning some kind of an air offensive to relieve Rommel. . . .

I have cut across liaison lines to make it perfectly certain that the British were duly warned—but they probably know a good deal about it. . . .

Certain of the allied war plans are already pretty well forward; but I do not set them down here. It is interesting to see that in one respect, some earlier judgment out of this office was corroborated: the North African economic plan, which I physically pushed through the Department over vigorous resistance of a great many people here and of the British, has been renewed. Prospects for getting some results out of this are looking up and if the German air attack on North Africa fails, we may find ourselves considerably better off there. . . .

Meanwhile, and on December 24, a nasty little incident upset things. Admiral [Emile] Muselier, a Free French officer proceeding out of Canada to Halifax with three corvettes and the French submarine *Sercouf*, landed at the islands of St. Pierre and Miquelon and proceeded to take over in the name of De Gaulle. Of itself, this means practically nothing; but we had already entered into an agreement with Admiral [Georges] Robert in Martinique (he is also High Commissioner for the other French territories in the New World) agreeing that the *status quo* would not be disturbed, in return for which he agreed to maintain these territories on a basis of complete neutrality. We had likewise urged on Vichy that we had scrupulously respected their rights and expected them in return to decline to surrender the French Fleet or North African ports or otherwise move any further in collaboration with Germany. We know that [Admiral Jean François] Darlan [Vichy French Minister of Marine] had intrigued against us and, in fact, had sold out to the Germans but our own attitude here had been instrumental in making Marshal Pétain stand up in his boots and decline to give the Germans everything they have been asking. By consequence, it is no fun at all to have a Free French filibusterer upset the apple cart. What is worse, we learn that De Gaulle had given assurance to the British that no such act would take place; but that he withdrew that assurance some days ago—which is another way of saying that the British knew about this and were perfectly agreeable to it despite the fact that they say they had nothing to do with it and knew nothing about it. The Canadian position is that they are shocked and surprised; nevertheless we have every reason to believe some of the Canadians knew it too. . . .

I have been reviewing the possibilities for action in the State Department now that the fighting forces have the real brunt of responsibility. To me it seems that we have a limited number of jobs we can do. They are more or less in order of importance:

(1) The problem of getting the greatest possible collaboration for the Allies out of Vichy, France—the best we can do there is to hold the line, at least for the time being; later we might have a real government there which would give us some assistance. Bracketed with this is

(2) The North and West African situation which really revolves around the possibility of leadership. General Weygand might be such a leader; possibly also Admiral [Jean] Esteva [Resident-General in Tunisia].

(3) The problem of taking the best possible advantage of the Italian situation. There is practically universal hatred of the Germans by Italy; their armies have been beaten in the field; the whole thing now is a captive government. The question is, what kind of force can be engendered to complete the Italian detachment.

(4) Maintenance and strengthening of the bonds (such as they are) between Turkey and the Allies.

(5) Some more intensive work on Arabia and the Arab problem, which has to include not only Saudi Arabia but the Arabian sentiment in North Africa.

(6) Spain and Portugal. I doubt very much can be done here. The Germans either will or will not go into Spain, as they choose, and I doubt whether the attitude of the Spanish Government makes much difference.

(7) We may get some work done in India to increase supplies there.

(8) There is the constant run of South American work.

Assessing the order and importance of the jobs is itself troublesome.

It seems now that we would be on the defensive in the Far East for a period of time, namely, the time needed to build up combined naval, air and troop concentrations sufficient to take the offensive. . . .

We have not in this Department a Far Eastern mentality. We are pretty well set to handle the possibility of Germany's dropping out of the picture and a general reverse in Western European affairs. We have assumed, without knowing, that if you take the Germans and Italians out of the picture, the Japanese will be fighting alone and we shall have nothing to do but concentrate on wiping the Japanese off the map.

Last night, after Christmas was cleared away . . . I got to thinking of this last. The more I think about it, the more worried I get. For the logic of the situation would then be that Russia should change sides. She cannot, as I see it, make a deal with Germany under existing circumstances, nor does she want to. On the contrary, the defeat of Germany would leave Russia the only substantial military power on the continent and she will exploit that position to the utmost. . . .

Memorandum, December 29, 1941

Last night at dinner at my house the question of St. Pierre and Miquelon came up. I made the opening since I knew that both Jacques Maritain [theologian, philosopher] and Alexis Léger [former Secretary-General, French Foreign Office] had been advising the De Gaulle representatives in the United States. Léger had been outspokenly and emphatically critical of our policy to other people. Maritain had confided that the De Gaulle delegation knew nothing whatever about the proposed seizure until after it happened.

Léger said that it was an impossible situation; that French public opinion would see only one thing, namely, that the United States, faced with a choice between a German-dominated Vichy and an anti-German De Gaulle, had chosen Vichy. This would confuse and puzzle the De Gaullists, and would lend support to the tottering government in Vichy. He thought that over a period of months the result of this "mistake" would be very grave. He had no official position which entitled him to say this but since the question had come up, he was now expressing his point of view.

I said that the seizure of St. Pierre and Miquelon had raised an issue which was fundamental in the American system and had violated American public order. For many years we had been insisting that no forcible movement directed from outside could be permitted to take place in this hemisphere. If we ever allowed that kind of thing to get started, there would be endless sore spots which would be taken advantage of by somebody.

Léger interrupted to say this was not a question of change of sovereignty but merely of internal politics.

I said that that meant precisely nothing. Hitler and everyone else had been rigging up "national" parties which were really their puppets; any such movement would always masquerade as a true "national" movement. Were this to be permitted, no one could feel safe. Under the American public order, Haiti, whose Minister [Fernand Dennis] was present, could and did feel as safe as the most powerful of nations; but if forcible moves were permitted, every weak government would promptly wonder when its turn might come. In this case there was not even the slender justification of military advantage to be urged for the move.

The Haitian Minister and Dr. [Camille] L'Herisson promptly agreed. "Disorder for all of us," the Minister said, "would be the last word in disaster."

Léger contended that there was no need of "appeasing" Vichy by preventing De Gaulle from seizing St. Pierre and Miquelon, since Vichy was really controlled by French public opinion.

I observed a trifle grimly that French public opinion had not stopped Vichy very much so far as I could see; and that regrettable as it undoubtedly was, the De Gaullists had not succeeded in establishing themselves very heavily in French public opinion thus far, either in unoccupied France or in North Africa. But the main ground which made it impossible for us to ignore the incident was the fact that for the first time in many decades a force directed from outside had tried to interfere with the internal integrity and peace of the American hemisphere.

Léger said that the plebiscite seemed to settle the matter.

I said that no one could give much credence to a plebiscite conducted twenty-four hours after a military occupation under the guns of a commanding military force. Too many plebiscites had been held in just that fashion and everyone had declined to recognize them. I asked what Léger would think of a plebiscite conducted in the north of France under the guns of German occupation. To this Léger made no answer except to insist that probably the plebiscite reflected the real will of the islands, and that he thought public opinion would be very much confused.

I said in that case the job was to explain things to public opinion, and not to permit a grave error in fear lest public opinion would not understand the matter. I thought actually that American public opinion would understand the situation far better than Léger supposed; and that the best thing the De Gaullists could do would be to stop trying to deal with American problems on the basis of European nations.

December 30, 1941

The day's news, of course, was all bad; the Japanese are steadily plowing ahead with a big, prepared offensive. . . . I suppose the greatest safety is the fact that even in the days of airplanes the Pacific is a wide place; and behind that width you do have time to build up a very considerable striking power.

This morning to work on the proposed Joint Declaration, which includes the covenant not to make a separate peace. It seems that Winston Churchill was anxious that the Free French should be included. The President turned him down. The Russians stepped in and made a couple of changes in the drafts. They included, after the words "the struggle for freedom", the words "in their own countries, as well as in other countries", which might apply to the subjugated countries of Europe, and might equally apply to a forthcoming world revolution. They dropped out, before the covenant not to make a separate peace, the words "to continue war". Whether these changes have any significance, I cannot say. Lord Halifax, who came in to see me about the final wording of the draft, asked why the changes were made, and when I told him that the Russians were responsible, he asked whether there were any significance; and I could only answer that, unhappily, he could guess that as well as I.

Apparently the Secretary did a good bit of very close in-fighting. When the declaration was proposed, the President simply handed it to [Soviet Ambassador Maxim] Litvinov, who went off and presently cooked up an entirely separate declaration of his own, which had nothing about anything in it, but merely explained why Russia was going to fight Hitler.

It did not say a word about a separate peace. He was about to issue this statement when the Secretary caught him and steered him back into the Joint Declaration. His government has now authorized him to sign it, so I think a really great danger has been avoided—so far as words mean anything in these days.

The British likewise approve some little operations of mine with the Thai Minister, and so he will presently become a Free Thailander, still recognized as the Thai Minister, following the precedent of the Dane. He is an honest and patriotic youngster and I hope things go well with him.

We have, after a long period of time, succeeded in getting the Brazilians to close down LATI, the Italian air line to South America, and the only remaining German air line there, Condor. It is a good haul. The British, for some strange reason, seem much pleased. They made a point of coming down and telling me so.—But that is by way of amendment (though they did not say so), for I am not supposed to be popular at the British Embassy.

January 1, 1942

I have been at work on gathering in the signatories for the Joint Declaration, which I suppose really is the Charter of the Grand Alliance of the Second World War. To date, the score is nine American republics and a stack of European governments-in-exile, together with the Big Four —being the United States, Great Britain, U.S.S.R. and China.

A series of amusing incidents have happened. Halifax wanted to represent all of the British Commonwealth of Nations; and we let him do that; so far, two of them have vigorously objected, namely, Canada and Australia. He also wanted the heading of the document to recite a list of nations but to group together the United Kingdom and the self-governing dominions; but the self-governing dominions went right ahead self-governing and said they wanted the order alphabetical, and no British nonsense about it. Incidentally, I think we probably have boosted the constitutional status of the Empire of India, which now appears as a signatory. . . .

At all events, aside from Canada and Australia, who have not as yet got full authority from their governments, they are all sitting like ducks in a row, and I suppose tomorrow we shall have a grand signing party of some kind.

A New Year's party last night at the house of Evelyn Walsh McLean —her great estate, called "Friendship," which is now ending its plutocratic life and about to become a housing project for unmarried girls who are living in the District of Columbia. Knowing that our boys were being killed by hundreds in the Philippines and that probably Manila was even then being sacked by Japanese troops, I had less than no appetite whatever for this third act finale of the Lucullan luxury developed in the later plutocratic period. We drank to a happy New Year and sang "Auld Lang Syne" and three minutes later I was up to my neck in the politics of the North Baltic, for Hjalmar Procopé, the Finnish Minister, was nervously wondering whether the German line had not broken and whether the

Russians might not be coming into his country. I wanted to comfort him, but found little chance of doing it. The Finns misjudged the military situation; they ought to have made peace two months ago, when Secretary Hull urged them to; now they have hardly a hand to play and will find themselves once more with their backs to the wall, alone in a world of great powers who have all the cruelty engendered by terrific stress.

I am going to try to figure out a way to fish them out somehow—and took some comfort from the fact that Major Loy Roberts [Great Britain], who was along, genially shook hands with the Finn (despite the fact that they are at war) and said to me that he knew Finland and would be damned if he felt like letting them go by the board—a fine, decent people. . . .

Also, the infernal affair of St. Pierre and Miquelon. We told the Free French they had no business filibustering on our shores; and a string of propaganda has been circulated in the newspapers, chiefly, I suspect, of English origin, indicating that by not signing the Free French we are playing the game of Vichy, therefore the game of Berlin. For the life of me I can't make any sense out of it. . . .

Churchill is pushing the President to whitewash and sanctify De Gaulle and generally repudiate the Havana Convention, which outlaws force and filibustering in this hemisphere, and so on; and the President is caught in a cleft stick. What Churchill is not telling him, of course, is that he, Churchill, secretly authorized the De Gaulle filibustering expedition and the De Gaullists were probably on his neck when they suddenly discovered that they had run up against the United States. . . .

We are also looking for an Italian free movement and the only person in sight seems to be Carlo Sforza. He is not ideal, and his anti-clerical views will make trouble, but I see nothing else. . . .

This is all very amusing, this picking of Prime Ministers and Emperors, and so forth, from the angle of Washington, but I vaguely suspect that when the game opens up we will find that there are some stout-hearted and two-fisted men actually on the ground who will see to it that they are the real governors and will tell everybody so, in no uncertain terms. These "free movements" really are psychological spearheads, more than anything else. There are not many Masaryks to be seen among the exiles here. . . .

January 3, 1942

The Grand Alliance of the present war is now made; the final form of the draft Joint Declaration was approved at the White House, and the President has called it "Declaration by United Nations". Then he and Winston Churchill and Litvinov and [Chinese Ambassador] T. V. Soong signed it at the White House; the document came over to me on the morning of January 2nd. The representatives of twenty-two nations thereupon signed it in my office. The Czech, [Vladimir] Hurban, was so moved that he could hardly hold the pen, and I had to make him walk around the room two or three times until he got steady enough to put his name on it. Sir Girja Shankar Bajpai signed the document "The Government of India, by" etc. He later telephoned to say that on re-reading his instructions he was directed to sign merely, "India", and authorized me to erase the words "Government of"; Mr. Savage [assistant to Long] and I thereupon did, under that authority. The Canadian came in last; he had been waiting for telephonic authorization from Mackenzie King. It was a good job all around—and may to some extent offset the fall of Manila.

The actual situation, of course, is not as good as the document. A despatch indicates that Stalin talked to [Wladyslaw] Sikorski, the Polish Premier, and indicated that if the Poles and the Russians would work together they would be able at the close of the war to "disregard Great Britain and the United States"; and without question Stalin pushed [British Foreign Secretary Anthony] Eden very far in his talks at Moscow. Theoretically, Eden made no commitments, but in diplomacy there is always that half light which can ripen into a commitment or no commitments, depending on the understanding of the parties. . . .

January 6, 1942

Saturday, January 3rd. We were mopping up after the Declaration by United Nations, which is assuming its true historic place. It will need a lot of fighting and victories before it becomes a reality in the larger sense.

The problem of adherence by representatives of movements which are not governments came up at once. Savage and Hackworth had a bright idea and proposed, instead of exchanging notes all around, to issue a short press release on the subject; which we did.

Before doing so, I went over to the White House and found the President alone, in front of a mountain of work. . . .

Then because I think he wanted an excuse to stop working, he leaned back and spun a few yarns. Under seal of secrecy he told how he had got the Russians to accept the words "religious freedom" in the Declaration. He said that he had encountered opposition from Litvinov but finally had had an idea. He had then called in Litvinov; had told him that he, the President, had been under great attack after the Atlantic Charter was signed because religious freedom had been left out; that he recognized the Russian position but he hoped the Russians would help him. On the other hand, he had thought of something that might help them. "Freedom of religion" were the words generally used, but those contemplated that everybody had a religion—whereas the Soviets in their constitution included both freedom to have a religion, and freedom to oppose religion as well. For this reason he suggested changing the words to "religious freedom", which meant freedom to have a religion or not to, as one saw fit. Litvinov accepted the idea and cabled his Government; at all events, the Russian Government authorized him to sign.

Likewise, he said, he had been worrying about what to call this business. He had noticed that Churchill, in his speech before Congress, had fumbled with the words "allied nations" and then had called them "associated nations". The President had been mulling this over. He had finally got a bright idea and had himself rolled into Winston Churchill's room, where Churchill was taking a bath. He then proposed that this group be called "the united nations", because they were united in a common purpose. If it led to a greater degree of working together, so much the better. Churchill turned the matter over in his mind and finally said he thought the President had got the answer; whereupon the President wrote out the heading, "Declaration by United Nations", and so it stands—and will stand in history for a good long while. The President did not call to Churchill's attention the analogy to the "United States"—a name worked out by a somewhat similar process of mind in 1776. . . .

Sunday, January 4th. A bad day, and more coming after it. The St. Pierre and Miquelon business is going badly, largely because a great number of half-informed liberals, and, I regret to say, some of the British propaganda agencies as well, have been pounding the State Department, and particularly the Secretary, because he declined to accede to the forcible seizure of St. Pierre and Miquelon. . . .

Monday, January 5th. Yesterday was an almost solid day of St. Pierre and Miquelon. It is curious to be working over a row kicked up over two no-account islands, when there is a whole wide world in peril; but there is more to it than that. The German Government shows signs of breaking with Vichy and it just may be that things will begin to break our way in North Africa. For that reason, there is no particular point in flying in the face of Vichy at this time. Meanwhile, we have to get our own case stated—which we have not done. The Canadians and the British show signs of fixing things up; but I am not clear whether the British really intend to go through with it. They put De Gaulle in there and I think they propose to keep him there, if they can. It is bad business all around.

January 6. The President made his budget speech today. He made the very definite statement that we were going to fight until there was a complete end of militarism in Germany, Italy and Japan. "Most certainly we will not settle for less."

January 9, 1942

For the last three days we have had a flood of proposed "adherences" to the Declaration by United Nations. The terms of the announcement permitting "appropriate authorities" representing nations silenced by German occupation to adhere are such that they permit any organization to claim representation, and we have had everyone except the South Tyrol Yodelers' League sending in an "adherence". . . .

I plan to let everybody go ahead and announce that they accept the principles of the Declaration, and after a while get out a press release thanking them all for their kindly acceptance of the principles and saying that we will proceed in due time to the appropriate study of the organizations which can be said to be truly representative.

St. Pierre and Miquelon are still burning questions. The Secretary is taking a horrible beating from the so-called liberals who know nothing about it and yearn to have him break relations with Vichy. This would be fatal. Yesterday morning, in a meeting on the subject, when it developed that the situation was about the same as usual, he told a Tennessee story. A traveler, he said, came to a little town in Tennessee and put up for the night, and the next morning started on foot for another town twenty-five miles away, and was directed to take a short cut over the mountain and so forth, which he proceeded to do. At nightfall, having gone through the various short cuts and plowed through endless brush, he found himself in the same town. "At least," said the traveler, "I am holding my own." . . .

I am likewise having a lot of trouble with the foreign language groups in the United States. The leaders from overseas want to do a lot of proselyting and general politics in the United States; and in many cases we sympathize. On the other hand, the first and central interest of any proper United States authority must be to see to it that the United States is not fragmentized or Balkanized by disputes between groups. . . . Some of the governments-in-exile want us to give lists of all of the immigrants into the United States so that they can start in recruiting them for army service, etc.—which would be fatal. . . .

January 21, 1942

I said to the President that questions were being asked in connection with Allied High Command decisions which we could not answer. . . . I wondered whether some arrangement might not be worked out by which the State Department knew at least as much as was useful in those problems.

The President promptly said that he thought this was a good idea and probably essential. . . .

While I was with the President he told me a number of things regarding the formation and the operation of the Allied High Command. He said naturally it would have to be evolutionary. They had an agreement with Winston Churchill by which the decisions in the ABDA (American, British, Dutch, Australian) area of the Far East were to be made primarily here; decisions in the European theatre primarily by the British. In practice this meant that in each case there would be two copies of the despatch to be acted on, an action copy which in the ABDA area would come here; the carbon would forthwith go to London. In theory action could be taken here only on military matters and in case of emergency, but the prime responsibility for acting lay here. But, said the President, this did not altogether work out. . . . It seemed to him as though there would be quite a number of quick-action despatches, as things were actually falling.

In anything affecting political or state matters, of course, this Government could not and would not act until the British reaction had been ascertained and some agreement reached. The line might be a difficult one to draw. . . .

I talked to the President . . . about Bill Donovan [Coordinator of Information]. I said it would be of help to us if we knew exactly what picture the President had of Bill's functions. He wanted to get into South America and I understood that the President had vetoed that; and he wanted to get into the United States via the alien or foreign language groups here. The President said he thought Bill was doing a pretty good job on propaganda and something of a job in terms of intelligence. He did not want him in Canada or in South America; and he did not want him inside the country. His picture of Donovan was that of a war operations agency operating by propaganda and intelligence, etc.; but in no event was Bill to operate in the United States.

I said I thought this would help a lot because Bill had got crossways of the Attorney General and Secretary Hull, and so forth.

I talked to the President . . . about the St. Lawrence. I wanted to know what the final decision would be, so that we could clear up. He said that . . . he had carefully examined the proposed Rivers and Harbors Bill in the light of present circumstances. In that bill there were a considerable number of projects which had been certified as of immediate military necessity by General Marshall and by Donald Nelson [Head, War Production Board].

The list would include the St. Lawrence. . . .

Within a few months, it became clear that construction of the St. Lawrence project could not be completed in time to assist the war effort. Congress authorized an appropriation in 1954, and the Seaway opened in 1959.

January 24, 1942

The row of the State Department over St. Pierre and Miquelon is dying down somewhat. . . . We went to Mrs. Eugene Meyer's for a little reception. There was Field Marshal Sir John Dill, here in connection with the British high command. We discussed St. Pierre and Miquelon, unoccupied France and North Africa. . . . I suggested that we were given responsibility for North Africa by the diplomatic route, and I thought that perhaps we had better change our policy. It might be well to go all out for De Gaulle and turn over responsibility for France and Africa to the British. . . . Dill at once said that we shouldn't do it and that the matter ought to be settled. I said that I thought it would be a bad thing to do, myself, but in view of the attacks and certain calls for impeachment of the Secretary, I thought that we might have to. . . . Dill said that the situation is so nicely balanced, as we knew, that [a change of U.S. policy] might be disastrous. I said I was very much afraid of that. But I gathered that the British had found it politically expedient to take the opposite tack in Canada and by consequence in the United States, and I did not think that we could, or, for that matter, cared to, find ourselves in opposition. Dill grunted, and looked disturbed. Later, it seems that something happened to quiet things down, which means at least partly that the British propaganda about this dropped it like a hot cake. (Note: The British claim they have no propaganda.)

. . . Briefly, the British, through their military intelligence people, proposed just before Welles went to Rio [for the Conference of Foreign Ministers of the American Republics] that they should assist us in working up a series of Latin American coup d'états. They specifically mentioned, I believe, the Argentine, to [Laurence] Duggan [Adviser on Political Relations]. We turned the idea down promptly. Meanwhile, however, the British, through Donovan and other people, had taken a hand in the Chilean situation. Again bluntly, they proposed to use a large amount of money to bribe or buy the election. . . . The Secretary of State talked to the President about it and he vetoed the idea. But a number of people needled [Vice President] Henry Wallace about it and he talked to the President. I gathered that the idea was still turned down. Then Sir Ronald Campbell came in to see me. Among other things, he indicated that if we didn't want to do it perhaps we would give them a clear field and let them go ahead without assistance. I told him emphatically that I would have no part of it and that, frankly, I doubted whether the British Government could handle the Chilean situation well enough to carry out any such operation with success—if there were no other reasons against it, which there were.

The prize of the whole proceedings was last night. Sumner has been running the Rio Conference pretty much on his own, without any consultation. The reports come in later. We were staying by a pretty solid resolution calling for an immediate break with the Axis powers. The line-up was 19 to 2, Argentina and Chile being the holdouts. But apparently Chile came in with a minor modification which we were content to accept, though I think the Argentinians expected to monkey with it. We are pretty clear that Acting President [Ramón S.] Castillo has made commitments to the Italians and probably also to the Germans, which he is not telling the world about. Accordingly, all hands were for standing right up to it and letting Argentina go off on the loose if she wished.

Last night I was at dinner with Hume Wrong [Canadian Minister and Counselor] when, half way through, a telephone call came from the Secretary. He was almost heart-broken, and I left the dinner table and went forthwith to his apartment. The radio commentators had given the text of a new compromise proposal drafted presumably to take care of the Argentinians, which really cut the heart out of the whole position. Welles was announced as having accepted it. The commentators were apologizing for the situation and it looked bad. Duggan joined us. The Secretary was a thoroughly angry man. He indicated that he thought Sumner had been undermining him; that he had gone over his head to the White House; that he had worked up the Rio Conference without getting authority either from the President or from Secretary Hull, each thinking that he had arranged it with the other. He intimated that a lot of things were going to change. Duggan and I tackled the job of trying to salvage the situation, for we both agreed that the revised resolution was disastrous. We might, of course, hold the nations in line, or most of them, despite the resolution; but our moral leadership at the conference had been lost. Thereupon the Secretary picked up the telephone and called Welles in Rio. It was a violent conversation. He said, in substance, that neither he nor anyone else had given Sumner carte blanche to go to Rio and give away the whole thing; that the result was that we had taken a terrific diplomatic beating, with incalculable loss to our future position. . . . He then suggested that they connect the President—which they did. . . . The Secretary put before the President his view, which was that the effect of the revised resolution was to permit each nation to act individually; that if this was all that anyone was to get, there had been no need of a Rio meeting at all; that all hands had agreed that we would take a solid position and stay by it, even if Argentina stayed out; that this position had been reversed without consultation. . . .

The President, after hearing the statement and hearing what Welles said (which of course I do not know) seemed to think that the best thing to do was to let well enough alone and make what we could out of it—which I think probably, in the light of a night's sleep, was good judgment.

The Secretary then called [Ambassador] Caffery in Rio to try to get the general situation, and discovered what indeed we had suspected, that the other nations lined up for the original, or strong, resolution were angry and hurt and felt that they had been let down, in favor of Argentina, who had been the least cooperative of the lot.

As I heard the conversation wear on (the Secretary had even got to the point of starting to draft a cable superseding Welles as our representative in the Rio consultation), I felt that several careers were ending that night—quite likely including my own.

Along past midnight, Duggan and I left to get a stiff drink, which represented my sole remaining idea of a tangible approach to the situation. For it is obvious that now there is a breach between the Secretary and Sumner which will never be healed—though the Secretary will keep it below hatches to some extent. Life in this Department under those circumstances will be about as difficult as anything I can think of.

Also, I was heart-broken because Sumner is one of my best friends, and I could not take any view except that, in accepting the pretty miserable compromise, he had given away a strong position, and lost a large amount of the tremendous force of American unity and of United States leadership, and probably compromised (though I think not irretrievably) our whole position. We shall have to take back the territory bit by bit. And I remembered the passionate words of Dr. [Carlos A.] Pardo, Counselor of the Argentine Embassy, "Do not let Welles accept a Geneva formula. If he does, it will be the end of United States leadership and then of Welles, and Ruiz Guinazú will be the greatest Foreign Minister Argentina ever had." I was foolish enough to laugh at the prospect, though I passed it on to Welles by cable, with the Secretary's full approval. . . .

An interminable series of strange and dramatic things. Shall we, and can we, get [President Manuel] Quezón [of the Philippines] out from the Island of Luzon? If we don't, will not the Japanese make him a Quisling? Can we get out [General Douglas A.] MacArthur and his family? Or [U.S. High Commissioner Francis] Sayre and his family? Can we work out the proper Venezuelan participation in the defense of Aruba and Curaçao? I think we can. Can we steer our way through the so-called "free movements" in the United States, which are developing all the eccentricities of Balkan politics?

Possibly, but it will be tough going.

February 1, 1942

This has been a bad week. Welles has been away and the Secretary has been in bed. Following the blow-up with Welles in Rio a week ago, he came to the office on Monday but was nervously and spiritually torn to pieces, to a point where his doctor kept him in bed. He emerged Friday to go to the Cabinet meeting, but this was about all.

Unless the situation is very carefully handled we shall have a repetition of the relations which prevailed when Stimson was Secretary of State and Castle was Under Secretary. Welles is not unscrupulous, as Castle was; his ambition is driving, but I think he would not be actively disloyal. On the other hand, the Rio incident did raise a square question as to who is the real Secretary of State. In cabling the President in defense of his course, Sumner intimated that there had been a major decision of policy which he had agreed on with the President without reporting to Secretary Hull —at all events, Secretary Hull has no recollection of it.

. . . I propose, therefore, tackling Sumner as soon as I can get hold of him and trying to bring some kind of a working relationship between the two men. It will be difficult. Sumner is really preserving a direct line of power through the White House, irrespective of the Secretary; the Secretary will be satisfied with nothing less than cutting that off. The difficulty is that no single human being could cover all the ground; and the Secretary is slow in making up his mind, sometimes, it has seemed to me, in situations that call for rapid action. But his judgment is far better than Sumner's. Sumner, on the other hand, will move like a shot in all situations. It is essential that the values of both be preserved.

At all events, for the last week I have had the combined work of the Secretary's office, Welles's office, and my own. . . .

We have had no end of a row, though it was all covert, about the new act on Registration of Foreign Agents. This was drawn in the Department of Justice.

. . . there also has been a silent indication from the British Intelligence that they want the Act killed, because they want to protect a very considerable espionage here which they have, and which they do not like to talk about. But no one has given us any effective reason why there should be a British espionage system in the United States. . . . Meanwhile, we have held a meeting between the F.B.I., the British Intelligence and the Canadian Intelligence, representatives of State (myself), the British Embassy and the Canadian Legation, in an endeavor to work out a smooth liaison system between the British Civilian Intelligence and our own. . . .

I have been doing a little work on post-war settlements, although frankly the situation in the Department is so chaotic that it is difficult to work at all. Some members of the Department have information, others not, and nobody is letting go of any. I have seen the report of the Eden-Stalin conversations. . . . It is plain that, as usual, the Russians have no faith in the British; at the same time they have considerable ideas of their own; the British, I think, are prepared to accede to the Russian view.

Apparently the honest diplomacy of saying all support for Russia in Russia; no support for any imperialism anywhere; a straightforward, clean-cut arrangement which will prevent any nation on your border from becoming a focal point of attack against you, is not quite good enough for the British diplomacy. . . .

February 5, 1942

I have read with interest the report of negotiations which have taken place between the Soviet and British Governments since the outbreak of war between Germany and Russia in June 1941.

It would appear that there is now outstanding a request of Stalin's that an alliance should be created between Great Britain and the Soviet Union which should continue in effect not only for the duration of the war but for the post-war period as well. . . .

As I see it, we shall have to face two facts. The first is that the smaller countries in Eastern Europe cannot exist as isolated units. They will be dominated by someone—either Russia or Germany, in the sense of being within the shadow of an overmastering military power.

I see no reason why we should object to their being within the orbit of Russia, provided we were assured that the U.S.S.R. would not use this power to subvert the governments, and set up a regime of terror and cruelty among the peoples—in other words, deal with the situation as they dealt in the Baltic countries. There should be some basis of adjustment whereby the safety and international interest of the U.S.S.R. will be assured without their claiming to dictate the method of life, cultural development and the type of civilization to be enjoyed by these countries.

This is, indeed, the chief distinction which exists between a power which seeks world domination and a power which does not.

In the interest of honesty I should favor the taking of some appropriate opportunity to have direct conferences, preferably with Stalin. I think the straightest way of putting it is to say we would go to any length to safeguard the U.S.S.R., but that neither we nor anyone else could undertake to carry on a war to enable another power to force its language, civilization and way of life on other peoples. We had been able to achieve a perfectly satisfactory result in the Western Hemisphere which safeguards all legitimate military and economic and even cultural interests, at the same time leaving nations as weak as Costa Rica or Honduras with the feeling that they are entirely free and entirely safe. We have been successful in excluding foreign powers from abusing the liberty of these weak people. Upon the willingness of the strong powers which must emerge to use a like policy with the weaker nations which surround them, must depend the evolution of a sound future relationship.

Experience in the present war ought to prove to the U.S.S.R. that the idea that all parts of the world are at war with her is so much rot. They are not; and such hostility as there is would die at once upon the cessation by the U.S.S.R. of their propaganda and espionage and under-cover activities in other countries.

On Monday Sumner returned from Rio. He had not got the Secretary's telegram of congratulations. I saw him early and then had lunch with him.

He had not as yet seen the Secretary and he went thereafter to talk to Mr. Hull at his apartment.

On Tuesday we went to work again on Franco-American relations. This situation is deteriorating rapidly. The seizure of St. Pierre and Miquelon after the President had given his word there would be no substantial change removed the one moral dike which had held Pétain from caving in completely. . . .

February 13, 1942

Mr. Tamm, of the F.B.I., called up today with a piece of information which is at once amusing, disturbing and irritating.

When the Department of Justice bill on registering foreign agents came up, the British Intelligence and espionage service here had been unhappy about its passage. They had interested the British Embassy in the matter, nominally on the ground of protecting the British information service.

I had not felt like recommending a veto of the bill and had told them so, suggesting they work it out by regulation with the Attorney General. . . .

Tamm told me that last week their people had discovered a British Intelligence man named Paine operating in New York. His purpose was to "get the dirt" about me and then through various channels, one of them being Pierrepont Moffat, and a couple of newspapers, to force my removal from the State Department. The F.B.I. had watched this to a point where they had conclusive proof and then had called in the head of the British Intelligence. They told him that they wanted Paine out of the country by six o'clock "or else"; in which case they would arrest him promptly and go right to it. [William S.] Stephenson had said first, weakly, that Paine had been a long time in the United States; to which they replied that that made it worse; he ought to know better; and Stephenson had then professed surprise and horror that any of his men should do such a thing, and had finally put Paine on the plane for Montreal, and that was that.

It developed that the only dirt they had dug up so far was a column about having twin bath tubs in our house.

This would be amusing if it did not illustrate the precise danger which is run from having these foreigners operate. I plan to call the British Embassy and tell them that I am sufficiently experienced not to be influenced by this kind of thing, but that I think they should take it up with Lord Halifax and arrange to have this kind of thing stopped.

February 16, 1942

[Adrien P.] Tixier came in, representing the Free French movement. He wished to serve notice on us on behalf of General De Gaulle that if we took any defense measures in respect of Martinique, General De Gaulle expected to be consulted and to participate.

I told him that the Monroe Doctrine had been working here for a hundred years, and that the job of keeping order in the Hemisphere was strictly an American system; that we settled these things by discussion and I hoped that they would talk before they started any more adventures; and that anyway these things had to be timed so that they had a good effect. . . .

Of course the point is that our very stiff representations to Vichy have as yet gone unanswered and for all I know we may be breaking relations with Vichy at any time. . . . The devastating thing is that in spite of the liberals, the logical thing for us to do is to try to keep the French fleet immobilized as long as we can—to declare war or otherwise smashing up Vichy does not seem to be the way to do it.

February 24, 1942

A day and a half at the farm, during which time I put in some heavy thinking, while trudging over the bleak fields incompletely covered with snow, and trees bent with a driving north wind. The thinking came to this:

The present war probably always was a people's war; but it has certainly become so on all fronts since the loss of Singapore. Our reliance now has to be on the Chinese people for resistance; on the Indian people putting up a resistance, if they can be galvanized into doing so; on the Russian people, who are already doing so; on the little people of Europe; and on our own people as they get going. In this spectrum Britain falls into her place; and it is by no means the dominant place. Gone is the ideal of the "English speaking world"; and on dead reckoning, the era of Anglo-American operation will be pretty short. . . .

Anyhow, pursuing the idea of a people's war, it becomes obvious that we must take the Atlantic Charter and the Declaration by United Nations as the charter of these two great attempts; and we must do what we can about them. This is going to mean a very real change in the entire scheme of things. Of necessity it brings us into some conflict with the imperial conception of the Far East; but as far as I can see the British strength has lain not in the Empire, but in the Commonwealth. Briefly, we must look for common denominators, which must take in Chinese, and Burmese, and Indians, and Malayans, and Javanese, and so forth, as well as white sahibs and plantation owners. An Australian remarked to a Colonel with whom I had lunch today that he had been evacuated from Penang and that no Malayan had offered to help him with his baggage when he went down to get on the boat. But, said the Australian, there was no reason in the world why he should. The boat was limited to white people, leaving Malayans and Chinese to the tender mercies of the invaders; and after all, these people had nothing to defend but their own exploitation. . . .

How to translate all this into mechanisms, or to assemble the existing mechanism, so that we have common ideas seems to be the intellectual problem for the next three months. Without this we shall never get that swift support that we need for the military objectives, but will always be dragging by the heels an imperialist system which has done great things in its time but seems now to be merely in the nature of a preparation for something else.

I talked these things over with Beatrice, who seems to see some pattern to them, and we shall try to see what we can do. . . . I likewise agreed to make a radio speech in respect of the United Nations pact, starting off a series, and will try to set the keynote along the lines of what can be done. . . .

Since the Communist paper has taken a shot at me and I already have my troubles with the British Intelligence, I do not think that it is advisable to get into any more trouble at the moment than is absolutely essential. Navigating the rapids in the next few months is going to be difficult, if not impossible, and it will require pretty careful steering to remain both honest and American, and at the same time see that all of the interests which have marched together are kept together, going in the same direction and for an ultimate victorious, and I hope somewhat idealistic, end.

February 28, 1942

This has been a violent week. Much of it was consumed by continuing to construct the intelligence net which is beginning to cover the entire hemisphere. Fletcher Warren and Freddie Lyon have just been in reporting progress which is doing pretty well. This is one case where cooperation between State and FBI is working out beautifully. . . .

We have been working on a production mission to India to increase their war effort. Plainly, now that Singapore has fallen, the British are beginning to do some thinking about India. Why should India defend a freedom she hasn't got? Therefore, Stafford Cripps [Labour member of the British War Cabinet] and the liberals are yelling for dominion status for India, and I suppose some sort of solution probably will result. At this point our production mission suddenly assumes the status of a major political gesture. The interesting thing about it is that apparently the Indian Government—which in practice means the British—want it very badly and very quickly; at all events, they cabled Bajpai approving the idea, welcoming the mission, hoping it got started fast, and praying for immediate publication of a communiqué. . . .

March 10, 1942

Matters have been moving here.

After considerable amount of work, we have got appointed and have launched the mission to assist India. Louis Johnson is heading it and he will be High Commissioner, or diplomatic representative, at Delhi in due time. This brings him back into the picture after a long absence. I am very glad of it. . . .

At the instance of the Navy, a Joint Intelligence Board has been set up under the guns of the Allied High Command, which is sitting here in Washington. I am appointed on it, representing State. Whether we can do anything remains to be seen. My first preoccupation has been the defense of the Middle East, especially Syria. I presume the Army and Navy people have already gone over this thoroughly, but I am not taking anything for granted. . . .

The feeling is growing here—I confess I share it—that the strategy of the war ought to be that of Scipio. We cannot indefinitely fritter our forces away all over the globe. On the other hand, it is fairly plain that France and Europe are very lightly held, partly because of the losses in Russia and partly because of the German concentration for a drive towards the Middle East. This would seem to indicate pooling things together and letting go straight into the Netherlands and Germany. The Germans apparently are committing everything they have in a triple-pronged attack, via south Russia to Rostov and the Caucasus, via air and water from Crete and Cyprus into Syria, and via Libya with a reinforced army for Rommel, to Suez. This would head up towards a battle like that which has occurred recurrently throughout history on the plain of Esdraelon near the famous Armageddon. I doubt if air will altogether change that classic geography.

Frankfurter is continuing his intrigue to throw out Mr. Hull, who continues ill in Miami, though he is getting better. His candidate to replace Mr. Hull is Acheson. It has now got into the columns and I suppose we may see developments. I am not altogether clear how this will work out.

March 21, 1942

Our own mission [to India] is moving up in the world. Louis Johnson started out as head of the mission and now he has been appointed personal representative of the President at Delhi with the rank of Minister. Henry Grady is heading the mission. . . .

A second item of work had to do with the committee to set up peace terms. It seemed to me that if Hitler can start wars before beginning hostilities, we ought to be able to start a peace before an armistice—naturally, the kind of peace that we want. This business of evolving peace machinery so that it will be actively useful in winning the war is an interesting problem. Of the four sub-committees, I am a member of three and chairman of one; and in my sub-committee we are plugging away at a number of things, all of them with ulterior motives.

We started to think about an organization for relief; decided that it ought to draw its authority from the United Nations; therefore decided to recommend calling a meeting of representatives of the United Nations to authorize such an outfit. This will give reality to the United Nations, which in practice have only met twice: once when the President called all hands in and told them about the proposed Declaration; second, when they streamed through my office to sign up, on January 2nd. I think we can give it reality by giving the representatives things to do. . . .

Next, they will need a resettlement service to take care of prisoners of war, of returning refugees, of displaced populations, and perhaps to work on the problem of transplanting great minorities.

Third, there ought to be an outfit aimed at reconstruction, in the nature of mobile engineering units accompanied by a call on materials, who can do the preliminary work of construction or reconstruction, as the case may be.

And fourth, there will have to be a bank capable of seeing that money is never an obstacle to movement of goods—if you have the goods to move.

Transport is the other question, but I have not thought that out yet. . . .

On the Washington guerrilla front, it seems that Frankfurter has over-reached himself and his intrigue to upset Secretary Hull and put in Acheson has become generally known. I rather think that there will be a vigorous backfire before very long.

A curious by-product in public opinion is the increasing insistence by Congressmen and Senators that the United States no longer defer to British leadership, but that we assume leadership ourselves. This collides with an exactly similar feeling (as far as I can make out) by the British Dominions. At all events, all of the Dominion representatives with whom I have had contact have urged that they wish direct relations with us.

I rather think we have broken the back of the principal German spy rings in South America. I should like to do as well by one or two of them that must be operating in American ports. But it is one thing to break a gang and another to have it stay broken.

March 28, 1942

An over full week. Perhaps the high point was the visit of General Sikorski, the Polish Prime Minister. I met him at the station when he arrived; and had a chance to chat with him the following evening at the dinner at the Polish Embassy.

He is here on a flying visit to see President Roosevelt. He knows the Russians have been pressing the British for a territorial deal; that the British have said they would not deal without us; and that the Russians are now pressing them to make a separate and bilateral arrangement.

Sikorski hoped to be assured that the President would not enter into any such transaction. He has received these assurances. Before this, there was quite an elaborate discussion of the matter. Welles talked to the President about it and before that, I talked to Welles. The President, in talking to Welles, summed it up and said, "To enter this transaction would mean that I tear up the Atlantic Charter before the ink is dry on it. I will not do that." . . .

A couple of meetings of the committees regarding peace.

I have at length got the general viewpoint across that the background has to be United Nations and not Anglo-British.

In the economic committee we have at least agreed on economic negotiations which consider three points: (a) open trade, which we hope to get; (b) a financial institution which will take care of the needs of various governments (notably Britain) in terms of exchange, if open trade does not and cannot supply enough; (c) a kind of world surplus commodities corporation which can buy surpluses and put them where they ought to be. Naturally it is more than merely buying surpluses. It consists really of having a mechanism which will undertake to be a balancing factor in case normal exports or normal markets for exports do not appear to be working out. This balances the program in my own relief committee which is now pretty well stabilized, by which the United Nations will construct: (a) a mechanism for relief; (b) a mechanism for resettlement; and (c) a mechanism for more or less short range (3 to 5 years) reconstruction.

As an Englishman put it, the formula appeared to be food, men, materials. I suppose this will do until we give it more concrete form as I hope we shall be able to do. This would have to derive its authority from representatives of the United Nations who would have to meet in advance of the armistice, probably in some kind of meeting here. In the political committee we debated how this ought to be done, and this morning I think came to a tentative decision. It would have to be a meeting of representatives of the United Nations—an executive committee of some kind, presumably composed of the four great powers (United States, Britain, Russia, China) and four or five more representatives of the other legions to indicate that this was a solution by consent as well as by force. . . .

April 4, 1942

Saturday evening: a stiff week.

The British have a draft treaty with the Soviet Government under which they recognize the Soviet right to the Baltic provinces. They want us to say "aye" to that. Apparently the President moved in to try to ameliorate the condition of these unhappy people, and as a result Sumner tackled with Lord Halifax the job of at least giving the right to these populations peaceably to resettle. I am afraid of it, because I think this will be construed as a recognition by us of a pressure deal which condemns about three million people to death. I put my views in the record in the form of a memorandum to Sumner; he is answering it, saying, in substance, I expect, that we were faced with a *fait accompli*. I am afraid this is true. I am also afraid that every British politician will get behind us and insist that we, in substance, did it. . . .

The military intelligence work is coming along fairly well; the Joint Intelligence Committee looks as though it might get somewhere. If we are careful in using our contacts with the submerged countries (as, for instance, Poland), we ought to be extremely well informed. . . .

April 14, 1942

The London radio announced early this morning that Laval had become Prime Minister of France, which means in practice that the Germans have got what they wanted. I am still not clear that Darlan can or will deliver the French Army or the French Fleet. Pétain is shoved aside and a German puppet has everything that is left of unoccupied France. . . .

What all this comes to is that our long, desperate and (frankly rather hopeless) rear-guard action to prevent Germany from seizing the last vestige of power in France is now over. At least we held them off for nearly two years. . . .

April 25, 1942

A conference between the Secretary, Atherton, Norman Davis and myself. We have to do something now about Martinique. We could either send a mission and try to talk Admiral Robert into sense, or send warships and shoot up the place. We decided to arrange a mission. . . . Robert must see that we cannot have collaboration with Germany behind our own lines in the Caribbean.

Dinner night before last at the Russian Embassy. It was strictly an American, State Department party, and in some ways it was grimly humorous. Wallace was there, and so was Sumner; naturally there was no hint of the fact that Sumner Welles and Acheson have been fighting Wallace's Board of Economic Warfare tooth and nail. Frankfurter was there and so was Acheson; never a hint that Frankfurter has been intriguing to fire out the Secretary, Sumner and, of course, me, and put in Acheson instead. General Marshall was there and he, thank the Lord, has no wars with anyone. . . .

I have made arrangements to furnish Litvinov with such information as we get which might be of help to the Russians in their war with Germany. There is every reason for doing this, from all points of view. The Russians and the Japanese are, however, talking "strict neutrality" to each other, which is all right as far as it goes except that neither of them really believes in what the other says—and I am not sure that I blame them. . . .

I got hold of Robert Sherwood, who is doing propaganda work for Colonel Donovan. I endeavored to make a deal with him to get to work on an all-out political propaganda campaign against Germany. I put in a memorandum . . . [dated April 23] it may prove to be all wrong. . . .

Memorandum, April 23, 1942

Political-Propaganda Campaign
Directed Toward Germany

I believe that the time is due (if not overdue) for an all-out political campaign to upset the Nazi Government in Germany. The conditions appear favorable, and there is a very fair chance of a successful outcome. On the other hand, the risk is negligible.

Underlying Conditions

. . . Although the German armies are successful in the military sense, the underlying situation appears to have deteriorated to a point where defeat or disintegration seems almost certain unless peace is made. . . .

It would seem therefore that the failure to achieve victory in 1941 means that a German victory over Russia in 1942, even if achieved (which I doubt) would be fruitless, much as was the German victory over Russia in 1917.

A second factor lies in the losses to the German army. . . . The deaths on the Russian front have been so widespread and are so widely known in Germany that there is already evidence leading to the belief that contingents sent to the east consider that they are probably condemned to death. Already the morale factor in that sense is beginning to deteriorate.

A third factor is the obviously growing concern of Germany at the British bombing. This, relatively ineffective in the year 1941, has begun to be extremely serious in the west of Germany. . . . In larger part, it has at length proved to Germany that her civilian population is not immune from direct military attack.

Political Factors

The political factors implicit in this situation are more obscure, but such evidence as we have indicates that they are beginning to be active.

It is fairly well established that one group of German generals has been actively canvassing the possibility of a change of government so as to place Germany in a better position to make peace. This is not to indicate that I think any kind of peace could be made with the German militarists —which I think would be disastrous. . . .

Catholic sources continually report the search for the nucleus of a non-Nazi Government. Originally it seems they were thinking of a military clique; later advices speak of their attempt to set up a civilian group based on the old civil servants who have survived.

Finally, we have indisputable evidence of the growing corruption and disorganization of the German administrative and second-string machinery. General Sikorski reported his ability to purchase, in German-occupied Poland, arms sufficient to equip 4 divisions. . . .

In German-occupied Europe the political situation is increasingly adverse. . . .

Outline of Political Campaign

I believe that the political campaign should be built up as follows:

1. The President should make a statement [announcing] that there was no desire to massacre or wipe out the German people; and that they would be included in the peace plans. This could, and I think should, be based on the phrase in the Atlantic Charter stating that the advantages of the post-war plans should be available to vanquished as well as victors.

The statement would have to call for something more than mere elimination of the present German Government. It would have to call for the elimination of the Nazi rulers, and for rigid and severe justice executed against Gestapo and S.S. units, and against the agents of inhuman oppression in the occupied countries. . . .

2. This statement, once made, should be hammered into Germany for a considerable period of time by radio, through the neutral press, etc.

3. The actual situation of Germany ought to be stated over the radio in the simplest possible terms. I myself would favor the textual use of parts of the Staff plan of 1940, with its dismal predictions for 1942. . . .

4. The rising might of the British, the Americans and the Russians ought to be put on the air. . . .

5. Certain of the better authenticated incidents such as the killing of German wounded by Germans rather than bringing them home for hospitalization, ought likewise to be stressed. . . .

Combined with this there should be a development over the radio of the thesis in the Atlantic Charter: freedom from want, freedom from fear, and a continuous and renewed insistence that Germans freed from Nazi slavery would be included in the program.

6. The inevitability of the British and American air and military forces attacking every individual German town ought to be carried on. . . .

April 27, 1942

To the Secretary's office where we talked over a variety of things; Hull is in good working form.

A long meeting of the Joint Intelligence Committee and a variety of military questions. The more I see of General Strong, the better I like him. He is a sound, solid citizen.

April 28, 1942

This started in bright and early in connection with Martinique . . . we called in Admiral [F. J.] Horne [Vice Chief of Naval Operations], who had worked with Admiral Robert, High Commissioner there; likewise General Strong, Captain Schuirmann, Atherton and [Samuel] Reber [Assistant Chief, European Affairs]. The decision was taken to send a mission to Martinique backed up by adequate economic and military forces, and try to make a deal.

The group withdrew to my room and we dictated a memorandum . . . which the Secretary signed and sent along to the President. This ought to provide some method of action. . . .

An evening party for the boys in F.C. [Foreign Communications] at [J. Daniel] Hanley's house. They have every right to celebrate. I think they are directly responsible for smashing the Rio spy ring, and, given time, will clean up on some more things.

F.C. is now the nerve center for a pretty large region: there are detectors for the secret radio stations; there is the short-wave network which is just coming into being; there are diplomatic privileges in the Embassies and generally speaking, the South American service is coming along.

April 30, 1942

Robert Sherwood, Taylor and Duel came in to see me. With them was Jimmy Warburg. We tried to hatch out a general program of political warfare and the beginning of an all-out campaign against Germany. I expressed my theory that Germany is really much worse off than anybody knows; that they have got to win this summer but winning means making a peace with us. Otherwise they would be in bad shape.

Getting started depends partly on being able to get clearance to publish some of the documents in the case and partly on the President's willingness to make some kind of statement. Sherwood said he thought the President was getting into a frame of mind to do so. I hope to get a little further with this. . . .

Tixier came in to see me today. He was just back from London, where he has been dickering with De Gaulle. . . .

Tixier also wants to centralize all negotiations with the colonies here in Washington. He says this will avoid a separatist movement in Africa. Incidentally, it would centralize power in Tixier—though he did not stress that point. . . .

And yet I feel that we cannot allow the movement to go to pieces. De Gaulle's name is current throughout the world, and so is the Lorraine Cross. If the movement splits up in the various colonies, our enemies will make full use of that fact. So the net problem is to take this handful of political incompetents and still put them together into something that can be useful. A tough job. . . .

The State Department is trying to solve its difficulty with the Board of Economic Warfare. Acheson tried to oust the Vice President of his job and the Vice President's counter-attack nearly knocked us overboard. This was silly; but the Department always starts that way—as Sumner tried to knock out Nelson Rockefeller. But we succeeded in maintaining ourselves as friends and I believe now things are entirely cooperative in that direction. Certainly we mended our row with the FBI and that is working very well; so I do not despair of the BEW.

Lunch with the President. He was in a quiet and friendly mood, in excellent spirits and moving along with entire serenity. He told a lot of stories over the trout and eggs Benedict. When he was in Germany, the very best meals you could get at the little inns were trout caught in the brook behind the inn, and the little German spotted deer. . . .

He then opened up the subject that was apparently on his mind. He asked whether I had any views as to whether the time had come to try to make some distinction between the Nazi gang and the German people, and to accelerate the process of political change there.

I told him that I was more optimistic than our Staff people, and than most of the Department. . . .

The President said that he himself was of that view. . . . He said there was such an amount of increasing talk from various angles in Germany that he was beginning to believe that something could be done about it. . . .

. . . He said Felix Frankfurter had been at him to broadcast in French, and in Spanish, and possibly in German, so that people there could hear the sound of his own voice. He had rather steered away from doing this, since once he started he thought he would have to keep on. I told him I thought he was exactly right; this would be the last, and not the first, step in the main-line campaign. He asked me to keep on considering the matter, which I said I would do.

He discussed a little the resolution of the row that has been going on between the State Department and the Board of Economic Warfare, saying that the matter was perfectly simple: the State Department had the right to conduct foreign relations; the Board of Economic Warfare was the procurement agency, and Jesse did the financing. He personally saw no reason for it. I told him that there had been some ambitious men over here and that probably was the result.

We reverted then to the subject of political warfare. I asked whether he had finally come to an arrangement on the Donovan outfit. He said that, as I perhaps knew, he had been trying to get a brigadier-generalship for the Colonel; after which he was thinking of putting him on some nice, quiet, isolated island, where he could have a scrap with some Japs every morning before breakfast. Then he thought the Colonel would be out of trouble and be entirely happy. The rest of it would have to be re-integrated somehow. I had some ideas on that subject, but decided to keep them to myself.

He then played a little discursively over the problem of eastern Europe. He said that he would not particularly mind about the Russians taking quite a chunk of territory; they might have the Baltic republics, and eastern Poland, and even perhaps the Bukovina, as well as Bessarabia. I said the Atlantic Charter had something to say about that; and anyhow I hoped he would not be getting generous with Scandinavia. He laughed and said certainly not. He said that he and Churchill had agreed not to discuss in any sense the possibility of a German collapse, because the whole attitude ought to be to talk on the pessimistic side, lest anyone get the idea the war would be easy. But he himself could not escape the feeling that we are drawing towards the conclusion.

I raised the question of New York politics. He said that he had gone over the situation. Lehman did not want to run again: quite bluntly, he was sick of Albany. He had himself "invented" Jack Bennett, to whom Farley was pledged, but Jack could not win. . . . He had to consider that there might be one man who could work things out. This was Owen Young, who would have considerable strength among the business people and the voters. "He is not," says the President, "your type of liberal and mine. But he is a man who is more liberal at sixty-eight than he was at fifty-eight." . . .

May 2, 1942

Some discussion in the Territorial Committee as to whether or not Germany should be partitioned. The general thought seems to be running along the line of possible division into three parts. Somehow or other, that doesn't quite set up to me; I think political tides will be running in Europe so fast and so muddy that a unified Germany will almost happen of its own weight. Anyhow, the thing that you want is not a weakened Germany (it might not stay that way), so much as a re-educated Germany which will be a balancing and peaceable force in the world. After all, there will be Russia. Sumner is building his entire hopes on the effectiveness of the world organization. My own guess is that the world organization will take a long time to get up steam, though I am entirely in accord that we should do our utmost to make it work. . . .

May 4, 1942

This began with the Free French and kept on with the Free French most of the day. . . .

A long meeting of the Joint Intelligence Committee. Then a tragic little call from [Etienne] Boegner [son of Pastor Boegner]. Tixier, while he was in London, succeeded in firing him from the Free French Delegation, along with Raoul de Roussy de Sales [journalist]. This breaks Boegner's heart, because to him it simply makes a dictatorial government, and he proposes to go to London and try to have it out with General De Gaulle.

Rumors have been reaching me that there is a general revolt in the Free French Committee in New York. I don't know how it will work out. . . .

May 5, 1942

To the Secretary's office this morning where we started to work on a formula which might resolve the Free French situation. . . . The urgency of the matter which the Secretary has been insisting on was proved, for the British landed on Madagascar this morning. As is usual with military movements, I knew nothing about it—in line with my rule of having no military information except in connection with a certain job on which I may be working. . . .

May 7, 1942

Bright and early on orders for Admiral [John H.] Hoover. These have to be carefully thought out; every instinct should be for diplomatic rather than military action. And yet you cannot leave a Laval collaboration center inside the American Caribbean defense area.

May 12, 1942

To New York, where I had dinner with David Dubinsky [President, International Ladies' Garment Workers' Union]. . . . Then over to the *Times,* where were Arthur Sulzberger, President Conant and Anne McCormick. We went down to The Times Hall and there delivered ourselves of speeches. The subject was "Books in Wartime". Conant discussed exclusively a huge number of Federal scholarships for boys to go to college so that they might become officers. (I calculated the war would have to last about six years to make this program valid—but let it go.)

I was talking, on my father's advice, about the literature of information and the literature of power, chiefly Aeschylus and De Quincey. Later, I said grimly to Conant that he ought to be talking about literature and Aeschylus and I about Federal arrangements. What is the use of being the President of Harvard if you cannot exercise the spiritual and intellectual leadership which goes with it. . . .

May 13, 1942

Meanwhile the Free French have shown up; and they are protesting like anything because (a) they were not consulted about military operations, and (b) they were not offered the government of Martinique. I said grimly to Tixier that he had a young revolution going on in New Caledonia and they had better learn how to govern the islands they had got before they started seeking a few more. . . .

I went home late to dinner where was the Prime Minister of Norway [Johan Nygaardsvold], and Morgenstierne—now Ambassador—and [Maximilien] Steenberghe [former Dutch Cabinet member]. The ultimatum to Martinique had expired at eight o'clock but we did not know what had happened. . . .

A fascinating evening—ridden to a degree.

At the close of it, the watch officer telephoned. A cable had come in from Martinique. Admiral Robert had agreed to dismantle the warships, and the negotiations as to the remaining points were continuing. In other words, we were over the hump. I slept comfortably for the first time in some days. Killing our people in an attack on Frenchmen, or killing Frenchmen, seemed to me about the most useless form of activity.

The Martinique matter which is now on the way to settlement does make it possible to work out eventually some sort of peace in respect of West Africa and perhaps even France itself—but these are wild hopes.

May 19, 1942

Negotiations from Martinique seem to be coming along fairly well. . . . But the Free French are rather furious because they wanted the island turned over to them. I can't quite see it—in spite of all the fulminations of the liberal journals, there seems to be no real reason to kill a lot of Frenchmen for the sole purpose of putting a De Gaullist in as Governor of Martinique. By evolution, the island ought to get to that phase, if things happen normally. If they don't, the less said about it the better. . . .

A little work today on the interminable problem of India. Louis Johnson is coming home. He has not been a howling success there, but he has done the best he could. I don't know that anyone could have been a success. . . .

June 20, 1942

I have not made any diary entries for a long time. An endless march of detail, urgent rather than important, has taken most of my time, and if I contributed anything to history I should have difficulty in knowing what it was.

Sumner had about caved in when the Russians demanded a treaty promising them territory in Europe. This was not that he liked it; he had fought it quite hard. But he had about agreed to accept a *fait accompli* and I am afraid may have advised the President so to do. At that point Cordell Hull got back in town and picked up—and I was cordially glad to see him. He waded into the situation forthwith; and as a result Molotov first visited Churchill; then came to the United States; was there met with a pretty solid front; and got the treaty which is now a public record and which is a frank arrangement to cooperate—and we mean business about that; but did not extort promises inconsistent with the Atlantic Charter, with our honor, and with the whole United Nations picture.

The newspapers say that Molotov flew over in a Russian bomber of a design which astonished our air men. This is true, but only remotely so. The bomber was seven years old and, as General Strong observed, Molotov is "more courageous than he to go up in that crate." . . .

Mr. Welles has made a couple of speeches laying out post-war plans. The difficulty with the speeches is not that they were bad—in fact they were excellent. But they should have been made either by the Secretary or by the President, and there is, accordingly, an increase in tension between Mr. Hull and Sumner. I don't know what the end of all this will be; it was forecast at the Rio Conference. . . .

New York politics have bobbed up. Jim Farley came in to see me prior to seeing the President. He said they had the votes to nominate Bennett and what was anybody going to do about it. I said that I thought the Labor Party and my gang might not take him. Jim said that would just mean defeat. I said that was as broad as it was long: so might Bennett. Apparently he talked the same way to the President, who declined to commit for Bennett. Thereafter Wendell Willkie's man, Walter Mack, got in touch with me; so did the American Labor Party; so did Harold Moskovit; so did La Guardia. All hands about agreed to nominate a third man on the American Labor Party ticket, and go to it—unless, of course, the Democrats cave in and nominate someone sensible. The Willkie people are just as angry with Dewey as we are against Bennett, so it looks like a pretty kettle of fish. La Guardia is obsessed with the idea that I ought to run for Governor; I don't plan to do any such thing. . . .

Berle had assessed the situation in a memorandum to the President on June 19, stating that the Labor party and Young Democrats

. . . would take [Senator James] Mead, with some enthusiasm, Owen Young (with less enthusiasm). . . . I have asked them not to use my own name in this connection.

Mayor La Guardia would support any of the foregoing. If need be, he would lead a third party ticket himself. . . .

The split is real, and not artificial. You cannot make the American Labor Party and the independent Democrats swallow an isolationist ticket.

June 24, 1942

Things are going badly in the Department. The Secretary and Sumner are farther apart than ever—in this case I am afraid it is so definitely Sumner's fault as not to be arguable. Briefly, he committed the fatal mistake of speaking as though he were the Secretary of State, when there is an alive and very active Secretary of State in the immediate vicinity. The Secretary thereupon went to work to clear the decks; and Sumner on his part has been retaliating by getting control of all the Department machinery he can. This bodes no good for anybody concerned, and least of all for me. . . .

June 27, 1942

News from the Near East is not good. . . .

Churchill has been here, staying with the President. The discussions were secret and I only know that Churchill exhibited great confidence—though just why I can't say. The conversations were principally military. My best guess is that they will be opening a second front fairly soon. Even talk of a second front will probably assist the Russians somewhat. The Russians as usual are putting up a magnificent holding fight at Sevastopol and around Kharkov. . . .

In a memorandum to Hull, July 1, 1942, on the Middle East, Berle recommended enlarging the economic program to North Africa; strengthening the civilian air structure of French Equatorial Africa and the Belgian Congo; strengthening U.S. connections with Saudi Arabia, Iraq, and Syria, after having ascertained that Ibn Saud was prepared to grant landing rights in Saudi Arabia; and getting technical assistance to the government of Iran, where money would probably be required. He concluded:

. . . until we are prepared to put military force into the Middle East we must rely in large degree on the relations we have with the local populations.

I think if all of these things could be done without delay, we might avoid a collapse in the Middle East following the seizure of the Nile Delta —a result which, unless prompt measures are taken, is only too possible.

July 21, 1942

I have just finished a political job, which ill accords with the detached status of the State Department.

Jim Farley proposed to nominate Bennett for Governor of New York. He also proposed to control the New York delegation in 1944, using the State machine for that purpose. The complexion of this varied from middle-of-the-road Democrats to the Christian Fronters; and anyhow, the movement was against the President. . . .

The President did not like it . . . it seemed to all of us that the logical opposite candidate was Jim Mead.

On Friday last (July 17) the President at length gave McIntyre a green light and we went to work to get up an invitation to Senator Mead to become a candidate for Governor. Over the week-end we got quite a lot of signatures, chiefly up-state mayors; and I got authority to sign the names of the Labor Party people. We also put in two or three from down here, to show that the Administration favored the move.

We likewise got a similar letter from Senator Wagner. It was interesting to see the timid ones run for cover: Herbert Bayard Swope, Nathan Straus, Owen Young, etc. They wanted the President to declare, first—whereas we wanted to take it off the President's neck.

This afternoon, in Senator Mead's office, we finished up the letters, the releases, etc. The schedule is that these will appear in the newspapers tomorrow; Mead will announce his candidacy tomorrow morning; will call at the White House in the afternoon; be formerly pledged, probably on Friday. Governor Lehman will announce his support, I presume on Thursday, and this takes Charlie Poletti [lawyer] out of the race.

It seems amusing, and a little futile, to be working on politics in the middle of a big and strenuous time. . . .

It will continue to be an extremely nervous and anxious summer— but I feel that the Germans will not quite get there.

The Russians are keeping up the agitation for a second front. I think they are right—and do not know the military considerations which have prevented its being established already.

The tension in the Department continues. The Secretary is taking a hand in administration, for the first time. This may help.

In a memorandum of July 13 to Roosevelt, Berle endorsed

[a plan] worked up jointly by State and O.S.S. [Office of Strategic Services] (Donovan) to set up the equivalent of an Arab Bureau, based on Beirut or Damascus and equipped to put up the real political fight against the Axis in Syria and Iraq. This plan is now before the Combined Chiefs of Staff. . . .

The chances are probably not better than one in four: but the risk (the lives of a few good men, and perhaps five million dollars) are small, against the possible loss of Syria and Iraq to Axis-controlled Arab governments. . . .

July 25, 1942

I have been trying to push the group that was to go to Arabia; and making some progress, though I wish it were faster. . . .

. . . The much abused North African economic accord has been rescued, once more. A little group in the Board of Economic Warfare, and some in the State Department, have been fighting it, despite the fact that the policy had been laid down by practically all responsible people; it is difficult to get anyone to realize that, were relations broken off, we should do far more than this, solely for the purpose of getting the Intelligence and other services into that area.

In New York politics the pot is still boiling merrily. The letter asking Senator Mead to run came out in due course; Senator Mead thereupon announced his candidacy; President Roosevelt thereupon blessed it. This was followed immediately after by a large blast from Jim Farley. . . . It is going to be a stiff fight; I think we shall win. If we do not, I propose to have the American Labor Party nominate La Guardia and go ahead and break it up. I should rather have Dewey win on a split ticket now than have a patched-up business which would mean a split Democratic Party in 1944, just at the time when reaction would be most dangerous. . . .

A meeting of the J.I.C. [Joint Intelligence Committee], with a really very pessimistic estimate of the war situation by General Strong. Roughly, he envisages the loss of the Russian Caucasus and the loss of the Middle East, and the probable loss at the same time of India, and a hemispheric war following. I came away from there feeling pretty blue; but pulled myself together when I remembered that the Military Intelligence were always pessimistic about these things; what they never reckon on is that last punch which both the British and the Russians seem to deliver when they are really up against it. On balance, I think I still stick to my prediction that the summer campaign will come within a hair's breadth of making it, but not quite. At least we can check by one prediction, namely, that by August 1st Rommel will start a full-fledged center attack on the British position at El Alamein and break through, cutting the British army in two. . . .

I have been trying to give some direction to the Joint Intelligence Committee. It seems to me that, increasingly, we must get an intellectual direction to the war. I do not see that the British are supplying any; and our people have been pretty modest. Ultimately there has to be something more than a mere general defensive strategy; and I am inclined to think that the quicker we get at it, the better. . . .

We are working on a proposed international stabilization fund and bank, which is really a revolution in international finance—revolutions come easily these days. I think we can do some business along this line.

July 29, 1942

I am still anxious to do something about a second front. I gather that nothing much is doing. My impression is that the British want something done in one place, and our people in another; and that the result is to paralyze action. This is a pity. While I doubt if the Russian situation is as black as it is being painted, if we do not make some move, ourselves, pretty soon, I think a good many people will decide that it is because we cannot—and then we shall be—in trouble. . . .

I have been up to the gullet in economic organization of peace, and attach to this diary the rough outline plans which I want to have the Committee consider (they are heads for suggestion, rather than actual proposals), but it all seems rather vague and far away, in the light of existing circumstances.

July 27—Memorandum "Post-War Economic Mechanisms of the United Nations."
I. Basic Considerations of Economic Organization.

. . . The economic operations of the United Nations should be guided by certain general principles set out through their constitutive documents which should be an elaboration of the "freedom from want" of the Atlantic Charter. . . . Thus, in granting loans or assisting internal development of any unit, the United Nations Bank should be instructed to consider, among other things, whether the constitutive state:

1. Is able to preserve public order;

2. Observes a humane and tolerant race policy and has achieved a reasonable protection of races within its borders;

3. So handles its economic affairs as to diffuse the benefits of economic development widely among its population, rather than concentrating the advantages among a few;

4. Is handling its affairs so that they are not a menace to the security of their neighbors.

The foregoing is by way of illustration; the same principle should be followed throughout the various mechanisms.

II. Contemplated United Nations Economic Organisms.

A. The United Nations should contemplate setting up four major organisms, namely:

1. A financial and capital exchange organism.
2. A transport and communications authority.

The transport authority functions should be to assure the freest possible transport and communication by land, sea and air. . . .

3. A raw materials administration.

This should undertake to facilitate to countries needing them, a selected list of raw materials when and to the extent that private arrangements for such raw materials break down. . . .

4. A food administration.

I suggest that the detail of working out a food administration be worked up by Mr. [Paul H.] Appleby [Under Secretary] of the Department of Agriculture, who has been studying this matter. . . .

III. Security Considerations.

On each of these organisms a representative of the security organism of the United Nations should sit. His business should be to guide the operations of these various mechanisms so that where threat to security appears, appropriate controls may be promptly introduced.

IV. Consideration should be given to the possibility that the heads of these organisms, together with certain outside representatives, might constitute an Economic Council of the United Nations.

August 11, 1942

A brief vacation at the farm. Most of it pitching hay. The hay at least will be good for something eventually. The country was very lovely.

Just prior to leaving, a directive came down from the President asking that food be expedited to France, and that the North African economic plan should go through without further delay. I am glad of this, because there has been a settled campaign of sabotage against that plan. . . .

A special meeting of one part of the J.I.C. The determination to do something in the nature of a second front has been reached. I am glad of the decision and of the nature of it, since it vindicates some of the thinking that some of us have been doing here for a good while. . . .

August 18, 1942

A couple of days which were relatively easy by Department standards. I have been occupied with two things. One was working chiefly with the Secretary, Green Hackworth, Atherton and Dunn on a possible statement by the President involving a plan to gather and perpetuate the evidence against individuals in Europe and Asia guilty of atrocities. This is partly due to the desire of the Dutch Government to do something to head off the continued German massacre of hostages there. It is partly an elaboration of my own feeling that some such step might check some individuals in the Axis countries from carrying on their sheerly terroristic and sadistic activities. The proposal is to appoint some outstanding American to get and classify evidence and preserve it for future reference, accompanied by a statement that guilt is personal. Arthur Sweetser [former League of Nations advocate], among others, is impressed with the idea.

The second was an attempt to get forward with the economic organization of the United Nations and parallel economic organization of the states in Europe which emerge from the German occupation. I am attaching a copy of my memorandum on the proposed Raw Materials Administration; likewise a copy of the tentative proposal regarding arrangements with the East European Federation, which is serving as a kind of experimental guinea pig in the thinking.

Last night, at Sumner's suggestion, Mr. [Frank Lidgett] McDougall [Economic Adviser] came to dinner and with him Paul Appleby. McDougall is advising Stanley Bruce of Australia [Representative of Commonwealth Government in United Kingdom War Cabinet], who is now perhaps the most intelligent man in London. I went over step by step some of these ideas, telling him I thought a United Nations Bank was a probability; so also was a United Nations Transport Authority more or less clearly indicated; I thought we might have a Raw Materials Administration (we were committed to one) and that I thought there might also be a Food Administration. . . .

August 22, 1942

. . . things have been happening on the New York political front. Dubinsky called up yesterday to offer me the Labor Party nomination for Governor. I told him I would hardly move into that unless the President asked me to do it. I also told him I did not think the President would ask. . . .

This morning La Guardia telephoned. I agreed to meet him at the White House after he had seen the President. . . . Fiorello said the President had indicated great interest: he definitely wanted the Labor Party to go forward and whip Farley; he said that he could not ask any Federal official to do it, or make any promises of reappointment, let alone grant leave of absence for the purpose; whoever did it would merely have to rely on the general situation—that is, on an understanding, without a given word. At all events, this was what Fiorello deduced from the conversation. . . .

Having stated this, Fiorello thereupon offered me the nomination. He said that the Labor Party is in convention and can't find a candidate. I said that there was nothing doing, and as Fiorello did not press it very hard, I gather that he felt this was all right. . . .

August 24, 1942

Sunday morning La Guardia called up. The Labor Party met in convention and finally nominated Dean Alfange. . . .

October 27, 1942

Assuming that the President will have to make a statement sometime in the next month or two, covering pretty explicit peace terms, I think that the statement will have to be built up somewhat as follows. As it lies in my mind, there will be a European revolution, in any event, as soon as the lid is taken off. The revolution will either be on Stalinist lines or it will be along liberal and individualist lines, depending on how bluntly the problem is stated. Roughly speaking, most of the west of Europe, like the United States and Britain, propose a revolution which shall increase the stature of individuals; the Communist position, like the Nazi position, submerges them.

Likewise, there will be an Asiatic revolution which will probably be on more nationalistic lines. There, political freedom is still the main issue.

Therefore, after the statement of the situation, point one has to be a statement of philosophy: the philosophy of the revolution of the individual. Without this, any mere kit of devices is meaningless.

The second major fact appears to be that in Europe there must be an organizing principle. Russia might supply that organizing principle—but only by force, and it would not last. Britain might supply that organizing principle, but her stock of moral credit is low. We obviously are not going to supply a permanent organizing principle. Therefore, we are bound to try to create an organizing principle in the west of Europe, arising out of a cooperative group of nations. I think, therefore, that point two of the address must be an insistence that the price of freedom is the abandonment of hatreds and the willingness to work together.

To achieve this involves the setting up of territorial units which permit a maximum of cultural and individual freedom of development. Men seek to realize themselves by communicating ideas and making them effective. They do this best in groups of the same language and habits of thought. By consequence, point three, which is really a territorial point, must be that of delimitation of boundaries for the purpose of culture, forms of life and social structure which will best accomplish this end. In large measure, this had been achieved before the war—for while the Versailles Treaty was bad enough in plenty of ways, it can be said that it accomplished a greater realization of these groups than had ever existed in the world. A sub-point under this must deal with those territories in which there can be no fragmentation and where races simply have to live together. As to this, there is a single option: either races will learn to live together or they disappear.

This paves the way for a statement of the organizing principle which must be fostered and protected by the United Nations. A west European regional bloc of some sort has to be achieved. This must include our enemies—Germany and Italy—as rapidly as a situation can be brought into existence by which they again become peaceful members of the family of nations.

In large measure, the problem of general security must be dealt with if any of these groups are to survive.

In consequence, point four must deal with the creation of a general security mechanism on a global basis; a sub-point under this must be the setting up of regional units. West Europe might be used as a specific example: pretty much everything from Poland westward would have to join in a European League of Nations of some sort.

On the Asiatic side, a somewhat similar situation prevails, except that the geography is different. China and India present two great powers; Australia and Japan likewise; the territories of Indo-China, Thailand, the Indies, and so forth, have to be worked into some sort of a cooperative system.

Reference has to be made to the Middle East—I have not yet tried to think that through.

There is a special and tremendous question regarding Africa—which will have to be dealt with but is difficult to figure out.

We have our own family of nations in the Western Hemisphere which requires no change.

So much for politics.

On the economic side, I think that the President has to take the bull by the horns and come flat out for a United Nations Economic Council. This I think will have to have certain defined agencies, notably: an Agricultural Authority, which must include handling of problems of food and nutrition, agricultural marketing and other practical matters; an International Bank, connected with an International Development Authority, which must take care of stabilization of currency, short-term credits, and arrange for long-term capital movements; an International Labor Authority—an adaptation of the ILO; an International Transport Authority—which probably would have fairly limited application; an authority for international movement of commodities—more especially raw materials, though not necessarily so; and an International Health Authority.

Each of these should be so set up that it can stand on its own bottom —so that if one of them does not work out, the remainder will continue in existence and function. They should be so handled that even if they do not work on a global basis, they can work on a partial basis.

October 29, 1942

DISCUSSION OF FRENCH TERRITORY

[prepared on eve of North African landing]

The considerations which should affect the decision in the matter of any occupied French territory are these:

1. What effect [will] the choice of a French administration have upon resistance of French allies to the United Nation force?

Should we choose to recognize General De Gaulle, and invite him to administer reoccupied French territory the effect would appear to be as follows:

(a) In North Africa, to cause perhaps increased resistance. This is not a mere surmise. . . .

The conclusion is inevitable, that in North Africa and West Africa, the bulk of the officials, and of the Army would be inspired to resist an American, Anglo-American or United force.

(b) In unoccupied France the situation is not clear. . . .

Nevertheless, a considerable element in the civilian population would follow anyone who offered them freedom from the oppressed measures forced upon them by the Germans through Laval. . . .

(c) In occupied France it is fairly plain that the civilian population would probably follow De Gaulle or indeed any non-Laval French leader. . . .

2. What is the best means of maintaining peace, order, and a favorable atmosphere for military operations in reoccupied territory?

On the foregoing analysis this plainly turns on the area selected for reoccupation.

If the area selected is in Africa, then it would seem plain that the De Gaullists should be left out of the picture completely for the time being and that the Army should endeavor to secure the cooperation of the civilian officials as it proceeds. . . .

Were the territory selected for reoccupation in the North of France, probably it would be useful to have it understood that a De Gaullist representative might act as political adviser; but it should likewise be understood that general proscription would not be allowed. . . .

Were the area selected in unoccupied France, it would probably be best to make no announcement for the time being, but to deal with those political leaders who emerge. . . .

November 9, 1942

This is the first entry in this Diary in a long time, partly due to the fact that I have been up to my neck in plans for the military invasion of North Africa; and I wished to have nothing in writing about it. If any advance information were derived from anywhere on that score, I did not wish it to be from any scrap of writing in my possession.

Nevertheless, the North African invasion is, in a sense, the culmination of a set of ideas running over a period of two years. Almost exactly two years ago, I got sufficiently excited to start the long campaign, which began by our sending [Robert] Murphy, then Counselor of Embassy at Vichy, to Africa, followed by negotiations for an economic agreement with North Africa under cover of which we could and did send in control officers and increased the staffs of our consulates. These men, as the records will show, endeavored not only to spread propaganda, but to establish the closest connections with the local leaders there. . . .

The tail end of the operation is marked by some of the wildest arrangements outside of Tom Sawyer's famous plans to deliver Jim, the Nigger! Thus, through Vichy we had a plot going to deliver General [Henri] Giraud out of France and plant him in North Africa. He actually arrived at Gibraltar about the time when the occupation was ready to start, and succeeded in getting into a violent argument with General [Dwight D.] Eisenhower as to whether he or Eisenhower should be in supreme command! This, apparently, they settled up yesterday. Meantime, we had the plot going in Algiers to clap the Vichy French leaders in jail. This one, I gather, worked. Darlan was there, partly to inspect and direct the defense, and partly because his son is dying. Darlan, it seems, was the first to advocate the capitulation of Algiers. . . .

Behind this was still a second line of possibility based on various relations we have guardedly opened with the Berber and Riff leaders, and with the Sultan of Morocco, and now with the Bey of Tunis.

But of course our major reliance was on the swift moving operation of our arms. Taken altogether, it is a very gaudy story with not much left out.

At the last, and when Eisenhower was leaving London, we had to put out that he was coming home for consultation—a job the War Department finally handed me. I tried to leak this in every direction. If it had been something we wanted to keep secret, the State Department would have leaked like a sieve! This time, however, it kept its mouth shut. Finally, I had to get McDermott to get a group of men to start talking out loud in the news room, after which it hit the front page with smooth certainty.

Last night [Counselor S. Pickney] Tuck telephoned from Vichy that Laval had broken relations. We completed the process today. I drafted a couple of statements for the President and for the Secretary. The President redrafted mine, cutting it to one-third and making it infinitely better.

Mackenzie King from Canada is afraid France may declare war, which would upset his French Canadians. He therefore proposes to get out a statement saying they now consider the Vichy Government as dissolved and it is, therefore, no longer a legal entity. This will mean that if France declares war, he will say there is no government there to declare war. I think it is a good scheme and we will work it out in the morning. . . .

We are now coming to the point where we have to think hard about Italy. In this file will be found record of conversations I have had with . . . Italian Socialist underground leader [George] Gentili, who represents [Emilio] Lussu, and probably represents what contact we have in Italy. Everything I get indicates that the Italians are very frightened. If we can move fast enough and our political warfare is well enough done, we may be able to blast Italy out of her position sometime in the not distant future. I propose to make a speech on Saturday night looking towards that end. In this regard, I am rather embarrassed. The Italian underground has said that if I would give them my personal word that Italy will not be subjected to a punitive peace, they will go forward. The Atlantic Charter pretty nearly rules out a punitive peace in the normal sense of the term so I think I can do it, but I have told them repeatedly one does not build on a personal word. . . .

There are more things to do in the day than I have time for.

November 16, 1942

Saturday. Various jobs, chiefly intelligence and a meeting of Welles's Committee on Political Post-War Settlements, in the morning. . . .

Then to New York, there to make a speech on Italian affairs. It merely recited the Atlantic Charter and the appropriate paragraphs of Secretary Hull's speech, but it was enough to satisfy the Italian Second Internationale socialists and their friends to throw in their lot with us. We have, of course, been working with the army and the ecclesiastical hierarchy; but this taps another line of support, a line of support the British apparently wanted and were unable to get.

Sunday. Chiefly plain and fancy loafing.

The North African adventure continues to go well, but we are in the damnedest fight there ever was at Guadalcanal. . . .

The British and American forces are nearing Tunis. Darlan seems to be a prisoner at our headquarters and is changing sides. He is angling for the French Fleet in arranging for the delivery of the North African armies and administration. . . .

Monday. Tixier, representing the Free French, came in, very much upset. He thinks we have recognized Admiral Darlan and pointed out that Darlan condemned De Gaulle to death as a traitor, and so forth. He also brought up a point I ought to have thought of—namely, the liberation of the Free French prisoners held in North Africa. I told him that Darlan had the conventional status of the leading authority in North Africa and we were recognizing him for the purpose of capitulation. We had, so far as I knew, no political commitments. . . .

Sir Ronald Campbell showed up and explained why the British thought it was unwise to make any political declarations to the Italians. He agreed that a political declaration of keeping the pledge of the Atlantic Charter was all right, since it did not go beyond the statements already made. Specifically, they did not wish to commit to Sforza.

I did not tell him that reciting the Atlantic Charter by an American was quite sufficient to get the adherence of groups in Italy who had declined to accede to the British position because, fundamentally, they do not believe generalities when the British talk about them, and they do believe our statements. . . .

To Hull, November 16, 1942

The handling of the French Government in North Africa is, at the moment, largely determined by the Military Command; and the factors are still obscure. I express an opinion only with hesitation; but feel that certain observations are justified at this time.

If use is being made of Admiral Darlan merely to give legitimacy to the government of General Giraud, and to draw into the picture the remaining elements of possible military and governmental resistance in North Africa, then the temporary use of Darlan as apparent governing authority in North Africa can be defended.

But if it is planned to recognize Darlan as a permanent integral or major factor in French North African government, then I am very clear that immediate difficulties will flow from it. These are, in order:

(a) The immediate feeling by the Fighting French authorities in

French Equatorial Africa and the Cameroons, that they are being betrayed. . . .

(b) For what weight you may wish to give it, a large part of the press, both conservative and liberal, will probably attack everyone concerned for setting up what they will term a "semi-Fascist" government in French territory. Darlan was active in forming the Pétain government along Fascist lines; his emergence will be taken as indicating that the State Department favors continuance of such a government. The accusation will be distorted and unjust; but will have enough color behind it to make trouble.

My own impression is that the desirable thing to do is to use Darlan merely as a temporary vehicle of succession, turning actual governmental authority over to more trustworthy elements as rapidly as possible. Even this is not without danger. . . .

(c) I presume the attitude of the British has been ascertained on the point, so I do not comment on that side of the matter. Acceptance of Darlan would seem to be contrary to all of their previous statements on the subject; and he is a confirmed Anglo-phobe.

(d) Finally, it would seem almost essential that we promptly get at the business of trying to unify, as well as we can, the fragments of French authority which now rule New Caledonia, the Cameroons, French Equatorial Africa, Madagascar and Syria, in the name of De Gaulle and the French government which is set up in Algiers and in Morocco. . . .

I do not know the discussions which led to the reappearance of Darlan. The reports of the situation on the ground are being transmitted entirely through military sources. It may be that there are elements in the situation which would change the picture as given by the press and our own cables. Darlan's character, past associations and history, of course, cannot be changed.

November 18, 1942

The repercussions from the Italian speech Saturday night continue to come in; I gather that as propaganda it worked out all right. It also, however, set out their national atmosphere towards Italy—one of friendship towards the people, though unvarying hostility to the Fascist Government and their Nazi masters. It may conceivably be of some help. . . .

A considerable amount of thought on the post-war economic readjustments here. The closer you get to the problem, the more difficult it becomes.

November 21, 1942

Yesterday, a Committee meeting in my office. We got started on what may be ultimately the germ of a European economic plan.

Briefly, the idea is to see whether we can start to recreate the many clashing national economies in Europe, with separate exchange, tariffs, transport, and so forth, or whether we take advantage of the fact that the Germans have wiped the slate clean, and try to see that they begin to fuse as an economic region with reasonably open trade barriers, reasonably open transport, and reasonably open agricultural and other, similar arrangements.

We have to settle this rapidly, because as soon as our troops land on the soil of the continent, we shall either permit the governments-in-exile to move in and start shoving for their individual interests, or we will have to try to guide the occupations into something like a continuous and working arrangement.

I likewise got started on how we will handle Tripoli. The North African invasion has gone a lot better than I, personally, thought it would, with the result that we may be in Tripoli in a few weeks. We have no Italian arrangements set up in respect of Tripoli, and indeed no Italian personalities to work with, in the same sense that we have French. It looks to me like a military government and nothing else but, for the time being. . . .

ECONOMIC POLICY IN REGARD TO WESTERN EUROPE

. . . The first problem of the West European plan is, therefore, a determination as to whether we steer in the main for highly nationalized economies or for a high economic common denominator for the region.

The Possibility of a Unified Western Europe.

There is a good deal to be said for the conception of an economically unified western Europe. There are also grave difficulties. . . .

Possible Line to be Taken if United Nations Undertake to Construct West Europe as a Whole.

In the event that the United Nations undertake to construct west Europe as a whole, it would seem that the most promising line would be for them to choose the smallest possible number of economic functions and undertake to make these an economic common denominator. Among the functions which would thus have to be considered are:

  (a) The creation of a customs union within the area.
  (b) The creation of a transport union within the area.
  (c) Possibly the creation of a monetary union within the area, or, in the alternative, the construction of a financial institution capable of relieving the stresses occasioned by lack of international currency.
  (d) The creation of a communications union.

In addition to these four, there are others which might come under consideration, although under open trade it might be possible to allow a natural grouping based on the mere results of trading and commercial operations.

A combined agricultural administration to effect a more or less uniform agricultural policy would likewise have to be considered.

November 25, 1942

At the moment, the government of North Africa lies, as far as I can see, entirely in the hands of General Eisenhower, who is reporting to the War Department, which in turn is probably reporting to the President. Everyone thinks the situation is terrible, but I don't; I think it merely reflects the fact that our forces are spread out along the north coast of Africa, and the civil government of the African Empire will have to wobble along as best it can until they get around to combing it out. Substantially, Darlan is giving orders and other people are obeying them—which saves our people from having to send detachments all over North Africa. . . .

About all we can do at this stage of the game is to keep on thinking about it and get all the information we can. Plainly, Darlan will not do for any length of time; there is very great bitterness in England against his reappearance, and the policy ought to be the construction of an *ad hoc* military government, after which Darlan should be allowed to slide gently down the current of history. . . .

November 28, 1942

Thursday, November 26. Thanksgiving. A long conference this morning in the Secretary's office, chiefly about North Africa and the North African Government. . . . Darlan's appearance was of course a pure accident; the army had expected to work primarily with Giraud. As Lieutenant General [Mark] Clark, who had to handle the matter, put it: "I have two king pins (Giraud and Darlan) but I will wiggle out of this somehow." He actually did wiggle out of it by accepting the fact that Darlan alone could deliver North Africa (which Darlan did) and by inducing Giraud to accept an active command of the French forces which are now going into battle against the Germans in Tunis. Eisenhower's letter asking the President to accept the situation is a masterpiece; he pointed out that unless the French troops laid down their arms he would have to detach perhaps sixty thousand men to tackle occupation jobs all over the place, and abandon the drive on Tunis and Bizerte; and I gather only God could tell whether the Arab tribes would rise. Anyhow, the President, not unnaturally, accepted it, though he later issued the statement that we had no political commitment to Darlan, as hell broke loose in England and in liberal and pro-De Gaullist circles in the United States. . . .

Friday, Nov. 27. News came in of the sinking of the French fleet. We have only a dim knowledge of the circumstances. But apparently it is the last word in complete drama, if the radio tales are half true.

I have been hard at work trying to develop plans for political warfare in Italy.

Nov. 28. Tixier came in today. . . . It was a strange, violent and emotional sort of conversation; indeed, with justification. Darlan, in the eyes of the De Gaullists, is a traitor; and he did condemn De Gaulle to death. Now he has the power, for the time being, and maybe for some time; while De Gaulle, who fought not wisely perhaps, but certainly as well as he could, feels that he may be asked to take second place.

The Secretary tells me that De Gaulle is coming here. . . . Certainly his adherence made as much trouble for us as good. But I do not consider this as any kind of a spirit to re-establish France; and will do what I can.

December 3, 1942

Lunch with Professor (now Commander) Sam Morison. He was on the *Brooklyn* with the fleet when it went into Casablanca. The *Brooklyn* was in action for nine hours, and the story was nothing if not dramatic. For one thing, the President's appeal to Frenchmen was broadcast exactly one hour before they landed, and I gather the fleet had a low opinion of it. However, the Frenchmen didn't wake up. The surprise was therefore complete. There were some minor scandals. The sixteen-inch shells fired by our men landed on the battleship *Jean Bart*—first-class gunnery; but the shells failed to go off. The Admiral of the French fleet later thanked our Admiral for sending blank shells indicating that he could have sunk the *Jean Bart* if he had wanted to, but was trying to be decent about it. I hope nobody disillusioned him! . . .

December 15, 1942

Yesterday, some work on the forward political plans. The staff officers of course have been doing some thinking, and I some talking with them. But however it goes it seems to me that the jugular vein of the German resistance is somewhere in Central Europe, and by consequence, the affairs of Yugoslavia and Hungary as well as Italy are of vital importance to us. . . .

To the Twentieth Century Fund board of directors meeting; it is, in general, an up and coming and upstanding board, and I have always enjoyed it. Francis Biddle was in excellent form, and one way and another we had a gay and happy time. There are some good men still left in the world, though they are not always apparent. . . .

December 18–22, 1942

In Canada. 34 degrees below zero.

A very pleasant visit with Pierrepont Moffat, who was unfortunately laid up with a game leg. I saw pretty much all of the Canadian personages, and tried to get them up-to-date on the state of the nation. This accomplishes nothing except that it keeps the Canadians aware of the fact that we are not forgetting them.

Ottawa is full of yarns about the Darlan matter. One of them is that we delayed landing in North Africa for two weeks until we could complete arrangements with Darlan. I don't know that facts have anything to do with this, but I said the date, November 7, had been fixed by the Almanac because the tide and the moon happened to be right that day.

Arranged to revamp the Joint Canadian-American Economic Committee.

December 24, 1942

A meeting of the Joint Intelligence Committee, working on Russian and German capabilities and so forth; coming out of the meeting we heard the news of Darlan's assassination. . . .

December 28, 1942

The North African situation continues to hold the center of the stage. We made diplomatic representations asking the British would they please calm down their gloating over Darlan's assassination—and they finally had sense enough to do this. Otherwise they would have come perilously close to convicting themselves of the assassination. Actually, it seems to have been done by a half-crazy young Frenchman who had been worked up into a state of hysteria by the anti-Pétain, anti-Darlan propaganda. He was convicted and shot by court-martial, which was the obvious and sensible way to deal with the case; had anyone made a state trial out of it we might have split North Africa from end to end.

Assassinations are not things to rejoice about. I think people who like them are far too likely to get their belly full before this is over. . . .

Meanwhile, the British have been doing their damndest to get an arrangement by which De Gaulle is in charge in North Africa. De Gaulle was supposed to come here and Secretary Hull has gone to bat asking that his trip be delayed, as I hope it may be. If they let Giraud alone for a few days or weeks, I think that he will probably prove to be the common element in the situation, and as he has more standing than De Gaulle this may prove the solution. It may be noted that our own plan was to build things about Giraud in North Africa at least, and hope that we might gradually get some unity in the situation by that route.

There are intrigues in all directions in this business, and one has to move carefully.

The Yugoslav situation is not much better, with the Russians backing the Partisans and the British, as nearly as I can find out, backing General [Draja] Mihailovich; I myself am hoping we can work out an accord there which should be in the nature of a Popular Front government, but it is close going.

Still working on Hungarian affairs. Unhappily, it is clear that anything we do which would effectively help us to win the war will probably perpetrate the bitterest and filthiest kind of attack from the [Eduard] Beneš [of Chechoslovakia] propaganda machine here. . . .

January 1, 1943

. . . a meeting of the Joint Intelligence Committee yesterday. Behind the reasoning [of resulting memorandum] is this:

By reason of North Africa and other military operations, the Germans are now "contained". But the fortress of Europe is not cracked. Further, the shipping losses have been so great that we have not built up that vast reserve of shipping permitting us to send to Europe an overwhelming mass of men and supplies capable of defeating the enemy on the mainland of Europe. We probably can gradually produce a more or less overwhelming air force, but this by itself is not enough.

We can of course simply sit down and besiege the continent of Europe. But in that case, probably the Russians would be increasingly under pressure, since their food situation will be difficult this year and next year may be very bad; their supply lines to the United States are relatively small, and they will have taken a terrific punishment. To remain quiescent, therefore, inflicts on them an almost intolerable burden.

Also, the peripheral populations such as Poland, Czechoslovakia, Yugoslavia, Greece, and in almost equal degree ultimately Norway, Holland, Belgium, and France will be more or less rapidly threatened with extermination. Certainly this is true of Poland and of Greece, and will be importantly true elsewhere. A siege of Europe may mean condemning whole nationalities to slow or swift death.

If, therefore, we adopt the principle of attack, it must be attack by relatively small, highly organized and highly armed forces, timed to coincide with political and military developments inside the fortress of Europe. In practice, this means a shift of allegiance of all or part of the Hungarian Army, and all or part of the Bulgarian Army or of fragments of the Rumanian Army, or any combination of these units. With this, of course, would go the popular risings and guerrilla operations which are already being carried on importantly in Yugoslavia and to less extent in Albania. Conceivably also there might be some major development in Italy, though this seems to be unlikely.

But if we are to get any of these things done, we have to start organizing now. The lines are hanging out in all directions, which we can use if we wish. Many of them result from contacts which I made in the Department; and the problem is to develop them so that they are available to the fullest extent practicable in achieving a victory.

The existence of such contacts gave us the information on which we could base a decision as to whether we would invade North Africa; and having decided to invade North Africa, these contacts made a swift victory possible. I believe we should tackle the same job now.

January 4, 1943

A fairly long conversation with Sumner. Churchill is coming here pretty soon and this may obviate some of the difficulties. I was pushing for an all-out accord with the British on major political policy. We are at odds now, because the British seem to be bent on a rule or ruin policy. The De Gaulle–Giraud controversy reflects in large measure the desire of the British Foreign Office to have a public government of their own in North Africa, and there is an undercurrent of latent resentment that the United States appears in the area as a political factor at all.

I wanted Sumner to go to London on a special mission to try to work out some of these questions. But as Sumner says, Churchill's advent here means that they will be handled direct.

The antagonism between Secretary Hull and Mr. Welles makes a good deal of difficulty; the Secretary resents Sumner's going to the White House too much but as he does not go very much himself, this leaves the President at the mercy of unskilled advisers like Bullitt, etc.; and things naturally go at 6's and 7's. But there is not much to be done about it. . . .

January 12, 1943

I suppose the big strategic decisions are probably being made now and far away. Roughly, the great issue is whether we push for victory in

1943 or whether we besiege the fortress of Europe. Ultimately, the decision must be taken on grounds of physical necessity which, I suppose, in practice comes down to ships. By consequence, you will have to multiply military possibilities by political possibilities to get any result at all. . . .

General Sikorski tells me he thinks that he can make an arrangement with Stalin which will stick. When I asked him whether Stalin was to be trusted, he said, of course not, but one could trust circumstances, and they would set up a kind of balance which he thought would make possible the working up of reasonable and fair relations.

Sikorski is bitter [about] Beneš, who, according to him, has tried to play both ends against the middle, and sacrifice the rest of the small powers in order to be a favorite little brother to the Soviets. Regrettably, there is a good deal of evidence to support this.

Our own work here, as I see it, has to form four lines:

(1) The consolidation of the various possibilities which exist in Central Europe. This means: an all-out attempt to resolve the civil war presently raging in Yugoslavia between the Croats and the Serbs, or, if you like, the Partisans and the Yugoslav government-in-exile, or between a revolution stimulated by Russia and a nativist movement headed by the Serbs; the organization of some all-out Hungarian resistance; the attraction of some fragments of Rumanians (Rumania is in such disorder it is difficult to see how anything can be done there); and an endeavor to crack the Bulgarian situation.

If we can combine any substantial number of these elements the invasion of Southeast Europe should be possible.

(2) The slow and steady evolution towards a unified France. General De Gaulle has now laid down his terms—unification of French forces if he is at the head of them, otherwise not. General Giraud would like to be recognized as the provisional government. I do not see that he is any great French leader either. Possibly out of the lot we can develop some real leadership, though the proposal to call the legislature in Algiers as a political theater of selection does not to my mind seem very intelligent. It is being pushed from London.

(3) The working out of a common political policy with the British (I hope that may be done this week), and

(4) The working up of some sort of economic policy for pre-armistice and post-war use.

This last will be extremely difficult because American sentiment is becoming increasingly nationalist and increasingly impatient of arrangements built to assist foreign nations.

January 13, 1943

I began the day with the Secretary and Atherton. [H. F. A.] Schoenfeld, our Minister in Helsinki, is back and has been talking with the Secretary. As a result of this, and some other problems, the Secretary believes we should get closer to the Russians in all matters of governments-in-exile. The problem is how to establish closer contact. Atherton and I then adjourned to get up a memorandum. As I see it, this may be the opening towards a closer relationship with Russia, which I think is all to the good. . . .

Lunch with Schoenfeld. He gives a fascinating account of the Finnish position. He thinks the Finns may back out of the war, but not immediately. They claim, of course, not to have taken an active part in the summer campaign, but they have nevertheless tied up twenty-two Russian divisions which were badly needed elsewhere. He raised with me, too, the question of closer relations with Russia, thinking that mere contact and continuity would help, as a starter. I think he is right. . . .

Then [Peter] Bergson came in, to discuss the horrible fate of the Jews —and it is horrible, indeed. Our own reports show some hundreds of thousands massacred in Kaunas; with even the Gestapo executioner finally going mad, as a result.

February 2, 1943
    . . . The preponderance of the evidence leads to the belief that the Germans had a chance to save the bulk of their forces by drastic withdrawal in November, but that since they could not do this, they are now compelled to withdraw in Russia over a wide front with far heavier losses, both in men and matériel, than they had anticipated. In the Joint Intelligence Committee, the American staff members regard this mood as over-optimistic; but then our staff people have persistently under-estimated Russian capabilities. . . .

The President and Churchill went into the North African situation and apparently supported our own view of it, namely, that this is a big empire and political evolution has to go slow. General De Gaulle seems to like the President, but is furious against Giraud, and his people here are intriguing in all possible ways against the Giraud people so that nothing like a happy marriage is in prospect.

Finally, the long, slow shadow of the coming European revolution is projecting itself pretty much everywhere. The Russians may have abandoned their general imperialistic view; and many well-informed people believe that they have. I hope so. But I feel bound to say that from the angles of the stuff that comes over my desk, every disposition seems to have been taken to create the largest fifth column possible everywhere; and that measures are promptly taken to try to discredit or eliminate all figures in Central Europe and, to less extent, in Western Europe who show any indication that they will not be subservient to the Russian idea. . . .

Meanwhile, Ray Atherton and I have firmly recommended an endeavor to try to reach an understanding with the Russians, and I hope this is going forward. Whether an understanding is possible of course remains to be seen. I should be happy if the Secretary would delegate this to Sumner Welles, who, I believe, would be as likely to get a result as anyone. I am very clear that if we finally reach the continent of Europe without some pre-arranged understanding, there will be a very fair chance that the conflict will take an entirely different form.

It is a big picture and difficult to understand.

Politically the Administration is losing ground all over the country. The President is personally popular; the Administration, if one can put it that way, is not. Secretary Hull seems to be the only one who really preserves an unimpaired position; and he, of course, is under continuous and rather vicious attack by left-wing circles, as are we all.

February 24, 1943

The Secretary is ill again, and Sumner is taking over. . . .

Anthony Eden will be here, probably on Saturday, and I imagine the real preliminaries as to political arrangements in Europe will be discussed. The clash, of course, will be on Russia. While the Russians have said very little overtly, their activities in propaganda and otherwise here make it clear that they propose a revolution practically all over Europe— and the revolution will have all the trimmings attached—terror included. . . .

The rest of the time, working on possible Canadian-American and other negotiations for the preliminaries of an aviation agreement. This is, in its way, busy work, since the fundamental difficulties lie closer at hand. . . .

Draft for Hull, March 10, 1943

Re: Balkan Policy

This Government has been receiving a number of communications that certain groups in the so-called "satellite states", namely, Hungary, Rumania and Bulgaria, would like to establish channels of communication with the State Department for the purpose of discussing a possible shift from the side of the Axis to the side of the United Nations. In handling these tentatives the Department has consistently endeavored to secure all possible information, but has declined to enter any discussions. Since most of the individuals thus seeking to establish contact plainly have in mind protection against a possible Russian invasion, the Department has made it clear that this Government intended loyally to maintain its alliance with Russia and would not be party to any anti-Russian intrigue.

In the event of the landing of a United Nations force on the continent of Europe, the problem will arise whether any of the possibilities apparently available should be used for purposes of political warfare. . . .

It is the view of this Government that elements desiring to assume an anti-Axis position must do so without receiving definite pledges from the United Nations, and must rely on the general pledges contained in the Atlantic Charter. Plainly, a shift from the Axis to the United Nations side will put these elements or their governments in a somewhat better position at the close of hostilities than would be the case if they continue to be enemies to the end.

It is the view of the Department that the governments of these countries, as and when they are liberated, must be chosen by the free act of the peoples of these countries, and that the policies adopted should, within the limits of possibility, be directed toward creating conditions in which such free choice can be made. . . .

April 10, 1943

One of the principal reasons for Eden's visit was to try to determine the relative positions of Russia, Britain and the United States. The British are very clear that they cannot swing their position alone—which, of course, is true. They are not clear whether we will stay with them, and under our Constitutional practice there is no way by which any assurance can be given. They had a 20-year treaty of military assistance with Russia —which is designed to give them a chance to re-insure their position (to use Welles's phrase) by hitting into a Russian alliance. This is not defined in the sense that certain questions are still open for discussion: notably, the arrangement of Eastern Europe. . . .

To Roosevelt, April 19, 1943

As perhaps you know, the British Government invited me to go to England last December. This is partly an *amende honorable* for an unpleasant incident in which the British Intelligence was involved, some time ago. At that time, Secretary Hull thought it was inadvisable, and so did I.

Mr. Anthony Eden repeated the invitation when he was here; and I have taken it up with the Secretary. He sees no objection, but believes it should be determined upon by you. I therefore ask leave to go to England for a couple of weeks, at the earliest available opportunity.

There are excuses for going: notably, to get their thinking on problems of aviation and investment, and on possible collaboration in labor policy. These are, as I say, excuses. The real reason is that no senior officer of this Department has been out of Washington since 1940,—aside from Sumner Welles's trip to Rio. I have a feeling that State Department thinking would be helped by some contact with the thinking in London. If on the way back it were possible to come through North Africa and Dakar, so much the better.

May 12, 1943

The fighting around Tunis and Bizerte is now substantially over. Nothing but mopping up remains. The next operation has already commenced, and I suppose we shall have news of it at any time. I hope it goes well.

I today started arrangements to prepare for possible occupation of the Dodecanese—and I suppose eventually Crete, though that will take more time.

Churchill is in Washington. The issue is whether the United States will take over Italy; our General Staff is adamant against it, feeling that there is nothing to be got by the occupation of Italy except the liability to feed a dependent population:—better leave that to the Germans. I am not clear that it will work out that way. I think the Germans will hand us Italy on a gold plate.

The possibility of an Italian government is uppermost. Sumner Welles believes that Lord Rennell [Major-General Francis James Rennell Rodd, Civil Affairs Administration for Middle East, East Africa, and Italy] is anxious to push in someone like [Count Dino] Grandi—which is no good. The British have turned thumbs down on Count Sforza. I asked Sumner whether he and I were going to get the blame for that—the fact, of course, being that he had been rather hoping for a liberal government in Italy, which might possibly be worked out. But Sumner thinks the British want control of Italy, as part of their complete control of the Mediterranean.

It is pretty plain that the second front will be in the Balkans. I am not clear whether the Russians would like this.

The President has OK'd my trip to England, and wants to talk to me first. As soon as I get back, after a week's rest in the country, we can do this; there is not much chance, anyhow, of seeing him, until Churchill gets out of town.

May 26, 1943

Dinner at the Mayflower with Lord [Frederick James] Leathers [Minister of War Transport]. . . . He said that the Churchill-Roosevelt conference had at length reached some square decisions and he had accordingly spent all night and then some in working out the shipping and other facilities, which I gather run both through 1943 and 1944.

He likewise told me that he expected to have the air transport job dumped in his lap. I said we would look forward with pleasure to contact with him because I expected that this would have to be discussed in the not distant future. We talked generally about the nature of the problems involved.

Yesterday, a quiet although busy day, with considerable happening. The next military move I suppose will happen in the not too distant future. I am inclined to guess that the American Command may be perpetuated.

Diverse secret but certain advices make it plain that Winston Churchill has finally got a clear picture of the activities of some of the De Gaullists here, and finds them intolerable, as we do. I am in hopes that this may lead to a clearer approach to the whole situation. Fortunately for De Gaulle, causes are sometimes greater than men, but the problems are here just the same. . . .

Last night, over a quiet drink with Sumner Welles, he told me that the program of assistance to the Chinese had been pretty well deferred; he was very much worried about it. He feared the Chinese would crack. So do I.

The Comintern is dissolved, but there have been four or five coincidences in four or five days—one in which Communist sources asked Sumner to intervene and assist in the release of some Communist cell leaders in various parts of this Hemisphere. We happen to know from intelligence reports that Browder, who was engaged in some of these requests, regards Sumner as a fool and an easy mark. Sumner is of course fully informed as to what is going on. . . .

June 15, 1943

To the Treasury, where Harry White and I opened an informal conference consisting of about 16 delegations, relating to monetary stabilization. Again, the experts talked, but it boils down to some pretty simple issues: shall we try a joint stabilization fund operation? Can we use it to give value to our gold? Since other countries have not gold, can we let them multiply their limited resources of that metal by adding a certain amount of their own currency and bonds? Having done this, can we agree on sane exchange rates to begin with, and a sane procedure for changing rates thereafter?

The significance of the meeting was not what it said, but that it was the first more or less democratic procedure for dealing with this sort of thing. . . .

To Hull, June 18, 1943

We have before us an overture from General Franco to enter into an agreement supplying his Government with certain arms and armament matériel. In my considered opinion . . . sale of military equipment to Spain is unnecessary either to preserve Spanish neutrality or to assist in safeguarding our forces in North Africa. In any case, we have better use for the equipment. Such sale could only amount, now, to strengthening one political group in Spain against another. . . .

June 19, 1943

Three days ago, the negotiations in Algiers looked as though the De Gaullists had so arranged matters that they would entirely control the French Army in North Africa. They did this by secretly changing the voting power of the National Committee on Liberation so as to give them a majority; accompanied with this was De Gaulle's demand for an arrangement virtually reducing Giraud to a figurehead. This was supposed to pave the way for a "purge"—nominally of officers favorable to Fascism but actually, of course, designed to strengthen the political grip on the Army. Since this will be the army that enters France, the real stake was military control of liberated France.

At this point the Secretary got sufficiently excited to urge the President to block it. He likewise urged that Churchill be at least equally active in the matter.

It so happened that Churchill was getting pretty suspicious of De Gaulle himself. At all events, Richard Law [Parliamentary Under Secretary of State for Foreign Affairs], when he was here, observed that De Gaulle was getting to be embarrassing; so also did Lord Leathers, and I have heard it from other British sources.

The result of this was that yesterday we got by cable the confidential directive of the British Government to the British press. It said in substance that Churchill had lost confidence in De Gaulle; that De Gaulle had Fascist and dictatorial tendencies; that he had posed first as a bulwark against Communism and now as the representative of the Communist forces; and that the press should stop slanting their news from Africa in favor of De Gaulle. It will be interesting to see how the result plays out there.

The British have been paying approximately 60 million dollars a year to General De Gaulle. They now are transferring this payment to the Committee on Liberation in its collective capacity. They hope that the French Empire can be self-supporting when it is unified. It is likewise rumored that De Gaulle has been receiving very large funds from the Russians. This last has not been verified.

I thought I was going to England in response to Anthony Eden's invitation. But Mr. Hull got very mournful about it, not only because there is a great deal to do here, but really because he is a little worried and afraid when anyone gets active. He is hardly to be blamed in view of the fact that during his 10 years almost everybody has tried to be Secretary of State over his head: Moley, Hopkins, Wallace, and so on. But it makes life a little difficult. I am writing Halifax and Eden.

There is, however, a valid reason for not going now that the monetary stabilization talks are beginning to be active; likewise, aviation matters are coming to a high state of boil.

June 22, 1943

Dr. Nahum Goldmann [of the Jewish Agency for Palestine] came in to see me, to raise two points.

First, he wanted to know whether the State Department could not now take the lead in getting the appointment and an announcement of the commission to try crimes against civilians—with special reference to Germans who had committed atrocities in connection with the Jewish massacres.

I said that this matter was before the President and that I did not see that there was anything further the State Department could do.

Second, he said that they had been canvassing the matter of Palestine, in London. They were now convinced, from interviews with British officials, that Britain was prepared to abandon the doctrine of the White Paper—which in any case closed Palestine to immigration beginning April next. He said that there was general agreement that if the United States would take joint responsibility this would ease matters greatly. He wondered whether we could not initiate a move to that effect.

I said that I had always dealt with extreme frankness in this entire Jewish matter, and I wished to continue to do so. There were many elements to be considered in connection with any move by the United States to assume joint responsibility for Palestine—a responsibility she had declined to assume in the days of President Wilson. But one of the most potent reasons was the simple fact that this Department had no right to assume responsibilities in Palestine—or for that matter, elsewhere overseas—until it was assured that the public opinion of the country and the

Congress of the United States was prepared to go through with the obligations accepted. Assumption of joint responsibilty meant pledging the United States to use men and money, and perhaps force, in that region. Only the Congress of the United States could give us the authority to make good on any responsibility assumed. Until this preliminary question was settled, it did not seem to me that we were in any shape to initiate such move.

. . . Quite irrespective of the personal feelings of any of us, the assumption of overseas responsibilities by the United States was a historic decision of such importance that it had to be most carefully considered, and done in the knowledge of full support by the country.

July 10, 1943

Secretary Hull told me yesterday that the President had offered him control of a variety of overseas economic affairs, notably relief, rehabilitation, and so forth. He told me that he had turned down the whole thing. I suppose this probably is necessary: They are controversial and not much can be done about them. If he had had them in the first place, and had staffed them, perhaps something could be done. . . .

We are endeavoring to work out with the British some method of reducing the tension between the Russians and the Poles and perhaps getting them to re-establish relations. But General Sikorski's death does not help. At the Requiem Mass for him today I was thinking that Sikorski, as a man, had been able to bridge the huge gaps between the positions which Poland must somehow bridge to continue as a nation; and there is no replacement for him. Possible replacements are dying by hundreds in the German concentration camps. Unfortunately, we have pretty clear evidence of this; the eyewitness account of Karski, an escaped member of the Polish underground, given by the Polish Ambassador to Loy Henderson, [Elbridge] Durbrow [European Affairs], [Charles E.] Bohlen [European Affairs] and myself last Wednesday night, makes this all too abundantly clear.

We landed in Sicily at dawn this morning. I hope that it goes well. The crucial question is what view the Italians will take of an invasion on their own soil.

General Giraud is in town. The foreign policy of the United States in connection with Africa is under vivid attack, principally by Lippmann and that group of papers. This is worrying the Secretary. Not having had any active hand in playing the political end since the landing last November, I cannot judge too well whether it was played well or ill; but I do know that the tactics of the De Gaulle group have been anything but truthful or honorable. Unless De Gaulle, as a man and a leader, is a great deal better than the methods his people are using, the Secretary is entirely right in judging him too dangerous to be astride our line of communication.

July 28, 1943

On Sunday, the 24th, after a dull morning in the Department, I went canoeing on the Potomac with Rudolf [Berle] and Beatrice. In the late afternoon we put in at Sycamore Island, where Mr. Kessler, of the Department of Agriculture, was spending Sunday. He said that the radio had reported the resignation of Mussolini. I telephoned the Department to find out that the source was Radio Roma, and concluded that it was authentic; later, discovering that [Pietro] Badoglio had formed his government. There seemed to be nothing to be done about it at the time, and we ate a quiet meal by the river, considering that the climax of one act of the drama was taking place. But that it was the end of the road seemed out of the question; Italy has no such significance for Germany in this war as did Austria in the previous war.

In the morning with the Secretary on various matters; some discussion of Italian affairs. The Secretary in excellent form: he seemed to think that matters were beginning to clear up. The problem of the attitude towards the King and Badoglio was discussed a little; he was fairly clear that we ought not at this time to take any hand in breaking down such structure as there was. He said that while it was likely that Badoglio would want to make peace, the problem of withdrawing the Italian divisions from Yugoslavia and the outlying positions was a staggering one. I observed that even the doctrine of unconditional surrender contemplated that somebody would make the surrender; it seemed to me that the ignominy of surrender ought to be tied as firmly as possible to a Fascist tail, rather than have that burden thrown on some new government, which we might wish to encourage.

That night the OWI, following a direction by Jimmy Warburg [Deputy Director] and Russell Barnes [radio division], came out with a string of broadcasts designed to undermine the King and Badoglio. This is really because Russell Barnes and Jimmy Warburg are following an extreme left-wing line in New York, without bothering to integrate their views with the Department of State.

Tuesday morning again we met in the Secretary's office; the Secretary was obviously hurt and angry. He telephoned the President about it, with the result that two hours later the President, in his press conference, repudiated the OWI broadcast as not expressing American policy. That at least is one way to get unity in American war agencies.

Today both the Yugoslav [Constantin Fotitch] and the Greek Ambassadors came by, to get whatever impressions they could of the Italian affair; plainly, both were beginning to see the possibility of liberation and, I might add, the possibility of getting even with their respective neighbors, Bulgaria and Hungary.

On Sunday morning likewise there was published the Moscow Manifesto of the Free German Group. This may be the Soviet bid for domination of the post-Hitler German government. I sat down with Durbrow, of the Russian division, and a string of documents to take account of stock. The Soviets, through their ambassador in London, have served notice upon the Greeks and Yugoslavs that nothing must be done in the Aegean area without first consulting Russia, intimating that Russian interests might run to the Adriatic. There is of course the Communist Manifesto already promulgated in Greece, and the active Communist-led Partisan movement in Croatia.

There is not anything very much in Italy. . . .

The Soviet Government is already the guide, philosopher and friend of Beneš and the Czechs.

When to this combination is added the Free Polish Committee now equipped with a Polish Red Army, and the possibility of a similar movement in Germany, it looks as though the Russian claim is pretty thoroughly staked out. Certainly there has been no abandonment of the desire for a Communist-led revolution in Spain.

This may be bracketed likewise with the very active movements which are going on in Latin America. Oumansky, the principal artist at this kind of thing, is in Mexico [as Ambassador]; a meeting dominated by [Vicente Lombardo] Toledano [Mexican labor leader] is about to be held in Cuba; and other tie-ups of less importance are going on up and down the coast, two notable ones being in Chile and in Peru. I should gather that the preliminary phases of the world revolution are tolerably far forward.

We are at work on the outline of three or four speeches for the Secretary, designed to be an authoritative exposition of American policy. The time is surely ripe.

August 5, 1943

On Saturday we met in the Secretary's office to consider some of the possible questions of an Italian Armistice: the Secretary was not so clear that anybody would ask for one.

It was pretty plain that we were running into very heavy weather. Contrary to a prior tacit understanding, the British, instead of making a joint statement with us to the Russian Government as to the outlined intent, had made its own statement, leaving us to deal separately with the Russians in that regard. (People do forget that there was a twenty-year military alliance between Britain and Russia: but whether this extends to matters of this kind, I am not clear.)

The Italians asked that Rome be made an open city; a matter for the Army, primarily, but their conditions would amount to denying transportation rights to the Allies, thus insuring a safe line for the Germans in the north of Italy. In other words, Rome was not to be an open city as long as it was of advantage to the Italians to use it militarily, but was to become an open city as soon as it became of advantage to the Germans to have it so. I am pretty clear that the result will be some more bombing of Rome before we are through.

Monday and Tuesday, an everlasting amount of work on the infernal question of the French. Over the weekend the Committee of National Liberation in Algiers did a typical French political stunt: they unified the command, De Gaulle handing over with great fanfare command of the troops to Giraud. At the same time, however, they cooked up an arrangement by which the Committee of Liberation and a subordinate committee, the Committee of National Defense, was to have control over the army in command: substantially enabling it to fire General Giraud. Meantime, we are supposed to equip 300,000 French troops, under a command we do not know, and with commitments which we have not been told.

On Wednesday we rounded up. The British had previously been advised of our proposed formula of recognition; they proposed a much fuller formula, which included ratification of all prior commitments of the French National Committee sitting in London: we do not know what these are. The message contained an intimation that the British and the Russians might go ahead and recognize, anyway, irrespective. There was considerable discussion and various points of view expressed; Sumner being of the view that we had best stick strictly to a firm statement of our military rights, and let it go at that; Jimmy Dunn and some of the rest feeling that we ought to see what we can make out of the Committee, but try to restore the balance. The Secretary said, forthrightly and bluntly, that when it came to equipping 300,000 men commanded by a group of people who had demonstrated a bitter enmity toward the United States, and without even any arrangement for a unified command, he could not see it. When somebody suggested that maybe the simplest thing would be to accept the *fait accompli* which the British and Russians might produce, he switched off and said: "You remind me of Davey Crockett's coon. Davey shot a hundred and five bears in a season and his reputation spread so that whenever he came to a tree the coon came down and rolled over at his feet, to save him the trouble of shooting."

The general view is that we ought to accept a part of the British formula but stick to our own insistence that all of this must be subject to the necessary overriding military authority of the Allied Command.

Following out a line of thought which I had canvassed with Chip Bohlen and Durbrow on Sunday, I held out for an evening with Stalin's "Foundations of Leninism" and a string of reports. They certainly set up a program for a first-class bid for domination of a fair proportion of the world. . . .

I note two historical points of interest: first, that this follows very much the tactical pattern blocked out by Stalin in his book; second, that it is not unlike the great ambition of the Tsar Alexander after the Napoleonic wars. Tsar Alexander did substantially dominate the situation for a couple of years, after which Russia withdrew into herself. But he had developed no such foundation of support within the countries which he sought to dominate. . . .

Further, as I see it we may be really at grips with this situation inside a very short time. If Hitler goes overboard, and the next thrust is in the Balkans, we shall then have not office calculations to deal with, but actual contact of American armed forces with armed forces actually a part of this great arrangement; and the attitudes will have to be taken by them in the field. As the Secretary put it when someone urged immediate action: "Full steam ahead in a thick fog."

September 1, 1943

I have read of Cabinet crises in other countries; have lived through the Cabinet reorganization when [Harry] Woodring resigned, Stimson was appointed Secretary of War and Louis Johnson had to retire. But the

State Department crisis has been more poignant and unhappy than anything I have yet encountered.

On August 18, Secretary Hull left for Quebec taking with him Jimmy Dunn, his principal adviser. Sumner became Acting Secretary. The next three days were as dull as anyone could wish, for all the work and the drama were at Quebec. Had they approached the Russian situation? If so, how? Who would do it? And against this background were huge military decisions.

. . . [Sunday] morning I got a telephone call from Sumner asking whether I expected to be in the Department. I arranged to meet him at five o'clock Sunday afternoon, which I did. He was clearing his desk, dictating letters of farewell, and was tired out. He said that he had submitted his resignation and that on the previous Monday (August 16) he had talked to the President and the President accepted it. He added that he never would forget the extremely kind words which the President had said to him in respect to his many services to the United States. He was now leaving for Bar Harbor and asked me to assume charge. He had talked to the Secretary by telephone at Quebec and Hull had agreed. We spent a few moments recalling old times, and how we had worked in the new field in '33 and nearly got shot together one night in Habana; and had had many adventures since.

I then tried to persuade him to stay here until the Secretary got back. I told him I thought the story could not fail to get out if he left then. Both in his political interest and every other interest I hoped that he would stay by. Sumner thought he could not; best get away. The Secretary would announce the acceptance of his resignation when he reached town the following Thursday; there would be a week of unpleasant and difficult comment then complete obscurity.

I said I thought that the retirement would be temporary in any event because men of his experience and ability did not and could not stay out of service very long.

Sumner said that the President had proposed sending him to Russia. I said I hoped that he would go. This was the biggest situation ahead to meet; an unresolved relationship with Russia could only mean a head-on collision later on. "It would mean more in five years", said Sumner. I said I thought that getting at this job is essential and that there was little time left. "It is five minutes of midnight", said Sumner. "If the situation runs much longer it will be insoluble." That, I argued, was precisely the reason I thought he should accept the Russian mission. He said he could not go. He said he could only go with the full confidence and support of the Department. This, in view of the resignation which had been occasioned by Mr. Hull he obviously would not have. I said I was by no means sure of that; the interests were too big; the stakes too great for personalities to enter the situation. If he had not already declined it I urged him to keep his mind open on that point. This he said he would do.

And so I said farewell and left him, in a dusty, sunlit office, in an empty building, finishing, as he believed, his stormy but brilliant career.

The next morning I devoted a little attention to the somewhat surprising job of being Acting Secretary of State without allowing anyone to find out. I cancelled the press conference, and the traditional announcement of the Secretary's or Acting Secretary's diplomatic appointments for the day. Fortunately, not much was happening and it was fairly simple. On Tuesday, some question was asked where Sumner was and we answered that he had been unwell and had returned to Bar Harbor for a few days' rest. But that night, Leon Pearson, over the radio, announced Sumner's resignation, thereby exploding all of the many rumors which had been floating about the press, since the New York *Times* and Arthur Krock had blasted into the situation some weeks previous. The Wednesday morning newspapers failed to carry it, but the afternoon newspapers were talking in scared headlines.

Almost at once the left-wing press in the United States began to make Sumner a hero. They spoke of him as the only friend of Russia in the Department; the sole bulwark against a Fascist State Department; they opened a general attack all along the line on everyone else notably Breckinridge Long, Jimmy Dunn and myself, and, to some extent, Secretary Hull, whom they have not hitherto attacked. This was ironic, because the intelligence reports picked up instructions from a couple of Communist Party secretaries in the Mid-west to the effect that the time had come now to open up a Communist attack on Mr. Hull and also Mr. Welles—the latter we had been expecting for some time since Lombardo Toledano had been incautious enough to mention the problem when he was recently in Cuba for the meeting of the C.T.A.L. [Confederation of Latin American Workers, of which he was president]. But I gather the directive so far as Sumner was concerned was promptly withdrawn. Also, from the kind of publicity coming out it sounded probable to me that Sumner had once more confided either in Drew Pearson or some other of his friends and they, without attributing it to him, were repeating what he had said. The attack had given tongue by the time Mr. Hull returned to Washington; and he reported that the President was not coming back until the latter part of the week and possibly not until the following Monday. Actually, this was what happened; in the meantime, the entire situation remained in ferment. I was reported as having threatened to resign if Breckinridge Long were appointed Under Secretary—which, of course, was pure foolishness; generally things were getting pretty confused. Drew Pearson began a one-man campaign to convict the entire State Department of "wishing to see Soviet Russia bled white," together with any other nonsense he could think up; and the New York *Tribune* and other papers of that kind began to insist that the State Department had no foreign policy and intimated that the only capable man in it was gone. It seemed to me that it was my job to try to keep the work rolling and got out.

The President got back on the thirtieth and he lunched with the Secretary. Mr. Hull had been supporting Sumner's mission to Russia but he said, with entire correctness, that nobody could go representing the United States in that capacity if it were assumed that he was an antagonist of Russian cooperation acting alone against the wishes of the entire Department and that he thought Sumner ought to make a statement repudiating the support of the left-wing press. The President agreed to have

Sumner to the White House on Thursday, the second of September, and talk matters over with him; but the next thing I heard was merely a newspaper notice that Sumner had cancelled his reservation from Bar Harbor to Washington. He may, however, come back. But I am afraid the damage is done.

The strange thing about it is that Sumner, in his talk with me when he turned over charge, recognized perfectly the danger that this would happen; and the last thing he wished to have happen was to become the representative of a left-wing group fighting the State Department. Something must have gone on. . . .

Behind it all, of course, is the matter of a Senate investigation of a couple of unpleasant incidents that I find it impossible to believe—but whose fame has been industriously spread [by Bullitt] to others of Sumner's enemies.

This situation has all the elements of tragedy. It overshadows incidents which are in their way dramatic: The desire of the Greek emissaries in Cairo to dethrone the King of Greece; the seizure of the Danish Government by Germans, the Danish scuttling of the fleet and King Christian's declaring himself a prisoner; the affair of the Italian armistice terms (primarily military drama), and so forth, all of which had been over my desk for the past three days. It seems the British are in the process of committing themselves to the restoration of King George in Greece; our specialists think it means political upheaval and perhaps even civil war if he goes; also, we are not yet in that close consultation in regard to Danish matters, which is really required if all is to go smoothly in view of our own great interest in Danish Greenland.

As a result, Mr. Hull is now solely in control of foreign policy, at a time when something has to be said decisively and he, himself, has to say it. I, therefore, have been urging him to accelerate his idea of making a speech and to avoid that the speech should be a collection of academic statements and shall contain the outline of a pretty clear-cut program. The Russian matter, meanwhile, is being dealt with in London where [Soviet Ambassador Ivan M.] Maisky and Eden and [U.S. Ambassador John G.] Winant are conferring. Based on the actions of the Soviet Government that I can see happening so far, not much progress has been made. If the Communist activities here and in Latin America, especially Cuba, Mexico and Peru, are any guide, they have quite other plans. It must be our task to try to get to an understanding if we possibly can, provided that in doing so we make no sacrifice of principle. One Munich in a decade is enough. If the Soviet Government is a Government of good will we shall see.

September 3, 1943

A pleasant chat with Sir Alexander Cadogan [Permanent Under-Secretary of State for Foreign Affairs]. This was general, because he merely came in to pay his respects. He is here with Churchill and I expect they are working on a variety of things. They are up to their necks in this Russian business. There is now some reason to believe that talks will take place; the question is where. The British very much want to have them on British territory.

A two-hour lunch with Averell Harriman, who will undoubtedly be one of the men we send to Russia. He asked about the Welles matter; I expressed my hope that it could still be worked out that Welles could go to Russia; but pointing out the difficulties that stand in the way. More bluntly, Welles's adherents had put him in the position of being the only champion of Russia in the State Department, and to send him would be equivalent to intimating that the State Department was pursuing an anti-Russian policy. Possibly this could be cleared up by appropriate statements all around—though I am not sure that the Secretary would agree.

Harriman is not in accord with the way General [John H.] Burns and the rest of them have been handling the Lend-Lease arrangements with Russia. He thinks that instead of telling them what we will try to do, we ought to be blunt and tough; state a rock bottom minimum and then beat it if we can. He also feels that when the fault lies with the Russians— as, that they cannot lift the cargoes we lay down in Archangel or Persia— we ought to raise hell about it. He says that the policy of soft and encouraging statements permits us always to be maneuvered into the position of being in the wrong—having encouraged hopes we could not fulfill, etc. . . . I think he is right.

He feels that to find a formula with the Russians would be of the extremest difficulty; but he says he is incurably optimistic. . . .

September 7, 1943

On Saturday night Alvin Johnson was in town and we had dinner together. I was glad to see him, since among other things he came to say that my friends were standing by me. At the moment, friendship is a rare article in this village. In substance, his thesis was that the State Department had a tremendous power over the situation and did not know it; and that the public was getting wrathy because it realized that fact. The country wanted to know what was going to be done to it, and felt that a great deal more could be told than is being told. This is true. A lot of mystery goes on which is wholly needless.

I told him I was worried, myself, since I did not mind being "expendable" in connection with the war effort, but I did mind assuming public responsibility for decisions—or still more, indecision and failure to move—when I could not affect the situation. This of course was the real difficulty between Secretary Hull and Sumner Welles. Both men were entirely sincere, and from their point of view both were quite right. As to being of any use in explaining the situation, obviously I could not do that without general approval; membership in a foreign office does end your freedom of speech. I thought, however, that the next few months would tell the story and a firm decision could then be reached. Alvin Johnson said that he was pretty clear that this was about the timing; he thought the Germans would not crack up until the Fall of 1944, with Japan following pretty close after.

I asked the philosophic question which had been on my mind. Many of us represent a rather vigorous moderate development which has nothing in common either with the chauvinism of the Right or the sheer tyranny of the Left. Were we doomed to be ground out of existence as the Liberals and Social Democrats have been? Alvin answered that the war had created a middle class in the United States larger than it had ever seen before; and that, assuming that the Government of the time had brains to prevent perennial unemployment, the United States had the greatest basis for a moderate and evolutionary development that any country had ever provided. . . .

September 11, 1943

Saturday evening, at a dinner meeting of the Social Science Research Council [in New York] which was merely a round table discussion of the State Department. I told everyone to ask any question they liked: the sky was the limit. It wound up as a discussion not of foreign affairs, but of philosophical values. The values of free life and the free mind and soul as against those either of the left or of the right. . . . The Germans have taken Rome and it looks as though the Italians will be actually fighting them within a short time. Badoglio, some of his government, and apparently the King, seem to be inside the Allied lines; I don't have information but I imagine they are in Sicily. . . .

Today, at work trying to get the policy on the Mediterranean clear. There is no knowledge as to who the new Under Secretary of State is to be.

Memorandum for the files, September 13, 1943

There was a meeting this morning in the Secretary's office. . . . The problem was to see whether we could not get some clarification of policy between this Government and the Government of Great Britain—also the Government of Soviet Russia—in the Mediterranean area east of Italy; and possibly also in the Near Eastern area lying between the Eastern Mediterranean and the Indian Ocean and the Persian Gulf. . . .

In strict confidence, the Secretary observed that Mr. Churchill at Quebec had said that he was not going to be a party to setting up left-wing governments all over Europe; and that the Secretary indicated his own suggestion that the Soviet Government be informed as to endeavor to work out a field of common action. Apparently he also does not feel like letting himself be a party to a set of dispositions on purely ideological grounds. I made the point that we ought to have a clear line of policy. If we had nothing to do east of the Adriatic we ought to know that. If, on the other hand, we had policies we wanted to make good we ought to be in a position to carry them out.

The Secretary, likewise, said he thought we ought to make a point to the British that we did not want these Balkan countries to fall back into and the old "trench" to which they had been condemned by British and French policy. Without being starry-eyed he thought we might consider practical measures which might make them more really capable members of the Community.

September 16, 1943

We have been receiving information purporting to state the negotiations between Germany and Russia for a separate peace which began last spring. The Japanese are endeavoring to stimulate this result. In this respect, we know the information to be accurate. . . .

Yesterday, a rather dull day enlivened by the first meeting of the Anglo-American group discussing stabilization and monetary arrangements. Lord Keynes, Lionel Robbins, Professor [Dennis Holme] Robertson and a couple of others were the negotiators for the Britishers. Harry White did the negotiating for the Treasury. It was an interesting conference. Keynes opened cleverly, I thought, by explaining that the British Labour party was inalterably opposed to getting themselves into a position in which the social or budgetary policy of Britain could be limited or overthrown by rigid currency arrangements such as attachment to the gold standard. It is in a way the formal statement of the revolt of the socially conscious classes against the Central Bank oligarchy of the Twenties.

January 6, 1944

There have been no entries in this Diary for a long time. This has been due partly to the fact that some of the work on which I was engaged had to do with military movements which I did not care to put on paper at all; partly to excessive occupation; and partly to the fact that the events of last summer were pure tragedy. As the Department became too small for both Sumner Welles and Secretary Hull, the difficulties of all of us were extreme. It so happened that Sumner Welles's resignation was put in (though not accepted) and he actually left while Mr. Hull was at Quebec —leaving me Acting Secretary of State.

And it so happened that when his successor, Ed Stettinius, was finally appointed, Mr. Hull was away resting, preparatory to going to Moscow; and I was Acting Secretary when Stettinius entered the Department.

The fundamental conflict which led to Sumner's resignation might have been kept under control had there not been an endless series of intrigues against him by a number of people, notably Bill Bullitt. A somewhat grim feature was the intercepted order of the Communist Party. In December 1942 they had given orders for personal attacks on Jimmie Dunn and Ray Atherton. In February 1943 they included me in the list—perhaps as rather a chief target.

Just before Sumner's resignation the Communist Party orders were to go all out against the entire Department, including Cordell Hull and Sumner Welles. Immediately after Welles's resignation was announced the order was changed—Welles was to be named a hero and the attack was to be centered on Cordell Hull.

It is perhaps an even grimmer irony that the Moscow Conference was one which Sumner had been urging for some time, and the method of procedure was substantially that which had been worked out in a committee of which he was chairman. At the time of his resignation he told me he was offered the headship of the mission to Moscow. I urged him to take it; but he felt that he could not go without the full support of the Department, which he was very clear he would not have. He thought the end would be obscurity for him. I thought not.

But in any event it was a top rank personal tragedy of Greek proportions.

In late December a coup d'état by some Bolivian Army officers threw out the government of President [Enrique] Peñaranda. The secret information we have makes it perfectly clear that this was planned in Buenos Aires by the Buenos Aires military government in consultation with the Nazi intelligence people. A debate in the Department ensued, Duggan and [Philip W.] Bonsal [Chief, American Republics] feeling that they wished to be cautious; and the Secretary feeling that the time had come to get tough. I thought the Secretary was right and still do. We accordingly declined to recognize the new government. The Committee for Political Defense at Montevideo proposed consultation between the American republics before recognition should be had in cases of revolution, to ascertain that such revolution was not engineered by forces outside of the continent, or as a result of intervention by another country. All hands accepted this except, of course, Argentina. Two days ago Argentina threw down the gauntlet by recognizing the Bolivian junta—which is now a coalition of the younger Bolivian Army officers and the Bolivian equivalent of the Nazi party (M.N.R.). . . .

Though I have not been in on the discussions, I must say that the play-off from the Moscow Conference is worrying me. On its face, it was an agreement of four powers to cooperate in winning the war and in keeping the peace after the war. It has been assumed to be recognition of Russia's paramount interest in Eastern Europe. This is to be effected by partisan movements of the type of Tito [Josip Broz] in Yugoslavia. Some unhappy souls are beginning to speak of an "Eastern Munich". I certainly hope not, for if that is true many of us have a date with death sometime in the next twenty years.

January 10, 1944

Secretary Hull assigned to me the job of getting up negotiations for the air bases required by the United States after the war. The military specifications are of course worked up by the Joint Chiefs of Staff. One way and another, it is quite a proposition, and in a sense tends to delimit what might be called the "American Empire"—except that we do not propose to make it an empire. It is a vast sweep, and presents some problems (e.g., Dakar) of peculiar difficulty.

We are rapidly coming to grips with Argentina. The evidence is now conclusive that the Army crowd there, headed by [Juan] Perón, and through the secret society known as the G.O.U., financed and handled the plot to take over the Bolivian Government, and proposes to execute another similar plot in Chile and in Peru, and probably also in Paraguay and Uruguay. They are working hand in glove with the Germans in all this. By consequence, the Secretary is prepared to go to ultimates. The difficulty, as usual, is that the British draw twenty-five percent of their meat supply from there, and that Argentine wheat will come in handy.

Yesterday at lunch with the Brazilian Ambassador [Carlos Martins] and [Carlos Martins Valentim] Bouças, of the Brazilian Production Committee, the Brazilian point of view was forcefully presented: they think the matter has to be sweated out and we had best get to it.

We have laid down some, at least, of the evidence we have for the benefit of the rest of the American republics so far as Bolivia is concerned, and the plan is to follow it up with a statement on Argentina, following which we will call Ambassador [Norman] Armour home.

There is a cruiser standing by at Montevideo, and the Chilean angle is covered. We are of the view that the Argentine Government does not represent the bulk of the Argentine people, and the difficult thing is to take a stiff stand against these Argentine buccaneers without antagonizing the Argentine people to a point where they will support this crowd. The particular and putative Mussolini in the lot is Colonel Perón, who has been using money lavishly to foment disorder and who proposes to set up an Argentine-controlled Fascist bloc running as far North as Peru. . . .

January 18, 1944

The State Department reorganized Saturday. The precise purpose of it is unclear and the plan is a sloppy, botched job; I do not fare too well myself, though events have a habit of transcending organization charts.

It seems I have shipping and radio as well as aviation assigned to me in the new layout. We got to work on them this morning.

The Soviet troops have crossed the boundary of Poland; the Soviet Government proposed that the Polish Government (which, of course, it does not recognize) should be reconstituted with men "friendly" to the Soviet Government, and that its boundary in Poland be fixed at or near the Curzon Line. Anthony Eden induced the Polish Government in London to make a reasonably conciliatory answer, asking the British and American Governments to mediate. We sent to the Soviets offering our good offices; but, alas, the cable was delayed two days in transmission and before it got there the Soviets had issued a thumping rejection of the Polish offer. Yesterday they likewise published in *Pravda* a rumor (which I believe to be a lie) that the British had a couple of agents dickering with the Germans for a separate peace. The thing is a mess and will increase everybody's difficulties. It is a great pity; for Russian relations had just begun to get on a good footing here and all that was needed was a show of self-restraint on the part of the Soviets in dealing with a country which at the moment is completely helpless.

Actually, there is a good deal to be said for the Russian position since a line something like the Curzon Line would have been fixed at Paris in 1919 if there had been any way to fix it—which there was not. . . .

This morning, more work on the acquisition of air bases. . . .

Secret Memorandum, January 24, 1944

The attached cablegram from Algiers suggests that in the case of an early capture of Rome the King should be allowed to pay a short visit to Rome accompanied by Badoglio. . . .

The sending of the King and Badoglio to Rome in advance of other political leaders will be taken—widely—as a plain indication that the Allied Governments are supporting the King and Badoglio and are endeavoring to give them a chance to consolidate the position before anyone else arrives. Judging from the information at hand about the men who have gathered around the King and Badoglio, which include men like [Filippo] Naldi (probably one of the worst types connected with Mussolini, and who now bobs up as Chief of Press Service) full use will be made of the opportunity.

The proposal that the King dicker with the Rome party leaders while all others are excluded, is hardly tenable.

If we are to act on [the Counselor of the U.S. Mission at Algiers, Selden] Chapin's recommendation (which obviously comes not from him but from [British Minister of State at Algiers, Harold] Macmillan) the line ought to be that within a few days after occupation of Rome, Badoglio, Sforza, [Benedetto] Croce, and the rest of them all go to Rome and there state their positions in conferences with leaders, and publicly as circumstances may then permit, and set up a reorganized government. . . .

I do not believe that Allied authorities in Italy should be allowed to use their own discretion as they request. The matter is of too high policy to delegate.

We have never been clear whether the British do not really hope to reestablish the Savoy dynasty with Badoglio as Premier. I see no reason why the Department should accept criticism because we have "gone along" with a policy of this kind. . . .

January 24, 1944

Probably as a direct result of the conversation in my library on January 21, President [Isaías] Medina [Angarita, of Venezuela] asked if I could see him at Blair House. . . . After speaking to Secretary Hull, I did this. President Medina wished to know whether we could make more precise the general line of information contained in the memorandum sent by us to all of the consulting American republics opposing recognition of the present Bolivian Junta.

Accordingly, I went over the salient points of that memorandum, adding somewhat to the detail of them. . . .

In response to a question as to whether similar activities were going on elsewhere, I said that we had reason to believe that from Argentina similar moves had been made in the neighboring republics, though I had not any reason to believe they had attained a great measure of success. Likewise answering a question, I said that we had no information indicating any movement going on in Venezuela. . . .

I said there was ample evidence making it clear that intrigues proceeding from Argentina and particularly from an influential Argentine group presently represented in the government there, and tied in with German activities, were going on in the southern continental area.

President Medina thanked me and said that in his view the most essential thing now was to preserve and safeguard the unity of the Hemisphere. This was the first tenet of his policy.

I said it was likewise uppermost in our thinking. In handling this Argentine and Bolivian matter, indeed, our desire was to seek means by which we could restore the unity of the Hemisphere—rather than permit any group to break it up. . . .

February 22, 1944

The other more dangerous and difficult thing comes to me, as usual, from the bottom and not from the top. The Joint Intelligence Committee has been asked to consider a variety of operations in addition to the cross-channel operation. I do not set them down here. My fear is that this is a move towards substitution for the cross-channel operation. Now the Russians believe that at Moscow and Tehran a definite commitment for a cross-channel operation was taken; and I think that obligation simply has to be kept. Whether it was a mistake to take on the obligation, of course, is another question, but that problem no longer exists. But consequently we are trying to work out the situation so that any peripheral operation there be in aid of the cross-channel business.

It is the old gambling game. They say bad things about the State Department, but at long last in every case the political operations have proved the way by which the door was opened through which attack could be made against the Nazis. So it was in North Africa, Sicily, Sardinia, Italy. And so it is again.

Our intelligence reports show steady intensification of revolutionary movements in South America. These are assuming a European pattern. The pro-Nazi Army groups are endeavoring to stiffen their power: they hold Argentina and are trying to hold Bolivia. They are active in Colombia, Peru, Chile. The Communists, on the other hand, are strengthening their forces; the meeting of the C.T.A.L. in Montevideo on February 25 is for that purpose. Again it is the movement of the two extreme factions against the middle—with blood either way.

June 10, 1944

Yesterday, a heavy debate in the Policy Committee about Albania, then a meeting with the President. . . . The President was in excellent form, though obviously a little weary with a great deal of work. He said that the military affairs were going as well as could be expected but "it was a long walk from Normandy to Berlin". He had to proceed on the assumption that the war would go on for some time. He also reckoned on the possibility of a German collapse. . . .

Evening, a dinner at the Polish Embassy, again for the Polish Prime Minister [Stanislaus Mikolajczyk]. A very interesting conversation with

General Stanislaw Tabor, the Assistant Chief of Staff of the Polish Underground Army. The history of the Polish Underground State, with a cabinet, courts, schools, army, et cetera, functioning only at night and in the daytime appearing to be quite ordinary workers, shop keepers, and so forth, will furnish one of the amazing stories of the present war.

June 13, 1944

Monday, June 12. It seems that over the week end a mess blew up in Italy. Badoglio was unable to form a cabinet; [Ivanoe] Bonomi was asked by Prince Umberto to form one; he invited Sforza and others. The British General [Frank M.] MacFarlane, went to Bonomi and said that the Allies, meaning Britain and the United States, objected to Sforza. We at once protested, since we like Sforza. Eden in London says it was done without instructions, but, knowing Winston Churchill's violent dislike of Sforza, I am not sure that this is true. Subsequently Churchill cabled orders that any Italian government ought to be approved by the Allies. We don't agree with that either. Sforza, not unnaturally, asks just why the first anti-Fascist government should be disapproved by the Allies when they cheerfully approved a lot of Fascists under Badoglio. It is a cogent question.

At work with the Parliamentary Secretary of the British Ministry of Economic Warfare, who rejoices in the name of Dingle Foot, in connection with getting some more relief supplies into German-occupied territory. The British are prepared to go part way on feeding prisoners in camps. They do not want to send food into civilian populations. . . .

The controversy over Bolivian recognition is getting to be considerable.

Secret material likewise makes it clear that the controversy over recognizing De Gaulle's Committee as the provisional government of France is becoming extreme. Mr. Hull takes the position that this is entirely a presidential matter and is backing away from it.

June 23, 1944

Some more facts about the British proposal to divide Eastern Europe into spheres of influence with Soviet Russia have turned up. Halifax first came in and talked to the Secretary quite generally about it. This was followed up by a direct cable from Churchill to the President saying that the British had proposed that the Soviets take a sphere of influence in Rumania and Bulgaria, the British a sphere in Greece and Yugoslavia. He said that they had proposed this to the Soviets and the Soviets had inquired whether the United States had been consulted. Hence Churchill's cable.

Since European affairs are supposed to be on a tripartite basis, of course, we should have been consulted. And it appears that the British proposed a secret deal with the Soviets which was blocked by the Soviets insisting on consultation with the United States—very decently.

Subsequently Halifax, who had been pressing for an answer to his note asking our assent to this arrangement, changed his line and asked that we do not answer it, saying that nothing had happened except a very general chat about possibilities had between Anthony Eden and the Russian Ambassador, [Feodor] Gusev, in London. This does not go along with the Churchill cable, but such are the ways of diplomacy.

We, of course, are dead against spheres of influence or tripartite partitions or anything of the kind.

My private opinion is that the proposal was designed to implement a half understanding made between the British and the Russians shortly after Russia was attacked in 1941. This was before we were in the picture. The attempt was made to capitalize on a pre-war arrangement somewhat as the Europeans cashed in on the secret treaties of 1916 made before our entry into the war and expected us to assist in implementing them—which, in fact, we actually did in the Versailles Treaty. This time, at least so far, we have not made the same mistake.

Yesterday a quiet day, with air matters and one thing and another; dinner at home with Charles Taussig. We agreed that when the hostilities were over the best thing for both of us would be to get away for some considerable period of time into an atmosphere which would differ from Washington.

Preparations and plans well forward for the International Monetary Conference at Bretton Woods. I have some slight disappointment at being out of it, having worked for two years on the preparations.

July 3, 1944

We still have no reply from the Russians as to whether they will come and talk about setting up a League of Nations.

Eighteen out of twenty countries have withdrawn their Ambassadors from Argentina. On our recommendation, the President has approved virtually guaranteeing the security of Paraguay and Uruguay, who are afraid of reprisals. This would have to be done by air.

The matter of exchanging spheres of influence (Russia taking Rumania, Britain taking Greece) appears to have come out not so well. We turned the thing down flat. At our suggestion, the President cabled Churchill. He got back a pretty hot answer, Churchill urging that the President trust him, and finally suggesting that in any event they ought to work along these lines for a brief period, reviewing it every three months or so. Though I have not seen the text, I gather the President's answer accepted this for a short-run proposition. I hope it all works out, but I must say that the outlook is not pleasant.

We are getting off a military mission to Tito, but this whole Tito business worries me. There are still six million Serbs, and Tito's genial observation that he will come to an understanding with them by invading Serbia and settling their hash looks to me more like a civil war than anything else. Further, I think the Soviet Union eventually will decline to sponsor a civil war. Tri-Slovak rows are now part of their plan. . . .

July 6, 1944

Ambassador Armour got here the day before yesterday. We had a powwow in the Secretary's office. The Secretary feels that the time for appeasing Argentina is past, and that we ought to take a firm and direct position on Argentina's non-cooperation in inter-American defense and solidify the entire hemisphere on this basis. Norman Armour would like to stipulate some conditions which, if fulfilled, would entitle this regime to recognition. Most of us feel, I think, that this regime is really trying to play up a Fascist Government and that any statement of conditions would simply be used to get the best trade possible, after which the old course would be pursued. In other words, it was like the situation which confronted Britain and the other European countries when Hitler started his policy of going as far as he could go and getting it considered; then waiting for a while and then going a little farther.

. . . Maintaining of peace is no longer a distant job for somebody else's League of Nations. It is a present job for the United States and the American group of nations.

July 28, 1944

Equally, on the continent of Europe, thanks at least in part to our own lack of vigor and thanks partly to the military situation, I can only say that we are being angled out of any major voice. The Soviets have taken the lead in forming a new Polish government and there is nothing we can do about that. There is a preliminary indication that they expect to take the same lead in the Danish picture. They have a Free German Committee in Moscow and nobody else has anything in respect of Germany, so that, as far as appears, they have the extremely favorable market for new German regimes pretty thoroughly cornered.

Winston Churchill's romantic desire to placate the Soviets led him to gamble heavily on Tito, and we more or less backed out of the situation. The replacement of the American high command by British in Italy has substantially given the British a major hand in that theater, though certain grudging concessions have been made to our own desire for more or less democratic, liberal government. The British have been backing De Gaulle to the limit, and there is now no question in my mind that he will attempt to establish himself as virtual dictator of France and that if he ever gets in the saddle he will be dislodged only by force. The recent British note in respect of Iraq suggests that the British claim economic preponderance there and have already claimed political preponderance.

The other side of the picture is that both of the other powers have strong and defined objectives. Our general one, namely a Europe which will be peacefully minded and generally make its inhabitants happy, seems too diffuse. Further, the number of Americans who have become passionate partisans of some country other than their own is amazing; and the complaissance of the American Government in respect of foreign pressure as to the type of American and his actions as representing American interests is, to my mind, amazing. If we are not careful we shall reach the position where the only American representatives who are in a position to act do so because they are supported by some foreign propaganda machine. This is where a certain type of State Department Foreign Service official shows up at his worst. He has long since learned that if he stands up to a situation and gets into a row about it he is wrong, irrespective of

the fact that the row might be in legitimate and honest defense of a legitimate and honest American interest. By consequence, when he sees trouble
approaching, he slides away from the point—having learned by long experience that it is the safest thing he can do.

The question, to my mind, is what an over-all League of Nations
organization is worth if it merely sits on top of an underlying situation in
which every country except our own is pursuing national interests with a
ferocity equalled only by war itself.

In reading Sumner Welles's book [*The Time for Decision*], I was
impressed with the new evidence of the futility of war books by any figure
in them. Such a book almost inevitably has the author for its central
character and figure; whereas the one certain thing about this business is
that whatever any individual was doing was parallelled, duplicated or
affected by a great many other individuals at the same time. The central
ego figure is permissible to an autobiographer, because that is what autobiography is for; but it diminishes the utility of a book on general subjects, however learned and experienced, as this one was. In one respect,
the book was scarcely straightforward. This in its defense of the Soviet
policy up to and through the German attack on Russia in 1941. . . .

The published account is, of course, in line with the general policy,
and probably to publish the facts would have done no good; but I do not
think that misleading accounts are either necessary or useful. A good deal
simpler theory would have been that the Soviets, having been attacked in
1919, invaded in 1920, generally kicked around for some years, finally
excluded at Munich in 1938, considered that they had nothing whatever
to hope for from the Western powers and therefore were jolly well taking
care of themselves. . . .

August 28, 1944
Monday, August 21. Back from two weeks in the Berkshires—the
second week principally spent with the children tramping in the hills
with a knapsack. On the last day, between Washington Mountain and
October Mountain, high in the hills, we came on an old chap who was
lining out wild bees. He knew every curve in those hills, and I envied him
whole-heartedly. . . .

The Dumbarton Oaks conference opened today; I am not on this
crew and sorry about that; but, as I see it, the words they write on a piece
of paper are far less important than the actual relationships achieved in
the next few months. Water cannot rise higher than its source; if sound
relationships are achieved, the new League of Nations will be a success.
But if not, this will be merely a mustard plaster on a series of open
wounds. So it was at Paris; so it is again. Two prime problems are handling the nascent civil wars in Greece and Yugoslavia. . . .

Thursday, August 24. It looks as though the Allied push into France
is succeeding beyond our wildest dreams. . . . To the airport on cookie-
pushing duty to meet the President of Iceland [S. Bjoernsson] and his
Foreign Minister [Villajalmor] Thor—the latter an old friend of mine
since I had negotiated with him the economic agreements for the supply

of Iceland in 1941 when we went in. Thence to the White House for tea with the President; the conversation chiefly on fishing and such like. The President, I thought, was not up to his old form; in older days he would pump so much vitality into everybody present that the effect was like a couple of glasses of champagne. Not so now, though he still is more vigorous than most men who are twenty years younger.

August 25. It is said that the Germans have been chased out of Paris by a *levée en masse* of the Parisian population. The American Armies could have taken the town any time in the last few days but they rightly have been heading for the German Armies rather than merely taking territory. The situation is not clear.

Saturday, August 26. To St. Matthew's Cathedral to a Te Deum for the liberation of Paris. I went out of love and not out of politics; but the emotional lift had to come out of our own heads and out of companionship with Beatrice, who likewise went for love. The Irish priests who chanted the Te Deum, not very well, added a few words on the significance of France, but as they based these words entirely on St. Louis and the Crusades, and the explorations of Marquette and Joliet in the Middle West, it hardly connected with the time. But I was remembering the great service on Christmas Eve 1918, in Notre Dame, when the First World War was over, and wondering what tides of emotion, brave and terrible, splendid and tender, must be released in Notre Dame now. For it is now clear that while the first report of the liberation of Paris was premature, General [Omar] Bradley promptly released General [J. P.] Leclerc and the French division, together with a quite adequate number of troops of his own to go in and clean up. This they did, to the wild and enthusiastic acclamation of the Paris crowds. There is life in that; and also death; and who knows whether it would be discriminate as to who lives, and who dies.

It is now clear that the Bulgarians are likewise suing for an armistice; and the entire house of cards is coming down. Whereas the Rumanians have to negotiate primarily with the Russians, the Bulgarians, who are not at war with Russia, have to negotiate with the British and ourselves. And this precipitates the entire problem of the Balkans, which will be on us almost overnight.

The President has determined that no American troops are to be in the Balkans and has so instructed [Ambassador] Lincoln MacVeagh. The question is, therefore, whether we can affect the Balkan situation very much—for my observation is that in the present state of affairs in Europe your writ runs just as far as your army of occupation goes and no farther. In our case not even so far, since we have too often let the British write our writ for us. The question, therefore, is this: Not being able to affect the Eastern Mediterranean much, should we not flatly dissociate ourselves from responsibility for it? . . .

If we are in the Balkans, we have little choice save simply to underwrite the British in this regard. Perhaps it would be better not to assume responsibility where we do not have power.

August 29, 1944

While the Dumbarton Oaks Conference is proceeding (I have no information as to what is going on), some situations in Europe are worrying me a great deal.

The Warsaw uprising was an attempt by the Polish underground to throw out the Germans, believing that the proximity of the Russian armies was sufficient to make the attempt successful. The Soviet armies did not liberate Warsaw; and Soviet press despatches berated the underground for rising without previous arrangements with the Soviet armies, and accusing the Polish Government-in-exile of starting this for political purposes and thus betraying their men to their death. The facts appear to be that some two days before the uprising the Soviet-sponsored Polish Council of National Liberation broadcast from Moscow a general appeal for a levee en mass; this being done, if I recall correctly, August 16 or 17, the Soviet Army did not liberate the city; I am not clear whether this was a design or merely that the Russian advance had spent itself to a point where the Germans could check them. It is probably true that the Polish underground wanted to show that they, too, were fighting the Germans, instead of being pro-German fascists in accordance with the accusations of the Soviet propaganda. The uprising also demonstrated the existence of a peaceful Polish underground, which the Soviets had denied. The Soviets have given them no help; the British are attempting to assist them by air; and I personally feel that we ought to do everything we can to assist likewise, if only on straight military and humanitarian grounds. I should not be prepared to conclude that the Soviet armies had deliberately left the underground to be exterminated by the Germans; it was pretty clear, however, that the propaganda service has been substantially condemning these people to death with a gusto which does not make pleasant reading.

This has to be considered along with the reports of Latvian massacres, analagous to the reports of Lithuanian massacres—neither of which can be accepted as wholly reliable—but the picture building up is frightening.

This contrasts with a really very moderate policy towards Finland, and a moderate policy towards Rumania—at least as far as the declarations and diplomatic moves go.

When you get old and skeptical you are interested not in what the governments say they are doing but in what their people actually are doing on the ground. The solution of this would be a free press so that we could get reliable news accounts—instead of having the whole of the Eastern situation shrouded in complete secrecy. . . .

[Ambassador] Spruille Braden, who has been back here, tells me of a little incident the night of the election of [Ramón] Grau San Martín in Cuba a few weeks ago. Apparently the majority which Grau received was a surprise both to Batista, the outgoing President, and to Grau himself. The Army junta behind Batista had been so convinced that Batista would win and that they would be in power that they were not set for this; they promptly held a meeting designed to take over the power and set up a government. Braden was dining with a prominent American resident of Havana, Johnson, the drug man. One of Grau's men burst into the garden where they were seated and told them of this, asking Braden to intervene at once. He said he would not touch it until the facts were verified; but an hour or so later they were verified, and Braden in the meantime had gone over to where a number of these Army officers were. He stated to one of them that he would not intervene in the situation at all except by non-intervention. Specifically, the United States recognized the existing government and would recognize Grau as soon as he was inaugurated; and would not recognize anybody else nor any group that seized the government by force; and there ought to be no misunderstanding about it at all. According to Braden, he made it pretty solid and added that anybody could figure out exactly what that would mean when taken in all its implications. The Army junta thereupon thought better of the idea and abandoned the plan.

When Braden told me this I laughed and asked whether he had sought instructions of the Department or whether he had reported it. He said there were some things you had better not ask instructions about, and as for reporting, he had told me and proposed to tell it to the Secretary if he got a chance, and let it go at that. There are other ways of diplomacy than the Departmental cable and instruction. . . .

September 23, 1944

Early this week, discussing the Dumbarton Oaks Conference with the Secretary, he commented concisely: "It has blown up". He ascribed this to two things, a deep suspicion by the Soviets of the British, and the fact that Senator [Arthur H.] Vandenberg [R., Mich.] proposed to make an issue out of any arrangement to use force to keep the peace without prior consent of Congress. The other parties to the conference apparently objected on the ground that an assurance so qualified was no assurance at all.

Beneath this, of course, is a deep and almost insoluble problem. The Soviets are contesting with the British for domination in the whole area of the Eastern Mediterranean and east through the Persian Gulf. To the British, it is a matter of their life line; cut it, and they are out of the Far East, shrinking to an Atlantic power. To the Soviets, if there is not access to warm water, which means not only to the Mediterranean, but to the entrances to the Mediterranean and to the Persian Gulf, they are still an enclosed power.

This probably underlies the row at Dumbarton. The precise issue is whether, when aggression is alleged, the decision to take action against the aggressor must be by unanimous vote which shall include the vote of a member of the Council (i.e., a great power) even though that power is the nation charged with aggression. This, of course, would give any great power the right to veto use of the proposed world machinery if it decided to become an aggressor. Should the clause emerge this way, the Dumbarton agreements would be little more than a holy alliance. . . .

Somewhere a voice must be found for the voiceless: the little people who fought in our fight, and are being condemned to death by our common victory. I am rapidly getting to the point where I have had all of this I can take. But until the Germans are beaten, we have to follow the rule either to be quiet or to be helpful. . . .

The new list of diplomatic appointments is out. It is not a strong set of appointments, to put it mildly. . . . Adding it all up, however, we are a first-rate power putting on a third-rate act, at a time when Europe would give a great deal if we would take rank and right and decision comparable to our military power. For the fact is that our diplomatic influence is not greater than our direct military power; and that it is circumscribed to a degree.

I thought that the play-off as this war closes would be as bad as that after the war of 1914. I am blunt to say it seems worse. Major Farish's death (he had been in Yugoslavia, and was killed early this month) hit me between the eyes, because he had borne such eloquent testimony to the kindliness of the little people on all sides of the Yugoslav question, and their invincible faith in the United States.

Berle submitted the following report to the State Department's Policy Committee on September 26, 1944. It resulted from the Department's announcement on January 15, 1944, of "far reaching changes in the organization . . . designed to free the Assistant Secretaries from administrative duties," to enable them to "devote the greater part of their time to matters of important foreign policy." Members of the Policy Committee, created at that time, were Hull, Stettinius, Berle, Acheson, Long, G. H. Shaw [an Assistant Secretary], Hackworth, Pasvolsky, the directors of the twelve Department offices (ex officio), and an executive secretary.

PRINCIPAL PROBLEMS IN EUROPE

The collapse of German resistance envisaged as a possibility by the European Office in its memorandum of July 15 has now become a probability. December 1, 1944, is estimated as the latest probable date by the British Joint Intelligence Committee and likewise by the Joint Intelligence Committee of the United States.

With that collapse, substantially the entire congeries of European problems will be presented in various phases as action matters. These detailed aspects will have to be solved in the light of general policy. This comment is prepared with that central fact in mind.

Introduction

Diplomacy may be rated by the ability of a country to obtain acceptance of its point of view beyond the area in which it can obtain such acceptance by command and, if need be, the direct application of force. Were our diplomacy limited, therefore, to the areas in which we exert direct command, it would rate at, say, zero, increasing its rating as the American point of view can be projected beyond those areas. Normally the diplomacy of a great power shrinks to zero towards the edge of military defeat, and falls to a minus quantity when defeat places affairs in the hands of its enemies.

We have ideals and ideas as to what we would like to see happen in the entire continent of Europe. Because in some measure these depart from the ideas of our allies, they have not been pressed during the period of war, lest division be created. Some of the powerful reasons for not pressing our points of view will disappear with the defeat of Germany. Others will remain, notably the strong desire to enlist the Soviet Union in the war against Japan, and the desire to collaborate with our allies in building a world organization, provided this can be done without sacrifice of essentials. But we cannot sacrifice the reputation of the United States for a large degree of moral approach to problems, as contrasted with the cynical approach of power politics. To sacrifice this would undoubtedly endanger the likelihood of the American public's adopting a plan for world organization, and equally would endanger the success of such an organization when formed. Both of these factors entered powerfully into the failure of the United States to go into the League of Nations, and the failure of the League as constituted.

The United States, in respect of certain principles, is bound to assume responsibility where and to the extent that she has power to act militarily or diplomatically.

Where she has not power to act but can express a view without endangering greater interests, she is bound to do that.

Where she cannot act in the situation, and cannot affect the situation by expression of her views, she should make it perfectly clear that she does not accept any responsibility for the situation.

As the second most powerful armed force on the continent, and a major participant in a huge common victory, public opinion generally will tend to hold the United States jointly responsible with the other victors for everything that goes on in Europe, except as a definite limitation has been made clear. The conduct of the war was obviously a joint matter depending on closely coordinated decisions of strategy and operation. In perfection, the measures following the collapse would likewise be joint and coordinated, in which case the United States would have roughly equal power and also equal responsibility with all of the major allies. Yet it is already plain that we will not exercise power in a number of thorny situations. In respect of those, it would seem that the Department must not only consider, but, as rapidly as circumstances make it possible, state the policy it is attempting.

Assumptions

Upon the German collapse, the following assumptions seem warranted:

(1) The Soviet Army will be the most powerful on the European continent, and will occupy Europe up to a line which is substantially the longitude of Berlin and running south to the border between Yugoslavia and Italy. The southern limit of this occupation will probably be from the south boundary of Bulgaria westward to the Adriatic, possibly dividing Albania.

(2) The Army of the United States will be the second most powerful on the continent of Europe but, aside from the zone of occupation agreed upon in Germany, will have physical occupation only of lines of commu-

nication and ports. Elsewhere the American forces will have turned over responsibilities so far as possible to local governments which are, in fact as well as in name, free to take decisions.

(3) The British forces will be either third or fourth in size, depending on the number of French forces which are organized and armed, but they likewise will only occupy the assigned sector in Germany, together with ports and lines of communication.

(4) The French forces will be fourth, or possibly third, in strength, and will eventually occupy Germany up to the Rhine.

(5) Politically, the Soviet Government will have governments acting in substantial compliance with their desires in Poland, Rumania, Bulgaria, Czechoslovakia, and Hungary.* Such governments may also exist in Yugoslavia, Austria and Greece. On the collapse of Finland, a like government will exist in Finland, possibly also in Norway and Denmark, although the degree of influence in both places will be far less than in the other countries named. There will likewise be a powerful move to upset the government of General Franco, with a growing degree of Soviet influence there. These and other similar political arrangements will expand the Soviet influence far beyond the area in which she could exert actual military force.

(6) The British will be able to secure a large measure of compliance from the Governments of the Netherlands and Belgium, Denmark, Portugal and Greece. The degree of her influence in France and Italy, and ultimately in Spain, is problematic, though she will make a strong attempt to have the senior voice in both countries and she would seem to have a fair chance of succeeding in the case of France, and possibly in Italy. In view of the Far Eastern war, there will be a powerful bond of common interest between the British, the French, the Netherlands, and, to some extent, the Portuguese to maintain their position in the Pacific, as well as with Belgium to maintain her African position.

(7) The degree of American influence in the situation will tend to diminish, though it will be maintained for a time through the hope of economic assistance. The United States has not yet become the protagonist of any set of ideas or set of policies which would give rise to great influence in Europe on doctrinaire grounds.

* Marginal note by Berle: "Albania?"

American Troops and Representation

(a) It is understood that the President does not wish to engage American troops east of Italy and the American zone of occupation in Germany. A possible exception is a token participation in the occupation of Austria. Substantially, the absence of American military forces on the southern shore of the Mediterranean, and from the Balkans east to Iran, may be taken for granted.

(b) In those areas in which American troops are not in occupation, the United States will have missions which either share in the work of Allied Control Commissions to carry out the terms of armistice or have direct representation with the local governments. These will be similar;

will have little actual voice (whatever the nominal situation) in the actual policies on the ground; and whatever influence they have will turn upon the general prestige of the United States, the powers of persuasion of the individuals, and the possible but fading hope of large scale economic assistance.

The Underlying Problem:
The Eastern Mediterranean and the Middle East

This is not technically a part of Europe, but the European scene cannot be divorced from the actual situation in the Eastern Mediterranean and the Middle Eastern countries lying between the Mediterranean and India.

From intelligence and other data at hand the conclusion seems warranted that:

The Soviet Union proposes to extend her influence south to the Persian Gulf throughout its entire length, and westward to the Mediterranean, roughly as far west as Cairo, though this last is a distant objective. They propose to have an influence analogous to that which the British now have in Iraq and the Levant States, and to extend their influence in Turkey. Their policy as to Saudi Arabia is still obscure.

This must be taken in connection with the Soviet policy of extending its sphere of influence to the Adriatic through Rumania, Bulgaria, and Yugoslavia; and the probability that they will secure by some method an entry into the Aegean Sea, either through Turkish territory, or through Thrace. As long as the latter was done through friendly agreement, few problems would be raised; but the Soviet doctrine that the governments must be "friendly" is still obscure. If it is meant that these governments must not engage in intrigue against the Soviet Union there could be no possible objection; if it is meant that, by subsidizing guerrilla or other movements, virtual puppet governments are to be established, a different situation would prevail.

The foregoing has set up an unresolved conflict between the Soviet aspirations and the British aspirations. The British see a threat to the empire life line, cutting them off from their Far Eastern interests including India, and reducing Britain from the status of a world power to the status of a strong Atlantic power. Taken in connection with the British economic situation, many Englishmen regard this as a life and death issue.

It is hardly too much to say that if a third world war is now being generated, the breeding ground lies exactly in this area. Given the present British view of their essential interests, the British will have to be tenacious in this regard and they will consider that while the Soviet Union undoubtedly has a power interest there, it is not vital to Soviet life. Consequently the British will be unlikely to recede.

It may likewise be assumed that the British attempt to exclude the United States from the Middle East will continue, which is presently going on despite official denials in Whitehall and perhaps contrary to the personal policy of Winston Churchill. In spite of many attempts to work out a different set of attitudes, there appears to have been no major change in British measures taken on the ground. The British assumption appears to be that in any major conflict arising out of this region, the United States necessarily will come to the support of Britain, irrespective of the fact that we shall have been excluded from the area (save perhaps a grudging acceptance of our oil interests in Saudi Arabia); and British reasoning is further buttressed by the oft repeated statement that the United States can hardly expect to be admitted to that area unless she is prepared to join in the "obligations" entailed by it and be prepared to station troops continuously in that part of the world for police and other similar purposes. The British rightly assume that the United States at this time is not prepared to maintain such forces there.

European Policy in this Background

Against this background, the suggestions made in the memorandum of EUR, under reference, would have to be judged. If the foregoing assumptions are approximately correct, the problem is less that of giving all possible aid to the Army, than that of adopting those policies and implementing them by those measures which are most likely to result in a balanced and peaceful cooperative solution, giving hope of a long plateau of peace.

Secondarily, the policies and the measures must be adopted so that the United States shall be in the best position to deal with the situation should the unsolved conflict between the British and Soviet Union reach an open issue—a possibility which may not come to a head for a period of years, but which cannot be discounted. The solid fact is that despite the negotiations in progress at Dumbarton Oaks, there is no visible diminution of the moves and countermoves on the ground, or of the tenacity with which both sides are pursuing nationalist objectives. Power politics is continuing between these countries today on the pattern made nauseatingly familiar by the Axis in 1935–1939.

The American Policy

1. *The General Objective.* Accepting, without discussion, the self-limitations placed on the use of American force and American influence east of Italy, it seems that we have to draw a careful line of policy based on the tools we shall actually have in hand.

East of Germany, the task of the American representatives, whether they are diplomatic, military, or economic in character, should be the continuous attempt to resolve differences between the major contending forces. It is believed that the major doctrine which can be invoked for this purpose is primarily that of a humanitarian interest in the individual populations of the countries concerned. A Soviet "sphere of influence" in these areas operated in somewhat the same fashion as we have operated the good neighbor policy in Mexico and the Caribbean area would be no threat to anyone, and would raise no essential conflicts since it would not conflict with the basic interests of the peoples of these countries, nor with the operation of the British life line and the only casualty would be the attempt at economic exclusiveness sought by certain elements in the British Government. In this aspect it would make relatively little difference to us or perhaps to anyone else who had the dominant position; a British sphere of influence similarly operated would likewise be little threat to the Soviet Union. But the basic concept behind such a policy is first the elimination of these countries as a center of power politics, and second a basic concern for the rights and situation of the populations of the countries involved. Both of these conceptions provide a possible ground on which the contending forces could meet in friendship without conflict. To secure their application, however, does require a modification of the ruthlessness of British commercialism and the ruthlessness of Soviet nationalism.

It would follow that the men sent out should have this sort of indoctrination and the task to which they turn their hands should be informed in this sense. The Department should support them in these matters by all possible diplomatic means. A campaign of this sort should be conceived in terms of years, since the only clear chance lies precisely in the decade or so needed before the major contending parties recover to a point where their domestic situation has been recouped to a point permitting them to resume their desire to expand.

2. *Prompt and Careful Elimination of Political Responsibility.* The situation by which the United States appears as a joint proponent of policies which she does not control should be promptly ended. The present policy in the Eastern Mediterranean is not being affected by the view of the United States; yet it is labeled "Anglo-American". Some steps have already been taken to clear up the situation. Propaganda has been issued by one or another joint psychological warfare station in the name of both countries; the British freely use the American name in association with their own in respect of policies distinctly their own. If care is not taken at once we shall find ourselves made jointly responsible for a situation in Greece which in practice is being determined by the Middle Eastern Command and carried out by British propaganda and intelligence officers; and for policing eventually by troops brought to Greece under British command; and for commercial policies largely carried out under the control of the British representation in the Middle East Supply Center.

We need not withhold support from such policies as go along with the basic command but we should as rapidly as possible get clear of the situation in which we are plastered with responsibility for endless incidents about which we know little and over which we have still less control. When we know about and like these policies, we can always say so. But if the British and the Soviets elect to work out their difficulties in Yugoslavia by sacrificing the Serbian population which revolted and fought the Germans at our insistence the least we can do is make it clear that this is their work and not ours; and bear in mind the mess the British got into in the same part of the world after the Napoleonic war when they sacrificed the Greek insurgents to Ali Pasha of Tepelini; we should be well advised to effect a graceful withdrawal as soon as we can; to endeavor to conserve the good will of both populations without being involved in responsibility for a political solution which apparently we cannot greatly affect.

Equally, if the Soviet Union elects to achieve her desire to get into the Eastern Mediterranean by sacrificing the Greek population of Thrace, we can make it clear that we are not in that situation either.

These are merely illustrations: the principle is general.

3. *Participation in Control Commission and Armistice Commission Work.* Except where the United States is taking active part in the work of the commissions and subcommissions set up under the Allied Control Commission and similar bodies, very great caution should be observed in authorizing participation by our representatives. In Germany where there is joint occupation, we would presumably take representation on all commissions; but in Eastern Europe where our representation is more or less nominal, and where we are not prepared to follow our hand with the full weight of such influence as we may have, it would seem desireable to play out.

In general we should want to be in a position of having our participation sought, and granted rather rarely, rather than that of having our participation taken for granted while our influence is not great.

4. *Public Information.* Our representatives should be under standing instructions to procure the greatest flow of public information from these countries to the United States. In one sense, the United States will be for some time a continuous battleground between contending international propaganda machines for sympathy and influence; and the only corrective possible is that of a free flow of information to the American press, as well as to the Department and Government agencies. The public cannot form any intelligent opinion capable of supporting any Department policy in the absence of impartial reporting.

A notable illustration is the effect which was produced by such reporting as was done of the Warsaw rising under General [Tadeusz] Bor [Komorowski]. Some help was eventually got to this beleaguered band after it became clear that the conscience of the world simply would not forgive their being sacrificed.

5. *Continuous Opposition to Closed Zones.* Standing instructions likewise ought to be issued to our representatives to oppose the setting up of "closed" systems, whether of commercial intercourse, or barter trade, or manipulation of exchange, or travel, et cetera. In general, the attitude ought to be taken that the United States, as a great power which has played a decisive part in the present conflict, cannot be in the position of having its citizens under restrictions not applicable to those of the greatest power in the region.

6. *Return of Exiles.* In respect of the return of individuals in exile from the United States or areas controlled by the United States to these countries our general position should be that *prima facie* anyone who wishes to go has a right to go. Having committed ourselves to the proposition that these countries are entitled to a government of their own choosing (with certain distinct reservations should the governments be Nazi or Fascist) there is a concomitant obligation to permit exiles to return to

their countries and submit whatever views they have to the public opinion of that country.

7. Except where we have direct obligations as an occupying power, we should withdraw from civil affairs commissions and military government commissions as rapidly as is possible.

All the foregoing seems dictated by the essential decision not to attempt to use military force in certain areas, coupled with the fact that we have not yet been able to achieve relations with our principal allies giving effect to our views by a process of argument.

8. *Certain Points of Application.* Despite the foregoing there are certain main line interests of the United States which should always be preserved and forwarded with every means at our command. These are the essential interests of a free access by communications, by air landing and transit rights, by the rights of our shipping to call at ports. These rights, if maintained with vigor, can, in my judgment, be obtained and held. It will need all of the influence of the Department to do this. But our representation in all of these countries can and should take the position that it is inadmissible for any ally to deny to us in any area peaceful access for peaceable communications and transport.

This is not primarily a commercial interest, though in the United States it is commonly so conceived. These thin lines are likely to be the only real lines through which we can maintain contact with and exert some influence over the underlying situation. They will be essential whether the problem is forwarding the work of whatever results from the Dumbarton Oaks Conference; or forwarding a generalized good neighbor doctrine which may avoid the conflict between two major powers. At the moment there appears to be no other leverage. The commercial interests, though they are important in some respects, are incidental to the maintenance of the general moral and diplomatic position which we should have, and which we will need, if we are not to be caught between the unresolved British and Soviet forces in respect of which there is no accommodation as yet in sight.

9. *Application to the Middle East.* If the conclusion above expressed is right, namely, that the Middle East and Eastern Mediterranean have to be taken together, certain specific application must be made to the Middle East.

(a) *Ethiopia.* It should be remembered that the conscience of the world was shocked by the Hoare-Laval Treaty designed to cut up Ethiopia. We cannot be in the position of assenting to the absorption of Ethiopia. The irony is too obvious, since it would merely be said that the conscience of the world was shocked when the French assented to an Italian seizure; but that this conscience promptly died when a politer form of seizure was carried out by someone else. The principal of equal access probably will be sufficient.

(b) *Iran.* Substantially the same obligation applies to Iran, though the irony is less obvious. Again equal access probably is the major solution; in practice this means putting into effect the high principles of the oil agreement, the maintenance of air and communication rights, and the maintenance of the principle of open commerce, and of free rights of travel by our citizens.

(c) *Saudi Arabia.* In Saudi Arabia where we have very substantial interests, we should not bow out of the picture. In substance, there we should play a part equal to that of any other power, and accept similar obligations.

It is my considered judgment that in the Middle East if a firm position is taken, the British will accede to it. For in the long run, all their calculations are based on the assumption that should they ever clash with the Soviet Union, the United States will be on the British side. This is not an assumption we should encourage; but unless we are hopelessly soft in our attitude, the British Government will hardly care to take the risk involved in a continued exclusionist policy.

Conclusion

Although we are possessed of very great force, there appear to be reasons convincing the senior officers of the Government that it cannot be used to extend our influence in Europe and the Middle East. Nevertheless the hope of survival of one great power, and a considerable portion of the hope of economic reconstruction of another great power, depends on the assumption that the United States will support them, politically in the one case, and economically in the other.

It would seem that while we are pushing for world organization, we should not let ourselves be taken for granted in either situation.

As the war ends, elements of pure force, which are now dominant in great parts of Europe and the Middle East, will tend to recede. At that time, influence will depend far more on the attitude of the populations than on the fire power of the victorious Allies mobilized in the district.

We have not, by manipulating our troop movements, created a *status quo* representing our ideas, and others, by their troop movements, are creating situations along the lines of their national interest. But the outstanding fact about these situations is that they are created by force, and that there is no particular reason to believe that they would remain once force is withdrawn. Yet nothing is more certain than that much of the force will have to be withdrawn by Britain and by the Soviet Union, as well as ourselves. It is at that time that American influence should grow if our work is well done. It is likewise at that time that any world organization worked out will get its first real chance to function.

To Hull, October 10, 1944

One of the White House assistants called up today to ask whether I would make a couple of campaign speeches in New York and Massachusetts. You are aware of the fact that New York appears now to be close.

I said I was entirely willing to do anything I could and would be glad to make any speeches, but that you had been a little unhappy about having State Department men do any talking, and I therefore would consult you. I should be glad to have your views.

I think any speeches made would have to be made on a high line, rather than normal political bickering. They could not, as I see it, be of any major influence except among the 150,000 independent votes in New York and a few similar votes in Massachusetts, both of which this year are on the fence.

Hull, not wishing to express any views, left the matter entirely to Berle.

To Roosevelt, October 12, 1944

At Charleston last Saturday, Governor Dewey [campaigning for the Presidency] misquoted a personal memorandum of mine date May 23, 1939 to the Temporary National Economic Committee, in a surprisingly dishonest effort to claim that your Administration was secretly trying to set up a Communist system.

To do this, he ripped a single sentence from a section dealing with the dangers of a closed capital market. One of the dangers set out was the fact that if capital did not flow into necessary enterprise, the Government would be compelled to enter direct financing of activities supposed to be private. If this happened, "Over a period of years, the government will gradually come to own most of the productive plants of the United States"—this being just what we wanted to avoid. Governor Dewey put this sentence forward as the doctrine advocated, though the entire memorandum showed the exact contrary.

He then built a speech on the theory that this was "your program". The record shows not only that this was not your program, but also that it was not anyone's program. In the circumstances this was a clear attempt to play fast and loose with the American public.

The program actually advocated was clearly stated just three paragraphs later:

"In a democratic organization of economy, the obvious end should be to permit and require private initiative to do as much of the work as it can, consistent with maintaining the national economy on a reasonably even flow, distributing the burdens and benefits meanwhile that no class will be unduly favored, no class unduly burdened, and a maximum of opportunity be provided for everyone to use his abilities usefully with corresponding reward. It is the definite function of the financial system to make this possible at all times."

Governor Dewey knows me quite well. He asked and got my help in getting him the independent nomination which made possible his election as District Attorney in New York. We served together for two years in New York City. He knows, as does everybody else, that, while I want a finance system that takes care of little people as well as big, I have never been a Communist.

On October 10 and 11, 1944, a number of newspaper correspondents noted that the statement had been taken out of context. Richard L. Strout, in the *Christian Science Monitor,* added: "This is only a footnote to a political campaign. Mr. Berle has been under bitter and almost constant Communist attack. He is a favorite target of the 'Daily Worker.' Candidates have to take a good deal of material supplied to them by research workers. But the latter can't be too careful in what they select and in the long run they injure rather than aid their employers by tearing quotations out of context."

October 21, 1944

Night before last a Congressional letter which I sent along through to Secretary Hull came back with the concise note from [Cecil] Gray that the Secretary was not able to transact any business. Yesterday morning Ed Stettinius told me that he had gone to the Naval Hospital and that, quite frankly, it looked as though he would not be better for a considerable period of time. He himself was going up to New York with the President to hear his speech to the Foreign Policy Association and that was that.

This takes the Secretary out at one of the most complicated periods in American diplomatic history. Just to add to the gaiety, last night a Guatemalan revolution broke out, with much shelling and some loss of life. The eventual armistice which led to the retirement of the provisional President, [Federico] Ponce, was signed in our Embassy, which was the neutral meeting place selected by the participants, and the whole Diplomatic Corps, including our man, signed as witnesses. I think this is probably all right. . . .

A meeting with the four top political men, Dunn [Acting Director, Special Political Affairs], Armour [Director, American Republic Affairs], Grew [Director, Far Eastern Affairs], and Wallace Murray [Director, Near Eastern and African Affairs], to try to determine our course of action in the conflict arising between Britain and Russia in the Balkans and the Middle East. I think that the Moscow agreement between Churchill and Stalin probably gets us over this hump; but I do not yet know what happened. As nearly as I can make out, the British recognized a predominant Russian sphere of influence in Bulgaria; they got what they thought were concessions in Yugoslavia, and took the dreary Polish controversy along another step. But I am afraid things are patched up rather than settled. . . .

Berle went to Chicago as chairman of the International Air Conference on November 1, 1944 (see Part VI). On November 26, Hull resigned. The Department was reorganized, and Stettinius became Secretary of State. Berle then resigned, but subsequently agreed to accept the ambassadorship to Brazil and was a delegate at the Inter-American Conference in Chapultepec, Mexico.

February 20, 1945, Mexico City

A long talk with [Ambassador George S.] Messersmith, who emphasized two things about the Conference: (1) The Inter-American system must be strengthened and not diluted by world organization. It can join the world organization but must not be destroyed by it. (2) The economic issues are of first importance. Further talks with some of the economic people but I gather from Nelson [Rockefeller, Assistant Secretary] that I should be working more on military affairs. They need working on; and General [Stanley D.] Embick, who is here, is an old friend. At work on various Resolutions, etc. and seeing people. Stettinius came in in the afternoon; a very fair turn-out; I went along to greet him, and Secretary [Pedro Leão] Velloso [Acting Minister for Foreign Affairs, Brazil] came in with his wife. Apparently for a first flight he had an extremely good time.

February 21, 1945
Committee meetings all over the place and the customary early conference confusion but I think it will sort itself out without trouble.

It is evident that there are two groups in the American Delegation: the group that thinks entirely globally and knows little about the hemisphere, and the group that thinks about the hemisphere first and global matters second. I do not know whether they will come in contact or not. The Conference was opened in the Chamber of Deputies by President [Manuel] Avila Camacho; a good short session. Very imposing with Mexican uniforms, etc. I added some gayety in the proceedings because my car blew out a tire on the way to the Chamber.

February 22, 1945
The opening session for speeches; [Ezequiel] Padilla [Mexican Minister for Foreign Affairs] made one of the best speeches I have ever heard (and I have heard a goodly lot) and Stettinius answered with a speech whose content was excellent although Padilla had him beaten for form. Then three mortal hours of succession in speeches. At the close of which I went back to the Hotel and there found a reporter from the Washington *Star* and we went out to have a sandwich and coffee preparatory to bed.

February 27, 1945, Mexico City
The real issues are beginning to show up. They were produced frankly, and came by indirection.

Uruguay and Colombia both introduced declarations which in effect constituted neutral guarantee by all the American Republics against aggression by any one of them, including guarantee of frontiers. This was aimed at the Argentine.

Thereupon Leo Pasvolsky and others objected, on the ground that it committed the United States to the use of force, whereas at the Dumbarton Oaks conference they had agreed that no one should be allowed to use force without consent of the World Council. This would mean that the United States and others could not prevent Argentina from seizing Uruguay without the consent of Britain and Russia—who at that moment might be backing Argentina. It would also introduce European diplomacy into every inter-American dispute.

At this point Generals Embick, Strong, [Robert LeGrow] Walsh and [Kenner] Hertford blew up, pointing out that the hemisphere is now in military entity; and that by breaking up the unity of the hemisphere, except with European consent, we sacrificed a military entity capable of defense. Europe and especially Russia make no such sacrifice. . . .

Naturally, I want both the unity of the hemisphere and its right to act in its own affairs without European diplomacy; and also the broad establishment of the Dumbarton Oaks arrangement that we can get consistent with this. I do not see that we can or should sacrifice the hard-won liberty of the hemisphere from European disputes and intrigues as a down payment for the right to participate in world organization.

This view at least is shared by a number of people. [Raúl R. ("Eddie")] Chibas of the Cuban Delegation (whom I have last seen as a young student who voted against Machado, and at his house Sumner Welles and I argued the American case at a dramatic session of the directorial estudiantil in 1933—he is now a Senator) was forcibly expounding this view last night. The Brazilians want the Monroe Doctrine lock, stock and barrel and make no secret of it. The Uruguayans think that the British would throw them to the Argentines. The rest of South America simply thinks we don't know what we are doing—and I must say I think they are right.

March 1, 1945, Mexico City

My own committee assignment, the First Commission, has to do with war criminals and war cooperation. There were no problems and we are cleaning up without difficulty. [Thomas C.] Mann, the youngster from the State Department, is excellent, and I therefore shifted to the main problem which is the Declaration of Chapultepec.

This rolled up almost spontaneously. It constituted a joint guaranty of everybody's territorial integrity and a joint obligation to resist any aggression inside the Americas as well as outside. Few people here realize the real drive behind it. It is terrific. The American nations think that Dumbarton Oaks means that any little dispute in the Hemisphere will be thrown into the proposed World Council, whereupon Britain, Russia, France, etc., would start stirring around in the Continent. Now the Continent has spent its entire history fighting to keep European imperialism out—and they are not going to go back over this trail if they know it. So they propose the tightest union here.

If we miss it, they probably will make that Union themselves, perhaps under European leadership.

The difficulty is that Senators [Warren] Austin [R., Vt.] and [Tom] Connally [D., Tex.], who are here, are worried lest the Senate will not approve a declaration which may commit us to use of force to keep the hemispheric peace—and on that may toss away the greatest unity the Hemisphere has yet seen.

The other difficulty is that some of the Dumbarton Oaks people, like Pasvolsky, know nothing of the Hemisphere, care less, and would like to see the regional situation broken up. The Army, Generals Embick, Strong, Walsh, Hertford, and Admiral [Harold Cecil] Train, want to see the regional situation thoroughly integrated. I cordially agree.

March 6, 1945, Mexico City

The Act of Chapultepec was formally passed by the Plenary Session today; of course it was really adopted by the full Committee three or four days ago. Behind it is a story not altogether pleasant in some respects.

The Uruguayan and Colombian proposals noted under date of February 27 were brought together by a subcommittee. The resulting document they christened "The Declaration of Chapultepec". It was briefly reported on by my old friend Luis Anderson [Foreign Minister, Costa Rica] merely as a matter of information to the full meeting of Committee no. III as a basis for discussion. The Committee, without more, stampeded for the Resolution lock, stock and barrel. It did guarantee frontiers; it did promise the use of force. It did multilateralize the Monroe Doctrine. But Pasvolsky had succeeded in infecting Senator Austin with the idea that the American regional organization ought to be broken up, and he feared that the Act of Chapultepec was a violation of some vague agreements still unexplained to the public made at Moscow or at Yalta, or lying below the surface of Dumbarton Oaks. Also in certain respects the Declaration was defective; a majority of countries could pledge all countries to the use of force. I was sitting in the Committee but decided to let Austin handle the situation since only in that way would he ever appreciate the strength of the drive behind this new organization. He blocked the adoption of the Declaration by acclamation, saying that there had not been time to study the English text although he was in full sympathy with its purposes.

Then we went into session at the American Delegation. Meanwhile our newspapermen had been pretty well posted. For if we had rejected this out-stretched hand, either the American Nations would have formed a union of their own, leaving us out of it, or they might have gone into intrigues either with Europe or Argentina.

The ensuing debates in the Delegation were pretty hot, but Rockefeller joined with me in urging that we meet the situation; and so did George Messersmith. Pasvolsky attempted an intrigue with Stettinius, whose cheerful ignorance remains the amazement of all hands; and he was about to succeed when the American press opened up. Lippmann's article was especially significant. After a brief struggle the Pasvolsky party withdrew from the field and Warren Austin went to work. He cured the defects in the Delegation by skillful use of the war powers and the Declaration was redrafted as the "Act of Chapultepec" in its present form.

It was so reported out, and the subcommittee and the Committee agreed; and it is being handsomely acclaimed as a milestone in inter-American relations.

What is not known is that arrangements have already been made to cut it to pieces at San Francisco by insisting on the right of the World Council—which in practice means the European powers with ourselves—to determine when, whether and on what circumstances the Act may be used. This, of course, would mean that the world is a straight, holy alliance, Metternich style; and I discover by a chance remark from Stettinius that this was discussed between Stalin and Roosevelt, Stalin rather insisting that we ought to get tough with the hemisphere or else permit the World Council to do so—in this case of course meaning himself. I have endeavored to take a few simple measures to see that the San Francisco meeting at least knows what it is about—but this is not an altogether easy thing to do—and anyway I shall be in Rio. . . .

The last question up (aside from economics) is Argentina. As to that, Padilla would like to declare a straight antagonistic attitude against all "non-democratic states"—leaving anybody to decide what a democratic state is or is not according to his fancy. The Communists would ex-communicate every state which did not meet their views irrespective of its form of government as they are now trying to ex-communicate Switzerland.

This seems impracticable: and anyhow you cannot legislate democracy into a country—certainly not if the country is to be free. It would undoubtedly lay the basis for a left-wing imperialism as dangerous and terrible as the right-wing imperialism; people soon forget that historically revolutions are imperialistic. After various discussions the pen finally came into my hand and we drafted a formula which is presently under discussion. This is designed courteously to hold open the door to Argentina when she shall have by action, as well as by word, carried out the principles on which the American nations have been working for some years past—but so drawn as to be a very strong hold that performance is expected. This would be an impossible policy were it not for the fact that by the Declaration of Chapultepec we have guaranteed frontiers, we have agreed to use our force against aggression, and to maintain a common attitude; so that Argentina's militaristic and imperialistic policy is now blocked in all directions. She can, as I see it, only make war at once—a practical impossibility—or contemplate the complete sterility of her policy until such time as she gets ready to change it. . . .

Meditating, I think that this Conference, or more accurately the American part in it, was saved by the fact that the newspapermen knew what to do when they were told to do it and performed valiantly. This influenced an American Delegation whose head is singularly sensitive to that kind of thing to do what was necessary at the right time. But suppose no-one had been around to tell the pressmen—or the pressmen had not been capable enough to use the information!

March 14, 1945, Washington
The Mexico City Conference closed with the loud fanfare of klieg lights but the heart of it worked out about as we had hoped, namely:

the recognition that peace-keeping within the Americas is a matter for the American nations, implemented by guarantee of territorial integrity and direct obligation of all hands to assist therein;

the recognition of a variety of subordinate but highly important matters, including necessity for free transmission of information, for the elimination of Axis agents and return of war criminals;

finally, and perhaps as important as anything else, the reorganization of the Pan American Union so as to make its council a true American League of Nations.

There were likewise a good many resolutions about economics, but I have not followed them closely enough to have an opinion or to know whether they are really important or merely words.

Berle summarized the importance of the results of this conference in a lecture at the Air War College, Maxwell Field, Alabama, on February 13, 1956.

. . . In point of fact, the Act of Chapultepec (now the Treaty of Rio de Janeiro) was almost forced on an unwilling United States by nineteen of the twenty other American republics (Argentina being at the moment absent) and it was finally accepted by the American Government owing to strenuous efforts by Mr. Nelson Rockefeller and Senator Warren Austin, the American naval and military delegates and the [lecturer].

The incident should have ended there. The United Nations Conference convened in San Francisco on April 25, 1945. The American delegation did not include anyone who had been at Chapultepec. The proposed United Nations charter did not include any recognition of regional groups. The text of the charter indeed would have outlawed the arrangement made at Chapultepec. It was then discovered that the Latin American countries were unable to vote for it. Mr. Nelson Rockefeller was summoned to assist in getting their votes; he pointed out that the American word given after full deliberation had not been kept. Ultimately by enlisting the aid of Senator Vandenberg he was able to compel the inclusion in the charter of the United Nations Article 51 which provides:

"Art. 51. Nothing in the present Charter shall impair the inherent right of individual or collective self-defence if an armed attack occurs against a Member of the United Nations, until the Security Council has taken the measures necessary to maintain international peace and security."

And again

"Art. 52. 1. Nothing in the present Charter precludes the existence of regional arrangements or agencies for dealing with such matters relating to the maintenance of international peace and security as are appropriate for regional action".

It is under these clauses that the Treaty of Rio de Janeiro, the North Atlantic Treaty Organization, and other similar agreements now exist.

The struggle in the American delegation at San Francisco appears to have been violent. President Roosevelt, who had finally determined the point in favor of the Chapultepec agreement, of course, was dead. Secretary Stettinius apparently had been induced to agree that the Chapultepec agreement should not be carried out. President Truman was too recently in the situation to have been well informed about it, and the State Department had been entirely reorganized. The persistence of Mr. Rockefeller and of Senator Vandenberg eventually carried the day; and as a result the present structure of American foreign policy has taken form.

March 14, 1945

On return to Washington from the Mexico conference I put in to see the President and, on Monday (March fifth), Stettinius, Velloso, and I, with Ambassador Martins, saw him for half an hour; after which I lingered for half an hour longer. The President is tired and getting old. His trip to Yalta obviously aged him a good deal. He was telling the assembled group about his trip back from Yalta and how he had sent a destroyer to bring King Ibn Saud up from Jiddah, the King arriving in a tent on the forward deck of the destroyer with a gold chair set for him and six slaves. They apparently talked over the Palestine business, the President saying that they arrived at nothing at the moment though he hoped that he had begun to lay a base for the eventual solution of the problem. Ibn Saud made the point that he had no trouble with native Palestine Jews but the immigration from Europe was more than he could cope with and if things went wrong the millions of surrounding Arabs might easily proclaim a Holy War and then there would be no end of trouble. He likewise said that he hoped General [Getúlio] Vargas would be reelected President but did not want to take any hand in it lest it do more harm than good. Vargas had a world point of view and had done the best he could with the situation, his dictatorship being a result of the wide illiteracy in the country. Obviously it was a great day in Velloso's life. Afterwards we had a real chat. I told him that Mexico City represented partly a jolt from the fear lest the World Council designed by Dumbarton Oaks should import European diplomacy into the Hemisphere; the American republics had no reason to trust European diplomacy whether it be Russian, French, or British. The President at once cordially agreed. He said, that, so far as he could see, Churchill was running things on an 1890 set of ideas; that after he had talked to Ibn Saud literally hundreds of British Intelligence agents swarmed out of the landscape to try to find out what he said to Ibn Saud, and Ibn Saud said to him it would have been simpler if Churchill had asked him and Churchill indeed had wanted to go along with the President lest British imperial interests be threatened. He said he had in mind that the Hemisphere had to be better protected and, partly because of this, he had vetoed the sending of Leo Pasvolsky to San Francisco; "he would get lynched out there"; and I added that he had nearly got lynched at Mexico City. We talked some generalities and I wished him good fortune. He was obviously unhappy about certain of the settlements he had had to make in Yalta but saw no escape from the fact of the situation. . . .

In a speech at Kalamazoo College, May 26, 1965, Berle summarized his views on Yalta.

I had been opposed to [the meeting at Yalta]. Perhaps because one of my jobs was liaison with the intelligence services, it was clear to me that the Soviet Union had lost interest in cooperating with the British and Americans—and probably also with the French. Stalin was playing a Soviet hand against the field, and the Soviet Union intended if possible to dominate continental Europe. Her people were using for that purpose the Communist-organized underground movements everywhere, from Warsaw to Paris. They had already pushed their armies beyond pre-war Russian frontiers. Increasingly it was plain that where the Russian armies stood, there the Russian power—and Communist organization—would stay. . . . So I thought the Yalta conference and its underlying motive— necessity for redeploying the American troops in Europe to the Far East against Japan—would lead to trouble. Partly at least because of this, I left the Senior Assistant Secretaryship of the State Department and had gone as Ambassador to Brazil.

As it happened, I returned to Washington just after Roosevelt had returned from Yalta, and went to see him. He was ill and tired. He put up both arms and said: "Adolf, I didn't say the result was good. I said it was the best I could do." I put my arm around him and tried to make laughter. He wanted to talk. He explained patiently that he had got the Russians' word for reconstitution of the countries under Russian occupation. There were to be free elections. They were to choose their own governments. True, this was only an agreement. But the Chiefs of Staff were pushing the need of taking American forces out of Europe and deploying to Japan. Since, therefore, we would not push troops into the area, we must rely on the Russian word. Also the Chiefs wanted Russian participation against Japan in the final drive.

I thought—and President Roosevelt knew it—that the Russians could be of little help against Japan anyway and that the Japanese even then were seeking ways and means of ending the war. Therefore, no sacrifices need be made to assure Russian cooperation. The President knew—and so did I—that Assistant Secretaries of State, especially in wartime, do not override the cold calculations of the military chiefs. They are responsible for the results, and for the lives of hundreds of thousands of men under their command. Even then, Roosevelt was mulling over the methods, persuasions and pressures by which the Soviet Union might be induced to keep its word in Central Europe.

VI

1944

February 17, 1941

We settled up the internal administration of the Department with Welles. Acheson draws the blockade and economic defense work; I will have finance, aviation, and a variety of other things. Secretary Hull is ill and the strain on Sumner is getting very great indeed.

To Hull, September 9, 1942

I feel that the best interests of the Department would probably be served if the responsibility for aviation were shifted from my office to one of the other Assistant Secretaries. . . .

(1) In April of this year I raised the question of handling aviation either as a separate division, or under an aviation adviser analogous to our petroleum adviser. . . .

(2) In June of this year the Department declined to accept this view, and decided that it preferred to keep aviation within the section of International Communications but would endeavor to staff a section, and equip it with a capable assistant chief. . . .

(3) Three months have now passed. We have no assistant chief. . . .

The situation is at an impasse.

Behind the difficulty is a difference in conception.

I feel that aviation will have a greater influence on American foreign interests and American foreign policy than any other non-political consideration. It may well be determinative in certain territorial matters which have to do with American defense, as well as with transportation matters affecting American commerce, in a degree comparable to that which sea power has had on our interests and policy. We should, accordingly, study our territorial relationships, certain of our international objectives, and certain phases of our diplomatic strategy, in view of this rapidly developing, and perhaps decisive, element. . . . We cannot remain unconcerned as to location of airports, present and post-war control of those airports, and arrangements by which they are controlled and maintained.

In this conception we ought to be doing a great deal of original work in considering, planning and developing policies, and acting consistently with the conclusions reached.

The opposing conception is that other agencies will bring matters to the attention of the Department as they may arise, and that the Department will give them more or less routine consideration. . . .

For six months I have endeavored to resolve the problem, without success. Only recently, the legal Vice President of Pan American Airways was seriously urged by the Department as assistant chief in charge of aviation and in control of that section, despite the fact that one major issue in the proceeding is whether our foreign relations in respect of aviation shall be largely controlled by that company for its private profit, and that a Senate investigation is in progress.

January 2, 1943

The British seem to have formulated some air proposals relating to distribution of civil transport after the war. Thanks to the dunderheadedness of this Department in not arranging a setup that had an effective air man in it, we are pretty helpless. I talked to the Secretary and got authority today to work up an interdepartmental group with the help of [Assistant Secretary Robert] Lovett (War Department), [Assistant Secretary Ralph A.] Bard (Navy) [later replaced by Artemus Gates], [Under Secretary] Wayne Taylor (Commerce), and Welch Pogue (Civil Aeronautics Board), and draft proposals of our own. I think we will get a good deal done that way. . . .

This interdepartmental group evolved into a working committee, which also included Wayne Coy, Assistant Director of the Budget. On April 30, 1943, it sent the following report to Hull:

Your Advisory Committee on Aviation met on April 29th and agreed on the essentials of a first report. . . .

(1) There is a wide and rapidly growing tendency throughout the world to work out arrangements excluding American civil aviation from post-war landing rights and routes. . . .

(2) The Committee feel that the best interests of the United States are served by the widest generalization of air navigation rights. This is the historic American position. . . .

Our principal bargaining point consists in ability to grant or deny entry into the United States. After careful review of all factors, the experts have with substantial unanimity reached the conclusion that American aviation is better off if an understanding can be reached by which our planes are granted entry into the countries willing to enter a general agreement; in return for which we would accept entry of the planes of the signatory countries into the United States.

(3) The generalized agreement, it is the experts' belief, should likewise include the right of an innocent commercial plane to pass through the air of any of the signatory countries, subject, however, to the right of the signatories to block off certain areas for purposes of military security.

(4) The Committee and their experts further believe that to avoid

destructive competition, a generalized agreement should provide for the creation of a regular "conference" to set rates, analogous to the shipping "conferences" which set the "conference rates" for ocean passenger and freight service.

(5) The Committee tackled the tough question as to whether American foreign aviation after the war should be in the hands of a monopoly company (Pan-American Airways), or whether it should be divided among a number of American companies. Due note was taken of the fact that this is going to be a hot political issue, because of the strength of the lobbies of the various contending parties.

The Committee—one member dissenting—was of the view that American foreign aviation is too big a proposition for any single company; and that the monopoly principle used by other countries has in general produced inefficient service. It therefore proposes apportionment among a selected number of airlines, granting to each a particular zone in which it might be dominant. . . .

(6) If the recommendation of the Committee be accepted, namely, that negotiations for a general air agreement be commenced, then the procedure would seem to be as follows:

We should ask the British and the British Dominions and India to name experts who could confer with us here in Washington; and we should make a similar request of Russia and China.

We should, as discussions go on, keep the other American republics having an interest in the subject carefully and closely informed of the progress of discussion, and invite them to submit ideas.

The heart of a general navigation agreement would have to rest on agreement between the United States and the British Empire and Commonwealth of Nations; it may fairly be assumed that once this agreement is reached, practically all countries in the world (with the possible exception of Russia) would accede.

A subsequent report, August 31, 1943, of the Advisory Committee emphasized the conflict between Pan American's desire for a monopoly of air traffic and the desire of sixteen other commercial airlines, which favored free competition, worldwide freedom of transit in peaceful flight, and private ownership of U.S. aviation, backed by the government in the acquisition of civil and commercial outlets.

British and U.S. aviation experts had already agreed that without a general understanding neither would negotiate agreements exclusive or discriminatory against the other.

November 11, 1943

The President requested [a meeting with Berle, Lovett, Pogue, Stettinius, and Hopkins].

He stated that he had begun to discuss aviation policy with Prime Minister Churchill at Quebec and he expected to go on doing so at their coming meeting. He had considered the various problems of policy and wished to state the policy he wanted followed. Reading from a memorandum which he said he had himself prepared . . .

(1) Germany, Italy, and Japan were not to be permitted to have any aviation industry or any aviation lines, internal or external. This involved policing these countries.

Their external traffic would be handled by the lines of the other countries. Internal aviation could be handled by a company or companies to be formed by the United Nations. . . .

(2) As to aviation in other countries: The President felt that each country should have ownership and control of its own *internal* aviation services. . . .

(3) The scope of [American] international aviation was too great to be trusted to any one company or pool. He said that certain companies— to speak frankly, Pan American—wanted all of the business, and he disagreed with Trippe. . . .

(4) and (5) . . . there remained open the question of ownership by the Government of an interest in the various lines contemplated under this policy . . . he thought there was no need of such ownership under the proposed plan, except as the Government might have to own, initially, lines going to places in which the traffic could not support a company . . . but always on the understanding that if ever a private line was prepared to bid for the route, the Government would promptly retire from the business.

(6) As to air and landing rights . . . he wanted a very free interchange . . . he thought planes should have general right of free transit and right of technical stop—that is, the right to land at any field and get fuel and service, without, however, taking on or discharging traffic. . . .

(7) . . . there should be no general party or conference about aviation until the time was right to call a United Nations conference. Talks with Britain and other countries could be handled quietly as a part of the preparatory discussion.

(8) The President considered that there would have to be a United Nations conference on aviation and probably a United Nations organization to handle such matters as safety standards, signals, communication, weather reporting, and the incidental services which went with airports; and also to handle the problem of competitive subsidies or rates. . . .

February 22, 1944

The last few days, working on two separate jobs, although they sound the same: the development of a post-war civil aviation policy; and the collection of a string of bases designed to take care of United States security after the end of the war.

The former has now resolved itself in conferences to be held with the British and some, or perhaps all, of the Dominions; the British want all of them; we should prefer Canada only. Likewise, conversations with the Russians if they wish to join, and probably the Chinese. The lot are designed to lead up to a United Nations conference later this year.

The British Government is talking of open flying generally throughout the world, but nervously expressing the hope that we will control competition.

But the Department reports make it perfectly plain that behind that the British shipping companies and the BOAC are trying to rig up blocs under cartel arrangements with the continental Europeans designed to exclude the United States from the whole European area. The British plan apparently is to get participating rights to fly in South America, the Pacific, and China; and access to the United States; meanwhile, to exclude us from the continental European area and the Mediterranean routes—and presumably also the Near East. It will be quite a battle when it comes. . . .

On the base side, we have got a tentative indication from Brazil that they will go along, which would take care of our Brazilian bases. Joe McGurk [American Republics Division] thinks the Mexicans will join. I have no worries about the Central Americans. The bases in the Japanese mandated islands, the Marshalls, Colombia, Marianas, we will not negotiate for; I hope we shall simply go out and take them. We shall have some negotiations to do with a few British islands.

The tough job will be with the French. We need some bases on the Society Islands and the Marquesas; likewise one at Dakar and Casablanca, in Africa; and, of course, we should like some in the Cape Verde Islands, the Azores, and the Canaries. I think we can get a base in Ascension without trouble.

Just as soon as we get reasonably started in Brazil and Mexico, I propose to go to work in Canada. With good luck, we might have the whole program fairly well implemented by the first of July; after which I would feel that we had gotten out of this war reasonably safe.

Memorandum, March 6, 1944

The Soviet Ambassador [Andrei A. Gromyko] came in to see me at my request. I said that I wished to give him, for his information, the present state of exchanges regarding exploratory conversations on aviation. . . .

I said . . . the British Government had assented to the suggestion of exploratory conversations between us, the British, the Chinese if they cared to join, and Canada, but had asked that in that case the other British Dominions should be present, namely, Australia, South Africa, and New Zealand. We had responded that, while we were glad to do that, if the Australians, South Africans, and New Zealanders were present, there was no legitimate argument why other countries, including South American countries, as well as the Netherlands, the French National Committee, and others, should not be present, since they had equal interest.

In consequence, we had proposed a series of bilateral conversations commencing with the British, the Soviet Union, the Chinese, and the Canadians, to be followed right up by conversations with the necessary South American countries and the necessary European countries, all preparatory to a United Nations conference to be held later in the year. This proposal was presently outstanding with the British Government, and we had not yet received a reply. . . .

The Ambassador asked if I had any idea of the possible date of a United Nations conference. I told him that I did not see how we could know that until the exploratory conversations had gone forward; we had rather hoped that it might be this summer.

The Ambassador thanked me for the information and said that it might be necessary for them to consider what men they would send. He asked who would handle it on our side. I told him that we had asked Ambassador Grew to head up the group for the United States; he would be assisted by technicians and others. The Ambassador asked whether I expected to join, and I said that I probably would be on hand to be of whatever help I could. . . .

On March 11, 1944, Hull wrote a memorandum headed "Aviation Conversations" for Roosevelt. It read:

"After various preliminaries, the British now have come fairly close to our projected method. They suggest a quiet trip by Berle to London, stopping in Canada en route. Discussions to be for the purpose of exchanging views but without making commitments. It is considered probable they would not object to our keeping the Soviets informed, and discussing with them at about the same time either in London or Washington, equally without commitment.

"If you approve, I contemplate authorizing Berle and either Pogue or [Edward] Warner [Vice Chairman] of C.A.B. to go to London as quietly as the newspapers will let them, in about ten days, to hold such discussions, exchange views, make no commitments, and report back. Could you let me have your views?"

Roosevelt returned it with the comment, "OK And let the Soviets know."

Memorandum, March 21, 1944

The Soviet Ambassador came in to see me at his request. He said that he had word from Moscow that the Soviet Government would be glad to have conversations with the United States in respect of post-war civil aviation. They have named their delegation. . . .

I said I was gratified to see that he would be on the delegation and asked whether the others were already here. He said all were here except General [Ivan Y.] Petrov and Colonel [Pavel Fedorovich] Berezin. These two would be coming along soon. They could not arrive earlier than ten days; he understood, however, that they were leaving Moscow shortly. . . .

Berle and Warner flew to London on March 29, 1944, stopping in Montreal on the way at the request of the Canadian Government. Informal conversations were held in London, with Lord Beaverbrook, Lord Privy Seal, presiding. Berle also discussed these matters with Churchill. The joint statement, released April 7, stated that

"(1) Sufficient agreement between them had been reached to justify the expectation that final dispositions can be reached at an international conference;

"(2) Government of Soviet Union and other governments would likewise enter into conversations prior to such conference; and

"(3) International control should govern a considerable field of technical matters."

The British favored an international authority with power to fix rates, frequencies, etc. The Americans felt that the international authority should deal only with technical matters related to air traffic.

Memorandum, June 10, 1944

The President asked Senator [Bennett Champ] Clark [D., Mo.], Mr. Pogue, and myself to meet him at the White House on June 9. . . . The Senate Committee had been working now for some time, and the President wanted to know what the prospects were of getting an agreement.

Senator Clark said that the Subcommittee was pretty well divided . . . the first question they had to solve was whether we would proceed on a chosen instrument monopoly theory, or whether we would have the more traditional form of regulated competition. The active members of the Committee, he thought, were favorable to the chosen instrument theory, though [Ralph O.] Brewster [R., Me.] only had committed himself. The other members, Mead, [Hattie W.] Caraway [D., Ark.], and [Harold H.] Burton [R., O.], had not indicated a position. [Josiah W.] Bailey [D., N.C.], he thought favored the chosen instrument, though Bailey had been very judicial throughout. Senator Clark said that he himself wanted to follow whatever policy the President decided. Generally speaking, he did not favor the chosen instrument.

The President said that he himself had rather felt that the best policy was to have chosen instruments in particular fields . . . [he] favored different lines assigned to different routes and zones. Senator Clark seemed generally to agree. . . .

From the discussion the following facts became clear:

(1) Senator Clark personally will follow the President's line; he does not know whether he can carry the Subcommittee, though he will have a substantial group in it.

(2) He recognizes the necessity of getting into action during the summer; believes that Brewster and the Pan American interests will raise a row in any event unless they get what they want.

The President said that he had discussed this matter a little with Stalin at Tehran in the general sense that Soviet planes desiring to fly over American territory ought to have the right to land and refuel, though not to take on and discharge passengers or cargo; we would want equivalent rights in the Soviet Union. Stalin thought something could be worked out.

In respect of Hawaii, the President said that the right to land and refuel ought not to be had at Honolulu. There were plenty of other points, especially on the Island of Hawaii itself, which could be made available for these landings. He noted that General [Henry H.] Arnold thought there should be at least three lines across the Pacific Ocean for safety reasons.

June 23, 1944

The past four days have seen a phase of the struggle to get control of American foreign aviation which is reminiscent of the old Gould-Vanderbilt railroading tactics. We know that Trippe of Pan American Airways negotiated with [Alfred Cecil] Critchley of BOAC when Critchley was in the country some months ago. They agreed, roughly, that Pan

American would have the cream of the North Atlantic traffic; and would stay out of the continent of Europe, BOAC staying out of South America except for a limited entry. Critchley had no authority to make this agreement and Beaverbrook suspected him and had him shadowed by the British Intelligence. The report of the deal reached Beaverbrook via the Intelligence . . . and it was later confirmed by Critchley, whereupon Beaverbrook directed that it all be called off. But, so far as the two groups are concerned, both appear to have endeavored to carry it out if they could.

So far as America was concerned there were some obstacles, and one of them was the fact that there was no law conferring all American aviation on Pan Am. My own consultations with the Senate subcommittee, headed by Bennett Champ Clark, have been really my own assertion of the right of the United States to its international aviation, against the thinly concealed but active campaign by Pan Am, whose stooge in the committee is Brewster of Maine, to secure, by some means, a subcommittee report favoring the chosen instrument theory and conferring on Pan Am the right to handle American air interests in foreign negotiations.

They did not make as much progress in the subcommittee as they expected—partly because Clark, whom they had counted on, declined to go along and finally decided to stay with the President. . . . The independent airlines got busy and started a campaign throughout the country. Bennett Clark came back by airplane from St. Louis—which was not on the program. A number of the Senators thought to have been lined up declined to go along with the program, so that a majority of the subcommittee could not be had. Yesterday morning, when Panair counted noses, they did not have enough, and the scheme failed. . . .

The preparatory conversations in respect of air matters are going forward. The Soviets have still to state their views. The Chinese in general are in accord with us and are quite prepared to grant routes and landing rights to us, but on the side, Chang Kai-ngau, who used to be Minister of Communications and is here talking for the Chinese, tells me that Chungking hopes for help in building up their internal system. Help means a present, or substantially that, of 300 Douglas DC-3's and 200 of the big DC-4's—a kit of planes which would give even the United States, in its present state of development, about half again more service than it now has. Certainly the price is not low.

To Beaverbrook, June 29, 1944

The situation regarding conversations with the Soviet representatives is this:

The Soviet representatives are proceeding in a leisurely manner, taking time out between discussions to go over American airfields and American technical processes of control, licensing, signaling, and so forth. They are really combining the technical with the general conversations. My present guess is that in another two or three weeks these conversations should be concluded though I cannot guarantee this because the Russian group is controlled by instructions from Moscow. . . . They tell me they have no instructions as yet to proceed to London. . . .

Thus far, the Soviet representatives have said very little as to the attitude of their Government. I gather that they are, in principle, agreeable to the setting up of a world organization which shall have considerable competence in the technical fields covered in our conversations in London.

The Soviet Government appears, however, to be very clear in its determination not to yield what they consider sovereign powers, though our present impression is that they would accept a world organization with reporting and advisory functions in respect to economic and commercial matters. . . .

It is clear that the Soviets do expect to fly internationally; and that they want to have their ideas taken into consideration in connection with general air settlements. I think they intend to admit a limited number of foreign air lines into Soviet territory, granting use of their airfields for that purpose. . . .

They would likewise be interested in knowing whether there were disagreements between the British and United States Governments; and we have told them that the British point of view favored a far stronger world organization, with far wider authority than we would be prepared to accept. We have said that in other matters such as the definition of cabotage, the maintenance of equilibrium between available transportation and the traffic desiring to use it, and in the general desire to have freer passage rights than existed previously, we were generally in accord.

In accordance with our understanding that the result of conversations shall be available to all hands, I will keep you advised as matters develop, and the Soviet group understands this.

Memorandum, June 30, 1944

I refer to Lord Halifax's conversation with Secretary Hull on June 29, and his aide-mémoire which requests American support for the allocation to the Soviet Union of four heavy air transport craft. The British applied to the Munitions Assignment Board for these aircraft, planning to transfer them to the Soviet Government. The Board ruled that they would await a direct application from the Soviet Government; the British wished to contest this. They asked that, on British application, the Munitions Assignment Board transfer four American aircraft to the Soviets. . . . The British wish an air route into Moscow. This route will be, in effect, a commercial route. We are likewise seeking an air route into Moscow, both from the North across Scandinavia, and from the South, from Tehran.

The British finally secured Soviet consent to British air entry into Moscow provided, (1) the British would grant reciprocal flying rights for the Soviets into England, and (2) the British would provide American planes which the Russians could operate in this airway. The British themselves expect to use American aircraft on their part of the route. In effect, therefore, the British propose to set up a British-Moscow air route with lend-leased American planes, and propose to equip the Russians to set up a Moscow-Britain air route with American planes; the consideration for the transaction appears to be American planes which the British will get and give to the Soviets.

Meanwhile, we have not as yet got any air entry into the Soviet Union. . . . We see no reason, if American planes are to be used to establish quasi-commercial services, and are to be given away to buy Russian air rights, why we should not have our air rights considered at the same time. In other words, if the Russians want American planes, they can get them from us. We have no objection to having the British get air rights into Moscow, but we want air rights, too. . . .

If the Soviets apply to the Munitions Assignment Board for American planes, presumably they will get them. But in that case it will be plain that the planes came from the United States and by United States desire. . . .

This is the background of the Halifax note. My thought is that we should tell the British that we are glad to help them with their air entry into Moscow, but that we want the same or similar rights for the United States. The handing over of such planes as the Soviet Union may need could be arranged jointly for the whole transaction.

It would be well to obtain Harriman's opinion on this.

July 4, 1944

General Bissell, Chief of Military Intelligence, called up today. He and Admiral Schuirmann had before them the question of whether the Truman Investigating Committee should be allowed to release publicly the data concerning the Pan Am airport contracts, particularly those in South America. It will be recalled that some months ago the War Department sent over the data on these, collected at the request of the Truman Committee, with a letter stating that there was no objection to their being disclosed from the military point of view but they wished to know whether State had any objection. At that time we answered that we thought the material should be released to the Truman Committee, but would request that they hold it in executive session until such time as the Brazilian air base negotiations, then pending, were completed. Subsequently, when those negotiations were completed, I telephoned the counsel for the Truman Committee, stating that these negotiations were completed and that, from our point of view, we saw no further reason to insist on the secrecy of the data.

General Bissell, who stated frankly that there was pressure on him from Pan American, asked whether or not we did not wish to continue our injunction of secrecy on the ground that Pan American interests might be prejudiced. I said that quite frankly I did not want the State Department to be responsible for concealing the facts here. They were not too creditable to the company. The company had been paid for building the air fields and had got, as additional compensation, the exclusive right to the use of the fields and installations after the war—in other words, the reversion of some 38 millions of dollars' worth of work as soon as the war was over.

General Bissell said that there had been an oral understanding between the War Department and Pan Am at the time the contracts were made that they would be kept secret. I said that was a matter for them to consider, since we had not been a party to it. . . .

Bissell said that one of the considerations was that they did not want the enmity of big American companies while we were trying to win the war. I said that, frankly, that reason did not appeal to me too much; whenever a company had engaged in a discreditable transaction, of course enmity would result from disclosing it. But I did not see that that, by itself, made a very good reason. If, of course, there was some military reason for withholding the information that was another thing. Bissell said that [Thomas] Burke, now working for Export, was stirring up the situation and he did not like that. I told him I did not like it either. It was frankly a case of a commercial war between two companies and I wanted no part of it. . . .

Bissell concluded by asking whether I would call up the Truman Committee and say that, in stating that the information was available for release, I was speaking only for the State Department and not for War and Navy. I said that I had no objection to that because the State Department never undertook to speak for other Departments.

Bissell indicated that he and Schuirmann had agreed that the data about the Pan Am contracts ought not to be made public.

July 6, 1944

Dinner last night with the Russian Aviation Mission—General [Leonid G.] Rudenko, General Petrov, Colonel Asaieff [P. N. Asseev?], General Berezin and so on. It was in Tommy Corcoran's old house on Garfield Street, and was highly convivial. The young captain-interpreter fell on Beatrice's neck saying over and over again again that our house was the only home he had entered in Washington in two years. We must do more about this. Knowing no Russian, I played the first 15 moves of a chess game with Petrov, who liked it. I think he was getting ahead of me when we went in to dinner.

Memorandum, July 21, 1944

Lord Beaverbrook and Richard Law [Minister of State] came to Washington for conversations on oil and aviation.

At lunch with Lord Beaverbrook today, he gave his ideas as to the possible course of civil aviation matters. He said that he was under instructions to maintain the desire for a strong international body which could regulate civil aviation matters. He was fully aware of our position, which was that we could not assent to this. I gathered, however, from the conversation that at an appropriate time the British Government will recede from its position. Lord Beaverbrook, indeed, indicated that there would have to be several days' battle at an international conference before this would be achieved.

He said that he thought the situation had progressed to a point where the parties really interested ought to sit down and begin talking about routes in advance of an international conference. We had stated what we wanted; the Netherlands had stated what they wanted. The British would be able to lay down a map on relatively short notice. Probably the other parties principally interested could do likewise. His idea was that we first talk routes, and not talk frequencies. Frequencies could be left for a later stage,—possibly an international conference. Routes, especially at this stage of the game, he thought would have to be determined by reasonable give and take between all parties interested—a thoroughly flexible arrangement which could develop as events move forward.

I told him that in the more recent conversations, especially with the Netherlands, somewhat the same idea had been expressed. I would tell him very soon whether he had better send for his route experts while he was here. In any event we should like to know what their plans were, since we had already stated our own.

July 29–30, 1944

Following is a report of a rather fantastic weekend.

[Saturday] morning at seven o'clock I went to the airport to leave with Beaverbrook for New Brunswick, where we were to meet Clarence Howe, the Canadian Minister of [Munitions and Supply]. This was designed to be all party, though we had a little business to transact. General [Harold L.] George kindly gave us a plane and we sailed away; but the plane also contained [Ralph] Assheton and Law, and Beaverbrook's gentleman's gentleman, Nockles, who belongs in a P. G. Wodehouse novel except that he makes Jeeves look like a piker. Just as we were floating over New Brunswick, it suddenly dawned on me that this was a sentimental place; Richard Law's father, Bonar Law, besides being Prime Minister of England, was born in New Brunswick . . . Beaverbrook, though actually born in Ontario, was likewise a New Brunswicker . . . there is a little streamlet known as Beaver Brook, which is where the title comes from. We flew over Wrexton and duly saw Dick Law's grandfather's Presbyterian Church; were met by all the village gentry at Chatham, where we congregated in front of the two-story building where Beaverbrook had his first job; then floated through Newcastle past Beaverbrook's father's Presbyterian parsonage and further in the direction of the New Brunswick woods, winding up at the camp of one Sir James Dunn, who runs the Algoma Hotel Company and has relatively recently acquired a lovely girl, I should think thirty years his junior, as a wife, whom everybody calls Christopher. She is English by accent and manner; only an occasional slight shift in point of view revealing the fact that she is racially Greek. Tall, slender, obviously under instructions to keep out of the way while three members of the British Cabinet (Assheton, I suppose, rates that, though the title is Secretary of the Treasury), a ranking Canadian Cabinet Minister, C. D. Howe, an American Assistant Secretary of State, Sir James Dunn, a doctor who was a house guest, and the omnipresent and amazing Nockles proceed to put in what was left of a Saturday afternoon and night, all of Sunday and a fair proportion of Sunday night on a combination party and discussion of some proportion.

The whole thing from beginning to end was dominated by the abounding bounce, gaiety and endless vitality of Beaverbrook, who seems to have cooked all this up mostly for the fun of it. Sir James seems to have been likewise a bare-fisted New Brunswick boy who came up the long hard road to British land and British baronetcy along with the Beaver; and his camp, which is twenty miles from anywhere, in the middle of the New Brunswick woods, is on land which his grandfather used to cut masts for British and New Brunswick ships.

Appropriately, the party began by the Lady Christopher bringing out some champagne which Sir James declared to be the best in the world, along with some brandy reported to be the same . . . likewise a bottle of whiskey. The Beaver had brought along some caviar, whiskey and other miscellaneous drinks and things, all of which Nockles served up with apparent gusto. The Beaver was in rare form. He went over every stick and stump in New Brunswick from Chatham to the Bay of Chaleur, all of which he had known in his youth, and there was no question but that he was having the time of his life. Law, somewhat more restrained, obviously was a little subdued in the presence of his Presbyterian ancestors, and having an amazing time making his conscientious, kindly and reserved emotion bracket with the sky-writing ebullience of the Beaver. . . .

I should add that this began at lunch, which was appropriately served, on this Alice-in-Wonderland schedule, at a quarter past six, after which we separated. I continued the argument with the Toronto doctor while attempting to cast a fly line for some trout. We met up with Assheton, who had been off looking for a beaver dam, where we continued happily, and encountered the Beaver (I mean his lordship) with Lady Christopher sitting on top of a beaver house under some spruce trees. Dick Law, I believe, had meanwhile gone off to fish down the stream.

I got in a few solid minutes with Howe during the evening, bringing him up to date on the aviation conferences had with the Russians, with the Netherlanders, and New Zealanders and so on; after which we joined the group which had by now foregathered in the big room in Dunn's camp, with Nockles keeping a stiff upper lip and serving another round of a new kind of champagne reported to be better than ever. Sir James was dividing his verbal shots between the most glorious sagas of New Brunswick I have ever heard, and a comparison of the best whiskey in the world with the best champagne in the world, both of which were flowing around in considerable quantity.

Finally somebody decided it was time for dinner (the Lady Christopher had arranged it for eight and it was then 11:15), whereupon we adjourned to the dining room and had a most marvelous meal. I don't think I have had better champagne. At all events, over the coffee we proceeded to take up the broad subject of economic reconstruction and how much the Government would have to support the situation; bracketed with accounts of politics in the high old days, especially in New Brinswick, and Sir James certainly put us all to shame on his memories of the precise dates and opponents in the campaigns of Grover Cleveland and James G. Blaine.

My best recollection is that everyone started for bed at about two o'clock. . . .

Sunday morning I rolled out at seven o'clock, likewise a fishing rod, and started to explore the little lakelet (crystal-clear—a little bit of water made by damming a cold New Brunswick stream at the foot of a river; the camp stands on a bluff which is cleared, fishing on the other, which is covered with spruces). The trout were running small; I caught but did not kill. . . .

And so the day proceeded. There was a serious piece of conversation about aviation; not knowing how to start a serious discussion in the perpetual and magnificent merry-go-round, I decided to do it by an angle shot, began with C. D. Howe, later tackling Dick Law and trusting (fortunately rightly) that one of them would repeat it to the Beaver. We later picked up the discussion on the rebound in the plane. . . .

I was so anxious to digest this cascade of shimmering intellectual splendors that I got a little time off in the afternoon and fished up the stream and down the stream and then back up again, counting with pregnant delight every needle on every spruce and identifying every northern flower. . . .

Thereupon we went at the question of British (and also American) policy orientation again. Assheton got more conservative by the minute, Sir James Dunn rather more taciturn and a little more humorous; the Beaver reminded me somewhat of Sunday in Gilbert Chesterton's novel, *The Man Who Was Thursday,* drawing everyone into a kind of maelstrom of warm-hearted and enthusiastic discussion, below which was a discernible flavor of direct political purpose. . . .

Dinner (scheduled at eight) actually was at ten. At half-past eleven, we got into a couple of cars and exactly at midnight we arrived at the main road. Precisely at that moment the Beaver decided that the news of the day was of highest importance. The car radio drawled out the news of the American break-through in Normandy, the Russian troops approaching Poland, the cut-off in the Baltic, and the slow moving of the line in Italy. This was like wine, or rather more of it, to the Beaver, who explained that we were witnessing the greatest drama in history; after which we drove down the main road, occasionally missing a skunk at close range. At Newcastle we got out and inspected Beaverbrook's ancestral parsonage and considered the imminent danger that the occupants thereof would run us in for attempted burglary. But we decided that C. D. Howe, as a Canadian Cabinet Minister, could possibly get us out of trouble. Then over the bridge of a river which Beaverbrook described as "one of the great rivers of the world"—the Mirimichi; we stopped in the middle of the bridge while the Beaver explained what happened when the old ferry broke loose. I recalled a childhood line about it which the Beaver later made me write down for his memory book.

Losing our way, we eventually debouched on the Chatham airport at 2:15, where Beaverbrook and C. D. Howe were taken in tow, and Assheton, Law and I put in for some bunks at the students' training camp there. Nockles was very solicitous and then vanished in the darkness. . . . At all events, we cleared away, getting up to a brilliant dawn, and sliding into Hyannis a little after nine, where Dick Law went off to see his sister. . . .

Memorandum, July 30, 1944

Over the weekend I had an opportunity to discuss the general situation on aviation with Mr. Richard Law and Lord Beaverbrook. I said that we were aware that the British airlines, and in particular the B.O.A.C., were making every effort to move out, to acquire landing rights, and to develop commercial intercourse. This was not the declared policy of the British Government, but the fact was that the B.O.A.C., under the guise of the Army Transport, had been doing just this. There was no dissent from this statement. . . . Equally, our own commercial lines disliked the position in which they found themselves, that they could not move out; our Air Transport Command was a purely temporary matter and would vanish at the end of the war. . . .

Accordingly I wondered whether the thing to do was not to have an understanding that both sides would move out in an orderly fashion, obtaining landing rights along the lines of the routes they wanted, but in no case attempting to exclude the other or prejudice the position of the other. The British already knew the routes we wanted, because the Civil Aeronautics Board had announced them some weeks ago and thus placed their cards on the table. We had a general idea but not a detailed idea of the British routes.

I said that if this plan were considered, each of us ought to keep the other informed of what they were doing and the friendliest basis ought to prevail. We knew that the British wanted landing rights in Brazil; and we did not propose to try to prevent them. They knew that we wanted landing rights in the Mediterranean and the Middle East, and I assumed that they would not try to prevent us either.

Both gentlemen thought this was not a bad idea and I gathered they were wiring London on the point. . . .

Mr. Law, who obviously was giving the matter more concentrated thought, said he wanted to think this over likewise. I gathered the idea appealed to him.

Memorandum, August 2, 1944

Yesterday, at the conversations with the Russian civil aviation officials, they produced [a] memorandum which undoubtedly was telegraphed them direct and verbatim from Moscow.

The Soviet scheme, as outlined, is virtually this:

The Soviet Union wants all operation of air routes in Soviet territory to be carried on by Soviet planes and Soviet fliers. They propose that international aviation across Russian territory shall be conducted by having the lines of other countries end at agreed points, at which points the Soviet planes and fliers will pick up the traffic. The traffic would then be carried into or across Soviet territory; and the Soviet line would then meet the lines of other countries at a point or points on the other side of Soviet territory. The international agreements would consist of arrangements to coordinate the arrival of American and other planes at the fixed points and the pick-up there of the traffic by the Soviet lines.

This, of course, amounts to a closed Soviet system. . . .

This is not fatal to a scheme of world aviation if all of the other countries get together, since it would be possible to make a reasonably satisfactory world aviation system with the Soviet Union left out, or rather, remaining as a great closed enclave. . . .

But the general significance seems to me very great. It suggests:

(a) That the Soviet Union still considers her major advantage to lie in a closed and self-conducted commercial system;

(b) That she has made a slight advance, but only a slight advance, in the direction of admitting the rest of the world to her territory in the fashion usual with other countries . . . by admitting passengers and cargo. . . .

(c) On the territorial side it is of interest that the Soviet Union considers her Near Eastern terminus at Cairo. In substance this would mean that no commercial plane headed for Russia would come east of Egypt. . . .

(d) It would appear that at present the Soviet Union is not interested in a northern contact. . . .

In view of the very real importance which the Secretary attaches to non-autarchy, and the fact that we base much of our hope for the future on open trade and open relations, I rather feel that we ought not to accept this position of the Soviets as final. But it is clear that effective argument will have to be made in Moscow rather than in Washington. . . .

. . . As matters stand now, the three positions are:

(1) The Russian position looking towards a closed area, but with agreements permitting entry of persons and goods (but not planes) into it.

(2) The British position calling for general transportation lines, controlled and allocated by international authority; and

(3) The American position looking to generalized rights of transit and landing, preferably under a regulated competitive system, conforming to our general commercial policy. In this last respect, we have kept the door open for regulatory controls, in view of the strong opposition in certain quarters in the United States to a truly open system.

August 25, 1944

I got the aviation groups together to try to round up on the possibility of an international conference, since we have about concluded our exploratory work. We can either try to shoot the whole idea with an international conference; or try to make interim arrangements. Either will be difficult. In the meantime, we have to get something like civil aviation ready in the event of a general German collapse in Europe. My own feeling is that the mechanics of civil relief ought to be established at the absolute earliest moment, so that healthy sentiment can grow again. . . .

The State Department extended an invitation in September 1944 for an international air conference to all members of the United Nations, nations associated with the United Nations in the war, and the European and Asiatic neutral nations. The Danish Minister and the Thai Minister could attend in their personal capacity. The conference was to be held in the United States in the near future.

To Hull, September 19, 1944

U.S. REPRESENTATION AT THE CONFERENCE ON CIVIL AVIATION

It would appear desirable to get the delegation to the Civil Aviation Conference chosen as soon as practicable, so that we can bring them together from time to time for discussion and general education. . . .

The Senate presents a problem. . . . Bennett Clark has been defeated in the primary. . . . Brewster has in fact committed himself in public to a plan under which United States, Britain, Russia, and China will "declare themselves trustees of the air for all countries" and exclude all other countries; which makes his position as a negotiator extremely difficult.

An ideal slate on the public side might therefore look somewhat as follows:

Senator Bailey, Senator Vandenberg or Senator [Wallace H.] White [R., Me.]; Congressmen [Clarence F.] Lea [D., Cal.] and [Charles A.] Wolverton [R., N.J.]; Mayor La Guardia or Eric Johnston [President, U.S. Chamber of Commerce]; Chairman Pogue, Assistant Secretary [William] Burden and your designee from State.

September 23, 1944

We are coming along with preparatory work for the aviation conference. Senator Bailey, with his usual consideration and courtesy, tells me that the Senate Committee will not make any move pending the conference, and that in any event the time is not right for legislation. This means that he will not permit Senator Brewster and the Pan American lobby to try to embarrass the situation. Since the Congress is adjourning until November 14, we shall have a relatively clear field ahead and by that time I think we shall have a new situation.

Memorandum, October 9, 1944

Mr. Michael Wright [Counselor of the British Embassy] came in and we discussed civil aviation. I gave him the general draft of the plans. . . . I likewise inquired what the change in civil air authorities in England might mean. I said I had heard on the radio that Lord Swinton had become Minister of Aviation, leaving Beaverbrook out. Wright said that Beaverbrook had entered civil aviation believing that it could be triumphant and quickly done; actually it had proved difficult and thorny, and he had been trying to drop it. He had now succeeded. . . . My real wonder was whether the British doctrine had now gone in for a closed sky and exclusive arrangements, or whether they were maintaining the general cooperative understanding reached between Churchill and myself.

Wright said that he thought there would be no change in policy.

Memorandum, October 23, 1944

The Soviet Ambassador said that he would head the Russian air delegation, and that the men who took part in the air conversations before would be here as delegates. . . . His general manner intimated that he hoped that we would have close working relations in this Conference.

At the close of the interview I told the Ambassador that the British had already opened negotiations to explore a method of compromise between their position and ours. The Ambassador asked what the reply was, and I told him that we had stuck on an international organization which should be consultative and fact-finding, and possibly even recommendatory, but that we were not prepared to go any farther than that, and indeed could not.

"In other words, you are staying on the same position you took during the conversations," said the Ambassador. I said we were.

Later, on December 7, 1944, Berle reported to Roosevelt:

All of the governments accepted this invitation with the exception of Saudi Arabia. Among the governments accepting was the Government of the Soviet Union, a copy of whose acceptance is in the files of the State Department. In this document notation was made that the Soviet Union decided to accept despite the fact that the neutrals were included as well as belligerents, no doubt in recognition of the fact that certain neutrals, notably Sweden and Portugal, held a geographic position requiring their action if world aviation lines were to be opened. Subsequently, the Soviet Union withdrew its acceptance on the ground that Spain, Portugal, and Switzerland were included in the Conference.

On October 27, 1944, Roosevelt designated Berle chairman of the U.S. delegation to the International Civil Aviation Conference, scheduled to open on November 1 in Chicago. The delegation included Senators Bailey and Brewster, Assistant Secretary Burden (Commerce), Pogue, and La Guardia (Chairman, U.S. Section, Permanent Joint Board on Defense, Canada-U.S.). Assistant Secretaries Lovett (War) and Artemus Gates (Navy), and Warner were consultants. Stokeley W. Morgan, Chief, Aviation Division, State Department, was Secretary General. The following, dated November 1 to 27, were memoranda sent to the State Department.

November 1, 1944

The International Civil Aviation Conference was opened this afternoon, the formal steps going reasonably well. . . .

Lunched with Lord Swinton directly on arrival. He stated with great frankness and bluntness the British point of view, namely, (1) that they were not prepared to discuss routes now; (2) that they were prepared to discuss the principles of the Civil Aviation Convention; (3) that they wanted an international control resulting in an equitable division of traffic.

To my question what they meant by equitable division of traffic, he answered that they wanted an arrangement by which each country had the right to carry the traffic which embarked within it—or an amount of the traffic measured by that. I observed that this was a reversion to their proposal that controls be applied dividing traffic between Britain and the United States on a fifty-fifty basis. This, in effect, meant diverting part of American traffic out and in to British lines. Swinton said that, in effect, it meant that, but why was that not fair? I said that this really came down to a request by Britain to us to assign part of American traffic to support British aviation, and I thought it was as impossible now as when it was broached last spring. Swinton then dropped the subject. . . .

November 2, 1944

The second day of the Civil Aviation Conference was devoted primarily to organization and to the statement of the positions of the countries principally interested in aviation. . . .

This afternoon the United States stated its position in a speech which I read after it had been cleared by the United States delegation and endorsed by Senator Bailey. Senator Brewster did not dissent, though he has made a general statement of his position as the opposition member. . . .

[Berle asserted:]

"The use of the air has this in common with the use of the sea: it is a highway given by nature to all men. It differs in this from the sea: that it is subject to the sovereignty of the nations over which it moves. Nations ought therefore to arrange among themselves for its use in that manner which will be of the greatest benefit to all humanity, wherever situated.

"The United States believes in and asserts the rule that each country has a right to maintain sovereignty of the air which is over its lands and its territorial waters. There can be no question of alienating or qualifying this sovereignty.

"Consistent with sovereignty, nations ought to subscribe to those rules of friendly intercourse which shall operate between friendly states in time of peace to the end that air navigation shall be encouraged, and that communication and commerce may be fostered between all peaceful states.

"It is the position of the United States that this obligation rests upon nations because nations have a natural right to communicate and trade with each other in times of peace; and friendly nations do not have a right to burden or prevent this intercourse by discriminatory measures.

"No greater tragedy could befall the world than to repeat in the air the grim and bloody history which tormented the world some centuries ago when the denial of equal opportunity for intercourse made the sea a battleground instead of a highway. . . ."

The British delegation stated its position in a speech by Lord Swinton. . . . The Canadians thereupon did likewise. . . .

The important fact was that the Canadian delegation attempted to find middle ground between the British and the United States. They thus endorsed the proposition of free competition in the air, suggesting that a provisional group of routes be established by common consent, together with the provisional number of round trips per week on each route. . . .

November 4, 1944

Last night the Chicago *Tribune* carried a display front page story nominally coming from Washington but actually obviously written here. . . . It was designed to show that attempts were being made to give away more than was necessary of the United States position, which, however, had been stopped by some valiant battling in the Delegation. . . . The disturbing fact was that a member of the Delegation must have gone almost immediately from the room and worked up the story with the Chicago *Tribune*. The Delegation in general was furious, but in view of the identity of the individual probably nothing can be done about it.

Mr. White was kind enough to take up the general campaign with the press and discovered that almost the entire press room here was equally angry at what they considered was a piece of unethical journalism, as well as bad conduct in the Delegation. They apparently caucused and agreed to pay as little attention to the Chicago *Tribune* story as possible.

November 6, 1944

Over the weekend the British had reconsidered their position regarding establishment of traffic quotas for airplane traffic. Apparently they decided it was untenable.

I give herewith the analysis of the situation to date:

(1) The issue as to whether civil aviation should be worked out through collaboration, or through mere anarchic agreements made by strength or force, is now settled. The plan will be for international collaboration.

(2) The question as to whether there shall be a wide exchange of needed transit and landing rights, or an attempt to favor some and limit others, is in general settled. There will be a wide exchange—not freedom of the air, but the established custom of exchange between friendly nations.

(3) On the question of establishing minimum rates, their appears to be universal agreement that minimum rates must be established. . . .

(4) The toughest issue has been whether an attempt would be made to condition all the foregoing on agreement to a system of international traffic quotas—a scheme by which a given amount of traffic would be assigned to each country irrespective of whether it could take the traffic by ordinary economic processes or not. The British held out for international quotas—of course proposing one very unfavorable to the United States.

The United States and Canada and others violently opposed this. The question is still formally at issue—and is the toughest issue in the Conference.

However, over the week-end the British re-examined their position. They really abandoned it, and have sent us word that the British White Paper is a statement of view rather than a defined position. They are now proposing a scheme of free competition coming much closer to the Canadian plan—as set out above. This is the real "break" in the Conference; for with this matter disposed of, the rest can move along more or less smoothly.

(5) The issue of whether the international organization should have "power" or whether it should be a consultative body: On analysis this issue ceases to be very frightening. Lord Swinton tonight over cocktails agreed with me that for the interim period that authority had to be consultative in any event. . . .

(6) The problem of routes and actual landing rights: The British originally said they were not here to discuss routes and had no authority. I accepted that without question and proceeded to get acceptance in principle of transit and landing rights everywhere in Europe that I could, as has been shown by previous memoranda. We have now reached the position where people are coming to us and asking us that we run American lines into their countries. . . .

Tonight Lord Swinton said that, while he had not authority to talk routes now, he expected, of course, to make arrangements for this substantially at once and these would be forthcoming after the Conference. I propose to follow this up and get as far with it as I can. . . .

In result: The Conference has now been going for six days. The major issues have been met and cracked with a minimum of public debate, largely because the British receded from their position directly they got the feel of the situation. The balance of this question will really consist of putting the solutions into form. There will remain a ghastly ten days of agreeing on texts. If my analysis is correct, the climax has been reached and passed. . . .

November 9, 1944

The present indication is that the Delegation will be able to agree upon a policy, with the exception of Senator Brewster. Unhappily, the evidence is now pretty convincing that in certain instances at least he has communicated the Delegation's decisions to Mr. Samuel Pryor, who is one of the lobbyists of Pan American Airways and who is also feeding the Chicago *Tribune*. . . .

November 18, 1944

Outline of the American Position

The American position at the International Civil Aviation Conference has been:

(1) This is the Twentieth Century.

(2) In the air there is no excuse for an attempt to revive the Sixteenth and Seventeenth Century conceptions by which transportation pioneers first got exclusive concessions, widened those by political influence to great blocs of territory, and then negotiated with each other for advantageous arrangements, to the exclusion of a great part of the world. In other words, there is no excuse for a modern air British East India Company or Portuguese Trading Monopoly or "Spanish Main" concep-

tion. Instead, we propose a system of mutualized permissions to use the air without prejudice to sovereignty, like the mutualized permissions to use coastal waters and seaports, and permitting to all countries the chance to get into the air.

(3) Nor is there any excuse for quotas or limitations which eventually can only work towards either cartels or national combinations to benefit themselves at the expense of other countries. All countries should be free to use the air, and the shippers and passengers should be able to choose the airlines they wish; and the airlines should be able to put on as many planes as needed to carry the traffic. Therefore, there should be no control of plane frequencies,—except that we would accept a rule that airlines should not increase their frequencies unless their planes are running reasonably full.

(4) The rules of the air should be so clear that an international authority does not exercise power, but rather keeps track of the observances of these rules. The power to enforce the rules should always be the power of the countries involved; but they must consult when problems arise. The international authority thus becomes ministerial and not dispositive.

(5) The world-wide conception of through routes and the right to communicate throughout without undue hinderance, but with reasonable consideration for the position of local traffic systems, is essential if the conception of one world at peace is to be maintained. We are thus endeavoring to write the charter of the open sky.

To Stettinius, November 18, 1944

This is merely a note, the only moral of which is that politics is nasty.

Brewster has been reporting right along to Pan American Airways and before the election he tried, as you know, to make trouble. Pan American Airways tied up with the Chicago *Tribune* in this respect, but the campaign is dying now that the election is over. At the same time, to add to the gayety of nations, he got the idea that there had been a protest from the War Department to the State Department, in connection with our plans. He then got hold of the Junior Counsel for the Truman Committee, of which he is a member, and asked him to demand all of the confidential correspondence between State and War from the War Department. The Junior Counsel did so; and the War Department thereupon answered that they could not release confidential correspondence with State unless the Secretary of State agreed. . . .

I then tackled Brewster, who is here. He promptly and shamefacedly said that this related to a different investigation, had nothing to do with us, and could, of course, await the end of the Conference. So the matter is left until we get back. It is a nasty piece of business; for it is hard enough fighting things out with the British, without having a member of your own Delegation, who announced that he is in the opposition, try to make political capital out of interior affairs, and to use an investigating committee set up for something else at the same time. It just happens that my connections with the Truman Committee, now the Mead Committee, are very close, strong and intimate, so they will not permit the process to be abused. But I think it is the first time in the constitutional history of the country that a member of an American Delegation, seeking to torpedo his own Delegation at the behest of a private interest, this time Pan American, has attempted to embarrass the Delegation by a press campaign and a Senate investigation at the same time. It is not a pretty story, but equally it is not any cause for concern. The War Department and the Navy Department, both of whom were consulted in the matter, propose to support us up to the gullet. . . .

November 26, 1944

There has been an interruption in reports, largely due to the fact that all of us were working under great strain, and wholly unpredictable claims on our time. This report merely attempts to sketch the salient points of the narrative to date.

Up to Sunday morning, November 19, it looked as though the British and we were close to an agreement. They had conceded the so-called "Four Freedoms" (transit, technical stop, embarkation from the country of origin to any other, embarkation from any other country to the country of origin). The discussion therefore ranged about the so-called "Fifth Freedom"—the right to pick up traffic at intermediate points. We had insisted that in this regard traffic should find its natural level, and while we were content to accept a starting quota, if additional traffic offered, the line should have the right to increase its frequencies through the process of "escalation"—adding additional planes when planes were running at 65% load factor, which in operating language means substantially full.

Late Saturday night or early Sunday morning, it developed that the British considered that escalation should not be applicable to this intermediate or "Fifth Freedom" traffic, whereas our people had proceeded on the steady theory that escalation would apply to this traffic. We thought this was a radical change in position on the part of the British, occasioned by news they had had from London. The British say it was a misunderstanding by our experts of what their experts said and thought. Naturally I find it difficult to accept this in view of the very clear statements made by Mr. Warner, Vice Chairman of the Civil Aeronautics Board, and the men who are working with him, who insist that they raised this point three times to the British experts, notably [Winfred Charles George] Cribbett [Assistant Under Secretary of State, Air Ministry] and [Major John Ronald] McCrindle [Deputy Director-General, B.O.A.C.]; but we all of us agree that this is not a case for recriminations, for such things are bound to happen. My private opinion is . . . that Swinton is ill-prepared, not having been in civil aviation very long, and he also tends to be arrogant and inflexible, not having quite appreciated the difference between the atmosphere of the coast of the Gulf of Guinea and that of the shores of Lake Michigan. Most of his European colleagues are in despair about it; but publicly the relations are on a basis of complete and almost exaggerated courtesy and cooperation. . . .

When on Sunday it became apparent that there had been disagreement, Swinton took the position that he was bound by instructions, that he could make absolutely no change, that he would be grossly misleading us if he said that he could change his Government's position, and that was that. I said that under the circumstances it seemed that further discussion was hardly useful, and that we had best go ahead with the work of the Conference, leaving the difference to general debate. . . .

The plenary session of the three committees duly met under my presidency and took a turn which some of us had foreseen but which was surprising in its intensity. I made a speech indicating what we had done and stating the nub of the differences still between us, not as a controversy but as a tough problem for which neither of us had yet been able to find a solution.

Lord Swinton followed with a speech along very much the same lines. Thereupon the Canadians, who have steadily supported our general point of view and have been anxious to get to accord, proceeded to blow the lid off. [Herbert James] Symington [President, Trans-Canada Air Lines], Acting Chairman of the Canadian Delegation, said very bluntly that agreements on technical matters and on air navigation law, and so forth, meant nothing if agreements permitting air transport were not to go forward; that he thought the difference was capable of solution and that was what everybody wanted. He favored the Conference going right on with its work until a solution was reached. His speech was pretty definitely directed against Lord Swinton, with evidence of a desire to slide out of the whole matter as gracefully as he could. I acknowledged by saying that if I thought there were any hope of getting to an agreement I was prepared to keep the Conference here until Christmas. Surprisingly the Canadians were followed by the Australians, who took somewhat the same line; likewise the New Zealanders, though with less emphasis; also two or three of the European delegations. When the last one had been heard, to close the debate I recognized Mayor La Guardia. He accurately recognized the terrific applause given the Canadian speech as a mandate of an unrecorded vote, which was what it was. Accordingly, he stated with his usual picturesqueness and force that it was pointless to make arrangements for airfields if you had no planes which could fly into them, and alluding to escalation, said that an escalator clause ought not to become an emasuclator clause. The applause which followed Mayor La Guardia's speech was as great or greater than that which had followed Symington's speech, since it was taken as an indication that the United States Delegation wanted to go along as far as possible to reach an agreement; and therewith the meeting closed.

In view of the fact that one or two of the newspapermen thought that this represented a difference between La Guardia and myself, I should like to report that Mayor La Guardia said exactly what I should like to have said except that it came with a far better grace from him than from the President of the Conference. It was, in fact, a good completed lateral pass. . . .

The precise issue between the two plans is not technical but fundamental. The British formula provides for a limited right to run planes from one country to another—the right being limited on the traffic between the homeland (say, New York) and each point along the route (say, New York-Lisbon, New York-Madrid, New York-Athens, New York-Cairo on a route running from New York to Cairo through these points). This would mean that there was a steadily diminishing right to run planes which could not ever be increased even though there might be healthy local traffic between, let us say, Rome and Athens, and Rome and Cairo, which would support the route. In the opinion of our experts, the Dutch experts, the Canadian experts, and possibly most of the British experts, this arrangement would not make possible the operation of an economical self-supporting route. As Steenberghe, the Netherlander, put it to me, this is one way of guillotining the KLM. The Frenchmen know equally well that their ambition of a French line to Indochina dies with equal speed. The question everyone is asking: Given this situation, what else do the British propose to add to their traffic to make it economically self-supporting, and is that to be available to others? The only thing that anyone can see is that the British, through political influence in the Near East and in Europe, propose to add special permission to BOAC which will not be accorded to other companies. . . .

The British are putting on a stiff press campaign, I suppose to show that they are generally reasonable, and I suppose to try to put the responsibility for any failure to reach an accord on us. Not unnaturally, we are doing the same, vice versa.

I do not despair of pulling this thing out yet, though it is going to be close going at best.

November 27, 1944

The issues between the United States and the British Delegations came up for debate this morning. So that it should not create any public issue, we had the joint meeting in closed session. Lord Swinton presented the British plan; I presented the United States point of view, being careful, however, to leave open all possible doors for further adjustment. Lord Swinton based his case largely on the idea that the plan the British advocated was the only plan doing justice to small nations.

Thereupon the small nations proceeded to get up and state their views. The French supported the British (coming around to me and apologizing, saying that they had orders which they hoped eventually to reverse). In quick succession the Peruvians, the Mexicans, and all the Latin Americans supported the United States. The Netherlander, in an excellent speech, demolished the British position. The Swedes did likewise. The Belgians stayed somewhat on the fence but inclined to the American position. So also did the Greeks.

The Canadians declined to support the British position and proposed instead a plan leaning heavily towards the American side. They likewise stated that the British plan made it impossible to operate an air route.

The Australians supported the British; the New Zealanders, in an equivocal speech, defended the British for having put in their plan but indicated that they did not like it.

When the dust cleared away, the British had the support of the

French and Australians and no one else. The small nations have not all spoken as yet—some will speak tomorrow; but the great bulk of them have declared against the foundation of the British position. It is fairly clear that the break has come, for in this situation a plan whose only justification is its alleged protection for small nations, is simply blown out of the water.

The debate continues tomorrow. Lord Swinton for the first time in the Conference has asked me to lunch with him. At the moment things look as though we should reach a solution—but, of course, surprises always do occur.

During these crucial negotiations, the news of Hull's resignation, the appointment of Stettinius as Secretary of State, and the consequent reorganization of the State Department came over the radio, on November 27, 1944. In effect, this meant that all members of the State Department were expected to resign, and that Berle had no mandate to continue as chairman of the International Civil Aviation Conference.

Two days later, Berle received this telegram from Roosevelt:

"Harry [Hopkins] has told you of my desire to have you take over the embassy at Rio. You know fully the great importance of that post at this particular time and after reviewing many possibilities I have come to the conclusion that I need your ability and experience in that post in order to insure the proper carrying out of the program we now have before us in maintaining the whole hemispheric policy against the insidious influences of which you are aware. This is a vital job and a challenge, and your services are needed right in that particular job.

"Please let me know as soon as you can whether you will accept this appointment as I wish to proceed with the arrangements immediately before Congress adjourns, possibly soon, in order that we may be in a position as soon as possible to take care of the responsibilities we have in the whole inter-American system and the part we shall play in the forthcoming world organization."

Roosevelt, discussing with Churchill their controversy over postwar aviation, wrote the Prime Minister on November 30: "You say that the British Empire is being asked to put bases all over the world at the disposal of other nations. Of course it is. Would you like to see a world in which all ports were closed to all ships but their own or open to one foreign ship, perhaps two if they carried only passengers and cargo bound all the way from Liverpool to Shanghai? Where would England be if shipping were subjected to such limitations? Where would it be if aviation is? I am unable to believe that you do not want an agreement at this time.

"I cannot agree that the answer is to hold everyone back. It must be to go forward together."

To Roosevelt, December 1, 1944

Your extremely kind telegram of November 29 asks a very quick answer. This has been difficult to give here where the work has been so continuous as to leave no time for thought or for consultation with my family, who of course are in Washington. Under all the circumstances I feel that I cannot accept, though I much appreciate the confidence you place in me. The reasons can wait until I get back to Washington next week but they are very solid and would, I think, appeal to you. My congratulations on your choice of Under Secretary [Grew] since it is the man I would have urged myself as the best man in the country for the job.

December 2, 1944

Following the meeting on November 27, the United States Delegation reviewed its position and at length drew a simple document, in view of the disastrous reception which the Conference had given the British plan. We had in mind representations made by a good many small countries, notably the Scandinavians, that even the compromises we had been willing to make with the British were too restrictive to permit them to fly. We accordingly put in a simple plan under which each of the parties granted to the other all five freedoms, subject to a general right of the proposed Council and assembly of the Organization to listen to complaints, examine them and hold consultations thereon; and in extreme cases, to suspend a signatory from its privileges. The entire South American bloc in a meeting agreed that they would support this, though Brazil had certain reservations. China likewise wished it, as do certain of the European countries, notably the Netherlands. We put this in the following morning; but the debate was not the happiest since countries which had disagreed with Britain the day before were nevertheless not prepared to go all the way out, and the result was a session not very satisfactory from our point of view. However, the general feeling was that a clear line of principle had been presented, and the more people thought about it, the better they liked it.

During the past three or four days the Canadians were busy trying to see whether the Canadian compromise plan could not be accepted. The British flatly refused. . . .

Meanwhile Swinton had said that he was not convinced that under his instructions anything could be done further; they could not yield, and that the only thing to do was to move to refer all the disputed sections of the air transport agreement to the Council for further study. I was convinced myself that the game was over, especially because of the very definite answer which Churchill had sent the President, and I agreed to second the motion.

On Thursday, in a joint closed meeting of the Subcommittees of Committees I, III, and IV, this motion was made and I seconded it. Mayor La Guardia then gave notice that he reserved the right to speak at the Plenary Session of the three Committees which would approve the report of the Subcommittees.

Yesterday afternoon, accordingly, we had a Plenary Session, and thereafter a couple of surprises came thick and fast.

Mayor La Guardia made an eloquent plea for getting together with the British on something, saying that the Conference had not advanced air transport at all. If we could not reach agreement on five freedoms, why not try to agree on four, and if we could not agree on four, why not agree at least on two—freedom of transit and technical stop?

Lord Swinton, trying to remove himself from the difficult position of an obstructor, made an adroit speech, stating the position of the British, how they were opposed to pick-up traffic but did not wish to be judged in their own cause and had put in a plan based on the Canadian plan, but leaving it to the Council to decide whether pick-up traffic should be allowed; and finally said that if anyone should make a motion to incorporate the first two freedoms—transit and technical stop—he would state the position of his Government. He did this in a fashion which intimated that they would accept these two freedoms. . . . However, taking his words as indicating that they favored putting in the two freedoms, the Netherlands Chairman of Delegation, Mr. Steenberghe, at once got up and made a surprise motion to incorporate the two freedoms in the draft convention. This was immediately seconded by Syria, and at this point confusion broke loose.

I was presiding, it being a Plenary Session of the three Committees; and technically the Netherlands motion was out of order since we were discussing La Guardia's speech on Swinton's motion to adjourn discussion and leave the disputed questions to the Council. La Guardia had moved as an amendment that the matter be referred for the time being to the Executive Committee to be held in abeyance pending further efforts to get together. . . .

Thereupon Swinton got up and, reversing his previous positions, stated that Britain was prepared to grant freedom of transit and technical stop . . . and the Frenchmen thereupon moved for the adoption of a text which was literatim the text of the American proposal for a mutual grant of all five freedoms, except, of course, that it referred only to the first two freedoms. The Netherlands accepted this as a working text and we adopted it. . . .

When the discussion was over, the meeting had agreed to a separate document to run along with the main convention constituting a mutual grant of the two freedoms along with the right of the Council to review any abuses of them; and Britain, France, Canada, and the United States had announced that they were prepared to sign, as indeed the Latin American countries will also, along with a good many European countries. My impression is that this will become a practically universal document. We then adjourned and that is where the matter now stands.

The American position in voting in favor of a general exchange of transit and technical stop is, of course, historical; in the Habana Convention of 1909, Britain, France, the United States, and the Netherlands likewise advocated the principle and voted for it.

The drafting of the document is now going forward.

Aside from drafting points and any snags which may come up, the main work of the Conference is finished. . . .

Berle closed the final plenary session on December 4 with the following remarks:

As a result of the work of these and many other men, when we leave this Conference we can say to our airmen throughout the world, not that they have a legal and diplomatic wrangle ahead but that they can go out and fly their craft in peaceful service.

In humbleness we must offer thanks for the opportunity to work upon these great affairs. In giving that thanks we must remember that these machines that fly are still guided by humans, and, in that connection, we may properly be justified in recalling the words of David—King, Captain, and Poet:

"If I take the wings of the morning and dwell in the uttermost parts of the sea, even there shall thy hand lead me and thy right hand shall hold me."

The International Conference on Civil Aviation is adjourned.

The previous day Berle had dictated the following message to the White House confidential telegraph clerk:

With this, my resignation, go my most cordial good wishes to you, to Secretary Stettinius and to the new group who are now to take over in the Department of State.

Let me take this opportunity to thank you for your many kindnesses to me during the past twelve years, in which I have been connected with your administration, nearly seven of which have been spent as assistant under the leadership of Secretary Hull.

Particularly I must thank you for your offering me the ambassadorship to Brazil, a country for which I have the greatest admiration and affection. As Secretary Stettinius knows, acceptance of that embassy is not possible at this time.

With warm personal regards . . .

On December 4, 1944, Roosevelt answered:

"It is with great regret that I accept the resignation you sent to me by telegram yesterday as an Assistant Secretary of State, a post which you have filled with such distinction during the past seven years. I expect you, of course, to continue as head of the United States Delegation to the Civil Aviation Conference, the proceedings of which you have conducted with such skill and ability. As you suggest, upon your return from Chicago, we can discuss the new work which I am anxious for you to undertake and in which I especially need your outstanding abilities.

"You and I have been friends and have worked together for a long time, and I am eternally grateful to you for your never-flagging loyalty and cooperation."

December 6, 1944

SUMMARY: THE WORK OF THE INTERNATIONAL CONFERENCE ON CIVIL AVIATION

The International Conference on Civil Aviation has advanced civil air flying by at least twenty years.

Few people realize that, prior to this Conference, all the air was closed, except that over the high seas. No one had a right to fly anywhere outside the borders of his own country. Certain air companies had obtained extremely limited concessions permitting them to fly through and land in other countries through a system of concessions, like the old trading concessions of the colonial companies centuries ago.

The world was well on the way towards building up a few big air trading companies not unlike the British East India Company, the Dutch East India Company, and the old Spanish and Portuguese trading companies. These were always monopolies, always in politics, and were fruitful sources of imperialist wars. . . .

. . . [the] issue was whether countries would arrange among themselves to exchange friendly permissions to fly into and land in each other's countries so that commerce by air can begin to be as normal and peaceful as commerce at sea.

The Chicago Conference squarely faced this issue. It faced the problem in the same way that Hugo Grotius, the father of international law, faced the problem of the sea three centuries ago. It came to much the same answer.

First, an agreement was reached by which the countries of the world agreed to standardize their practices regarding airplanes, airports and air practices. As this is made effective it will mean that any airplane can fly with reasonable safety and reasonable ease from any airport in any country along any airway, to any airport in any other country. It will find similar practices, similar signal systems, similar standards, and similar aids to navigation. This is the same problem which the Civil Aeronautic Board and the Civil Aeronautics Administration in the United States had to view for our own country.

Likewise, the Conference adopted two documents, to be signed by the countries which desired to use them. One of them was proposed by the United Kingdom and is called the "Two Freedom Agreement". This agreement is a grant of the right to transit the air over the countries which sign it, and the right to land at designated public airports in such countries for the purpose of refuelling, repair and overhaul. . . .

In addition to that, the Conference proposed a second document, the so-called "Five Freedoms Agreement". The signers of this document grant each to the other the right to enter each other's countries, discharge passengers and freight, and take on passengers and freight. Of course, this permission applies only to foreign commerce, and does not permit any country to engage in the internal domestic traffic of another country. . . .

Finally, the Conference, realizing that many international problems would come up as a result of opening the air, created and set up an International Council. This Council keeps track of traffic statistics and general economics. It likewise registers all air agreements, and puts an end to the system of secret agreements which had prevailed heretofore. It likewise bans agreements between two countries discriminating against or excluding a third country, and thus prevents a great source of friction. In case abuses or hardship or injustice grow up, the Council can hear complaints, call the parties into consultation, and try to effect a solution. . . .

This is new in air history. It took two hundred years of squabbling and several major wars to get to this result on the sea.

To La Guardia, December 7, 1944

This is a personal line to express my very deep thanks for your kindness and help at the International Civil Aviation Conference. The job was tough in more ways than one, and if the result was successful, it was due principally to your own swift instinct, and to your wisdom in crystallizing the discussion at the right time and getting the result embodied in the agreements which look toward the freedom of the air.

I shall not forget your personal tenderness to me at a time which was necessarily one of personal perplexity. We have been working together through so many years that I do not believe this is going to be our last venture together. I hope all of them turn out as well.

December 23, 1944

I talked to the President for about one hour on December twenty-first. He renewed his request that I go to Brazil, agreeing that I should have a "return ticket" not later than V-E Day. He said that he thought this country would be in a jam at or prior to that time, arising out of economic problems and he thought he would want me here at that time in any event.

I told him that I thought this was essential, since I was by no means a career diplomat nor would I wish to become one; and that my reason for accepting his very kind offer now was that no one in war time could decline to accept any assignment which might be of service to the war effort.

He likewise readily agreed that I should come to Mexico to participate in the proposed Consultation of American Governments relating to post-war problems.

. . . He . . . asked if I would not report personally to him. He intimated that he expected to take very close personal charge of foreign affairs, and apparently had had some discussion with Ambassador Messersmith along this line. . . .

December 28, 1944

The attached telegrams [between Roosevelt and Berle, November 29, December 1, 3, 4] were sent, as the record shows. The President's acceptance was likewise drafted. As the President was in Warm Springs and these documents were dealt with at the State Department and the White House, I have no particular reason to believe that he personally functioned on them at all.

When they were getting ready to give out the documents, however, my good friend, Steve Early, moved into the picture. Expressing himself with his usual force, he said that:

(1) Nobody ought to have had a decision like that forced on him in the middle of the Chicago Conference;

(2) To release the documents in substance would put me on record as refusing something in wartime;

(3) Before releasing anything he wanted it taken up with me.

McDermott thereupon telephoned to Chicago and asked that the telegram of resignation be altered so that, instead of including a declination of the Rio post, it would include merely a statement that, in respect of another important post which had been offered, the decision could wait until the Chicago Conference was over. Alteration was thereupon made in Washington and the release was given out in that sense.

On returning from Chicago, I talked to Nelson Rockefeller. His general theory was that the Rio Embassy would have to be one of the pivotal points from which hemispheric policy was made, and he hoped that he and I together could work on hemispheric policy, joining in working up the Conference of American Ministers at Mexico City, etc. He fully agreed that the ambassadorship at Rio should have a return ticket attached to it, available on V-E Day.

I later talked to Stettinius, who readily agreed. Ed obviously felt a little guilty at having cut the ground out from under me at Chicago. . . .

At a meeting of the International Civil Aviation Organization on June 22, 1965, Berle gave this speech:

Twenty years ago at Chicago, I had the honor to preside over a congress of fifty-seven nations, convened to establish an international civil aviation organization. This we achieved. Establishment of ICAO realized one small part of Franklin Roosevelt's great dream of organized peace among nations. It was designed as a specialized agency, operating under the aegis of the United Nations, then projected only, but to become real at San Francisco a few months later. Its organization was planned so that it could function separately, irrespective, if need be, of the fate of the United Nations itself.

Two decades of history have established your success. . . . Lessons for the future can perhaps be drawn from [ICAO's] achievements.

We met in November, 1944. The Soviet Union, then the only Communist nation in the world, had engaged in preparatory conferences. Its delegation actually reached the United States. As the Chicago conference opened, the delegation was withdrawn, and the seat of the Soviet Union still remains unfilled. The "Cold War," as it is called today, had already begun. The incident would not be worth recalling save for a remarkable fact. Soviet aircraft today travel the airways of the world. . . . Though the Soviet Union has never formally adhered to the Chicago treaties and is not represented here today, yet its planes, pilots, and routines follow the body of rules agreed on by you. Other nations, not in existence when ICAO was born and also not parties to its charter, do the same. They do so because these rules, routines and practices represent technical reality. Adhering to them is essential to participation in the vast process of world communication by air.

But for the dominance of this body of rules, the air would once more become an impassable barrier. . . . At Chicago, powerful interests in some countries tried to take the air for themselves. They fought the principle of open skies with every weapon at hand. The principle that every country seeking access to the air had a right to it had to be fought for. Happily the Chicago conference accepted it, though only after a bitter struggle—whose honorable scars I still proudly bear.

This is true international supra-political, even supra-sovereign, law in action.

When we met in Chicago, commercial air traffic as now known scarcely existed. . . . Most commercial inter-continental traffic was blanked out by World War II. . . . At Chicago, we were dealing less with reality than with dreams.

We hoped then to organize the future. Today you govern the present, over an area coterminous with the inhabited earth.

History often deals ironically with early fears and preoccupations of men. . . . Let me call back some ghosts which gibbered through our discussions in Chicago.

The head of the pioneer American airline committed himself to the proposition that, in the then foreseeable future, 30 planes would adequately carry all commercial trans-Atlantic traffic. He was speaking of the DC-4s which today cower under the wings of great jet liners.

Because of that and similar estimates, it was claimed that by no possibility could trans-Atlantic traffic support more than two airlines. Our conference was seriously asked to limit trans-Atlantic aviation to American and British airships only and refuse passage to any other country. . . . Today, vast jets of all flags, without artificial trammels, set out every hour of the day and night to cross the seas.

Let us call up a more sordid little spectre. War conditions had for the moment made the United States the sole producer of large passenger and cargo aircraft. Dread was expressed that the United States, abusing this accidental monopoly of construction, would allow only Americans to secure planes, would prevent all others from developing air routes, would thus monopolize the airways. As President of the conference, I committed myself to a prophecy and a promise. First, I insisted that in a short span of time industrial countries wishing to do so would manufacture planes competitive—or more than competitive—with anything the United States could produce. Today, British, French, Russian and other plants turn out whatever craft their nation's interest suggests and are, I am clear, only beginning. Second, I promised that during the transition post-war period, American craft would be available on equal terms to any nations wishing to establish airlines. That also happened. As an American, I like to think that no country found obstacles because, for a period, they had to make use of American facilities while developing their own. For a brief time, the world was aloft on American wings—but not bound to them. Today, those that choose are aloft on their own. As an American, I am glad of it. . . .

Can we, perhaps, draw lessons from this vast, if silent, success?

Classic international law is conceived as a set of rules formally or informally consented to by nations, and derived from their will. We now see emergence of a parallel body of international law dealing with application and use of natural scientific principles. They are not made by sovereign consent. They are made by nature. . . .

Point by point, area by area, nature demands, and people insist on, recognition of her laws in those areas where the rule must be a common law or an indiscriminate death.

VII

1945

January 26, 1945

January 20. The President had his fourth inauguration; Beatrice and I took Alice and little Beatrice to the ceremony and afterwards they went to tea at the White House with Dean [Mildred] Thompson of Vassar. The ceremony was very short and extremely simple.

In the afternoon I was sworn in as Ambassador. Stettinius arrived, uninvited. Bob Jackson was good enough to come down from the Supreme Court to swear me in.

Monday, January 22. The Air Transport Command gave us a C-54 wherewith to transport our goods and chattels and three passengers, Beatrice, Miss [Louella J.] Livengood [Berle's secretary], and myself. We landed at Borinquen Field, Puerto Rico, just before sunset. . . .

January 23. A non-stop flight from Puerto Rico to Belém, which is on the banks of the Rio Pará and just on the edge of the huge Amazon-Pará swamp. . . .

We saw the sunset crossing the Amazon River, and a marvelous and fantastic scene it was. This is a very mighty river indeed; and it protects its banks well with hundreds of miles of almost impassable swamp. . . .

January 24. Arrived in Rio, where there was a small delegation at the Santa Cruz airport, whence we came down by Brazilian plane to Santos Dumont. Captain Luiz Sampaio, who piloted the plane, is an old friend of ours. At the airport there was a party of some proportions, chiefly old friends, including the Brazilian delegation from the Aviation Conference, and a whole raft of people. . . .

We went to the Embassy and in due time got some goods and chattels from the plane. Seeing this majestic pile, which would do credit to a California nouveau riche, pretty nearly ended my diplomatic career; the place was so rigged that it only half worked in any particular . . . the next morning it developed that the water system did not work after dark, so that (January 25) we could not get a bath, and we succeeded in keeping decent by sending a boy up the hill to bring water in buckets. . . .

. . . I would have sold the whole show for fifteen cents on the dollar and a free ticket home. We used the last of the bucket brigade to get my traveling suit pressed, after which I came down to tackle the Embassy, the first thing being a conference with all of the Brazilian press. Herbert

517

Moses, a Brazilian despite his English name, is President of the Press Association and was kind enough to come in and pay his respects and generally take charge; I tried to treat the conference as I would an American press conference and it seemed to go well. . . .

I went to work on the Embassy. The blunt fact is that Caffery [Berle's predecessor] ran it as a personal show with half a dozen men, most of whom have already been pulled out. . . .

Some curious facts . . . The Embassy has had nothing to do with Rockefeller's office . . . and I gather that they are not on particularly good terms with the FEA [Foreign Economic Affairs?]. . . .

It is said that President Vargas will call elections as soon as possible and will himself stand for re-election. This may happen quite soon. Actually there is a more or less dictatorial oligarchy, underneath which is a very strong current of opposition centering in the provinces of São Paulo and Santa Catarina, and possibly Rio Grande do Sul. The north of Brazil is, of course, a straight tropical colony without substantial independent life, as far as I can see. The opposition is or at least claims to be democratic, and because it is young, must eventually inherit the situation . . . indeed one's first impression is that the problems of the country are not dissimilar to those of the United States in 1880 or perhaps better 1900, though there are less human resources with which to meet it.

Thursday, January 25. Dinner with [Cecil M. P.] Cross [Consul General at] São Paulo and [Harold S.] Tewell [First Secretary] from the Embassy. I was trying to find out who knew anything about Rio other than the Granfinos (high society). But I drew a blank. Cross apparently knows São Paulo well; but the Embassy hasn't bothered much with it. In fact, the detachment of the Embassy from the life of what must be 98% of the population is surprising. Nobody could give me even a guess figure about the national income of Brazil.

January 26. This morning's papers carry the news of the death of Oumansky in a plane accident in Mexico. He was probably nourishing an anti-American revolution in Central America and was considered the most anti-American of the Russian group. I remember when Welles undertook to inform him about the projected German attack on Russia . . . he promptly informed Hans Thomsen, the German Chargé. . . .

Reading routine stuff at the Embassy (I am trying to read all of it until I catch the hang of this place). . . .

. . . The Brazilian newspapers were very kind in connection with the press conference we had yesterday [actually, 24th]; apparently they were much impressed by my answering a few questions "off the record", which, of course, is standard practice in the States. Here it has been unknown in the Embassy at least; and was—and rightly—interpreted as reposing confidence in the professional standards of the Brazilian newspapermen. It might be added that the reporting was excellent—considerably better than the American standards.

January 27, 1945
Saturday, not much doing. . . . going over this Embassy from top to bottom. . . .

In the late afternoon we knocked off and went to the beach beyond Copacabana: big surf pounding straight in from the sea; Beatrice and I enjoyed it thoroughly. . . .

January 30, 1945

More birthday greetings than I usually get, chiefly from Brazilians.

You cannot do anything now without being caught at it. Beatrice and I went to the beach for a dip before dinner. There were scatterings of people on the beach, none of whom had ever seen us. . . . A fisherman was hauling in his nets; and we swam over and did some hauling too; unfortunately having to leave before the fish came in.

This morning I heard that one of the American businessmen saw this and thought it was good stuff. It could just as well have been someone who thought it was terrible! . . .

In the afternoon, the ceremony of presentation of credentials. It is a terrible pity that Peter was not there, since you go with a motorcycle escort from the Palace guard, and find a regiment drawn up at parade; the regiment, resplendent in white uniforms, black hats with gold decoration and red pompons. . . . I presented my letters of credence [to the President]. I haven't any. They forgot them in Washington, and we cabled for some texts which we wrote out on a typewriter here. The President handed them to the Foreign Minister, who handed them to someone else, and they will not be seen or heard of again.

Getúlio Vargas is a quiet, solid, retiring man, who impresses me as being the common denominator of Brazil, at least partly because no leader of his caliber has emerged. In this respect he is in somewhat the position of President Roosevelt: not particularly anxious to seize power for its own sake, but by no means clear that anybody else can steer the country as well. Whether this is illusion on his part or fact, I cannot tell. He was very kind to me personally, and had been well briefed on what I had done. We talked about a variety of things, including the forthcoming Mexico City Conference and the campaign against illiteracy in Brazil. The conversation was in Spanish because my Portuguese is still not a going concern. I should like to know Vargas better. He gave me the kindest permission a Chief of State can give: an assurance that at any time I wanted to see him he would be available immediately. The older I grow, the more I realize that entree to the Chief of State is the greatest executive prerogative a man can have. Also, in many ways, the most dangerous. . . .

Thence at once to pay a call on the Minister of Finance, Souza Costa, an old friend of mine, who is in trouble with coffee. The Army wants a million bags of coffee at once; the stocks are said to be getting low in the States; the Brazilian Coffee Department had agreed to supply them; the speculators in São Paulo won't put the coffee on the market, hoping that the United States will raise the ceiling price on coffee. It won't. I told Souza Costa that we wouldn't, and that we wanted a million bags; which he will try to dredge out of the coffee people somehow.

On the other side of the story is the fact that there have been three short crops in a row, and this crop is short; this runs up the cost of coffee, and it is a fair question whether the ceiling price may not be below the cost of production.

I told Souza Costa that I would study the matter and see what we could do. Maybe a crop insurance plan with the cost split between us and the Brazilian Coffee Department might work. Nelson Rockefeller would, I think, be friendly to such an idea since he was the protagonist of making a grant to the Brazilian Government enabling them to subsidize their coffee growers. . . .

I must say that the more I get into this, the tougher the assignment looks. For the young intellectuals who are all for democracy are against the Government and want the United States to do something about that; the entrenched Government group know that they have cooperated with the United States during the war up to the limit; and I am afraid neither side will be particularly happy at a merely "neutral" or "hands off" attitude. The problem is to find and hold a moral position capable of comprehending all elements. . . .

. . . To the Foreign Office to see Velloso, who wants information on the Mexico City Conference. I told him that before I left Washington they were talking of three things:

(1) The inter-American system should assume primary responsibility for inter-American problems as against any world organization;

(2) Adoption of the Atlantic Charter as general inter-American policy;

(3) Regular consultation of Foreign Ministers, and coordination of the American system with anything that washes out of the Dumbarton Oaks agreements—which last, of course, we can't yet know.

I told him that on the economic side we were considering trying to handle purchases for rehabilitation of Europe in such fashion that they would also help to stabilize South American economy. . . .

February 6, 1945
. . . Then to the house where we were having a reception for the cultural relations group. These were a group of Brazilian authors and writers called in to meet [John Eugene] Englekirk [Professor of Spanish and Portuguese, Tulane University] a teacher of education who is going to be here for some time and who, thank God, speaks perfect Portuguese. . . . I hope we can translate "cultural relations" (a ghastly phrase) into something like straight, decent contact between educated people and giving the emphasis to education.

February 7, 1945
Considerable research on economics in this country. I am beginning to think that the problems are not the problems of inflation (as generally supposed) but the age-old problems of monopoly, bad marketing, overspeculation, and shortsighted finance. Inflation, of course, has something to do with it. We will get at this later. . . .

. . . to meet the Consuls from all the districts whom we had called to Rio for a conference. . . . I tried to give them in an hour what little I knew about the situation and arranged for a come-back when they could instruct me about Brazil.

February 8, 1945

. . . To lunch with the Canadian Ambassador [Jean Desey] who had kindly offered to introduce me to some of the intellectuals. . . . I met Francisco Campos (writer) there and two or three of the others. They all said that the soul of the country was dead and so forth and so on, and that nobody could get anything done. I agree that they are having a rough time, and the repressive policy of Vargas in this regard is wholly indefensible. But the terrible thing is that these people are not showing very much in the way of dead-weight lift for the masses they really want to serve. Again the problem of how to connect the intellectual with dynamic forces. . . .

February 9, 1945

. . . To the Foreign Office where Velloso had kindly invited their delegation to the Mexico City Conference to meet me. We talked Mexico City a few minutes, and then someone asked how to raise the standard of living. I pointed out that I had no right to intervene. However, since they had asked for a discussion on the subject, I opened up. My Portuguese was terrible and must have hurt everybody's ears, but for two mortal hours we talked Brazilian economics.

"Uma boa sabatina," said somebody at the end, and when I asked what that was, I found it to be the equivalent of a professor's seminar. I was busting into the high price policy of businessmen and saw Valentim Bouças [Brazilian businessman] grinning from ear to ear. He had been having a fight with the industrialists on this and was getting some powerful support from an unexpected quarter.

I likewise asked Velloso if he saw any reason why I should not receive Aranha [former Minister of Foreign Affairs], who wants to see me, and he said no.

February 10, 1945

Aranha came in at 10:30 and we talked for an hour. I got his views about Argentina. He thinks that Argentina is going places as do I, but did not think that staying away from there is doing anybody any good. Mainly he was talking basically about the problems of Brazil. He insisted that the Vargas Government's cooperation with us in the war had been due entirely to popular pressure, and was quite willing to agree that he had had a great deal to do with that pressure, as indeed he did. . . .

February 12, 1945

I have been giving a good deal of time to the Argentine affair, and the cables more or less summarize the conclusion.

Perón [War Minister, Vice-President; Berle had met with him on February 7] means business. He is building up his army, has made an armed camp of the Chilean frontier and the salient between Rio Grande do Sul and Paraguay; is shooting for a total army of 400,000, of which he expects to get 200,000 ready as soon as possible; has completely fascised the life of the country; there is no tangible opposition in sight. The bulk of the country is against him, but as they are silenced and cowed, nothing is going to happen. He is counting on the support of the British and is kidding us along, meanwhile standing ready to take advantage of any political opportunities in the surrounding states, unless and until he sees a chance of a military Putsch. . . .

. . . He has already a grip on part of the Chilean Government, and the unstable equilibrium there gives him a grand chance to maneuver. Suggested policy: at Mexico City, to build a high wall around Argentina, trying to make it clear that a military policy of this kind is going nowhere. This must mean a guarantee of frontiers, and a guarantee against aggression of any kind; and must be followed up by some kind of steps making it plain to Perón that any military adventures will mean trouble at once, and lots of it. Then with a sterile foreign policy they may turn to more peaceful pursuits. I am not optimistic about the result in any event. With the post-war slump, there will be disturbances and Perón will try to appear as the saviour of the continent from Communism, etc., etc., and we shall have a dreary business. . . .

February 15, 1945

Last night, unannounced, Major Juracy Magalhães arrived at the Embassy and asked whether I would see him. I had previously known that he wished to see me, and I had asked General [Hayes A.] Kroner [U.S. Military Attaché] to see whether General [Eurico Gaspar] Dutra [Secretary of War] had any objection. Dutra said he would leave it to my judgment, but replied that he had rather hoped not. It was therefore slightly embarrassing when Juracy showed up. It seemed, however, best to see him.

Juracy, who is a leading political figure in Bahia, where he was Interventor [governor], said he had come in to pay his respects and promptly started to talk Brazilian politics. He said he had come to town and President Vargas had offered him all sorts of posts in the government, including one or two cabinet posts, but he had declined to accept. He stated that he did not have any confidence in President Vargas, and that he and his group wanted a change of regime. He said that by this they meant a true reversion to democratic government, and not a mere change of men. . . .

. . . I said he realized, of course, that the United States Government could not intervene in local politics, nor could an Ambassador. We had no quarrel in the world with the Government of President Vargas, which had cooperated with us faithfully and wholeheartedly in international matters. Equally, we had no reason to believe that any government which might come in later would take any other line. I referred to a current story that the United States Government would intervene to prevent a change in government, and said that, of course, it was absolutely untrue: the non-intervention policy of the United States was well-established and would be scrupulously adhered to. . . . The United States, of course, was a democratic country, with democratic processes, and naturally trusted those processes, and we had full and complete confidence that the Brazilian people would find their own way towards democracy and a sound government. . . .

Juracy said he was proceeding to Florianópolis, where he is assigned, and we parted with expressions of mutual esteem.

Berle went to the Inter-American Conference in Mexico (see Part V) and returned to Brazil in March after consultation in Washington.

March 19, 1945

Trying to pick up the threads. As far as I can see, there is no real development in the political situation that you can get your teeth into. As appears from the wires to Mexico City, Vargas has opened up on the censorship (though the newspapermen tell me the censors still work when they feel like it). [Eduardo] Gomes has announced his candidacy but the opposition does not take it altogether seriously for the time being; the Government parties have announced the candidacy of General Dutra but they seem not to take that too seriously. . . .

March 22, 1945

Yesterday, a slew of work, relatively unimportant. I am trying to get the Embassy staff focused on some long-range work respectively on food, health, education, and price levels. . . . The stewing of the political campaign, focused entirely on personalities, is worrying me, and I am going to try to make a speech on the history of industrialization in the United States, letting the Brazilians draw their own parallel. We ought to be able to get some real economic discussion out of this campaign—or the last state of the country will be worse than the first.

Dinner last night with Sir Henry Lynch, an old British resident of Brazil; chiefly interesting because afterwards I had a chance to talk to the British Ambassador, [Donald] Gainer. He is a fine English gentleman, a Catholic, and almost inevitably, the talk fell on European problems. I was feeling low in my mind because I had been reading the European reports. These show that immediately after the Yalta agreements, [Russian diplomat Andrei] Vishinski came down to Rumania; without consulting the British and the United States, as was contemplated by the Yalta agreements, he threw out [Nicholas] Radescu as Prime Minister of Rumania and insisted on putting in [Petru] Groza, the Communist. The Communists may have two percent of the population of votes. . . . I am glad that our Government for once stood up in its boots and made a stiff protest. . . .

Gainer then raised the real shadow on his mind—as also on mine. Was this Russian business to go on indefinitely, or were we going to have to face up to a Russian menace not materially different from the German menace? I told him frankly that I did not know, having alternated between hope and fear in this matter. I had noted, as he had, the Russian shy at the Mexico City Conference and at the Chicago Aviation Conference. . . .

Gainer propounded the theory that prior to the Reformation, sovereignty had been limited by certain over-all moral conceptions embodied in the Catholic Church. He wished that the equivalent existed now. I said that I had been worrying about this myself; some sort of moral solvent was essential, else Dumbarton Oaks and the San Francisco Conference would be mere mechanics and paper without spirit. The American system at least was beginning to reach an agreement on main-line principles, which was why the American group of nations had life in it. Were we sure that the same thing was true of Europe?

To the office this morning; to work with Kadow and his group on food health program; likewise with [William Rex] Crawford [Cultural Relations Attaché], [Kenneth] Holland, Englekirk, and [Frank] Nattier [Rio Chief, Coordinator's Office] on vocational education. A brief talk with the Polish Minister—who raised ghosts from the night before. He said the Russians were systematically deporting great numbers of Poles from the area west of the Curzon Line, that 9,000 families had been deported to Siberia and Turkestan from Bialystok, and that three concentration camps were being built for the members of the Polish Underground who had fought the Germans. . . .

March 29, 1945

Nattier from the Coordinator's Office brought in their visiting expert, [Charles H.] Kline, and we got to work on a campaign to try to work up a popular demand for elementary education. This is a very un-Ambassadorial line of activity but with luck we might do some good. This country could have elementary education if it really wanted it—or at all events could have a good deal more than it has had heretofore.

Some unimportant stuff, and then [Paul C.] Daniels [Counselor] brought in [Roderic] Crandall, the Petroleum Attaché. He tells me that the Brazilians are thinking of changing their policy and opening the country to oil exploration by the American companies. This is all very well, but I want to see if we can't work out a somewhat better and safer method of oil concessions than has prevailed in Mexico, Venezuela, and Bolivia.

The difficulty is the familiar one in Brazil: a lack of capital, which is soluble because it can be overcome; and a lack of organizing ability, which at the moment seems almost insoluble. . . .

Another phase of the same problem followed at once: this was Kennedy, an American contractor who is building a line of railroads to take the Itabira iron ore down to the sea. The Export-Import Bank is financing the construction, thus solving capital. But the road is being built slowly because Brazilian contractors have alternate sections with the American contractors, and the Americans can get the work done vastly more quickly. This is partly due to the fact that they have better equipment; but even more due to the fact that while Brazilians individually make excellent mechanics, there is great difficulty in finding Brazilian foremen and supervisors who can direct the jobs—again the lack of ability to organize.

This may go back to a lack of elementary and vocational education; and thus connects the problem with the educational question which is first on the list. Fortunately a good many Brazilians are getting interested in it: for instance, Father [Roberto] Sabóia [de Madeiros] S.J. . . .

March 30, 1945

. . . It develops that last month when President Vargas was thinking of becoming a candidate to succeed himself there was much talk in the army of a revolt in favor of Eduardo Gomes. To stop this, Vargas finally asked the Secretary of War, General Dutra, to proclaim his own candidacy and got a few political people and a number of army men to support that candidacy. This probably was a maneuver, but it was taken seriously by a great many people, including at present General Dutra. The moderate groups are hoping that one or the other of the two, Gomes or Dutra, will retire, agreeing on a third candidate, thus providing a single solution. Should Vargas remain in the field or attempt to hold power, these groups believe that there will be an armed rebellion. There is considerable evidence to support that viewpoint. . . .

During the day a cable came in saying that the Department would propose on March 31 a resolution in the Pan American Union admitting Argentina to adhere to the Final Act of the Mexico City Conference. This in my judgment is a mistake. I had previously cabled recommending that the Department go slow; and now can merely cable my comments, which I have done. . . .

Telegram to Stettinius, Washington, March 31, 1945

The policy adopted by the Department regarding present Argentine situation would seem to have been settled. . . .

The decision having been taken, however, I should like to express the earnest hope that adhesion to the Final Act of the Mexico City Conference be not (repeat not) considered as adequate reason for exchanging Ambassadors, et cetera, unless and until a probatory period has elapsed, along the lines of the Brazilian suggestion. This seems to me urgent and important, but if that position is taken it should be made entirely clear to all other Latin American countries.

The urgency of this step is as follows:

A majority of Argentina does not like the present government, and will see in our acceptance of it a betrayal of their attempts to regain the historic Argentine liberties. This view will likewise be the view of most of the liberal elements in other South American countries. These elements, which are not by any means Communist in character, will be forced to the conclusion that their principal moral support comes from outside the Americas, and they are in a mood to look for that support if they do not get it from within the hemisphere.

Should Argentina be proposed as a possible signatory of the United

Nations, the Argentine problem at once becomes a matter of debate between the principal Allied powers, namely, ourselves, the Soviet Union, Great Britain, and China. This is a perfect forum for a non-American country to assume the leadership in a public issue affecting the Americas, making the most of the entire situation. Basically, no European power is really favorable to the unity of the Americas, and however the issue is cast, the maximum of damage to inter-American unity will be created.

Telegram to Stettinius, April 5, 1945

PERSONAL FOR STETTINIUS AND ROCKEFELLER.

Tewell, Daniels and I have reviewed the problems of personnel at this post. Following is a painfully blunt review of what has happened and where we are. . . .

Replacements have been incomplete, hasty and without reference to the needs of the post. . . . Personnel Board should also have in mind that the language of Brazil is Portuguese, and its second language, French. Spanish will get you meals at a hotel and the ill will of the Brazilians. . . .

Comparisons are not too useful; but according to last list Havana has 16 Foreign Service officers, Mexico 19, Argentina 15. We have 9, of whom two are being withdrawn. But we have three times the population and six times the territory of any other American post. . . .

This cablegram is a breach of old-style departmental form. But tentative venturing to hope and wonder, so dear to Department, hardly meets the situation. . . .

April 12, 1945

At about 6:45 p.m., John Burns, Third Secretary of Embassy, called up to say that the BBC had just announced the death of President Roosevelt; and within the next few minutes the confirmation came in. I did not have much heart to go through with the rest of the evening. We canceled the dinner and almost immediately afterward a steady stream of people, high and low, began to come to the Embassy to express their sorrow. Some were official but nevertheless real, like Foreign Minister Velloso; some were little people who had no shoes but merely came up to salute the Embassy and go away in silence. Some hundreds of students from the Faculty of Law came in; they were stopped at the gate by the guard; I sent word to have them admitted and met them under the portico with merely a few courteous words. . . . [Frank] García of New York *Times* and some of the American newspapermen; but there was nothing much to say, for the end of an American era had come and a new one had to open.

I do not yet think that the world realizes how great a man President Roosevelt was. The mere fact that he could make himself as much a personal friend of the little laborer in the Brazilian streets as he did of millions of Americans is a tribute to something more than politics. The great secret was the tremendous well-spring of vital friendship which he somehow communicated far beyond the borders of his own country. "This is the only man who thought of us," is the recurrent theme of the little people who do not make or read great phrases.

Through the long watches of the night, I tried to put together the series of pictures since I first saw him in 1918 and came to know him in 1932. The amazing fact was that he had an almost universal interest; there were few fields of knowledge with which he had not contact, many in which he was expert, but in all he had a vivid interest. This ran the whole scale from naval construction to the ability of white men to live in the tropics; from constitutional law to the history of coins. It is quite accurate to say that nothing human was alien to him.

For that very reason he was tolerant of many things which shocked me: the crude and bitter intrigues of the European powers, often directed against us; the corruption of some of his Tammany friends; the bickering and self-seeking which went on all around him. But more austerity would have prevented him from meeting all of the various conflicting forces, and dealing with each on its own terms instead of on preconceived premises. Looking back over twelve years of almost continuous crisis government, I think he would have been torn to pieces if he had not developed community with each of these forces or groups, and so made himself at all times the principal unifying element.

And yet—I am not sure that the providence of God may not have intervened to take him now. For himself, of course, it was best: he had come to the point where he could see clearly a certain victory; and the completion of the victory would be anti-climax. The division of forces within the country and within the great alliance is becoming vastly more acute; and the time may have been coming where this vast and gracious tolerance would have been no longer a unifying influence, but the instrument for betrayal, either of him or by him. For it seems to me that forces are again building up with which there cannot be compromise, just as they built up in 1938 and 1939, when the search for peace with Germany ceased to be a virtue.

Many found him puzzling; but this I think was due to their own limitation. He was a friend of nations, and also a friend of peoples. So his foreign policy not merely included friendship with other countries, but also friendship with the various classes, especially the large humbler classes who do not usually find expression in their governments. So his policies had not only length and breadth, but also depth, and brought into the consideration of current affairs problems which normally do not find the place to which they are entitled in foreign relations. This was exactly what he did in our internal policy, when he lifted the entire problem of the national economics into the responsibilities of the Federal Government in 1933. As a result, no President will ever be able to look at the Presidency again, either in its foreign or its internal implications, as did Presidents before his time.

I had the sense when I talked to him a month ago, returning from Mexico City, that he was working against time—that he knew that he was on the outer fringe of even his own unquenchable vitality; and that he was trying to tell me a great many things to have them on the record against the time when his own voice might be stilled. It is easy to imagine these things after the fact, but the picture is so clear that I do not think I am mistaken. He had not been happy about Yalta; and was trying to convince himself that the Russians would be satisfied if their outer barriers in Eastern Europe were secure; a feeling which I hope may prove to be true, though the current evidence is all against it. He was worried about the domestic situation, believing that V-E would find the country "in the biggest jam in its history"—these were his words—and that returning soldiers would insist on jobs and on their point of view, and would not be too finicky about whether they used constitutional methods in getting them. He was planning and gathering himself for some kind of a tremendous mass attack on the internal economic plan of the United States, and suggested that he thought America's internal safety would turn on her ability to solve the problem of readjustment. He said frankly that he had taken European affairs to himself; that he was not sure that Stettinius read all the documents he sent over to the White House; that he thought Jimmie Dunn, while inadequate, was growing, but that the principal responsibility would have to fall on him. Particularly he said he needed some rest.

And, in fact, this was what he searched for at Warm Springs. It was a swift, kindly and beautiful death, in full tide of activity, without preliminary struggle, in the place he loved best, and surrounded by the two or three people who probably loved him best in the world.

April 13, 1945

I have issued the appropriate orders to the Embassy and the Consulates and am arranging memorial service for the President tomorrow in the Embassy gardens. . . .

Telegrams, and visitors, come by thousands. A beggar stopped the Press Attaché in the street to weep on his shoulder; an old man, seeing the Military Attaché in an American uniform, stopped him to express a tremulous emotion. The little people telephone to the Embassy giving their names, saying that they are of no importance but wish to express their grief; we have set up a book for people who come to sign their names.

I have telegraphed to President Truman offering all support and offering my resignation if he wishes it; and have likewise telegraphed him personally to say that I have asked my friends in New York to give him all support. After all, they have been the balance of power in New York for twelve years and should be of help. I have wired La Guardia, David Dubinsky, and have asked Cuneo to get into action. . . .

I have had the pleasure of knowing Senator Truman, chiefly as Chairman of the Truman Committee. He investigated Pan American Airways and I gave him such help as I could, especially on the Brazilian base question; and he has been at dinner at our house in Washington. He is a modest, quiet, very industrious man, who never sought the offices he has. . . . I was told that as Vice President he had done very well; and the best recommendation of the man is that he rapidly grows in new responsibilities. . . .

April 17, 1945

Last evening Bill Wieland [special assistant] brought in a young leftist leader, Carlos Lacerda; a good honest boy, rather on the poetic side, and very active in anti-Administration politics. As usual, I asked him what his program was and drew a blank. He said quite concisely that they were not interested in programs; merely in throwing out the dictator. I said that was a pious idea but what for: was anybody in the middle of the street going to be better off? He said that in Brazil you first got power and then you studied it because no politician made programs. I then asked how it would do to have a group of younger men get together who did work on programs. My own observation had been that in the long run politicians only used ideas that other people worked up; in fact, if other people did not work them up, the ideas were not politically viable. He seemed to think there was something in this—but I do not know whether we made the point or not. If he can get a group of youngsters who have any ideas along this line he might be able to do something. . . . [A group of young men did organize themselves into a seminar and met with Berle at the Embassy regularly.]

. . . At work with Nattier and Englekirk, on a project for agricultural education—aimed to hit the grass roots. My difficulty with the Americans is something the same as with the Brazilians: everybody wants to get upstage and float into the high altitudes. . . .

. . . I understand now why the old missionaries got results. The moral rule under which they worked forbade them to try to jump at once from being corporals to being generals—whereas less devoted service, motivated in part by ambition, takes a man out of the most useful work he can do with terrible speed. . . .

In the evening, to see [Cândido] Portinari, the Brazilian painter. . . . He showed us four rather modernist studies of the underside of Brazil: a burial in the mato, a group around a dying child, a group of women working, and a couple of women washing clothes with a sick child between them. This was top-flight work . . . and what the pictures had to say was not propaganda, nor cartooning, but actual interpretation. The terror of it lay precisely in its truth. The mildest of the four—the women washing clothes—had a universal quality in it; nobody who sees it will ever be able to look at women washing by the streams again without doing a little thinking. I suppose great art consists exactly in portraying an unforgettable new dimension.

April 21, 1945

A holiday here, so I threshed some straw at the office. Luiz Carlos Prestes (leader of the Communist party) got his picture in the paper with me on the balcony of the American Embassy. I thought there would be trouble but the Brazilian reaction was different. Their general view was that it was a confession of weakness on Prestes' part: a real leader would not have need to get political prestige in a foreign Embassy. . . .

April 22, 1945

[In] the Sunday newspapers . . . it developed that the [Assis] Chateaubriand [newspaper] chain was putting on a huge campaign for a country-wide string of schools. They began this by a whole page on "Roosevelt and Education", to which I had contributed a little piece, not knowing the real objective. But, happily, what I had written went along with the design. . . .

April 23, 1945

The Chateaubriand chain has picked up from its "Roosevelt and Education" page and is now asking that a school be established in every prefecture as a memorial to President Roosevelt. They are quoting liberally from my brief article.

To the Foreign Office, where I gave Macedo Soares the general bill of fare: Argentina wants to join the United Nations; we are favorable, the Brazilian Government is favorable. I anticipate stiff objection from the Russians. I cleared with him the general outlines of the program for admitting Argentina to synthetic rubber; told him that I thought we ought not to give Argentina any rubber until she came in on a complete schedule of controls. . . .

West of the Export-Import Bank came in to talk of the Vale do Rio Doce Railroad. This is important because it brings Itabira ore down to the sea; and that ore probably would be a principal export to the new steel mills that United States Steel are planning on the Atlantic seaboard. This gives Brazil a good export, and in return the ships could bring coal which Brazil needs, thus providing an excellent exchange. . . .

I likewise got somebody started to Volta Redonda [steel mill], to look over the food situation there. The Volta Redonda management claims to be supplying its people with food at 40% below current prices simply by cutting out unnecessary and speculative middlemen. If true, this might be interesting and a pattern to follow. . . .

April 24, 1945

The regular press conference. This bunch of newspapermen are a good crowd. Since I don't have spot news, I try to fill them in on the background of what is going on so that they can write about it intelligently when the time comes. . . .

In the evening Sir Donald Gainer, British Ambassador here, brought in Sir David Kelly, who is Ambassador to the Argentine. I gave him the daylights of the situation as we could see it. Kelly was politely critical of our policy: said that, having decided not to recognize Argentina, we should have stayed by it and should have seen it through. Particularly he was unhappy about the wave of arrests in the Argentine. . . . I did not say that I thought Kelly was dead right—but of course he was. If we had kept our shirts on, the situation would probably have reversed itself. Now we are in the position of having to work with a government which is jailing the people who have stood by us through thick and thin. This is a case where Nelson Rockefeller, with the best intentions in the world, showed his inexperience. The unity of the hemisphere means a great deal; but you can trust the hemisphere if you stay by it.

Then a little group of artists—[Francisco] Mignone, the musician, and his wife; Portinari and his wife; Heitor [Villa-Lobos] and his wife; [Cultural Attaché] Carleton and Elizabeth Smith. There was considerable talk and a little music. Portinari, philosophizing on why intellectuals could not be politicians, was really fascinating.

There was a little ceremony as homage to President Roosevelt at the Engineering School at 5:00 o'clock. I went, saying nothing; a quiet little ceremony, very impressive.

April 26, 1945
. . . the local oil adviser of the Brazilian Government [came in.] This oil thing is on my mind. There is a good small field located in Bahia; there may be more oil up the São Francisco valley. There is undoubtedly a field in Paraná, but it will be long to explore. There is probably a great deal of oil in Amazonas, but a terrible job both of finding and getting it out. I understand the advisers are suggesting that the Brazilian Government continue their explorations in the São Francisco region, and I think they probably are right. As usual, the difficulty is to get the money for the work that does not show: geology, geophysics, and the drilling.

Of course, if the Brazilians wanted oil fast they could simply open the country to exploitation by the private companies. But that does something else besides get oil—and the something else is not too nice. . . .

April 27, 1945
. . . a young man named Mario Carneiro; he is active in a group of young men calling themselves the "Democratic Resistance". He gave me a copy of their statement of principles, but what he really wanted was to have a group study the essentials of state planning as we do it in the United States. We don't do much in the United States, but I have been trying to find some young men to talk to about handling obvious social and economic problems and this is a good place to begin. I like Carneiro, who seems a very good sort. The problem is how to do this sort of thing and still keep out of local politics.

April 28, 1945
Off to see the Itabira mine—it is an iron mountain and part of a huge ore reserve—perhaps the largest and richest in the world. It must get to the sea through the valley of the Rio Doce; they have a sixth-rate railroad, which is now being fixed up, but the work is not going satisfactorily.

Beatrice and Colonel [Ben W.] Barclay and I took the Beechcraft and first lost our way in the mountains of Minas—amazingly lovely but bad to explore by airplane. . . .

The next morning, with the Beechcraft to Valadares, where we met the boys who have been getting out the mica. Nobody had paid any attention to them for years and they were glad to be visited. We got into a jeep and headed outward for the nearest mine. This is the first touch of modern civilization in a wild and terribly backward neighborhood; and the touch has not gone very deep. The doctors have cleaned most of the malaria out of Valadares. . . . They are, however, getting mica, which is the important thing. . . . We started for Victôria, flying down the route of the railroad along the valley of the Rio Doce. In some places the railroading is pretty rough; and the old railroad looked like a shoestring somebody dropped. I later learned that the contractor had been paid by the mile, and naturally built as many miles as he could. The carrying capacity has to be doubled or tripled, after which the railroad can carry the ore to the sea, where both the British and the United States Steel want to buy all they can get, probably exporting coal in return.

At Victôria we circled the town and saw a monastery on top of a high hill, which Beatrice wanted to visit. Consequently, [Vice Consul V. Harwood] Blocker and his wife, who had waited angelically all afternoon at the airport, took us there on the way into town. . . .

To the Blockers' for dinner and the night; the Interventor, Santos Nieves, and his wife, and a lawyer and teacher, Dr. Braga [a public health physician] and his wife, came over to join us with two or three people in for a quiet dinner in an old-fashioned Portuguese house set on the side of a hill. Afterward the Bragas played, she at the piano, he with the violin. A lovely, quiet, gracious, informal evening. . . .

At the airport . . . John McClintock [special assistant to Rockefeller] back from the Argentine . . . He was not happy. Nelson, who had got the recognition pushed through a little too fast, was now on terribly thin ice, since he could not get the Argentine admitted to the United Nations—and Perón and his government was providing all possible ammunition for not being let into anything. . . . Late at night came the news that the Americans had pushed the invitation of Argentina to the San Francisco Conference and had carried it by a considerable vote, but the Russians and their satellites had voted no, and France had abstained.

May 1, 1945

Further news on the Argentine this morning is not reassuring. It seems that at the meeting at which the Argentine thing went through, [Russian Foreign Minister] Molotov had recited all of the American statements about Argentina; Stettinius got rattled; the various foreign ministers were saying that they thought they had to get home for urgent business. . . .

John McClintock and I drew the telegram on possible handling of the situation and sent it along. But I am frank to say it looks past praying for. There will be repercussions in all directions, not the pleasantest of which is that for the first time in 50 years we have opened a major American question to debate by the European powers, and the Russians accepted the challenge. If this does not mean trouble, I miss my guess.

Kline came in today, likewise back from Argentina; he confirms everything that McClintock says. Likewise [Francis A.] Truslow [President, Rubber Development Corporation] showed up, having finished up his rubber deal. He got everything he wanted and a little more. We give no crude rubber to Argentina. We settled for 3,000 tires, as against the 20,000 they wanted. We do give some synthetic. They agree that they will stop the contraband trade, keep prices down, regulate consumption, et cetera. . . .

I see the Europeans giving us a run for our money in South America. And I don't see San Francisco settling it. If the State Department does not pull itself together and start scoring some points on the right and not the wrong levels, we are going to be in trouble. I don't know what more I can do about it from here. Firing advice by cable is not much fun, and it is still less fun when you can say afterwards, "I told you so."

May 4, 1945

Wednesday, May 2. Cleaning up on the rubber agreement with the Argentine and reviewing the general situation. The European despatches are in, and matters divide themselves into two categories.

The first is pure drama and the question is whether it has more than dramatic value. Mussolini and his mistress trapped and killed like rats, with Italians defiling their bodies; and this is the end of the "Little Caesar". . . .

Hitler and apparently Goebbels reported dead in the ruins of Berlin. . . . One wonders whether these men would have liked their twilight of the gods if they had realized that it would be without flames and without music; nothing but the sordid end of criminals hunted to their holes.

This is the drama; it is victory without triumph.

The second category relates to the actual situation. I do not see it happily; and I am afraid for the United States.

The Soviet Union has taken, and is governing, by force, and unilaterally, Poland, Bulgaria, Rumania, Hungary, substantially also Yugoslavia and now Austria. . . . In the Middle East, she has come just short of challenging the British, save in Iran and Turkey where her challenge is open. . . . She agreed that she would not push these lines in Greece and confined herself merely to giving moral support to the ELAS-EAM group, leaving the British to crush them by arms. So that the British with the weak Greek Government are now holding forth in Athens. But she is continuing her intrigues with foreign groups in Greece, is surrounding Greece with further intrigues in both Bulgaria and Yugoslavia, and has already made of Greece a frail island in her growing empire. Meanwhile she is reaching into Italy, with Tito's claims on Trieste, and a firm foothold through [Palmiro] Togliatti [Communist party leader] in the Italian door. . . .

In the Far East she is maintaining a virtual state of civil war in China, powerfully aided, of course, by the mistakes of Chiang Kai-shek; her agreement to declare war on Japan will probably also be accompanied by claims for the southern part of the Island of Sakhalin; substantial control of Manchuria, probably also of Korea, and not impossibly considerably more besides. I am not informed as yet about her designs on India.

This is, quite concisely, an almost exact picture of the world Hitler proposed to create for himself—except that this is almost done.

Will we be free from challenge? There is every indication we will not; and that if we undertake to oppose this new concept of world empire, the Russians will challenge for the hemisphere. I do not believe that the very widespread organization in Mexico and South America is merely accident. Spot the incidents as they come: Oumansky's vast intrigue with Cárdenas in Mexico, which he was extending rapidly through propaganda and bribery in Central America: one of those bribed Mexican diplomats in Central America is now in Rio. Oumansky's death may have hindered the work, but is not likely to have ended it. In Montevideo two days ago a Communist mob attempted to force a Uruguayan paper to run up the Soviet flag, and rioted against the Chief of Police and the Uruguayan Minister of Interior because he had declined to control the press as the Soviet Government demanded. In Brazil, where there has been relatively little organization, there was a demonstration in Santos, the crowd having been issued Russian and French flags, and the quick and steady increase of Communist organizations acclaiming Russian victories —but no other; proclaiming Russian friendship—but no other; endeavoring to rate as Fascists all who disagree with them—is steadily going forward. None of these movements is capable of conquering the hemisphere. Continued indefinitely, they might, of course, divorce these countries from their traditional friendship with the United States. This undoubtedly is a primary aim. . . . The diplomacy of the group in the State Department has been so inept that we are likely to find ourselves defeated on the very battlefield of our greatest military victory. . . .

A third phase, that of rather ghastly burlesque. This is the San Francisco Conference. To this Conference was directed the idealist thought of the world: the hope that somewhere, somehow, by consultation, methods might be found through which the world might rid itself of its great ills. But alas, while San Francisco might change the mechanics, there is nothing of it to make conquerors into good neighbors, or to make men who seek domination into men of good will. And so, while the diplomats, the foreign offices, the armies and the underground organizations are consistently playing power politics with a ferocity greater than that of the Munich days, San Francisco spins words. . . . But the point is that the word without the spirit is dead; the spirit is certainly not proceeding along the line of words.

At 2:30 today, General "Hap" Arnold and Major General Walsh, along with quite a staff, came in from Europe via Natal; and after the usual band reception at the airport (very nicely done, with General Arnold reviewing the troops) we slid down a greased pole of state visits beginning with President Vargas and going on through the huge tomb-like structure of the Ministry of War. . . . General Arnold with his plane went through Europe, including the Rhine valley; he says the destruction of German cities is beyond measure complete, and that it will take 100 years to rebuild. I remember, however, John Stuart Mills's statement that the time needed to repair the ravages of war is always overestimated. . . .

May 3. To lunch at the American Chamber of Commerce, where I made an off-the-record speech, urging the American businessmen to lend a hand in the economic life of Brazil. Specifically, I hoped they would encourage more transportation which every Brazilian wants; and would likewise raise their wages before and not after they were forced to by the rising cost of living, especially where they knew that they were going to do it anyhow.

At 7:00 o'clock, presentation of medals at the Embassy residence, the same done very prettily by General Arnold, while a considerable group looked on; then by accident the flight crews of the General's plane showed up at the Embassy, when they were expected the next night. We promptly fed them drinks, and they seemed to be happy, though scared. The first one who thawed out was an Irishman named Foley who came from the Bronx. I was happy, being homesick for a New York accent. . . .

May 4 . . . Wieland brought in [Fernando] Tude Souza, the educational director of the *Diarios Asociados,* who has been running their educational page and doing one of the few jobs of "crusading journalism" that is being done here. . . .

Some interesting experiments are going on, notably the Institute of Puericultura at Bahia, organized by an energetic local government; this undertook to do the whole job from pre-natal care up through secondary school. Tude Souza agreed that the principal need was public sentiment that would demand some decent education, and he said with entire truth that he and Chateaubriand were doing their level best to get it.

The flight crews of General Arnold's party came over to the house for a mild party afterward. . . .

May 6, 1945

. . . I was thinking, as Arnold's plane pushed off into the night, that he had probably done as much as any one military man to win this war.

From Berle's speech at the Ceremony of Homage to President Roosevelt, Itamaraty, Brazil, May 12, 1945

Great men have two lives: one which occurs while they work on this earth; a second which begins at the day of their death and continues as long as their ideas and conceptions remain powerful. In this second life, the conceptions earlier developed exert influence on men and events for an indefinite period of time. Now, only a month after his death, we are seeing the beginning of his second, and perhaps greater, life. None of us can prophesy what its results will be; but few will deny that there is a continuing and beneficent spirit which will not cease to speak to a world in pain, with a voice of confidence, hope and wise and humorous counsel.

May 16, 1945

Tuesday, May 8. This is the day of victory celebration in Europe; wholly anti-climactic in many ways. At 10:00 we tried to pick up President Truman's broadcast but could only get Churchill's speech—which was simple, straightforward and moving. Press conference included a distinguished journalist, Felix Belair, down here representing Henry Luce and the *Time* group. I went over the international situation coldly, indicating that, while San Francisco was having a good time, the European powers and particularly the Soviet Union were moving their own or their satellites' troops and grabbing the territory. This seems to bother Belair, but he did not question the facts. The claim by Tito of Trieste seemed to stagger everyone. . . . Then a brief ceremony in the Embassy garden celebrating the victory, and reception to the American colony. . . .

Friday, May 11. A visit to the national motors factory which the Government is building out on the Petrópolis road; it is another one of these little cities which is being built around a factory. . . .

Saturday, May 12. I have been trying to make sense out of the reports from San Francisco. Apparently the boys at that Conference started to construct their world organization. The Soviets demanded a free hand against all ex-enemy countries—which they got. This is equivalent to a right to intervene, without bothering the world organization, anywhere in the Mediterranean as far west as Italy and Sardinia, and anywhere in Europe as far west as the Rhine. They also got a right to act under their security treaties—which are of course one with England, one with France, and one with Czechoslovakia—and maybe more that we don't know about. Perhaps it is under this that they are moving out to grab Trieste.

So far so bad; but when the Latin American nations insisted that equivalent liberty of action should be given to the inter-American group under the Act of Chapultepec, apparently the United States delegation wanted to block them. . . . The reaction here has been terrible. It was pointed out that we signed the Act of Chapultepec too and are now the first American nation to run out on Pan Americanism.

You could defend the subordination of all regional groups to a world group provided this was a general rule. I should be against it on practical grounds: the American countries can and do keep the peace; the European countries can't or at least don't. But the theory that all force could only be exercised by an amorphous world government at least is a tenable theory.

But when you have conceded the principle on the Continent of Europe—query: also the Continent of Asia?—and then deny it to the Americas, it is equivalent to throwing the American organization into the jackpot of European politics. I have subsequently read Walter Lippmann's defense of this—to the effect that the American system is not a real security system—and am frank to say that it makes no sense whatever. . . .

May 18, 1944

Some routine work and then luncheon with [Ernani] Amaral Peixoto [Governor of the State of Rio de Janeiro] and his wife, Vargas's daughter, and others at the residence. I asked Peixoto whether it was true that he had worked out an arrangement with Luiz Carlos Prestes, they having been old friends. He said he had. I asked him whether he thought Prestes was an honest Brazilian or whether he was the kind of Communist who follows the Moscow line irrespective. He said that his present feeling was that Prestes and his friends were following the Moscow line and probably could not break away. But he thought that in the long run no Brazilian group would remain subservient to a foreign power. . . .

. . . At dinner at the British Embassy, Gainer confided his very great fear of the Russian methods and operation. Not only is the Trieste situation extremely difficult, but news has come of their landing on Bornholm, one of the Danish islands. Taken together with their intrigue with the Danish Freedom Council, this rather confirms my feeling that the Russians propose to strike straight to the mouth of the Baltic Sea, as, in time, they will strike for the Straits of Gibraltar. All this is not a reassuring prospect. . . .

June 5, 1945

[Berle was called back to Washington for consultation. He flew] . . . in . . . a C-47, which we nicknamed "Jumping Charlie" because in rough weather it bounces! . . .

June 8, 1945

I camped in [Chief, Brazilian Affairs Philip O.] Chalmers' office in the State Department and went looking to see what was going on. What was going on was the damnedest mess I have ever seen in my life. Joe Grew [Under Secretary] is doing his best on European affairs, taking the line that he would like other people, notably the Russians, to keep their agreements. Hopkins is in Moscow, presumably trying to persuade the Russians to do the same thing and arrange for the next meeting of the Big Three. As far as I can make out, Stettinius, Rockefeller and the rest of the lot in San Francisco haven't a friend in the world. The Latin American section is being jumped on right, left and center for having favored Argentina. If they say this before they know the full extent of commitments made to Argentina, I wonder what they will say when they know the rest of the story.

June 11, 1945

President Vargas has ordered Ambassador Martins back from San Francisco to try to clean up on the general situation. I made an arrangement accordingly to see him at cocktail time and proceeded to do so. Apparently things were in a worse mess than I thought; for Martins, who is stable and able, was a hurt and angry man. He had had a violent session with Rockefeller and told him that while they had been friends for years, he was through with him and that the State Department's word was no longer any good. Apparently certain agreements had been made very casually about supporting Brazil for the chairmanship or the position of relator in one of the committees, and thereafter, equally casually, the United States had shifted its support to Chile. . . . The Argentine oil agreement, which is now known, had made things still worse. Further, neither Stettinius nor Rockefeller would talk over anything with either Velloso or Martins except in company with [Guillermo] Belt, the Cuban Ambassador, Galo Plaza, the Ecuadoran Ambassador, and the representative of Bolivia. . . . Finally, in connection with coal, agricultural machinery, et cetera, the Brazilians had promises that they would be taken care of after the victory in Europe. Victory in Europe is past, and they are told they can have nothing, but the Argentines appear to get what they need.

Fortunately I had been working at this all day in the Department. I had worked myself into a right royal rage. . . . It was not assuaged when Joe Grew told me that he had been so busy on European affairs that he did not know anything about these things but assumed that they must have been okayed by somebody in the Latin American section. There isn't any Latin American section; my old friend [George] Butler, who was Second Secretary and I believe now First Secretary in Lima, is sitting there holding down the desk. Avra Warren has been trying to run things from San Francisco; and he has been more interested in the Ambassadorship to Argentina . . . than anything else. The net result is that these agreements have been negotiated without any coordination, everybody trying to get what they wanted and giving Argentina anything she asked for. . . .

. . . I told Martins that I felt as badly about it as he did; and the next morning made a date to see President Truman.

June 12, 1945

They have a fancy arrangement between the White House and the State Department that no foreign or American diplomat is to see the President except in the presence of the Secretary of State. Accordingly, Joe Grew came along to the White House. I dislike this rule; it made me angry. I do not need a guardian and do not want a spy. Joe Grew is of course a gentleman and personally I can get along with him.

I talked to the President about my personal arrangements coming to a quite satisfactory conclusion from my point of view. He tells me that they are having a conference in Rio in October for the purpose of drawing a treaty which will give effect to the Act of Chapultepec, and he wanted me to work on that.

I told him exactly what I thought of the whole Argentine business— the beginning, the middle, and the end; and he wound up by saying he felt exactly the way I did about it. I gathered that he simply had not got his hand on the thing in time. He was interested in Brazil particularly, and he told Mr. Grew and myself to go ahead and do anything we could to equate the Brazilian situation with the Argentine. He further told me that he wanted to reinforce the Inter-American system. . . .

Thereafter I saw every official I could find in Washington. . . .

June 13, 1945

I saw Admiral Land and asked for more ships. I am hoping to get some for the Santa Catarina coal. . . .

I likewise talked to Wayne Taylor and hope that I have got the financing of the São Francisco River project started at last. We will know more about that later. This is an attempt to do something roughly analogous to the TVA in the São Francisco valley; it could also supply [the entire Northeast].

July 8, 1945
[Back in Rio] . . . we took the car and went off to Teresópolis; and spent Sunday taking a 30 kilometer walk through the little national park, climbing Pedra do Sino, the dominant peak in the range there. The weather was perfect; the scenery as beautiful as any in the world; the Brazilian director of the park, whom we did not wish to bother, nevertheless gave us some pack horses and on the little log shelter half way up the mountain he had the Brazilian and American flags displayed. I loved it.

July 15, 1945
This job is an endeavor to cobble up an endless series of economic arrangements, no one of which is spectacular but failure of any of which will mean a progressive breakdown in the economy of the country. I cannot speak too highly of the endless patience and cooperation of the Brazilians. . . . Clearly any governmental measures we take must have as their principal base raising the standard of living of the masses of Brazil, and in order to do that we have to get the materials to work with. . . .

I felt impelled to get myself in trouble and probably have done so. The Russian demands in the Middle East, which include virtual control of Turkey plus the Aleppo district, and virtual control of Iran with an obviously dominant position in Arabia, mean the end of the British Empire roughly east of Italy—though they might hold Egypt. We could be philosophical about this: the United States is not in the business of underwriting European colonial systems. But they would also have control of economic resources, notably oil, capable of making everything in Europe dependent on them, except as we supply from this hemisphere.

. . . the Lord knows neither the British nor the local governments have done much for their populations beyond the 19th Century service of giving a degree of public order and a limited amount of justice. But the evidence does not seem to me convincing that the Russians would do any better; and the power politics they are using to force their position plainly violate any process by which we might hope to get freedom from fear, let alone freedom of information, in this world. Further, the concentration of power in the hands of a single country does not normally lead to progress. Its historical result has commonly been oppression and eventually war.

Accordingly, I stuck my neck out and telegraphed such views as I had to President Truman. . . .

TO SECSTATE WASHINGTON—SECRET—FOR THE PRESIDENT AND
SECRETARY OF STATE, JULY 13, 1945

Following views on present Russo-British-Near Eastern crisis are offered at risk of giving unasked advice. In this connection reference is made to my memorandum dated [September 26] 1944 addressed to State Department Policy Committee foreseeing substantially this situation and suggesting we form our views, and report of subcommittee to discuss this matter.

It is my judgment that USSR objective is to control entire Middle East, Egypt included. At time of USSR air conversations their delegation proposed joint US-USSR line with US operation as far as Cairo, after which USSR would carry on, in accordance with carefully worked out Moscow instructions. Steady progress in this direction is indicated by direct moves through Iran and Turkey plus reported request for Aleppo and other moves. Without even crossing Suez, entire oil supply of Western Europe (other than that from Western Hemisphere) would be in hands of USSR leaving Western Europe dependent on grace either of USSR or of US for essential materials for civilian life and for national defense. In view of fact that British Empire now is major organizing factor in Western Europe, question is squarely posed whether, under all circumstances, we wish to defend her position. In this connection following considerations seem outstanding:

(1) National interest: undoubtedly USSR will exclude every vestige of American communications and authority. Though less violently, British have followed similar policy in respect to aviation, communications, and other matters. Only immediate question is whether "keep off" sign is written in Russian or English. Obviously this limited and exclusively irritating fact is minor in entire situation. Imperial position of British is capable of evolution along lines we understand, and at bottom does have certain respect for principles of justice and freedom, though in economic matters especially these principles are often violated. With British we are able to discuss the problems and probably could make arrangement now for continued evolution in Middle and Far East of group of free cooperative nations along line of British Commonwealth or present American nations system.

(2) Policy of USSR in this regard is obscure as yet. While undoubtedly there is sincere USSR interest in welfare of masses, which have not progressed much under British hegemony, as yet we have no evidence that social changes imposed by USSR force will result in any real human advance outside USSR borders. Net result to date outside USSR has been warfare, cruelty and misery, without evidence that new crystallization will give anyone material benefit. Usually spontaneous revolutions uncover unrestricted layer of capacity in local population, as happened in Soviet Union. Historically revolutions superimposed from outside do not usually have this result. Effect of turning over Middle East and probably Far East with it to USSR control will apparently exchange slowly evolving process guided by British thought with which we can communicate for violent change exclusively guided by USSR thought with which as yet we have established no effective communication and which shows many signs that such communication is not desired.

(3) Substantial absorption by USSR of British position from Mediterranean eastward places huge military and economic resources in hands of single power, almost, though not quite, enabling it to dictate to remainder of world, as it is unnecessary to point out. Geopolitics of Nazis

were designed to realize this dream in German hands; now USSR is on threshold of realizing it with power in her possession. It is at least open question whether power thus obtained would be friendly or not. USSR espionage, propaganda and organization in South America are following lines very similar to German lines in 1936 and 1937; they are ignoring US with whom obviously no present quarrel is desired, which was German policy from 1937 to 1940. Nevertheless all machinery is being set up to cause major embarrassment should US policy diverge from interests of USSR.

(4) To estimate temporary tactical position it is necessary to determine USSR Far East intentions. In my view USSR will not and cannot make arrangements supporting Japan. Irrespective of what we do, they will maintain their force on Manchurian border and the tacit threat of releasing Japanese Manchurian troops against us has been used to secure concessions already. Without technical military advice I hesitate to venture opinion, but my distinct impression is that present strategic position in Pacific has probably dissipated likelihood that Japanese force in Manchuria could now be used effectively against US even if Japanese fear of USSR thrust was removed. Also, USSR proposes inevitably in any case to seize territory and position equal to or greater than her position prior to Russo-Jap war, and she will come into conflict with Chinese masses as well as Japanese eventually.

(5) Also, it is difficult to escape feeling that USSR is in no condition to force issues despite enormous façade, and there is propaganda that USSR armies are most powerful universally. Position of USSR resembles French position at time of Versailles Treaty when speaking in light of deployed armies France undertook to create French Europe as far east as Ukraine; but soon found that internal condition of France did not permit continued deployment of troops on which their influence was based at that time. Consequently entire structure collapsed upon withdrawal of troops. It is my belief that somewhat the same situation exists now in connection with USSR position. It is an outstanding fact about revolutions based on fifth column and social movements stimulated from outside that they have never yet been successful except when supported by adjacent or occupying troops, whether initiated by France after last war, or by Germany and USSR in present war.

(6) In addition, moral aspects of present situation closely approximate moral aspects German policy from 1933 until the defeat of Hitler. Same tactics are used: violent propaganda, smear accusations, portrayal of other peoples' patriotism as criminal or reactionary, financing of fifth columns, stimulated disorders, street terrorism, ultimately direct territorial and occupation demands. Such tactics give no present prospect development of eventual good neighbor policy enabling us to realize world of good neighbors pledged to mutual respect, mutual cooperation and mutual maintenance of peace, which is our principal national interest. Nothing has been gained and much may have been lost if we are merely going into another cycle like that between 1919 and 1939.

(7) In conclusion, I believe we should at once and as purely inde-

pendent decision state forcefully that present policy of unilateral expansion has become intolerable, not because we guarantee British Empire but because we went to war to stop world order in which this sort of thing continually happens. Continuance of USSR unilateral expansion would mean that we should have to implement promises implicit in Atlantic Charter, agreed to by USSR, indicating support of British at present. We propose as substitute international good neighbor policy which affords full freedom of economic passage and access to everyone, with imperialist ambitions renounced by all. We should discuss independently with British evolution of imperial system we are now being asked to save, towards cooperative grouping of independent nations possibly on lines of British Commonwealth with certain definitely recognized duties including open door and recognition that they will be judged by extent and degree to which their governments devote themselves to raising standards of living of their people and respect neighbors' rights. We could cooperate with British on this platform, which is in substance that of Atlantic Charter, and would be glad to have USSR join if they accepted this basis.

It seems to me that any other policy would involve us in same rearguard action American diplomacy unsuccessfully fought against Germany from 1937 onward, with the final result of our joining the European war primarily because otherwise we should have had to fight alone, but with collateral result of supplying underlying force to support European imperialisms which are of little interest to US. Should present Soviet policy continue, it is difficult to escape conclusion that we would eventually be forced into same position again, with same outcome.

July 15, 1945

Being Sunday, the family went walking in Tijuca and climbed Pedra Bonita. On top there was a little club of excursionists who recognized us, made coffee at their camping ground, and we generally had a good time.

July 18, 1945

General [Mark] Clark, Commander of the Armies in Italy, with General [Willis D.] Crittenberger and General [Donald W.] Brann are in town as guests of the Brazilian Government to help welcome the return of the Brazilian Expeditionary Force. Clark is a story-book soldier; he has what it takes, has a first-rate head, and he looks the part; he is handling himself extremely well. There is no question that the Brazilians like him, and he has crowds to greet him wherever he goes, like a first-class movie star.

This morning General [João Batista] Mascarenhas [de Moraes, head of the Brazilian Expeditionary Force] came in with the first contingent of the Brazilian troops, to be greeted by everybody from President Vargas down. I went along and behind the ceremonies got hold of the two First Lieutenants who are here with a platoon of American mountain troops who served with the Brazilian Force and who are here to join the party. They are two good boys, and we shall see something of them before they get out of town.

Last night we had a cynical aftermath of the United States Government's trading with Argentina. As will have been seen, when Avra Warren worked up the recognition of Argentina and opened the door for economic trading, we handed the Argentines 500,000 tons of oil while maintaining to Brazil that we didn't have any to give to her. The Department and FEA have been trying to defend this singularly shabby deal ever since.

Last night President Vargas sent me confidential word that the Argentines have demanded 10,000 rubber tires from Brazil (these being tires which Brazil is under contract to deliver to the United States). In return, Perón had offered to deliver gasoline which he knew Brazil needed, this being of course the gasoline our boys had thoughtfully handed him while denying Brazil. As a piece of minor cynical diplomacy this takes the cake.

Yesterday, also, a meeting with the Brazilian Planning Commission. They want to get reparations from Germany in the form of factories—which I think is a little imaginative; but I told them that there was an endless amount of stuff in the way of surplus material which could be used, and if we knew where it was and what the Brazilians wanted and could connect their need with the waste which otherwise will take place in Army surplus, we ought to get some useful things done.

August 7, 1945

Saturday, July 28. Beatrice and I, along with Captain W. R. Cooke, U.S.N., Lieutenant Gordon B. Whelpley, U.S.N.R., and Captain Samuel J. Skousen, U.S.A., started on a trip around the Amazonian region of Brazil. We left Rio in Captain Skousen's Beechcraft for Belém, stopping at Barreiras, where we found a squadron of photography boys making a map of Central Brazil, and left them a turkey from General Mark Clark's reception the night before. Then to Carolina on Rio Tocantíns for gasoline; there were a couple of tame emus, which look much like ostriches, running around the airport. Thence to Belém, where we stopped the night at the little French pension of Madame Garré; and had a reception at the club given by Consul and Mrs. [Randolph A.] Kidder. A nice little party.

Sunday, July 29. Got a little chance to walk around the town; and then over to help dedicate a new wing of the [Serviço Especial de Saúde Pública] laboratory where they are training laboratory assistants to make laboratory analyses and verify diagnoses in the Public Health stations. SESP has 27 stations ready to open in the Amazonian region—a small bite at a huge problem. Then out on the river in an RDC [Rubber Development Corporation] boat. . . .

Monday, July 30. Collecting some more RDC people and Consul Kidder, we started up the Amazon, this time in a Grumman amphibian accompanied by a PBY Catalina. We went first to Altamira, a little town just above the Falls of the Xingú River; the whole town was out to meet us; we saw the school and the little Prefecture, and the road that RDC is building around the Falls of the Xingú. . . .

Thence to Santarém, where we had delayed proceedings. There is one of the loveliest schools that I have yet seen on a height of land overlooking the junction of the Tapajós and the Amazon. I think it was originally started for something else. We also saw the new hospital which they are building there and which is almost done; but the problem is even more doctors and nurses than it is hospital buildings. SESP is working at it.

Thence to Belterra where we passed the night. This is on the Tapajós; the Ford Company has a rubber plantation there, which, with the other Ford plantation 90 miles up the river, is the only organized rubber plantation in the Amazon. All other rubber work is merely gathering wild rubber. The Ford manager there tells me that they have the problem licked, and that they can produce rubber in competition with Asia provided the price does not go much below fifteen cents a pound. . . .

Tuesday, July 31. Left Belterra and arrived in Manáos. The Grumman hit a buzzard circling into the Manáos river landing and smashed a windshield. We were very nicely received, taken to the square where the Manáos band played the National Anthems; a new note was introduced when it played "amen" after the "Star-Spangled Banner." . . . In the evening a party for the *granfino* socialites at the Rio Negro Club, which is an extremely luxurious place with a beautiful dance floor. Large numbers of the populace were banked up outside to see the *granfinos* come and go; after we got through with the receiving line, I went out to the fence and shook hands with everybody I could get hold of, beginning with a couple of policemen, a couple of school teachers, et cetera, and generally tried to get below the high society in Manáos.

Manáos has possibilities; obviously not very well developed. The RDC has built an airport there; it is a bad job and we have to fix it. There were some Redemptorist priests in town who are actually doing the missionary work up the river, and I gather having their hands full. They are trying to organize schools. Nice American boys . . .

Wednesday, August 1. By direct flight from Manáos to Pôrto Velho, over the huge jungle.

This Amazonian forest is impressive both for what it is and for its huge size; the whole region is as large as all Western Europe. I should think it would be the last region to be tamed by man; the forest is unmaliciously impregnable; never hurrying, never stopping, capable of absorbing into itself inside of two years any scar that man can make on it. What is inside of it no one yet knows. It defends itself economically; its riches, though vast, are so scattered that they cannot be organized as we like to organize things; a square mile of timber will have fifty different kinds of trees in it, none grouped so as to be capable of easy exportation.

To Pôrto Velho at noon, where we were met by one of the most impressive characters I have run into yet—Colonel Aluizio Pinheiro Ferreira. He is presently Governor of the Territory of Guaporé. . . . He was the son of a little Pará farmer, Bragança; one of 11 brothers. He was appointed to the military school and finally got to be a second lieutenant. At this point the revolution broke out—I think in 1921; he says that he didn't like politics but it may have been that he was on the wrong side. At all events he packed up and got out; went to Guajará and there lived among a friendly tribe of Indians. He worked as a rubber gatherer, or *seringueiro;* and made a living at it. . . . In due time the dust died down, and he went back into the Army, always having frontier posts.

There is a railroad from Pôrto Velho to Guajará-Mirim around the Falls of the Madeira, connecting 1,000 miles or so of navigable Madeira above with 600 or 800 miles of navigable Madeira below. This railroad had been built at terrible cost of life and money by an American company; its operation had not paid; it had then been taken over by a British company; and in 1931 or thereabouts was abandoned. Vargas, coming in, nationalized it and appointed Aluizio as director. The railroad is all there is in Guajará-Mirim—aside from roving Indians who even now come in and shoot up the railroad workers once in a while with bows and arrows; and the occasional rubber gatherers. Its business consists of picking up the rubber balls which are brought down the rivers on launches or rafts to the railroad line, whence they are shipped to Pôrto Velho; and then down in boats to Manáos. Anyway Aluizio made this railroad run; principally with his two hands. When we saw it, it was in good working order, with locomotives, cars, a machine shop which functions, etc. In 1943, President Vargas created the Territory of Guaporé and made Aluizio Governor of it—Guaporé being a very large jungle attached to a very small railroad.

Aluizio fed us a huge lunch of turtle meat (the "poor man's beef", they call it) which was extremely good; showed us the roads he is building, largely with machinery supplied by the RDC; and in the afternoon there was a parade in our honor. This was all of the school children, the territorial guard—except that they were in blue jeans. Aluizio explained that he had no particular military problems so he had organized them into a corps of engineers and was using them to build roads, etc. There was also a small corps of federal troops doing military service there; and in conclusion was a parade of all the road machinery they had, a couple of tractors, some road scrapers, a moving derrick, etc. It was amazing, and the dust was hideous. But it was very impressive. Somebody was trying to do something and doing it. Obviously this is not the whole story—we were only seeing the upper side of it. But you did get the sense that Aluizio knew his job. Somebody asked whether this organization was Fascist or not. My own feeling was that it was much more in the style of our early semi-militarized frontier posts in the United States. There is no question that this bunch like Aluizio.

We had the house of one of the people in Pôrto Velho; their hospitality is simple. They fire the family out of the best house in town and put you in. The house is as big as a minute, and I suppose the family is taken care of somehow.

Thursday, August 2. Abandoning the Grumman for the time being, we went on the gasoline car down the whole line of the Madeira-Mamoré Railroad. . . .

This was 365 kilometers on a railroad whose grade is not too good;

stopping from time to time. At Abuna we had the school children out for us and then went over to dedicate the electric light plant—a small unit about as big as an automobile engine, also got through the RDC; but it gives light to the town. Then they served lunch, and we saw the school children, etc.; I tried to take particular pains to talk to the teachers. Some of these school teachers in the little rural schools are probably the real heroines of the frontier. . . .

There was a dinner that night, in the railroad station [in Mamoré]. Aluizio does not go in for residences and interventorial palaces. He hasn't time and would rather put the money into roads. The Prefect was there but his wife was not; later we found that she was doing cooking across the square and sending the food to the station by a line of territorial guards. Other territorial guards were organized to work on the table; and they started to sling the hash, but Aluizio was trying to teach them how it should be done. We promptly and enthusiastically cooperated in teaching everybody to pass the plates on the left, etc.; Aluizio insisting that the proper thing to do was to tell them how it ought to be done because they got relatively few chances to learn. After dinner we called loudly for the Prefect's wife, who was the real heroine; and generally had a first-rate time.

Friday, August 3 . . . Then the Grumman took off for Trinidad, Santa Cruz and Corumbá, flying over Bolivian territory. . . . Finally [the bush pilots] were thoroughly lost and headed west to pick up their direction, which they only did when they finally sighted the Andes Mountains. This gave them enough direction to get back to Santa Cruz, where we landed, but it was too late to try to make Corumbá. Since I had no right to be on Bolivian territory at all, I decided to keep dark and Beatrice and I strolled around town with the local manager of the RDC, stopping for a drink with him at the airport, which had been constructed by the Germans and later taken over when we had the line nationalized. . . .

Saturday, August 4. Up very early hoping perhaps to make Rio by nightfall. But the bush pilots are simply not up to it. . . . The engines were not warmed up. We started off, as it later turned out, with the generator said to be in bad shape. The flight to Corumbá was routine flying; the weather was good and you cannot miss it with anything like navigation. And the bush pilots did not miss it. But when they got to Corumbá somebody got rattled, they made a bad landing, ran off the end of the field, and the Lord Almighty personally intervened. The end of the field was closed by a barbed wire fence instead of a stone wall and beyond that a road, and beyond that a line of trees. The barbed wire fence wrapped itself around our left wheel, bringing the plane to a right-angle turn in the middle of the road. Otherwise we should have fried in burning gasoline. The occurence was dramatic because General Mascarenhas de Moraes was just arriving from Peru where he had been helping to inaugurate the new Peruvian President; and the entire territorial army was lined up to meet him and play the anthems, etc. They were going to play one for us but tactfully decided this was no occasion to celebrate. At all events, we climbed out of the plane looking and feeling quite foolish, and toddled over to the airport where we shook hands with everybody and promptly claimed a couple of seats on the Pan Air do Brasil plane taking General Mascarenhas de Moraes into Rio. . . .

Upon climbing into the Pan Air plane, the Brazilian pilot made a perfect run through Mato Grosso to Campo Grande, where there was a little welcome to the General at the airport which they kindly took us in on . . . and thence to São Paulo. . . .

Sunday, August 5. Up bright and early and once more the Pan Am pilot made a perfect flight through somewhat difficult weather into Rio, landing with a grace and perfection which makes it clear that Brazilian pilots can be as good as any in the world. . . .

September 3, 1945

Sunday, September 2. The Japanese duly surrendered and so the war, whose end we have already celebrated, may be fairly said to be over. Whatever the doctrine, Grew's final diplomacy worked, and the Japanese armies seem actually to be surrendering. This has saved an endless number of lives.

The Third Inter-American Conference on Radio Communications will meet tomorrow and the bulk of the delegates got here today; we got them together at the house. Most of the work is technical, which does not affect me very much, but we can fire a shot for additional liberty of information.

In a world of atomic bombs, liberty of information, and eventually a general body of common doctrine which binds people, is about all we can do. . . .

September 20, 1945

I have been stewing a good deal recently and the result of it is not very satisfactory.

The Council of Foreign Ministers is meeting in London, and to all intents and purposes it is a secret session. Nobody is laying down plans or demands for the scrutiny of world opinion, and it is becoming the familiar territorial bargaining match.

The mechanics of manipulating world opinion by propaganda have vastly improved since the crude days of Versailles when people merely bribed occasional editors or circulated handsomely printed propaganda pamphlets. Actually now, in every country, there is a group of people manipulating opinion, monopolizing sympathizers, and bringing political pressure to bear within the country. These are brought into action to support various claims of one sort and another.

I do not see that the powers have undertaken to agree on any set of principles which should govern their territorial and political action. In other words, they are acting quite frankly on the doctrine of self-interest, territorial, political and economic. All this adds up to a clash and not an agreement. Relative weakness, fear of immediate destructive force, and so forth, will restrain undue insistence for a time. But this is not permanent.

In terms of direct territorial clash, the Russians have now unveiled their demand for the Middle East. They are asking military bases in the Dodecanese, and, it is said, but not confirmed, a port on the Red Sea, as well as a voice in Tripoli. This last is probably for bargaining purposes.

The French are at length frightened; Léon Blum [Socialist leader] has at last got the idea of a Western European family of nations; and is encountering again Russian opposition.

We on our side will negotiate here in October a treaty implementing the Act of Chapultepec; but I should not be surprised to find that this too, in some fashion, is regarded as a threat to Russian security. We shall know more about this by the end of October.

I have not yet seen that anything the State Department is throwing up has mental or moral characteristics capable of dealing with this. Nor would it be certain that, if they did have such ability, the Congress would let them get it into action.

The greatest danger in the situation is that as yet we have developed no means of communicating with the Russians. That is to say, we cannot get the truth about what goes on within the Soviet Union, nor can we state the truth as to what is going on in our own countries. This leaves it an open season for the Soviet hater on the one side and the Soviet propagandist on the other, and score adds up to something looking much more like a clash than an agreement, unless some way is found of bridging the chasm, and none has yet appeared. Obviously there are now only two major powers in the world—the United States and Russia. Both are anxious not to quarrel, but the Russian ambition is still apparently as limitless as Hitler's. . . .

There is . . . a cable sent to the Department giving the present complexities of the Brazilian situation. Vargas, by not entering the lists as a candidate for President, has foreclosed himself from any legal method of perpetuating his own power. He is being pressed, however, to continue the dictatorship by the Communists on the one hand, who are making great propaganda for a constituent assembly—with the implied continuance of the present government while it deliberates; and by the office-holding group or "Queremistas" on the other. This fact is driving both the opposition candidates, Gomes and Dutra, into a common camp, and probably with them the Army.

Elections mean a politically conservative and economically reactionary candidate—either Gomes or Dutra would be that—under the form of democracy.

Perpetuation of the dictatorship means absence of democracy, a popular President with the support of the masses, and probably an Army revolt.

We are being pressed to declare against continuance of the dictatorship—which perhaps we should do if, as and when there is real reason to believe that Vargas will not go through with elections. But, while this satisfies the principle, it probably prevents any immediate progress towards much-needed economic reform.

As my thinking now runs, we had best ask for democracy and get it, even though its first act is to make what appears to be a mistake—relying on popular force to correct that mistake. This will not satisfy the Left, despite its clamors against the dictatorship—for the Left has been notoriously opportunist, and while it damned Vargas as a dictator, it will damn, still more, any interference with its plan to make use of him while it can. . . .

The other night I had an evening visit from the head of the Philips electric light bulb cartel. We did some intelligence work for the Army through some of his connections and got some really useful material on the German movements which were of value in beating the Nazis. . . .

September 23, 1945

To church and then to climb Pico da Tijuca. Coming down from there, a tea at the Fontes house where President Roosevelt stayed.

To the Embassy to find that Spruille Braden [U.S. Ambassador to Argentina] had just arrived at the airport and was on his way up. . . .

I told him that after much sweating I had come to the conclusion that the only way to have democracy was to have it; and that the United States was beginning to be expected to express a view. We took time out to consider and got a night's sleep.

October 1, 1945

President Vargas asked me to go to Guanabara Palace at 7:00 o'clock on the evening of September 28. . . .

He first raised the question of the activation of the base agreement. . . . There were two questions at issue: the first, the activation of the base agreement with a Brazilian-American commission; the second, on a lower level, the appointment of someone to deal with [U.S. General Ralph] Wooten [Foreign Liquidation Commission] in connection with the property. . . .

He next brought up the question of the civil air agreement.

I told him that the civil air agreement was not a condition of returning the bases. We had no government-to-government agreement authorizing the use of these fields for civil aircraft; but the fact was that these fields were the principal line of communication between our two countries. It therefore seemed useful at this time to open the question so as to have an orderly settlement of affairs. All previous arrangements have been by agreement between the Brazilian Government and some private airline. The President asked what effect the Chicago accords had on this. I told him that in Chicago we believed in free air; the Brazilian Government had not accepted this as yet but preferred bilateral agreements; and we were accepting the Brazilian point of view and suggesting that bilateral accord be worked out. The President raised a question about the aviation meeting in Montreal; I told him this was primarily to work out technical matters and organization but did not involve necessarily acceptance of the Chicago accords. The President asked whether the bilateral accord could be on a reciprocal basis. I told him that we assumed of course it would be on that basis; Brazil might have some difficulty because the Chicago accords provided transit rights all the way through, as, for instance, across the Guianas and the Caribbean countries which Brazil would have to negotiate for separately outside the Chicago accords in order to get full transit rights through to the United States. I said of course we should be glad to help on this. The real reason for liking the principle of freedom of air was that it saved the endless complications of negotiating with every country over which an airplane had to pass. The President nodded and seemed satisfied.

The President then raised the question of 2,000 tires for Argentina. He said I could speak quite frankly, that we were talking as friends. I told him that we had offered to cancel the rubber agreements, in which case Brazil could deliver 2,000 or any other quantity of tires. But to give permission for 2,000 tires was troublesome. Other Latin American countries had quotas which were still unfilled: the Ecuadoran had been in my office only the previous day begging for more tires. Further, the Argentine price of tires was merely ten times that of the Brazilian, and 2,000 tires did not settle the Argentine question. It looked to me as though a couple of Argentine officials proposed to get the tires from Brazil at the Brazilian price and sell them in Argentina at the Argentine price and make a brutal profit. The President grinned and then said that the Brazilians intended to send two ships to Argentina asking wheat; the Argentines at first said they could not load them unless Brazil exported auto trucks which Brazil declined to do, and then had asked for 2,000 tires. He asked what I thought. He said at the end there might not be bread in Brazil.

I said that quite aside from the 2,000 tires, Brazil was far too great a country to have to act under threats of that kind. I would promptly explore with the American Government the possibility of shipping wheat to Brazil. Brazil might do as she pleased about buying Argentine wheat but she ought not to be in the position of negotiating with Perón under threat of being deprived of an essential foodstuff. The President seemed very much relieved. . . .

In discussing Perón, the President gave me an opening to talk a little about our thought regarding the internal situation in Brazil. I told him that I approached this with the greatest of hesitation but that one could not be as close to the situation as we were without seeing a great many things, and that the Brazilian situation would be very closely watched in the United States. We had admired as acts of great statesmanship his putting Brazil back on the democratic rails, and doing thereby what General [Agustín P.] Justo in Argentina had been unable to do. He had been kind enough to invite me to hear his speech of September 7 declining to run again; a speech which was forthright, direct and honest, and we had not taken any stock in his enemies who had tortured this speech into the exact opposite of what it said. We now saw various groups talking about a coup d'état in exact opposition to a policy which would place Vargas on a par with the greatest statesmen of South America.   –

Vargas then said that he did not propose to be a candidate. There were two reasons, both good. One was that he said he would not and he had respect for his word. The second was that he was tired; and he proposed to leave while he had the affection and applause of his people, and not to stay until he went out with either their hatred or their indifference. For this reason he was going through with elections and he had made that plain. The agitation for a *constituinte* was coming along next week but he would resolve that.

I then told him that I had thought of saying something and showed him the manuscript of what I expected to say. He read it and asked one question: whether this meant we were opposed to a *constituinte*. I told him certainly not, though speaking as an individual I did not recall any case where a constituent assembly had been able to take over executive power; that of course was a matter which Brazilians themselves would decide. . . .

We talked a little about the Communists. The President said rather grimly that the Communists knew very well that the masses were with him and not with them; that all they wanted was a chance to organize and that their real goal was 20 or 30 years ahead. . . .

As we left it, I think our views were clear about the base activation agreement; about the arrangements for the base property; about the civil air accord. The President indicated he wanted the tire matter given a little more study, which I agreed to do. . . . He said that this was the end of a government and he was putting things in order.

As previously, I got the sense of a tired, sincere man struggling with many forces, no longer anxious for great power, caught to some extent in the shackles of his past.

October 6, 1945

Saturday, September 29. I went to Quitandinha with Beatrice, where there was a small and dull luncheon of the Government-controlled *Sindicato dos Jornalistas;* at the close of which I made the speech [which Vargas had seen].

It is going to cause a good deal of political comment and in a sense takes the Embassy off the pedestal and puts it into the firing line.

It is made on the theory that everything the Brazilian Government has done to date has been done in good faith and it rejects the charges of the enemies of the Government that the Government is secretly fomenting a Fascist coup d'état. I personally think this is true; but it is very difficult to wrestle with the grim fact that probably the worst elements in the Government are proposing a coup d'état, and that many of the men behind it were most active in opposing the United States and cheering Italian Fascism in 1937.

The Communists are stringing along with it, though obviously this cannot be any permanent alliance.

Further, every friend of the United States has been making friendship with the United States friendship also with the democratic process, and it is this which has enabled us to represent with truth Brazil as a country moving towards democracy. The Government has followed this line throughout—barring the activities of the *Queremistas* who are, as stated, men who were the backbone of the Fascist Party in 1937.

Anyhow it is done, and that is that.

[Excerpts from the speech follow.]

Never were relations between Brazil and the United States closer than they are today. Brazilian events are widely and thoroughly reported in America, with constant and growing interest. Through nearly a century and a half our two countries have thought and worked together. Now we have fought together in the battle for human freedom. The long friendship is bound with common sacrifice of blood.

Brazilian affairs interest the entire world; but they are most closely watched by the millions of American friends of Brazil who make up the public opinion of the United States. That public opinion has rejoiced over the steady Brazilian determination to develop and use the institutions of democratic government, and has acclaimed the steps taken by the Brazilian Government to reach the goal of constitutional democracy.

The United States thus warmly welcomed the establishment and safeguarding of freedom of information and free press within the country, as wartime dangers died away.

It welcomed, too, political amnesty, and freedom of political organization granted to all except the Nazi group, which of course had forfeited its right to political organization through its announced intention to betray democracy whenever it could gain power.

The United States welcomed the free organization of political parties, for the purpose of carrying out free elections. Brazilians, at this moment, enjoy every right of political organization and discussion which we have in the United States.

The pledge of free Brazilian elections, set for a definite date, by a Government whose word the United States has found inviolable, has been hailed with as much satisfaction in the United States as in Brazil itself. Americans have not agreed with some who tried to misrepresent straightforward pledges and declarations as insincere, or as verbal trickery. . . .

The happiness with which this steady march towards constitutional democracy has been welcomed is based on American experience. We have learned that the only way to be a democracy is to practice democracy.

Monday, October 1. To Santos with the family. . . . We had a very pleasant and quiet time.

But Santos was prepared for a coup d'état on October 3; the Army had been alerted and was setting up machine guns around the airfields, etc. . . .

Wednesday, October 3. To Rio. We had hoped to go either to Rio Grande do Sul or to fish for dorado in São Paulo. But there were complications; with the big push for a coup d'état, thinly disguised under the name of *Constituinte,* I felt I had better be in Rio.

During the evening [Cecil] Cross [U.S. Consul] telephoned from São Paulo saying that the meeting in São Paulo had been a flop—partly because the Army had vigorously stated that it wanted no nonsense; and partly because it was raining. Meanwhile the meeting had been held here in Rio. For some hours special trains were running in from surrounding parts of the country, and free fare and meals were provided to those who came in. Query: Who is paying for all this? They met and made speeches and somewhere between ten and fifteen thousand people gathered. They went to the Guanabara Palace, where President Vargas made an address reaffirming his desire to preside over elections and transfer the power to his duly elected successor; but adding that if the people really wanted a *Constituinte,* of course their desires had to be satisfied.

I still think he means what he says and is not engaged in double talk. His enemies do not give him credit for this.

Thursday, October 4. There has been a great deal of newspaper discussion of the speech, many groups liking it, others attacking it violently. The attacks come almost exclusively from two extremes—the extreme Left (Luiz Carlos Prestes attacked it in a speech in Pôrto Alegre stating the Communist view) and the extreme Fascists, headed by Viriata Vargas [brother of Getúlio], attacking it on the ground that it is the kind of Yankee imperialism which is victimizing Franco and Perón. How these two will put themselves together I can't possibly see. . . .

I have been in a good deal of mental turmoil because, being natively a timid soul, I don't like to get into political controversy and always torment myself with wondering whether I did the right thing. For the speech is being referred to as the "atomic bomb that ended *Queremismo*". The many hundreds of telegrams and the very kindly support which has been accorded by most of the press are perhaps the best answer; but primarily I think diplomacy has changed. The public opinion in any country is necessarily a factor in the affairs of every other country; the worst thing a diplomat can do is to leave anyone in doubt. Certainly if on October 3 these boys had pulled off their coup d'état and the tide of public opinion in the United States had dealt with it as it dealt with Perón, our situation would have been strikingly unpleasant. But this form of diplomacy means that the easy life of the diplomat is gone forever.

Friday, October 5. Two things have happened in the realm of foreign affairs that are worrying me.

The first is Dean Acheson's rather summary calling off of the Pan American Conference in Rio because Argentina is being naughty. . . .

The second is that the Conference of the Five Foreign Ministers in London has broken up. . . .

. . . the coincidence of the two events makes bad reading. The American world cannot get together; and at the same time the five principal world powers cannot get together. If this situation is not pulled together somehow, not much is going forward. News that the new League of Nations is being formed with Stettinius as Secretary and a seat in the United States just becomes a comic footnote.

I had cabled the Department saying that I hoped the Rio Conference would not be indefinitely postponed; but this is unasked advice and probably will get little attention.

October 8, 1945

Saturday, October 6. The Department cabled to know whether Brazil would enter a consultation in respect of the Argentine situation, and Velloso today gave me the answer; Brazil would; would do so by diplomatic channels; believed nobody ought to take unilateral action while the consultation was going on; and hoped the United States would sign a bill of particulars stating wherein we thought Argentina had violated the Act of Chapultepec. All of this is reasonable and good sense.

Velloso told me that the President was somewhat irritated at my speech but that on further explanation, especially through Velloso, he had agreed that it was meant in friendly spirit and so the incident was closed. I told Velloso that I had bet my own personal career on defending the Brazilian administration in the United States and thereby vastly ameliorating its press; and that if the enemies of President Vargas had turned out to be right and he was really planning reestablishment of the dictatorship, not only would there have been trouble in the United States from public opinion but my own position would have been impossible. Velloso understood that perfectly because he follows the American press. At all events we are riding into easier water.

Doing a thing like this is like using up your capital. Obviously it can be done very, very rarely. To date the results seem to justify the act.

There remains the underlying and solid question. There has got to be a genuine popular movement in Brazil which influences affairs, events and governments. Plainly the ex-Fascists who are getting up the *Queremista* movement represent nothing of that sort of thing. . . . The Communists are not strong enough or representative enough to call such a popular movement into existence; the democratic parties still are principally weak; the only thing I can see is the continuance of a free press, growing experience and working democratic machinery, and the evolution over a year or so of a real and representative popular movement based on labor and so far as possible the peasants and small agriculturists. The manufacturing classes are talking of doing something about it. . . .

October 30, 1945

Yesterday (October 29) the revolution took place and the Vargas Government fell.

What happened was a third crisis, and this proved to be too much.

On October 3 demonstrations for *Constituinte*, which implied continuance of the dictatorship, had been scheduled; and the Army had objected. My own speech of September 29 was designed if possible to head off violent moves in either direction. The good sense of President Vargas prevailed and he told the demonstrations that he was not going to depart from the democratic path he had marked out.

After a brief period of quiescence, however, the dictatorship parties started again, planning a Queremista demonstration for Friday, October 26, and a Communist demonstration for Saturday, October 27. The chief agitation was Queremista, and they had lots of money and were spending it. . . .

Apparently the Generals had been increasingly coming to the conclusion that Getúlio was not playing it on the level. Nevertheless as far as I could find out they stuck to the general theory that they would encourage him to go through with elections.

I should think it may have been due to their pressure that he called off the Queremista demonstration for October 26 and rather wet-blanketed the Communist attempt to march on Guanabara Palace on the 27th. At all events, both days passed quietly without any trouble; on Sunday, October 28, we went to church and then to [Brazilian businessman] Drault Ernanny's for lunch in Gavea, and then quietly home.

Monday, October 29, developed nothing of interest during the morning. But about noon a strange and ugly rumor began to run around: the President had made a Cabinet change. He had eliminated João Alberto as Chief of Police, making room for him by displacing [Henrique] Dodsworth as Prefect of Rio de Janeiro and putting João Alberto in his place. João Alberto apparently had been told that he would have more power as Prefect and had accepted this. Dodsworth, the Prefect of Rio, had been provided for by offering him the Ministry of Foreign Affairs—which Dodsworth had sense enough to decline. The explosive end of it was that the vacant Chieftainship of Police had been filled by none other than Benjamim Vargas [brother of Getúlio]!

. . . Even to the little people in the street Benjamim was a symbol of graft and corruption. This may have been unjust: I don't know. But in this job what people think is what counts.

The rumors of these changes spread and apparently were confirmed and then the whole set of fireworks went off! The Generals insisted on meeting . . . and [delivered] an ultimatum. They wanted Getúlio's resignation. Meanwhile apparently the local garrison at Vila Militar had decided to go along with the Generals, and slowly began to move into town. An abortive move during the afternoon to fire Goes Monteiro and replace him with a supposedly pro-Getulian, General Plaquet, failed, it is said, because Plaquet declined. . . .

There seems to have been a dramatic session in the Palace, with Getúlio offering to negotiate. He would withdraw Benjamim and get back to a Cabinet status. But unfortunately the naming of Benjamim had finally convinced the Generals that the Government program of democratic institutions was a deception, and that the Palace really was planning a coup d'état under the Queremistas and the Communists as support. So the Generals insisted on resignation instead. . . .

. . . [I] went on down town. Daniels, [Reginald S.] Kazanjian [Second Secretary], and [Hugh H.] Clegg [FBI], some of the other men were there. They had confirmation of the story; the Getulian age was apparently at an end. We got off our telegraph reports; and decided to turn in. The city was moving about as usual, though there was a battalion of troops around the Catete Palace and another one around the entrances to Guanabara Palace, and some tanks, et cetera, had just moved into the Praia Flamengo when I left. (*Note:* This morning all of the battalion tank crews were peacefully asleep on the grass, having, I gather, sat up all night.)

In the early hours of the morning it developed that the President's resignation had transmitted power to the President of the Supreme Court, [José] Linhares, in accordance with the terms of the 1937 constitution. I gather pretty much everybody thinks well of Linhares; he had delayed taking the Presidency until he could consult his colleagues in the Supreme Court, and they promptly told him to go ahead.

We have news that the Minister of Labor, Marcondes Filho, is under house arrest, also Agamemnon Magalhães; and that Luiz Carlos Prestes has disappeared. Apparently the Army took the Communist archives to the Ministry of War for examination. I hope and I am taking some steps to try to see that the political liberty and rights of the Communist Party are respected. There was temporary interruption in cable and telegraph traffic, which seems to have opened up in the early morning, though some of the newspapermen complain that there is censorship of their outgoing despatches. We have tried to convey word delicately that that is a poor idea. For the rest, the town is rather calmer than a beach party after clambake, everybody going about their business. There is a rumor that some of the syndicates had wanted a general strike, but apparently that died. The Communists seem to have given orders that their people were to stay absolutely quiet.

At lunch I mentioned to my friend Father Sabóia de Madeiros, a Jesuit priest, that I felt it would be very unfortunate if they suspended the rights of the Communist Party. He vigorously and violently agreed, adding that if they put Prestes in jail he would be the first to write an article against this. He said as an active opponent of Communism himself, the worst thing they could do was to drive it underground. Communism, as he saw it, would have to be fought by argument and by action and not by suspension. I cordially agreed, adding that the Communists had a good many ideas that might profitably be adopted.

As a revolution, if it is that, this was the quietest thing I have yet seen. I am told that two shots were fired, the same being at a Lieutenant in civilian clothes who was walking with his girl and declined to halt when a sentry tried to stop him for identification; the first shot knocked the heel off the girl's shoe; the second one nicked the Lieutenant in the calf of the leg; they tied it up and he went home. These seem to be the casualties to date.

And yet—and yet . . .

There is a real tragedy in the fall of Getúlio. In his way he had done more for the country than any President. Had he carried out his announced program, he would have been the greatest statesman in South America. Had he run as a candidate, he would have been elected. But when, with a rather disreputable Palace gang, he tried to continue his dictatorship, even the support of the Communists could not convince the little people that he was so much their champion that they should support him as dictator—though they did support him as a man.

With typical calm, when the resignation and other arrangements were duly agreed on, it is reported that he said to the Generals: "Gentlemen, since you seem to have everything arranged now, I suggest that we all go to bed." I think that as history draws away from Vargas he will loom larger, as a figure, and his virtues will be remembered, as his vices will be forgotten. His real trouble is that during the 15 years of his uninterrupted rule a new generation has come along: a generation which wanted to have its say, and felt that it was not getting that opportunity under a dictatorship. Fifteen years is a long time, and the young men cannot be denied. . . .

Anyhow we are beginning a new phase; and my first concern is to try to see that it represents the masses of Brazil at least as well and if possible better than did Getúlio. But I shall not say a word against Getúlio; for he was loyal to us, and kind to me; and his fall merely demonstrates that the Machiavelli prince ruling by skill and guile is a pretty weak thing after all. He could only repeat the tactics he used in 1930 and 1937; but the current of time, tide and world opinion, and the surge of the new generation had altered circumstances; and the old magic no longer worked.

There is always an element of tragedy in the end of an administration. This one had in general dealt well with its people. It had been, in general, humane. As dictatorships go, it was about as good as one is likely to find. But the weaknesses of dictatorship in the long run outweigh its strengths; for it still is true that power corrupts and absolute power corrupts absolutely; and the strength of Getúlio was being eaten away in a thousand ways which perhaps he never knew. . . .

November 1, 1945

The new Government has formed itself of men of standing and general respect. Linhares is perhaps not a great lawyer but has been an honest and capable President of the Supreme Court. He now becomes President of Brazil—probably few people knew of him and in any event it is the position more than the man, but I think he has good common sense. Velloso continues in the Foreign Office, and I am very glad. . . .

The place is as calm as a millpond on a still afternoon, and reports from the outlying regions indicate the same thing, which I consider pretty good, since getting into the detail of dictatorial government (including outlying States) must be a pretty tough job.

I was worried about the possibility of violent reaction here, especially since on the night and early morning of the 30th Army officers were arresting Communists and Labor leaders and turning them over to the police for detention. It was rumored that they had arrested Luiz Carlos Prestes, but this seems not to be the fact. They took him down to the War Ministry for brief questioning, and let him go, after which he promptly flew the coop and disappeared. Apparently he moved fast from place to place and they never did catch up with him. I have some wires from Communist sources in New York asking me to use full influence for his "liberation", which of course I can't do.

Being worried, I dropped by Velloso's apartment last night and asked to see him. I told him that I had no right of course to interfere, but that as an old friend I wanted to express the hope that the Government would stop any anti-Communist campaign and would liberate the leaders and set the thing going as long as they kept the peace. I said I thought it was bad business for the new Government, giving it an appearance of weakness, whereas in fact it was in excellent shape. . . .

Velloso promptly agreed; said that the officers of the regional command had been a little excited but that the Government's policy was to reestablish the Communist Party and he would find a way of getting word to headquarters. On account of that or otherwise, the Government began releasing Communist leaders this morning, and I suppose they are all out of the jug by now; and the patrols were withdrawn from the Communist headquarters. It is said that the Communist paper, *Tribuna Popular,* will appear tomorrow as usual.

I am not altogether sure that the Army officers may not have had more to justify their action than I thought at first. At lunch today [Jorge] Costa Neves [Professor of Portuguese for the Berles] gave a pretty circumstantial account of the Queremista plot. It seems that they planned to have a general strike immediately following Queremista and Communist demonstrations. This was originally planned for October 3; postponed to October 27; and the final date was set for November 5. Demonstrations were to be held after which everybody was to strike, tying up water, electricity, light, transportation, banks, and so forth. This was to continue a suitable length of time, after which Vargas was to step in and yield to the urgent demand of the people by postponing elections and proclaiming that there would be a *Constituinte* at some future time. Immediately afterward he was to arrest Gomes and Dutra and dispose of any opposition.

To do this required the help or at least the passivity of the police, so Vargas approached João Alberto, his Chief of Police, on the subject. For once in his life, João Alberto decided not to go along; whereupon Vargas shifted him to the Prefecture of Rio, put Dodsworth in as Minister of Foreign Affairs, and named Benjamim Vargas, Queremista and grafter, as Chief of Police. . . .

For the rest, principally people calling to know whether we are going to "recognize" the new Government. This includes the Papal Nuncio, the Australian Minister, the Canadian Ambassador, and the Dominican Ambassador. I have already expounded to the Department my own view that this is not a change of government but rather a continuance of the old, the constitutional lines of succession having been followed and the Army having moved not to overthrow the constitution but to protect it. The State Department has adopted this view and is circulating the other American republics hoping to put itself in a position to announce continuance of relations without new recognition, on November 3. So far, so much. . . .

Memorandum to the State Department, November 13, 1945

I called today on President Linhares by arrangement made through the Foreign Office.

I took occasion to compliment him on the rapid and effective way in which he had organized his new Government and on the public praise which had been accorded his Cabinet appointments. He thanked me courteously and said that for him the Presidency was a sacrifice; he had never expected it; he proposed to hold office some eight or ten weeks, during which time he hoped to have elections fairly held, a new President installed, and the Congress elected and organized. . . .

[Berle brought Linhares up to date on the various matters discussed with former President Vargas: agreements on rubber, wheat, northeast air bases, surplus material, development of Paulo Afonso power. . . .]

The conversation was informal and very friendly throughout; I had of course known Linhares before and we have been on the friendliest of terms; so that the contact was extremely easy.

November 24, 1945

The life of any Ambassador is incomplete without a scrimmage with the international oil people, and my turn has come. On November 10 I received a telegram from the Department which was plainly dictated by representatives of Standard Oil Company of New Jersey and Atlantic Refining Company—probably the former. The drift was that [Vice President Orville] Harden of Standard Oil of New Jersey and Nave of Atlantic Refining [?] had gone to Washington to ask the Department to intervene. The Brazilians were about to grant authorization for the construction and operation of a couple of refineries, to be built under Brazilian Decree-Law 395 of 1938 and Decree-Law 4071 of 1939. These laws prevented non-Brazilians from owning or directing refineries. The companies seem to have made representations that the result of this would bring about Brazilian "monopoly" of marketing and refining oil. . . .

. . . So their simple solution was to get the Department to send a cable instructing me first to consult with the representatives of the companies and then enter into Brazilian conversations saying that the provisions of preventing foreigners from going into refining ought to be opened. In any event, we ought to get the Brazilian Petroleum Council to postpone action granting concessions for refineries. Almost shockingly, the instruction suggested that I add that Brazil was getting public loans from the United States, that this Government in future would examine the borrower's commercial policy more closely and that it was hoped that the narrow nationalism of Brazil would change—the implication being that unless they came to time, the policy of economic cooperation between our two governments might change.

This was getting pretty far off base and I came back hard. This was partly because I knew the story.

The Brazilians are too nationalistic and merely keeping foreigners out is not a healthy way of going at it. On the other hand, they don't want Brazilian oil in the ground, or refined marketing, to fall into the control of the foreign cartels. I respect this, and so does everybody else who has watched the results of oil policy in Mexico, Colombia, and Bolivia. This was the thrust behind the two decree-laws.

Nobody did anything as far as I can discover during the last six years. Brazil made a weak and pitiful attempt to drill her own oil in Bahia and has a little experimental refinery going there. It has not got far as yet. . . .

Six or seven months ago the Brazilian Petroleum Council opened applications for permits to build refineries and market refined products. Only Brazilian groups, under the law, could bid on these concessions. The Petroleum Council required that the applicants should show that they had available a supply of crude oil. At this point the local representatives of the Standard-Shell-Texas-Atlantic group merely smiled. Crude was not available from anybody except through them and they weren't selling. So they sat quiet and did nothing.

They would not have smiled if they had known as much as we did in the Embassy. For a new sail had appeared on the horizon in the shape of a knowledgeable gent by the name of Coghill, formerly Petroleum Adviser to FEA, and now representative of Gulf Oil Company. . . .

What Gulf actually did was to buy a half interest in an oil marketing concern, the Corrêa Castro Company. Foreseeing the end of the war—or perhaps just after the victory—they went to work with one group of Brazilians who were proposing to put in for an oil concession—the so-called Ypiranga [now Ipiranga] group. They were helped in this because one of the interests in that group is the Guinle clan, and my friend Guilherme Guinle told me he had discussed the possibility of Brazilian-American partnership in oil development with Standard, and they had treated him rather arrogantly. He therefore was predisposed to do business with Gulf.

Gulf looked at the decree-laws and then worked out the following. They said they would help Ypiranga build their refineries, giving them experts and so forth. They would advance to Ypiranga $5,000,000 against Ypiranga's notes, to be paid off in 10 years. They would supply Ypiranga with crude. They would likewise go partners with Ypiranga in the job of marketing the refined product. . . .

What must have happened was that Standard and the rest of them got wind of this; the Standard and Atlantic representatives at once headed for New York; they then got the lobby division of Standard to descend on the Department, and they descended on two nice but not very hefty boys in the Department, namely, Charlie Rayner [adviser on Petroleum Policy], whom I know from personal contact in the Department, and [John] Loftus [Chief, Petroleum Division], whom I do not know. The rest followed in order.

Shortly after I got this telegram, in quick succession the Gulf man, Coghill, the Standard man, [Paul J.] Anderson, and the Texas [?] man, Nave, wanted to come in to see me, separately, which they did. . . .

I told them that a threat of economic sanctions if Brazil was naughty enough to put up Brazilian-owned refineries was to my mind playing with high explosives. If any such policy as that were adopted and were ever known, it would blow everybody concerned clear out of the water. I hoped, accordingly, that the Department would withdraw that phase of the telegram.

I told them that I thought that American capital could be useful in the refining industry in Brazil, but that I did not see how we could invade the sovereignty of Brazil to the extent of telling them they must not put up any refineries unless and until Americans were permitted to have an interest in them. Partnership arrangements could be useful since Americans could supply the crude, and also had the technical ability. I asked whether they were really hostile to any refining in Brazil.

The Standard man said very frankly that they did not want refining in Brazil but that they thought it had to come. They estimated that the new refineries under contemplation alone would save Brazil $16,000,000 annually in foreign exchange which would be needed. He would be content with a minority interest but apparently his people wanted complete financial control. The Atlantic man followed the lead of Standard; the Gulf man individually took the position that the whole thing was wrong but officially he simply declined to support the full-fledged Standard view. I worked out a memorandum of the conversation . . . and later gave them all copies. Everybody said yes, the Standard man saying he thought it had been a constructive conference. I hoped we were getting somewhere. . . . I brought the conference to a close with a sense of duty well done. The meeting was held on November 17, and I reported in three cablegrams to the Department which I thought would put the matter to rest. This was merely naive.

On November 19 I got another telegram from the Department. It was obvious that the oil representatives had reported the conference of November 17 to their home offices and their home offices were not pleased. . . .

I received that telegram on November 20 and sat on it on November 20 and 21. I didn't like it. In broad outline it reaffirmed the instruction the Department had telegraphed on November 10 which was to barge in, tell Brazil to hold up giving concessions to Brazilian-owned refineries unless and until they opened up their laws so that Americans could own them. Without saying so, it reinforced the position of the Shell-Standard-Texas group, which had thus far blocked Brazilian refining by the simple process of declining to supply any crude to refineries they did not own. The only escape Brazil has had from this stranglehold is the Gulf-Ypiranga arrangement, and it was perfectly plain that whether or not the Department knew it (and more things happen by accident than by ability in that Department) the Standard proposed to block Gulf, using the diplomatic machinery of the United States. To do this they proposed a really shocking invasion of the sovereignty of Brazil, and a shocking protection of an essentially monopolistic cartel agreement, probably informal, which has had extortionate profits, and has been and is in a position to tax every Brazilian. I was thinking of the little Brazilian in the streets and the fields who has to buy rice and beans and clothing, most of which are transported by truck, and one element in the high price of food is precisely this high price of gasoline. I was thinking of the little people in the interior who burn kerosene oil and go dark when they don't have it and can't afford it. I was thinking, too, that the time had come when Brazil cannot pay out many millions in foreign exchange to companies who wanted to refine somewhere else: it takes a lot of sweat in the cotton fields, the coffee plantations, and elsewhere to produce goods that will have to be sold abroad in order to pay this huge bill. I was thinking that God knows that Gulf is no lily-white angel and the Mellons who control it have not been more socially enlightened than Standard. But if Gulf and the Standard group compete, the little fellow has at least a ten thousandth of a ghost of a show, whereas now he has none at all. I was thinking that if refineries and refined products are in Brazil and in Brazilian hands, while there may be Brazilian monopolists—and are—at least the money is in Brazil and Brazil can deal with the situation; where if it were in foreign hands, we are heading right into another mess like the Mexican and Bolivian messes. I was thinking, too, of something else. All we have to do is to be intransigent about it and sometime or other somebody else will emerge with oil to sell. The Soviet Union will have lots of oil to sell. Having affronted Brazilian independence, wounded her pride, and safeguarded an oppressive cartel, what would prevent a Soviet representative from coming in and offering both to finance and supply with crude oil a Brazilian refining industry? Indeed what would prevent them from putting into the picture a flock of captured German oil technicians to run them? And what would prevent them from campaigning against the United States on the ground that their Embassy was merely an agency of "colonizing capital"? . . .

Likewise on November 23 Coghill dodged around to say that the company representatives here had decided they wanted a new meeting with me but it was no go unless Gulf joined. He had declined to join. They apparently had cables evidencing the further contact of their companies with the Department. I took time out to think some more and still am.

The United States is the last great capitalistic country in the world. I should think this sort of monkey-business was forcing the whole situation towards socialism about as fast as could be done. If there ever is a move in the United States analogous to the movement of the British Labour Party in England, it would pretty nearly put the oil industries at the head of the list for early nationalization. I should think these fellows had better be pretty careful.

December 7, 1945

Sunday, December 2, was election day. I went around with Drault Ernanny in his car and visited 20 or 30 of the polling places. I never saw better run election in my life, though the early comers had to wait a good long while before they voted. There was absolutely no question that this was as fairly done as a country could do it—certainly in Rio; and I have seen plenty of worse elections in the United States.

The exciting aspect was the attitude of the people. They were free and they were happy and they liked it. They had waited a long time to express their opinion and now they were having their chance. As for peace, the children played by the election booths, and the people in line sat around and swapped gossip, and nobody was doing much electioneering, and if anybody asked anyone how they voted, the answer was usually a triumphant: "This is a secret ballot." Women voted in very great numbers—the first time they had really had a serious voice in affairs. . . .

On Monday, December 3, the country was principally rejoicing in having carried off the best election in South American history, rightly feeling that its prestige had moved up several pegs. However, on Tuesday when the first returns began to show General Dutra winning, the young liberals who had supported Gomes were feeling very sad. They felt that they had borne the burden of the fight for democracy—and they are right; and the old guard was slowly edging into power. Actually they are lucky, for they will have a strong representation anyway, and a government wrestling with postwar problems is likely to have a rough time. It is the opposition that has all the luck. At the end I should gather Vargas swung his strength to Dutra, probably on the simple calculation that the Dutra group are far less likely to dig into some of the financial scandals of the old regime.

The oil business continues to wobble along. The lawyers for Standard have indicated to the State Department that they were going to buy into one of the Brazilian refineries for which permits were to be granted. The State Department still wants the Embassy to prevent Brazil from granting these concessions. But, in the meantime, another sail has heaved over the horizon in the shape of Standard Oil of California (not in the Jersey group) which also wants to sell and is quite prepared to back a couple of groups if it gets a chance. The Department cabled me that we ought to tell the Brazilians not to build refineries as long as their laws refused to allow foreigners to own and control refineries—basing this on Article 6 of the Economic Charter of the Americas agreed to at Mexico City which has a clause providing for free movement of capital. I am cabling back asking if the Department will also guarantee free access to supply of raw materials by any buyer, and compliance with Article 4 which agrees that there will not be combinations in restraint of trade. I think I see a chance to resolve this by not doing anything except getting the Brazilians to agree that the permissions to grant refineries, when granted, will not constitute vested rights but will be subject to any change in Brazilian laws later adopted. This will keep things fluid for a while, but will not prevent Brazilians from going ahead and getting their refining industry, which they badly need.

The Department reiterated its order to prevent Brazil from granting concessions. Berle cabled on December 12, 1945:

Since I expect to be in Washington by Tuesday of next week, there will be time for discussion which I hope may prevent Dept from making very grave mistake. In honesty I should add that I personally would not wish my name to appear in connection with the proposed representation and cannot make it with the sincerity which alone might make it successful. . . .

On December 21, 1945, Berle discussed the petroleum situation at a State Department conference. The Departmental memorandum concluded: "Following further discussions of the varying points of view surrounding this general subject, Mr. Rayner stated that while he felt that a liberalization of laws could more readily be affected if such liberalization preceded rather than followed the granting of refinery permits he would bow to the Ambassador's view that such a course might be more prejudicial to the ultimate goal than were the granting of refinery permits be allowed to pass without comment and steps taken thereafter to urge the desired liberalization."

December 13, 1945

Last night I went to the graduation of the Law School, the patron saint of the occasion being Franklin Roosevelt. I must say that I got a real thrill out of being saluted as the "Ambassador of Democracy". Of course these are all the young intellectual liberals—and the majority has gone against them because General Dutra's election would be about equivalent to MacArthur on the Republican ticket, while the youngsters are New Dealers. But I got a real sense that in this brief interlude Brazil has had a chance to breathe and to think and to hope.

Will the chance last long? I wonder. There is considerable reason to believe that Vargas proposes to reestablish himself in power and has been driving a bargain with Dutra looking towards that end. Dutra thought he was much weaker than in fact he is. On the other hand, his people are opening tentatives with the Gomes forces for a government of national union.

The Army would revolt and push in Gomes at the drop of a hat. One pro-Gomes man asked me how the United States would regard that, and I told him I thought it would be regarded very badly indeed. But that will not help much if in fact Vargas or some of the other boys try to stage a pushover.

My guess is that they will try—because this is what Vargas did in 1930 and he seems to be repetitive in his patterns. But I should question, whether the same thing would happen. In 1930 he had the Army; and now apparently he does not. Instead he is taking the leadership of the so-called labor party and if he stays by that for a while he can perform a very valuable service to the country.

I walked a little around Rio yesterday and today. This is a sweet city, fragrant and tender, a kind of graceful iridescent jewel; worthy of more love than these politicians give it.

To Secretary of State James F. Brynes, February 1, 1946

Ambassador La Guardia and I yesterday attended the ceremony of inauguration of General Dutra as President of Brazil. This took the form of a very brief session of the Electoral Court presided over by the Chief Justice of the Supreme Court, which declared its finding that under the law General Dutra had been elected President by a majority of votes and that he was entitled to become President on taking the oath of office. He thereupon swore to maintain the constitution and laws of the United States [of Brazil] and to defend the integrity and independence of Brazil. The Electoral Court thereupon, and in the presence of all, declared him elected President of Brazil, and all present signed the act.

This concluded the ceremony, which lasted altogether about 21 minutes.

President Dutra thereafter made a brief radio speech, text of which is being sent separately to Dept. Among other things he announced his determination to maintain a democratic form of government in Brazil; and to cooperate with the United Nations and particularly with the nations of America, especially with the US.

Formal reception followed.

For what it is worth, the Brazilian protocol authorities assigned first place, as is usual, to the representative of the Vatican; and second place to the delegation of the US, thus rather emphasizing the American precedence.

The form of the ceremonies appeared to emphasize the constitutional quality of the regime and the fact that it represents the popular will. This has likewise excited the attention of a good many newspapers in other parts of Latin America, whose comments are prominently re-published in Rio this morning. There is no question that Brazil is priding herself on having resumed her place among the constitutional nations of the world and that she is getting considerable prestige in other parts of the continent on that account.

To Truman, February 6, 1946

When in December 1944 President Roosevelt requested me to take the American Embassy in Rio, I asked and he agreed that this be considered war service and that at the close of the war I might return. You were kind enough to confirm this understanding when we talked over Brazilian affairs in June 1945.

I was deeply appreciative of the suggestion that you made in December 1945 that I remain indefinitely at Rio; but equally grateful for your kind agreement to release me after the new Brazilian Government had been installed. I therefore now submit my resignation to take effect on my return to the United States.

To Brazil and Brazilians I am indebted for one of the happiest and most interesting years of my life. . . .

February 11, 1946

The Brazilian incident is almost over for me.

I got to the United States in time to spend one day in Washington, December 22, and then went to Massachusetts. I had not quite two weeks in the snow; and returned to Washington to get into some Department work and to see President Truman. We then confirmed the plan made earlier to pull out as soon as the Dutra Government was duly installed. Before that, and on New Year's Eve, La Guardia and I dined at Judge Seabury's, where the old group who took over the government of the City of New York on January 1, 1934, met to say farewell to the passing of the La Guardia regime in New York City. It wasn't altogether a gay occasion; though old friends are always glad to get together.

Since La Guardia had been named as Special Representative of the President to the inauguration of General Dutra as President of Brazil, we drafted a Flying Fortress off General [Laurence S.] Kuter; cabbaged

Major General Bob Walsh and Admiral [Marshall R.] Greer as military aides, and with them, Phil Chalmers and Colonel [Paul V.] Betters of the Association of Mayors (nominally Secretary to La Guardia), Beatrice and I came along down here fast. All was quiet along the January River, as far as I could see; and indeed the inauguration festivities moved along without serious break.

One very happy thing was that on the last day of the Linhares regime, the Government of Brazil gave Beatrice the decoration of the Cruzeiro do Sul.

They were kind enough to offer me one too, but I can't take it until after I am out, and maybe nobody will remember it then. [The decoration was awarded in 1949.]

The Government also sent the new aircraft carrier *Franklin D. Roosevelt* to visit Rio during the ceremonies. We don't usually do this, but the British sent the *Ajax* and the Argentines sent a cruiser, so that we might as well show up. The *FDR* is a 46,000 ton carrier with a complement of 120 planes, and is distinctly impressive. We invited General Dutra and the new Brazilian Government to go aboard her one day when we went out of the harbor, launched the planes, shot the cannon, and generally had quite a time. To imagine those planes loaded with atomic bombs gives something to think about.

As usual I have been tangled in my mind because the next phase of life will be at once interesting and difficult. Difficult, because I cannot tell how private life will set for a while, and I have no mind for any more second-string Government jobs. Interesting, because getting back into the life of the United States, and I hope private life for a time, will be of first-rate importance. . . .

Press release, February 8, 1946

As I am not a career diplomat, only a long-standing affection for Brazil and Brazilians led to my acceptance of the mission. I arranged with President Roosevelt, and later with President Truman, that my mission here should only cover the period of the close of the war and the period of initial economic readjustment thereafter. This phase is substantially over. Of many experiences in Government service, this has been the happiest; and the many friendships made here are more than ample reward for a year's work. I am sincerely grateful to the many friends in public and private life who have helped and inspired me personally, and who have cooperated in the common cause of deepening the traditional friendship between our two nations. Returning to the United States, I shall continue to do everything in my power to forward the cause of Brazilian-American friendship, which is so deeply satisfying to both our peoples, and which is now a vital necessity in world affairs.

It is perhaps appropriate to review, briefly, some of the work of cooperation carried on through this Embassy between Brazil and the United States. Modern diplomacy must deal with relations between peoples as well as with relations between governments. The object of inter-American diplomacy must always be to improve the welfare of peoples, since in the

American family of nations the welfare of one is the welfare of all. This requires practical measures even more than eloquence.

A year ago the greatest single problem was that of transport. Because of the war, supplies of gasoline were limited, and trucks, busses and other needed transport material could not be had. The United States was the only source from which such material could come.

By agreement between our Governments, arrangements were made for manufacture of 10,000 trucks and busses.

A thousand of these were delivered in Brazil before the first of December last year; more have been delivered since. These were needed to transport food and goods to markets and stores so that people have been able to continue to buy the things they need.

A second question was that of oil and gasoline. A year ago there was no gasoline for private cars, and not enough even for economic purposes. Even during a serious phase of the war cooperative action of our two Governments made possible delivery in Brazil of greater quantities of gasoline.

Arrangements were made by which part of this could be used to save a considerable amount of rice in Goiás. Thereby the supply of food in certain of the great centers of Brazil was increased, and further rise in prices was avoided.

More recently, arrangements were made to provide transport for gasoline in order to assist in harvesting wheat in Rio Grande do Sul.

Before the war ended, a special allotment was secured making it possible to supply gasoline to private cars. Directly after the victory over Japan, further arrangements were made, so that gasoline could be had at will. The situation was thus ameliorated before the war ended, and made normal within a few weeks after victory.

Through the generous cooperation of Brazil and the Brazilian sailors, the Brazilian Merchant Marine had been placed at the disposition of the Allies during the war. A large part of this merchant fleet had been sunk in the war effort.

After negotiations between the competent authorities of the two Governments, arrangements were made for the construction of a new and modern merchant fleet substantially replacing with more modern ships the vessels lost in the war. Through the Export-Import Bank financial arrangements have been completed and during the present year new and modern ships now under construction will be delivered to Brazil, to sail under the Brazilian flag.

The war prevented repairs and new supplies of railway cars and railway engines. Arrangements were made to increase the supply of coal for the Brazilian railways and to finance the construction of new rolling stock for the Brazilian railways.

All of these measures, including motor trucks, merchant ships, railway material and the like during the coming months should progressively ameliorate the economic situation of Brazil, as the supplies of food and manufactures in Brazil can be transported more freely throughout the country to supply the needs of the Brazilian people.

During the war Brazil, like the United States, was a country under attack. Contributing generously to the common defense of the hemisphere, the Brazilian and United States Governments cooperated in the development of air bases and defense forces in those parts of Brazil most likely to be attacked. It is now known that the Nazi Government had planned such an attack.

These defense arrangements involved the stationing of American troops along with Brazilian troops, working in close friendship and harmony with the Brazilian Army under arrangements between the Brazilian General Staff and the General Staff of the United States. Twenty-four hours after our common victory, measures were begun for the prompt withdrawal of these troops, except where technical men might be needed to maintain installations until the Brazilian authorities assumed charge. The number of American troops was promptly reduced. From approximately 11,000 in Brazil at the time of the victory over Japan, they have now been reduced to approximately 1,300. These are technical air transport elements only, whose task is to maintain installations to be turned over to Brazilian authorities in accordance with plans which are being worked out. Rarely in history has such an evacuation been carried out with greater speed. Arrangements for continuing cooperation are being developed in case it should again be necessary to defend the American hemisphere.

The Governments of Brazil and of the United States have long agreed that every assistance should be given towards industrialization of the continent. Cooperation with Brazil is being continued with technical financial assistance to bring to completion the great Brazilian steel mill of Volta Redonda, now nearing completion. Further progress has been made on the railway of the Vale do Rio Doce which will open up the enormous iron ore reserves of Itabira. Preliminary studies have begun looking towards the production of electricity at the falls of Paulo Afonso, so that this magnificent natural resource may be made available to the Northeast of Brazil.

Arrangements have likewise been made between our two Governments for increased exchange of technical information, and making technical training available to Brazilian citizens in both industry and agriculture. Two agreements have been signed for the creation of vocational schools. One group of these schools is designed to give training in agricultural technique. The other group is to give vocational training in industry. Industrialization is not merely a matter of building factories, but also of having trained staffs available for their operation.

At the close of the war, Brazilian civil aviation had at its disposal not more than 50 civil airplanes for transport of passengers throughout the country. The only source of planes was the United States, which of course had devoted its entire airplane industry to war purposes. Directly after the common victory, by agreements between the two governments and with the Brazilian internal civil aviation lines, arrangements were made substantially to double this number of planes. Thirty additional passenger planes have now been delivered and are in operation by Brazilian companies over Brazilian airways. These, with other planes which will arrive, are steadily ameliorating the crisis which prevailed earlier in Brazilian internal aviation.

Nothing is more important in international cooperation than public health. The United States is grateful for the Brazilian cooperation in our common arrangements to prevent African fevers from crossing to Brazil on the airline between Natal and Dakar. The danger which at one time existed that air communication between Brazil and Africa might bring foreign diseases has now been overcome. But the year has seen also a steady progress in a more direct attack on disease and the resulting misery. A joint Brazilian-American enterprise, under Brazilian direction, the Serviço Especial de Saúde Pública, not only continued to work, but during the past year opened 28 new hospitals and stations in Pará and Amazonas; and in addition has carried on work in other parts of Brazil.

These measures, and many others not enumerated here, are proof that cooperation between our two countries is no matter of diplomatic mystery. They were inspired and supported, in both countries, by the warm friendship of two great peoples. Diplomacy, properly considered, is cooperative international action for the welfare of peoples, and modern diplomacy, like modern government in general, must be chiefly concerned with improving the conditions of the masses, so that the benefits of improved technique shall be available to all.

This was, and is, the conception of international relations fostered and maintained by President Roosevelt, and enthusiastically carried on by President Truman—and Brazil has given every evidence of sharing and cooperating in applying that conception for the general welfare of nations.

February 21, 1946

The publication of the American Blue Book on Argentina was the principal explosion of the week. Released in Washington and likewise here a few days ago, it has ripped things wide open.

The book is an up-to-date revised version of the document I had made up for the Mexico City Conference out of the material we had then accumulated. At that time the Army would not permit us to release it— and rightly, because it would have compromised sources of valuable information. Now it is augmented by a few captured German documents and by further information. The whole thing, of course, adds up to direct proof that the Argentines, under German leadership, plotted to assist the Germans where they could, and in aid of this to subvert the governments of several neighboring American countries, and that it was contemplated that Perón and his friends would be used as the Quislings to organize a Nazi South America.

First effects here were that the new Spanish Ambassador appointed to Brazil, [Eduardo] Aunós, was implicated. João Neves da Fontoura [Minister of Foreign Affairs] called me to the Foreign Office to say that they had suggested to the Spaniards that they withdraw Aunós. The Spanish, typically Castilian, first said the idea had occurred to them; then they proceeded to rear on their hind legs and refuse to withdraw him; whereupon

Neves da Fontoura canceled the agrément. Meanwhile there was a debate and a row in the Constituent Assembly. This morning Aunós is reported as having "resigned"—he having got as far as Curaçao.

The Communist Party line—which is of course a part of Russian strategy—has been that this is a capitalistic maneuver of the United States to embroil Brazil in a war with Argentina. The Brazilian Communists are supporting Perón. The Argentine Communists have not been.

What is not known yet is the fact that the Soviet Government is already flirting with Perón. At all events, on or about February 15 the Soviets requested transit visas for five members of a Soviet trade mission to Argentina. This was just before the Blue Book came out.

My own impression is that the Soviets will quite cynically exploit any advantage they can get by tying up with Perón if they think they can. Horribly, cynically, and terribly, the Soviet policy is approximating the German policy: exploit any center of thought or action which may make trouble either for Britain or for the United States. The American Communists, like William Z. Foster, see this and are guiding themselves accordingly. Some of the South American Communists, more sincere and more frank, are patiently trying to discover a principle. For instance, Argentine Communists, like Rodolfo Ghioldi, when they find out that they have been sold down the river to a Nazi group, may well wonder where all this is taking them.

Many expressions of warm sympathy and friendship by Brazilians for us as we get closer to departing. Yesterday at a medical meeting an entirely unknown lady got up to say that she had had a scholarship from the United States to train her to teach Brazilian children; that the United States had never asked anything of her since; and she gave to Beatrice an old family ring merely as an expression of gratitude [to the United States.]

. . . I wondered whether it was fair to leave now; but the short answer is that there never is a logical time to leave government service. Certainly so far as I am concerned the United States Government made it as clear as possible that they did not need me to run their affairs a year ago in December when they fired me as Assistant Secretary of State; they certainly did not do anything further to maintain the situation when they rearranged the State Department staff, promoting Acheson and Braden; so I think that it is absurd to be sentimental about it. This Government is not very clever about using men, though now it is finding that men are what they really need. . . .

VIII

1946~1959

March 15, 1946

On Tuesday, March 12, I saw President Truman. It was in the nature of a leave-taking but we hashed over a great many other things. He made some kind remarks about my work in South America and spoke about the difficulties he is having at home. He said that he had decided on a policy toward Russia; to keep every agreement we make and to expect them to keep every agreement they make. He is not looking to another meeting of the Big Three. He is ready to have it but was not prepared to go out and beg for it. He thought that the Russians were bluffing in the sense of not being willing to risk a new world war; but that they would carry on local aggression unless world opinion stopped them. He hoped to do this through the United Nations Organization; beyond that he could not see.

I urged him to have his intelligence people get up the best estimate that they could of Russia's present potentialities (which they should have done but did not do at Yalta). He said that at Yalta the Russians had apparently deceived President Roosevelt who was ill and also Harry Hopkins. I said that Ed Stettinius did not have enough brains to meet the situation, with which he cordially agreed. . . . He implied without saying so that he considered the State Department unduly weak; but he considered that President Roosevelt's policy of trying to run the State Department himself was hopeless. He proposes to get men who could do the job and delegate power unto them. . . .

As in the case of our previous meeting, I had the sense of a very fine, clear-thinking man who has more head than many around him. What he has not got—or perhaps circumstances have not given it to him—is the ability to dramatize things. I should think anyone who worked for him would feel on much safer ground than anyone who worked for FDR—for he stands by his men until the last gun is fired. . . .

March 19, 1946

We spent the day at Oberlin. This was because Alice thinks she wants to go there but for me it was dropping quietly and without shock into an old family atmosphere. [Harold S.] Wood, Vice President of the College, took us around; President [Ernest Hatch] Wilkins, whose grandfather was a deacon in my Father's church, had us to lunch during which we talked

573

over all known problems. It was fascinating and emotionally luxurious to tackle international problems through the eyes of a college president whose great love is Romance Languages, and especially through the eyes of Dante.

I think the United States has been traveling largely on the strength it got from the Calvinist movement which flowered in New England in my Father's generation. That movement should never die out. No individual could deny responsibility and start looking out for himself alone. So the whole community pitched in. Is there enough of that or its equivalent to take us through the next big jam?

Oberlin was so much a seat of that tremendous although sometimes narrow sense of responsibility that I was glad Alice has decided to go there.

Through the week the Russian crisis mounted. Mentally I placed a little note about Kurdistan. This is because Rudolf and some of his men got hold of a map indicating a Kurdish state, taking in northern Iran, Turkey and Iraq and including the head of the Persian Gulf. This, of course, would be the beginning of a real invasion of the Middle East.

The Soviets asked that the UNO meeting scheduled for March 25 be delayed to April 20. This was probably in order to complete the revolution already well advanced in Iran; control of that government would give the Soviets the South as well as the North; and apparently to permit them to develop further a Kurdish revolt which appeared this week in Iran.

March 22, 1946

Apparently alarmed by the tremendous reaction and by Truman's prompt refusal to delay the UNO meeting and his insistence that this was not a matter for Big Three negotiation but for world opinion, Stalin came out with a statement that no nations want war; this of course is true and it is always true. Hitler used to say the same thing but it leaves open the second barrel of Hitler's gun—which is that anyone who wants to defend against invasion wants war. The solid gain is the Russian agreement to come into the UNO session.

Truman comes out of this so far as a much bigger figure. As the only man in Washington who kept his head and did straighter thinking than anyone else.

March 23, 1946

Today La Guardia has just been chosen to head the UNRRA as a successor to Herbert Lehman. Called me up to go over the situation. We have been partners in a good many enterprises before; and this looks like another. . . .

For the next few years Berle made only occasional diary entries.

November 6, 1946

The election returns are in, which merely confirm what anybody could see coming. The New Deal dissolved with Roosevelt, and the country is voting for another shot at the laissez-faire economy. It is a vote against the Administration rather than a vote for anyone in particular.

President Roosevelt, just before his death, said that the country would be presently in the worst economic jam that it had ever seen, and that great masses of men, including veterans, would want things fixed up and not care too much about constitutional methods. . . .

My guess is that by the end of next year we shall see a very disturbed political picture. By the law of their being, the Republicans cannot undertake to meet it, since they are pledged not to get into the game. It will be a nice question whether the country imposes responsibility on the Republicans as the party in power, or on Truman as President. In the Hoover days, they pinned their difficulties on Hoover himself. The election of 1948 will come along before the situation is cleared up. This is going to take a lot of careful thinking and a good deal of planning. It will also be different in kind; in 1920–1921, the financial problems were uppermost; in 1947, the problem will be one of distribution. Political repercussions are unpredictable.

November 19, 1946

On Friday, November 15, the heads of a number of Italian-American societies came to see me at my house. They were members of the Committee for a Just Peace for Italy and they included Eddie Corsi, John Salterini and a variety of other people. Their real question was of the attitude to take towards the Italian treaty which is emerging from the meeting of the four Foreign Ministers in New York.

I said they had a grave decision to make: whether to accept the treaty or to oppose its ratification. The basic defect of the treaty is that it is really an endeavor to adjust between the Western democracies and the Soviet Union, over the corpse of Italy. A second defect is that it cannot be judged except as part of a whole European settlement.

Specifically, the Trieste settlement is impossible and cannot last: it would make a Balkan Danzig. The reparations cannot be paid by Italy—unless we lend Italy the money—that is, pay them ourselves. We are tired of that. The disarmament of Italy is stupid unless surrounding countries, namely, Yugoslavia, under Russian influence, likewise is disarmed and this has not happened. The whole business looks to me like an arrangement to get the West out of Italy—after which the Russians rip it to pieces. This, by the way, is very much what has happened in Iran as a result of the half-settlement reached last May.

The Italian-Americans felt exactly the same way, but wondered what the Italian Government would be. They likewise felt that if there were objections they should be made as a part of a general American position, and not as a part of a race bloc—which is extremely good sense.

I volunteered to consult the Italians, and on Sunday, November 17, went over to cocktails with Max Ascoli. I there met [Alberto] Tarchiani, the Italian Ambassador, likewise a couple of other members of the Italian delegation and a former secretary of Count Sforza who is now with the Italian Embassy. They all said that Italy would be better off without any treaty than with the one that is going on; that Italy herself could not start a rebellion against the four powers; that the only possibility was to hope that there would be some movement started here. I know, of course, that this leaves the Italian-Americans unprotected with nothing but an assurance that their feelings would be welcomed by their Italian brethern.

It was finally left that Corsi and I would endeavor to get going an American Committee on a just peace and that we would try to work out an appropriate statement requesting that the Italian treaty, in its present form, be not signed; or, if signed, that it be not ratified and that action on it be delayed until the whole European settlement is made. Then we can judge.

It should be noted that this differs from what we did after Versailles. Then we threw over the whole arrangement. Now we can decently stay by the United Nations and oppose the piece-meal settlements which are plainly power politics and not peace.

December 11, 1946

The sudden death of my old friend Cimon Diamantopoulos [Greek Ambassador to the U.N.] was a real shock. Not the most brilliant man in the world, but one of the most honest and patriotic; a good servant of Greece. We struggled through many things together, from the time when Greece was attacked, and I was able to force an unwilling Navy to send some Grumman airplanes to them (they never got there in time, but eventually did good service for the British in the Near Eastern fighting), through the time when Greece was starving and Athens living on garbage shipped from Istanbul; through the time when we resisted attempts of the Russian Army in Bulgaria to tear northern Greece into pieces; through the time when we finally forced the evacuation of troops from Thrace; and so on down. He had been in my house forty-eight hours before his death.

Monday, December 9. Thence to Columbia for some work on the new case book. Then out to dinner. . . . The group, chiefly bankers and such, were talking foreign affairs. I am no friend of Russian imperialism; but by the time they got through, I was about ready to run up the Hammer and Sickle myself. That is the devil of this whole business. Apparently you must choose between a popular revolution already battered by Russian imperialists, on one side; and well-dressed black reaction on the other; and I do not see that the little people will get a break either way.

May 13, 1947

Last night I accepted the Chairmanship of the Liberal Party. Under any dead reckoning, this is foolish. I could sit here and maintain a technical status as a Democrat, get occasional plush appointments from the State Department, and grow old with dignity and leisure. But the political wilderness has some attractions.

The Liberal Party has been quarrelling with La Guardia. The first job must be to compose that quarrel. This will take time; but men like La Guardia and Dubinsky and what is left of the [Sidney] Hillman [d. 1946; President, Amalgamated Clothing Workers] group, and Walter Reuther [President, United Automobile Workers], and [Luigi] Antonini [President, Italian-American Labor Council] and the rest of them must work together. This will be a long, tough and difficult job.

So far as ideas are concerned, we have a clear monopoly. The Labor Party cannot have an idea unless it is okayed by the Communists. Neither the Democrats nor the Republicans have any ideas at all. We have to draft the program.

So far as politics is concerned, this is about like being elected Chief Engineer of a vacuum cleaner. Some things may shift rapidly.

When Hillman in 1944 had supported the Communists in gaining control of the American Labor party, Dubinsky and the party's right wing formed the Liberal party.

June 3, 1947

It is plain now that the [Henry] Wallace third party movement is a Russian movement, despite the huge number of fuzzy-heads who, of course, are no more Russian than I am. They want to punish Truman for the Truman Doctrine; and a penny-pinching Republican administration, heavily isolationist, if possible, is their best bet. We shall have the whole campaign of '37–39 over again—with an obbligato of small European countries falling while we talk. Not so nice.

July 3, 1947

Tuesday night David Dubinsky had dinner with [Giuseppe] Saragat, the new leader of the Italian Socialists, who has broken away from [Pietro] Nenni and the Communist united front. With him was [Matteo] Matteotti, son of the deputy whom Mussolini murdered. It was quite a dinner and David wound up by arranging a contribution of $100,000 to the expenses of Saragat's Party. These Social Democrats stick together.

It was of some interest that two State Department men, Sam Reber and young [Walter C.] Dowling, showed up at the dinner. There were times when no State Department man would have dared to touch an Italian-American meeting.

Saragat told me that their estimates showed 200,000 Communists more or less armed in various parts of Italy, capable of taking over at any time. The government, he thought, could count on not more than 75,000 carabinieri. He put the case in a nutshell. He said that a democracy in time of peace found it almost impossible to deal with Communists who carried on war even in peacetime. The state was bound by rules of war in peacetime; the Communists could and did act as though they were an army. "To spend one-half of your life fighting the Fascists' dictatorship, and the other half fighting a Communist dictatorship, is not amusing", he commented grimly. He expects trouble in the Fall. . . .

Molotov in a matter of form broke up the Paris Conference on the Marshall Plan. This time, however, the Russians end with considerable loss of face. Almost no one could defend their position, except on a straight "rule-or-ruin" basis. Molotov's final speech—Europe must "take the consequences" is, in diplomatic language, a threat to shoot the works.

Hitler used to talk like that. My impression is that the Russians mean what they say and we shall have disturbances all over the Continent as the year wears on.

July 9, 1947

Went to Washington yesterday to talk with the President. . . .

I told the President that various groups and interests aligned with the Liberal Party like his domestic policy and like his foreign policy and were not going into the wilderness with Henry Wallace. I told him it would be almost impossible to bring these groups into camp if he had not vetoed the Taft-Hartley Bill.

He said the Taft-Hartley Bill was the worst piece of legislation to come before him yet. He had had it studied and had studied it himself and the more he studied it the worse it got. . . .

In answer to a question of mine, he said that he thought this was the worst Congress since the Civil War. It has been a special-interest Congress right through, both on the big issues and on the little ones. He was trying to stick right to the Democratic platform which he had a good deal to do with writing and that was all that he could do and exactly what he ought to do.

I told him that I thought that the old Roosevelt crowd had to get out. A good many of them thought they knew more about being President than he did. He said that a good many of them had run themselves out. And cited numerous examples. He said: "You know I never asked you to leave the Government. If you had wanted to stay, you would be here yet." I said that I thought I could be of more use on the outside than on the inside. He said that the Brazilian job had stood up very well. I said that I thought it was in better shape than some others at least. . . .

. . . Home by plane after some legal work, to find a bunch of children from the liberal Young Voters' League. Their general point was that we ought not to be merely anti-Russian—with which I cordially agree. I tried to explain to them that what we were really trying to do was not to make a third party but to make a second party and that before long we would have to be the second party or take over the Democratic Party. . . .

July 25, 1947

Yesterday, July 24, I went up to Riverdale to see Fiorello. He was sitting in the sun, in the little garden in back of his house. We talked of the state of the Union, re getting some of the historic American progressive sentiment going and of concentrating progressive force in districts where it had a chance to win; and of the fact that anybody who was a member of the 80th Congress is guilty of something until he proves an alibi. He talked at some length with [Secretary of State George] Marshall just before his operation; and thought well of him but was amazed how little he knew of the food and agricultural organization, and of economics generally. . . .

I suppose the two best-known names throughout the entire world in this generation are Franklin D. Roosevelt and Fiorello La Guardia; so a generation passes and I am getting old myself.

To the Twentieth Century Fund where Max Thornburg [foreign industrial consultant] was back from Turkey. His story was surprising to say the least. He arrived in Turkey about the same time the State Department boys had showed up to work out a program of economic aid to Turkey. He naturally asked them what surveys they had made, or were making. They answered: "None" and had no resources or machinery to make any. Finding [Thornburg] was making one, [under a grant from the Twentieth Century Fund] they promptly seized on it, gave him an office in the Embassy and agreed to use his [study]. In addition to his survey work, he had had a string of conferences with cabinet ministers leading up to an arrangement by which the Turkish Government . . . agreed to let a certain amount of private enterprise function in place of the horribly corrupt, inefficient, state monopolies and concessions. . . . Apparently his investigation and report are to be used not only by the American Government but by the Turkish Government and our military mission as well. This is one case where inserting a little brains into the situation at the right time produced exactly the right result and I am glad we sent him. We likewise made preliminary arrangements by which the Caribbean Commission can make use of the services of Fred Dewhurst [Twentieth Century Fund economist] as economic consultant for the survey they are making.

Dinner at the Century Club with Fred; then home to a lonely glass of beer and unhappily thinking about Fiorello, and then to bed.

On Wednesday, July 23, we formally organized the Liberal Party. Considering that 407 delegates from all parts of the State showed up in hot weather, there must be some interest in this. What we can make out of it, I do not yet see; but it is bound to be useful.

November 28, 1947

On Wednesday, Harry Uviller [from the Liberal party] telephoned me. He said that the United Nations' plan to partition Palestine and create a Jewish state was shy one vote, Haiti having abstained.

On Thanksgiving morning, Dr. Nahum Goldmann, who is "Man Friday" [for Chaim Weizmann's Jewish delegation], came in to breakfast. We went over the situation. He thought that this vote was essential if the scheme was to go through.

Last night I cablegrammed President [Dumarais] Estimé of Haiti substantially as follows:

"Haiti apparently has deciding vote on Palestine question at United Nations Assembly Friday. Hope you can telephone instructions to your delegation to vote for plan as recommended by majority, as magnanimous gesture by leading representative of an oppressed race to the oppressed Jewish race. Your personal intervention in the matter will receive world-wide acclaim in a righteous cause. Adolf A. Berle, Jr."

I today received the following cablegram:

"Président de la République a reçu votre cable relatif à Palestine Stop Instructions nécessaires passées à Délégation Haitienne.

Manigat."

It would seem this was determinative.

January 19, 1948

On Tuesday, January 13, I went to see the President . . . the Liberal Party had asked me to see him. We were glad of the doctrine of his state of the nation message.

Now that Wallace had declared himself, the time had come to arrange cooperation between the Democratic Party and the Liberal Party. I said that it seemed to me that the control of New York lay with about a million independents who were not interested much in the Democratic organization; our job was to try to energize them; otherwise Henry Wallace would.

Specifically, I asked if the President would make arrangements for me to see Senator [J. Howard] McGrath [D., R.I.] of the Democratic National Committee and for him to make arrangements in the state. I said I preferred for them to come from the President.

The President was very courteous. He said he would be glad to do that. . . .

I said it was hard to tell what the city Democrats would do. . . . They would coldly estimate what was to their advantage without estimating where it led. The President nodded vigorously and said that was exactly true. . . . I said that, while labor was for him, I was not clear that organized labor would deliver votes though their support was useful. The President said yes; gathering in votes was something he had been doing all his life. Labor was a dangerous opponent to have but was not so good on the positive side. He was perfectly aware that the degree to which the liberal vote turned out would be crucial in New York. . . . McGrath likewise had a fair general knowledge of the situation. The conversation was in substance a repetition of my conversation with the President. McGrath promptly telegraphed to [Paul E.] Fitzpatrick [State Chairman] and to Flynn of the National Committee. . . .

On Monday, January 19, 1948, because a special election is to be held in the Bronx to fill the seat vacated by the election of [Benjamin J.] Rabin to the Bench, it was decided that we should seek a conference with Ed Flynn to see if we could join on a Democratic-Liberal candidate. I was pretty clear that Flynn would have none of it, but we were bound to make the attempt. . . .

As to state and city-wide matters, he thought cooperation was possible, but this was not his business—it was Fitzpatrick's.

As to the Bronx, it was his view that the Democratic Party should not combine with anyone. . . .

Also on January 19, 1948, Congressman Richard M. Nixon (R. Cal.), chairman of the Sub-committee on Legislation of the Committee on Un-American Activities, asked Berle to give his views to the committee on proposed legislation to outlaw the Communist party. Berle replied: ". . . The matter you have in hand is of very great interest, and I am glad you are giving it such careful attention."

MEMORANDUM OF TESTIMONY
OF A. A. BERLE, JR.
BEFORE THE HOUSE COMMITTEE ON UN-AMERICAN ACTIVITIES,
WEDNESDAY, FEBRUARY 11, 1948,
WASHINGTON, D.C.

1. I oppose legislation to outlaw the Communist Party at this time because it is both unnecessary and ineffective.

The Communist who registers as a member of the Communist Party, and is known as such, is not effective. Public opinion knows him for what he is, distrusts what he is doing, and declines to support him.

Communists are more dangerous when they are under cover than when they are exposed. These do not register as members of the Communist Party. In New York, for example, a good many of them are actually registered in the American Labor Party, where they dominate its policies. Legislation to outlaw the Communist Party would thus have no real effect on Communist political activities; they would simply move, as a body, into some other group which they considered they could control. . . .

2. It likewise seems to me that the McDonough Bill (H.R. 4581) would likewise be of very little effect. It would be necessary first to define a "Communist". The word "Communist" has been applied as an epithet to any reformer for half a century. . . . In my own thinking, I define a Communist as a member of the Communist Party or as an individual intellectually or emotionally so under control that he will at all times follow in the Communist Party line as laid down by Moscow.

It would be perfectly possible for a man to be philosophically a communist—for instance, in the early Christian sense—and have nothing whatever to do with Moscow Communism. . . .

The real difficulty with which we are struggling is the fact that certain groups of people have become more loyal to a foreign government— namely, that of the Soviet Union—than to the United States; and this, far more than any social doctrine they may hold, is the real danger. A man could be a perfectly good American and still believe in a civilization without private property—though I should disagree with him. He cannot be a good American when he places the foreign interests of the Soviet Union ahead of the interests of the United States, and in the event of a clash of interests would consider himself bound in all cases to follow the policies and instructions laid down by that government.

3. The Mundt Bill (H.R. 4422), or its companion bill, which proposes that the Communist Party or any groups controlled by it be required to register with the Department of Justice as agents of a foreign principal comes closer to being a practical solution. This rests on the proposition that the Communist Party (despite legal disclaimers) in fact is so controlled by a foreign government that both the party itself and its subsidiaries and "front" organizations are in essence agents of the Soviet government. In my judgment, the assumption, at present, is substantially

correct as applied to the Communist Party in the United States. I question, however, whether further legislation is really necessary. It seems to me that the Attorney General could hold an administrative inquiry, develop all of the facts, and make an administrative finding with respect to the Communist Party; and he could hold similar inquiries with respect to the various subsidiary or "front" organizations. I am by no means clear that a legislative declaration of this kind would be wholly effective if it did not provide for such a determination, since it might be held to deny to citizens equal protection of the laws, or to be the equivalent of an attainder law. The Foreign Agents Registration Act, if it does not provide for such an immunity, could be enlarged to make such provision. The Communist Party, or any group, would, of course, have the right to court review—as they should.

I take this opportunity to suggest likewise review of the legislation which vests consuls with the power to grant or deny visas for entry to the United States to Communists. . . . The visa procedure is not a very good defense . . . there are a great many persons who have at one time or another been members of Communist parties who are actually our best friends. These include persons who have become disillusioned with Russian policy. . . . Again there are, especially in South America, a great many young men and women who are merely intellectual Communists—persons who actively wish to better social conditions. . . . One of the groups in Brazil most friendly to the United States had at one time been a member of local Communist parties but split off in protest. . . .

5. Finally, it should be noted that the United States, without abandoning its traditional institutions, has many times met similar threats. . . .

Overt acts against the United States such as espionage, sabotage, or conspiracy to do these things or any other unlawful act are, of course, governed by existing legislation. The present circumstances do not suggest any basis for hysteria or ill-considered action. They do suggest that public opinion should be steadily and fully informed and that, when so informed, the American public takes care of the situation and of itself very well.

August 9, 1948
Last week, one Whittaker K. Chambers testified before the House Committee that there was in existence a Russian underground group including Alger Hiss, his brother, Donald Hiss, and various others. He stated that he told the story to me in late August of 1939, but that nothing was done about it.

I confirmed to the newspapers that Chambers had talked to me in 1939 [September 2], though we did a great deal about it. I did not give them any further statement on the subject.

Chambers had been a member of the Russian secret group in New York. He told me that from these contacts he knew that a Marxist study group had been formed including the Hiss boys and some others; that these would go underground and be of use to the general Russian scheme.

Chambers had left the Communist underground in 1935, and subsequently had changed his name to Chambers. His information about the Hiss boys was two years cold at least when he gave it to me. He struck me as being a sincere man who was telling the truth as he saw it but emotionally much involved. He did not tell me directly that he knew Alger Hiss to be a member of the Communist Party, nor did he relate his own connection with Hiss's wife.

There was no evidence sufficient to base a conclusion as to Hiss's underground associations.

The Hiss boys were later of the appeasement faction of the State Department. Anything that went through their office leaked, usually to Drew Pearson. . . .

August 18, 1948

The [Karl] Mundt [R., S.D.]-Nixon-[J. Parnell] Thomas [R., N.J., Chairman] Committee yesterday had the Senior Editor of *Time* (Chambers) meet Alger Hiss. Chambers had testified that he knew Hiss as a member of the Communist Party and as a member of the underground back in 1935. Hiss denied that he had ever met Chambers. I thought Hiss was telling only a technical truth, because Chambers was probably operating under a different name in 1935.

Hiss said he recognized Chambers as one "Crosley" with whom he had been friendly and to whom he had sub-let his apartment. The question is whether Hiss when he denied knowing Chambers knew or did not know that Chambers was his old friend Crosley. I personally think he did. I think, too, that when we get to the bottom of it we will discover the true Communist in the Hiss family is the wife either of Alger or Donald Hiss.

It seems possible now that the Committee will call me. All I have to say is that Chambers told me the story, in less detail, in 1939 and did not directly accuse Hiss of being in the Communist Party. As a result of that, I worked steadily at organizing an effective counter-espionage group, including Fletcher Warren, Fred Lyon, Jack Neal, Win Crane, and others, and developing a high state of activity in the F.B.I., and in getting the Foreign Agents Registration Act passed, and in strengthening the passport control, and so forth. One result was that we prosecuted Earl Browder for false statements in his passport application. . . .

All of this may make some noise but is not really important.

September 3, 1948

Yesterday Alex Rose and I went down to Washington and got the signatures of Senator Barkley and President Truman to the formal acceptance of the Liberal Party nomination. President Truman was very cordial and very confident. Nothing of importance happened and I was not too anxious to have any.

I was not happy about the splash headline publicity given to my testimony before the House Committee on Un-American Activities. The testimony was voluntary—that is, they requested it and I did not put them to the trouble of a subpoena. I hated to appear to be in the "red baiting" business, and did my best to segregate people who had an intellectual interest in Communism and the people who were emotionally involved in some fashion. For that reason, in answer to the Committee's questions, I explained that Hiss was in favor of a much more complacent policy towards the Soviet Union than I was, therein following the lead of his immediate superior, Dean Acheson, but that honest men might differ on this subject and did, since it turned at least in part on the degree to which we might need Russian support in the invasion of Japan.

The question ended there, and I was glad it did. . . . My private opinion is that Hiss was pretty deep in something or other in the early days; nevertheless I am not prepared to think that he maintained these obligations after he had got into a position of influence. In other words, he was not a traitor. The Committee hearings do seem to suggest that he is a liar—but this is a matter he can settle with St. Peter.

September 7, 1948

. . . Unless everything is forgotten, the next move will be that somewhere, sometime, people will start inquiring as to what people were doing in the State Department in 1944 and 1945. As to 1945, I cannot answer. I was in Brazil and Mexico. In 1944, I can only give the substance of the memorandum of September 26, 1944, which about states the case. But if anyone should ask me if I dissented from Roosevelt's decision at Yalta, I should be obliged to say that it was a closed case: nobody foresaw then that we would have the atom bomb or that Japan would suddenly cave in.

And how—oh, how—to explain that opposition to Russian expansion is opposition to expansion and not to Russia. The Russians will have to settle their own government, Communist or otherwise. But if they slop over into other parts of the world, it becomes an attack on world law, and therefore on peace, and therefore on the only real national interest we have, which is a peaceful world. We opposed German expansionism and now Russian and I hope we shall be patriotic enough to oppose expansionism in the United States.

To Arthur Schlesinger, Jr., September 29, 1948

I haven't a spare copy of my remarks to the Thomas Committee. I was called on three hours' notice to discuss the spectacular and not very important Hiss case for no better reason than that Chambers told me the story about Hiss in 1939. The question naturally came up as to the division of opinion in the State Department in 1944, at which time some of us estimated that the Russian policy would be about what it has proved, and pressed for a clear-cut plan as to how to meet the resulting problem.

This is about the story. The fact, of course, was that at the time the indications became clear (Summer of '44), Mr. Hull was ill and retiring; Mr. Roosevelt was likewise ill (about October, 1944); Mr. Stettinius knew very little about things in general, and Harry Hopkins, ill but energetic, became the dominant and deciding factor. In the ensuing play-off, practically everyone with experience in foreign affairs was eliminated from policy-making; and the failing President was left almost alone—unless the Generals can be said to have been some support—for even as great a man as President Roosevelt could not be expected to know everything by mental telepathy.

In which connection, I make one observation. The inexperienced men pay great attention to the statements and perhaps sincere intentions of the high personalities in foreign affairs. The experienced men invariably cross-check to modify by the most meticulous collation and analysis of the material showing what is happening on the ground. The actual conduct of an irregular contingent in Yugoslavia might be a better guide to real intentions than a formal statement of the Russian and British Governments. This does not necessarily mean insincerity in chieftains; but even dictators are more or less prisoners of the machines they have created; and I suppose all of us are prisoners of the philosophy which animates us. The Communist line, from its own point of view, has been perfectly consistent. The issue which had to be met at Yalta was not the problem of a series of local arrangements—but the problem of meeting, and, if possible, changing the course of a long and powerful movement. . . .

Whether that could have been met in the early part of 1945 remains a historical "might-have-been". I cannot even say, honestly, that the attempt made was unwise, or that the things done were necessarily unjustified. I can say that the justification would have to depend on a clear-cut intent and plan to follow right up so that the concessions made constituted steps towards a real understanding and adjustment—rather than ineffectual sacrifices on the altar of appeasement. If there was such a plan, it died with Roosevelt when he died in 1945; our own sketches for such a plan, of course, had been eliminated when the State Department was reorganized in the Fall of 1944.

December 1, 1948

The Liberal Party: 1948–1949 Position

Analysis of the election returns nationally [following Truman's election] shows:

a) Wherever a New Deal candidate was running he was elected, particularly everywhere north of the Mason-Dixon Line. Where the Democrats ran "conservatives", they lost.

b) Further, the President regularly ran behind the ticket. The liberal forces carried him—not he them. Many Liberals split the ticket. . . .

c) The kernel of influence for the future rests in Congress. There is a strong liberal bloc, whose voting strength entitles it to be heard there, and whose popular vote gives it even greater weight.

d) The question as to what the national liberal party of the future will be is settled for the time being. It will be the Democratic Party; third party notions are out.

The Liberal Party in New York demonstrated:

a) That it has approximately 300,000 votes in the state—though it cast only 226,000 for the President. This is still enough to be a balance-of-power position in the next state election—not enough to assume leadership, as a right.

b) Since alliance with the Republicans is plainly impossible at present, this means its principal position is as a pressure group on the Democratic Party.

c) . . . the Democratic Party is itself in bad shape. . . .

The Liberal Party now: On this layout, the Liberal Party has to choose between two alternatives (there are no others). It must either

a) Frankly and promptly enter the Democratic Party and then see what happens. This would be a maneuver very difficult to execute without breaking up the solid nucleus of a couple of hundred thousand votes (and possibly more) which we do have, or

b) Immediately take an independent stand on something in which its ideas and vitality can be made serviceable. . . . In pracitce, the only field of movement it has is the municipal campaign.

It seems to me that the Liberal Party ought to decide, now, if it proposes to spear-head a movement for a non-partisan liberal government of the city of New York. This means that it ought to decide now that it will oppose O'Dwyer [for mayor]. . . . If a suitable slate can be agreed upon with the Republicans (which must mean liberal Republicans committed not to use the city as a basis for operations against the national government), we should do that. If we are unable to do that, we should resolve now to name an independent slate. . . . If we make a strong enough show, we should then be entitled to ask Democratic consideration in the state. . . .

January 12, 1949

The Acheson appointment as Secretary of State made a good deal of trouble. Many people tend to resent his own part in the policy of appeasement from 1944 to the enunciation of the Truman Doctrine in 1947. He was also the sponsor of Alger Hiss, now under indictment for perjury.

I testified before the House Committee [September 1948] and referred to the fact that Acheson was one of the leaders of the "appeasement" group at that time. When his appointment was announced, this was immediately remembered, and various Republicans presumed that I would spearhead an opposition to his confirmation.

Yesterday, on [brother] Rudolf's excellent advice, I telephoned Tom Connally, Chairman of the Foreign Relations Committee, and told him that I had no intention of doing any such thing. I could either testify or telegraph that an honest difference of opinion would not in my judgment justify withholding confirmation. . . .

Connally thought it was handsome, said so and apparently forthwith called up Acheson, who was relieved for a variety of reasons.

The situation is not without drama. The personal antagonisms of

Acheson's staff to me were unexplained and bitter during my term of office. Acheson, as sponsor for the two Hiss boys, is in a vulnerable position—which is obviously worrying him. It is difficult for me to believe that he did not at least tacitly permit the bitter personal campaign which his associates carried on inside the State Department; though I question whether he knows that much of this was fed to the New York papers from his office through Elizabeth Bentley, who recently confessed that she was mixed up with some Soviet espionage or propaganda schemes. . . .

Telegram to Connally, January 12, 1949

I telegraph you because my name has been mentioned as a possible witness in connection with the confirmation of Acheson as Secretary of State. I do not oppose his confirmation and no implications to that effect are warranted.

It is true that in the fall of 1944 I and others forecast an expansionist Russian policy along lines now familiar to everyone, and urged that we formulate an American policy to meet it then. It is likewise true that I had no confidence that the Russian expansionism could be altered by a policy of wide concessions. Mr. Acheson like other men in the government at that time felt otherwise under the conditions then prevailing. As I have repeatedly stated the matter was one on which honest men could differ, and I have never felt that divergence on this question reflected on the competence or loyalty of men who went along with the policy then adopted. All this is matter of common knowledge and public record, which I could only repeat. I also feel strongly that confirmation proceedings should be as swift as possible. This is no time for an interregnum, and the next Secretary of State should take office under conditions giving him the best possible chance of complete success for which he has my best wishes.

June 2, 1949

I lunched yesterday with Judge Seabury, who is anxious that Nelson Rockefeller should take the candidacy for Mayor.

David Dubinsky's position is briefly that he doesn't want to settle anything until the situation clears up, i.e., until we know whether the draft of O'Dwyer is getting anywhere. It is obviously synthetic. He wants to preserve to the last the chance that the Democratic Party will come through with a man capable of making a first-rate Mayor. . . .

Last night Raul Fernandes, Minister of Foreign Affairs of Brazil, dined with me with Eugenio Gudín [Brazilian economist and banker]. This was an intimate [evening]. . . . [Fernandes] said that he had talked with everyone in Washington and no one knows Latin America exists with the single exception of old Cordell Hull. . . . [He] had tried to explain that the economic situation of South America in general and Brazil in particular was headed downward and, of course, they have no support analogous to that of the Marshall Plan. It was a long session, filled with many thoughts and personalities and the only outcome was our own agreement we had to get started on an economic program for Latin America cast in lines large enough to open up the whole situation.

I did not debate the difficulties. I am struggling with them. I know them all well.

June 13, 1949

Last night the Policy Committee of the Liberal Party met regarding the Mayoralty. No decision was reached. . . .

I got excited and stated that, rather than see the Party go along with some Democratic hack who would be servant to the machine, I would run myself; but I did so with the profound and earnest hope that nobody takes me up on it. Actually the sentiment for working out something with the Democrats is so strong that if they, the Democrats, have the sense of a goose their man will get our endorsement. This would mean, in substance, their nominating somebody like Ferdinand Pecora or possibly [District Attorney] Frank Hogan, etc. or young Bob Wagner. . . .

. . . were such a man nominated it would be very difficult for us to make a fight on principle—despite my personal feeling that such a man would be more likely to make terms with the Tammany machine than he would with us, and that it would be very difficult for us to go on building a party whose primary purpose appeared to be making careers for non-members. . . .

July 21, 1949

Last week the quadrennial convulsion that appears to be necessary to nominate a Fusion ticket took place. My difficulty was that the Liberal Party is unhappy outside the Democratic ranks. . . .

For O'Dwyer, having first withdrawn from the race, had simultaneously set up a "Draft O'Dwyer" movement. This was on May 25. The draft movement went badly and a few days later he cancelled it out—then, I think, he really intended to retire. . . .

Forthwith everyone treated the Mayor as out of it and white hopes began to appear on the Democratic side all over the lot. . . . Later O'Dwyer announced that he was going to run himself. . . .

. . . the conferees on a Fusion ticket met. This was the Seabury group represented by [William C.] Chanler, the Republican group represented by [Charles] Tuttle and George Mintzer, and the Liberals represented by Harry Uviller and me. From the list of possible Fusion candidates, Hogan promptly dropped out. Arrangements were made to meet with the five Republican county leaders and we went to it.

Time and fate having slaughtered all the others, the Republicans put forward [Edward] Corsi; we put forward Newbold Morris and my name. I stated that I did not want it but would take it if that would resolve an otherwise impossible situation and continued to argue for Morris. The five County leaders withdrew and an hour later came up with Newbold Morris. I found later that Tom Curran [New York County Republican leader] had wanted me. . . .

Anyway they took Morris on the understanding that the other two offices would be divided between the Republican Party and the Liberal Party. . . . We then nominated Harry Uviller [for Comptroller], who was promptly accepted and that game was over. . . . In the course of the process I put in a plea for Christian charity for Frank Hogan on the ground that he was more Flynned against than Flynning and got general agreement that he would be nominated for District Attorney.

Yesterday (July 20) to Washington to testify before the House Committee on Judiciary in connection with the change in the antitrust laws. The Committee seemed pretty much interested and we had a good time, though I did not see the universe shaking very much. Lunch with [Emanuel] Manny Celler [D., Brooklyn] and a couple of his Committee members; and chatted with Dave Coyle, the economic expert and various of the brethern.

September 29, 1949

Life Magazine has been interviewing various people who escaped from the Soviet Union. One of them, a Soviet Army Colonel, states that the Russian General Staff prepared plans for war against the United States in 1947, apparently with the acquiescence, if not at the orders, of a substantial part of the Russian Government.

This merely confirms my own analysis at the time. I thought that the Russian Government debated the question of war against the United States shortly after the proclamation of the Truman Doctrine, or perhaps a little before. It was touch-and-go what their decision should be. During this period the United States was walking like a somnambulist on the edge of the cliff.

The decision was apparently to attempt seizure of Europe by political revolutionary means instead—a decision probably reached about the time the Marshall Plan conversations were going on in Paris, say, July, 1947. The attempt was actually made in December, 1947, by a string of general strikes with the hope that they would be converted into civil war —as they were not.

The Soviet Union did not at that time have the atom bomb. Therefore they had no way "to take out" the American air bases which might have hindered the operation.

Today, they have the bomb.

November 9, 1949

We had our election last night.

The Liberal Party cast the largest vote in its history: 396,000 for Lehman, 372,000 for Morris. The Liberal Lehman vote made possible the election of Lehman [to the Senate]; without it he would have been beaten. . . .

In the city, however, the blunt fact is that the Republicans sold 220,000 votes away from Morris to O'Dwyer. . . . We had ample testimony during the day that this was going on . . . [otherwise Morris] would have been elected.

This probably reflects the work of Governor Dewey. . . .

November 10, 1949

. . . Even in a contest of relatively little interest—that for Judge of the Court of Appeals—we gave [Charles W.] Froessel 350,000 votes. This is balance-of-power with a vengeance. . . .

January 17, 1950

On the night of January 11, Roberto Marinho [owner-publisher of the newspaper *O Globo*] telephoned from Brazil to say that Vargas had issued a statement attributing his downfall to Wall Street, the control being exercised through Spruille Braden and the Department of State to me to make the Petrópolis speech [see diary entries for October 1 and 6, 1945]. Comment was asked. . . .

Subsequently apparently most of Brazil rose to deny the charge. . . . I declined to comment further. . . .

Nevertheless I dislike to be put in such a position in Brazil. The Petrópolis speech was good business. It did congratulate Vargas on his decision to hold free elections. It was shown to him and approved by him. But the fact was that Vargas was secretly planning a coup d'état to reestablish the dictatorship, thinly masked by a "Constitutional Convention" and of course this did not help that game at all. If, however, he had done so and gone on with his second plan of allying with Perón, the United States would have been in a rough spot. Also, the Brazilian Air Corps would have revolted and we might have had anything up to a civil war. Since the United States was operating the air bases, our position would have been extremely embarrassing.

The great majority of Brazil thought the speech was good business and that probably is the way to leave it. . . .

October 11, 1950

I went last night to the Brazilian Dinner. . . .

Leaving aside the usual diplomatic chit-chat, drama lay in the fact that for the first time in several years Sumner Welles made a public appearance. He greeted me with great warmth and great affection and we made a date to foregather after the dinner was over, which we did at the Knickerbocker Club. The last contact I had with Sumner Welles was when the Brazilian revolution against Vargas took place, and Sumner attacked me publicly at a bitterly dangerous time. But I bore no malice and he insisted that he had missed me very much. . . .

. . . He thinks Hull lied in print about him. I did not argue the fact but no one really cares about past disputes of statesmen. He named as the man he would like to see as next President [Senator] Paul Douglas [D., Ill.].

This morning I arranged to offer him radio time to speak on foreign affairs in support of Herbert Lehman.

November 2, 1950

The Puerto Rican group in the Liberal Party is very much upset at the attack on the President's life. . . . [On November 1 two Puerto Rican Nationalists attempted to assassinate Truman.]

The Puerto Rican colony has been split down the middle on the issue of "independence." The independence group, per se, is small though very fanatical. . . .

To Elmer Davis, December 20, 1950, in answer to a request for what Berle "actually said" to the Un-American Activities Committee about Acheson

. . . In answer to a question by Mr. [Harris] McDowell [D., Del.], I said to the Committee that Mr. Acheson and a group of men in the State Department had favored concession to Russian demands and that there had been a sharp division of opinion in the Department. In that same answer I added that honest men could differ on the subject: many people, including high officers of the Army, felt the same way about it at that time. The point I endeavored to make was that the "soft" position did not give cause for suspicion. This related to the period prior to January 1, 1945. A major argument then went that Russian aid against Japan was so urgently necessary that every concession should be made to assure Russian cooperation to save American lives. I wholly disagreed, believing that Russia was certain to move on the Asiatic mainland against Japan in her own Far Eastern interest; but I could quite understand the opposite point of view.

I should add that I have no first-hand knowledge of the motivations and methods of developing American policy subsequent to the period following the United Nations Conference, and have rigidly kept out of the ensuing controversy. Past motives and methods will be judged by history, and past policies measured by their results. At the moment, in view of present peril, the debate is out of order. When Winston Churchill was asked to attack the policies of Neville Chamberlain at the outbreak of World War II, he said, wisely, "When the present struggles with the past, we lose the future." . . .

January 15, 1951

On Friday, I had lunch with DeWitt Poole [Director, Foreign Nationalities Branch, Office of Strategic Services, 1941–1945]. Allen Dulles [Deputy Director, C.I.A.] asked him for suggestions in connection with the program Dulles is now taking over. . . .

What has happened, of course, is that the Government has, at length, discovered that you cannot meet a full-scale political warfare of the kind the Russians are waging against us merely by radio broadcasts of the "Voice of America." I have recommended that particular attention be paid to the Eastern Mediterranean. At the moment, we have sea power and not much else; but we can use that as our line of communications.

The State Department has accepted (if it did not indeed actively propose) the United Nations proposal for a "cease-fire" order, a condition of which is that the United States discuss all "Far Eastern questions," which, in practice, means pulling out of Formosa, and probably pulling the French out of Indo-China. This sets the stage for surrender on a grand scale. The New York *Times* is saying this morning that we cannot prevent all wrong-doing in this unhappy world, but should not sell our souls, which is just about right. . . .

January 16, 1951
   . . . something happened at Lake Success which will affect everyone's fortunes. Acheson instructed Warren Austin [U.S. Representative to U.N.] to agree to the so-called "cease-fire" plan in the United Nations. The cease-fire is all right, but included an agreement that the United States would "discuss" withdrawal from Formosa, and permit Russia and Red China to join in the peace treaty with Japan. This sets the stage for the surrender of the Far East on a scale which makes Munich seem like a tea party. This is not peace with dishonor, but dishonor without peace, and the military result will be, if this happens, that, if war finally comes, the outposts will be Dutch Harbor and Hawaii, and the Pacific Coast will get bombed to hell-and-gone. . . .
   I discussed briefly with Paul McNutt [former Ambassador to the Philippines] the results of the surrender of Formosa. He said (and it is the view of all of the men who know) that when the island line running from Japan to Borneo is broken, the whole line is in danger, and we are back about where we were on the day after Pearl Harbor. We must have the line in the Mediterranean. Even a top-flight fleet would have trouble in holding the Pacific, the Atlantic and the internal lines. Big trouble in the offing.

January 30, 1951
   Last week I spent most of my time in working with Nelson Rockefeller, Wallace Harrison [architect; Director of Planning, U.N.], Ben Cohen and B. Ruml on plans for the Point IV Program. . . .
   Yesterday, at the National Committee for a Free Europe, representatives of five groups of exiles—Polish, Rumanian, Bulgarian, Czechoslovakian and Hungarian—agreed on a draft declaration to be read in Independence Hall on February 11th, and which will serve as a spear-head of American policy. It is a minor miracle to get these representatives to agree on anything. . . .

February 14, 1951
   . . . In Haiti with the family for a little holiday from Thursday to last night. John Burns, my old Executive Officer in Rio, is Chargé d'Affaires there, and certainly gave us a good time.
   I met President [Paul E.] Magloire. He and the Army took over last May. This was because President Estimé, who wished to amend the Constitution so that he could succeed himself, had imported a little mob who wrecked the Senate Building, and is supposed to have marked a great number of the "Jaunes" for slaughter or mob violence. . . .

What actually happened was that he went to the Army barracks to ask the Generals for aid for his movements. Two said that they would obey orders; the third, Magloire, said he had taken an oath to support the Constitution of Haiti, and would do so. Estimé left. Magloire and the other two Generals quickly disarmed the Palace Guard. Estimé fled, along with the funds.

Dantes Bellegarde [distinguished elder statesman] was kind enough to delay his trip so that he could talk with me. I gave him the best briefing I could on the state of politics in the United States; and my own guess as to the world situation. I told him that we should work for the maintenance of the principle that the peace of peoples had been provided for through the United Nations and that they had to stick by the principle, compromising with facts when they could not enforce the principle. A very interesting and heart-warming talk. . . .

Also a jam-session with the boys in the Embassy. . . .

March 8, 1951

On Monday, March 5, I went to Albany to attend a meeting of some sixty legislators on Liberal Party policy. This was principally to oppose the Sales Tax and urge ratification of the St. Lawrence Waterway.

Since the meeting happened after the legislative session adjourned, I dropped in to listen to the Assembly. Irwin Steingut [D., Brooklyn] moved to give me the privileges of the floor, which was amusing. . . .

April 11, 1951

This morning the news had [General Douglas] MacArthur [U.N. Commander, Korea] being fired. The President is right; but I am not sure he has the political and moral strength of the country behind him in order to escape some terrible repercussions. The Far Eastern policy of the United States has not been so clear or conclusive, and the confidence in Acheson is not so great, as to ballast the move adequately. This could bring a move for impeachment as in Andrew Johnson's situation. Obviously in the next mainline struggle the primary issue will be the conception of authority of the government of the United States, no matter who is President. But the Lord knows how it will come out.

July 20, 1951

I appeared last night before the House Committee on Foreign Affairs [at the request of Congressman Jacob K. Javits (R., N.Y.)]. . . .

Everyone asked questions. I made the point that the Near East is rapidly going over the dam: the quickest possible action is needed.

This morning Herbert Cummings, who used to be in Istanbul and who has been working in Near Eastern affairs for the Department of Commerce, came in to see me enroute to the E&SC meeting in Geneva. He said that their information was that in six weeks the Egyptians will demand withdrawal of all British troops and start armed movement to take over the Suez Canal.

The noon papers carry headlines announcing the assassination in Jerusalem of King Abdullah of Transjordania. This is, very nearly, the last of the Hashimite rulers. I knew his brother, Emir Feisal, later King of Iraq, at Versailles. The work of Lawrence of Arabia is just about destroyed.

Adding up these various straws, my guess is that when the Russians make their big push, they will find an almost complete vacuum from Persia clear through to Ethiopia. I do not think there is time to organize. They will need a fleet in the Red Sea, and armed men in the Persian Gulf to stop this, if they can.

I am told Egypt would be glad to have the United States take over the British position though Egyptian sincerity is always dubious but I do not see any disposition in Washington to organize, or pick up, the equivalent of the pieces of the British Empire. FDR would have done it in his own way, probably throwing it into the United Nations.

Everything considered, it looks as though we were approaching nearer to the world show-down.

STATEMENT OF ADOLF A. BERLE, JR.,
FORMER ASSISTANT SECRETARY OF STATE
BEFORE THE HOUSE COMMITTEE ON FOREIGN AFFAIRS,
WASHINGTON, D.C., THURSDAY, JULY 19, 1951.

This statement is directed to the drafting of a Mutual Security Act of 1951 (Program for 1952). I am convinced that the House Committee should recommend that the Congress pass a Mutual Security Act along the lines of the Administration draft. In my judgment, certain changes could usefully be made in that draft. . . .

This brings us to the organization of mutual security. The point is highly controversial, and it has to be resolved partly on the question of expediency. The form of organization should be chosen which can be most rapidly activated and can most rapidly get into action. If the perfect, logical form of organization is not politically possible, the best possible alternative should be chosen. There is no way out of this: action seems to me essential.

In strict logic, security aid should be split. Military aid should be separately organized and administered. Strict relief operations—like that in Korea—should likewise be separately administered as is proposed. Economic assistance and Point IV aid should be a third division. Never should the military men be in a position to take resources needed for roads and put them into tanks, or vice versa. The two operations are parallel but they are quite different.

Also in strict logic, economic aid should be administered by an organization dependent on, but subordinate to, the Department of State. Traditionally the Department of State is not particularly good at administering huge enterprises. Equally, the Administrator of an economic program in a country cannot have a policy separate and distinct from that of the State Department; he cannot be in competition with the Ambassador. . . .

. . . This sort of work is not a matter for high negotiation in overstuffed palaces. It is a job of devoted men, working against time, and talking to the simplest and humblest of people in language they can understand, accompanied by deeds which they can see and appreciate.

Finally, I should like to express the hope that the portions of the Bill which deal with Point IV be isolated so that the Point IV Program emerges as a reality. . . .

As a matter of detail, I note that for the American republics $22 million is suggested for assistance. This strikes me as low. I believe it should be increased to at least $50 million, with appropriate authority to transfer. This is not asking a great deal. We cannot have literally millions of people living adjacent to the United States on the peon level without substantial hope of changing their position, and expect a stable situation between the Rio Grande and Cape Horn.

It ought to be made perfectly clear that the object of this Act is not to build up more huge agencies in Washington. The product, the end result, must be a peasant or an artisan in Burma, or in Iran, or in West Africa, or in Chile or Brazil, who sees that he is taking the first step, however short, towards getting benefits of the amazing industrial civilization and comforts of the twentieth century. One hundred first-class, able and devoted, though wholly obscure, operators in the field are worth a thousand administrators and sub-administrators, clerks and so on, in Washington. This is not to decry the able and devoted work done by many and many of these Washington men who do the work which furnishes the reputation and headlines for other people. It is to say that the man in the field who is doing a job is what this is all about.

Conclusion

I hope this Mutual Aid Bill will pass. I hope it will pass rapidly, accompanied by legislative and executive realization that we are approaching the greatest crisis in American national security we have yet encountered in our history.

September 12, 1951

The Liberal Party reports the [Rudolph] Halley campaign [for President of the City Council] getting underway under favorable auspices. In all events on his petitions (Liberal Party and a couple of independent petitions), they accumulated more than 90,000 signatures which is believed to be a record. The newspapers paid little attention to it; I do not know that means anything.

Some work yesterday and day before yesterday on the Free Europe University in Exile, which is getting underway and is likewise getting overtaken by events. I think we can work something out but the stress will be between those who want to make it a straight cultural welfare training school and those who want to make it a broader, long-range repository of ideas and culture. Included in this is the necessity of developing some ideas for the new organization of Eastern Europe.

The San Francisco Conference duly signed the Japanese pact [peace treaty]. It is regarded here as an achievement and undoubtedly has a certain psychological value. But in point of fact, the only eastern countries represented were Pakistan (good), Indonesia (good), and three states of Indochina. What do these represent? The big blocks of population in China and India were unrepresented. So that, except for Pakistan, San Francisco really deepens the rift between the western world and the mainland of Asia. Also, having learnt to take the Russian pronouncements seriously, Gromyko's insistence that this was a step towards Far Eastern war has to be taken into account. . . .

October 15, 1951

Week-end at the Berkshires; glorious weather. Roger Baldwin, Harold [Professor of Medicine (Neurology), Cornell University Medical College] and Isabel Wolff [painter] at the house. Saturday, a scramble on Mt. Everett through the day, then to dinner at Albert Spalding's. He had heard I wanted to hear Bach's "Chacone" again and after dinner played it for us in his living room.

In 1943, Albert Spalding spent an evening with us in Washington, dropped his music and went as public relations officer to American headquarters in the Italian campaign. I feared for his going (these assignments leave scars) and he thought he would never play the violin again. His work in Italy was brilliantly successful: it is one of the major reasons Italy is still friendly to us. He came back in 1945; considered, and decided he would try to play once more—a hard thing to do for a musician who has been out of it for some years. It was decided to make his second debut in Rio. He stayed with us in the Embassy; a crowded house saluted him at the Teatro Municipal; and he played the Bach "Chacone." It was a brilliant evening. I had never heard it before nor again until Saturday when four old friends met together on a Berkshire holiday at "Aston Magna."

Meanwhile, Egypt is blowing up with Egyptian claims to Suez. . . . I am remembering that in the preparatory diplomatic conferences for the Civil Aviation Conferences in 1944, the Russians proposed an end-to-end airline—the Russian end to meet the American end. We asked where the ends would meet. After deliberation they answered, "In Cairo."

November 7, 1951

Last night the City election showed Rudolph Halley elected on the Liberal ticket as President of the City Council. Since only 1,700,000 votes were cast this is a light skirmish with a main issue. Well over 1,000,000 did not register and did not vote. . . .

This will have some national repercussions. Obviously, neither the Republican nor the Democratic delegations from New York to the National Conventions will have too much weight as neither of them can definitely deliver a block of votes. Also we will have trouble supporting a Democratic candidate, for to support him we would have to support the very men who supported the narcotics peddlers and thieves who have been running in New York City.

I made arrangements on Friday and then again yesterday for Harry Culbreth of the Farmers Cooperatives Life Insurance Company to talk with Allen Dulles, about supporting the Italian cooperatives. We may get something done in Italy and in the European cooperative field as well.

November 9, 1951

Last night to dinner with Fred Dolbeare [of NCFE] and Henry Freney, who was at one time Foreign Minister of France in the early De Gaulle days. Freney is forming a "National Committee for a Free Europe," or its equivalent, in France, and wants liaison with us. He also wants, unquestionably, some financial help.

There are two elements in this. The first is that France claims a historic interest in organizing Eastern Europe and wants to get in on the act. The second is that Eisenhower is putting pressure on for a unification of Europe of some sort, and the two ideas can be combined. The head of the Committee is Paul Reynaud, and obviously has the backing of the French Foreign Office.

Our Washington friends have shipped it along to us.

What this comes to is the beginning of the diplomatic planning in the event (if, as and when it occurs) that Eastern Europe is opened up. The little question of where and when and how that will happen is by no means easily answered but there is no harm in dreaming.

A group of American citizens had, in 1949, organized the National Committee for a Free Europe, to wage psychological warfare against the East European satellite governments. Radio Free Europe, broadcasting from Munich, played the major part in the organization's activities and today is an acknowledged U.S. government station. Berle served on the Board of Directors from its beginning until 1963.

November 28, 1951

At a meeting of the National Committee for a Free Europe today, we took up the matter of starting broadcasts to the Baltic States; the State Department first insisted we do it, later backed water because the Voice of America wanted to do it. . . .

I stated off the record that unless the State Department was prepared to support a liberation of the Baltic States, I was opposed to broadcasting or starting movements which could only end in the slaughter of the people involved. For this reason I was opposed to NCFE's getting into it until a firm policy was made; I should question whether the Voice of America ought to go into it therefore with purely cultural propaganda broadcasts.

At the Board meeting of NCFE today, we took up the matter and decided to play "out". . . .

March 18, 1952

Today, President Truman's book, *Mr. President,* came out and splashed over the front pages. Byrnes denies the part of it which applies to him; Wallace denies the part of it which presumably applies to him. The fact of the matter is that there are endless items which unquestionably were honestly made by the President but do not jibe with some of the other things that were going on at the same time. The politicians will have a field day.

I have been worrying a little about Whittaker Chambers' book, and particularly about his account of telling the story of the Hiss case to me, after which he records me as going to the President and being told to jump in the lake. Read carefully, the book (as far as I have got it) is not in detail inaccurate, but the whole impression is wrong. At no time does he record what he said to me, and thus gives the impression that he told me everything he told many years later in the Hiss case. The fact, of course, was that he did not state anything he told me as personal knowl-edge—but as something he had heard about while in the Communist Party in New York. He did not even remotely indicate that he personally had been engaged in the operation. He did not charge individuals with espionage—they were merely "sympathizers" who would be hauled out later when the great day came. He would not take his story to the FBI. He would not even stand to it himself—he would not himself verify or stick to the story. He really wanted to see the President.

Further, under some cross-examination, he qualified everything to the point of substantial withdrawal. He also told of having fled the Party, and having been in fear of his life, spending a long time in flight and fearing armed attack, and so on. I thought I was dealing with a man who thought he was telling the truth but was probably afflicted with a neuro-sis.

I reported the substance of this, not to the President, but to McIn-tyre. This was because Chambers and Levine had sought an appointment with the President and had been "brushed off" in my direction to McIn-tyre, and the procedure was to report back to the official in the White House who had referred the job to you. I never did know what McIntyre reported to the President. I have vague recollections of having mentioned the matter to the President when shortly thereafter we were working on the Foreign Agents Registration Act, which was the real, tangible out-come of this, though there were plenty of other lines leading to it. I was struck with the fact that no law was violated by having foreign-controlled sympathizers around, and that in this respect the Nazi pattern of having propaganda agents was almost exactly the same as the Communist pat-tern, but there was no law against it.

Chambers, of course, did not tell the story of his own personal in-volvement with it until he testified before the House Committee, or the degree to which he had entered into espionage himself, and did not really come clean (if then) until he brought out the famous "pumpkin papers." At one of the Hiss trials, he was questioned more or less extensively as to whether he had told the story to me which he was telling at the trial and Chambers answered that he had not.

As the Chambers articles came out, they give the impression that I was quite all right and wanted to do something but had been blocked off by the President. This avoids a dispute with me, of course, but it is an unfair attack on the President. The question is whether to write some-thing about it now in defense of President Roosevelt. I have decided for the time being not to do this because it is a political year; there will be nothing but emotional reaction and no sound appraisal of the facts. Later we may be able to do something but now we should simply have all the hate-mongers and that kind of thing trying to twist and torture and otherwise mangle the facts. These are quite simply that the story as Chambers told it to me would not hold up against the reputation of any honest man.

March 20, 1952

. . . Later in the afternoon to meet Nelson Rockefeller, and Wallace Harrison. Nelson Rockefeller has fitted up a little house on 54th Street back of the Museum of Modern Art, to be a center for a very small and singularly esoteric group of serious thinkers. As Nelson said, if the capitalist system has any way of getting things done . . . the [five Rockefeller brothers] have access to it. . . . Now the question is whether you can get anything done for the benefit of the world with all that, and the house is designed to be an intellectual center. It is an old and not very beautiful house on the outside, with a couple of beautiful rooms fixed up by Wally Harrison, a nice kitchen which will eventually have a cook. The theory is that anybody can drop in to lunch there and discuss a few subjects from time to time. Nobody is to be invited as lunch guests without the consent of two members. The members consist of the Rockefeller brothers, Wallace Harrison, Beardsley Ruml and myself which makes it about the most esoteric group there is; and, of course, the tangential contacts run into many billions of dollars. What is really happening is that the old generation is passing, and the five Rockefeller brothers are increasingly picking up the burden of empire. But, though the private fortunes are large, this is not power in the sense of old J.D. They are struggling with the fact that there is no central intellectual concept and so no way of pushing ideas or physical development and no way of combining the two, and Nelson's always generous and always active mind is seeking some method of giving some intellectual and philosophical direction to this blob of influence and, occasionally, power inherent in their position. The fascinating thing is the range: it can run from philosophy in the Rockefeller Foundation to drilling oil wells or making fresh water out of sea water and irrigating the Sahara Desert.

This ought to be fun.

Of interest is the fact that after we got through discussing things and having tea and Dubonnet, the assembled thinkers-for-millions washed the dishes. This is revolution, American-style.

April 3, 1952

Most of the day was spent on matters concerning the National Committee for a Free Europe. This involved finishing up negotiating a labor contract, Executive Committee meeting, and then a very thrilling session with the Research Commission. They covered the basic material on which a federation of Eastern Europe could be erected: the maps of coal, iron, industry, etc., the transport lines and roads, the in-and-out trade, the ethnic and religious distribution, etc. It makes an impressive showing. I am thrilled with the beginning—this is the stage of large enterprise in which anything seems possible. Later, the disappointments begin. . . .

May 12, 1952

On Friday last, I had lunch with Nathan Straus. He is Treasurer of the [Senator Estes] Kefauver [D., Tenn.] campaign. He wanted me to join the "brain trust" and write speeches for Kefauver. . . . I told him this time before I committed to a President I wanted to know a few things: there was no point in my pitching in for a man again who would simply deliver the Democratic Party to its worst politicians, and its foreign policy to men who, however well meaning, were not much good at it, like Acheson. I rather think this may be the end of it, but you never can tell.

Actually, this is getting to the stage where everybody would like to send a boy around for the Liberal Party's money, brains and votes, on condition that we kindly commit suicide immediately after election.

To Michael Rogen, Secretary, Young Liberals, Forest Hills, N.Y., May 12, 1952 in answer to a request for Berle's views

Thank you for your courteous letter. I should hardly expect you to agree, off the bat, with the conclusions of anyone who had learnt foreign affairs the hard way.

You see, most of the United States is longing to be told that there is an easy way out. They would like to dethrone dictators like Franco and Perón but would not like to commit American lives or American money to that adventure. They would like to repel the menace of Russian Communism, but they do not like the sacrifices involved in joining in the defense of half the world. They have a feeling that a magic formula of words can do it, or that the persuasiveness of some diplomat can arrange it, and do not like to be told that none of these things have ever stopped an aggressor who had armies and was prepared to use them. Historically, peace over any area has been won by a process of struggle, cold or hot, resulting in sacrifices, before victory. The process of learning that you cannot have a square meal without paying the bill for it is always painful.

The best that statesmanship can do is to lay out enlightened universal objectives, and continuously work towards them by the best means available. Unhappily, paper constitutions like the North Atlantic Treaty Organization, World Federalism, or even the United Nations, are not self-realizing. They become real when they recognize underlying conditions and effect the desires of great masses of people. It is hard to learn that ideas become real slowly.

To Paul Douglas, May 21, 1952

I have been seeing and talking with a lot of people in the last few weeks. You are still their first choice for Democratic nominee for President. . . .

The reason, of course, is very simple. You are the one Democrat of great experience who could run without being burdened by the miserable record of ingrown political machines and bureaucratic corruption. In my considered judgment, you could defeat Eisenhower.

The burden on you would be inordinate; but political service is by hypothesis an invitation to tragedy rather than comedy. That seems to be the price for any faithful service to the public.

I propose to be at Chicago during the Convention. If matters open before then, let me know what I ought to do.

June 12, 1952

. . . to Williamsburg, Virginia, where the exiles from the Iron Curtain countries made a Declaration, and I made a ringing speech in favor of their getting together in a Mid-European regional federal union. . . .

June 27, 1952

Last night, a little meeting of some of the people in the Liberal Party. We agreed that we would tackle the theme of this campaign and the campaign of next year. The general idea is starting the twentieth century revolution—as an offset to the Marxian nineteenth century revolution. This is based on the probability that (if war has not happened) there will be huge surpluses of goods and no marketing machinery capable of moving them, and the clear need that they be moved. There is also the problem of assuring that the Constitutional rights run to the individual, as against any institution, private or public, that wields power tantamount to power of the state, however it gets that power.

There was also agreement that Liberals should stop being blind devotees of nationalism (Wilsonian style), irrespective of results. This came up apropos of some suggestions that we go all-out for the nationalism of Tunis. I said I was through supporting nationalist movements unless something else went alongside capable of assuring a modicum of protection for individuals, a modicum of capacity for defense, and a modicum of international arrangements capable of assuring an economic base. Mobs shouting for nationalism mean just nothing in the long pull and, anyway, who wants the Barbary States back?

July 1, 1952

To Charlottesville to make a speech, sharing the platform with Estes Kefauver. He wanted to talk and therefore invited me to travel up to Washington with him. . . .

Accordingly and in due time, we debouched on a cornfield which they call the University airport, and climbed into a Lockheed painted red on the nose (Kefauver's Staff irreverently call it, "Rudy, the Rednosed Reindeer") with "Kefauver for President" on one side of the plane, and sailed into the air narrowly missing a couple of hay-ricks on the way.

The talk was conventionally political. . . .

I told him I thought he ought to make a couple of solid speeches, of which the one he gave at the University was a good example. The stereotype was of the nicest fellow in the world with a coonskin cap who made friends at sight and the case now called for some more ballast. . . .

Realistically, it looks pretty tough for him. He has a considerable bloc of delegates—but the ones he does not have and must get will probably be controlled by the Truman machine and it will be stiff-going all the way.

July 15, 1952

. . . Yesterday morning I got a letter from [Governor] Adlai Stevenson. . . . For practical purposes, this puts him out. There comes a point where you have to lay down a bet or get out of the game and the opening of a Convention is that time. So I plan to see what can be done about Paul Douglas's availability and just support Kefauver as long as we can; and if that becomes hopeless, do everything to get Paul into the game. . . .

July 16, 1952

Last Friday night at the Affiliated Young Democrats, I ran into Jim Farley. He said he was going to the Chicago Convention, he had a few delegates ("Farley for President"), and he was going to have some fun. I asked if he was serious. He said, perfectly frankly, that he knew very well there was nothing in it but he was going to amuse himself and there were quite a lot of delegates who would vote for him. I said, "Whom do you really want?" He said, "Stevenson if possible, but otherwise, Paul Douglas." I said Paul Douglas would be my first choice though I would go along with Stevenson. . . .

Today (the 15th) I saw Mannie Celler, who is on the New York Delegation. He said that all of their group (chiefly the Brooklyn bloc) would vote for Harriman on the first ballot but didn't think he stood a chance of being either nominated or elected. Who next? They thought Kefauver was not the strongest candidate; would prefer Paul Douglas. I told Mannie that Douglas would stay with Kefauver as long as he had a reasonable chance. After that, Paul Douglas. . . .

July 17, 1952

Last night, the State Executive Committee meeting of the Liberal Party. The general sense of the meeting was that of the two declared candidates we should support Kefauver against Harriman. Individually, most of us know Harriman better and like him but he represents what the New York *Times* this morning calls "the Old Guard," that is, the Truman machine and probably is not a very effective candidate.

But if there were any chance to get either Douglas or Stevenson, the Party would prefer that. . . .

Dinner with a group of Jesuit Fathers . . . An interesting little dinner which touched on everything from corporations to Ambassadors to the Vatican. Stevenson's name came up. I observed that he had been divorced. The Jesuit host simply observed that unquestionably there would be a divorced man in the White House sometime and he did not see that it made much difference. It would not to Catholics, because he was not a Catholic. I observed that there were probably more Protestants who would be worried about this than Catholics.

July 28, 1952

I reached Chicago on Tuesday, July 22, and headed immediately for Paul Douglas' apartment. He said he thought the avalanche had begun and it would be Stevenson. . . . He is not too happy about Stevenson though he believes he will govern honestly and liberally, but will not be too militant in cleaning up the city machines though he will do his best in the area of his own responsibility; he believes him a little closer to Acheson than he (Douglas) likes. Stevenson had come to him and had asked him to speak on behalf of Acheson once or twice. Paul felt he could not do that because he had caught Acheson once or twice in what were in effect lies—statements factually correct but giving the opposite effect of what really happened. He said he thought he could have got the nomination himself had he campaigned for it. He decided not to do that and was supporting Kefauver right through. Actually, he thought Kefauver could not make it. I agreed to keep in touch: there will be a lot of work to do no matter who was nominated. He was very kind to me personally, adding that he knew that Acheson had stimulated the attacks on me when we were colleagues in the State Department and he did not like it.

Then, a little manoeuvring, and I then connected with David Dubinsky and Alex Rose and we went at it. The platform had come out nicely from their point of view.

I had previously connected with the New York Delegation via Aaron Jacoby and Emanuel Celler. They were sticking with Harriman on the first ballot and were clear that he could not win and were wondering what to do next. I proposed either Stevenson or Kefauver, whoever was working at the time. . . .

Tuesday night, however, came a fight on the rules of which we shall hear more later. The Harriman men—chiefly young Frank Roosevelt and Senator Lehman—centered their attention on a Civil Rights plank (which they got) and on a rule of the Convention which excluded from the Convention any delegation which did not sign a loyalty pledge. . . .

Tuesday evening on the floor three states declined to take this pledge —Louisiana, South Carolina and Virginia. Jimmy Byrnes was presiding and obviously he wanted to keep the Party together. Frank Roosevelt had mustered the Kefauver men—"the young mindless militants"—who had rallied around Kefauver and the Americans for Democratic Action group (not including, I am glad to say, [ADA Chairman] Francis Biddle). These became known as the "Young Turks."

First up was a request from somebody or other to know whether or not the three delegations—Virginia, South Carolina and Louisiana—were seated in this Convention or not, and whether they would participate. Sam Rayburn ruled, properly, that since they had refused to sign the loyalty pledge, they could not participate—though he had no objection to their sitting there. He obviously did this unhappily. . . .

This was a time when any sane bunch would have taken the substance for the fact. But the Young Turks were out of control. They really wanted to drive the Southern states out of the Party. The Delegation from Tennessee (Kefauver) and from Minnesota, nominally for [Senator Hubert] Humphrey [D., Minn.] but really for Kefauver, and . . . young Frank Roosevelt, circulated the floor. They were for grinding the nose of Virginia in the dirt and stamping on its neck. I sent word to the New York people to be sensible—not that it was really needed: they are politicians, and many of them crooks, and are therefore tolerant. At the close of it, the Maryland Resolution carried, with the Kefauver and Harriman extremists and the Young Turks howling bloody murder. This set the lines for the first ballot.

Meantime, however, the issue had really been settled. My friends in the New York Delegation had caucused, and had decided that they would break, preferably on the second but in any case on the third ballot. Fitzpatrick, Chairman of the New York Delegation, Harriman himself, and Roosevelt and Lehman were shouting, "never," but the politicos had learned a savage fact, namely, that Frank Roosevelt wanted to be Vice President and his idea was to make a deadlock if he could and wind up as Vice President on some ticket or other before selling Harriman out in the process.

. . . But word had at length come that Truman, after a vigorous rear-guard action, had agreed to accept Stevenson. The bloc of place holder Truman machine delegates could not dominate the Convention, nor could they get anyone they wanted and, indeed, Truman had sent word to his alternate at first to vote for Harriman; had later reversed that in favor of Vice President Barkley, and before the first ballot had cancelled that and had sent word to vote for Stevenson. I rang up Adlai and congratulated him. He said it was no cause for congratulations—he would have done his best to get out of it and he would take condolences or flowers for his funeral. He said now the question came up of a Vice President and what did I think. I said that the rumor was around that he would be asked to accept [Senator J. William] Fulbright [D., Ark.] or [Senator Richard B.] Russell [D., Ga.]. I said that our people would simply not accept the out-and-out Dixiecrat group though I personally had a very high opinion of Fulbright. He then gave several names, including Harriman himself, who he said was the only one he knew well at all; [Senator John] Sparkman [D., Ala.]; Oscar Chapman [Secretary of the Interior]. I said that he could accept without trouble Harriman, whom we knew and liked; Oscar Chapman, whom I knew and also liked; and I personally would accept and work for Sparkman though that was getting to the lower range of the possible. Sparkman is a first-class man but he had voted wrong on the Civil Rights legislation and the Negro group and the Liberals who support them would have a somewhat difficult time but I would endeavor to do it. I wished to urge, however, that the strongest man on the ticket would be Kefauver. Adlai said that Kefauver had behaved so erratically and wildly during the campaign that he, Adlai, entertained serious doubts that if he died Kefauver could administer the Presidency of the United States. . . .

David Dubinsky, Alex Rose and I went to breakfast with [Kefauver]. . . . I think by this time Kefauver had got past the stage of dead certainty that he was going to be nominated, though, of course, he did not admit it. I tried to make the point that what he needed now were friends, not enemies, and his Young Turks going around accusing Stevenson of being the Northern Dixiecrat were not much help to anyone. I adverted to the mimeographed sheet which had come out of his headquarters. Kefauver said this was without his knowledge and he would stop it and he went over the sheet taking out some of the nastier cracks about the people who were nominating Harriman and Stevenson and so forth, but he stuck to his belief that he was the only unbossed candidate and that the others were products of bosses and machines, etc. Actually, through the day, the Kefauver tactics were bitterer than ever, and we did not need to be told that a rift was developing between him and Stevenson and for that matter everyone but Harriman which could not be breached. . . .

On the first ballot, the avalanche did not avalanche. Kefauver got rather more than I expected; Stevenson did quite well but not as well as he might have. The favorite sons were getting their complimentary votes. In the main, however, it was as expected. The second ballot was no more conclusive than the first, Stevenson picking up a little strength and Kefauver likewise with the so-called "liberal" sentiment setting heavily in favor of Kefauver. But on cold analysis it was clear that Kefauver could not possibly get a majority: the Russell men, the Barkley men and the [Senator Robert S.] Kerr [D., Okla.] men could not go to him anyway, and his tactics had hopelessly alienated the Stevenson men, and, of course, Truman hates Kefauver's guts. Actually, since the President had said Stevenson on the third ballot, the lines were to be drawn there.

Kefauver had got a temporary gain from Soapy [Governor G. Mennen] Williams [D., Mich.]. Soapy had decided to shift to Stevenson but he was mad at the Stevenson men for not staying with the Young Turks and pasting the Virginia Delegation the previous night; so he took the surprising decision to punish Stevenson by giving a second ballot nominal vote for Kefauver. So no avalanche on the second ballot.

Then Kefauver had finally seen the handwriting on the wall. As the balloting began, for the third time, he had circulated word that he was withdrawing from the contest. He had wanted to get up and nominate Paul Douglas and Paul Douglas had undertaken then to refuse the nomination and ask instead that Stevenson be supported. But Sam Rayburn denied [Kefauver] the floor—this was really a nasty piece of business—retaliation for the Young Turks. The third ballot wore along until New York came along. At this point, Fitzpatrick got up and announced that the New York Delegation switched to Stevenson. He did this over the bitter opposition of Frank Roosevelt and he did it because if he had not made the announcement the Delegation would have broken anyway—this in accordance with their agreement with me. From there on the avalanche began to roll and when the dust cleared away, it was Stevenson. Actually, I think that the Federal men throwing in for Stevenson would have decided it anyway. . . .

Stevenson then came in and made his acceptance speech which was generally regarded as a masterpiece. It was a great comfort to have a literate man talking again. . . .

The next morning we foregathered. By now David Dubinsky and Alex Rose had steamed themselves up to a point where they really wanted Kefauver for Vice President though they recognized that he had made himself impossible. Why men who have decided that something is impossible will go ahead and break friendships, etc. for it, I cannot understand. But I kept quiet. In substance, Walter White and the National Association for the Advancement of Colored People, together with the Young Turks, had come to a conclusion. They wanted Kefauver. Failing that, they would take any Northerner. Otherwise, they would run, bolt and otherwise raise hell. David, Alex and I had breakfast with White and some of the others, so we know. I could not see it and said that we hoped for the best on Kefauver but that we ought to take any real liberal. But a decision had been reached that night about the Vice Presidency, probably at Adlai's house. After canvassing the lot, they decided on Sparkman, and Sparkman it was. David Dubinsky was saying that he could not go along and that the Liberal Party ought not to nominate Stevenson, and so forth. I was trying to exercise a moderating influence; Walter White the other kind of influence, and generally we were having a bad time of it. I still do not know how it will come out but I think wiser heads will prevail. . . . I thought Stevenson rather markedly tried to disassociate himself from Truman in the course of the proceedings. The Sparkman nomination was really an attempt to make reparation for the violence of the Young Turks who were really laying down the doctrine that no one south of the Dixie Line could be on a Democratic ticket. Whether the appeasement of the South will work, I do not know. . . . I am not yet clear whether the Stevenson candidacy has two sets of enemies: the Young Turks in the North, and the unreconstructed rebels in the South—or whether we can unify both wings. One difficulty is that he has no major organization to do it with—that being one of the weaknesses of a draft. . . .

There being no more to do, I left for Ann Arbor and spent a lovely Sunday with Alice and Clan [Crawford].

July 29, 1952

Adlai Stevenson telephoned this afternoon. He said that after our talk in Chicago he felt he ought to report events leading up to the nomination of Sparkman for Vice President. . . .

I thanked him for his kindness in calling and said that, as I told him, Kefauver was the best vote-getter but we could accept Sparkman. The Young Turks had whistled up a wind and this would take some selling but this could be arranged. The fact is that Adam Clayton Powell, the Negro attached to the New York Delegation, had walked out on the proceedings. Nevertheless, I thought things would work out. Men like David Dubinsky thought well of Sparkman but would have a problem because they had Negroes in their unions. . . .

To Stevenson, July 29, 1952

The immediate task here is reconciling the very large Negro vote in New York, and with them the larger bloc of independents and Liberals that feel for and with them, to the Sparkman nomination. The decision was sound: the South is part of the United States; encouraging Southern liberals is good; and the Southern Congressmen have to be brought into a working majority. As stated, I think acceptance of the nomination can be brought about, though not quite easily. The "Young Turks" around Kefauver (and some around Harriman) apparently wanted to start Reconstruction all over again and whistled up a wind. The labor leaders I work with—notably David Dubinsky and the garment trades—thus have a real problem. . . .

August 5, 1952

Second thoughts on Stevenson: he will be a moderate liberal. In practice, this means maintaining the status quo. He will try not to antagonize anyone. As to foreign affairs, I think it questionable whether he yet understands the situation thoroughly. This, of course, may prove untrue. . . .

August 13, 1952

The news from Iran is worse by the minute. [Premier Mohammed] Mossadegh came into power with the support of fanatical Mohammedans. Now in power, with the Shah reduced to a cipher, the Mohammedans have allied with the Communist Tudeh Party. Mossadegh demanded and got dictatorial powers—but the loyalty of the Army is in question. The United States and Britain are now reduced to endeavoring to support him—it is probable they cannot do it. Shan Sedgwick's [for many years New York *Times* correspondent in Greece and the Middle East] estimate that the Russians would be on the Persian Gulf by Christmas seems all too likely to come true. There will be, between Mossadegh's fall and the Communist take-over, a period of fanatic Mohammedan nationalism which will be short-lived.

The United States seems to have decided that it has no troops to spare and cannot use force. It will, therefore, make monkey-business with the southern tribes—a ghastly program for a great power.

What is worse, Iran is already set for a take-over of Iraq and the cutting up of that country between the Kurds and some of the other elements. Iraq, cutting straight across the Tigris-Euphrates Valley comes perilously close to Lebanon and Syria and the Mediterranean. . . .

The Truman Administration will go down in history as the Administration which lost the Far East. It will be lucky if it does not add to its record honors in losing the Near East as well. The only defense for them is that the Republicans would have lost it a little faster.

September 22, 1952

Landed in Europe August 21 . . . At Lisbon installations of Raret —radio station of Radio Free Europe . . . A few days in Munich going over installations . . . thence to Strasbourg—Collège de L'Europe Libre . . . I gave one lecture at the university in French and an evening seminar, but mainly it was straight organization work . . . the plane to New York, arriving the 17th [of September].

The Free Europe University in Exile, an affiliate of the National Committee for a Free Europe, was incorporated under the Education Law of the State of New York in 1951. Berle was Chairman of the Board. The corporation planned to provide "suitable educational facilities and instruction upon the level of college and postgraduate work for persons presently in exile from regions behind the Iron Curtain who, because of their non-citizen status in the countries of their sojourn, are unable to obtain adequate assistance and facilities; to maintain this institution financially; to carry on its operations in the United States and in foreign countries; and to operate branch offices in foreign countries as needed. . . ."

September 22, 1952

Monday, the 22nd, a date with Adlai Stevenson. This being at his request. I found a very tired man who writes his own speeches (he hasn't time but hasn't found that out yet), is somewhat jammed up with the New York situation which, however, is very badly mixed anyhow. He is optimistic but says that people only tell him good news.

This was merely to pass the time of day. He asked me to write some things for him which I agreed to try to do. . . .

Stevenson is likable and liked. But is a man of the head more than of the powerful personality; he probably has a clearer gift of analysis than Roosevelt but not that tremendous, blazing power of communication. In point of fact, it is anybody's guess how this campaign comes out. . . .

September 24, 1952

Stevenson asked me to send to him directly some drafts of things I thought ought to be said. . . .

Reflecting on it, my present feeling is this:

1. The campaign has been primarily defensive: no new measure has been proposed, no addition to any moral or intellectual impulse has been provided other than what may proceed out of Stevenson's own dryly humorous personality. Stevenson, in terms of somebody else, is a more literate, politically experienced man than Eisenhower; a man more sensitive to public ethics than Truman; a man more aware of the human problems than the Republicans; with a Democratic Party more willing to make headway against self-interest lobbies, and so forth. A really great campaign develops its own logic and its own spiritual impulses and correspondingly liberates forces in its own right.

2. Foreign Relations. These could be and I think should be stated in positive terms rather than negative. You do build up families of nations. You do slant the economic assistance needed towards the building of the

great regional federations. You do work towards making these regional federations as cleanly pure in terms of representing their peoples as possible. You do thus make them able to defend themselves—as a clean country like Finland did—and able to communicate their growing strength across the Iron Curtain.

You do maintain the strength of the United Nations as an instrument for bringing these great regional organisms into a common system.

You do not commit yourself to giving the kind of government we personally would like to every country outside the Iron Curtain, but you do make it clear that cooperation is easiest and most useful where the aim of the government is most clearly recognized as being simultaneous welfare and liberation of its people.

You build forces to maintain such a system against armed attack, and use force where necessary.

You do propose the principle of *Pax Gentium,* which is deeper and stronger than the mere peace of nations.

3. Domestic Economy. You do recognize quite clearly the facts of life in American economy: it is concentration, it is tremendous productiveness. You note that the technical progress is enormous, and indeed barely unveiled. You note that technical progress, scientific development is not in any sense "inventiveness": it is the heritage of a generation of thought and work. The accident of war research has led to a situation in which much of the new development has to be in the hands of the United States Government—not as a result of socialist theory—but as a result of defense needs. You state as a definite objective your intent to steer and direct this huge mass of new, going knowledge into civilian life and its enrichment as rapidly as possible, pointing out that dynamite, invented as a munition of war, has helped to construct a thousand projects and that it has destroyed few.

You do believe that with this there is a powerful instrument capable of ameliorating, if not preventing, economic depressions, and capable of assisting every nation or people willing to educate its youth. You say, in a word, that you tackle the job of the 20th Century Revolution, and you think that the Communist Revolution of the 19th Century really belongs in a museum.

4. Possibly, you really tackle the relationships between American industry and the American state. You try to assimilate them, what's more, to the business of economic service of the state rather than to mere money-making units, though you do not oppose their making money if they can. Try to push in the idea that the man making steel is working for the United States much more than he is working for Ernest Weir, or James Farrell; that men working on electronics are working for the United States as well as for RCA or GE, and these men are entitled to the same honor and subject to the same duties as public servants anywhere.

To Stevenson, October 1, 1952

On current reactions to date: you can keep on pitching the level of speeches high. At least in the cities, people like it.

Something has to be done to lift the campaign to a somewhat higher level. I have tried my hand in the memorandum enclosed which might be useful as a short section when you are discussing foreign affairs. It is a reasonable interpretation of the broad outlines of our foreign policy for the past three or four years, adopted substantially when Bob Lovett [Secretary of Defense; former Under Secretary of State] activated the Chapultepec agreements in Latin America and laid the foundation for NATO. I should be less than human if I resisted the temptation to note that these policies were violently opposed by most of the State Department from 1944 to 1947, or thereabouts, and those of us who wished them then were rather unkindly dealt with. But events sometimes impose truth. There is, I think, a clear pattern to follow. There is wide public demand for some outline of the pattern during this campaign and you are in an excellent position to do it. I do not think the obvious political arguments—that Eisenhower worked on NATO and so forth—need deter you. If he is lured into talking foreign affairs, all the better: he could start debating with [Senator Robert A.] Taft [R., Ohio].

To Stevenson, October 1, 1952

Regarding the New York situation:
You do not suffer from the split between the Democrats and the Liberals and about six subsidiary splits in the Democratic machine. . . .

This situation existed in FDR's time when he regularly carried the state. Separate organization of what is now the Liberal Party was, of course, his idea. . . ..

Anything you can do upstate will help. The St. Lawrence Seaway is the popular issue there: only the most liberal handling of electric power will assure the continued growth of the upstate counties.

There was excellent reaction to your speech last night.

October 17, 1952
Miguel A. Magaña came to see me today: he is with the United Nations and is Secretary General of the Democratic Revolutionary Party in El Salvador.

This party is presently in power.

He said that the government of El Salvador is thoroughly worried and unhappy about the situation in Guatemala. This is a Communist government, net: hardly even disguised. They captured on the border the documents shipped in from Moscow and headed for El Salvador via Guatemala, setting up organization to eventually seize El Salvador's government. They have likewise been intercepting steady shipment of arms into Guatemala; these arms were all Czechoslovak. (The Czechoslovaks steadily supplied arms for the guerrilla risings all over the world.)

He said that he had reason to believe that an attempt to overthrow the present government in Guatemala might be made as early as December of this year. He implied that this movement would have the sympathy and perhaps the direct support of the governments of Salvador and Honduras.

. . . Unquestionably, he wanted at least a sympathetic attitude by the United States Government. . . .

I told him that in my view the Communist government in Guatemala was a clear-cut intervention by a foreign power, in this case the Soviet Union. I personally did not consider the Communist movement there as an American movement at all. The social reforms and so forth which are needed can be very well done by indigenous movements or by American movements: here so-called social amelioration is nothing more than a selling argument for a Russian-controlled dictatorship. It seemed to me that there was perfectly sound ground for the United States to invoke the Act of Chapultepec and the Treaty of Rio de Janeiro, pledging all hands to defend against domination from without the hemisphere.

What this really comes to, of course, is that the Guatemalan Government, which is heavily Communist infiltrated, has made an attempt to seize the government of El Salvador, and has been temporarily blocked. The United States has temporized with the situation and the local neighbors are planning direct action. They rather hope we will welcome it.

I think we should welcome it, and if possible guide it into a reasonably sound channel. Certainly the Council on Foreign Relations the other night agreed generally that the Guatemalan Government was Communist, and that it was merely carrying out the plan laid out for it by Oumansky ten years ago.

I am arranging to see Nelson Rockefeller, who knows the situation and can work a little with General Eisenhower on it; I will endeavor to do the same thing for Stevenson.

Telegram to Stevenson, October 22, 1952

Can you not say something in your Eastern tour about the Western hemisphere and the other American nations? Wide comment in Latin American press indicates apprehension and worry because neither candidate has even alluded to the hemisphere. It would be sufficient to pay tribute to the half century spent in building the Pan American conception of the Good Neighbor policy and to the Treaty of Rio de Janeiro as forerunner of the European and Asiatic defense pacts.

Telegram to Stevenson, October 22, 1952

The principal chain of Brazilian papers asks a statement from you on Brazilian relations for publication. Am informed General Eisenhower is releasing a similar statement. Am airmailing possible statement to Arthur Schlesinger which might be used if you agree.

To Stevenson, October 27, 1952

You were kind enough to ask me what can be done about Indochina: I told you I wanted to study it. Attached, a brief memorandum. . . .

INDOCHINA POLICY

The Indochinese question is a large detail of a much larger picture. Public take-off for policy in Asia should be a square declaration by the President that U.S. policy is to assert emergence of an independent Asia, the West asking only that it shall not conquer its neighbors. Our record—independence for the Philippines, maintenance, despite conquest, of the independence of Japan, encouragement of independence for Indonesia—is excellent.

Special status must be given Malaya, which controls a major international waterway.

Before announcing general policy, detailed application, as in Indochina, must be well worked out.

ASSUMPTIONS:

(a) France cannot indefinitely defend her position in Indochina against a well-organized, general Indochinese opposition; still less when it is aided by Communist China;

(b) U.S., given present military commitments, cannot now commit to all-out participation in a war in Indochina which, like the Korean War, may be lost, but cannot be won without conquest or conversion of Communist China. Weakening Communist China's military potential and draining Russian military supplies does not compensate for American sacrifices and tends to bind China to the Soviet Union.

It follows the primary solutions must be political. . . .

Considerations:

1. Direct intervention by the U.S. in the Indochinese war would mean a second Korea, and might transmute present "limited" action into an unlimited war against China. . . .

2. Yet the present situation in Indochina, as well as in Korea, cannot continue indefinitely: either the wars have to be won, or we shall have to retire to a line which can be defended. . . .

3. There is doubt the French alone will successfully defend Indochina indefinitely. . . .

Any defense can be successful only if overwhelming Indochinese sentiment is wholehearted for defense—at the moment this is not the case.

4. The conclusion must be that a major political counter-force must be created which can and will do its own work, with some assistance from us. Apparently this force must base on Asiatic nationalism, built around India and renascent Japan. . . .

5. With this policy of direct promise of independence even military failure and eventual conquest by the Communist groups leaves the United States in better moral position than would unsuccessful defense of the French empire, or failure to move at all.

6. [Donald R.] Heath, our quite able Ambassador in Saigon, ought to be flanked by men who can work directly with the Indochinese people irrespective of their politics, placing the United States on the "right" instead of on the "wrong" side of the current national revolution. Here, [Ambassador to India and Nepal] Chester Bowles's advice would be good.

\# \# \#

In Indochina, as elsewhere, the problem is to make the Western World the best friend of legitimate anti-colonial nationalism. We did this in the Philippines and Indonesia, and appreciably in India. It could be done in Indochina. This could be made major policy, both for us and for Western Europe.

November 5, 1952

I listened to the election returns at the Liberal Party headquarters with David Dubinsky; it was almost exactly twenty years since I had watched the beginning of the era with Franklin Roosevelt.

Now we have a new one beginning. General Eisenhower as nearly as I can find out will try to govern with the help of the more intelligent side of American big business; he will quite soon find himself at odds with the extremist element in his own party. Politics is a tragic business at best.

A tiny detail in the general picture but of interest locally is the fact that the Liberal Party, casting about 460,000 votes for George Counts [author; Professor of Education] and more than 400,000 in New York City, becomes now a clear major factor in city affairs, so we shall have to go to work on a city ticket almost at once.

Granted reasonable luck in that, I am hoping to drop out of the Chairmanship of the Liberal Party after the city campaign.

In defeat, Adlai Stevenson becomes a very appealing character personally. He could not carry the burden of a rotten Truman Administration and a foreign policy which has made as big mistakes as can be made, and has had a disastrous seven years.

Probably in American political history the biggest fact is the shift of much of the Solid South, towards conservatism, from the Democratic Party. The Republican Party is once more, therefore, a solid conservative party; it remains to be seen whether the Democratic Party has the intelligence to make itself a clean, unified, moderate liberal party. . . .

To Stevenson, November 7, 1952

It is not often that a Presidential loser comes out of a campaign greater than when he went in, and still rarer that a defeat guarantees a prominent position in national life. Both of these happened to you and you owe it to the sincerity and honor of your campaign. On the personal side, you have every reason to be congratulated. . . .

November 17, 1952

On Thursday (November 13), at lunch C. D. Jackson [Vice President, Time Inc.] observed that he had to produce a "dynamic plan", promised by General Eisenhower during his campaign, designed to push the Russians back rather nearer their original quarters. He had contemplated a task force [which became the Jackson Committee] composed of Bill Jackson [lawyer; former Deputy Director, CIA], himself and myself but now discovered that Bill Jackson is in the hospital. "Our hero" volunteered to draft a tentative working paper as a mark to shoot at: but as Huckleberry Finn says, "not feeling brash." . . .

January 21, 1953

The Eisenhower Administration came in yesterday, the Truman Administration going out. It is interesting to note that it bases its claim to fame on its conduct of foreign affairs.

As to that:

(a) In the hour of victory, it wholly misconceived the Russian position, and ceded mid-Europe to the Communist power up to 1947.

(b) They misconceived the Communist position in Asia, losing most of the Asiatic mainland, the Korean war being the line of resistance.

(c) Until 1947, they fought tooth and nail against developing regional groups and alliances and were less than kind to those of us who sought to build them, first in the Western Hemisphere and then elsewhere, including Europe. This, indeed, was one of the grounds for the bitter struggle in the State Department in 1944–45.

In 1947–48, Lovett, who is not a fool, established the present basis, Acheson then being out of office. Coming into office in 1949, he reversed all previous positions, which was the right thing to do—and bases his claim to fame really on hard work, endeavoring to put into practice the principles he fought when they might have done the most good. Well, such is fame, and such is life. . . . Obviously we shall never know how much a different course would have prevented this damage; it is clear, however, that the policies we pursued during the three years after victory, and of victory, contributed mightily to unhappiness and the present national danger. . . .

February 16, 1953

A committee of the Twentieth Century Fund: [Professor John Kenneth] Galbraith [Harvard], [Professor Franz L.] Neumann [Columbia], [Professor David B.] Truman [Columbia], myself, met to see if we could get at a scientific development of political science, using economics as a take-off. A tough assignment and I could not see that it got very far.

February 17, 1953

Nelson Rockefeller telephoned. . . . Arrived at Cell 13 [13 West 54 St.; see March 20, 1952 entry] about 6:00, he came in agitated about the Latin American situation. Brazil is in debt for dollars and has no exchange; a loan has been arranged; the Eisenhower Administration has indicated that it may not go through with the loan; the Brazilian Ambassador can get nobody; he came to visit Nelson. Actually the situation was worse than we thought because the next morning some importer got out an attachment on the Brazilian reserve in the Federal Reserve Bank. At all events, things are going from bad to worse. Nelson called to find out if I could get the Eisenhower Administration to do something about it, working via the Jackson Committee. I said I would get to work on it—this means getting the Jackson Committee to work alongside of Nelson. But it is queer: the Republicans getting an opposition member to push policy through their own Administration. . . .

April 1, 1953

. . . I went to Central America with Beatrice and Peter [March 19–26]. . . .

Arrived in Nicaragua, we were met by my old friend, Luis Manuel Debayle. He is brother-in-law of the dictator, [Anastasio] Somoza. In 1936 he had mobilized his political adherents and thrown out his uncle who was President and put in his brother-in-law instead. I think the deal was that Somoza would stay one term and then Luis Manuel would succeed him; but Somoza stayed. . . .

Dinner at the club with a party of people including the American Ambassador [Thomas E. Whelan] and his wife. . . . Nobody in the American Embassy speaks Spanish; they rely on their Nicaraguan clerks. Naturally they have little political standing in the country though Ambassador Whelan gets on well with the palace and has some political shrewdness.

The next day, to León in the hills by gasoline car over the railroad. . . .

The old matriarch [Debayle's mother] is amazing. They gave us the courteous honor of a family dinner at which we were the only non-relatives; tongues gradually unlocked and the flood of dislike of the dictator and his corruption and his libertinism and so forth grew as the meal progressed. . . .

Next morning we walked around the markets and one thing and another; I was trying to pick up the reaction on the street. . . . [An] Englishman [whom we visited] set out the Somoza policy of monopolies, the result being that practically no one can sell any produce except to state monopolies owned by Somoza, naturally at the monopoly price. . . .

The next day to go over the Pan American highway with the American road builder, a good New Hampshire man by the name of Adams from Lincoln, N.H., and on the whole the most knowledgeable American I found in Nicaragua. Then to a cocktail party at the American Embassy; all Americans. . . . Luis Manuel and his wife the only Nicaraguans. Good fun but we might as well have been in Fargo as in Nicaragua. . . . Much talk about [José] Figueres in Costa Rica, who was thought to be a Communist. . . . I was sceptical; we decided to change reservations and go to Costa Rica.

Which next day we accordingly did, arriving at sunset. The difference between Costa Rica and Nicaragua is amazing: a thriving, up and coming little country, trim and well-kept as Latin American countries go; a contrast to the relatively down-at-heel condition in Nicaragua. . . .

March 24 . . . [I] immediately telephoned Dr. Figueres; he kindly sent his car and I went to his house. With him was Dr. [Gonzalo] Facio, lawyer and brain truster. . . .

The Somoza government considered Figueres a Communist. So did some of the men in the American Embassy. Since he is very likely to be the next President of Costa Rica, this was important. My connections with him through Padre [Benjamín] Nuñez [Costa Rican Ambassador to the UN] in New York did not suggest Communism and I wanted to find out.

I went straight to the bat. I said that I was in a wholly private capacity; like all Americans, I was worried about the Guatemalan situation. I said the United States could not permit a Kremlin-Communist government on this continent and had to undertake a policy. Of course, we expected American rights to be protected, including the United Fruit Company; but the United Fruit Company interests were secondary to the main interests. I had been told that Figueres' judgment was the best in Central America on it and wanted to know what he felt.

Figueres, having sized me up, was equally direct. He said that he and all his friends fully recognized that a Kremlin-Communist government in this hemisphere was impossible. Actually he and all his friends were grateful that the United States offered protection against that sort of thing. He had fought the Communists in Costa Rica; expected to continue to do so; was, if possible, even more concerned about them than we were because in Central America they can be a great danger. . . .

I said we hoped for a Central American solution. Obviously a brigade of Marines would do the trick at once but then we were back to the dangerous days and no one wanted military intervention. I had spent a good deal of my life liquidating the earlier ones, as he knew.

He said that he considered military intervention out of the picture— the real need was for a type of moral intervention in which the United States as a democratic power stood with democratic forces of necessity against Communist totalitarianism. He considered that there were two possible alternatives in Guatemala: to induce President [Jacobo] Arbenz, a weak, compromising citizen, to shift, throw out the Communists and put in a democratic government; or, alternatively, to await the appropriate time until elements in Guatemala were prepared to deal with the Communists by force. He thought the first ought to be tried though he made it clear that he had not too much hope from Arbenz. . . .

. . . He was clear Costa Rica could work with El Salvador. He did not think that Costa Rica could work with Nicaragua under present conditions. Somoza, he pointed out, was the symbol of corruption. His own people would leave him if he tried to tie up there. . . .

Generally speaking, his view was that the three or four Central American republics could pull themselves together, make a straight determination that a Communist government would not be permitted in Central America; let loose all of the propaganda they could and gather their own friends in Guatemala. . . .

Figueres said he was visiting the United States in May. He knew no one in the government except Tommy Mann. I said I hoped he would let me know when he was coming and I would try to see that he met some of the people.

#   #   #

Although it is alleged that America is not popular in Central America, I notice that ever present desire of every President there for the prestige of association with and support by the United States.

Memorandum to the Jackson Committee, March 31, 1953

The Guatemalan Problem in Central America.

Preliminary

The President's Committee is unquestionably fully informed about the situation prevailing in Guatemala and Central America. Accordingly no fact statement is here given. But if there is any gap in information, prompt summary report can unquestionably be had from the Department of State and from CIA giving the substance of the situation.

The Problem

Guatemala presents a genuine penetration of Central America by Kremlin Communism. While the President, Arbenz, claims not to be a Communist, he is estimated to be an opportunist and his government is, for practical purposes, dominated by Communists, both Guatemalan and from other parts of the hemisphere. . . . (The situation results from the careful advance planning done by the Russian Ambassador, Oumansky, during his lifetime and carried forward by his successors.)

Guatemala is apparently in the initial phases of a Communist take-over—that is, government penetration has been well effected; local organization in the country is fairly well advance; a substantial group of her intellectuals are under Communist control; probably arms are cached secretly at some points; though formal Communisation has not yet begun, the familiar initial stage of so-called "agrarian reform," etc., is now being carried forward.

There is, however, a gap. The Guardia (army) apparently has not been brought under control. There still is raw material (though divided) for a substantial opposition movement.

The precise problem is how to clear out the Communists.

The Alternatives

The United States cannot tolerate a Kremlin-controlled Communist government in this hemisphere. It has several possible alternatives:

(1) American armed intervention—like that of 1915.

This is here ruled out except as an extremely bad last resort, because of the immense complications which it would raise all over the hemisphere.

(2) Organizing a counter-movement, capable of using force if necessary, based on a cooperative neighboring republic. In practice, this would mean Nicaragua. It could hardly be done from Mexico, and neither Salvador nor Honduras appears strong enough, though they might help. . . .

Agreed Central American "Political Defense" Action

The course of action I should recommend is slower, less dramatic, but I think more complete. This is to work out a Central American "Political Defense" action, using the three states El Salvador, Nicaragua and Costa

Rica as chief elements, with what help can be obtained from Honduras. . . .

The key to such action, oddly enough, seems to be Costa Rica. There, according to general opinion, the summer's elections will result in putting in as President, José Figueres. He has been attacked by the Somoza government as Communist. Some of our Embassy people in Nicaragua (though they do not know him) regard him so. Reflections of this probably appear in the State Department reports. (Some of these reports need not be taken too seriously. In our Embassy in Nicaragua, for example, there is not a single senior officer who speaks Spanish fluently: they rely on bilingual clerks and their Nicaraguan help. Their contacts are thus limited.) I should judge him as an anti-Communist liberal Democrat about comparable with Senator Lehman of New York. Figueres has a strong hold on the younger intellectuals all over Central America; he is the recognized symbol of "democracy." Since he seemed to loom so large in this picture, I went to Costa Rica and saw him. . . .

Visiting him, I raised the question of the Guatemalan situation. He said he had been likewise worrying about it. He considered that if the Communists established themselves in Guatemala nothing in Central America would be safe, least of all his own group. He said he did expect to be elected President of Costa Rica. It was stated he could take it by force if not elected but he wanted none of that: for one thing, he did not need it. Once President, one of his first jobs was to see that the Communist and Peronist agitators got out of the country and stayed out.

As to Guatemala, he said that he thought Arbenz was not a Communist but that he was an opportunist and probably a fellow-traveller. . . . He said there were only two courses to pursue: either help along a movement to throw Arbenz out; or detach Arbenz from the Communists, and then staff his government for him. He believed in trying the latter first. . . . He wound up by saying that he was coming to the U.S. in May. I said I hoped to meet him then. It may be added that Figueres, American-educated, talks better English than most Americans. He obviously was in touch with such opposition elements as there were in Guatemala, in Nicaragua, and in Tegucigalpa.

I asked whether he thought of any immediate steps.

He said that he thought of one merely as a point of approach. The United Fruit Company was under heavy attack in Guatemala. This he considered merely a pretext for the Communists. There were plenty of issues between Central American governments and United Fruit but none that could not be worked out on a reasonable basis. He thought of getting together the three Central American governments in which United Fruit operates (this excludes Nicaragua) and endeavoring to bat out a common policy for the protection and handling and fair adjustment of interests with United Fruit, using this as a point of approach to get Honduras, El Salvador and Costa Rica together. . . .

I relate this at length because it is of some importance in working out a plan. Of the men who have or are likely to get popular support in Central America, Figueres is easily the most dynamic, and I should think the fairest-minded. As between betting on him and betting on a senescent dictatorship in Nicaragua, I should immensely prefer the one democracy which has made its way, has done its work on the whole fairly well, and has a large measure of popular respect and good will. . . .

The Method of Action

To carry out this plan or any similar plan some shifts in organization have to be handled up here.

There is not, in any of the Central American Embassies, a first-class student of Spanish-American affairs, or a man who is a figure in the hemisphere in his own right. This is no attack on the present Ambassadors. All have their qualities and do a better than average job in keeping on good terms with the governments to which they are accredited, inducing these governments to follow American lead in the United Nations, and so forth. But no American Embassy is close to the people of these countries; and no American representative has sufficiently gained their confidence and good will to be a political force in his own right.

Also, our five Central American Embassies act separately. They rarely, if ever, consult on matters of mutual interest. They only articulate their action through Washington. A theatre commander for a job like the Guatemalan operation does not, apparently, exist in Central America.

So the *first* job is to get a theatre commander for the operation. . . .

The job of local political organization should be split. Guatemala is an unfriendly country and our own people—or Costa Ricans or Salvadorians friendly to us—ought to go in and organize in the country. This would have to be sub-rosa. In the other countries whose governments will be brought to cooperate, the organization can be in the open and it should be done by nationals of those countries.

This last calls for a word. Two facts stand out:

(1) Propaganda without local organization to act on it is worthless. . . .

(2) Organization within a country must be organization of residents and nationals *of that country*. . . .

Second. A quiet understanding should be reached between the governments of Costa Rica, Salvador, Honduras and at least some powerful elements in Nicaragua. This last, I think, can be done.

Third. Some powerful Central American figure—I suggest Figueres—should be encouraged to take leadership and deal with the problem, all-out.

The result ought to be an organization of a party of Democratic Defense in the five Central American republics, taking as its first job the clearing out of the Communists in Guatemala.

April 23, 1953

Jack Javits would like to be Mayor. . . . I discussed it last night with David Dubinsky. We all agreed that Jack Javits, if he was prepared to go out and fight Dewey, would probably be the hero of the occasion and he probably would be elected. But leaving the Republican Party is like asking a Catholic to leave the Church.

May 5, 1953

Max Ascoli came in to dinner before his trip to Europe. He has been surveying the political scene and more especially [Senator Joseph] McCarthy [R., Wis.] and his friends. He has a notion that there is somewhere behind all this a growing unity of sorts which will eventually ferment into something closely akin to an American Fascist movement but he cannot locate it. There is a clear common line taken by parts of the Hearst papers and the upstate magazine, *The Freeman,* certainly the extremist veterans associations, and so on. . . .

May 25, 1953

Friday, May 22, Dr. Figueres met me at the Century Club for a farewell call (he was leaving for Costa Rica on Sunday). John McClintock, Assistant Vice President of United Fruit, and Kenneth Redmond, President of United Fruit, came in—at their request. The background was that John McClintock (an old friend of mine from State Department days) had received a telephone call from Tommy Mann, who is [Assistant Secretary of State for Inter-American Affairs] Jack Cabot's deputy in the State Department. They had been talking to Figueres [at the request of Berle].

The talk ranged over a wide number of subjects, but the primary question was Guatemala. Figueres said . . . he was prepared to assist an anti-Communist liberal movement in Guatemala.

He said the alternatives were either changing the mind of Arbenz, President of Guatemala, or changing the government. The last, quite bluntly, meant violence—i.e., a revolution. He had no idea of facing that question until the first question had been thoroughly explored. His idea was, therefore, straight political action. . . .

But, said Figueres, you might as well realize that Guatemala has been a military dictatorship for 150 years. Ultimately the Army controls things . . . [a liberal leader would need] not only the backing of an organized party but a situation in which the Army did not promptly throw him out. . . .

I said that possibly I could be of some help there. Guatemala was a member of the Inter-American organization: The Inter-American General Staff was created for the precise purpose of preventing invasion of the hemisphere either by military or by political action; Stalinist Communist infiltration like that going on in Guatemala was squarely within the line of aggression contemplated by the Act of Chapultepec and the Treaty of Rio. I said that it seemed to me that the American military mission and the Inter-American General Staff arrangements made at Washington furnished a line of contact with the Guatemalan forces for any proper action taken to protect the hemisphere.

Figueres agreed that this would be a line to explore. . . .

Figueres thought that the ultimate solution was creating better standards of living in Guatemala. He proposed to do this in Costa Rica. The talk then fell on the position of United Fruit. Delicately, he felt for some partnership arrangement with United Fruit—United Fruit did not seem very receptive. He then spoke of buying one of the United Fruit projects—United Fruit countered with the suggestion that it be distributed to small landowners. Figueres wisely dropped the subject there, saying that this was a matter which unquestionably could be negotiated. He likewise said that he hoped that practical men could discuss these matters in the spirit of give and take—if he became President of Costa Rica, he hoped that United Fruit would feel free to do so with him and, of course, he the same.

We parted with the usual expressions of mutual esteem.

Note added by Berle later: "I am very much impressed with Figueres. He looks to me like a first-rate, level-headed anti-Communist liberal."

May 29, 1953

Jim Farley wants a speech written for Colgate. I told him I would do it. . . .

David Dubinsky has agreed to write an article for the New York Times entitled "What is the Alternative to McCarthyism?"—he has a splendid article, except the alternative. He asked me if I would draft up something. I told him I would do it.

I have heard that C. D. Jackson wants some suggestions likewise for something Eisenhower will have to say on the subject of the unified world. Even the best public figure needs to have a scenario written for him but the real question is what to write.

June 2, 1953

Last night the officers of the Liberal Party interviewed Jack Javits as a possible candidate for Mayor. The problem is whether we get a Republican or an independent. Jack is trying to be both. . . .

June 26, 1953

Comment: It was perfectly clear to me that the Republicans were not prepared at this time to accept Mr. Javits and that they still wanted to keep the idea of Hogan open, and that they probably are unable to consider Mr. Javits at all, and that Mr. Tuttle was maneuvering to try to put the responsibility for a break on the Liberal Party. . . .

July 1, 1953

The Liberal Party City Convention met at 8:00. I reviewed the situation, carefully not tipping the scales. The rest of them reported that the Policy Committee had set on Halley. Not a single shot was fired for Javits. . . .

We are getting John Pelenyi [Professor of Political Science at Dartmouth College] as President of the Collège de l'Europe Libre in Strasbourg. . . .

September 22, 1953

RFE and NCFE have been having themselves a time. The second-in-command of the Polish Delegation, Dr. Marek Korowicz, a very respected professor of public law at the University of Cracow, defected almost as soon as he got here and put himself in our custody. He has been all over the newspapers since—and so has RFE. There will be more incidents of that kind during the next few months.

Of less spectacular but more fundamental importance is the fact that the research organizations now working out a possible standard for satellite countries as they emerge have it pretty well forward. We are studying all the angles for tieing them into a growing mechanism of united Europe —that is, the Council of Europe at Strasbourg, the European Payments Union, the European Defense Community [Jean Monnet's] steel and iron group, possibly the European Army, and so forth. This time at least we will not leave an empire adrift again, as we did after Versailles.

October 2, 1953

At NCFE matters are quietly moving along. Just as the idea of "East European Federation" exploded there and is now a national policy, the second idea exploded last Spring—integration of the European union—is likewise bearing fruit. The proposal now is to institute consultation with representatives of the West European powers. Some think this merely a form of approach towards a solution of boundary and other questions between Germany and the East European states. Others (of which I am one) want a real approach towards the European union solution. The danger of bilateral arrangements with Germany is that the Adenauer government may not last forever. As long as [Chancellor Konrad] Adenauer himself is in the saddle we should have a clear, moderate and forward-looking attempt at a solution. But we have seen German governments change their nature before. The debate is today in the Board of Trustees.

The municipal campaign—pretty uninspiring—is warming up. Truman endorsed Wagner [for Mayor] and Adlai Stevenson may do the same thing. I doubt if this would help Wagner much or affect the result. But it is a bit pathetic to see the fidelity with which these fellows hang on to the discredited wreck of the Democratic city machines.

October 28, 1953

Celebration of the declaration of Czechoslovakian independence (1918). This was a concert in Carnegie Hall preceded by a speech by Joe Grew and by C. D. Jackson. C. D. Jackson stated the policy of the United States: we were all for independence of these East European countries. But we also realize that they could not eat by themselves, and could not raise armies sufficient to deter invasion. Therefore they had to work together . . . the amusing thing to me was to see that some ideas conceived in a bathtub three or four years ago have now emerged as policy of the United States. This is not to say that we have got there yet.

1953

November 4, 1953

The election yesterday came out about as I had expected: the Liberal Party cast about 470,000 votes [for Halley]; Wagner was elected by a large plurality but still less than a majority of the total vote. Since the registration was low, a great many of the independents did not get into the act: the basic Liberal Party strength increased, but it still is not enough. . . .

I took my son, Peter Adolf, along to see the show, and meet the gang. He had all the drama of an election night: the tragedy of Halley bowing out, with hopes collapsed, but some good manners remaining. The feeling of the idealists who supported him: ideals don't die because they are defeated. The disappointment of the self-seeking politicians; the grim irony of old Jim Farley, first manager for FDR, Sr., hating the young son; the friendly informality of FDR, Jr., reminiscent of his father's charm, but covering young FDR's cold calculation as to where he stood; his friendliness due in part to the fact that he knew without being told the Tammany majority of New York was too small to make him Governor unless the Liberal vote stood alongside. The side calculations: maybe he would get it anyway; better be friendly to the leaders and see what happens.

Peter understood it as he went; I could explain it a little; he may not have use for the lesson but it makes for understanding of the universe. . . .

November 17, 1953

. . . On Monday, November 16, a telephone call came in from Robert Morris, Counsel to the [Senator William] Jenner [R., Ind.] Committee investigating Communism in government. He wanted to know if I had any slant on [Attorney General Herbert] Brownell's accusation that Truman knowingly appointed a spy, Harry Dexter White, to the International Monetary Fund. . . . I told him that as he knew I had no knowledge whatever of the White case. He intimated that he really wanted to sum up and get some conclusions. . . . Nobody really knows, yet, what the FBI said White had done.

Berle, who was Chairman of the Board of Trustees of the Twentieth Century Fund from 1947 to the time of his death, reviewed the Fund's objectives in November 1953.

The effects of intellectual work are, really, incalculable: an idea expressed in a piece of intellectual work, however little known, may have significant causative effect if it falls into the right hands. Nevertheless, historically, the intellectual work which has been most causative has attained a moderately, and sometimes an extremely, wide circulation. One crude test of the probable utility of the Twentieth Century Fund books and studies may be, therefore, quantitative.

We have had five books with sale or circulation of more than 30,000 each:

The Road We Are Traveling	(Stuart Chase)
Goals for America—A Budget of Needs and Resources	(Stuart Chase)
Democracy under Pressure	(Stuart Chase)
Where Is the Money Coming From?	(Stuart Chase)
U.S.A.: Measure of a Nation	(an illustrated summary of *America's Needs & Resources,* by Carskadon & Modley)

The last named, with 50,000 circulation, is apparently more widely read than any other publication of ours. With it, of course, should be bracketed *America's Needs and Resources,* which, though it sold only 22,000, is a large and expensive book, parts of which have been so widely used, repeated, copied and cited, that the actual circulation of its material far transcends the sales figure. . . .

Certainly the figures do suggest that the largest target, and the area of most acute interest, is in synthesis and generalization. Apparently what people of all grades of intellectual development (including the highest) are seeking most is the kind of thinking, writing and studying which organizes an area so that the reader can find its application to him or his group, and his own bearings in it. When the area is as great as the entire economic development of the country (*America's Needs and Resources,* or the Stuart Chase studies), there is very vivid interest—often almost pathetically poignant in intensity. . . .

The point is this. If yearning and demand are any guide, the need of today is for philosophic generalization. More precisely, the hope is that the multitudinous phenomena of life which more or less obtrude themselves on the consciousness of everyone are made to appear (so far as explicable) in harmony with some system of order in the cosmos—rather than mere meaningless happenings in cosmic anarchy.

It will at once be asked whether the Twentieth Century Fund either should or can profess faith or take as a premise that there is order or design in the cosmos. That matter has usually been left to philosophers or theologians. The answer must be that, if there is no order in the cosmos, if there are no principles which have at least a degree of validity, if no phenomenon is relevant to any other phenomenon, there is no particular reason for the Twentieth Century Fund's indulging in research at all. We would better spend our money giving every college student in New York a free ticket to a baseball game or the opera once a year, and let it go at that. Research of the type we have attempted assumes as a necessary (if tacit) premise that there is philosophic order; that phenomena are related; that by describing, classifying and analyzing, methods and principles can be deduced; and that such methods can indicate and verify principles and that such principles can be employed to guide action. . . .

Where we have sought to solve spot problems, we have, I think, made contributions whose causative effect is difficult to assess. Probably the work we did in 1935 relating to the securities market was of some assistance in getting the S.E.C. away to a start. Unquestionably [Max Thornburg's] *Turkey: An Economic Appraisal* in 1949, though it only sold 2,700 copies, powerfully influenced American policy in Turkey and contributed mightily to the outstanding success of policy there as contrasted to policy in other countries. . . .

The end and aim of the Twentieth Century Fund is, of course, not to produce best sellers but to be useful. Note, however, may be taken of the fact that the most useful studies and books have actually been or become in time best sellers—Adam Smith's *Wealth of Nations,* Hobbes' *Leviathan,* Locke's *Human Understanding* will do as illustrations. In specialized fields, attempt to derive general principles produces similar effect. To take one illustration where I have personal knowledge: my own book, *The Modern Corporation,* with a circulation over twenty years of perhaps 35,000, was in a field in which the Twentieth Century Fund did a far better scientific piece of work, *Big Business: Its Growth and Its Place* (2,500 copies). The contrast perhaps illustrates the point. The former was really oriented to the position of Americans in a shifting American society; it made guesses as to where the corporate movement might take us. The Fund study meticulously examined and accurately stated a case. But people were not interested in the case—save as the statement demonstrated the right of the commentator to work out his philosophy.

The illustration tends to point up the conclusion. What we ought to hope for in the case of any study, however specialized, is a philosophical "appreciation" of the place of men in their environment, and of the effect which the subject matter under study may exert in that environment as it affects men. The scholarly work of providing the facts is useful precisely as it permits this sort of generalization. . . .

Are scholars, and particularly those we know best, willing to attempt and able to carry out this generalization? . . . This, I suggest, is a major question before the Twentieth Century Fund if it is to develop major usefulness in the research field. . . .

Note: It may be remembered that practically every scientific (and in some measure, economic) design has been foreshadowed by some such intuitive or artistic hypothesis. . . . For that matter, Adam Smith's *Wealth of Nations* was almost an intuitive hypothetical sketch of a free market economy drawn against the background of a feudal system then moribund, based on large generalizations from observation of the relatively secondary mercantile life of eighteenth century towns. . . .

November 30, 1953

Early November 24 to take the airplane with Beatrice and little Beatrice to Iceland, there to marry her to Dean Meyerson. There was really no point in their waiting several months more solely to have the wedding in Grace Church in New York. . . .

. . . on Saturday afternoon, November 28, they were married in the Laurgarneskirkja in Reykjavik in the dim half-light of a sub-Arctic winter. The Lutheran minister, Rev. Dr. Gardar Svavarssen, under the gaunt little white roof of the old Lutheran church, performed the ceremony, beginning with an Icelandic invocation and a prayer of his own: "There are many nations but only one God in whom all must live." Then in painfully exact and singularly impressive English went through the familiar ceremony. An Icelandic choir sang a wedding hymn in Icelandic which is as lovely music as I have ever heard. So it was done before God and this company. The company was small but not without its picturesque: the American Minister, Mr. [Edward B.] Lawson, and his wife (an old State Department man); the Danish Minister, Mme. [Bodil] Begtrup and her husband; the retired Danish Minister to Russia Bjornsson; the Danish Counsellor, [Viggo] Christiansson and his wife; Brigadier General Ralph O. Brownfield, Commander of the American Base at Keflavik, and his wife; and one or two officers. Also three or four Icelandic friends, including two women in Icelandic costume, black with silver embroidery and white fittings—a striking combination of the highest rank Iceland has to offer—and the simplest of Icelandic life. After that, a little reception in a private room at the small but very well kept Hotel Borg, Scandinavian in its simplicity and its cleanliness, with such hospitality as we could arrange. . . .

All emotions were complicated. Here we were on the Arctic edge of the western world, where the Russian and the American power zones intersect. Twelve years ago I had been part of the process of taking over protection of Iceland and this queer substitute for empire that is the American system was now maintaining it. Only that morning American planes left Keflavik scouting for Russian fishing boats, lying with anti-aircraft guns and heavy armament to the northeast, as Dean was taking my daughter in pledge. So we waved farewell to them as the gray mist rolled in from the North Atlantic with, I think, a happy life ahead through an Arctic winter.

The President of Iceland, Mr. Asgeir Asgeirsson, invited us to his house—a beautiful, simple Danish farmstead on the point beyond Reykjavik. He had been a part of the Icelandic delegation of 1941—the British dumped the problem of Iceland in the American lap, and it came in my charge. He and another member of the Cabinet had been at our house for dinner that night, and little Beatrice, then ten years old, had been there to pass the crackers with the cocktails. Now, a singularly impressive old man, with a library that would give credit to any student, was gravely talking of the opposition to Americans in Iceland, his disagreement with the opposition and his hope that he could convince those Icelanders who are not Communist (20% of the vote is Communist) that their very existence depended upon being within some cooperative framework. Also to the American Legation where the Minister and all his staff are suffering from the perpetual fear of all missions in far-away places— the fear of being forgotten. Iceland is in fact one of the three or four major strategic points in the northern defense. But because it is not Paris or London or Rome no one thinks of it. In the last State Department reorganization even their radio operator was taken away, so that the Minister gets no current news except from Icelandic newspapers and from what he can pick up from other legations—unless General Brownfield is kind enough to send up from Keflavik, an hour from Reykjavik, the current news, which he gets from Air Corps wireless.

Iceland itself is fascinating. The population of 150,000 have much in the sense of higher education, better living and lower infant mortality; lowest tuberculosis and venereal rates. The doctor took us over some of the public schools; I wished there were anything as well set up in New York; and the children are better looked after medically than any children anywhere. The University is imposing, and the little museum interesting. But all of it is dominated by the great dark mountains, the endless gray sea, and the shriek of the sea gulls, overhung by the limitless gray mist.

And yet—this is one of the oldest continuous cultures in the western world. Since the 9th century, Iceland has had its own language, its own poetry, its own writing, its own art. Reykjavik is a tiny variation of Copenhagen, multiplied by Ireland.

February 9, 1954

The Foreign Operations Administration . . . asked the Freedom Fund, Inc. to work on a project for a European cooperative bank. Freedom Fund is really run by Murray Lincoln and Harry Culbreth, my friends in Columbus. Included in the contract is a "security risk" clause. They then asked that one of the men Freedom Fund has on the job—[Vincent] Checchi—be fired as a security risk. The contract when finally negotiated includes the right to have charges stated in a hearing where this request is made. Charges against Checchi were made, they being merely that he had associated with three people of allegedly "pro-Communist" tendencies, and may have shared their views.

I represented Freedom Fund, and Checchi as their employee, and looked into the three.

One of them, Kay Daniels, is private secretary to Hugh Gaitskill, ranking member in the British Labour Party. . . .

The second man, [Walter] Gaumnitz, is Associate Dean of the School of Business Administration at the University of Minnesota.

I went to Washington last Thursday, filed an Answer on behalf of Checchi, and told Morris Wolf, Counsel for FOA, that I hoped we would not have to try the case. . . .

I did not tell him that in the event we have to have a hearing, my plan is to have every newspaperman in Washington around to listen to the fun. My impression is that the University of Minnesota as well as the British Labour Party will be there with bells on.

If the charges amounted to anything—that is, if Checchi ever had been a Communist or pro-Communist, it would be different. This is mere nth degree nonsense. . . .

Radio Free Europe keeps on going and we are beginning to get the work there pounding towards a positive political orientation—regional unification for East Europe and the gearing in of East Europe to a unified Europe—that is, of course, if Europe can be unified to any degree.

Now a split in the organization. One-half wants a violent campaign strictly in American interest. The other and more intelligent half wants a more cautious, better thought-out campaign: that we are presently pursuing. . . .

February 27, 1954

Last night to the house for dinner were August Heckscher and Chris Sonne [Treasurer, Trustee of Twentieth Century Fund] and their respective wives. August is Chief Editorial writer for the New York *Tribune* and he had been getting a blow-by-blow account of the McCarthy-[Robert T.] Stevens [Secretary of the Army] row. As he saw it, Stevens had first protested against McCarthy bullying Army officers and directing them to disobey regulations. [August] had written a bitter editorial which appeared yesterday morning and another published today. Mrs. Ogden Reid, a close personal friend of President Eisenhower, had been very unhappy but had stood right by him. The whole thing is a bitter business. . . .

March 3, 1954

. . . Today, Cord Meyer came to lunch. It was interesting to see the boy who was starry-eyed at united world federalism now working at sober reality through the CIA.

We talked over various ideas.

He and I think everyone in Washington is worried about the McCarthy situation. . . . The next row will come as between McCarthy and [Secretary of State John Foster] Dulles, since one of McCarthy's stooges, Scott McLeod, has been both security officer and personnel director in the State Department. In practice this meant that McCarthy and not Dulles was directing Foreign Service and the careers of the men in it. This morning Dulles announced that he had relieved McLeod as Personnel Director though keeping him as security officer. McCarthy has immediately served notice that he will demand an explanation (why, or on what constitutional grounds, only the Lord knows) and when Dulles gets back from Caracas he will either have to fight or run.

Meanwhile an inter-American conference has been convened at Caracas. It looks to me like a green crew with the single exception of Fletcher Warren, Ambassador at Caracas, who knows the score. He writes me that we should pray for him every night—which is about all that can be done.

March 29, 1954

Wednesday night (March 24) to Puerto Rico to work on the corporation laws. This was chiefly working with the Attorney General, Dr. [José] Trias [Monge]. . . .

. . . Governor [Luis] Muñoz Marín lifted the party, so we motored out to his little country place, and had dinner in a thatched summerhouse while occasional tropical storms pounded down from the hills. Besides Dr. Trias there was a Spanish poet, Dr. [Tomás] Blanco, and Chief

Justice [Cecil] Snyder of the Puerto Rican Supreme Court; and as always in a Spanish-American discussion between friends, it got down to philosophy of government. Muñoz was trying to work out in his mind what Puerto Rico was and what else could be done and made the point that if countries are to survive, they have to give up something for the purpose of conserving the freedoms that they really need. He was trying to think of hierocracy of levels. Thus, every country has to be a member of a radio wave community, else nobody could use a radio. But it does not want to give up its freedom to determine what use should be made in the country of radio waves: for example, to decide whether radio and television should be developed commercially, as in America, or extra-commercially, as in Britain. It has also to be a member of some kind of economic union in order to be able to live; also of some sort of a regional defense arrangement to protect itself. And so forth. He said when anything came up in Puerto Rico he tried to think whether this was a case where the real interests of the island demanded that it should assert its autonomy or that it should join with others. . . .

He is a great friend of Figueres in Costa Rica; and advised him to go to the Caracas Conference (advice Figueres did not take) and he hoped to be of help. Here in Puerto Rico, the Anglo-Saxon civilization has met the Spanish-American civilization, mixed with Negro and some Indian, and the result is wholly successful. That ought to prove something to somebody and the question is how we can make it most useful.

The Government of the island of Puerto Rico is perhaps the most interesting place now in the American complex. They are tackling their problems, and moving fast and the standard of living is rising more rapidly than in any other place in the world though it has some distance to go. . . .

April 9, 1954

Jane and Andrew Carey back from Ethiopia because, may God forgive us, the Security Service of the Foreign Operations Administration decided that Andy was a security risk because he had married Jane. The real reason was that they had invited Adlai Stevenson to dinner. Well, I suppose so. These are two conservative Republicans who had behaved approximately like human beings. It makes you a bit sick.

May 3, 1954

To Chicago on April 21st to give the Rosenthal Lectures. They seemed to go well. Likewise a conference at the University of Chicago on very high philosophy.

To Ann Arbor to see Alice and so back to Great Barrington by air on Saturday morning.

Much doing at RFE. . . .

May 10, 1954

Last weekend, May 1 or 2, I was having a quiet week before going to Maxwell Field [to discuss the interrelation of the Air Corps with political warfare]. President Figueres of Costa Rica telephoned; he wanted me to come to Costa Rica to talk. . . .

On Tuesday I talked to the Air War College with some added guests, trying to put up a case for developing techniques which could be used in advance and in aid of non-Communist governments attacked by force. Obviously whatever the announced study, we were all talking about Indo-China. . . .

I took the thesis that atomic warfare was unpredictable in its results, therefore neither side would resort to it except for retaliation, and probably only there if we should have contests on a local scale and should be prepared for that as well as for the necessary deterrent weapon. But I had a horrible feeling that we were missing something here: this is accepting the twentieth century on hydrogen terms.

Berle flew to Costa Rica from Maxwell Field. Figueres was worried about a number of problems which Berle helped to resolve on his return to the United States.

May 10, 1954

Don Pepe [Figueres] is a man of whom I am becoming inordinately fond. A philosopher, rather than a politician, a man of delicate sensibility, recently married to an American wife of Danish extraction (she is learning Spanish and being the President's wife at the same time). He is struggling with the fact that politics is not all saving your soul but of getting viable arrangements—even if your soul suffers as a result.

May 17, 1954

Daniel Oduber, Figueres' European observer, came in to breakfast this morning. I told him . . . I had been in Washington and I had ascertained that

(a) the United States government is no party to any movement of Somoza's against Costa Rica and would vigorously object;

(b) that they think Somoza has no real intention of moving against Figueres; they may be mistaken about that, but they would move in some fashion to assist Costa Rica in case of violation;

(c) they are not able to do very much about the possibility that Somoza may supply money and so on . . . but Oduber and Figueres both are clear that the Costa Rican government can take care of these groups;

(d) the leaving of the American Ambassador was merely coincidental: he is probably already back in Costa Rica;

(e) United Fruit Company is quite satisfied with the way the Costa Rican government is negotiating and it is no party at all to any Nicaraguan move. But Oduber tells me in fact that the United Fruit Company has already reached an agreement with Costa Rica on very fair and favorable terms so everyone is quite happy. . . .

A lovely pair of May days in the Berkshires. It is hard to work in that weather.

May 28, 1954

The Costa Rican situation is moving rather rapidly. Recently a shipment of arms from Communist-controlled Stettin was discovered to have been landed in Guatemala. Probably there have been prior shipments. . . .

Costa Rica, however, made a move to refer the matter to the Organization of American States, indicating that it likewise thoroughly appreciated the Communist menace (and not saying too much about the Nicaraguan mess) and got at least a courteous and rather laudatory reply from the Department of State—a little gesture but I think enough. I will try to arrange something a little better later on. . . .

June 7, 1954

On Saturday evening (I was up in the swamp) President Figueres called the Farm. When I finally got to the telephone he merely had to say that Costa Rica had signed its revised agreement with the United Fruit Company on terms which were a fair compromise, that the situation was coming along extremely well, and he merely called up to say "Thank you for some help." . . .

This battens down one hatch—if the hatch is battened down. . . .

The United Fruit contract is a great satisfaction. It shows that people of common-sense and good temper can get together even though they start from opposite points of view. I like to remember that Figueres and the United Fruit Company first met when he was here before his election at the Century Club.

Last week two interesting little dinners: one with Herschel Johnson [Ambassador to Rio, 1948–1953] confirms my own opinion that our Embassy in Brazil is in very bad shape; the other with Robert Lang, Director of Radio Free Europe. I was trying to suggest the possibility of the politics of conversion. There is no question that RFE is now the recognized head of the non-Communist opposition in great parts of Central Europe and that it can force changes in the governments and the policies both in Czechoslovakia and Hungary. The question now is how best to use the power. . . .

June 11, 1954

Last night my son was graduated from Friends' School. It is always a very simple and moving ceremony. The youngsters went off to have a party and I went off to the night's work. . . .

. . . last Thursday we had a meeting of the Policy Committee of the Liberal Party. Many questions were raised as to what the future of the Liberal Party should be. It is clear that we

   (a) could not take them all as a unit into the Democratic Party;

   (b) have no moral right at the moment to fold up;

   (c) could not expect vast expansion;

   (d) should not get into an endless string of local contests where we could hardly affect the result.

My own thinking runs along the lines of endeavoring to make the Democratic Party hospitable to the idea of a broad coalition (that is, abandonment of the Truman idea of "regularity") and see if we can find a common-ground status. This, I think, is the thing to discuss with [Tammany Hall leader] Carmine De Sapio. . . .

June 16, 1954

At the Finance Committee meeting of the Twentieth Century Fund, Chris Sonne and Charley Taft were present. After the meeting we chatted over the [J. Robert] Oppenheimer matter. Chris indicated delicately that he was President of the National Planning Association which did have close relations with the government. He had to balance a good many points of view. It might be difficult for him to stay on the same Board of Directors (Twentieth Century Fund) that Oppenheimer was on. I told him I thought this might be carrying things too far but this was entirely matter for him to decide.

I asked the views of both gentlemen as to whether we ought to say or do anything in the event of an adverse finding by the A.E.C. (which I think will occur). I said with some emphasis that my own view was that we ought to go about our business as usual. Oppenheimer was one of the great scientists of the world. As to his loyalty and discretion, they have been attested. The question is whether somebody wants him in a government position making policy—but this is not a question that we ought to consider since we do not make government policy, or have much to do with secret documents, or particularly seek that kind of thing. Further, any hostile move towards Bob would make enemies in all directions— and, on the evidence, it would be an inhuman thing to do.

Charley Taft cordially agreed. He said this business of applying government security regulations in their extreme form to private associations was being carried to an absurd degree.

We generally agreed that so far as the Twentieth Century Fund is concerned, we would take the line that Oppenheimer was a great scientist and a valuable member of the Board, and we are not concerned with government policy and that we saw no present reason to take any action. . . .

June 21, 1954

The Guatemalan revolution broke out. . . .

The Arbenz government has followed the line of the Leninist handbook almost without a break. Its last importation of arms was from Russian sources and probably paid for by the Russians; on its arrival at Guatemala the arms were not put into the hands of the Army but were used at least in part to arm the Indians and peasants of the back land. As far as I can make out, at the moment, the Guatemalan army is sitting on the sidelines and there is no substantial resistance; on the other hand, the Army has not revolted and deposed the government either. So things could go either way. My guess from here would be that the revolutionary forces under [Colonel Carlos] Castillo Armas will eventually take Guatemala City, but will find an armed guerrilla movement raised against them, Huk-Balahap style, in the hills.

The Soviet-Russian line is that the United States is behind all this and is so because it hates the Indians. This is obviously a bid for support from Indian and pro-Indian groups all the way from Peru to Mexico.

Guatemala appealed to the Security Council of the United Nations. It ought to be remembered that Nelson Rockefeller and I vested the jurisdiction for peace-keeping first in the Inter-American organization; and that the United Nations is not supposed to come into it until after the Inter-American organization has failed.

June 22, 1954

I have been reading the newspaper accounts of the Guatemalan revolution. The present prospects for the anti-Communist forces do not seem to me bright. I think that a good deal of money has been used, and that attempt was made to build a purely military force, and that it was believed that the political orientation of the [Castillo] Armas group was towards a Somozan dictatorship. It takes more than that to make any Latin American revolution.

More importantly, this is probably the beginning of revolutions—Asiatic-style—in Latin America. The next major emphasis will probably come in Bolivia.

I telephoned Jack Javits and asked him to make a date with the new Assistant Secretary of State for Latin American Affairs, a Texas lawyer named [Henry F.] Holland. But the real difficulty is moral and intellectual: the present Administration is not able to energize any spiritual forces and without these, their money and their arms are not good for much.

June 28, 1954

The morning's news records that the President of Guatemala, Jacobo Arbenz, last night resigned and turned over the government to a Junta of Guatemalan Army officers. The position of the Guatemalan Army was always crucial in this business; they have disposed of Arbenz. What they will do next, I do not yet know. The leader of the insurgents, Castillo Armas, has insisted that the government must be turned over to him and my guess is that he stands a fair chance of getting there. . . .

July 1, 1954

In the evening [June 29] we dined with the Brazilian Ambassador to the United Nations [Ernesto Leme] and his wife, Hugo Gouthier [Brazilian delegate to the U.N.] and his wife. Naturally the talk fell on Guatemala. Gouthier had carried the battle in the Security Council of the United Nations . . . and handled [it] very well. He immediately moved to refer it to the Organization of American States. He buttressed this with copies of the speeches which the Guatemalan Foreign Minister, [Guillermo] Toriello, had made at the conference of Chapultepec in my committee there, insisting that the Inter-American organization must have primary jurisdiction over the hemisphere with no European interference.

Gouthier tells me that the Brazilian intelligence is that while the Russian arms have been widely distributed in Guatemala, the ammunition had been ordered through Switzerland and Germany and had been stopped. I was expressing my fear lest we should have guerrilla fighting in the hills.

Next day, June 30, to Washington to have lunch with Congressman Jack Javits and the Assistant Secretary of State for Latin American Affairs, Holland. The more I talked to Holland, the more I liked him. He is serious, learning his job, getting his baptism of fire. . . .

Javits wants Holland to announce a doctrine of hemispheric integration and back it up with added economic measures. I told Holland I was for this but we needed more than economics and military measures. Somehow we need to get a moral initiative and this problem was preoccupying me. . . .

On July 11, 1954, Figueres wrote to Berle after reading an article by Berle in the New York *Times Magazine*. He said, in part:

"Also, the new policy needed is double: a moral policy and an economic policy. On the moral field, we shall not go anywhere until the United States, as a leader, upholds an ideology. This ideology has to be Democracy. Unfortunately at this moment the opposite is true, in the minds of Latin Americans. The U.S. appears as the ally of tyranny and political vandalism. . . .

"On the economic aspect of Inter-American relations, I keep repeating that the logical help to Latin America, and one which will help the U.S. as well, is the stabilization of the prices of primary products. . . .

"Imagine what would happen to the hemispheric economy if the workers who produce the coffee and the tin could increase their purchasing power in harmony with the workers who produce the automobiles.

"In the matter of establishing branches of U.S. corporations in Latin America I am coming to the conclusion that we would derive nothing but benefits if a) the wage scales go up gradually, giving time for adjustments; b) the corporate taxes are paid in the country of operation. Maybe we could agree to a uniform corporate tax in the Latin American Republics, or in a group of them. This corporate tax should be lower than in the United States, as an inducement. . . ."

To Figueres, July 19, 1954

The problems you raise in your letter need full discussion but I am beginning to be clear about one thing. We should work up an economic system for the entire hemisphere—including price support mechanisms, wage policy boards and general stabilization machinery. This, on the economic side.

The moral side is something else, and I think calls for an extra-governmental group of some sort. . . .

July 19, 1954

On July 11 Padre Nuñez, presently Ambassador to the United Nations for Costa Rica, came up to spend the week-end with us. The Guatemalan matter is resolved for the moment—but the reaction has not been good. We eliminated a Communist regime—at the expense of having antagonized half the hemisphere. . . .

July 29, 1954

On Tuesday night, July 27, we got a message from Boscawen indicating that my father was ill. Beatrice and I motored up early next morning. My father had had a slight stroke: he is physically relatively well and able to get around and so forth; what has happened has been that a tiny blood clot has affected one part of his brain and while he can think clearly, he cannot connect words with thought beyond a certain amount. . . .

But it does draw finis to an intellectual career lasting three-quarters of a century. The sheer tragedy of seeing him among the books which he had loved, working out a single line of Greek tragedy and then, from memory, reminding himself of everything else in the play is something that belongs in heroic tragedy. He has meant a great deal to a great many people. At 89, it may not be irreverent to wish the end may not be lingering but swift; for his mind is working perfectly; only the search for speech presents a difficulty. When we left him last night, he did not yet realize what had happened and assumed, of course, that we would understand the code words he fitted into otherwise perfect sentences. Most pathetic was the paper in his typewriter. He was trying to write a letter to the editor of the Boston *Herald*. He struggled with various letter combinations and finally got it: "The Editor, The Boston *Herald*," and then stopped.

September 9, 1954

On August 27, Beatrice, Peter and I left for Costa Rica via Havana, arriving on the 28th. Matters meanwhile had been going well for Costa Rica. . . . But under cover of the Guatemalan incident, Somoza, the Nicaraguan dictator had mobilized his troops on the Costa Rican frontier, had raised a strong propaganda, some of it very vile, against Figueres and proposed apparently a straight military-political invasion. On one occasion a Nicaraguan force crossed the border but only robbed a bank. I had advised Padre Nuñez to take up with the American Government the possibility of sending American planes on a good-will tour. They actually sent a "good-will" mission of six cargo planes, but it was all that was needed: the United States was evidencing, tangibly, that it had no intention of sanctioning incidental nonsense. Also, the American Embassy in Costa Rica had strongly argued Figueres' case; and the American State Department had made it clear to Somoza that they did not (repeat "not") want any nonsense. So it had boiled down to a political dispute, with the immediate danger past. . . .

Costa Rica is a democratic republic, doing things quietly; none of the splendour and luxury which symbolizes some other Latin American governments. Wisely Don Pepe is spending his money on serious public services and not on splash. It is perhaps typical that on showing us to our bedrooms, he gave us the keys to the Casa Presidencial. At night the place was generally deserted; we could have "seized the Palace" all by ourselves.

Pepe grinned while observing this fact; Peter suggested that we would use all the Presidential telephones and see what happened. Pepe grinned again and said a great deal would happen but not for very long.

Thence presently to "La Lucha," Pepe's country house up in the hills. We were joined by my old friend, Arthur Schlesinger, who is also Stevenson's Brain Truster, likewise down for a visit. Around the fireplace (La Lucha being 6,000 feet up), we developed some large thoughts and great ideas. . . .

Pepe's opposition had accused him of being afraid to go through the streets of San José and Pepe had retaliated by taking occasion from time to time to stroll in the Plaza alone or with one secretary. Actually after a concert in the national theatre, Beatrice and Karen Figueres, and Peter, Pepe, Schlesinger and I strolled down from the theatre across the Plaza and to the principal coffee bistro on the corner (it is a wide-open little street), picked a table close by the street and sat there having coffee and soft drinks and chatting with any passerby we happened to know. Of course it is true that an assassin could kill him without difficulty. But I do not see that Pepe could cover himself up: this is a hazard of the Latin American politics. . . .

September 23, 1954

Averell Harriman, duly nominated by the Democratic Party, came to talk to the Liberal Party officers this morning. This is pure form since the Liberal Party can do nothing but go along with Harriman and indeed had made it clear that it preferred Harriman to Roosevelt for the Governorship. In the evening the Liberal Party convention at which I presided. Mr. Harriman was duly nominated along with his running mates. Franklin Roosevelt, defeated for the nomination by the action of the New York Democratic chieftains, finally caved in and took a poor nomination for Attorney General. Meanwhile the Republicans named Jack Javits, a Republican-Liberal Congressman for Attorney General likewise. So both men come into being via the Liberal Party. . . .

October 4–6, 1954

By bomber to Maxwell Field, doing a little talking on the diplomatic history of 1944–1950; and a pleasant and interesting contact with a fascinating institution. The Air War College is considering what to do with guided missiles and their absolute assumption that they will have an atomic airplane capable of indefinite flight within three years as per Buck Rogers come to life.

They are clear that the Russians are moving at least as fast if not faster than we. Last Spring their thinking ran to whether a preventative war was not the only way of protecting the United States—though this was strictly theoretical talk. I was glad to find that the thinking had considerably changed. I offered the necessity of thinking in a denomination of time beyond the atomic war. Five years after any victory in atomic war how is any victor going to be safe from a surprise attack from either the recovered enemy or some part of the globe that will no longer take a chance on international morality? That kind of logic would reply that you exterminate everyone else in the world lest he do to you what you have just done to your potential enemy. There was theoretical agreement on the point and we are beginning to get away on lines of political action instead.

One amusing footnote to history. One of the Air Corps colonels had been at the conference at which the 38th parallel was selected as the demarcation zone between Russians and Americans at the close of the Japanese war. They wanted a line; the orders were to get one fast; three or four officers looked for a good one and drew a straight line with a ruler on the map. The suggestion being relayed to headquarters, they looked for a good description of it, noticed it was close to the 38th parallel. No one remembered that this line had been used in an earlier diplomatic dispute between Japan and Russia, and that it was a line fraught with all kinds of evil significance.

Note: I have always wondered when any singularly stupid or unsuccessful thing happened whether there was not a far greater likelihood that it was chance rather than villany or design. . . .

October 8, 1954

Night before last Dr. Eugenio Gudín, an old friend, came in to dinner. He is presently Brazilian Minister of Finance; came for the Monetary Fund meeting; talked in Washington to [George M. Humphrey, Secretary of the Treasury] and Randolph Burgess [Under Secretary for Monetary Affairs] about Brazilian finances. Nobody was around from the State Department except [Under Secretary Walter] Bedell Smith, who is going out of office and young Herbert Hoover, who hasn't taken over as yet. So as usual the State Department was somewhere else when the South American problems knocked at the door. . . .

At all events Gudín bought himself a little time with a year's loan from the Federal Reserve Bank of New York—no favor since he pledged gold to get it—and has a staggering task of leading a country in full tide of inflation.

I said I would try to help in Washington and will. But he has a job to do at best.

The results of the Brazilian elections are not yet in but they indicate surprisingly enough that the pro-Vargas forces are getting handsomely trimmed. This, on top of a piece of drama—Vargas' suicide and letter—almost unparalleled in history. The Brazilian public has a more level head than some people suppose.

November 3, 1954

Election yesterday: it looked as though Harriman were in by a huge majority but he actually seems to have squeaked through by about a whisker. As always, when the Liberal Party makes a coalition the Liberal vote ran around 280,000 though I haven't the figures. . . .

Paul Douglas won in Illinois which is good news. . . .

Harriman will not be a serious contender for the Presidency. This is a situation looking for new men but where in the world are they? . . .

. . . Since no substantial issues were on the agenda, the best the public could do was to choose between the men. John Q. Public is the only hero in this situation.

November 9, 1954

Last night Pepe Figueres was kind enough to telephone: I had sent him a copy of the new book, *The 20th Century Capitalist Revolution,* and he was kind enough to telephone saying how much he liked it. This is Latin America for you.

The election is over, and Harriman seems to have won it, and that is that. I cannot say that I find anything to be particularly excited about. It is highly unlikely that it opens any possibility. My plan is to retire from the Chairmanship of the Liberal Party at some appropriate time—presumably about the time Harriman is inaugurated.

November 17, 1954

November 16. A friend of Manuel Debayle came in to see me. . . . He was going to Washington to try to interest the government in some sort of moral support against the dictatorship. I listened, merely expressing some question as to how far Americans could intervene in the affairs of another country. But he handed me a tab of matches which I kept as an exhibit. It says:

> "Walker-Zelaya
> –Somoza–
> Blood Bank Co. Ltd."

Walker was an adventurer-dictator, shot. . . . Zelaya was a dictator for years—barely rescued from a Nicaraguan mob howling for his blood. Somoza, of course, is there now. Either they are accusing these three dictators of having Nicaraguan blood on their heads; or they are suggesting something more sinister. Well this is Nicaraguan politics—not at its pleasantest.

November 17. Last evening to see David Dubinsky; we arranged for my resignation from the Chairmanship of the Liberal Party in early January as soon as Harriman has got through being inaugurated. David rather expects to retire a few months later. We both feel that it would be bad for everyone for us to retire at the same time.

This year the Party did not spend any money to speak of and did pretty well so that the Liberal Party has no debts.

The foreign situation is beginning to be disturbing—and not only disturbing but dangerous, though it will be six months before the newspapers get the follow significance. The Chinese mean business and contemplate attacking Formosa; they calculate that if they can take Formosa they will have Indo-China as a matter of course. The Russian aggression is light in Europe, but they are pushing their advantages in the Near East, especially Iran and Egypt. This sets up a real hot summer for 1955.

At Max Ascoli's request I wrote another article about the United Nations, advocating greater use of this institution. . . .

November 20, 1954

At a dinner party designed to be social but Mario Esquivel [Foreign Minister] and young Oduber and Ambassador Facio, all of Costa Rica, were guests. Afterwards and over the coffee, they said that the Nicaraguan danger to Costa Rica was once more near the boiling point. Specifically:

Former President [Otilio] Ulate [Blanco] and . . . Luis Carballo and former President [Teodoro] Picado (the last two now paid by Somoza of Nicaragua) joined in a common manifesto against Figueres. Camps of supposed exiles and Nicaraguan mercenaries had been set up along the border. At the same time the Communist cells in the United Fruit plant at Golfitos were being activated: the familiar combination of the extreme right and left. With no Army, Pepe would have a hard time controlling a thrust from the north and an uprising or political strike in the south and generally everyone was worried. . . . We worked out a plan of action: Facio was to get to the State Department pronto: unhappily Under Secretary Hoover and Assistant Secretary Holland are all in Rio where there is an economic conference and where they are making heavy weather. . . . It is, after all, up to the American Government to keep the peace in that area.

November 21, 1954

To Puerto Rico . . . to work on the Puerto Rico corporation law. . . .

In the evening, to the Fortaleza to have dinner with Governor Muñoz Marín, Trias Monge and two or three others. This was a glistening evening: Muñoz Marín is one of the few first-raters I have known as the parade goes by. Also the setting was dramatic: the loggia on top of the Fortaleza which is on the headland dominating the entrance to San Juan harbor.

I opened the discussion at once. I said that at my house in New York I had discussed Costa Rican matters with the Costa Rican Foreign Minister, Esquivel, their Ambassador, Facio, and the Party leader, Daniel Oduber. With their consent, I wanted to explain the dangers which Figueres thought were real. . . .

Muñoz Marín immediately arranged, first, to have a telephone call put through to Figueres in the morning, and, second, to give instructions to his representative at Rio de Janeiro, [Teodoro] Moscoso, to talk to the American Delegation there, notably Hoover and Holland. He was perfectly aware of the whole situation—obviously knowing more about it than I did.

Then we got into something else. The Caribbean Commission which Charles Taussig founded is now meeting in Trinidad; Trias Monge was going over to represent Puerto Rico. Muñoz Marín had been thinking over this strange situation in which many little sovereign nationalities worked in a region in which they could only exist as members of the region—defended by the forces of the United States, locked in a single economic system. He was, therefore, proposing to make the Caribbean

Commission the beginning of a true regional parliament of sorts and proposed, therefore, to make suggestions for change in the Commission. . . . In substance, it was to make the Caribbean Commission a kind of representative parliament in very elementary scale, dealing with the small but essential common elements on which all of the members of the Commission are dependent. . . . We tossed the idea back and forth across the dinner table for a couple of hours; it opened up a new range of possibilities to me and I think perhaps opens possibilities for development of Latin American policy which could be of major interest. . . .

I said good-bye and came down through the entrance courtyard with Trias Monge. . . . He suggested [my] coming [back] quite soon; and then after the conventional Spanish courteous phrases, added: "Muñoz Marín, too, is a lonely man"—meaning thereby that he needed the support of friends who understood things just as Pepe Figueres did.

The next day, more work on the Puerto Rico law; in the afternoon, a ride in a single-engine plane with Trias Monge to inspect the very impressive housing developments and water-power works which are growing up all over the island.

November 26, 1954

Padre Nuñez telephoned. . . . He thought the situation was getting more serious. Figueres was worried and was prepared if the Nicaraguans crossed the frontier to declare war. I was not sure the situation was that imminent because Somoza cannot be so foolish as to risk open hostilities. The State Department has put six jet planes "at the disposition" of Figueres; since there is no field, they are standing by at Tocumen Airport in Panama. This, of course, is not a gesture but a very powerful deterrent and the State Department is entitled to high marks for moving decisively.

Thinking the matter over, it seems to me that declarations of war have no place in the scheme of things. We had better get some new international law. I worked out a "declaration of armed breach of the peace," designating Nicaragua, or whoever it might be, as the peace-breaker and proclaiming a state of defense.

The next day I suggested this for study to Padre Nuñez and Esquivel; the theory being that war is outlawed both by the United Nations Charter and by the Organization of American States; and therefore what is called for is a declaration that the peace of the region has been broken and invoking all hands to defense. . . .

November 29, 1954

Daniel Oduber came to dinner. . . . The evening mentally scintillating with discussion on atom bomb policy. Undercover I tried to arrange that the Costa Ricans and Peruvians act as friends. Oduber said that the governments respectively of Colombia, Ecuador, Uruguay and some others had checked in to the Costa Rican Delegation at the United Nations, generally expressing their support of Figueres and their satisfaction that the State Department had moved in the matter with jet planes;

and offering to send planes themselves (if they have any, which I doubt). I asked Daniel to encourage these governments to check in with the Department of State and generally express their approval of the State Department policy. The poor old State Department has been getting more brickbats than bouquets from Latin America and it will hearten the boys to have some Latin American governments come around and tell them that they, for once, did the right thing.

December 1, 1954

Padre Nuñez telephoned. They had word from Costa Rica. The Nicaraguan incident seems to be liquidated and the game is over: no hits, no runs, no errors. Anyhow, if this proves accurate, as I think it will, we have stopped a possible armed raid without firing a shot or killing or imprisoning anyone—or allowing anyone else to do it. This is all you can ask of diplomacy.

To Henry Holland, December 1, 1954

Information reaching me this morning suggests that the latest difficulty between Nicaragua and Costa Rica has abated and perhaps liquidated. This is due, I think, to discreet but decisive action by the State Department at the right time. I write merely to say that I think the Departmental handling of this situation, for which you were responsible, deserves high marks.

Particularly heartening was the fact that a number of Latin American governments went out of their way to express to the government of Costa Rica their feeling that the situation had been well handled—one or two of them going to the length of saying that if the United States desired their participation in measures taken they would join the American government. My understanding is that some of them contemplated a similar statement to the State Department. Since the United States has had more brickbats than half-pennies from its hemispheric neighbors, it is good to find one situation in which there is substantial support for American policy and measures.

December 30, 1954

I took [yesterday] the proposed outline of the Summer Session at Robertsau and tried to remake it so that it might set up a first-rate philosophical synthesis of the ideal of the free world. Outlining it turned out to be a tremendous job: I never understood the allegory of Jacob wrestling with the angel (though I have no admiration for Jacob and know no angels) until I tried this one. Wrestling with an abstract idea is exactly what the Old Testament was talking about. . . .

Yet as the year closes, I have a feeling that the future has more in it than the past though I cannot see what kind of assignment with destiny it will be. . . .

Outline for Summer Session, Free Europe University in Exile, Robertsau, outside Strasbourg

The suggestions are made because it is increasingly clear that our difficulties at Robertsau are the same which we are finding all over the world.

The root difficulty is that the ideals of the free world, of which America is presently the proponent, are nowhere stated in doctrinal form, capable of being restated and applied everywhere.

Marxian Communism has a dogmatic base, surrounded by a body of doctrine capable of being packaged and repackaged for export more or less universally. The free world ideal is, in the opinion of the writer, far more appealing, more nearly universal, no less definite, and equally capable of statement—though it involves a conception of continuous evolution and change which Marxian dogma (like some religious dogmas) does not.

The proposal suggested in this memorandum is an attempt to see whether the Summer Session at Robertsau can be used to attempt a statement of free world ideals, and of the mechanisms by which its ideals are realized. Ideally, such a statement should be so cast that it could be used (with appropriate changes in emphasis) anywhere from Eastern Europe to Eastern Asia. Obviously this is not likely to be realized in one attempt. Yet, given the overwhelming evidence of the need for this, there seems to be solid reason for attempting the task. The Free Europe University in Exile is perhaps as good a starting point as any.

The first group to which any statement of ideals must appeal (if they are to be dynamic) is clear. Primarily, the men who make ideas and ideals effective are intellectuals; particularly, young intellectuals. Even the Communists know very well their primary appeal is not to the "masses"; it is to the men whose ideas guide masses. (In this respect, the Communists merely borrowed an idea originally worked out by St. Paul, which eventually translated itself into the Christian revolution in the Roman Empire.) This necessarily involves a very long view. But it is the long view contemplated now by most thinking Americans, and apparently, though tacitly, adopted by American foreign policy. Unless change is to take place by a more or less unlimited world war—ruled out by the present situation in weapons—the conception of combined intellectual and spiritual conquest, translating itself in time into political change, is the only apparent alternative. This does not exclude local armed conflicts; but the central conception must give meaning to local conflicts so that, as any conflict takes place, success in it becomes an item, building towards an ultimate solution, and, indeed, tends to indicate what result in any local conflict constitutes "success." . . .

In these countries there was and is a solid desire to share the economic and personal fruits of twentieth century technical progress. There was and is a passionate yearning to accomplish the transition without devastations of a new war. This implied and still implies some international organization of affairs which can keep a modicum of peace and order, and some national organization of affairs which takes account of individuals.

There was, and still is, a relatively large submerged class in these countries to whom change of regime means little if any change in the comparative misery of their daily life. Their apathy made possible the Communist take-over; their conscious participation could lead to Communist exclusion. These submerged groups are not as depressed as in the case of South American or Asiatic peons or coolies whose situation is so bad that they could not care less whether Communists or capitalists rule affairs: their lot is the same either way; their only interest, therefore, is to survive. But in substantial degree the status of the Mid-European worker and peasant offers illustration of a world-wide problem.

In a word, we have a relatively limited situation presenting most of the problems encountered in the disturbed areas of the world. This affords possibility of as good a laboratory test as one is likely to find.

First, the philosophical conception . . . the attached outline stresses the individual himself, and suggests statements and discussions on the ideal of the individual demanding construction of a world community of free individuals, each working towards his interpretation of a cosmic ideal of order. Philosophically, of course, this is the precise opposite of the Marxian materialism which denies both the cosmic ideal and substitutes materialism and consequently necessarily denies the significance of the creative individual. It substitutes merely a protoplasmic unit whose actions are part of the materialistic evolution of a group. What we have to do comes close to being a spiritual as well as a political statement. But so it should. Devotion of intellectuals is engaged, not by mathematical calculations, but by relating their thought to some overlying larger ideal. The young intellectuals are the men who really have carried the Communist revolution as far as it has gone; only a greater conception is likely to carry the twentieth century free world revolution toward its fruition. Necessarily this suggests the kind of men we have to seek. We shall be looking much more to philosophical leaders like Albert Schweitzer (a Protestant) or Archbishop de Andrea of Buenos Aires (a Catholic) or some of the great German or English rationalists—rather than to experts in political affairs or even in civil liberties.

Second, the methods by which the free world has attained and proposes increasingly to attain some degree of realization of these ideals . . . For example: (a) the history and realization of civil liberties . . . (b) the struggle for and results of free labor organization . . . (c) . . . international organization (discussion could be led by Ambassador [Eelco N.] van Kleffens, retiring President of the United Nations General Assembly and a member of the Institute of International Law at the Hague). . . .

To show what can be done when you really try, I would strongly suggest Governor Muñoz Marín of Puerto Rico. He is struggling precisely with the problem of the "separate state" to which sovereignty is an empty word. He has carried forward a truly revolutionary American experiment in Puerto Rico—a form of government which gives full rein to cultural nationalism, but also recognizes the necessity of pooled interests in economics and defense if the culture is to be maintained.

Flanking these general lectures, there might be meetings having to do with methodology. These could cover two distinct subjects: (1) the relative success of the free world (as contrasted with the non-free world) where a staggering case can be made; and (2) the means by which this success has been achieved and continues to move forward, not merely in aggregates but in actual liberation of individuals. This group of meetings ought to deal, not with dogma, but with ways and means. Nobody pretends that the same ways and means are necessarily appropriate in all places. . . .

Muñoz Marín came to Robertsau in the Summer of 1955 and revealed the "new world" to the Europeans.

January 3, 1955

To Albany December 31 with a trainload of old friends, including Sam Rosenman and Robert Sherwood along with David Dubinsky and others.

At 11:00 o'clock we went over to the Governor's Mansion. The same old Mansion but the dingy leatherette had been replaced by white paint. Regrettably, that too is already beginning to peel. At all events, a small group of guests had gathered to take over the Capitol. I noted with some sorrow that the average age was about 60. These were the young men of the Roosevelt Administration, now grown old. The only really young man I spotted was [Jonathan B.] Bingham, Governor Harriman's new Executive Secretary.

At midnight the band played "Auld Lang Syne", then [Judge Albert] Conway swore Harriman in; then the orchestra played "Happy Days Are Here Again". I kissed Mrs. [Thomas K.] Finletter (one of the Damrosch girls) and went over to the window, not wanting anyone to realize I could hardly see. The spirit and life that were Franklin and Eleanor were not there; nor the tempestuous drive of Fiorello; nor the undisciplined but intellectual idealism of the youngsters. I ran into Jim Farley; made my "Good Nights," and we walked back in the moonlight to the hotel, neither of us saying very much.

Saturday to lunch with Nelson Rockefeller. If the Republicans had any sense they would have nominated him and he would have been where Harriman is now.

Dulles had asked Nelson to take this new job—Coordinator of International Programs—because Dulles understands perfectly that he is merely putting out fires—if he is putting them out—and is on the defensive everywhere. He himself has no time to think and feels something is lacking, and expects Nelson to supply the miraculous element. Briefly the situation is this:

In Europe we have about held the line with an alliance held together by baling wire or less. In Asia we are just going down the greased slide.

Nobody has wasted any time on Latin America. And Latin America knows that trouble is coming up. The Colombo Powers have called a convention for April: this is frankly a conference of the non-white countries including Africa. A slow beginning of a Negro-Asiatic alliance throwing down the gauntlet to the white world.

Nelson felt and I cordially stimulated the idea that the real trouble here was philosophical and spiritual more than economic, material and political. There is no guide line to any political policy. Another dimension was needed. This dimension has to work out. I told him that we were working on this at Strasbourg and he asked to see the papers, which I am sending him. We agreed to work together on this from time to time to see what could be developed. We both agreed we are neither philosophers nor divines. This does not let us out. We are bound to do the best we can—with or without qualifications. Nelson asked if Eisenhower were a personality around which the thing could be gathered. At least, I hoped so. Privately, I rather doubt it. But there isn't anyone else.

Nelson was particularly worried about the position of Secretary Humphrey. These men see everything in banking lines. If you were "bankingly" good, you would be bankingly happy. But about 75% of the world is not affected by that. And banking happiness doesn't help much anyhow. . . .

January 13, 1955

Saturday, January 8. 4:00 o'clock this morning President Figueres telephoned from San José. He said that they had information a Nicaraguan invasion was impending. He hoped for help from the United States. Nothing had occurred as yet so there was not too much to go on.

Monday, January 10. Padre Nuñez telephoned to say that an unidentified band of men, presumably coming from Nicaragua, had come by water up the San Carlos River and had taken the city of Villa Quesada, about 50 miles south of the Nicaraguan border. The Costa Ricans had already demanded action by the OAS. . . .

Tuesday, January 11. Taking of Villa Quesada was confirmed. In the evening I telephoned Nelson Rockefeller, and told him the situation and asked that he get into this. He said he'd do the best he could. But I gather he has some hesitation about moving in on the Department of State. During the evening Padre Nuñez telephoned again saying that they were increasingly worried and were asking immediate help from the United States under Article 3 of the Treaty of Rio de Janeiro. This provides that an armed attack on any American state is an attack against them all; and that any state may decide for itself what assistance to give on the application of the state attacked. He said the State Department was still unsure whether this was an attack by another state and did not want to play "favorites" (as though the giving or withholding of peace were a matter of "favoritism"!).

Wednesday, January 12. Padre Nuñez' office telephoned to say that an unidentified plane or planes had machine-gunned the cities of Cartago and Turrialba. These planes were P-47 type and there is no airfield in

Costa Rica from which they could take off. A little later news came that a plane said to be Venezuelan had machine-gunned San José, and later had been shot down by a Costa Rican battery.

The Costa Ricans have armed Lacsa DC-3s with machine guns and are hammering back. Their militia has been called up and they are in contact with the forces at Villa Quesada.

I then telephoned Paul Douglas and got him about noon. He had already been grieving over this and prepared a telegram to the State Department which he will release but likewise he said he would talk to the State Department at once in the sense of asking prompt action under Article 3 of the Treaty of Rio de Janeiro. I telegraphed Dulles and said I thought Costa Rica ought to have such help and to [Senator] Wayne Morse [Indep., Ore.], asking him to get into the matter. . . . [Both Senators sent strong statements to the State Department.]

If the State Department knew its mind; if there had been an American Ambassador at Nicaragua to state that mind and be sure he would be believed, this could have been avoided. One cool, definite and decisive man in the State Department and a solid diplomatic warning in Nicaragua would, I think, have stopped this foolishness. I am not clear how far the Venezuelan government is involved. I am afraid more than we think.

In fairness to the State Department, they did today insist that the OAS reconvene and I suppose it is at work now. It has appointed a commission to inquire, shot it in the direction of Costa Rica and was going to await a report.

To Paul Douglas, January 14, 1955

Your statement was magnificent and I think your intervention at the Department of State materially helped it to take prompt and, as it seems to me, very wise action in the Costa Rican–Nicaraguan affair. As always, you are a present help in time of trouble.

Of greater significance and specific importance is the fact that the American peace-keeping machinery seems to have worked. I put a good deal of it together myself at the Chapultepec Conference and it is now embodied in the Treaty of Rio. But no machinery will work unless our government is prompt and intelligent in using it. At the present stage, it seems as though they have done this. There is always danger that diplomats will talk while force alters the situation. The danger seems to have been avoided in this case.

January 14, 1955

The peace machinery we put together at Chapultepec and later embodied in the Treaty of Rio de Janeiro seems to have worked. At least so it appears now. We know well enough that when fighting is going forward, the slow procedures of a commission of inquiry or of a debate by representatives of the American republics does not suffice to stop the killing. Accordingly anyone who is appealed to for assistance may, provisionally, render assistance.

The Costa Ricans appealed to the Organization of American States.

The OAS appointed a commission and sent it to Costa Rica. Costa Rica meanwhile appealed to the American republics for provisional emergency aid. The American Government did not act directly on this but sent Navy planes to observe, patrol and so forth. I do not know what orders were given to the air crews but cannot imagine they were expected to limit themselves to "observation" if actual shooting were going on. At all events there seems to have been no air action since.

It develops the chief of the operation is the son of ex-President Picado. This ex-President is at present a Secretary to Somoza in Nicaragua.

We have acted throughout on the premise that Figueres could handle matters on the ground because his people were solidly behind him. This seems to have been well-founded so far. Unless the invading column has heavy artillery or weapons this affair should be liquidated within the next few days.

On Wednesday night Ernest Cuneo dropped in; he has agreed to let us have some good publicity over the week-end. Then to dinner with Georges Henri Martin [Editor, *Tribune de Genève*], who is writing the story for the European newspapers. I am hoping that next week will be peaceful again. . . .

January 17, 1955

[Padre Nuñez and I were lunching together on the 15th. He] was for proposing a disarmament pact in Central America. We also discussed the question of what to do with the prisoners taken by the Costa Rica militia: to the Costa Ricans they are quite simply traitors and Figueres is being attacked for not hanging them out of hand. I said to Padre Nuñez it was easy for us to discuss the question in the tranquillity of the Century Club; Figueres had to contend with public opinion. But I thought that the same crowd that was thirsting for their blood would condemn him thirty days later; Pepe Figueres should say that Costa Rican justice was the greatest interest of the republic and keep them locked up safe for a while. Later he could either have them tried civilly, or release them, or follow Caesar's old method and arrange for the escape of most of them, and so on. There has been enough killing already.

While I was there [Fernando] Fournier, Vice Minister of Foreign Affairs, telephoned. He and the Costa Ricans were worried about Holland; they believed that he was watering down the resolutions in the OAS and was trying to get unanimity and not getting enough action. I told him that I would see what I could do but my own impression is that they were trying to do the right thing. (I did not feel it necessary to tell Fournier that Holland is having his troubles. Everything we are condemning Nicaragua for had, for all practical purposes, been done on our side in the Guatemalan affair last Summer and the Nicaraguan dictator, Somoza, knows it. So Holland is trying to stay behind the OAS and so would I if I were in his position.) In a meeting which began at 2:00 AM Saturday morning, the result was a resolution that squarely placed Nicaragua as the source of much of the arms and matériel used by the rebel forces.

Meanwhile in Costa Rica matters had taken a turn for the worse. A couple of planes with incendiary bombs had appeared over the northwest corner of Costa Rica. The ground troops seemed to be doing fairly well but have no defense against incendiary bombs. The Costa Ricans renewed their request for assistance.

Late Saturday night the OAS council met again in Washington, and in the small hours of Sunday morning voted to request immediate aid to Costa Rica. Holland had apparently got authority to offer to send planes immediately if the OAS wished it, as they did. He thereupon arranged to sell four American Mustang fighter planes and one transport plane for arms and spare parts to Costa Rica for a nominal amount: it is said, $1.00 a plane. Likewise the Costa Ricans bought a plane load of ammunition which was sitting at Miami. Then, an almost typical piece of bureaucratic snafu. Being a week-end, they could not find the right official to sign the license to allow shipment of these arms. While the fighting was going on, the plane load of ammunition in Miami and the Mustangs in Texas sat there awaiting clearance. . . . Apparently they tracked down the official sometime on Sunday and he completed the papers, and the planes got off Sunday afternoon. I suppose they are there now. . . .

I spent Sunday sweating: the battle was going on and there was nothing I could do about it, and so forth. Ernest Cuneo came through like a gentleman and Walter Winchell made a broadcast generally favoring American aid to Costa Rica and pointing up the danger that the dictators might get together here. So far as facts went, it was a cartoon but it probably will help. . . .

All things considered, I think the State Department has done about all that could be expected of it—except for one thing. There is no Roosevelt, and no Hull, to say in a clear, calm voice that there is to be law and peace in the hemisphere.

This is a good little historical illustration of how things happen. On the surface this is a border row between two countries and the issue is preventing filibustering backed by one country against another. Basically it is an issue between the dictatorial systems which are always frightened by democracy and an impetuous but perfectly sincere democratic liberal, passionately and perhaps sometimes rashly, trying to do the best he can for his own country and anxious to do something for the populations of the nearby countries. . . .

As of now: there are American observation planes "observing" for the OAS commission in San José. There are or should be four American fighter planes capable of smashing any air attack. There is presumably a plane load of ammunition for Costa Rica. All of this has been done under the authority of the law of the hemisphere, acting through OAS. There is public sentiment crystallizing in favor of Costa Rica. The fighting in the next few days will determine the issue. This is about all that one can do here.

January 26, 1955

On January 24, my father's ninetieth birthday and a party for the Harvard Club group at the house. Everyone enjoyed it, especially Father.

Tuesday, January 25. After a series of moves, the group in Costa Rica threw in the sponge and crossed back to Nicaragua. Apparently there was drama. The OAS in Managua interviewed Somoza; he lost his head and talked of war, and so forth; the OAS Chief, my old friend Luis Quintanilla, stood firm and Somoza backed down. . . .

January 29, 1955

My own sixtieth birthday and Alice and Clan, little Beatrice and Dean, together with some other people came to dinner. . . .

[President Figueres called.] I said that without information my impression was that the Department was preoccupied with the situation, especially with OAS; that Figueres' diplomatic victory had been complete and brilliant; that the problem now was so to handle it that it created the best possible conditions. Pepe said he would be glad to listen because he knew any counsel would be that of a friend, or words to that effect, and after some courteous words, we then hung up. (One has to assume that any such conversation was picked up by the Mexican and Nicaraguan Intelligence.)

Immediately thereafter, Frank Wisner [of CIA] called up. He said that he had made a date with Holland for 10:00 AM on Tuesday morning. I said that I would meet it. . . . He said that he thought Schlesinger and I ought to talk with Pepe afterwards. I said that was what I had in mind since it was difficult to work in any other way but we would see what we would do. I said I had no desire to get into the newspapers and so forth, but it seemed to me that the State Department had done its level best in this matter and was entitled to all the help I am capable of. Wisner thought Pepe believed Nicaragua was ready for a change; I told him I knew of my own knowledge that there was a substantial movement against Somoza but this was not my affair and probably not the affair of the United States either.

After dinner, I gave Padre Nuñez the general drift of the situation. He said he had been telling Pepe that it was more difficult to manage a victory than to manage a fight. I tried to outline both to him and to Frank Wisner the dual position in which Figueres was. As leader of the liberal movement which overpasses the boundaries of Costa Rica, he cannot haul down his moral advocacy of democratic government. As Chief of the Costa Rican state, he must be scrupulously correct in using the power of his government. There is a difference between moral action (the action of the party leader) and governmental action (the action of the Chief of State).

January 30. With the children; a lovely day. An excellent performance of *Twelfth Night* in the evening.

# # #

I have been considering the situation a little. We know, as previous entries in this diary show, that there is a group in Nicaragua who strongly wish Somoza would quit and permit political change. We also know that Somoza will not be dislodged except by force; he proposes to bequeath his kingdom to his son. We know, in his own family, there are men who would cheerfully head a move against him. It seems to me that probably only a main-line defection in the Nicaraguan Army would produce a change. We also know that Costa Rica is probably not in any position to bring off an effective change, that the United States has done about all it can safely do for Costa Rica at this time. But I don't like to get in the position of defending the Somoza dictatorship. On the other hand, I do want to defend the OAS which has proved its worth and proved the outer citadel of Costa Rican defense. . . .

February 1, 1955

Went to the Department of State. There were present Assistant Secretary Holland, Ambassador [John C.] Dreier (American representative on the Organization of American States), Frank Wisner, Arthur Schlesinger, Jr., and a couple of others.

The State Department had proposed to Somoza and to Figueres a rather naive reconciliation, they to meet at the border and shake hands. They thought it would be a good idea to have Vice President Nixon preside. This is pure ham; neither Somoza nor Figueres will admit that it was merely personal animosity that led their countries to war. It isn't, though it contributed. Somoza will say anything, and said he would do it and Figueres said he would not. The Department then called me to Washington to say they wanted my help to advise. After a little discussion, it was clear the problem had not been thought through. In a regular war there is a regular way of ending war, by a peace treaty. But there is no known way of ending an action such as this. The idea that I could persuade Figueres to accept a rather naive proposal by telephone was out and the upshot was that at the request of the Government I agreed to spend the weekend in San José with Figueres. The State Department is cabling the American Embassy covering authority. . . .

My present conception is that instead of a schoolboy act after a backyard scrap, we have both presidents declare their devotion to the law of the Hemisphere and their whole-hearted acceptance of the Organization of American States; and they each, without receding from his position on principle, declare that as chiefs of state their task must be to recreate friendly relations between their respective peoples. As tangible evidence, Somoza can open the Nicaraguan border so that trade and shopping and the other usual economic interchange can take place freely. On his side, Figueres can deal generously with the prisoners which he has.

Here there is a funny complication. When the Nicaraguan invading force withdrew and was interned by Nicaragua, they took with them some Costa Rican prisoners, who were prisoners of prisoners. So far as I know, this is a new one in international law, but we shall find a way through it. . . .

Then to see Nelson Rockefeller. He has Cordell Hull's old office now and I asked him if he saw ghosts. He was fired from his post as Assistant Secretary of State in that same office by Jimmy Byrnes, then Secretary of State.

He gave me the drift of what he hoped to do. I said I would work with him on the overall program; he agreed to be of help in the Costa Rica–Nicaragua matter; and so to New York and to bed.

February 7, 1955

Feb. 3 . . . [Arrived in San José.] I showed President Figueres the cablegram to the American Embassy asking me to explore possibilities of peaceful solution of the Nicaraguan–Costa Rican matter and likewise showed it to [Ambassador Robert F.] Woodward, who said he had not got it as yet but would in the afternoon. (I think he had got it and merely was not showing the hand.)

I told President Figueres that in Washington our Government was very much concerned to bring the Nicaraguan–Costa Rican trouble to an end: that there were many reasons for this, including the fact that no one could tell how serious the Asiatic situation might become, and there is, therefore, the most powerful interest in having the highest measure of peace within the hemisphere. . . .

. . . I said further that the United States Government considers that maintenance of the OAS was of top-flight importance; it was a new, young institution and if strained too far might either break up or be emasculated. . . . For that reason, any method of reducing the tension which could be found acceptable would be of the utmost importance; and that was what I had come down to talk about. . . .

President Figueres said he wanted to be entirely cooperative and much appreciated the attitude of our Government and we would get at this at once.

Woodward left, and we continued the discussion.

Figueres said that, unhappily, the situation was not one of a contest being overt. In point of fact, there was a modified state of war on the border and he was concerned that it might break out at any time (I learnt later that the grape-vine had accurately forecast the attack on Los Chiles). Figueres said that the idea of a meeting with Somoza had been broached, and that his predecessor and present opponent, Ulate, had offered to go and meet Somoza and a picture of Ulate with Somoza had been published in the Press. He said there had been immediate and violent repercussions of the kind to be expected in a war or near-war situation. . . .

. . . What were the immediate steps that could be taken to end the fighting.

President Figueres said that assuming Somoza really did not wish to keep up the conflict, there were a number of things. Six Costa Rican prisoners of the rebels were held in Managua. They could be released. Communications could be normalized so that LACSA planes could land in Managua as they were accustomed to do. The restrictions on commerce could be opened. . . .

I agreed to think things over and so did he and we broke off.

To dinner at the American Embassy, catching up on the situation as the Embassy saw it. The Ambassador indicated that the information reaching them rather confirmed the impression President Figueres gave me. . . .

On February 4, breakfast with President Figueres and Karen; it was their wedding anniversary. We started right in. I thought we were making some progress—that is, along the line that if immediate conditions of peace could be restored, then appropriate ceremonies could be worked out. The idea of shaking hands with Somoza was obviously not palatable to Figueres: the familiar argument was that this would appear to be betrayal of the democratic leadership of the continent. I pointed out that he was one set of things as Pepe Figueres and quite another set of things as Chief of State; that the phrase could be normalization rather than conciliation; that there was never any implication that he (or Somoza either for that matter) was abandoning his principles. . . .

But, at this point, an officer came in with word that the telegraph operator at Los Chiles had just reported the arrival of a regular LACSA civilian plane, had reported "Están atacando", after which the station had gone dead. The conversation stopped there and arrangements were made to send planes up to observe the place, and so on. . . .

. . . Some sort of force was occupying Los Chiles and the observation planes [sent by Figueres] had reported gasoline drums coming down the river from the Lake of Nicaragua. Figueres grimly observed [at dinner] that they did not grow on trees in northern Costa Rica.

We tackled conciliation again. Figueres said that it was one thing to conciliate if things really worked out; it was quite another to offer to humiliate himself without any guarantee that a result would be achieved. "I am expendable," he said, "but to be expendable you have to have reasonable certainty of a result corresponding to the expenditure." He, of course, has absolutely no faith in Somoza's word. He pointed out that they had acres of papers and agreements and declarations in connection with the OAS mission, but the fact was that there were still hostilities on the border and apparently they were continuing. . . .

. . . In the course of the day I found opportunity to go to the Embassy about 11:00 Friday morning (the 4th), sending a telegram which the Department has, and which I think is a fair summary of the situation as we saw it. The phrase that meeting with Somoza would be political suicide was, of course, Pepe's but I had cross-checked to see the probable truth in the statement. Every competent man with whom I talked agreed that this would be the case.

Saturday, February 5. Did some more talking at breakfast but during the night arrangements had been made for the mobilization of volunteers and the sending of a force to retake Los Chiles. Nobody was much interested in conciliation until the returns came in. Delegations of people from Cartago were pressing the President for action. One group of hotheads wanted to take one of the new planes and machine-gun Managua —Figueres had spent part of the night quieting them down, pointing out that kind of thing would be of no use whatever, and so forth. The Commandos took off. . . .

. . . The 25 prisoners [captured at Los Chiles] came to San José and were interrogated Saturday night. With this sort of thing going on, it is obvious that any talk about personal hand-shaking is out of the question. I arranged to take the Lacsa cargo plane that night. At 9:00 Pepe made a speech which he had been working on off and on during the day as circumstances changed. It wound up by being primarily an internal political speech directed against the Ulatistas and smashing then and there any idea of civil resistance.

To breakfast with Figueres, Karen and the baby; we went over the situation again. I pointed out the dangers to the United States abroad, now augmented by the fall of the Mendès-France government and the consequent pressure for a pragmatic solution so that I hoped that as and when conciliation became possible Pepe would do his best to give us some help. He said he would be glad to do anything within the range of the possible. He asked me to thank the American Government for its desire to effect conciliation and to express his whole-hearted desire to cooperate within any limits of possibility. He added that a pre-condition of any normalization of relations must be an actual state of affairs in which the northern border is at peace and that no conciliation which left Nicaragua free to organize and carry out periodic attacks would meet the situation. Conciliation under those circumstances would be a ghastly jest. He was re-enforced this time, of course, by the statements of the prisoners and the reports from the OAS men. . . .

At this point, Pepe having been up all night quieting down a group of extremists, I made him and Karen go back to the Presidencia. As the cargo plane was delayed, Ambassador Woodward kindly fed me some more breakfast. The Deputy Ambassador then telephoned to say that reports had come in of the gravest nature. We left our second breakfast and went down to the airport. It seemed that Colonel Flores had received information from Managua which he rated highly, indicating that Somoza had given word to [Calderón] Guardia that he expected to declare war on Costa Rica within three days.

The cargo plane left at 11:30 (the 6th), arriving at Miami about 6:00. . . .

Monday, February 7. I communicated to Frank Wisner, making arrangement to transmit documents, etc., this afternoon.

This is like the old days and in some ways the most foolish job I have tackled yet. But the Caribbean Sea has been to me what a mistress has been to other men and when she calls it is generally because she feels she is entitled to more attention than she has been getting. Her claims have been extravagant in the last few months. There is always a degree of delight in meeting her.

One of the rather glistening pictures is one of Pepe's bride, Karen. Of Danish parentage, and coming from Westchester, she has put her chin up and come through. It must be a difficult and lonely life. When she and Pepe came to the airport to see me off, she took her baby with her. Every woman in the airport suspended operations to look at the baby. This was not intended as a political gesture, as I know, but it couldn't have been better. If there is anything in this world Spanish-American women understand, it is a woman and her first baby.

February 8, 1955
In the course of the foregoing . . . Woodward gave me a little of the inside situation in the Department.

John Foster Dulles has a scunner against Figueres for his refusal to attend the Caribbean Conference. His instructions are flat: do nothing to offend the dictators; they are the only people we can depend on. Woodward is clear there will be no peace in Central America until Somoza is firmly told that he has got to stay inside his own borders and given appropriate incentive to do so—the inference being a clear intimation that he will be bucking the United States if he does not tranquilize things. He adds that there is a current in the Department that really does want to placate him and build up the dictatorships; Holland has gone as far as he can in bucking this to the point of getting himself in the dog-house; Jack Cabot suffered the same fate; the best opinion in the Department was that the high command was simply barking up the wrong tree. Woodward was really turning over in his mind whether the time had not come for him to resign and go political in protest. I told him I thought he ought not to do that: his responsibility was discharged when he had reported carefully and accurately. He had no use whatever for [Whelan's] reporting in Managua; was clear that nothing could be done through that avenue; that the best thing to do was to send a perfectly capable American to Managua to talk turkey to Somoza. . . .

I inquired whether it was certain that Foster Dulles took this view. He said it was: he himself had been at a Staff meeting where Dulles had laid down the policy with vigor.

I observed that the State Department had got out of the dog-house with their support of the OAS and Costa Rican democracy; that they had got out of it not only in the hemispheric press but in the American press and I could not see for the life of me why they would want to walk back in. . . .

March 4, 1955

Various things and contacts during the week. On Wednesday night to Harvard to the Committee to Visit the History Department. . . . I found it a very pleasant evening, with Crane Brinton (I review his books and he reviews mine. This makes for a unique relationship of mutual apprehension, tempered, at least on my side, by a very solid respect).

The next morning to Harvard—this in the nature of a sentimental journey. Peter and I went to chapel in the morning (my father had taken me to that chapel in 1909 when I was a freshman). With him to a course hideously named "General Education" something or other. It is nothing else than Philosophy I; my father had been Assistant to George Herbert Palmer in that course in 1890. If the world does not blow itself to fragments, Peter may be taking his son to chapel and attending with him lectures in Philosophy I in 1990. Then to a course in history which turned out to be more philosophy (the professor was talking St. Augustine). . . .

March 23, 1955

Fournier [Costa Rican Ambassador to the U.S.] came in for breakfast this morning. He has been now three months in Washington trying to negotiate a treaty of peace with Nicaragua. The State Department listens and says nothing. The Nicaraguan Ambassador, [Don Guillermo Sevilla-] Sacasa, butters him up and sends flowers to his wife. Fournier is disgusted and has a right to be. As usual, the State Department lifted itself up and took stiff measures when the fighting was on, and has walked away from making a real peace.

I am writing Holland about it but I learn that the real difficulty is that Dulles has told him he must not offend the dictators. So I suppose the next thing to do is to get Senator Douglas to say something about it in the Senate. This will make the State Department very angry but it may get some results.

April 2, 1955

Lunch with August Heckscher; his point was the reactionary or McCarthyite wing of the Whitelaw Reid family had won out so the *Tribune* had ceased to be a "liberal Republican" sheet and would probably become the organ of the reactionary wing, a sort of morning *World-Telegram-Sun*. As a result, August was thinking that he would have to pull out and I renewed my suggestion that he take the Directorship of the Twentieth Century Fund.

April 3, 1955

The midnight plane to Puerto Rico.

This was to act as Government expert witness in favor of the proposed new corporation law of Puerto Rico. . . . I opted to work in bad Spanish rather than good English because I thought it would help matters generally, and it did. At all events, after a little cobbling, we finished up, the Chairmen of both committees saying that the law would be passed this Session. On Wednesday night, the two committees and the President of the Senate and the President of the House gave me a dinner at the Rada —the first time in my experience in which committees before which you appeared gave a party in celebration of it. A very pleasant evening with much talk backwards and forwards as to the relative benefits of being a Senator or a Representative. The President of the Senate has just been elected President of the Puerto Rican Academy. The talk went all the way from Gilbert and Sullivan (Iolanthe) and the relative merits of the House of Lords to [Salvador de] Madariaga [Spanish diplomat, historian].

To dinner with Governor Muñoz Marín. I invited him to speak at Strasbourg this Summer and he accepted. And the talk wandered through to midnight with miscellaneous philosophical observations. Muñoz Marín has maintained himself in Puerto Rico and is beginning to spread out but has never been in Europe.

He said one very interesting thing. He said his majority in Puerto Rico was a steady 65%—the "beauty rest" mattress for a political leader. If it was more than 65%, he said, the job would be impossible—you could not be a common denominator for much more than two-thirds. If it were less, you would find it difficult to get the necessary measures through. He considered he had achieved an almost perfect balance on supporting opposition.

April 17, 1955

At Great Barrington, Harold and Isabel Wolff as guests. Harold has been out to California and there had interviewed the American prisoners brain-washed and released by the Chinese. Unquestionably he had done this for the United States Army, though he did not say so. They could not have got a better man.

He said that the men had been converted by a type of experience almost exactly described by William James in his book. The horrible thing about this was that conversion was used for purely political ends but in all other results the end was the same. The man was first stripped of his pride by all kinds of means and then cut off from all communication with any other part of society and then left to find a new spiritual home in the Communist movement; the result being so like a religious experience that you could not tell the difference. There is nothing new in the technique, Harold pointed out. It has been done since the days of the early Christians. There is no truth in the talk of secret drugs.

I asked what the answer to it was. He said by prevention—by maintaining any possible means of communication however slight so that the individual does not find himself completely cut off.

He also mused that Communist society invariably gathers men into groups as feudal society did. The free world of the democracies does not necessarily connect a man with any group. He also noted that there was only a limited kind of person available for conversion—usually the intellectual who has lost faith in the organization and principles of his own society, and who is on the edge of instability. These people convert easily.

We had reports on the Nazi conversion technique when I was Assistant Secretary of State. They told almost the same story.

April 18, 1955

At work with Peter Beers on the Strasbourg Conference this Summer.

At various jobs, then to dinner at Max Ascoli's house. Dag Hammarskjöld [Secretary-General, United Nations] there; I think Max's real and kindly idea was to bring Hammarskjöld and me together.

Among other things, Hammarskjöld was very outspoken on the Chinese question. He had been negotiating with the Chinese for the release of the American airmen (which he did not get) but was developing a good technical diplomatic method. His real object, of course, was to use the affair of the American airmen as a means of establishing contact in the hope of negotiating a possible settlement particularly in respect of Formosa.

His idea was that:

1. Chou En-lai [Premier and Foreign Minister of the People's Republic of China] is probably as ruthless a man as he had seen. On the other hand, he would be scrupulous in formal matters, keeping his word and so forth. His idea of getting out of a commitment would be to kill his opposite number—destroying a man rather than breaking form. "You

have to think of these people as you think of the figures in the Italian Renaissance," said Dag Hammarskjöld.

2. The ideological hold of Communism on China is small. The drive is far less that of idealism than of renascent nationalism. This shows itself in a number of ways but one of them is a vigorous dislike [of] the Chinese Communist Government [being] unduly dependent on the Soviet Union. On the other hand, an enemy is useful to them; and the United States as the least dangerous enemy (because it is farthest away) is therefore handy.

3. The Chinese Communists regard Formosa as Chinese and as closed issue—but not necessarily now. He said it was like the French insistence that Alsace and Lorraine were French after the War of 1870. It was a closed issue in their minds. On the other hand they did not intend to go to war for it. By consequence he thought that while they would keep up the assertion of title, they would not attack unless they and the Russians jointly considered it to their advantage to do so. He noted that their propaganda for the last ninety days had not stressed the recovery of Formosa. On the other hand, they cannot, of course, accept the notion that there is another Chinese Government—that of Chiang Kai-shek—in the field and doing business.

Like a well-trained diplomat, he considered that the situation could be managed by careful attention to detail and buying time for time. I gathered, though he did not say so directly, that he had very carefully maintained his contacts with the Peking Government. He was also expansive about the technical assistance program, which he considered had many possibilities.

April 20, 1955

Costa Rican–Nicaraguan negotiations are at a standstill. Fournier on returning to Costa Rica had found the Costa Rican Cabinet in an angry mood; they had worked out a line of policy which involved breaking negotiations with Nicaragua and had sent it along to the Ambassador in Washington but with the suggestion that before acting on it Facio discuss it with me. This is not the easiest position to be in. I went over the matter as best I could and by agreement with Facio wrote a letter to Figueres . . . [suggesting carrying out negotiations for a treaty of peace with Nicaragua through the OAS]. . . .

In the evening, a quiet little dinner party at the house and Jules Romains and his wife came to dinner, they having been referred to us by Professor Shotwell. It was interesting to see the old generation functioning in the present. It was Romains who for a split second lifted the thinking of Europe with his book, *The Men of Good Will,* in an attempt to make an appreciation of peace—what it is and can be. He is girding his loins for a last shot. He wants to write a book advocating a group of intellectuals with authority who can meet without reference to governments and try to set out a moral synthesis, at least of the free world.

This prompted Beatrice to say, "You intellectuals certainly don't think badly of yourselves. The F.E.U.E. is thinking of conquering the world by ideas in Strasbourg this Summer; you are thinking of trying to do it by a book in Paris." Romains answered that something very like this had held the thirteenth century together and he considered himself as able to do it as the thirteenth century boys. What is lacking in the twentieth century, he said, is courage.

June 10, 1955

Last night, Secretary Hammarskjöld of the United Nations to dinner at the house.

I congratulated him about the release of the American flyers held prisoners by the Chinese Communists and said that I was sure that this was due to his efforts. Without beating about the bush, he said that it was; and he had maintained the contact and had waited for the appropriate time to crystallize sentiment. He said Chou En-lai had been clear that they should be released but had had to have time to convince his own party—that is to say, the Communist group in China.

I said that logic should suggest that other releases could be made; I hoped that by the 1st of July we might have another batch. He said that he considered that it would happen within two weeks (that is by the 23rd of June). This was either a remarkable prediction or more likely an actual knowledge of what the plans are.

With us was Lewis Galantière [Counsellor, Free Europe Committee]. I turned the discussion then to the problem of resolving the problem of the Iron Curtain countries. I said that Americans were disturbed about it, partly because they had debts of honor there. Promises had been made to us at Yalta; and this was all we had to protect populations which had trusted us during World War II. Consequently, we cannot let go. I wondered whether a solution like that of Finland could not be worked out. Hammarskjöld considered this. He said that he thought the Iron Curtain situation would be a continuous source of trouble. The Finnish solution had been arrived at because Finland stood next to Sweden—a neutral country offering no threat to Russia but very costly if it was forced into war. Sweden could be strenuously and armedly neutral because behind her was Norway tied up to the West and with American bases. Consequently Finland was equipoised; it would cost Russia a great deal to seize Finland because of the danger involving Sweden and others. She would gain little by doing so. Further the Finnish population would never go along with Russian seizure. The question was whether this could be recreated in the other Iron Curtain countries.

I mused on the possibility of an arrangement, tacit or negotiated, namely, that as and when Germany is unified as it probably would be, nevertheless remaining within the NATO alliance, there was at least a silent understanding that Allied troops would not be stationed east of the Oder-Neisse line. Meanwhile, Hammarskjöld said this could not be negotiated; it would have to happen. If in fact the populations of these countries were, as they appeared to be, opposed to Russia, it probably would; the Russian position would get weaker, they would eventually decree freedom to these people to govern themselves. Hammarskjöld seemed to think this would take some time but it would be within the scope of the possible.

Hammarskjöld was kind enough to make a pleasant remark about my book [*The Twentieth Century Capitalist Revolution*]. I asked him whether the day might not come when the United Nations would issue a charter for corporations. For example, in connection with the proposed pool of atomic energy information that Eisenhower wants. He said at once that this was an entirely logical thing for them to do in certain limited aspects. I noted that the power to create a corporation has become one of the implied powers of the United States Government.

He described a couple of new wrinkles in diplomatic technique. In one committee it was obvious that the Russians and the rest of the world could not agree. Hammarskjöld was elected Chairman of the Committee. He then declared that the committee was a committee advisory to the Chairman and that instead of having votes on motion, he would hear the entire debate; he would then state his conclusion as to the result of the debate: that is, as to the committee's advice to him—and ask the committee to accept or reject it. The technique, he said, worked perfectly. It meant that he did not have an adverse vote on any particular proposition; that the conclusion thus proposed did not necessarily have to include a rejection of someone's position; that thus everybody's face would be saved. This was a new one on me and a trick worth remembering. . . .

June 17, 1955

Yesterday the inevitable Argentina revolt took place. This appears to have been an inside job by the Argentine Navy who planned an amphibious landing to seize Buenos Aires, accompanied by an air attack paralyzing resistance; simultaneously there were to be risings outside the capital. The air attack began; heavy seas prevented amphibious landing so that the small group who seized the Casa Rosada was left without support. The Army remained loyal to Perón. . . .

. . . Perón paralyzed the Army and made it his own; he was engaged in trying to paralyze the Catholic Church but he had never fully dominated the Navy.

Last night to dinner at my house was Rodolfo García Arias, Counsellor of the Argentina Embassy during the war; later Ambassador to Mexico; and my colleague in many diplomatic jobs. He is here on business but I surmise may have wondered whether something was likely to break loose. He tells me that the quarrel with the Church was nothing more than Perón's normal desire to control an institution; he had been slowly converging on this and finally had reached the point where the hierarchy reacted. Then he had followed his usual course of trying to prevent any independent meeting or organization.

The report today suggests that the revolution failed. . . .

Today, to "The Little Church Around the Corner," to the funeral of Walter Hampden. At the close of it [actor] Dennis King read the final death speech of Cyrano de Bergerac; an impressive, if unusual, end, but Walter Hampden, whom I had been seeing through my lifetime, had been a very great player.

I am increasingly concerned about the European diplomatic situation. Everyone is talking about atmospheric conditions between the East and West, but from a professional diplomatic point of view the map tells the story. Switzerland is a neutral bloc on top of Italy. By neutralizing Austria through the Austrian treaty (happily recommended by our State Department) another neutral point is established. The Russians obviously are asking for the same thing from Yugoslavia. The German bloc and the Italian bloc just cannot get together. They are divided by Switzerland, Austria and the Communist-held Czechoslovakia. The Russians move their troops 40 kilometres back to the Austrian border; the Allies are supposed to get to the other side of the Alps. If they can detach Yugoslavia, Italy is, for practical purposes, not reachable by any land line (the French line is bad). Greece and Turkey are detached from the NATO group. You would expect the Russians to be busy as beavers on the other side of Turkey. One of my diplomatic friends tells me they are infiltrating into Afghanistan very heavily; I surmise they are very active in Iran. In another six months this will be making headlines but apparently no one sees the strategy now.

July 7, 1955

Adlai Stevenson called on David Dubinsky to discuss Presidential probabilities. He wanted to know whether David and I thought he would be stronger as a candidate than Harriman.

I told David that my private opinion was neither could beat Eisenhower at the moment. My guess is Stevenson would make a better run, and would educate the American public more. But we are in an era like the second Coolidge Administration: the public wants to spend its money and be let alone, and is only mildly interested in being educated.

I am asking to be relieved of the Chairmanship of the Liberal Party tonight. . . .

July 13, 1955

Last night, a dinner tendered me by the Liberal Party. David Dubinsky presided; short speeches; a quiet, pleasant, sentimental evening. This is Louis Stulberg's [Vice President, ILGWU] doing. I told him I thought my departure ought to be done gracefully and he agreed and it was so done. In politics you only get what you ask for; the problem is to ask the right thing. But there is a solid bond of affection between these men who have carried whatever slender thread of desire for honesty and better government has continued constant in New York politics. . . .

July 15, 1955

Radio Free Europe is coming in for increasing attack in the German Press, chiefly from German nationalists. Yesterday talking with Whitney Shepardson [President, National Committee for a Free Europe], Lewis Galantière and Connie Egan [USIS aide in Brazil, 1945], I suggested that we begin to make an affirmation of political faith. This, it seems to me, could best be done by having Lucius Clay make a speech at some appropriate European festival, preferably the Free University of Berlin, talking straight Wilsonian lines and incidentally explaining why some millions of Americans had supported RFE. It is once more the theory that positive attack is best. Otherwise RFE in Germany will be done to death by a series of small bites without having affirmed itself. If we have to go out of Germany, we should go out with a bang, and not a whimper.

September 16, 1955

Peter decided that before he went back to college, he wanted a last shot at the mountains. So Saturday noon, he and I took the car; slept that night a mile out on the Long Trail; the next morning motored over to the foot of Franconia; went up to Liberty Spring where we left the duffle and climbed there. Back to sleep Sunday night. Monday, we went over the range, Haystack, Lincoln, Lafayette, then down to Profile Notch. Motoring, we had dinner at Tilton; then to Boston where I picked up the midnight train.

Peter, now strong and husky, did most of the work. I was content to feel at sixty I could still go over the range. I had gone over it first in 1912 or thereabouts, and taken Peter out when he was ten or eleven, then doing the work myself. This time I was getting it back. There may not be so many more week-ends when my son and I can climb together. He will be somewhere else; and 5,000 feet of mountain climbing is not as easy for me as it was forty years ago.

October 24, 1955

The national political pot is boiling though I am pretty far on the edges this time. I think Stevenson is the likely nominee but my instinct would be to work with Harriman, partly because he is nearer and a little franker in his personal relationships. Stevenson, an excellent man, has a quality of manipulating people with great skill rather than direct personal relations.

November 23, 1955

Monday the 21st, various things. Dinner with Bill Burden [President, MOMA Board of Trustees], thence to Latin American opening at the Museum of Modern Art. A dinner guest of Bill's was Hammarskjöld. He rather sought us out. I told him I thought the direction of affairs was headed for a main-line crisis in the Near East with the Soviet insistence on control of the Dardanelles and joint control of Suez. He said he agreed that was the direction; he was sure there would be a crisis sometime in 1956 though he could not tell the date. In dead secret he said that he has kept up his personal correspondence with Chou En-lai; he said that with typical oriental gesture the last eleven prisoners released by them were released, according to Chou En-lai's letter, as a birthday present to him (Hammarskjöld). As he observed, typical oriental diplomacy. He is keeping his personal line open because it may be needed later. He feels a similar, personal line might be needed to Moscow. . . .

Tuesday, November 22nd. I kept an appointment with Tom Finletter [lawyer; former Secretary of the Air Force]. He asked me to go on the

Stevenson Committee; I told him I was too old merely to go on name committees, and that my real interest was in foreign affairs. I knew, of course, there was a seminar for Stevenson (omitting any reference to the fact that I had not been invited) and said I did not know who was running their foreign affairs. Finletter said he thought Chester Bowles was. The upshot was that he asked me to come to the next seminar, probably to talk Latin America. He also agreed that before going on a committee I should talk with David Dubinsky. All this is putting your finger in the cog-wheel. Beatrice is dead against any more Washington adventures. For the end of this trail if it works (and it doesn't necessarily work) would be, of course, a Washington job of some sort. And I have come to the conclusion that unless it is a real assignment with destiny, more can be done here than there. . . .

December 5, 1955

Thursday, December 1. Lunch with Carlos Lacerda and we went over the Brazilian situation in great detail. Fundamentally they are afraid that [Juscelino] Kubitschek as President-Elect has promised the Ministry of Labor to the [João] Goulart group. These are Perón's comrades acting in alliance with the Communists. He also is afraid that Kubitschek has promised the Prefecture of Rio to Amaral Peixoto (he is married to Vargas' daughter) or perhaps to Vargas' son, Luthero. Since these two people were part of the conspiracy to murder Lacerda, his worry is natural.

That evening and Friday to Princeton for the meeting of the Twentieth Century Fund. We duly installed August Heckscher as the new Director, retaining Fred Dewhurst as Economic Adviser and giving him a first-rate European project. As a minor item, we gave a grant-in-aid to Jacques Maritain. This is to enable him to finish his book. We really did it so that the old man does not starve to death either in the streets of Paris or New York. Foundations do not do these things at all. I said it was silly to talk about ethics and then not do something about the man who had carried the play. Oppenheimer then moved the grant.

Sunday, December 4. Hugo Gouthier came in to lunch. He is a close adviser to Kubitschek; also paradoxically a close friend of Carlos Lacerda. I told him the substance of my talk with Lacerda. Gouthier said he had discussed these things with Kubitschek and he was clear Carlos was wrong. I told him I thought Kubitschek would either be the prisoner of the Communist-nationalist group or he would be their bitterest enemy; they would try to take over. Gouthier said he was clear this was true. . . .

In the evening, [Paulo] Bittencourt of the Brazilian *Correio da Manhã* came in. He was the chief anti-Kubitschek editor but steadily supported the insistence of the Army that Kubitschek be allowed to take office. I told him that I thought he was quite right. I explained the fear that this would let in the jungle via Amaral Peixoto or Goulart or both. Bittencourt said that he thought there was no danger and that he thought Carlos Lacerda was overstating the case. This is, I think, quite likely.

I added that if I had a chance I'd put in a word re State's policy, but there was no certainty they would take my advice. . . .

On Sunday also I sent a telegram to Tom Finletter as follows:

"Will be glad to join your committee for Stevenson. . . ."

This was in response to a call from Finletter asking me to join the committee; but my chat with him resulted in an invitation to join the "Stevenson's Seminar" chiefly to discuss Latin America. This takes place the 13th of December; we shall open up the whole foreign policy question before we get through.

In this respect the United States is in trouble. Whatever the result of the [Nikita] Khrushchev visit to India, it is clear they can count on India's neutrality in any push they make on either side of the Indian Ocean. Elsewhere and especially at the Naval Academy in Annapolis, I have expressed my feeling that they plan to shove for the Dardanelles and Suez next Summer. This could easily be by a sudden call for a conference to revise the terms of the Montreux Convention; I don't see what you are going to do to stop it as things are running now.

December 13, 1955

A meeting with the Stevenson group on foreign affairs; Finletter presiding. Among those present were

> Chester Bowles,
> Arthur Schlesinger,
> Oscar Chapman,
> Ben Cohen,
> Former Senator Bill Benton

I reported on Latin America. But by the time everyone had got through demolishing (a) NATO, (b) SEATO, (c) bases in Japan, (d) about everything else, I wondered whether this bunch had solidity enough to handle any situation. Their instincts are of the best. But this is a rough, tough, world.

I agreed to put in a memorandum on Latin America, which I hope does some good.

January 10, 1956

Lunch with Willard Barber, Counsellor of Embassy in Colombia, who is leaving to take the same post in Warsaw. He drew a terrible picture of the [Gustavo Rojas] Pinilla regime of Colombia; it began well and steadily went down-hill. It machine-gunned a student demonstration and tried to cover up by claiming it was "Communist." Barber was there and saw it; they weren't Communists. Further, the government had been militarized right down to the alcaldes of the little towns who were sergeants; also, as usual, the family and camp followers are richer. The Colombian Catholic Church he describes as, in the words of the Encyclopaedia Britannica, "The last survival of medieval ecclesiasticism." People are excommunicated right and left for reading the wrong newspapers, having the wrong ideas, and so forth. I remember [Alberto] Lleras Camargo's remark at dinner at our house; he said that in Colombia the Catholic Church had never had the advantages of Reformation. There is solid danger that the result may be a Spanish-type revolution—the most hideous of all.

Barber thought, as I did, that American diplomatists should be split into two classes: the career diplomat who sticks to orderly communication and does nothing else; the diplomat who goes straight in to the politics of the country and fights it out on principle. He jeopardizes his career if he does not win; he is "expendable" and is understood to be that. He can struggle against forces which seem to be heading towards disaster.

February 1, 1956

Sunday was my 61st birthday. C. D. Jackson came over to lunch. The Oppenheimer case came up. I told him that Lewis Strauss [Chairman, Atomic Energy Commission] was tagged with this as truly as was Bishop Cauchon tagged with the condemnation of Joan of Arc and nothing could be done about it. C. D. said this was not just. Lewis Strauss wanted quietly to discontinue Oppenheimer's contract without more. J. Edgar Hoover had, however, received a letter . . . accusing Oppenheimer of everything in the book. Hoover had sent this letter not only to the President and to Lewis but to "Engine Charlie" Wilson [Secretary of Defense]. That simple "valve-in-the-head" character, as C. D. described him, charged into the White House demanding Oppenheimer's head and he withdrew Oppenheimer's clearance, in effect publishing the situation to the world. Lewis had hoped to finesse the situation without a security trial but was pressed into the ensuing action. C. D. thinks Lewis unjustly dealt with and so, probably, he is.

C. D. made an excellent memorandum of the actual facts under date of October 12 to Henry Luce—it was an answer to the Alsops' column "We Accuse" but, of course, private memoranda are of little help in a public controversy. . . .

February 24, 1956

. . . Thence to Puerto Rico: nominally and really a holiday; actually a spectacular drama. . . . The same night we came in Pepe and Karen Figueres arrived for a state visit; Luis Muñoz Marín and Doña Inez were expecting us and treated us as part of the visiting party. . . .

The next day was Muñoz Marín's birthday; it was celebrated with a picnic at Luquillo Beach with the Legislature and high officials and others—and ourselves. Presently, however, Doña Inez sent word that she hoped Beatrice and I would move rather close to the Governor's party, which we did. We then, the beach party coming to its end, slipped in our cars off the beach and headed, at once, for a little sheltered cove far out on the Island, the so-called "Convento" where there was a little cabin. . . . Pepe was taut as a fiddle string and presently the truth emerged.

[Rómulo] Betancourt, the leader of the Venezuelan opposition to the dictator, [Marcos] Pérez Jiménez, had been given asylum by Figueres; at the State Department's urging he had left Costa Rica and been given asylum in Puerto Rico. When Figueres' state visit was announced, Holland had telephoned Muñoz Marín, asking that Muñoz Marín arrange for Betancourt to be away during Pepe's visit. Muñoz Marín had explained this and Betancourt was in the Virgin Islands. Muñoz Marín had no liking for this at all; it was a move to please the Venezuelan dictator, [Pérez] Jiménez; Pepe, of course, knew it (Betancourt had told him about it to explain his absence and everyone was thoroughly angry); they were angry for a good Spanish reason: the United States, claiming hegemony of the West, had been dictated to within its own borders by a two-cent dictator who could punish an enemy even within the United States borders. The Spanish expression used is sorry, colorful, classic and not pleasant.

At this point Doña Inez took control. She knew not only of Pepe's tremendously taut reaction. She also knew that Karen, a school-girl who had in two years become the wife of a foreigner, who is also the President of Costa Rica, had had one baby and expecting the second, found the going very hard indeed. . . . The combination was something which could have broken as sensitive a man as Pepe but here Doña Inez emerged as the wise and tender mother of the whole Caribbean Sea. Quietly she laid down the law to Muñoz.

Pepe wanted to send a telegram to Holland. "He must send it," said Doña Inez, "otherwise he will simply pound himself to a pulp." So he composed and we redacted a telegram to Holland telling him that this was no kind of thing to do.

Doña Inez put Karen on a cot in the shade of a palm tree—and Karen quietly and promptly went to sleep, and stayed asleep. We spent the entire day (Sunday) in the little cabin with no one around—except a couple of guards and FBI men patrolling in the background. . . .

Then in the sunlight we began to debate the whole question of Latin American policy. . . . The Betancourt incident was theoretically "secret" which meant that everyone from the students in Puerto Rico to the Argentine already knew about it. Muñoz Marín was in some difficulties. The University of Puerto Rico had given an honorary degree to Chief Justice Earl Warren and also to the Chief Justice of Spain in celebration of a new courthouse. The students had picketed the university against this recognition of Franco; Pablo Casals [Spanish cellist], who was in the Island, had promptly refused to accept an honorary degree Puerto Rico had offered him. Pablo as a personal matter had come to the Governor's reception and to a small dinner at which we were (and a lovely dinner it was) but had made it plain that he had refused to play in the United States after America had recognized Franco. . . .

We, all of us, agreed that the United States in some manifestation—government, if possible; private people, if not—ought to indicate where it stood.

Again Doña Inez intervened. She knew that I was scheduled to speak at the University of Puerto Rico. I had suggested that the University invite Pepe. . . . [She] asked that I . . . have Pepe come along with me in some fashion. This was really a move to ease the difficulty caused by the University's degree to the Franco Chief Justice. So through the day, beautiful, quiet, relaxing, with all of the edges of policy and personality coming up to the surface—indeed, being brought up to the surface—by Doña Inez—and resolved.

Monday morning, back in the hotel, I got a clean shirt and tackled

President [Jaime] Benítez [University of Puerto Rico]. He was very glad to arrange—and did arrange—that the following day Pepe and I should speak together at a meeting of the Faculty of Social Science. He likewise arranged a large meeting to be held this coming Friday for Pepe to talk to the students.

On Tuesday afternoon, we had an academic conference in which I gave some economic theory and introduced Pepe as an intellectual in his own right who was also a President; Pepe thereupon gave an excellent exposition of the reason his government had chosen a mixed instead of a socialist economy. The address was extremely well received; Pepe won the respect of the assembled academicians; I thought I could go to the formal State dinner and report to Doña Inez that it was a mission accomplished.

The net result of this was that Beatrice and I arrived at the State dinner in the Forteleza forty-five minutes late and then followed a dinner and evening that belongs in a story book. For the old Forteleza is a majestic Spanish castle and the State receiving rooms and dining rooms are beautifully proportioned. Afterwards a Puerto Rican string quintette played as well as any quintette I have ever heard and we adjourned in a luminous tropical night to the escarpment of the fortress for talk and a drink and talk again. Having to take a plane early the next morning, we left at 1:30; things were just getting started; Muñoz was prepared to talk and so was Pepe. Inez and Karen had wisely gone off to bed. But things were easier now. Just before dinner, Holland had telephoned Muñoz Marín. He had got Pepe's wire. He hoped (1) that it would not be published; (2) that Pepe would realize that the step was only to protect him (Pepe) from Venezuelan reprisals. I think that Holland really believed this. He was the only one in the hemisphere, however, that did. Everyone else believed it had been dictated by the oil interests. . . . I know that Holland has orders from Foster Dulles not to offend the dictators; he has done his best to help out when he could. He is not a free agent. So the best I could do was to say that someone was a damn fool, without saying who. Of course this will be out in the Latin press, probably *Bohemia*, anytime now. . . .

But the real experience of the trip (against a setting of sheer loveliness equal to anything in this world, heightened by the music of Handel and Haydn) was, of course, Doña Inez. This was great placidity; great understanding; great kindness; the most acute political judgment; a woman acting as a woman, and not as a politician.

Beatrice and I had sent her flowers for the State dinner, with an inscription, "To the Wise and Tender Mother of the Caribbean Sea." Said Doña Inez, "I think that was a love letter." Said we, "No doubt about it whatever."

We raised the problem, "How can you maul an American government into realizing that Latin Americans expect and demand that a senior power shall have some moral principles?" For, in the course of the conversation, came in the Uruguayan proposal that the Latin nations should unite by themselves, leaving out the United States on the ground that the United States is too amoral and too insensitive to be a safe ally. It was Pepe who argued against this with Muñoz Marín; it was Doña Inez who pointed out that America was not its government but the essential kindliness and decency of its people. It was Pepe who agreed but said that no one except those who knew the United States could know this. It was to me they left the job of trying to get something done about it. And I have been sweating it out ever since.

While there I asked Pepe whether he could take Peter on one of his plantations for a couple of months next Summer. It is time Peter got into the act and he has to know some Spanish. Pepe said he would be glad to do it.

I also tentatively opened the possibility that he might come to the Free Europe University in Exile in Europe. . . .

March 9, 1956

To Cambridge to the "Committee to Visit the History Department" at Harvard. They have been worried about educating enough Doctors of Philosophy in history to teach the tide of incoming students everyone expects in the next five or six years. Nobody seemed to want to tackle the question of why history should be taught at all. We shall get at that later.

After which to the Parker House for beer with Arthur Schlesinger, Jr. I agreed to join in a draft of Stevenson's foreign policy speech on April 21 before the Newspaper Publishers Association.

There is not much question now that Stevenson will be nominated but the Southern split on segregation is rapidly coming to completion and it will be a great struggle to hold the party together.

March 13, 1956

. . . My old friend Lou Mallace died last night. I had known him as a fifteen-year-old on the Lower East Side: the son of a junk man going nowhere; he could have been a gangster; and we became friends.

Against every kind of disadvantage he maintained headway and educated two children, giving them college degrees, and is dead of a heart attack at 50. It was a terrible blow to his family; one of the golden, unrecorded lives that belong in history and doesn't get there.

April 4, 1956

Just before he left for South America last week, Nelson Rockefeller called up and asked if I would do a job for him. "Tell me where we will be twenty years from now," he said, "and what the problems will be." He was thinking of a study somewhat like that on capital we got up a couple of years ago. I told him that no sane man would take an assignment like that. He said that was why he had asked me. I agreed to do the job.

. . . [Nelson has] access to the Republican Administration; the ability to command any expert on anything; the question is what to do with his life; and with the most magnificent "do-it-yourself" kit ever provided; only it has no plans or suggestions. I had somewhat the same experience— if one leaves out the money and that is not important because you can always get it if you want something badly enough. I have been trying to surround the problem.

It seemed to me that we should have not only something in the nature of an economic and social forecast in the selection of problems—but something also in bravura style appreciating the fundamental question. . . .

Tom Finletter called up and asked me if I would speak at the Stevenson dinner on April 25. Stevenson's campaign is going badly, with Kefauver the obvious popular candidate; I surmise that Finletter is disappointed. Privately I have difficulty in seeing how Stevenson could get nominated short of some miraculous showing he makes in California.

Being more accustomed to lone hands and lost causes than Finletter, my feeling is that you are never in trouble if you pick the best there is even if you get trimmed.

May 4, 1956

[The Stevenson dinner] . . . A political dinner, especially in a preconvention campaign, is black art. It is put together chiefly to see that all hands who should be represented are represented; who is there is more important than what is said and so forth. So Finletter (chiefly famous in the Truman Administration) represented one stripe of thought; I (Liberal), another; [Francis W. H.] Adams (former Police Commissioner of New York) spoke for the Irish Catholics; Anna Rosenberg (also of the Truman Administration), Jewish; and, of course, Adlai Stevenson. The high-priced political performers were, of course, Senator Lehman and Mayor Wagner.

James Farley was there. This shocked the Harriman forces. Being alone, David Dubinsky invited him to sit at the Liberal table which surprised people still more. They had a happy time.

To Stevenson, June 14, 1956

. . . Unemployment, reflecting cut-backs in automobiles and accessories, is showing in Michigan, Ohio, Indiana, and in Atlantic textile areas.

Because most Americans are in hock for instalments, impact is immediate; unemployment insurance won't pay them. There is no cushion of ownership which kept unemployed afloat for a year after 1929. . . .

It should be possible to point out that government, which bought time for banks, insurance companies and railroads in 1933, could buy time for individuals who through unemployment are in danger of losing cars, kitchens and houses in 1957.

Also to arrange credits permitting American production for countries like Morocco, Bolivia, and others which cannot make consumer goods and build capital at the same time, bringing employment back.

We could shift the concept of foreign aid to what Gunnar Myrdal calls "integration"—real building of international economy whereby American economy, with reasonably full employment, is not interrupted, while great areas dependent on us—for instance, Latin America—are in crises of want.

This is the real answer to the Soviet organization of an international economic and military system opposed to the free world.

The discussion thus moves a step forward from where Roosevelt and Truman left it.

July 15, 1956

Rio . . . We were enveloped in the gorgeous Brazilian hospitality. . . . We have friends in all camps and before we left, the President, Kubitschek, invited me to lunch. He was just back from the Panama Conference. There were only three of us—Kubitschek, his principal advisor, [Horácio] Lafer, and myself. He was perfectly frank about his own politics: he was trying to keep things under control; thought he had got the army pledged to a peaceful government. . . .

The fascinating part is the growth of the west. All the way from Amapá to the border of Paraguay, you see new cities rising. The little city of Ceres in Goiás was forgotten forest twelve years ago. Now it is an up and coming little town of 25,000 of shops, tile houses and so forth, and a Franciscan school (run by American priests) with 1,500 children in it. This appears to be typical of the whole Western belt. It is coming along like a shot and some day will dominate the life of Brazil.

Rio is all politics, and always was, but the interior cities are plowing along making things and trying to make money and making some gain on creating a middle class. In the short pull, I am a little worried, but in the long pull, there is no question that Brazil will be a very big, very powerful country; will make its appearance on the world scene in some ten or fifteen years. . . .

July 31–August 2, 1956

By plane to Africa where we had breakfast at Dakar. I had never seen it; had fought like the devil to get our fingernails into Dakar during the war; got it and then the airfield came from which we had reenforced the battle of El Alamein. Anyhow here we were, in a quite respectable airport which was in the worst snafu I had ever seen. Several plane loads of African Mohammedans making a pilgrimage to Mecca had showed up and things were in chaos. Some of them were stunning—six foot tall with white robes, looking askance at white men until you put your hands together and said, "Shalom" ("Peace be with you"), whereupon they reciprocated. They invaded the kitchen, the offices, the ladies' rooms and everything else and getting breakfast out of the place was a major operation. I tipped the boy in the bathroom a dollar; you would have thought I had given him the Island of Manhattan. The Near East begins at Dakar without any doubt.

Thence to Zurich and to sleep. We motored the next day to the kindly eighteenth century chateau and gardens of Robertsau.

There, August 2, they were just getting ready for the influx of students for the Summer Session. A good deal of the administrative work and some minor headaches but they were coming along well. . . . The students came in as though they were coming to an old home week; glad to be back and making no bones about it; taking care of the sixty-odd neophytes and generally having a wonderful time. I gave the opening lecture. This time in a different atmosphere because the mid-European revolution is beginning to get up steam. . . .

Whatever else we have done, we have got together a group of several hundred extremely able and extremely well-trained young men and women. On the night before we left, they were having their opening. Everyone singing his native songs and doing native dances against a background of the kindlier side of France and a general warm feeling.

But they want a philosophical lead from the United States. "How," they say, "can we blaze away at the Communist dictatorship in Poland and swallow a similar dictatorship in Yugoslavia?" One boy who had been terribly tortured in Yugoslavia raised the question and he meant it. I could only say that philosophically we went the whole way. Tactically, we were only attacking the Soviet domination for the moment because that was the immediate target. Some of the questions were embarrassing. . . .

Thence by plane to Geneva to spend the night with Georges Henri Martin. . . .

Obviously Suez was the main discussion. Everybody in Europe thinks we should have taken a stiffer stand in Suez—and I think so too at present. Maybe it will work out but I am not so sure. . . .

August 12–13, 1956

To New York. Immediately to Great Barrington to look at some green grass and sleep; the next night (August 13) to Chicago where the Democratic Convention was getting underway. Over to see David Dubinsky and things began to happen fast. . . . During the afternoon Walter Reuther came over to say that the Michigan delegation was declaring for Adlai. This was the beginning of the bandwagon. I went over to Adlai's suite in the Blackstone Hotel. . . . The usual group of adoring ladies. . . . Adlai and I went off in a corner and talked. It was the first time anyone would listen. He said he was grieved about Truman. He had watched him sacrifice a rather assured and gracious position for something that was shoddy at best. I said that I grieved about Harriman. He said he didn't. Apparently Harriman had done something like welching on an understanding. I commented that as a school teacher, I hated to see any good man lost. Then we got to the serious business of the Vice President. Adlai said he had no doubt about his nomination. The Vice Presidency was important. He wanted a man who could be of real help and take some work off his shoulders. I said that labor was solid for Estes Kefauver. There was no good in making any concessions to the [Senate Majority Leader Lyndon B.] Johnson [D., Tex.] group. He had the votes anyhow. . . .

The possibility of a Catholic, [Senator John F.] Kennedy [D., Mass.] or Wagner. I said not now. He said Sam Rayburn. I said this was delightful but not practical. My guess was Kefauver. Adlai said, swearing me to secrecy, that he was about at the Kefauver point. He did not want anyone to think that any deal had been made. He had made no deals. Sidney

Davis of the Liberal Party told me that Kefauver had come over to Stevenson of his own will without any reservation.

Ernest Cuneo tells me that the Lyndon Johnson crowd is angry about Kefauver but would accept Humphrey. Adding up the pluses and minuses, I think Kefauver will make it but it will be close going.

Not thinking of anything else to do now that the show is over, I told Adlai I would not bother him again until this organized bedlam had died down, and took a plane for New York. . . .

August 27, 1956

. . . —— came in to see me this afternoon at the request of Allen Dulles. . . .

I had given him the report received [in Rio] from Affonso Arinos [Brazilian Foreign Minister] that Perón had caused to be shipped $200,-000,000 in bar gold from Switzerland to Montevideo, presumably for use in revolutionary activities. He came in to say that the report had been verified—the amount was $100,000,000, not $200,000,000; there were two shipments of $50,000,000 each. . . .

He intimated that steps were being taken to see that the gold is immobilized so that it is not used to subsidize a revolution in Argentina. Let us hope so.

My son, Peter, came back from Costa Rica today. He has been living as a peon for six weeks; has lost 15 lbs. living on rice and beans. He had an amazing experience. He knows now what the underside of the world looks like.

He spent his last day there with President Figueres. During this time, President Figueres' youngest son, two and a half years old, fell into the pond, and was not missed until Peter went looking for him. The boy was almost drowned; Peter's artificial respiration work stood everybody in good stead so the boy came through all right.

September 24, 1956

Friday to Washington for a little brain-trusting for Stevenson with Arthur Schlesinger and Robert? Tufts and young Miller, formerly of the Union Theological Seminary . . . and now on Stevenson's staff. There is the equivalent of the [Commonwealth?] speech which Stevenson has to make next month and Schlesinger suggests I set up a draft. . . . Stevenson is tired. He observed that last time he had tried to do an intellectual job and it was not enough. This time he was trying to do both that and a political, but always feeling that he had never achieved a first-rate job in either. He thinks his chances of election are about even. I, of course, put in my oar on foreign affairs, using Latin America as a great laboratory and the theory that we had to work not only on nationalist lines but also on the internationalist layer. . . .

After lunch, work on some material including the old-age study which Stevenson is putting out. . . .

To Great Barrington over the weekend. . . .

During the evening the news came that Somoza had been shot. As usual in these matters, the assassin bungled the job. There will be hell to pay in Nicaragua.

I hastily reviewed the hand. Fortunately Figueres is in France, [Ramón] Villeda Morales [later President of Honduras] is here, and I am pretty clear Luis Manuel Debayle kept out of this; things are as safe as they can be made. The man who did the shooting was Rigoberto [Cabezas] López, a Nicaraguan; it happened in the city of León.

It would be death to say so in Nicaragua, of course, but anyone who has followed the career of Somoza would know almost without being told that something of the kind was certain to happen. It merely means that every honest democrat for miles around is accused as being an assassin.

October 22, 1956

Yesterday, October 21, the Honduran Army demanded that the Honduran dictator, [Julio] Lozano [Díaz], resign. The reason they gave was that he represented no popular support whatever.

The fact is that the man who has the greatest personal following in the country is Villeda Morales. . . .

. . . Villeda Morales, who probably had a majority of votes in the last election, was prevented from taking office by an intrigue in which American Ambassador [Whiting] Willauer was a party. Apparently the excuse was that Villeda Morales was a Communist which, of course, he is not. When he arrived here at my invitation he was duly introduced to a lot of people in Washington and elsewhere who I believe were satisfied. He returned at once to Costa Rica and the Lozano election referred to above was held. It seemed to me as though the only way he or any democratic group could get into Honduras was to shoot their way in. But apparently two of the three Army officers are American trained, disliked the position of using their guns to maintain a dictator and told the dictator to retire. . . .

Also over the weekend the Polish situation blew up. This, of course, is in part the outcome of seven weary years' work by R.F.E. The explosion took the form of a growing Titoist movement in the Central Committee of the Polish Communist Party. Under Stalin's influence, they had deposed and put in jail one [Wladyslav] Gomulka of Titoist leanings. On Friday, the majority of the Committee voted to take him out of jail and reelect him to the Central Committee along with some other adherents. On Saturday, Khrushchev, [Anastas] Mikoyan, [Lazar M.] Kaganovich and Molotov flew to Warsaw. . . . Attempt to move Russian troops from East Germany into Poland was met with resistance by the Polish troops and they retired. This morning it appears that the Gomulka or Titoist group are supreme in Warsaw.

A Titoist Poland is or at least can be an independent Poland. This does not make it a free Poland. R.F.E. has been giving the news and generally encouraging the proceedings, but without committing to the Gomulka type of government. Eventually we shall have to have some really free elections there. I have been watching closely with Connie Egan.

In larger aspect, this may be important. Russia has contact with Communist East Germany *only through* Poland. Cut that connection and the Russian power there becomes very much less. But there is a kicker in this. Germany, of course, wants back the territory east of the Oder-Neisse line, which was taken away from her and given to Poland by Stalin. All Poles, Communist and free, seem to think that they are entitled to the territory forever. The danger is that the Russians stir up East Germany to fight the Poles.

October 25, 1956

. . . It seems the day before yestérday, the Hungarian revolution, sparked by the students, demanded the return of Imre Nagy, supposed to be a Titoist and put in jail by the Stalinists. Nagy was released, took over the government. . . . [The Russians are] strafing Budapest with tanks, airplanes and troops. The Hungarian Communist troops or substantial chunks of them declined to go along; today the situation is unclear, though I hope to know more by evening via RFE monitoring station near Munich. I should give Nagy ten days to live, unless he takes refuge as a naked Quisling behind the Russian troops. It is not easy to tell whether he was bribed or otherwise corrupted in advance to betray the revolution. Anyhow, hell is to pay.

In Poland the revolution put in Gomulka, it paused there and Gomulka is negotiating with the Russians who have not used their troops.

Yet it is clear that both in Hungary and in Poland the guts of the revolution want not national Communist tyranny but real freedom. The fact that the Russians have used troops to shut down alleged friendly populations cannot but have repercussions everywhere.

A stiff day for R.F.E.

#   #

The Stevenson campaign in full swing. My fear is that he will almost make it. But not quite. At the moment, I cannot quite tell; the situation suggests that of 1948.

October 30, 1956

On Saturday, October 27, Connie Egan 'phoned to give the latest bulletins on the Hungarian uprising. . . . The Russians were shooting; the Hungarian army was fraternizing with the rebels but not doing much except to give them arms; the RFE group were wondering whether a cease-fire order could not be worked out.

I said that it looked as though the rebels were doing fairly well; whether we wanted a cease-fire order depended partly on whether the Russians were reenforcing their troops. If they were, cease-fire would end in slaughter. In that case, the way to do it was to get the Austrian govern-ment to intervene. Austria has a plain interest: she is unarmed and neu-tralized so that no one can be afraid of her.

On Monday, October 29, all day, a string of reports. As nearly as we could get it:

(a) The Russians are not reenforcing their troops;

(b) The two Russian divisions do hold Budapest, if it can be said to hold a city where any householder will shoot you if he can;

(c) The Nagy government . . . now is desperately seeking to deal with the rebels. But they want them to surrender their arms *after* which Russian troops will get out. Not unnaturally the rebels do not want to trust their lives to that crew. The United States Government people are, of course, trying to help with medical supplies, food, etc. I think the Hungarian rebels feel let down: they want guns. Walter Lippmann thinks we ought to settle for a Titoist regime. But that is not what the Hungarians want now. They would have settled for that last week—but Nagy, their Tito, called on Russian guns and the fat is in the fire.

Over Sunday, the United States and others put the question into the United Nations which debated all day Sunday and came up with very little.

Just as I opened my Seminar at Columbia yesterday, a student came in to say that the Israeli Army had crossed the Egyptian border. Hell alone knows where that will go to. The Israeli probably think that now is the precise moment in which to start a preventative operation: there is a certain grim luck in it but to bet the life of a nation on that kind of gamble seems hazardous in the extreme.

In the evening at dinner at my house Hugo Gouthier, Brazilian Consul General now headed for his first Embassy in Brussels, Max Steenberghe, head of the Catholic Party in Holland, an old friend; General [Willis D.] Crittenberger, now President of F.E.C; Carlos Chagas, Chairman of the Atomic Irradiation Committee of the United Nations, splendid Brazilian scientist. He is in trouble: the scientific evidence before the United Nations Committee fully supports Stevenson's position on the hydrogen bomb, but they cannot say anything for fear of being thought to have interfered in American politics. On the other hand, if they say nothing this will be ascribed by the other United Nations members to American political pressure.

October 31, 1956

Yesterday Lewis Galantière called up from FEC to say that the Nagy government had issued a radio broadcast promising free elections, the end of the one party system, a demand that the Russian troops move out, and generally acceding to all of the demands of the Hungarian revolution.

But there was some doubt as to whether the Russian troops had moved out or would move out until the revolutionaries came in. We thought the revolutionaries ought to hang on to their arms. There are also reports that the Russians are moving troops into the country via Czechoslovakia; the whole thing might be a trap. On the surface, however, it looked as though the revolution is complete. But the cost is fearful: there must be at least 30,000 wounded, and the Lord knows how many dead. Even children of ten and twelve joined in the fighting. The Hungarian Army came down on the side of the revolution.

I feel like a heel being safe in New York while the ideas we have been propagating have engaged the lives of so many men.

#

The Mid-East blew up. This is not something I have worked at. But it may connect later. The facts were that the Israel Army mobilized and crossed the Egyptian border, striking towards the Suez Canal. A very short time after that Britain and France without consulting the United States issued an ultimatum to the Egyptians and the Israeli saying that if both sides did not withdraw to ten miles from either side of the Canal, the British and the French would mobilize to protect the Canal. Israel promptly accepted the ultimatum; the Egyptians rejected it; and I suppose the British and French troops are moving in now. . . .

November 5, 1956

A violent week-end. Chagas spent it with us.

It really began Thursday night at dinner with Jaime de Barros [Brazil's Permanent Representative to the UN] saying fare-well to Gouthier, departing to take the Brazilian Embassy in Belgium. [Cyro de] Freitas Valle of the Brazilian Delegation to the United Nations came in late and left early. The United Nations Special Assembly was debating the Near East problem created by the invasion of Suez by the British and French.

We, all of us, agreed:

(1) NATO alliance very nearly dead. Whether it can be restored or not is a problem. Obviously we cannot be in a defensive alliance if any party can go into a warlike operation without consultation.

(2) United States is in a queer position. Realistically the French and British are right. They may restore some order to the East. But we are opposing them, and Israel, in favor of [Gamal Abdel] Nasser [President of Egypt] and the Arabs who are technically right, while the British are technically wrong. Our artillery is legally right, realistically pointed in the wrong direction.

(3) This could be a severe weakening of the United Nations.

(4) During the week-end, for practical purposes R.F.E. was receiving and picking up the calls of the Nagy government in Hungary as it desperately struggled with the situation. Our own information was that Russian troops were pushing in from Carpathia and over the Czech border—which proved correct. By Saturday it was clear that the Russians had enough force in Hungary to swamp it.

Sunday morning news came that they had struck, organizing a puppet government around [Janos] Kadar. We could pick up and furnish the American Delegation with the facts, or at least the Hungarian government's pronouncements on the subject. But it was all words against Russian artillery.

Sunday evening, two debates. The American resolution on Hungary, voted in the Security Council, went before the United Nations. It carried 50 to 7. But the grim fact was not only the Soviet bloc voted against anything being done but also that all of the Asians excepting the Philippines and Pakistan abstained.

When the dust died down, the Russian-Asian bloc including the peripheral States were outside the breastworks. The Bandung Conference group, in other words, in spite of the Russian ferocity in Hungary, would rather do nothing than go on record against it. Not reassuring.

This morning the question is whether we should recognize the Russian government in Hungary. I telephoned no; certainly not now. The second, whether we should try to construct a government in exile. We want to think this over. I just don't know how this would cut.

But probably the events will keep on moving.

The election is tomorrow. It looks to me as though Stevenson is likely to be beaten, but it is not quite as sure as one thinks. Some new driving forces are entering the situation; Lord knows how they will cut.

November 14, 1956

The blunt fact is we . . . struck out. The Hungarian revolution won. During that forty-eight hours the United States government should have made a gesture showing its presence if only by a few plane loads of supplies for the sick and wounded. Either it was too lethargic to act or frightened lest action be bad politically, since it might be thought that the government was involving the United States in another conflict. Now the Russians have paralyzed the country with tanks. . . .

December 5, 1956

Got to the bottom of some of the troubles of RFE. It was accused of having broadcast inflammatory incitements to the Hungarian rebellion. I can find no proof that this happened. But I do find that Radio Madrid, giving time for Hungarian broadcasts to the Habsburg Monarchists, did so. There was also a Communist station broadcasting in Hungary from East Germany; it is said to have used the RFE call letters and, of course, acted as *Agent Provocateur*. There is a third station, operated by some Hungarian exiles, which may have done the same thing though I know little about it. It is claimed that our mutual friends in Washington had nothing to do with the last two. But I am not dead sure. . . .

January 3, 1957

We have been having a couple of meetings for the Rockefeller Brothers Fund; they are studying foreign affairs hoping that their new foundation will tackle it in a large way. It is not easy; everyone likes to be very intellectual. Actually, there is a long, strong pull of emotion underlying foreign affairs which has to be met in its own terms, and quite often it gives the lie to the best planning of experts.

This is proving the case in the Hungarian revolution where RFE and some of the rest of us are under attack. The Communist paper in Budapest of December 19 insists that I was largely responsible for the revolution. It would be a compliment of sorts if true—but of course is not. (Though I am too old to be romantic, there were times in the Hungarian revolution when I should have been happier on the barricades than sitting quiet here; then to watch the United States walk away from it as though our very existence had not provoked it, was to me shocking. They did not have to go to war; but they might have thrown some solid shot into the United Nations debates and at least declared where we stood.) . . .

Anyhow the target for 1957 is to get the big book on corporations finished. A little pot-boiler book on foreign affairs [*Tides of Crisis*] is in way of being published and should be out about February or March.

January 7, 1957

. . . I talked with Allen Dulles. He was kind enough to give me a little time during one of his visits to New York.

I raised two questions in regard to R.F.E. One was whether the time has not come to take the government into the private operation. I told him the responsibilities were great; this could happen in other areas as it did in Hungary; we could not deliver government support, and I wondered whether the time has not come to disregard the fiction that this was strictly private. This for a leisurely solution. I added that government is a lot more flexible than a private instrument. Government could be opportunist, opt for Tito tyrannies as a matter of tactics, whereas men committed to freedom in government could not desert their essential premises.

Second, I said that it would make life easier for all of us if the United States Government would state its "cold war" aims. That is, present a picture of the kind of solution it would regard as good in Central Europe. This, of course, would mean that neither side proposed to use the strip as a military take-off point, and would recognize that Europe never would be at peace if either the East or the West had military control over it—and made use of it for that purpose. Allen said he thought the idea was a good one and would go to work on it. . . .

January 9, 1957

Yesterday all day at the Rockefeller Brothers Fund meeting on foreign affairs.

. . . we agreed that we had better find out where we were going. Everyone has to put 300 words on their idea of Utopia on paper in the next couple of weeks. It ought to be an interesting collection of stuff. [See May 17.]

I was also told [by Dean Rusk who had been talking with the State Department] that the reason for the sudden excitement about the Middle East lies in the fact that the Russians have been arming and stirring up the Kurd strip. It is nice that they finally learned about the Kurdish strip; it has been a private red flag of mine for some years.

March 27, 1957

Having been a happy guerrilla, in the last three weeks [traveling in Central America], three or four foundations have discovered that they could not exist without my valuable advice. The result has been a series of continuous meetings with high level talent of one sort or another, much discussion, frequently brilliant, and whether anyone is better off on that count I cannot say.

Thus:

(1) The Fund for the Republic has seven and a half millions unexpended; doesn't know what to do with it; proposes the relation of private

government, corporations, labor unions, to civil liberties, and have asked me to serve on the consulting committee. I said I would, and I am sorry. But we may get some work done.

(2) The Rockefeller Brothers Fund. This is an attempt of the five brothers to set up a foundation which will be as meaningful as the great Rockefeller Foundation set up by their grandfather. They have had a set of panels working on the principal problems of American foreign affairs in a series of meetings. I am on the Overall Panel as well as on the Foreign Policy Panel; the job now is to pull the assembled stuff together and see whether we can make anything out of it. Everybody from Lucius Clay and the Continental Can Company to President [James R.] Killian of M.I.T. and all manner of intellectuals and experienced men in between appear in these discussions; Nelson Rockefeller is Chairman but administration lies heavy on Dean Rusk, President of the Rockefeller Foundation.

(3) The Rockefeller Foundation. This is having a high-level committee survey legal philosophy and science in the hope of getting some kind of a philosophical statement on the map in the political science field. This is difficult and they are making heavy weather.

(4) The Committee on Human Ecology. This revolves around Harold Wolff at the Cornell Medical School and is really an attempt to see whether behaviour and science can be brought together in economic matters. I am frightened about this one. If the scientists do what they have laid out for themselves, men will become manageable ants. But I don't think it will happen. As Harold Wolff says, nature has a happy habit of making a long snout at the scientists and telling them to start over again.

(5) And of course the Twentieth Century Fund which is so much smaller and so much better than the rest of them that it almost comes under the heading of fun.

(6) There has also been a labor negotiation for F.E.C. (I don't know whether it will blow up or work out) and a raft of work. . . .

May 8, 1957

An ungodly amount of work for the Rockefeller Fund. I deserted the ship for Tuesday and Wednesday meetings and will pick up with Dr. [Henry] Kissinger [Harvard] to help draft the report. . . .

Draft report for the Rockefeller Brothers Fund, May 17, 1957

THE AMERICAN AFFIRMATION

Faith, which modern students like to call a "value system," is the driving force in all societies. History, at all events, records no society without a value system; no strong society without a value system firmly held and followed; no enduring society whose values did not have a measure of universal validity.

These value systems, past and present, have invariably centered upon religion. Time may produce a society whose value system expresses itself in non-religious terms—a rationalist's religion, if you choose, and this has yet to occur . . . by ironic paradox, Communist organization draws much of its strength from Christian doctrine which it officially denies; and some of which it averts.

America, perhaps more than any other society, exemplifies this unfailing historical imperative. It was formed around a series of religious movements, giving dynamism to its evolving political organization. The Protestant Reformation stamp runs straight across the northern tier of the United States. Missionary Catholicism gave form and frame to the Southwestern third of the American union. Wesleyan Baptist and Church of England power brought together the Central and Southern area, as Quakers gave substance and permanency to Pennsylvania. Later immigrant movements merely added to this emotional and spiritual heritage the Mormons of Utah, Roman Catholics, Irish and Italian, in the Northeast; Jewish tradition on the Eastern coast and in the Midwest centers. To state an American outlook without recognizing this foundation would be a negation.

Derived from and surrounding the core of religious faith, there is an ethical system. Guiding the actions of men in society and of the lesser divisions of society, and of the national or international organization of society. Men who claim not to acknowledge religious faith, nevertheless follow an ethical system. From it are derived the judgments of what we call "public opinion," sometimes flowing freely, sometimes apathetical. Men in public life, politicians, governments must act along the lines of this value system whether they choose or not. Violation of its values eventually entails defeat. Internationally violation may involve destruction.

June 20, 1957

Some full days, chiefly foundations, and last night the meeting of the Alumni of the Princeton Graduate School. This at the instance of my old friend [Professor] Alpheus Mason. . . .

Mason tells me some odd things about his *Life of Harlan Stone*. The Frankfurter boys have all been going for it—not as a book but on the ground that Harlan Stone didn't amount to much. Felix Frankfurter has inspired this. . . .

. . . Some of the letters [from Frankfurter to Stone] Mason wanted to print in the biography; Felix asked him not to. After they were returned to the Library of Congress, apparently Felix had them sealed until 1974.

July 1957

Chiefly three weeks' vacation in Great Barrington.

August 28, 1957

[Rómulo Betancourt and Roberto Sánchez Vilella came for a weekend, August 3–4, to Great Barrington.]

Betancourt was talking about the coming conference of South American diplomats to be held in Puerto Rico sometime in the Fall. We blocked out the possibility of a draft pronouncement which Rómulo will write up.

Muñoz Marín's delegate [Roberto Sánchez Vilella, later Govenor of Puerto Rico], had something else on his mind. Muñoz Marín wants me to go on the Council on Higher Education. . . . It is the kind of thing one should stay out of. But being constitutionally unable to stay out of trouble, and likewise wishing to stand by my friends, I sent word I would accept. But it looks tough.

Left New York on Sunday, August 4: left for Strasbourg via Zurich. There followed a stiff week, for the Collège de l'Europe Libre has been under fire and there is a lot to do. Also we need a new President—my old friend John Pelenyi is now ill and is 72 years old and has to retire.

Meeting the Hungarian students was not easy. I did the best I could with it. Jacques Freymond of the International Institute at Geneva came in to give some lectures. He was splendid as always. Analyzing the Western situation he said that the Western Powers complex was gradually disintegrating, but the Eastern complex was equally disintegrating. The question was which would disintegrate faster. Unhappily he is right on both scores and it looks as though the Western disintegration was going with extreme rapidity. . . .

. . . Thence [August 25] . . . to the Hague and to call on Hugh McClure-Smith, Australian Ambassador in the Netherlands. He repeated almost verbatim what [Joseph M. A. H.] Luns [Netherlands Foreign Minister] had said. He said that when the British proposed to join the Canal Users Association in the Suez crisis on the suggestion of John Foster Dulles, [Prime Minister] Eden in Parliament, wishing to copper-rivet the job, had used in his speech the exact text of the message sent by the State Department to him on the subject. Commons accordingly voted it, whereupon Dulles walked out on the Association. This was underscoring what Luns had said. . . .

An item in my mind:

The Poles are allowing students to go out to Western Europe freely. I arranged to take ten of them into the College. Unquestionably they are Polish Communists; unquestionably they are not Russian Communists; we had better meet them than exclude them.

September 24, 1957

The Honduran election took place on Sunday. Ramón Villeda Morales and his Liberal Party got clear majority of a constituent assembly.

[Roy R.] Rubottom, Assistant Secretary of State, congratulated the military junta on holding a fair election; it was a good move.

A constitution will be prepared and presently a President elected on October 22. If all goes well, Ramón will thus become President. . . .

September 25, 1957

. . . My son Peter came back late Sunday night. He had been in British Columbia; had staked out a claim to some land on a lake which is half-way between Vancouver and the Yukon; and came back to file his claim in the provincial capital of Victoria, after two weeks in the untracked bush. Apparently he ran afoul of some small regulation but the old-timers including the Surveyor General were struck by the two boys (Peter Wilde was with him) who had slugged on beyond the settled area. This seemed to them good pioneering; also better than the soft generation who wanted to pioneer by automobile; the boys may get their land. It was a good stiff piece of well-organized camping and a good job of quick, administrative understanding. Both boys had the time of their lives. . . .

October 3, 1957
Everybody from the four seas is in town attending the United Nations session. Life is beginning to be complex. Also these damn foundations are making trouble. The Fund for the Republic committee is publishing a presentation of mine as a pamphlet. This is all right as far as it goes. But you get the sense of an outfit clutching at pieces of your work for their purposes while they ought to be getting together an eventual book.

The Rockefeller Bros. Fund is in somewhat the same situation: a lot of high-priced talent unable to think consecutively or sort out their material. I have drafted the Panel I report and working on a redraft. But again, why do it? Other people want an intellectual project generally for their own purposes and in most of these cases it means nothing but sticking a lot of names of men on my work. However, I suppose I shall have to note that ideas take their way irrespective of the name tacked on them. . . .

November 25, 1957
Bill Wieland telephoned from the State Department last night. He is off to Cuba to see whether anything can be done to bring the Cuban revolt to any kind of an orderly conclusion. It is rough going. Anti-intervention is all right up to a point. But we are responsible for keeping order in the hemisphere quite aside from the proprieties, and a rather bolder policy in that regard seems indicated. . . .

I have put in quite a bit of time on the Fund for the Republic. All I have been able to contribute so far is a picture of the economic power in a free society.

The trouble is that each of these jobs involves a mortgage on one's mind and time and there is not time to do the underlying thinking. The assumption that because you have done some studying you can sound off on any subject is a mistake.

December 9, 1957
It was a quiet week-end.
The Puerto Rican Senate seems to have confirmed my appointment to the Superior Council of Education. . . .

December 31, 1957
Monday before Christmas, Roger Baldwin called up. Mr. [Povl] Bang-Jensen was with him. They asked me to represent Mr. Bang-Jensen. He came down here Christmas Eve and I agreed.

Bang-Jensen was Secretary of the Committee appointed by the Assembly of the United Nations to investigate the Russian reprisals in Hungary following the revolution last year. He became increasingly disturbed. There was a division in the Secretariat of the committee as to whether the committee should take a strong line or a weak one. Bang-Jensen became convinced that his immediate superior, [W. M.] Jordan, wished to have a weak report and therefore attempted to prevent some information from reaching the committee and therefore causing difficulties. Whether he was right or wrong, I do not know.

Things came to an issue when the report was admitted by the Assembly. Bang-Jensen was asked to turn over his papers including the names of the Hungarian witnesses. These had testified anonymously, making a condition that their names should not be disclosed to anyone, including the Secretariat of the United Nations (nor the secretary of the committee). The committee agreed. Bang-Jensen refused to turn over the list and was suspended from his job in the Secretariat of United Nations. Dag Hammarskjöld then appointed a committee to inquire into Bang-Jensen's conduct as Deputy-Secretary of the committee. The inquiring committee's chairman is Ernest Gross. It is in that position that the matter comes to me. The issue is split. There is the problem of the list. There is also the problem whether Bang-Jensen made unjustified charges against his associates in the Hungarian committee.

The case has some interesting technical angles. If witnesses cannot testify anonymously in matters of this kind, the United Nations will have a hard time getting testimony from here on. On preliminary go-around, I think we ought to be able to negotiate a respectable arrangement—if not, to ask the United Nations to take up the matter of the list with the World Court and ask for an advisory opinion. But this is only a preliminary conclusion.

The newspapers are on this case and would like to make a bigger thing out of it than perhaps is wise. . . .

January 24, 1958
Bang-Jensen's case has been up. The list of witnesses will shortly be destroyed in his presence, in mine and an officer of the United Nations.

The United Nations Committee was acting very stupidly. They would like to issue statements reflecting on Bang-Jensen and then become annoyed when he comes back and answers them. If this is an internal matter to the United Nations Secretariat, it should be kept internal. If the newspapers and the public are to be the judges, they have to expect all sides to be presented. It ought to be kept an internal matter—but the United Nations people seem anxious to get into the press. In that case I cannot prevent Bang-Jensen from doing likewise.

Re: Bang-Jensen

January 24, 1958, 3:50 pm.
At 2:30 PM this afternoon I went to the office of Bankers Trust Company, 455 Park Avenue, and there met Mr. [George] Fluhr. I delivered to

him an envelope which, in fact, contained nothing but an old report of the Banque Nationale d'Haiti, and requested that it be given to the guard who should accompany me to the United Nations building, who was to deliver the envelope to me there on my receipt. The purpose of this was merely to provide the added protection of a guard. At 2:35 PM Mr. Bang-Jensen came to the Bank accompanied by a friend of his who left him there. This friend had formerly been an associate of his in the Danish diplomatic service in Washington.

Mr. Bang-Jensen, the guard and I then debouched on Park Avenue, took a taxi cab and went to the United Nations Building. We were met at the door by a United Nations security officer who was expecting us. He, Bang-Jensen and I, and the Bankers Trust Company guard then went to the office of Dr. [Dragoslav] Protitch [Under Secretary of the UN]. The Bankers Trust Company guard thereupon delivered the envelope to me (containing only the Banque Nationale d'Haiti report) against my receipt, and left. Mr. Bang-Jensen, Dr. Protitch, the United Nations security officer and myself then went to the roof of the United Nations Building where there was a small incinerator. Mr. Bang-Jensen produced two sealed envelopes which were then and there burnt in the presence of Dr. Protitch, Mr. Bang-Jensen, the security officer and myself. I added the dummy envelope for good measure.

We then went back to Dr. Protitch's office, and Mr. Bang-Jensen then and there signed a statement. . . .

We then left, accompanied by the security officer. We stopped at the reception desk to ask Mr. [Bruce] Munn, President of the United Nations Press Association, to come downstairs. Mr. Bang-Jensen thereupon gave him the . . . statement for release.

Nothing further happened except that the representative of the United Nations Hungarian Radio passed by accidentally, and Mr. Bang-Jensen gave him a copy of the release, and I exchanged a few courteous words with him.

The burning was complete by 3:07 PM, and we left the Building not later than 3:20 PM, or thereabouts.

January 31, 1958

Last evening, Betancourt came in to dinner alone. But the house was pretty well populated by telephone. President Figueres of Costa Rica called up; so did various Venezuelan friends, for the Venezuelan government is in full tide of organization.

The two principal factors are Betancourt himself and Jovito Villalba who was elected President in the Venezuelan election but was forcibly prevented from taking office by the fallen dictator, Pérez Jiménez. Betancourt is a boyhood friend of Villalba. . . .

The parties have agreed that the current junta shall retain power for about eighteen months, choosing a non-partisan chief of state, and that thereafter hold elections. Though he makes no announcement, Betancourt himself plans to run. Probably Villalba does too. There has been talk that they should combine on a single candidate as was done in Colombia but no one really thinks of doing this.

American interests will not be disturbed although Betancourt plans to go into the bookkeeping of the American companies to see whether they have paid the agreed share of their profits to the government under the existing contract. . . .

He does not think Venezuela is well advised merely to acquiesce when American import of her oil is restricted. I pointed out that Venezuela was less ruthlessly restricted than the American oil fields, where the allowed extraction of oil is rigidly held down when supply outruns demand. Betancourt's idea is that some sort of general stabilization arrangement should be worked out, treating the oil problem as a whole—at least between Venezuela and the United States. . . .

March 26, 1958
Friday, March 14. [To Costa Rica] . . . To La Lucha for a wonderful extended weekend [with President Figueres]. There is nothing lovelier than the Central American upland and Pepe and I covered the district thoroughly. He will have control of the new Costa Rican Congress despite the election of his opponent, [Mario] Echandi. He is bitter because Echandi, immediately after his election, was invited to the United States with some ostentation whereas the United States has made it steadily impossible for Pepe to visit the country, officially or otherwise. At lunch at the Embassy (Woodward had left and Willauer had not got there). The Staff gave me the line that it was now the policy of the United States to invite President-Elects only. I was suave about it; Beatrice (there being only Americans present) suggested they tell it to the Marines. . . .

To meeting of the Little Institute (over which Padre Nuñez also presides) composed of the leaders of Pepe's party. This is a kind of Fabian Club of Costa Rica. They are developing courses of instruction for leaders in the various fields of economics, public administration, and so forth. . . .

Of more immediate importance is the fact that the price of coffee has been kept at a tolerable level up to now but may collapse at any time. That may break a number of countries, including Costa Rica, just as these countries were broken in the American recessions of 1921, 1931 and 1938. This is one thing the American government ought to get to work on at once and no nonsense about it.

March 19 to Tegucigalpa where we slid quietly and easily into the arms of President Ramón Villeda Morales and his wife. . . . President Villeda discussed his various plans; he proposes to give first place to roads and schools, and is wondering where to begin. . . .

Next morning with the Minister of Natural Resources (taken out of the Honduran Army; he was a Colonel) to Comayagua, the original Spanish capital of Honduras . . . the reason for going was to have a look at the new road being built. A very good job once it gets some oil on it; and a really big irrigation dam which is slowly getting itself finished; and a government agricultural station where a couple of American experts from Texas and Cuba were working at things like home economics and agricultural methods. . . .

To visit the Minister of Education, Juan Ramírez Bahía, a Mayan

Indian who comes up to my shoulder and who is as square as the King of Diamonds. He has taken over, having left the Supreme Court. They have a good many things started but I am not sure that the organization can carry through.

Somewhere there is a job for an American foundation to help. . . .

To lunch the next day with Ambassador Willauer. This was a three-some: Beatrice and the Ambassador and myself. . . . He claims to have originated the idea that the American military aid should be given by the Army engineers and by training the Honduran Army officers in engineering . . . if they are equipped only with road-building machinery they cannot do much in the way of revolutionary activities. I did not discuss the origin of this idea: I have been making propaganda for it in the State Department for some years but congratulated him on a brilliant result. . . .

. . . Thence by TAN to Miami and Puerto Rico [to attend the meeting of the Education Council].

This was interesting. I spent half a day at the University attending classes like any student; then spent some time with the Secretary of the Superior Council. . . . We are going to build a College of Liberal Arts; try to get some scholars there and move up. . . .

Then home to finish up the Garment Workers strike; more especially, the Southern mills with Jonathan Logan [textile manufacturer] and David Dubinsky.

March 31, 1958

Governor Muñoz Marín and Doña Inez spent Saturday and Sunday with us at the Farm. This was strictly loafing but some good talk.

Muñoz Marín made two observations. He said that "Capitalism was bad semantics and called up the old money-lender picture." The "profit motive" likewise suggested grasping exploitation. Neither of these really described the system we had.

He also said that the results of space operations diminish nationalisms. If you "triangulate" not only the moon to the United States but to Russia, with one leg in the United States and the other in Russia, the triangle was so thin it made Russia and the United States so small that they might as well be working together. . . .

April 2, 1958

Bill Wieland from Washington to pass the night and to discuss the Cuban situation.

I asked Governor Muñoz Marín and his wife to come over for breakfast and we went at it this morning.

(1) Batista's government is on its way out.

(2) Fidel Castro is a personally brave man but interested only in power. He was one of the organizers of the Bogotá riot; rather boasts of his killing; intends to be top dog in Cuba; and has no social program. The description is much like that of [Rafael] Trujillo [in the Dominican Republic] when I knew him as a young man. . . .

The Governor, Wieland and myself then explored possibilities. At the close of it, our conclusion was to try (1) a short declaration by a group of liberals, chiefly Latin Americans (maybe a few Americans) calling for an end to sheer bloodshed; and attempting to give the Cuban people a real chance to state their want. Muñoz Marín will try his hand at drafting, and (2) statements of support of such a program would then be forthcoming from a number of liberal governments in Latin America. Pepe Figueres and his friends in Venezuela, possibly Colombia and elsewhere, would jointly support such a move. (3) The State Department and the government of the United States would likewise come through with some support. Then: (4) the OAS might be invoked. We should probably be playing by ear.

As intermediate step, we would find and encourage the relatively few men who offer some hope for an honest to God social program. The two men mentioned, Felipe Pazos and Pepín Bosch, both of whom have been in Fidel Castro's movement, but apart from it. . . .

May 13, 1958
Two vignettes. The week-end of April 27 to Puerto Rico for a meeting of the Council of Education.

At the end of the day we wound up on the Convento Beach with Muñoz Marín and his wife. . . . Isaac Stern, the violinist, and his friend, an oboe player, in bathing suits and shorts greeted us. As the sun went down, we sat in bathing suits on the beach. Stern got his violin and played the second movement of Bach's "Chaconne" to an obbligato of little waves breaking on the beach. Albert Spalding had played the "Chaconne" at Rio when he returned from his Italian expedition. This was movement, and friendship, and scenery—a high point in any emotional experience.

The following evening, after the Council meeting, which was bitter, to hear Pablo Casals, now 82, play a cello at the Festival. The old man was in excellent form and obviously enjoying it. . . .

Friday at Tarrytown with Nelson Rockefeller, Stacy May [of the Rockefeller Foundation] and a few others to discuss the economic report. I said the nineteenth century was not going to return and we had to get away on a new international New Deal. Apparently all hands were convinced and I have a lot of work to do. . . .

May 8 to Grace Church for the funeral of Samuel Seabury. There were not a great many people there. I was remembering that Seabury in his day had worn New York City like a glove, had made the La Guardia Administration, and probably had done more to bring this city out of a mess than anyone with the possible exception of La Guardia himself.

He hated Roosevelt and Roosevelt hated him. I had the rare privilege of being a friend of both. . . .

June 10, 1958
The first and only award I have ever gotten was given me by the Inter-American Association for Democracy and Freedom. This is something like being given a birthday party by your children. We are all old

friends. This organization is small and the treasury is non-existent but this small group of people working together did get things done.

Saturday to Nelson Rockefeller's birthday party with Beatrice and Peter, and Peter's Harvard tutor, Professor Zeph Stewart. . . .

Someone alluded to Nelson's political aspirations on the Republican ticket. Whereupon the band played in quick succession: "East Side-West Side" and "Happy Days Are Here Again," the first the anthem of Al Smith, the second that of Franklin Roosevelt. I was seeing ghosts. . . .

July 2, 1958

Nelson Rockefeller called up. He has announced his candidacy for nomination for Governor. I had already told him I could not support him: I had supported Harriman before and I could not change my party loyalties any more then he could. He telephoned to say this made no difference. We are going to have a great deal to do together however it came out, and wanted nothing to break an old friendship. . . .

July 4, 1958

The Council on Foreign Relations called. The Council is financing people to go to Africa to get them interested. Would I go? I said I thought Council members ought to do that but I was not committing to any trips just now.

With sadness we are arranging to end the Collège de l'Europe Libre this year. . . .

July 9, 1958

To Washington last night to dine at the Army and Navy Club with Bill Wieland and Assistant Secretary of State Rubottom.

Their worries were three.

(1) Thirty-odd Americans and a Canadian are still held by the Castro rebels. Fidel Castro wants to release them; his brother does not. I agreed that I would try to see whether Betancourt and Pepe Figueres could not bring some influence to bear.

(2) The government of Venezuela is for the time being in the hands of a rather weak, rather ambitious man, [Wolfgang] Larrazábal. He would probably like to be President. He has appointed representatives of all of the parties, including the Communist Party, as an advisory council. The boys foresee a quiet, elaborate Communist infiltration. . . .

(3) The government is thinking now of the idea of stabilizing coffee price for the time being but, of course, this is only buying time. The Brazilian financial situation could not be worse: they have money enough for only one month's importations; after that as far as they could see the economy shuts down. . . .

August 25, 1958

To Europe on July 27 to open the closing session of the Collège de l'Europe Libre at Strasbourg. Everyone is sorry to see it shut down and so am I too but there is nothing else to be done. (Note: we will have educated about 1,000 youngsters and given emergency relief to 200 Hungarians in addition.) Statistically these boys are making an astonishing record. Two of the lecturers at this year's seminars were an Assistant Professor at the University of London and at the University of Copenhagen. Both were graduates of the Collège. The breakdown of where they all land shows that more than half of them are doing well and a respectable percentage are already showing signs of distinction. So something got done though not as much as I had hoped.

Just before leaving (specifically on July 27) I dictated a memorandum for C. D. Jackson to be used in connection with Eisenhower's proposed speech to be made at either (1) the Summit conferences or (2) the United Nations, depending on how Lebanon worked out. It was the United Nations, and Eisenhower made the speech. While in Europe I received [a] cable from C. D. Jackson which showed he had drawn heavily on the memorandum. "The stock of International Brain Trusters, Inc. rapidly rising." Returning, the newspapers note that he had been called back to Washington to handle the Khrushchev correspondence.

Apparently as a result of our quiet confabulation, the government decided (1) to tackle the Arab problem as a group problem instead of individually; and (2) to propose a really solid regional job and (3) to tackle squarely the question of "indirect aggression." The European reaction was good. I was in a tiny town in France, Savoie, walking in the Alps when I got C. D.'s cable. But I also got some Paris papers. They all said the speech was fine. It might not succeed but at least Eisenhower had the courage to tackle it. I like to hope that it contributed to the favorable result in the United Nations. The Arab League did get together; the United States policy was to favor it; and the Arabs acted without Russia. Now the question is whether the boys can follow up—not so easy. . . .

August 27, 1958

. . . The problem was whether the Governor and the Mayor run the show or does Tammany Hall; and Tammany Hall won [nominating Peter J. Crotty for Attorney-General of New York].

August 29, 1958

Finletter, as expected, refused to run independently for the Senate (no surprise, that). The Liberal Party convention reconvened, would have stampeded for an independent candidate. Dubinsky, Rose and I arranged to have the question put over for a week, urging sober consideration. Specifically I pointed out that the effect of an independent nomination would be to elect [Kenneth] Keating. . . . Could we really afford to throw away a more or less Liberal Democratic vote (Hogan's) because we were, rightly, angered at Tammany Hall's control. . . .

The general sentiment in the committee I think agreed with mine, that we will have to take Hogan. We won't like it. I think De Sapio and Tammany Hall by their high-riding arrogance are doing their best to elect Nelson Rockefeller. He really hadn't much of an issue until they handed him this one.

September 17, 1958

Cecil Cross came to see us over the weekend. He was Consul General in São Paulo when I was there. Now, retired, he is colonizing a couple of land grants in the Brazilian frontier—one at Goiás, another in Mato Grosso. Beatrice has some land in each of these and they may serve as foundations for discoveries for Peter later on.

Peter, who was also there, was back from British Columbia, where he has staked out a land grant halfway between Vancouver and the Yukon. As a result the tropical frontiersman was comparing notes with the Far Northern frontiersman and the results were interesting. If Peter can swing both, no one can accuse him of not having hemisphere-wide interests.

Quemoy-Matsu temporarily reached an angle of rest with negotiations in Warsaw. I personally agree with Truman and the Administration. They could not yield to a little shooting and a lot of yelling without provoking more shooting and more yelling a little later. We ought not to be in Quemoy and Matsu at all: this is yesterday. It does not follow that we can get out quite so simply on that account. . . .

But I do not forget that I felt this way about it in 1939—the result was a war and the war settled nothing. Would staying out have produced a worse result? Nobody can tell.

October 16, 1958

My son went off to start his service as 2d lt. with the Air Force; this means that he is a man grown, on his own. He reported for duty on October 15 at Wichita Falls. This is somewhat of a milestone in all our lives; the last child leaves home.

\#   \#

The tough line on Quemoy and Matsu has worked out. It has also opened a split in the Democratic Party. Acheson and those opposed were attacking the Administration for standing up hard to the combined Chinese-Russian attack. Truman with a much sounder instinct twice wrote that this was a case where the country ought to stand with the President. The net result was that the Chinese finally put into effect a unilateral "cease fire" arrangement and we equally unilaterally agreed to stop convoying supplies. Unquestionably the next will be to work out a quiet withdrawal from Quemoy and Matsu and still holding Formosa. This will require putting a lot of pressure on Chiang and, of course, marks abandonment of any thought of reconquering China for Chiang. This is not giving up much. I don't think he ever had a chance.

In South America, things are moving. Betancourt has declared his candidacy; somewhat surprisingly the United States government has come to the conclusion that the best thing that could happen was his victory. This is quite a change from the days when, under Holland as Assistant Secretary, State kicked him around. . . .

The Cuban situation is still a puzzle. The country is in opposition to Batista but the Castros offer little. . . .

November 5, 1958

Yesterday, election day. To the Liberal Party headquarters, then to C. D. Jackson's—solidly Republican—then back to the Liberal Party where Harriman, now defeated, gracefully and sportsmanlike, bowed on the way out.

Nelson is elected by a landslide and drags in a ticket with him. It was a personal victory: the party did not do so well. It leaves him now a leading contender for the Republican nomination.

Beatrice and I telegraphed him congratulations last night. Wallace Harrison left to go over to his apartment—I thought of going too but thought better of it.

My own emotions were mixed. A warm personal friend of mine now takes a position of national leadership. In that he cannot have friends beyond a certain amount. Personal considerations will always have to yield to political necessities, and they should. Nelson will immediately be fought by the conservative elements of his party.

The Democratic Party meanwhile makes a national sweep in the Congress. But there is not a man in the party who has a solid national position.

December 9, 1958

Yesterday, my son, Peter, came of age. I sent off the accounting of his trust fund and one thing and another; it may be useful to him but his real equipment lies somewhere else. For I am remembering as a child he lived in Washington through the war. He stood with the then Brazilian dictator, Vargas, reviewing the Brazilian and American troops coming back from the Italian campaign. He stood to the King's health in Government House in Jamaica at a dinner for one of the last of the Victorian princesses. Later, we left him on the River of the Dead in Goiás and told him to find his way to Rio which he did. He was then fourteen years of age. He was with Pepe Figueres in Costa Rica when the Nicaraguan crisis was brewing and later he worked as a peon on one of Pepe's plantations. He has harvested wheat across the United States. He has gone alone into the wilderness north of British Columbia and south of Alaska and has made the first ascent of a mountain there and built a cairn of rocks as evidence. In the course of this he got at least the outline of an education including honors in economics at Harvard and the best economic scholarship they had to offer at Oxford, though he did not take this up.

Now he is at new adventures as a lieutenant in the Air Force. He finds the world a smiling, friendly place, largely because he is himself a friend. It is not bad equipment.

#

. . . The Venezuelan elections were held. On Sunday my friend Rómulo Betancourt was elected though by somewhat narrow majority. . . .

Anyhow, between Colombia, Venezuela, Costa Rica and Honduras, with friends elsewhere, we have a fairly good galaxy of governments composed of exiles who at one time had few friends except Beatrice and me. . . .

December 29, 1958
December 18—to Alvin Johnson's 80th birthday celebration at the New School. He has done well.

For the Christmas holidays to Great Barrington. Cold and sunny: a perfect Currier & Ives day with all the children skating on the pond.

Peter home from Shepard Air Base at Wichita Falls. They have put him in Strategic Intelligence: a very useful assignment because he is learning the realities and not the theories of this atomic warfare problem.

The young are dealing with atomic warfare as we used to deal with the Day of Judgment. Above the pulpit in the Congregationalist Church was a scroll: "Prepare to meet thy God." The theory was that it might happen at any time. These youngsters take the same view of life. . . .

December 27. Yesterday, Jim Perkins [of the Carnegie Foundation] asked me to lunch and I went. The result was disturbing.

He asked me what I wanted to do with the rest of my life and I said I had been mulling this over without a conclusion. He said that I was recognized as one of the creative minds in America and the question was how to make it useful. . . .

I told him I was going to Greece the end of February and I would sit for a couple of days at Delphi where the oracle is and maybe come up with an answer. . . .

December 29. Nelson Rockefeller came to dinner; no one else except Tod and Beatrice. We went over an entire range of things. From here out, he has to be careful of his friendships. I told him I thought that he would be running for President whether he liked it or not; currents of events are not easily denied.

We were discussing the affairs of the State: Nelson wants to improve its economic conditions but that raises the question of how you direct unlimited productivity (which we have) into the areas where it won't go. Taxation is one of the ways but not the best. Municipal authorities like Moses' empire, says Nelson, have the same characteristics that the old tyrannous tycoon corporations did. Somehow this has to be reduced to order. And a lot of other things besides.

Nelson is a man without a party. The Democrats are a party without a man. Stevenson's stock is rising chiefly because there is no one else to do anything about it (except possibly Humphrey).

Betancourt is now elected President of Venezuela. When after the election Nelson was there he was invited by the Embassy to a party. They asked him whom he wanted to see. He reeled off a list, including Betancourt, and some of his men. The Embassy was shocked. They said they didn't have truck with any of that kind of people.

January 6, 1959
To Scarsdale, to assist in giving the Scarsdale Bowl to my brother. It was about time that Scarsdale recognized appropriately the fact that they had been getting, for a long time, some very devoted and effective service.

To James Perkins, February 11, 1959

I have not forgotten our luncheon. . . . It was disturbing for a number of reasons; it was generously intended, in contrast to the more usual polite invitations to throw one's mind and work into someone else's organizational pot. . . .

A precise question is posed. What supporting frame-work assists individual creativeness, specifically in the field of political science? Obviously in that field creativeness is a vital necessity. Crowding of population, intense technical and economical development and rapidly widening scientific horizons combine to demand or perhaps impose better ordering of politics, certainly as the price of advancing civilization, possibly as the price of survival.

"Politics" is used here in the Greek sense and to that field I address myself. It includes ethics, economics and law, all of these being operative. It does not necessarily include history, sociology and anthropology, these being, so far, primarily descriptive. Their material may and surely should serve the politician or political scientist; but the sociologist or historian need not decide anything. Nothing requires practitioners in these disciplines to bet other people's lives on their conclusions.

\# \# \#

Personal limitations aside, there is respectable evidence for the proposition that intellectual creativeness in the field of politics is a product (or by-product) of the creator's conflicts with reality. . . .

. . . Machiavelli would not, and could not, have written *The Prince* had he not been Undersecretary of State of Florence.

Keynes could not have tackled economic theory had he not been hurt at Versailles and sweated with the British Labour Party. On the reverse side, the experience of the Institute for Advanced Study at Princeton seems to confirm the observation. They have been immensely fertile in mathematics, the natural sciences and history. Their political scientists and economists needed, apparently, something more than a luxurious and secure palace of thought. I conclude that you are not likely to get creative intellectual work from men who have been merely abstracted from the conflict with power which politics implies.

Does teaching and student contact supply this element? It helps: your man is a little less isolated than if he were sequestered in a tower of ivory. . . . When the teacher can admit students to some sense of collaboration, as working on a problem when the work may influence action, the results are immensely productive. The student, under those circumstances, then ceases to be merely a student; he hopes also to participate in influencing events. Pedantic experience is chiefly of value because it compels some acknowledgment at least of the teacher's philosophical premises and systematization of his ideas. . . . Can anyone make a system of his thinking—except in retrospect? It is possible to maintain philosophical premises without great change through a lifetime. But it is impossible to maintain unchanged a system of thinking and political application—

unless you are prepared to commit to a tyranny, as do the Russians, forcibly reducing change in social thinking to the barest attainable minimum. Obviously in the end, changing facts and uncontrolled new thinking obtrude on the surmised theory, upset the tyranny and force a new phase. . . .

What can be worked out of this? In my case, there is plenty of institutional machinery at hand. Dean [William] Warren thinks I should take a research professorship at the Columbia Law School. . . .

The result ought to be a workshop rather than a typical academic seminar. Nobody could guarantee, and I should be the last to predict, what would come out of it. . . . This is particularly true because a shop of that kind ought to tackle problems which any sane analyst would know were impossible of solution. It ought to throw minds not at neatly circumscribed classified questions now so dear to academic project-makers but against the largest, most vital, and least soluble enigmas, setting its lance above mischance in Roncesvalles of its own devising.

The temptation is great to indicate the glory and terror involved in the questions really worth attempting. Our period of history combines casual acceptance of cruelty and the sordidness of bazaar chaffering with the majesty of great music. In counterpoint, it sets the tremendous theme of the necessity of power and its organization against the infinitely delicate, far deeper contratheme of the preservation of man as the only instrument capable of seeking eternal values and playing ape to his own dreams. If he cannot prove the existence of an eternal principle of order, he can posit it; and by positing it, create it. The fact that it has been posited is itself unchangeable, and is creative, and the derivations drawn from it guide events. Creation is not dressing up dolls and pushing them around in interesting combinations. Its essence is that the thing created is stronger than the creator. . . .

. . . I am off to consult the oracle at Delphi, hoping for more light, and will talk with you on my return. This is as far as my thinking has gone.

March 17, 1959

February 19. With Beatrice to Athens. . . . [Then] to Delphi where we stayed for forty-eight hours. Although the weather was cold, it was lovely. From the stadium above Delphi, we saw two of the eagles of Zeus making a long dive of 3,000 feet into the Gulf of Hephaestos. . . .

I duly consulted the oracle at Delphi but it returned the same answer that it always does. Its first piece of wisdom is to know what you are all about (a free translation: the Greek is "understand thyself"). The second piece of wisdom is don't overdo it—again a free translation (—the Greek is "everything in moderation"). Beatrice was reading Herodotus and I was reading Thucydides and we kept it up right through. . . .

March 5 . . . The following evening on the plane to Ankara where [Ambassador] Fletcher and Willa Warren met us. . . .

The next day in the other direction—to Pergamum. This was something. Alexander the Great had tossed this part of the world at one of his generals who could build a city there, with his own palace on top. He had an even better view than the Aegean. It was a princely palace overlooking the rolling Anatolian plains with the mountains far away. Here, too, was a temple of Zeus—once more, power—. You got a sense that the idea of power as the greatest principle in the world had come out of the Caucasus, or maybe the Hindu Kush, and then became Zeus or Ammon or Marduk and had only encountered something modifying it when it hit the Greeks who also believed in wisdom—the Athena of Athens—and beauty, Apollo—and then, of course, the Muses which you find at Delphi.

Anyhow, this boy, Attalus, believed in power. He held that city and that province for Alexander. After Alexander's death, as the empire broke up, and his descendants were overthrown, and recognizing that the Romans had greater power, Attalus willed it to Rome. It was the second largest city in the Roman Empire—as attested by a theatre which holds 30,000 people. Today there is nothing but a grubby little village, surrounding a huge basilica built by Justinian and Theodora for their favorite saint, whose name I believe was Helen. . . .

Like Ephesus, this city is dead. The game is over. Zeus had lost his capacity and there was nothing left to replace it. But while it was a going show, it certainly was a remarkable one. . . .

April 6, 1959
. . . Jacques Maritain's sister is very ill and her expenses have bankrupted him. I shall try to see what I can do. Old age can be a great tragedy.

They are having a meeting of the liberal group in Costa Rica the week of the 13th and I think I had better go, though it is not handy. . . .

Also several of us will be determining policy. Fidel Castro's bitter attack on Pepe means only one thing. The extremists—Communist or otherwise—want to take charge of the liberal revolution in Latin America and make it into a bloody Mexican-style social revolution instead.

A social revolution certainly has to be operated but I cannot see that we need the waste of a Mexican or the current Bolivian or Cuban-type revolution. They are generally betrayed at the end. Revolutions are like wars—always wasteful, usually unpredictable, necessary only in the last resort.

In addition, this revolution would be anti-American and I am pretty certain would produce more harm than good—with the possible exception of the tiny remaining dictatorships like the Dominican Republic. The job can be done without that in Nicaragua. I do not know about Paraguay. This we will discuss in Costa Rica.

This is the old gambit: the extremes both of the left and of the right trying to blank out the liberals and after the blank out the only certain thing is that there is a new dictatorship. This kind of thing has not even the merit of honest Communism which does propose to do something after the revolution is over.

April 13, 1959
By plane to San José [Costa Rica.] . . .

April 15, 1959
Pepe [had gone] to Cuba on the triumph of Fidel Castro. He had every right to be thankfully received. The reception was rather cold; when he did speak and said that the future of these countries lay with the United States, a pro-Communist claque made some trouble. This was followed by Fidel Castro's automatic response against him and later by a speech widely reported in the newspapers attacking Pepe. The speech was so solidly a Communist line that it amounted to a tip-off. Immediately thereafter all the pro-Communist elements supported Fidel but violently attacked Betancourt, Pepe, [Lleras] Camargo [President of Colombia] and pretty much everyone else. They were now much more bitter against the democrats than against the dictatorship, the reason being they were not anti-American but pro-Russian. The extent of the attack shocked and alarmed Pepe somewhat. I told him I was unhappy about it but not surprised, having been watching this for a long time. . . .

April 20, 1959
Home for a quiet couple of days at the Farm.
Fidel Castro has been in Washington. In appearance before the Foreign Relations Committee and in radio addresses he contrived to say the exact opposite of what he had been saying in Cuba. There he said that Cuba would be neutral between any struggle between the United States and Russia; here he said Cuba could not be neutral; she would keep her obligations under the Treaty of Rio de Janeiro.
There he said he was campaigning against election. Here he said he would have elections in three or four years (what does that mean?). There he said that Cuba must be defended against Yankee imperialism. Here he said he wanted foreign investment and would respect American interests. All Cuba needed was a social reorganization. Here he completely denied any Communist influence in his government which simply is not true.
I think Castro is irresponsible, saying whatever he thinks will please his audience. Or he means one of the two sets of things he has been saying. My impression is that his spontaneous reactions in South America are more accurate than here. He is drawing the picture of a revolutionary who wants to change conditions in his own country, against the obvious fact that they need changing. But we have heard this before.

May 20, 1959
Wednesday, May 6. Some work and to a reception at the Harvard Club for Pepe Figueres.
Thursday, May 7. Roundtable at the Council on Foreign Relations. I introduced Pepe Figueres. The general idea seems to be that Castro is a Western democrat and not some other kind of dictator but he stated frankly he was pessimistic.
Friday, May 8 . . . In the evening Luis Manuel Debayle and Pepe Figueres at my house. The problem was to try to see whether a peaceful transition of the Somoza regime could be arranged. The two men talked

and there was a basis for negotiation—though there were plenty of details left unsettled. . . .

June 8, 1959

Wednesday, 27 May. The Rockefeller Bros. Fund is finishing up its report on foreign affairs—Heckscher, Kissinger and I seem to be the penholders.

Friday, 29 May. Contact with Luis Manuel Debayle and also with Figueres. It is still possible to negotiate the Nicaraguan thing but it does need a nudge from the State Department to Somoza. The State Department seems totally unwilling to act.

In the evening to Ann Arbor to spend a day with Alice and her husband and children and thence to Chicago and on to Yankton, arriving Sunday the 31st. The following day I got an honorary LL.D. and made the Commencement address. This was strictly sentimental: they gave a degree to my father in 1894 and my mother worked as a teacher at the Indian reservation a little to the north as a mission school teacher. The present head of that mission, a Congregationalist minister by the name of Workentine came down. He is discouraged about his work with the Sioux Indians. The American policy broke up any structure the Sioux had themselves—and he has not been able to put any other structure under.

. . . The college has 300 students; the best conservatory of music in the vicinity; and succeeded in having the services of an excellent English conductor who put on a splendid performance by the conservatory orchestra of Handel's "Acis." Generally an interesting sentimental journey and a good look at the South Dakota prairie which we had never seen. Beatrice thought them splendid.

July 6, 1959

. . . To the Berkshires for the weekend. My son Peter got engaged to Lila Field Wilde and he couldn't do better. . . .

July 9, 1959

Today Dr. [Eugene A.] Gilmore came in. Beatrice and I knew him when he was Counsellor of Embassy at La Paz, Bolivia; now he is Counsellor of Embassy in Cuba. . . .

We went over the Cuban situation. The American policy at the moment is to do nothing and raise no unpleasant questions, fearing that this would simply irritate Castro. But the situation deteriorates. Gilmore fears also that Latin America as a whole is slowly lowering its estimate of American power and coming to believe that the senior power in the region is the Soviet Union. . . .

July 15, 1959

To Puerto Rico to dine at Muñoz Marín's kindly fortress and to a staff meeting of the Superior Council. . . .

Muñoz Marín is daily more disillusioned about Castro. . . .

July 22, 1959

To the farm for a longish week-end, chiefly taken up with Peter finishing the hay and somewhat grumpily carrying out his duties as newly announced fiancé of Lila Wilde. This is very much an engagement of county aristocracy—so he has to cover a bit of ground.

Beatrice and I left him on Monday morning. He will be on his way now to Manila and a year and a half or so of service in the Far East in the Air Force Command. . . .

October 2, 1959

Monday, September 7. To Geneva, where we were met by Georges Henri Martin . . . and next morning to a session of *Rencontres*. The following day we opened up for business—a full-dress debate between Jules Moch [former French Minister of the Interior and, later, Minister of Defense], defending the classic Socialist theory of the organization of the European State, and myself expounding, and to some extent defending, the American system—in Jacques Maritain's words, "neither capitalist nor socialist but something of both."

. . . The audience was surprised, and some of it pleased, to find an American speaking French, acting like a gentleman, and quoting Goethe, and a considerable head of steam was developed. . . .

I thought I held up my end: the newspapers at least gave courteous, if somewhat grudging, acknowledgment (breaking down the stereotype of the material American takes a little time). . . .

Intellectually, I was making a case for capitalism making its own heritage when united with democracy. . . .

[September 15] . . . and then by plane to Brazil (Lisbon, Recife, São Paulo). At São Paulo, we were in the hands of the Federation of Industries of São Paulo. Shifting from French to Portuguese, I gave two lectures in São Paulo and met a bunch of students there through the initiative of Consul General [Ralph J.] Burton. We also met the new Governor of São Paulo, [Carlos Alberto] Carvalho Pinto, a former professor and first-rate. Also his Secretary of Agriculture and general Brain-Truster, José Bonifácio, and the younger crowd that are coming up in the State of São Paulo. This was impressive. . . .

[September 24]. The last day, to lunch at the Foreign Office by invitation of the Foreign Minister [Lafer]—very official. The Mello Franco clan was represented by Chagas and [Jayme] Chermont; there also was Affonso Arinos (a Mello Franco) whose political star is very much on the rise. . . . Assis Chateaubriand told some of the old stories including my famous speech that in legend (though not in fact) ended the dictatorship. Affonso confirmed the fact that I had shown it to Vargas and got his approval first. Additional testimony. Lafer gave a toast that couldn't have been nicer.

This was one of those things that happened. It may have been a breach of diplomatic form. But the Brazilians did not resent it as "intervention" but appreciated it as a contribution to history and here was the

Foreign Office saying so with bell, book and candle. It is true the old Vargas crowd was not there. They wouldn't agree.

Friday, the 25th. Arriving at Caracas after an all-night run from Rio. This is almost 3,000 miles in a single hop straight across the Amazon swamp. Unfortunately, it was night-time. We went directly to President Betancourt's house, "Altamira", a charming suburb overlooking Caracas, and spent three days with him. . . .

Betancourt has a couple of things on his mind. He has his economic problems—but they can be swung. The oil revenue is good enough for that. But he has to get public participation to do things by organizing through his party the agricultural people all through the districts. He is attacking the problems of a country half-medieval agriculture and half-modern industry and oil. He is also worried that the American Ambassador [Edward J. Sparks] repeated the old canard that he had been a Communist. The fact is that he had been in a Communist group in Costa Rica as a student and had never been a member of the party and then had been cured and never involved in this since.

September 27. To Bogotá, Colombia . . . we spent a stiff day Monday looking at the University of the Andes as guests of . . . Jaime Samper, and [Vice-Rector] Hildebrand. The latter has a father teaching at Princeton, an Irish-English wife, nine children and is perfectly charming. I thought I was back in the convocation of ancestors who built universities on faith: Oberlin and Yankton. This was exactly the same thing. They gave a luncheon for us at the Jockey Club. Samper is an aristocrat, not a teacher. He had been engineer in the light company for years and his wife was connected with the Cabot family of Boston. There were Cabots there, most of them because they are trustees of the University. We saw the University from top to bottom: quite literally: it runs right up the side of the mountain outside Bogotá. It has one new building in it, thanks to Nelson Rockefeller, and an old and beautiful convent that had been the women's jail. They do a smashing good job. . . .

One of the trustees is Secretary General of the Presidency. We were colleagues at the Conference of Chapultepec and helped to draw the famous Act. We thereupon went over to the palace where we visited with President Lleras Camargo—a brief visit because we had not sent word ahead. He is working twenty hours a day. He, like Rómulo, has his State well in hand, just as everyone agrees Rómulo Betancourt is firmly in the saddle in Venezuela. We gave him Rómulo's greetings and because we had expressed a desire to see him the old Foreign Minister López de Mesa came over to the palace. . . . We had a pleasant chat with a fascinating man whose mind is like a diamond point. But he said a little sadly that the almanac was beginning to be aggressive towards him now—meaning he was growing old.

Thursday, September 29. To New York, arriving four hours late because the plane blew out a tire in Jamaica. No adventures.

We had arranged to go all around the Atlantic Ocean in twenty-six days.

IX

1960~1961

January 20, 1960

The suicide, unless it was murder, of Bang-Jensen is having after-effects. Senator [Thomas J.] Dodd of Connecticut [D.] wants to investigate but the question is, what? He has hired an investigator whom I know —David Martin. Martin came in and wanted to find out about the matter. I told him that aside from Bang-Jensen's feeling that the United Nations was insecure he had provided no facts—either because he had none or because whatever he knew he could not tell.

As to the suicide itself: Forty-eight hours are uncounted for. He left his house on a Monday morning; was found dead two or three days later but obviously had been alive [for most of that period]. It also is true that simulated suicide as a cover for murder is one of the standard tricks in the Russian book. That, of course, does not prove it was murder. . . .

Yesterday, also, Allen Dulles called me. The report is that Bang-Jensen eight times tried to see the C.I.A. but was refused. The fact was that Ambassador [Henrik] de Kauffmann had an intimate dinner at his Embassy for Allen Dulles and invited Bang-Jensen. They talked for half an hour but, Dulles says, Bang-Jensen expressed his fear about the security of the United Nations but gave no definite information to go on. Allen, of course, is not responsible for the security of the United Nations. . . .

January 24, 1960

By jet to California . . . The Center for Democratic Studies is trying to do abstract research on the theory of government. . . . They are working on some theories of mine relating to the popular consensus.

February 2, 1960

I tried to start writing a book about power—but made heavy weather of it. I will start at a later date.

On Saturday, Governor Pat Brown came in with a set of economists from the University of California. He wanted to do some theoretical thinking. So did we. I thought myself that instead of the Governor asking questions of his experts, they were asking questions of the Governor as to what they were all about.

In the course of these proceedings I evolved a theory.

An economy does not run merely by satisfying the individual needs of its people. It will not run fast enough, at that rate, to get much done. There has to be a second, non-personal motivation. The Catholic Church supplied that in the days of the Spanish Empire—the Santa Barbara Mission and its companions all up and down the Coast were an illustration. Probably the Communist state organization does the same thing. At present, California is running, not on taking in its own washing, but on an added increment: the armament business. This may not last forever. Historically, there have been three observable non-personal motives which have stimulated economy: a religious organization (for example, the Mormons in Utah), an imperial motivation (for example: the Spanish or the Napoleonic Empires); a defense motivation (our present situation). To this might be added the variety of social religion, which is present-day Communism.

The idea is worth exploring. It means, economically, that people have to work not only for the things they consume, but for something else that they don't consume, and the motive is either a great enthusiasm or a great compulsion. Maybe something of both. . . .

In the course of this I achieved a sixty-fifth birthday and the calendar becomes aggressive. [Robert] Hutchins [President, The Fund for the Republic] would like me to go out there to live, there is no possible reason for me to do anything of the sort. . . . I should rather spend the last few years meeting and, if need be, fighting with reality than in anyone's palace by the sea.

Monday, February 1. The Rockefeller Foundation has had some ideas. They would like me to run a meeting at the Villa Serbelloni some time next summer. On a limited shot that might be rather fun.

February 2, 1960

Bill Wieland telephoned from the State Department. The Dominican Republic is blowing up. The plots against the dictator there are serious and he has responded in classic fashion—with unlimited terror and torture. In each day a family discovers that some member of it has vanished, and the torture chambers of the old fortress are said to be full. . . .

Lunch with the Argentine Ambassador [Emilio Donato del Carril] to the United Nations and his two economic advisors, [Alejandro] Orfila and [Roberto T.] Alemán. He wants an economic study from the Twentieth Century Fund, quick but helpful. The position is this.

On the advice of its best economists and the encouragement of the United States, Argentina stopped her inflation, reduced her public expenditures, balanced her budget and started to live at a lower economic level which she can afford. But this also meant great unemployment, considerable hardship, dissatisfaction and political opposition. . . .

The questions are thus two: How can you give a lift to Argentina within a short time? And how can you make enough people in the United States and Argentina believe that the situation will straighten out so that they start up business again and get going?

[President Arturo] Frondizi does not put it this way. But what he is really saying is, "Demonstrate that the private property system will work fast enough to make it politically viable—or else shut up and let the socialists have it." . . .

February 12–13, 1960

A stiff two days in the Superior Educational Council in Puerto Rico. . . .

Some Caribbean gossip. The recent revolt in Venezuela seems to have been financed by the falling Dominican dictator, Trujillo, who also has financed some trouble in Cuba. On the other hand, Castro has been helping the troublemakers in Honduras and in Panama. As neither is able to handle the affairs in his own country, they are not doing too well abroad. But the Russians are now boring into the Cuban situation, and my belief is that they will all be full of Communists in six months. The situation is bound to explode before too long.

February 17, 1960

Yesterday to Washington for work-out. A lecture and two hours of seminar at the National War College on Latin America. Pretty much everyone I ever knew was there. The ghastly fact was that most of the men, including ranking officers, had no more idea of Latin America than I have of Tibet.

Then to lunch at the Labor Department. . . . We were spading over the question of economic planning. . . . [Secretary James P.] Mitchell said, a bit grimly, that party lines made no difference at this point. Any sane administration had to be thinking of it. On the other hand, the Congress was invariably opposed.

I forebore to press the point. A President who is willing to use some of his political capital can put measures forward and get them through. A President who is content to sit and let nature take its course will get nothing through. But you could hardly ask a Cabinet officer to comment on his own President.

. . . Drinks in the afternoon with Bill Wieland. They are slowly proposing to close in on Castro—by offering to negotiate everything and then taking him up on his desire to be clear of the United States. This could be done, in part, by so handling the sugar quotas that the profit derived from it is used in part for the determination of American claims for confiscated property.

Obviously, the substantial question—are they allying to the Communist world—remains. I am pretty clear they are and that the real head of the island is Che Guevara.

To speak at the Cooperative Forum in the evening . . .

Home to sleep and needing it. This was about equal to having seven hours of classes in a row.

February 26, 1960

Here some strange things. Trujillo in Santo Domingo has been trying to arrange revolts in a number of countries. He apparently supplied the money for a plot by a group of army officers to overthrow Betancourt.

Some American military mission officers sat in with them, apparently without knowledge of the American Ambassador, Sparks. [Harry] Hermsdorf finally got a list of the Venezuelan officers, and he took it to Betancourt who had known something was going on but not exactly who or where. Thereafter, Betancourt clamped down, arrested the whole lot, and liquidated the conspiracy by sending some of the men abroad, and otherwise handling the matter with finesse. . . .

March 1, 1960

Eisenhower is making the right noises in Latin America. Unhappily, he seems not to be in control of his own government. The Navy landed several contingents of Marines in Santo Domingo, nominally in routine, but really to shore up the Trujillo government. They did this without clearing with the State Department.

March 4, 1960

To India House to lunch with Virginia Prewett [columnist] and Carlos Urrutia, Guatemala Consul General here and just appointed Ambassador to the Organization of American States. We were seeing whether we could get some combined Caribbean policy in case Castro starts some armed adventures. Cuba has bought some jet planes from the Russians and some other miscellaneous material. He does not need these arms for Cuba, and one of his targets is Guatemala. . . .

At three o'clock Phil Bonsal, presently American Ambassador to Cuba, came in. He vaguely hopes that with enough patience and time the Cuban government will be reasonable. It need not necessarily be a private capitalist government. I agree with him that we may well have a socialist government in Cuba—perhaps it ought to be socialist. But I do not think these men will deny themselves the luxury of being enemies of the United States. This can only mean eventually that we take some sort of action which makes it impossible for a Cuban government to play around with either Russia or China.

March 9, 1960

Formal lunch to celebrate the eightieth birthday of James Shotwell and his book *The Long Road to Freedom*. I remember first meeting Shotwell in December, 1918, as we were getting the American delegation to the Versailles Peace Conference organized.

March 10, 1960

Commission on Money and Credit. This is getting into a mess: a million dollars spent on research and none on finding out what they want to do. . . .

Drove in with David Rockefeller. He thinks that the year 1960 on the whole would be a good one. . . .

March 18, 1960

Oppenheimer is anxious to have Twentieth Century Fund finance some scientists to work on problems of disarmament. The problem is whether we can get it far enough along. . . .

March 21, 1960

. . . The news is not good. There will be Russian armament in Cuba probably in May. Castro has already bought 120 millions of arms and has more than Batista ever had. With the Russian planes, he can attack the mainland. His first target will be Guatemala. The Guatemalans have been advised but I cannot find effective counter-measures taken. . . .

April 28, 1960

April 1. Beatrice and I went to Paris to see the tulips out behind Notre Dame and to see Paris again. We put up at a tiny hotel on the Quay des Grands Augustins with a view of Notre Dame from our window. There was no objective in this, merely a holiday.

But as always there was some work to be done. I presented in French a thesis to a little group called "Prospectives" headed by Gaston Berger. He used to be Director of Higher Education in France. This is a group about equally composed of very high-priced intellectuals and very heavy-weight industrialists searching for directions in civilization. The thesis presented was little more than a reworking of the Felix Adler Lecture, namely, that to keep a modern economy running there had to be a sub-stantial factor of effort devoted to purely altruistic or, at all events, non-personal, effort. Since I used the Cathedral at Chartres as one illustration, they liked it. . . .

We lunched with Jacques Rueff, who is now the chief economic ad-visor for De Gaulle. He is drawing the second economic plan for the Fifth French Republic—classic but interesting. He is trying to liberate the French from the endless limits and restrictions which have been built up through the years, applying to everyone from agriculturists to hairdress-ers. He wants to turn production loose. He is working to make an entity out of the Common Market and is openly outspoken in condemning Eng-land for not joining. . . .

April 18. To a little conference at the Council on Foreign Relations with Hugh Gaitskill. He was giving the British side of the European Common Market picture. Speaking with great frankness he said:

1. Britain was not prepared for unification of Europe. They had been fearing it and fighting it for so many centuries that they did not like it.

2. They were still pretty distrustful of the Germans.

3. He thought they could go farther working with if not joining the Common Market. (The necessity of staying with the British Common-wealth countries was overdone.)

4. He did not see that the Summit Conferences could make any con-cessions to Khrushchev and thought there would be fireworks in May; he

recognized that the left wing of the Labour Party wanted agreement badly. He was not optimistic about the Labour Party's return to power. I got the sense of a man of great good will who did not quite know where he was going. . . .

April 21. [To Pittsburgh] . . . I led off with a debate with [Friedrich A. von] Hayek, trying to forecast the corporation as a neutral but powerful instrument of society twenty-five years hence: the real questions being philosophy and the ultimate controls lying outside corporations which would become instruments like a government agency.

April 22. Bright and early to Columbus, there to dedicate the new Ohio State Law School. A pleasant occasion—I shared the platform with Judge [Charles E.] Clark, formerly Dean of the Yale Law School, and a lot of friends. That same night to New York, to pick up the LAV plane to Venezuela.

April 23. Arrived at [Venezuela] . . . went down to Maracay to attend a meeting of the Inter-American Conference on Democracy and Freedom.

My estimate is this was a mess. Frankly the pro-Communist left has terrorized the non-Communist center which dared not raise a word against Castro or for the United States, or for liberty, that might cut into the Castro type of thing. Pepe Figueres and I introduced a project which summed up the high point. I had to leave on the 26th after talking with Betancourt, Galo Plaza of Ecuador, and Paz Estenssoro of Bolivia. . . . I don't like the feel of this. The men are all right but the Communist left can haul out a mob any time it likes—reminding me vaguely of the situation in the French Revolution before the Terror. A little revolution, promptly stamped out, in Venezuela lent background though it was not serious. . . .

April 26. A stiff session in the War College on the handling of cold wars . . . the outline paper is the first analytical paper on the cold war in our literature (note: the Russians have a great many). After which they gave a little luncheon for me and as a delicate attention had a tape recording of my son Peter's presentation of the Indonesian situation to a group of high brass and Embassy people at Clark Field a couple of weeks ago. I thought he did a competent job. . . .

So I am home after a spell of trouping. I had had enough though I am afraid more is coming.

Beatrice came in later in the evening. She had been at the De Gaulle dinner and I gathered having an extremely good time.

May 3, 1960
Morning to Washington on some FHA business. In the afternoon [name unknown] who is writing the life of Bang-Jensen came in. I gave him some atmosphere, whatever I could, because it is serious. . . .

But it is increasingly clear that the Bang-Jensen death was not and has not been cleared up. He left home on Monday and on Thursday was found dead but was dead only twelve hours. What happened in the meantime nobody knows. Simulated suicide is one of the oldest tricks in the intelligence book. Anyhow, Bang-Jensen has become a symbol in certain respects.

May 5–6, 1960

Twentieth Century Fund meetings in Princeton. This is all right but the Fund is almost too respectable. We ought to get into a first-rate row about something. Foundations sit on a very padded cushion.

May 10, 1960

The Committee on Money & Credit. These people talk about all issues except the important ones. Money and credit should be so handled that nothing is settled on purely financial grounds—only on grounds of productivity. Money and credit are merely to get things going, to take product and labor from here where it is to there where it is needed. . . .

May 17, 1960

Final meeting of the Over-all Panel of the Rockefeller Bros. Committee. We had before us a report on democracy which will duly come out and which I fathered but it lacks something and I don't know what. Democracy has more in it than syllogistic logic.

My admiration for Laurence Rockefeller mounts. . . .

May 18, 1960

To a lunch with the Newspaper Guild where I got a "Page One" Award. Sitting next to me was John L. Lewis and I have had previous acquaintance with him. But he was all smiles and velvet and we chatted and nobody said a word about his negotiations with Hitler. He has done a great deal for a great many people.

May 22, 1960

Peter got back from the Philippines and was met by his fiancée, Lila. We had breakfast at 19th Street and forthwith left for Great Barrington for a week until he was married.

Peter is a 1st Lieutenant, "eight foot tall" and dressed in khaki. He has been fighting the cold war in more ways than he can tell about. He volunteered for special service in Cambodia (that is to say, guerrilla warfare) and did not go because it was called off. He knew all about the U-2 flights. He thinks we are getting clobbered in the cold war because it has been a policy of pure opportunism. Any enemy of our enemy is a friend of ours and in that way you can make discreditable friends. He thinks the Chinese would take over South Viet Nam in time; and that the shaky governments we are propping up play one side against the other to their own advantage. He has a low opinion of Syngman Rhee in Korea (he has just departed this political life), Ngo Dinh Diem in Viet Nam—their governments are cruel and corrupt; not easily distinguishable from the enemies they are fighting. Indonesia he thinks is in the wash. The Communists want it but the Indonesians have been systematically expelling the Chinese as they did the Dutch. This pushes Indonesia farther away from Communist China. The Chinese, Peter thinks, are the most unpopular people in all Asia, Communist or not. They stick to each other, speak their own language, regard other people as savages. They can handle property and organize affairs. Like Jews, they accumulate the economic power and don't share it.

Peter says, sadly, he expects to live to see the day we fight a major war with China, as they are quite as capable of making anything that we are and this will be a war of extinction.

Our job is to discover ways by which that does not happen.

Peter also has a low opinion of the Army and government machinery. Second-rate men, without contact with the country, trying to give advice and settle things and they frequently know very little about it.

We talked about the Summit conference. It is pretty plain that the Summit conference failed before it started—the only question is how. . . . On the other hand, the failure tended to strengthen the Chinese, who are now openly attacking Khrushchev and the extremist faction. Khrushchev reacted as did Hitler. While insulting the United States, he declared for a singularly modest line in Moscow and is slowly reshuffling his government with a view to getting rid of his enemies.

From now on, the world picture has three elements: the West, the Soviet and the Chinese and each is different.

May 29, 1960

Win and Kitty Crane gave a party for Peter and Lila at Chilton House. I had been there to see Senator Crane first in 1912. All the Berkshire community was there and it had a kind of old world flavor about it you find usually in novels about the old South of the plantation palace days.

May 30, 1960

Peter and Lila were married at Trinity Church in Lenox. Followed a reception at High Lawn, a great palace built for a favorite Vanderbilt great-granddaughter, specifically for great ceremonies. About half of the company assembled were great families: the rest were the farmers and workmen with whom Peter or Lila or both had worked since childhood. A lovely day and everyone extremely happy and Lila radiant.

I came back to our farm. I ought to have been as happy as they and wasn't. I went to look at Peter's room and could only think that now there was nothing to do but dismantle it—he would never come back. His first big trout mounted on the wall, his .22 rifle, a handful of odd souvenirs, the Harvard shingle, the little trophies from childhood to young manhood, all had meaning. There were no longer the children of the house in that homestead. The void was great and I was 65 years old.

And yet I know this happened when Priam sent Hector off to the wars and that if it had not happened life would have been unhappy. This is simply one of the great moments of life like birth and death, honorable and natural and not accomplished without pain.

The pair are off on their wedding trip, coming back briefly to New

York, then off to the Philippines for nearly a year. It will be rough and tough and they will love it. They plan to get a Landrover and cross Singapore and the Burma Road to Europe. It's great to be young. But not particularly comfortable.

June 1, 1960

The India Consul General brought in a Mr. Mazundar who is Secretary of the Department India has to run corporations. We talked of everything, including the Far East and corporations, and the accumulation of capital and whether you can use corporations to do this. These were both literate, thoughtful men. I don't know that I can help. They want to use corporations in the Indian State. We do not allocate resources. India must. We shall have to very soon ourselves. But having a great many the problem is not pressing. India has not enough and has to make her capital go where needed. . . .

June 8, 1960

Professor [Jean] Gottman is writing *Megalopolis* for the Twentieth Century Fund and he came in to visit. Some of his new findings on the make-up of a city are interesting, but the real thrilling part is the change in make-up of urban society. I think, if we can get away from statistics, this book may make some history. . . .

June 14, 1960

Peter and Lila came back to Great Barrington for the week-end and are here today. A little dinner party for them tonight.

June 16, 1960

The A.Y.D. [Affiliated Young Democrats] want me to speak at their convention tomorrow night. Meanwhile, Agnes [Mrs. Eugene] Meyer wants me to sign a pro-Stevenson petition. John Saltonstall [of Massachusetts] wants me to sign a pro-Kennedy petition. Abe Fortas [lawyer, Under Secretary of the Interior 1942–1946] would like me to come out for Lyndon Johnson though he doesn't believe Lyndon can be nominated. . . .

Still worse in the Caribbean, Cubans are making more trouble than mere words. I have two reports: that late in July they will announce that they have concluded an agreement by which the Soviet Union can establish a base in Cuba; and, this may be another version, that on the occasion of Khrushchev's coming visit they will announce that they are within the Warsaw Pact or that the Soviet Union will say that any aggression against Cuba will mean war with the Soviet Union. This is the end of the Monroe Doctrine. I think they are hoping to shift arms to the Caribbean littoral and start an Asian pattern. The United States appears not to have any clear-cut end or aim; is not in real motion; is unpredictable in action and really appears not to know what it wants, can do and will do. This is like a shirt without starch. Only bad fortune can happen: it gets no breaks. And we can only hope that the other side will make mistakes.

June 28, 1960

June 18–19. Reasonably quiet week-end at the Farm. Meditated on the state of the universe and didn't like it.

June 21. In the evening a seminar for the younger liberals. Pleasant: but one wonders whether this is the way you swing things today.

June 22. A luncheon by the Liberal Party in honor of Reinhold Niebuhr [theologian]. As he was ill and could not come, we had a talk without him. It had its significance. It signified that the labor movement can work with intellectuals like Niebuhr. Thirty-odd years ago the chief paper of the labor movement, then the New York *Call*, printed an editorial bracketing a book by my father with one of Reinhold Niebuhr's, and others, under the title, "To hell with Applied Christianity." A generation later, everyone having worked together with great fidelity, we were paying tribute to Reinhold Niebuhr on his retirement.

The Kennedy headquarters called up and asked me if I would join in signing an intellectuals' liberal appeal for Kennedy. Ken Galbraith, Arthur Schlesinger, and others, are signing. I said that I didn't throw over old friends so rapidly, though I would support Kennedy if he were nominated.

Privately, I think Kennedy will be nominated—but one cannot yet tell. Alex Rose insists he has a majority of delegates signed up but I think not, though he is close.

June 23. At lunch with Senator Kennedy, Alex Rose, David Dubinsky, and about twenty of the Liberals. Kennedy was asking for their support in New York if and when he is nominated.

He made a good impression. This was partly because of a certain honesty. Someone attacked him about his stand at the time of the McCarthy furor. He gave his record—which was one of having dodged the issue —partly because he was ill for some months during it. He wound up by saying that in the light of hindsight it was not so good. He could and should have done more. But that was it. There was no point in denying it. He could have gone in for the kill and did not. If he had tried to make out that he was all right all the time, we would have lost all use for him.

Since I sat close to him at lunch, we talked of Latin America. He asked me if, in the case of his nomination, I would work with him on Latin American affairs. I said of course I would: I was very much worried about the situation because I thought the cold war would be loosed on this continent if somebody did not move fast. He had read an earlier article of mine in *The Reporter* and liked it.

The Cuban news is getting worse by the minute. I believe there will be a revolt attempted in a month or so. Also I have reason to believe (the information comes from L'Herisson) that Castro has cobbled up a working agreement with [François] Duvalier, now dubiously president of Haiti. Duvalier will demand a great deal of relief from America, make a show of not getting it, and then entertain some Soviet offers with Castro's people acting as intermediaries. (A couple of days later the preliminary methods actually appeared.) Meantime Castro sent back to Haiti anti-Duvalier Haitians supporting [Gaston] Jumelle, who is here. He has also imprisoned some of the anti-dictator men of Nicaragua, notably [Benjamín] Lacayo [Sacasa].

What is really going on is an attempt to paralyze the democratic movement, leaving only pro-Communist and pro-dictator forces in the field. In the meantime, both in Haiti and in Nicaragua, the dictators will be eliminated and pro-Communist groups will immediately endeavor to seize the government. It is the old prewar game of the right and left extremists combining to paralyze the liberal groups and then fight it out among themselves. . . .

June 29, 1960
Some miscellaneous work on possible manuscript on "Power."

July 4, 1960
We got the full news of the bomb plot against Rómulo Betancourt. This was a highly professional job, flown in from the Dominican Republic.

July 5, 1960
The Brazilian Ambassador (Freitas Valle) and the Guatemalan Consul General [Carlos] (Urrutia) were at dinner the other night. I was examining whether they would support arms control to blank out force moves in the Caribbean—they would like it but, as always, would like America to do it, reserving the privilege of throwing bricks at her. My own estimate is that this Caribbean situation is spear-heading a mainline attack on the United States probably worldwide. I am beginning to be upset.

July 6, 1960
The American Molasses Company is resetting its plans since the Cuban quota will be cut. The Castro government is expropriating American sugar mills and likewise insisting it is an act of aggression for the United States not to continue a quota situation giving Cuba the higher price—in other words, subsidizing them for their enmity.

A country can expropriate American interests within its territory. What it cannot do is to expropriate the American consumer as well. . . .

To Averill Harriman's house for cocktails where were Senator Fulbright and Bill Benton, David Lilienthal and others. Harriman is pledged to Kennedy.

Half the men in the room were running for Secretary of State. My own feeling is a little simpler. A man capable of holding that job ought to be smart enough not to want it if he can avoid it.

July 7, 1960
The anti-Castro Cubans (not Batista men but the men who really made Castro's revolution) are now mostly in the United States and are

unifying themselves under the leadership of [Aureliano] Sánchez Arango and [Manuel Antonio de] Varona. . . .

The United States government now has black and white evidence that Trujillo in the Dominican Republic organized the bomb plot against Betancourt. He is rather more badly wounded than the newspapers make out.

I think if we knew all the facts we would find the Castro government has a temporary working agreement with Trujillo. They are quite prepared to let him wipe out the Democratic leaders in the Caribbean if he can do it. After that, the Communist group will move in on those countries and throw out Trujillo, at leisure. . . .

If the United States is doing anything, I don't know what it is.

July 8, 1960

A violent week-end. Not so far as I was concerned. We went to the Farm and thence to see my father at Kinderhof; back to the Farm. On Sunday, God forgive me, I poured coffee at the social hour after Church and went to lunch. Nothing could have been more banal. Meanwhile the heavy guns were going.

Last week, following the expropriation of the oil refineries in Cuba, President Eisenhower now duly authorized by the Congress, cut out the Cuban preferential sugar quota. . . . The oil companies retaliated by insisting that the Cuban airlines pay cash for any gasoline they get when they get it. This is not surprising because they had been supplying oil to Cuba which wasn't paying for it and Cuba owed them about $27 million. They also said that no tanker could carry Russian oil to Cuba and expect any business from them. The Soviet Union answered that they would supply the tankers.

Khrushchev then made a speech in which he said that any American intervention in Cuba would be answered by rocket bombs from Russia, noting that they had fired one in the Pacific at a 13,000 km distance. So far, routine—but then came a real body blow.

One of the leaders of the Majority (practically the only) political party in Mexico made a speech in the Congress stating that in a struggle between Cuba and the United States, Mexico would side with Cuba. This was cheered to the echo. It startled even this lethargic administration into action.

Eisenhower issued a statement on Saturday. He said that the United States would not tolerate setting up of a Communist satellite in the Western Hemisphere. Simultaneously he gave orders to set up a Marshall Plan for the hemisphere (an old hope of mine though I imagine he got it from others). I imagine it is one more of these study-but-save-the-dollar jobs. . . .

At the same time, Betancourt in Venezuela squarely demanded from the O.A.S. retaliatory, or punitive, action against Trujillo, who is now proved to be the instigator of the plot against Betancourt's life.

Castro called a big meeting for Sunday, asking a million and a half people to listen in. It wound up in anti-climax. He had "pneumonia" and didn't show up. From his sickbed he made a rather weak speech, all things considered. . . .

The real danger to the United States is considerable. Mexico stays with Castro for political reasons; a good many other countries will do so, too. Since the situation in Southeast Asia is anything but safe, we may find ourselves pretty much limited to North America and the waning allegiance of Western Europe. The climax cannot be too far off.

Congo got her independence from Belgium and promptly fell apart. It is now black-white race rioting to continue until all the whites are expelled. . . . If this goes on, empire will look very good indeed by comparison.

July 14, 1960

During the night the radio reported the nomination of Kennedy at the Democratic Convention in Los Angeles.

This morning, to meet Professor Archibald Cox of Harvard Law Schoool, presently on fulltime duty with Kennedy, at the Century Club. Kennedy had asked Cox to get into touch with me without specifications. I told him that Kennedy had asked whether I would work on Latin American affairs and I said that when he was nominated I certainly would help him against Nixon. I asked Cox to note and make it plain to Kennedy that I did not wish to be committed until after July 29 since my personal relations with Nelson Rockefeller were such that I would not wish to be in the position of campaigning against him. . . .

Cox wanted several things. First. The Senator is holding some unannounced seminars to discuss various problems. He hopes to have one on foreign affairs at Hyannisport. . . . I said . . . I would be glad to join.

Second. He asked if I would generally help along as consultant on speeches and policy declarations. I said I would be glad to do this; obviously I will have to know a little more about Kennedy's own ideas.

Third. He hoped I would try to work out the outline of a Latin American policy. This has not been a region to which Kennedy has given much thought. I said I would be glad to do that, though by now it was tied into the world situation. I thought the situation would be considerably worse before it was better; what with Cuba, rapidly deteriorating situation in Haiti, and the danger of turning on the Cold War in the mainland.

Fourth. The Senator would have to make one speech for the Liberal Party in New York . . . perhaps I could think about a draft. Possibly, this time it had best be foreign affairs rather than the usual speech on labor and domestic policy—the conventional in labor politics. I said I would be glad to do this.

There was no point in going into my own emotions with Cox. Khrushchev is going to carry the Cold War as close to America as he can. The weakness of the current government will mean that the situation will be worse as the campaign goes on. We will need somebody with a touch of Winston Churchill. I would back Kennedy, an untried young man, as against Nixon, not much older but a representative of policies which have failed. There is no point now in wondering whether Kennedy ought to be different or not. It is clear that he would like, as Roosevelt did, to gather in as many different segments as he can. Whether he has Roosevelt's genuine capacity for using [different people] and at the same time to give assurance and courage to people that are rapidly becoming frightened— one cannot yet tell.

July 19, 1960

Marquis Childs came in. He wants an article for his column on Latin American affairs. For some reason my stock in that quarter is going up.

Whether it should, I don't know. The problem is not at all the same as that we met with Franklin Roosevelt. Briefly:

1. The Communists under Russian influence have been organizing all over South America. These are small groups, chiefly centered in international classes with a cadre of highly trained professional agitators. And an apparently unlimited supply of inflammatory propaganda probably printed in Moscow. Included in the apparatus is the fact that they have bought a good many of the newspaper men.

Following the failure of the Summit conferences in May, a high-level decision was taken in Moscow, probably in consultation with Peiping, to turn on the Cold War. The Communist strike in Italy was designed to spark a revolution. The similar demonstrations in Japan probably did not hope to achieve that result, though they may have hoped to start a long chain reaction. The Cuban situation unquestionably was timed in part to produce this end; so I think was the attempt to turn the Congo mess into demand for Russian troops. This is presently the theory of the United States government.

2. So far as the Caribbean situation is concerned, the United States cannot make up its mind whether it will behave like a great Power, or will stand aside and let events take their course, and is somehow coming to a position where it is actually afraid to defend, fearing it will be accused of "imperialism." Yet it has in its hands all needed tools. Defense of the hemisphere is the fixed principle.

3. It is beginning to appear that the Communist hard-core running Castro's government went too far in yelling for Khrushchev. It was, of course, all right with Khrushchev; he is carrying the Cold War straight into the enemy's camp. But the rest of the hemisphere reacted like a shot. Or at least most of it did. I am still not sure how far the organizers of the inter-American movement (presently it is more anti-American than pro-Communist) have been able to persuade anyone that they not only do not want the United States as senior Power but do want Russia.

4. But there is a vacuum here. A sympathizer with Communism or anti-American group at once allies himself with that organization and goes to work. People who do not want Communism have no defined program for a better social structure and no one with whom they can join. . . .

Clearly the whole base of these relations has to be recanvassed. For one thing our foreign affairs machinery must include not only the diplomat who talks to the palace but an actual organization on the ground.

July 25, 1960

Spent a lovely week-end at the Berkshires. Max Ascoli is also up there; just back from the Los Angeles convention. He is supporting Kennedy and thinks the Convention did the best it could. He also thinks well of his young campaign coordinator, [Theodore C.] Sorensen.

Meanwhile, Nelson Rockefeller's fortunes have taken a rather dramatic shift. It slowly dawned on the Republicans' high command that with Rockefeller really off the boat they were in trouble. Especially since Lyndon Johnson is on Kennedy's ticket, they cannot have too much hope of bringing the Solid South into camp. Nixon thereupon visited Rockefeller, probably hoping to get him to accept the V.P. He must have learned that Rockefeller cannot take any position on the ticket unless the party is going to support his ideas. So Nixon agreed to support them—thereby practically reversing himself on practically everything. The newspapers today suggest that the Republican platform committee is not having this. So Rockefeller—and presumably Nixon—is fighting for a set of policies outlined by Nelson himself.

Some of these policies are directly drawn from the Rockefeller Bros. Commission report. Particularly, insistence on regional confederations. This had its origin in some work of mine and I am somewhat amused to find a piece of thinking which originated at least in part here now become an issue on which the Republican party is asked to pledge itself.

Nelson has taken himself off the hook. Nixon, the factual candidate, has associated himself with the Rockefeller proposals. If these imply criticism of Eisenhower, then Nixon and the majority have agreed to go along. If Nixon wins, Rockefeller can claim he has at last pushed things in the right direction; if Nixon loses, Rockefeller is the logical candidate for '64. It was a good hand, well played.

My own guess is that no matter what they do, the country will swamp Nixon. Their estimate is that he will say anything for a dollar and swear to it for five. This last incident tends to confirm the impression. Though I wholly disagree with them on pretty much everything, I get amused at seeing the hard-core Roosevelt-hating [Senator Barry] Goldwater Republicans come to the same opinion of Nixon that much of the country has. I understand they cut off his money.

September 22, 1960

This resumes after a lapse of several weeks spent chiefly at the farm with the grandchildren.

My colleague Professor [Richard N.] Gardner was working this Summer at Rand and I went down there for an afternoon. It is frightening. These boys calculate cold war, retaliation, etc. up to a decimal point. They are for raising the stakes of atomic warfare to its real limit—spending some twelve billion dollars on an ultimate bomb which would blow up the entire globe and threatening to use that as the ultimate deterrent. This is really the mathematics of double-or-quits. They fail to take into account that after the fourth or fifth redouble, the risks involved outweigh any possible advantage.

Men attached to this type of reasoning, I think cease to be mentally normal. They are severely logical within limited premises—but cease to make the rational adaptation to human life needed. . . .

September 13, the Liberal Party duly named Kennedy and Johnson and I was Honorary Chairman of the platform committee. The following night at the Liberal Party Dinner both Kennedy and Stevenson spoke. Because of the Catholic issue we had Reinhold Niebuhr introduce Kennedy—a stroke of genius, I think. The speeches were good. I discerned a couple of paragraphs of a speech I wrote for Kennedy which found their way into his but it was his own job and a better one than mine. The campaign is slowly getting off the ground: I should say it was not better than an even chance for Kennedy. The Catholic issue is more talked about than the really great issues up in the campaign—economic motivations, planning, to use a bad semantic word, and the growing catastrophe in foreign affairs.

On Thursday, September 15, the F.B.I. came in to see me. They are investigating Roy Rubottom and Bill Wieland for the State Department, the charge being that they turned over Cuba to Castro. In point of fact, this appears to have been started by Trujillo, the Dominican dictator, who has money and uses it in Washington. . . . I think I satisfied the F.B.I. man that Wieland from the very beginning had sized up Castro as a megalomaniac and that our real failure was not being able to organize the responsible elements in Havana to take over. . . .

September 20 . . . I have arranged to make a speech in support of Kennedy probably about October 10 with a large hook-up. . . .

The American Assembly just called up and asked me to make the opening address of the American Assembly on "The Secretary of State." This is flattery but less so when you know the circumstances. They had saved this spot for President Eisenhower. . . . So they asked me instead. I said I would. . . . Obviously it would be interpreted *inter alia* as my bid for a high State Department job if Kennedy is elected. As this is doubtful, we need not lose any sleep.

The most heartening thing is to see the way the United Nations has for the time being closed up the Congo situation. Everyone is giving Dag Hammarskjöld well-deserved bouquets. He has done well, acted courageously and staked his own career on it. The solid support of the Arab and African nations is heartening.

But I think a special bouquet ought to go to the ex-stenographer turned army colonel, [Joseph D.] Mobutu, who finally flattened both [Patrice] Lumumba and [Joseph] Kasavubu and undertook to bring a modicum of order out of chaos. This came under the heading of good luck for Hammarskjöld. Yet it must be remembered that good luck comes to men who are trying to go somewhere; bad luck to people who merely flap around or stand still.

Also from this United Nations meeting is emerging something else; in its own peculiar way, frightening. The breach between the Russians and Chinese is growing wider and now is obvious. The African bloc is crystallizing not around ideological lines but around racial lines. "Down with the white man." The Arabs are joining them in that. The Chinese position I do not know. The Russians themselves are the victims of this racism which they themselves started in Africa. We shall have, pretty soon, not one cold war but two or three: Communist against non-Communist; Negro against White; possibly Asian against them all. The mills of the gods of hatred may grind slowly but they grind terribly.

Strangely, the Russians, cold war and all, are closer to the European West than they are to this sort of thing though they have blood guilt in starting it. I should think we are seeing the dim forerunners of a vast realignment. For when the show-down came in Africa, the Russians withdrew not, I think, because of the words in the United Nations but because they were quite simply regarded as white.

The problem then arises: what can be made out of the African complex. It could dissolve quite easily into primitive tribalism which the imperial system of the nineteenth century interpreted and somewhat organized, and restrained. But it did not change the fundamental pattern.

October 27, 1960

. . . To join the receiving group for Kennedy at the Garment District. There was a vast throng of people as far as one could see. Anyone's estimate is as good as the next man's. I should say a couple of hundred thousand. . . .

It was interesting to see that Kennedy did develop a personal communication and communicated enthusiasm. . . .

October 31–November 3, 1960

Various tasks, not very important, chiefly writing things previously committed for.

One of them is a memorandum on confederation. Nelson Rockefeller wants to work on that beginning as soon as the election is over, and he has Henry Kissinger to work with him and he wants me alongside.

A good deal of incidental campaigning. . . .

November 7, 1960

Election eve. To dinner with David Rockefeller and a bunch of African representatives speaking various languages and obviously enjoying the Rockefeller hospitality. Appeared on TV though it had been recorded previously. The election round-up for the Liberal Party.

November 8, 1960

Election Day which I spent reading in libraries. In the evening to Liberal Party headquarters, then to Max Ascoli's. At 1:00 AM we decided it was not worth while staying up.

November 9, 1960

Kennedy apparently elected though the vote is terribly close. . . .

November 10, 1960

Projects Committee of the Twentieth Century Fund. Then downtown to work. To preside at the Foreign Relations Council meeting for

José Figueres. Dinner then at my house for Jules Romains and Figueres and a party of other people.

Pepe feels that much of Latin America is already lost: the combination of hotheads with quietly organized Communists waiting to take over may be invincible.

November 15, 1960

A little meeting at Rockefeller Center to discuss the problems of international confederation. Nelson Rockefeller came in, very tired, wondering how he emerged from the late campaign in feeding Nixon to New York.

November 17, 1960

Lunch with José Bonifácio Nogueira, Secretary of Agriculture of the State of São Paulo. He is drafting a program of agricultural reform in São Paulo. He had visited Washington, observing bitterly that they didn't know what it was all about—they merely wanted to peddle farm surpluses. Yet agricultural reform must be the basis of any South American policy. . . .

November 18, 1960

About 8:00 o'clock Helen Lyons [nurse] telephoned that my father was taken ill during the night and had not recovered consciousness. At 11:30 he died. We left at once for Boscawen.

November 19, 1960

On Saturday we had the funeral in Concord—merely for the family and a few acquaintances, planning to hold a memorial service in New York later.

Then to Arden House where there was a conference on science, health and religion at which I gave a paper. This on account of Harold Wolff, who wanted it very badly. If there was anything Father would not have liked, it would have been to shut down business on account of his funeral. The paper related to certain philosophical or perhaps religious assumptions that were made by social scientists although they do not usually recognize that fact. It seemed to go well.

November 20, 1960

More conferences at Arden House, then to New York in the afternoon. Thence to Newark where I was on T.V. . . .

November 22, 1960

Lunch with Dr. Spijkermann of Philips and some work on the antitrust case. At 6:30 to make one of those foolish parish speeches at Trinity Church—pure sentiment. I have been working in the Trinity Church area for forty years and it seemed ungracious to refuse a hand on their community program. . . . Then, by airplane to St. Louis to make a University address at Washington University. . . .

This was in the Washington University Chapel; beginning with singing the Washington University song, an old German love song in fact, and the University choir sang Bach's B Minor Mass. So far as I was concerned, they could have suspended all other proceedings and kept on singing. We were talking of planned economy. Thereafter, lunch with the Economics Department and some good talk and then talked with some of the students in the afternoon.

November 25, 1960
. . . Ted Sorensen telephoned. He is Kennedy's Man-Friday and organizer. He asked if I would be the head of a small task force to report in the latter part of December to Kennedy on Latin American affairs. The others are Robert Alexander of Rutgers University, Lincoln Gordon of the Harvard Business School and Ted Moscoso of Muñoz Marín's staff [Economic Development Administrator, Puerto Rico]. I said I would do this.

This, of course, is it: they want a set of suggestions on the things that will come up right away; not a study in depth but what to do next. There are all kinds of "snags." These run all the way from the Navy in the Caribbean intercepting attacks on the mainland from Cuba, a touch-and-go situation in Venezuela, Brazilian exchange and about everything else.

This does not necessarily mean that the same group will take over in State, but it suggests that we will have the first guess when the Kennedy Administration comes in in January.

Since election I have been wondering whether I would be asked to work in Latin American affairs in the new government or whether I would be left out. If I were not asked, my vanity would be wounded—but my relief would be extremely great. As between pangs of wounded vanity or the salve of relief, I wonder which would win. Anyhow my vanity is now salved; relief will come if we do not have to go to Washington—of course it does not follow from being asked to report on policy but is quite likely.

The trouble with this kind of assignment is that it should have come ten years ago. There is no hiding the fact that at 65 one does not field as many tennis balls as at 55 or 45.

November 29, 1960
Lecture at Senior Seminar of the State Department.

December 2, 1960
. . . Professor Robert Alexander of Rutgers came in. He was one of the men designated by Sorensen who also was designated with [Professor Arthur P.] Whitaker of [Pennsylvania]. We cantered over the ground to be covered by the Task Force.

As it emerges this Task Force is supposed to do three things.

(1) It is the "shadow section" of the State Department to advise Kennedy in case of emergency during the interregnum in case he needs any advice. This dies, of course, on January 20. Probably earlier if a Secretary of State is appointed. He may have other notions.

(2) It is supposed to draw up a list of the steps to be taken immediately on January 20.

Orders to be given or considered.

In the inaugural speech; a suggestion as to the next step in Latin American affairs.

(3) It is supposed to indicate the lines of a dramatic revitalization of Latin American relations. . . .

December 5, 1960

Work: [Professor Arturo] Morales-Carrión [University of Puerto Rico] to lunch at the Century. I wanted him on the Task Force on which also is Ted Moscoso; both ought to be members.

Afternoon at Columbia teaching school.

December 7, 1960

The Task Force got together. A. Whitaker, Lincoln Gordon, Robert Alexander, Morales-Carrión and Ted Moscoso. Sorensen's Assistant, [Richard N.] Goodwin, sat in. . . . Moscoso had come all the way from Puerto Rico, which was nice of him.

We agreed:

Kennedy ought to say something quick to allay the fear that he has forgotten about Latin America. Agreed that Muñoz Marín will send him a telegram. Kennedy will answer it. This is strictly general. Morales-Carrión will arrange for the Governor to send us the text. . . .

Venezuela is the hinge to the situation. We need Rómulo Betancourt to keep the thing in line. That way we may be able to avoid a major cold war in the Caribbean littoral.

So our hope is Betancourt and it is not so long ago, as this journal will disclose, that the United States Government was trying to hound him all over the hemisphere. And now Harry Hermsdorf died of cancer a month ago so that we cannot be sure that Rómulo will be well guarded. I am turning over in my mind asking Muñoz Marín to send some guards: his men know how but Muñoz Marín needs protection himself. Anything goes in this game, and neither Trujillo nor Castro scruple about making it go.

December 10, 1960

TV late Saturday night, a broadcast on Latin America. This was before an audience of about 500. The prime question was Cuba. One-third of the audience were Cuban exiles; another third, Communists or sympathizers; both loaded for bear. The remainder were uncommitted. A heavy police detail was there to prevent rioting after the show. My opponent was to have been C. Wright Mills, who has degenerated from being a capable though rather left-wing opinionated Professor of Sociology [Columbia] into a ranting propagandist. He was to have been the champion of the Castro regime, but he got a heart attack—partly I think because he was frightened—and had reason to be. His book, *Listen, Yankee,* written after a couple of months in Cuba, where he had never been, was derived from interviews in Spanish, which he does not know, with refusal to ascribe identity to the sources thereof; really a piece of noisy propaganda and not even good, so I was ready to plaster him.

In his place came Congressman Charles O. Porter [D., Ore.], an old friend of mine, and on the wooly-headed side. The result was a not uninteresting debate with a lot of questions from the audience, mainly loaded. But it did not allow for really good presentation of the issues and one always feels a sense of frustration.

December 10 continued. To take Raúl Prebisch [Argentine economist] out to breakfast. This pursuant to instructions from Senator Kennedy's office. Whether this was a brush-off in my direction or a real desire to have me talk to Prebisch about his plan for Latin America, ECLA [United Nations Economic Commission for Latin America], I do not know. I have known him many years ago and was glad to see him again.

He said the whole job was to give economic and social content to the idea of freedom, and that a strong statement by Kennedy along those lines would be a great deal of help to him. He was all for Betancourt. In his view this was an historical moment and required everyone to get on board. I observed that I would be 66 in January. He registered shock, adding that he was about to become 60 himself and had thought of retiring then to write books.

ECLA contemplates a closed common market for Latin America. I asked whether the United States might come in on it—opening its own markets now to Latin American manufacture against their commitment to reduce their tariffs on our manufactured goods over a period of X years. This brought him up all standing (he is alleged to be anti-American) and he thought it would be wonderful. He made the point that the United States must stop making out that its entire policy is to increase a field for investing its capital. I observed a little bitterly that I thought we should need all the capital we had at home as things were going now.

By chance a couple of days previously I had been at a meeting of Nelson Rockefeller's group on "Confederation". Stacy May had made the suggestion I had thus transmitted to Prebisch.

December 14, 1960

Various jobs and to the Chase National Bank where were David Rockefeller, Frazer Wilde [life insurance executive], Per Jacobsson, of the International Monetary Fund. We talked over the gold drain. David Rockefeller wondered whether the United States could guarantee to the central banks in other countries that deposits left here would be repaid in dollars equal in value to the present. This he thought would stop all out-flow.

December 16, 1960

Afternoon to the Twentieth Century Fund where the Task Force on Latin America worked up a preliminary report for Senator Kennedy. . . .
A long, stiff session.

December 17–18, 1960

To the Farm, taking Arturo Morales-Carrión with us. On Sunday evening, Arturo and I drafted the final form of the telegraph report. . . .

But under cover of this, of course, was a minor personal matter. Rumours have been circulated that I might be appointed Assistant Secretary of State for Latin American Affairs. Enough of them circulated so that I was fairly clear the subject had been discussed and the "leak" was possibly in the nature of a trial balloon. Goodwin and I talked about it after the Friday meeting. I told him I was too old for Assistant Secretaryships; that it called for a high-level desk; that the things that would be done to me in the job were singularly unpleasant; in any event, a major mistake had been made in the past twelve years by running Latin America from a third-string office. Goodwin said that the times were so serious that it called for everyone to sacrifice himself and go to work. I said I had made that speech so many times myself and had made it so often to other people, I could recite it by heart. But the thing that mattered was whether you could get something done. He said the appointment would be popular both in the United States and in Latin America.

I had the sense that if I had said I would accept the job then, I could have had it. But at my time of life, it seems to me that it calls for a first-string job or none. In the evening I was reading Winston Churchill's second volume of the history of World War II (p. 4, *Their Finest Hour*). He said it is always a mistake to tackle a first-rate proposition from a subordinate position.

So the fact is that a third chance at a historical moment has come—and probably gone—chiefly because I shall be 66 my next birthday. A subordinate position must be held by a younger man, and I estimate that they will not set up a first-string position. I can, I think, do more for the human race (it cannot be much in any event) with my own thinking and writing than from a second-string job in Washington.

Telegram to Sorenson, December 18, 1960

Taskforce Latin America suggests following for immediate action. Area now major and active cold war theatre with outcome in serious doubt. Continued inaction may entail grave risk.

One: Bill setting up State Department Undersecretaryship Western Hemisphere thus ending stepchild status of this area in US policy.

Two: Bill appropriating five hundred million for interAmerican development fund implementing [Under Secretary of State and incoming Secretary of the Treasury C. Douglas] Dillon's Bogotá pledge.

Three: Venezuela Colombia key countries needing open support. Direct Sectreasury work out prompt emergency financial support Betancourt government.

Four: Transfer Sparks but with dignity. Promote Counsellor [Allan] Stewart to Ambassador Caracas.

Five: Send personal representative unpublicized trip consulting

Puerto Rican government enroute to explore with Betancourt and Lleras Camargo possible combined policy and corrective action respecting Dominican Republic and Cuba, including possibility of combined center Caracas or Bogotá for propaganda and other activities. This might become nucleus for hemispheric wide democratic progressive front for social development and ideological and political defence against Communist and Castro attacks.

Six: Directive Defense Department in conjunction CIA prepare orders for unpublicized operation preventing shipment arms and guerrillas from Cuba Santo Domingo and elsewhere into other Latin American countries. Plan should envisage possible multilateralization with Venezuela Colombia possibly others who might wish to join.

Seven: Remove Whelan from Embassy Nicaragua. New Ambassador should be capable of negotiating peaceful organization of a transition government.

Eight: Directive Secstate work out plan for Haiti with a view to organizing transition group and then reconsidering aid to Duvalier.

Nine: Directive Secstate prompt high level consultation Brazil regarding Ecuador Peru dispute. In Quito especial precautions should be taken in respect of Interior Secretary [Manuel] Aranjo Hidalgo.

Ten: Directive Secstate convene interdepartment group to draft long range economic plan preferably based ECLA liberalized to include US with undertaking to set up relations between ECLA group and OECD, and stepped up program of aid and consideration plans to stabilize prices key agricultural and mineral exports. Have Puerto Rican representative in group, and avoid commitment of administration of such plan to Panamerican Union Secretariat.

Eleven: Sugar quota action already requested by outgoing Administration appears adequate but power should be given President eliminate Dominican quota arranging compensation for sole American company involved if legislatively feasible. Restoration Cuban Dominican quotas should be made possible when situations change.

References are to incoming Cabinet officers. Paragraph Five suggested by Morales-Carrión and not fully discussed though disagreement unlikely. Other recommendations unanimously agreed by Alexander, Gordon, Whitaker, Carrión, Moscoso and myself.

January 6, 1961

December 19, 1960. Had lunch with Sánchez Arango, former Minister of Education in Cuba. He has no use for the Miami Front. I understand he has gone back to Cuba. It is quite likely he will get killed; he knows that. Then to a class at Columbia.

December 20. Lunch with former Ambassador Hugo Bethlem of Brazil. A friend of Jânio Quadros [President-elect, Brazil], he is setting up an institute to try to educate the Brazilians as to what a good educational system is. This is one of the really strong types produced by the Brazilian Army. He was General before going as Ambassador to Pakistan and other places. An interesting man.

To a lecture at Columbia . . . then the University Club where the Free Europe Committee was having a dinner and Allen Dulles was there. He said he understood I had turned down the Assistant Secretary of State-ship in Latin American affairs. I said I had not; it had not been offered; I thought I could get it if I wanted it; but if St. Michael the Archangel had that job it would take the State Department only two weeks to cut him down to bureaucratic size. Anyone else they could deal with in a week. I gave a very brief review of Latin American affairs to the assembled multitude at his request. Odd, for he ought to know all about it and I am a private citizen. After that they debated; I don't know exactly what.

December 21. To a Faculty meeting of the Columbia Law School. The problem was continuing the work in legal history. I was all for it—heavily supporting my old friendly enemy, Julius Goebel, who is retiring. It came out all right.

December 25. Christmas in the classic New England tradition: snow, sleighing, skating on the pond and troops of youths and maidens coming after skating for hot wine and coffee; reading the Christmas Carol on Christmas eve; to church on Sunday, more skating and so forth. . . .

December 29. To Puerto Rico for a meeting of the Task Force on Latin American Affairs. We were thoughtfully invited to the inauguration by Arturo Morales-Carrión, who besides being Undersecretary of the State of Puerto Rico was Chairman of the Committee on the Inauguration of Muñoz Marín. So we all got free tickets. We took [Dean Emeritus] Mildred Thompson along with us. . . .

December 30. The Task Force convened. Went into session. Started again on Saturday. Adjourned with a quite respectable document Saturday night, December 31. Sunday, January 1, 1961, we loafed. January 2 we got a stenographer and started copying. At 10:30 we went over to the inaugural: simple, splendid, some inspiring words by Muñoz Marín. . . .

Max Frankel, *Times* correspondent in Cuba, came over for a drink on Sunday. He tells me the mystique is out of Castro. Waiters and taximen and so forth will shout disapproval. A good many men working the propaganda mills and other spots spouting anti-American venom are really hiding anti-Castro refugees in their cellars. He said that, as the firecrackers went off in celebration, here it meant a celebration; there it meant killing. Bombs were exploding every night.

I saw two other men: Felipe Pazos and Manuel Ray [Cuban exiles; former Castro officials]. Pazos had been a member of the student government in Havana in 1933 which "tried" Sumner Welles and myself through one blazing night in 1933, in the revolt against Machado. This represented "the 26th of July Revolution" that is still fighting—against Castro. Then to the Fortress for the last night. Dinner with the Governor and a small group of friends; as always, fascinating and interesting. The Governor and Inez were educating Goodwin of Kennedy's staff. . . .

January 6. I met President-Elect Kennedy at the Carlisle Hotel slightly after 10:00 A.M. today. Theodore Sorensen sat in. I gave him the report; and asked him to read a summary, "The guts of it". . . .

Sorensen said the report was a liberal education in Latin American affairs; it was hard-hitting; he liked it. Then we started to talk. The conversation lasted an hour and a half—more time than I had expected. JFK was called to the telephone and I offered to go: time is valuable. Sorensen said, no—the Senator was obviously enjoying it. So we had a long chat.

Kennedy was listening while we were talking. It may be that he knew a great deal more than he suggested but he listened: a good attribute in a President. I think the field is new to him and he is studying it.

I pointed out that we had said nothing about Cuba, feeling that this ought to be a solo. I said that the Task Force had asked me to say that it could not be asked to advise where it could not know the facts. Specifically, aid and assistance to forces hostile to Castro in Cuba should be based on one of three situations: (a) a state of affairs menacing the United States in which self-defense was the operating principle; (b) a threat to the safety of other American countries, in which case the United States would act, presumably on request; (c) action authorized or approved preferably by the O.A.S. but in any case by a multilateral group in accord with the rather settled law of the hemisphere. All of these involved estimates of fact which would have to be made by a President.

Personally I said that we were in a situation in any event. The "26th of July" revolution was a legitimate, perhaps necessary reaction to a messy state of affairs. This revolution had been aborted by Castro; it should succeed and our line should be to aid its success.

The talk ranged widely over many things, mainly covered in the report. The President-Elect discussed one or two points himself. He seemed convinced that Latin America needed better representation in government than a mere Assistant Secretary of State. Sorensen observed that that particular job had been downgraded and something ought to be done. He speculated whether our peculiar position in Latin America would not justify giving recognition to the region not given to other regions. I said it could be done if someone identified with Latin American affairs had been appointed to a top post. This, however, was over the dam since the two top positions had been filled with men identified with other regions. So it seemed to me some act of state—creation of a new position and so forth—was in order. . . .

He then said he hoped I could work in his Administration and asked if I had seen Dean Rusk [incoming Secretary of State]. I said I had an appointment with him for Sunday. He very kindly said he hoped I could be with him. . . .

THE GUTS OF IT

Background:

Full-scale Latin American "cold" war is underway. A bloody guerrilla phase active in Cuba threatens to spread to all other Caribbean countries. Objective: quiet quarantine of Cuba, support and defend other key points: Venezuela (prime battleground) and Colombia, and by diplomacy gain support of Mexico. Social revolution is inevitable; it must be dissociated from Communism and its power politics.

Organizational steps:

1. A U.S. political command post; (a) for operation purposes; (b) as affirmation of American interest in Latin America.

2. An area-wide political instrument: an "international" of American democratic-progressive parties, supported by extra-official American interests (A.F. of L.-C.I.O., possibly others, with one or two unofficial American representatives). Such a group is already forming. It should have American financial support: it would off-set the alliance of Russian-Chinese directed Communist, Castro-left, and "united front" parties. Substantial progress could be made by end of March, 1961.

Political steps:

1. Stabilization of social revolution at left-of-center (substantially the Betancourt plan in Venezuela, modeled on Muñoz Marín's Puerto Rican experiment. Level will vary in different countries). U.S. cannot support dying dictatorships (Dominican Republic, Haiti, Nicaragua, Paraguay) or plutocracies—or any group including Communist parties.

2. *Cuba.* (A.A.B. only) The "26th of July" revolution has the sympathy of U.S. It is incomplete, and should succeed. Castro aborted it; he is now dictatorial obstacle to be removed like Batista. Castro is probably in trouble now.

The present "Miami Front" is not impressive. A better nucleus (because presently in Cuba) is the Chibas group. Don't fall for a phoney Castro peace move, due anytime after January 20.

3. All-out support for Betancourt in Venezuela.

4. Continue sanctions against Dominican Republic. Stimulate organization of a take-over group when Trujillo falls.

5. Fire Whelan and negotiate a transition government in Nicaragua which wants just this.

Economic steps:

1. Prompt support of an Inter-American common market plan. Choice lies between the Montevideo Treaty plan (excluding U.S.) and ECLA (excluding U.S. but into which U.S. could go). Politically rather than economically it is desirable U.S. should be in such a plan, however distantly.

2. Appropriation for and implementing of Bogotá program by Inter-American Development Bank. (A tail-end intrigue by which Cutler proposes to maintain his control with [Thomas G.] Upton as virtual executive officer must be cleared out. American representatives should be acceptable to Dillon and Rusk.)

3. Stabilization of key commodities, using "buffer stock" plans where feasible.

January 8, 1961

At about 1:00 Dean Rusk and I had lunch at our house with Beatrice. . . . (The three of us the only people there.) Dean Rusk said they wanted me in the Administration on Latin American affairs. He asked how I felt about being American representative in the O.A.S. I said I thought there was nothing in it: it was peripheral and I would rather be working somewhere else. He wondered then about the title of "Ambassador at Large" and about the possible title of "Presidential Assistant."

I said there was no good blinking the real problem. The real work of policy was done in the long, slogging, day-by-day medium of the State Department. Extraneous jobs, however be-spangled with titles, didn't do the job—and no one knows that better than Latin America. Nelson Rockefeller had had that job and it didn't work.

Rusk said Kennedy planned to fill the White House, whereas in these other cases this was not the situation. I said I knew that and I thought that temporarily the title plus transmission from the White House would work—but it was only a temporary solution and a personal one. This was the only time I would have the chance to state the case and I had better state it with all the force I could, however inconvenient. This is a continent and a half with 200 million people in it; crucial to us. Either you staffed to handle it or you didn't. As they had complimented me by asking my views, I could state what it takes to do the job. I thought I convinced Dean Rusk as I thought I had convinced Kennedy. But they were not sure whether they could do it. We left it that I would have sent over to Dean Rusk a copy of the Task Force report which I did by telephoning Goodwin on Monday, January 9.

There we left it. They are studying the matter.

As always, these things are half personal and half organizational. On the personal side, Rusk was kind enough to say that all roads led to me: I said this was unhappily true and it was a scandal. There ought to be more Americans whose names meant something in Latin America. This was one reason I did not wish to waste the name on a meaningless position. I said I would take any presidential job if the Administration would equip to tuning up to do the job.

I do not know whether they will decide to do this or not. They are likely just learning how touch-and-go the whole situation is. If Cuba cannot teach them, I don't know what can. There is always a wonder.

January 10, 1961

. . . Lunch with Ambassador Freitas Valle who represents Brazil at the United Nations. This was mainly to swap the time of day.

He tells me President-Elect Quadros sailed yesterday from Lisbon to Brazil by ship. Nobody yet knows what kind of a government he will organize. His economic problems are staggering, and it looks as though inflation has finally reached the stage where they would have to gallop through the whole German *impasse*.

He thought Castro would have to be stopped by force eventually; that the Americans would have to use the Marines; it is too bad they hadn't done it earlier. Public opinion, he said, and criticism would die down, and the job would have been done. I said that Latin America wanted Castro stopped and wanted the luxury of criticizing us. Anyhow, it couldn't be done now. I thought the President should say that if the Cubans were waiting for invasion, they would have to wait for a long time, and offer to send some coffee over to the boys in the trenches.

January 18, 1961

This morning Pepe Figueres came for breakfast. He will shortly be leaving for the F.A.O. conference in Rome. He has coordinated the Social Democratic front which includes parties in power in Bolivia, Venezuela, Costa Rica, and the Aprista in Peru. I suspect that he has been very deeply in the operations of what is going on in Cuba. In fact the Cuban situation is civil war; the Russians are arming and organizing the Castrista forces; and the anti-Castro Cubans are organizing themselves and seeking and I assume getting help from the United States. The training field at Guatemala reported in the papers was accurately described. As Pepe says, it is not a question of how much hardware the Russians give the Cubans. It is a question whether Cubans will want to shoot them at other Cubans.

Then to see Muñoz Marín. He was about to see the [President-Elect]. . . .

During the day Dean Rusk telephoned to ask whether it would be thinkable to appoint Franklin D. Roosevelt, Jr. as Assistant Secretary of State for Latin American Affairs. I told him it would be fatal. . . . Muñoz Marín and Pepe had both talked about it today. Kennedy wants to do something for him. Apparently he has offered other jobs which he has declined, wanting this. . . .

One of the U.A.W. men, [Bernard] Rifkin, brought in four Cuban labor men, presently in exile, who analyzed the Cuban situation. They think the largest block of people in Cuba are the Auténtico—represented by [Antonio] Varona. Another 20% are the "30th of November" people represented by Manuel Ray. Fidel Castro has about 20% of Fidelistas—not Communists but blind followers of Castro—and 20% of Communists. But there must be, more than anyone estimates, a large number of Cubans who are simply sitting around and hoping and not doing much. All of them make a point that the Batista Army men ought to stay out of this: no Cuban will fight under the leadership of army men who took their liberties away in Batista's day. The difficulty of doing the work of bringing all elements together for a common purpose is perhaps typified by this group: they do not work with the labor groups and have a splinter of their own.

January 19, 1961

I went to Washington on the midnight train and had breakfast with Dean Rusk. He said in substance that they were in difficulties with Latin America (this is an understatement). They want me to work on these matters and were proposing that I head up a task force to try to handle the pressing questions of policy, drawing in the representatives of the Joint Chiefs of Staff, the Pentagon, the Assistant Secretary of State and C.I.A. and so forth. This would be on an emergency basis—say for six months and I would spend two or three days (it actually would be three or four) in Washington each week. I said I would do this; I would try to frame it around some definite basis. I said I had no interest in any third-rate titles (I think a first-rate job ought to be created with some fanfare; otherwise the less said about it the better. Obviously the latter was easier so he agreed to it). I am not sure whether this is great wisdom or great foolishness. It will wind up I am afraid as usual with a great deal more responsibility than power and a great deal more aggravation than recognition. . . .

Leaving him I went over to the Army & Navy Club and rang up Bill Wieland. He is under the heaviest kind of attack, but it mainly starts from the old Batista crowd who are also working somewhat with the Trujillo crowd. . . .

But it is a nasty Washington. I had a chance to tell Rusk that I thought he ought to have a look at this. It was an assassination job and not serious business.

January 23, 1961
. . . Dean Rusk telephoned and wanted me in Washington. . . .

January 24, 1961
In the morning to the State Department; the Secretary had already gone into a Staff meeting. I was feeling like a cat in a strange garret. Then it turned out that Dean Rusk's secretary and general nurse was Mildred Livingood. She used to be my secretary when I was in Washington. She greeted me like an old friend.

The job is slowly materializing. They are creating an interdepartmental Task Force. I will be consultant or something of the kind as head of that. It has jurisdiction over the Assistant Secretary of State for Latin American Affairs and I hope over some other things too. Thereupon, going into lunch all of the old State Department men now in top positions greeted me like a long-lost friend. Some were professional motions in which diplomats specialize. Some flattery. I remembered Dean Swift: "Praise is the product of present power." They gave me an office three doors down from Dean Rusk and keys to the secret elevators. Ensued the usual waiting period for something to happen so I got hold of some of the men who really know the score and got some information. . . .

. . . Present estimate is that eight governments may go the way of Cuba in the next six months unless something is done. I have been trying to wrap my mind around Cuba. The A.R.A. handles routine well. But apparently stops right there. We have better information on the national situation in these countries at 70 Pine Street [Berle's New York office] than they do. And, of course, a great deal more direct contact with the men. . . .

January 25, 1961
Muñoz Marín and Arturo Morales-Carrión dropped in. We are arranging for Arturo to come to the Department as Deputy Assistant Secretary of State and working out a worth while job for him. . . .

The President's press conference was Wednesday night (25th). He came into Rusk's office on his way down, greeted me very courteously and said he was glad I was coming to work. And went off downstairs for the first television press conference in history. I saw it in Rusk's office on a television set built by Philips, and on which you changed channels with a remote control apparatus. We go in for toys even in top government.

January 26, 1961

Goodwin sent to me the State Department suggestions on Latin America for inclusion in the President's State of the Union message to be delivered on January 30. He thought it lacked zest. I thought it had the sex appeal of a Lynn Haven oyster, and we wrote. We have already sent along the President's Latin American statement for *Life International,* which I suppose comes out with a splash next week.

The danger of things like this is lest you undermine the Secretary of State's position. I have therefore taken care that everything I do with the White House goes to him simultaneously so that he can object. Presently we will work out a routine so that it goes across his desk first; at the moment, deadlines have to be met. (Remembering that Sumner Welles and Hull came in two because Welles communicated directly with the White House, I shall see the routine is set up.) Later, of course, this made trouble between Hull and the President. House (not that my position is comparable) was the reason Wilson was not on terms with his Secretary of State Lansing. Also the Secretary needs to be fortified.

I made a list of immediate questions that seemed to me emergency questions and was horrified to find nobody had any real thinking done on any of them—except, of course, the army, whose solutions are the last thing you do—to be avoided if possible.

While I was there the El Salvadorian government blew up. We did not even have an Ambassador in San Salvador. [Murat W.] Williams was promptly shipped down there. What he is expected to do when he gets there, he doesn't know and neither does anyone else. They simply do not know the men in these countries, what they are all about, nor whom to call on.

Rómulo Betancourt has sent here the brother of his Finance Minister (formerly governor of the Caracas Federal District). We are to talk on Sunday.

January 30, 1961

By midnight to Washington; put up again at the Army & Navy Club. To the State Department and started right in. Many of the men I have known for some years came in, notably Ted Achilles, Counsellor of the State Department; Mann, Assistant Secretary of State for Latin American affairs; and a number of others. Some work about the announcement which we are making as indefinite as possible. Whatever your job, power in Washington is seized by conquest. . . .

January 31, 1961

More talk with various people and gathering information. The Quadros government takes over in Brazil. My old friend Affonso Arinos

Mello Franco, is Minister of Foreign Affairs. This increases the personal stance since I am fortunate enough to be friends with him, and a number of the Cabinet, as well as with President Lleras Camargo, Betancourt, Villeda Morales, and a number of the other men. On the personal time there is not much trouble.

Brazil will be as nearly bankrupt as a government can be. We are trying to get out some help. But getting anything done in the Department is about like running a presidential primary, followed by nomination, followed by campaign.

The President's liaison man, Goodwin, who worked on the Task Force with us, has been kind enough to keep contact and has offered the White House artillery as we need it.

[George S.] McGovern, head of the Food for Peace organization, wants to send a mission to Latin America. We also are sending some messages to [Adolfo López] Mateos of Mexico and generally setting up some contacts.

I hope we can make good on some of the impressions we are creating. This reminds me of a Wisconsin friend of mine who said the idea was to throw a good bluff and then make the bluff good.

February 3, 1961

A string of telephone calls and visits during the last couple of days. Aside from certain interests manifested by the newspapers, they are mainly old friends, or people wanting jobs, or people wanting help in connection with business matters pending in Latin America. High point in humor was somebody who asked me if I would take 60 days off to settle the Turkish problem. I could only think Turkey has been a problem during the last three centuries and the compliment lacked sophistication.

Washington snowed in. To New York to get some shirts and spend the weekend. While in New York I got a report from some friends of mine about the situation in Haiti and also Colombia. Haiti, as far as I can determine, will dissolve into anarchy at any time. The problem is what will happen then.

February 6, 1961

Some work with Goodwin at the White House; with [Robert] Kingsley of the International Petroleum Company in connection with the University of the Andes; and with Muñoz Marín. There were also the usual formal visits from various Ambassadors.

February 7, 1961

The problem of Cuban exiles is beginning to be difficult. We are arranging to have them all see Phil Bonsal.

Some economic work with Lincoln Gordon; general go-around with Ted Achilles and Assistant Secretary Mann. We are slowly getting the information lined up. The question is what to do about it.

February 8, 1961

A White House meeting was held with pretty much everyone interested in the Cuban question. The discussion ranged over all points and the situation is anything but nice.

We agreed that our own favor ought to go to the younger, more idealistic groups; and that our hope should be that the revolution of the 26th of July, aborted by its Communist turn, could be brought back to its original ideals.

February 10, 1961

The problem of doing something about Representative Charles Porter is up. He is one of the few Congressmen very interested in Latin America. Senator [Mike] Mansfield [D., Mont.] wants him taken care of. His proposal to give Guantánamo back to the Cubans on the television the other night, unhappily, does not help.

The feeling is growing that we best clear our policies with Rómulo Betancourt and Lleras Camargo. I am arranging to go down next week. But this is back to the 19th Street dinner table. Through the years we have been discussing these things when this particular confluence of power was never remotely thought of.

Double-spaced and underscored is the terrible obvious thought of the Cuban Revolution which, in turn, connects with everything in the hemisphere. Cuba was entitled to the social revolution—so are a great many other countries in Latin America. Fidel Castro, however, was not satisfied with this. He wanted, also, a quarrel with the United States—he calls it "liberation." Herbert Matthews [of the New York *Times*] makes the point that this is inevitable and natural.

February 16, 1961

The continuing agonizing appraisal of the Cuban situation goes on. Briefly, it is clear that the Cubans are building up arms at a tremendous rate—and the Russian and Czech technicians (otherwise, officers in disguise, though some are really technicians) are arriving by the planeloads. I should guess there were about 3,000 in the Island.

Castro, a week ago, said he intended to export his revolution. In fact, he has been building up for this, sending arms and technicians to other points for future reference. The Communists have said the year 1963 is their target year to take over South America. Everyone here thinks we are in the odd situation of being prevented from doing anything because action by us would be illegal; the other side, of course, can do what it pleases.

Lunch yesterday with Herbert Matthews—for the first time it seemed to me that he had really slid over the Marxism watershed, though he does not admit it to himself. Briefly, his thesis is:
   (1) There will be a revolution in South America. (In this respect, he may be right.)
   (2) There can be no revolution except one directed by the Com-

munist forces. (In this respect, I hope we can prove him wrong.)

(3) The United States cannot resist this; nor accept it.

I asked him whether the United States was expected to commit suicide with the alternative of creating a military empire. He said realistically we create a military empire. (The result leaves us, as he sees it, without much of anything except to be surrounded by a Communist world—after which the ensuing war might be disastrous.)

This is the fallacy of the limited premise. It is our job to impart a few other ones—and I think we can do it. Anyhow, we propose to try. He is still pretty romantic about Castro. He would like to think "Castroism" is different from Communism—whereas I am clear that it is merely a thin veneer for propaganda purposes. His point is that we should think of Latin America as an "uncommitted" area. Well, perhaps, but international politics is a long tangled road and I do not think we are bound by historical inevitabilities.

Home to Nelson Rockefeller's house. He has kindly let us use his until we get our own.

Completing arrangements for a trip to South America next week— back to the dinner table circuit with Betancourt—Lleras Camargo—then to Brazil. Then, I hope, returning home. This is no time to be away.

February 26, 1961

After a day at the Farm, we came to New York, expecting to leave on Monday, February 26, for Venezuela, Colombia and Rio. . . .

February 27, 1961

On KLM to Caracas. We were met at Aruba by the Consul and some of the staff and also a nice representation from the government (Dutch) of Aruba. In course of conversation, it was mentioned by the Representative from the government that a KLM plane came in there from Europe with about 60 Russians, Czechs, Chinese technicians—with women—who stayed overnight and took the next plane out to Cuba. This has been going on for quite a while. We arrived that evening at Caracas; went directly to the President's house and stayed there. . . .

The next morning a long conversation with Betancourt. We wasted no time in preliminaries. We have been discussing them for many years. I asked him about economics. He stated that the outline of his policy was the [Tomás Enrique] Carrillo Batalla [Venezuelan economist] plan. . . .

We then went to the Caribbean problem. I said we had to be braced for a general Caribbean crisis. This would include the Dominican Republic, where reports were more and more harrowing. . . . Finally, to Cuba. I stated the facts and left with him a copy of a confidential (though by no means Secret) compilation made of the various activities of the Cuban government.

Betancourt said that in case things blew up, he was prepared to act. He believed that he would act together with Colombia but in any event was prepared to move in himself. He was thinking of the Navy and Venezuelan arms. . . .

Betancourt considered he had the Venezuelan situation pretty well in hand. The occasional riots usually supposed to be pro-Communist (two occurred while we were there) were small matters and of no great significance. The last serious plot was an uninspired affair.

Economically, while he had temporary difficulties, he thought the long-range problem was not bad. The country had paid off 1,200,000,000 in debts of one sort or another, had reduced its currency and credit supply by about 26%. The Batalla plan contemplated expanding the currency again to the tune of about one-half the currency credit contraction. On the other hand, the closing out of a substantial part of the public works program had thrown about 300,000 men out of work: this was a problem. He wanted money to reemploy these men. I said that in handing his requests to us, I hoped that these would be capitalized—that his development money would be used for the public works and not a mere budget deficit. Our people always disliked to give financial assistance merely to meet budget deficits.

He seemed to think this was an entirely feasible way of handling it.

As to the continent in general, he thought it would be a good idea to see what hemispheric support could be had for meeting the Cuban-Dominican situation jointly. He authorized me to give his views to President Lleras Camargo of Colombia though he would send his own Ambassador with instructions to talk with President Lleras. . . .

March 1, 1961

By afternoon plane (BOAC) to Bogotá. A pleasant flight: we were met by the Chargé ([Milton K.] Wells) and went immediately to the Bogotá Embassy. As there was no Ambassador, we were king of the castle, and a very lovely castle it is.

We went to dinner with the President and his Foreign Minister, [Julio César] Turbay [Ayala]: an intimate dinner, mainly devoted to discussing philosophy. It was a pleasant respite. President Lleras observed it was a continuation of the dinners we had had at 19th Street, and indeed we picked up where we left off—discussing the philosophy of power. The palace is one from which Bolívar once escaped by jumping out of a window: a splendid, rather feudal historic building, but Lleras would prefer I think to live in his own house.

March 2, 1961

Next morning to the palace where Turbay and I started our conversation. I had had the benefit of an excellent briefing from Wells and his staff on some of the problems that came up. Among the less important ones were:

1. The Colombians had asked for some small arms and helicopters. The danger to Colombia is not, he said, formal invasion but guerrilla attacks. He felt that the negotiations (one year and a half) had been much delayed. I told him I would look into the matter when I got back. . . .

2. They were having trouble in the matter of loans made to Colombia. For example, the EXIM Bank had opened a grant for housing. . . .

3. He had hoped the Inter-American Development Bank would be more flexible than the EXIM Bank but the preliminary questionnaire they had received drove everybody wild.

4. We talked of the enclave cities—the bandit-held towns . . . it was a stituation wide open for energetic Communist infiltration—easy from the Cuban side—and he was worried. His army was being trained by the American mission to study the invasion on the Normandy Beach but this had nothing whatever to do with meeting bandits in the high hills.

Then we tackled the Caribbean crisis. I presented it as I had to Rómulo. . . .

Lleras agreed. He said that he was perfectly aware of the fact that if Castro ever got loose, Colombia as well as Venezuela would be the next targets. He assumed that Target No. 1 would be Colombia. He had resolved not to do anything meaningless like merely breaking relations with Castro which would accomplish absolutely nothing. But he said that he was in no position to head a movement to deal with the situation—if the OAS would go along, or a consultation of foreign ministers evidenced substantial support something could be done. This he considered would depend on Brazil where Quadros was a mystery. . . . If we had to confront the situation and did so, I hoped that we could count on his sympathy. I got the impression that we could certainly count on that and certainly on more active aid as the situation developed.

I left to go over to the University of the Andes where they gave me an honorary doctorate. My old friend, former Foreign Minister López de Mesa, made the speech. He is a great Latin purist, but I had to make one first and I hope my Spanish did not make him writhe. . . .

. . . We went over for a final formal meeting with the President. At this interview Wells was present as well as Turbay. In the course of it Turbay produced an idea. He said that what we really need is a green light to deal with Cuba. He said that if an American country puts itself outside the discipline of the hemispheric machinery, this might give that freedom of action. He wondered whether we could have the Ad Hoc Committee of the O.A.S. send a note to the Cubans to know whether they were or were not accepting the obligations of the hemispheric system— meaning that they would cut their relations with the Communist bloc, accept a democratic procedure and so forth. I left out the machinery and followed his idea. In that case I suggested they could not claim the benefits of non-intervention and other agreements. Turbay struggled with this for a moment and I put the question to Lleras. He said at once that quite obviously a country that did not acknowledge the obligations on one side of the bargain could not claim the benefits on the other. I note this for future reference, having underscored the point a couple of times. . . .

All night to Rio, arriving there on Tuesday. After a couple of hours' sleep at our old Embassy in Rua São Clemente, we went down to the Foreign Office. There were the Minister of Foreign Affairs and the new Secretary General (former Brazilian Ambassador to Cuba, [Vasco] Leitão da Cunha), the Finance Minister, Clemente Mariani, and Jim Chermont— along with several others. We started in on finances. . . .

Then we tackled the Caribbean crisis. I made the same presentation I had in Colombia and Venezuela; I asked their views on the subject. After detailed examination of the facts, Cunha—himself just back from Cuba—said that their intelligence exactly agreed with mine. Whatever Castro had been in the beginning, now he was a prisoner of a Communist government. . . .

It was obvious they had no instructions from Jânio Quadros.

It really added up that they did not feel they wanted to do anything though they were in entire agreement that something had to be done. . . .

Up early next morning to get a plane to Brasília. We arrived about 10:00 o'clock and went at once to the President's Office, this a very simple room, in the Planalto Palace, and started in with the now famous interview.

Quadros could not have been more frank. After a few minutes in which we sparred a bit, during which I presented President Kennedy's greetings, and so forth, he squared away. He said he had inherited Brazil in a shocking condition; the government was insolvent. Worse, it was demoralized. There was corruption everywhere you looked. He was having the country make enormous sacrifices. He said he would be the most unpopular man in Brazil pretty soon and he meant it. He was prepared to sacrifice everything to get this situation pulled around. So he was preparing to send [Walther] Moreira Salles to break the ground followed by Mariani, to get the business done. I said we had discussed this at the Foreign Office and would give it consideration. He thanked me for the $100 million. He said this was generous and kind. He said he was refusing it because he wanted the whole package. $100 million was nothing in comparison to his necessities. He would rather do the whole job at once. I let it go at that. Then I made the presentation about the up-coming Caribbean crisis. Though I did not know it at the time he had been briefed about it the night before. He agreed with the analysis but pointed out that this meant immediate conflict with the left-wing in Brazil. He felt they could put on an opposition which would paralyze his government. He therefore could not do very much. I said this of course left us to meet it and I did not see how we could walk away from our responsibilities. He wondered whether we could not delay this business for a year and a half during which time he could meet his own State problems and get things in his hands—but I said foreign affairs would not always give the luxury of time—or we should look to have it ourselves. Since we were getting no where I said that I hoped we could count on his sympathy if the moment came. He said that his first principle was cooperation with the United States; that he considered the integrity of the hemisphere essential to everyone; that defense of a Christian civilization had to be the ultimate interest of all of us, and that he was speaking about himself and his State with the utmost frankness. I personally believe it. We left after a couple of hours of this on the most friendly terms after a very frank and very cordial discussion though it did not solve any problems of ours.

Since we did not wish to talk to the press I left by the private elevator and went to lunch with [Ambassador] Cabot who was present at the interview. A couple of newspaper men came by and I said it was the custom in our country when a visitor talked with the President to leave it to the President to say anything.

March 3, 1961

After a huge hike of intercontinental proportions, we finally made it to New York. . . . I went down to the Overseas Press Club where were my Haitian friends meeting at the invitation of Frances Grant [Secretary-General, Inter-American Association for Democracy and Freedom]. There were Dr. [Camille] L'Herisson, [Gaston] Jumelle, [Daniel] Fignolé, and Jacques Leger, representing four separate groups. We had an hour or two, chiefly talking the possibility of turning our efforts to unifying our terms for Haiti. . . . On Saturday, March 4, the New York *Times* came in. Dispatch had a story about a row in Rio which was, of course, untrue. It seemed that immediately after I left the President's office announcement had been made that Marshal Tito had accepted an invitation to visit Brazil. Since immediately before my visit announcement had been made that Brazil had hoped to include the admission of China on the UN Agenda, the announcement looked like a slap in the face for the United States; and the assumption was made that Quadros and I had discussed these matters, disagreeing violently. On the other hand, it is entirely possible that the announcement was made in an attempt to convey to the left wing and national elements in Brazil the impression that Quadros had been very stiff and offensive—currying favor with the left at our expense. The State Department theory is that this was exactly what was meant; I am not so sure. But the lid blew off. . . .

March 6, 1961

. . . Meantime a Cuban note has been sent around proposing that the friendly nations in hemisphere (friendly to Cuba, I suppose) mediate the dispute between the United States and Cuba. It pays the dubious compliment to me of saying that I was training several thousand men in Guatemala for the Cuban invasion force. I have been on the job about three weeks, so I must be a pretty good trainer.

The trouble with all this infernal business is that it prevents work on real problems. The fact is that we are fighting a cold war without a coordinated command. This is the cold war of the hemisphere—and not a fight with words, either. If I get out of this with a whole skin, I shall be lucky.

My estimate is that there will be a major climax over Latin America, like the climax when Communism sought to take all Europe in 1947. I think this will come fairly soon. The Caribbean will explode. We shall have to act. Attempt will be made to promote revolutions in every continent. And the battle is joined. A particularly weak spot is Ecuador. I think the others will come through.

March 7, 1961

Report to President Kennedy at 10:00 AM. He is kindly, reserved, unflustered. The technique is so opposite to that of Roosevelt that I have to hold on to myself. He asked that a courteous letter from him to President Quadros be drafted, and this has been done.

A lot of miscellaneous, more or less routine work but it all added up to the weakened position of the hemisphere.

March 8, 1961

The Cuban problem is pushing itself into the picture. Meanwhile the President is having his big Latin American speech drafted for him. Dick Goodwin is doing this job and doing it very well.

March 9, 1961

To the House Committee on Foreign Affairs in the morning. A very full session, well attended, in which [Under] Secretary [George] Ball, Lincoln Gordon and I made the presentation. Everybody was genuinely interested and I tried to cool down the newspaper allegation that Brazil had treated us very coolly. But when asked directly whether I thought the Inter-American machinery was important to the United States in defending against the Cuban intrusion as cutting-edge of Communist invasion of the hemisphere, I could only answer honestly, "no". . . .

We are really getting ready for the President's speech and for his message recommending that the $500,000,000 promised by President Eisenhower but thoughtfully left as a tab for us to pick up now has to go forward. I thought we did fairly well.

March 11, 1961

Theoretically a day off. Actually, mostly a standard day, straight through. Endless discussion about the everlasting question of Cuba. As to this, my own feeling is crystallizing. Sooner or later we are going to have to meet the Cuban question head on and it ceases to be matter of diplomacy and is rapidly getting to be one of force. This will precipitate and crystallize all of the Communist forces in the hemisphere—against the United States. The President's speech on Monday ought to give his conception. If possible, I should like to lock the Communists into the position of revolting against this type of Marshall Plan as they did in 1947 when they lost.

I think we had best precipitate the climax. I can't see that it will be infinitely less if we wait and we ought to have the battle on our ground instead of on theirs but it will be frightening when it comes. . . .

March 12, 1961

My difficulty is that the hemispheric machinery is shot. The thing that existed in the old days is no longer there. Recognition of the fact is the only constructive thing you can do. How we pick up the pieces is something else. Later this week we can estimate on the hand.

March 22, 1961

A great deal of work, interrupted by the fact that we are before the House Committee on Appropriations, hoping to get the $500 million promised by the last Administration to the Inter-American Bank. If we don't get it our name will be mud. The Committee Chairman is spending a great deal of time on it, most of it almost meaningless heckling of Linc Gordon, who ought to get a medal of merit for keeping his temper. The last Administration took long chances in leaving us to pick up the tab.

The reaction to President Kennedy's speech of March 13 is all good (Communists aside). What is really happening is a slow separation of the democratic and liberal elements from the extremists of both sides. The situation will be precipitated into a main-line climax when the Cuban situation breaks open. It can hardly avoid breaking open before too long. . . .

The result of my Brazilian visit is a little amusing. The false statements in the press of a quarrel between President Quadros and myself precipitated a barrage of publicity in Brazil, almost entirely in favor of me and Beatrice, which was touching fifteen years after we had been there. They said in essence: "What do you mean by doing this to our best friends?" Our denials caught up with the press, and I think things are moving quietly now. . . . My own view is that a group of pro-Communists tried to create an incident, hoping to split the country apart, putting Quadros into their camp. It failed. . . . Brazilians like diplomats; but what they want most is friends.

The Brazilian Ambassador to negotiate the debt situation is in town —Walther Moreira Salles. He couldn't be nicer, and we are getting to work on his problem as rapidly as we can.

We have come to the conclusion that the Hemispheric machinery which we have spent years in building up is of no use in the coming climax. We will go ahead as best we can. The job is more political on the street than it is diplomatic in the chanceries.

March 28, 1961

We are arranging to send Mann as Ambassador to Mexico. His Second-in-Command, Mr. [Wymberley] Coerr will be Acting.

The Haitian meetings are going well in New York. We may have the making of something that is promising, as and when the time comes. We hope to get started the end of next month on the Dominican situation.

Meanwhile we are really holding together, unhappily, and desperately—situations which fundamentally ought not to be held together. Without going into competition with St. Peter I should estimate that Trujillo would be more at home in hell than in a presidency. The Haitian situation is really a combination of incompetence, corruption and the incapacity of anyone else to organize something better.

Meanwhile the Laos situation has built up to its inevitable crisis. . . .

Simultaneously the Congo situation has been rolling along. . . .

The third and biggest crisis, of course, is in Cuba. I have been working steadily at various matters, all of them ultimately aimed at bringing together a variety of organization capable of fighting the cold war in the hemisphere on any terms proposed. Regrettably, we are less well prepared than Brazil.

The strange thing is that the populations of these countries have very little to do with it in spite of the noise made about them. Apparently cold wars are fought with a handful of people who are prepared to create disorder, use force, make noise, and more or less paralyze the rest of the population, into staying out of it. Occasionally, of course, there is a break, for someone: there was in Cuba when Castro virtually sold out the revolution to the handful of Communists around him—whereupon the Russians and Chinese proceeded to push in with arms and forces.

This is very much like the wars of the Reformation.

I have been trying to arrange today (the 28th) to get an appropriate script which can be used for doctrine. The American Revolution has done more for more people than anything else: but it has not a single book like Karl Marx's *Manifesto* or the Epistles of St. Paul. . . .

President Kennedy has had more rough crises thrown at him in the first sixty days of his Administration than any President since Lincoln. In FDR's case, in 1933, the crisis was internal. Therefore within American control. Further FDR had complete control of the Congress. President Kennedy does not. The Republican–Southern conservative coalition can in extreme cases mobilize a bare majority in the House—enough to defeat the President. So we do not have anything like the control or the tools to work with.

It is difficult to make anyone see how dangerous the hemisphere situation is. Still less that the sugar legislation giving the President right to fix sugar quotas, or the appropriation to make good the pledge made by the last Administration at Bogotá for $500 million for the Inter-American Development Bank are really part of the economic mobilization one needs to fight a cold war.

There are no diary entries for the month of April 1961. On April 17 the commando expedition of Cuban exiles landed at Cuba's Bay of Pigs. As the invasion ran into trouble, Kennedy sent Berle and Schlesinger to Miami to see Miró Cardona and Tony Varona of the Cuban Revolutionary Council. At Berle's suggestion, the Cubans flew to Washington and discussed the situation with the President.

Memorandum, May 3, 1961

The Cuban affair is now completed and it is therefore appropriate to state my own view on the situation in respect to it though only for this record.

Shortly after I arrived here (really picking up full-scale duties about the 20th of February) the realities of the Cuban situation became perfectly clear.

For all practical purposes, Cuba had become a Communist satellite, without formal declaration of that fact being made. This in part was in fulfillment of the program decided at the Communist Party Congress in 1959, directing that the Cold War front be set up in Latin America.

Castro, meanwhile, had taken himself out of the Inter-American system in every way that he could short of completing the formalities. By a declaration on September 2, 1960, he had openly attacked the O.A.S. and everything it stood for. By a speech in March 1961 he openly declared his intention to export his revolution in all ways—in that he obviously had support of the Sino-Soviet bloc. Many months ago he had denounced the Treaty of Rio de Janeiro in a speech though not in formal act. During 1959–1960 in fact he had attempted attacks on a number of neighboring American States including the Dominican Republic, probably Haiti, Panama and Nicaragua. Were this merely Cuban, one might be philosophical. But Cuba is the spear-head of the Sino-Soviet bloc and is obviously a serious threat. A clash of some kind was inevitable sooner or later.

My own feeling was that it was best to have the clash come earlier rather than later. The other American republics in general were not facing up to the situation. Some sectors of their public opinion did not know that Cuba was now in effect a Sino-Soviet tool. Some sectors suspected but did not wish to know. Some knew but wished to play that the problem was not there. A great many sectors including the politicians and intellectuals wished to hide behind cloudy unrealities. The doctrine of "non-intervention" was used as an excuse for not facing the savage fact that high intentions, good words and even good deeds would not stop Cold War activities carried on with agitation, money, bought demonstrations, and surreptitious organization of guerrillas with arms. To leave this situation without clarification merely meant that the process would go on. Then circumstances would probably be created which might require much larger military action.

Reports that Russian MIG 15s and Russian destroyers were on the way to Cuba added to the severity of the situation.

Various meetings were held with the President at the White House. . . . These meetings, attended by [Allen] Dulles and [Richard M.] Bissel [Deputy Director for Operations] and others for CIA; Secretary [of Defense Robert S.] McNamara and General [Lyman L.] Lemnitzer and Joint Chiefs of Staff; by McGeorge Bundy [Special Assistant to Kennedy] and not infrequently Arthur Schlesinger of the White House; by Dean Rusk and Thomas Mann, then Assistant Secretary of State for Latin American affairs; and myself for State. The proposals of CIA were expounded. They were already very far forward.

My own opinion was generally not asked though on three occasions I stated a view.

At the first meeting I suggested that the United States instead of acting covertly should act as a great Power. Since Castro's government was no longer in the OAS, Lleras Camargo's observation [was] that Castro could not claim the benefits and immunities of the American agreements against intervention at the same time that he denounced the system and violated all its principles and obligations. The rights of these treaties automatically lapse under those circumstances. Neither the Cuban people, nor the United States, nor any other country has given up its capacity to act when a member of the regional collective security group becomes an aggressive enemy of that group. Still less can he claim that the agreements creating that group protect him against the action of any one of them.

Of more importance was the fact that failure to act in these circumstances would have implied acceptance of the dictatorship Castro had fastened on them by the Cuban people and by the United States, and possibly by the American system as a whole. Obviously there was no such acceptance. In these circumstances unless some men are prepared to risk their lives for the cause of freedom of their country, freedom dies without a whimper. In this sense was Byron's famous sponsorship of the Greek expedition at Missolonghi. My own thinking on this has been better expressed by Salvador de Madariaga than I can express it myself.

Referring to great power in action, it would make clear the fact that this is now a front in the Cold War, a fact that seems to have escaped the notice of most of the American commentators.

This suggestion about no follow-up was not therefore discussed.

CIA and the Joint Chiefs of Staff presented various methods. Their final one assumed the virtually unopposed landing, capable of establishing a beach-head and an opposition government for Cuba.

Subsequently some sort of meeting was held in Miami at the close of which a revolutionary front was agreed on, namely, Miró Cardona, Manuel Ray, [Manuel] Artime, Carlos Hevia and Varona. Sánchez Arango had been asked to join but did not. All known Batistianos had been filtered out. The CIA asked my opinion on this group. I said I thought it was as representative of the revolution of the 26th of July as could be expected though I regretted Sánchez Arango's absence from it.

At a subsequent meeting, the plan was discussed. By this time President Kennedy had made it clear that he would not back it with American forces. I had difficulty with this but the President had made known his decision and we had no further discussion on the point.

The Joint Chiefs of Staff and the CIA thought the plan for getting ashore was a sound one. Thereafter the success of the expedition depended entirely on its support within Cuba.

As it presented itself then, the operation was substantially a Commando operation—getting into Cuba with a relatively small group of trained men—in other words, doing exactly what Fidel Castro had done. The Joint Chiefs and the CIA were sure they would get ashore without opposition, and that adhesions would come automatically.

I did not dissent though two elements were absent: willingness of the United States to assume responsibility and willingness to assume a Cold War front levied against the United States would imply that America would use force if need be.

My final connection with it (there were subsequent meetings at which final decision was made which I did not attend) was with Miró Cardona in Washington when he was received by Ambassador Bonsal and myself and merely stated his plans for our information. Later I was asked to see him and did see him alone at my house. . . . My principal task was to tell him that decision had been taken not to use American force.

Subsequently I met him . . . in the Century Club in New York with A. Schlesinger and again we stressed the fact that as this went forward American forces would not be used although American help would be given. It would be very frankly a Cuban group who wished to strike a blow for the freedom of Cuba which had been taken from them. I am clear that Dr. Cardona understood this though I think he believed that in case of necessity American force would come in as a matter of political sequence. Both Arthur Schlesinger and I tried to disabuse him of this idea. At that time I think that final decision to go ahead had been taken though I do not know when or by whom.

A good deal of information has subsequently appeared in the newspapers as to the handling of the force, plans, etc., about CIA. I had no connection with any of this and no knowledge other than that it was presented at the earlier meetings at which I was.

I feel bound to say, however, that I should not be hostile to any plan which gave a group of Cubans, especially those who fought the revolution of the 26th of July and had been betrayed into the Soviet camp, a chance to speak their piece on Cuban soil. The problem is whether this plan gave them such a chance. Both the Joint Chiefs of Staff and the CIA were clear that it did. There is nothing more shocking in this than there was in support given by most of American public opinion to Fidel Castro when he was doing the same thing in the struggle against Batista. There cannot be a double standard in these matters.

The handling of the expedition itself, its leaving and so forth, though not its destination, were, of course, top secret. I knew nothing about them and did not wish to.

May 11, 1961

Some long days. The Venezuelans are in town negotiating a loan to help out Rómulo Betancourt. The Brazilians are in town finishing up on the loan to help out Quadros. Pepe Figueres is in the south taking soundings for a league of pro-democratic parties. The Cuban situation continues to be debated backwards and forwards.

Duvalier has made himself dictator of Haiti by the simple process of holding a one-name one-ballot election and claiming he has been re-elected for six years. The Dominicans' dictatorship is tottering to an eventual fall. The fleet is in the Caribbean. . . .

May 15, 1961

The problems are coming thick and fast. Yesterday at the Senate Committee: they used me quite kindly. They asked some questions about the Cuban operation which I could not answer not having much to do with that end of it. Obviously the real drive there was to put in troops and we, they think, should have done so earlier—this is not true of Senator Morse but the feeling is perfectly clear. We were within a hairsbreadth of a straight war operation a few days ago.

Now the next phase. In Haiti Duvalier (legally elected) has just re-elected himself by the simple process of putting his name (illegally) on a ballot for the election of Congress. He proposes to inaugurate himself on the 22nd for a further period of six years (this makes him frankly a dictator). We called the United States Ambassador [Robert] Newbegin in for consultation. The immediate problem is whether he goes back to attend the inauguration and blesses it or whether he stays here. If he goes back, we are hooked in another one of these dictatorships—Duvalier really rules with a group of mobsters ("Tontons Macoutes"); if we do not he may try to inaugurate a Castro-type infiltration. We think that one or two of his Ministers ([Paul] Blanchet) is really a Communist agent. This would hook us into another Castro situation. If we bless him, it may be a slow process. If we don't, it may be a quick one and any hint of Communist take-over there will mean American occupation as matter of course.

The Dominican Republic presents somewhat the same picture: Trujillo is moving towards his fall. There will be attempts made for Communist infiltration there. Neither there nor in Haiti is there any popular interest in Communism: it is strictly an outside job. But Trujillo has nothing more to hope from the United States and knows it. He has exported money in all directions; he will try a last fling at the left. Again the problem is working out something like decent governments.

The Organization of American States, long entrusted to work out these situations, is now useless. Brazil is trying to sit on the fence. Mexico is indulging day-dreams and it may be that General Cárdenas wishes to close his career by conducting Mexico into the Communist combination. The others talk a good deal but are not willing to take very firm stands on anything. It is tragic for me having spent much time in building up the O.A.S. to find it now not merely useless but a handicap to the only practical action which can be taken, which is action by the United States.

As far as Haiti is concerned, the dictatorship, to my way of thinking, should not be recognized, and merely getting about the job of constructing something promptly looks intelligent. We may have to move fast and it may well be that the touchstone of the Caribbean may not be Cuba but the island of Hispaniola.

May 17, 1961

The agreement to send Ambassador Newbegin back to attend the "inauguration" of Duvalier has been decided by the Under Secretary [Bowles]. This, I think, is a moral mistake of the first order and will plague everyone. It comes pretty close to being the last surrender of principle to expediency that has yet been done. I have fought this thing all the way up.

May 23, 1961

A good deal of work, though a good deal of question whether it gets anything done. The Brazilian financial operation was announced a couple of days ago. It is one of the most generous I think in history. All it did was to provoke an extremely snide speech from Affonso Arinos. I think we are right in not letting Brazil go bankrupt irrespective of its current attitude in foreign affairs. It does not buy friendship. But Brazilian politicians can create enmity and this is what they are doing. If they cannot be helpful, they ought to quit.

The general situation is frightening. The Laos affair has come out badly. The Geneva negotiations are anything but successful—a stalling match during which any Communist force, though it has nominally ceased fire, will go as far as it can. The Russians are increasingly meddling in Latin America. Their Embassy here is talking to and taking the Latin American countries (with which they have no formal relations) to lunch and saying action in Cuba may mean war. They advocate therefore a peaceful solution—whatever that means. Their emissary, [Aleksei] Kosygin, is going about in Latin America presumably establishing contacts for future references. Immediately, the situation in Haiti is coming to a boil. . . .

The disarmament negotiations are going badly and one result is we are likely to resume atomic testing. Just what is accomplished by this I do not know. . . .

In all these situations our only answer is direct use of force. But in each case we hitch a little closer to a little war which may prove to be a big one in the end.

One can only hope that in the cold war this is a low moment. Luck has to change sometime. It feels very much as Europe did in 1938.

I have been seeing some interesting people. [Ramiro] Prialé, second in command of the Aprista [APRA] Party, in to dinner Sunday night (May 21); a very able politician, seeing Europe and the United States for the first time. The run of average Latin American politicians is substantially improved by his appearance in it. He is very much for a league of pro-democratic parties, and talks of the meeting in July to make it stick. This of course is also a project of my own.

Castro has offered to trade prisoners for bulldozers. This is a propaganda stunt with all sorts of nasty overtones. Dick Goodwin organized a committee headed by Mrs. Roosevelt to trade on the point. . . .

May 26, 1961

There was great division of opinion in the State Department as to what to do about Duvalier of Haiti and his prolongation of his own term. . . .

Popular position was of course to have the Ambassador attend; giving the whole thing our blessing. . . .

Eventually the middle course was arrived at. The Ambassador stayed here; the Chargé attended and said nothing. The danger of the situation frightened the wits out of the Acting Assistant Secretary of State Coerr. There was some validity to his argument—but it is quite as dangerous to get caught as protagonist of Duvalier as it is to risk his displeasure. After all, we are contributing 25% of the Haitian budget as well as any capital improvement that is going on there—and Duvalier is really trying to run the country with armed thugs.

. . . If we have to choose between the present (Duvalier) and the future (the good-will of the people of Haiti) I would rather play for the future though it is a singularly difficult picture.

The difficulty of this State Department is that it will always come down on the side of the *status quo*.

May 31, 1961

On Friday night of last week to Great Barrington, there being nothing much on the schedule. Not that there was not plenty of work—but other people are doing it and not wanting much help from me.

Returning this morning came the news that late last night report had come in that Trujillo had been assassinated. During the day the news was confirmed, though it is still secret. This seems to have been an inside job done by the Army men—at least I suppose so—I don't know. And the puppet President, [Joaquín] Balaguer, is carrying on for the moment. Obviously this situation will not last very long—the bottle was uncorked and almost anything can happen.

In accordance with the contingency plan worked out earlier, the ships are standing by but I hope they will not be needed. Nobody can tell yet who will try to seize power. I do not see that we can influence the situation immediately. Probably the thing to do is to watch developments. Fortunately [Henry] Dearborn who is there as Consul is a first-rate citizen who knows the score well and has enormous courage. Likewise his wife, an Ecuadorean. . . .

We still do not have an Assistant Secretary for Latin American Affairs though this may be developed within the next two or three days.

Meanwhile the President is in Paris and then on to Vienna to see Khrushchev.

Castro's attempt to trade prisoners for tractors (I don't think he meant it seriously) was of course taken up. Dick Goodwin at the White House stimulated the formation of a "Tractors for Prisoners" committee which went to work. The result seems to have swept Latin America; offer to sell human beings for machinery hit everybody the wrong way. . . .

While at the Farm I did a good deal of thinking. It is not altogether happy. Historically the decision to do something about Cuba will, I think, prove to have been a sound one. The immediate result should be to serve notice on everybody, not least on the Russians, that mixing with the Western Hemisphere could produce an explosion. They might therefore withdraw for the time being. (a) This is evidenced by the interview on the 16th between the Soviet Counsellor of Embassy and Arthur Schlesinger. The Soviet Counsellor wanted to know whether the United States would negotiate with Castro. Schlesinger merely asked what there was to negotiate about; (b) The fact that about then the Soviet Embassy began to withdraw some technicians (this apparently has been subsequently reversed); (c) The very casual, and possibly unintentioned observation made by one of the Soviet Foreign Office men to our Embassy in Moscow that they did not take Castro seriously, believing that in a year or so he would be out or we would have moved in. They appear surprised that we did not push troops right in;

(d) The relative restraint of Castro at the time of the assassination of Trujillo—this, of course, is apparent rather than real. We had the Dominican Republic ringed with ships. What Castro did was to issue a call for all Dominican exiles to meet in Cuba. Actually from 1959 on, anti-

Trujillo Dominican exiles had been organizing in Cuba. The group broke up when Castro imposed on them a Dominican Communist leader.

Obviously this does not mean that the Communist front authorized and the Communist Congress organized in Moscow in 1959 is not going forward, underground, ideologically and so forth. It merely means that for the time being there will be a lull in the push from Cuba and that Castro himself does not seem like too good an instrument.

June 5, 1961

On Friday, June 2, I was requested to attend a meeting at 11:30 in respect of the Dominican Republic situation. There were several possibilities. First, the group that were endeavoring to overthrow Trujillo might take over the government—or take over a piece of territory and set up an independent government in the Republic. In that case the United States would have been glad to assist. In fact there were small units which apparently attempted to do so. But the repressive measures—they seem to have been ferocious though silent—paralyzed the opposition. As night drew on, it became clearer that the Trujillo dictatorship was merely succeeded by the old clique—Ramfis [Rafael Trujillo], Johnny Abbes and [Arturo] Espaillat. Taken together they are pretty nearly the lowest form of life in government, which is saying a good deal. They have been trying to sell themselves to the Communists who were, however, smart enough not to buy them. The nominal President, Balaguer, has the legal position but not much else.

On Saturday, June 3, working at the Department. The decision of the previous night had been that there should be a high level briefing. Press conferences were to be set for next morning and I was elected. But as the situation was unclear, having of a conference had not been decided. So on Saturday morning I was conferring with the assembled multitude as to what to say and wondering whether anything should be said. Then Goodwin of the White House telephoned to say that the press conference had been announced for 12:45. Meanwhile Alex Johnson, Bowles's Deputy, had taken charge of it for Bowles, who is Acting Secretary of State (Rusk and the President being in Paris). The White House policy was to build up a case against the Ramfis group. Bowles's policy was to talk only diplomatic relations of the O.A.S. We had Bowles telephone Rusk in Paris on the sound ground that you allow no one to come between the President and the Secretary of State. The line was accordingly fixed for discussing chiefly diplomatic moves while emphasizing that we did not think well of the Rafael [Trujillo, Jr.] successor dictatorship. So we shoved over to the White House at 12:45 and I duly performed, trying to cut a fine line between the President's obvious desire to lay a base for motion, and the Secretary's obvious desire to keep a diplomatic channel. I think we did as well with the situation as could be, given the situation. At all events, the Sunday morning press was reasonably representative of what happened.

Meanwhile the diplomatic front had been boiling with Arturo Morales carrying the ball. It took the form of a proposal to send a committee of the O.A.S. to visit the Dominican Republic—the Committee to be in fact a special committee of the permanent committee organized at San José last August to follow up on the Dominican Republic and decide whether it is ceasing to be a threat to the hemisphere.

Its presence, however, may cool down the epidemic of arrests and tortures going on in Santo Domingo City.

Our Consul General there, Dearborn, is apprehensive that someone may try to build up a case for the United States cast as assassin. This, of course, is not true; we knew of the plots and counter-plots and this was all —though it was I imagine quite clear that we sympathize with any effort to get rid of the Trujillo regime and obviously had no use whatever for an anti-American line such as that followed by the Elder Trujillo, the Younger Trujillo and Johnny Abbes.

The Soviet propaganda line is curious this morning: it says that the United States is mourning Trujillo, a friend of American monopolies.

The situation winds up badly. There will be another period of dictatorship by the most cutthroat elements going. We will wind up represented as tolerating it—though God knows everyone wants nothing better than an excuse to go in and blow it off the map. As always in a dictatorship, the Communists will organize a quiet underground as best they can, waiting for a period of disorder when they can take over. Meanwhile the relatively few elements that can take over will be annihilated horribly by Ramfis, Abbes and Co—meanwhile we have an Ambassador in Haiti burning to appease Duvalier.

The one thing that apparently is not allowed in this business is getting squarely alongside of some respectable moral forces and being able to implement those by force where an opposite group has force in its hand. Nobody around here seems much interested in escaping from that dilemma except myself, and it is another case where careful attention to the presumed rules of the game provides an exact result of what you do not want. . . .

Monday, June 5. Quiet. Arturo [Morales-Carrión] is getting ready for today's meeting with the O.A.S. He thinks he has everyone lined up with the possible exception of Chile and Ecuador. For once the Mexicans are with us but their effort is negligible. The Committee from O.A.S. will go there. Everything on the surface will be smooth as silk. No one will show them the prisons or the torture chambers and no visitors will dare to say a word unless they be immediately assassinated or arrested. Noises will even be made about "free" elections. But how anything like a respectable reorganization of government can be had while the Trujillo family controls the situation and the Chief of Police is capable of slaughtering anyone who dissents, I do not easily see.

This looks to me as though there will be a main-line explosion after a while. There must be so many people with a blood feud going on here that one can only look forward to some plots and counter-plots and more killing before things are over. And, in the next round, we will be meeting a somewhat similar situation in Haiti. . . .

June 6, 1961

This morning an early meeting at the White House. Colonel [Robert D.] Heinl [Jr.], who heads the military mission was giving us his view. He thought that there was no effective opposition to Duvalier, bad as the government was; that the only force for stability was the Army; that his mission was doing its best to educate all of the Army people—officers and enlisted men alike; but unlike State he thought we could put pressure on Duvalier by dominating the budgetary support. He said Duvalier had no interest whatever in building up the country unless some graft could be obtained from it. And that he was slowly building the black hatred of whites as well as their mulatto opponents.

O.A.S. special committee on the Dominican Republic yesterday voted to send a special committee of O.A.S. to Dominican Republic. It will leave tomorrow the 7th and arrive in Santo Domingo the next morning. I don't know what it will find except the polished top of a severely repressive dictatorship.

June 15, 1961

The Dominican case is beginning to be strange. The OAS is sending a commission to see whether sanctions should be lifted. As though Ramfis Trujillo would be apt to tell them very much. Meanwhile, we have the whole fleet in the Caribbean waiting for a revolution which might happen and probably will not.

This does not look good.

June 16, 1961

Sevilla-Sacasa and Tachito [Anastasio] Somoza [son of the Nicaraguan dictator] came in. I made a speech, saying we had no faith in dictatorships and we were hoping that the regime would democratize itself.

June 17–19, 1961

In Puerto Rico to attend the meeting of the Superior Council on Education.

The night before to dinner with the acting Governor, Roberto Sánchez. There is a large Dominican apparatus of some kind in P.R. which has to be dealt with somehow. I think they were hoping for a revolution on the fall of Trujillo. It didn't happen; and now they are sitting there. This is a difficult problem for the P.R. Government.

For the first time, a tiny exhibition of Communist-Castro organization has appeared in the University of Puerto Rico. So far it is scarcely a fly-speck. A couple of students are beginning to agitate for joint control of students along with the professors. This, of course, is the classic Communist gambit.

The Communists are making a common cause with the Fidelistas and we shall have this problem presently emerging.

Meanwhile there has been a good deal of newspaper attack on the alleged interference on the "clear lines" of authority in Latin American affairs. This is a triple attack on the Latin American Task Force, of which I am Chairman; on Richard Goodwin; and on Arthur Schlesinger. At bottom it is probably more an attack on the President than on the individuals. It obviously has a focal center; I suspect it is not far from the present Department.

Behind it is really the growing division of opinion in the government. There are people who want something done; and those who want to stop short and play around with words. Division of the Department is evident; it is very like the division we had in 1944—would we cooperate with the Russians or would we try to check their all too evident imperialism? This time it is will we really meet the "Cold War" or will we simply talk and hope that a white soul and good intentions will protect us. I plan to make an opportunity to talk it over with the Secretary of State and the President as soon as possible. Obviously if we are merely going to let Latin America go with sweet phrases, I had best be somewhere else.

June 22, 1961

The Task Force this morning. Unhappily all variety of bureaucratic sabotage in ARA is showing up. No surprise. We know it but it makes life unpleasant and difficult. The Task Force has had admirable cooperation from all the other departments.

July 6, 1961

Some work on various matters and a chat with Edward Kennedy who is going on a trip to Latin America. He wants to go as a private citizen. ARA does not like the idea at all and wants to take him over.

July 7, 1961

To the White House with Dean Rusk as agreed. I handed in the final report of the Task Force and asked its discharge. The President was very frank and very kindly; he observed, "these fellows really object to my being President"—which, of course, is true. He said that he was entirely disillusioned about the "old pros" in the State Department; their capacity to deal with situations. He asked if I would stay on as consultant, to which I agreed and hoped that I would work out a good propaganda-educational program and stand by to be a help when needed. I told him I would defend the Cuban adventure even as it came out. He grinned wryly and said that I would have trouble in court proving it. I said that the historical evidence was not in, and that if the action had not taken place in April, we would have been right there fighting it out with troops at summer's end. . . .

Thence to spend the week-end in the Berkshires.

To Kennedy, July 7, 1961

I transmit herewith the report of the Task Force on Latin America whose creation you directed shortly after your inauguration.

The Task Force was conceived as a mechanism of transition. With the appointment of the new Assistant Secretary of State for Latin American Affairs, the period of transition has substantially ended. . . . Under your leadership, the new direction of policy, I am convinced, offers good opportunity and prospect of success. I therefore ask that the Task Force be now discharged.

Prior to your inauguration, you constituted an informal group to report on Latin American policy. That group made one suggestion not yet acted on. It proposed the creation in the Department of State of the post of Undersecretary of State for Latin American Affairs. This would provide a high level straight line channel through the Secretary of State, by which the widely scattered activities of the government affecting Latin American affairs could be coordinated. This recommendation I venture to renew. Management of hemispheric affairs, comprising a continent and a half organized as a regional alliance, is a huge task. It is difficult to carry out so great an enterprise from a subordinate bureaucratic position.

The Task Force report suggests enlargement of the education-information-propaganda effort. . . .

Let me pay special tribute to the effective cooperation and support of Assistant Secretary of the Treasury John M. Leddy and Assistant Secretary of Defense Haydn Williams. We are indebted to both for their wisdom and unstinting effort.

With the discharge of the Task Force, my own assignment comes to an end. Please feel free to call on me if at any time hereafter I can be of assistance.

July 11, 1961

More cleaning up work (there is a good deal). Press conference relating to the general work of the Task Force by way of cleaning up; and to find that the defense paper passed by the Task Force had been held up by ARA; so also had been the Caribbean defense arrangements—Mr. Coerr. This can be very dangerous.

July 12, 1961

Fished the defense paper out of ARA and sent it along to the White House. . . .

Dinner for the newly appointed Assistant Secretary of State for Latin American Affairs, Robert Woodward. I think he will be good. At all events, he knows the score. Unlike ARA, he understands the democratic forces as well as the governmental forces since he started Ambassadorial life in Costa Rica in the time of Pepe Figueres.

July 13–14, 1961

Some work in New York, leaving for Columbus, for a Nationwide meeting. Beginning to pick up once more the lines broken last January. They are all there: plenty of them; no difficulty in picking up. This is not a case of finding a job but of preventing jobs from finding me.

July 18, 1961

The news from Brazil is anything but happy. Jânio Quadros seems anxious both to make trouble for the United States (which has just saved his hide) and play up to the Communist and quasi-Communist countries. It may be that he really does intend to make Brazil into a variety of Yugoslavia. I doubt if he can do it. It is becoming increasingly hard to remain a friend of Brazil on this record.

July 24, 1961

July 20. Well, it is perhaps a good time to take a holiday, so we will go to Honolulu, then to the Philippines and get Peter and Lila [who went to Japan with us] to Hong Kong; to India to see [Ambassador] Ken Galbraith; to Africa; and thence home where a couple of books need to be written as well as the current run of academic work picked up. An "around-the-world" trip has one advantage: there is plenty of time to think in the airplanes. Beatrice enjoys travelling and her enthusiasms are always a joy to watch.

July 21. A time of cleaning up the office and getting out after a six-month adventure in Washington in the Kennedy Administration. So far as the public record goes—and political standing with it—I am getting out with a whole skin and a few bouquets. . . .

Individually I am leaving with a sense of personal defeat. The Latin American policy has, I think, taken a new turn—but the bureaucratic elements which can slaughter the new policy are still active. In leaving I am really shirking a fight against bureaucracy and finding that at this stage in my career I have less desire to use up energy and enthusiasm in that kind of thing than one needs to emerge successful. The fact is that the last three months the ARA has been directed by an unpleasant little bureaucrat named Coerr. . . . It took the form of gathering bureaucrats, inducing them to leak to the press in an attack on any Presidential influence on policy and possibly the attempt to bring influence to bear on the White House itself.

In quiet times, this would have been merely monkey-business as usual. Conducted against the background of a rising national crisis in which our own fate and the fate of much of the word is at stake, this sort of thing assumes far more evil character. (One remembers the treason of elements in the British army in the Ulster affair in 1914; this helped to decide the Germans to start World War I on the ground that the British government was divided and unable to act. A similar intrigue in 1943-44 again headed by Acheson led to the almost fatal blunder by which the Russians assumed control of Middle Europe.) In this case the intrigue was partly based on personal ambition, partly a desire to wipe out the old element by becoming dominant in the Department of State, and maintaining a hard-line in the Berlin crisis. I happen to agree with the hard-line doctrine; anything else is merely waiting for a more devastating crisis later. It does not make Washington an easy place to live in. In part, of course, this is merely the normal six-month upheaval which frequently takes place if the Administration is changed, bringing in a new party, new policies. The bureaucrats who have been built up during the previous Administration see themselves threatened, and rationalize in the strangest way actions which are at bottom defensive of their own power.

A clean-cut is the best personal policy and I have taken it, following with a month's holiday during which Beatrice and I will go around the world. But I cannot say I take much satisfaction in it. On the other hand, I am not quite sure that I have what it takes to move into the kind of superlative risk-taking required in the next phase. Equally, I am not quite sure that I shall be let off it. I have a feeling that destiny has taken a rain-check instead of giving me an honorable discharge and that a few months or maybe a year or two later in somewhat changed circumstances the issues will have to be met again.

To Mrs. Sumner Welles, September 27, 1961

In grief, not unmingled with pride, I send my sympathy on the occasion of Sumner's death.

I owe him many personal debts of gratitude. We were colleagues, allies and friends through the bitterest struggles of the United States. We lived together during the passionate and bloody Cuban Revolution of 1933. We were lunching together when the attack on Pearl Harbor took place. We worked together during the agonizing days of World War II. He was Acting Secretary of State when he retired, and (Mr. Hull being absent) turned over the Department of State to me as next in line of rank. During all those unhappy and often terrible times we were friends and I like to think that friendship did not waver in later clouded years, and like Franklin Roosevelt, I am unable to forgive his enemies. The United States owes a great deal to his integrity, his courage and his skill. Some of this the country knows about, though much of its obligation it never will know. There are countless men, some in high places, who owe their careers to him and who, like myself, are grieving now.

His was a noble contribution to America in time of trial and stress. All of us wish his talent and genius could have been liberated to meet the problems assaulting us now.

Some of us remember even more poignantly the kindly, understanding, even tender comrade-in-arms, always strong in support and sympathy.

Like a great galleon, he has completed a great voyage—prelude perhaps to newer more splendid adventures. The chains of causation he set in motion move on steadily and productively. To the man and the friend, we can now do no more than offer a loving farewell.

October 2, 1961

A day in Washington and a few moments with Dean Rusk—he is endeavoring to negotiate the Berlin mess and meanwhile the Department is going wild. An evening with Schlesinger and Goodwin. These boys are in it up to the neck. Meanwhile Peter came home and I arranged for him to see Schlesinger and [Kennedy's adviser on military affairs General]

Maxwell Taylor's outfit so that he could give some of the facts of life about warfare in southeast Asia, notably Viet Nam. It looks to me like a lost cause there.

Then came the news of Dag Hammarskjöld's death and crisis in the United Nations. A few days later Sumner Welles died. I went to his funeral in St. Bartholmew's on Friday, September 29. This is a clear-cut change in generation. Sumner Welles was only three years older than I and he belonged to the past. Allen Dulles resigned as head of the CIA. . . .

Meanwhile the Berlin crisis is unresolved. I do not think there will be war this time. My fear is that the arrangements by which they get around it this time may make war certain a year or so from now—as did Munich. Not necessarily, but the danger is great.

Meanwhile, estimating on the hand. The Russians are at their zenith now. They have been unable to convert the Iron Curtain countries to Communism. They have been unable to maintain their own primacy in the Communist world. The Chinese are contesting and the Yugoslavs have broken away. They have not been able to house their own people by acceptable Western standards and probably cannot do it as long as they devote most of their effort to military affairs. There they have reached a remarkable position. It is their only real claim to capacity by comparative standards. If they are unable to convert this into a diplomatic victory, or tó fight a victorious war, they are condemned as they would see it to shrinking somewhat and really doing a job of developing their own country and their own people. In all conscience this is enough, and they could do it well. But they would not be masters of the world. The pressure—in absence of diplomatic victory—to risk military adventure must be considerable. But the Chinese are on the eve of exploding nuclear bombs and treading closely on their heels.

On the other hand, war with us, even if they won it will leave them wide open to the Chinese. Not an easy situation for anyone—and the stakes are unlimited both ways. For all of us.

I am also convinced that the United States in dealing with the new countries is mainly indulging a set of myths self created. Certainly the realities of Africa and Asia are anything but those we hear about here.

October 9, 1961

René Fiallo came in to see me. His brother-in-law is head of the Unión Cívica in the Dominican Republic. He thinks his brother-in-law (whose name is Villato) has now a large popular following.

They think that unless Ramfis and the rest of the Trujillo tribe are expelled from the Dominican Republic, there will be an explosion, bloody. The present policy is not decisive. It is blamed on deLesseps Morrison, present Ambassador to the Organization of American States.

Villato wants a conference in San Juan with Muñoz Marín and me and hopes to get a clear declaration from the United States that it will not support any government which is directly or indirectly controlled by the Trujillo tribe—who must leave. I do not know whether this will happen. I agreed to pass the word along to Muñoz, who is in town and I will talk to the State Department or Goodwin.

The American project of election with a couple of "tame" opposition parties means, René thinks, a bloody revolt before too long. . . .

On Friday at Freedom House Award, [Mayor] Willy Brandt [of West Berlin] made his now famous declaration about Berlin, "The wall must come down." At the subsequent session at which I spoke I sat next to Henry Kissinger, who has been in on the conference surrounding the Berlin business. Kissinger thinks Rusk is a weak man and the whole thing is headed for the kind of compromise which sets up a bigger crisis later. A variety of Munich in fact. My fear runs along the same line. Rusk is a good man and a wise man but not a strong man. We did not dare take the gamble of a strong policy on Cuba which at least would resolve the situation. I do not know that we will take the far less difficult gamble of a strong policy in the Dominican Republic. The stakes in the Berlin crisis are a million times greater; yet the will to lay it on the line seems to be the only possibility of avoiding a temporary solution which may turn out to be disastrous in the end.

November 30, 1961

The Berlin crisis is turning out badly—far worse than most people realize. By cutting Berlin in two (the famous wall of last August) the Russians pretty well paralyzed the future of the city of Berlin as a whole. The United States and the allies did not react by requiring its destruction. The evidence coming in now suggests that a little nerve would have stopped the maneuver. . . . So Lippmann is already beginning to talk about relinquishing West Germany. This is exactly what went on before Munich. It leads finally to an ultimate concession after which further retreat is impossible—after which war is inevitable. We have really bought a "Munich Year" as Neville Chamberlain did in 1938 and as a result late in 1962 or 1963 will be dangerous in the extreme. Henry Kissinger has been in the government; he is leaving it, and will say why in the *Reporter*.

As to Latin America. The last of the Trujillo dynasty have finally fled from the Dominican Republic. The plan, much as I left it as I left the Department, is being implemented. That is, American force in overpowering scale is present in the hope that it will not have to be used. The tail end of the Trujillo government under Balaguer is keeping order and trying to make a peaceful transition to the next stage . . .

But there is present a Communist cold war element, of course working with Castro. This crowd had expected to take over and start killing when Trujillo fell. Balked of their prey partly by the moderates under Fiallo and partly by fear of American force, they may be brought under control. At the moment, the issue is in doubt. . . .

The Organization of American States is by now nothing but a farce. President Lleras Camargo of Colombia has asked the OAS to do a very simple thing: define an essential basis of the Inter-American system—and everyone is making piddling excuses for not doing anything. I think this results from political fear in the respective administrations in these countries—but of course it may reflect a real desire to break up the Inter-American system and eliminating the United States. Meanwhile, of course, collecting whatever cash can be realized through the Alliance for Progress.

In result we are really back to 1936 when the Nazis made a bid to dominate the continent as the Communists are doing now, and by about the same methods—inside revolutions financed from outside. We did pull this out, though it took several years of hard work in which Nelson Rockefeller and I took the leading part. Can it be done again? The task for us was eased—strange as it may seem—by the war of Germany against Britain and later against the United States. War narrows and clarifies immediate issues. This time probably that kind of war will not occur until the very end and it may not come together.

There have been shake-ups in the State Department—Bowles is out, has a nominal job as advisor; is paid off in sweet and meaningless words. Goodwin goes to the Latin American Division in State. This is good for the Latin American Division but he will have rough going. Walt Rostow goes to planning in State. He might as well have the job of night watchman on Mount Washington.

. . . Dean Rusk's position should be somewhat strengthened; he becomes primary channel to the White House, working presumably with McGeorge Bundy there. The President in theory gets trusted men at some crucial points in State. But essentially he has not yet conquered the State Department bureaucracy; only Rusk has the direct power to do that—and he can hardly have any time for it. Ball, the second in command, is essentially a Stevenson man and not a Rusk man. The President is not out of the woods yet.

Some extremely good evenings at the house. Last night, Denys de Rochemont, now, I think, one of the first philosophers in Europe (he is Swiss) along with Harold Wolff, Bill Burden and Norman Eddy [Minister of East Harlem Church]. Talk on the death wish and other things. Harold insisted that the greatest enemy of personality was a meaningless feeling that nothing had significance at all. De Rochemont came fairly close to my position: there is order in the cosmos and if you cannot apprehend it, then you make one inside of your head. I pointed out that this was straight Goethe but he got it from the 83rd Psalm.

To Richard Goodwin, November 28, 1961

This is a line to wish you good luck in the new job. I gather that the President is putting his own men into State so that it shall, as it should, reflect his views more than the views and delaying tactics of a bureaucracy whose tenacity is not justified by its record of success. I am happier about Latin American affairs with you there.

You may encounter some difficulties. Unless the system has changed in the last few months, the Department had some bad habits. The "Assistant" designated for you, depending on the man, may be either an assistant or something else. That is, he may be reporting on everything you say, you do and you write to someone else. Your secretary is instructed to listen in and take notes of your telephone conversations. When you find out, it is explained that this is to save your time so that you need not make records. Later some of this stuff begins to appear in the Washington gossip columns. And so forth. Dillon put a stop to the wire-tapping in Treasury and it may have happened in State though I think not. . . .

Also you are limited by one principle. The close relationship between the President and the Secretary is of first importance. So you have to guard and strengthen that relationship at all points. This may be personally costly to you since it means subordinating your close and fertile personal relationship with the President to strengthen Rusk's position.

December 11, 1961

Last night some young people at the house. One of them was young [Mauricio] Nabuco who stated the Brazilian view with certain intensity. "We don't want to be 'yes-men' to the United States." "What do we have to do with Cuba?" "Occupy it as Russia occupied Hungary and don't bother us with something not our concern." "Why do you want our help?" I said that we had thought an Inter-American system existed in which these matters were matters of common concern. If not, then, of course, we would have to do whatever we had to do. He made some observation about an independent foreign policy. I asked if he wanted to be independent of our buying coffee? He argued the case: the United States needed Latin American products. I pointed out that we could buy coffee in Africa and had sugar enough for ourselves. He thought we needed the oil of Venezuela. I told him we preferred to buy in Venezuela and had more oil here in the undeveloped oil base on the Canadian border and oil shale enough for many years. I doubt that he believed this. The pathetic notion that the United States would go to pieces without their supply, a fallacy of Latin Americans, is a difficulty here. Since his father is counsel for Bethlehem Steel and American interests, he thought perhaps not unnaturally that the United States was defending property. I told him if we lost 10 billions of investment in Latin America in the context of a national production of 550 billions, it would hardly be noticed. But I doubt if I made much impression.

The Castro declaration of Communism is, of course, a main theme of conversation. Many say it embarrassed Communists all over Latin America who hoped to conceal their actual colors until later. This is probably true. But my impression is that Castro wished to precipitate out-and-out Communist revolution all over the hemisphere and I am not sure that he may not have done so. He knows, as Americans cannot, the steady driving attempt to take over the underside of Ecuador. Here, we watch the Cabinet. There, they watch the police stations, local school system, local Sub-Ministry office, and so forth, whose impact on the people is far greater than anyone in a police office in Quito. Castro probably wants more Russian support than he is getting. In effect, the lines are drawn for attempt at revolution all over the place. I see no way now to avoid the sheer horror proceeding from a civil war over large areas. Nabuco's other remark was interesting. "You," he said, "are interested only in the Caribbean." I said certainly. The Caribbean countries owe their existence either to the American system or the United States—no one else will defend them—certainly not Brazil. Further, they are strategically necessary to the United States: we would have to defend them in defending ourselves. We have a choice outside the Caribbean; but the military master of the Caribbean has been the master of the New World; and there is no Latin American nation that can take up the job, and for our safety we cannot permit any European country to do so. . . .

December 29, 1961

We passed the Christmas holidays at Great Barrington: a very white Christmas with many children, coming to ski, to toboggan, and seeking hot chocolate, hot coffee and mulled wine. . . . Externally it could not have been happier.

Below the surface I was unhappy. For it seems to me that we are approaching Munich and if it goes wrong war is inevitable sooner or later. I relieved my mind by writing an article, "The Great Divide," which I think Max Ascoli is going to print. But I think it may make me more controversial than ever. I am already in controversy in several places including Brazil; there is a strange feeling that one ought to be somehow mediating between forces which are essentially not susceptible of mediation. I think the Communist power bloc intends the destruction of the United States—they say so, and mediation at this point is negotiating for our own existence.

This is the last working day of the old year and it has not been a good one. Externally in terms of personal life and the progress of the children, prosperity, and all external family matters, it could not have been happier. The diabolic pounding of international affairs, accompanied by enough knowledge of them to know what is involved, has made it one of cognate agonies.

The expedition into the government was both a mistake and a failure. A mistake because I did not bargain for the position of power consistent with the responsibility assumed. Or at least the degree of responsibility attributed to me. Endeavor to protect the position of Dean Rusk who is a good man but I think weak, by protecting the close working relation with the White House perhaps saved his situation; otherwise I think would have weakened him. Having only a peripheral idea of the Cuban situation, I nevertheless took everything that came.

Months later, my appraisal of the Cuban situation is this. What we did is entirely lawful and consistent with international law and with our treaties; indeed was a fulfillment of a debt we had undertaken to protect the hemisphere against aggression. Many commentators . . . thought not. In retrospect the Cuban action which rates as a fiasco was probably one of the few intelligent things we did. It was noted in the Soviet Union and possibly in China that they had met the threshold of armed action and overtly at least pulled in their horns. It will not last; they will try again.

Probably in the unreduced disorderly lands between Colombia and Panama and spreading south to Ecuador. But at least we gave it check. Failure to have reacted probably would have meant open warfare by now. But it is only check and not solution. The Alliance for Progress is a good platform to campaign on—nothing more than a platform. The fact is that the State Department bureaucracy unready, inefficient, even in its own way corrupt, but, with the President and me in between, probably would have made effective action. It takes about a year for a President to take control of his own machinery. To get out with as few wounds as I did was probably the best that could be hoped for; but I assume that it is an end of political matters.

In any event it cannot be construed as a success.

The trip around the world—a logical exit—taught us a great many things, chiefly that much of what we read here is not based on fact. Certainly this is true of Africa. But this is merely peripheral to the main problem of policy.

Arrived home I attempted to work on two books and at present overcomplicated the situation by assuming responsibility for a third. The first, of course, is the attempt to analyze power—a long range job on which I have made a start but not much more. The second was attempt to describe and analyze the American system which at present arrived at a state which shows that Marxism and Socialism is in a nineteenth-century museum. I have made some progress, Max Ascoli is at present looking at it as a friend.

The manuscript on Latin American affairs for the Council on Foreign Relations is approaching completion. I hope to have it finished in January. But as the total output of the year's work, my 67th year in fact, I cannot figure the output as impressive. Probably I should be thankful that a year of relative failure has been accompanied by so much happy personal relations.

On the satisfactory side, there is gradually an increasing understanding of what the real issues are in Latin America and elsewhere. And perhaps enough ground-work laid so that we can finish some jobs next year.

My conclusions as to the present state of affairs are adequately stated in a copy of the article I wrote, "The Great Divide," . . . I think Henry Kissinger at Harvard agrees with this; he had planned to leave the government service; had been induced to withhold his resignation for the time being; he is struggling with the usual difficulty: should he stay in and try to influence events or get out and use his freedom to state what he thinks. Being vindicated by history is cold comfort.

I should be wiser than I will be if in the coming year I stick to academic economics and political science. There is, however, a difficulty. All the best academic work in the world counts for nothing if the essential integrity of the American system is not preserved.

X

1962~1971

January 15, 1962

Lecturing at Columbia solidly from 10 in the morning to 7 at night. And then home.

Israel Klabín [Brazilian businessman] was in town and came down for a late dinner . . . it was heart-warming to talk with him. . . . He notes that the anti-American campaign is dying down; it is beginning to cease to be fashionable. . . .

January 19, 1962

. . . The ex-Foreign Ministers in Brazil got out a manifesto attacking the stand of the Goulart government for trying to be "neutral" in the Cuban matter. This was sparked by Israel Klabín's uncle, Horácio Lafer, who was Foreign Minister under Kubitschek. The press is supporting that position. . . .

This morning Virginia Prewett (Mizelle) telephoned me. The Brazilian Foreign Office telephoned her (they have been reading her columns). They said they were modifying their stand and were coming closer to the American position. Not quite close enough, I think—they duck the main issue. . . .

Pepe Figueres telephoned me this morning. We are arranging to visit him the end of February in Costa Rica. I told him the Nicaraguan government would not intervene in favor of Calderón Guardia—this on the assurance that Luis Manuel Debayle had given me. Pepe thinks his man, [Francisco José] Orlich, will win the presidency and can only be stopped by military power. If the Nicaraguans are out of it, there will not be any trouble.

The question now is whether on that slender base I can bring Pepe and Luisito [Luis] Somoza together at the end of February. Since Luisito's father tried to kill Pepe a couple of times, this may not be too easy. Perhaps we can arrange it in Guatemala or Honduras. . . . Nothing would make me happier than to have some of the democratic and liberal forces in Brazil team up with the democratic and liberal forces in Central America. With the friendships already existing between Betancourt and Figueres we would begin to have some permanent contacts and machinery around the Caribbean littoral.

The hole, of course, is that strip of Colombia lying just east of the Panama Canal—bandit country—and probably busily being organized by the Communists.

January 25, 1962

On Saturday I was at the Farm peaceably pulling some thoughts together for another chapter of the book on the American system. The telephone rang: it was Dick Goodwin from the White House. The boys were just getting off for Punta del Este and he wanted any last thoughts. Considering the hand weak in other respects, they were proposing to try to throw Cuba out of OAS as a substitute for general breach of diplomatic relations.

I cordially approved and told him I hoped they would get by with it. . . .

Meanwhile the Communist camp was not idle. They attempted two revolutions: one in Venezuela and another in Guatemala. Betancourt got the first in hand rapidly and I think [Miguel] Ydígoras [Fuentes] is on the top of the second. Both were, I am sure, Chinese jobs though it is difficult now to tell which of these is sparked from Moscow and which from Peking. Obviously a successful *coup* on the mainland would make Punta del Este look like a sewing circle.

I told Goodwin I felt like the famous remark of Henri Quatre to Crillón: "Go hang yourself, Crillón. We fought at Vancouleurs and you weren't there." Actually I know something else. This is another time and another generation and another set of people both in U.S.A. and L.A. Better let the younger men do it.

On the 24th, which would have been my father's 97th birthday, a review group went over my manuscript on Latin America. They liked it; suggested certain changes in emphasis which were good. Generally I think it will go over well here—raising some hell in Latin America. I think the time has come to talk facts and not fiction if we are to make anything happen at all and the manuscript when published may help. Or may not —we shall know later. [*Latin America—Diplomacy and Reality,* 1963.]

. . . Meanwhile we are cobbling up a trip to Central America. This will be difficult. The Central Americans know that their lives depend on being defended from the straight-way drive against them via Cuba and they have fixed faith neither in the Inter-American system nor in the resolution of the United States. They all want assurance of the American position. As I represent nobody but myself I cannot give any.

January 31, 1962

The morning of the 30th there was a CBS program on Franklin Roosevelt's birthday. He would have been 80. Samuel Rosenman, Rex Tugwell and I chatted over TV about old times. The drama is now 30 years old. It seemed to me like yesterday. We are almost the last survivors of the Rooseveltians.

January 31. The Punta del Este conference is ending. I think it came out fairly well. That is, the United States got

(a) A declaration that an overseas Communist regime was incompatible with the hemispheric system. Everybody joined but Cuba.

(b) An agreement directing the O.A.S. to throw Cuba out of the O.A.S. 14 votes cleared it. The big ones, Argentina, Brazil, and some smaller ones, Chile, Bolivia, abstained.

(c) An agreement on arms control. Probably also, though not in the papers, understandings for bilateral arms pacts with the various countries that stood with us.

The papers say this is a defeat; the hemisphere split, etc. The fact is the line-up is much as it was in the beginning of World War II. The hemisphere will not split and stay split. . . . One should not expect results too soon. But my guess is that in a reasonable period of time (possibly two years) they will all be together. I do not think we could have done this if we had not made a clear issue. First, by tackling Cuba last spring and, second, by having the Punta del Este conference. The six Central American countries would have walked out if the O.A.S. had been unable to meet.

February 6, 1962

Luis Manuel Debayle telephoned today. Pepe's candidate, Orlich, seems to have won the Costa Rican elections. This makes it more necessary than ever that some cooperation be established between Costa Rica and Nicaragua. . . .

February 14, 1962

To lecture on Latin American affairs at the National War College. Between periods a message came that Harold Wolff, in Washington on a defense conference, had been taken ill and was in the N.I.H. Hospital. I got clear of the War College as soon as I could (unkind to them; it was a very interesting session) and headed for the hospital. But he . . . had lost consciousness. He was in the hands of two of his former students; they were turning all of the batteries of the government and medical science to work for him to try to give him a fighting chance. Specifically they lowered his body temperature to a point where life barely goes on while they tried to clear up the occlusion. I never did see him again conscious. Isabel [his wife] and Helen Goodell [an associate] came down; presently Beatrice.

We kept up the vigil for two days, asking Father Paul Harbrecht to come by, which he kindly did. . . .

March 14, 1962

Harold Wolff never did regain consciousness. He died while we were in Mexico City. So passed a great scientist and a very dear friend. I miss him at once for I should have liked to tell him the story and to have him give his wise and kindly insight of an involuntary Macbeth like Luisito Somoza, who cannot hold on without being a villain or let go without danger. The drama of power which he and I have discussed through the years is at its peak. —The man who best understood the brilliance and the terror of that drama was Harold himself.

February 20–March 12, 1962 were spent in Central America. Berle sent a copy of the following entries to Goodwin.

February 20. Two dinner parties in Mexico City: one, some older people generally of the conservative party. A second with some younger friends of [our hostess]—"the young intellectuals". They represent a chaotic conglomeration of views, running from Marxism to a variety of Christian Socialism; all talking at once; all anxious to change the *status quo;* all agreed that the United States isn't what it ought to be; nobody clear what they really want of it. The complete absence of American intellectual leadership was the most striking factor; the university in Mexico they consider as essentially Marxist, [while they are] looking for other leads.

Mexico is really suffering from a one-party dictatorship which has lasted since the days of Cárdenas. Like the Southern Democratic organizations in the South, it makes for a certain stability: the issues are settled within the party. But it sacrifices men, develops little doctrine and at the moment the party is split. . . . There is capital flight, largely because of the Mexican vote at Punta del Este, a good deal of feeling that the López Mateos government is slowly delivering the country into the hands of the Communists which may or may not be true. Actually Mexico is probably rather more prosperous than usual, a prosperity marred by the corruption of its government and the irresponsibility of much of its upper class.

February 24. To Guatemala. We went there because I had been asked by the Guatemalan government to take a job of organizing its economic plan. I declined the retainer but said I would be glad to help. We put up at the Casa Presidencial—a large, solid office-like building around the corner from the cathedral. The President [Ydígoras Fuentes] himself stayed at the Casa Crema next door to the military barracks. . . . We had the presidential bedroom. In Arbenz' time, he had had the window blocked with a steel plate so that bullets could not get through. On the long corridor beside the patio leading to the dining room were the bullet marks resulting from the assassination of Castillo Armas and there were a couple in the wall of the State Dining Room. President Ydígoras did not have them blocked up. At a State dinner he gave for us the day before we left he pointed to the two bullet holes. "These are the watching eyes," he said somewhat grimly. I said, "The sword of Damocles."

. . . Ydígoras (whose wife, Doña Mary, is five feet high, oblong, an Indian, as nice as she can be and with the Indian shrewdness well built in) explained his own situation. The extreme right, who were also black Catholics, were against him. He had countered: *Mater et Magistra.* He had incorporated the last Papal Bull in his speech, but . . . these people consider that the last three Popes were Communists.

He went on to point out what he had to do. He had to build a substructure for the country. He had to add to his capital. He had to increase its productivity. But he had to satisfy an underpaid urban population and the Indian population was hardly getting a break. He personally thought the Indian villages were more progressive in matters of education than anyone else.

Thereafter we dove into the economic planning. . . . I put in three days sweating it out. . . .

. . . We saw the Minister of Economics, the President of the National Bank, etc. I got a raft of figures, some meaningful, some not, planning to try to get things going in New York on return.

. . . The President seemed to appreciate my having come there (which is fair enough) and I pointed out to him that I worked for no government except my own for money but had worked for many governments and would work for his for love.

A brief talk with the American Ambassador there. He, a careerist, recently arrived from Pakistan of all places. The bureaucracy of Washington lies heavy on all these men. One of the underlying questions is what institutions in Guatemala can be relied upon to do a job rather than to waste the money. . . .

. . . It really means splitting the funds to be allocated to Guatemala between infra-structure work (roads, electricity), social expenditure (schools and public health) and something to meet the needs of the workmen in Guatemala City—housing. Land reform comes into this but land reform is a tough proposition.

While we were there and after my talk with Ydígoras, he issued a variety of decree: directing the reorganization of Guatemalan economic affairs along the lines carried out in Puerto Rico by Muñoz Marín and Ted Moscoso, and appointed Roberto Alejos as Presidential representative directed to do the job. This makes him in effect the second man in Guatemala. I immediately suggested that he might want to visit Puerto Rico and have a look at the thing in action and volunteered to wire Muñoz. This proving agreeable I wired Muñoz asking if he would invite Roberto Alejos to Puerto Rico and give him a short course. He promptly answered that he would be glad to do so. . . .

From Guatemala City to San José on February 28. There we were met by Pepe Figueres and it was old home week for us all. His party has just won the election. Orlich will be President but he is in Europe; Pepe and the Ministers he will have designated on May 1 were working like nailers. The previous or conservative government left things in bad shape. It was not crookedness; just bad management. Having over-spent their budget and with the low price of coffee, they found themselves about $30 million short and their credit not too good. Taxes have to be raised; this will reduce the standard of living. They have a really stiff job. On the other hand, it is only money. The institutions are there and reasonably sound. The infra-structure of the country is reasonably well taken care of. Pepe paid for most of his public improvements as he went along so the total national debt is not out of proportion. . . .

Then on March 5 to Tegucigalpa . . . There we were guests of President Ramón Villeda Morales, and he could not have been nicer. Also we found a hard-working American Ambassador, [Charles] Burrows, whom I have known for years in the State Department. He is a real person and on excellent terms with the President. . . . During my visit came confirmation that Honduras had been allocated $29 million which will help. . . .

When Ramón Villeda Morales came in we thought him a good, honest well-intentioned man but questioned whether he was strong enough to swing it. Well, he was. He has got more done in the last five years than all the Honduran governments in the last thirty. It still is only a breakthrough and not fully accomplished. Starting from scratch, you cannot do much. But he had a small electricity project finished and now had the money in hand for the big one. He had built a net of roads and a substantial chunk of them were macadamized. He had fixed up the market (Lord knows it needed it) and he had just inaugurated a system of social security: the first in Honduran history. Everybody, he said, wanted to be his successor. His term ends in about two years. . . .

. . . I took occasion to tell Villeda Morales that I had talked to Pepe and that I intended to talk to Luis Manuel on behalf of the Nicaraguans; that the formula was a pacific solution but it concealed a great many difficulties. This is because it is better to tell everybody what you are doing than to let them guess. Even telling them, there are going to be wild guesses as well.

Thence by TACA to Managua, arriving March 7. Luis Manuel, wisely, had played it way down. So he and his wife met us at the airport, but with an addition: a man in khaki with five stars. It was Tachito Somoza. We greeted each other kindly and courteously and without fanfare. I thanked him for coming to meet us and we left at once for a little coffee finca owned by Luis about fifteen miles out of Managua on the crest of a height overlooking the Pacific. . . .

. . . [Luis Manuel] explained how things were working in Nicaragua. . . . Elections will be held in February 1963. . . .

. . . Luisito Somoza inherited the presidency, the power, the property and the country when his father was assassinated. The government is commonly considered illegitimate—that is, without any popular mandate from the people and Luisito has inherited that situation.

The opposition seeking democracy, popular mandate and talking in terms of liberalism nevertheless inherits the Chamorro name, the reaction of the Conservative Party and its general reputation. Not too good for either side. One gets a sense of both men being caught in circumstances created by neither.

On the evening of March 9, somewhat late (he had been adjudicating a land dispute), Luisito Somoza and his wife came alone to Luis Manuel's finca. We had dinner and talked until three o'clock in the morning. . . .

. . . I said it was an impertinence to come into someone's country and talk politics. Luis said, "We know you." "We would be glad to have any ideas you have." I said he had two problems: the first was to legitimatize his government by getting a clear popular mandate. In this case it was not only necessary but to get one in such fashion that everybody recognized it. His second was to do it in such fashion that the result was recognized by all hands and the defeated side would accept the result and devote itself to political rather than military opposition if they wished to continue. . . .

Luisito was very generous in saying that he appreciated that and that this was what he hoped to do himself. He said somewhat pathetically that the problem of his own future and Tachito's was somewhat enigmatic. He could not succeed himself; was not too clear whether his successor would be recognized as independent if Tachito remained head of the army; on the other hand, Nicaragua had progressed perhaps more than any other country and he did not propose to have this progress wrecked by civil strife if he could prevent it.

I wanted to congratulate him on the progress Nicaragua had made. I had seen some of it in a day and a half and even without statistics the Nicaraguans now had a net of paved roads comparable to an American state. The country was electrified everywhere. Light manufacture had come in and it was growing. The land question I could not guess although there were apparently 78,000 small fincas in the country: a substantial increase. The financial condition of the country seemed good. The crops were diversified. There was little question that the country economically was better off than it had been.

Luisito went on to say that the workmen were on the whole satisfied. Their labor code was working well. The workmen were beginning to be more interested in wages than in politics; strikes were comparatively few; he himself had worked at that more consistently than at anything else. (I am prepared to think that this is substantially true. The cross-check one habitually makes—the number of people with shoes; the state of nutrition of the children; the prevalence of a school system; the number of teachers in normal schools; the number of small factories running—and so forth—generally suggests that in the past five years this has been a primary preoccupation of government.)

At the end . . . we spoke of the policy of the United States. He said that they were Americanized in Nicaragua and had to be. Their business was to stick with the United States, come thick or thin. There was nobody else to stick with. . . .

It developed that [on March 8 Fernando] Agüero [the opposition candidate] had wanted to talk with me but he would not come to Luis Manuel's house. . . . I did not want to give the impression that I was refusing to see him by talking with the dictator. . . . His mediary appeared . . . we talked for half an hour. He is perhaps the closest man to Agüero and has the burning, intense quality of so many of these men and also is a man of cultivation and discernment.

I said I would be very glad to talk to Agüero but I thought best not to do it in Nicaragua. I was not here for intrigue but merely to discuss matters with Luis Manuel, my old friend. If, however, Agüero should be in the United States, my house was always open to him and I intensely wished the pleasure of meeting him. Little was said about political terms. . . .

Prior to meeting the President, I had tried to see the American Ambassador. This, Friday at noon. At 11:30 he was not yet out of bed—so I saw the Counsellor, [Louis F.] Blanchard, instead. A nice, hard-working Foreign Service boy doing his best. The Ambassador, Aaron Brown, had a night of it with the Rotarians and others. . . .

This may be unjust to the Ambassador; Latin American parties can be stiff and it takes practice to go through a night of banqueting and show up in the office for business hours next morning.

April 13, 1962

To Columbus for a meeting of the Board of Nationwide.

U.S. Steel had announced its increase in price on the heels of the wage settlement. [Howard Edwin] Isham who is on the Nationwide Board used to be finance officer for Steel. I nominated Steel as the damn fool of the year. Isham said private enterprise was making a necessary stand; all industry would fall in behind Steel; that Kennedy had made the mistake of his career. I said we had met that kind of thing in Roosevelt's time and they hadn't a chance.

April 14–16, 1962

. . . By plane to Puerto Rico. . . . We went not to the castle by the sea but to Dorado Beach—very lovely but not as much fun. There were Dick Goodwin, [Assistant Attorney General Nicholas] Lee Katzenbach, who replaces [Deputy Attorney General Byron R.] White, who went on the Supreme Court, Heckingher of Justice, as well as Muñoz Marín, Trias, [Abreu] Palanco [Santiago], and [Heriberto] Alonzo. Later, Arthur Schlesinger. We were discussing the possible evolution of the Estado Libre de Puerto Rico. I am Chairman of the committee but the other boys do the work. Splendid.

April 20, 1962

Luis Manuel Debayle and José Figueres met at our house in Nineteenth Street at 11:00 A.M. for conversations which lasted through and after lunch. . . .

A great many angles were discussed one way or another in entire and great friendliness. Don Pepe asked Luis to assure President Somoza that he had no personal animosities against him whatever. Luis Manuel gave like assurance to Pepe. . . .

It was left that Pepe when he had done a little discussing would communicate either with Luis Manuel or with me as might seem convenient and we would take the discussion another step forward.

Both sides knew, though it was not said, that Pepe's position in this matter is powerful. He not only has the cachet of a great democratic leader and a reputation for great honesty, he has a power position as well. No armed revolution could possibly succeed in Nicaragua without having a friendly base on Costa Rican territory, from which it could get the arms and other matériel necessary to carry on its campaign. Even then it would be stacking up against a pretty competent Nicaraguan army. Without that support, it would be folly to try. It would be highly intelligent to work along the lines that were being discussed.

After that, Pepe and I left for the Easter week-end at Great Barrington: pleasant, good weather, no cares.

May 8, 1962

Working on Guatemalan plan. In the evening four Brazilian students, sent up here by an international committee came in to dinner. They are Christian Socialist—that is, Catholic and not Communist. But the line they peddled was the straight Communist line. . . . How do you fight incessantly against pure myth? The girl was sure the American experts working for the Brazilian government oil commission were there to prevent that commission from discovering any oil. The boys were sure every American concerned made 30% profit a year. They distrusted all American enterprise in Brazil, but when I suggested we had better keep out American capital, they thought any such action would constitute "sanctions." This meaningless, unfriendly, malicious nonsense is intensely irritating but it is topped by their dislike of stating any constructive program. The fact probably is that they dislike what exists, without knowing what they want, and blame the situation on the United States.

May 10, 1962

To the political meeting of the Liberal Party with my friend Moskovit . . . I told him that I rather planned to vote for Rockefeller [for Governor].

May 16, 1962

A little work on east Europe and then an evening with the Honduran students sent up here by Ambassador Charles Burrows. They turned out as nice a lot as I have met in a long time and took the taste of the crypto-Communist Brazilian students out of my mouth. Not because of their views but because they were obviously being crooked about their connections.

My mind has not been at rest. I don't know why. Partly it is working on Guatemalan plans without real faith in the situation or too much faith in my capacity to do it. Partly it is an inability to come to grips with the peace-war issue, particularly as it presents itself in Latin America.

May 23, 1962

Kissinger is going to Brazil as guest of the Government of Brazil (God knows why) and I have been giving him some letters. The more I find out about the Goulart Government the less I think it amounts to anything.

University of the Andes Foundation meeting at the Harvard Club last night, and then to preside at a little dinner at the Council on Foreign Affairs given for the Secretary of the Organization of American States, José Antonio Mora. He exploded an idea in the one place where ideas are very likely to be buried. He thought the OAS might get off the ground if besides having a meeting of diplomats they had a lower house where the members of parliament met as politicians and could talk without inhibition.

May 28, 1962

The stock market smash began to assume titanic proportions today. This does not mean that stock prices are unduly low. They would have seemed high two years ago. The words and music, however, are exactly the same as they were in 1929, namely,

1. Something is wrong.
2. Only paper profits have vanished, no real change.
3. Business is fundamentally sound.
4. Kennedy by slapping down Big Steel has impaired investor confidence in everything; therefore, he is liable.
5. The government should keep rigidly out of it.
6. The government should get into it with both feet.

Reflecting on this nevertheless I am beginning to be concerned. It is true that the $40 or $50 billion drop in paper values does not change anything fundamentally. Nevertheless it does alter the habits of people. A man who thinks he has $10,000 stuck away will do one set of things; a man who thinks he has $5,000 will do a different set of things; the man who has nothing to fall back on will do something else. We have been urging wide stock distribution. The stock exchange thinks (perhaps a little optimistically) that 15,000,000 Americans hold stocks. In that case there will be 15,000,000 people feeling poorer tonight than they did three weeks ago. They won't buy so much. Sooner or later we will have some business repercussion.

So it proved in 1929 though it was not so much change in individual habits as sudden tightening of the belt by all the business companies who stopped making expenditures. This time I think business will be less panicky.

The second round of crash after 1929 was due partly to the belt tightening by business corporations but still more to the fact that the banking system was involved. This time the banking system is not or at least should not be so involved: margin requirements are far higher, banking losses ought to be practically negligible. Nevertheless we must assume that there are weak spots. Some banking group somewhere will have either violated the law or circumvented it and now will be in trouble. The involution of any bank at once involves other banks and, of course, confidence in all banks. It will be two or three months before such a weak spot is discovered. When it does, this time the government ought to follow the policy of allowing no bank to close its door. Let the FDIC take it over at once, keep it open, merge it if necessary, and see that all deposits are promptly met. They can put the right people in Leavenworth Penitentiary without closing the bank itself.

September 24, 1962

. . . to the Brazilian Delegation to U.N. reception. According to one of my friends, Communist infiltration is going on apace in the Goulart Government. . . . I don't like the feel of things at all in Brazil.

September 25, 1962

Breakfast with Nelson Rockefeller. I gave him a copy of the statement [see below] to be issued. . . . A very warm, friendly little political meeting; with twenty-five years of friendship behind it.

He blocked out a bit his own ideas both as to the State and Federal governments. He is clear that by private handling of credit, you can get sufficient money to do anything worth doing; he has got authority to pick up a billion dollars for middle income housing and is asking five billion which he will probably get in this election referendum. He is working out an elaborate State plan to give loans on 2% interest to build factories in areas where unemployment is high. He is arranging credit so that anyone with $200 together can buy a cooperative apartment—now—the down payments in cooperatives sponsored by labor unions and others are too high, for the really poor people. He wants planning and lots of it—Federal as well as State.

I thought we were not out of the woods yet on economics and he had better stay by the state planning.

He wanted my estimate of Kennedy. I said I thought Kennedy thought and worried too much and too deeply—thus impairing capacity for action. An uncomplicated common-sense reaction like Truman's was frequently safer. He wondered whether Kennedy did think. I thought the trouble was not that he did not think but that he thought too much. I had every sympathy for him. He is personally warm, friendly and sensitive. And, remembering the terrible mistakes of life and death involved in possible war, one can only sympathize with him in the kind of agony over decisions.

Draft of statement, September 24, 1962

I intend to vote for reelecting Governor Nelson Rockefeller as Governor of New York.

Twenty-five years of close personal friendship and collaboration are undoubtedly contributing factors. But the reasons are deeper. Nelson Rockefeller has made a splendid Governor, is entitled to reelection on his record, and the State of New York and its people will be better off if his administration is continued.

Nationally I support and will continue to support the Democratic administration. This is a state election and in state and local elections, I have steadily been a Liberal and independent. In the case of the governorship, I disagree, with regret, with the conclusions reached by my friends in the Liberal Party.

October 1, 1962

A little dinner for [M. W.] Holtrop, representing the Netherlands at the I.M.F. meeting. With him we had Oren Root, Banking Commissioner of New York; Arthur Burns [Chairman, Council of Economic Advisers, 1953–1956], and a couple of others. The talk was good. Burns made a point that Kennedy had succeeded in gaining the enmity of the business community although he was right. The violence with which he tackled the steel industry—though he was right in his position—followed by his speech at Yale on the economic kits on which businessmen were working —again, sound doctrine—were so put that it excited fear rather than confidence. I defended the President on the ground that the businessmen provoked him intolerably. Burns agreed with that, but said—I am afraid unanswerably—that the business of a president was not to respond with human understandability but to get the result. Tactics, not his doctrine, was what Burns called for.

I said my impression was that Burns had left the Eisenhower Administration because he wanted much more active measures taken than the Administration was willing to take. Burns confirmed this. . . .

The diary has been suspended for the summer. For the month of July we had the grandchildren with us at the Farm. Thereafter leaving for a month in Europe. . . .

In his château near Paris, Louis de Bourbon Busset showed me the last entry in Paul Valéry's notebook, made just before his death. "The idea of love was never associated with God until the advent of Christ." True, amazing, profound. Busset was Valéry's closest friend. . . .

October 13–14, 1962
. . . Principal job in hand is to get the manuscript for the new book, presumably to be called "The Economic Republic" in shape. Meanwhile on October 10, the Latin American book, *Latin America: Diplomacy and Reality* was duly published and had some reviews. . . .

Charles Poore's [New York *Times*] was very good. . . .

October 23, 1962
Days full of foreboding spurred by the announcement that the President would make a statement last night at 7:30. This was the Cuban statement—announcement of the blockade. Technically the statement was beautiful. It not only used apt diplomatic language with force but it also mentioned the Latin American cities as well that were most likely to be effected by missiles if the Cubans started to shoot them from the bases they had established.

It happened that the Channel 13 engagement came up immediately after the rebroadcast of the President's speech so several of us went to work on it over TV. Kenneth Thompson (Rockefeller Foundation) and Joe Newman (Chief Editor of the *Herald Tribune*) among others. I was supporting for all in sight. . . .

This is reprise on the Bay of Pigs business and this time there will be no charges that somebody weakened at the crucial moment.

But this does mean that the American public faces the fact that nuclear war is possible and may have to be faced—God save us all. On the other hand, failure to act meant we should have to face it later and in worse position. The President could not have delayed it. There is no point in arguing that he might have done it earlier. In any event he has gained the support of the American public. (No "Fair Play for Cuba" phoney committees this time; nor fuzzy-headed intellectuals' statements.) . . .

The hole in these arguments about Cuba is they assume Cuba is the actor. But the major actor is the Soviet Union, shoving an arms salient into the Western Hemisphere. Cuba could not do this, nor is Cuba important in it.

Later that evening the Council of the O.A.S. approved the American action. This would not have been possible a year and a half ago. The Alliance for Progress may be in administrative difficulties, but it presents a clear-cut alternative to the Russian operation and the Latin Americans are coming to prefer it.

October 25, 1962

We went to the Metropolitan Opera. *Andrea Chenier*. Beautifully done. Against the background of present crisis, it was fascinating.

October 26, 1962

Working on the manuscript and to the farm for a weekend with [Edouard] Morot-Sir [French Professor of Philosophy] and his wife, Jacqueline, and his daughter, Catherine. During the day came the break: Khrushchev's agreement to dismantle the bases if we would call off invasion.

Later it became apparent that there was an unclear clause. I think Kennedy meant merely to call off the invasion for the time being if the Russians would dismantle the bases under inspection. Castro of course bellowed that inspectors would have to fight their way in.

October 29, 1962

More talking. I debated the legality of the Cuban blockade at the Columbia Law School. The Student Forum (the international law club) invited [Professor] Quincy Wright [international law] and me and I thought I backed him into saying that self-defense was entirely within the determination of each power, and that you did not have to wait until you were killed by a nuclear bomb to establish the fact that defense was necessary. He is a nice old man but I think carrying nineteenth century legalistics into the area, where they do not apply.

I never was fonder in my life of Art. 51 in the Charter of the United Nations, nor gladder that it was there (Nelson Rockefeller's personal achievement) and that exactly similar language is in the treaty of Rio. "The inherent right of individual or collective self-defense."

On October 24, Jules Romains was briefly in town. We had a dinner party for him—Jacques Barzun [Dean of Faculties and Provost of Columbia University], the Burdens, the Carleton Smiths, Roger Baldwin, Mary Rockefeller. It was a lovely and fascinating evening. It is true that men of good will are far back in the early history of the twentieth century. Romains at 78 is no longer a great influence in affairs. But no one can take away from him the fact that for a few brief moments he pulled Europe together. It did not stay together but this helped to pull it together later as it is pulled together now. The 19th Street house at this point at its brilliant best.

November 20, 1962
Thursday, November 2. At the Air War College, Maxwell Field, for the annual lecture.

I made a prediction: that the Soviet imperial push reached its farthest point with Cuba and would now begin to recede: ever so slowly and with great danger. The break after the President's October 22 statement and Khrushchev's agreement to withdraw the nuclear rockets from Cuba probably set the high water mark. On the other hand, withdrawal of missiles from Cuba did not end the Cuban crisis. That could not be ended as long as the Communists actually controlled the territory.

In point of fact as negotiations wear on I am frightened. Russian diplomats are cleverer than we and trying to build up a situation in which they once more interpose Cuba as a sovereign entity to mask their own operations. They will go right on attacking the other Caribbean countries —Venezuela and Guatemala. . . .

Wednesday, November 7. Election was yesterday. Having split my ticket and supported Rockefeller, I am in political isolation again: the Liberals don't like it and I imagine the White House still less, though I supported the President in all national votes. The White House would like to destroy Rockefeller as a possible rival. I think he is their best insurance policy. . . .

Then over to WABC theoretically to comment about the election returns. It amounted to putting in a couple of comments over TV every once in a while. . . . I cannot see that the Congress has changed much. On the other hand, it was perfectly clear that the entire nation was supporting the President on Cuba. They had done this though everyone was frightened. The possibility of rockets going off was very real, or seemed so. This success has bolstered the President nationally, and enormously. The problem is whether he could exploit the victory; that is far less certain.

For myself, I am old enough not to want public office so am quite capable of accepting the situation. On the other hand, if anyone wants me they will want me not for political reasons but for something I can do— if anything. But I think my forward career will be intellectual rather than political and maybe it is as well that way. The six months in Washington last year left me wondering whether I could stand the gaff when every decision may cost thousands of lives. Twenty years ago it was easy.

Saturday, November 10. Eleanor Roosevelt died Thursday night. On Saturday we went to the funeral at a little church in Hyde Park and down to her grave in the rose garden of the old house. I had seen that house first in May 1932; a generation and an era had passed.

For this funeral was distinctly the end of an era. Present was President Kennedy, most of his family; President Eisenhower. In the pew with us, Henry Wallace; behind him, Jim Farley; across, Senator Lehman; the great and lesser great figures of the New Deal. Now old and white-haired they were—and perhaps I with them—visibly going over the horizon line which divides politics and history. . . .

This was a gray and storm-racked sky and crowded roads. Eleanor Roosevelt was a great and gallant woman whose title, "First Lady of the World," was given spontaneously by everyone, and had more legitimacy than any imperial title. We could only say "Good-Bye."

November 21, 1962

The Cuban crisis seems to have stabilized. The Russians are taking out their missiles and also their airplanes. It still leaves them with a small army in Cuba, control of the territory, no inspection, a capacity to make infinite trouble. A half-done job.

December 4, 1962

Incidentally Henry Kissinger insists that the government did mean to negotiate Turkey against Cuba as a "fall back" position in case of necessity. All I can say is that I think some of the government was for that. . . .

I think the Communists will hold on to Cuba; will play things very smooth until next fall or possibly next January and suddenly explode army operations designed to take over both Guatemala and Venezuela. Then hell will break loose.

January 10, 1963

The last two weeks in December, a long struggle to get the manuscript of the next book—"The American Economic Republic"—buttoned up and ready for printing. It is off now. I have never had a manuscript edited before. The publishers were kind enough to edit this one. The girl that corrects grammar has a modern twist. Wherever she sees a relative clause beginning with "which," she springs on the "which" like a cat landing on a mouse and changes it to "that." Well, all right. The publishers think the book is good—better than I think it is. But then after writing a book you always want to begin over, write it again and write it better. Temptation to be resisted, else nothing ever gets finished.

January 3, 4, 5, 6. To Puerto Rico to stay with Muñoz Marín at his kindly castle by the sea and Beatrice was enormously glad to be there again. . . . There is a movement to change the legislation so that the University of Puerto Rico will be more Latin American than it is; probably Communist-inspired.

Thence to a meeting of the Presidential committee to clarify the Puerto Rican compact so that it can be submitted to another plebiscite. . . . It was agreed that we would ask the President to appoint a presidential commission to meet with an equivalent Puerto Rican commission, redraft the compact as needed; and then ask Congressional legislation serving it up for a plebiscite.

January 25, 1963

A radio show at CBS chiefly talking about the Communist intentions in Cuba.

Thereby a bit of a tale. I had been insisting that there was not enough attention paid to the actual military capabilities of the Russians and the Castroites and that they intend to attack the American mainland after a suitable period for build-up. I should expect the attack to come in Guatemala and Venezuela. On January 21 a speech of Blas Roca [Francisco Calderío] was reported. It spelled out in deadly detail that they intend to try to seize Venezuela and equipped with the resources of Venezuelan oil and iron "we will set Latin America afire." They mean just that. There are two understrength Russian divisions in Cuba and they are probably expecting to recruit. There will be hell to pay unless I miss my guess though the timing is difficult to work out. Since Betancourt's administration (and also Ydígoras Fuentes') ends in January of 1964, one can expect the attack to come just about then.

January 29, 1963

My birthday . . . This evening a party at the house. This was a party to end all parties, with Carleton Sprague Smith and Gilbert Highet [Classics Professor, Columbia] explaining the Renaissance songs and singers. They were singing the Odes of Horace in various musical forms. . . .

February 11–15, 1963

Week spent entirely at the University of Michigan, Ann Arbor. . . . The occasion for going was to give the Cook Lectures. In reality they were a preview of the forthcoming book, *The American Economic Republic*. They seemed to go well. At all events the small auditorium at Rackham Hall was filled to capacity through all four and people seemed to like them. The idea of presenting the American system as a thing (as we present the Communist system) seemed to surprise some and please others and all went well. At all events, Dean Allan Smith of the Law School which provides for these lectures seemed to think so.

And, of course, some time with Alice and Clan and the grandchildren who are growing up with extreme speed.

March 12, 1963

February 19. To dinner at Max Ascoli's where was a German observer at the United Nations (not Ambassador—Germany is not a member).

Max is thoroughly off the Kennedy Administration: he has come to think they are really Bonapartists. This is slightly overdoing it. The danger is not Bonapartism. It is disintegration.

February 21. To New York University where they presented a gold medal to Rómulo Betancourt and we had a chance for a brief chat. His State visit here has been a great success. I remember the old days when they were trying to chivvy him out of the hemisphere and I could not forebear grinning.

February 22. To Tarrytown, where Nelson Rockefeller was having a formal lunch for Betancourt with a lot of distinguished guests and a chance to talk with Rómulo. He thinks he will come out all right in Venezuela; the Communists are reduced to a very small force but they are terrorists and can do a lot of damage. They are now a small isolated group merely endeavoring to raise hell. He apparently had a good talk with Kennedy. . . .

Increasingly it is clear that Kennedy did negotiate with the Russians about Cuba; did get a half agreement to withdraw some troops; did impliedly at last accept a Russian force of greater or less strength in Cuba —in a word, was jockeyed into the position of agreeing to permit a Russian force in Cuba. This will raise hell as it increasingly comes out.

March 11 . . . Peter telephoned. He and Lila have a son. They have named him Adolf Augustus. He will be the fourth of the name in the United States, though there were plenty before that time in Germany. So I suppose some of the dynastic hopes of my father may possibly be fulfilled. Peter is very happy and I imagine Lila too.

March 29, 1963

March 13. At Williamsburg, Virginia, at a conference called by the Brookings Institution for twenty-five heads (presidents or treasurers) of labor unions, and Willard Wirtz, presently Secretary of Labor (I knew him when he was Professor of Law at Northwestern). A lot of old friends of mine, including Emil Mazey of the Auto Workers union. The conference had two "themes." One was how to control strikes which are beginning to be absurd—the longshoremen's strike, the newspaper strike, and a railroad strike coming up. I proposed that we try a median line. Where the rate of pay is so low that the workers have a claim on society then anything goes. But above that line the unions themselves ought to establish a strike analysis committee and the union contemplating a strike ought to take out a license. That is, it ought to submit the matter to the strike analysis committee for determination whether the issue involved was worth the mess. If it did not get it, the labor movement would not support the strike, would cross picket lines and so forth. Otherwise, I said, there will be a shot-gun law for compulsory arbitration or putting unions under the anti-trust laws or cutting into their right of representation and the unions will be back where they started before the Wagner Labor Act. In the old days they had a social cause. Now at the upper limits they have simply a power position on which their people want to capitalize.

Much frank talk and I thought it went well.

March 19 . . . The first of two lectures at City College. Then the beginning of a hassle with the city government. My old friend Joel Landres, who was in my Settlement House club in 1920 (when I lived at Henry Street), has one of several businesses which may be wiped out if the new fancy, expensive and plush civic center is put there at City Hall without adequate compensation to the business destroyed. . . .

March 26. Meanwhile I have been doing a good deal of thinking about Cuba. If my analysis is right, the situation is really ghastly.

After the confrontation of October 22 last,

(a) some understanding—tacit—was reached that we would not interfere with the Communist regime in Cuba,

(b) likewise an understanding that "some" (but not all) Russian troops would be withdrawn from Cuba. In practice this amounts to acceptance of the continued Russian occupation of Cuba,

(c) a simultaneous withdrawal of our rockets in Turkey,

(d) no asurance of any kind that an attempt would not be made to export the Communist revolution (with Russian financing and arms) to the mainland of South America. We paralyze ourselves and leave the Russians freedom to work with anything except perhaps missiles—only, of course, until they get ready next time. Meanwhile we leave all our friends around the Caribbean littoral naked to the winds.

March 28. [Leonel] Cisniega Otero, Liberal candidate for President of Guatemala, came by. [He] thought the United States ought to take a position in this election. "If you are merely contemplative, you are lost. You have a power position and you cannot run away from it." I asked about non-intervention. He said it was stupid to talk non-intervention when Russian financed parties were attacking the United States.

I was careful to say nothing. I thought, however, he was right—but when the United States favored a candidate it generally favored the wrong one. The United States favored Larrazábal in Venezuela in preference to Betancourt; and couldn't have been more wrong.

March 28. By shuttle to Boston, there to visit Peter and Lila and have a look at the new heir apparent.

He has big hands like Peter and a long head—I think rather resembles my son, Peter Adolf Augustus.

Peter has been elected head of the student Democratic club at the Harvard Law School and he aims to get into politics fast and furious. He would do well at it.

April 29, 1963

A surprising interview with a man . . . who is writing a doctoral thesis on my life and thought. For one thing, one discovers more dissent and criticism than one supposed—and unhappily some of it justified. It is supposed to be both amateur economics and amateur political science. I don't mind about political science. There is no such discipline. All thinking is amateur. On the other hand, technical economics is not my competence. I am merely trying to introduce a new premise. Perhaps instead of grousing, I should be happy it has done as well as it has.

June 2, 1963

To Wesleyan University at Middletown, Connecticut, there to get an honorary degree and make a commencement address—which I did with some trepidation. This is one of the few real honorary degrees I have had. It was suggested by Dr. Henry Allen Moe [trustee] and he asked the privilege of presenting me with it as an old friend; and for a moment, the illusion of being home again was complete. The citation must have been written by Henry Moe himself—who else would know about my grand-father's exile, or the device, *Fortis et Dulcis,* under the oak leaves and the bee which are our family crest.

June 6, 1963

Returning from lunch, I picked up an afternoon newspaper. Its front page carried terribly bitter news. My very dear friend Henrik de Kauff-mann, Ambassador from Denmark and for practical purposes all of Denmark during the invasion and World War II, was in Copenhagen dying of cancer. To save him his final agony, his wife, Charlotte, an American, also a very dear friend of ours killed him and then killed herself.

Henrik was the most gallant of them all. This diary may record that when the Germans invaded Denmark he reached my office very early in the morning (I had been up all night). We agreed there would be a Denmark if only it was in his head and mine. He said he was going on the air and announced that he would not take instructions from the Danish gov-ernment now under Hitler's captivity and he expected to be dismissed at once. This he did, and he was dismissed. Meanwhile I got hold of Presi-dent Roosevelt. Roosevelt observed that there was such a thing as duress. We had recognized de Kauffmann as envoy from a free Denmark and we would go on recognizing him as Ambassador of a free Denmark now that his country was in the hands of a German army. We worked out a method by which the Danish funds were frozen and paid them to him to maintain the costs of his embassy and other work. I saw him last Fall and was look-ing forward to seeing him when he came again this year. Mercy killing is no crime—suicide in Denmark is no crime either. The death of the two, though terrible, still has the gallantry of the old Danish nobleman whose courage was limitless and whose manners invariably impeccable.

I remember him coming to Woodley for dinner. There was snow on the ground; a pair of skis on the porch and a tempting hill. He excused himself for a moment; put on the skis; made a perfect run down the hill and came in as the dinner guests were assembling, barely flicking a snow flake from his ankle.

And I was with him at Fredriksborg Castle where his father and his grandfather had served the king. He was at home there—and I hope he and Charlotte are at home now with God.

Various jobs and then to the Farm, leaving on Saturday with Peter— June 8 through June 16—for the far north of British Columbia. The ar-rangements worked perfectly. Out of respect to the old man, Peter got a little airplane to fly into Copley Lake instead of slugging the ten miles through trailless forest. The weather could not have been better. The fishing was superb. And the untouched wilderness, the lakes, the hills and the little rivers indescribably beautiful. A cow moose and calf came into camp one night and there were bear around though we could not see them. For the rest, it was sun and cloud and sun and blue sky and blue water and the endless stretches of spruce woods which stretch uninter-rupted from there to the edge of the tundra.

Peter took as good care of me as though I had been a five year old, and

I am afraid I didn't pull my weight in the expedition. But he loved every moment of it and so did I.

The fish, rainbow trout, are so many and so hungry that if you did not get a strike every third cast you would change your fly. Our capacity to catch was limited by our capacity to eat (who kills fish for the fun of killing). . . .

On Saturday we slogged out through the woods, with Peter's compass, and taking advantage of moose trails when they were going our way. The compass tells you where to go but invariably when you take a bearing it tells you to go through the worst mash of windfalls. With Peter acting as guide, however, the difficulties were minimized and anyhow he was carrying 70 lbs. against my 30.

We talked a good deal. He is taking Harvard Law School more seriously than it deserves; actually it is a good, technical, rather sterile, institution just now, which has wandered after false gods and not found good new ones. Also he is beginning to get up in government opinion. When he gets through with his summer work in the White House staff, there will be a considerable clutch for him in governmental circles. And yet he must learn a trade before he gets mixed up in the governmental Moloch.

. . . This was one of those golden interludes that happen once in a lifetime. Peter and I have been out in the White Mountains when he was seven years old. Now the White Mountains seem like a child's holiday to him; nothing less than an Asian archipelago or the vast emptiness of the Northwest attracts him. He thinks less of crossing the continent and heading toward the Arctic Circle than I did of walking fifty miles to climb the Franconia trails.

September 19, 1963

I have been away on vacation for all practical purposes since the 1st of August. Until August 29, we had the grandchildren at the Farm in Great Barrington and enjoyed them very much. Many historic events happened during the period but not by any action of mine.

During that period, however, my son Peter entered history for the first time. He is putting in the summer in Washington (nominally, to the White House), "Food for Peace" and also as reserve officer at the Pentagon. He was working on the policy in Laos—his old stamping ground in Asia. The chief of the crew working on it was Mike Forrestal, son of the late James Forrestal, and as Peter said, he got the job because he was one of the few men in Washington who had ever been in Laos. The time had come for a revision of policy. He gathered the data, worked out the data with Forrestal and at length was invited to the White House where the President envisioned the next phase of the policy, reading from Peter's memorandum. He had thus been all the way from the bottom to the top and (though it is comparatively unimportant in the world picture) had counselled the policy, persuaded the government committee and at length saw it adopted as the policy of the United States.

I suggested to him that he make a very careful memorandum as to how these things happened: both for his own protection, for possible use when history catches up with southeast Asia and as a case study. Roughly it equals some of the work that I did about his age when I was at Versailles. They want him to take a job in Washington next year; he wants to learn his trade first: he is right.

. . . by plane to Caracas, there to stay with Rómulo Betancourt from September 13 to September 18 and to see three sets of developments there: (1) the agriculture around Maracay; (2) The huge industrial development in Guayama (where the Caroní joins the Orinoco) and finally to look at politics and urban development including slum clearance in Caracas.

Venezuela is really impressive. They have secured the kind of break-through the Communists dream about and don't have. . . . Venezuela already produces 70% of the manufacturing products consumed there. The real income of the people has jumped by 30 or 40% since Betancourt took over. There is a school and a teacher in it for every child. . . .

The installation of the U.S. Steel (subsidiary: Orinoco Mining Company) to ship ore and Venezuelan Steel Company to produce rolled and finished steel are enormous and moving fast. Modern industry in situations like this can do what the European princes used to do when they built their castles, except that this produces something. The electric generating plant—wholly Venezuelan—is as good as anything we have here, planned and so beautifully kept that you could give a formal dinner party in it.

Rómulo has got together a lot of young Venezuelans well trained, straight and patriotic who are working like nailers. The next election is coming up, in December. The night before we left Rómulo gave us a dinner party, including the government candidate, Dr. [Raúl] Leoni, who will probably be elected—my guess 40 to 45% of the vote, with two men running neck and neck for second place. . . . The Ambassador, Allan Stewart, was there as well as several others. . . .

. . . Actually the Communist movement is limited to a handful of people who have resorted to terrorism and sabotage. . . . They have no support among the unions, among the army, among the business or among humbler people. It is a small group of intellectuals plus some mercenaries, unable to organize a serious military movement. At the moment their whole plan is to try to prevent elections: this they cannot do.

The big meeting of the government party, Acción Democrática, was scheduled for the evening of the 13th—that is, when we got there. A chap calling himself chief of operations published in the newspaper a letter forbidding the meeting, saying that it had not been authorized and that they would sabotage the meeting, presumably with bombs. The Acción Democrática mobilized anyway, many thousands of people turning out in a wild rainstorm. One bomb went off and the security police answered, killing three Communists and that was the end of it. . . . But it looks to me as though Rómulo has got it made. And on the economic and social side he has secured a victory comparable to that of Muñoz Marín in Puerto Rico—but it has been gruelling for him, and the guards with machine guns are around everywhere—not that we saw any hostility but no one was taking chances on the Communist outfit (FALN) trying to do anything. As far as I could see, they don't try. I was impressed—and I am old enough not to be impressed without reason.

I think the achievement is irreversible. I mean by that that I do not think anything short of a foreign invasion could change the current of the country.

On the other hand the situation both in Colombia and in Ecuador is sloppy and dangerous and Brazil at the moment is a mess.

I was re-enforced in my conclusions: you need not only economic measures but you must also be prepared to defend. Betancourt says the Alliance for Progress has worked well in Venezuela. Its impact is about equal to the capacity of the recipient country to organize and get going. In Venezuela, they were able to do so. . . .

One thing is clear in the American scene. The Goldwater boom is moving. It is less personal than a ground swell of reaction, and is bound to play a major part, first in the Republican nomination (Rockefeller losing ground right along) and second in the election. A sort of plebiscite on the New Deal. But everyone will find that the New Deal simply cannot be reversed. . . .

September 30, 1963
Classes opened at Columbia; this is the 16th year of the seminar.

November 22, 1963
I went downstairs for a sandwich. The waitress came over to tell me that President Kennedy had been shot but was supposed to be still alive. Later the news of his death was verified.

This is terrible. It is always true that the President of the United States can be killed by a man prepared to sacrifice his life in the process. But we are not accustomed to that. I can only hope that the man turns out to be a madman—not a white racist boiling up out of the extreme rightist perimeter.

Kennedy may not have been one of our greatest Presidents. But he certainly was one of the most sensitive, well informed, and hardest working. In a painstaking, possibly over-intellectualist way, he sought moderate solutions and so far as I know never was bitter or vengeful. While he solved few problems, he was always working on the right side of civilized solutions and many of the people attacking him will soon wish they had him back.

Internationally the moment is going to be one of great danger. But [in the Communist propaganda view,] the "dirty reactionary capitalists" could only unite to kill a man . . . who sought to bring peace with or concessions to the Communist view. . . .

I am heartsick about it. . . .

December 3, 1963
The Kennedy assassination and the evil melodrama of the killing of the assassin has left a weight on all of our minds and there is no point in expounding on it. The impressive fact was the almost uninterrupted

movement of the Federal system, despite tragedy. Anywhere else, there would have been instability. . . .

The outstanding news was the success of the Venezuelan election on Sunday. Betancourt's man, Raúl Leoni, is the leader. . . . The terrorist campaign turned out to be a bluff. They killed one or two people and made a little trouble but the wholesale threat of murder to voters turned out to be so much wind.

Meanwhile Betancourt's government has uncovered a cache of arms coming from Cuba. I gather they were brought near the Venezuelan coast by a large ship and taken off by a small one, buried in the sand and dug up by Betancourt's men. The evidence is said to be conclusive.

Perhaps now someone will believe that this terrorism is not a Venezuelan indigenous movement. It is a Fifth Column attack financed, armed and trained from Cuba. Since their cry was "Death to Americans," it is plainly aimed at us. Some day Americans will get over being sentimental about movements which call themselves "revolutions" which in this case totally misstates the case.

December 5, 1963

. . . I have had a crisis of conscience. Lyndon Johnson's most intimate friend is Abe Fortas; if I want to move toward the White House I can do it through him. I want to help. But I don't want to get caught in a second-string Washington job. I don't know whether I could take it. My instinct is to offer my help, discuss it with Abe Fortas, and not push.

December 6, 1963

[The relationship with Venezuela is] the most brilliant achievement of the Kennedy administration—I like to think that I contributed as much as anyone to the administration's backing of that particular situation. I am happy it worked out.

December 12–13, 1963

The Twentieth Century Fund meeting . . . The Fund somehow succeeds in maintaining extra-political connections without really trying. Jim Rowe formerly with Truman is now working with Lyndon B. Johnson. Ken Galbraith, leaving the White House, as Ambassador to India, nevertheless worked with Johnson on his speech to the Congress. . . .

To Lyndon B. Johnson, December 16, 1963

Let me congratulate you on your swift and direct initiative in Latin American affairs. Centralizing command was the first recommendation of the Task Force appointed by President Kennedy in 1961. For the job, we wanted Tom Mann whom you have now appointed. But at that time he (rightly, I think) did not wish to accept. He will do extremely well.

I hope he may also have the title of Undersecretary as soon as may be. He will need it. . . . The next year in Brazil, Santo Domingo, Haiti and Guatemala will be anxious enough. . . .

December 31, 1963

The year ends and I cannot regard it as a very successful one. I thought *The American Economic Republic* which came out in the spring was good. It seems to have had only a moderate success with the usual 10,000–15,000 copies. Optimism is not popular this year. But the chores got done in one form or another and my name is current; but it is difficult to isolate anything achieved of great importance. In other respects the year was happy. The children are doing well. Perhaps at 68 being healthy and prosperous is enough. I have an obstinate feeling there is another climactic period ahead—though how, where and in what context I cannot tell. The area of greatest danger and of warmest friendships remains in Latin America. The country of refuge remains France. If it were not for Beatrice and her endless warm contacts, I think life would be rather grim. . . .

We expect to see the New Year in with Max Ascoli.

January 10, 1964

Dinner in New York; Mr. [Richard W.] Greenebaum brought in Gregory Wolfe who is to head up the Peace Corps in Brazil. The Peace Corps will have a rough time there. This last is because people do not realize what a cold war is. The whole end and aim of the cold war is not to do something for the people of Brazil or any other country but to drive out any American influence anywhere if possible. The Goulart government is quite likely to team up with the Communists. Simultaneously it will insist that any suspension of American foreign aid is aggression(!).

January 13, 1964

The last of the seminar and some various odd jobs. Tomorrow I shall be mobilizing for the big course in corporations at Columbia which I expect to give next semester though for the last time.

I don't know whether the time has come to take up Lyndon Johnson's invitation to go down and talk to him about things. He has a man to talk to him now. Tommy Mann is saying nothing at the moment and endeavoring to saw some wood. He has a rough row to hoe. . . .

January 20, 1964

To the School of Journalism of Columbia to begin a series of lectures on the economics of the United States. A sane man would not take that on. I am chiefly summarizing the arguments made in *The American Economic Republic*. . . .

February 6, 1964

Last night to dinner were Laurance Rockefeller and Ambassador [Roger] Seydoux—De Gaulle's representative at the United Nations. . . . I said I thought the United Nations was breaking up, and the next phase of America would be isolationism—not in the next four years but thereafter.

Seydoux said he had the same view of the United Nations. He said France had always been sceptical. . . . He asked whether I found isolationism rising; I said I did. Americans read newspapers and the kind of publicity we are getting does not dispose the everyday American to keep on with altruism whose only result is insult.

Seydoux said his father had been one of the founders of the old League of Nations and this was tragedy. I said we would have to set the intellectual atmosphere for what will succeed. We could not expect that great countries would allow their destinies to be determined by votes of minor African demagogues with nothing behind them. The job now was to try to re-set the stage so that the next stage would be stronger—as indeed the United Nations has proved stronger than the old League of Nations.

France, he pointed out, and De Gaulle had always been rather sceptical about the United Nations (as Clemenceau was of the old League). Nevertheless it is difficult to see how the world could get on without organization.

A fascinating if pessimistic evening. Today comes an invitation to accept an LL.D. from Columbia—this is one result of going Emeritus. Columbia does not give honorary degrees to active members of the faculty. I am honored—my own university, Harvard, has scarcely recognized my existence. Life does odd things.

February 7, 1964
. . . Castro has announced that he is cutting off the water supply of Guantánamo, demanding immediate return of four Cuban fishermen who invaded Florida waters and fished there. They apparently did it purposely. They radioed Havana they were in United States waters. Florida seized the boats. . . .

This morning the *Times* carried a telephoned advance statement of an editorial warmly supporting the Cubans in Pravda (Moscow). The timing suggests that there had been consultation between the Cubans and the Russians.

In this case it seems difficult to avoid the conclusion that the United States had better get ready for another "confrontation" like that of October, 1962. . . .

Obviously this is not disconnected from the Panama affair. That also was a minor incident aggravated to crisis proportions by the Russian-Cuban machine.

Finally, deserters from Cuba in the past month have been bringing in news of increased Russian activity there. It leaks to the public via the Pentagon. The Pentagon is obviously leaking this stuff intentionally.

This morning, Ed Joyce of CBS, has asked me to go on his show at 1:15 and I intend to do so with some misgivings. The moral question is obvious. My own sense is that we had better make the issue and stand right up to it, though it does mean great risks. Nobody, of course, has given me responsibility for this kind of thing. I should shut up and let things take their course or, inversely, is there a moral duty not to add to a danger which is likely to grow in any event.

My own solution is to say what I think and it may be the wrong one.

March 27, 1964

The Venezuelan government was kind enough to invite us to the inauguration of President Leoni; academic engagements at Columbia prevented Beatrice and me from accepting. I think we were missed. Backing the Betancourt government was one of the contributions I made to the Kennedy Administration; the most successful thing that was done in Latin American affairs. . . .

Abe Fortas tells me that the internal organization of the government at the time of Kennedy's death was incredibly bad. . . . Perhaps in the providence of God, Kennedy died at the right time for his reputation. Historically his administration will go down as great poetry but not as political achievement. Poetry as well as political achievement are needed in historical development; but both are needed, and it will fall into the hands of a politician like Johnson to put in the substructure.

April 2, 1964

March 31 was a dramatic evening.

[Alberto] Byington [Brazilian businessman] came in for dinner. Last November he had likewise come in for dinner alone and had laid out the plan he had for mobilizing Brazil to prevent a Goulart dictatorship. His plan was to mobilize (a) the grass roots, (b) the business associations, (c) the free labor unions and (d) the state governments if they could be induced to work together. Byington is, of course, a Brazilian: descendant of one of the Southerners who left the United States for Brazil at the close of the Civil War.

He had come here to make some final arrangements. Specifically he had bought on his own credit a shipload of oil to make sure the Brazilian Navy would be able to function. He had sent off his wife by the afternoon plane to Rio with secret word as to the plans. At 6:00 o'clock or thereabouts the radio carried the news that the Brazilian army was in motion. . . .

Goulart had been moving Army officers to other commands, working with his precious brother-in-law, [Leonel] Brezola, and had mobilized some 20,000 troops in commands loyal to him in Rio. Probably he intended to finish with Carlos Lacerda [Governor of new state of Guanabara at the time] as a first step.

Byington was, of course, worried whether the plan would go through on schedule and whether his wife when she landed in Rio would be arrested. He laid out the plan. Through the evening, we watched it work out with almost clock-work precision.

The Army plan had been worked out by General [Humberto] Castelo Branco, [Chief of the War College]. Using units he knew had been unhappy about Goulart's probably projected dictatorship, he had worked out combined action with three of the four army groups. . . . He had also activated the political and other elements. . . .

The theory was that a unit would move southward towards Rio from Minas—that happened on the night of March 31. Another would move towards Rio from São Paulo. They would assault Rio—and have Carlos Lacerda take refuge within one or other anti-Goulart army lines. Goulart himself was in Rio.

The move came off in order but Carlos Lacerda did not take refuge. He barricaded his palace, mobilized the state police and a few people favorable to him, seized after a brief tussle the Copacabana fort and prepared for a siege. . . .

Also according to plan, the principal governors declared against Goulart. . . . By the end of the evening [April 1] Goulart, whose men had seized the radio station, had had enough—Carlos Lacerda retook it. As the movement snowballed, Goulart went to Brasília by commercial plane. There, of course, he found the Army group in control, waited, took another plane for Pôrto Alegre. But the next morning most of the Army units declared against him and he vanished. . . .

As it turned out, Byington's wife was met at Campinas by a large contingent of police (they were in control) and Byington's son-in-law, Paulo Egidio Martins. . . . So it was an escort, not arrest.

April 15, 1964

Some work at Columbia and Twentieth Century Fund and then to the house, Rómulo Betancourt, now leaving his presidential post in Venezuela after the most brilliant record in recent times, dined alone with us in New York. He had dined alone with us just before he ended his exile to go back to Venezuela to form his government. . . . He had been invited by *Life*. They wanted him to write articles on "Why I am not a Communist." He tried to tell them he was not a Communist all right, but any article would be on the positive values of democracy not on a negative dislike of Communist tyranny. . . .

. . . Much talk on the philosophy of things . . .

. . . Rómulo, rightly, is going to loaf across the United States, and get his mind sorted out. Leaving power is like falling off a ten-story building and landing on a brick wall. It takes about six months to get over the shock. Even when you are well adjusted, it is a jar as I have reason to know.

May 11, 1964

A good deal of miscellaneous work. Partly an attempt to explain the Brazilian revolution—it becomes increasingly clear that that country avoided a Castro-style take-over by a matter of days. Whether the new revolution can make the social changes needed is now a great problem. I have been on the air and I have written for the *Reporter* but the old "right-or-left" controversy goes on.

To San Juan for a meeting of the Consejo. . . .

And the usual magic evening—the great blue mountains, the deepening purple sea and the lights of Luquillo across the harbor. . . .

Former President of Honduras, Ramón Villeda Morales, is in town for a little speech tonight and I am introducing him. The 19th Street crowd has to stick together, even when they are out of office.

The Twentieth Century Fund voted a little grant to Jim Shotwell. I doubt if it will ever be fully executed because he is slowly dying of an incurable disease and being near 90, the end cannot be too far off. But he was very happy and I am glad of that.

May 12, 1964
More classes . . .
Carlos Lacerda is to be in town on June 18 and I am to preside over a little meeting for him at the Council on Foreign Relations. . . . The Brazilian revolution probably is the break-through in the Cold War in Latin America. This does not mean that the war is over.

May 20, 1964
May 16–17. The week-end of the 16th–17th at the Farm: the loveliest of May mornings I think I have ever seen.
May 18. To speak at the National Association of Mutual Funds. An attempt to put over the idea that the savings banks ought to be a poor man's trust company instead of a mere put and take operation.
In the evening two Brazilians came to dinner: Eudoro Villela [Brazilian banker] and Paulo Egidio Martins; later also Max Ascoli. Paulo was a member of the General Staff group that directed the revolutionary operation in São Paulo. As he states it, the speech of Goulart on March 13 proposing the expropriation of private property in Brazil really triggered the operation, especially when followed by his rather obvious attempt to cook up a mutiny of sergeants, corporals and lower officers to displace the officers in the Brazilian Army. He holds Goulart responsible for an earlier rising of sergeants in Brasília. The sergeants rising was an old trick of the Cuban Dictator, Batista.
Goulart also had planned to paralyze the country by use of his control of the oil monopoly (Petrobrás) and his control of labor unions. He had already given a blank order that all rediscount privileges of all São Paulo banks were suspended: forcing an attempt to collect in a short time all the outstanding bank loans of all of the companies. The result would be, of course, general bankruptcy in the business world, control of all movement (which would then stop oil and gasoline) and simultaneous attempt to take the army. Consequently it was decided to move on March 31.
Three Communist groups were involved in it: Chinese, most active in some of the rural areas; the Soviet Union, wanting a more gradual approach; and the Titoist group (chiefly intellectuals) stressing the "nationalist" philosophy. . . .
As Paulo and Max Ascoli analyzed it this was primarily the middle class based revolution. The younger officers did not propose to vanish to please the sergeants. The rank-and-file knew very little about it. The businessmen, the small contractors, the housewives, the Catholic laity and most of the people did not relish the idea of being banged around by a Goulart-Brezola police state and they wanted nothing to do with the Communists. Practically as soon as they moved, the Goulart machinery

fell apart. The government-controlled labor unions immediately after refused to obey any orders. A strike called in Rio and elsewhere failed to materialize. The state is getting away on a new tack: the problem is whether it will be able to meet the economic and social problems by measures which do not bear too brutally on the poorer and lower class. This, of course, will be the test.

June 8, 1964

May 26. Lunch with [William] Jovanovich, head of Harcourt, Brace. He wants me to do a book on power. . . .

Jovanovich is an interesting man. He has made a success of Harcourt, Brace but he fundamentally values his position as an intellectual. He made one observation. He thinks the outbreaks of juvenile violence result from the desire of these kids to be something in a civilization which does not make assertion of individuality easy. You can always have a momentary illusion of power by using violence.

June 2. Columbia Commencement; I got handed an LL.D. and value it. Most honorary degrees are the results of political office and notoriety of some sort. This was not true of the LL.D. Henry Allen Moe presented to me at Wesleyan last year—that was a kind of courteous appreciation of intellectual friendship. But the Columbia degree did result from a lifetime of teaching and writing. It was, I think, an earned degree—and I am grateful for it. It had to be passed by a Faculty committee and I am told the vote was unanimous—whatever that means. In the evening, a minor celebration at 19th Street. Carleton Sprague Smith put together a very lovely program of music—and a great many people came in. This was strictly Beatrice's doing—it was a variety of Lucullan culture which closed the day. . . .

The following evening Israel Klabín came in. He is here with his wife from Brazil. The stories of the last night in Rio before the revolution (March 31–April 1) are dramatic. . . . The army let [Goulart] go—they must have controlled the airport. This is typical: Brazilians as a rule do not like to kill. One of the professors in the University of São Paulo was taken into custody by the anti-Goulart police. Another professor went immediately to the station demanding the release of his colleague. The revolutionary police head asked whether he would vouch for his imprisoned colleague; he said he would. Then he was shown some captured intelligence lists. The pro-Communist Goulart men had been told off each to kill or otherwise dispose of some enemy. The imprisoned professor had been assigned to kill the professor who was—in all good faith—trying to intercede for [him.]

In Goiás, committees had been set up to divide land, meaning thereby to seize all the plantations there and distribute them to their followers. It would then become very rapidly a Castro-type affair.

Here, of course, there is something of a campaign to say that the revolt was a counter-revolution of reactionaries—merely to stop the mild agrarian reforms proposed by Goulart. This is the standard build-up for a Communist revolution—and somehow the United States always seems to fall for it. The same build-up was made for Mao in China, for Castro in Cuba. . . .

June 9, 1964

Carlos Chagas came in this morning and is staying at our house. He told us some of the history of the Brazilian revolution. He says the revolution was a double revolt: (a) against the open Communist drive; and (b) against the immense corruption which has continued in Brazil ever since the second Vargas administration, uninterrupted (save for a few weeks under Quadros). It was this last that really led to the proscription yesterday of Kubitschek. . . . Goulart's plan was perfectly clear. He wanted to be a variety of Perón, using the Communists. . . .

June 18, 1964

. . . Later to the Council on Foreign Relations to preside over a meeting for Carlos Lacerda. Lacerda in excellent form; apologizing for nothing; staying right with it; giving his side but generally taking the view that the Brazilians were going through with their revolution whether the Americans liked it or not. They had had all they wanted of governments aligned with corruptionists. . . .

July 1, 1964

June 20, Saturday. To the Dominican Republic via Puerto Rico. . . .

June 21, Sunday. A little time cruising around Santo Domingo City. To mass at the Iglesia Mercedes and to Boca Chica for lunch at a popular little tavern and a swim in the sea. Returning to the hotel, we found an invitation from the President's secretary, Fabio Herrera, to dine with him at the best little restaurant in the city—Nina's. Across the restaurant was the President, Dr. [Donald] Reid Cabral, with his wife and with Francisco Aguirre, editor of the *Diario Las Américas,* and the Dominican Ambassador to the United States, [Antonio de] Bonilla Atiles. Herrera obviously was asked to be courteous to us and to look us over but both Bonilla and Aguirre knew us from old times and presently came over and fell on our necks. I had been of some help to Bonilla at the time of the fall of Trujillo. We presently joined the President; after dinner went to his house and talked until midnight.

He is the most appealing Dominican I have met in years. Son of a Scotchman, Reid, who was manager of some of the Royal Bank of Canada branches in the Cibao, who married a Dominican—he is more Scotch Presbyterian than Dominican. . . .

Having discovered he was with a sympathetic man, the President opened up. His government is not legitimate, resting only on the army and the police. He wants to make it legitimate. He is therefore seeking personal touch with the entire republic—but as he has no party, it is individual. When the *coup* ended [Juan] Bosch's government, the United States cut off all aid—but still worse, the Puerto Ricans, who had been helping, simply shut down. He has been trying to maintain work started by them.

Also he is a bit afraid of the Haitians. That half-savage government, probably in close league with Castro, every once in a while makes trouble on the frontier dividing the two countries. His policy is to try to keep it quiet—but with a dictator like Duvalier, you never know. I told him that if Castro plus Duvalier made a dive in that direction I thought the only recourse the United States had was to move in whatever force was necessary to repel the attack and so make it a *fait accompli*. Cabral breathed a sigh of relief. He said he would sleep easily if that would happen. I said I couldn't be sure that would happen; it was my opinion. He said it was enough that some well placed American thought so; at least he would not have to fight a combined Haitian-Communist threat alone. He also wanted badly to know what the Puerto Ricans thought. Home to bed about 1:00 A.M.

June 22, Monday. The President rang up in the morning . . . inviting us to go with him . . . to the town of San Juan de Magaña to dedicate a school. . . . Motoring along with him and a Colonel who is his aide and a sergeant-chauffeur. For practical purposes this was going unarmed. Unexpectedly we stopped at Banica for a sandwich (Cabral had had no breakfast) at 12 noon. School was out and five minutes later about forty school boys showed up at the door of the little restaurant. The Colonel let them in by sections. It seemed they wanted to have the former headquarters of Trujillo's party—a substantial building—converted into a school. The President sat on the restaurant table and talked with them, seriously and sympathetically. He said he would come back that way with the Secretary of Education and have a look at it and see what could be done. The boys were talking with him as directly as though they were talking to their local alcalde. About twenty minutes later, in fact, the alcalde and city council turned up to meet the President—the school boys beat them to it by half an hour.

Thence to San Juan de Magaña in the hills [near the Haitian frontier].

. . . There he dedicated a big school house, the first product of the Alliance for Progress. No other American showed up. The President said very little, the Secretary of Education (a woman) made a very good speech. . . .

June 23, Tuesday. We motored to La Romana where I had started my Latin American career in 1918. . . . One of the old men in the Records Office, Pagán, was still there . . . and greeted us. We looked around the Central a bit and then motored back to town. I remembered in the old days before there was a road it took ten hours fighting mud to make that trip—if you made it—and in the rainy season you went by launch or by sailing boat.

The President invited us to a little dinner—the Hollywood Restaurant. He was a fair target for anyone who wanted to shoot him; nobody did.

I asked whether he controlled the army. He said he did. He had thrown out two colonels last week and the army had taken it without a murmur. They had been doing a little plotting on the side. . . .

June 24, Wednesday. The President called us in the morning. . . .
We went to the palace where he was: the same office where more than one
man had been killed outright by Trujillo. I would have liked to examine
it for secret peep-holes, electronics and the inevitable concealed hole from
which machine gun fire could sweep the place but it seemed hardly tact-
ful. At any rate I really doubt that anything of that kind is going on now.
We got into the President's car and went along to the air force base at
San Isidro. This was squarely in the hostile camp of Reid Cabral's opposition. . . . An air force cabal had seized and imprisoned the first council
of state including Juan Bosch.

I remembered a similar visit with Rómulo Betancourt when he had
first taken power in Venezuela. He took us alone to the military club,
again walking straight into the camp of his possible enemies.

. . . The commanding General, [Elias] Wessin y Wessin, one of the
authors of the *coup* against Bosch, could not have been nicer. I took occasion to say that I thought Reid Cabral was doing a very honest and conscientious job. He nodded vigorously. He said they proposed to support
him. . . .

Then out to a development on one of the former Trujillo properties
where they are building houses and making the army do the work. The
theory is that as enlistments run out, they allow the retiring soldier to buy
one of these houses at a very favorable price—increasing the housing supply and, of course, tending to keep the enlisted men happy. As the labor is
army labor, and the materials not too expensive and the land is owned by
the government, the price is low. . . .

June 25, Thursday. We went on our own to Santiago de los Cabal-
leros. . . . We met there a Bishop who is forming a new university,
Madre y Maestra (a translation of the papal bull). . . . This is a real
Dominican educated in various places including Canada. He means to
have a school going there if it is the last thing he does. He has done about
two million dollars work on it already and means to get more from the
proprietor of a very prosperous rum business. . . .

June 26, Friday. We motored across the island via San Pedro to Hato
Mayor, a poor hill village where we had lunch in one of the real old-style
"hotels," that was like the old days. Two tables, some beans and rice on a
charcoal fire in the room behind; a couple of rooms to let upstairs; a tiny
room giving on the street and an occasional chicken wandering in. Then
over the hills and down to the sea on the edge of Samaná Bay; open country, cocoa, coffee, some rice, cattle, and a bit of rain forest like a sample
of Brazil. . . .

Reid Cabral said rather wistfully that he wanted some way of meeting
Muñoz Marín. I said that I would see what could be done. We went out
and had a late dinner at a little restaurant giving on the Malecón with a
full moon. About the only thing that Trujillo did that I approve of was
building the Malecón.

Sunday, June 28. Our last day, and we went way up in the mountains
to Constanza. This is intended as a mountain resort—but not many people
go there. There we found a dozen or more of the Peace Corps who had

assembled to discuss the cooperative move in R.D. They are a good lot. But they are discouraged. They said there is no honest government anywhere. The police and the army run the show. Nobody wants to do anything. Everyone wants a government job and no work. Generally they were discovering what the inside of Latin America really is. I said Puerto Rico looked like this when I first knew it in 1918. Now it is one of the garden spots of the world. . . .

Next morning bright and early to Puerto Rico but Muñoz Marín in the States . . . [To] Roberto Sánchez Vilella who is Acting Governor . . . I stated the Dominican case. I said: Reid Cabral is as good and progressive a man as you will ever find in Santo Domingo. He has no party behind him. He is trying to build something so that he is not wholly in the hands of the army and police. I thought the Puerto Ricans would guide him. He wanted to meet the Puerto Ricans. Roberto Sánchez Vilella said this is a power vacuum, threatening explosion. It is not good, leaving the scene either to the army, [Police Chief] Belisário [Peguero] or the Communists. . . .

July 2, 1964

To see President Johnson. I had very little to say except to commend him warmly, first for getting his legislation program through and, second, for his handling of Latin American affairs. He was right about Brazil. I told him the Dominicans hoped to have some help from the Puerto Ricans tending to stabilize a difficult situation there.

The President was very courteous and very kind. . . .

Later, Johnson signed the Civil Rights Act in a brief and moving ceremony and the remarks were excellent. He is playing things down in a low key, obviously knowing that the Republican convention will nominate Goldwater; every kind of extremist force will be released; the going will be rough.

I had the sense that Johnson is much like Roosevelt though in less universal, lower key. He has no illusions about the size of the job on his hands.

July 30, 1964

Muñoz Marín is not enthusiastic about any meeting with Reid Cabral. . . .

Goldwater is now duly nominated; he has written out of the Party everyone who does not go along with him; this means throwing out men like Nelson Rockefeller as well as Senator Keating. The worst elements in American reaction have their day. . . .

Goldwater has picked up Milton Friedman, the economist of the University of Chicago, straight out of the old *laissez-faire* group. He will make the campaign a referendum on everything that has happened since Roosevelt was elected in 1932, and his crowd means to go for broke.

I don't think it can be done but I do think they will come closer than we could wish. These balls of hate, emotion, prejudice, frustration, come to gather unbelievable headway. While I think Johnson will win, I think we will also find . . . [a] large body of activist reactionary currents of public sentiment going with him (Goldwater).

I am talking with David Dubinsky to see whether—and where—I can be of any use in the picture. . . .

During the month we have had three race riots in New York: in Harlem, in Brooklyn, in Rochester. We have also had an additional run of Negro intellectuals tending to justify it. I mention LeRoi Jones for one. They seem merely nihilist, going nowhere and throwing overboard the wiser counsels of Martin Luther King. In other words, they are trying to stage a variety of revolution, not for something but for nothing. The effect is to release purely hoodlumism, looting, anti-white violence with no program of any kind.

September 21, 1964

. . . Peter was putting in what was amusingly called "Military Reserve Duty" in Washington. This meant he was assigned to the Viet Nam Task Force headed by Mike Forrestal and working in the State Department. There was not a single State Department regular working on it. The regulars have sized up the Viet Nam situation as all bad luck and so Peter and Mike Forrestal were reporting to the President and at the same time [Peter was] doing a few parachute jumps to keep his hand in. This is shortest hop from the line to the extremely top staff I can think of. It means that at 26 years, he has seen the process all the way from the poor [man] in the rice paddies of Southeast Asia to the White House machinery.

He had taken his last vacation with his wife going around the world with emphasis on Southeast Asia, visiting Nepal and thence going to Siam and Laos and along the fighting front. . . . This meant that when he got back to Washington he was an expert on Southeast Asia—he had been there and nobody else had. Well, it's all in a night's work.

He is now starting his clerkship in the office of Lloyd Garrison where he will stay for a while.

Politics are moving. Robert Kennedy has got the [New York] nomination for United States Senate. But he and his people are already developing the machinery to make him President in 1968 or possibly 1972. The tension, to put it mildly, between the Kennedy crowd and President Johnson is obvious for anyone to see. It looks to me as though Bobby Kennedy is setting up the kind of situation that Teddy Roosevelt set up against Taft back in 1912.

The Liberal Party dinner this week will have Humphrey as well as Kennedy there—with a major speech scheduled for Humphrey and Kennedy will try to blitz the affair. Abe Fortas who is counselling the President tells me that Kennedy was all set to blitz the convention for nomination as V.P. but he was out-maneuvered; doesn't like it; and has developed almost a hatred for Johnson.

The President has assigned to Humphrey the job of taking over the machinery of the Democratic Party—which is mostly in Kennedy's hands —in the next four years. Knowing Johnson, I predict that he will succeed but there will be repercussions in all directions. The two party system will shift and the political chassé forecast by La Guardia is taking place now. There will be stormy seas.

September 23, 1964

To C. D. Jackson's funeral. I shall miss him. As Eisenhower's Brain Truster he was friend to Roosevelt's Brain Truster. We worked together on R.F.E., on European refugee matters in Strasbourg, at the Collège de l'Europe Libre. He was always understanding, gay, acute. Somewhat swift in his judgments, I could never induce him to support Pepe Figueres. . . . His wife, Gracie, was devoted throughout.

October 1, 1964

I started work on a book on power; cannot say I like the beginning.

My worry is this. There can be no structure of power—and equally no structure of society—without some system of ideas—a philosophy of the good life and of the good society. In the United States, the consensus on both points appears to be decaying at the edges. The intellectuals and artists who should be contributing it are not doing so either. They are making wails of despair or preaching the doctrine of disintegration without alternative, or are fooling around with any kind of authoritarianism which presents itself. A great deal of the country, of course, is not, plowing along much as usual. But intellectual currents sooner or later reach into the heart of the structure.

Along the line of my own specialty—the evolution of the property and industrial system—increasing reliance is being placed on an intellectual system. Corporations do not have power; property is chiefly paper; the government, being democratic, will ultimately reflect ideas. Given the strains on the system as population piles up, and certain problems are not met, we could have a period of vivid disturbance if not dissolution ten or fifteen years from now. At that time the strains unless they have been met would be intolerable. Moral structure will be weaker than today. We have no doctrine of power which could be interposed instead—assuming we would want to do it. The problem of all this is in this book in which theory, fact and forecast must be mingled in about equal degree.

I have been asked to join the committees both for Kennedy and for Keating. I am already on some committees for President Johnson. I greatly dissent from Kennedy's tactics in invading New York. He is tied up with the worst elements in the New York Democratic machine and obviously is proposing to make a power base from which he can run for President. On the other hand in the Senate he will vote right and it is by no means clear that he can make the power base.

Keating on the other hand may be right but I owe him nothing. Is there sufficient reason to desert the party for him? He came out flatly against Goldwater, which took courage. On the other hand, had he stuck with Goldwater he would have gone down to certain defeat so that more than idealism entered into his decision. My conclusion is simply to stay quiet without interrupting such little degree of regularity which I have and vote as I please.

October 15, 1964

. . . To the Waldorf-Astoria, there to meet President Johnson. This is a form of political currency. I was appointed member of the Liberal Party Committee to escort him. . . .

The President was very kind to me—said I had given him a great deal of help in Latin American affairs. I said I didn't think so—he said he knew it. And we tootled over to Madison Square Garden a half hour late. It was a great affair and he joked over the Khrushchev matter [ousted from control of Russia]. It forecast a more serious speech in the works.

The President really means what he says about the Great Society. This is a dream. He is trying to liberate a series of projects which will give it reality. Obviously the Great Society is a huge ideal. Specific projects will merely put in pier after pier after pier on which it can be built.

November 2, 1964

. . . A little belated ceremony for Professor Shotwell's 90th birthday . . .

In the quiet way of an intellectual, Shotwell has had a quiet influence on his time. He helped put together the League of Nations. It died. But out of the ashes, the United Nations rose. The United Nations seems to be on the verge of trouble but if it should fall it would have to be reinvented.

The foreign situation is going from bad to worse. As the Communist world breaks up, so the West European world is breaking up. I ascribe this chiefly to the romantic egotism of De Gaulle, and hope I am right. If so, and De Gaulle passes on to his reward, the rift will not be as great as if it were really fundamental difference.

Also I think that as Russia is increasingly divorced from the headship of the Communist world, it will become increasingly imperialistic. Not by the ideological route but by straight classical armed—and intrigues—action. Increasingly things are looking like Europe in 1911 with a devastating chance of 1914 to follow.

November 4, 1964

Elections were yesterday. . . . In the New York contest Kennedy won from Keating by a majority of 700,000 but Johnson won over Goldwater by 2,000,000. . . . After dinner, a little television and discussion of the election over Channel 13. Among those there, my old friend Norman Thomas, now past 80 and a very young professor of political science at MIT, Dr. John Saloma, a contemporary of my son at Harvard. He wants to make a progressive Republican Party and it looks to me as though he has a tough job on his hands.

November 6, 1964

Yesterday (the 5th) to take a seminar at the School of Journalism at Columbia University to teach budding journalists a little about the economic struggles in Washington and the deep issues of economic reconstruction.

In the evening to Columbia where Virginia Prewett was getting a Cabot medal for Latin American reporting along with a number of other people. Afterwards, back to 19th Street with the Venezuelan Ambassador, [Enrique] Tejera París, and Virginia and three or four others for a champagne toast to Virginia.

Venezuela is still doctrinaire; will not recognize Brazil or the Dominican Republic or other countries whose governments did not occur by election. This is all very well but frequently ignores the substance for the form. . . . The Bolivian revolution is in full swing with Paz Estenssoro fired out by the army he himself organized. Yet it must be admitted that in the latter end Paz Estenssoro had first extended his own hold on office and second had been unable to keep the peace. There is an unpredictable equation. When dictatorship is the only alternative to chaos any country will accept dictatorship any time.

November 14, 1964

November 9. In the morning a seminar for visiting Venezuelan journalists. . . . It rapidly turned into a discussion of the internal Venezuelan affairs because they were representatives of a number of parties other than the government.

As always, the question was raised "how can the country function if it does not agree on its objectives?" I tried to make the point that a democratic government does not have to agree on objectives—that all points of view take part in political life. All that the parties do agree on are practical measures taking the country along through a current hitch. . . .

November 11–12. Montreal . . . for a seminar on Latin American affairs at Sir George Williams University. . . .

It became clear to me that the difficulty in the debate arises from the confusion of two distinct situations. One is the social question: is there need for a bloody revolution in Latin America? Quite separate from that is the fact that there is also a great power struggle for control of territory —in this case, the Russian push into the Caribbean. I tried to point out that one could sympathize with a revolution and still be dead opposed to have the Great Powers make colonies of Latin America. Since the same debate probably will occur at St. Louis next week, it was a good staging ground, for it is clear that the propaganda boys are hard at work in all the universities. By confusing the situation as they do, they make more progress than they have any right to [achieve]. . . .

December 1, 1964

To the Assembly of the Captive European Nations where I got awarded for service to the captive nations. I do not think it deserved but

I was glad to salute these nations submerged by the Soviet Union as a result of the Yalta agreements. I did my best to give them some hope still staying within the State Department line. . . .

Then home to dinner. Nelson and Happy Rockefeller came, also my son Peter and Lila; also Georges Henri Martin and his wife and Morris Abram [lawyer] and his wife. Nelson . . . admitted he had had a rough go and had taken a beating. But he also steamed up with the possibilities of New York; the organization of an enlarged state university here; and the chance of presenting a full scale program even to a hostile legislature. A very good evening: warm, friendly and so forth. I told Nelson there was a strategy of defeat as well as of victory and both of us had seen both in the course of a long life. . . .

Nelson is not finished because he does not think he is finished. So he won't stop.

I should add that on Friday, November 27, Carlos Lacerda in town. . . . He likewise dropped by my daughter Alice's show in New York. When Brazilians do things they do them in style. The Ambassador showed up, so did Lacerda which is all you can ask of one country. The show was good, at all events she sold eight pictures and got a commission for another one.

December 2, 1964

Lunch with Roger Baldwin discussing proposed conference in the Virgin Islands on a new organic act for those tiny colonies. Tonight I have to go to Washington to open a high priced conference at Catholic University which I suppose will be something of a show and not much else. Looking back one wonders whether these speeches are worth anything but still I suppose one should keep it right up.

December 16, 1964

Leaving for Aix-en-Provence to get a degree of honorary doctor from the University of Aix-Marseilles. . . .

January 8, 1965

. . . Washington is pretty occupied about the situation in the Dominican Republic. Theoretically elections are to be held this fall. Reid Cabral has no party behind him even though he has a good deal of personal support. The old Trujillo crowd, possibly headed by Balaguer, or possibly by some of the old cohorts in Santo Domingo, are grouping. . . . The nearest thing to a popular party is headed by the displaced President, Juan Bosch, in exile in Puerto Rico. Some people in Washington think it possible to negotiate an agreement between Reid Cabral and Juan Bosch along the lines of the Lleras Camargo agreement in Colombia. . . .

January 14, 1965

Columbia Law Review was kind enough to dedicate its issue to me. . . . This was one of the kindliest things that has happened to me in a long time and I am grateful. We had a dinner at 19th Street for the administrative board of the *Law Review* and contributors. [Stephen] Grant [the editor] made a little speech of presentation and I said "Thank you" to the Review. Paul Harbrecht among others came up to spend the weekend with us.

It was very happy to have Grant make as his principal point that he and the other 240 men in the corporation section last year had had the best time of their lives. My preference for using Nym, Bardolph and Pistol and Sir John Falstaff as figures in the hypothetical cases seems to have excited a great deal of Shakespearean interest. I am not so sure how much corporation law they learned.

January 18, 1965.
The American Ambassador to the Dominican Republic, [W. Tapley] Bennett, is in town—called me up and came down for a morning appointment at 19th Street.

. . . He is trying to support the Reid Cabral government and wants liberal help, fearing lest everyone be tabbed as supporting a military junta. I said I would help if I could.

I said that I had an opportunity to try to negotiate an arrangement with Bosch and Reid Cabral and asked what he thought. He said in substance it is a good trick if you can do it. Juan Bosch, he said, from Puerto Rico had been agitating to overthrow Reid Cabral and Reid Cabral had been hoping the United States would expel Juan Bosch from Puerto Rico. So it looks like a bad hand to play. Well, there is no harm in trying.

. . . As I conclude my seventieth year, I find that I still have zest for these adventures though probably wisdom would suggest going slow on some of them.

January 25, 1965
Yesterday, January 24, was the 100th birthday of my father, born 1865, a few months before the assassination of Abraham Lincoln. He died six years ago. He spanned a century of American history, world history, covering about the greatest changes since the Renaissance.

The immigrant, my grandfather, Protas, established a bridge-head enough to enable his son, my father, to get an education and enter the causative processes of the United States. The third generation—mine—is the one that can enter the causative group to the extent of its capacity. I did—and if I was not more causative, it was my fault and not anyone else's.

Yesterday, Winston Churchill died. I remember meeting him on three or four occasions—chiefly in Washington. But particularly on my trip to London in 1944. Lord Beaverbrook took me around to visit him at 10 Downing Street. We talked civil aviation and the international air agreements—the reason I was there. I don't think they interested Winston Churchill as much as his love affair with Tito of Yugoslavia. "You must permit me my romantic attachment to Tito," he said. I said, rather grumpily, that I hoped his affection would be returned but wasn't sure. Church-ill merely grunted and went on a little. He did not say so, but he was clearly hoping to detach Yugoslavia from the Russian combination which he even then feared though he was committed to working with it.

My daughter Alice had asked me to bring her a stone from London being bombed. I told this to Churchill. He took me out to the little garden in back of 10 Downing Street whose walls had been demolished by the German bombs. He said he was pretty clear that they were endeavoring to get him when they bombed 10 Downing Street. He picked up one of the stones and said, "Give her this from me." . . . [He added] that the little girl was right in remembering the historic defense.

This was the eve of D-Day; the invasion of France. We were all reasonably clear then that the war would be won though it was not certain until the effective landing in Normandy a short time later.

They say Churchill will be the last of this kind of hero. I wish I could be sure. My uncertainty is because the forces of break-up seem almost irresistible. The United Nations flounders from futility to futility. . . .

Nor are we much better at home. The Democrats with a tremendous mandate in New York are unable to organize a legislature and they sit. Balkan politicians could do no better in messing things up. Whatever the mandate, it was not given to do this. Probably something else is going on. The federal system is increasingly centralizing. At this rate, in another fifteen years, state governors will be nothing more than the governors of French Departments.

In Europe we are having a duel between the forces of disunion led by General De Gaulle in his attempt to recreate the glory of France and the force of union. And in Asia it is no question that the United States is steadily losing a war in Viet Nam and the consequences of that loss are almost impossible to foresee. . . . Is there any common element which can be emphasized and struggled for tending to reduce the possibility of an international struggle of super-Homeric proportions?

January 29, 1965
Last night, a low life political meeting of the A.Y.D. I issued a clarion call to stop the legislature deadlock which is wrecking the Democratic Party in Albany. As far as I can see, nobody paid the slightest attention to it. . . .

Today was something different. Just why the seventieth birthday should be occasion for congratulating the subject, I don't know; he was not responsible for being born and gave precisely no help to making the years go by. They do that anyway. But in honor of the occasion the Twentieth Century Fund under the direction of August Heckscher organized a luncheon of the Twentieth Century Fund Board members and old friends. . . .

Ken Galbraith said a few words and so did some others and so did I but the important fact was the amount of sheer power and achievement in the intellectual world contained around that table. Dick Goodwin came up from Washington, and a telegram from the President of the United States arrived—unquestionably drafted if not sent by Dick—it was a Brain Truster's tribute to a Brain Truster over the signature of the President. We Brain Trusters understand these things . . . an anthology of my various opera [was got] out by August Heckscher. I am not sure that I recognize myself in this. The words are wonderful. A good editor and enough words and anything can be done—and it seems to me that A.H. did it.

More party tonight after which things will once more settle down and I shall be glad of it. The quality of being present at your own funeral cannot wholly be eliminated, it is like the death-head which used to be exhibited at medieval banquets.

February 5, 1965

Nelson Rockefeller stepped in to settle the legislative impasse at Albany. We had chatted it over at my birthday party. I told him the state had to have a government and he was Governor of it: if the Democrats could not organize the legislature by their party members, sooner or later he was going to have to see it done by using Republican votes. Nelson said he had been thinking of this himself. He did not want to let the Democratic Party off the hook since he wanted them responsible either for accepting or rejecting his legislative program but he could not leave the state in anarchy. So he settled it by having Republican votes elect the former minority leader [Joseph] Zaretski as Senate majority leader, and the former majority leader in the Senate, [Anthony J.] Travia, as Speaker.

February 9, 1965

A pleasant but inconsequential week-end while the heavy guns were beginning to go off in South Viet Nam. The Russian Prime Minister Kosygin was in Hanoi (North Viet Nam) at the time. There is thus a confrontation in United Nations of the three great powers—United States, China, Soviet Union. This seems to be heading up a three-powered negotiation—unless it escalates into a main-line war.

I do not see that President Johnson could have done anything else than what he did. To run away from a bad situation would simply mean having the whole pack fall on us (and on him) all the way from Japan to Malaysia. No negotiation could take place without convincing these people that they had to deal. For once I agree with Lippmann. In guerrilla warfare, we probably cannot match them without full-scale war effort. On the other hand, they are in no position to meet reprisals from the fleet. There is enough balance to produce a negotiated position—though it is difficult to see how anything more than a short time agreement can be maintained without a permanent maintenance of naval and air power in the region. Never mind how we got here—here is where we are.

The Cuba missile crisis in 1962 was an incident by the side of this.

Judging from the newspapers, the Russian reaction has been a bit restrained.

Meantime the United Nations is paralyzed, since they have not yet solved the problem of voting rights and the whole business of world order theoretically maintained though it seems to be disintegrating. It is not a good prospect.

February 9, 1965
Beatrice and I have been invited to observe the Honduras elections on the 16th and we are going. . . .

February 24, 1965
Beatrice, Frances Grant and I were official observers of the Honduran election, held to legitimatize the government established by a military *golpe,* headed by Colonel [Osvaldo] López Arellano. It is axiomatic that you can never win an election against a military government—and this one proved it.

The government had agreed with the American Embassy that it would hold fair and free elections, as a condition precedent to being recognized. It was recognized, and these were the elections. It was a beautiful exercise on how to steal an election.

. . . The government clamped down on all visas unless there was special permission from Fidel Durón who is Foreign Minister. . . . Beatrice and I came in without difficulty. The whole School for Democracy had asked admission (run by Pepe Figueres in Costa Rica) and were denied entry.

On proper application we were given observers' cards and thereupon observed the election which took place on February 16. We scattered, looking at about twenty polling places in the city and several outside, within an hour's motoring distance of the capital. . . . A couple of newspapermen, one from *Time* Magazine; one from CBS; and others, having more transport (airplane and such) went down to the provinces. I chased down rumors of rough stuff in the city, finding them untrue. They traced down some of the rumors in the provinces and verified them. What happened was the government made a show-case of the capital district (it is the Department of Francisco Morazán) but did a nice job of intimidation and obstruction out in the bush. The CBS man found twenty of the opposition party in jail. . . . In one Department, Olancho, the liberals withdrew because of obstruction. The habit is to bring the voters from the rural districts in big trucks to the voting places—otherwise they wouldn't get there. The government used government trucks and tried to prevent any other trucks from coming in, and succeeded. There were, for example, towns in which the liberals have always had a majority where there were no liberal votes or only a few.

We were courteously treated which is all we could ask personally though we obviously made the government a little bit nervous. The day after, I saw Ramón Villeda Morales. The real question was whether the liberals would at once go into revolution or stay with it. The election was not for a president but for a constitutional assembly. He had elected 30 as against the government's 34, with a number in doubt. Obviously the margin was closer than the government intended it should be.

With a great deal of soul-searching, I advised him not to go into revolution but to exploit to the full the sounding board of the constituent assembly until the government began to clamp down, making this impossible. . . .

Before giving this advice to Ramón Villeda Morales, I talked with the American Ambassador [Burrows]—it is his view also, though he had the same view I did on the stolen election.

Unhappily the Communists won either way. The one thing that could have made trouble for them would have been a liberal election; the liberals could then have thrown them out. Now they will lead the resistance against military government, whose constituent assembly will elect López as constitutional president. The going is going to be rough.

Honduras is about twenty years behind any other Central American country, which is saying a good deal. A military government would be of very little help. What is more—as was the case of Cuba—the extremists lead the opposition and the moderates are slowly squeezed to pieces. . . .

On February 22, back to New York. I cannot see we accomplished anything on this trip; only in a long lifetime I have learned that when the Caribbean calls, it is wise to go.

Meanwhile, new development: Tom Mann has been made Undersecretary of State. This is the recommendation the Task Force made to Kennedy which he never carried through. The new Assistant Secretary of State for Latin American Affairs is Jack Hood Vaughan, whom I do not know. He is clearly one of Johnson's men and one result is to diminish the capacity of the little internal intriguers in the State Department to run things.

The second is the approximation of Russians and Chinese. . . . They will make all the trouble possible for us before fighting each other. I get the sense that we are crossing a water-shed in foreign relations, and the next phase may see a very grim struggle indeed. Since the United Nations is clearly unable to cope with anything, we are back to 1933 politics. It is all right to say the world will live together in a generation. The question is how you get from here to there without blowing it up.

March 31, 1965

I have been wanting to see President Johnson; he has written me a kindly letter though I think the signature is stamped (a good idea; he hasn't time for everything). But I cannot see that I have any brilliant ideas or wisdom to offer. Bluntly, Viet Nam, if we let go, we will probably let the Chinese invasion into all of Southeast Asia including India. This means that everyone will be yelling for the entire American war effort to protect India at the cost of immense loss of life. On the other hand, bombing to create a situation capable of being negotiated will have to go on a long time. The bombing of our Embassy in Saigon yesterday does not help.

Also the waters in the United States against this kind of thing are rising. I would be happier if I did not spot a good many demonstrations which are pretty plainly Communist organized—like the one at Queens

College the other day; like the organized "teach in" movements. Not that all these people are Communists. But the Communist propaganda seems to be able to co-opt an adequate number of adherents chiefly drawn from the intellectual world. They are, however, having some trouble raising the waters against Johnson, thanks to his immensely brilliant speech on the occasion of the Selma demonstration.

Politics in New York are as low as they can get. We have a legislature that could not organize. Having organized, they are unable to pass a budget . . . neither Democratic nor Republican can organize now. Can the Liberals do anything? I really think not. Some kind of scandalous climax is likely to resolve the situation. Perhaps Peter can organize the rescue party.

April 7, 1965

Various jobs. The waters are slowly rising on Viet Nam. The same group of intellectuals with additions and subtractions for age and death want an immediate pull out in Viet Nam that wanted a truce with Hitler at the time of Munich and no engagements in Greece in 1946, and even getting out of Korea (though there they didn't have a chance to organize, being caught off guard) and hands off Cuba in 1961. Practically all of them are as sincere as could be. They are as honest as they are ignorant. I would be happier if I did not think that below this there was a well-conceived Communist propaganda job. We know this was true in Cuba in 1961 and there is good reason for believing such influence was there in 1939–1940. My reason for suspicion is simple. Always they raise the cry that the United States is opposed to Communist power. They never raise a cry in opposition to any Communist aggression. Because of the McCarthy affair, it is unfashionable to suggest Communist influence. McCarthy yelled that everyone was a Communist—whereas in fact at least 99% of them were not Communist: they were pacifists, innocents, or the like.

Yesterday, lunch with Bill Jovanovich and his editor, [William B.] Goodman, on the power book I am trying to write. Jovanovich suggested a possible form which I will try to work out. The problem is not what to say but how to say it. For power

(a) is not visible to the personality that has it;

(b) is an experience not only of princes but of policemen and school teachers and in fact everyone;

(c) is a legitimate part of personality;

(d) is devastating if unbalanced by a philosophy; and

(e) if used for purposes irrelevant to that for which power is needed.

So at intervals I find myself trying to write a poem, a novel, a study in psychology, a study in political science and a study in history. To combine all that is difficult. Goethe could write a poem: *Faust;* Machiavelli could write a how-to-do-it book: *The Prince.* Max Weber could write a study in social science. (His at least covers a universal principle.) Nobody so far as I can see has found it necessary to write all of them together. But unless that is done, the job is not well done.

Bill and I agree this book ought to be a classic or not written. Quite an assignment.

May 25, 1965

This has been an unhappy month—spoiled by the Dominican crisis. I have been seeing ghosts. I fought the Dominican occupation as far back as 1919 and campaigned to get it ended and worked with Francisco Peinado to liquidate it in 1924.

Nevertheless I find myself supporting it this time and I wrote what I thought in an article in the *Reporter* (May 20). This in face of practically all the liberal community in the United States and I gather a good many of my Latin American friends. I plan to defend President Johnson over WABC later this week.

On April 24, a cabal of officers voted to overthrow the Reid Cabral junta backed by General Wessin y Wessin. Nominally they did so to restore the constitutionally elected President, Juan Bosch, who had been in exile in Puerto Rico for a couple of years. The motives of these officers can only be guessed at. Some of them, like [Francisco] Caamaño Deñó, came out of the old Trujillo regime, had been working with Belisario Peguero (police general), which led it to be assumed that they had no dealings with the three Communist groups—one Castrista, one Moscow, one Chinese, actively functioning in the Dominican Republic, but as the Reid Cabral government fell, all forces were released. By the end of the day, the Dominican government was literally up for grabs. The Communist boys by this time were in it up to the neck—nominally for Bosch, really, of course, for themselves. With a large Cuban army within easy reach of the Dominican coast and the disorganization of affairs in the Dominican republic, they could have taken over.

And I am convinced intended to unless it was stopped. On January 15, *Diario Las Américas* obtained a report of the Latin Americans meeting in Moscow. Their Soviet hosts affirmed the sacred duty of the Soviet people to support a cold "war of liberation" in Dominican Republic, Guatemala, Venezuela and Colombia. Indications are that the Communist guerrillas in all those countries were being activated.

The army revolt had been set for June 1 but had been precipitated because Reid Cabral discovered it and took measures to eliminate the officers involved. The rising was thus premature. Immediately a Dominican mob alleged to be Communist by the witnesses who later escaped surrounded the Embajador Hotel where a few hundred Americans had been concentrated for safety and possible rescue. The American Ambassador called for troops to save their lives. The head of CIA reported to the President that a Communist take-over was a serious possibility. I do not know the other influences bearing on it in Washington but the President decided to send troops and did so.

I think he was right. If a Castro-Communist grab had taken place in the Dominican Republic, pretty much the whole Caribbean would have been ablaze, and the whole position would have been impossible. This was a risk I think the President could not afford to take. . . .

Thereafter he called in the O.A.S., virtually asking them to take charge. As usual, they talked a great deal and only nerved themselves to action three weeks later.

Also, as usual, neither the State Department nor the Embassy was really prepared to deal with the situation rapidly. Reid Cabral—the most honest man in the group—had been eliminated. In any case he was heading up an illegitimate government. The Marines arrived in time to stop the fighting. The Embassy was not well enough informed about men, and apparently wobbled in its search for a provisional government. One of its mistakes was to call out [Brigadier General Antonio] Imbert [Barreras] one of the assassins of Trujillo, whose probable intent was to replace Trujillo with himself. Present American policy came down on the side of endeavoring to restore the constitutional government. Bosch, however, had pooped out. He did not go back to head his revolution but "resigned" leaving the local army group to choose its leaders, and choose Caamaño Deñó—himself an army officer. After some fighting a truce was cooked up and now it seems to stick. After a little time, it probably will be possible to evolve a government. . . .

So far as the bulk of the three and a half million Dominicans are concerned, I am clear that they want not to have their throats cut in a civil war; they do not like American soldiers in their republic but prefer it to the kind of civil war they unquestionably would have had without them.

One good thing has come out of this so far. Three days ago the O.A.S. under American prodding was able to work up a joint O.A.S. force—Brazilian, Nicaraguan, Costa Rican and some Hondurans (1200 of them are already in the island). They also worked out a single command under General [José Joaquím de Sá Freire] Alvím, a Brazilian officer who served with Mark Clark in Italy. The O.A.S. thus is beginning to assume reality instead of being a courageous and futile talk fest. . . .

But the formula holds—anyone can put troops into a place but it takes a political genius to deal with the ensuing situation and get them out.

Meanwhile all good little intellectuals and good little liberals mightily aided by Communist propaganda are damning the President. What would they have said if he had sat by to let everything go over the dam into Russian hands is another story. . . . My little liberal friends forget that only a year and a half after the Bay of Pigs the Russians were installing an atomic missile base in Cuba, and the United States had to go to the threshold of a nuclear war to prevent it. The play-off may have obviated the danger of a nuclear missile site but it did leave the Russian-Cuban combination in a position to start wars of liberation all around the Caribbean—as they did in Venezuela and propose to do again. . . .

All the same, what with my memories of the Dominican occupation in the old days and the Bay of Pigs and so forth, it gives me a sick feeling at my stomach. I am glad I was not on the firing line in Washington though it is clear that I know more about the Dominican Republic than most of the people operating there.

1965

May 28, 1965

May 26. To Kalamazoo, to make a speech in memoriam for President Roosevelt. Afterwards, discussion with students. Awfully good crowd. This is a small school, originally Baptist and retaining some of the flavor which made those denominational colleges great schools. My daughter, Alice, and her husband, Clan, came over. Alice has some pictures showing in two or three places and seems very happy. . . . Back to the White House about 1:00 PM and presently to lunch with the President.

He wanted to talk about Santo Domingo and about the whole story. He was happy that I had written the article for the *Reporter*. . . . He gave me his picture of what was going on. In part, of course, this was a recapitulation. He had acted partly on instinct (as a man in that position would and must) from day to day. He felt the press had not got the thing straight. He had not consulted the O.A.S. but had consulted the O.A.S. peace committee. It had come up with nothing. He also had consulted fourteen Latin American governments. There is no question of legality; the Embassy had twice been begged by the Dominican junta to send military assistance. (He forthrightly showed me the telegrams; the date of both being April 28.) First a member of the military junta had called the Embassy and asked for 1200 Marines to be sent to stop the Caamaño Deñó revolt. . . .

Still later that day the newly formed junta (all that was left of the Wessin-Reid government) had presented a formal note stating that the revolutionary movement was then directed by Communists and was committing excesses against the population including mass assassinations and sackings and was under constant instructions to continue the warfare broadcast from Havana and stating that the country would be converted into another Cuba. They therefore requested "with responsibility and in categoric manner that United States Government lend us its unlimited and immediate military assistance so that such grave situation may definitively be controlled." At this point the 400 Americans concentrated in the Hotel Embajador were under fire.

Then Bennett telephoned the President. The President said Bennett was underneath his desk and the bullets were going through the window above. The President struggled with the situation for three days and then ordered the landing.

I told him that he was dead right and could not fault it except possibly in bringing out Imbert, on which the President did not comment. He gave me then the formulation of what they had accomplished. . . . Would I not think things over, come back next week with a new approach to it. I said that the question was not what happened in April but how we come out of the situation now. He said that was the precise point. Then he brought up a submerged iceberg. He said we were getting closer and closer to the outer wing of fortresses of Hanoi from Saigon and that our air people might be meeting Russian MIGs (war planes) any time. It was clear that he saw—as I did—two icebergs (possibly three) slowly converging with the possibility of all-out war as a result.

He was tired out; we were through lunch; and went into the bed-room as he undressed and put in for some sleep and I cleared out, he having told [Jack] Valenti [adviser to Johnson] to arrange for me to come down sometime next week and I wished him good fortune.

A tactical mistake. They were giving me the red carpet treatment: a White House car and the White House plane back to New York. It was actually quicker to take a taxi and catch the dear old shuttle. . . .

. . . to WABC for taping up a debate with [Professor] Hans Morgenthau [University of Chicago]. I was defending the President. To my surprise, Morgenthau did not protest. He even stated the case more strongly for the Dominican invasion than I did, assigning much weight to the fact that the Russians were present in the Caribbean via Cuba.

Thence home to dress and immediately to go to the last part of Balanchine's splendid performance of *Don Quixote* at the State Theatre. A brilliant gathering giving some of the gaiety and glitter one sometimes gets in Europe.

Home and to bed, having had three and a half hours sleep in the last 40 hours. I am getting a bit old for that kind of thing.

And a considerable amount of emotional grist as a result of the talk with the President. Though he played it down, the President obviously thinks we are in the penumbra of what would be World War III. So do I. He was asking me to be an adviser on policy. One can easily overdo one's position when this kind of thing happens. But better overdo it than underdo it. Somebody may take what you say seriously. . . .

Politically, of course, the President is concerned. The wholesale revolt of intellectuals—the so-called "teach in" debate in which Hans Morgenthau took the lead against American policy followed by a large though motley collection of professors—does present a problem. But his real concern is with the underlying indications: Johnson is no war-monger yet does not want to arrive at a Munich. So he is looking for advice.

To enter history again, however modestly, is I suppose a compliment. In my case, having entered history (albeit very modestly) two or three times, the sensation is not one of exhilaration—perhaps if I had been thirty years younger. History is implacably reaching in my direction—though the stakes for good or evil especially for evil are greater perhaps than they have ever been in human history. This needs a very clear head but it keeps you wakeful.

June 4, 1965
I cooked up and sent off a memorandum to the President. . . .

Last night (June 3) first to preside over meeting of the Council on Foreign Relations at which the Brazilian Ambassador, my old friend Juracy Magalhães, spoke about the Dominican crisis. Brazil supported us flat out. Said the doctrine of non-intervention did not have applica-tion to the new status. It had 1200 troops to join the Inter-American force.

Juracy himself had had to act in the O.A.S. before he could get in-structions from his government. Later, his government came through and approved. But, he said to me privately, the Spanish Americans were all against. He had denounced them roundly and eventually the United States had carried their motion for an Inter-American force and participation by a vote of two to three.

Thereafter to the dinner of the Inter-American Committee for Democracy in honor of Rómulo Betancourt. All our old friends were there, Latin American and American. Of interest was the fact that both Bobby and [Senator] Ted Kennedy [D., Mass.] turned up, to make a few remarks—critical of the United States. Arthur Schlesinger made a speech—guardedly concealing some of his criticism. . . .

Betancourt himself disapproved of the American action and said so. Muñoz Marín has always tried to lift the discussion to a plane to comprehend both points of view and nearly achieved it. . . .

Life is odd. I began in the Dominican Republic—under an American occupation which I disliked—in 1918. In a sort of spiral trajectory, I am coming towards the end of my life once more working on the Dominican Republic, this time defending an occupation. Then, any American was an enemy in Latin America until the contrary was proved. It may work out this way again, and it makes me unhappy.

But the difference is obvious. Now a great hostile power is squarely planted in the Caribbean—namely, Cuba. The alleged revolutions in every case are used by that power to establish a position in which eventually they plan to attack the United States. At this point the locus of power becomes important. The incapacity of the Latin Americans to govern themselves, let alone take a hand in world politics, compels the United States to take care of itself and incidentally, it may be added, the Latin Americans however much they dislike it.

The one great power outside the United States is, of course, Brazil —Brazil accordingly understands the logic. But it is a hideous situation.

Memorandum for the President, June 3, 1965

The Dominican Occupation and Cold War in the Caribbean

Summary

I. *Santo Domingo*

Stick to the plan to organize an interim government, preferably through O.A.S.; thereafter a plebiscite and an election. . . .

Increase the Peace Corps; have the Seebees or army engineers start public work construction and offer jobs to the mobs cooped up in Santo Domingo City.

II. In other Latin American countries intensify Alliance for Progress work. . . .

Get a real propaganda service going. This recommendation was made to President Kennedy. He never tackled it. The Voice of America is good but talks only excellent Castillian to the educated. Leave it as is, but flank it with a low grade service. Talk at the popular level is needed. Our people could learn by listening to the Cuban Radio broadcasting to Cubans, Dominicans and others. Needed is insistent repetition of a few simple ideas, of which the "Yankee" is a symbol: better houses, more food, better jobs, a chance for the children; unlimited opportunity. No more killing—and so forth. The Santo Domingo little people want these things.

III. *The world-wide basis*

Plan to renew the "dialogue" with the Communist empires as soon as appropriate occasion offers. . . .

It would be presumptious for me to braintrust. The major premises . . . are, of course, indicated.

(a) The world is on collision course for World War III—as usual, after a lapse of twenty years since the last war. Yet it is a war nobody (save perhaps the Chinese) really wants.

(b) We consider wars of "liberation" as any other kind of war—the name does not change them—though initially carried on by propaganda, commandos and guerrillas. . . . Communists did not invent this technique. Hitler used it; Tsarist Russia used it in the Balkans before World War I. Seven centuries ago, Genghis Khan used the technique, and so did Julius Caesar. . . .

The United States proposes not to be trapped by that ancient imperialist technique. We have the right to consider "wars of liberation" as attacks on other countries. In the Americas, they give rise to the right of individual or collective self-defense. America stands for self-determination of peoples. But "self-determination" is not to be picked up by handfuls of men with tommy guns. Guerrillas which have seized a national palace do not speak for "the people." Terror, not popular will, then does the talking.

(c) The United States is engaged now in a far bigger war even than World War II or World War III. We intend to conquer race discrimination, disease, ignorance. We are engaged in a campaign to abolish poverty. We intend, not to use the proletariat to seize empire, but to end proletarian misery throughout the world. . . . Half a century of comparative experience shows the United States under its system can produce more, and can do more for more people than any of the Communist systems have done. But that is matter of local choice: each country will make its own institutions; if some want systems not based on individual ownership, that is their right.

(d) On the other hand, the United States must act if, under cover of fomenting social revolution, the real purpose is to set up countries as armed enemy staging grounds designed ultimately to attack the United States. We have not forgotten Cuba, or the missile attempt of 1962. We read the propaganda supplied to these revolutions from Moscow, Peking and their substations. We know quite well that enmity to the United States, not benefit of the inhabitants of these countries, is the real objective.

Our design must be to end this warfare before—from being regional —it escalates into catastrophe.

A great deal more needs saying. There will be plenty of chance to say it. This dialogue would be essentially a dialogue of power opened by a United States prepared, if need be, to deal in power—aimed toward a constructive purpose.

June 23, 1965

June 4 to June 7. At Great Barrington. House guests were Rómulo Betancourt and Muñoz Marín along with his police guard. . . . The garden was beautiful and the weather fine. The three of us discussed the failures of the world and came up with a memorandum. . . . Whether it will make much difference, I do not know. Current events are moving too rapidly. The Dominican crisis dominates the Latin American scene. . . .

But in academic circles the tide is rising heavily against President Johnson. This is partly due to emotion—the men making the most noise know the least about the situation; partly, I suspect, to some behind the scene propaganda manipulation. We won't have accurate knowledge of that for a long time. In this war, as in other wars, foreign propaganda services are working overtime. As usual, they involve a great many holy innocents.

It is like the 1930's. Extremists on the one side, ranging all the way from Marxists to pacifists unite in attacking the center. So, of course, do the extreme rightists—John Birch Society types, and so forth. Max Ascoli and I had dinner together and considered that we were rapidly becoming the last survivors of evolutionary democracy.

On July 27, 1965, Ambassador Tapley Bennett wrote to Berle from Santo Domingo: ". . . [I] have had the privilege of going through your article on "A Stitch in Time" from the May 20 issue of *The Reporter*. It is as clear and perceptive as anything I have seen written on the issues involved in this situation. . . . There are some intractable forces here, and it is very frustrating for [Ambassador] Ellsworth Bunker [Representative to O.A.S.] and all of us to have such a long delay in getting a provisional government established and the country back to work. However, I agree with the conclusion in your article that, while we have many problems as a result of our intervention in the Dominican Republic, they are less dangerous than the problems we would have faced had we stood aside in April."

To Bennett, August 3, 1965

. . . I have no apologies to make for the *Reporter* article to which you kindly refer.

I do not add any comment. . . . I do hope, however, that while the present situation is going on, we can take measures to equip and open the schools—and keep open whatever schools are going, and if possible underwrite the tiny crops and so forth around the countryside. . . .

September 21, 1965

Some work on the "Power" book but not much.

To Brazil on August 19. A week in Rio. Beatrice was godmother at the wedding of the daughter of Carlos Chagas. . . . In Brazilian custom, this makes you a member of the family. . . .

I had an hour with the Brazilian Foreign Minister, Vasco Leitão da Cunha, at his suggestion. He had been Brazilian Ambassador to Cuba and had been with the government when I made my fateful and unsuccessful trip to Rio just before the Bay of Pigs. He was the only one that knew the score. He was kind enough to say that I was the only one who had really called the turn, saying that there would be an explosion in Cuba, another in the Dominican Republic and a third in Haiti. He pointed out that the Haitian one had not happened yet but could in time. He wanted me to tell President Johnson that there ought to be contingency planning in case Haiti blew up. Also Uruguay; they think it will. Since Brazil and the United States have been working together on the Dominican occupation through the O.A.S. he feels we should consult quite often as to policy. He does not want a Brazil-American Axis but points out that we are the two biggest elements in the situation and pretty much must work together. . . . When I got back, I wrote to President Johnson, transmitting the message, and I have reason to believe he got it.

In Rio, we spent a day with Carlos Lacerda. Governor of Guanabara, he is the only man in Brazil now with a personal following all over the country. His work in Rio has been amazing. The new water works would command engineering respect anywhere. The rebuilding of Rio is beautifully done. Rio has handled the battle of the twentieth century against the eighteenth with more success and less sacrifice of beauty than any other city in the world. . . .

Then we were guests of the Paulo Afonso Electric Light Company on a sentimental journey to the falls of Paulo Afonso. I had been there in 1945 with a then official in the Vargas regime, Apolónio de Salles, who wanted to use the huge cataract to make electricity. I had been instrumental in getting him a loan from the American government to start work. Then the place was a single town in a vast desert with a tiny dumpy village where we stayed. Now there is a city there. The electric light company supplies power to the whole Northeast—altogether some 453 big and small cities and towns. It is a government-owned company along the lines of the TVA and claims to be self-supporting. This is an impressive job of construction. The Northeast may blow up as American liberals love to hope but it does have the beginnings of the material structure for its reconstruction. . . . Thence to Goiás where we were guests of the Coimbra Bueno clan. Three of their children are presently in the United States and going to school but under our care so it was a sort of reciprocal job. We saw the state from the bottom—the little squatters on the big farms—all the way through the capital—Goiânia—and Brasília. Twenty years ago this was a forest state with little in it except mud huts and occasional buildings. Now it is sprouting small cities like Davenport, Iowa, the forest has been burned off (alas) and it has become a great producer of rice and cattle. . . .

To Recife where we saw Gilberto Freyre [distinguished Brazilian scholar] and friends. . . .

September 29, 1965
Several days at work writing and thinking of the book on power I am trying to write. The job is a combination of trying to put a fence around space and picking up a basket full of eels with one arm.

October 8, 1965

. . . That afternoon to Toronto, there to represent the American point of view at a Teach-In. I declined the invitation but my old friend Escott Reid, formerly of the Canadian Foreign Office and now Master of a new college at Toronto University, asked me to come which I did out of respect for him. (He is the son of a Presbyterian minister; prays before class as he did before Foreign Office conferences; and is a wonderful man though sometimes I think unrealistic in his judgment of events.) Teach-Ins were conceived in sin. They really amount to Communist and pro-Communist demonstrations in universities, in which the real Communists, the crypto-Communists, and the fellow travellers join to belabor America, particularly about Viet Nam and the Dominican Republic.

The University of Toronto tried to reduce it to a civilized discussion by authorizing the arrangement, providing a first-rate Chairman, and generally bringing it within the frame work of more or less orderly discussion. I sympathize with this approach and so went, not expecting to enjoy it.

The evening performance (October 8) was a debate between the Editor of *Pravda* and my Columbia colleague—expert in Soviet theory . . . Zbigniew K. Brzezinski. This was good. The *Pravda* man behaved himself well, talked theory, obviously was not trying to insult Americans. Brzezinski performed brilliantly and the result was pretty good. Notable was the *Pravda* editor's concession that the Soviet Union had made a mistake in seizing Hungary at the time of the Revolution of 1956.

The next morning, I took over but did not fare so well. A Dominican named Lockwood (obviously from the British West Indies) and the former Prime Minister of British Guiana, Cheddi Jagan, were theoretically debating Latin America. Lockwood claimed he is a Social Christian. This is a concealed Communist, using the "Christian" so as not to repel Catholics. Jagan, of course, is straight Communist. It really amounted to a lot of abuse of the United States coupled with explanation of the Marxist theory. . . .

I made, and thought I established, the difference between moving in to defend against "indirect war" operations and non-intervention where the revolution was indigenous. Both of my opponents dodged this question. They want the advantage of indirect war carried from outside and the doctrine inhibiting anyone else from moving in for the defense.

Intellectually, however, we did get an idea of the waters rising around the United States all over. The picture in fact carried on for twenty years the United States would be defending itself. Jagan said quite openly that their ultimate attempt was "to change the social structure of the United States," i.e. have a revolution.

Externally the facts are not quite as black as their fantasies. For the fact is that the Russians are at odds with the Chinese though they are trying to play both ends against the middle. The Viet Nam war is slowly forcing re-examination of tactics on the Chinese. The Dominican invasion did stop the active prosecution of direct war in the Caribbean. It is one thing to carry on "indirect wars" when you are trying to seize small, weakly organized and weakly governed countries. It is another thing to try to seize them if you expect to meet the force of the United States so we may get back to a basis of reason and common sense. . . .

October 25, 1965

I have been on the air with a speech supporting [John V.] Lindsay [Republican candidate for mayor of New York] in the coming election. I wasn't much interested in the campaign until the Conservative candidate, [William F.] Buckley, began to become a major element in it. It would be much easier to remain quiet, getting credit for being an orthodox Democrat and not complicating relations with Johnson.

My difficulty is that in the Democratic Party I cannot see any heir to the sceptre but Bob Kennedy. The Democratic Party has been slowly destroying itself though Johnson will win the State.

October 29, 1965

Three days ago, Castelo Branco put out a decree dissolving Brazilian political parties, authorizing him to reorganize them, and to take away part of the jurisdiction of the Brazilian Supreme Court. This last because two of the justices appointed by Goulart are alleged to be Communist.

What it means is that the next President will be elected by Congress and not by popular vote. Castelo Branco disqualifies himself: he is not making himself a dictator. The "revolution" in Brazil plans to perpetuate itself. They are going to wipe out the last vestiges of the Vargas machine who are squarely behind Kubitschek.

I can understand what is going on—and Brazil being Brazil, it will work itself out peacefully and perhaps even fruitfully. But when one abandons elective processes and superimposes another type of political organization, nobody can tell what will be the next phase. . . .

November 19, 1965

November 17. President Johnson convened a group in Washington on November 16. . . . There were present government men, university men, representatives of organized labor, leaders of various sectors of the Negro Civil Rights movement. Among them were a number of "far out" personalities. The problem of bringing the American Negro population into equality, economic and social so that civil rights should be meaningful was the precise subject.

The problem was attacked constructively by most; but the "far out" men presently coalesced. They had little interest in social engineering or political engineering. . . . Presently it was clear that some of them really wanted the luxury of a chaotic disorder. Such chaos had emerged during the past months in Birmingham, Alabama, in Harlem, New York, in Los Angeles, California, and elsewhere. Emotionally they were planning another lot of chaos as Marat and the Paris Commune had done in September 1793. One suspects that like Marat they themselves hoped to be catapulted into fame. Like some of the artists and intellectuals, they saw an emotional satisfaction in developing an uncontrollable whirlwind—

but hoped to fill the temporary power vacuum by assuming a measure of power themselves.

Chaos, I thought, is never too far away. In a sense, these, like Marat and his friends, proposed to liberate the formless, meaningless, ruthless, monsters of older times. Zeus had fought them at Pergamum; could not destroy them—could merely imprison them far below the surface, guarding them not by thought but by power.

November 18. The Comptroller of the State of New York, Arthur Levitt, came to lunch along with Leo [Cyril] Brown [S.J.; educator, labor economist, St. Louis University]. He really wants to work on how to connect state government and municipal government with the federal revenue. I agreed it had to be done; told him this was probably the beginning of the revolution which would end the importance of state government. I asked him to think out what decision-making functions he wanted to allocate to the state and municipal governments—and how far federal standards must limit its decisions. His next step is to try to call a conference of experts on the subject and come up with a trial balance. I told him that AFL-CIO were proposing to ask the federal government to take over and pay for the capital budgets of the cities. This would add to employment; give lots of work to union members; and, incidentally, lots of plunder for corrupt states like, say, Massachusetts.

December 28, 1965

Last night the father of the Brazilian children, Jerónimo Coimbra Bueno, turned up. He is staying at the house which is now full of Brazilians. . . . They are all lovely people which makes possible what would otherwise have been a very agitated time. . . .

We shall spend New Year's at the farm.

December 29, 1965

Considerable activity but very little done. . . .

Columbia asked me to give the Dean's Day speech on Latin America: it takes place on February 5, 1966. It is to be a defense of American policy. This counters all of the intellectual thinking going on around here.

I have been increasingly unhappy as I watch developments. The imperial left applies a double standard: one for the United States; another for the enemies of America. Many of them don't say so but really would like to break up the American organization. . . . Of more difficulty are the muddled liberals who don't say so and probably don't feel that way but are willing to join any movement to discredit the United States.

I could keep out of this mess. I am not responsible for what has been done in the State Department or Viet Nam. I could quite peaceably stay out of the fray and live a quiet life. It seems ignoble to have convictions and some knowledge of the (L.A.) situation and simply sit quiet, while a silly discussion goes on.

Arthur Levitt is still working on a commission to revise finances of the state of New York. Robert Kennedy wants to take over. Both of them are against Rockefeller. They want me to go along with Kennedy. I want to be of help. I don't want to be a cog in the wheel of self-seeking ambitions of Robert Kennedy. I don't want to sacrifice my friendship with Rockefeller—but I am not of his party . . . so I am playing along with these boys.

January 5, 1966

On Monday, January 2, we motored down from Great Barrington and attended the funeral of Camille L'Herisson [Haitian public health physician]. This was a brave man, dying in exile after doing his best for his country and his kind. We had been friends for perhaps thirty years. He was a "jaune" who had endeavored to collaborate with the "noir" at the time of President Estimé. He had seen his best friend, [Gastron] Margron, make the same attempt and die for his pains. L'Herisson insisted that he was poisoned by Estimé's men. Later, L'Herisson was exiled by Duvalier—and died before the situation was reversed. I shall miss him.

Meanwhile a transit strike has tied up the city. Lindsay, the new Mayor, is behaving as most people think he ought to—and I do not like it. . . . He is playing a quiet role in the negotiations with the Transit Union. What he ought to do is say that we are coming to the end of collective bargaining where the greater public interest is involved. . . . This is a very nice man and what is needed is a very strong man. But most people do not feel this way about it.

I have accepted membership in the committee constituted by Arthur Levitt with the benevolence of Bobby Kennedy to work out division of federal and state taxes. We shall work it out before we get through in some fashion although there is too much politics for my liking. The political situation in New York is getting more and more tangled. . . . I shall have something to say on my own. Naturally I want to keep things as clear as I can for my son, Peter.

President Johnson is taking all kinds of moves to try to stimulate peacekeeping moves in Viet Nam. I have no hope whatever of this—and I am not sure he has. But he can say to the country and to the world that he did the best he could and that it was Hanoi and the Chinese who turned him down.

Writing away at the "Power" book. It is tough going.

January 16, 1966

To Mexico City where we stayed for three days with Blanca Espinosa de los Monteros. A little sightseeing . . .

January 18, 1966

Thence to Nicaragua where we stayed with Luis Manuel Debayle. We saw everything there was to see. The big power project at Tumas is working now, and there is electricity all over the place. On the other hand the Pacific port of Corinto is only one jump ahead of the old tumbled-down rat-infested tropical ports of old times.

The son of old Tacho Somoza, Tachito, is General of the army. He came in to chat with me. For some reason, they treat me with enormous respect though I have not been a friend of their dictatorship. He made several points. First, he had converted the army into a professional army. He did not allow any officer to go into politics. Second, he had tried to influence social legislation. The social standards were now higher than any other country in Central America. This is true.

Third. He was trying to induce the political opposition (the "conservatives") to set up their political party and establish their political machinery. . . . The elected President, René Schick, had had a free hand; he had not interfered.

Fourth. The army had not taken too much of the country's substance. Its expenses accounted for 17% of the budget; but in that 17% was included the police expenses of the municipalities. . . .

This is Tachito. He is candidate for president; will almost certainly be elected in 1967; meanwhile the Somozas are the power behind the throne and everyone knows it. They have been moderately intelligent.

A chat also with [Francisco] Lainez, president of the central bank. He is essentially a John Stuart Mill economist; he believes in the free market. The prosperity of Nicaragua he attributes to the expansion of cotton. . . . Much of this is exported to Japan in return for Japanese machinery, motor cars and such like. They have been joining in the Inter-American common market. . . .

. . . The best economic analysis was given to me by José Debayle, who is Manuel's son. He is managing a couple of their farms and the new milk plant they put up. I asked what made Nicaragua begin to change as change it has in the past five years. . . . First, José said, about 100 youngsters educated abroad came back to Nicaragua, were not impressed by politics, and went to work to produce. This they were doing. Cotton, milk, cheese, textiles, manufactures, and so forth. They work with American companies but were increasingly anxious that Nicaraguan industry should be owned by Nicaraguans.

Second. The government had changed and the stealing had stopped. This meant that men who worked got what they worked for.

Third. The Inter-American common market had given a higher perspective on commercial possibilities.

Fourth. The Alliance for Progress (Nicaragua has had about $54 million) had freed local capital for business; before, it was taken in large measure for infra-structure.

Finally. There had come cotton. . . . Later the American Counsellor of Embassy analyzed matters and came about to the same conclusion. The intellectual and moral factors were if not decisive at least singularly important.

These were immensely pleasant days; the unfailing hospitality of Luis Manuel Debayle puts our quieter hospitality here to shame. A lovely few days.

February 2, 1966

The President ordered resumption of the Viet Nam bombing twenty-four hours ago. I wrote him yesterday expressing confidence—not that this means anything but expresses my emotion.

As in the case of the Dominican Republic, he had to weigh the risks of non-action—unlimited killing by the Vietcong—with the risks of action: the growth of military operation. American intellectual opinion declines to face the consequences of non-action. So did European and American intellectual opinion refuse to face the consequence of non-action in the early 30's when the Nazi-fascist combination was moving forward under cover of local nationalist movements (Austria, Czechoslovakia). I can understand their feeling. There ought to be a better way of solving these things than force. What do you do when the other side does use force?

The tricontinental congress in Havana made overt what all of us have known: the force movements in Latin America are not local but are being supported from outside. They were in fact imperialism under its usual disguise. If these were allowed to be successful, a couple of years from now, we should certainly have to face a general war condition in Latin America. . . .

Last night a very pleasant dinner at the August Heckschers—chiefly about art. A pleasant interlude in a difficult world.

February 24, 1966

Teaching school and then to Washington to tape a TV film commemorating the 25th anniversary of the signing of the treaty between the United States and Denmark covering the defense of Greenland. . . .

Oddly, the Voice of America though it helped the Danes make up the script took no interest in this at all. I should have thought it was a good piece of propaganda.

While broadcasting, I thought that this Greenland incident is a splendid illustration of what power is and how it is made. Henrik de Kauffmann, fired as Ambassador, might have meant nothing. One more exile in Washington. Actually, we continued to recognize him as Ambassador. This gave him a position but position only. Power needs an institution. The only institutions were the Greenland councils—rather less impressive than the village board in Scarsdale. But they were the only territory Denmark had not under occupation. So we treated them as though they were the nation of Denmark and de Kauffmann as though he were the senior authority. They accepted him as though he was senior authority and so he was virtually Governor of Greenland. Money we could arrange by freeing Danish assets and used them to pay de Kauffmann's expenses and Greenland's needs. On that slender base the treaty was made giving us an air base during the war, later turned back, and a great many other operations—eventually the authority of Henrik de Kauffmann to deal with an important factor—a great many Danish ships were afloat when the German attack came. There was a vacuum; de Kauffmann occupied it; there were rudimentary institutions, these were developed. There were economic needs. These could be handled with assistance from the United States government. The moral authority of the position enabled de Kauffmann to maintain a Danish fleet in being. The whole went back to Denmark after the war.

Back from Washington on the Pennsylvania. Train broke down twice on the way to New York. Before that a snack at the Savarin restaurant. No one to clean up the early dishes; a holiday staff. Half the food out. One gets the sense of an America beginning to decay in certain activities; some of them, like transportation, essential. The difficulty is simply that the work at the bottom is not being done or is not being well done. It is also a part of the increasingly evident signs of coming inflation. Can this, and its incidental results, be headed off, or do we have to take a bad crack. America is like a child that sometimes needs to be spanked. I am afraid we are in for it. . . .

March 11, 1966

Yesterday, the announcement of David Dubinsky's retirement as head of the ILGWU. This is a great man with a great career behind him—I don't think his life is over. . . .

My son, Peter, is announcing his candidacy for the Democratic nomination for Congress in the 17th Congressional District—Lindsay's old district. He is running on a platform of support for President Johnson. . . .

April 25, 1966

Without asking me, Bill Warren put in to extend my teaching assignment at Columbia. There is a mandatory retirement at age 70. They beat the devil around the stump for the current academic year. The Law School wanted to extend it beyond that time. The Trustees voted no: and they were right. Either you have a retirement date or you don't and if I had been voting, I would have voted against it.

Nevertheless in a sense, it does put an end to a connection which has been continuous since 1927—with time and leave of absence out for wars and spells of government service. Since I never committed all my time to the Columbia Law School, they would have been within their rights if they had terminated the arrangement at any time. As fate worked out, Columbia and not the traditional Harvard has been my intellectual home —and no university could have been more tolerant and kindly.

It will not be difficult to fill up next year, so retirement does not mean the usual vegetation while waiting to die that it does for some men. The real problem is whether at this point one's thinking remains significant. There is always a sneaking fear that one has said everything one has to say.

May 4, 1966

To Princeton to a meeting of the Advisory Committee on the Department of History. A really delightful occasion. We had a little debate as to whether anyone learns anything from history. The general conclusion: they don't. They merely try to avoid the mistake made last time; and repeat the mistake they had made the time before that.

June 22, 1966

. . . Other things are happening too. Arthur Schlesinger is Kennedy's chief confidant. After a spell of power with JFK, he wants another round and expects to get it with Bobby as indeed I think he will. But power is a bitch-goddess. . . .

The combination of some power and a great deal of publicity forced on a man does strange things to him unless he has enormous tensile strength.

June 30, 1966

June 28 was Primary Day and Peter was running. He lost. Jerome Wilson got some 16,000 votes; Peter got around 7500. That was that.

It was an honorable loss. When he entered the fight it was open—a straight question between him and Wilson. Thereafter the movement to nominate [Samuel J.] Silverman for Surrogate in protest against a joint Democratic-Republican nomination of [Arthur G.] Klein for that office stirred up the waters. Bobby Kennedy was induced to take over the Silverman campaign. . . .

He then, at the instance of some Democrats, in the 17th Congressional District, put Jerome Wilson on the same line as Silverman. This left Peter fighting alone, with neither Tammany nor Kennedy support—on his name alone. In point of fact, he ran ahead of Klein, the regular Democratic candidate in the district. The loss is bitter but not I think crushing. At his age—28—you can take that sort of thing. Included in the deal, Alex Rose threw the Liberal Party nomination to Wilson and against Peter and helped to secure the Silverman-Wilson nomination. This was a rather spectacular act of dirtiness to me and means my usefulness in the Liberal Party is over. It likewise precipitated a crisis in the ILGWU with Stulberg and perhaps also Dubinsky. . . .

September 16–25, 1966

Plane to Warsaw to attend a meeting of the International Political Science Association. . . . For two days we knocked around Warsaw with our Polish friends, free as far as I could see from any surveillance. One does not talk in hotel rooms and especially not in the Europejski. This is a first-rate hotel with all the trimmings: very expensive, primarily used for foreigners and one suspects that the police know everything about who is there and what he is doing and who he sees and what he says. Our Polish friends did not talk freely to us until we were outside in the street or in the car.

I saw too many ghosts in Warsaw to be happy. I had been handling affairs at State at the time of the Warsaw rising in 1944. The Russians then had signalled the uprising; then stood aside while the Nazis massacred the Poles to the last man. Then moved in and installed their own government: the government still in power. No Pole has forgotten this. . . . I could only grieve for my friends who died in the uprising. And also for those who died in the massacre by the Germans when they destroyed Warsaw. They literally levelled it. . . . Today it stands rebuilt according to the old patterns almost brick by brick. . . .

We went to the opening night of the Warsaw Opera. They played *Faust*. In deference to Communist thinking, they eliminated a good deal of the cathedral scene. Nor did the populace repel Mephistopheles by presenting the crosses of their sword hilts. Nor does Margaret ascend to heaven—there not being any in Communist theory. She faded away into an abyss of slowly vanishing light. The staging was excellent, the voices not bad. But a play depending on the contest between the devil and God is pretty much empty if you eliminate God. Apparently they believed in the devil. The audience was subdued—did not know when to applaud. It was filled by workers in factories who every so often get a trip to Warsaw.

Distribution of culture is perhaps the best thing the Communists have done. . . . There are schools and children in them and illiteracy has practically disappeared. On the other hand, Big Brother is always watching and no one forgets it. We were told that to get an apartment in the new construction requires influence; promotions, jobs, practically everything is visaed by some party functionary. The control is not quite total.

On Sunday we went to mass at one of the reconstructed old churches. . . . After the mass closed, everybody got up and sang a hymn, "We Want Our God," which is practically a political demonstration.

We were taken aback by seeing a huge statue before the Mayor's palace of Feliks Dzhershinsky, the blood drinker of the Stalin regime. He was born in Poland so the Communists put up a monument to him. Every once in a while at night someone goes out and colors his hands with red paint. If I recall correctly he was in charge of one of Stalin's main purges; was said to be fond of children while killing hundreds of thousands.

Sunday night, September 18, to Jablonna Castle.

This is an eighteenth century villa built for the Poniatowski family, now taken over by the state. The International Political Science Association, guest of the Polish government, held its meetings [there]. . . . The co-Chairman of the session was Professor [Charles Edward] Lindblom of Yale, as a courtesy to the Americans. Ehrlich, head of the Polish delegation, opened with a head-on talk on my own paper which had been previously submitted. He wanted to know why I was optimistic about the fate of the American economy and cited some of my observations in *The Modern Corporation and Private Property*. I answered he was talking of the pre-Roosevelt era and gave the facts and figures as to the American experience. I also pointed out that under the antitrust laws we could and did dissolve monopolies which was why there were none. . . . The Russian delegation moved in with a statement of good Marxist doctrine. Immediately the Jugoslavs jumped on the Russians. The Poles tried to conciliate a little between the two. The American, English and French delegations were guarded and courteous, trying to avoid disputes and in the main succeeding. Talk rippled around the table for two days. I don't think anyone got anywhere.

Off the record, things were different. We made friends with Ehrlich and with some of his colleagues. Likewise with a couple of the younger Poles. They asked questions and we answered them. I asked questions, developing the fact that the Communist Commissar was second-in-command of every factory and passed on the personnel. No American manager would swallow that. If he was responsible for performance, he picked staff. Ehrlich said, "I cannot answer that." . . .

After three days of this we escaped and went down to Cracow. This is a jewel among cities. The order was given to destroy it as Warsaw had been destroyed but the instructions were not carried out. I did not find out why. The city is intact. Beautiful palaces, now museums. We met two professors at the University of Cracow: one of them a young man . . . really beating against the gates of Marxian control. . . . When safely out in the bush where no one could overhear, he said simply it was a question of how many lies one could deliver. I said don't break here unless the result is worth the sacrifice.

The Polish economy is viable: the country goes. The huge iron works and artificial city built 20 kms. away from Cracow is grandiose and impressive. But the people are not happy and their life allows for little escape. A professor will perhaps have a meal at the good restaurant in Cracow once in a year. Six months salary will buy an overcoat. The workers are probably better housed than before: but their tenure depends on their standing with the Communist political chief and somehow they seek a spontaneous expression. The peasants are the best off. In the revolution of 1956, they succeeded in keeping their lands though they were excluded from social security and other benefits. But they grow their food and sell it to the cities and are prosperous. They won the round.

Sunday, September 25 . . . When we finally landed in Zurich and changed for Geneva, we stretched. Life in the Iron Curtain countries has its limitations and I suppose you could get accustomed to it but it is stifling, unhappy and at the end of six months I personally would go crazy.

. . . And I am all for Freymond's desire to keep a line open. Even though ghosts stalk street corners, there comes a time when you have to forget in order to see what can be done with the new organization. Below all governments are people.

January 16, 1967
Just before Christmas time, I went to a party at [lawyer] Sam Gates's apartment and [met] John Oakes . . . head of the editorial page of the New York *Times*.

I told him that they were underestimating Johnson. He might be wrong but this was an honorable man and a big not a small situation. He said: "If you can write what you think in 750 words, I shall print it on the editorial page of the *Times*. I mean that seriously."

I took him up and wrote it and he honorably published it on January 14.

Saturday morning, the White House called—Walt Rostow [Special Assistant to Lyndon Johnson] speaking. He said the President and Mrs. Johnson had read it at breakfast and wanted to thank me for it. I thanked him for calling and wished the President luck. Being jaundiced about this sort of thing, I recognized Presidential form C (Form A is an invitation to the White House; Form B, the President calls himself; Form C, one of his aides does). I should say this is about what it is worth. The

President has not too many friends around here anyway. And still fewer get into the New York *Times*.

This morning comes a telegram of appreciation.

From the New York *Times*, January 14, 1967

Topics: Appraisal of L.B.J. by an Old New Dealer
By Adolf A. Berle

Though President Lyndon B. Johnson may, as pundits say, be in for a spell of stormy political weather, conclusions from the 1966 Congressional elections can be overdone. In 1964 Republicans bolted from Goldwater to Johnson by millions. In 1966 they returned to the fold, perhaps restoring hairline party balance by which President Kennedy defeated Mr. Nixon.

But, since the Camelot era, President Johnson introduced a new element. He launched an irreversible tide in American politics inescapably bearing his stamp. Irrespective of press popularity, or opinions of his "style," or the barring of Camelot castles to him, his conception of the Great Society must dominate the political scene for years to come.

Meant What He Said

Johnson was one of a very few to realize that the impulses of Franklin Roosevelt's New Deal had achieved themselves. A new phase transcending mere economics was overdue. Christening it "The Great Society," Johnson blocked out its goals.

Credibility gap or not, he meant what he said. Civil rights, of course. A Southerner, he took the Negro side, converting ideas into measures. Abolition of poverty, plainly possible in a country providing an average income of nearly $3,000 for each American. But that means taking poverty out of people as well as people out of poverty.

A society of beauty, wiping out ghettos, redeveloping cities, cleansing air and streams, cleaning foul highway borders. But that requires liberating and canalizing reservoirs of local energy. A society in which no student must forgo education for want of funds. But that calls for vast increase in schools and universities. A society whose business and labor understand economic planning well enough to cooperate in handling prices, profits and wages. But that calls for a changed conception of business.

Translation of American capacity to give full bank accounts into ability to cause civilized cultural achievement. But that requires intellectuals and artists to conceive, propose, execute. As in the case of the New Deal, criticism of the Great Society is bitter—but perhaps headed for similar oblivion.

Battle is joined on all fronts. President Johnson should, and does not, have support of many intellectuals who would seem to be his natural allies. Perhaps because of his proletarian experience, he dealt in realities rather than in unassailable abstractions.

After the Dallas tragedy, he met coolness from some who identified their finest hours exclusively with President Kennedy. In fact, President

Johnson did more than continue the Kennedy direction. He opened the gates to a new vista; and these cannot be shut by friend or foe. Already his ablest competitors pay him the compliment of imitation—as did Gov. Nelson Rockefeller on Jan. 2 in proposing the "Just Society."

The War in Vietnam

In fiscal policy—to tax or to abandon Great Society spending—the issue comes to this: Will the prosperous insist on saving today at cost of a drab and dangerous tomorrow, or will they—as they can without hardship—assume the costs for tomorrow's America as well as the far from crushing costs of Vietnam? The President is saying they must.

Johnson's really controversial decision—his handling of the Vietnamese war—was that of a big man. At time of involvement, Moscow and Peking were working together. Indonesia was in the Chinese orbit. War was making in Malaysia. To enter Indochina was dangerous; to stand aside meant risking world balance at incalculable peril. Today, the Soviet Union is at odds with China, Indonesia is back in the United Nations, the Malaysian war is liquidated.

Johnson's decisive Dominican action seems to have reduced to minor scale Russian intrigues in the Caribbean. Balance is again emerging, and the Vietnam problem seems moving toward manageable dimensions, offering possibility of peace and disinvolvement without tossing Southeast Asia overboard.

Dissident Democratic Governors and reputed rivals are realizing that in 1968 any Democrat will have to run on the record, achievements and conceptions of Lyndon Johnson's Great Society. They cannot do otherwise. These will be the stuff of the next campaign.

Winning or losing, the President emerges as a towering figure. He is not a great politician; his local connections are absurdly weak. He is not a romantic image. The brilliant court and flashing pennons of Camelot are not his.

Trace-Lines of the Future

But neither is he an Andrew Johnson, vulnerable to attack by misguided idealists. Rather, with dogged determination, using what tools he has, and denied the help of some who should have been with him, the small-farmer's son become President has plotted out in his Great Society the contours and trace-lines of the next major social development in America.

Be the outcome triumph or tragedy, as an old New Dealer I am clear that to underestimate him is a historical mistake of the first order.

February 3, 1967

Various matters, chiefly working on the book with occasional interruptions . . .

January 26 to attend a reception at the Brazilian Embassy for [Marshal Artur da] Costa e Silva, President-elect of Brazil. Many old friends there. But I do not like these visits to old stamping grounds. For some years I was master in that field: to be one of the audience is not a pleasant sensation. Rather like a ghost haunting a lifetime residence.

To New York and some work. On January 31 we were invited to a White House reception, the occasion being the unveiling of a Roosevelt portrait. But the same day Juracy Magalhães, the Foreign Minister of Brazil, came to town and wanted a quiet evening with us. He is a very old friend. . . . So we cancelled the White House invitation (which is supposed to be very bad form indeed) and took care of Juracy.

Among other things, we discussed the coming meeting of American Presidents. Juracy said there was a good deal of opposition to the idea; no one quite knew what to do about it. . . .

The telegram [inviting Berle to discuss the program for this meeting] is a classic of State Department English. It says, "We are now at a key point in our preparation for the proposed meeting of American Presidents . . ." and "would like some advice." When you don't know where you are going, any point is a key point. . . .

This is going to make for a stiff conference. . . . I think that [Sol] Linowitz [the new American Ambassador to the O.A.S.] wanted the meeting on February 6. The State Department bureaucracy did not want to be interrupted—and circulated its paper without bothering him. Whether Dean Rusk was a party to this, I do not know.

The United States has a great many critics and some enemies—State Department bureaucracy lies somewhere between the enemies and the critics.

Meeting of the Kennedy-Levitt Committee on Federal-State taxation: my son, Peter, did all the work.

My schedule is in a jam. I have three Carpentier lectures at Columbia beginning March 18. And on April 20 the Penrose Lecture at the American Philosophical Society meeting—standing in for Jean Monnet, who was scheduled but could not come. I also want to get the book done. I am beginning to feel very inadequate.

The Carpentier lectures were published under the title *Three Faces of Power*. The lecture delivered at the American Philosophical Society, entitled "The Laws of Power: An Approach to its Systematic Study" received the John Lewis Prize by the Society.

February 7, 1967

Yesterday to Washington in a storm and eventually to the State Department at 4:30 . . . Those present besides myself were Douglas Dillon, George Harrar [President, Rockefeller Foundation], Father [Theodore M.] Hesburgh [President, Notre Dame], David Rockefeller and others.

Lincoln Gordon presided. He laid on the table the documents which had already been circulated to the Embassies. The proposed agenda takes in everything including the kitchen stove but few definite agreements could be reached on any of the points. . . .

All of us made a few observations—none of them very pointed. I called out Hesburgh, who put in a plea for some more discussions of education and agriculture. I suggested we ought to take the dollar sign off Inter-American conferences.

David Rockefeller hoped there would be a study group looking towards (a) monetary policies—a step towards balance of payment and stabilization of currencies; and (b) an agreed code regarding treatment of foreign investments. . . .

After that the meeting discussed somewhat aimlessly and then went home.

I came home with David Rockefeller, George Harrar and Douglas Dillon in a private plane supplied by Time Inc.—Rockefeller's plane is being repaired. . . .

Unhappily the situation is clear. The bureaucracy had already cooked up its elaborate agenda. It has no desire whatever to get outside advice. The President on the other hand had indicated his desire to Sol Linowitz. Linowitz had got up the list so the meeting was held. But by that time the agenda had gone out and not much could be done.

As I cleared out, Linowitz asked me to write him a letter—which he would arrange to get to the President. I said I would do this. . . . When I was in the Kennedy Administration, I refused to act at the White House except through the Secretary of State. The net result was that I got little done. This time there is a pipeline to the White House for whatever it is worth and I will use it.

The State Department bureaucracy has been systematically making trouble for Lincoln Gordon. He responded by getting himself a job as President of Johns Hopkins University, a graceful exit. Their next target will be Linowitz. They offered him a couple of Cabinet posts—he wants to stay where he is; I shall try to give him a little help. The President likes him because he talks very much as Johnson does and not at all as the State Department bureaucrats do. But then the State Department bureaucrats hate everyone from the President down for some reason—regarding them as vast irrelevancies.

February 16, 1967

The radio broadcast the news of Bill Bullitt's death—it is all over the newspapers this morning. I meditated during the night. I met Bill Bullitt first at the Versailles Peace Conference; from our office he went on his famous mission to Lenin and got an agreement; came back; was repudiated by Lloyd George, who had sent him; and Wilson refused to receive him. Bullitt was bitter: later handed over his records to a Senate Committee.

Still later, Franklin Roosevelt asked me about him before sending him to Russia as Ambassador. I told him I thought he had a right to be bitter. The government cut his throat and not the other way. And Roosevelt appointed him.

His dispatches from Russia and later as Ambassador to France came to my desk. Returning home after the German conquest, he entered into an intrigue against Sumner Welles—helped circulate the story that Welles was a homo; and eventually forced Welles out. I was senior and took over the Department when Sumner resigned.

Presently President Roosevelt came back and I went over to see him. He said Bullitt had just been there. That on Bullitt's entry he had appointed himself St. Peter. Two men came up: Sumner Welles, and after chiding him for getting drunk, Roosevelt let him in. The second was Bullitt. After paying due tribute to what Bullitt had done, St. Peter accused him of having destroyed a fellow human being and dispatched him to Hell.

The President said to me a bit naïvely: "I don't think Bill will ever forgive me." But so far as I know they never met again.

Nor did I meet Bill Bullitt again. Well, of other people's sins, let those who are sinless judge. Bullitt was flashing, effective, ego-filled, knight-errant. What it all came to in addition to human progress, I don't know. Sentimentally I found it difficult to forgive his destruction of Sumner Welles, who also went bitter and died in his bitterness.

March 8, 1967

On Saturday, March 4, I was at the farm in Great Barrington, meditating on the fact that 34 years ago we had moved into the White House with Franklin Roosevelt. The previous evening, Walt Rostow had called asking me if I could meet him at his house in Washington on Sunday, March 5. I agreed to do so. . . . There were present Milton Eisenhower, President of Johns Hopkins, formerly doing Latin American affairs for his Presidential brother; Tom Mann, who preceded me in Latin American affairs in the Kennedy Administration; Jack Vaughan who had also done Latin American affairs; a White House aide whose name I did not get; Linc Gordon, about to become President of Johns Hopkins; myself.

The subject was the script for President Johnson's operations at the forthcoming meeting of Latin American Presidents . . . (Montevideo, April 12). Linc stated the agenda agreed on at the Foreign Ministers conferences which had just ended. . . . Vaughan thought that the President should bear more heavily on the needs of education, etc. Everyone agreed that he should give as good an assist as he could to the Latin American Common Market.

I added that I thought they needed to consider a whole new revamping of the course of trade. The Latin American Presidents had brains enough to know that a few million dollars in grants were not going to solve their problems. What they really needed was what Keynes had recommended twenty years ago: a stabilization of prices and trade arrangements between the underdeveloped countries and the developed countries. . . .

Factually I have in mind a world commerce organization like the World Monetary Fund (IMF). It ought to buy all surpluses over national production at fixed prices, and distribute this surplus to the countries which needed them most. This is a real revolution. I told Walt Rostow —who agreed—that if something of the sort were not done two or three years from now we might be seeing a world recession comparable to that of 1929. . . .

. . . My son, Peter, is expecting his third child any time. Last night, March 7, was Lila's birthday; it was a question whether it would be celebrated at our house or at the hospital but the baby waited and we had a pleasant party. Among those present was Christopher Crane, nephew of Winthrop Crane and a fast friend of Peter's. This makes three generations of friendship between the Crane family and ours.

April 18, 1967

I gave a class in Arthur Schlesinger's seminar. I didn't think the seminar amounted to much but had an amusing time with Arthur.

He, Kenneth Galbraith, George Backer and some others have been having conversations with Hubert Humphrey. . . . Clearly the object was to establish better relations with the intellectual community and with the Kennedy crowd. Schlesinger was reporting by telephone to Bob Kennedy while I was there.

I gathered that it had been somewhat stormy; Schlesinger had got a bit excited but had found the Vice President cordial and thoughtful.

Schlesinger says the Vice President constitutionally cannot disagree with the President else it almost comes to the point where he has to resign—as Calhoun did. Accordingly they give Hubert credit for staying with his Chief, irrespective of his private views. I am not sure he is right about that.

Schlesinger believes that Johnson will be beaten next election by a Republican who will thereupon make peace—the analogy is to the election of Eisenhower and the end of the Korean war. I am not sure that I agree.

In the evening to see a brilliant performance of Tolstoy's *War and Peace*. It raises all the questions—not least, whether anyone in international affairs knows what he is doing or what he may expect as a result. Certainly no one expected World War I or for that matter World War II to turn out as it did. . . .

Luis Somoza, formerly President of Nicaragua and now succeeded by his brother, Tachito, died suddenly and I am permitting myself a letter of condolence, to his brother. Had Luis not been a Somoza, he would have been a first-rate developer of Central America. . . . He could not, of course, lift the burden of the dictatorial position his family occupies, neither can his brother.

June 6, 1967

Yesterday, war broke out between the Arabs and Israelis. There could have been no other outcome. . . .

If this were merely an Arab-Israeli matter, it would be bad enough. Actually if Nasser wins the Russians will take over everything from the Persian Gulf to the Red Sea. If he fails, they will wait and try it again.

Max Ascoli telephoned this morning. He is beside himself: thinks Johnson was almost criminal and weak in not landing some force and otherwise getting into the picture.

Actually the stakes are enormously high: a third world war could easily result. All the same I think it would have been safer if we had stationed a ship or two in the Suez Canal in some appropriate place and announced that in the interest of world peace we would guard the freedom of the waterway. We have no legal right to do this—but I don't see that legalistics play much part in any of this.

My immediate forecast is reasonably optimistic. I think the Israeli will go straight to the Suez and hold it; and probably occupy enough of the Sinai peninsula to open the Aqaba Strait. I don't think the Russians will move in. Equally how long the Israeli can hold the position, I do not see. . . .

This is a nice way to spoil a pleasant June.

June 22, 1967

The Rockefeller party at Tarrytown [June 9] was the last word in color and splendor. The guest list was mixed: Cardinal Spellman, Bobby Kennedy, Tom Dewey, to take a few. There were also some family friends which is why Beatrice and I were there. It was a splendid spectacle: the gardens were lovely and it had a Renaissance quality about it which has not been characteristic of recent years. Nelson in fine form.

Working away at the book on power with some disappointments: it is a difficult book to finish.

Meanwhile, the Israeli have cleaned up the Arabs—as I thought they would—but now the question is what to do with the Middle East. More world wars have started there than in any other area. . . . This time the Russians obviously intend to influence the Arabs; we are assumed to be backing the Jews—morally but not diplomatically and the whole thing has been thrust into the inept proceedings of the United Nations.

January 17, 1968

I have been preoccupied about the possibility of confrontation between the United States and the Soviet Union. This preoccupation is six months old and now is beginning to emerge in the papers. At length it has been discovered that after the Israeli war, the Russians undertook to move naval and other strength into the Arab States on a large scale. Sometime they will invite the United States to leave and if successful the Soviet Union will have Europe in a vise—East Germany and Berlin on the north, the Mediterranean on the south—and the United States will be back to the Atlantic line. What the United States will do when the confrontation comes up is not clear to me—I don't think they will like it. Israel would then be at the mercy of the Russian-Arab combination.

March 21, 1968

I went on a vacation trip, beginning at Kansas City, of all places—some lecturing to a regional association of colleges: Baker College, Tarkio College and Kansas City University (in Kansas City). Then to the University of Miami to give three days of seminars to some third-year students at Miami Law School. Thence to Venezuela where we put up at an excellent hotel, the Avila, and went over to see President Leoni. I asked him whether his party and the Acción Democrática could unite. He said briefly, "no."
. . . He is not worried about a military coup. Nor is he worried about the

Cuban expedition: says they are now limited to about 70; of whom about 37 are holed up hiding—a police problem.

Then with a delightful young man, Dr. [José Antonio] Rangel, in the President's plane to visit the Orinoco and Caroní developments. I had seen them when they were nothing but pampa just after the Cerro Bolívar mine was discovered. Then a few years later as the operation was in action, and the government steel plant had been opened on the banks of the Orinoco, and the Caroní electricity had begun to develop—now they are great cities—Puerto Ordaz with 100,000 people, a country club colony and (believe it or not) a key club for lunch. More importantly, the program (Rangel is in charge) is for an orderly rather than disorderly development. There as elsewhere people are leaving the country and flocking into the cities—squatting where they can. Now the government provides for this in advance. Tracts of land are set aside; a squatter is assigned an area—I should guess 30 metres square. The government puts up four posts and a tin roof for him to squat under. They tell him he can build that into any kind of shack he wants but it must be on the back of the lot because he is expected to build a good house on the front of the lot. . . . The construction of the good house is financed by very low rate government loans—and the squatters in the area are organized to cooperate in building each other's houses—virtually free labor. . . . There is also city planning, some provision for artistic and musical expression, etc.

Since the entire area is booming—everything from steel to aluminum and other industries—it may be they will construct an industrial system that has design and esthetics as well as productivity. They have only scratched the surface of the resources within ready transport distances of the Orinoco River ports.

To Monte Sacro, an old plantation once owned by Bolívar and now by Nelson Rockefeller for three days loafing and walking in the high hills. . . .

Meanwhile the United States has been in some turmoil. I never felt less relevant. In most national crises I have had something to do. Here I don't because I don't know what ought to be advocated. The Viet Nam war is going badly—of course, we ought to get out but the problem is how to do it—as the *London Economist* notes, getting out has far wider consequences than cutting losses in Viet Nam. The next result may be explosive—enemies who win exploit their victories.

Bobby Kennedy calculated that he could not get the nomination away from Johnson so he stayed out. Thereafter [Senator Eugene] McCarthy [D., Minn.] challenged, running for nomination in New Hampshire and the result was a brilliant success. Thereupon Kennedy seeing the crowd starting down the road decided he ought to lead it and announced his candidacy. At a Twentieth Century Fund meeting a few days ago, Arthur Schlesinger, who is doing the negotiating for him, said that the policy was for Kennedy to help McCarthy, not fight him, though he, Kennedy, expected McCarthy to help him in a state where Kennedy was challenged. This was a quiet way of beating McCarthy, and nobody knew it better than McCarthy. Meanwhile the President himself has been as inept in dealing with local politics, parties, and so forth, as a President can be. He simply isn't there.

The strength of the presidency is such that I think he may very well win the nomination if he really wants it; he might pull out though I doubt it. But this looks to me more and more like 1912 when Taft won the nomination and was promptly defeated by Woodrow Wilson.

Who the Republicans will take, I cannot tell yet. Nelson Rockefeller is about to announce his own candidacy. Nixon has already set up an enormous number of delegates but I think must win on the first ballot in the Republican convention else he may lose to a Rockefeller-[Ronald] Regan combination or equivalent.

My difficulties are great. I have very little respect for Kennedy. It is clear that McCarthy cannot get the nomination. I like the President but think he is a lost cause. My preference would be for Rockefeller if he gets the nomination—I don't know that he will. If he does and runs against the President I shall have a division of loyalty, for Johnson with all his limitations has done his honest best. On the other hand, a new man could extricate America from her difficulties more easily than Johnson—and Nelson is probably the best equipped man in the country to do it and is a close personal friend. My personal decision would not be of great importance but I shall feel like a slacker until it is made. It cannot be made now until we see what the alternatives are.

April 1, 1968
. . . To the farm in Great Barrington. Winthrop Murray Crane II, son of the old Senator and father of my associate and friend, Winthrop Murray Crane III, died; to his funeral in Dalton. This was the death of a hereditary duke of the Berkshires and the succession of another.

The grandfather was my father's friend, the father and grandson, my friends and my son's friends. A long history.

Reached New York last night at 9 PM and listened to the President. He is dropping out of the Presidential race. From the highest motives—he thought he personally was a divisive force and wanted the country to unite itself. I think he is wrong. We shall have an interregnum now for nine months and unless I miss my guess every international crisis will be precipitated, from Viet Nam to Venezuela. . . .

Rockefeller better get into the act: he is the nearest thing to a common denominator we now have.

October 2, 1968
An ironic, interesting fact. My old friend Arthur Burns, of the Twentieth Century Fund board, has been asked by Nixon to draw a program for economic legislation. Burns asked me if I would join in drawing the program. I said I was supporting Humphrey. Burns said he understood that perfectly but the problems would be the same. I said I would go along. The United States government has to work well, no matter who is running it.

Harcourt, Brace has scheduled the *Power* book for the fall of 1969. I am sorry—I should like to get the damn thing into print.

January 9, 1969

Harvey Schwartz, Vice President of IBEC [International Basic Economy Corporation], and Mr. [Robert Helander], also IBEC (Peruvian Vice President), had lunch with me. We may be moving into a very big crisis indeed.

The new military government of Peru expropriated Standard Oil of New Jersey's subsidiary—the Talára Oil fields. Under the present law—the "Hickenlooper Amendment"—all American aid and the American sugar quota has to be cut off within six months—actually, in April. In combination, Peru will be flattened. Practically all local sentiment is against the United States and might be stirred to violent action if the amendment is used. The Peru government talks about throwing all Americans out within forty-eight hours. Given the sentiment elsewhere in the continent—Chile, Bolivia, possibly Brazil—we may see a clear break-down of Inter-American relations. Everything is moving toward the crunch—and Nixon has not even been able to appoint an Assistant Secretary of State for Latin America to meet it. Under the Hickenlooper Amendment, the precedent is to wiggle but there is no reason to assume Nixon will want to use the possibility he has or that Congress will let him if he does.

I suggested that we throw the matter into the O.A.S. and perhaps also the World Court and then take the view that the matter is still in litigation. Whether the Peruvians will accept that I cannot say nor are the IBEC boys optimistic. They think the Peruvian Generals want a big issue and they can precipitate one.

To Henry Kissinger, January 13, 1969

Amid more pressing situations, a South American matter comes to head in April.

Peru's military government last October expropriated the properties of a Standard Oil (New Jersey) subsidiary. Under the Hickenlooper Amendment cancellation of foreign aid (less important) and of her crucial sugar quota is due next April. Peru will suffer. But both the nationalist right and the Marxist left (there is little effective center) yearn for a Nasserite anti-American campaign. Ensuing political reaction could produce seizure of all American properties there (Grace & Co., CERRO, IBEC, several banks). The movement could spread to other South American countries—Chile, perhaps Brazil.

Wriggling out, perhaps by throwing the matter into the World Court, is dubiously possible. The American companies hope we will do this. On the other hand, unless a self-respecting instead of a blackmail relation is reached, confrontation will have to take place sometime.

You may wish to get a crew working on the problem.

April 18, 1969

We had our own baptism of fire at Columbia a year ago. Interestingly at Columbia, the Law School had very little part in it—didn't like it.

It is interesting to note the Harvard students talk about "violence"— apparently it was not "violent" for them to move into University Hall, pick up the Deans and physically throw them out of the building, but it was violent to bring in the police.

I know enough about revolutions, however, to know that neither truth, fairness nor decency has anything to do with positions people take.

The whole thing is sickening, besides being unnecessary.

I am clear that deep in the background is a small group of organizers working primarily as political warfare agents for Maoist Communism. This is not surprising: we are in a variety of Cold War with Communist China, though the Vietnam war is point of contact. The unhappy point is that the political warfare boys (who keep secret and keep silent) are able to develop as much receptivity for their ideas as they have among students who haven't the foggiest idea of the origin of the business.

The student strikes are now highly organized, with a central group which is hardly conscious of what is going on, but is well financed and able to ship propaganda and organizing agents all over the country. While Harvard is on strike, we have some trouble at Columbia, some at Queens College, some at New York University and some at Rutgers, New Jersey, not to mention a great many other parts of the country. While the obvious object is to force action in favor of North Viet Nam, the long-range end is to weaken the United States, for reasons we can only guess at.

November 12, 1969

There were three buildings bombed in New York the night before last. I am afraid this is the beginning of a bit of urban terrorism with which we have been familiar in South America and I knew at one time in Paris. The context suggests that this is a small group of people working in somewhat the same way that the urban terrorists work in other parts of the world.

The United States is, for the first time in many years, encountering a real revolutionary movement though it has its own peculiarities and is less likely to succeed than elsewhere.

December 18, 1969

On December 14 to Santa Barbara for a meeting on constitution-alization of procedures of certain administrative agencies and particularly those of A.E.C. I put in a paper suggesting a council of economic advisers and the development of a concerted attack on this avalanche of technology which is swamping American society. A conference crystallized around that nucleus. . . .

The conference itself developed two facts: (1) "ecology"—meaning thereby air pollution and general blasting of resources is rapidly replacing the Viet Nam war as the cause of unrest, in many universities. I could not understand it until I came into Los Angeles on a plane. Los Angeles is already almost unlivable because of the smog; (2) that, surprisingly, violence is accepted among a number of respectable men as a way of getting things done—except that none of them has figured out what gets done when violence has run its course.

The Center was kind to me personally and invited me to come out for a month later in the year. I doubt if I can do it.

. . . Professor V. Petrovsky, attaché at the Soviet embassy to the United Nations, is the political scientist attached to that delegation. He came in to see me today to discuss certain ideas on power—and I gave him a copy of my book, *L.A.: Diplomacy and Reality*. He also presented a couple of questions from the Soviet papers relating to my work and insisted that the two best-known political scientists in the United States were Ken Galbraith and myself. Well it takes all kinds to make up a world.

Petrovsky is writing a book on political science and power and he showed me his outline and it is in many respects surprisingly close to my own.

January 14, 1970

Last night there came to dinner Sumner Welles's son, Benjamin. He is writing the life of his father and gathering various impressions. He will want to see papers later. We discussed many things but particularly his father's resignation from the Department in 1943. He brought with him and read to me a letter from Sumner Welles to his wife, Mathilde, describing his interview with President Roosevelt just before he resigned and turned over the Department to me: the President was in Quebec and Cordell Hull was away. The letter was immensely moving. It relates the growing jealousy of Hull to Welles, beginning at the time when the President supported Welles against Hull when Welles was head of the delegation to the Conference at Rio de Janeiro. . . . I had been with Cordell Hull when he telephoned the President asking him to reverse Welles's position at Rio—and Roosevelt had decided to support Welles because he was the man on the ground.

January 29, 1970

My 75th birthday. What to do with an obviously diminuendo in range of possibiities not to mention energy and activities during remaining active years is a problem. A little more so sincere it is scarcely possible to deny that *Power* has not been a resounding success.

It seems clear that we are in the preliminary stages of a depression—not of a recession or a minor turn-down but a real dislocation. It will not be on the same scale as that of 1929 but it will be bigger than anything we have had since the war and will require at least as much inventiveness as was evident in the days of the New Deal.

At some point, the political situation will become fluid—that is the government will begin to try to meet the situation. I don't know that the Nixon government will be any less amenable to ideas than any other. We shall probably come out with some machinery able to direct the national capacity towards meeting the national priorities, and able to override some of the special interests—including some branches of organized labor which at present stand in the way. My impression is that the deepening difficulties will not work to the benefit of the famous New Left which has not been able to articulate any ideas of the civilization it wants or where it is going.

Whether I have any skills to be useful in this situation I don't know. Unlike most of the current operators, I have been there before—at the exact opposite stage of the cycle.

A birthday party tonight with some good music organized by Carleton Sprague Smith. A great many old friends.

April 6, 1970

I am more unhappy about the state of the world. The blacks occupied the University of Michigan; the University of Michigan settled by agreeing to rearrange their curriculum to meet the blacks' demand. This means that any teacher anywhere can be denied time to teach his course. A somewhat similar row went on at the Harvard Law School. At the University of California (Santa Barbara) the place was almost closed down. My lecture at the State University at Buffalo on April 1 was cancelled because the State University at Buffalo is under martial law. 45 faculty members sat in at the administration building and the president rightly had them arrested but it may mean that the university cannot continue. Another group has occupied Mount Holyoke College. This is like a variety of rebellion exercised against any academic institution where there is a group that can be mobilized. In every case it was the white radical, especially junior members of the faculty, that were able to bring them off. Something has got to be done somewhere.

Victor Reisel says that in May there will be a whole storm of bombing of banks. They burnt the branch bank of the Bank of America at Santa Barbara a couple of weeks ago. Meanwhile Lindsay is making speeches about "whittling away of freedom." I would say that freedom to do anything has grown. Apparently resistance to force is considered oppression. This is so much nonsense.

May 12, 1970

A couple of days ago the construction workers charged a "peace" and radical demonstration in front of City Hall. . . . It was a right-wing mob and when it met some young hippies, a few people shouted "Heil Hitler," and went pretty mad.

Then they went for Mayor Lindsay and probably couldn't find him. Two observations:
1. Nixon cannot govern;
2. Probably Mayor Lindsay can't either.
This looks like trouble ahead.

The demonstration on Friday, May 8, was a mixture of riot for peace and extreme radicals. The construction workers were apparently organized the day before and came out and charged them.

A friend of mine, Mr. Neisser of the F.C.C., came in to lunch. He said he was frightened: all this resembled 1931 in Germany just before the Hitler take-over.

May 26, 1970

Yesterday (May 25) Alfred Hayes, President of the Federal Reserve Bank of New York, invited a number of businessmen and myself for a meeting, followed by lunch. Theoretically this was to increase communications between the Bank and the business community. It turned out to be a very urbane presentation of the fact that the Federal's policies were not working well and that they needed help. They presented a set of charts and figures. One set of figures threw at me something I had already discovered. The standard non-financial corporations of the country have been borrowing; in 1969 alone they borrowed very heavily indeed. Fair enough: but something over $40 billion, spent for plant and expansion—or perhaps for buying other companies—consists of short-term commercial paper either held by banks or in the open market. It had been assumed these notes would be paid by issuing or selling stocks or bonds.

When it came my turn, I asked whether any provision was made for taking care of these obligations. . . . The question was not answered—vague thinking that individual investors would buy bonds and pay off these notes. This, of course, is absurd: some bonds would be bought but not that much. Later at lunch, it came my turn to sound off. I said they had better organize an R.F.C. and be quick about it. . . .

The government recognizes we are on the eve of a depression if not already there. How far it will go no one knows. I pointed out that liquidity was the job of the Federal government—at least in crisis—and when markets do not function the Federal government had to. This time—unlike 1933—we have savings; we do not have overhanging inventory; we do have purchasing power in the hands of the public. The job is to mobilize these and stop the kind of nonsense there is now.

Returning from the Federal Reserve Bank, I discovered that the stock market had gone off 20 points while we were talking. Probably there will be greater liquidation in the next few days.

Bond market financing at 10% is not the answer. No manufacturing company can pay 10% for its money and still make a profit without inflation.

Everyone was for wage and price control. This is not an answer, merely a sticker while some real action is being devised.

I remembered that in 1933 the Federal Reserve Bank of New York was itself broke. They didn't have gold enough to support their operations. They ran up the white flag. Randolph Burgess [New York Federal Reserve Bank] took me out to dinner at the Bankers Club and confessed during dinner. He wanted me to get the incoming Roosevelt Administration to go to work on it. Then we were struggling with deflation; now, inflation; but it still can be done.

November 4, 1970

The campaign of 1970 is over. Most interesting to me was my son's fate. Running as a Democrat for re-election to the Assembly of the State of New York, he carried a small Manhattan district by more than 3-to-1 though both [James] Buckley [Conservative candidate for Senator] and Rockefeller carried it on the Republican and Conservative tickets at the same time. This meant it was a personal victory for him.

Generally it is a pretty indecisive campaign. Except in New York there was general reaction against the New Left and also against the extreme right. This is as it should be. New York is a pressure cooker but getting farther away from reality. . . .

Nationally the swing is slightly to the Democratic side. That is usual: the party in power commonly loses in mid-term elections. What this will look like two years from now is anyone's guess.

January 12, 1971

Yesterday to Washington where a so-called leadership group was assembled, first at the White House and then at the State Department. The plan is to gather a non-partisan group who will support the foreign policy of the United States (i.e., the President and particularly his White House adviser, Henry Kissinger).

They did an honest job of briefing and I think are telling what they hope to do. It is not very impressive: play all foreign affairs down. But it is also clear that they are worried. Nobody knows how the Middle East crisis is coming out.

January 20, 1971

Last night Bill Jovanovich was here to dinner. I told him that I had taken on Travis Jacobs to do the editing. He was familiar with some angles of it already.

Soon after, Berle went to Puerto Rico, where he gave his last lecture, at the Faculty of Law of the University of Puerto Rico, on February 5. He returned to his home on 19th Street, in New York, and there died of a massive cerebral hemorrhage on February 17, 1971.

Index

841

INDEX

INDEX

INDEX

851

INDEX

INDEX

INDEX

INDEX

INDEX